한 권으로 끝내는

해커스
토익
800+ plus

해커스 어학연구소

실시간 토익시험 정답확인&해설강의
Hackers.co.kr

한 권으로 끝내는 해커스 토익 800+ LC+RC+VOCA

토익,
한 권으로
목표 달성하세요.

취업, 졸업, 공무원 시험, 승진…

여러분의 멋진 꿈을 향해 가는 길에 토익 점수가 걸림돌이 되어서는 안 되겠죠?
《해커스 토익 800+》는 여러분이 다른 중요한 일들에 더 집중할 수 있도록,
꼭 필요한 내용만으로 토익 목표 점수를 빠르게 달성할 수 있게 구성되었습니다.

CONTENTS

책의 특징과 구성　6
토익 소개　8
800+ 정복 학습 플랜　10

LC

PART 1

PART 1 소개

| DAY 01 | 사람 중심 사진 | 16 |
| DAY 02 | 사물/풍경 중심 사진 | 22 |

PART 2

PART 2 소개

DAY 03	의문사 의문문: Who, What/Which	32
DAY 04	의문사 의문문: Where, When	36
DAY 05	의문사 의문문: Why, How	40
DAY 06	일반 의문문 및 부정 의문문	44
DAY 07	선택 의문문 및 부가 의문문	48
DAY 08	제안/제공/요청 의문문 및 평서문	52

PART 3

PART 3 소개

DAY 09	주제/목적 및 화자/장소 문제	60
DAY 10	요청/제안/언급 및 문제점 문제	66
DAY 11	이유/방법 및 특정 세부 사항 문제	72
DAY 12	다음에 할 일 및 의도 파악 문제	78
DAY 13	시각 자료 문제	84
DAY 14	대화 상황	90

PART 4

PART 4 소개

DAY 15	문제 유형	100
DAY 16	음성 메시지 및 회의 발췌	106
DAY 17	공지 및 관광 안내	112
DAY 18	연설 및 강연	118
DAY 19	방송 및 보도	124
DAY 20	광고 및 소개	130

RC

PART 5

PART 5 소개

DAY 01	명사와 대명사	140
DAY 02	동사	146
DAY 03	to 부정사, 동명사, 분사	154
DAY 04	형용사, 부사, 비교 구문	162
DAY 05	전치사	170
DAY 06	접속사	176
DAY 07	관계사	184
DAY 08	최신 빈출 어휘	188
DAY 09	최신 빈출 어구	196

PART 6

PART 6 소개

DAY 10	문맥 파악 문제: 문법	204
DAY 11	문맥 파악 문제: 어휘	210
DAY 12	문맥 파악 문제: 문장	216

PART 7

PART 7 소개

DAY 13	주제/목적 및 육하원칙 문제	226
DAY 14	Not/True 및 추론 문제	232
DAY 15	의도 파악, 문장 위치 찾기, 동의어 문제	238
DAY 16	이메일/편지 및 메시지 대화문	246
DAY 17	양식 및 광고	252
DAY 18	기사 및 안내문	258
DAY 19	공고 및 회람	264
DAY 20	다중 지문	270

시험장에도 들고 가는 토익 기출 VOCA 별책

DAY 01	PART 1 기출 어휘	DAY 11	PART 5&6 기출 어휘
DAY 02	PART 2 기출 어휘	DAY 12	PART 5&6 기출 어휘
DAY 03	PART 2 기출 어휘	DAY 13	PART 5&6 기출 어휘
DAY 04	PART 2 기출 어휘	DAY 14	PART 5&6 기출 어휘
DAY 05	PART 3 기출 어휘	DAY 15	PART 5&6 기출 어휘
DAY 06	PART 3 기출 어휘	DAY 16	PART 5&6 기출 어휘
DAY 07	PART 3 기출 어휘	DAY 17	PART 7 기출 어휘
DAY 08	PART 4 기출 어휘	DAY 18	PART 7 기출 어휘
DAY 09	PART 4 기출 어휘	DAY 19	PART 7 기출 어휘
DAY 10	PART 4 기출 어휘	DAY 20	PART 7 기출 어휘

| 실전모의고사 별책
| 온라인 실전모의고사 Hackers.co.kr
| 해설집 정답·해석·해설 책 속의 책

책의 특징과 구성

01 LC, RC, VOCA를 한 권으로 완성!

LC
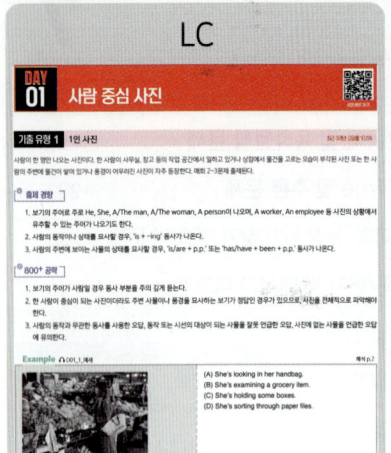

RC
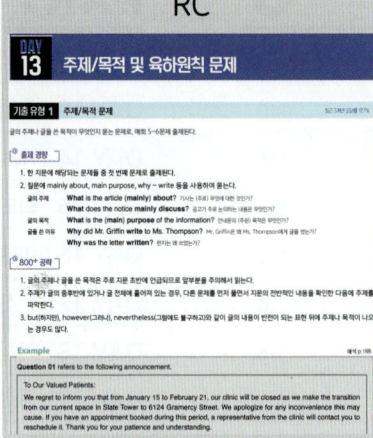

VOCA

02 토익 최신 출제 경향 완벽 반영!

출제 경향 / 800+ 공략

최신 토익 기출 유형을 철저히 분석한 출제 경향을 확인하고, 이를 바탕으로 목표 점수를 효과적으로 달성할 수 있는 공략을 익힐 수 있습니다.

기출 공식

PART 5의 핵심 문법을 담은 기출 공식을 학습합니다. 추가로, 고득점 포인트로 심화 내용을 학습하여 고난도 문제에도 대비할 수 있습니다.

빈출 표현

각 기출 유형마다 자주 등장하는 표현을 한 눈에 확인하여 시험에 나올 단어를 효율적으로 암기할 수 있습니다.

03 풍부한 문제 풀이로 실전에 철저하게 대비!

토익실전문제

매 기출 유형마다 학습한 내용을 실전 형태의 문제에 바로 적용하여 학습이 잘 이루어졌는지 점검할 수 있습니다.

HACKERS TEST

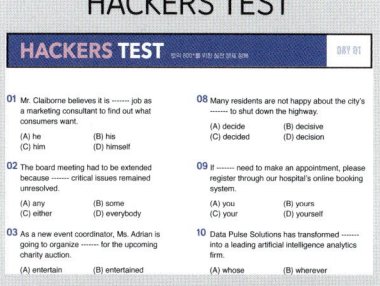

각 DAY에서 학습한 내용을 종합적으로 점검해보며 실전 토익에 필요한 실력을 다질 수 있습니다.

실전모의고사

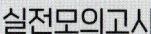

토익 경향이 완벽하게 반영된 실전 모의고사를 통해 실전 감각을 한층 더 키울 수 있습니다.

04 다양한 부가 학습자료와 상세한 해설로 확실하게 복습!

단어암기장

핵심 어휘를 정리한 단어암기장과 MP3로, 이동할 때나 자투리 시간에 효율적으로 단어를 암기할 수 있습니다.

받아쓰기 & 쉐도잉 워크북

교재에 수록된 핵심 문장을 복습할 수 있는 받아쓰기 & 쉐도잉 워크북으로, 토익 리스닝 점수를 단기에 대폭 향상할 수 있는 기본 실력을 갖출 수 있습니다.

해설집

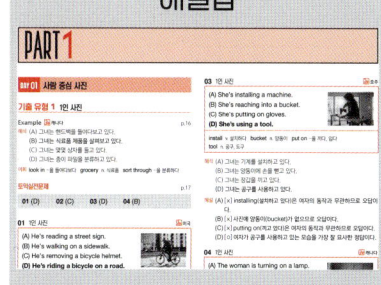

정확한 해석과 해설로 문제를 확실하게 이해할 수 있습니다. 오답에 대한 상세한 설명을 통해 틀렸던 문제의 원인을 파악하고 보완할 수 있습니다.

책의 특징과 구성 **7**

토익 소개

■ 토익이란 무엇인가?

TOEIC은 Test Of English for International Communication의 약자로 영어가 모국어가 아닌 사람들을 대상으로 언어 본래의 기능인 '커뮤니케이션' 능력에 중점을 두고 일상생활 또는 국제 업무 등에 필요한 실용영어 능력을 평가하는 시험입니다. 토익은 일상생활 및 비즈니스 현장에서 필요로 하는 내용을 평가하기 위해 개발되었으며, 다음과 같은 실용적인 주제들을 주로 다루고 있습니다.

- 협력 개발: 연구, 제품 개발
- 재무 회계: 대출, 투자, 세금, 회계, 은행 업무
- 일반 업무: 계약, 협상, 마케팅, 판매
- 기술 영역: 전기, 공업 기술, 컴퓨터, 실험실
- 사무 영역: 회의, 서류 업무
- 물품 구입: 쇼핑, 물건 주문, 대금 지불
- 식사: 레스토랑, 회식, 만찬
- 문화: 극장, 스포츠, 피크닉
- 건강: 의료 보험, 병원 진료, 치과
- 제조: 생산 조립 라인, 공장 경영
- 직원: 채용, 은퇴, 급여, 진급, 고용 기회
- 주택: 부동산, 이사, 기업 부지

■ 토익 시험의 구성

구성	내용	문항 수	시간	배점
Listening Test	PART 1 | 사진 묘사 PART 2 | 질의 응답 PART 3 | 짧은 대화 PART 4 | 짧은 담화	6문항 (1번-6번) 25문항 (7번-31번) 39문항, 13지문 (32번-70번) 30문항, 10지문 (71번-100번)	45분	495점

Reading Test	PART 5 | 단문 빈칸 채우기(문법/어휘)
	PART 6 | 장문 빈칸 채우기(문법/어휘/문장 고르기)
	PART 7 | 지문 읽고 문제 풀기(독해)
	    - 단일 지문(Single Passage)
	    - 이중 지문(Double Passage)
	    - 삼중 지문(Triple Passage)
		30문항 (101번-130번)
		16문항, 4지문 (131번-146번)
		54문항, 15지문 (147번-200번)
		- 29문항, 10지문 (147번-175번)
		- 10문항, 2세트 (176번-185번)
		- 15문항, 3세트 (186번-200번)
			75분	495점

Total	7 PARTS	200문항	120분	990점

■ 토익, 접수부터 성적 확인까지!

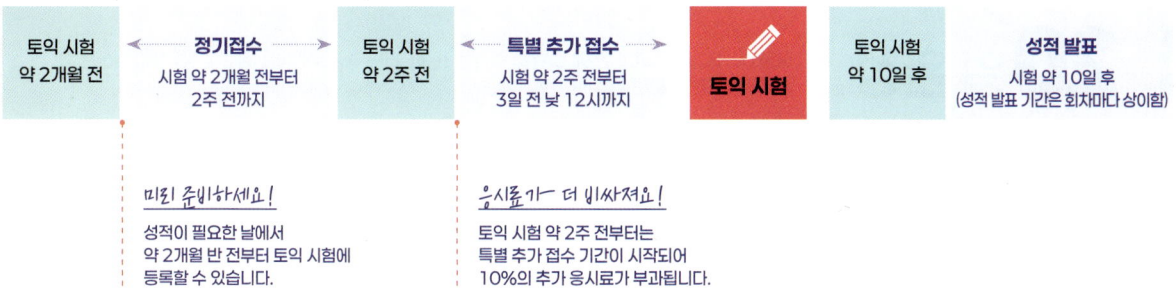

1. 토익 접수

- 인터넷 접수 기간을 TOEIC위원회 인터넷 사이트(www.toeic.co.kr) 혹은 공식 애플리케이션에서 확인하세요. 정기 토익은 시험 약 2개월 전부터 접수가 가능하며, 특별추가 접수 기간에는 정기접수 기간 응시료에서 10%가 추가된 응시료로 접수할 수 있습니다.
- 추가 토익 시험은 2월과 8월에 있으며 이외에도 연중 상시로 시행되니 인터넷으로 확인하고 접수해야 합니다.
- 접수 시, jpg 형식의 사진 파일이 필요하므로 미리 준비해야 합니다.

2. 토익 응시

- 토익 응시일 이전에 시험 장소 및 수험번호를 미리 확인합니다.
- 시험 당일 신분증이 없으면 시험에 응시할 수 없으므로, 반드시 ETS에서 요구하는 신분증(주민등록증, 운전면허증, 공무원증 등)을 지참해야 합니다. ETS에서 인정하는 신분증 종류는 TOEIC위원회 인터넷 사이트(www.toeic.co.kr)에서 확인 가능합니다.

3. 성적 확인

성적 발표일	시험일로부터 약 10일 이후 (성적 발표 기간은 회차마다 상이함)
성적 확인 방법	TOEIC위원회 인터넷 사이트(www.toeic.co.kr) 혹은 공식 애플리케이션
성적표 수령 방법	우편 수령 또는 온라인 출력 (시험 접수 시 선택) *온라인 출력은 성적 발표 즉시 발급 가능하나, 우편 수령은 약 7일가량의 발송 기간이 소요될 수 있음

800+ 정복 학습 플랜

20일 완성

매일 LC, RC, VOCA의 한 개 DAY를 학습함으로써, 더욱 확실하게 목표 점수를 취득하길 원하는 학습자에게 추천합니다.

1일차	2일차	3일차	4일차	5일차
☐ LC　DAY 01	☐ LC　DAY 02	☐ LC　DAY 03	☐ LC　DAY 04	☐ LC　DAY 05
☐ RC　DAY 01	☐ RC　DAY 02	☐ RC　DAY 03	☐ RC　DAY 04	☐ RC　DAY 05
☐ VOCA DAY 01	☐ VOCA DAY 02	☐ VOCA DAY 03	☐ VOCA DAY 04	☐ VOCA DAY 05

6일차	7일차	8일차	9일차	10일차
☐ LC　DAY 06	☐ LC　DAY 07	☐ LC　DAY 08	☐ LC　DAY 09	☐ LC　DAY 10
☐ RC　DAY 06	☐ RC　DAY 07	☐ RC　DAY 08	☐ RC　DAY 09	☐ RC　DAY 10
☐ VOCA DAY 06	☐ VOCA DAY 07	☐ VOCA DAY 08	☐ VOCA DAY 09	☐ VOCA DAY 10

11일차	12일차	13일차	14일차	15일차
☐ LC　DAY 11	☐ LC　DAY 12	☐ LC　DAY 13	☐ LC　DAY 14	☐ LC　DAY 15
☐ RC　DAY 11	☐ RC　DAY 12	☐ RC　DAY 13	☐ RC　DAY 14	☐ RC　DAY 15
☐ VOCA DAY 11	☐ VOCA DAY 12	☐ VOCA DAY 13	☐ VOCA DAY 14	☐ VOCA DAY 15

16일차	17일차	18일차	19일차	20일차
☐ LC　DAY 16	☐ LC　DAY 17	☐ LC　DAY 18	☐ LC　DAY 19	☐ LC　DAY 20
☐ RC　DAY 16	☐ RC　DAY 17	☐ RC　DAY 18	☐ RC　DAY 19	☐ RC　DAY 20
☐ VOCA DAY 16	☐ VOCA DAY 17	☐ VOCA DAY 18	☐ VOCA DAY 19	☐ VOCA DAY 20
				☐ 실전모의고사

*학습이 완료된 DAY에 체크(√) 표시를 하세요.

한 권으로 끝내는 해커스 토익 800+ LC+RC+VOCA

빠르게 10일 완성

점수가 쉽게 오르는 LC부터 집중 공략해서, 더욱 빠르게 목표 점수를 취득하길 원하는 학습자에게 추천합니다.

1일차	2일차	3일차	4일차	5일차
☐ LC DAY 01-05	☐ LC DAY 06-10	☐ LC DAY 11-15	☐ LC DAY 16-20	☐ RC DAY 01-03
☐ VOCA DAY 01-03	☐ VOCA DAY 04-06	☐ VOCA DAY 07-08	☐ VOCA DAY 09-10	☐ VOCA DAY 11-12
6일차	**7일차**	**8일차**	**9일차**	**10일차**
☐ RC DAY 04-06	☐ RC DAY 07-09	☐ RC DAY 10-14	☐ RC DAY 15-18	☐ RC DAY 19-20
☐ VOCA DAY 13-14	☐ VOCA DAY 15-16	☐ VOCA DAY 17-18	☐ VOCA DAY 19	☐ VOCA DAY 20
				☐ 실전모의고사

*학습이 완료된 DAY에 체크(√) 표시를 하세요.

실시간 토익시험 정답확인&해설강의
Hackers.co.kr

한 권으로 끝내는 해커스 토익 800+

PART 1

DAY 01 사람 중심 사진
DAY 02 사물/풍경 중심 사진

◀ 음성 바로 듣기

교재에 수록된 모든 음성을 다운로드하거나 바로 스트리밍하여 더욱 편리하게 이용해보세요.

PART 1 소개   사진 묘사 (6문제)

주어진 4개의 보기 중에서 사진을 가장 잘 묘사한 보기를 고르는 파트이다. 문제지에는 사진만 제시되며, 음성에서는 4개의 보기를 들려준다.

최신 예제 및 풀이 방법

[문제지]

1.

[음성]

Number 1.
Look at the picture marked number one in your test book.

(A) The man is opening a file cabinet.
(B) The man is wearing glasses.
(C) The man is typing on a computer.
(D) The man is leaning over a counter.

Step 1 사진 유형 파악하기
보기를 듣기 전에 사람의 유무 및 수에 따라 사진 유형을 확인하고, 사람의 동작/상태 또는 사물의 상태/위치와 관련된 표현을 미리 연상한다.

Step 2 보기 들으며 오답 소거하기
특히 동사 부분에 주의를 기울여 문장을 끝까지 듣는다. 정답이 이미 앞선 보기에서 나온 것 같더라도 반드시 모든 보기를 듣는다. 들으면서 다른 보기 내용과 혼동하지 않도록 확실한 정답에 O, 확실한 오답에 X, 헷갈리는 보기에 △를 표시하면서 오답을 소거해 나간다.

Step 3 정답 고르기
사진의 상황을 가장 잘 묘사한 보기를 정답으로 고른다. 헷갈리는 경우에는 표시해 둔 O, X △를 확인하여 답을 빠르게 고르고, 다음 문제의 음성을 들을 준비를 해야 한다.

최신 출제 경향

6개의 문제 중 사람 중심 사진이 평균 4~5문제로 출제 비율이 상당히 높으며, 사물/풍경 중심 사진은 주로 후반에 평균 1~2문제 출제된다. PART 1 보기에는 현재진행 시제(be + -ing)가 가장 많이 사용되지만, 최근에는 현재완료 수동태(have/has + been + p.p.)가 고난도 문제에 사용되는 비율이 높아지고 있다.

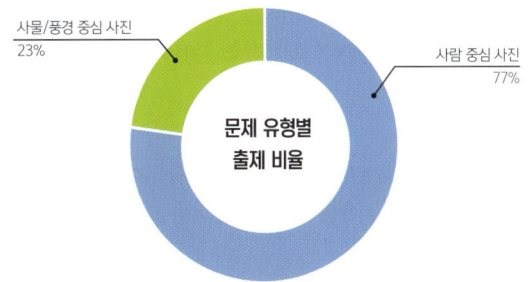

800+ 학습 전략

자주 출제되는 사진 유형과 오답 트릭을 익힌다.
PART 1에는 크게 사람 중심 사진과 사물/풍경 중심 사진이 출제되는데, 사람 중심 사진의 출제 비율이 높으므로 집중해서 학습해 둔다. 특히, 사람 중심 사진에서 사람의 동작과 무관한 동사를 사용하는 오답이 높은 비율로 등장하므로, 이와 같은 오답 트릭을 학습하면 정답을 정확하게 고를 수 있다.

사진 유형별로 자주 등장하는 표현을 암기한다.
PART 1에 사진 유형별로 자주 등장하는 표현들을 암기해 두면 더욱 쉽고 정확하게 음성을 들을 수 있다. 최근에는 사진 속 사람이 하고 있는 동작의 의도를 설명하거나 사람의 시선을 다양한 동사로 표현한 문장이 정답으로 자주 출제되고 있으므로, 관련 표현을 꼼꼼히 암기한다.

DAY 01 사람 중심 사진

기출 유형 1 1인 사진
최근 3개년 오답률 10.5%

사람이 한 명만 나오는 사진이다. 한 사람이 사무실, 창고 등의 작업 공간에서 일하고 있거나 상점에서 물건을 고르는 모습이 부각된 사진 또는 한 사람의 주변에 물건이 쌓여 있거나 풍경이 어우러진 사진이 자주 등장한다. 매회 2~3문제 출제된다.

출제 경향
1. 보기의 주어로 주로 He, She, A/The man, A/The woman, A person이 나오며, A worker, An employee 등 사진의 상황에서 유추할 수 있는 주어가 나오기도 한다.
2. 사람의 동작이나 상태를 묘사할 경우, 'is + -ing' 동사가 나온다.
3. 사람의 주변에 보이는 사물의 상태를 묘사할 경우, 'is/are + p.p.' 또는 'has/have + been + p.p.' 동사가 나온다.

800+ 공략
1. 보기의 주어가 사람일 경우 동사 부분을 주의 깊게 듣는다.
2. 한 사람이 중심이 되는 사진이더라도 주변 사물이나 풍경을 묘사하는 보기가 정답인 경우가 있으므로, 사진을 전체적으로 파악해야 한다.
3. 사람의 동작과 무관한 동사를 사용한 오답, 동작 또는 시선의 대상이 되는 사물을 잘못 언급한 오답, 사진에 없는 사물을 언급한 오답에 유의한다.

Example D01_1_예제
해석 p.2

(A)   (B)   (C)   (D)

(A) She's looking in her handbag.
(B) She's examining a grocery item.
(C) She's holding some boxes.
(D) She's sorting through paper files.

해설
(A) [x] looking in(들여다보고 있다)은 여자의 동작과 무관하므로 오답이다.
(B) [o] 식료품을 살펴보고 있는 여자의 동작을 가장 잘 묘사한 정답이다.
(C) [x] 여자가 상자(boxes)를 들고 있지 않으므로 오답이다.
(D) [x] 사진에 종이 파일(paper files)이 없으므로 오답이다.

정답 (B)

Possible Answers
Some boxes have been filled with produce.
몇몇 상자들이 농산물로 채워져 있다.
A woman is standing in front of a display stand.
여자가 진열대 앞에 서 있다.

1인 사진에 자주 나오는 필수 표현 🎧 D01_2_표현

사람의 동작 및 시선

1 He's **holding** a water bottle. 그는 물병을 들고 있다.

2 A man **is wiping** a window **with** a cloth. 한 남자가 천으로 창문을 닦고 있다.

3 A person **is emptying** soil **from** a pot. 한 사람이 화분에서 흙을 비워 내고 있다.

4 A worker **is kneeling down on** the floor. 한 작업자가 바닥에 무릎을 꿇고 있다.

5 An employee **is assembling** a display case. 한 직원이 진열장을 조립하고 있다.

6 She's **looking at** a laptop screen. 그녀는 노트북 화면을 보고 있다.

7 He's **examining** a clothing item. 그는 옷을 살펴보고 있다.

8 A man **is inspecting** an electrical device. 한 남자가 전자기기를 살펴보고 있다.

9 A woman **is browsing through** store shelves. 한 여자가 매장 선반을 훑어보고 있다.

사람의 옷차림

10 He's **adjusting** his glasses. 그는 안경을 고쳐 쓰고 있다.

11 She's **rolling up** her sleeves. 그녀는 소매를 걷어 올리고 있다.

12 A worker **is wearing** a safety vest. 한 작업자가 안전 조끼를 착용하고 있다.

주변 사물의 상태

13 A bike **is propped against** a wall. 자전거가 벽에 기대어 놓여 있다.

14 Luggage bags **have been piled on** a cart. 짐 가방들이 카트에 쌓여 있다.

토익실전문제 🎧 D01_3_실전

토익 문제 이렇게 나온다!

01

(A) (B) (C) (D)

02

(A) (B) (C) (D)

03

(A) (B) (C) (D)

04

(A) (B) (C) (D)

정답·해석·해설 p.2

기출 유형 2 2인 이상 사진

최근 3개년 오답률 10.3%

두 명 이상의 사람들이 나오는 사진이다. 사람들이 야외에서 이동하거나 대중교통을 이용하는 사진, 사무실이나 공장 등의 작업 공간에서 일하고 있는 사진, 물건을 구경하거나 식당에서 식사를 하는 사진 등이 자주 등장한다. 매회 2~3문제 출제된다.

출제 경향

1. 여러 사람을 공통적으로 묘사할 때는 보기의 주어로 They, (Some) people, The men, The women이 나온다. 여러 사람들 중 한 사람만 묘사할 때는 One of the men, One of the women, One of the people, The man, The woman이 주로 나오며, Workers, Customers, Musicians, Diners 등 사진의 상황에서 유추할 수 있는 주어가 나오기도 한다.
2. 사람의 동작이나 상태를 묘사할 경우, 'is/are + -ing' 또는 'has/have + p.p.' 동사가 나온다.
3. 사람의 주변에 보이는 사물의 상태를 묘사할 경우, 'is/are + (being) + p.p.' 또는 'has/have + been + p.p.' 동사가 나온다.

800+ 공략

1. 보기를 듣기 전에, 사진 속 사람들의 공통된 동작이나 개별 동작을 파악한다.
2. 주변 사물이나 풍경을 묘사하는 보기가 정답인 경우가 있으므로, 사람들 주위에 무엇이 있는지도 파악해야 한다.
3. 서로의 동작을 바꾸어 설명하거나, 개별 동작이 모두에게 해당하는 것처럼 묘사한 오답에 주의한다.

Example 🎧 D01_4_예제

해석 p.2

(A) (B) (C) (D)

(A) Some folders have been left on a chair.
(B) Some shelving units line the walls of a room.
(C) One of the men is standing in front of a computer monitor.
(D) One of the women is holding a piece of paper.

해설
(A) [x] 사진에 폴더(folders)가 없으므로 오답이다.
(B) [x] 사진에 선반(shelving units)이 없으므로 오답이다.
(C) [x] standing(서 있다)은 남자들의 동작과 무관하므로 오답이다.
(D) [o] 종이를 들고 있는 한 여자의 동작을 가장 잘 묘사한 정답이다.

정답 (D)

Possible Answers
People are meeting in an office space.
사람들이 사무실에서 만나고 있다.
A computer monitor has been set on a desk.
컴퓨터 모니터가 책상 위에 설치되어 있다.

2인 이상 사진에 자주 나오는 필수 표현 🎧 D01_5_표현

모임·무리

1 They're **seated side by side** on a sofa. 그들은 소파에 나란히 앉아 있다.
2 The men **are attending** a presentation. 남자들이 발표에 참석하고 있다.
3 The women **are facing each other**. 여자들이 서로 마주 보고 있다.
4 Some people **are gathered** in a meeting room. 몇몇 사람들이 회의실에 모여 있다.
5 Customers **are waiting in line** at a clothing store. 고객들이 옷가게에서 한 줄로 기다리고 있다.
6 Musicians **are performing** in a square. 음악가들이 광장에서 공연을 하고 있다.

대화·인사

7 They're **chatting** in a group. 그들은 무리를 지어 이야기를 하고 있다.
8 The women **are having a discussion**. 여자들이 토론하고 있다.

이동 동작

9 They're **strolling along** a beach. 그들은 해변을 따라 거닐고 있다.
10 One of the men **is climbing up** a ladder. 남자들 중 한 명이 사다리를 올라가고 있다.
11 The workers **are moving** a piece of furniture. 작업자들이 가구를 옮기고 있다.
12 Some people **are entering** a building. 몇몇 사람들이 건물로 들어가고 있다.

주변 사물의 상태

13 Some shop windows **are being washed**. 몇몇 상점 창문이 닦이고 있다.
14 Bicycles **are lined up along** a platform. 자전거들이 플랫폼을 따라 줄지어 있다.

토익실전문제 🎧 D01_6_실전

01

(A)　(B)　(C)　(D)

02

(A)　(B)　(C)　(D)

03

(A)　(B)　(C)　(D)

04

(A)　(B)　(C)　(D)

정답·해석·해설 p.2

HACKERS TEST

DAY 01

🎧 D01_7_테스트

01

(A) (B) (C) (D)

02

(A) (B) (C) (D)

03

(A) (B) (C) (D)

04

(A) (B) (C) (D)

05

(A) (B) (C) (D)

06

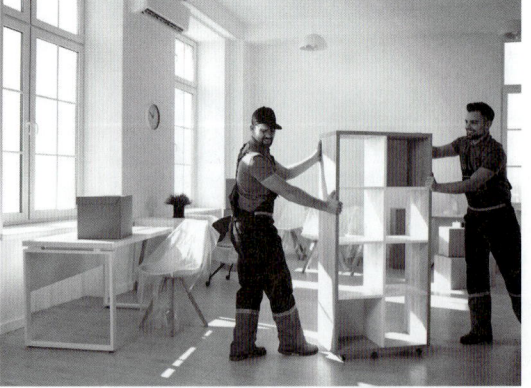

(A) (B) (C) (D)

07

(A)　　(B)　　(C)　　(D)

08

(A)　　(B)　　(C)　　(D)

09

(A)　　(B)　　(C)　　(D)

10

(A)　　(B)　　(C)　　(D)

11

(A)　　(B)　　(C)　　(D)

12

(A)　　(B)　　(C)　　(D)

DAY 02 사물/풍경 중심 사진

기출 유형 1 실내 사진

최근 3개년 오답률 16.7%

실내 공간의 사물이 중심이 되는 사진으로, 가구가 배치된 방이나 물건들이 놓인 작업 공간 또는 상점이 자주 등장한다. 매회 1~2문제 출제된다.

출제 경향

1. 집, 사무실, 식당이나 상점 등의 내부 모습이 주로 나오며, 의자나 테이블은 furniture(가구), 연필이나 메모지는 office supplies(사무용품)로 포괄하여 나타내는 표현이 나오기도 한다.
2. 사물의 상태를 묘사할 경우, 'There is/are', 'is/are + -ing', 'is/are + p.p.' 또는 'has/have + been + p.p.' 동사가 자주 나온다.
3. 사물의 위치를 묘사할 경우, 'is/are + 전치사구' 형태의 문장도 사용된다. 이때 on(~ 위에), underneath(~ 아래에), by(~ 옆에) 등의 전치사가 사용된다.

800+ 공략

1. 보기를 듣기 전에, 사진 속에 보이는 사물의 상태와 위치를 나타내는 표현을 미리 연상한다.
2. 사람이 없는 사진에서 사람을 나타내는 표현(people, worker 등)을 사용한 오답에 유의한다.
3. 사람의 동작을 묘사하는 'is/are + being + p.p.' 동사를 사용한 오답에 유의한다. 단, is/are being displayed(진열되어 있다), is/are being stored(보관되어 있다) 등의 표현은 사물의 상태를 묘사할 수 있음을 알아둔다.

Example 🎧 D02_1_예제

해석 p.5

(A) (B) (C) (D)

(A) A cushion has been placed on an armchair.
(B) A potted plant is hanging above a window.
(C) Some paintings are being removed from a wall.
(D) Some books have been laid on the floor.

해설
(A) [o] 쿠션이 안락의자 위에 놓여 있는 모습을 가장 잘 묘사한 정답이다.
(B) [x] 화분이 창문 위에 달려 있지(hanging above a window) 않으므로 오답이다.
(C) [x] 사람의 동작을 묘사하는 'are being p.p.'를 사용한 오답이다.
(D) [x] 책들이 바닥에 놓여 있지(laid on the floor) 않으므로 오답이다.

정답 (A)

Possible Answers
A picture frame is hanging on the wall. 그림 액자가 벽에 걸려 있다.
Some books are being stored on shelves.
몇몇 책들이 선반에 보관되어 있다.

실내 사진에 자주 나오는 필수 표현 🎧 D02_2_표현

사물의 상태

1. Some chairs **have been placed in a circle**. 몇몇 의자들이 원 모양으로 놓여 있다.
2. A picture **is attached to** a wall. 사진이 벽에 붙어 있다.
3. Some notices **are pinned to** a bulletin board. 공지 몇 장이 게시판에 핀으로 고정되어 있다.
4. Some items **are displayed** for sale in a shop. 몇몇 제품들이 판매를 위해 상점에 진열되어 있다.
5. Some light fixtures **have been hung from** the ceiling. 몇몇 조명 기구들이 천장에 매달려 있다.
6. The curtains **have been pulled shut**. 커튼이 닫혀 있다.
7. Some boxes **have been stacked on top of each other**. 몇몇 상자들이 차곡차곡 쌓여 있다.
8. Some papers **are scattered** on a desk. 책상에 종이들이 흩어져 있다.
9. The furniture **is reflected in** a mirror. 가구가 거울에 비치고 있다.
10. A storage closet **has been left open**. 수납장이 열려 있다.

사물의 위치

11. There are some boxes **beside** a photocopier. 복사기 옆에 상자 몇 개가 있다.
12. There is a lamp **between** the seats. 의자들 사이에 램프가 있다.
13. Some office equipment is **underneath** a desk. 몇몇 사무용 기기들이 책상 아래에 있다.
14. There is a potted plant **on the edge of** a seating area. 좌석 공간의 가장자리에 화분이 있다.
15. A trash can is located **next to** the front door. 쓰레기통이 현관 옆에 위치해 있다.
16. A small table has been put **in the middle of** a room. 작은 탁자가 방 한가운데에 놓여 있다.

토익실전문제 🎧 D02_3_실전   토익 문제 이렇게 나온다!

01

(A) (B) (C) (D)

02

(A) (B) (C) (D)

03
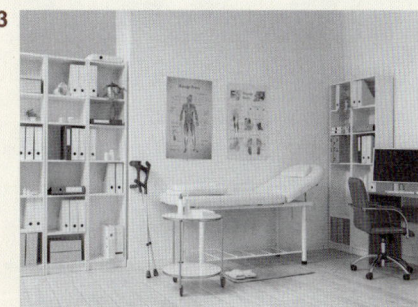
(A) (B) (C) (D)

04

(A) (B) (C) (D)

정답·해석·해설 p.6

기출 유형 2 　 야외 사진

최근 3개년 오답률 19.6%

야외 공간의 풍경이나 주변 환경이 중심이 되는 사진으로, 강가, 공원, 도로, 공사 현장 등의 사진이 자주 등장한다. 매회 1~2문제 출제된다.

출제 경향

1. 강, 공원 등의 풍경이나 공사장, 광장, 주차장 등 건물 외부의 모습이 자주 나온다.
2. 풍경과 사물의 상태를 묘사할 경우, 현재 시제 동사, 'is/are + -ing', 'is/are + p.p.', 'has/have + been + p.p.' 동사가 나온다.
3. next to(~ 옆에), near(~ 근처에), along(~을 따라서), in front of(~ 앞에) 등의 부사나 전치사가 자주 사용된다.

800+ 공략

1. 보기를 듣기 전에, 사진 속에 보이는 풍경과 사물의 상태, 위치를 나타내는 표현을 미리 연상한다.
2. 사람이 없는 사진에서 사람을 나타내는 표현(person, worker, driver 등)을 사용한 오답에 유의한다.
3. 사람의 동작을 묘사하는 'is/are + being + p.p.' 동사를 사용한 오답에 유의한다. 단, is/are being blocked(가려져 있다), is/are being cast(드리워지고 있다) 등의 표현은 사물의 상태와 풍경을 묘사할 수 있음을 알아둔다.

Example 　 🎧 D02_4_예제

해석 p.6

(A) Some umbrellas are being folded.
(B) Tablecloths are draped over the tables.
(C) Shadows are being cast on a patio.
(D) Some chairs have been arranged around a fountain.

(A)　(B)　(C)　(D)

해설
(A) [x] 사람의 동작을 묘사하는 'are being p.p.'를 사용한 오답이다.
(B) [x] 사진에 식탁보(tablecloths)가 없으므로 오답이다.
(C) [o] 안뜰에 그림자가 드리워지고 있는 모습을 가장 잘 묘사한 정답이다.
(D) [x] 사진에 분수대(fountain)가 없으므로 오답이다.

정답 (C)

Possible Answers
An outdoor seating area is unoccupied.
야외 자리의 자리가 비워져 있다.
A stone wall separates a dining area from some trees.
돌담이 식사 공간을 나무들로부터 분리하고 있다.

야외 사진에 자주 나오는 필수 표현 🎧 D02_5_표현

강·호수·해변

1. Some boats **are tied up to** poles. 몇몇 배들이 기둥에 묶여 있다.
2. Several buildings **overlook** a lake. 건물 몇 채가 호수를 내려다 보고 있다.
3. A row of umbrellas **stretches along** a beach. 일렬로 늘어선 파라솔들이 해변을 따라 펼쳐져 있다.

공원·들판·정원

4. A field **is surrounded by** a fence. 들판이 울타리로 둘러싸여 있다.
5. There are picnic tables **positioned side by side**. 피크닉 테이블들이 나란히 놓여 있다.
6. A path **is covered with** fallen branches. 길이 떨어진 나뭇가지들로 덮여 있다.
7. A gardening hose **has been hung on** a rack. 원예용 호스가 걸이에 걸려 있다.

교통수단·도로

8. Some vehicles **are parked** in front of houses. 몇몇 자동차들이 집 앞에 주차되어 있다.
9. Some cars **are stopped** at an intersection. 몇몇 자동차들이 교차로에 멈춰 있다.
10. Some lines **have been painted on** a road. 길 위에 선들이 그려져 있다.

공사 현장·공장

11. Boards **are piled on top of each other**. 판자들이 차곡차곡 쌓여 있다.
12. Some scaffolding **is erected at** a construction site. 몇몇 비계가 공사 현장에 세워져 있다.
13. Some tools **have been covered with** a tarp. 몇몇 공구들이 방수포로 덮여 있다.

토익실전문제 🎧 D02_6_실전

토익 문제 이렇게 나온다!

01

(A)　(B)　(C)　(D)

02

(A)　(B)　(C)　(D)

03

(A)　(B)　(C)　(D)

04

(A)　(B)　(C)　(D)

정답·해석·해설 p.6

HACKERS TEST

DAY 02

🎧 D02_7_테스트

01

(A)　(B)　(C)　(D)

02

(A)　(B)　(C)　(D)

03

(A)　(B)　(C)　(D)

04

(A)　(B)　(C)　(D)

05

(A)　(B)　(C)　(D)

06

(A)　(B)　(C)　(D)

07

(A)　　(B)　　(C)　　(D)

08

(A)　　(B)　　(C)　　(D)

09

(A)　　(B)　　(C)　　(D)

10

(A)　　(B)　　(C)　　(D)

11

(A)　　(B)　　(C)　　(D)

12

(A)　　(B)　　(C)　　(D)

실시간 토익시험 정답확인&해설강의
Hackers.co.kr

한 권으로 끝내는 해커스 토익 800+ LC+RC+VOCA

PART 2

DAY 03	의문사 의문문: Who, What/Which
DAY 04	의문사 의문문: Where, When
DAY 05	의문사 의문문: Why, How
DAY 06	일반 의문문 및 부정 의문문
DAY 07	선택 의문문 및 부가 의문문
DAY 08	제안/제공/요청 의문문 및 평서문

◀ 음성 바로 듣기

교재에 수록된 모든 음성을 다운로드하거나 바로 스트리밍하여 더욱 편리하게 이용해보세요.

PART 2 소개 — 질의 응답 (25문제)

주어진 질문이나 진술에 가장 적절한 응답을 고르는 파트이다. 문제지에는 질문과 보기가 제시되지 않으며, 음성에서는 질문과 3개의 보기를 들려준다.

최신 예제 및 풀이 방법

[문제지]	[음성]
7. Mark your answer on your answer sheet.	Number 7. Who is leading the sales seminar on Monday? (A) Yes, leaders should be organized. (B) I heard it's going to be Mr. Johnson. (C) Because the seminar was canceled.

Step 1 질문 유형 확인하기

질문의 첫 단어를 반드시 들어 질문 유형을 확인한다. 특히 가장 출제율이 높은 의문사 의문문은 가장 처음에 언급되는 의문사만 들어도 대부분 정답을 선택할 수 있으므로 질문 유형을 반드시 제대로 확인하고, 나중에 헷갈리지 않도록 의문사를 적어 둔다.

Step 2 보기 들으며 오답 소거하기

반드시 모든 보기를 끝까지 듣는다. 들으면서 다른 보기 내용과 혼동하지 않도록 확실한 정답에 O, 확실한 오답에 X, 헷갈리는 보기에 △를 표시하면서 오답을 소거해 나간다.

Step 3 정답 고르기

질문에 대한 가장 적절한 응답을 정답으로 고른다. 헷갈리는 경우에는 표시해 둔 O, X △를 확인하여 답을 빠르게 고르고, 다음 문제의 음성을 들을 준비를 해야 한다.

최신 출제 경향

25개의 문제 중 의문사 의문문이 평균 11문제로, 비교적 쉽게 풀이할 수 있었던 의문사 의문문의 출제 비중이 점차 감소하는 추세이다. 최근에는 전형적인 응답 패턴이 없는 평서문의 출제 비율이 높아졌으며, 정답으로 간접 응답이 많이 사용되고 있어 체감 난이도가 많이 올라갔다.

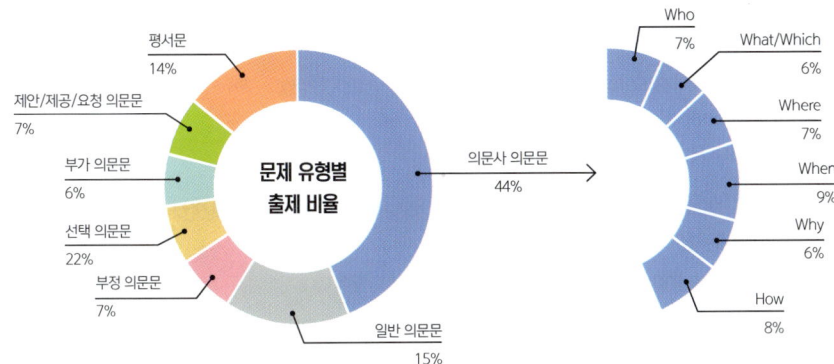

800+ 학습 전략

🔍 각 질문 유형의 전형적인 정답을 익힌다.
PART 2에 출제되는 다양한 질문 유형에는 각 질문별 전형적인 정답이 있으며, 이를 익혀 두면 정답률을 높일 수 있다. 예를 들어, who 의문문에는 사람 이름 외에 직위·직책이나 부서명도 정답으로 자주 출제되는 것을 알아 두면 실전 시험에서 문제를 더욱 정확하게 풀 수 있다.

🔍 헷갈리는 오답에 유의한다.
PART 2에는 발음이 유사하거나 의미가 다양한 단어를 사용한 오답, 질문에 쓰인 단어를 통해 연상할 수 있는 단어를 사용한 오답, 의문사 의문문에 Yes/No로 대답한 오답이 자주 등장하므로, 정답과 헷갈리지 않도록 유의한다.

🔍 간접 응답의 예시를 알아 둔다.
우회적인 응답, 모른다는 응답, 되묻는 응답, 제3자의 결정이라는 응답과 같은 간접 응답이 최근에 정답으로 점점 더 많이 사용되고 있는 추세이므로, 이들의 예시를 학습해 두면 더 많은 문제를 맞힐 수 있다.

DAY 03 의문사 의문문: Who, What·Which

기출 유형 1 Who 의문문
최근 3개년 오답률 12.9%

Who 의문문은 특정 업무의 담당자나 행위의 주체를 묻는 의문문으로, 매회 2~3문제 출제된다.

출제 경향 및 800+ 공략 D03_1_예문

1. 사람 이름, 직위·직책, 부서명, 대명사를 사용한 응답이 정답으로 주로 출제된다. 정답에 take care of(처리하다, 책임지다), manage(관리하다), handle(처리하다) 등 업무를 담당하는 것과 관련된 표현이 자주 나온다는 점을 알아 둔다.

   Q. **Who** approved the revised budget for the project? 프로젝트의 수정된 예산을 누가 승인했나요?
   A. **Ms. Lopez** did. Ms. Lopez가 했어요. [사람 이름]
   A. **The financial director** took care of that. 재무 책임자가 그것을 처리했어요. [직위·직책]

   Q. **Who** should I talk to about the software update? 소프트웨어 업데이트에 대해 누구에게 이야기해야 하나요?
   A. **The IT department** will handle that. IT 부서에서 그것을 다룰 거예요. [부서명]
   A. **I** can help you with that. 제가 도와드릴 수 있어요. [대명사]

2. '모른다' 또는 '이미 완료되었다'라는 의미로 간접적으로 답변하는 응답도 정답으로 자주 출제된다. 이때 I'm not ~ 또는 No one을 사용하기도 한다는 점을 알아 둔다.

   Q. **Who**'s supposed to review the contract? 누가 계약서를 검토하기로 되어 있나요?
   A. **No one** in my department. 제 부서에서는 아무도 안 해요.
   A. It has **already been signed**. 그것은 이미 체결됐어요.

3. 사물의 소유자를 묻는 질문에 해당 사물이 있는 장소로 응답하기도 한다.

   Q. **Who** has some spare batteries? 누가 여분의 배터리를 갖고 있나요?
   A. Check **the cabinet** next to the printer. 프린터 옆에 있는 수납장을 확인해 보세요.

Example D03_2_예제
해석 p.10

(A)   (B)   (C)

Who is in charge of ordering the vehicle parts for the assembly plant?
(A) Jonas manages that.
(B) One that's fuel efficient.
(C) To finish the assembly.

해설
(A) [o] Jonas가 그것을 관리한다며, 누가 자동차 부품 주문을 담당하는지 언급했으므로 정답이다.
(B) [x] vehicle(차량)에서 연상할 수 있는 fuel efficient(연료 효율이 좋은)를 사용하여 혼동을 준 오답이다.
(C) [x] 질문의 assembly를 반복 사용하여 혼동을 준 오답이다.

정답 (A)

Possible Answers
I'm not sure about that. 저는 그것에 대해서 잘 몰라요.
We should ask the facility manager. 시설 관리자에게 물어봐야 돼요.

토익실전문제 D03_3_실전
토익 문제 이렇게 나온다!

01 (A) (B) (C)   02 (A) (B) (C)   03 (A) (B) (C)   04 (A) (B) (C)

정답·해석·해설 p.10

기출 유형 2   What·Which 의문문

최근 3개년 오답률 21.2%

What 의문문은 시간, 비용, 종류, 의견 등 다양한 정보를 묻는 의문문이며, Which 의문문은 다수 중 하나를 선택하게 하는 의문문이다. 매회 1~2문제 출제된다.

출제 경향 및 800+ 공략 🎧 D03_4_예문

1. What 의문문은 뒤에 오는 명사 또는 동사에 따라 시간, 비용, 종류, 의견 등을 묻는다. What 뒤의 명사 또는 동사를 반드시 듣고 무엇에 대한 정보를 묻고 있는지 파악해야 한다.

   Q. **What time** do we have to arrive for the seminar? 우리가 세미나에 몇 시까지 도착해야 하나요? [시간]
   A. At **10 A.M.** 오전 10시요.

   Q. **What** is the **price** of the ticket? 티켓 가격이 얼마인가요? [비용]
   A. It's **20 dollars.** 20달러예요.

   Q. **What kind of beverages** should we prepare for the meeting? 회의를 위해 어떤 종류의 음료를 준비해야 하나요? [종류]
   A. **Coffee and tea** are usually a good choice. 커피와 차가 보통 좋은 선택이에요.

   Q. **What** do you **think of** the new vacation policy? 새로운 휴가 정책에 대해 어떻게 생각하시나요? [의견]
   A. It seems **reasonable.** 합리적인 것 같아요.

   Q. **What**'s the **process** for submitting my expense report? 제 경비 보고서를 제출하기 위한 절차가 무엇인가요? [특정 정보]
   A. You **can e-mail it to** Jenna in the finance department. 재무 부서의 Jenna에게 이메일을 보내시면 됩니다.

2. Which 의문문은 뒤에 오는 명사를 잘 들어야 한다. the one, both, either를 사용한 응답이 정답으로 자주 출제된다.

   Q. **Which** of these **hotels** do you recommend? 이 호텔들 중 어느 것을 추천하시나요? [선택]
   A. **The one** near the train station. 기차역에서 가까이 있는 것이요. [둘 중 하나 선택]
   A. **Both** have great reviews. 둘 다 후기가 좋아요. [둘 다 선택]
   A. **Either** would be suitable. 어느 쪽이든 적합한 것 같아요. [둘 중 하나 선택]

Example 🎧 D03_5_예제

해석 p.10

(A) (B) (C)	What is the topic of the upcoming workshop? (A) No, in Room 102. (B) That's my favorite shop. (C) Management skills.
해설 (A) [x] 의문사 의문문에는 No로 응답할 수 없으므로 오답이다. (B) [x] workshop – shop의 유사 발음 어휘를 사용하여 혼동을 준 오답이다. (C) [o] 경영 기술이라며 워크숍의 주제를 언급했으므로 정답이다.	**정답** (C) **Possible Answers** Didn't Ivan tell you about that? Ivan이 그것에 대해 당신에게 말하지 않았나요? I won't attend it this time. 저는 이번에 참석하지 않을 거예요.

토익실전문제 🎧 D03_6_실전

토익 문제 이렇게 나온다!

01 (A) (B) (C)   **02** (A) (B) (C)   **03** (A) (B) (C)   **04** (A) (B) (C)

정답·해석·해설 p.10

HACKERS TEST

DAY 03

토익 800+를 위한 실전 문제 정복

🎧 D03_7_테스트

01 Mark your answer on the answer sheet. (A) (B) (C)

02 Mark your answer on the answer sheet. (A) (B) (C)

03 Mark your answer on the answer sheet. (A) (B) (C)

04 Mark your answer on the answer sheet. (A) (B) (C)

05 Mark your answer on the answer sheet. (A) (B) (C)

06 Mark your answer on the answer sheet. (A) (B) (C)

07 Mark your answer on the answer sheet. (A) (B) (C)

08 Mark your answer on the answer sheet. (A) (B) (C)

09 Mark your answer on the answer sheet. (A) (B) (C)

10 Mark your answer on the answer sheet. (A) (B) (C)

11 Mark your answer on the answer sheet. (A) (B) (C)

12 Mark your answer on the answer sheet. (A) (B) (C)

13 Mark your answer on the answer sheet. (A) (B) (C)

14 Mark your answer on the answer sheet. (A) (B) (C)

15 Mark your answer on the answer sheet.   (A)   (B)   (C)

16 Mark your answer on the answer sheet.   (A)   (B)   (C)

17 Mark your answer on the answer sheet.   (A)   (B)   (C)

18 Mark your answer on the answer sheet.   (A)   (B)   (C)

19 Mark your answer on the answer sheet.   (A)   (B)   (C)

20 Mark your answer on the answer sheet.   (A)   (B)   (C)

21 Mark your answer on the answer sheet.   (A)   (B)   (C)

22 Mark your answer on the answer sheet.   (A)   (B)   (C)

23 Mark your answer on the answer sheet.   (A)   (B)   (C)

24 Mark your answer on the answer sheet.   (A)   (B)   (C)

25 Mark your answer on the answer sheet.   (A)   (B)   (C)

26 Mark your answer on the answer sheet.   (A)   (B)   (C)

27 Mark your answer on the answer sheet.   (A)   (B)   (C)

28 Mark your answer on the answer sheet.   (A)   (B)   (C)

정답·해석·해설 p.11

DAY 04 의문사 의문문: Where, When

기출 유형 1 Where 의문문

최근 3개년 오답률 15.3%

Where 의문문은 장소, 위치, 방향, 출처에 대해 묻는 의문문으로, 매회 1~2문제 출제된다.

출제 경향 및 800+ 공략 🎧 D04_1_예문

1. 장소, 위치, 방향, 출처를 나타내는 전치사구나 부사, 장소를 나타내는 표현 등을 사용한 응답이 정답으로 출제되며, 간접 응답도 정답으로 자주 출제된다.

   Q. **Where** is the product launch being held? 제품 출시 행사는 어디에서 열리나요?
   A. **At the Grand Hotel downtown.** 시내에 있는 그랜드 호텔에서요. [장소/위치]

   Q. **Where** is the nearest bus stop? 가장 가까운 버스 정류장은 어디인가요?
   A. Turn **right** at the corner. 모퉁이에서 오른쪽으로 도세요. [방향]

   Q. **Where** did you borrow this book from? 이 책을 어디에서 빌렸나요?
   A. **From the public library.** 공립 도서관에서요. [출처]

   Q. **Where** do we keep the sample products? 우리가 샘플 제품들을 어디에 보관하죠?
   A. They were all distributed already. 이미 그것들은 모두 배포되었어요. [간접 응답]

   Q. **Where** should we take the clients for lunch? 우리가 점심 식사를 위해 고객들을 어디로 데려가야 할까요?
   A. I heard it will be a group of 10. 10명으로 구성된 그룹이라고 들었어요. [간접 응답]

2. 물건이 어디에 있는지 묻는 질문에 그 물건을 가지고 있거나 위치를 알고 있는 사람으로 응답하기도 한다.

   Q. **Where** can I pick up the printed flyers? 인쇄된 전단지를 어디에서 받을 수 있나요?
   A. **Michael** already collected them. Michael이 이미 그것들을 가져갔어요. [사람]

3. 질문에서 'Where + be동사/조동사' 뒤에 이어지는 명사와 동사를 반드시 들어야 한다. 특히 질문이 길어질 경우 뒷부분을 정확히 파악해야 정답을 고를 수 있다.

Example 🎧 D04_2_예제

해석 p.16

(A)   (B)   (C)

Where can I buy a new toaster for my kitchen?
(A) Try Mina's Appliances.
(B) A new cookbook.
(C) I need some flour.

해설
(A) [o] Mina's 가전제품점에 가보라고 장소를 언급했으므로 정답이다.
(B) [x] 질문의 kitchen(주방)에서 연상할 수 있는 cookbook(요리책)을 사용하여 혼동을 준 오답이다.
(C) [x] 토스터를 어디에서 살 수 있을지를 물었는데, 이와 관련이 없는 밀가루가 필요하다고 응답했으므로 오답이다.

정답 (A)

Possible Answers
Didn't you buy one a year ago?
1년 전에 한 개 사지 않으셨나요?
I'll text you a link.
제가 링크를 문자로 보낼게요.

토익실전문제 🎧 D04_3_실전

토익 문제 이렇게 나온다!

01 (A) (B) (C)   02 (A) (B) (C)   03 (A) (B) (C)   04 (A) (B) (C)

정답·해석·해설 p.16

기출 유형 2 | When 의문문

최근 3개년 오답률 11.8%

When 의문문은 어떤 일이나 행동이 일어나는 시점을 묻는 의문문으로, 매회 2~3문제 출제된다.

출제 경향 및 800+ 공략 🎧 D04_4_예문

1. 시점을 나타내는 전치사구, 접속사, 부사 등을 사용한 응답이 정답으로 출제되며, 간접 응답도 자주 출제된다.

   Q. **When** is the board meeting rescheduled for? 이사회 회의가 언제로 다시 일정이 잡혔나요?
   A. **March 15**. 3월 15일이요. [특정 시점]
   A. **Next Monday**. 다음 주 월요일이요. [특정 시점]

   Q. **When** can you provide the details for the upcoming workshop? 다가오는 워크숍에 대한 세부 정보를 언제 알려주실 수 있나요?
   A. **Probably by** the end of this week. 아마 이번 주 말쯤에요. [불확실한 시점]
   A. **Once** the venue is confirmed. 장소가 확정되면요. [불확실한 시점]

   Q. **When** does the art exhibition open? 그 미술 전시는 언제 시작되나요?
   A. **It is listed on the Web site.** 웹사이트에 나와 있어요. [간접 응답]

   Q. **When** will the company retreat be held? 회사 야유회는 언제 열릴 것인가요?
   A. **Management is still deciding.** 경영진은 아직 결정하고 있어요. [간접 응답]

2. When 의문문의 정답에 시간/날짜를 나타내는 숫자 표현이 사용된다는 특징을 이용하여, 개수/장소 등에 숫자를 사용하여 혼동을 준 오답에 유의한다.

   Q. **When** is the shipment supposed to arrive? 수송품이 언제 도착하기로 되어 있나요?
   A. **Four containers.** 컨테이너 4개요. [개수로 답한 오답]

3. 질문이 영국식 또는 호주식 발음으로 출제될 경우 Where와 When의 발음이 비슷하여 의미를 혼동할 수 있으므로 충분히 연습을 해두어야 한다.

   Q. **When** can you meet with me to discuss the budget? 예산을 논의하기 위해 저와 언제 만나실 수 있나요?
   A. **135 Bedford Street.** Bedford가 135번지요. [When을 Where로 혼동했을 때 선택할 수 있는 오답]

Example 🎧 DAY 04_5_예제

해석 p.16

(A) (B) (C)

When is the concert starting tonight?
(A) On Whitehead Avenue.
(B) At seven o'clock.
(C) About 20,000 people.

정답 (B)

해설
(A) [x] 콘서트가 시작하는 시점을 물었는데, 장소로 응답했으므로 오답이다.
(B) [o] seven o'clock(7시)이라는 특정 시점을 언급했으므로 정답이다.
(C) [x] 질문의 concert(콘서트)에서 연상할 수 있는 관객 수와 관련된 20,000 people(2만 명의 사람들)을 사용하여 혼동을 준 오답이다.

Possible Answers
Let me check the ticket. 제가 티켓을 확인해 볼게요.
Didn't you look on the Web site? 당신은 웹사이트를 확인하지 않았나요?

토익실전문제 🎧 D04_6_실전

토익 문제 이렇게 나온다!

01 (A) (B) (C) 02 (A) (B) (C) 03 (A) (B) (C) 04 (A) (B) (C)

정답·해석·해설 p.16

HACKERS TEST
토익 800+를 위한 실전 문제 정복   DAY 04

🎧 D04_7_테스트

01 Mark your answer on the answer sheet.   (A)   (B)   (C)

02 Mark your answer on the answer sheet.   (A)   (B)   (C)

03 Mark your answer on the answer sheet.   (A)   (B)   (C)

04 Mark your answer on the answer sheet.   (A)   (B)   (C)

05 Mark your answer on the answer sheet.   (A)   (B)   (C)

06 Mark your answer on the answer sheet.   (A)   (B)   (C)

07 Mark your answer on the answer sheet.   (A)   (B)   (C)

08 Mark your answer on the answer sheet.   (A)   (B)   (C)

09 Mark your answer on the answer sheet.   (A)   (B)   (C)

10 Mark your answer on the answer sheet.   (A)   (B)   (C)

11 Mark your answer on the answer sheet.   (A)   (B)   (C)

12 Mark your answer on the answer sheet.   (A)   (B)   (C)

13 Mark your answer on the answer sheet.   (A)   (B)   (C)

14 Mark your answer on the answer sheet.   (A)   (B)   (C)

15 Mark your answer on the answer sheet.   (A)   (B)   (C)

16 Mark your answer on the answer sheet.   (A)   (B)   (C)

17 Mark your answer on the answer sheet.   (A)   (B)   (C)

18 Mark your answer on the answer sheet.   (A)   (B)   (C)

19 Mark your answer on the answer sheet.   (A)   (B)   (C)

20 Mark your answer on the answer sheet.   (A)   (B)   (C)

21 Mark your answer on the answer sheet.   (A)   (B)   (C)

22 Mark your answer on the answer sheet.   (A)   (B)   (C)

23 Mark your answer on the answer sheet.   (A)   (B)   (C)

24 Mark your answer on the answer sheet.   (A)   (B)   (C)

25 Mark your answer on the answer sheet.   (A)   (B)   (C)

26 Mark your answer on the answer sheet.   (A)   (B)   (C)

27 Mark your answer on the answer sheet.   (A)   (B)   (C)

28 Mark your answer on the answer sheet.   (A)   (B)   (C)

정답·해석·해설 p.17

DAY 05 의문사 의문문: Why, How

기출 유형 1 Why 의문문

최근 3개년 오답률 10.9%

Why 의문문은 특정 행동 및 사건에 관련된 이유를 묻는 의문문으로, 매회 1~2문제 출제된다.

출제 경향 및 800+ 공략 🎧 D05_1_예문

1. Because (of) 또는 For를 사용한 응답이 거의 매회 정답으로 출제된다. 질문에서 Why와 함께 주어, 동사를 반드시 듣고 무엇에 대한 이유를 묻고 있는지 정확히 파악하면 쉽게 풀 수 있다. 간접 응답은 다른 의문문에 비해 정답으로 거의 출제되지 않는다.

   Q. **Why** are you taking the day off? 왜 오늘 휴가를 내시나요?
   A. **Because** I don't feel well. 몸이 좋지 않기 때문이에요.
   A. **For** a medical checkup. 건강 검진 때문이에요.

   Q. **Why** are the store hours being changed? 왜 매장 영업 시간이 변경될 건가요?
   A. Let me ask our manager. 저희의 관리자에게 물어볼게요. [간접 응답]

2. Because나 For 없이 이유를 설명하는 응답도 정답으로 자주 출제된다.

   Q. **Why** can't you participate in the charity event? 당신은 왜 자선 행사에 참여하실 수 없나요?
   A. I already have other plans. 저는 이미 다른 계획이 있어요.
   A. The quarterly report is due on the same day. 분기 보고서가 같은 날 마감이에요.

3. Because와 For로 시작하는 보기가 한 문제에 모두 나오는 경우도 있으므로 Because와 For만 듣고 정답을 고르지 않도록 주의한다.

Example 🎧 D05_2_예제

해석 p.22

(A) (B) (C)

Why did you move to New York City?
(A) Because I found a job here.
(B) Yes, a few weeks ago.
(C) Let's move to a quieter location.

해설
(A) [o] 여기에서 일자리를 찾았기 때문이라는 말로 뉴욕시로 이사한 이유를 언급했으므로 정답이다.
(B) [x] 의문사 의문문에는 Yes로 응답할 수 없으므로 오답이다.
(C) [x] 질문의 move를 반복 사용하여 혼동을 준 오답이다.

정답 (A)

Possible Answers
I needed a change. 저는 변화가 필요했어요.
For my new position. 제 새로운 직책을 위해서요.

토익실전문제 🎧 D05_3_실전

토익 문제 이렇게 나온다!

01 (A) (B) (C)   02 (A) (B) (C)   03 (A) (B) (C)   04 (A) (B) (C)

정답·해석·해설 p.22

기출 유형 2 How 의문문

최근 3개년 오답률 17%

How 의문문은 방법, 의견, 기간, 수량 등을 묻는 의문문으로, 매회 2~3문제 출제된다.

출제 경향 및 800+ 공략   🎧 D05_4_예문

1. **How로 시작하는 의문문은 방법, 의견, 상태를 묻는다.**
   Q. **How** can I reserve a rental car? 렌터카를 어떻게 예약할 수 있나요? [방법]
   A. Use the rental company's mobile app. 렌트 업체의 모바일 앱을 사용하세요.
   Q. **How** was the conference in Amsterdam? 암스테르담에서의 학회는 어땠나요? [의견]
   A. Very informative. 매우 유익했어요.
   Q. **How** is the traffic on the highway? 고속도로의 교통 상황이 어떤가요? [상태]
   A. It's pretty heavy this morning. 오늘 아침에는 꽤 혼잡해요.

2. **'How do you like ~?', 'How do you feel ~?', 'How did ~ go?'와 같은 표현을 사용하여 의견이나 상태를 물을 수 있다.**
   Q. **How do you like** the cafeteria food? 구내식당 음식은 어떤가요? [의견]
   A. It's better than I expected. 예상했던 것보다 더 좋네요.

3. **How 뒤에 형용사나 부사가 붙어 기간, 빈도, 수량, 가격을 물을 수 있다.**
   Q. **How long** are you going on vacation? 당신은 휴가를 얼마나 오래 가실 건가요? [기간]
   A. For two weeks. 2주 동안이요.
   Q. **How often** does the airport shuttle leave? 공항 셔틀버스는 얼마나 자주 떠나나요? [빈도]
   A. Every 20 minutes. 20분마다요.
   Q. **How many** people signed up for the seminar? 세미나에 몇 명의 사람들이 신청했나요? [수량]
   A. There are 14 altogether. 총 14명이요.
   Q. **How much** will the repairs cost? 수리는 얼마의 비용이 들까요? [가격]
   A. They'll be around 300 dollars. 약 300달러일 거예요.

Example 🎧 D05_5_예제

해석 p.22

(A) (B) (C)	How did you know about this hotel? (A) December 15 and 16. (B) I saw an ad on social media. (C) At the pool.
해설 (A) [x] 이 호텔에 대해 어떻게 알았는지를 물었는데, 날짜로 응답했으므로 오답이다. (B) [o] 소셜 미디어에서 광고를 봤다며 이 호텔을 알게 된 경로를 언급했으므로 정답이다. (C) [x] 질문의 hotel(호텔)과 관련 있는 pool(수영장)을 사용하여 혼동을 준 오답이다.	**정답** (B) **Possible Answers** My friend stayed here last summer. 제 친구가 지난 여름에 여기에서 묵었어요. The last conference was held near there. 지난번 학회가 그곳 근처에서 열렸어요.

토익실전문제 🎧 D05_6_실전

토익 문제 이렇게 나온다!

01 (A) (B) (C)   02 (A) (B) (C)   03 (A) (B) (C)   04 (A) (B) (C)

정답·해석·해설 p.23

HACKERS TEST

DAY 05

토익 800+를 위한 실전 문제 정복

🎧 D05_7_테스트

01 Mark your answer on the answer sheet. (A) (B) (C)

02 Mark your answer on the answer sheet. (A) (B) (C)

03 Mark your answer on the answer sheet. (A) (B) (C)

04 Mark your answer on the answer sheet. (A) (B) (C)

05 Mark your answer on the answer sheet. (A) (B) (C)

06 Mark your answer on the answer sheet. (A) (B) (C)

07 Mark your answer on the answer sheet. (A) (B) (C)

08 Mark your answer on the answer sheet. (A) (B) (C)

09 Mark your answer on the answer sheet. (A) (B) (C)

10 Mark your answer on the answer sheet. (A) (B) (C)

11 Mark your answer on the answer sheet. (A) (B) (C)

12 Mark your answer on the answer sheet. (A) (B) (C)

13 Mark your answer on the answer sheet. (A) (B) (C)

14 Mark your answer on the answer sheet. (A) (B) (C)

15 Mark your answer on the answer sheet.   (A)   (B)   (C)

16 Mark your answer on the answer sheet.   (A)   (B)   (C)

17 Mark your answer on the answer sheet.   (A)   (B)   (C)

18 Mark your answer on the answer sheet.   (A)   (B)   (C)

19 Mark your answer on the answer sheet.   (A)   (B)   (C)

20 Mark your answer on the answer sheet.   (A)   (B)   (C)

21 Mark your answer on the answer sheet.   (A)   (B)   (C)

22 Mark your answer on the answer sheet.   (A)   (B)   (C)

23 Mark your answer on the answer sheet.   (A)   (B)   (C)

24 Mark your answer on the answer sheet.   (A)   (B)   (C)

25 Mark your answer on the answer sheet.   (A)   (B)   (C)

26 Mark your answer on the answer sheet.   (A)   (B)   (C)

27 Mark your answer on the answer sheet.   (A)   (B)   (C)

28 Mark your answer on the answer sheet.   (A)   (B)   (C)

정답·해석·해설 p.23

DAY 06 일반 의문문 및 부정 의문문

기출 유형 1 일반 의문문
최근 3개년 오답률 16.6%

Do, Have, Can/Will/Should 등의 조동사나 Is, Was, Are, Were 등의 Be 동사로 시작하는 의문문으로, 특정 사실을 확인하거나 의견을 묻는 의문문이다. 매회 3~4문제 출제된다.

출제 경향 및 800+ 공략 ♫ D06_1_예문

1. Yes/No를 사용한 후 부연 설명을 추가한 응답이 주로 정답으로 출제된다. Of course(물론이죠), Sure(그럼요), Sorry(죄송해요), I don't think so(저는 그렇게 생각하지 않아요) 등 Yes/No를 대체하는 표현도 정답으로 자주 출제됨을 기억한다.

   Q. **Have** you finished designing the posters? 포스터를 디자인하는 것을 끝내셨나요?
   A. **No**. But I'm almost finished. 아뇨, 하지만 저는 거의 끝났어요. [No를 사용한 응답]

   Q. **Is** there enough time to go to the bank? 은행에 갈 충분한 시간이 있나요?
   A. **Sure**, we can go now. 그럼요, 우리는 지금 가면 돼요. [Sure를 사용하여 Yes의 의미를 전달한 응답]

2. Yes/No를 생략한 응답도 출제된다.

   Q. **Do** you want some coffee while you wait? 기다리시는 동안 커피를 드시겠어요?
   A. That would be nice. 그거 좋겠네요. [Yes를 생략한 응답]

3. 질문의 중간에 의문사가 포함된 간접의문문이 출제되기도 하며, 이때 해당 의문사에 대한 응답이 정답으로 출제된다.

   Q. Can you tell me **where** the office supplies are stored? 사무용품이 어디에 보관되어 있는지 알려주실 수 있나요?
   A. In the storage room on the second floor. 2층 창고에요.

4. Be 동사 의문문의 경우, be going to와 be -ing는 미래 시제를 나타낸다는 것을 알아 둔다.

   Q. **Are you going to** attend the workshop tomorrow? 내일 워크숍에 참석하실 건가요?
   A. Yes, I'm planning to go. 네, 저는 갈 계획이에요.

Example ♫ D06_2_예제
해석 p.28

(A)　(B)　(C)	Do you want to order some dessert? (A) It is out of order again. (B) No, I'm too full. (C) At Table 11.
해설 (A) [x] 질문의 order를 반복 사용하여 혼동을 준 오답이다. (B) [o] No로 디저트를 주문하지 않겠다는 것을 전달한 후, 배가 부르다고 부연 설명을 했으므로 정답이다. (C) [x] 디저트를 주문하겠냐고 물었는데, 11번 테이블이라며 관련이 없는 내용으로 응답했으므로 오답이다.	**정답** (B) **Possible Answers** Of course. I'll have ice cream. 물론이죠. 저는 아이스크림을 먹을게요. Let me look at the menu. 메뉴를 볼게요.

토익실전문제 ♫ D06_3_실전
토익 문제 이렇게 나온다!

01 (A) (B) (C)　　02 (A) (B) (C)　　03 (A) (B) (C)　　04 (A) (B) (C)

정답·해석·해설 p.28

기출 유형 2 부정 의문문

최근 3개년 오답률 22.8%

'조동사/Be 동사 + not'으로 시작하는 의문문으로, 자신이 알고 있는 사실의 진위 여부를 확인하거나 자신의 의견에 동의를 구하는 의문문이다. 매회 1~2문제 출제된다.

출제 경향 및 800+ 공략   D06_4_예문

1. 확인하고자 하는 사실이 맞는 말이거나 의견에 동의하면 Yes로, 사실을 부인하거나 의견에 반대하면 No로 응답한 후 부연 설명을 덧붙인 응답이 정답으로 출제된다. Yes/No를 생략한 응답도 출제된다.

   Q. **Doesn't** this bus go to Mayflower Park? 이 버스는 Mayflower 공원에 가지 않나요?
   A. **Yes**. It's the final stop. 네. 그곳이 종점이에요. [Yes를 사용한 응답]
   A. **No**. You need to take the blue line bus. 아뇨. 파란색 노선 버스를 타셔야 해요. [No를 사용한 응답]

   Q. **Don't** you have the card key? 당신은 카드키를 가지고 있지 않나요?
   A. It's in my bag. 그것은 제 가방 안에 있어요. [Yes를 생략한 응답]

2. Shouldn't we로 시작하는 부정 의문문은 제안을 나타내므로 이에 대해 수락하거나 거절하는 내용이 정답으로 출제된다.

   Q. **Shouldn't we** ask for help with this project? 이 프로젝트에 대해 도움을 요청해야 하지 않을까요?
   A. Yes, that's a good idea. 네, 좋은 생각이에요. [제안 수락]
   A. I believe we can handle it on our own. 우리가 스스로 처리할 수 있을 거라고 믿어요. [제안 거절]

3. 부정 의문문은 간접 응답이 정답으로 출제되면 난도가 높아지므로 질문과 보기를 끝까지 듣고 그 의도를 정확히 파악해야 한다.

   Q. **Aren't we** meeting this afternoon to discuss the marketing plans? 우리 오늘 오후에 마케팅 계획을 논의하기 위해 만나는 거 아닌가요?
   A. There's a leadership seminar from 1 P.M. 오후 1시부터 리더십 세미나가 있어요. [간접 응답]
   A. Didn't you get the message from the manager? 매니저로부터 메시지를 못 받으셨나요? [간접 응답]

Example D06_5_예제

해석 p.29

(A)   (B)   (C)

Aren't you going to give a presentation today?
(A) It was very interesting.
(B) Yes. Right after lunch.
(C) I got you a present.

정답 (B)

Possible Answers
There might be some last-minute adjustments.
막바지 조정이 좀 있을 수도 있어요.
The meeting has been canceled.
회의는 취소됐어요.

해설
(A) [x] 질문의 presentation(발표)에서 연상할 수 있는 interesting(흥미로운)을 사용하여 혼동을 준 오답이다.
(B) [o] Yes로 오늘 발표를 한다는 것을 전달한 후, 점심 식사 직후에 그것을 할 것이라는 부연 설명을 했으므로 정답이다.
(C) [x] presentation – present의 유사 발음 어휘를 사용하여 혼동을 준 오답이다.

토익실전문제   D06_6_실전

토익 문제 이렇게 나온다!

01 (A) (B) (C)   **02** (A) (B) (C)   **03** (A) (B) (C)   **04** (A) (B) (C)

정답·해석·해설 p.29

HACKERS TEST

DAY 06

🎧 D06_7_테스트

01 Mark your answer on the answer sheet. (A) (B) (C)

02 Mark your answer on the answer sheet. (A) (B) (C)

03 Mark your answer on the answer sheet. (A) (B) (C)

04 Mark your answer on the answer sheet. (A) (B) (C)

05 Mark your answer on the answer sheet. (A) (B) (C)

06 Mark your answer on the answer sheet. (A) (B) (C)

07 Mark your answer on the answer sheet. (A) (B) (C)

08 Mark your answer on the answer sheet. (A) (B) (C)

09 Mark your answer on the answer sheet. (A) (B) (C)

10 Mark your answer on the answer sheet. (A) (B) (C)

11 Mark your answer on the answer sheet. (A) (B) (C)

12 Mark your answer on the answer sheet. (A) (B) (C)

13 Mark your answer on the answer sheet. (A) (B) (C)

14 Mark your answer on the answer sheet. (A) (B) (C)

15 Mark your answer on the answer sheet.   (A)   (B)   (C)

16 Mark your answer on the answer sheet.   (A)   (B)   (C)

17 Mark your answer on the answer sheet.   (A)   (B)   (C)

18 Mark your answer on the answer sheet.   (A)   (B)   (C)

19 Mark your answer on the answer sheet.   (A)   (B)   (C)

20 Mark your answer on the answer sheet.   (A)   (B)   (C)

21 Mark your answer on the answer sheet.   (A)   (B)   (C)

22 Mark your answer on the answer sheet.   (A)   (B)   (C)

23 Mark your answer on the answer sheet.   (A)   (B)   (C)

24 Mark your answer on the answer sheet.   (A)   (B)   (C)

25 Mark your answer on the answer sheet.   (A)   (B)   (C)

26 Mark your answer on the answer sheet.   (A)   (B)   (C)

27 Mark your answer on the answer sheet.   (A)   (B)   (C)

28 Mark your answer on the answer sheet.   (A)   (B)   (C)

정답·해석·해설 p.29

DAY 07 선택 의문문 및 부가 의문문

기출 유형 1 선택 의문문   최근 3개년 오답률 15.2%

두 가지 선택 사항을 or로 연결하여 제시하며, 둘 중 하나를 선택하도록 요구하는 의문문이다. 매회 2~3문제 출제된다.

출제 경향 및 800+ 공략 🎧 D07_1_예문

1. 선택 사항은 주로 단어와 단어, 구와 구, 의문문과 의문문의 형태로 제시된다. 두 가지 선택 사항 중 하나를 선택하거나, 둘 다 선택 또는 둘 다 선택하지 않는 응답이 정답으로 출제되며, 간접 응답도 출제된다.

   Q. Are you going to book the hotel **downtown** or **near the airport**? 호텔을 시내에 잡으실 건가요, 아니면 공항 근처에 잡으실 건가요?
   A. **The downtown hotel** is more convenient. 시내 호텔이 더 편리해요. [둘 중 하나 선택]
   A. **Whichever one** that provides breakfast. 조식을 제공하는 어느 것이든요. [둘 중 하나 선택]
   A. **Both** are fine with me. 둘 다 저에게는 좋아요. [둘 다 선택]
   A. **Neither location** meets my needs. 어느 곳도 저의 요구를 충족시키지 못해요. [둘 다 선택하지 않음]
   Q. Does Heather belong to **the sales team** or **management team**? Heather는 영업팀 소속인가요, 아니면 경영팀 소속인가요?
   A. Don't you work with her? 당신은 그녀와 함께 일하지 않나요? [간접 응답]

2. 선택 의문문에는 Yes/No로 응답할 수 없지만, 두 개의 의문문을 연결한 경우에는 Yes/No로 응답할 수 있음을 알아 둔다.

   Q. **Are you busy**, or **can you give me some feedback** on the proposal? 바쁘신가요, 아니면 제안서에 피드백을 좀 주실 수 있나요?
   A. Yes, I can do that. 네, 저는 그것을 할 수 있어요.

3. 'Should we A or B(우리 A해야 할까요, 아니면 B해야 할까요)?'의 형태로 묻는 선택 의문문에 대해서는 Let's(~합시다)로 시작하는 답변이 정답으로 자주 출제된다.

   Q. **Should we drive** to the grocery store **or walk** there? 우리 식료품점에 차를 타고 가야 할까요, 아니면 걸어가야 할까요?
   A. **Let's** just walk. 그냥 걸어갑시다.

Example 🎧 D07_2_예제   해석 p.34

(A) (B) (C)	Can I use this coupon online or only in the store? (A) We accept it on our Web site. (B) A coupon for 5 percent off. (C) The network has been restored.
해설 (A) [o] Web site(웹사이트)로 온라인에서 사용할 수 있음을 선택했으므로 정답이다. (B) [x] 질문의 coupon을 반복 사용하여 혼동을 준 오답이다. (C) [x] store – restored의 유사 발음 어휘를 사용하여 혼동을 준 오답이다.	**정답** (A) **Possible Answers** I'm afraid it has expired. 유감이지만 그것은 만료되었어요. Let me ask my manager. 관리자에게 물어볼게요.

토익실전문제 🎧 D07_3_실전   토익 문제 이렇게 나온다!

01 (A) (B) (C)   02 (A) (B) (C)   03 (A) (B) (C)   04 (A) (B) (C)

정답·해석·해설 p.34

기출 유형 2 부가 의문문

최근 3개년 오답률 15%

평서문 형태의 진술문에 덧붙여 사용되며, 사실을 확인하거나 의견에 동의를 구하는 의문문이다. 매회 1~2문제 출제된다.

출제 경향 및 800+ 공략 🎧 D07_4_예문

1. 진술문이 전달하는 사실이 맞는 말이거나 의견에 동의하면 Yes로, 사실을 부인하거나 의견에 반대하면 No로 응답한 후 부연 설명을 덧붙인 응답이 정답으로 출제되며, 간접 응답도 출제된다.

   Q. The kitchen faucet is leaking again, **isn't it**? 부엌 수도꼭지가 또 새고 있죠, 그렇지 않나요?
   A. **Yes**. I'll call the plumber. 네. 수리공을 부를게요. [Yes로 응답]
   A. **No**. It seems fine. 아뇨. 괜찮아 보여요. [No로 응답]

   Q. The lights are still on in the office, **aren't they**? 사무실에 불이 아직 켜져 있죠, 그렇지 않나요?
   A. It's probably just the hallway lights. 아마도 복도 불일 거예요. [간접 응답]
   A. I think someone is still working. 누군가 아직도 일을 하고 있는 것 같아요. [간접 응답]

2. 부가 의문문으로 right, correct, don't you think 등이 붙기도 한다.

   Q. The prototype will be ready by next Tuesday, **right**? 견본품이 다음 주 화요일까지 준비될 거죠, 그렇죠?
   A. **No**. We need more time. 아뇨. 저희는 시간이 더 필요해요. [No로 응답]
   A. I thought you wanted it by Thursday. 저는 당신이 그것을 목요일까지 원하시는 것으로 생각했어요. [간접 응답]

3. 진술문이나 부가 의문문에 not이 있든 없든, 긍정적인 응답일 경우에는 Yes로, 부정적인 응답일 경우에는 No로 답한다는 것을 기억한다.

Example 🎧 D07_5_예제
해석 p.35

(A) (B) (C)	You moved into a new apartment last week, didn't you? (A) At Mary's house. (B) Yes. Everything went smoothly. (C) If all the furniture fits.
해설 (A) [x] 질문의 moved(이사했다)와 관련 있는 house(집)를 사용하여 혼동을 준 오답이다. (B) [o] Yes로 지난주에 새 아파트로 이사했음을 전달한 후, 모든 것이 순조롭게 진행되었다는 부연 설명을 했으므로 정답이다. (C) [x] 질문의 apartment(아파트)에서 연상할 수 있는 furniture(가구)를 사용하여 혼동을 준 오답이다.	**정답** (B) **Possible Answers** It's been a busy week with the move. 이사로 바쁜 한 주였어요. Well, it's much closer to my work. 음, 제 직장과 훨씬 더 가까워요.

토익실전문제 🎧 D07_6_실전
토익 문제 이렇게 나온다!

01 (A) (B) (C)   02 (A) (B) (C)   03 (A) (B) (C)   04 (A) (B) (C)

정답·해석·해설 p.35

HACKERS TEST

DAY 07

토익 800+를 위한 실전 문제 정복

🎧 D07_7_테스트

01 Mark your answer on the answer sheet.   (A)   (B)   (C)

02 Mark your answer on the answer sheet.   (A)   (B)   (C)

03 Mark your answer on the answer sheet.   (A)   (B)   (C)

04 Mark your answer on the answer sheet.   (A)   (B)   (C)

05 Mark your answer on the answer sheet.   (A)   (B)   (C)

06 Mark your answer on the answer sheet.   (A)   (B)   (C)

07 Mark your answer on the answer sheet.   (A)   (B)   (C)

08 Mark your answer on the answer sheet.   (A)   (B)   (C)

09 Mark your answer on the answer sheet.   (A)   (B)   (C)

10 Mark your answer on the answer sheet.   (A)   (B)   (C)

11 Mark your answer on the answer sheet.   (A)   (B)   (C)

12 Mark your answer on the answer sheet.   (A)   (B)   (C)

13 Mark your answer on the answer sheet.   (A)   (B)   (C)

14 Mark your answer on the answer sheet.   (A)   (B)   (C)

15 Mark your answer on the answer sheet.   (A)   (B)   (C)

16 Mark your answer on the answer sheet.   (A)   (B)   (C)

17 Mark your answer on the answer sheet.   (A)   (B)   (C)

18 Mark your answer on the answer sheet.   (A)   (B)   (C)

19 Mark your answer on the answer sheet.   (A)   (B)   (C)

20 Mark your answer on the answer sheet.   (A)   (B)   (C)

21 Mark your answer on the answer sheet.   (A)   (B)   (C)

22 Mark your answer on the answer sheet.   (A)   (B)   (C)

23 Mark your answer on the answer sheet.   (A)   (B)   (C)

24 Mark your answer on the answer sheet.   (A)   (B)   (C)

25 Mark your answer on the answer sheet.   (A)   (B)   (C)

26 Mark your answer on the answer sheet.   (A)   (B)   (C)

27 Mark your answer on the answer sheet.   (A)   (B)   (C)

28 Mark your answer on the answer sheet.   (A)   (B)   (C)

정답·해석·해설 p.35

DAY 08 제안/제공/요청 의문문 및 평서문

기출 유형 1 제안/제공/요청 의문문
최근 3개년 오답률 16.6%

상대방에게 제안, 제공, 또는 요청하는 의문문이며, 주로 Why don't you(we), How about, Do you want me to, Can(Could) you, Would you 등으로 시작한다. 매회 1~2문제 출제된다.

출제 경향 및 800+ 공략 🎧 D08_1_예문

1. 무엇을 하자고 제안하거나, 무엇을 해주겠다고 제공하는 의문문에 대한 수락 또는 거절하는 내용의 응답이 정답으로 출제되며, 간접 응답도 자주 출제된다. Sure(물론이죠), No problem(문제 없어요), That's a good idea(좋은 생각이에요)와 같이 제안을 수락하는 전형적인 표현도 정답으로 자주 출제됨을 기억한다.

   Q. **Would you like me** to send you the updated report? 제가 업데이트된 보고서를 보내드리기를 원하시나요? [제공]
   A. That would be great, thank you. 그래 주시면 정말 좋겠네요, 고마워요. [수락]
   A. That won't be necessary. 그러실 필요는 없어요. [거절]

   Q. **How about** visiting the new bookstore downtown? 시내에 새로 생긴 서점에 가보는 게 어때요? [제안]
   A. When do you plan to go? 언제 갈 계획이에요? [간접 응답]
   A. I didn't know it had opened. 그것이 열었는지 몰랐어요. [간접 응답]

2. 제안이나 제공, 또는 요청한 사항을 이미 완료했다고 응답하는 경우 과거 시제를 사용한 응답도 정답이 될 수 있다.

   Q. **Can you** take a look at this revised document? 이 수정된 문서를 봐주시겠어요? [요청]
   A. I already **checked** it in the morning. 저는 아침에 그것을 이미 확인했어요.

Example 🎧 D08_2_예제
해석 p.40

(A)   (B)   (C)

Would you like us to send you a product list?
(A) I returned that item yesterday.
(B) Yes. I'd appreciate that.
(C) A tour of the facility.

해설
(A) [x] 질문의 product(제품)와 관련 있는 item(물건)을 사용하여 혼동을 준 오답이다.
(B) [o] Yes라는 말로 제안을 수락한 후, 그렇게 해주면 고맙겠다는 부연 설명을 했으므로 정답이다.
(C) [x] 제품 목록을 보내주기를 원하는지를 물었는데, 시설 견학이라며 관련이 없는 내용으로 응답했으므로 오답이다.

정답 (B)

Possible Answers
Could you e-mail it to me? 제게 이메일로 보내주시겠어요?
I already have one. 저는 이미 하나를 가지고 있어요.

토익실전문제 🎧 D08_3_실전
토익 문제 이렇게 나온다!

01 (A) (B) (C)   02 (A) (B) (C)   03 (A) (B) (C)   04 (A) (B) (C)

정답·해석·해설 p.40

기출 유형 2 평서문

최근 3개년 오답률 17.3%

의문문이 아닌 형태로 주로 정보 제공, 문제점 언급, 제안/제공/요청, 의견 전달, 감정 표현, 칭찬 등의 의도를 전달하는 진술문이다. 매회 4~5문제 출제된다.

출제 경향 및 800+ 공략 🎧 D08_4_예문

1. 평서문의 의도에 따라 추가 정보 제공, 수락/거절, 동의/반대, 감사를 전달하는 응답이 정답으로 출제된다.

   Q. I think the concert tickets are already sold out. 콘서트 티켓이 이미 다 팔린 것 같아요. [정보 제공]
   A. Actually, a few seats are still available. 사실, 아직 몇몇 좌석이 구매 가능해요. [추가 정보 제공]

   Q. Please arrive 10 minutes before your scheduled appointment. 예약된 시간의 10분 전에 도착해주세요. [요청]
   A. OK. I will make sure to arrive early. 알겠습니다. 일찍 도착하도록 할게요. [수락]

   Q. Feel free to borrow my laptop for the presentation. 발표를 위해 제 노트북을 자유롭게 빌리셔도 돼요. [제공]
   A. Thanks, but I'd prefer to use my own device. 고맙지만, 저는 제 기기를 사용하는 게 더 좋겠어요. [거절]

   Q. The office should start a flexible working schedule. 사무실은 유연 근무제를 시작해야 해요. [의견 전달]
   A. Yes, I agree completely. 네, 전적으로 동의해요. [동의]

   Q. You did an excellent job on the product design. 당신은 제품 디자인을 훌륭하게 했어요. [칭찬]
   A. Thank you for noticing my efforts. 저의 노력을 알아채 주셔서 감사해요. [감사]

2. 의문문을 사용하여 추가 정보를 요구하는 응답도 정답으로 출제된다.

   Q. My computer has been running unusually slow today. 오늘 제 컴퓨터가 평소보다 유난히 느리게 작동하고 있어요.
   A. Did you try restarting it? 재부팅 해 보셨나요?

3. 평서문은 질문의 초점이 되는 부분이 없어 문장 전체의 내용을 이해해야만 정답을 선택할 수 있으므로 문제를 끝까지 주의 깊게 듣고 내용과 어조를 통해 의도를 파악해야 한다.

Example 🎧 D08_5_예제

해석 p.41

(A) (B) (C)

Let's host a charity fundraiser next month.
(A) Yes, it was last month.
(B) I'd be happy to try some.
(C) Good, I'll come up with some ideas.

해설
(A) [x] 질문의 month를 반복 사용하여 혼동을 준 오답이다.
(B) [x] 다음 달에 자선 모금 행사를 개최하자고 했는데, 이와 관련이 없는 몇 개를 먹어보겠다고 응답했으므로 오답이다.
(C) [o] Good이라는 말로 제안을 수락한 후, 아이디어를 생각해보겠다는 부연 설명을 했으므로 정답이다.

정답 (C)

Possible Answers
I'm not sure if we have the budget. 우리가 예산이 있는지 확실하지 않아요.
Have you searched for a venue? 장소는 찾아보셨나요?

토익실전문제 🎧 D08_6_실전

토익 문제 이렇게 나온다!

01 (A) (B) (C)   02 (A) (B) (C)   03 (A) (B) (C)   04 (A) (B) (C)

정답·해석·해설 p.41

HACKERS TEST

DAY 08

토익 800+를 위한 실전 문제 정복

🎧 D08_7_테스트

01 Mark your answer on the answer sheet. (A) (B) (C)

02 Mark your answer on the answer sheet. (A) (B) (C)

03 Mark your answer on the answer sheet. (A) (B) (C)

04 Mark your answer on the answer sheet. (A) (B) (C)

05 Mark your answer on the answer sheet. (A) (B) (C)

06 Mark your answer on the answer sheet. (A) (B) (C)

07 Mark your answer on the answer sheet. (A) (B) (C)

08 Mark your answer on the answer sheet. (A) (B) (C)

09 Mark your answer on the answer sheet. (A) (B) (C)

10 Mark your answer on the answer sheet. (A) (B) (C)

11 Mark your answer on the answer sheet. (A) (B) (C)

12 Mark your answer on the answer sheet. (A) (B) (C)

13 Mark your answer on the answer sheet. (A) (B) (C)

14 Mark your answer on the answer sheet. (A) (B) (C)

15 Mark your answer on the answer sheet. (A) (B) (C)

16 Mark your answer on the answer sheet. (A) (B) (C)

17 Mark your answer on the answer sheet. (A) (B) (C)

18 Mark your answer on the answer sheet. (A) (B) (C)

19 Mark your answer on the answer sheet. (A) (B) (C)

20 Mark your answer on the answer sheet. (A) (B) (C)

21 Mark your answer on the answer sheet. (A) (B) (C)

22 Mark your answer on the answer sheet. (A) (B) (C)

23 Mark your answer on the answer sheet. (A) (B) (C)

24 Mark your answer on the answer sheet. (A) (B) (C)

25 Mark your answer on the answer sheet. (A) (B) (C)

26 Mark your answer on the answer sheet. (A) (B) (C)

27 Mark your answer on the answer sheet. (A) (B) (C)

28 Mark your answer on the answer sheet. (A) (B) (C)

정답·해석·해설 p.42

실시간 토익시험 정답확인&해설강의
Hackers.co.kr

한 권으로 끝내는 해커스 토익 800+ LC+RC+VOCA

PART 3

DAY 09 주제/목적 및 화자/장소 문제
DAY 10 요청/제안/언급 및 문제점 문제
DAY 11 이유/방법 및 특정 세부 사항 문제
DAY 12 다음에 할 일 및 의도 파악 문제
DAY 13 시각 자료 문제
DAY 14 대화 상황

◀ 음성 바로 듣기

교재에 수록된 모든 음성을 다운로드하거나 바로 스트리밍하여 더욱 편리하게 이용해보세요.

PART 3 소개   짧은 대화 (39문제)

두세 사람의 대화를 듣고 각 대화와 관련된 3개 문제의 정답을 고르는 파트이다. 문제지에는 하나의 질문과 4개의 보기로 구성된 39개의 문제가 제시되며, 일부 문제는 시각 자료가 함께 제시되기도 한다. 음성에서는 대화와 이에 대한 3문제의 질문을 들려준다.

최신 예제 및 풀이 방법

[문제지]	[음성]
33. Why does the man say, "There are a lot of details"? (A) To offer reassurance (B) To show agreement (C) To discuss a complaint (D) To indicate concern	Questions 32 through 34 refer to the following conversation. W: Zack, can you send me the file for our latest accounting report? I want to review it before our presentation on Friday. M: Sure. I'll send it to you by e-mail right now. As for Friday, how about we go over the presentation together beforehand? There are a lot of details. W: I'm open to that. Let's discuss it later this afternoon in the conference room. In the meantime, I'll set up the projector for us to use. Number 33. Why does the man say, "There are a lot of details"?

Step 1 문제 내용 파악하기
대화를 듣기 전에 질문의 핵심 어구를 미리 읽고 밑줄을 쳐서 대화의 어느 부분을 중점적으로 들어야 할지 파악한다. 특히 시각 자료가 제시된 문제라면, 문제와 시각 자료를 함께 확인하면서 시각 자료의 종류와 내용을 파악한다.

Step 2 대화를 듣는 동시에 정답 고르기
정답을 마킹할 시간을 따로 주지 않으므로, 대화를 들으면서 미리 파악해 둔 문제에 대한 정답의 근거를 확인하여 정답을 바로 고른다. 3개의 문제에 대한 정답의 단서가 대화 안에서 순차적으로 나오므로, 한 문제의 정답을 고르면 바로 다음 문제의 정답의 단서를 주의해서 들을 준비를 한다.

Step 3 다음 지문의 문제 내용 파악하기
3개 문제의 질문을 들려주는 동안, 다음 지문의 문제 내용을 미리 파악한다.

최신 출제 경향

39개의 문제 중 특정 세부 사항을 묻는 문제가 가장 많이 출제되며, 화자/장소 문제도 꾸준히 높은 비율로 출제된다. 시각 자료 문제는 3문제가 고정으로 출제되는데, 최근에는 표나 차트 외에도 쿠폰, 지도와 같이 다양한 시각 자료가 출제된다. 대화 상황은 회사 생활과 일상생활이 골고루 등장하지만, 회사 생활이 조금 더 높은 비중으로 등장한다.

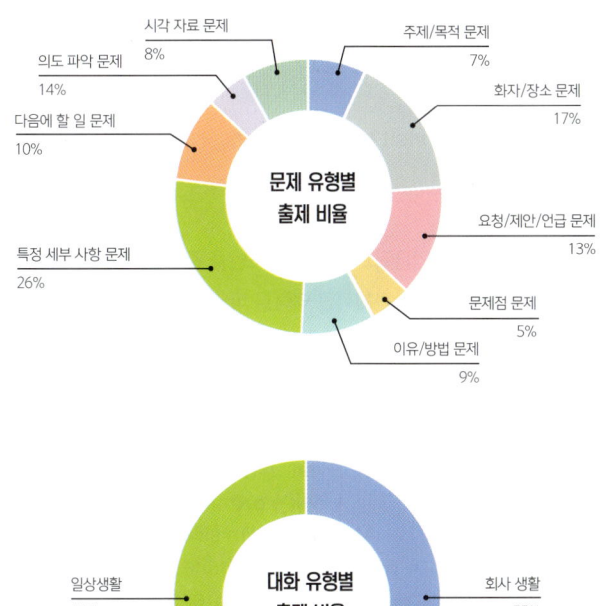

800⁺ 학습 전략

🔍 문제 유형별 풀이 공략을 익힌다.
PART 3에 출제되는 문제들의 각 유형별 풀이 공략을 익혀 두면 실전 시험에서 문제 풀이를 하는 것이 쉬워진다. 예를 들어, 주제/목적 문제의 정답의 단서는 주로 대화의 초반에 언급되므로 대화의 초반을 집중해서 들으면 정답을 쉽게 찾을 수 있다.

🔍 대화 유형별로 자주 등장하는 표현을 암기한다.
PART 3에 대화 유형별로 자주 등장하는 표현들을 암기해 두면 더욱 쉽고 정확하게 음성을 들을 수 있다. 특히, PART 3에서는 일상에서 사용 가능한 대화가 출제되므로 관용적인 구어체가 많이 등장하는데, 이들은 미리 암기하지 않으면 의미를 파악하기 어려우므로 확실히 암기해 둔다.

DAY 09 주제/목적 및 화자/장소 문제

기출 유형 1　주제/목적 문제

최근 3개년 오답률 13.6%

화자들이 이야기하고 있는 주된 내용을 묻는 문제로, 매회 2~3문제가 출제된다.

출제 경향

1. 한 대화에 해당되는 세 개의 문제들 중 주로 첫 번째 문제로 출제된다.
2. 주로 다음과 같은 질문을 사용한다.

　주제　**What** is the conversation **mainly about**?　대화는 주로 무엇에 관한 것인가?
　　　　What are the speakers **mainly discussing**?　화자들은 주로 무엇에 관해 이야기하고 있는가?
　목적　**What** is the **purpose** of the call?　전화의 목적은 무엇인가?
　　　　Why is the man **calling**?　남자는 왜 전화를 하고 있는가?
　　　　What is the **purpose** of the woman's **visit**?　여자가 방문한 목적은 무엇인가?

800+ 공략

1. 주제 및 목적과 관련된 내용은 주로 대화의 초반에 언급되므로 대화의 초반을 주의 깊게 듣는다.
2. 대화의 초반에서 주제 및 목적을 파악하기 어려운 경우 전체적인 맥락을 파악하여 정답을 선택한다.

Example 🎧 D09_1_예제

해석 p.47

| 01 What is the conversation mainly about?
　(A) Organizing a grand opening
　(B) Preparing for a promotion
　(C) Finalizing a price quote
　(D) Choosing a business location | Question 01 refers to the following conversation.
W: Ryan, **have you finished arranging the items for next week's promotional event**?
M: **Not yet.** I'm still organizing the display racks and attaching the tags with the reduced prices.
W: We need to ensure everything is ready before Friday. Maybe I should ask another staff member to assist you.
M: That won't be necessary. I'm pretty sure that I'll be able to finish all the preparations by tomorrow afternoon at the latest. |

해설 주제 문제　　　정답 (B)

대화의 초반에서 여자가 남자에게 "have you finished arranging the items for next week's promotional event?"라며 다음 주 판촉 행사를 위한 물품 정리를 끝냈는지 묻자 남자가 "Not yet."이라며 아직 못 끝냈다고 한 후, 판촉 행사 준비에 대한 내용으로 대화가 이어지고 있으므로 (B)가 정답이다.

빈출 정답 단서와 패러프레이징　🎧 D09_2_표현

다음은 주제 문제에서 정답 단서와 함께 나오는 표현과 정답 단서가 패러프레이징된 예시이다.

단서와 함께 나오는 표현	대화 지문	질문 및 정답
1 I'd like to discuss ~ / I want to talk about ~ ~에 대해 이야기하고 싶습니다	M: I'd like to discuss a marketing collaboration between our companies. W: Certainly. Do you have any specific initiatives in mind? 남: 저희 회사들 간의 마케팅 협업에 대해 이야기하고 싶어요. 여: 물론이죠. 생각하고 계신 구체적인 계획이 있으신가요?	질문 What is the conversation mainly about? 대화는 주로 무엇에 관한 것인가? 정답 A business collaboration 사업 협력

다음은 목적 문제에서 정답 단서와 함께 나오는 표현과 정답 단서가 패러프레이징된 예시이다.

단서와 함께 나오는 표현	대화 지문	질문 및 정답
2 I'm calling to ~ ~하기 위해 전화드립니다	W: Tom, I'm calling to check if you have time to work on the new product package design. M: I've just finished my current project. 여: Tom, 신제품 패키지 디자인 작업을 하실 시간이 있는지 확인하기 위해 전화드려요. 남: 현재의 프로젝트를 방금 마쳤어요.	질문 Why is the woman calling? 여자는 왜 전화하고 있는가? 정답 To give a work assignment 업무를 주기 위해
3 I'm interested in ~ ~에 관심이 있습니다	W: What can I help you with today? M: I'm interested in loan consultation. 여: 오늘 무엇을 도와드릴까요? 남: 대출 상담에 관심이 있어요.	질문 What is the purpose of the man's visit? 남자가 방문한 목적은 무엇인가? 정답 To discuss a loan 대출을 논의하기 위해

토익실전문제　🎧 D09_3_실전

주제 문제

01 What are the speakers mainly discussing?
(A) A reservation
(B) A review
(C) An opening
(D) An advertisement

02 What problem is mentioned?
(A) The service is poor.
(B) The atmosphere is uninviting.
(C) The food is overcooked.
(D) The menu is limited.

03 What does the man suggest doing?
(A) Preparing a meal
(B) Tasting a new dish
(C) Making an online post
(D) Meeting with an employee

목적 문제

04 What is the purpose of the woman's visit?
(A) To purchase some plants
(B) To arrange a group tour
(C) To apply for volunteer work
(D) To take a gardening class

05 What does the man say the woman should do first?
(A) Fill out a document
(B) Talk to a supervisor
(C) Go through a manual
(D) Present some identification

06 Why is the woman unavailable on weekends?
(A) She needs to lead a class.
(B) She travels frequently for business.
(C) She has a part-time position.
(D) She has to attend workshops.

정답·해석·해설 p.47

기출 유형 2 화자/장소 문제

최근 3개년 오답률 14.7%

화자들의 직업이나 근무지/부서, 그리고 대화가 이루어지고 있는 장소를 묻는 문제로, 매회 6~7문제 출제된다.

출제 경향

1. 한 대화에 해당되는 세 개의 문제들 중 주로 첫 번째 문제로 출제된다.
2. 주로 다음과 같은 질문을 사용한다.

   화자   **Who** most likely is **the man**? 남자는 누구인 것 같은가?
   Who are **the speakers**? 화자들은 누구인가?
   Where do **the speakers** most likely **work**? 화자들은 어디에서 일하는 것 같은가?
   What industry/department does **the woman work in**? 여자는 어느 업계/부서에서 일하는가?

   장소   **Where** most likely are **the speakers**? 화자들은 어디에 있는 것 같은가?
   Where is the conversation most likely **taking place**? 대화는 어디에서 일어나고 있는 것 같은가?

800+ 공략

1. 화자 및 장소와 관련된 내용은 주로 대화의 초반에 언급되므로 대화의 초반을 주의 깊게 듣는다.
2. 특정 직업이나 장소와 관련된 여러 표현들을 통해 화자의 직업이나 대화 장소를 유추한다.

Example 🎧 D09_4_예제

해석 p.48

01 Who most likely is the man?
 (A) A delivery person
 (B) A news reporter
 (C) A tour guide
 (D) A restaurant employee

Question 01 refers to the following conversation.

M: **Thank you for calling Bella Bistro. How may I help you today?**
W: **I'd like to make a reservation for 7 P.M.** Are there any tables for six people available then?
M: Let me check . . . It appears that we are fully booked at 7. However, we should be able to accommodate a group of that size at 7:45. Would that be OK?
W: That seems fine. Please make the reservation under the name of Katherine Miller.

해설 화자 문제

정답 (D)

대화의 초반에 남자가 "Thank you for calling Bella Bistro. How may I help you today?"라며 Bella 비스트로에 전화해 줘서 감사하다고 한 뒤, 어떤 도움이 필요하냐고 묻자, 여자가 "I'd like to make a reservation for 7 P.M."이라며 오후 7시에 예약하고 싶다고 한 것을 통해 남자는 식당 직원이라는 것을 알 수 있다. 따라서 (D)가 정답이다.

직업·근무지/부서·장소를 나타내는 표현 🎧 D09_5_표현

화자의 직업을 나타내는 빈출 표현과 관련 키워드

1 salesperson / sales representative 영업 사원	product / merchandise 제품 stock the shelves 선반을 채우다	demonstration 시연 in stock 재고로	sales strategy 판매 전략
2 receptionist (호텔, 병원 등의) 접수원	room reservation 방 예약 reschedule 일정을 변경하다	book 예약하다 patient 환자	appointment 예약
3 journalist 기자	article / story 기사	column 칼럼, 정기 기고란	deadline 마감 기한
4 property manager / real estate agent 부동산 중개인	leasing office 임대 사무소 lease 임대차 계약	property 부동산 tenant 세입자	accommodate 수용하다

화자가 일하고 있는 근무지/부서를 나타내는 빈출 표현과 관련 키워드

5 construction 건설	building plan 건축 계획	building material 건축 자재	renovation 개조
6 shipping 운송	cargo ship 화물선 overseas 해외로, 해외의	ship 선적하다 behind schedule 예정보다 늦게	package 소포
7 accounting 회계부	calculate 계산하다 expense report 경비 보고서	travel reimbursement 출장비 환급	
8 human resources 인사부	job description 직무 기술서 prepare a contract 계약서를 준비하다	job offer 일자리 제안	candidate 지원자

대화가 이루어지는 장소를 나타내는 빈출 표현과 관련 키워드

9 bus terminal / train station 버스 터미널/기차역	buy a ticket 표를 사다 depart 출발하다	change a seat 좌석을 바꾸다 board 탑승하다	miss 놓치다 delay 지연시키다
10 manufacturing plant 제조 공장	assembly line 생산 라인 electricity 전기	factory 공장 automated equipment 자동 장치	machine 기계
11 museum / art gallery 박물관/미술관	exhibit / display 전시	painting 그림	sculpture 조각상

토익실전문제 🎧 D09_6_실전

토익 문제 이렇게 나온다!

화자 문제

01 Who most likely is the man?
(A) A technician
(B) A salesperson
(C) A receptionist
(D) An architect

02 Why does the man apologize?
(A) A conference was delayed.
(B) A service is unavailable.
(C) A tool was misplaced.
(D) Incorrect information was shared.

03 What does the woman ask about?
(A) A discounted price
(B) A device's location
(C) Meal options
(D) Operating hours

장소 문제

04 Where is the conversation most likely taking place?
(A) At a bus terminal
(B) At a train station
(C) At an airport
(D) At a taxi stand

05 What is mentioned about the Belmont Inn?
(A) It renovated its rooms.
(B) It is hosting a trade show.
(C) It recently opened.
(D) It has affordable rates.

06 What will the man do next?
(A) Request a refund
(B) Attend an event
(C) Make a reservation
(D) Buy a ticket

정답·해석·해설 p.48

HACKERS TEST

DAY 09

🎧 D09_7_테스트

01 What are the speakers mainly discussing?
(A) A trip itinerary
(B) A training program
(C) Event preparations
(D) Award recipients

02 What does the woman ask about?
(A) How much a product costs
(B) Where a meeting will be held
(C) How many invitations should be printed
(D) Whether a manager will attend

03 What does the man say he will do this afternoon?
(A) Draft a report
(B) Contact some coworkers
(C) Make an announcement
(D) Attend a meeting

04 Why is the man calling?
(A) To cancel an order
(B) To purchase a membership
(C) To make an appointment
(D) To ask about a location

05 What does the woman say about her business?
(A) It was recently opened.
(B) It offers durable goods.
(C) It has several branches nationwide.
(D) It is conveniently located.

06 Why will the man be out of town on the weekend?
(A) A business exposition is being held.
(B) A private event is scheduled.
(C) A cultural festival is taking place.
(D) A company workshop is planned.

07 What industry does the man most likely work in?
(A) Security
(B) Construction
(C) Transportation
(D) Education

08 Why does the man want to meet with the woman?
(A) To discuss a job opening
(B) To describe a service
(C) To explain a contract
(D) To negotiate a price

09 What information will the woman most likely provide next?
(A) A business name
(B) A departure time
(C) Some contact information
(D) Names of workers

10 Where is the conversation taking place?
(A) At a hardware store
(B) At an accounting firm
(C) At a grocery store
(D) At an educational institution

11 What does the woman say about the fee?
(A) It can be refunded in some cases.
(B) It is reduced for a limited period.
(C) It must be paid once a month.
(D) It was introduced very recently.

12 What will the man most likely do next?
(A) Check a calendar
(B) Install some software
(C) Cancel a payment
(D) Complete some paperwork

13 Where are the speakers?
 (A) At a charity event
 (B) At a grand opening
 (C) At a trade show
 (D) At an award ceremony

14 What did Rachel find most inspiring about the previous event?
 (A) A video
 (B) A speech
 (C) A performance
 (D) A demonstration

15 What information does the man want to find in a brochure?
 (A) The name of a presenter
 (B) The topic of a talk
 (C) The time of a presentation
 (D) The location of a venue

16 Who is the woman?
 (A) A town official
 (B) A consultant
 (C) A journalist
 (D) A business owner

17 According to the woman, what will be built in Chicago?
 (A) A shopping complex
 (B) A sports facility
 (C) A community center
 (D) A manufacturing plant

18 What is located on a table?
 (A) Some name tags
 (B) Some pamphlets
 (C) Some registration forms
 (D) Some sample products

19 Where most likely are the speakers?
 (A) In a clinic
 (B) In a hotel
 (C) In a restaurant
 (D) In a spa

20 What problem does the woman mention?
 (A) A payment was not sufficient.
 (B) A reservation was canceled.
 (C) A space is currently in use.
 (D) A facility is not large enough.

21 What does the woman offer to do?
 (A) Change a booking
 (B) Post a photograph
 (C) Give a partial refund
 (D) Provide a free item

22 Why is the man calling?
 (A) To track a shipment
 (B) To correct a mistake
 (C) To complain about staff
 (D) To confirm a work deadline

23 What does the woman say recently happened?
 (A) A company merger was finalized.
 (B) An inspection was conducted.
 (C) An application was updated.
 (D) An online order was canceled.

24 What will the woman do next?
 (A) Send a document
 (B) Change some dates
 (C) Check some machinery
 (D) Negotiate a contract

DAY 10 요청/제안/언급 및 문제점 문제

기출 유형 1 요청/제안/언급 문제

최근 3개년 오답률 13.9%

화자들 중 한 명이 상대방에게 요청 또는 제안한 사항이나 특정 대상에 대해 언급한 사항을 묻는 문제로, 매회 5~6문제 출제된다.

출제 경향

1. 요청/제안/언급 문제의 질문에는 화자들 중 한 명, 즉 남자 또는 여자가 항상 등장한다.
2. 주로 다음과 같은 질문을 사용한다.

요청	**What** does the man **ask for**? 남자는 무엇을 무엇을 요청하는가?
	What does the woman **ask** the man to do? 여자는 남자에게 무엇을 하라고 요청하는가?
제안	**What** does the woman **suggest** doing? 여자는 무엇을 할 것을 제안하는가?
	What does the man **suggest** that the woman do? 남자는 여자가 무엇을 할 것을 제안하는가?
	What suggestion does the man make? 남자는 어떤 제안을 하는가?
언급	**What** does the woman **say about** the mobile app? 여자는 모바일 앱에 대해 무엇을 말하는가?

800+ 공략

1. 질문에 언급된 화자(남자 또는 여자)의 말을 주의 깊게 듣는다.
2. 요청하는 내용은 Can(Could) you, Would you, I'd like you to 등의 표현 다음에 나오는 내용을 반드시 듣는다.
3. 제안하는 내용은 Why don't you/we, I suggest/recommend, You should 등의 표현 다음에 나오는 내용을 반드시 듣는다.
4. 언급하는 내용은 질문의 say about 뒤에 나오는 핵심어구가 언급된 주변을 들으면서 정답의 단서를 파악한다.

Example 🎧 D10_1_예제

해석 p.54

01 What does the woman suggest doing?
(A) Booking a facility tour
(B) Arranging a boat ride
(C) Attending a cultural event
(D) Watching a theater performance

Question 01 refers to the following conversation.

M: Good morning. I'll be staying at your resort for a few days, and I'd like to arrange an activity for Saturday.
W: Since our resort is located close to the sea, we offer a number of water-based activities.
M: That sounds fun, but I'd rather do something related to the culture here.
W: Then, **there is a traditional dance festival this weekend**. You'll have the chance to dance with locals. **Why don't you attend this festival?**

해설 제안 문제 　　　　　　　　　　　　　　　　　　　　　　　　　　　　　　　　　정답 (C)

여자가 "there is a traditional dance festival this weekend"라며 이번 주말에 전통 춤 축제가 있다고 한 뒤, "Why don't you attend this festival?"이라며 이 축제에 참여하는 게 어떻겠냐고 제안했으므로 (C)가 정답이다.

빈출 정답 단서와 패러프레이징

다음은 요청/제안 문제에서 정답 단서와 함께 나오는 표현과 정답 단서가 패러프레이징된 예시이다.

단서와 함께 나오는 표현	대화 지문	질문 및 정답
1 Can(Could) you / Would you ~? ~해주시겠어요?	M: Our company has a variety of office furniture. W: **Could you** send me the product catalog? 남: 저희 회사는 다양한 종류의 사무용 가구들을 보유하고 있습니다. 여: 제품 카탈로그를 제게 보내주시겠어요?	질문 What does the woman ask the man to do? 여자는 남자에게 무엇을 하라고 요청하는가? 정답 Provide a product catalog 제품 카탈로그를 제공한다.
2 Why don't you / we ~? ~하는 게 어때요?	W: How should we advertise our upcoming exhibition? M: **Why don't we** create a short video clip showing the artworks? 여: 우리의 다가오는 전시를 어떻게 홍보해야 할까요? 남: 전시품들을 보여주는 짧은 영상을 제작하는 게 어때요?	질문 What suggestion does the man make? 남자는 어떤 제안을 하는가? 정답 Making a video 영상 만들기

다음은 언급 문제에서 정답 단서가 패러프레이징된 예시이다.

대화 지문	질문 및 정답
3 M: I'm impressed with our updated **mobile application**. W: Really? I find it complicated to use because there are too many functions. 남: 저는 업데이트된 우리의 모바일 애플리케이션이 인상 깊어요. 여: 정말요? 저는 너무 많은 기능이 있어서 사용하기 복잡해요.	질문 What does the woman say about the **mobile app**? 여자는 모바일 앱에 대해 무엇을 말하는가? 정답 It is difficult to use. 사용하기 어렵다.

토익실전문제

01 What department do the speakers most likely work in?
(A) Design
(B) Accounting
(C) Public relations
(D) Human Resources

요청 문제
02 What does the woman ask the man to help with?
(A) Updating a policy
(B) Training new employees
(C) Editing a report
(D) Creating presentation slides

03 What will the man do tomorrow?
(A) Send an e-mail
(B) Bring an invoice
(C) Sign some documents
(D) Travel to a conference

04 What are the speakers mainly discussing?
(A) A new textbook
(B) A field trip
(C) A group project
(D) A university policy

언급 문제
05 What does the man say about the museum?
(A) It provides several art classes.
(B) It is nearby.
(C) It includes a new facility.
(D) It will be relocated.

제안 문제
06 What does the woman suggest that the man do?
(A) Print out some materials
(B) Arrange transportation
(C) Make a phone call
(D) Submit a detailed plan

기출 유형 2 문제점 문제

최근 3개년 오답률 12.3%

화자가 겪고 있는 문제점이나 화자가 걱정 또는 염려하는 사항을 묻는 문제로, 매회 2~3문제 출제된다.

출제 경향

1. 한 대화에 해당되는 세 개의 문제들 중 첫 번째나 두 번째 문제로 자주 출제된다.
2. 주로 다음과 같은 질문을 사용한다.

   What problem does the man mention? 남자는 무슨 문제를 언급하는가?
   What is the woman **concerned(worried) about**? 여자는 무엇을 걱정하는가?
   What is the man **having trouble with**? 남자는 무엇에 어려움을 겪고 있는가?
   Why is the woman **worried(concerned)**? 여자는 왜 걱정하는가?

800+ 공략

1. 대화에서 but, however, unfortunately, worried, concerned 등 부정적인 표현이 언급된 다음을 주의 깊게 듣는다.
2. 질문에 특정 화자(남자 또는 여자)가 언급되는 경우 해당 화자의 말에서 단서를 파악한다.
3. 주로 문장 형태의 보기가 출제되는데, 정답의 단서가 자주 패러프레이징되는 것에 유의한다.

Example 🎧 D10_4_예제

해석 p.56

| 01 What problem does the woman mention?
(A) A device is malfunctioning.
(B) A Web site is not working.
(C) A parking area is closed.
(D) An item was damaged during delivery. | Question 01 refers to the following conversation.

M: Good morning. What can I do for you?
W: Hello. **I got this smartphone a month ago, but it stopped working this morning.** It keeps shutting down after I use it for a few minutes. So I brought it to this service center.
M: Hmm . . . I'll need a few days to determine exactly what is wrong with it. I'll contact you once I figure out the problem. Could you leave your e-mail address?
W: Of course. Let me write it down for you. |

해설 문제점 문제 정답 (A)

여자가 "I got this smartphone a month ago, but it stopped working this morning."이라며 스마트폰을 한 달 전에 구매했는데, 오늘 아침에 작동을 멈췄다고 하였다. 따라서 (A)가 정답이다.

빈출 정답 단서와 패러프레이징 🎧 D10_5_표현

다음은 문제점 문제에서 정답 단서와 함께 나오는 표현과 정답 단서가 패러프레이징된 예시이다.

단서와 함께 나오는 표현	대화 지문	질문 및 정답
1 The problem is (that) ~ 문제는 ~입니다	W: We've just received a bulk order for 150 of our new sneakers. M: **The problem is that** we don't have enough employees to handle such a large order. 여: 방금 우리의 새 운동화에 대한 150개의 대량 주문을 받았어요. 남: 문제는 우리가 그렇게 많은 주문을 처리할 충분한 직원들이 없다는 거예요.	질문 What problem does the man mention? 남자는 무슨 문제를 언급하는가? 정답 A staff shortage 인력 부족
2 I'm concerned (worried) about ~ ~에 대해 걱정됩니다	W: **I'm worried about** the poor lighting in the exhibition hall. M: Don't worry. I'll take care of it by tomorrow. 여: 전시장의 조명 상태가 좋지 않아 걱정돼요. 남: 걱정 마세요. 제가 내일까지 해결하겠습니다.	질문 What is the woman worried about? 여자는 무엇을 걱정하는가? 정답 A lighting issue 조명 문제
3 but / however 하지만	W: You're working on a marketing report for Mr. Thompson, right? M: Yeah. I've still got a lot to do, **but** the report is due tomorrow morning. 여: 당신은 Mr. Thompson을 위한 마케팅 보고서를 작성하고 있죠, 그렇죠? 남: 네. 저는 여전히 할 것이 많은데, 보고서는 내일 아침까지예요.	질문 Why is the man concerned? 남자는 왜 걱정하는가? 정답 A deadline is approaching. 마감일이 다가오고 있다.

토익실전문제 🎧 D10_6_실전

토익 문제 이렇게 나온다!

01 Where does the man work?
 (A) At a department store
 (B) At a law firm
 (C) At a travel agency
 (D) At a publishing company

문제점 문제
02 What problem does the man mention?
 (A) A document includes an error.
 (B) A message was not received.
 (C) An event has been delayed.
 (D) An assistant is not available.

03 What does the woman say she will do?
 (A) Return to her office
 (B) Speak to an employee
 (C) Check a warranty
 (D) Make a reservation

문제점 문제
04 Why is the woman worried?
 (A) A lifeguard did not attend training.
 (B) A visitor has been injured.
 (C) Some weather conditions are poor.
 (D) A facility will need more staff.

05 What is mentioned about Diana Harris?
 (A) She disagrees with a proposal.
 (B) She is not at work today.
 (C) She will not fulfill a request.
 (D) She has filled out a form.

06 Why does the man say he will make an announcement?
 (A) To praise some workers
 (B) To clarify a policy
 (C) To ask for volunteers
 (D) To apologize for a mistake

정답·해석·해설 p.56

HACKERS TEST — DAY 10

01 Why is the man calling?
(A) To change an appointment
(B) To confirm an order
(C) To ask for a payment
(D) To request a refund

02 What does the woman say about the company's logo?
(A) It will appear on a Web site.
(B) It is currently too small.
(C) It includes several images.
(D) It has been changed.

03 What will happen next Monday?
(A) An order will be shipped.
(B) A meeting will be held.
(C) A payment will be made.
(D) An invoice will be sent.

04 Where does the woman most likely work?
(A) At a parking facility
(B) At a rental agency
(C) At a car dealership
(D) At a repair shop

05 What does the woman recommend?
(A) Replacing some parts
(B) Having a car towed away
(C) Selecting a different model
(D) Comparing some options

06 What did the man write on a form?
(A) A pickup time
(B) A telephone number
(C) An e-mail address
(D) A price estimate

07 What problem does the woman describe?
(A) A presentation was canceled.
(B) A room is occupied.
(C) A device is malfunctioning.
(D) A request was denied.

08 What does the man suggest doing?
(A) Notifying a supervisor
(B) Contacting a coworker
(C) Placing an order
(D) Changing a venue

09 What will the woman most likely do next?
(A) Speak with a manager
(B) Review some material
(C) Update a Web site
(D) Check a schedule

10 Where does the man work?
(A) At a furniture store
(B) At a grocery store
(C) At a gardening shop
(D) At an advertising firm

11 What motivated the woman to visit the business?
(A) She saw an advertisement online.
(B) She heard about it from a colleague.
(C) She was satisfied with a previous purchase.
(D) She read about it in a newspaper.

12 What does the man ask the woman to do?
(A) Visit a Web site
(B) Order additional supplies
(C) Provide an image
(D) Take measurements

13 What industry do the speakers most likely work in?

(A) Technology
(B) Publishing
(C) Film
(D) Tourism

14 What does the man say about Proto Construction?

(A) It has received prestigious awards.
(B) It has successfully renovated many buildings.
(C) It has operated for several decades.
(D) It has multiple branches overseas.

15 What does the woman ask the man to do?

(A) Conduct an interview
(B) Submit an article draft
(C) Rewrite a proposal
(D) Participate in a press conference

16 What is the conversation mainly about?

(A) A medical facility design
(B) A public relations initiative
(C) A performance evaluation
(D) An upcoming health fair

17 What does Emily say about Mr. Greer?

(A) He was recently promoted.
(B) He earned an advanced degree.
(C) He is retiring soon.
(D) He is organizing a party.

18 What will the speakers most likely do on Monday?

(A) Train some employees
(B) Review an application
(C) Negotiate a new contract
(D) Take a group photograph

19 Why is the man calling?

(A) To question a recent charge
(B) To discuss a problem
(C) To schedule a home repair
(D) To confirm a mailing address

20 What does the woman suggest doing?

(A) Substituting a material
(B) Redesigning a logo
(C) Consulting an expert
(D) Opening an additional location

21 What does the man want to do?

(A) Add lighting fixtures
(B) Visit a factory
(C) Inspect a sample
(D) Cancel an order

22 What did the woman do this morning?

(A) She posted a schedule.
(B) She checked some inventory.
(C) She contacted some customers.
(D) She called a shipping company.

23 What problem are the speakers discussing?

(A) A supplier has increased its prices.
(B) Some negative feedback was submitted.
(C) Some equipment is not working.
(D) A product is underperforming.

24 What will Lucas do next?

(A) Revise a store catalog
(B) Arrange product display
(C) Purchase an electronic device
(D) Give a demonstration

DAY 11 이유/방법 및 특정 세부 사항 문제

기출 유형 1 이유/방법 문제

최근 3개년 오답률 16.5%

어떤 일이 일어난 이유 또는 화자의 감정과 관련된 이유를 묻거나, 방법 또는 수단을 묻는 문제로, 매회 3~4문제 출제된다.

출제 경향

1. 이유 문제는 문장 또는 To 부정사구의 보기가 나오며 정답의 단서가 자주 패러프레이징 된다.
2. 방법 문제는 'By -ing(~함으로써)' 형태 또는 From으로 시작하는 보기가 나온다.
3. 주로 다음과 같은 질문을 사용한다.

   이유 **Why** was the man **surprised**? 남자는 왜 놀랐는가?
   Why is the woman **unavailable on Tuesday**? 여자는 왜 화요일에 시간이 안 되는가?
   Why does the man **apologize**? 남자는 왜 사과하는가?
   What is the **reason for** a delay? 지연된 이유는 무엇인가?

   방법 **How** can the woman **get/qualify for** a discount? 여자는 어떻게 할인을 받을 수 있는가?
   How did the man **learn about** the store? 남자는 어떻게 상점에 대해 알게 됐는가?
   How will the speakers **get to** the airport? 화자들은 어떻게 공항에 갈 것인가?

800+ 공략

1. 이유 문제에 대한 단서는 대화에서 주로 because (of)(~ 때문에), due to(~ 때문에), since(~이므로)의 다음이나 so(그래서)의 앞에서, 또는 목적을 나타내는 to 부정사(~하기 위해서)의 내용에서 파악한다.
2. 추가 정보를 얻는 방법을 묻는 문제에 대한 단서는 대화의 후반에 자주 언급되므로, 마지막 부분을 주의 깊게 듣는다.

Example 🎧 D11_1_예제

해석 p.62

01 Why does the woman apologize?
(A) A call was not returned.
(B) A product is defective.
(C) A meeting started late.
(D) A discount is not available.

Question 01 refers to the following conversation.

W: Kendrick, **sorry to delay our meeting** . . . I had an unexpected phone call.
M: No problem. Well, I requested this meeting to discuss the second branch of our grocery store. That branch is doing poorly despite the discounts we have been offering to celebrate its opening.
W: I know. What do you think about distributing flyers in the neighborhood?
M: Let's give it a try.

해설 **이유 문제** 정답 (C)
여자가 "sorry to delay our meeting"이라며 회의를 지연시켜서 미안하다고 했으므로 (C)가 정답이다.

빈출 정답 단서와 패러프레이징 🎧 D11_2_표현

다음은 이유 문제에서 정답 단서와 함께 나오는 표현과 정답 단서가 패러프레이징된 예시이다.

단서와 함께 나오는 표현	대화 지문	질문 및 정답
1 I'm sorry / I apologize for ~ ~해서 죄송합니다/~에 대해 사과드립니다	W: I sent a text message to confirm today's appointment, but I didn't receive a response. M: I apologize for not getting back to you. 여: 오늘 저의 예약 확인을 위해 문자를 보냈는데, 답변을 받지 못했어요. 남: 회신을 드리지 못한 것에 대해 사과드립니다.	질문 Why does the man apologize? 남자는 왜 사과하는가? 정답 He failed to send a response. 답장을 보내지 못했다.
2 I was surprised because ~ ~해서 놀랐습니다	M: Did you book the flight ticket to Bangkok? W: No. I was surprised because the price has gone up a lot since last month. 남: 방콕행 비행기표를 예약하셨나요? 여: 아니요. 가격이 지난달부터 많이 올라서 놀랐어요.	질문 Why was the woman surprised? 여자는 왜 놀랐는가? 정답 The ticket price has increased. 티켓 가격이 올랐다.

다음은 방법 문제에서 정답 단서와 함께 나오는 표현과 정답 단서가 패러프레이징된 예시이다.

단서와 함께 나오는 표현	대화 지문	질문 및 정답
3 You can ~ if you - 당신이 -하시면 ~할 수 있습니다	M: I heard that your bakery is holding a special promotion today. W: Yes. You can get a free cookie if you spend over 15 dollars. 남: 당신의 제과점이 오늘 특별 판촉 활동을 한다고 들었어요. 여: 네. 15달러 이상 구매하시면 무료 쿠키를 받을 수 있습니다.	질문 How can the man qualify for a free item? 남자는 어떻게 무료 제품을 받을 자격을 얻을 수 있는가? 정답 By spending a certain amount of money 특정 금액을 소비함으로써
4 ~ recommended / referred ~가 추천했습니다/소개했습니다	M: Who told you about our furniture store? W: My colleague recommended your store. 남: 저희 가구점에 대해 누가 말해주었나요? 여: 제 동료가 당신의 상점을 추천했어요.	질문 How did the woman learn about a store? 여자는 어떻게 상점에 대해 알게 됐는가? 정답 From a coworker 동료에게서

토익실전문제 🎧 D11_3_실전

이유 문제

01 Why was the woman surprised?
(A) A schedule was changed suddenly.
(B) A contest had many participants.
(C) A new policy was announced.
(D) A business has closed down.

02 What does the man's company make?
(A) Sporting goods
(B) Food products
(C) Kitchen utensils
(D) Cookbooks

03 What will the woman do tomorrow?
(A) Create a new dessert
(B) Send some samples
(C) Go to a branch
(D) Review a proposal

04 What is the purpose of the man's visit?
(A) He is applying for a job.
(B) He needs help with moving.
(C) He wants a consultation.
(D) He has a complaint.

방법 문제

05 How did the man learn about the woman's company?
(A) From a Web site
(B) From a publication
(C) From a TV commercial
(D) From a local business owner

06 What will the woman show the man?
(A) A floor plan
(B) Some photographs
(C) Some 3D models
(D) A cost estimate

정답·해석·해설 p.62

기출 유형 2   특정 세부 사항 문제

최근 3개년 오답률 13.8%

대화에서 언급된 다양한 세부 사항에 관련된 사실을 묻는 문제로, 매회 11~12문제 출제된다.

출제 경향

1. 특정 세부 사항을 묻는 문제로 다음과 같은 문제들이 자주 출제된다.
   - 현재 화자가 준비하고 있는 일, 또는 과거에 일어난 일을 묻는 문제
   - 화자가 문의하는 정보 또는 상기하는 것을 묻는 문제
2. 특정 인물의 신분이나 직업을 묻는 문제도 출제되는데, 대화에 등장하지 않은 제3자의 인물이 언급된다.
3. 주로 다음과 같은 질문을 사용한다.

특정 세부	**What** happened **last year**?	작년에 무슨 일이 일어났는가?
	What did the man **recently do**?	남자는 최근에 무엇을 했는가?
	What does the woman **ask about**?	여자는 무엇을 문의하는가?
특정 시기	**When** does the man **expect to be available**?	남자는 언제 시간이 될 것으로 예상하는가?
특정 장소	**Where** did the woman **find the man's résumé**?	여자는 남자의 이력서를 어디에서 찾았는가?
특정 인물	**Who** is **Frank Cortez**?	Frank Cortez는 누구인가?

800+ 공략

1. 대화에서 질문의 핵심 어구가 언급된 부분을 주의 깊게 듣는다.
2. 세 명의 대화에서 같은 성별을 가진 화자들에 대해 묻는 문제, 또는 세 명의 화자 중 한 명의 이름을 언급하고 그 사람이 한 말에 대한 세부 사항을 묻는 문제도 출제되므로 화자를 구분해서 들어야 한다.
3. 정답의 단서가 자주 패러프레이징됨을 기억한다.

Example   ∩ D11_4_예제

해석 p.63

01 What happened last summer?
(A) A corporate merger was finalized.
(B) A new branch opened.
(C) A workspace was relocated.
(D) Additional workers were hired.

Question 01 refers to the following conversation.

W: Mr. Choi. You've been with our company for about a month now. How are you finding it?
M: It's great. I especially like the office layout. It makes it easy to focus on my work.
W: I'm glad to hear that. **We moved into this office last summer.** Many of the staff have said that their productivity has increased since then.
M: Interesting. By the way, is the lunch meeting with the senior managers still on for today?
W: Yes. You should be in the lobby at noon.

해설 특정 세부 사항 문제   정답 (C)
여자가 "We moved into this office last summer."라며 작년 여름에 이 사무실로 이사했다고 했으므로 (C)가 정답이다.

빈출 정답 단서와 패러프레이징 🎧 D11_5_표현

다음은 특정 세부 사항 문제에서 정답 단서와 함께 나오는 표현과 정답 단서가 패러프레이징된 예시이다.

단서와 함께 나오는 표현	대화 지문	질문 및 정답
1 recently / yesterday / last + 시점 ~ 최근에 / 어제 / 지난 ~	M: Have you seen our **recently** modified company logo? W: Yes. It looks friendlier than before. 남: 저희 회사가 최근에 변경한 로고를 봤나요? 여: 네. 이전보다 더 친근하게 보여요.	질문 What did the speakers' company **recently** do? 화자들의 회사는 최근에 무엇을 했는가? 정답 It changed its logo. 로고를 변경했다.
2 send / provide / e-mail / text 보내다/제공하다/이메일을 보내다/문자 메시지를 보내다	W: This apartment meets all of my requirements. I'm very interested in renting it. M: I'll **e-mail** you a copy of the contract to review. 여: 이 아파트는 제 모든 요구 사항을 충족합니다. 저는 매우 임대하고 싶어요. 남: 검토하실 수 있도록 계약서 사본을 이메일로 보내드릴게요.	질문 What is the man going to **send** to the woman? 남자는 여자에게 무엇을 보낼 것인가? 정답 A legal agreement 계약서
3 remember ~ ~을 기억하세요	W: Just **remember**, JK Air only allows one piece of carry-on luggage. M: OK. I'll make sure to pack light. 여: JK 항공사는 한 개의 기내 수하물만 허용한다는 것을 기억하세요. 남: 알겠어요. 가볍게 짐을 싸도록 할게요.	질문 What does the woman **remind** the man about? 여자는 남자에게 무엇을 상기시키는가? 정답 A luggage restriction 수하물 제한

토익실전문제 🎧 D11_6_실전

01 Why is the woman calling?

(A) To make a job offer
(B) To reschedule an appointment
(C) To discuss a replacement
(D) To change an interview date

02 Who most likely is Richard Hammel?

(A) A politician
(B) A copywriter
(C) A conference organizer
(D) A magazine editor

03 What does the woman ask the man to do?

(A) Attend a meeting
(B) Submit some documents
(C) Look through applications
(D) Call a potential candidate

04 Where is the conversation most likely taking place?

(A) At a service center
(B) At a research laboratory
(C) At an electronics store
(D) At a business exposition

05 What did Echo Incorporated recently do?

(A) It won an industry award.
(B) It hired more employees.
(C) It developed a new product.
(D) It expanded overseas.

06 What does the woman ask about?

(A) A free product
(B) A discounted price
(C) A business location
(D) A delivery date

HACKERS TEST

토익 800+를 위한 실전 문제 정복   DAY 11

🎧 D11_7_테스트

01 What are the speakers mainly discussing?
(A) Choosing a new director
(B) Replacing equipment
(C) Planning a charity auction
(D) Increasing compensation

02 Why is the man concerned?
(A) Some team members are unavailable.
(B) A training manual is outdated.
(C) A production goal might not be met.
(D) An area is too small.

03 Why will the woman contact the supervisor?
(A) To request some more workers
(B) To talk about an installation schedule
(C) To ask when a report is due
(D) To explain why a change was made

04 Where is the conversation most likely taking place?
(A) At a café
(B) At a supermarket
(C) At a stationery store
(D) At a shipping company

05 What does the woman say about some staff?
(A) They were recently hired.
(B) They have food allergies.
(C) They work only the morning shift.
(D) They will be dispatched abroad.

06 How can the woman get a discount for future orders?
(A) By signing up for a membership
(B) By visiting on a specific day
(C) By showing a coupon code
(D) By using a mobile application

07 Why is the woman calling?
(A) An appointment should be rescheduled.
(B) A receipt must be revised.
(C) A delivery arrived early.
(D) A worker is late.

08 What does the man apologize for?
(A) He did not contact a customer.
(B) He did not cancel an order.
(C) He charged the wrong amount.
(D) He forgot to bring some tools.

09 Who is the man most likely waiting for?
(A) A truck driver
(B) A repairperson
(C) A sales clerk
(D) A courier

10 What is the conversation mainly about?
(A) A construction project
(B) A staffing change
(C) A press conference
(D) A training initiative

11 Why does the man suggest changing a plan?
(A) To get special benefits
(B) To address a customer's complaint
(C) To ease a work burden
(D) To align with current trends

12 What does the woman ask the man to do?
(A) Make a reservation
(B) Contact an employee
(C) Recommend an application
(D) Create an account

13 What kind of business did the men open?

(A) A housekeeping service
(B) A fitness center
(C) An office supply store
(D) A catering company

14 How did the men learn about the woman's business?

(A) From a brochure
(B) From an online advertisement
(C) From a former colleague
(D) From a radio advertisement

15 What information will the woman provide next?

(A) Pricing details
(B) Branch locations
(C) Service periods
(D) Employee names

16 Where is the conversation most likely taking place?

(A) At a technology firm
(B) At a convention center
(C) At a warehouse
(D) At a medical facility

17 Why will the man be unable to attend a conference?

(A) He has a schedule conflict.
(B) He failed to register in advance.
(C) He was not invited.
(D) He cannot arrange transportation.

18 What does the woman offer to do?

(A) Modify a list
(B) Fill out some forms
(C) Call a supervisor
(D) Take some notes

19 What is the purpose of the woman's visit?

(A) She needs to purchase a gift.
(B) She wants to exchange an item.
(C) She is looking for a specific employee.
(D) She is taking a tour of a building.

20 What does the man say about Dove Fit?

(A) It is holding a sale.
(B) It is being renovated.
(C) It has been relocated.
(D) It has changed a policy.

21 Where will the woman most likely head?

(A) To a parking lot
(B) To a changing room
(C) To a subway station
(D) To an information desk

22 What department does the man most likely work in?

(A) Marketing
(B) Accounting
(C) Engineering
(D) Information Technology

23 What will the speakers' company do in the spring?

(A) Open an overseas branch
(B) Replace a department head
(C) Release a new product
(D) Launch an online service

24 What does the man say should be provided by tomorrow afternoon?

(A) A form
(B) A manual
(C) A schedule
(D) A photo

DAY 12 다음에 할 일 및 의도 파악 문제

기출 유형 1   다음에 할 일 문제

최근 3개년 오답률 15.2%

화자가 다음에 할 일 또는 미래에 일어날 일을 묻는 문제로, 매회 3~4문제 출제된다.

출제 경향

1. 한 대화에 해당되는 세 개의 문제들 중 주로 마지막 문제로 출제된다.
2. 주로 다음과 같은 질문을 사용한다.

   What will the woman **do next**? 여자는 다음에 무엇을 할 것인가?
   What will the man most likely **do next**? 남자는 다음에 무엇을 할 것 같은가?
   What does the woman say she will **do in the afternoon**? 여자는 오후에 무엇을 할 것이라고 말하는가?
   What will **happen next month**? 다음 달에 무슨 일이 일어날 것인가?

800+ 공략

1. 주로 대화의 마지막 부분에 단서가 언급되므로 대화의 마지막 부분을 주의 깊게 듣는다.
2. will, be going to 등의 미래 시제나 later, next, after 등의 미래와 관련된 표현이 포함된 문장을 주의 깊게 듣는다.

Example 🎧 D12_1_예제

해석 p.70

| 01 What will the woman do next?
(A) Speak with a colleague
(B) Put up a notice
(C) Sign a rental agreement
(D) Make an appointment | Question 01 refers to the following conversation.

W: Erik, are there any apartments for rent in Fosh Tower? I was speaking to a potential client named Sylvia Miller, and she's interested in moving into the complex.
M: Let me check . . . Uh, there are three apartments available in that complex right now.
W: Are they currently occupied?
M: No. They're empty, so you can show them to her whenever you like.
W: Perfect. **I'll contact Ms. Miller to set up a time for her to view them.** |

해설 다음에 할 일 문제   정답 (D)

대화 마지막에 여자가 "I'll contact Ms. Miller to set up a time for her to view them."이라며 Ms. Miller에게 연락해서 아파트 매물을 보러 올 일정을 잡을 것이라고 했으므로 (D)가 정답이다.

빈출 정답 단서와 패러프레이징 🎧 D12_2_표현

다음은 다음에 할 일 문제의 정답 단서와 함께 나오는 표현과 정답 단서가 패러프레이징된 예시이다.

단서와 함께 나오는 표현	대화 지문	질문 및 정답
1 will / be going to ~ ~할 것이다	M: We should start planning for the company retreat next month. W: I'll draft a list of the supplies we need. 남: 우리는 다음 달 회사 야유회를 계획하는 것을 시작해야 해요. 여: 우리가 필요한 용품들의 목록 초안을 제가 작성할게요.	질문 What will the woman do next? 여자는 다음에 무엇을 할 것인가? 정답 Make a list of supplies 용품 목록을 만든다.
2 let me ~ 제가 ~할게요	W: It seems like we'll have more people visiting our booth than expected. M: We won't have time to go out for lunch. **Let me** order some sandwiches. 여: 우리 부스에 예상보다 더 많은 사람들이 방문할 것 같아요. 남: 점심을 밖에 나가서 먹을 시간은 없을 거예요. 제가 샌드위치를 주문할게요.	질문 What does the man say he will do next? 남자는 다음에 무엇을 할 것이라고 말하는가? 정답 Order some food 음식을 주문한다.
3 next ~ / later ~ / 특정 시점 다음 ~에/이따 ~에	M: The printer in our office doesn't seem to be working. W: A technician will be coming **later this afternoon**. 남: 우리 사무실의 프린터가 작동하지 않는 것 같아요. 여: 기술자가 이따 오후에 올 거예요.	질문 What will happen in the afternoon? 오후에 무슨 일이 일어날 것인가? 정답 A technician will arrive. 기술자가 도착할 것이다.

토익실전문제 🎧 D12_3_실전

토익 문제 이렇게 나온다!

01 Why is the man calling?
 (A) To request technical assistance
 (B) To question a charge on a bill
 (C) To cancel an online order
 (D) To complain about a late delivery

02 What does the woman ask for?
 (A) An account number
 (B) A mailing address
 (C) A business name
 (D) An order number

다음에 할 일 문제
03 What will happen tomorrow?
 (A) A payment will be refunded.
 (B) A shipment will be delivered.
 (C) Maintenance will be performed.
 (D) Operating hours will be extended.

04 Where most likely do the speakers work?
 (A) At a bookstore
 (B) At a legal firm
 (C) At a recruiting agency
 (D) At a publishing company

05 What suggestion does the woman make?
 (A) Revising a schedule
 (B) Working over the weekend
 (C) Requesting additional staff
 (D) Ordering more supplies

다음에 할 일 문제
06 What will Michael most likely do next?
 (A) Participate in an event
 (B) Confirm a meeting
 (C) Promote a book
 (D) Contact a manager

정답·해석·해설 p.70

기출 유형 2 의도 파악 문제

최근 3개년 오답률 18.2%

대화에서 언급된 문장에 담긴 화자의 의도나 뜻을 묻는 문제로, 매회 2문제가 출제된다.

출제 경향

1. 인용어구는 화자의 의도에 따라 긍정적/부정적 의도 또는 그 외의 의도를 나타내거나 구체적인 맥락을 나타낸다.
2. 다음과 같은 질문을 사용한다.

   Why does the man **say**, **"My flight is about to leave"**?
   남자는 왜 "제 비행편이 곧 출발할 거예요"라고 말하는가?
   What does the woman **imply/mean** when she **says**, **"look at the company calendar"**?
   여자는 "사내 달력을 보세요"라고 말할 때 무엇을 의도하는가?

800+ 공략

1. 정답의 단서는 질문의 인용어구 주변에서 자주 언급되므로, 해당 인용어구의 앞뒤를 주의 깊게 듣는다.
2. 강세나 어조도 문맥을 파악하는 데 단서가 될 수 있으므로 인용어구를 주의 깊게 듣는다.
3. 인용어구에 쓰인 표현은 문맥에 따라 의미가 달라질 수 있으므로 맥락을 잘 파악해야 하며, 표현의 일차적 의미를 이용한 오답 보기에 유의한다.

Example 🎧 D12_4_예제
해석 p.71

01 Why does the man say, "You sent just three staff last time"?
(A) To compliment a team
(B) To question a decision
(C) To provide encouragement
(D) To request assistance

Question 01 refers to the following conversation.

M: I'd like to discuss the budget for your team's upcoming Hong Kong business trip. I've reviewed the funding request you submitted yesterday. You sent just three staff last time.
W: **Some of the new employees will accompany us on this trip for training purposes.** Will it be a problem?
M: **Your budget exceeds the maximum amount** allowed for business trips. You need to find a way to cut costs.
W: Hmm . . . The Doyle Hotel is offering a 30 percent discount this month. Maybe I can book our rooms there.

해설 의도 파악 문제
정답 (B)

여자가 "Some of the new employees will accompany us on this trip for training purposes."라며 신입 직원들이 교육 목적으로 이번 출장에 동행할 예정이라고 하자, 남자가 여자에게 "Your budget exceeds the maximum amount"라며 예산이 최대 금액을 초과한다고 하였다. 이를 통해 남자가 "You sent just three staff last time"이라고 말한 이유는 더 많은 직원들이 이번 출장에 가는 결정에 의문을 제기하기 위함인 것을 알 수 있다. 따라서 (B)가 정답이다.

빈출 인용어구와 정답 보기 🎧 D12_5_표현

다음은 인용어구의 의도에 따라 자주 출제되는 정답과 예시이다.

의도에 따라 자주 출제되는 정답	대화 지문	질문 및 정답
긍정적인 의도 To support / agree with a suggestion 제안을 지지/동의하기 위해 To give(offer) reassurance 안심시키기 위해 can / be able to ~ ~을 할 수 있다 be willing to ~ ~을 할 의향이 있다	W: There's a continuous paper jam error message on the printer. M: I've dealt with similar situations before. Just open the back cover of the device. 여: 프린터에 계속 용지가 걸렸다는 에러 메시지가 떠요. 남: 제가 이전에 비슷한 상황들을 다뤄본 적이 있어요. 장치의 후면 뚜껑을 여세요.	질문 Why does the man say, "I've dealt with similar situations before"? 남자는 왜 "제가 이전에 비슷한 상황들을 다뤄본 적이 있어요"라고 말하는가? 정답 To offer reassurance 안심시키기 위해
부정적인 의도 To reject a suggestion 제안을 거절하기 위해 To express doubt / concern 의구심/우려를 나타내기 위해 cannot / be unable to ~ ~을 할 수 없다	M: I need the final version of the contract. Could you e-mail it to me later this afternoon? W: Mr. Akio needs to review the changes. He will do that tomorrow. 남: 저는 계약서의 최종 버전이 필요해요. 이따 오후에 제게 이메일로 보내주실 수 있나요? 여: Mr. Akio가 변경 사항을 검토해야 해요. 그는 내일 그것을 할 거예요.	질문 What does the woman mean when she says, "Mr. Akio needs to review the changes"? 여자가 "Mr. Akio가 변경사항들을 검토해야 해요"라고 말할 때 무엇을 의도하는가? 정답 She cannot fulfill a request. 그녀는 요청을 이행할 수 없다.
기타 의도 To make a suggestion 제안을 하기 위해 To confirm an assumption 추정을 확인시켜주기 위해 To correct some mistakes 실수를 정정하기 위해	W: The launch of our company's new electric scooter is scheduled for May 15, right? M: The product will be released on May 10. 여: 우리 회사의 새로운 전동 스쿠터의 출시가 5월 15일로 예정되어 있죠, 그렇죠? 남: 그 제품은 5월 10일에 출시될 거예요.	질문 Why does the man say, "The product will be released on May 10"? 남자는 왜 "그 제품은 5월 10일에 출시될 거예요"라고 말하는가? 정답 To correct a mistake 실수를 정정하기 위해

토익실전문제 🎧 D12_6_실전

토익 문제 이렇게 나온다!

01 Why did the woman hire the man's company?

(A) To inspect a building
(B) To perform renovations
(C) To take some photographs
(D) To prepare for a company retreat

의도 파악 문제
02 What does the woman mean when she says, "I like the distinctive appearance of the chandelier"?

(A) She wants to change her decision.
(B) She needs to get some feedback.
(C) She is impressed by some progress.
(D) She is willing to pay extra.

03 What will the man send the woman tomorrow morning?

(A) A revised schedule
(B) Some design samples
(C) A cost estimate
(D) Some contact information

04 According to the woman, what is taking place today?

(A) A festival
(B) A conference
(C) A fundraising banquet
(D) An award ceremony

의도 파악 문제
05 Why does the man say, "we partner with a taxi company"?

(A) To announce a change
(B) To justify a decision
(C) To make a suggestion
(D) To correct a misunderstanding

06 What will the woman most likely do next?

(A) Wait near an entrance
(B) Return to a room
(C) Contact a business
(D) Evaluate a report

정답·해석·해설 p.71

HACKERS TEST

DAY 12

🎧 D12_7_테스트

01 What problem does the man mention?
 (A) An item is damaged.
 (B) A Web site is not working.
 (C) An order has not arrived.
 (D) A billing statement is incorrect.

02 What does the woman ask about?
 (A) A customer name
 (B) An order number
 (C) A method of payment
 (D) A date of purchase

03 What will the man most likely do next?
 (A) Download an order form
 (B) Check an exchange policy
 (C) Call a delivery person
 (D) Place an item in a designated spot

04 Why is the man calling?
 (A) To arrange an initial interview
 (B) To provide information about an apartment
 (C) To ask about requirements
 (D) To schedule home repairs

05 Why does the man say, "It's close to a metro station"?
 (A) To request assistance
 (B) To praise improvements to a system
 (C) To correct a mistaken assumption
 (D) To offer reassurance

06 What does the woman ask the man to send?
 (A) An event invitation
 (B) A tracking number
 (C) An employment contract
 (D) A residential address

07 What are the speakers mainly discussing?
 (A) A corporate event
 (B) A hotel opening
 (C) A business trip
 (D) A training workshop

08 What concern does Peter point out?
 (A) Some menu options are not available.
 (B) A project may be understaffed.
 (C) A space must be cleaned.
 (D) Some food is expensive.

09 What will happen next week?
 (A) An award will be given.
 (B) A company will move to a new location.
 (C) A report will be reviewed.
 (D) A press conference will take place.

10 Where is the conversation taking place?
 (A) At a gift shop
 (B) At a supermarket
 (C) At an airport
 (D) At a restaurant

11 What does the woman say she just tried to do?
 (A) Place an order
 (B) Use a device
 (C) Find a document
 (D) Make a payment

12 What does the man mean when he says, "today is less crowded than usual"?
 (A) An issue has been resolved.
 (B) The woman's concern is not valid.
 (C) An estimate has been updated.
 (D) The woman's request is not reasonable.

13 What is the reason for a delay?
(A) Mechanical issues occurred.
(B) Weather conditions are poor.
(C) Several staff members are absent.
(D) Some information was incorrect.

14 Who are the speakers scheduled to meet with?
(A) An inspector
(B) A client
(C) A former colleague
(D) A family member

15 What does the woman say she will do?
(A) Download an application
(B) Purchase a ticket
(C) Send a message
(D) Provide a link

16 Where do the speakers most likely work?
(A) At a retail outlet
(B) At an electronics store
(C) At a photography studio
(D) At a movie theater

17 What does the woman mean when she says, "That is in just half an hour"?
(A) She is asking for more details.
(B) She wants to change a seating request.
(C) She is doubtful about a suggestion.
(D) She is able to adjust her schedule.

18 What does the woman ask the man to do?
(A) Announce a change
(B) Reserve a venue
(C) Perform an inspection
(D) Assist a colleague

19 What type of product does the speakers' company make?
(A) Clothing
(B) Office furniture
(C) Sports equipment
(D) Appliances

20 What does the woman ask about?
(A) Event venues
(B) A guest list
(C) Product samples
(D) A user manual

21 What will the woman most likely do next?
(A) Read a brochure
(B) Present a plan
(C) Contact a manager
(D) Update a Web site

22 Where most likely do the speakers work?
(A) At a dining establishment
(B) At a department store
(C) At a manufacturing facility
(D) At a consulting firm

23 What did the speakers' company do last year?
(A) It conducted online training.
(B) It hired some employees.
(C) It transferred some staff members.
(D) It held an advertising workshop.

24 Why does the woman say, "they went through our normal orientation process"?
(A) To show disagreement
(B) To indicate satisfaction
(C) To inquire about a process
(D) To offer confirmation

DAY 13 시각 자료 문제

기출 유형 1 표 및 그래프

최근 3개년 오답률 15.1%

대화에서 언급된 내용 중 질문과 함께 제시된 표 또는 그래프와 관련된 사항을 묻는 문제로, 매회 3문제 중 2~3문제 출제된다.

출제 경향

1. 상품명과 가격이 나열된 리스트, 업무 일정표, 회사의 매출 그래프 등의 시각 자료가 주로 출제된다.
2. 주로 다음과 같은 질문을 사용한다.

   Look at the **graphic**. Which model does the man **recommend**? 시각 자료를 보아라. 남자는 어떤 모델을 추천하는가?
   Look at the **graphic**. What is the **amount** the woman **will pay**? 시각 자료를 보아라. 여자가 지불할 금액은 얼마인가?

800+ 공략

1. 주어진 표 또는 그래프를 보고 무엇에 관한 내용인지 빠르게 파악한다.
2. 대화에서 변경 사항, 최고·최저 항목 등의 특이 사항이 언급될 경우 시각 자료의 해당 항목 주변에서 정답의 단서를 파악한다.

Example 🎧 D13_1_예제

해석 p.77

01 Look at the graphic. Which brand will the woman most likely buy?
(A) Bongo Fashion
(B) West Coast Apparel
(C) Luna Beachwear
(D) Sunny Clothes

Question 01 refers to the following conversation and product list.

W: Steve, our company is sending me to Bangkok next week to participate in a marketing convention. I plan to stay a few extra days and visit some beaches, so I need your opinion on some sun hats.
M: Which hats are you considering?
W: These ones are available online. The hat from Bongo Fashion looks great, but it's too expensive.
M: **I think you should get the one for 25 dollars.** It's very stylish.
W: **Yeah, I like that one too.** Now, I just need to create an account on this online shopping site so that I can place my order.

정답 (C)

해설 시각 자료 문제

제시된 제품 목록의 정보를 확인한 후 질문의 핵심 어구(woman ~ buy)와 관련된 내용을 주의 깊게 듣는다. 남자가 "I think you should get the one for 25 dollars."라며 25달러짜리를 사라고 제안하자, 여자가 "Yeah, I like that one too."라고 했으므로 Luna Beachwear의 모자를 구매할 것임을 알 수 있다. 따라서 (C)가 정답이다.

표 및 그래프 형태의 시각 자료

다음은 자주 등장하는 표 및 그래프 형태의 시각 자료이다.

표

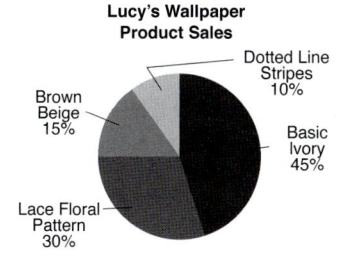

0.5 Ton	1 Ton
$550	$980
1.5 Ton	2.5 Ton
$1,300	$2,200

→ 크기가 1.5톤이면 충분하다고 한다면, 지불할 비용은 1,300달러 임을 알 수 있다.

Date	Room	Instructor
March 1	203	Simon White
March 2	204	Joshua Walz
March 3	205	Claire Lee
March 4	206	Mitch Marks

→ 수업을 3월 4일로 옮겨 달라고 한다면, Mitch Marks가 이끄는 수업에 참석할 것임을 알 수 있다.

그래프

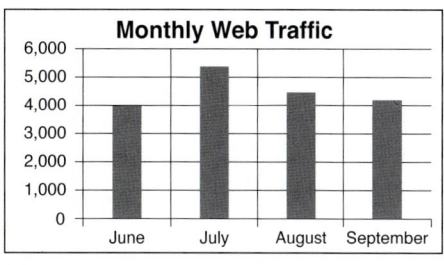

Lucy's Wallpaper Product Sales
- Basic Ivory 45%
- Lace Floral Pattern 30%
- Brown Beige 15%
- Dotted Line Stripes 10%

→ 가장 잘 팔리는 벽지를 보여 달라고 한다면, 판매율이 45%로 가장 높은 Basic Ivory를 보여줄 것임을 알 수 있다.

Monthly Web Traffic

→ 웹사이트 방문자가 가장 적은 다음 달에 프로모션을 했다고 한다면, June(6월) 다음 달인 July(7월)에 프로모션을 했음을 알 수 있다.

토익실전문제 D13_2_실전

토익 문제 이렇게 나온다!

SAVALL MOTORS TEAMBUILDING WORKSHOPS	
Speaker	Topic
Logan Jenkins	Staff Communication
Betty Graham	Trust in the Workplace
Aubrey Hammond	Training New Workers
Carson Filby	Team Efficiency

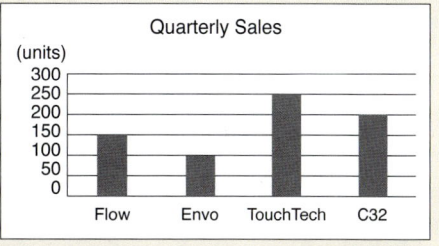

Quarterly Sales (units)
- Flow: 150
- Envo: 100
- TouchTech: 250
- C32: 200

01 Why was the woman unable to attend an event?

(A) She needed to assist a manager.
(B) She was away on a business trip.
(C) She had to meet with an important client.
(D) She had to complete an assignment.

02 Look at the graphic. Who led the workshop the man participated in?

(A) Logan Jenkins
(B) Betty Graham
(C) Aubrey Hammond
(D) Carson Filby

03 What will be posted online?

(A) Videos
(B) Transcripts
(C) Maps
(D) Schedules

04 Where do the speakers most likely work?

(A) At a manufacturing plant
(B) At a retail shop
(C) At an advertising firm
(D) At a television studio

05 What will the woman send the man?

(A) The annual sales report
(B) The customer survey results
(C) The quarterly expense report
(D) The product development plans

06 Look at the graphic. Which brand is going to be discounted?

(A) Flow
(B) Envo
(C) TouchTech
(D) C32

기출 유형 2 약도 및 기타 시각 자료

최근 3개년 오답률 13.5%

질문과 함께 제시된 약도, 노선표, 탑승권, 쿠폰 등과 관련된 사항을 묻는 문제로, 매회 3문제 중 1~2문제 출제된다.

출제 경향

1. 상점 및 시설 안내도, 거리 약도, 자리 안내도, 노선표, 탑승권, 쿠폰 등의 시각 자료가 주로 출제된다.
2. 주로 다음과 같은 질문을 사용한다.

   Look at the **graphic**. **Which room** will the meeting **take place in**? 시각 자료를 보아라. 어느 방에서 회의가 진행될 것인가?
   Look at the **graphic**. **Which number** does the man say is **incorrect**? 시각 자료를 보아라. 남자는 어떤 숫자가 맞지 않다고 말하는가?

800+ 공략

1. 시각 자료가 안내도 및 약도일 경우, 각 보기 주변에 있는 주요 장소의 위치를 파악한 후, between(~ 사이에), next to(~ 옆에), across(~ 건너편에), in front of(~ 앞에) 등의 위치나 방향을 나타내는 표현을 주의 깊게 듣는다.
2. 생소한 형태의 시각 자료가 나올 경우, 어떤 종류의 시각 자료인지 빠르게 파악한 후, 시각 자료에 나타난 각 상세 항목이 언급된 주변을 주의 깊게 듣는다.

Example D13_3_예제

해석 p.79

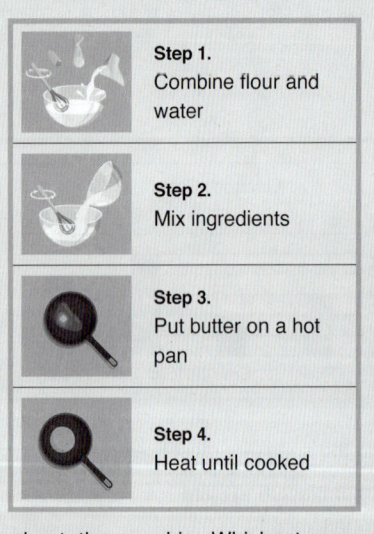

Step 1. Combine flour and water
Step 2. Mix ingredients
Step 3. Put butter on a hot pan
Step 4. Heat until cooked

Question 01 refers to the following conversation and recipe.

M: OK, we're done setting up the equipment for the cooking class. We should go over the recipes. Students are going to begin arriving in 45 minutes.

W: Yes, here's the pancake recipe that we're going to use. **But we have to change one of the steps slightly. Some students don't eat dairy, so we should use oil instead of butter.**

M: **Oh, you're right.** I'm going to get the ingredients that we will need from the storage room.

01 Look at the graphic. Which step must be changed?
(A) Step 1
(B) Step 2
(C) Step 3
(D) Step 4

정답 (C)

해설 시각 자료 문제
제시된 요리법의 정보를 확인한 후 질문의 핵심 어구(be changed)와 관련된 내용을 주의 깊게 듣는다. 여자가 "But we have to change one of the steps slightly. Some students don't eat dairy, so we should use oil instead of butter."라며 한 단계를 변경해야 된다고 한 뒤, 몇몇 학생들이 유제품을 먹지 않아서 버터 대신 오일을 사용해야 한다고 하자, 남자가 "Oh, you're right."이라며 여자의 말이 맞다고 한 것을 통해 버터가 필요한 Step 3가 변경되어야 하는 것임을 알 수 있다. 따라서 (C)가 정답이다.

약도 및 기타 형태의 시각 자료

다음은 자주 등장하는 약도 및 기타 형태의 시각 자료이다.

약도

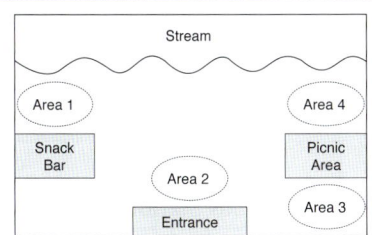

→ 화자가 간단히 먹을 snack(간식)을 사고 있을 테니 그 앞에서 만나자고 한다면, Area 1에서 화자들이 만날 것임을 알 수 있다.

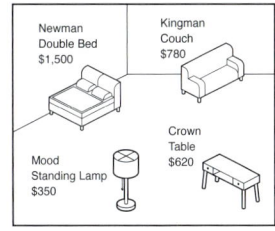

→ 화자가 소파를 구매하고 싶다고 한다면, Kingman 브랜드의 제품을 구매할 것임을 알 수 있다.

기타 시각 자료

→ 화자가 할인율을 변경해야 할 것 같다고 한다면, 10이라는 숫자를 변경할 계획임을 알 수 있다.

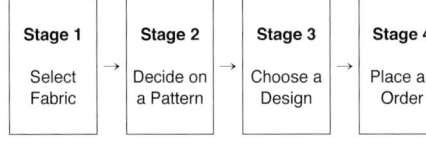

→ 화자가 패브릭과 패턴을 모두 결정 완료해서, 다음 단계를 시작할 것이라고 한다면, 다음 진행할 단계는 Stage 3임을 알 수 있다.

토익실전문제

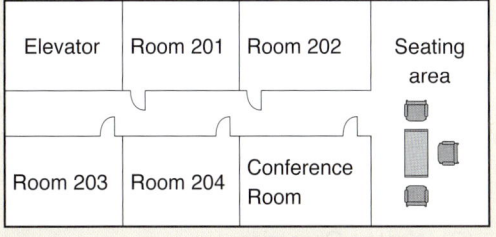

Boarding Pass	Business Class
Destination: Sydney Departure Date: 24 May 6:30 P.M.	Seat: B-07 Gate: C42

01 What is the purpose of the woman's visit?

(A) She is conducting an interview.
(B) She is touring a property.
(C) She is inspecting a workspace.
(D) She is applying for a job.

02 Look at the graphic. Where is the woman going to visit?

(A) Room 201
(B) Room 202
(C) Room 203
(D) Room 204

03 What does the man ask the woman to do?

(A) Secure some belongings
(B) Contact a manager
(C) Provide contact information
(D) Complete an evaluation form

04 What type of event are the speakers invited to?

(A) An art exhibition
(B) A trade show
(C) A shareholders meeting
(D) A press conference

05 What topic does the man say he will discuss?

(A) Facility modifications
(B) Product improvements
(C) Government programs
(D) Company policies

06 Look at the graphic. Which information has been changed?

(A) Business Class
(B) 24 May
(C) B-07
(D) C42

HACKERS TEST

Swift Auto Rentals

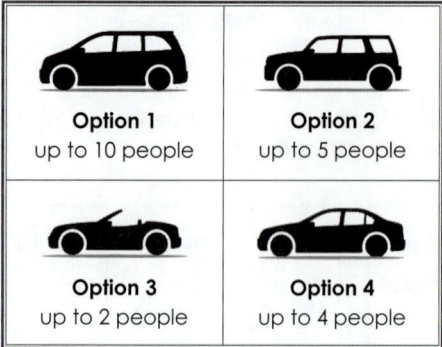

Customer	Delivery Time
Gibbs Market	9:00 A.M.
Star Gas Station	9:45 A.M.
Black Bird Café	10:30 A.M.
Weston Groceries	11:15 A.M.

01 Why is the woman visiting Seattle?
(A) To open a branch office
(B) To inspect some properties
(C) To meet with customers
(D) To attend an industry event

02 Look at the graphic. Which option does the man recommend?
(A) Option 1
(B) Option 2
(C) Option 3
(D) Option 4

03 What does the woman want to pay extra for?
(A) Hotel pickup
(B) Vehicle repair
(C) A navigation system
(D) An insurance policy

04 What problem does the woman mention?
(A) A bill has not been paid.
(B) An order is incorrect.
(C) A store has to close early.
(D) A shipment did not arrive.

05 What does the man offer to do?
(A) Provide some product samples
(B) Extend a due date
(C) Return to a storage facility
(D) Arrange a discount

06 Look at the graphic. Where does the woman work?
(A) Gibbs Market
(B) Star Gas Station
(C) Black Bird Café
(D) Weston Groceries

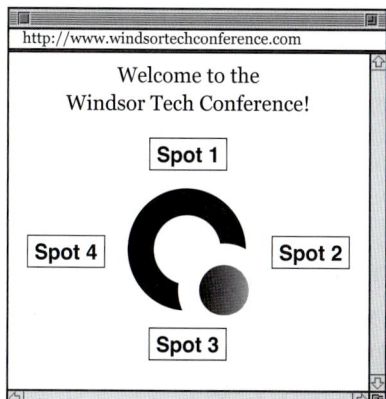

Finley Department Store Directory	
Floor 1	Cosmetics
Floor 2	Clothing
Floor 3	Electronics
Floor 4	Sporting Goods

07 Look at the graphic. Where does the man want to place a registration button?

(A) Spot 1
(B) Spot 2
(C) Spot 3
(D) Spot 4

08 What did the man make this morning?

(A) Manuals
(B) Questionnaires
(C) Invitations
(D) Nametags

09 What does the woman request?

(A) Delaying a task
(B) Expanding an event
(C) Preparing a contract
(D) Downloading a file

10 Why does the man want to visit a department store?

(A) To purchase a product
(B) To request a refund
(C) To exchange an item
(D) To pick up an order

11 What does the woman offer to do?

(A) Make a reservation
(B) Provide a ride
(C) Pay for a meal
(D) Find information online

12 Look at the graphic. Which floor is closed this weekend?

(A) Floor 1
(B) Floor 2
(C) Floor 3
(D) Floor 4

DAY 14 대화 상황

음성 바로 듣기

기출 유형 1 회사 생활
최근 3개년 오답률 14.2%

회사 업무·행사·사무기기 관련 등 회사에서 접하는 상황이나 마케팅·판매·재정 관련 등 구체적인 회사 업무에 대한 대화로, 매회 7~8개의 대화가 출제된다.

출제 경향

1. 회사에서 흔하게 접할 수 있는 상황과 관련하여 다음과 같은 대화들이 출제된다.
   - 문서 작성 및 발송, 업무 기한, 회의 및 프리젠테이션 일정, 파일 정리, 고객 응대에 관한 일반적인 회사 업무 관련 대화
   - 사무기기의 작동 오류 및 수리, 사무용품 주문 및 위치 문의, 시설 보수 및 안전 점검 작업에 대한 사무실 관련 대화
   - 채용, 퇴임, 업무 평가, 승진, 전근, 출장, 직원 교육, 회사 야유회 등 인사 및 사내 행사 관련 대화
2. 특정 부서에서 하는 구체적인 업무와 관련하여 다음과 같은 대화들이 출제된다.
   - 상품 마케팅 전략, 제품 홍보, 물품 배송 등 마케팅 및 판매 업무 관련 대화
   - 예산 수립, 비용 절감, 자금 조달, 사업 확장 등 재정 관련 대화

800+ 공략

1. 대화 초반에서 구체적인 대화 상황을 파악하는 것이 중요하다.
2. 회사 생활과 관련된 다양한 표현들을 알아 둔다.

Example D14_1_예제
해석 p.84

01 What is the conversation mainly about?
(A) A business report
(B) An office machine
(C) A new manager
(D) A policy change

02 Why does the woman want to copy a report?
(A) To submit it to a supervisor
(B) To send it to a client
(C) To discuss it in a meeting
(D) To prepare for a presentation

03 What will the woman most likely do next?
(A) Order some supplies
(B) Return an item
(C) Review a document
(D) Go to a storage area

Questions 01-03 refer to the following conversation.

W: Paul, ⁰¹**do you know what's wrong with the office photocopier?** ⁰²**I'm supposed to give a copy of this report to my manager** by 2 P.M., but the machine isn't working.
M: Well . . . If you're trying to make color copies, the ink may have run out. The last time I used the printer, there was a message saying that the color ink cartridge would need to be replaced soon.
W: I need to make a color copy. Have you ever replaced an ink cartridge?
M: Yes. ⁰³**There should be a new ink cartridge in the supply room. If you bring it, I'll help you replace the one in the copier.**

정답 01 (B) 02 (A) 03 (D)

해설
01 [주제] 대화의 초반에 여자가 남자에게 "do you know ~ the office photocopier?"라며 사무실 복사기에 무슨 문제가 있는지 아냐고 물은 뒤, 복사기에 관한 대화가 이어지고 있으므로 (B)가 정답이다.
02 [이유] 여자가 "I'm supposed to give ~ to my manager"라며 관리자에게 보고서를 제출해야 된다고 했으므로 (A)가 정답이다.
03 [다음에 할 일] 대화의 마지막에 남자가 여자에게 "There should be ~ the one in the copier."라며 비품 보관실에 있는 새 잉크 카트리지를 가지고 오면 교체하는 것을 도와주겠다고 했으므로 (D)가 정답이다.

회사 생활 관련 대화에 자주 나오는 필수 표현 🎧 D14_2_표현

회의 및 문서 작성

1 review a report/proposal 보고서/제안서를 검토하다	3 complete the paperwork 서류 작업을 완료하다
2 travel reimbursement form 출장비 환급 양식	4 expense report 경비 보고서

인사 및 사내 행사

5 convention / conference 대규모 회의/학회	9 trade fair/show 무역 박람회
6 training session 교육 활동	10 recruitment 채용
7 company retreat 회사 야유회	11 fundraiser 기금 모금 행사
8 luncheon 오찬 모임	12 charity auction 자선 경매

사무기기

13 routine update 일상적인 업데이트	15 instruction manual 사용 안내서
14 access 접근하다, 접속하다	16 malfunction 오작동하다

마케팅 전략 및 홍보 수단

17 product demonstration 제품 시연	20 launch 출시하다
18 advertising strategy 광고 전략	21 promotional efforts 판촉 활동
19 marketing budget 마케팅 예산	22 expand one's product line 제품군을 늘리다

매출 증가 및 감소

23 profit 수익	25 sales figures 매출액
24 increased competition 치열해진 경쟁	26 decline in sales 판매 감소

토익실전문제 🎧 D14_3_실전

토익 문제 이렇게 나온다!

01 Where most likely do the speakers work?

(A) At a convention center
(B) At a marketing firm
(C) At a phone service provider
(D) At an electronics manufacturer

02 What does the man express relief about?

(A) Well-trained employees are available.
(B) The woman has met a project deadline.
(C) Customer reviews are generally positive.
(D) The woman made a suitable selection.

03 What information does the man ask the woman to include?

(A) A promotional price
(B) A model number
(C) Features of products
(D) Guidelines for a refund

04 What field do the speakers most likely work in?

(A) Finance
(B) Transportation
(C) Law
(D) Healthcare

05 What does the woman imply when she says, "It will be almost an hour long"?

(A) A speech will be informative.
(B) Some issues were addressed.
(C) A conference was extended.
(D) Some revisions are needed.

06 Why will the woman leave the office early today?

(A) To visit a service center
(B) To take a certification exam
(C) To get a medical checkup
(D) To attend an industry event

정답·해석·해설 p.84

기출 유형 2   일상 생활

최근 3개년 오답률 13.1%

쇼핑·편의 시설·주거 관련 등 일상 생활이나 여행·여가 관련 등 다양한 여가 생활에 대한 대화로, 매회 4~5개의 대화가 출제된다.

출제 경향

1. 쇼핑이나 편의 시설 이용, 주거 관련 등의 일상적인 상황과 관련하여 다음과 같은 대화가 출제된다.
   - 상점에서의 물건 구매, 환불이나 교환 요청 등의 일상적인 쇼핑 관련 대화
   - 도서관이나 우체국 이용, 미용실 서비스 예약, 병원 진료 예약, 은행 업무 등 편의 시설 이용 관련 대화
   - 이사 또는 집 보수 공사, 부동산 투어 등 주거 관련 대화
2. 여행이나 여가와 관련하여 다음과 같은 대화가 출제된다.
   - 항공편 및 숙박 예약, 여행 일정, 공항 및 호텔 이용 관련 대화
   - 공연 또는 전시회 관람, 티켓 예매, 수업 등록 관련 대화
3. 팟캐스트의 진행자와 게스트 간의 대화가 출제된다. 주로 지역 사회 이슈나 게스트의 최근 업적 등에 대해 이야기한다.

800+ 공략

1. 일상 생활 대화는 출제될 수 있는 주제가 매우 다양하기 때문에 대화 초반에서 정확히 어떤 상황인지 파악해두면 수월하게 문제를 풀 수 있다.
2. 물건 및 부동산 구매, 교통수단 및 편의 시설 이용, 항공편, 숙박 시설, 표 구매와 관련된 표현들을 알아 둔다.

Example 🎧 D14_4_예제

해석 p.85

01 Why was the man late for the appointment?
(A) He went to the wrong building.
(B) He was stuck in a traffic jam.
(C) He forgot to bring a document.
(D) He was confused about the date.

02 What does the woman inquire about?
(A) A rental period
(B) A monthly fee
(C) An availability date
(D) A contract term

03 What does the woman say she will do?
(A) Reschedule a tour
(B) Take some pictures
(C) Compare some properties
(D) Meet with a tenant

Questions 01-03 refer to the following conversation.

M: Hello, Ms. Parker. ⁰¹I'm very sorry that I arrived late for our appointment. I got confused about which house I was supposed to show this morning and went to a different one.
W: It's fine. I just got here a few minutes ago myself. Um, ⁰²this house is available to rent on March 1, right? My current lease agreement ends on February 28.
M: Correct. You can even move in sooner, if you like. It's currently vacant.
W: That's good to know. Oh, ⁰³I'm planning to photograph the interior of the house as you show me around. I assume that won't be an issue.
M: Of course not. Let's begin the tour, then.

해설

정답 01 (A) 02 (C) 03 (B)

01 [이유] 남자가 "I'm very sorry that I arrived late ~. I got confused about which house I was supposed to show this morning and went to a different one."이라며 보여주어야 할 집을 혼동해서 다른 집으로 가서 늦었다고 했으므로 (A)가 정답이다.
02 [세부] 여자가 "this house is available to rent on March 1, right?"이라고 했으므로 (C)가 정답이다.
03 [다음에 할 일] 여자가 "I'm planning to photograph the interior of the house as you show me around."라며 집의 내부 사진을 찍겠다고 했으므로 (B)가 정답이다.

일상 생활 관련 대화에 자주 나오는 필수 표현 🎧 D14_5_표현

쇼핑

1 purchase 구매하다	5 get a refund 환불받다
2 register for membership 멤버십에 등록하다	6 lifetime warranty 평생 품질 보증
3 custom order 주문 제작	7 checkout counter 계산대
4 price quote 가격 견적	8 in stock 재고가 있는

주거 및 부동산

9 renovation / remodeling 보수 공사	12 leaking 누수
10 complex 단지, 복합 건물	13 property tour / room tour 매물 구경
11 interior decoration 인테리어 장식	14 move out 이사를 나가다

교통수단 및 편의 시설 이용

15 fee 요금, 수수료	18 make an appointment 일정을 잡다
16 commute 통근	19 aisle seat 통로 좌석
17 mechanical problem 기계적 결함	20 compartment 칸, 객실

여행 및 여가 활동

21 car rental 자동차 대여	24 accommodation 숙소
22 craft 공예	25 confirm a booking(reservation) 예약을 확정하다
23 upcoming exhibit 다가오는 전시회	26 newly released film 새로 개봉한 영화

토익실전문제 🎧 D14_6_실전

토익 문제 이렇게 나온다!

01 Who most likely is the woman?

(A) An author
(B) A politician
(C) A librarian
(D) An architect

02 What does the woman say was difficult about a project?

(A) Making a tight deadline
(B) Finding a suitable partner
(C) Meeting public expectations
(D) Raising adequate funds

03 What will happen on June 17?

(A) A facility will open.
(B) An announcement will be made.
(C) A festival will be held.
(D) A regulation will change.

04 Why is the man calling the woman?

(A) To describe a new company policy
(B) To change an appointment
(C) To schedule a home repair
(D) To inquire about catering

05 What does the man say about the Coolmax 78?

(A) It is a recently released model.
(B) It is energy-efficient.
(C) It is offered at a discount.
(D) It is gaining significant popularity.

06 What will the woman receive later?

(A) A list of items
(B) Contact information
(C) Account access
(D) A survey link

정답·해석·해설 p.86

HACKERS TEST

🎧 D14_7_테스트

01 What type of event are the speakers mainly discussing?
(A) A grand opening
(B) A city festival
(C) A company outing
(D) A product launch

02 According to the man, what will some attendees receive?
(A) A photo
(B) A meal voucher
(C) A clothing item
(D) A membership card

03 Why is the woman going to travel to Boston?
(A) To give a speech
(B) To attend a convention
(C) To visit a family member
(D) To interview for a position

04 What type of business do the speakers work at?
(A) A garden store
(B) A moving company
(C) A landscaping service
(D) A construction company

05 What does the man say about the project?
(A) It will begin in a few more days.
(B) It could finish earlier than expected.
(C) It requires additional workers.
(D) It was interrupted by severe weather conditions.

06 What does Ms. Lowery ask for?
(A) An updated schedule
(B) A site blueprint
(C) A list of supplies
(D) A budget report

07 What did the man do this morning?
(A) He repaired his mobile phone.
(B) He met with a client.
(C) He went to the service center.
(D) He made a business call.

08 How did the woman learn about the art fair?
(A) From a colleague
(B) From an online review
(C) From a newspaper advertisement
(D) From a local business owner

09 What does the woman say about Greener Park?
(A) Its parking lot is small.
(B) It is convenient to public transportation.
(C) It has hosted several festivals.
(D) Its facilities are under renovation.

10 What is the conversation mainly about?
(A) A factory relocation plan
(B) A remodeling project
(C) A recruitment plan
(D) A press conference

11 What does the woman mean when she says, "we submitted our request three weeks ago"?
(A) A job opening will be posted soon.
(B) A decision is taking longer than expected.
(C) A project can carry on as originally planned.
(D) A work schedule has already been changed.

12 What will the woman probably do next?
(A) Contact a manager
(B) Negotiate a contract
(C) Review an office budget
(D) Draft a training manual

Community Health Seminar Schedule		
Speaker	Topic	Time
Jim Bartley	Preventive Heart Care	8 A.M. – 9 A.M.
Adrian Smith	Balanced Diet Strategies	10 A.M. – 11 A.M.
Carlos Fernandez	Exercise Rehab for Seniors	11:30 A.M. – 12:30 P.M.
Yi Lang	Coping with Stress	2 P.M. – 3 P.M.

13 Look at the graphic. Which topic is the man going to cover?

(A) Preventive Heart Care
(B) Balanced Diet Strategies
(C) Exercise Rehab for Seniors
(D) Coping with Stress

14 What does the man ask the woman to do?

(A) Distribute some materials
(B) Test some equipment
(C) Print out a document
(D) Prepare for a safety inspection

15 What information will the woman most likely provide later?

(A) An event venue
(B) Addresses of businesses
(C) Names of participants
(D) A time estimate

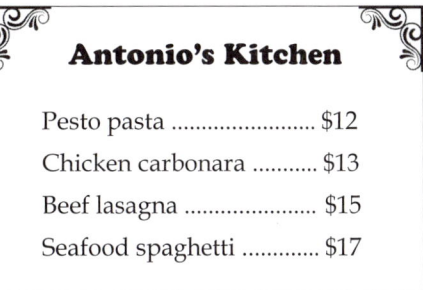

Antonio's Kitchen

Pesto pasta $12
Chicken carbonara $13
Beef lasagna $15
Seafood spaghetti $17

16 Why is the man late?

(A) A parking spot was unavailable.
(B) A meeting was delayed.
(C) A road was inaccessible.
(D) A restaurant was hard to find.

17 What does the woman say about the daily special?

(A) It is served with a free beverage.
(B) It is a newly introduced dish.
(C) It is based on a family recipe.
(D) It is available only on weekdays.

18 Look at the graphic. How much will the man's meal cost?

(A) $12
(B) $13
(C) $15
(D) $17

실시간 토익시험 정답확인&해설강의
Hackers.co.kr

한 권으로 끝내는 해커스 토익 800+ LC+RC+VOCA

PART 4

DAY 15	문제 유형
DAY 16	음성 메시지 및 회의 발췌
DAY 17	공지 및 관광 안내
DAY 18	연설 및 강연
DAY 19	방송 및 보도
DAY 20	광고 및 소개

◀ 음성 바로 듣기

교재에 수록된 모든 음성을 다운로드하거나 바로 스트리밍하여 더욱 편리하게 이용해보세요.

PART 4 소개   짧은 담화 (30문제)

하나의 담화를 듣고 각 담화와 관련된 3개 문제의 정답을 고르는 파트이다. 문제지에는 하나의 질문과 4개의 보기로 구성된 30개의 문제가 제시되며, 일부 문제는 시각 자료가 함께 제시되기도 한다. 음성에서는 담화와 이에 대한 3문제의 질문을 들려준다.

최신 예제 및 풀이 방법

[문제지]

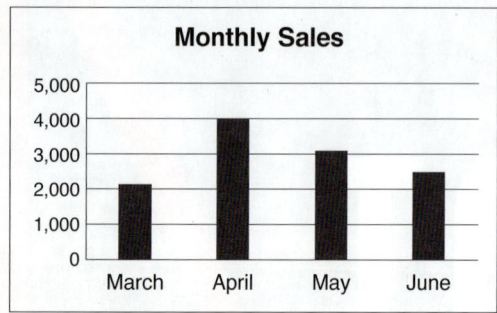

73. Look at the graphic. When was a product reviewed?
(A) March
(B) April
(C) May
(D) June

[음성]

Questions 71 through 73 refer to the following excerpt from a meeting and graph.

Good morning, everyone. I've called this meeting to talk about the performance of our recent marketing strategies. Last quarter had some surprises for us. One month in particular is of interest, as a prominent blogger—Stacy Meadow—positively reviewed our MusicBeat headphones. During that month, sales jumped up to 4,000. I believe her review contributed to the sudden boost in sales. So starting next month, we'll begin reaching out to popular Internet bloggers to ask them to review our products. My hope is that their reviews will drive our sales.

Number 73.
Look at the graphic. When was a product reviewed?

Step 1 문제 내용 파악하기
담화를 듣기 전에 질문의 핵심 어구를 미리 읽고 밑줄을 쳐서 담화의 어느 부분을 중점적으로 들어야 할지 파악한다. 특히 시각 자료가 제시된 문제라면, 문제와 시각 자료를 함께 확인하면서 시각 자료의 종류와 내용을 파악한다.

Step 2 담화를 듣는 동시에 정답 고르기
정답을 마킹할 시간을 따로 주지 않으므로, 담화를 들으면서 미리 파악해 둔 문제에 대한 정답의 근거를 확인하여 정답을 바로 고른다. 3개의 문제에 대한 정답의 단서가 담화 안에서 순차적으로 나오므로, 한 문제의 정답을 고르면 바로 다음 문제의 정답의 단서를 주의해서 들을 준비를 한다.

Step 3 다음 지문의 문제 내용 파악하기
3개 문제의 질문을 들려주는 동안, 다음 지문의 문제 내용을 미리 파악한다.

최신 출제 경향

30개의 문제 중 PART 3과 마찬가지로 특정 세부 사항을 묻는 문제가 가장 많이 출제된다. 담화는 유형별로 골고루 등장하지만, 음성 메시지 및 회의 발췌가 꾸준히 가장 많이 출제된다. 그 중 음성 메시지에서는 주문 내역을 확인하는 내용, 회의 발췌에서는 직원들에게 업무를 요청하는 내용이 최근 높은 비율로 등장하고 있다.

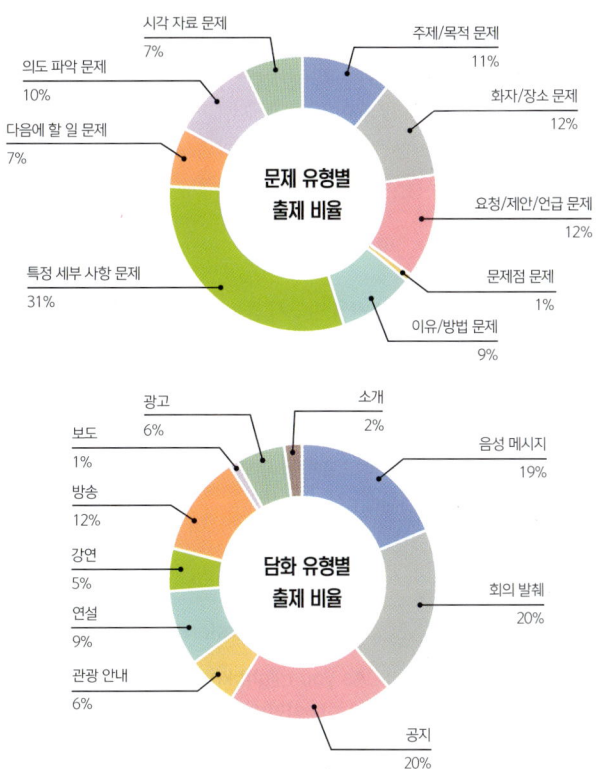

800+ 학습 전략

🔍 **문제 유형별 풀이 공략을 익힌다.**
PART 4에서는 PART 3에 출제되는 문제 유형이 동일하게 출제되며, 크게 전체 지문 관련 문제와 세부 사항 관련 문제로 나누어 학습할 수 있다. 특히, PART 4의 세부 사항 관련 문제는 질문 자체가 긴 경우가 많으므로, 질문을 빠르고 정확하게 이해하는 연습을 해야 한다.

🔍 **담화 유형별로 자주 등장하는 표현을 암기한다.**
PART 4에 담화 유형별로 자주 등장하는 표현들을 암기해 두면 더욱 쉽고 정확하게 음성을 들을 수 있다. 특히, PART 4에서는 구나 절로 연결된 긴 문장들을 연속해서 읽어 주는데, 관련 표현들을 많이 알아 두면 이 문장들을 듣는 즉시 이해할 수 있다.

DAY 15 문제 유형

기출 유형 1   전체 지문 관련 문제   최근 3개년 오답률 15.5%

지문의 주제 또는 목적, 화자/청자, 장소와 관련된 내용을 묻는 문제로, 매회 7~8문제 출제된다.

출제 경향

1. 한 지문에 해당되는 세 개의 문제들 중 주로 첫 번째 문제로 출제된다.
2. 주로 다음과 같은 질문을 사용한다.

주제	**What** is the **main topic** of the talk?	담화의 주제는 무엇인가?
목적	**Why** is the speaker **calling**?	화자는 왜 전화를 하고 있는가?
화자/청자	**Who** most likely is **the speaker/listener**?	화자/청자는 누구일 것 같은가?
	Where does **the speaker most likely work**?	화자는 어디에서 일하는 것 같은가?
	Where do **the listeners work**?	청자들은 어디에서 일하는가?
장소	**Where** is the **talk taking place**?	담화는 어디에서 이루어지고 있는가?

800+ 공략

1. 정답의 단서는 지문의 초반에 자주 언급되므로, 지문의 초반을 반드시 듣는다.
2. 화자의 신분이나 직업은 I am(저는 ~)이나 As(~로서) 다음에 자주 언급되는 점, 청자의 신분이나 직업은 지문에서 언급된 장소 및 회사명/부서명을 통해 유추해야 하는 점을 기억한다.
   ▶ 신분이나 직업을 나타내는 표현은 LC DAY 09(p.63)에서 자세히 다루고 있다.
3. 장소는 지문에 직접적으로 언급되는 경우가 많으므로, 지문의 초반을 주의 깊게 듣는다.
   ▶ 장소를 나타내는 표현은 LC DAY 09(p.63)에서 자세히 다루고 있다.

Example 🎧 D15_1_예제   해석 p.92

01 Where do the listeners work?
(A) At a grocery store
(B) At a restaurant
(C) At a cooking school
(D) At a kitchenware store

Question 01 refers to the following excerpt from a meeting.

As you might know, **we've recently hired some new staff at our restaurant**. Accordingly, I've just posted an updated work schedule on the bulletin board in the break room. One more thing . . . the chef has added some new dishes to our lunch menu, including chicken noodle soup and a mushroom panini. Don't forget to recommend these to customers. OK, back to work, everyone.

해설 청자 문제   정답 (B)

질문의 Where, the listeners work를 통해 청자들이 일하는 곳을 묻는 문제임을 알 수 있다. 지문의 초반에서 화자가 "we've recently hired some new staff at our restaurant"이라고 한 말을 통해 청자들이 식당에서 일한다는 것을 알 수 있으므로 (B)가 정답이다.

빈출 정답 단서와 패러프레이징

다음은 전체 지문 관련 문제에서 정답 단서와 함께 나오는 표현과 정답 단서가 패러프레이징된 예시이다.

단서와 함께 나오는 표현	담화 지문	질문 및 정답
1 I'd like to discuss ~ ~에 대해 논의하고자 합니다	In this online session, **I'd like to discuss** how leaders inspire and guide their teams. 이 온라인 세션에서는, 리더들이 어떻게 그들의 팀에 영감을 주고 지도하는지에 대해 논의하고자 합니다.	질문 What is the main topic of the talk? 담화의 주제는 무엇인가? 정답 Leadership techniques 리더십 기술
2 I'm calling to ~ ~을 하기 위해 전화드립니다	**I'm calling to** confirm that our technician will arrive at your office at 10 A.M. tomorrow to repair the printer. 저는 저희의 기술자가 귀하의 사무실에 내일 오전 10시에 프린터를 수리하기 위해 도착할 것임을 확정하기 위해 전화드립니다.	질문 Why is the speaker calling? 화자는 왜 전화를 하고 있는가? 정답 To confirm an appointment time 예약 시간을 확정하기 위해
3 As ~ ~로서	**As** the mayor, I'm excited to see new opportunities emerging for businesses. 시장으로서, 저는 기업들에게 떠오르는 새로운 기회를 보는 것에 들떠 있습니다.	질문 Who is the speaker? 화자는 누구인가? 정답 A city official 공무원

토익실전문제

01 What business is being advertised?
(A) A supermarket
(B) A repair shop
(C) A gardening store
(D) A plumbing company

02 What happened in February?
(A) A seasonal sale was concluded.
(B) A company received an award.
(C) A shop opened additional branches.
(D) A government program was launched.

03 What does the speaker suggest doing?
(A) Entering a contest
(B) Writing a review
(C) Subscribing to a channel
(D) Signing up for a publication

04 Who is the speaker?
(A) A company president
(B) A journalist
(C) A receptionist
(D) A department manager

05 According to the speaker, what is impressive about the listener?
(A) He is honest.
(B) He is an effective leader.
(C) He has good communication skills.
(D) He has a lot of work experience.

06 What is included in an e-mail?
(A) A company introduction
(B) Position details
(C) Meeting times
(D) A delivery address

기출 유형 2 세부 사항 관련 문제

최근 3개년 오답률 16.1%

지문의 세부 사항과 관련된 내용을 묻는 문제로, 매회 22~23문제 출제된다.

출제 경향

1. PART 4에서 의도 파악 문제는 매회 3문제, 시각 자료 문제는 매회 2문제가 고정으로 출제된다.
2. 문제 유형별로 주로 다음과 같은 질문을 사용한다.

요청	**What** does the speaker **ask** the listeners to do?	화자는 청자들에게 무엇을 하라고 요청하는가?
제안	**What** does the speaker **recommend doing**?	화자는 무엇을 할 것을 권하는가?
언급	**What** does the speaker **say about the Evergreen Park**?	화자는 Evergreen 공원에 대해 무엇을 언급하는가?
이유	**Why** does the speaker **apologize**?	화자는 왜 사과하는가?
방법	**How** can the listeners **use the service**?	청자들은 어떻게 서비스를 이용할 수 있는가?
문제점	**What problem** does the speaker mention?	화자는 무슨 문제를 언급하는가?
특정 세부 사항	**Where** will some **equipment** most likely be **used**?	몇몇 기기는 어디에 쓰일 것 같은가?
다음에 할 일	**What** will the listeners probably **do next**?	청자들은 다음에 무엇을 할 것 같은가?
의도 파악	**Why** does the speaker say, "**These things change frequently**"?	화자는 왜 "이것들은 자주 바뀌어요"라고 말하는가?
시각 자료	Look at the **graphic**. **Which area** was recently **added**?	시각 자료를 보아라. 어느 구역이 최근에 추가되었는가?

800+ 공략

1. 세부 사항 관련 문제는 질문이 긴 경우가 종종 있으므로 질문을 빠르고 정확하게 파악하는 연습을 해야 한다.
2. 질문의 핵심 어구를 먼저 확인한 후, 지문에서 질문의 핵심 어구가 언급된 부분을 주의 깊게 듣는다.
3. 요청/제안 문제와 다음에 할 일 문제는 지문 후반부에 단서가 나오므로 마지막까지 집중해서 듣는다.

Example 🎧 D15_4_예제

해석 p.93

01 What does the speaker ask the listeners to do?
(A) Update a document
(B) Work additional hours
(C) Wear protective gear
(D) Review a manual

Question 01 refers to the following excerpt from a meeting.

Before we finish our meeting, I have an important announcement for all assembly line employees. Senica Shoes, the firm that hired us to make their sneakers, has informed us that it needs these products one week earlier than the date we originally agreed on. To deal with this situation, **I'm asking everyone to work an additional two hours each day next week**. Of course, you'll receive extra pay for those additional hours.

해설 요청 문제

정답 (B)

질문의 What, ask를 통해 화자가 요청하는 것을 묻는 문제임을 알 수 있다. 지문의 후반에서 화자가 "I'm asking everyone to work an additional two hours each day next week"이라며 모든 직원들이 다음 주에 매일 추가로 2시간을 일할 것을 요청한다고 하였으므로 (B)가 정답이다.

빈출 정답 단서와 패러프레이징

다음은 요청/제안 문제에서 정답 단서와 함께 나오는 표현과 정답 단서가 패러프레이징된 예시이다.

단서와 함께 나오는 표현	담화 지문	질문 및 정답
1 please ~ ~해주세요	Now, **please** take a moment to share your opinion in our poll on employee satisfaction. 이제, 잠시 시간을 내어 직원 만족도에 대한 투표에 여러분들의 의견을 공유해주세요.	질문 What does the speaker ask the listeners to do? 화자는 청자들에게 무엇을 하라고 요청하는가? 정답 Participate in a poll 투표에 참가한다.
2 recommend / suggest / ask 권장합니다 / 제안합니다 / 요청드립니다	I highly **recommend** checking customer reviews before starting on your marketing proposal. 여러분의 마케팅 제안서를 시작하기 전에 고객 후기를 확인할 것을 매우 권장합니다.	질문 What does the speaker recommend doing? 화자는 무엇을 할 것을 권하는가? 정답 Reviewing customer feedback 고객 의견 검토하기

다음은 문제점을 묻는 문제에서 정답 단서와 함께 나오는 표현과 정답 단서가 패러프레이징된 예시이다.

단서와 함께 나오는 표현	담화 지문	질문 및 정답
3 Unfortunately / But / However 안타깝게도 / 그러나 / 하지만	Yesterday, you ordered 25 of our headphones. **Unfortunately**, our current inventory shows that we can only provide 15. 어제, 당신은 저희의 헤드폰 25개를 주문했습니다. 안타깝게도, 저희의 현재 재고는 저희가 15개만 제공할 수 있다는 것을 보여줍니다.	질문 What problem does the speaker mention? 화자는 무슨 문제를 언급하는가? 정답 An order cannot be fulfilled. 주문이 이행될 수 없다.

토익실전문제

01 According to the speaker, what is the problem?

(A) A room is currently locked.
(B) A device is malfunctioning.
(C) An image needs editing.
(D) A document is inaccessible.

02 Why does the speaker want the work to be done quickly?

(A) She must finish a report.
(B) She would like to print a document.
(C) She has to give a presentation.
(D) She needs to confirm a budget.

03 What will the speaker send to the listener?

(A) A password
(B) An e-mail address
(C) A copy of the contract
(D) A model number

04 Who most likely are the listeners?

(A) Software developers
(B) Hotel receptionists
(C) Mechanical engineers
(D) Sales associates

05 What does the speaker suggest?

(A) Decreasing a budget
(B) Reducing the number of ads
(C) Adding new features
(D) Using a different application

06 What does the speaker mean when she says, "they'll be trained over the next two weeks"?

(A) Assistance will not be available immediately.
(B) Company policies were updated.
(C) A meeting is going to be postponed.
(D) A venue is not ready to be used.

HACKERS TEST

🎧 D15_7_테스트

01 What is the broadcast mainly about?
(A) Traffic congestion
(B) A government program
(C) Highway construction
(D) A building renovation

02 What does the speaker say about the Harborview Expressway?
(A) It is connected to the Bayport Bridge.
(B) It has been closed for a community event.
(C) It requires payment of a fee to use.
(D) It is undergoing unscheduled repairs.

03 What does the speaker suggest that the listeners do?
(A) Call a hotline
(B) Take an alternative route
(C) Avoid the downtown area
(D) Use public transportation

04 Who most likely is the speaker?
(A) An office assistant
(B) A computer repairperson
(C) A course instructor
(D) A security guard

05 According to the speaker, what will be provided free of charge?
(A) An educational book
(B) A career consultation
(C) An online membership
(D) A software program

06 What does the speaker request that the listeners do?
(A) Change a password
(B) Create a system account
(C) Apply for some positions
(D) Sign in to a system

07 What type of business do the listeners most likely work for?
(A) A hotel chain
(B) A food catering service
(C) A market research agency
(D) A moving company

08 Why does the speaker say the work will be difficult?
(A) The event will have many attendees.
(B) The event will be held in an unfamiliar venue.
(C) The company is understaffed.
(D) The preparation time is insufficient.

09 What will Erica do before the meeting tomorrow?
(A) Order an item
(B) Contact a client
(C) Conduct a survey
(D) Prepare a list

10 Why is the speaker calling?
(A) To offer assistance with an assignment
(B) To provide information about a service
(C) To inquire about purchasing an item
(D) To request involvement in an event

11 What does the speaker mean when she says, "You have captured many images of mountains"?
(A) She expects a project to be approved.
(B) She wants to buy one of the images.
(C) She thinks the listener's work is suitable.
(D) She wants the listener to take pictures of something else.

12 According to the speaker, what can be requested by e-mail?
(A) A list of participants
(B) A map of a venue
(C) A sample of a product
(D) An estimate of costs

13 Where do the listeners most likely work?

(A) At a bank
(B) At a graphic design firm
(C) At a law office
(D) At an electronics store

14 What problem does the speaker mention?

(A) A request has been denied.
(B) A delivery has been delayed.
(C) A client has complained.
(D) A cost has increased.

15 Why does the speaker say, "This will become part of our daily routine"?

(A) To encourage others to attend some events
(B) To explain a change to a work schedule
(C) To stress the importance of some changes
(D) To promote a healthy lifestyle

---

16 Where most likely is the announcement being made?

(A) At an art gallery
(B) At a trade show
(C) At a shopping mall
(D) At a sporting event

17 What does the speaker say about the event participants?

(A) They come from various countries.
(B) They are selling merchandise on-site.
(C) They received help from volunteers.
(D) They had to pay an admission fee.

18 What does the speaker recommend doing?

(A) Making a reservation
(B) Watching a video
(C) Wearing a nametag
(D) Listening to a lecture

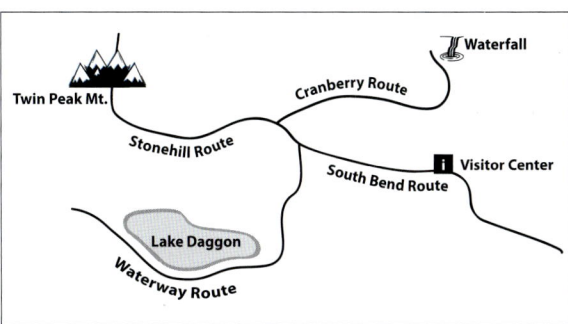

19 What does the speaker say about Fairwood Park?

(A) It is near a major city.
(B) It is promoting a restoration project.
(C) It was recently expanded.
(D) It has many uncommon animals.

20 Look at the graphic. Which is the easiest route?

(A) Stonehill Route
(B) Cranberry Route
(C) South Bend Route
(D) Waterway Route

21 What is available on the application?

(A) Parking passes
(B) Trail information
(C) Photos of park wildlife
(D) A shuttle service schedule

DAY 16 음성 메시지 및 회의 발췌

기출 유형 1 음성 메시지

전화에 남겨진 녹음 메시지로, 업체에서 고객에게 남긴 메시지, 고객이 업체에 남긴 메시지, 개인이 동료에게 남긴 메시지 또는 업체의 자동 안내 메시지가 등장한다. 매회 1~2개의 지문이 출제된다.

출제 경향

1. 지문이 시작되기 전에 telephone message 또는 recorded message로 지문의 종류가 소개된다.
2. 음성 메시지의 목적, 화자의 신분이나 직업, 청자가 할 일 등을 묻는 문제가 자주 출제된다.
3. 다음과 같은 상황이 자주 출제된다.
   - 상점 직원이 배송 지연 및 재고량 부재 등의 주문 관련 정보를 제공하거나 주문 내역을 확인
   - 행사장이나 레스토랑 예약을 위해 고객에게 필요한 추가 정보를 문의
   - 상점이나 회사에 영업시간 외에 연락한 고객을 위해 영업시간 정보를 제공

800+ 공략

1. 음성 메시지의 처음 한 두 문장에서 화자와 청자가 누구인지와 화자가 음성 메시지를 남기는 목적을 파악한다.
2. 다양한 상황에서의 음성 메시지와 관련된 표현들을 알아 둔다.

Example ∩ D16_1_예제

해석 p.99

01 Why is the speaker calling?
   (A) To discuss an upcoming promotional event
   (B) To provide information about a business location
   (C) To notify a customer about a completed task
   (D) To provide a reason for a billing mistake

02 What does the speaker ask the listener to do?
   (A) Visit a business
   (B) Pay a balance
   (C) Send a measurement
   (D) Meet with a supervisor

03 What does the speaker offer for an additional fee?
   (A) A private consultation
   (B) A product upgrade
   (C) An extended warranty
   (D) A delivery service

Questions 01-03 refer to the following telephone message.

This is Amanda from Leroy's Formal Wear. ⁰¹**I'm calling to let you know that the suit alterations you requested last week are now finished.** ⁰²**We'd like you to come into the shop and try the suit on to confirm that it fits.** That way, our tailor can make changes if necessary. Once any final adjustments are made, you can either return to pick up the suit or have it sent to your residence. Please note that ⁰³**we charge an additional 15 dollars for delivery**. Thank you.

정답 01 (C) 02 (A) 03 (D)

해설

01 [목적] 지문 초반에서 "I'm calling to let you know that the suit alterations ~ now finished."라고 하였으므로 (C)가 정답이다.
02 [요청] 화자가 "We'd like you to come into the shop and try the suit on to confirm that it fits."라고 하였으므로 (A)가 정답이다.
03 [세부] 화자가 "we charge an additional 15 dollars for delivery"라고 하였으므로 (D)가 정답이다.

음성 메시지에 자주 나오는 필수 표현 🎧 D16_2_표현

업체에서 고객에게 남긴 메시지

1 This is – calling from ~. ~에서 전화드리는 저는 –입니다	**This is** Sophia **calling from** Waldorf Furniture. Waldorf 가구점에서 전화드리는 Sophia입니다.
2 This is – returning your call. 회신 전화드리는 –입니다.	**This is** Steven Miles **returning your call**. 회신 전화드리는 Steven Miles입니다.
3 confirm the date 날짜를 확정하다	Please **confirm the date** of your vehicle service appointment. 귀하의 차량 서비스 예약 날짜를 확정해 주십시오.

고객이 업체에 남긴 메시지

4 I'm calling about ~ ~에 관하여 전화드립니다	**I'm calling about** a recent purchase I made online. 저는 제가 온라인으로 했던 최근 주문 건에 관하여 전화드립니다.
5 place an order 주문하다	I'm calling to **place an order** for custom uniforms for our team. 저는 저희 팀을 위한 맞춤 유니폼을 주문하기 위해 전화드립니다.
6 call me back 저에게 다시 전화해주세요	Could you **call me back** so we can discuss the itinerary? 여행 일정을 논의하기 위해 저에게 다시 전화해주실 수 있을까요?

업체의 자동 안내 메시지

7 You have reached ~. ~에 전화하셨습니다	**You have reached** Cedar Kitchen, Houston's number-one spot for contemporary cuisine. 현대적인 요리를 위한 휴스턴 제일의 장소인 Cedar Kitchen에 전화하셨습니다.
8 apologize for the inconvenience 불편에 대해 사과하다	**We apologize for the inconvenience** and appreciate your understanding. 불편에 대해 사과드리며 이해해 주셔서 감사합니다.

토익실전문제 🎧 D16_3_실전

01 What type of products does the business repair?
 (A) Computers
 (B) Vehicles
 (C) Appliances
 (D) Instruments

02 Why will the business be closed on Friday?
 (A) For an inventory count
 (B) For a branch relocation
 (C) For a training session
 (D) For an equipment installation

03 What special benefit does the speaker mention?
 (A) A gift certificate
 (B) A complimentary service
 (C) An extended warranty
 (D) A price reduction

04 What information did a friend tell the speaker about?
 (A) Available courses
 (B) Membership fees
 (C) A facility's operating hours
 (D) An instructor's schedule

05 Why does the speaker say, "I've been doing yoga for six months"?
 (A) To show her dedication
 (B) To highlight an achievement
 (C) To explain a decision
 (D) To indicate her uncertainty

06 Why is the listener asked to contact the speaker?
 (A) To confirm a payment
 (B) To arrange a meeting
 (C) To get access to a building
 (D) To provide event updates

정답·해석·해설 p.99

기출 유형 2 회의 발췌

회의에서 직원들에게 다양한 정보를 전달하는 담화로, 업무 관련 세부 사항, 회사 방침 변경, 고객 의견 공유에 대한 내용이 자주 등장한다. 매회 2~3개의 지문이 출제된다.

출제 경향
1. 지문이 시작되기 전에 excerpt from a meeting으로 지문의 종류가 소개된다.
2. 화자나 청자가 속한 회사의 업무 분야, 요청 사항, 청자가 할 일 등을 묻는 문제가 자주 출제된다.
3. 다음과 같은 상황이 자주 출제된다.
    - 업무를 요청하거나 새로운 업무에 대한 세부 사항을 전달
    - 회사의 변경된 방침을 소개하며 이를 숙지하도록 조언
    - 상품 또는 서비스에 대한 고객 의견을 공유하며 해결 방안을 제시

800+ 공략
1. 지문 초반에서 어떤 종류의 회사인지 파악하면 전반적인 회의 상황을 수월하게 이해할 수 있다.
2. 회사 업무, 회사 방침, 고객 의견 및 고객 서비스와 관련된 표현들을 알아 둔다.

Example 🎧 D16_4_예제
해석 p.100

01 Where does the speaker most likely work?
    (A) At a furniture store
    (B) At a sports stadium
    (C) At an electronics company
    (D) At an insurance firm

02 Who is Darrell Bedford?
    (A) An athlete
    (B) A musician
    (C) An author
    (D) A model

03 What does the speaker ask Haley to do?
    (A) Recruit some personnel
    (B) Sign some documents
    (C) Book an event space
    (D) Install a security device

Questions 01-03 refer to the following excerpt from a meeting.

⁰¹**Let's discuss next week's launch party for our latest tablet computer.** I have some good news. ⁰²**Darrell Bedford, the popular musician who appears in our commercial**, is coming to the event. This will definitely attract a lot of attendees. So ⁰³**we need to hire additional security guards to make sure everything goes smoothly. Haley, please take charge of this task**, and give me a status update before the end of the day.

해설
정답 01 (C) 02 (B) 03 (A)

01 [화자] 지문 초반에서 "Let's discuss next week's launch party for our latest tablet computer."라고 한 것을 통해 전자제품 회사에서 일하고 있음을 알 수 있으므로 (C)가 정답이다.
02 [세부] 화자가 "Darrell Bedford, the popular musician who appears in our commercial"이라고 하였으므로 (B)가 정답이다.
03 [요청] 화자가 "we need to hire additional security guards ~. Haley, please take charge of this task"라고 하였으므로 (A)가 정답이다.

회의 발췌에 자주 나오는 필수 표현

회사 업무

1 kick off ~ ~을 시작하다	We're ready to **kick off** our digital advertising campaign. 우리는 디지털 광고 캠페인을 시작할 준비가 되었습니다.
2 come up with ~ ~을 제시하다, 생각해 내다	You need to **come up with** lists of potential companies that we should get in touch with. 여러분들은 우리가 연락을 취해야 할 잠재적인 회사들의 목록을 제시해야 합니다.
3 take charge of ~ ~을 담당하다	Mr. Daniels will **take charge of** developing the new accounting software. Mr. Daniels가 새로운 회계 소프트웨어를 개발하는 것을 담당할 것입니다.
4 top priority 최우선 사항	Customer satisfaction is our **top priority**. 고객 만족이 우리의 최우선 사항입니다.

회사 방침

5 per company policy 회사 정책에 따라	**Per company policy**, all employees must complete the annual compliance training by the end of the month. 회사 정책에 따라, 모든 직원은 이 달 말까지 연간 규정 준수 교육을 완료해야 합니다.
6 as of ~ ~부터	**As of** next month, we will adjust our expense reimbursement guidelines to streamline the process. 다음 달부터, 절차를 간소화하기 위해 우리는 경비 상환 지침을 조정할 것입니다.

고객 의견 및 고객 서비스

7 receive feedback 의견을 받다	We've **received feedback** from one of our major clients. 우리의 주요 고객들 중 한 명으로부터 의견을 받았습니다.
8 meet customers' expectations 고객의 기대에 부응하다	We need to continually make changes to **meet our customers' expectations**. 우리의 고객들의 기대에 부응하기 위해 우리는 지속적으로 변화해야 합니다.

토익실전문제

01 What type of event is being planned?
 (A) A sports competition
 (B) A music festival
 (C) A theater performance
 (D) A company picnic

02 What problem does the speaker mention?
 (A) A stage needs to be repainted.
 (B) There is inadequate security.
 (C) There is insufficient seating.
 (D) An entrance fee is too high.

03 What will Tanya most likely do today?
 (A) Meet with a client
 (B) Purchase an item
 (C) Confirm a start time
 (D) Check a budget

04 Where do the listeners most likely work?
 (A) At an appliance store
 (B) At an auto repair shop
 (C) At a marketing firm
 (D) At a car manufacturer

05 Why does the speaker say, "It seems there are many new products on the market"?
 (A) To request a list of competitors
 (B) To suggest a product
 (C) To explain low sales
 (D) To ask for feedback

06 What does the speaker say he will do?
 (A) Edit a document
 (B) Talk to an executive
 (C) Reveal a product design
 (D) Approve an advertisement

HACKERS TEST

DAY 16

🎧 D16_7_테스트

01 Why is the speaker calling?
(A) To offer employment
(B) To arrange a transaction
(C) To publicize a service
(D) To schedule an interview

02 What does the speaker want the listener to do?
(A) Train a staff member
(B) Attend an orientation
(C) Give a presentation
(D) Head a design team

03 What did the speaker send to the listener?
(A) An employee manual
(B) A legal agreement
(C) A progress report
(D) A cost estimate

04 What type of business does the speaker work for?
(A) A construction company
(B) A sporting goods outlet
(C) A recreational center
(D) A marketing firm

05 What has the speaker's company been asked to do?
(A) Conduct a survey
(B) Work on a project
(C) Test a product
(D) Inspect a facility

06 What does the speaker say he will do?
(A) Correct some information
(B) Update a chart
(C) Contact a client
(D) Perform some research

07 What is the meeting mainly about?
(A) A competitor
(B) A merger
(C) Sales figures
(D) Branch closures

08 What does the speaker mean when she says, "people like to shop at well-known stores"?
(A) A customer has provided feedback.
(B) Employees will be asked to make suggestions.
(C) A marketing effort has been a success.
(D) A challenge should be expected.

09 What will be sent out later in the afternoon?
(A) Travel itineraries
(B) Performance evaluations
(C) Work assignments
(D) Pay statement

10 How did the speaker learn about a business?
(A) By talking to a friend
(B) By watching television
(C) By reading a newspaper
(D) By checking an e-mail

11 What does the speaker imply when he says, "there are leaves all over my backyard"?
(A) He forgot to do a task.
(B) He is not satisfied with a service.
(C) He is interested in a discount.
(D) He is doubtful about a suggestion.

12 Why is the speaker unavailable this afternoon?
(A) He will be out of town on business.
(B) He has to see a doctor.
(C) He is going to visit his family.
(D) He has to talk to a customer.

13 Who most likely is Oscar Juan?

(A) A curator
(B) An artist
(C) A critic
(D) A magazine editor

14 What does the speaker say will be special about an exhibit?

(A) It will involve online interactions.
(B) It will feature a digital artwork.
(C) It will include a talk by an expert.
(D) It will showcase valuable items.

15 What will the listeners most likely do next?

(A) Plan some activities
(B) Take some measurements
(C) Watch a presentation
(D) Visit a center

16 Where does the speaker work?

(A) At a real estate agency
(B) At a law firm
(C) At a publishing company
(D) At an accounting firm

17 What does the speaker ask the listeners to leave?

(A) An invoice number
(B) Contact information
(C) An appointment time
(D) User reviews

18 What did the speaker's company recently do?

(A) It changed its operating hours.
(B) It launched a new service.
(C) It updated its work policies.
(D) It posted a job advertisement.

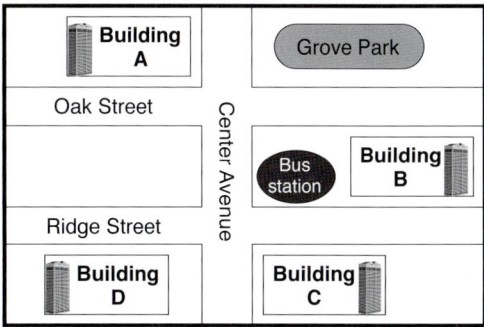

19 Look at the graphic. Where will the company's new office be located?

(A) In Building A
(B) In Building B
(C) In Building C
(D) In Building D

20 What are the listeners reminded to do tomorrow morning?

(A) Set up some furniture
(B) Get an identification card
(C) Check some prices
(D) Move some equipment

21 What will be shared after the meeting?

(A) An office directory
(B) Product designs
(C) A building address
(D) Parking regulations

DAY 17 공지 및 관광 안내

기출 유형 1 공지

화자가 청자들에게 새로운 사실이나 변경 사항에 대한 정보를 공지하는 지문으로, 사내 공지, 교통수단에서의 안내, 시설물 관련 안내가 자주 등장한다. 매회 1~2개의 지문이 출제된다.

출제 경향

1. 지문이 시작되기 전에 주로 announcement 또는 notice로 지문의 종류가 소개된다.
2. 공지의 목적, 공지를 하는 장소, 화자의 신분, 청자에게 요청하는 것, 미래에 일어날 일을 묻는 문제가 자주 출제된다.
3. 다음과 같은 상황이 자주 출제된다.
   - 회사에서 직원들에게 시설 점검 및 보수 공사 일정을 안내하거나, 새 정책 및 사내 행사 등의 소식을 알림
   - 상점에서 고객들에게 할인 및 특별 행사에 대한 정보를 제공
   - 교통수단에서 출발·도착 시간 및 경로 안내, 지연 일정 등에 대해 알림

800+ 공략

1. 지문 초반에서 공지가 이루어지는 장소와 공지의 목적이 언급되므로 집중해서 듣는다.
2. 사내 공지, 교통수단 관련 공지, 시설물 이용 안내와 관련된 표현들을 알아 둔다.

Example   🎧 D17_1_예제   해석 p.106

01 Where most likely is the announcement being made?
   (A) At a banquet hall
   (B) At a theater
   (C) At a museum
   (D) At a convention center

02 Why has the event been delayed?
   (A) Some guests are not present.
   (B) There is a technical problem.
   (C) Some performers are not ready.
   (D) There is a seating shortage.

03 What does the speaker suggest doing?
   (A) Looking at some displays
   (B) Making a reservation
   (C) Reading through a program
   (D) Inquiring about future shows

Questions 01-03 refer to the following announcement.

May I have your attention please? ⁰¹**This evening's performance** was scheduled to begin at 8 P.M. ⁰²**Unfortunately, we are experiencing some technical issues with the lighting system, so there will be a short delay.** ⁰¹**The play is now expected to begin** at 8:30. We sincerely apologize for the inconvenience. In the meantime, ⁰³**please feel free to check out the special displays in our lobby about this performance**. Thank you for your patience.

해설   정답 01 (B) 02 (B) 03 (A)

01 [장소] "This evening's performance", "The play is now expected to begin"이라고 한 것을 통해 연극이 공연되는 극장임을 알 수 있으므로 (B)가 정답이다.
02 [이유] "Unfortunately, we are experiencing some technical issues ~, so there will be a short delay."라고 하였으므로 (B)가 정답이다.
03 [제안] "please feel free to check out the special displays ~ about this performance"라고 하였으므로 (A)가 정답이다.

공지에 자주 나오는 필수 표현

🎧 D17_2_표현

사내 공지

1 **remind A to ~** A에게 ~하라고 다시 알려주다	We would like to **remind** everyone **to** submit their monthly performance reports by Friday. 모두에게 금요일까지 월간 성과 보고서를 제출할 것을 다시 한번 알려드립니다.
2 **will be implemented starting ~** ~부터 시행될 것이다	A flexible work schedule **will be implemented starting** next month. 유연 근무 일정은 다음 달부터 시행될 것입니다.
3 **fill in for ~** ~를 대신하다	Timothy Chen will **fill in for** the project manager who is currently on sick leave. Timothy Chen이 현재 병가 중인 프로젝트 매니저를 대신할 것입니다.

교통수단 관련 안내 방송

4 **routine maintenance check** 정기 유지 보수 점검	Departure has been delayed because a **routine maintenance check** is taking longer than expected. 정기 유지 보수 점검이 예상보다 더 오래 걸리고 있기 때문에 출발이 지연되었습니다.
5 **proceed to ~** ~로 가다	All passengers traveling to Washington, please **proceed to** Track 4A. 워싱턴으로 가는 모든 승객분들은 4A 트랙으로 가주십시오.

시설물 이용 안내 및 공지

6 **adjust hours** (영업) 시간을 조정하다	We will be **adjusting** our store's **hours** for the holiday, closing one hour early. 저희는 공휴일에 매장 영업 시간을 조정할 것이며, 한 시간 일찍 닫을 것입니다.
7 **stop by ~** ~에 들르다	To sign up for a membership, **stop by** the information desk. 멤버십을 신청하기 위해서는 안내 데스크에 들르세요.
8 **If you need assistance with ~** ~과 관련하여 도움이 필요하시면	**If you need assistance with** payment, please approach our cashier. 결제와 관련하여 도움이 필요하시면 저희 계산대로 가주세요.

토익실전문제

🎧 D17_3_실전

토익 문제 이렇게 나온다!

01 Where do the listeners most likely work?
 (A) At a pharmacy
 (B) At a warehouse
 (C) At a service center
 (D) At a retail outlet

02 What is the goal of the training session?
 (A) To reduce waste
 (B) To increase productivity
 (C) To improve safety
 (D) To encourage teambuilding

03 What does the speaker ask the listeners to do?
 (A) Read a manual
 (B) Suggest topics
 (C) Inspect a worksite
 (D) Report accidents

04 What has caused a delay?
 (A) A weather complication
 (B) A reservation error
 (C) A mechanical issue
 (D) An unexpected stop

05 Where most likely are the listeners?
 (A) At an airport terminal
 (B) On a commuter train
 (C) At a ticketing office
 (D) On a passenger plane

06 What does the speaker say some staff will do?
 (A) Serve some refreshments
 (B) Help connecting passengers
 (C) Pass out some forms
 (D) Offer partial refunds

정답·해석·해설 p.106

기출 유형 2   관광 안내

관광이나 견학, 시설물 관람 시 가이드가 앞으로의 일정이나 진행 순서를 설명한 후 청자들에게 요청하는 사항을 전달하는 담화이다. 매회 1개 정도 출제된다.

출제 경향

1. 지문이 시작되기 전에 주로 tour information 또는 talk로 지문의 종류가 소개된다.
2. 여행·관람·견학의 목적이나 장소, 청자에게 요청하는 것, 청자가 할 일을 묻는 문제가 자주 출제된다.
3. 다음과 같은 상황이 자주 출제된다.
    - 유적지, 동물원 등의 관광지에서의 여행
    - 미술관, 동물원, 박물관, 극장에서의 관람
    - 공장이나 기타 시설물에서의 견학

800+ 공략

1. 도입부의 인사말에서 장소에 대한 정답의 단서가 주로 언급되므로 지문의 초반을 집중해서 듣는다.
2. 지문의 후반부에서 청자들에게 요청하거나 당부하는 사항이 자주 언급됨을 기억한다.
3. 여행, 관람, 견학과 관련된 표현들을 알아 둔다.

Example   D17_4_예제

해석 p.107

01 What is the site famous for?
  (A) Challenging trails
  (B) Tropical plants
  (C) Wild animals
  (D) Rock carvings

02 What does the speaker tell the listeners to wear?
  (A) A nametag
  (B) A helmet
  (C) A backpack
  (D) A jacket

03 What does the speaker mean when he says, "several other tour groups are here today"?
  (A) Some equipment is unavailable.
  (B) Access to an area is restricted.
  (C) A route will be changed.
  (D) There may be some delays.

Questions 01-03 refer to the following tour information.

Welcome to Grandview Canyon. ⁰¹**This site is famous for the beautiful images of animals carved into rocks** thousands of years ago. As we hike along the trail, ⁰²**wear the protective headgear you were given**. Otherwise, you might be injured by a falling stone. I should also mention that, um . . . several other tour groups are here today. ⁰³**Please be patient if we get stuck behind a slow-moving one.** OK, let's begin.

정답 01 (D) 02 (B) 03 (D)

해설

01 [세부] "This site is famous for the beautiful images of animals carved into rocks"라고 하였으므로 (D)가 정답이다.
02 [세부] "wear the protective headgear you were given"이라고 하였으므로 (B)가 정답이다.
03 [의도] "Please be patient if we get stuck behind a slow-moving one."이라고 한 것을 통해 다른 투어 그룹들이 많아서 일정이 지체될 수도 있음을 의도한 것임을 알 수 있으므로 (D)가 정답이다.

관광 안내에 자주 나오는 필수 표현

여행 안내

1 **feel free to ~** 자유롭게 ~하다	**Feel free to** take photos without using a flash in the aquarium. 수족관 내에서 플래시를 사용하지 않고 자유롭게 사진을 찍으세요.
2 **follow the safety regulations** 안전 규정을 준수하다	Please **follow the safety regulations** throughout our mountain hike. 저희의 등산 동안 안전 규정을 준수해주십시오.
3 **updated itinerary** 업데이트된 여행 일정표	Our tour has an **updated itinerary** featuring additional sunset viewing opportunities. 저희의 투어는 추가적인 일몰 감상 기회를 특별히 포함하고 있는 업데이트된 여행 일정표가 마련되어 있습니다.

관람/견학 안내

4 **recently renovated** 최근에 보수된	The second floor features a **recently renovated** art gallery. 2층은 최근에 보수된 미술 갤러리가 있습니다.
5 **temporary exhibit** 한시적 전시	Our **temporary exhibit** will run from May 15 to July 30, offering visitors a chance to explore this unique collection. 저희의 한시적 전시는 5월 15일부터 7월 30일까지 진행될 것이며, 방문객들에게 이 특별한 컬렉션을 살펴볼 수 있는 기회를 제공합니다.
6 **admission to ~** ~로의 입장	**Admission to** the laboratory is restricted to authorized personnel only. 실험실로의 입장은 승인된 직원들에게로만 제한되어 있습니다.
7 **hands-on experience** 체험형 경험	The interactive, **hands-on experience** allows visitors to directly engage with our scientific exhibits. 상호작용할 수 있는 체험형 경험은 방문객들이 저희의 과학 전시에 직접 여여할 수 있게 합니다.

토익실전문제

01 Where most likely are the listeners?
(A) At a town hall
(B) At a sports arena
(C) At a history museum
(D) At a public library

02 According to the speaker, how can the listeners learn more about a topic?
(A) By listening to a recording
(B) By reading a publication
(C) By attending a lecture
(D) By visiting a Web site

03 What are the listeners reminded to do?
(A) Complete a survey
(B) Leave beverages outside
(C) Post some photographs
(D) Avoid touching items

04 According to the speaker, what will the listeners see?
(A) Buildings
(B) Statues
(C) Vehicles
(D) Plants

05 What is available on the boat?
(A) Area maps
(B) Refreshments
(C) Battery chargers
(D) Guidebooks

06 What does the speaker ask the listeners to do?
(A) Remain in their seats
(B) Store some luggage
(C) Show their tickets
(D) Put on safety gear

HACKERS TEST

DAY 17

토익 800+를 위한 실전 문제 정복

🎧 D17_7_테스트

01 Where is the announcement being made?
(A) In a subway station
(B) In a real estate office
(C) In an apartment complex
(D) In a research laboratory

02 According to the speaker, what will happen tomorrow afternoon?
(A) Some machinery will be replaced.
(B) A parking lot will be shut down.
(C) Some guidelines will be distributed.
(D) A system test will be performed.

03 What does the speaker recommend doing?
(A) Visiting an office
(B) Registering in a program
(C) Checking a pamphlet
(D) Turning off some computers

04 Who most likely is the speaker?
(A) A professor
(B) A tour guide
(C) A real estate agent
(D) A podcast host

05 What does the speaker say is unique about a facility?
(A) Its size
(B) Its design
(C) Its history
(D) Its function

06 What does the speaker remind the listeners to do?
(A) Take care of belongings
(B) Attend a performance
(C) Remain with a group
(D) Purchase souvenirs

07 Why does the speaker apologize?
(A) She arrived late.
(B) She forgot to send out an announcement.
(C) A room is too small.
(D) A class will end earlier than expected.

08 What will the speaker do next?
(A) Show a video
(B) Give a demonstration
(C) Distribute a manual
(D) Set up a machine

09 What does the speaker mean when she says, "the fabric is stored in the back cabinet"?
(A) An order arrived on time.
(B) An organization accepted a donation.
(C) A suggestion has been applied.
(D) An issue has been addressed.

10 What is the focus of the tour?
(A) Farming
(B) Business
(C) History
(D) Science

11 What does the speaker say is available in the lobby?
(A) Brochures
(B) Pictures
(C) Refreshments
(D) Maps

12 What will the listeners probably do next?
(A) Eat a meal
(B) Board a vehicle
(C) Listen to a talk
(D) Meet an architect

13. Where most likely is the announcement being made?

(A) At a sports stadium
(B) At a fitness center
(C) At a train station
(D) At a medical clinic

14. According to the speaker, what caused a delay?

(A) A technical malfunction
(B) A heavy storm
(C) A late arrival
(D) A traffic accident

15. What does the speaker say will happen later?

(A) Autographs will be signed.
(B) A ceremony will be held.
(C) Questions will be answered.
(D) An interview will be conducted.

---

16. Where will the listeners most likely go first?

(A) To the ticket office
(B) To the visitor's center
(C) To the photography hall
(D) To the building lobby

17. Who most likely is Gonzalo Ruiz?

(A) A caterer
(B) A sculptor
(C) A curator
(D) A guide

18. What are the listeners asked to do?

(A) Gather in a location
(B) Form a line
(C) Check a timetable
(D) Buy a pass

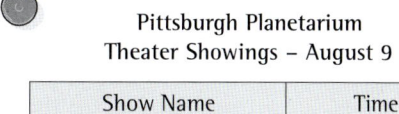

Pittsburgh Planetarium
Theater Showings – August 9

Show Name	Time
Stars and Planets	9 A.M. – 10 A.M.
The Northern Lights	10 A.M. – 11 A.M.
Traveling Through Space	11 A.M. – 12 P.M.
Views of Earth	1 P.M. – 3 P.M.

19. Who most likely are the listeners?

(A) Volunteers
(B) Facility visitors
(C) Class participants
(D) Trainees

20. Look at the graphic. Which show was canceled?

(A) *Stars and Planets*
(B) *The Northern Lights*
(C) *Traveling Through Space*
(D) *Views of Earth*

21. Where can the listeners receive some free items?

(A) At a gift shop
(B) At a garden
(C) At a front desk
(D) At a main entrance

DAY 18 연설 및 강연

기출 유형 1 연설

모임 또는 시상식에서 지식·인물에 대한 정보나 소감·감사를 전달하는 지문으로, 사회자가 환영 인사로 청중을 맞이하면서 발표자를 소개하거나 행사의 주요 순서를 소개하는 식으로 진행된다. 매회 1개 정도 지문이 출제된다.

출제 경향

1. 지문이 시작되기 전에 주로 speech 또는 talk로 지문의 종류가 소개된다.
2. 화자나 청자의 신분, 행사 장소, 화자가 전달하는 특정 정보, 인물에 대한 세부 정보를 묻는 문제가 자주 출제된다.
3. 다음과 같은 상황이 자주 출제된다.
   - 시상식, 퇴임식, 자선 행사 등의 행사에서 인물을 소개하거나 소감 및 감사 인사를 전달

800+ 공략

1. 도입부의 인사말에서 화자나 청자의 신분 및 행사 장소에 대한 정답의 단서가 자주 언급되므로 지문의 초반을 집중해서 듣는다.
2. 모임 및 행사와 관련된 표현들을 알아 둔다.

Example 🎧 D18_1_예제

해석 p.113

Questions 01-03 refer to the following speech.

We are here tonight to celebrate the anniversary of the Yorkville Medical Facility. **01 As a member of the board of trustees, it is my honor to speak before you all.** Exactly 100 years ago, this hospital first opened its doors to the public. **02 In its early years, the facility only had 10 doctors. But now there are well over 75, plus numerous nurses.** Over time, the Yorkville community has come to appreciate our high-quality care. Dinner will be served shortly, but **03 first, Dr. Lily Driver is going to give a short talk** on the history of the Yorkville Medical Facility. **03 Please welcome her to the stage.**

01 Who is the speaker?
   (A) A board member
   (B) A regional supervisor
   (C) A head doctor
   (D) A security guard

02 What does the speaker say about the Yorkville Medical Facility?
   (A) It was funded by local donors.
   (B) It was recently relocated.
   (C) Its construction took longer than expected.
   (D) Its staff has expanded over the years.

03 What will most likely happen next?
   (A) A song will be performed live.
   (B) A speaker will take the stage.
   (C) A short film will be shown.
   (D) A parade will be held.

정답 01 (A) 02 (D) 03 (B)

해설

01 [화자] "As a member of the board of trustees, it is my honor ~ you all."이라고 하였으므로 (A)가 정답이다.
02 [언급] "In its early years, the facility only had 10 doctors. But now there are well over 75, ~."라고 하였으므로 (D)가 정답이다.
03 [다음에 할 일] "first, Dr. Lily Driver is going to give a short talk"라고 한 뒤, "Please welcome her to the stage."라고 하였으므로 (B)가 정답이다.

연설에 자주 나오는 필수 표현 🎧 D18_2_표현

사내 모임에서의 연설

1	conduct the session 세션을 진행하다	An HR representative will **conduct the session** on our company's new onboarding process. 인사부서 담당자가 우리 회사의 새로운 온보딩 프로세스에 대한 세션을 진행할 것입니다.
2	move on to ~ ~로 넘어가다	Today, we'll **move on to** the packaging phase. 오늘은, 포장 단계로 넘어갈 것입니다.
3	refer to ~ ~을 참조하다	During the presentation, I'll be **referring to** the latest research findings. 발표 동안, 저는 최근의 연구 결과들을 참조할 것입니다.

공식적인 행사에서의 연설

4	on behalf of ~ ~을 대표하여	I am honored to be here at this year's Consumer Electronics Show **on behalf of** Lifan Industries. 저는 Lifan사를 대표하여 이곳 올해의 가전제품 전시회에 있게 되어 영광입니다.
5	invite ~ to the stage ~를 무대로 모시다	Now, without further ado, I'd like to **invite** Mr. Jenkins **to the stage**. 이제, 더 이상의 지체 없이 Mr. Jenkins를 무대로 모시겠습니다.
6	keynote speaker 기조 연설자	Our **keynote speaker** for this event, Dr. Heidi Balina, is one of the leaders in the field of solar energy research. 이번 행사의 기조 연설자이신 Dr. Heidi Balina는 태양 에너지 연구 분야의 선두주자들 중 한 명입니다.

토익실전문제 🎧 D18_3_실전

01 Where most likely is the speaker?
(A) At an art gallery
(B) At a convention center
(C) At a library
(D) At a shopping mall

02 According to the speaker, what does the pamphlet contain?
(A) Upcoming publications
(B) Lists of designers
(C) Names of presenters
(D) Workshop details

03 What can the listeners do at Edwards Hall?
(A) Purchase some books
(B) Pick up a conference badge
(C) Listen to a story
(D) Watch a documentary

04 What type of event is taking place?
(A) A trade fair
(B) A retirement party
(C) An award ceremony
(D) A theater opening

05 What does the speaker praise Daryl Meyers for?
(A) Studying famous building designs
(B) Inventing a popular device
(C) Experimenting with new materials
(D) Creating an innovative design

06 Why is Daryl Meyers going to give a talk?
(A) To describe his career
(B) To acknowledge his coworkers
(C) To praise an architectural firm
(D) To discuss future projects

기출 유형 2 강연

화자가 청자들에게 다양한 주제에 대해 강연을 하는 지문으로, 전문가의 설명, 사내 업무 처리 방법 설명, 시설 이용 절차 안내와 같은 내용이 자주 등장한다. 매회 1개 정도 출제된다.

출제 경향

1. 지문이 시작되기 전에 주로 instructions, talk 또는 lecture로 지문의 종류가 소개된다.
2. 강연의 주제나 목적, 화자나 청자의 신분, 업무 처리 방법, 청자가 다음에 할 일을 묻는 문제가 자주 출제된다.
3. 다음과 같은 상황이 자주 출제된다.
   - 교육, 건강, 스포츠, 여가 활동, 문학 작품, 영화 등 다양한 주제에 대한 전문가의 설명 및 강연
   - 출장 허가, 업무 절차, 스케줄 근무 신청 절차, 새로운 급여 시스템에 대한 설명
   - 도서관, 공원 등의 시설물 이용 관련 절차 안내

800+ 공략

1. 다양한 주제의 강연이 나올 수 있으므로 초반부를 반드시 듣고 강연의 주제를 파악한다.
2. 사내 업무 처리 절차 설명, 시설 이용 안내, 전문가의 설명에서 자주 나오는 표현들을 알아 둔다.

Example 🎧 D18_4_예제

해석 p.114

01 Who most likely is the speaker?
(A) A photographer
(B) A gallery owner
(C) An instructor
(D) A machine operator

02 What can the listeners take home?
(A) An artwork
(B) A brochure
(C) A certificate
(D) A photo

03 What does the speaker remind the listeners to do?
(A) Use some tools carefully
(B) Purchase some souvenirs
(C) Rearrange some tables
(D) Leave some items

Questions 01-03 refer to the following instructions.

Welcome, everyone. My name is Lana, and ⁰¹**I'm going to be teaching you how to paint nature scenes this evening**. Since many of you are new to painting, I will guide you through each step of the process. The class will last for approximately two hours, and ⁰²**you may take your painting home** with you afterward. Um . . . ⁰³**just make sure to place the aprons and equipment on the table near the classroom door before you head out**. Any questions so far?

해설   정답 01 (C) 02 (A) 03 (D)

01 [화자] "I'm going to be teaching you how to paint nature scenes this evening"을 통해 화자가 강사임을 알 수 있으므로 (C)가 정답이다.
02 [세부] "you may take your painting home"이라고 하였으므로 (A)가 정답이다.
03 [세부] "just make sure to place the aprons and equipment on the table ~ before you head out"이라고 하였으므로 (D)가 정답이다.

강연에 자주 나오는 필수 표현

사내 업무 처리 절차 설명

1 keep in mind 명심하다, 고려하다	**Keep in mind** that all products must undergo quality checks. 모든 제품들은 품질 확인을 반드시 거쳐야 한다는 것을 명심하세요.
2 pass around ~ (여러 사람이 보도록) ~을 돌리다	Please **pass around** the updated employee manuals. 업데이트된 직원 매뉴얼을 돌려주세요.

시설 이용 방법 설명

3 be familiar with ~ ~에 익숙하다	Our fitness instructors **are familiar with** proper weight training techniques. 저희의 피트니스 강사들은 적절한 웨이트 트레이닝 기법에 익숙합니다.
4 take advantage of ~ ~을 이용하다, 활용하다	Event organizers should **take advantage of** our conference facilities. 행사 기획자들은 저희의 콘퍼런스 시설을 이용하셔야 합니다.

전문가의 설명 및 강연

5 be committed to ~ ~에 전념하다	I **am committed to** advancing renewable energy technology for a greener future. 저는 더 친환경적인 미래를 위해 재생 에너지 기술을 발전시키는 데 전념합니다.
6 take a look at ~ ~을 보다	I'd like you to **take a look at** this chart analyzing social media usage across generations. 세대별 소셜 미디어 사용을 분석한 이 차트를 보시기 바랍니다.
7 give an overview of ~ ~에 대한 개요를 설명하다	Today, I'll **give** you **an overview of** the new tax laws. 오늘 저는 새로운 세법에 대한 개요를 설명할 것입니다.

토익실전문제

01 What type of photography will the speaker discuss?
(A) Flower
(B) Fashion
(C) Food
(D) Travel

02 What does the speaker say is the most important consideration?
(A) The types of light sources
(B) The locations of objects
(C) The brightness of colors
(D) The number of background items

03 What will the speaker do next?
(A) Distribute handouts
(B) Set up a device
(C) Move a table
(D) Print images

04 What is the topic of the workshop?
(A) Soil quality
(B) Pest control
(C) Garden design
(D) Flower selection

05 What will the listeners do after lunch?
(A) Watch a video
(B) Take a test
(C) Inspect a site
(D) Try a technique

06 According to the speaker, what will the listeners receive?
(A) Gardening tools
(B) Protective gear
(C) Hiking equipment
(D) Storage containers

HACKERS TEST

01 What is the main purpose of the talk?

(A) To introduce a guest speaker
(B) To inform attendees of a change in schedule
(C) To provide an overview of a workshop
(D) To describe a new shop concept

02 Who most likely are the listeners?

(A) Business owners
(B) Job applicants
(C) Interior decorators
(D) Advertising executives

03 What will the listeners do in the afternoon?

(A) Ask questions of a guest speaker
(B) Take part in group activities
(C) View examples of past displays
(D) Tour a department store

04 Who most likely is Ms. Littleton?

(A) A marketing consultant
(B) A financial advisor
(C) A department manager
(D) A personal assistant

05 What does the speaker say about the publicity campaign?

(A) It has increased business.
(B) It earned the company an award.
(C) It exceeded its budget.
(D) It was conducted on social media.

06 What will most likely happen next?

(A) A speech will be given.
(B) A picture will be taken.
(C) An introduction will be made.
(D) A winner will be announced.

07 Who most likely are the listeners?

(A) Focus group members
(B) Orientation attendees
(C) Job applicants
(D) Company shareholders

08 What does the speaker mean when she says, "there are some forms on the table in front of me"?

(A) Research will be conducted.
(B) The listeners should print a file.
(C) The listeners have to take a test.
(D) Paperwork must be completed.

09 According to the speaker, what was changed?

(A) A venue
(B) A presenter
(C) A topic
(D) A timetable

10 What is the class mainly about?

(A) Native plants
(B) Agricultural methods
(C) Local ecosystems
(D) Environmental risks

11 How is today's class different from what the instructor planned?

(A) It will feature a guest speaker.
(B) It will involve more students.
(C) It will be finished early.
(D) It will be held indoors.

12 What will the speaker do next?

(A) Install applications
(B) Turn off lights
(C) Distribute photographs
(D) Collect assignments

13 What is the speaker mainly discussing?

(A) Guidelines for a presentation
(B) Rules for reimbursement
(C) Directions to a venue
(D) Requests from clients

14 According to the speaker, what should be included in a report?

(A) Quarterly budgets
(B) Sales forecasts
(C) Meal costs
(D) Trip details

15 Why would the listeners visit a Web site?

(A) To leave suggestions for supervisors
(B) To sign up for a workshop
(C) To obtain a copy of a document
(D) To register for an employee benefit

16 What is the speaker surprised about?

(A) The number of participants
(B) The size of a venue
(C) The length of an event
(D) The availability of tickets

17 What will happen in a few minutes?

(A) An organizer will be introduced.
(B) An award will be given.
(C) A tour will commence.
(D) A demonstration will begin.

18 Why does the speaker say, "Please stop by the information desk in the lobby"?

(A) To indicate that an item is available
(B) To explain how to get assistance
(C) To specify where to buy a ticket
(D) To state the location of an employee

Carter Award for Best Novel Nominees

Kevin Peterson	Jose Gomez
This Old Life	*Win It All*
Beth Anderson	Tara Choi
Fallen Leaves	*Away from Home*

19 Look at the graphic. Who won the award for best novel?

(A) Kevin Peterson
(B) Beth Anderson
(C) Jose Gomez
(D) Tara Choi

20 What motivated the speaker?

(A) The feedback of an editor
(B) The advice of an instructor
(C) The support of a friend
(D) The example of a colleague

21 What is mentioned about the speaker's book?

(A) It was featured in an article.
(B) It includes illustrations.
(C) It has been translated.
(D) It is based on real events.

DAY 19 방송 및 보도

음성 바로 듣기

기출 유형 1 │ 방송

라디오나 TV, 팟캐스트를 통해 전달되는 지문으로, 교통 방송, 일기 예보, 초대 손님 인터뷰가 자주 등장한다. 매회 1개 정도 출제된다.

출제 경향

1. 지문이 시작되기 전에 주로 broadcast 또는 podcast로 지문의 종류가 소개된다.
2. 방송의 주제, 교통이나 날씨에 대해 언급한 사항, 초대 손님의 정보, 청자가 할 일을 묻는 문제가 자주 출제된다.
3. 다음과 같은 소재가 자주 출제된다.
   - 교통 방송에서 도로의 공사 및 사고 상황 전달, 교통 체증 소식 전달, 우회 도로 안내 등
   - 일기 예보에서는 날씨 정보 제공, 날씨 상황에 따른 대비책 안내 등
   - 팟캐스트에서 초대 손님(guest)을 소개하는 인터뷰 등

800+ 공략

1. 방송의 주제를 나타내는 정답의 단서는 주로 focus on(~에 중점을 두다), discuss(~에 대해 이야기를 나누다) 뒤에 나오는 것을 염두에 두고 듣는다.
2. 교통 방송, 일기 예보, 인터뷰에 자주 나오는 표현들을 알아 둔다.

Example 🎧 D19_1_예제
해석 p.120

01 What is the broadcast mainly about?
   (A) Travel
   (B) Art
   (C) Health
   (D) Sports

02 According to the speaker, what did Dr. Khan recently do?
   (A) She wrote an article.
   (B) She attended a conference.
   (C) She launched a radio show.
   (D) She received a degree.

03 What can the listeners find on a Web site?
   (A) A cooking video
   (B) A talk transcript
   (C) A meal plan
   (D) An event schedule

Questions 01-03 refer to the following broadcast.

You're listening to *Our Society*. I'm your host, James Ash. ⁰¹**In today's show, we'll be focusing on the health effects of the typical American diet**. I'll be discussing this topic with nutrition specialist Omani Khan. ⁰²**Dr. Khan will talk about her article, which was recently published in *Health Today Magazine*.** ⁰³**On our Web site, you can find her ideal weekly meal plan for adults.** Please feel free to check it out.

정답 01 (C) 02 (A) 03 (C)

해설

01 [주제] "In today's show, we'll be focusing on the health effects of the typical American diet."라고 하였으므로 (C)가 정답이다.
02 [세부] "Dr. Khan will talk about her article, which was recently published ~."라고 하였으므로 (A)가 정답이다.
03 [세부] "On our Web site, you can find her ideal weekly meal plan for adults."라고 하였으므로 (C)가 정답이다.

방송에 자주 나오는 필수 표현 🎧 D19_2_표현

교통 방송

1	take an alternative route 대체 도로를 택하다	Due to heavy traffic on Highway 101, drivers are advised to **take an alternative route**. 101번 고속도로에서의 교통 정체로 인해, 운전자들은 대체 도로를 택할 것이 권고됩니다.
2	be closed for repairs 보수 공사로 폐쇄되다	North Avenue **is closed for repairs** from 9 P.M. tonight until 5 A.M. tomorrow morning. North 도로가 오늘밤 9시부터 내일 아침 5시까지 보수 공사로 폐쇄됩니다.
3	road conditions 도로 상황	Drivers are advised to check the **road conditions** before traveling through mountain passes during a snowstorm. 운전자들은 눈폭풍 중 산악 지역을 통과하기 전에 도로 상황을 확인할 것이 권고됩니다.

일기 예보

4	it is expected to ~ ~할 것으로 예상되다	**It is expected to** drop below freezing throughout the region by midnight. 자정에는 전체 지역이 영하로 떨어질 것으로 예상됩니다.
5	a chance of ~ ~의 가능성	According to the National Weather Service, there is **a chance of** light rain this evening. 기상청에 따르면, 오늘 저녁에 약한 비가 올 가능성이 있습니다.

인터뷰

6	be joined by ~ ~와 함께 하다	To help us better understand, we **are joined by** Tara Hong, the marketing director at Top Consulting. 우리가 더 잘 이해하도록 돕기 위해, Top 컨설팅사의 마케팅 부장인 Tara Hong과 함께 합니다.
7	a frequent guest 자주 오는 게스트	I'm pleased to welcome Mr. Bernard, who is **a frequent guest** on our show. 우리 방송에 자주 오는 게스트인 Mr. Bernard를 맞이하여 기쁩니다.

토익실전문제 🎧 D19_3_실전

01 What industry is the podcast about?
(A) Agriculture
(B) Construction
(C) Energy
(D) Aviation

02 Why has a policy been changed?
(A) To address customer complaints
(B) To reduce operating expenses
(C) To meet a safety standard
(D) To prevent a facility closure

03 What is included in the report?
(A) A summary of benefits
(B) A calculation of expenses
(C) An overview of regulations
(D) A comparison of companies

04 Why did Townsend become famous recently?
(A) It opened a tourist attraction.
(B) It was featured in a movie.
(C) It hosted an international event.
(D) It launched a marketing campaign.

05 What are residents unhappy about?
(A) High prices
(B) Excessive noise
(C) Traffic jams
(D) Air pollution

06 According to the speaker, what can the listeners do on a Web site?
(A) Download an app
(B) Complete a survey
(C) Read a report
(D) Check a map

기출 유형 2 보도

사회 전반에 걸친 소식을 전하는 지문으로, 경제, 비즈니스, 교육, 환경과 관련된 내용이 자주 등장한다. 매회 출제되지는 않으며 가끔 1개의 지문이 출제된다.

출제 경향

1. 지문이 시작되기 전에 주로 news report 또는 report로 지문의 종류가 소개된다.
2. 보도의 주제, 기업 상황에 대해 언급한 사항, 지역 사회 봉사·교육 신청 방법, 다음에 일어날 일을 묻는 문제가 자주 출제된다.
3. 다음과 같은 내용이 자주 출제된다.
   - 생산과 소비, 업계 매출 및 수익, 합병 소식과 같은 경제·비즈니스 관련 보도
   - 지역 사회의 일자리 안내, 자선 단체 소식, 봉사자 구인, 도심 환경 개선과 같은 사회 관련 보도

800+ 공략

1. 지문 흐름에 특별한 패턴이 없어 난도가 높으므로, 문제를 먼저 파악하여 핵심 내용을 집중해서 듣는다.
2. 경제·비즈니스, 사회 전반과 관련된 표현들을 알아 둔다.

Example   🎧 D19_4_예제   해석 p.121

01 What is the main topic of the news report?
(A) A community festival
(B) A street closure
(C) A traffic congestion
(D) A policy change

02 According to the speaker, what are riders required to do?
(A) Wear safety equipment
(B) Stay on city sidewalks
(C) Avoid riding after dark
(D) Register their devices

03 What does the speaker mean when she says, "there are still long lines outside stores selling these products"?
(A) Buyers demanded a refund.
(B) Some instructions were not followed.
(C) An event was delayed.
(D) The restrictions did not affect sales.

Questions 01-03 refer to the following news report.

⁰¹Now for a report on the city's recently announced adjustment to its policy on motorized scooters. Many people in Belleview have started riding these. However, after a few riders were injured in the last few weeks, the city council decided yesterday that ⁰²/⁰³riders must wear helmets and use bicycle lanes only. The council also set a speed limit of 15 kilometers per hour for the devices. ⁰³Despite all this, there are still long lines outside stores selling these products.

해설   정답 01 (D) 02 (A) 03 (D)

01 [주제] "Now for a report on the city's recently announced adjustment to its policy"라고 하였으므로 (D)가 정답이다.
02 [세부] "riders must wear helmets"라고 하였으므로 (A)가 정답이다.
03 [의도] 질문의 인용어구 앞에서 여러 규제들을 언급했고, 그럼에도 불구하고 "그 제품을 파는 가게들 밖에는 여전히 긴 줄이 있다"라고 말한 것은 규제들이 판매에 영향을 주지 않았다는 의미이므로 (D)가 정답이다.

보도에 자주 나오는 필수 표현

경제·비즈니스

1 go ahead with ~ ~을 추진하다	The city is **going ahead with** its plan to create small business support programs. 시는 소규모 기업 지원 프로그램을 만드는 계획을 추진하고 있습니다.
2 according to ~ ~에 따르면	**According to** the government's Web site, the annual city festival will be held next month. 정부 웹사이트에 따르면, 연례 시 축제가 다음 달에 열릴 것입니다.
3 In local news 지역 소식에서는	**In local news**, Passion Sportswear is throwing a party today to celebrate its one-year anniversary. 지역 소식에서는, Passion 스포츠 의류사가 창립 1주년을 기념해 오늘 파티를 개최합니다.

사회 전반

4 promise to ~ ~할 것을 약속하다	The project **promises to** bring thousands of jobs to the community. 그 프로젝트는 지역사회에 수천개의 일자리를 가져올 것을 약속합니다.
5 in progress 진행 중인	Construction of the new community center is currently **in progress**. 새로운 주민센터의 건설이 현재 진행 중입니다.
6 convert A into B A를 B로 개조하다, 전환시키다	The city council approved the sale of the old warehouse to a local builder, who will **convert** it **into** apartments. 시의회는 지역 건설업자에게 그 오래된 창고를 매각하기로 승인했는데, 그는 그것을 아파트로 개조할 것입니다.

토익실전문제

01 What is the news report mainly about?
- (A) The development of a suburb
- (B) The implementation of a toll
- (C) The expansion of a street
- (D) The construction of a bridge

02 What problem does the speaker mention?
- (A) A schedule will be altered.
- (B) A budget will be exceeded.
- (C) A tax will be increased.
- (D) A project will be canceled.

03 What will happen on May 25?
- (A) A public meeting
- (B) A city election
- (C) An opening ceremony
- (D) A charity fundraiser

04 What is the news report mainly about?
- (A) A corporate merger
- (B) A business expansion
- (C) A security measure
- (D) A payment process

05 Why does the speaker say, "Now, around 20 major retail chains use it"?
- (A) To suggest a solution to a problem
- (B) To show the growth of a trend
- (C) To identify the source of a technology
- (D) To indicate a reason for a change

06 What did Ms. Lewis do last month?
- (A) She published a book.
- (B) She gave a speech.
- (C) She released a report.
- (D) She organized an event.

HACKERS TEST

DAY 19

🎧 D19_7_테스트

01 Who is Marcia Gray?
(A) An actress
(B) A dancer
(C) A musician
(D) An athlete

02 Why would the listeners visit a Web site?
(A) To read messages
(B) To post a review
(C) To watch videos
(D) To register for a class

03 According to the speaker, what did Ms. Gray recently do?
(A) She opened an academy.
(B) She received an award.
(C) She appeared on television.
(D) She published a memoir.

04 What has caused the delay?
(A) Timetable conflicts
(B) Insufficient funds
(C) Contract issues
(D) Venue renovations

05 According to the speaker, why were some fans concerned?
(A) They were uncertain about a new conductor.
(B) They expected performances to be canceled.
(C) They were given inaccurate information.
(D) They experienced issues placing orders.

06 What are the listeners advised to do?
(A) Listen to an album
(B) Contact management
(C) Buy tickets early
(D) Download an application

07 What is the broadcast mainly about?
(A) Economic forecasts
(B) A city election
(C) Successful small companies
(D) Bad weather

08 Why does the speaker say, "it will probably last a short amount of time"?
(A) To offer reassurance
(B) To request help
(C) To express disappointment
(D) To finalize a plan

09 What will the listeners hear next?
(A) An interview
(B) An advertisement
(C) Sports updates
(D) Business news

10 What is Diego Franco known for?
(A) Tutoring students
(B) Collecting donations
(C) Making investments
(D) Promoting businesses

11 What will the speaker ask Mr. Franco about?
(A) A musical performance
(B) A fashion show
(C) A museum exhibit
(D) A sports competition

12 What does the speaker encourage the listeners to do?
(A) Create a social media account
(B) Help set up equipment
(C) Find information online
(D) Contact an event organizer

13 According to the speaker, what will finish soon?

(A) A park cleanup
(B) A store expansion
(C) A construction project
(D) A city festival

14 What does the speaker imply when she says, "But this is about to change"?

(A) She hopes there will be more bus stops.
(B) She wants streets to be safer for cyclists.
(C) She predicts few drivers will use the road.
(D) She thinks there will be less traffic.

15 What will the speaker do next?

(A) Interview a resident
(B) Inspect a site
(C) Speak with a city official
(D) Join an opening ceremony

16 What is the broadcast mainly about?

(A) Renovations to a plant
(B) Preparations for a convention
(C) A manufacturing agreement
(D) A corporate merger

17 What does the speaker say about Health Bites?

(A) It will remain in production.
(B) Its price will increase.
(C) It will include different ingredients.
(D) Its packaging will change.

18 According to the speaker, what will happen later this week?

(A) A press conference will take place.
(B) A new factory will open.
(C) Information will be made available.
(D) Staff will be trained for new positions.

Weather forecast			
Thursday	Friday	Saturday	Sunday
🌧	☁	☁	💨

19 What does the speaker say about Karma Birds?

(A) They are performing for the first time at an event.
(B) They will be playing in the morning.
(C) They declined to use one of the stages.
(D) They are the most popular band.

20 According to the speaker, what has been changed?

(A) A performer
(B) A location
(C) A start time
(D) An entrance fee

21 Look at the graphic. Which day is the event being held?

(A) Thursday
(B) Friday
(C) Saturday
(D) Sunday

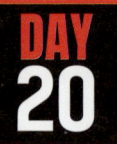

광고 및 소개

기출 유형 1 광고

제품이나 서비스, 또는 사업체를 홍보하는 지문으로, 전자기기, 가구 등의 제품 광고나 조경/수리 등 서비스 광고가 자주 등장한다. 매회 1개의 지문이 출제된다.

출제 경향
1. 지문이 시작되기 전에 advertisement로 지문의 종류가 소개된다.
2. 광고되고 있는 대상, 제품 또는 서비스의 특장점, 혜택 이용 방법 등을 묻는 문제가 자주 출제된다.
3. 다음과 같은 소재가 자주 출제된다.
   - 신제품 출시, 할인 혜택, 제품 특장점 등을 소개하는 제품 광고
   - 보상·보험 제도, 수리 및 공사 등을 소개하는 서비스 또는 업체 광고

800+ 공략
1. 지문의 초반에서 무엇이 광고되고 있는지 반드시 듣는다.
2. 강조하는 특징이나 기능을 묻는 문제가 두 번째 문제로 자주 출제되므로 중반부에서 이를 놓치지 않고 듣는다.
3. 제품 광고, 서비스/업체 광고와 관련된 표현들을 알아 둔다.

Example 🎧 D20_1_예제   해석 p.127

01 What is Stinson Woodworking known for?
    (A) Using modern styles
    (B) Offering competitive prices
    (C) Providing fast deliveries
    (D) Fulfilling custom orders

02 According to the speaker, what does Stinson Woodworking provide customers?
    (A) Free items
    (B) Product guarantees
    (C) Expedited shipping
    (D) Discounted prices

03 What can the listeners find online?
    (A) Pictures of products
    (B) A list of prices
    (C) Directions to a branch
    (D) A schedule for a store

Questions 01-03 refer to the following advertisement.

Stinson Woodworking is proud to offer the finest handmade tables and chairs in the state. ⁰¹**Our independent shop has a reputation for taking custom orders**, and all of our items are one of a kind. Moreover, ⁰²**we ensure our customers' satisfaction by providing a 10-year warranty** on everything that we produce. For further details about Stinson Woodworking, ⁰³**you can visit our Web site. There you will find images of some of the chairs and tables** that we made in the past.

정답 01 (D) 02 (B) 03 (A)

해설
01 [세부] "Our independent shop has a reputation for taking custom orders"라고 하였으므로 (D)가 정답이다.
02 [세부] "we ensure our customers' satisfaction by providing a 10-year warranty"라고 하였으므로 (B)가 정답이다.
03 [세부] "you can visit our Web site. There you will find images of some of the chairs and tables"라고 하였으므로 (A)가 정답이다.

광고에 자주 나오는 필수 표현
🎧 D20_2_표현

제품 광고

1 tired of ~ ~에 진저리가 나는	**Tired of** struggling to find important documents in your home office? 당신의 홈오피스에서 중요한 서류들을 힘들게 찾는 것에 진저리가 나시나요?
2 best of all 무엇보다도	**Best of all**, the ergonomic design ensures that you will never experience neck or back pain. 무엇보다도, 인체공학적 디자인은 여러분이 목 또는 등 통증을 결코 경험하지 않게 해줍니다.
3 a special deal 특별 할인	We're offering **a special deal** on ski resort packages. 저희는 스키 리조트 패키지에 대해 특별 할인을 제공하고 있습니다.

서비스 및 업체 광고

4 interested in ~ ~에 관심이 있는	Are you **interested in** turning your hobby into your own business? 당신의 취미를 당신의 사업으로 변화시키는 것에 관심이 있나요?
5 specialize in ~ ~을 전문으로 하다	We **specialize in** eco-friendly home renovation and design services. 저희는 친환경적인 주택 개조와 디자인 서비스를 전문으로 합니다.
6 be proud of ~ ~을 자랑스럽게 생각하다	We **are proud of** delivering cutting-edge technology solutions for businesses. 저희는 기업들을 위한 첨단 기술 솔루션을 제공하는 것을 자랑스럽게 생각합니다.
7 at affordable prices 적정한 가격에	We provide high-quality graphic design **at affordable prices**. 저희는 고품질의 그래픽 디자인을 적정한 가격에 제공합니다.

토익실전문제
🎧 D20_3_실전

01 What does the Mason Vista Institute teach?
 (A) Customer service
 (B) Driving
 (C) Sales techniques
 (D) Programming

02 What is mentioned about the program?
 (A) It involves an entrance exam.
 (B) It is held during evening hours.
 (C) Its class sizes are limited.
 (D) Its success rate is very high.

03 What is offered to graduates?
 (A) Photo session
 (B) Job search assistance
 (C) Online workshop
 (D) Educational facility access

04 What is being advertised?
 (A) An accommodation facility
 (B) An event venue
 (C) A travel agency
 (D) A dining establishment

05 What does the speaker emphasize about the bus?
 (A) Its size
 (B) Its schedule
 (C) Its cost
 (D) Its comfort

06 According to the speaker, why should the listeners make a booking this month?
 (A) To receive a gift
 (B) To get a discount
 (C) To avoid a rush
 (D) To obtain an upgrade

기출 유형 2 소개

주로 인물에 대해 소개하는 지문으로, 신입 직원이나 전근하는 직원을 소개하거나 행사에서의 연설자 등을 소개하는 내용이 자주 등장한다. 매회 출제되지는 않으며 가끔 1개의 지문이 출제된다.

출제 경향

1. 지문이 시작되기 전에 introduction으로 지문의 종류가 소개된다.
2. 소개의 목적, 소개하는 인물의 신분, 작품에 대해 언급한 사항, 청자에게 요청하는 것을 묻는 문제가 자주 출제된다.
3. 다음과 같은 소재가 자주 출제된다.
   - 신입 직원, 전근하는 직원, 은퇴하는 직원 소개
   - 학회에서의 연설자, 책의 저자, 예술가 소개

800+ 공략

1. 지문의 초반에서 누구를 소개하는지 반드시 듣고 소개하는 대상에 대해 언급하는 점을 주의 깊게 듣는다.
2. 인사 이동, 행사와 관련된 표현들을 알아 둔다.

Example

01 Why was Jenna MacArthur hired?
   (A) To serve as an assistant
   (B) To counsel students
   (C) To promote a college
   (D) To lead a department

02 What will Ms. MacArthur speak about?
   (A) A popular course
   (B) Some exam details
   (C) Some planned changes
   (D) An administrative duty

03 What does the speaker imply when he says, "He has the schedule for next week's workshop"?
   (A) There's a new research project starting.
   (B) There's more information to be shared.
   (C) The class will be postponed.
   (D) Some volunteer speakers are needed.

Questions 01-03 refer to the following introduction.

[01]**I want to introduce Jenna MacArthur, who's been selected to lead our school's biology department.** She was a biology professor at Raymount University, and we are excited that she has decided to join our school. In a few minutes, [02]**Ms. MacArthur is going to speak about some adjustments she's going to make to our department**. [03]**But first, please give your attention to Mr. Dryson.** He has the schedule for next week's workshop.

해설

정답 01 (D) 02 (C) 03 (B)

01 [이유] "I want to introduce Jenna MacArthur, who's been selected to lead our school's biology department."라고 하였으므로 (D)가 정답이다.
02 [세부] "Ms. MacArthur is going to speak about some adjustments she's going to make to our department"라고 하였으므로 (C)가 정답이다.
03 [의도] "But first, please give your attention to Mr. Dryson."이라고 한 것을 통해 공유될 정보가 더 있음을 알 수 있으므로 (B)가 정답이다.

소개에 자주 나오는 필수 표현 🎧 D20_5_표현

인물 소개

1 contribute to ~ ~에 공헌을 하다	Professor Rodriguez actively **contributes to** sustainable urban development projects. Rodriguez 교수는 지속 가능한 도심 개발 프로젝트에 적극적으로 공헌합니다.
2 be promoted to ~ ~로 승진하다	Mr. Park **was** recently **promoted to** chief of the West Port Fire Department. Mr. Park은 최근 West Port 소방서장으로 승진했습니다.
3 be in charge of ~ ~을 담당하다	She'll **be in charge of** communications with international clients. 그녀는 해외 고객들과 의사소통하는 것을 담당할 것입니다.
4 thanks to ~ ~ 덕분에	Ms. Finn has been awarded this honor **thanks to** her volunteer work in the city. Ms. Finn은 시에서 그녀의 자원봉사 업무 덕분에 이 상을 수여받았습니다.
5 be responsible for ~ ~에 대한 책임이 있다	John Williams **is responsible for** optimizing supply chain efficiency. John Williams는 공급망 효율성을 극대화하는 것에 대한 책임이 있습니다.

토익실전문제 🎧 D20_6_실전

토익 문제 이렇게 나온다!

01 What is Ms. Park known for?
(A) Working with foreign musicians
(B) Receiving positive recognition
(C) Giving lessons to students
(D) Performing at charity concerts

02 What will Ms. Park most likely talk about?
(A) Her recent album
(B) Her new book
(C) Her career change
(D) Her upcoming tour

03 What does the speaker plan to do after the interview?
(A) Play a recording
(B) Perform a song
(C) Give away a ticket
(D) Introduce a guest

04 What will Mr. Lee talk about?
(A) Online security
(B) Software updates
(C) Customer loyalty
(D) Training techniques

05 Where do the listeners most likely work?
(A) At a financial institution
(B) At a medical facility
(C) At a law office
(D) At an insurance firm

06 What will the speaker do next?
(A) Give a presentation
(B) Distribute a document
(C) Describe a process
(D) Check a list

정답·해석·해설 p.129

HACKERS TEST

DAY 20

🎧 D20_7_테스트

01 What is being advertised?
(A) A sporting goods store
(B) A fitness center
(C) A pottery studio
(D) A community college

02 According to the speaker, what has recently been updated?
(A) A price list
(B) A class schedule
(C) A refund policy
(D) A company regulation

03 How can the listeners get a free item?
(A) By registering by a deadline
(B) By attending an event
(C) By bringing a coupon
(D) By posting a photo online

04 Who most likely is the speaker?
(A) A business owner
(B) An event organizer
(C) A keynote speaker
(D) A contest judge

05 What did Mr. Nolan receive?
(A) A letter of recommendation
(B) A business award
(C) A government loan
(D) A job offer

06 Why should the listeners download an application?
(A) To communicate with other participants
(B) To access a map of a venue
(C) To read transcripts of a speech
(D) To find information about activities

07 What type of business is being advertised?
(A) An interior decorating firm
(B) An insurance company
(C) A residential cleaning service
(D) A real estate agency

08 How is the speaker's company different from its competitors?
(A) It has multiple branches.
(B) It has a mobile application.
(C) It provides delivery service.
(D) It offers free initial consultations.

09 What is available for the rest of the month?
(A) Express shipping
(B) Free membership
(C) A promotional discount
(D) A gift certificate

10 Where most likely do the listeners work?
(A) At a distribution center
(B) At a consultancy firm
(C) At a retail store
(D) At a fashion company

11 What task will Mr. Larson be responsible for?
(A) Creating some products
(B) Repairing machines
(C) Training some staff
(D) Maintaining a facility

12 What is Mr. Larson scheduled to do today?
(A) Review records
(B) Perform an evaluation
(C) Meet employees
(D) Give a presentation

13 Where is the introduction being made?

(A) In an office
(B) In a laboratory
(C) In a warehouse
(D) In a showroom

14 Who is Scott Baily?

(A) A salesperson
(B) A technician
(C) A researcher
(D) A designer

15 What are the listeners requested to do?

(A) Buy some equipment
(B) Submit a document
(C) Clean an instrument
(D) Share some information

16 What is being advertised?

(A) A storage facility
(B) A repair shop
(C) A retail outlet
(D) A travel agency

17 Why does the speaker say, "These are only available to members"?

(A) To express satisfaction
(B) To explain a process
(C) To justify a decision
(D) To provide motivation

18 What does the speaker say will happen next month?

(A) A new service will be launched.
(B) An overseas branch will open.
(C) An annual sale will be held.
(D) A business will relocate.

Age Group	Annual Sales
16-25	$8 billion
26-35	$6 billion
36-55	$4 billion
56-65	$2 billion

19 What type of product is being discussed?

(A) A board game
(B) A food storage bag
(C) A beverage
(D) A snack

20 According to the speaker, what was recently changed?

(A) A company logo
(B) Packaging
(C) Flavoring
(D) A brand name

21 Look at the graphic. Which is the fastest-growing age group of customers?

(A) 16-25
(B) 26-35
(C) 36-55
(D) 56-65

실시간 토익시험 정답확인&해설강의
Hackers.co.kr

한 권으로 끝내는 해커스 토익 800+ **LC+RC+VOCA**

PART 5

DAY 01	명사와 대명사
DAY 02	동사
DAY 03	to 부정사, 동명사, 분사
DAY 04	형용사, 부사, 비교 구문
DAY 05	전치사
DAY 06	접속사
DAY 07	관계사
DAY 08	최신 빈출 어휘
DAY 09	최신 빈출 어구

PART 5 소개 — 단문 빈칸 채우기 (30문제)

한 문장의 빈칸에 알맞은 문법 사항이나 어휘를 4개의 보기 중에서 골라 채우는 파트이다. 30문제를 약 11분 내에 끝내야 PART 7에서 시간이 모자라지 않으므로, 각 문제를 20~22초 내에 풀어야 한다.

문법

최신 예제 및 풀이 방법

101. Mr. Gonzalez must make a ------- between accepting the promotion and pursuing a new career path in a different industry.

    (A) decide
    (B) decision
    (C) decided
    (D) decisive

Step 1 문제 유형 파악하기
보기가 어근은 같지만 형태가 다른 단어들로 구성되어 있으므로, 문법 문제임을 알 수 있다.

Step 2 빈칸 주변이나 문장 전체의 구조 파악하기
빈칸 주변이나 문장의 전체적인 구조를 통해 빈칸에 적합한 문법적 요소를 정답으로 고른다. 만약 구조만으로 풀 수 없는 경우, 문맥을 확인하여 정답을 고른다.

최신 출제 경향

30개의 문제 중 평균 20문제가 출제되며, 특히, 명사, 대명사, 형용사, 부사의 자리를 묻는 문제가 꾸준히 높은 비율로 출제된다. 자리 문제는 비교적 쉽게 나오는 편이지만, 최근에는 보어 자리에 명사와 형용사를 구별하여 채우는 문제처럼 난이도가 높은 문제도 종종 출제되고 있다.

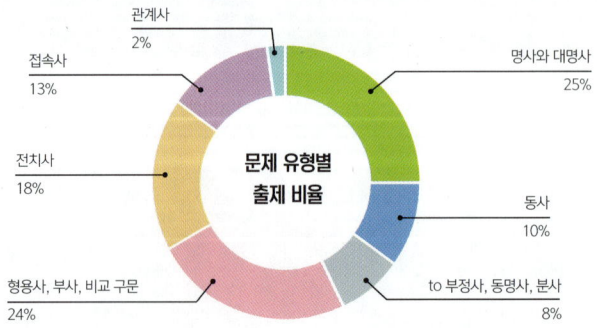

문제 유형별 출제 비율
- 관계사 2%
- 접속사 13%
- 전치사 18%
- 형용사, 부사, 비교 구문 24%
- to 부정사, 동명사, 분사 8%
- 동사 10%
- 명사와 대명사 25%

800+ 학습 전략

🔍 **자주 출제되는 문법을 익힌다.**
PART 5에 특히 자주 출제되는 문법을 확실히 익혀 두면 PART 5에서 문제 풀이 시간을 많이 단축할 수 있고, 절약한 시간을 PART 6와 7을 풀이하는 데 활용할 수 있다.

어휘

최신 예제 및 풀이 방법

102. The city planners aim to ------- the abandoned warehouse district into a vibrant cultural hub.

(A) classify
(B) stimulate
(C) transform
(D) specialize

Step 1 문제 유형 파악하기
보기가 같은 품사의 다양한 어휘들로 구성되어 있으므로, 어휘 문제임을 알 수 있다.

Step 2 빈칸 주변이나 문장 전체의 문맥 파악하기
문맥을 확인하여 그 문맥에 가장 적합한 어휘를 정답으로 고른다. 만약 문맥만으로 풀 수 없는 경우, 빈칸 주변의 단어와 어구를 이루는 어휘를 정답으로 고른다.

최신 출제 경향

30개의 문제 중 평균 10문제가 출제되며, 어휘와 어구 문제 중 대부분은 어휘 문제로 출제된다. 어휘 문제는 명사, 동사, 형용사, 부사가 거의 비슷한 비율로 출제되므로, 모든 품사를 골고루 학습해야 한다. 어구 문제는 출제 비율은 낮지만 평균 오답률이 조금 더 높은 편이며, 최근에는 동사 관련 어구가 가장 많이 출제되고 있다.

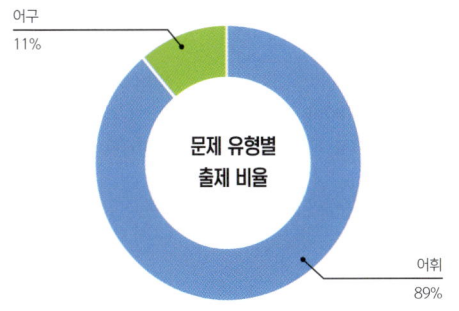

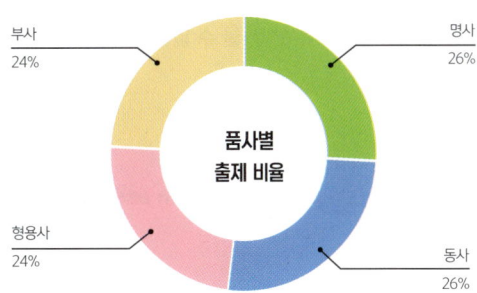

800⁺ 학습 전략

🔍 **자주 출제되는 어휘 및 어구를 암기한다**
PART 5에 특히 자주 출제되는 최신 기출 어휘 및 어구를 암기해 둔다. 특히 어구는 정확히 알아 두면 실전 토익에서 매우 빠르게 문제를 풀 수 있어 시간 단축의 핵심이 된다.

DAY 01 명사와 대명사

출제 경향 매회 4~5문제
최근 3개년 오답률 15.9%

1. 명사 사람, 사물, 장소, 개념 등의 이름을 나타내는 말이다.

기출 공식 1 명사는 주어, 목적어, 보어 자리에 온다.

주어 **Admission** to the national museum is free on Sundays. 국립 박물관의 입장료는 일요일마다 무료이다.
목적어 A number of stores offer **promotions** during the holiday season. 많은 가게들은 연휴 기간 동안 판촉 상품을 제공한다.
보어 Jen Wong is the **manager** responsible for supply chain optimization. Jen Wong은 공급망 최적화를 담당하는 관리자이다.

기출 공식 2 명사는 주로 한정사⁺, 형용사, 분사 뒤에 붙어 나온다.

Centis Tech accelerated its **growth** by opening a new branch. Centis Tech사는 새로운 지사를 열어서 그것의 성장을 가속화했다.
A project's success depends on effective **cooperation** among team members. 프로젝트의 성공은 팀원 간의 효과적인 협동에 달려 있다.
With the bank's app, users can make automated **payments**. 은행 앱으로, 사용자들은 자동화된 결제를 할 수 있다.

⁺한정사: 명사의 의미를 한정해 주는 것으로, 관사, 수량 형용사, 소유격, 지시형용사가 있다.

기출 공식 3 자주 출제되는 가산 명사와 불가산 명사

• 가산 명사는 반드시 앞에 한정사가 오거나 복수형으로 쓰인다.

approach 방법, 접근법	detail 세부 사항	increase 증가	regulation 규정	strategy 전략
appointment 약속	document 서류	opinion 의견	responsibility 책임	solution 해결책
compliment 칭찬	employee 직원	option 선택지	request 요청	subject 주제

The board is reviewing (**option**, **an option**, **options**) for the upcoming merger. 이사회는 다가오는 합병을 위한 선택지를 검토하고 있다.

• 불가산 명사는 앞에 부정관사 a/an이 올 수 없고 복수형으로 쓰일 수도 없다.

access 접근	assembly 조립	equipment 장비	information 정보	luggage 수하물
advice 조언	clothing 의류	funding 자금	knowledge 지식	merchandise 상품
approval 승인	consent 동의	furniture 가구	lending 대여	seating 좌석 (배열)

Most Neft Furnishing's furniture needs (**an assembly**, **assemblies**, **assembly**). 대부분의 Neft 가구점의 가구는 조립이 필요하다.

토익실전문제

토익 문제 이렇게 나온다!

01 The biggest concern for the HR department is a ------- of qualified candidates.
(A) short   (B) shorten
(C) shortage (D) shortly

★최빈출
02 Opticore Financial has been searching for a suitable ------- for its new office.
(A) locate   (B) locatable
(C) located   (D) location

03 The employee transferring from Singapore was asked to prepare necessary ------- regarding his work visa application.
(A) document   (B) documents
(C) documented   (D) to document

04 The project manager finally got ------- to hire three senior software developers.
(A) approval   (B) approvals
(C) approve   (D) approves

정답·해석·해설 p.135

기출 공식 4 — 자주 출제되는 사람명사와 사물/추상명사

사람명사	사물/추상명사	사람명사	사물/추상명사	사람명사	사물/추상명사
analyst 분석가	analysis 분석	coordinator 진행자, 조정자	coordination 합동, 조화	manufacturer 제조업자	manufacture 제조업, 제조
applicant 지원자	application 지원, 신청서	distributor 판매자, 유통 업자	distribution 분배, 배포	negotiator 협상가	negotiation 교섭, 협상
architect 건축가	architecture 건축(술)	employer 고용인 / employee 피고용인	employment 고용	occupant 입주자	occupancy 점유 / occupation 직업
assistant 조수, 보조원	assistance 원조, 보조	facilitator 조력자, 협력자	facility 시설	owner 소유자	ownership 소유권
attendee 참석자	attendance 출석	founder 설립자	foundation 설립, 재단	performer 연주자	performance 연주, 실적, 성과
consultant 상담가	consultation 상담 / consultancy 컨설팅사	inspector 검사자	inspection 검사, 정밀 조사	producer 생산자	production 생산 / product 생산품
consumer 고객	consumption 소비	instructor 강사, 가르치는 사람	instruction 교육	subscriber 구독자	subscription 구독, 가입
contributor 공헌자	contribution 기여, 공헌	investor 투자자	investment 투자	supervisor 감독자	supervision 감독

At the partnership meeting, Mr. Amadi proved that he was a skilled (**negotiation**, **negotiator**).
제휴 회의에서, Mr. Amadi는 그가 숙련된 협상가임을 입증했다.

기출 공식 5 — 자주 출제되는 복합 명사(명사 + 명사)

application form 신청서
arrival date 도착일
conference room 회의실
confidentiality policy 보안 정책
confirmation number 예약확인 번호

customer satisfaction 고객 만족
distribution center 물류 센터
expiration date 만기일
interest rate 금리, 이율
investment advice 투자 조언

keynote speaker 기조연설자
product description 제품 설명서
product line 제품 라인, 제품군
reference letter 추천서
repair work 복구공사

retail sales 소매 판매
safety regulations 안전 규정
sales representative 판매 사원
shipping charge 운송비
tourist attraction 관광 명소

The (confirming, **confirmation**) **number** will be sent to your e-mail address. 예약확인 번호가 당신의 이메일 주소로 보내질 것입니다.

토익실전문제

01 ------- will have to turn off their mobile phones during the presentation to avoid any disruptions.

(A) Attends (B) Attendees
(C) Attending (D) Attendances

02 Maison Luxe's new product ------- features sustainable materials developed with environmental scientists.

(A) line (B) lined
(C) to line (D) lining

03 The university decided to make an ------- in laboratory equipment in order to enhance its research capabilities.

(A) invest (B) investment
(C) investor (D) invests

04 The botanical garden, which houses more than 3,000 species of plants, serves as both a research center and a tourist -------.

(A) attract (B) attractive
(C) attraction (D) attracting

2. 대명사
동일한 명사가 반복되어 쓰이는 것을 피하기 위해 명사를 대신해서 쓰는 말이다.

기출 공식 6 격에 맞는 인칭대명사를 고르는 문제가 출제된다.

주격 Mr. Sung found out that **he** would be relocated to Tokyo. Mr. Sung은 그가 도쿄로 전근될 것을 알게 되었다.
목적격 If the clients show interest, we can schedule a meeting with **them**. 고객들이 관심을 보인다면, 우리는 그들과의 만남을 잡을 수 있다.
소유격 Applicants should contact **our** recruitment team by e-mail. 지원자들은 저희의 채용팀에 이메일로 연락해야 합니다.
소유대명사 (소유격+명사) Most presentations were boring, but **yours** was creative. 대부분의 발표는 지루했지만, 당신의 것은 창의적이었습니다.

기출 공식 7 재귀대명사는 목적어 또는 부사 자리에 온다.

- 목적어가 주어와 같은 사람/사물을 지칭할 때 목적어 자리에 재귀대명사를 쓴다.
  Ms. Schmidt considers **herself** qualified for the leadership position. Ms. Schmidt는 스스로가 그 지도자 자리에 자격이 있다고 여긴다.

- 주어나 목적어를 강조하기 위해 강조하고자 하는 말 바로 뒤나, 문장 맨 뒤에 재귀대명사를 쓴다.
  Though the graphics are outdated, the game **itself** is entertaining. 비록 그래픽은 구식이지만, 그 게임 자체는 재미있다.

- 재귀대명사 관련 관용 표현

  by oneself (= on one's own) 혼자서, 혼자 힘으로   in itself 그 자체로, 본질적으로
  for oneself 혼자 힘으로, 자신을 위해   of itself 저절로

  The entrepreneur should not try to manage all aspects of a business **by himself**.
  그 기업가는 혼자서 사업의 모든 면을 관리하려고 해서는 안 된다.

기출 공식 8 지시대명사 those의 다양한 쓰임

- 앞에 나온 복수 명사를 대신해서 사용한다. 단수 명사를 대신할 때는 that을 쓴다.
  Evergreen Inn's facilities are as hygienic as (that, **those**) of a luxury hotel. Evergreen 여관의 시설들은 호화 호텔의 것들만큼 위생적이다.

- 복수 명사 앞에서 지시형용사로 쓰여 '저 –, 그 –'라는 의미를 갖는다. 단수 명사 앞에는 that을 쓴다.
  Only (that, **those**) departments showing growth will receive additional funding. 성장을 보이는 부서들만 추가 자금을 받을 것이다.

- 관계절, 분사, 전치사구의 꾸밈을 받아 '~한 사람들'이라는 의미로 쓰이며, 복수 취급한다.
  (These, **Those**) who wish to purchase tickets can do so online. 표를 구매하기를 희망하는 사람들은 온라인에서 할 수 있다.

토익실전문제

01 The people who introduced ------ at the real estate seminar were all experts in their fields.

(A) they   (B) their
(C) themselves (D) their own

02 The design of the new air conditioner model is more sophisticated than ------ of the previous version.

(A) that   (B) what
(C) those   (D) them

03 The workshop on Thursday is intended for ------ interested in pursuing a career in the IT industry.

(A) that   (B) those
(C) who   (D) whose

04 We would like to recognize ------ contribution in making this program successful.

(A) she   (B) her
(C) hers   (D) herself

기출 공식 9 자주 출제되는 부정대명사/부정형용사

one	정해지지 않은 단수 가산 명사를 대신한다. 복수형은 ones로, 정해지지 않은 복수 가산 명사를 대신한다. If you need a business consultant, get **one** who specializes in your industry. 만약 당신이 사업 컨설턴트가 필요하다면, 당신의 산업을 전문으로 하는 컨설턴트를 구하세요.
another	'이미 언급한 것 이외의 또 다른 하나'라는 의미이며, 단수 취급한다. One benefit of the training program is skill development, and **another** is the networking opportunity. 교육 프로그램의 한 가지 혜택은 기술 개발이고, 또 다른 하나는 인적 네트워크 형성 기회이다.
other(s)	'이미 언급한 것 이외의 것들 중 몇몇'이라는 의미이다. others는 복수 취급하는 대명사로만, other는 형용사로만 쓰인다. Some clients prefer digital communication, while **others** still value face-to-face meetings. 몇몇 고객들은 디지털 소통을 선호하는 반면, 다른 고객들은 여전히 대면 회의를 중요하게 여긴다.
the other(s)	'정해진 것 중 남은 것 전부'라는 의미이다. 남은 것이 단수일 때는 the other, 복수일 때는 the others를 쓴다. Ms. Jenson prepared two copies of the contract: one for the vendor and **the other** for the legal department. Ms. Jenson은 계약서 두 부를 준비했는데, 한 부는 공급업체를 위한 것이고 나머지 한 부는 법무부를 위한 것이다.
most	'대부분(의)'라는 의미이다. Some company events take place with strict dress codes, but **most** take place with business casual attire. 몇몇 사내 행사는 엄격한 복장 규정으로 진행되지만, 대부분은 비즈니스 캐주얼 복장으로 진행된다.
neither/ either	neither는 '둘 다 아닌 것', either는 '둘 중 어느 하나'라는 의미이다. 형용사로 쓰일 때 뒤에 단수 명사가 온다. Both the accounting department and finance department restructured their operations, but **neither** was effective in the long term. 회계 부서와 재무 부서 둘 다 운영 구조를 개편했는데, 둘 다 장기적으로 효과적이지 않았다.
some/any	some은 '몇몇(의), 약간(의)'라는 의미로 쓰이며 주로 긍정문에 쓰인다. any는 '몇몇(의), 조금(의)'라는 의미로 쓰이며 주로 부정문, 의문문, 조건문에 쓰인다. any가 긍정문에 쓰이면 '어떤 ~라도'라는 의미를 갖는다. Most workers commute by bus, but **some** take their own cars. 대부분의 근로자들이 버스로 통근하지만, 몇몇은 그들의 차를 탄다. If you have **any** concerns, don't hesitate to speak up. 만약 우려 사항이 조금이라도 있다면, 말하는 것을 주저하지 마세요.
none	'아무도, 아무것도'라는 의미의 대명사로만 쓰인다. **None** of the initial prototypes were suitable for mass production. 초기 견본들 중 아무것도 대량 생산에 적합하지 않았다.

고득점 포인트 –thing, –body, –one으로 끝나는 대명사 뒤에는 'of the + 명사'가 올 수 없다.
(**Somebody**, Some) of the projects still need thorough risk assessment. 몇몇 프로젝트는 여전히 철저한 위험 평가가 필요하다.

토익실전문제

01 When choosing a monitor for graphic design, select ------ that has high color accuracy and resolution.

(A) one (B) ones
(C) other (D) none

02 Even though Mr. Evans and Mr. Ivanov are experienced, ------ of them performs well under pressure.

(A) any (B) nobody
(C) many (D) neither

03 Some occasions demand immediate action, while ------ allow time for consideration.

(A) one (B) most
(C) another (D) the other

04 If ------ of the power systems shut down, facility operators should follow the emergency protocol.

(A) anything (B) only
(C) any (D) each

HACKERS TEST

DAY 01

01 Mr. Claiborne believes it is ------- job as a marketing consultant to find out what consumers want.

(A) he (B) his
(C) him (D) himself

02 The board meeting had to be extended because ------- critical issues remained unresolved.

(A) any (B) some
(C) either (D) everybody

03 As a new event coordinator, Ms. Adrian is going to organize ------- for the upcoming charity auction.

(A) entertain (B) entertained
(C) entertains (D) entertainment

04 During the office renovation, ------- had to work from home temporarily.

(A) employ (B) employee
(C) employees (D) employs

05 Instead of throwing away the old books, Inkwell Books decided to donate ------- to a local library.

(A) it (B) their
(C) them (D) themselves

06 The arrival ------- for the replacement furniture order is next Monday.

(A) date (B) dated
(C) dates (D) dating

07 The trained sales ------- remained professional despite working extended hours during peak season.

(A) assist (B) assistance
(C) assisted (D) assistant

08 Many residents are not happy about the city's ------- to shut down the highway.

(A) decide (B) decisive
(C) decided (D) decision

09 If ------- need to make an appointment, please register through our hospital's online booking system.

(A) you (B) yours
(C) your (D) yourself

10 Data Pulse Solutions has transformed ------- into a leading artificial intelligence analytics firm.

(A) whose (B) wherever
(C) its own (D) itself

11 Dr. Cruz showed some ------- when invited to speak at the conference, but he ultimately consented.

(A) hesitate (B) hesitant
(C) hesitation (D) hesitated

12 Among the restaurants in town, the only ------- that can accommodate up to 300 guests is Grand Palace.

(A) one (B) none
(C) most (D) others

13 Mr. Hawthorne was awarded a bonus for his ------- to the company.

(A) contribute (B) contribution
(C) contributor (D) contributed

14 Special discounts are available for ------- who book their vacation packages three months in advance.

(A) them (B) those
(C) which (D) either

15 Gasmark International agreed to a five-year contract with a possible ------- of five more years.

(A) extend
(B) extensive
(C) extension
(D) extended

16 The retail giant is going to relocate its largest ------- center to meet growing customer demand.

(A) distribute
(B) distribution
(C) distributed
(D) distributable

17 One candidate pledged to reduce campaign spending, but ------- declined to limit expenses.

(A) whoever
(B) other
(C) others
(D) themselves

18 Annual vehicle ------- are mandatory in most states, so drivers must ensure their cars meet required standards.

(A) inspects
(B) inspectors
(C) inspected
(D) inspections

19 ------- of the recommended changes were implemented in the final version.

(A) One
(B) None
(C) No one
(D) Nothing

20 The senior architect was given ------- to oversee one of the Greene Foundation's projects.

(A) authority
(B) authorize
(C) authoritative
(D) authoritatively

21 The actual temperature during the heatwave differed from ------- in the weather prediction model.

(A) only
(B) those
(C) that
(D) including

22 Ms. Wynn ------- developed the curriculum for advanced courses based on her 24 years of teaching experience.

(A) she
(B) her
(C) hers
(D) herself

23 The misleading product ------- on the company's Web site resulted in numerous customer complaints.

(A) describe
(B) description
(C) descriptive
(D) describing

24 The environmental agency shared the ------- that air quality levels had significantly improved.

(A) inform
(B) informed
(C) information
(D) informations

25 The research team conducting ------- with genetic modification techniques showed promising results.

(A) experimented
(B) experimental
(C) experiments
(D) experimentally

26 Financial ------- working at Quantum Analytics are helping companies navigate their investment strategies.

(A) consults
(B) consultants
(C) consultations
(D) consultancies

27 The government used the money that it received from a ------- with Habro Chemical to restore polluted waterways.

(A) settle
(B) settled
(C) settlement
(D) settleable

28 Kenneth Publishing will give a bonus to ------- in the firm who suggests an effective way to reduce operating costs.

(A) those
(B) other
(C) none
(D) anyone

DAY 02 동사

1. 동사의 형태 동사는 동사원형, 3인칭 단수 현재형, 과거형, 현재분사형, 과거분사형의 형태를 가진다.

기출 공식 1 조동사 뒤에는 동사원형이 온다.

- 조동사(will/would, may/might, can/could, must, should) 뒤에는 동사원형이 온다.
  Local businesses can (**worked**, **work**) together to reduce operational costs.
  지역 사업체들은 운영 비용을 줄이기 위해 함께 일할 수 있다.

- 조동사처럼 쓰이는 표현들 뒤에도 동사원형이 온다.

| ought to ~해야 한다 | had better ~하는 게 좋다 | would like to ~하고 싶다 | used to ~했었다, ~하곤 했다 |
| have to ~해야 한다 | be able to ~할 수 있다 | be going to ~할 것이다 | |

Following each session, participants had better (**taking**, **take**) time to summarize key discussion points.
각 세션 후에, 참가자들은 주요 논의 사항을 요약하는 시간을 가지는 게 좋다.

기출 공식 2 제안·요청·의무의 주절을 뒤따르는 that절에는 동사원형이 온다.

제안·요청·의무를 나타내는 동사, 형용사, 명사

동사	suggest 제안하다	request 요청하다	ask 요청하다	require 요구하다	insist 주장하다
형용사	essential 필수적인	imperative 필수적인	necessary 필요한	important 중요한	
명사	advice 조언, 충고				

Mr. Murray suggested that his team (**held**, **hold**) a meeting to discuss the project timeline.
Mr. Murray는 프로젝트 스케줄을 논의하기 위해 그의 팀이 회의를 할 것을 제안했다.

It is essential that the software (**is**, **be**) tested thoroughly before its release.
그 소프트웨어가 출시 전에 철저히 테스트되는 것은 필수적이다.

기출 공식 3 명령문은 주어 없이 동사원형으로 시작된다.

Please (**puts**, **put**) your name and contact information on the top of the application form.
신청서 상단에 당신의 이름과 연락처를 기재해 주세요.

토익실전문제

01 Developers of the VisionTech program should ------- feedback from users to make necessary improvements.

(A) gather (B) gathers
(C) gathered (D) gathering

02 Ms. Paige's advice was that the marketing strategy ------- a social media component.

(A) including (B) included
(C) includes (D) include

03 It is imperative that data ------- accurately to ensure reliable results all the time.

(A) analyzes (B) is analyzing
(C) analysis (D) be analyzed

04 To design new product packaging, ------- a color scheme that matches the brand identity.

(A) chose (B) chosen
(C) choose (D) choice

2. 수일치
주어와 동사의 수가 일치하는 것으로, 현재형에서 단수 동사는 동사원형에 -s를 붙이고 복수 동사는 동사원형을 그대로 쓴다.

기출 공식 4 주어의 수에 맞는 알맞은 동사를 고르는 문제가 출제된다.

- **단수 취급하는 주어**: 단수 가산 명사, 불가산 명사, 고유 명사, 동명사구, 명사절
  The supplier (**provide**, **provides**) high-quality materials for many companies. 그 공급업체는 많은 회사에 고품질 자재를 제공한다.
  Keeping diaries (**help**, **helps**) students enhance their writing skills. 일기를 쓰는 것은 학생들이 그들의 쓰기 실력을 향상시키는 것을 돕는다.

- **복수 취급하는 주어**: 복수 가산 명사, 명사 and 명사
  Workers (**is**, **are**) told to adhere to safety protocols during their shifts. 근무자들은 근무 중에 안전 수칙을 고수할 것을 요청받는다.
  Quality and price (**determines**, **determine**) consumer purchasing decisions. 품질과 가격이 소비자의 구매 판단을 결정한다.

고득점 포인트 주어와 동사 사이에 있는 수식어 거품은 동사의 수 결정에 아무런 영향을 주지 않는다.
The town [with many historic tourist sites] (**offer**, **offers**) free tours. 많은 역사적인 관광지가 있는 그 동네는 무료 투어를 제공한다.

고득점 포인트 주격 관계절의 동사는 선행사와 수일치한다.
Those who (**is**, **are**) looking for new jobs should update their résumés. 새로운 일을 찾고 있는 사람들은 그들의 이력서를 갱신해야 한다.

기출 공식 5 주어로 쓰이는 수량 표현

- **단수 취급하는 수량 표현**

one/each (+ 단수 명사)	the number of + 복수 명사 ~의 수	anybody, anyone, anything	nobody, no one, nothing
every + 단수 명사	somebody, someone, something	everybody, everyone, everything	

  Every product on the shelf (**are**, **is**) marked with a price tag. 진열대에 있는 모든 제품은 가격표로 표시가 되어있다.

- **복수 취급하는 수량 표현**

many/several/few/both (+ of the) + 복수 명사	a couple/variety of + 복수 명사	both + 명사 + and + 명사
a number of + 복수 명사 많은 수의 ~	명사 + and + 명사	

  A number of companies (**competes**, **compete**) for the government subsidies. 많은 수의 회사들이 정부 보조금을 두고 경쟁한다.

- **of 뒤의 명사에 동사를 수일치하는 표현**

  all, most, any, some, half, a lot, lots, part, the rest, the bulk, percent, 분수 + of + 단수/불가산 명사 + 단수 동사 / 복수 명사 + 복수 동사

  Half of the residents (**disagrees**, **disagree**) with the city's new tax plans. 주민의 절반은 그 도시의 새로운 세금 계획에 동의하지 않는다.

토익실전문제

01 Reducing tuition fees ------- a critical step towards making education more accessible.
(A) is (B) are
(C) have been (D) being

02 Each car engine ------- different depending on its make and model, especially when accelerating or running at high speeds.
(A) sound (B) sounds
(C) sounding (D) soundly

03 Based on HR statistics, only 20 percent of employees ------- advantage of the company's wellness program.
(A) take (B) takes
(C) is taking (D) taken

04 The new app that ------- users to manage their finances is now available for download.
(A) allow (B) allowing
(C) allows (D) allowance

3. 동사의 종류
동사에는 목적어가 필요하지 않은 자동사와 목적어가 필요한 타동사가 있다.

기출 공식 6   전치사가 있으면 자동사, 없으면 타동사를 고른다.

의미	자동사 + 전치사	타동사
말하다	speak to ~에게 말하다 talk about ~에 대해 이야기하다 talk to ~에게 말하다 account for ~에 대해 설명하다	mention 언급하다 discuss 의논하다 instruct 지시하다 explain 설명하다 address 말을 하다
답하다	reply to ~에 답장하다 react to ~에 반응하다 respond to ~에 답변하다	answer 대답하다
동의/반대하다	consent to ~에 동의하다 object to ~에 반대하다 agree with(to, on) ~에 동의하다	approve 승인하다 oppose 반대하다
참가하다	participate in ~에 참가하다	attend 참석하다
따르다	adhere to ~을 고수하다	obey 따르다
도착하다	arrive at ~에 도착하다	reach 도착하다
기다리다	wait for ~을 기다리다	await 기다리다

The shopper (**mentioned**, **spoke**) to the customer service team about the refund process.
그 쇼핑객은 환불 절차에 대해 고객 서비스팀에게 말했다.

The HR team will (**talk**, **discuss**) the problem with the legal department.
인사팀은 법무팀과 그 문제에 대해 의논할 것이다.

기출 공식 7   목적어가 하나인 3형식 동사와 목적어가 두 개인 4형식 동사를 구분하는 문제가 출제된다.

3형식 동사 + 목적어(that절)	4형식 동사 + 목적어1(~에게) + 목적어2(that절)
say / mention / announce (to someone) that 말하다 suggest / propose / recommend (to someone) that 제안하다 explain / describe (to someone) that 설명하다	tell someone that 말하다 inform / notify someone that 알리다 assure / convince someone that 확신시키다

The financial advisor (**told**, **recommended**) that the company diversify its investment portfolio to minimize risks.
재무 고문은 위험을 최소화하기 위해 회사가 투자 포트폴리오를 다각화할 것을 제안했다.

The landlord (**announced**, **informed**) the tenants that there would be maintenance work.
집주인은 세입자에게 유지보수 작업이 있을 것이라고 알렸다.

토익실전문제

01 The department head was asked to ------- for the unexpected increase in expenses.
  (A) explain   (B) account
  (C) address   (D) await

02 Mr. Taylor's boss ------- his request for an extended deadline on the report.
  (A) approved   (B) agreed
  (C) objected   (D) reacted

03 The airline ------- the passengers that the flight had been delayed due to the storm.
  (A) said   (B) described
  (C) notified   (D) mentioned

04 Our customer service team will ------- to your inquiries within 24 hours.
  (A) answer   (B) respond
  (C) obey   (D) instruct

4. 능동태와 수동태
능동태는 주어가 행위의 주체가 되며, 수동태는 주어가 행위의 대상이 된다.

기출 공식 8 | 목적어가 있으면 능동태, 목적어가 없으면 수동태를 쓴다.

The organization (**is provided**, **provides**) grants to outstanding researchers. 그 단체는 뛰어난 연구원들에게 보조금을 제공한다.
The equipment that (**installed**, **was installed**) last week is now fully operational. 지난주에 설치된 장비는 이제 완전히 사용할 수 있다.

고득점 포인트 4형식 동사의 수동태 뒤에는 목적어 중 한 개가 남으며, 5형식 동사의 수동태 뒤에는 목적격 보어가 남으므로, 아래 동사들 뒤에 명사가 있는 것을 보고 바로 능동태를 고르지 않도록 주의한다.

4형식 동사	give, send, grant, show, offer, guarantee 등
5형식 동사	consider, call, elect, name, make 등

Mr. Shin **was given** a raise after the successful project. Mr. Shin에게 성공적인 프로젝트 이후에 임금 인상이 주어졌다.
Meditation **is considered** an effective measure to reduce stress. 명상은 스트레스를 줄이는 효과적인 방법으로 여겨진다.

기출 공식 9 | 자주 출제되는 수동태 관용 표현

- **수동태 동사 + 전치사**

be pleased/delighted with ~을 기뻐하다	be credited with ~으로 명성을 얻다	be interested in ~에 관심이 있다
be associated with ~과 관련되다	be disappointed at ~에 실망하다	be devoted to ~에 헌신하다
be satisfied with ~에 만족하다	be surprised/alarmed at ~에 놀라다	be dedicated to ~에 헌신하다
be finished with ~이 끝나다	be shocked at ~에 충격을 받다	be tired of ~에 싫증나다
be equipped with ~을 갖추고 있다	be involved in ~에 관여하다	be based on ~에 근거하다
be covered with ~으로 덮이다	be engaged in ~에 관여하다/참여하다	be concerned about/over ~을 걱정하다

The majority of students **are engaged in** various extracurricular activities.
학생들 중 대다수는 다양한 방과 후 활동에 참여한다.

- **수동태 동사 + to 부정사**

be invited/requested to ~할 것을 요청받다	be advised to ~할 것을 권고받다	be prepared to ~할 준비가 되다
be required/urged to ~하도록 요구받다	be intended to ~을 위한 목적이다	be supposed to ~하기로 되어있다
be reminded to ~하라는 말을 듣다	be expected to ~할 것으로 기대되다	be scheduled to ~할 예정이다
be encouraged to ~하라고 권고받다	be allowed/permitted to ~하도록 허가받다	be projected to ~할 것이라 예상되다

Children aged five and under **are allowed to enter** the museum free of charge.
5세 이하의 아이들은 박물관에 무료로 들어가도록 허가받는다.

토익실전문제

01 The university ------ experts from various fields in order to strengthen its academic programs.

(A) recruit (B) recruited
(C) was recruited (D) recruiting

02 Employees' performance should be regularly ------ to assess their productivity.

(A) monitor (B) monitoring
(C) monitored (D) to monitor

03 The entire office ------ to attend the celebration of the company's 50th anniversary.

(A) is invited (B) invited
(C) invitation (D) inviting

04 Ms. Bianchi was ------ at the poor quality of the product she recently bought online.

(A) disappoint (B) disappointing
(C) disappointed (D) disappointingly

5. 시제 동사가 각각 다른 형태로 동작이나 상태가 일어난 시간을 표현하는 것이다.

기출 공식 10 현재/과거/미래 중 알맞은 시제를 고르는 문제가 출제된다.

- 현재 시제(동사원형 (+ -s))는 현재의 상태나 반복되는 동작, 일반적인 사실을 나타내며, 아래 표현과 함께 자주 쓰인다.

| usually 보통 | often 종종 | regularly 정기적으로 | every 매 ~, ~마다 | these days 요즘 |

Local volunteers **organize** community clean-ups every month. 지역 자원봉사자들은 매달 지역사회 청소를 조직한다.

- 과거 시제(동사원형 + -ed)는 이미 끝난 과거의 동작이나 상태를 나타내며, 아래 표현과 함께 자주 쓰인다.

| yesterday 어제 | last 지난 ~ | ago ~ 전에 | in + 과거 연도 ~년에 |

Last year, the city **witnessed** record-breaking temperatures during the summer. 작년에, 그 도시는 여름 동안 기록적인 온도를 목격했다.

- 미래 시제(will + 동사원형)는 미래에 일어날 일을 나타내며, 아래 표현과 함께 자주 쓰인다.

| tomorrow 내일 | next 다음 ~ | by/until + 미래 시간 표현 ~까지 |

The shipment of new furniture **will arrive** tomorrow morning. 새로운 가구 배송은 내일 아침에 도착할 것이다.

고득점 포인트 시간이나 조건을 나타내는 종속절에서는 미래 시제 대신 현재 시제를 쓴다.
The project will proceed once management **approves** the budget. 운영진이 일단 예산을 승인하면 그 프로젝트는 진행될 것이다.

기출 공식 11 진행 시제의 쓰임과 형태를 묻는 문제가 출제된다.

- 현재진행 시제(am/is/are + -ing)는 현재 시점에 진행되고 있는 일을 나타낸다.
At present, the research team **is working** to develop a new battery. 현재, 연구팀은 새로운 배터리를 개발하기 위해 노력하고 있다.

고득점 포인트 현재진행 시제는 예정된 일이나 곧 일어나려고 하는 일을 표현하여 미래를 나타낼 수 있다.
Ms. Leroy **is traveling** to London for a business trip next Monday. Ms. Leroy는 다음 주 월요일에 출장을 위해 런던으로 이동할 예정이다.

- 과거진행 시제(was/were + -ing)는 특정한 과거 시점에 진행되고 있던 일을 나타낸다.
Mr. Singh **was writing** an e-mail when the power suddenly went out. 갑자기 정전이 되었을 때 Mr. Singh은 이메일을 작성하고 있었다.

- 미래진행 시제(will be + -ing)는 특정한 미래 시점에 진행되고 있을 일을 나타낸다.
At the summit, world leaders **will be discussing** trade regulations. 정상회담에서, 세계 지도자들은 무역 규제에 대해 논의하고 있을 것이다.

토익실전문제

☆최빈출

01 Urban Thread ------- a pop-up store next week to showcase its upcoming jacket and coat collection.
(A) open   (B) to open
(C) opened   (D) will open

02 If our new 700Q headset ------- successfully, our market share will significantly increase.
(A) will launch   (B) launching
(C) to launch   (D) launches

03 The speaker ------- key concepts when the microphone stopped working.
(A) explains   (B) is explaining
(C) was explaining (D) were explained

04 An advanced security system is ------- in the building to enhance safety.
(A) install   (B) installation
(C) installment   (D) being installed

기출 공식 12 완료 시제의 쓰임과 형태를 묻는 문제가 출제된다.

• 현재완료 시제(has/have + p.p.)는 과거에 시작해서 현재까지 영향을 미치는 일을 나타내며, 아래 표현과 함께 자주 쓰인다.

since + 과거 시간 표현 ~ 이후로
since + 주어 + 과거 시제 ~한 이후로
for + 기간 ~ 동안
recently 최근에
up to now 지금까지
in/over/for/during the last/past + 기간 지난 ~ 동안

The city **has hosted** the marathon every year since 2008. 그 도시는 2008년 이후로 매년 마라톤을 개최해 왔다.

고득점 포인트 현재완료진행 시제는 현재까지도 그 동작이 진행되고 있다는 의미가 더해진다.
The sales team **has been receiving** calls about the product all day. 영업팀은 그 제품에 대한 전화를 하루 종일 받고 있다.

• 과거완료 시제(had + p.p.)는 과거의 특정 시점 이전에 발생한 일을 나타내며, 아래 표현과 함께 자주 쓰인다.

by the time + 주어 + 과거 시제 ~했을 즈음에
before + 주어 + 과거 시제 ~하기 전에
when + 주어 + 과거 시제 ~했을 때

The gift shop **had closed** by the time Carlos arrived at the mall. Carlos가 쇼핑몰에 도착했을 즈음에 기념품 가게는 닫았다.

• 미래완료 시제(will have + p.p.)는 미래 특정 시점 이전에 발생해서 미래의 그 시점에 완료될 일을 나타내며, 아래 표현과 함께 자주 쓰인다.

by the time + 주어 + 현재 시제 ~할 즈음에
by + 미래 시간 표현 ~ 즈음에
by the end of + 미래 시간 표현 ~ 말까지

The companies **will have signed** the contract by the end of this week. 그 회사들은 이번 주말까지 계약서에 서명해 있을 것이다.

토익실전문제

토익 문제 이렇게 나온다!

01 The Local Lift Foundation ------- financial support to local businesses over the last 30 years.

(A) provision (B) has provided
(C) will provide (D) to have provided

02 The HR department ------- hundreds of applicants before they selected the final candidates.

(A) screen (B) screening
(C) had screened (D) will screen

03 The electronic devices ------- to the manufacturer for replacement since the engineering team identified a critical flaw.

(A) to return (B) will have been returned
(C) has returned (D) have been returned

04 David Chen, a winner of multiple international design awards, ------- innovative architecture for 20 years.

(A) was designed (B) are designing
(C) has been designing (D) will be designed

정답·해석·해설 p.141

HACKERS TEST
DAY 02

01 Please ------- your expense reports with all necessary receipts attached.

(A) submit (B) submitted
(C) submits (D) submission

02 Many of the volunteers ------- raise funds for local charities and non-profit organizations.

(A) is helped (B) helpful
(C) helps (D) help

03 Apex Gas ------- to delay its rate increases at the request of the Fairfax City Council.

(A) reached (B) agreed
(C) reminded (D) approved

04 The measure ------- sugar consumption by placing a higher tax on sweetened beverages.

(A) will reduce (B) will be reduced
(C) reducing (D) is being reduced

05 Ms. Ko ------- a comprehensive training program for new employees last year.

(A) develops (B) development
(C) is developing (D) developed

06 The menus that Chef Sandy will create ------- going to include vegetarian options.

(A) is (B) are
(C) to be (D) has been

07 The business owner was advised to ------- a lawyer regarding the compliance issues.

(A) consultant (B) consult
(C) consultation (D) consulted

08 All customer service calls are ------- to ensure quality control and maintain service standards.

(A) record (B) recorder
(C) recorded (D) recording

09 Samir Patel is a passionate street artist who ------- vibrant murals around the country.

(A) paints (B) painters
(C) paint (D) painting

10 When you ------- at the conference center, please check in at the front desk, where our staff will help you locate your meeting room.

(A) arrival (B) arrive
(C) will arrive (D) to arrive

11 The release of the new action film will ------- due to some editing adjustments.

(A) delay (B) delaying
(C) be delaying (D) be delayed

12 The partnership between the two major companies ------- a month ago.

(A) renewal (B) are renewing
(C) was renewed (D) is renewed

13 New staff members ought to ------- the orientation program before starting their regular duties.

(A) completion (B) completing
(C) complete (D) completed

14 According to a recent report, Nine East Mall ------- to a new location by next winter.

(A) has moved (B) moving
(C) moved (D) will move

15 A couple of events taking place in the historic town square ------- local traditions with folk dance performances.

(A) celebration
(B) celebrate
(C) celebrates
(D) is celebrated

16 ------- your account by clicking the verification link sent to your e-mail.

(A) Activate
(B) Activation
(C) Activated
(D) Actively

고난도
17 The organizing committee ------- refreshments to all attendees at the conclusion of the upcoming seminar.

(A) served
(B) will be serving
(C) will be served
(D) was being served

18 The national science museum ------- interactive workshops focusing on robotics since last December.

(A) hosting
(B) to be hosting
(C) will host
(D) has been hosting

고난도
19 Users of Era Bank ------- to change their passwords after their data was accessed by hackers.

(A) instruct
(B) will instruct
(C) was instructed
(D) are being instructed

고난도
20 The university requests that visitors ------- their identification cards to enter certain campus buildings.

(A) presented
(B) presenting
(C) present
(D) presentation

21 The reporter ------- interviews with climate change researchers at next week's environmental summit.

(A) to conduct
(B) will be conducting
(C) conducted
(D) was conducting

고난도
22 Biomira Cosmetics ------- that they would launch a new vegan skincare line for sensitive skin types.

(A) announced
(B) told
(C) continued
(D) convinced

23 Mr. Martinez ------- Integra Systems at the technology exposition tomorrow.

(A) represent
(B) is representing
(C) representation
(D) had represented

고난도
24 The newly unveiled ------- for the office renovation are both modern and functional, reflecting current workplace trends.

(A) designer
(B) design
(C) designed
(D) designs

고난도
25 First-time customers of Vitaro Organic grocery store ------- discounts on their first purchase of $30 or more.

(A) offer
(B) offering
(C) are offered
(D) are offering

26 The president of Sparks Entertainment ------- major organizational changes last week.

(A) reveals
(B) revealing
(C) revealed
(D) has revealed

27 Contractors working on high-rise buildings are ------- to undergo safety training and wear protective gear.

(A) required
(B) requiring
(C) requires
(D) requirement

고난도
28 The author ------- her manuscript more than three times before she started sending it to editors.

(A) was revised
(B) had revised
(C) is revising
(D) has to revise

DAY 03 to 부정사, 동명사, 분사

출제 경향 매회 1~2문제
최근 3개년 오답률 20.5%

1. to 부정사
'to + 동사원형'의 형태로, 명사, 형용사, 부사 역할을 한다. 수동형은 'to be + p.p.', 완료형은 'to have + p.p.'이다.

기출 공식 1   to 부정사는 명사, 형용사, 부사 자리에 온다.   출제율 ↑

- **명사: 주어, 목적어, 보어로 쓰인다.**
  The team hopes **to increase** productivity with regular meetings. 그 팀은 정기적인 회의로 생산성을 올리길 희망한다.

  고득점 포인트   to 부정사는 진주어와 진목적어로도 쓰인다.
  It is important **to communicate** clearly with your supervisor. 당신의 상사와 명확하게 소통하는 것은 중요합니다.
  The latest update will make it possible **to automate** routine tasks. 최신 업데이트는 일상적인 작업을 자동화하는 것을 가능하게 할 것이다.

- **형용사: 명사를 뒤에서 꾸민다.**
  Titan Manufacturing makes an effort **to reduce** its environmental impact. Titan 제조사는 환경 영향을 줄이려는 노력을 한다.

- **부사: 완전한 절 앞뒤에서 목적, 이유를 나타낸다. 목적을 나타낼 때 to 대신 in order to를 쓸 수 있다.**
  The security guard checks IDs **(in order) to verify** employee access rights.
  경비는 직원 접근 권한을 확인하기 위해 신분증을 확인한다.
  The sales team was surprised **to achieve** their annual target in just eight months.
  영업팀은 8개월 만에 그들의 연간 목표를 달성해서 놀랐다.

기출 공식 2   to 부정사를 목적어로 가지는 동사

want to ~하길 원하다	would like to ~하길 원하다	agree to ~하기로 동의하다	manage to ~을 해내다
wish to ~하길 소망하다	aim to ~할 것을 목표로 하다	refuse to ~할 것을 거절하다	try to ~하려고 노력하다
hope to ~하길 희망하다	decide to ~하기로 결정하다	decline to ~할 것을 거절하다	attempt to ~하는 것을 시도하다
need to ~해야 하다	offer to ~할 것을 제안하다	fail to ~하기를 실패하다	pretend to ~인 척하다
desire to ~하길 갈망하다	plan to ~할 것을 계획하다	tend to ~하는 경향이 있다	hesitate to ~하기를 주저하다
expect to ~하길 기대하다	promise to ~하기로 약속하다	afford to ~할 여유가 있다	intend to ~을 의도하다

Mary Garcia, the chief technology officer, <u>plans</u> **to retire** next month. 최고 기술 책임자인 Mary Garcia는 다음 달에 은퇴할 것을 계획한다.

토익실전문제   토익 문제 이렇게 나온다!

01 The goal of the educational reform initiative is ------- equal learning opportunities for students.
   (A) provides   (B) provided
   (C) to provide   (D) to providing

02 Nexus Enterprises introduced flexible working hours ------- promote work-life balance among its employees.
   (A) due to   (B) in order to
   (C) owing to   (D) instead of

★최빈출
03 Small businesses are expanding their digital marketing strategies ------- with larger corporations.
   (A) to compete   (B) competitive
   (C) competes   (D) competition

04 Dr. Laurent would like ------- an international conference on global health innovations.
   (A) organize   (B) organizing
   (C) organizes   (D) to organize

정답·해석·해설 p.144

기출 공식 3 to 부정사를 목적격 보어로 가지는 동사

want 목 to ~하길 원하다	expect 목 to ~하는 것을 기대하다	get 목 to ~하게 하다	allow 목 to ~하도록 허가하다
need 목 to ~하는 것이 필요하다	persuade 목 to ~하도록 설득하다	cause 목 to ~하게 하다	permit 목 to ~하도록 허가하다
ask 목 to ~하라고 요청하다	convince 목 to ~하도록 설득하다	advise 목 to ~하도록 권고하다	forbid 목 to ~을 금지하다
invite 목 to ~하라고 요청하다	compel 목 to ~하라고 강요하다	encourage 목 to ~하도록 권고하다	warn 목 to ~하라고 경고하다
tell 목 to ~하라고 말하다	force 목 to ~하라고 강요하다	remind 목 to ~하라고 상기시키다	enable 목 to ~할 수 있게 하다

The public library system allows patrons **to reserve** up to three books online.
공공 도서관 시스템은 고객이 온라인으로 책을 세 권까지 예약하도록 허가한다.

기출 공식 4 to 부정사와 함께 자주 출제되는 명사

ability to ~하는 능력	need to ~할 필요	chance to ~할 기회	tendency to ~하려는 경향
attempt to ~하려는 시도	claim to ~하다는 주장	opportunity to ~할 기회	time to ~할 시간
authority to ~할 권한	decision to ~하겠다는 결정	plan to ~하려는 계획	way to ~할 방법
capacity to ~할 능력	effort to ~하려는 노력	right to ~할 권리	willingness to ~할 의향

The accounting department needs time **to process** end-of-month transactions.
회계 부서는 월말 거래들을 처리할 시간이 필요하다.

기출 공식 5 사역동사⁺의 목적격 보어 자리에는 to 부정사가 아닌 원형 부정사가 온다.   오답률 ↑

Let Horizon Travels (~~to take~~, **take**) care of your backpacking trip through Southeast Asia.
Horizon 여행사가 당신의 동남아시아 배낭여행을 책임지도록 하세요.

고득점 포인트 help의 목적격 보어 자리에는 원형 부정사와 to 부정사 둘 다 올 수 있다.
It is well-known that positive feedback helps employees (**to**) **build** confidence.
긍정적인 피드백이 직원들이 자신감을 쌓는 것을 돕는다는 것은 잘 알려져 있다.

고득점 포인트 '목적어가 목적격 보어 되다'라는 수동의 의미로 해석되면 목적격 보어 자리에 p.p.가 온다.
Mr. Park had his blood pressure (~~measure~~, **measured**) during his annual physical examination.
Mr. Park는 연례 건강검진 동안 그의 혈압이 측정되게 했다.

⁺사역동사: 다른 사람에게 어떤 행동을 하게 하는 동사로, make, have, let이 있다.

토익실전문제

☆최빈출

01 The complimentary shuttle service enables tourists ------- the beautiful beaches along the coastline.

(A) explore   (B) exploration
(C) are exploring   (D) to explore

02 World Bridge Airways has announced the plan ------- new international routes.

(A) adds   (B) to add
(C) will add   (D) additionally

03 The experienced coach helped the young athletes ------- their potential.

(A) develops   (B) to develop
(C) developed   (D) development

04 The museum had all of the ancient artifacts ------- in chronological order, which the visitors found interesting.

(A) displays   (B) to display
(C) displayed   (D) to be displayed

정답·해석·해설 p.144

2. 동명사
'동사원형 + -ing'의 형태로, 명사 역할을 한다. 수동형은 'being + p.p.', 완료형은 'having + p.p.'이다.

기출 공식 6 · 동명사는 주어, 목적어, 보어 자리에 온다.

주어	**Listening** actively is crucial for effective communication. 적극적으로 듣는 것은 효과적인 의사소통에 중요하다.
동사의 목적어	Tech experts recommend **updating** software regularly. 기술 전문가들은 소프트웨어를 정기적으로 업데이트하는 것을 추천한다.
전치사의 목적어	Pat's Café remains popular by **creating** new beverages every month. Pat's 카페는 매달 새 음료를 만들어서 인기를 유지한다.
보어	In an emergency, the first step is **finding** the exits. 비상 상황에서, 첫 번째 단계는 출구를 찾는 것이다.

기출 공식 7 · 동명사를 목적어로 가지는 동사

enjoy -ing ~하는 것을 즐기다	consider -ing ~할 것을 고려하다	give up -ing ~하는 것을 포기하다	deny -ing ~한 것을 부인하다
suggest -ing ~할 것을 제안하다	finish -ing ~하는 것을 끝내다	postpone -ing ~할 것을 연기하다	mind -ing ~하는 것을 꺼리다
recommend -ing ~하는 것을 추천하다	quit -ing ~하는 것을 그만두다	dislike -ing ~하는 것을 싫어하다	avoid -ing ~하는 것을 피하다

Successful leaders avoid **making** impulsive decisions through comprehensive risk assessment.
성공적인 지도자는 종합적인 위험 평가를 통해 충동적인 결정을 내리는 것을 피한다.

기출 공식 8 · 동명사와 to 부정사를 모두 목적어로 가지는 동사

| 의미 변화가 없는 동사 | like 좋아하다
love 사랑하다
prefer 선호하다 | hate 싫어하다
begin 시작하다
start 시작하다 | continue 계속하다
propose 제안하다 |
| 의미 변화가 있는 동사 | remember -ing ~한 것을 기억하다
remember to ~할 것을 기억하다 | forget -ing ~한 것을 잊다
forget to ~할 것을 잊다 | regret -ing ~한 것을 후회하다
regret to ~하게 되어 유감스럽다 |

The scientist said she prefers **conducting[to conduct]** field research in remote locations.
그 과학자는 외딴 지역에서 현장 연구를 수행하는 것을 선호한다고 말했다.

The project manager forgot **sending / to send** the critical update to all team members.
그 프로젝트 관리자는 중요한 최신 정보를 모든 팀원들에게 보낸 것을 / 보내야 하는 것을 잊었다.

토익실전문제

01 ------ advanced security systems helps defend corporate networks from potential cyber threats.
(A) Installing (B) Being installed
(C) Installs (D) Install

★최빈출
02 Environmental conservation teams are implementing innovative ways of ------ endangered species using tracking technologies.
(A) protect (B) protects
(C) protecting (D) protective

03 Mr. Lee is considering ------ the current project management approach to improve team productivity and collaboration.
(A) restructure (B) to restructure
(C) restructured (D) restructuring

04 BioGenix started ------ financial problems when key research funding was withdrawn by major pharmaceutical investors.
(A) has (B) had
(C) have (D) having

정답·해석·해설 p.145

기출 공식 9 — 동명사는 명사와 다르게 목적어를 가질 수 있다.

Ms. Patel plans on (**publication**, **publishing**) a new book on sustainable urban development.
Ms. Patel은 지속 가능한 도시 개발에 대한 새로운 책을 출판하려고 계획한다.

(**Management**, **Managing**) cross-cultural teams requires a deep understanding of implicit cultural norms.
다문화 팀을 관리하는 것은 암묵적인 문화적 규범에 대한 깊은 이해를 요구한다.

기출 공식 10 — 자주 출제되는 동명사 관용 표현

- **동명사구 관용 표현**

  go -ing ~하러 가다
  on -ing ~하자마자
  It's no use -ing ~해도 소용없다
  spend + 시간/돈 + -ing 시간/돈을 ~하는 데 쓰다
  have difficulty(trouble, a problem) (in) -ing ~하는 데 어려움을 겪다

  be busy (in) -ing ~하느라 바쁘다
  be worth -ing ~할 가치가 있다
  keep (on) -ing 계속 ~하다
  feel like -ing ~하고 싶다
  cannot help -ing ~하지 않을 수 없다

  The workers **are busy** (to assemble, **assembling**) wireless communication devices.
  작업자들은 무선 통신 기기를 조립하느라 바쁘다.

- **전치사 to + 동명사**

  contribute to -ing ~에 공헌하다
  look forward to -ing ~하기를 고대하다
  object to -ing ~에 반대하다, ~에 이의를 제기하다
  lead to -ing ~의 원인이 되다

  be committed to -ing ~에 전념하다
  be dedicated to -ing ~에 헌신적이다
  be devoted to -ing ~에 헌신하다
  be used to -ing ~에 익숙하다

  The research team **is looking forward to** (present, **presenting**) their groundbreaking findings.
  그 연구팀은 그들의 혁신적인 연구 결과를 발표하기를 고대하고 있다.

토익실전문제

01 The doctor mentioned that ------- moderate amounts of dark chocolate might help reduce the risk of cardiovascular diseases.

(A) consumes
(B) consumed
(C) consuming
(D) consumption

02 Educational innovators suggest ------- an adaptive learning system that personalizes education to each student's needs.

(A) create
(B) creating
(C) creation
(D) creative

03 The local entrepreneurship foundation is committed ------- start-up capital to emerging technology ventures.

(A) will grant
(B) grants
(C) to granting
(D) granted

04 Mr. Alvarez is having difficulty in ------- with the overseas team due to time zone differences.

(A) coordinate
(B) to coordinate
(C) coordinates
(D) coordinating

3. 분사
현재분사(-ing)와 과거분사(p.p.)가 있으며, 형용사 역할을 한다.

기출 공식 11   분사는 명사를 꾸미는 자리나 보어 자리에 온다.

- **명사를 앞이나 뒤에서 꾸민다.**

   Each team should take their lunch break at the **designated** time.
   각각의 팀은 지정된 시간에 점심시간을 가져야 한다.

   Everyone **attending** the conference was asked to wear name badges.
   회의에 참석하는 모든 사람은 이름표를 착용하라고 요청받았다.

- **주격 보어나 목적격 보어로 쓰인다.**

   Many diners said that the new restaurant downtown was **charming**.
   많은 손님들은 도심 지역의 새로운 식당이 매력적이라고 말했다.

   The antivirus software keeps users' personal information **protected**.
   바이러스 방지 소프트웨어는 사용자의 개인 정보가 보호된 상태로 유지한다.

기출 공식 12   부사절 접속사 없이 시간, 이유, 조건, 연속 동작을 나타낼 때 분사구문⁺을 쓴다.   오답률 ↑

시간   **Entering** the ancient temple, visitors should remove their shoes.
고대 사원에 들어갈 때, 방문객들은 그들의 신발을 벗어야 한다.
= When visitors enter the ancient temple, they should remove their shoes.

이유   **Being** analytical, Ms. Wallace quickly identified the flaw in the report.
분석적이기 때문에, Ms. Wallace는 보고서의 오류를 빠르게 찾았다.
= Because Ms. Wallace was analytical, she quickly identified the flaw in the report.

조건   **Guided** by the manual, users can repair the equipment themselves.
설명서에 의해 안내된다면, 사용자들은 그 장비를 직접 수리할 수 있다.
= If users are guided by the manual, they can repair the equipment themselves.

연속 동작   Mr. Davis visited clients in Asia, **securing** three major contracts.
Mr. Davis는 아시아의 고객을 방문했고, 세 개의 주요 계약을 체결했다.
= Mr. Davis visited clients in Asia, and he secured three major contracts.

고득점 포인트   분사구문의 뜻을 분명하게 해주기 위해 부사절 접속사가 분사구문 앞에 올 수도 있다.
When **working** with tight deadlines, prioritize tasks based on their importance.
마감일이 촉박한 상태에서 일할 때, 중요도에 따라 작업의 우선순위를 정하세요.

⁺분사구문: 부사절에서 접속사와 주어를 생략하고 동사를 현재분사형으로 바꾼 것이다.

토익실전문제

01 The company policy mandates that only ------- employees handle hazardous materials.

(A) train   (B) trains
(C) to train   (D) trained

02 Young professionals found the international conference quite -------, gaining new insights on emerging industry trends.

(A) engage   (B) engaging
(C) engages   (D) engagement

03 ------- extensive experience in marketing, Ms. Petrov was able to lead successful product launch campaigns.

(A) Has   (B) Had
(C) Having   (D) Has had

04 Since ------- the new strategy, Innova Logistics has significantly improved its operational efficiency.

(A) implements   (B) implemental
(C) implementing   (D) implementation

기출 공식 13 능동을 나타내면 현재분사, 수동을 나타내면 과거분사를 쓴다.

(~~Completed~~, **Completing**) his groundbreaking research, Mr. Kaya published a paper in a prestigious scientific journal.
혁신적인 연구를 마무리한 후에, Mr. Kaya는 권위 있는 과학 저널에 논문을 게재했다.

Please update your personal information on the HR document (attaching, **attached**) to the e-mail.
이메일에 첨부된 인사 문서에 당신의 개인 정보를 업데이트해 주시기 바랍니다.

고득점 포인트 분사가 감정을 나타내는 경우, 꾸밈을 받는 명사가 감정의 원인이면 현재분사, 감정을 느끼는 주체이면 과거분사를 쓴다.

The latest market research showed (disappointed, **disappointing**) results for the new product.
최신 시장조사는 신제품에 대한 실망스러운 결과를 보여줬다.

The investment analyst was (surprising, **surprised**) by the unexpected market trend.
투자 분석가는 예상치 못한 시장 동향에 놀랐다.

기출 공식 14 자주 출제되는 '분사 + 명사' 표현

현재분사 + 명사	과거분사 + 명사
opening remarks 개회사	preferred means 선호되는 수단
existing equipment 기존 설비	proposed plan 제안된 계획
missing luggage 분실된 수하물	qualified applicant 적격인 지원자
lasting impression 오래 지속되는 인상	experienced technician 숙련된 기술자
leading expert 선도적인 전문가	accomplished writer 뛰어난 작가
presiding officer 의장, 감독관	detailed information 상세한 정보
promising recruit 유망한 신입 사원	written consent 서면 동의
challenging project 힘든 프로젝트	reserved space 지정된 구역
remaining work 남아 있는 일	attached document 첨부된 서류
qualifying test 자격시험	damaged item 손상된 물건

(Opened, **Opening**) remarks will outline the critical challenges in renewable energy.
개회사는 재생 에너지의 주요 어려움을 개략적으로 설명할 것이다.

Ms. Taylor complained about the (damaging, **damaged**) item upon delivery.
Ms. Taylor는 배송 직후 손상된 물건에 대해 항의했다.

토익실전문제

01 The military facility was strategically positioned in a ------- area of the mountain range.

(A) seclude (B) secluded
(C) secluding (D) seclusion

02 ------- by the World Health Organization, the vaccine will be distributed to the public at a low cost.

(A) Approved (B) Approval
(C) Approving (D) Approves

03 Pearl Marina Resort offers a ------- experience to families looking for a peaceful beachfront getaway.

(A) please (B) pleasure
(C) pleased (D) pleasing

04 With her confident presentation, the candidate left a ------- impression during the final interview.

(A) lasted (B) lasting
(C) lastly (D) later

HACKERS TEST

DAY 03

01. Green Bite aims ------- its plant-based product range with nutritious meat alternatives.
    (A) broaden
    (B) to broaden
    (C) broadens
    (D) broadened

02. The luxury hotel offers exclusive access to premium spa facilities and welcome snacks to ------- guests.
    (A) registered
    (B) registers
    (C) registration
    (D) register

03. The foundation helps underprivileged students by ------- scholarships and mentorship opportunities.
    (A) provide
    (B) provided
    (C) providing
    (D) to provide

04. Despite heavy marketing, ------- sales of the winter collection forced Nordic Edge to cut prices.
    (A) disappoint
    (B) disappointingly
    (C) disappointed
    (D) disappointing

05. Ms. Angler left her consulting firm ------- take a position at a leading investment bank.
    (A) with
    (B) as long as
    (C) for instance
    (D) in order to

06. ------- August 1, the national park will implement new conservation measures for wildlife habitats.
    (A) Begin
    (B) Begins
    (C) Beginning
    (D) Beginner

07. Please photograph the ------- appliance before contacting our customer service team for immediate assistance.
    (A) damages
    (B) damaged
    (C) damaging
    (D) damage

08. The park ranger asks the hikers ------- the local environment by staying on marked trails.
    (A) to respect
    (B) will respect
    (C) respects
    (D) have respected

09. A ------- expert in marine biology, Mr. Shimizu has spent 20 years studying coral reef ecosystems.
    (A) led
    (B) leading
    (C) leads
    (D) leader

10. The building manager was ------- that energy costs dropped considerably after installing LED lights.
    (A) surprise
    (B) surprisingly
    (C) surprises
    (D) surprised

11. Urban Bridge Canvas is dedicated to ------- young artists by connecting them with potential buyers and galleries.
    (A) supports
    (B) supporting
    (C) supportive
    (D) supported

12. Sage & Spice is going to introduce online ordering services ------- revenues through deliveries.
    (A) increase
    (B) increases
    (C) to increase
    (D) increasingly

13. Mr. Marchetti turned in the ------- loan documents to the bank yesterday morning.
    (A) completes
    (B) completed
    (C) completing
    (D) completion

14. The diagnostic tool helps mechanics ------- engine problems without the need for disassembly.
    (A) identified
    (B) identifying
    (C) identify
    (D) identification

15 Investors may want ------- diversifying their portfolios, especially in uncertain market conditions.

(A) considering
(B) to be considered
(C) considerable
(D) to consider

16 Residents are urged to stay ------- of evacuation procedures during hurricane season.

(A) informed
(B) informing
(C) information
(D) informatively

17 The app guides users in deciding which insurance plan ------- by giving personalized recommendations.

(A) buy
(B) buying
(C) to buy
(D) buyer

18 A number of commuters have complained about frequent train delays ------- their work schedules.

(A) affect
(B) affecting
(C) affection
(D) affected

19 Professor Klein permitted her graduate students ------- laboratory equipment for their research projects.

(A) borrow
(B) borrowed
(C) to borrow
(D) would borrow

20 Those ------- to submit their artwork for the exhibition should follow the specified size requirements.

(A) wishes
(B) wishing
(C) wished
(D) wish

21 The museum curator had some ancient relics carefully ------- by experts before sending them on an international tour.

(A) restoration
(B) to restore
(C) restore
(D) restored

22 A folder ------- sensitive financial records disappeared from the accounting department last week.

(A) contain
(B) containable
(C) contained
(D) containing

23 Wellness World Gym regrets ------- valued members that membership fees will be adjusted from next quarter.

(A) notify
(B) notifiable
(C) to notify
(D) notification

24 Verdure Rentals is a new and innovative business ------- in electric bike rentals and eco-friendly tours.

(A) specialize
(B) specializing
(C) specializes
(D) specialization

25 Tickets ------- on mobile devices are automatically added to your digital wallet for seamless check-in at the gate.

(A) purchase
(B) purchaser
(C) purchased
(D) purchasing

26 The experienced project leader excels at ------- tight deadlines while keeping team morale consistently high.

(A) managing
(B) managed
(C) management
(D) manages

27 Jeff Blackwell was the first one ever ------- three consecutive championships in the regional chess tournament.

(A) win
(B) to win
(C) won
(D) winner

28 Since ------- its manufacturing systems, the automobile factory has doubled its production efficiency.

(A) upgrade
(B) upgraded
(C) upgrades
(D) upgrading

형용사, 부사, 비교 구문

출제 경향 매회 5~6문제
최근 3개년 오답률 15.1%

1. 형용사 명사의 성질 또는 상태를 한정하거나 설명해 준다.

기출 공식 1 형용사는 명사를 꾸미는 자리나 보어 자리에 온다. 출제율 ↑

- 명사를 앞에서 꾸민다.
  Consumers praise this **reliable** washing machine for its durability. 소비자들은 내구성 때문에 이 신뢰할 수 있는 세탁기를 칭찬한다.

- 주격 보어나 목적격 보어로 쓰인다.
  The beginner course is **suitable** for students new to the language. 초급 과정은 그 언어를 새로 접하는 학생들에게 적합하다.

  고득점 포인트 보어가 주어나 목적어를 설명해 주면 보어 자리에 형용사가 오고, 주어나 목적어와 동격 관계를 이루면 보어 자리에 명사가 온다.
  The news app keeps citizens (**information**, **informed**) about current events. 뉴스 앱은 시민들이 시사에 대해 알고 있게 해준다.

기출 공식 2 빈칸 뒤의 명사를 보고 알맞은 수량 표현을 고르는 문제가 출제된다.

- 가산 명사 앞에 오는 수량 표현

단수 명사	one 하나의	each 각각의	every 모든	another 또 다른	a single 하나의	
복수 명사	one of ~ 중 하나	both 둘 다의	a few 몇 개의	numerous 많은	various 다양한	a number of 많은
	each of ~의 각각	many 많은	few 거의 없는	several 여러 개의	a variety of 다양한	a couple of 몇몇의

(**Each of**, **Each**) participant must register online before the seminar. 각각의 참가자는 세미나 전에 온라인으로 등록해야 한다.

- 불가산 명사 앞에 오는 수량 표현

a little 적은	little 거의 없는	less 더 적은	much 많은	a great deal of 많은	a large amount of 많은

Tech companies show (**many**, **much**) interest in data privacy technologies. 기술 기업은 개인정보 보호 기술에 많은 관심을 보인다.

- 가산·불가산 명사 모두의 앞에 오는 수량 표현 (단, all, more, most, lots of, a lot of, plenty of, a wealth of, other는 가산 명사와 쓰일 때 복수 명사 앞에만 올 수 있다.)

no 어떤 ~도 -아니다	more 더 많은	some 몇몇의, 어떤	lots of 많은	plenty of 많은	other 다른
all 모든	most 대부분의	any 어떤	a lot of 많은	a wealth of 수많은, 풍부한	

Without exception, **all** workers should wear safety helmets on construction sites.
예외 없이, 모든 작업자들은 공사 현장에서 안전모를 착용해야 한다.

토익실전문제

토익 문제 이렇게 나온다!

최빈출

01 The local charity organization has ------- supporters who volunteer on a weekly basis.

(A) act (B) active
(C) actively (D) action

02 Pixel Matrix is ------- for not only editing photos but also developing graphic designs.

(A) use (B) using
(C) useful (D) usefully

03 ------- items on display are over a century old, requiring special preservation methods.

(A) One (B) Each
(C) Much (D) Several

04 It is essential that ------- department align with the company's overall objectives.

(A) both (B) each
(C) various (D) a number of

정답·해석·해설 p.149

기출 공식 3   형태가 비슷하지만 의미가 다른 형용사

acceptable 받아들일 만한, 만족스러운	accepting 받아들이는	dependent 의존적인	dependable 믿을 수 있는	profitable 유리한, 이익이 되는	proficient 능숙한
admirable 칭찬할 만한, 훌륭한	admiring 감탄하는	diagnostic 진단의	diagnosable 진단할 수 있는	prospective 장래의	prosperous 번영하는
appreciative 감사하는, 감사의	appreciable 상당한	economic 경제의	economical 경제적인, 절약하는	reliable 신뢰할 수 있는	reliant 의지하는
beneficial 유익한	beneficent 인정 많은	exhaustive 철저한, 완전한	exhausted 기진맥진한, 탈진한	respectable 존경할 만한	respective 각자의
careful 세심한, 조심스러운	caring 보살피는	favorable 호의적인	favorite 가장 좋아하는	responsible 책임이 있는	responsive 민감하게 반응하는
considerable 상당한, 중요한	considerate 사려 깊은	impressive 인상적인	impressed 감명받은	seasonal 계절적인	seasoned 경험이 많은
comparable 필적할 만한	comparative 비교의	informed 정통한, 알고 있는	informative 유익한	successful 성공한, 성공의	successive 연속의, 상속의
comprehensible 이해할 수 있는	comprehensive 포괄적인, 종합적인	personal 개인적인	personable 매력적인	understanding 이해심 있는	understandable 이해할 만한

Organic farming is (proficient, **profitable**) for small-scale farmers in the region.
유기농 농업은 그 지역의 소규모 농부들에게 이익이 된다.

기출 공식 4   자주 출제되는 'be + 형용사' 표현   오답률 ⬆

be about to do 막 ~하려고 하다
be acceptable to + 명사 ~에게 수용 가능하다
be aware of ~을 알고 있다
be available to do ~할 수 있다

be available for ~이 가능하다
be capable of ~할 능력이 있다
be comparable to + 명사 ~에 필적하다
be consistent with ~과 일치되다

be critical of ~에 대해 비판적이다
be eligible for/to do ~에 대한/할 자격이 있다
be responsible for ~에 책임이 있다
be willing to do 기꺼이 ~하다

Ms. Li is (capability, **capable**) of designing visually stunning user interfaces.
Ms. Li는 시각적으로 멋진 사용자 인터페이스를 설계할 능력이 있다.

토익실전문제   토익 문제 이렇게 나온다!

01 Renewable energy legislation has a ------- effect on reducing carbon emissions throughout the country.

  (A) consider   (B) considerate
  (C) considerable   (D) consideration

02 Gentle Giant's professional movers will carefully pack and transport ------- belongings to your new residence.

  (A) person   (B) personal
  (C) personable   (D) personally

03 The new eco-friendly sunscreen is expected to be ------- to environmentally conscious consumers.

  (A) accept   (B) to accept
  (C) acceptance   (D) acceptable

04 The financial analyst is ------- of the company's recent management decisions regarding cost-cutting measures.

  (A) critics   (B) criticize
  (C) critical   (D) critically

정답·해석·해설 p.149

2. 부사
형용사, 부사, 동사, to 부정사, 동명사, 분사, 문장 전체를 꾸미며, 주로 '형용사 + -ly'의 형태를 가진다.

기출 공식 5 부사는 문장 안에서 다양한 자리에 온다.

위치	예문	해석
일반동사 앞	The judge **carefully** considers all the evidence before sentencing.	판사는 선고하기 전에 모든 증거를 신중하게 검토한다.
동사+목적어 뒤	Researchers monitored the whales **continuously** for five years.	연구자들은 5년 동안 고래들을 지속적으로 관찰했다.
be동사 뒤	The city is **widely** known for its exceptional cuisine.	그 도시는 뛰어난 요리로 널리 알려져 있다.
조동사 뒤	Your subscription will **automatically** renew at the end of the month.	당신의 구독은 월말에 자동으로 갱신될 것입니다.
형용사·부사 앞	Influencer marketing has become **increasingly** popular.	인플루언서 마케팅은 점점 더 인기 있어졌다.
전치사·접속사 앞	The airline changed the flight details **shortly** before departure.	항공사는 출발 직전에 비행 세부 사항을 변경했다.

기출 공식 6 비슷한 형태를 갖고 있지만 의미가 다른 부사

hard 열심히, 힘들게	late 늦게	close 가까이
hardly 거의 ~않다	lately 최근에	closely 긴밀하게, 밀접하게
high (높이·목표) 높게	short 짧게, 못 미치게	near 가까이
highly (위상·평가·금액) 높게, 매우	shortly (시간상으로) 얼마 안 되어	nearly 거의

Living in New York, Ms. Thompson (**hard**, **hardly**) drives. 뉴욕에서 살기 때문에, Ms. Thompson은 운전을 거의 하지 않는다.

기출 공식 7 시간 부사와 빈도 부사

- 시간 부사는 문장을 해석해서 문맥 또는 쓰임에 맞는 것을 고른다.

already 이미, 벌써 (긍정문)	ever 전에 (부정문, 의문문)	later 그 시간 이후에 (시간 표현 바로 다음에 온다.)
still 여전히, 아직 (긍정문, 부정문, 의문문)	ago 전에 (시간 표현 바로 다음에 온다.)	thereafter 그 이후에
yet 아직 (부정문), 이미, 벌써 (의문문)	once 한때 (막연한 과거의 시점을 나타낸다.)	since 그 이후로

The organization was founded 20 years **ago**, advocating for equal education.
그 기관은 평등한 교육을 옹호하며 20년 전에 설립되었다.

- 빈도 부사는 '얼마나 자주' 일이 발생하는가를 표현하며, 보통 일반동사의 앞 또는 조동사나 be동사의 뒤에 온다.

always 항상	almost 거의	often 자주	frequently 종종	usually 보통	once 한 번
sometimes 때때로	never 결코 ~않다	hardly/rarely/seldom/scarcely/barely 거의 ~않다			

Government regulations **sometimes** affect businesses by imposing restrictions.
정부 규제는 제한을 부과함으로써 때때로 기업에 영향을 미친다.

토익실전문제

01 The company's new application, CollabFlow, is ------- designed to enhance productivity in remote work environments.
(A) specify   (B) specific
(C) specificity   (D) specifically

02 ------- responsible individuals start retirement savings early and make consistent long-term investments.
(A) Finance   (B) Financial
(C) Financially   (D) Finances

03 Prism Solutions ------- values employee innovation and creative problem-solving approaches.
(A) high   (B) highly
(C) higher   (D) highest

04 Dr. Erikson ------- speaks in meetings, except when the topic directly involves his field of expertise.
(A) seldom   (B) almost
(C) yet   (D) well

기출 공식 8 강조 부사

강조 부사	강조하는 대상	강조 부사	강조하는 대상
just/right 바로	before, after	quite 굉장한	a/an + 명사
only 오직	전치사구	quite 꽤	형용사/부사
just 단지	전치사구	nearly/almost 거의, just 꼭, very 매우	원급
well 훨씬	전치사구	much/even/far/a lot 훨씬	비교급
even ~조차도, ~까지도	단어나 구	by far/quite/very 단연코	최상급

Mr. Keith received an important e-mail **right** before the conference. Keith씨는 회의 바로 전에 중요한 이메일을 받았다.
Digital design tools have made graphic creation **much** easier. 디지털 디자인 도구는 그래픽 제작을 훨씬 더 쉽게 만들었다.

고득점 포인트 only와 just는 명사구를 강조할 수도 있다.
Only the system administrators can modify the core network infrastructure. 오직 시스템 관리자만이 핵심 네트워크 인프라를 수정할 수 있다.

기출 공식 9 동사, 형용사, 분사와 함께 자주 출제되는 부사

동사 + 부사	부사 + 형용사	부사 + 분사
work collaboratively 협동하여 일하다	widely different 크게 다른	continuously operating 계속 운영하는
grow significantly 크게 성장하다	surprisingly large 놀라울 정도로 큰	temporarily closed 일시적으로 닫은
respond promptly 즉각적으로 대응하다	completely functional 완전히 작동하는	reasonably priced 합리적으로 가격이 매겨진
proceed cautiously 조심스럽게 진행하다	entirely dependent 전적으로 의존하는	heavily influenced 심하게 영향받은
participate actively 적극적으로 참여하다	potentially risky 잠재적으로 위험한	urgently required 급히 필요한
review thoroughly 철저하게 검토하다	easily accessible 쉽게 접근 가능한	accidentally damaged 실수로 파손된

The marketing and sales departments should **work collaboratively**. 마케팅과 영업 부서는 협동하여 일해야 한다.
The satellite was not **completely functional** after launch. 그 위성은 발사 후 완전히 작동하지 않았다.
The west wing of the hospital is **temporarily closed**. 병원의 서쪽 병동은 일시적으로 닫혔다.

토익실전문제

01 The legendary artist's private collection will be displayed ------- for a day at the city's most prestigious museum.

(A) quite (B) very
(C) only (D) far

02 The smart kitchen appliance is automated enough for ------- a novice chef to prepare elaborate gourmet meals.

(A) even (B) right
(C) well (D) soon

03 Customer service representatives are trained to respond ------- to ensure high client satisfaction.

(A) prompt (B) prompts
(C) promptly (D) prompting

04 Solar Drive's newest electric vehicle is not only eco-friendly but also ------- priced for sustainable transportation.

(A) reason (B) reasoned
(C) reasonable (D) reasonably

3. 비교 구문 둘 이상의 대상을 수량이나 성질 면에서 비교하는 구문이다.

기출 공식 10 as와 as 사이에는 원급이 온다.

The virtual assistant handles customer inquiries <u>as</u> **efficiently** <u>as</u> a human agent.
그 가상 비서는 인간 상담원만큼 효율적으로 고객 문의를 처리한다.

고득점 포인트 '~만큼 많은/적은 -'을 나타낼 때 'as + many(much)/few(little) + 명사 + as'를 쓴다.
The space mission's primary objective is to gather **as much knowledge as** possible about black holes.
그 우주탐사 임무의 주요 목표는 블랙홀에 대한 가능한 한 많은 지식을 얻는 것이다.

고득점 포인트 as ~ as 사이의 형용사/부사 자리는 as ~ as -를 지우고 판단한다.
During the match, the boxer's reflexes were as **quick** as lightning. 경기 동안, 그 복싱선수의 반사 신경은 번개만큼 빨랐다.
→ During the match, the boxer's reflexes were (~~quickly~~, quick).
The young engineer completed technical designs as **precisely** as his boss. 그 젊은 엔지니어는 그의 상사만큼 기술 설계를 정확하게 완료했다.
→ The young engineer completed technical designs (~~precise~~, precisely).

기출 공식 11 than 앞에는 비교급이 온다.

The seminar's Q&A session will be **briefer** <u>than</u> the lecture portion.
그 세미나의 질의응답 시간은 강의 부분보다 간략할 것이다.

고득점 포인트 '~보다 덜 -한'을 나타낼 때 'less + 형용사/부사 + than'을 쓴다.
The modern apartment is **less spacious than** traditional houses.
현대적인 아파트는 전통적인 집보다 덜 널찍하다.

토익실전문제

최빈출

01 The bank tried to keep the waiting time for customers as ------- as possible by installing additional ATMs.

(A) short (B) shortly
(C) shorter (D) shortest

02 The number of smartphone users worldwide is ------- than ever before, thanks to affordable mobile technologies.

(A) high (B) highly
(C) higher (D) highest

03 Flex Factory offers better membership benefits ------- any other fitness center in the neighborhood.

(A) as (B) even
(C) than (D) so that

04 Group travel packages, which often include accommodation and transportation, tend to be ------- expensive than individual bookings.

(A) a lot (B) less
(C) rather (D) few

기출 공식 12 최상급은 the 뒤와 아래 표현들 앞에 온다.

- **of + 비교 대상**
  Ms. Roberts seemed the **most ambitious** of the five candidates.
  Ms. Roberts는 다섯 명의 후보들 중 가장 야심 차 보였다.

- **in + 비교 범위**
  Legacy Boulevard is the **most heavily** congested road in the city.
  Legacy대로는 도시에서 가장 혼잡한 도로이다.

- **that절**
  The recent leadership transition was the **most significant** management shift that the company has experienced.
  최근의 대표직 전환은 회사가 경험한 가장 중요한 경영진 교체였다.

기출 공식 13 자주 출제되는 다양한 비교급 표현

more than + 명사 ~ 이상
less than + 명사 ~ 이하
no longer than 길어야 ~이다
no longer 더 이상 ~않다
for a later time 나중을 위해

no later than 늦어도 ~까지
no sooner ~ than ─ ~하자마자 ─하다
other than ~ 이외에도
rather than ~보다는
would rather ~ than ─ ─하느니 차라리 ~하다

Employees are required to submit their expense reports **no later than** the 15th of each month.
직원들은 늦어도 매월 15일까지 그들의 비용 보고서를 제출하도록 요구받는다.

토익실전문제

01 In maintaining good health, the ------- factor is consistency in healthy lifestyle choices.
(A) importantly
(B) more importantly
(C) importance
(D) most important

02 Of all customer service issues, shipping delays are the ------- common complaints in e-commerce businesses.
(A) both
(B) most
(C) either
(D) between

03 Modern readers increasingly choose e-books ------- the printed version due to convenience and instant access to thousands of titles.
(A) upon
(B) even
(C) rather than
(D) at any rate

04 The express train to the airport will take no ------- than 30 minutes, even during peak hours.
(A) long
(B) longer
(C) longing
(D) longest

정답·해석·해설 p.151

HACKERS TEST — DAY 04

01 Velocic International ------- responds to clients' inquiries all the time.

(A) very (B) quickly
(C) ago   (D) so

02 News of the oil spill got ------- attention before videos about it were spread on the Internet.

(A) few   (B) little
(C) many (D) a single

03 Garnet Mobile's ------- offer for new customers promises 30 percent off the first three months of service.

(A) specializing (B) specializes
(C) special   (D) specially

04 At the construction site, workers will be ------- monitored by an on-site safety inspector.

(A) regular   (B) regularly
(C) regularity (D) regulation

05 The warehouse staff organize incoming shipments as ------- as they can during peak seasons.

(A) efficiently (B) more efficient
(C) efficiency   (D) most efficiently

06 The decorator recommends making ------- use of white paint to lower costs.

(A) extensive   (B) extension
(C) extensively (D) extend

07 Blue Scale Industries ------- hires new employees based on their innovative thinking and adaptability.

(A) once (B) enough
(C) most (D) always

08 In addition to restaurants, points earned on the Aviato Card are ------- at certain retail establishments.

(A) redeeming (B) redeemable
(C) redeem   (D) redeems

09 Relivium Pro is ------- more effective at reducing headache symptoms than other brands.

(A) signify   (B) signifier
(C) significant (D) significantly

10 The company focuses on building long-term relationships ------- pursuing immediate profits.

(A) whether   (B) so that
(C) rather than (D) as long as

11 Since Mr. Weiss has ------- booked tables at Sandro's Italian, there is no need to look further for a party venue.

(A) already (B) still
(C) later   (D) forward

12 Stratedge Advertising has gained ------- recognition than its competitors in the mobile advertising industry.

(A) great   (B) greater
(C) greatly (D) greatest

13 Sparta Foundation's mentoring program has proven to be ------- to students.

(A) inform   (B) informs
(C) informative (D) information

14 The bookcase is designed to be ------- attached to the wall with a set of special screws.

(A) secure   (B) security
(C) securely (D) secured

15 The renovation project required ------- less funding than similar projects completed in neighboring cities.

(A) right
(B) very
(C) further
(D) much

16 Small business owners are ------- for government grants during economic recovery periods.

(A) eligible
(B) eligibility
(C) eligibly
(D) eligibleness

17 Customer feedback is the ------- part of product development and improvement.

(A) essence
(B) most essential
(C) essentially
(D) more essentially

18 ------- recognized architects will design sustainable housing for growing urban communities in the country.

(A) Nation
(B) National
(C) Nationally
(D) Nationality

고난도
19 The workshop aims to effectively enhance participants' ------- skills through practical exercises.

(A) supervise
(B) supervises
(C) supervised
(D) supervisory

20 Dr. Sharma measured the chemical compounds ------- and repeated her experiment multiple times.

(A) accurate
(B) accuracy
(C) accurately
(D) more accurate

고난도
21 At the start of ------- session, the yoga instructor guides students through gentle breathing exercises.

(A) every
(B) all
(C) other
(D) much

고난도
22 Ms. Valdez, the legal assistant at Paramount Legal Solutions, works ------- with lawyers and clients.

(A) close
(B) closer
(C) closely
(D) closure

고난도
23 The tracking device has uses in wildlife conservation ------- its primary function as a pet monitor.

(A) since
(B) other than
(C) moreover
(D) in order to

고난도
24 The CEO tried to keep the majority of shareholders ------- about the current financial situation.

(A) knowledge
(B) knowledgeable
(C) know
(D) known

25 Due to the massive fires, some agricultural products became ------- hard to find in grocery stores.

(A) relate
(B) relative
(C) relatively
(D) relativity

고난도
26 Aether Airways is serving ------- three destinations during the initial phase of their international expansion.

(A) only
(B) quite
(C) many
(D) including

27 Queensland Holdings has satisfied its investors by ------- generating positive returns over the last decade.

(A) consistent
(B) consistency
(C) consistently
(D) consist

고난도
28 Modern facial recognition software is more ------- than human memory for identifying individuals in large crowds.

(A) relying
(B) reliable
(C) reliant
(D) relies

정답·해석·해설 p.152

DAY 05 전치사

출제 경향 매회 3~4문제
최근 3개년 오답률 18.2%

1. 전치사 명사 앞에 와서 장소, 시간, 이유 등을 나타낸다.

기출 공식 1 | 시간과 장소를 나타내는 in/on/at을 구분하는 문제가 출제된다.

• 시간 전치사 in/on/at

in ~에	+ 월, 연도, 분기, 계절, 세기, 아침/오후/저녁	on ~에	+ 날짜, 요일, 기념일
in ~ 후에	+ 기간 표현	at ~에	+ 시각, 시점

The new semester's orientation will take place **on** Monday. 새 학기의 오리엔테이션은 월요일에 열릴 것이다.

• 장소 전치사 in/on/at

in ~에, ~ 안에	+ 국가, 도시, 마을, 공간 안의 장소	at ~에	+ 지점, 번지
on ~에, ~ 위에	+ 표면 위, 층, 거리		

An exercise area specially designed for the elderly was built **in** the park. 노인을 위해 특별히 설계된 운동 구역이 공원에 지어졌다.

• in/on/at 관용 표현

in	in advance 미리, 사전에	in time 때맞추어, 이르게	in place 제자리에, 적소에	in a timely manner 시기적절하게
on	on time 제시간에, 제때	on a regular basis 규칙적으로	on the waiting list 대기자 명단에	on/upon arrival 도착하는 즉시
at	at once 즉시, 동시에	at least 적어도	at the latest 늦어도	at one's expense ~의 비용으로

기출 공식 2 | 자주 출제되는 시간 전치사

출제율 ▲

since ~ 이후로	from ~부터	until/by ~까지	before/prior to ~ 전에	+	시점 표현 (1 P.M., May 등)
for/during ~ 동안	within ~ 이내에	over/through/throughout ~ 동안, ~ 내내		+	기간 표현 (two hours, holiday 등)

Pinnacle Capital's stock price has not changed **since** last month. Pinnacle Capital사의 주가는 지난달 이후로 변하지 않았다.

고득점 포인트 for는 숫자를 포함한 기간 표현 앞에 와서 '얼마나 오랫동안 지속되는지'를, during은 명사 앞에 와서 '언제 일어나는지'를 나타낸다.
The patient will be monitored in the hospital **for** three days. 그 환자는 3일 동안 병원에서 추적 관찰될 것이다.
Visitors can use the east entrance **during** the renovation. 방문객들은 보수 기간 동안 동문을 이용할 수 있다.

고득점 포인트 until은 '상황, 상태가 계속될 때까지'를, by는 '행동이 완료될 때까지'를 의미한다.
The university library is accessible to students **until** 6 o'clock. 대학 도서관은 학생들이 6시 정각까지 이용 가능하다.
All project reports must be submitted **by** 6 o'clock. 모든 프로젝트 보고서는 6시 정각까지 제출되어야 한다.

토익실전문제

토익 문제 이렇게 나온다!

01 Terra Motors' revenue exceeded $50 million ------- the last quarter, setting a new record for its annual growth.
(A) at   (B) in
(C) to   (D) up

02 The electronics store offering the latest gadgets can be found ------- the third floor of Lakeline Mall.
(A) for   (B) on
(C) off   (D) onto

03 Buyers can conduct a thorough property inspection ------- seven days of signing the contract.
(A) while   (B) since
(C) even   (D) within

★최빈출
04 The keynote speaker, Mr. Sealey, is expected to arrive ------- 10 A.M. for the conference.
(A) by   (B) on
(C) until   (D) into

정답·해석·해설 p.154

기출 공식 3   자주 출제되는 위치 전치사

• 위치 전치사

above/over ~ 위에	behind ~ 뒤에	within ~ 내에	around ~ 주위에
beneath/under ~ 아래에	between/among ~ 사이에	inside ~ 안에	past ~을 지나
beside/next to ~ 옆에	near ~ 가까이, ~ 근처에	outside ~ 밖에	opposite ~ 건너편에, ~ 맞은 편에

Important research samples are stored **inside** the white cabinet. 중요한 연구 샘플은 하얀색 캐비닛 안에 보관된다.

• 위치 전치사 관용 표현

above	above one's expectations 기대 이상인	
over	have the edge/advantage over ~보다 유리하다	
under	under the direction of ~의 지시에 따라	under construction 공사 중인
	under new policy 새로운 정책하에서	under investigation 조사 중인
between	a difference/gap between A and B A와 B의 차이	
within	within walking distance of ~에서 걸어갈 수 있는 곳에	within the limits of ~의 범위 내에서
around	around the world 전 세계에	around the corner 길모퉁이를 돌아, 위기를 넘겨, 임박하여

기출 공식 4   자주 출제되는 방향 전치사

• 방향 전치사

from ~에서, ~로부터	toward(s) ~ 쪽으로, ~을 향하여	into ~ 안으로
for ~을 향해	through ~을 통과하여	out of ~ 밖으로
to ~로, ~ 쪽으로	along ~을 따라서	across ~을 가로질러, ~의 전역에 걸쳐, 건너편에

Luxury resorts are positioned **along** the shore of the tropical island. 열대 섬의 해안을 따라서 호화로운 리조트가 위치해 있다.

• 방향 전치사 관용 표현

from	from A to B A부터 B까지	from one's viewpoint ~의 관점으로 보면	
to	to the point 적절한	to a great extent 상당한 정도까지	to my knowledge 내가 알기로는
along	along the side of ~의 측면을 따라		
across	across the nation 전국에, 전역에 걸쳐	across the street 길 건너편에	
out of	out of date 시대에 뒤진, 구식인	out of season 제철이 아닌	out of order 고장 난
	out of room 공간이 부족한	out of reach 손이 닿지 않는	out of stock 재고가 떨어진

토익실전문제

토익 문제 이렇게 나온다!

01 The contract dispute ------- the company and its supplier was successfully resolved through mediation.

(A) after   (B) along
(C) until   (D) between

02 The critically acclaimed theater performance was staged ------- the direction of Ms. Kennedy.

(A) among   (B) under
(C) behind   (D) opposite

☆최빈출

03 Modern Living Designs will be closed ------- November 20 to November 25 for seasonal inventory reconfiguration.

(A) from   (B) outside
(C) near   (D) under

04 The vaccination program was systematically implemented ------- the entire nation to combat the pandemic.

(A) beside   (B) out of
(C) across   (D) beneath

정답·해석·해설 p.155

기출 공식 5 — 자주 출제되는 다양한 전치사

이유 전치사	because of ~때문에	due to ~때문에	owing to ~때문에	on account of ~때문에
양보 전치사	despite ~에도 불구하고	in spite of ~에도 불구하고	with all ~에도 불구하고	notwithstanding ~에도 불구하고
제외 전치사	except (for) ~을 제외하고 but for ~이 없(었)다면	besides ~외에 instead of ~대신에	aside from ~외에는 apart from ~외에는	without ~없이
부가 전치사	in addition to ~에 더해서	besides ~에 더해서	apart from ~에 더해서	plus ~에 더해서
기타 전치사	about ~에 관하여 regarding ~에 관하여 in regard to ~에 관하여 concerning ~에 관하여 as for ~에 관해 말하면	like ~처럼 unlike ~과 달리 for ~을 위해서 by ~에 의해, ~함으로써 with ~과 함께, ~을 가지고	throughout ~전역에, ~도처에 through ~을 통해서 as ~로서 against ~에 반대하여, ~에 기대어 beyond ~보다 뛰어난, ~이상으로	following ~에 이어 amid ~의 한 가운데

Mr. Zhou missed out on the investment opportunity **due to** a lack of funds.
Mr. Zhou는 자금의 부족 때문에 투자 기회를 놓쳤다.

In spite of its aggressive marketing campaign, Noxel Fabric struggled to attract younger customers.
공격적인 마케팅 캠페인에도 불구하고, Noxel Fabric사는 젊은 고객을 유치하는 데 어려움을 겪었다.

The management sent a detailed memo **regarding** the upcoming organizational restructuring.
경영진은 곧 있을 조직 개편에 대한 자세한 회람을 보냈다.

기출 공식 6 — 아래의 의미로 쓰이는 of가 출제된다.

의미상 A가 동사, B가 주어인 경우	launch of the new item 새 물품의 출시	departure of the ship 배의 출발
의미상 A가 동사, B가 목적어인 경우	unveiling of the new model 새 모델의 발표	advertising of goods 상품의 광고
A와 B가 동격인 경우	a chance of rain 비가 올 확률	the idea of online promotion 온라인 홍보에 대한 생각
A가 B의 소속, 부분인 경우	the weight of the machine 기계의 무게	this part of the country 그 나라의 이 지역

고득점 포인트 of가 문장 맨 앞에 오면 among(~ 중에서)의 의미를 가지며, 뒤에 복수 명사가 온다.
Of all the communication methods, the Internet is the most revolutionary in human history.
모든 통신 방법들 중에서, 인터넷은 인류 역사상 가장 혁명적이다.

토익실전문제

01 ------- inclement weather, the championship baseball game was rescheduled for the following weekend.
(A) Although   (B) Because of
(C) In spite of   (D) Except for

02 Cutting-edge VR gaming systems continue to gain popularity among tech-savvy consumers ------- the high cost.
(A) until   (B) against
(C) despite   (D) owing to

03 ------- adding interactive elements, teachers are able to increase student engagement in online learning platforms.
(A) Within   (B) Under
(C) Of   (D) By

04 Freight companies strategically plan vehicle loading based on the weight ------- individual packages and the total shipment.
(A) as   (B) of
(C) about   (D) among

기출 공식 7 자주 출제되는 두 단어 이상으로 이루어진 전치사

as of + 시간 ~부터, ~부로	in favor of ~에 찬성하여	on behalf of ~을 대신하여
such as ~과 같은	in terms of ~에 관해서는	as a part of ~의 일환으로
according to ~에 따르면	in light of ~을 고려하여	as a result of ~의 결과로
contrary to ~에 반해	in the event of ~의 경우에	regardless of ~에 상관없이
in place of ~을 대신하여	in charge of ~을 책임지고 있는	resulting from ~으로 인한
in response to ~에 응하여	in exchange for ~의 대신으로	compared with ~과 비교하여

As a result of the scheduled renovations, the museum temporarily suspended its exhibits.
예정된 보수의 결과로, 박물관은 전시를 일시적으로 중단했다.

기출 공식 8 동사, 명사, 형용사와 함께 자주 출제되는 전치사

- **동사 + 전치사**

depend/rely/count on(upon) ~에 의존하다	comply with ~을 따르다	transfer A to B A를 B로 옮기다
account for ~을 설명하다	consist of ~으로 구성되다	congratulate A on B A에게 B를 축하하다
prepare for ~을 준비하다	belong to ~에 속하다, ~의 소유이다	praise A for B B에 대해 A를 칭찬하다
be recognized for ~으로 인정받다	contribute to ~에 기여하다	supply/provide A with B A에게 B를 공급/제공하다
specialize in ~을 전문으로 하다	credit A to B A를 B의 공으로 돌리다	associate A with B A를 B에 관련지어 생각하다

When **preparing for** market expansion, companies must conduct a risk assessment.
시장 확장을 준비할 때, 기업은 위험 평가를 수행해야 한다.

- **명사 + 전치사**

access to ~에의 접근, 출입	a solution to ~에 대한 해결책	a dispute over ~에 대한 논쟁
a cause/reason for ~의 원인/이유	a problem with ~의 문제	a discount on ~에 대한 할인
a demand for ~에 대한 요구, 수요	a lack of ~의 부족	an effect(impact/influence) on ~에 대한 영향

Mobile banking apps provide convenient **access to** banking services.
모바일 뱅킹 앱은 뱅킹 서비스에 대한 편리한 접근을 제공한다.

- **형용사 + 전치사**

responsible for ~에 책임이 있는	equivalent to ~과 동일한	adjacent to ~에 인접한
eligible for ~에 대한 자격이 있는	identical to ~과 동일한	familiar with ~에 익숙한
grateful for ~에 감사하는	comparable to ~에 필적하는	consistent with ~과 일관된

Java Roasters, **adjacent to** the mall, offers shoppers a relaxing atmosphere.
쇼핑몰에 인접한 Java Roasters는 쇼핑객에게 편안한 분위기를 선사한다.

토익실전문제

01 ------- the survey results, flexible working hours significantly increase employee satisfaction and productivity.

(A) Because (B) In addition to
(C) According to (D) In place of

02 All occupants must immediately evacuate the building using designated emergency exits ------- fire.

(A) contrary to (B) in the event of
(C) in order that (D) in exchange for

03 The consulting firm provides clients ------- detailed market analysis reports to help them make informed investment decisions.

(A) at (B) for
(C) to (D) with

04 First-time homebuyers are eligible ------- special loan programs with lower interest rates.

(A) on (B) by
(C) for (D) from

HACKERS TEST

DAY 05

토익 800+를 위한 실전 문제 정복

01 The CEO delivered an inspiring speech ------- the ceremony marking the company's 25th anniversary.

(A) above (B) beside
(C) between (D) during

02 Heavy traffic begins to build up on the main highway into downtown ------- approximately five o'clock.

(A) at (B) on
(C) for (D) up

03 ------- the growing demand for delivery services, Swift Go has hired over 1,000 new drivers nationwide.

(A) Toward (B) Although
(C) Owing to (D) Now that

04 *Starlight Fractals* by Mr. Kazuka will be distributed to all major bookstores ------- Barton to Fort Bend.

(A) among (B) when
(C) between (D) from

05 ------- the cost of solar panel installation, homeowners are trying to embrace it as a renewable energy solution.

(A) Before (B) During
(C) Despite (D) Though

06 Ms. Potter works at Wallace's Used Books every day ------- Sunday.

(A) around (B) except
(C) across (D) within

07 Mr. Robertson sought the advice of financial experts ------- choosing which stocks to purchase.

(A) according to (B) before
(C) through (D) far from

08 Digital payment methods have become the default transaction option ------- young consumers.

(A) among (B) against
(C) onto (D) beneath

09 Metro Vista Mall visitors can enjoy various activities, ------- indoor gaming and virtual reality experiences.

(A) whereas (B) about
(C) such as (D) likewise

10 ------- expanding its regular hours, the childcare center now conveniently provides weekend care services.

(A) Whether (B) In order to
(C) Except for (D) In addition to

11 The office supply cabinet adjacent ------- the copy machine contains extra paper and toner cartridges.

(A) as (B) to
(C) off (D) into

12 Techspire Dynamics has developed more than 50 innovative software programs ------- its founding a decade ago.

(A) since (B) throughout
(C) except for (D) even though

13 The maintenance team will not be able to fix the elevator ------- tomorrow morning.

(A) until (B) while
(C) lately (D) without

14 Find all our stores ------- you by using our interactive location map either on the Web site or on our mobile app.

(A) out of (B) along
(C) near (D) next

15 Mr. Cory called a meeting to address employees' concerns ------- the revised policy on work hours.

(A) regarding
(B) around
(C) among
(D) throughout

16 ------- sending out packages, hazardous materials must be properly labeled and certified.

(A) By the time
(B) Past
(C) Prior to
(D) Aside from

17 Mirado Bakery had to raise the prices of some goods ------- an increase in the cost of ingredients.

(A) as of
(B) due to
(C) such as
(D) besides

18 Staff members at Fasheng International are entitled to discounts ------- online Chinese language courses.

(A) of
(B) on
(C) into
(D) like

19 Shoppers can get double reward points on all purchases ------- the promotional period.

(A) among
(B) throughout
(C) between
(D) to

20 Ms. Brooks was recognized by the director ------- being able to handle difficult customer complaints.

(A) for
(B) about
(C) within
(D) outside

21 ------- the initial forecast, the tropical storm shifted direction and spared the coastal communities entirely.

(A) On behalf of
(B) Provided that
(C) Contrary to
(D) As soon as

22 The ancient temple remains well-preserved ------- the dry desert climate and minimal human interference.

(A) so that
(B) for example
(C) out of
(D) because of

23 The news that producer Joel Manning had resigned from Harper Studios spread ------- the entertainment industry.

(A) across
(B) above
(C) onto
(D) between

24 All participants must pay a $50 deposit that will be returned at the end ------- the four-day trade show.

(A) into
(B) in
(C) for
(D) of

25 ------- some technical difficulties, the space mission achieved all its primary objectives ahead of schedule.

(A) During
(B) In spite of
(C) In favor of
(D) Nevertheless

26 Artificial intelligence applications have revolutionized healthcare diagnosis ------- the last few years.

(A) since
(B) until
(C) over
(D) nearly

27 ------- the closure of the regional distribution center, we are looking for a new logistics partner.

(A) According to
(B) In case
(C) In light of
(D) In spite of

28 The construction of the waste treatment facility was paused ------- local community protests.

(A) such as
(B) on account of
(C) opposite
(D) in order that

DAY 06 접속사

출제 경향 매회 2~3문제
최근 3개년 오답률 16.9%

1. 등위접속사와 상관접속사
단어와 단어, 구와 구, 절과 절을 대등하게 연결한다. 이때 상관접속사는 두 단어가 서로 짝을 이루어 쓰인다.

기출 공식 1 알맞은 등위접속사를 고르는 문제가 출제된다.

| and 그리고 | or 또는 | but 하지만, 그러나 | yet 그러나 | so 그래서 | for 왜냐하면 |

Climate change affects land **and** sea temperatures worldwide. 기후 변화는 전 세계 육지와 바다 온도에 영향을 미친다.

고득점 포인트 so와 for은 절과 절만 연결할 수 있으므로, 단어나 구를 연결하는 자리에는 정답이 될 수 없다.

They rushed to prepare the presentation, **for** the client was arriving in an hour. (O)
고객이 한 시간 후에 도착하기 때문에, 그들은 발표를 서둘러 준비했다.

The new micro-apartment offers affordable **so** practical living solutions. (X)
새로운 초소형 아파트는 저렴하고 실용적인 주거 솔루션을 제공한다.

기출 공식 2 상관접속사의 알맞은 짝을 고르는 문제가 출제된다.

both A and B A와 B 모두	not only A but (also) B = B as well as A A뿐 아니라 B도
either A or B A 또는 B 중 하나	not A but B = B but not A = (only) B, not A A가 아닌 B
neither A nor B A도 B도 아닌	

La Piazza provides **both** digital **and** printed menus for their customers. La Piazza는 고객을 위해 디지털과 인쇄된 메뉴를 모두 제공한다.

기출 공식 3 등위접속사나 상관접속사로 연결된 주어와 동사의 수일치를 묻는 문제가 출제된다.

B에 일치시키는 경우	A or B neither A nor B	either A or B not only A but (also) B	not A but B
항상 복수 동사를 쓰는 경우	A and B	both A and B	

Competitors and suppliers (**influences**, **influence**) pricing strategies in the market.
경쟁업체와 공급업체는 시장에서의 가격 전략에 영향을 미친다.

Not only the manager but also the employees (**participates**, **participate**) in weekly meetings.
관리자뿐 아니라 직원들도 매주 회의에 참여한다.

토익실전문제

☆ 최빈출

01 Dr. Sanchez is retiring on June 30, ------- his replacement will not be arriving until August.

(A) or (B) nor
(C) but (D) for

02 Sophia Anderson is a renowned marine biologist ------- a founder of Ocean Guard Initiative.

(A) and (B) but
(C) so (D) nor

03 For their convenience, participants can register for the business conference ------- online or at the venue.

(A) both (B) neither
(C) as well (D) either

04 The director and the actor ------- that the script needs revision before filming begins.

(A) agree (B) agrees
(C) agreeing (D) agreement

정답·해석·해설 p.159

2. 명사절 접속사 문장 안에서 주어, 목적어, 보어 역할을 하는 명사절을 이끈다.

기출 공식 4   that과 whether는 명사절을 이끄는 접속사 자리에 온다.

- that은 '~라는 것, ~라고'라는 의미이며, 전치사의 목적어로는 쓰일 수 없다. 동사의 목적어로 쓰인 that절의 that은 생략될 수 있다.

주어	**That** smartphones have become essential in our daily lives is not surprising. 스마트폰이 우리의 일상에 필수가 된 것은 놀랍지 않다.
목적어	Mr. Kumar said (**that**) the research findings exceeded initial expectations. Mr. Kumar는 연구 결과가 초기 예상을 뛰어넘었다고 말했다.
보어	The issue is **that** rural areas lack access to specialized medical care. 문제는 지방이 전문 의료 서비스에 대한 접근이 부족하다는 것이다.

- whether는 '~인지 아닌지'라는 의미이다.

주어	**Whether** the treatment works effectively varies from patient to patient. 치료가 효과가 있는지 없는지는 환자마다 다르다.
목적어	The beta test will see **whether** the new app can maintain stable performance. 베타 테스트는 새 앱이 안정적인 성능을 유지할 수 있는지 아닌지 볼 것이다.
보어	The customer's concern was **whether** the repair would be done quickly. 고객의 걱정은 수리가 빠르게 끝날 것인지에 대한 것이었다.

고득점 포인트 명사절 접속사 if도 whether와 같은 의미이지만, if절은 주어와 전치사의 목적어 자리에 올 수 없다.
(**If**, **Whether**) the conference will be held virtually or in person has not been decided.
회의가 가상으로 개최될지 직접 개최될지는 결정되지 않았다.

기출 공식 5   동사나 형용사와 함께 자주 출제되는 that/whether

동사/형용사 + that	say that ~라고 말하다 state that ~라고 말하다 mention that ~라고 언급하다 suggest that ~라고 제안하다 report that ~라고 보고하다	inform+사람+that ~라고 알려주다 remind+사람+that ~라고 상기시키다 assure+사람+that ~라는 점을 보장하다 convince+사람+that ~라는 점을 납득시키다 be confident that ~을 확신하다	be aware that ~을 알고 있다 be glad that ~해서 기쁘다 be afraid that 미안하지만 ~이다 be sorry that ~해서 유감이다 be sure that ~라고 확신하다
동사 + whether	see whether ~인지 아닌지 보다 know whether ~인지 아닌지 알다 ask whether ~인지 아닌지 묻다	determine whether ~인지 아닌지 결정하다 decide whether ~인지 아닌지 결정하다 wonder whether ~인지 아닌지 궁금해하다	

The airline **informed passengers that** their flight was delayed. 항공사는 승객들에게 그들의 비행편이 지연되었다고 알려줬다.
The analyst can't **determine whether** the market will improve next quarter. 분석가는 시장이 다음 분기에 나아질지 아닐지 결정할 수 없다.

토익실전문제
토익 문제 이렇게 나온다!

01 The most innovative feature of Work Flow Hub is ------- it automatically eliminates background noise during video calls.

(A) as   (B) that
(C) thus   (D) whether

02 ------- crops thrive depends on soil conditions, weather patterns, and proper irrigation methods.

(A) If   (B) Either
(C) Whether   (D) Often

03 Recent market analysis suggested ------- small businesses adopting AI technologies saw a 30 percent increase in operational efficiency.

(A) that   (B) this
(C) then   (D) there

04 Please let the travel coordinator know ------- you prefer a window or aisle seat for your flight.

(A) until   (B) which
(C) whether   (D) while

정답·해석·해설 p.159

기출 공식 6   의문사는 명사절을 이끄는 접속사 자리에 온다.

- who, whom, whose, what, which는 의문대명사로 명사절을 이끌며, 그 자체가 명사절의 주어, 목적어, 보어 역할을 하므로, 의문대명사 뒤에는 주어, 목적어 또는 보어가 없는 불완전한 절이 온다.

  The board will decide **who** will receive the annual innovation award at the event.
  이사회는 행사에서 연례 혁신상을 누가 받을지 결정할 것이다.

- whose, what, which는 의문형용사로 뒤에 온 명사를 꾸미면서 명사절을 이끌며, '의문형용사 + 명사'가 명사절의 주어, 목적어, 보어 역할을 하므로, 그 뒤에는 주어, 목적어 또는 보어가 없는 불완전한 절이 온다.

  The IT supervisor asked **whose laptops** needed immediate security updates.
  IT 관리자는 누구의 노트북에 즉각적인 보안 업데이트가 필요한지 물었다.

- where, when, how, why는 의문부사로 명사절을 이끌며, 의문부사 뒤에는 빠진 것이 없는 완전한 절이 온다.

  The residents didn't know **when** the severe storm would hit their town.
  주민들은 언제 심한 폭풍이 그들의 마을을 강타할지 몰랐다.

기출 공식 7   '의문사/whether + to 부정사'도 명사절 자리에 올 수 있다.

what + to 부정사 무엇을 ~할지	which + to 부정사 어떤 것을 ~할지	when + to 부정사 언제 ~할지
who(m) + to 부정사 누구를 ~할지	where + to 부정사 어디에(서) ~할지	how + to 부정사 어떻게 ~할지
whether + to 부정사 ~할지 안 할지		

The CEO can't decide **who(m) to promote** for the executive leadership position.
최고경영자는 누구를 임원 직책으로 승진시킬지 결정할 수 없다.

기출 공식 8   자주 출제되는 복합관계대명사   오답률 ↑

whoever (= anyone who) 누구든 간에   whatever (= anything that) 무엇이든 간에
whomever (= anyone whom) 누구든 간에   whichever (= anything that, anyone who) 어느 것이든 간에, 어느 사람이든 간에

Vantage Design Group will design **whatever**(= anything that) your company needs.
Vantage Design Group사는 당신의 회사가 필요로 하는 무엇이든 간에 설계할 것입니다.

고득점 포인트   whatever와 whichever는 뒤에 나오는 명사를 꾸미는 복합관계형용사로도 쓰일 수 있다.
Whichever color Mr. Jenkins chooses will be used in the new corporate logo.
Mr. Jenkins가 선택하는 어떤 색상이든 간에 새로운 기업 로고에 사용될 것이다.

토익실전문제   토익 문제 이렇게 나온다!

★최빈출

01 The moderator announced ------ topics candidates would discuss during the televised debate.

(A) as   (B) who
(C) which   (D) that

02 The director confirmed ------ the budget meeting would be held after consulting with all department heads.

(A) what   (B) who
(C) when   (D) whose

03 Vince Scott, a certified industrial safety instructor, will explain ------ to operate the new equipment safely.

(A) how   (B) why
(C) what   (D) whom

04 ------ conducts the orientation should keep in mind that new employees need clear and practical guidance.

(A) Whatever   (B) Whoever
(C) Whose   (D) Anyone

정답·해석·해설 p.160

3. 부사절 접속사 문장 안에서 시간이나 조건 등을 나타내는 부사 역할을 하는 부사절을 이끈다.

기출 공식 9 자주 출제되는 시간을 나타내는 부사절 접속사 출제율 ↑

when ~할 때
as ~할 때, ~함에 따라
while ~하는 동안

before ~하기 전에
after ~한 이후에
since ~한 이후로

until ~할 때까지
by the time ~할 때 쯤이면, ~할 때까지
even as 마침 ~할 때

once ~한 후에, ~하자마자
as soon as ~하자마자

No photography is permitted **after** the show begins. 공연이 시작한 이후에 사진 촬영이 허용되지 않는다.

고득점 포인트 시간을 나타내는 부사절 접속사 다음에는 미래를 나타내기 위해서 현재 시제를 쓴다.
The manufacturing process will not finish until quality control (**will approve**, **approves**) the products.
품질 관리팀이 제품을 승인할 때까지 제조 과정은 끝나지 않을 것이다.

기출 공식 10 자주 출제되는 조건을 나타내는 부사절 접속사

if 만약 ~이라면
in case (that), in the event (that) ~에 대비하여, ~의 경우
as long as, providing (that), provided (that), on (the) condition that, only if 오직 ~하는 경우에만

assuming (that) 만약 ~이라면

unless (= if ~ not) 만약 ~이 아니라면

Students can't graduate **unless** they complete all required courses. 만약 학생들이 필수 과정을 모두 이수하지 않는다면 그들은 졸업할 수 없다.

고득점 포인트 조건을 나타내는 부사절 접속사 다음에는 미래를 나타내기 위해서 현재 시제를 쓴다.
If the system (**will fail**, **fails**), the backup generator will be activated. 만약 시스템 장애가 발생하면, 예비 발전기가 작동될 것이다.

기출 공식 11 자주 출제되는 양보를 나타내는 부사절 접속사

although, though, even though 비록 ~이지만
even if 비록 ~일지라도

whereas, while ~한 반면에

Some prefer visual learning methods, **while** others learn better through hands-on experience.
일부는 시각적 학습 방법을 선호하는 반면에, 다른 사람들은 실습 경험을 통해 더 잘 배운다.

토익실전문제 토익 문제 이렇게 나온다!

01 Pure Origins is planning to release new premium thermal turtlenecks ------- winter arrives.

(A) during (B) before
(C) whereas (D) even though

02 The subscription can no longer be refunded ------- it is activated and the initial 24-hour trial period has elapsed.

(A) yet (B) unless
(C) which (D) once

03 ------- you order the cleaning supplies before noon, they will be delivered the next business day.

(A) If (B) In order to
(C) Then (D) As well as

04 ★최빈출 ------- the developers tried new methods and conducted extensive testing procedures, the results showed minimal improvement.

(A) Unless (B) Although
(C) So that (D) Since

정답·해석·해설 p.160

기출 공식 12 자주 출제되는 다양한 부사절 접속사

이유	because, as, since ~이기 때문에	now that ~이므로	in that ~라는 점에서
목적 및 결과	so that, in order that ~할 수 있도록	so/such ~ that - 매우 ~해서 -하다	
기타	except that, but that ~을 제외하고는	as if, as though 마치 ~처럼	given that, considering (that) ~을 고려했을 때, ~을 고려하여

The construction was postponed **because** the material costs were too expensive.
자재비가 너무 비쌌기 때문에 공사가 연기되었다.

Ricky's Pasta expanded its kitchen **in order that** chefs could handle more orders.
Ricky's Pasta는 주방장들이 더 많은 주문을 처리할 수 있도록 주방을 확장했다.

기출 공식 13 자주 출제되는 복합관계부사

복합관계부사	장소·시간·방법의 부사절	양보의 부사절
wherever	~하는 어디든지 (= at any place where)	어디로/어디에서 ~하더라도 (= no matter where)
whenever	~하는 언제든지 (= at any time when)	언제 ~하더라도 (= no matter when)
however	어떻게 ~할지라도 (= by whatever means)	아무리 ~하더라도 (= no matter how) *이때 however 뒤에는 형용사나 부사가 온다.

Quality control inspectors intervene **wherever**(= **at any place where**) there is a problem with production standards.
품질 관리 검사관은 생산 기준에 문제가 있는 어디든지 개입한다.

Wherever(= **No matter where**) tourists venture, they must respect the local customs and traditions.
관광객들은 어디로 가더라도, 현지 관습과 전통을 존중해야 한다.

However(= **No matter how**) difficult the negotiations get, both parties should remain respectful at all times.
협상이 아무리 어려워지더라도, 양측은 항상 공손함을 유지해야 한다.

고득점 포인트 복합관계대명사도 부사절 접속사로 쓰일 수 있다.

whoever 누가 ~하더라도 (= no matter who)
whatever 무엇이/무엇을 ~하더라도 (= no matter what)
whichever 어느 것이/어느 것을 ~하더라도 (= no matter which)

Whoever(= **No matter who**) provides medical care, patient confidentiality must be maintained.
누가 의료 서비스를 제공하더라도, 환자의 기밀은 유지되어야 한다.

토익실전문제

01 The new highway project is expected to impact downtown businesses ------ parking on Main Street will be limited.
(A) besides (B) though
(C) because (D) in order that

02 Please describe the system error issue in detail ------ our IT team can diagnose the problem.
(A) instead (B) whatever
(C) given that (D) so that

03 ------ the network enhancements across all regional offices have been done, teams will be able to work remotely.
(A) As if (B) In fact
(C) In case of (D) Now that

04 ------ students join the course, they have access to all previous content, making it possible for late enrollees to review past materials.
(A) Whoever (B) Whenever
(C) Regarding (D) Moreover

기출 공식 14 부사절 접속사는 절 앞에, 전치사는 구 앞에 온다.

부사절 접속사	전치사	부사절 접속사	전치사
while ~하는 동안	during ~ 동안	in case (that), in the event (that) ~에 대비하여, ~의 경우	in case of, in the event of ~의 경우에
by the time, until ~할 때까지	by, until ~까지	except that, but that ~을 제외하고는	except (for), but (for) ~을 제외하고는
as soon as ~하자마자	on(upon) -ing ~하자마자	given that ~을 고려했을 때	given ~을 고려했을 때
since ~한 이후로	since ~ 이후로	whether ~에 상관없이, ~이든 아니든	regardless of ~에 상관없이
unless 만약 ~이 아니라면	without ~이 없다면, ~없이	as if, as though 마치 ~처럼	like ~처럼
because, as, since ~이기 때문에	because of, due to ~ 때문에	so that - can ~, in order that - can ~ ~할 수 있도록	so as to + 동사원형, in order to + 동사원형 ~하기 위해서
although, even though 비록 ~이지만	despite, in spite of ~에도 불구하고		

The Crystal Palace Hotel offers complimentary spa access (**during**, **while**) the guests are staying.
Crystal Palace 호텔은 투숙객이 머무는 동안 무료 스파 이용권을 제공한다.

The maintenance team does not handle non-emergency repairs (**while**, **during**) evening hours.
유지보수 팀은 저녁 시간 동안 긴급하지 않은 수리를 처리하지 않는다.

토익실전문제

토익 문제 이렇게 나온다!

01 The city has prepared additional snow removal equipment ------- heavy snowfall is expected throughout December.
(A) because (B) because of
(C) instead of (D) except that

☆최빈출
02 The family restaurant continues to serve its traditional recipes ------- some changes to modern dietary trends.
(A) since (B) nevertheless
(C) in spite of (D) even though

03 Mr. Matthews arrived at the office an hour early ------- he could prepare for the board meeting.
(A) unless (B) according to
(C) in order to (D) in order that

04 Nexusphere's cloud service delivers consistent performance ------- users' geographic location, supporting global business operations.
(A) whether (B) due to
(C) regardless of (D) except that

정답·해석·해설 p.161

HACKERS TEST — DAY 06

01 Please turn off all electronic devices and refrain from talking ------- the show begins.

(A) when
(B) next
(C) where
(D) what

02 ------- demand for the new bag has been high, most retailers could soon run out of stock.

(A) Even if
(B) Unless
(C) Although
(D) Because

03 Survey respondents said they preferred listening to ------- audiobooks or podcasts on their way to work.

(A) either
(B) both
(C) every
(D) neither

04 The news reported ------- the city council finally approved plans for a new public park.

(A) those
(B) what
(C) that
(D) there

05 Refunds will not be issued ------ the product is returned in its original packaging.

(A) even
(B) therefore
(C) unless
(D) since

06 Eterna Motors decided to build a new factory ------- construction costs were soaring.

(A) such as
(B) notwithstanding
(C) as though
(D) even though

07 Branson Pictures is known for producing several low-budget ------- successful films.

(A) nor
(B) as
(C) but
(D) for

08 ------- Greg Larson pays for his unpaid charges, his phone service cannot be reconnected.

(A) Despite
(B) Until
(C) From
(D) Because

09 The audit will determine ------- the company complied with financial regulations in the past fiscal year.

(A) until
(B) whether
(C) even
(D) though

10 ------- Saffron Ember has moved to a larger location with an expanded kitchen, it can serve twice as many diners.

(A) In fact
(B) In case of
(C) Despite
(D) Now that

11 Ms. Piquet revised the presentation format ------- the complex data could be visualized more clearly.

(A) so that
(B) instead of
(C) as if
(D) in contrast

12 Due to the system upgrade, clients cannot access their online accounts ------- transaction histories.

(A) but
(B) or
(C) so
(D) both

13 The property manager must not enter residential units ------- written consent from tenants.

(A) about
(B) unless
(C) without
(D) against

14 ------- your payment is being processed, please do not refresh or close this browser window.

(A) Still
(B) During
(C) While
(D) Regarding

15 ------- some might regard security measures as unnecessary, they protect employees and company assets.

(A) After
(B) Because
(C) Except for
(D) Though

16 Not only the CEO but also board members ------- in annual shareholder meetings.

(A) participate
(B) participates
(C) participant
(D) participation

17 Train service between London and Manchester will resume ------- the damaged railway tracks are replaced.

(A) due to
(B) as soon as
(C) unless
(D) in order to

18 The firefighters are trying to figure out ------- caused the massive warehouse explosion last night.

(A) it
(B) that
(C) what
(D) where

19 Mr. Davis will consider both bathroom and balcony renovations ------- the budget allows it.

(A) in case of
(B) so as to
(C) up to
(D) only if

20 The downtown apartment was surprisingly inexpensive ------- its prime location near public transportation.

(A) while
(B) given that
(C) since
(D) considering

21 The store implemented a 20 percent price reduction, ------- more customers started shopping there.

(A) such as
(B) by
(C) so
(D) that

22 Union Apex Bank enhanced its verification process ------- its digital banking services could be accessed more securely.

(A) based on
(B) in order that
(C) as though
(D) according to

23 The electric company immediately sends out a repair crew ------- a major problem is reported.

(A) as if
(B) whereas
(C) during
(D) whenever

24 Customer feedback was positive about the product quality, ------- reviews were negative regarding the pricing.

(A) whereas
(B) unless
(C) likewise
(D) whatever

25 The culinary tour in Bangkok consists of local market visits -------- street food adventures.

(A) for example
(B) in case
(C) as well as
(D) thus

26 Lumeo Enterprises remained profitable ------- the fact that market conditions were challenging.

(A) although
(B) nevertheless
(C) in spite of
(D) as a result of

27 The firm has a backup server containing a duplicate set of records ------- the main server should ever fail.

(A) because of
(B) in the event that
(C) as long as
(D) now that

28 The textbook comes in digital and print versions, so learners can choose ------- format they like.

(A) both
(B) who
(C) however
(D) whichever

DAY 07 관계사

1. 관계대명사
접속사와 대명사 역할을 하여 관계대명사절을 이끌며, 관계절은 절 앞의 명사를 꾸미는 형용사 역할을 한다.

기출 공식 1 빈칸 앞의 선행사⁺와 빈칸 뒤에 오는 것을 보고 알맞은 관계대명사를 고르는 문제가 출제된다.

선행사 \ 빈칸 뒤에 오는 것	주어가 없는 불완전한 절	목적어가 없는 불완전한 절	선행사가 소유하는 명사
사람	who	who, whom	whose
사물·동물	which	which	whose
사람·사물·동물	that	that	–

The gym offers personalized workout programs for members (**which**, **who**) are new to exercise.
그 헬스장은 운동이 처음인 회원들을 위한 맞춤형 운동 프로그램을 제공한다.

The marketing strategy (**who**, **which**) the analysts recommended doubled customer engagement.
분석가들이 추천한 마케팅 전략은 고객 참여를 두 배로 늘렸다.

The author (**who**, **whose**) novels redefine modern romance is celebrating her 20th year in publishing.
소설이 현대 로맨스를 재정의하는 작가가 출판 20주년을 맞이한다.

고득점 포인트 전치사 뒤 목적격 관계대명사 자리에 who와 that은 올 수 없다.

Dr. Carlson is a senior lab technician with (**who**, **whom**) researchers can discuss experimental protocols.
Dr. Carlson은 연구원들이 실험 규약에 대해 함께 논의할 수 있는 선임 실험실 기사이다.

The software update about (**that**, **which**) the developers spoke yesterday will launch next month.
어제 개발자들이 이야기한 소프트웨어 업데이트는 다음 달에 시작할 것이다.

⁺선행사: 관계절의 꾸밈을 받는 명사이다.

기출 공식 2 수량 표현 + 관계대명사

one	all	some	several	much	half			
each	both	any	many	most	none	+ of +	whom / which / whose + 명사

Meridian Insights has 50 employees. + **Some of them** work remotely from different countries.
→ Meridian Insights has 50 employees, **and some of them** work remotely from different countries.
→ Meridian Insights has 50 employees, **some of whom** work remotely from different countries.
Meridian Insights사는 50명의 직원이 있는데, 그들 중 몇몇은 다른 나라에서 원격으로 일한다.

토익실전문제

토익 문제 이렇게 나온다!

☆최빈출

01 Ms. Sharma is the candidate ------- is best suited for leading the company's global expansion project.
(A) who   (B) which
(C) where   (D) whose

02 The century-old brick building ------- was damaged by a storm last year has been fully restored.
(A) them   (B) that
(C) what   (D) whoever

03 Marcus Stormfield, a rising artist ------- paintings explore deep human emotions, is gaining international recognition.
(A) that   (B) whom
(C) whose   (D) where

04 The Grotto Haven is known for its underground cave rooms, all of ------- maintain a naturally cool temperature throughout the year.
(A) whom   (B) which
(C) that   (D) their

정답·해석·해설 p.165

2. 관계부사 접속사와 부사 역할을 하여 관계부사절을 이끈다.

기출 공식 3 선행사의 종류에 따라 각각 다른 관계부사가 쓰인다.

선행사	관계부사
장소 (place, building, country 등)	where
시간 (time, day, year 등)	when
이유 (the reason)	why
방법 (the way)	how *the way와 how는 둘 중 하나만 써야 하며, the way 뒤에는 in which를 쓸 수 있다.

The lounge area **where** employees take their breaks includes a comfortable sofa.
직원들이 휴식을 취하는 라운지 공간에는 편한 소파가 있다.

Early spring is the time **when** many companies reassess their marketing strategies and budget allocations.
이른 봄은 많은 회사들이 그들의 마케팅 전략과 예산 배분을 재평가하는 시기이다.

Its innovative design was the reason **why** the building won multiple architecture awards.
혁신적인 디자인이 그 건물이 여러 건축상을 받은 이유였다.

The expert explained **the way** (**in which**) / **how** hackers breach secure networks.
전문가는 해커가 보안 네트워크를 어떻게 침해하는지 설명했다.

고득점 포인트 관계부사는 '전치사 + 관계대명사'로 바꿔 쓸 수 있다.
The lobby **where**(= **in which**) the guests check in is located on the third floor. 투숙객들이 체크인하는 로비는 3층에 위치해 있다.
June 1 is the day **when**(= **on which**) the construction officially starts. 6월 1일은 공사가 공식적으로 시작하는 날이다.

토익실전문제

01 Friday is the day ------- most shopping malls extend their opening hours for late-night shoppers.

(A) why (B) when
(C) what (D) whom

02 Ms. Roberts, a successful Broadway producer, renovated the old theater in the suburban town ------- she grew up.

(A) which (B) what
(C) when (D) where

03 A poor Internet connection was the reason ------- the virtual conference had technical difficulties.

(A) who (B) which
(C) why (D) how

04 The nutritionist suggested some ways ------- people can maintain healthy eating habits while traveling abroad.

(A) who (B) how
(C) what (D) in which

HACKERS TEST

DAY 07

토익 800+를 위한 실전 문제 정복

01 Willow Cove Resort offers special discounts to guests ------- stay longer than a week.

(A) who
(B) some
(C) when
(D) which

02 The conference room ------- executives hold their weekly meetings features state-of-the-art presentation technology.

(A) which
(B) where
(C) from
(D) in

03 The policy ------- management implemented last quarter has significantly improved overall workplace productivity.

(A) who
(B) what
(C) they
(D) that

04 Cloud Guard Elite is a software program ------- protects sensitive business information from cyber threats.

(A) whose
(B) which
(C) whoever
(D) something

05 September is the month ------- Sunnyvale Orchard harvests its signature organic apples.

(A) who
(B) why
(C) when
(D) which

06 Visitors ------- parking permit does not match their vehicle registration are advised to update their records.

(A) whom
(B) that
(C) which
(D) whose

07 Complimentary meal vouchers are available for volunteers who ------- the community service orientation.

(A) attend
(B) attending
(C) attends
(D) attendance

08 The government imposed new travel -------, which affected international flights immediately.

(A) restricts
(B) restricted
(C) restrictive
(D) restrictions

09 The workshop will demonstrate ------- strategic keywords can make your résumés stand out.

(A) how
(B) anything
(C) who
(D) whenever

10 The experiment will be led by two scientists, both of ------- have decades of experience in the field.

(A) them
(B) whom
(C) whose
(D) which

11 For working parents, having a daycare center ------- is close to their workplace is incredibly beneficial.

(A) who
(B) itself
(C) that
(D) them

12 Travelers can discover stunning architecture and historic sites ------- they explore the streets of Barcelona.

(A) as
(B) unless
(C) which
(D) during

13 Hincey Skincare's makeup remover wipes away cosmetics without causing irritation for ------- with sensitive skin.

(A) who
(B) that
(C) those
(D) whose

14 The walkway ------- the main terminal and the international gates stretches for nearly half a mile.

(A) connects
(B) connecting
(C) connection
(D) connectivity

15 The architect to ------- the award was given designed sustainable buildings across two continents.

(A) that (B) which
(C) what (D) whom

16 Developing strategic marketing campaigns is one of the critical tasks ------- which Ms. Lemoine is responsible.

(A) on (B) for
(C) from (D) because

17 The research showed the way ------- cultural differences shape consumer preferences and purchasing behaviors

(A) how (B) in that
(C) in which (D) whatever

18 Every package that ------- late automatically receives a 50 percent refund of shipping costs.

(A) delivers (B) delivering
(C) delivery (D) is delivered

19 Revone Clinic assists patients ------- need physical therapy with customized rehabilitation programs.

(A) all (B) who
(C) which (D) whoever

20 Mr. Kowalski is an ------- from apartment 4B who regularly helps maintain the community garden.

(A) occupy (B) occupant
(C) occupation (D) occupancy

21 Ms. Benson got offers from three investment companies, none of ------- were located near her residence.

(A) who (B) where
(C) that (D) which

22 Users of ReTouch Studio 2.0 are reporting an error that ------- occurs while processing large image files.

(A) frequent (B) frequents
(C) frequently (D) frequency

23 Managers ------- plan to implement new software systems should provide adequate training for their staff.

(A) some (B) who
(C) which (D) whose

24 The marketing director is sure ------- the company's new wireless earphone, WavePods, will attract younger consumers.

(A) of (B) that
(C) those (D) whom

25 The HR team will coordinate a training session during ------- new hires will learn about company policies.

(A) who (B) that
(C) which (D) through

26 The manufacturer recalled a number of cars ------- with faulty airbag sensors for immediate safety inspections.

(A) equips (B) equipment
(C) equipping (D) equipped

27 The company merged several departments ------- staff members had overlapping responsibilities and duties.

(A) whose (B) that
(C) what (D) whom

28 The concert hall ------- many opera singers perform is undergoing renovation to improve its acoustic system.

(A) when (B) whom
(C) whose (D) at which

DAY 08 최신 빈출 어휘

출제 경향 매회 10~11문제
최근 3개년 오답률 21.4%

아래는 PART 5에 정답으로 가장 자주 출제된 최신 어휘들이다. PART 5에 출제되는 더 많은 어휘는 VOCA(시험장에도 들고 가는 토익 기출 VOCA) DAY 11~16에서 다루고 있다.

기출 공식 1 최신 빈출 명사

access	접근	opportunity	기회
adjustment	조정, 적응	option	선택권, 선택
advancement	발전, 진보	organization	기구, 단체, 조직
budget	예산, 비용	package	소포, 상자
collaboration	협력	policy	정책
committee	위원회	portion	일부, 부분
cost	비용	position	위치, 일자리
deadline	기한	priority	우선 사항
decline	감소, 하락	promotion	홍보 (활동), 승진
dedication	헌신	proposal	제안(서), 제의
durability	내구성	registration	등록
enrollment	등록, 등록자 수	regulation	규정, 규제
expense	비용, 경비	renovation	보수(공사)
feedback	의견, 반응	restriction	제한
initiative	계획	source	출처, 근원
location	위치	spread	확산, 전파

기출 공식 2 최신 빈출 동사

acquire	얻다, 인수하다	install	설치하다
address	다루다, 연설하다	launch	출시하다, 개시하다
allow	허락하다	lease	대여하다, 임차하다
announce	발표하다	notice	주목하다, 의식하다
attend	참석하다	offer	제공하다
balance	균형을 맞추다, 가늠하다	operate	작동하다
commence	시작하다	perceive	~라고 여기다, 인지하다
consult	상담하다, 상의하다	postpone	연기하다, 미루다
demonstrate	보여주다, 시연하다	predict	예측하다
determine	결정하다, 확정하다	provide	제공하다
divide	나누다	recruit	모집하다, 채용하다
enlarge	확대하다, 확장하다	require	필요하다, 요구하다
ensure	보장하다	serve	일하다, (음식을) 제공하다
expand	확대되다, 확장되다	specify	명시하다
feature	특별히 포함하다, 특징으로 삼다	submit	제출하다
increase	증가하다	summarize	요약하다

기출 공식 3 최신 빈출 형용사

accurate	정확한	impressive	인상적인
adequate	충분한	lively	활발한, 활기 넘치는
available	이용할 수 있는, 가능한	mandatory	의무적인
brief	간단한, 짧은	obvious	분명한, 확실한, 명백한
compelling	설득력 있는, 강렬한	optimistic	낙관적인
complex	복잡한	original	원래의, 독창적인
confidential	기밀의	permanent	영구적인
convenient	편리한	popular	인기 있는
current	현재의, 통용되는	potential	잠재적인, 가능성이 있는
distinct	독특한, 별개의	primary	주된, 기본적인
effective	효과적인	rigorous	철저한, 엄격한
entire	전체의	substantial	상당한
exact	정확한	supplemental	보충의, 추가의
exceptional	우수한, 특출한	upcoming	다가오는, 곧 있을
extensive	광범위한, 대규모의	valid	유효한, 타당한
ideal	이상적인, 완벽한	various	여러 가지의, 다양한

기출 공식 4 최신 빈출 부사

accordingly	(상황에) 부응해서, 맞춰	heavily	(정도가) 심하게, 아주 많이
actively	적극적으로, 활발하게	immediately	즉시
approximately	거의	independently	독립적으로, 자주적으로
carefully	주의 깊게, 신중하게	mostly	대부분, 주로
clearly	또렷하게, 분명히	normally	보통, 정상적으로
completely	완전히	occasionally	가끔
considerably	상당히, 많이	perfectly	완벽하게, 완전히
correctly	똑바로	precisely	정확하게
currently	현재, 지금	promptly	즉시, 지체 없이
diligently	열심히, 부지런히	rapidly	급격하게, 빠르게
directly	직접, 곧장	significantly	상당히, 크게
elsewhere	다른 곳에서	specifically	명확하게, 분명히
entirely	완전히, 전적으로	temporarily	일시적으로
formerly	이전에, 예전에	thoroughly	철저히, 완전히
fortunately	다행스럽게도	unexpectedly	예기치 못하게
frequently	자주, 흔히	widely	널리, 대단히

HACKERS TEST — DAY 08

01 May 25 is the ------- for purchasing early-bird tickets to the summer music festival.

(A) attitude (B) comment
(C) deadline (D) description

02 Residents of the Hillside area consist ------- of students from the nearby Morgan College.

(A) namely (B) frequently
(C) publicly (D) mostly

03 Mr. Mattson began the presentation by passing out a ------- outline of his speech topic.

(A) constant (B) brief
(C) talented (D) potential

04 Car buyers have a vast array of ------- to choose from in the electric vehicle market.

(A) abilities (B) options
(C) incomes (D) exchanges

05 The research institute is currently ------- scientists specializing in biotechnology.

(A) rising (B) recruiting
(C) realizing (D) earning

06 Registration for the upcoming conference is now ------- on the official event Web site.

(A) available (B) capable
(C) decisive (D) comparable

07 Alpine Solutions' labor ------- are low thanks to its strategic outsourcing locations in Southeast Asia.

(A) costs (B) tickets
(C) schedules (D) inputs

08 Though the main actors performed their roles -------, the musicians were not good.

(A) equally (B) occasionally
(C) perfectly (D) simply

09 The instruction manual explains in several languages how to ------- the photocopier.

(A) print (B) operate
(C) reveal (D) overlook

10 The ------- of the old hotel were successful, and it now looks quite modern.

(A) locations (B) advantages
(C) renovations (D) productions

11 Primordial Technologies spent $50,000 in four months, which was half of its ------- advertising budget for the year.

(A) eager (B) entire
(C) reliant (D) adjacent

12 ------- considered the leader in computing innovation, Frye Systems has not had a new product in years.

(A) Necessarily (B) Formerly
(C) Eventually (D) Wisely

13 The sharp ------- in consumer spending has forced many retail stores to close nationwide.

(A) decline (B) merger
(C) replacement (D) commitment

14 The architect ------- the revised blueprints for the residential tower to the city planning department.

(A) taught (B) invented
(C) replaced (D) submitted

15 The special coupon is ------- only when shoppers spend more than $30 on their order.

(A) valid
(B) accurate
(C) efficient
(D) significant

16 Public health officials recommend wearing masks in public spaces in order to stop the ------- of the virus.

(A) break
(B) interior
(C) spread
(D) location

17 Customers who ------- a prompt reply to their problem can start an online chat with an AI assistant.

(A) constrain
(B) release
(C) provide
(D) require

18 The project's ------- goal is to lower manufacturing costs, although the board hopes to increase productivity as well.

(A) adverse
(B) primary
(C) fluent
(D) neutral

19 Veran Tech announced a new ------- in computer software that prevents hacking.

(A) destination
(B) advancement
(C) moderation
(D) qualification

20 All details about the new product have been ------- concealed to prevent information from leaking.

(A) lastly
(B) hopefully
(C) remotely
(D) thoroughly

21 The antibiotic created by BioPharmin has proven to be an ------- treatment for infectious diseases.

(A) assembled
(B) impartial
(C) effective
(D) intimate

22 Lumeva Apparel will ------- a business partnership with leading European fashion designers.

(A) announce
(B) issue
(C) consist
(D) reduce

23 Dr. Abalkin was requested to cite the ------- of the data in his recently published research paper.

(A) plan
(B) reply
(C) source
(D) trade

24 Medical professionals double-check each patient's record to make sure the diagnosis is -------.

(A) probable
(B) accurate
(C) remarkable
(D) fortunate

25 Since privacy is ------- guaranteed in modern digital platforms, users must proactively protect their own personal data.

(A) rarely
(B) widely
(C) readily
(D) publicly

26 Harvina Alliance is the ------- that transforms vacant city lots into productive community gardens and farms.

(A) adjustment
(B) organization
(C) leadership
(D) neighborhood

27 Additional soil testing will help ------- the most appropriate location for planting the endangered species.

(A) overcome
(B) deserve
(C) determine
(D) combine

28 Beemz Cable will ------- stop the service of any customer whose bill is overdue.

(A) instinctively
(B) positively
(C) mutually
(D) immediately

29 The government's military strategy is strictly ------- and will not be shared with unauthorized personnel.

(A) different
(B) frequent
(C) dominant
(D) confidential

30 Start-up founders should ------- solicit mentorship from experienced industry professionals.

(A) extremely
(B) lightly
(C) densely
(D) actively

31 The free coding workshop requires prompt ------- since only twelve seats are available.

(A) payment
(B) registration
(C) submission
(D) certification

32 To ------- outstanding quality, Royal Carat's every diamond is examined by certified gemologists.

(A) conclude
(B) arrange
(C) ensure
(D) foresee

33 In response to economic challenges, Aviara Air will make ------- changes to its operational cost management.

(A) chaotic
(B) inaccessible
(C) exclusive
(D) substantial

34 Home insurance may not cover ------- related to flood damage unless specifically added to the policy.

(A) expenses
(B) challenges
(C) displays
(D) reports

35 The event organizer raised the stage platform so that performers were ------- visible to the audience.

(A) tightly
(B) clearly
(C) eagerly
(D) commonly

36 Howell Corporation's decision to replace its CEO is ------- as a sign of positive change by many investors.

(A) charged
(B) determined
(C) perceived
(D) instructed

37 The sales team conducted personalized consultations with ------- customers to understand their specific requirements.

(A) paid
(B) secure
(C) potential
(D) profitable

38 The manager ------- approves all purchases, but exceptions can be made for items less than $50.

(A) relatively
(B) greatly
(C) normally
(D) patiently

39 Security personnel found the missing ------- in an abandoned storage room at the airport.

(A) worries
(B) packages
(C) locations
(D) responsibilities

40 The apartment ------- windows that stretch from floor to ceiling, offering breathtaking city views.

(A) features
(B) designs
(C) sounds
(D) establishes

41 The warehouse staff ------- counted the returned items to process refunds and update inventory records.

(A) politely
(B) carefully
(C) arguably
(D) spaciously

42 The board praised Ms. Russell's ------- to improving workplace safety standards in manufacturing facilities.

(A) adaptation
(B) distribution
(C) dedication
(D) deduction

43 Innovative product design contributed to Artisan Furnishings' ------- growth in recent years.

(A) involved
(B) favorite
(C) assembled
(D) impressive

44 Drivers should show their passport and international driving permit to ------- a rental car abroad.

(A) fulfill
(B) qualify
(C) lease
(D) place

45 The restaurant Ms. Alunga frequently goes to was ------- booked, forcing her to choose an alternative dining option.

(A) broadly
(B) completely
(C) kindly
(D) annually

46 At Sophus Industries, sustainable production is the top ------- across all our technological centers worldwide.

(A) honor
(B) priority
(C) revenue
(D) position

47 All new employees must take a ------- training program to understand the company's core ethical values.

(A) mandatory
(B) curious
(C) lacking
(D) strong

48 The prestigious university is ------- accepting applications for its upcoming summer research program.

(A) vividly
(B) recently
(C) currently
(D) exactly

49 Construction can ------- once the city council grants the final building permits.

(A) originate
(B) maximize
(C) acknowledge
(D) commence

50 Mr. Kumar developed a detailed ------- for integrating artificial intelligence into manufacturing processes.

(A) question
(B) proposal
(C) merger
(D) line

51 Modern agricultural practices can reduce water consumption ------- by utilizing underground water storage.

(A) richly
(B) adversely
(C) previously
(D) considerably

52 The expanded library is going to ------- abundant study spaces for the university students.

(A) provide
(B) propose
(C) reach
(D) accept

53 Proximity to local attractions and affordable pricing make Elysian Hotel an ------- accommodation for tourists.

(A) abstract
(B) indifferent
(C) ideal
(D) excessive

54 The finance committee allocates ------- of the budget to each department.

(A) objects
(B) salaries
(C) portions
(D) patterns

55 The newsletter is mailed to subscribers weekly, ------- recent trends in the media industry.

(A) admitting
(B) implementing
(C) relieving
(D) summarizing

56 The scholarship application system is so ------- that it needs to be simplified for students.

(A) complex
(B) successive
(C) considerate
(D) favorable

57 Seculen Digital's outdoor security cameras are designed with ------- in mind to withstand any weather conditions.

(A) durability
(B) enthusiasm
(C) freshness
(D) proximity

58 The volunteers worked ------- to provide essential resources to communities affected by natural disasters.

(A) completely
(B) extremely
(C) previously
(D) diligently

59 The board appointed Mr. Salman to ------- as a temporary director until a replacement is found.

(A) hire
(B) serve
(C) drive
(D) describe

60 Meadowfire Grill boasts ------- dishes prepared by chefs with decades of culinary experience.

(A) severe
(B) productive
(C) estimated
(D) exceptional

61 Noise pollution and a lack of affordable housing are some of the problems of ------- populated cities.

(A) solely
(B) evenly
(C) heavily
(D) nearly

62 In addition to providing the model number, customers requesting a refund must ------- the date of purchase.

(A) accept
(B) propose
(C) specify
(D) insist

63 It has become ------- that the business will improve its profitability by the end of the year.

(A) attractive
(B) honest
(C) obvious
(D) inclusive

64 Safety ------- must be followed by researchers conducting chemical experiments in the laboratory.

(A) ceremonies
(B) departments
(C) constructions
(D) regulations

65 Ms. Wright will ------- recurring customer complaints in the meeting with service team leaders.

(A) address
(B) respond
(C) function
(D) complete

66 The device comes with ------- instructions that explain advanced features not covered in the basic manual.

(A) eager
(B) supplemental
(C) promising
(D) temporary

67 The employee manual ------- describes the process for requesting an extended leave of absence.

(A) consequently
(B) immediately
(C) specifically
(D) accidentally

68 Local artists can take advantage of the art fair weekend as the ------- to sell more paintings.

(A) candidate
(B) preference
(C) impression
(D) opportunity

69 After months of negotiations, Alpha Core Systems has ------- Digency Networks for $975 million.

(A) divided
(B) acquired
(C) achieved
(D) reacted

70 Shipping companies have to send tracking information ------- to customers for transparent package monitoring.

(A) distinctly
(B) basically
(C) directly
(D) reasonably

71 After years of publishing print books, Inkspire Press plans to shift ------- to digital formats.

(A) entirely
(B) famously
(C) commonly
(D) internationally

72 Mr. Thorne convinced the committee to adopt his strategy by making a ------- argument about its potential advantages.

(A) fortunate
(B) compelling
(C) reputable
(D) talented

73 When giving presentations, researchers have to ------- a thorough understanding of the subject matter.

(A) arrange
(B) demonstrate
(C) initiate
(D) substitute

74 Job interviews should allow ------- time for candidates to fully express their qualifications and experiences.

(A) constant
(B) adequate
(C) receptive
(D) perpetual

75 Biblio Books started an online ------- in order to encourage sales of its newly launched e-book collection.

(A) contact
(B) information
(C) volume
(D) promotion

76 Freelance writers need strong skills to work ------- without immediate editorial supervision.

(A) shortly
(B) particularly
(C) certainly
(D) independently

77 The app developers are actively seeking user ------- before releasing the next update.

(A) feedback
(B) access
(C) conclusion
(D) quality

78 The rocket launch is scheduled ------- at 2:37 P.M., with mission controllers monitoring every second.

(A) infinitely
(B) hourly
(C) precisely
(D) absently

79 Art galleries often maintain ------- exhibitions of renowned artists to provide consistent access to famous works.

(A) complex
(B) succinct
(C) hesitant
(D) permanent

80 As the mayor of a tourist town, Mr. Venturi must ------- the needs of locals and those of visitors.

(A) balance
(B) waive
(C) overcome
(D) expose

81 Astralis Technologies developed a ------- cybersecurity solution that no other company could successfully imitate.

(A) chronic
(B) cautious
(C) distinct
(D) determined

82 The city's water conservation ------- aims to reduce residential water consumption by 30 percent within two years.

(A) permission
(B) alternative
(C) initiative
(D) allocation

83 Online banking services will shut down ------- due to critical system maintenance and security updates.

(A) greatly
(B) carelessly
(C) fairly
(D) temporarily

84 The city council favors ------- the business district so that entrepreneurs will be encouraged to start small businesses.

(A) enveloping
(B) enlarging
(C) relieving
(D) constraining

DAY 09 최신 빈출 어구

출제 경향 매회 0~1문제
최근 3개년 오답률 21.6%

아래는 PART 5에 정답으로 가장 자주 출제된 최신 어구들이며, 각 어구들의 형태를 정확하게 학습해 둔다.

기출 공식 1 최신 빈출 명사 어구

a range of	다양한	meeting agenda	회의 안건
a selection of	다양한, 엄선된	on an annual basis	해마다
a series of	일련의	press release	보도 자료
a study on	~에 대한 연구	quality standards	품질 규격
a tendency to	~하는 경향	regular duty	정규 업무
a variety of	여러 가지의	safety protocol	안전 규약
admission fee	입장료	sales figures	매출액
age requirement	나이 제한	sales projection	판매 전망
confidence in	~에 대한 신임	strong connection with	~과의 견고한 관계, ~과의 강한 관계성
contact information	연락처	supervisor position	관리직
expiration date	(식품의) 유효 기간	take a precaution	예방책을 마련하다
hiring process	채용 절차	to one's knowledge	~가 알고 있는 바로는
in its/their entirety	전부, 통째로	tourist destination	관광지
in recognition of	~을 인정하여	training session	교육 과정
in response to	~에 응하여	travel arrangement	여행 준비
job opening	공석, 채용 공고	vacation request	휴무 신청

기출 공식 2 최신 빈출 동사 어구

comply with	~을 지키다, ~에 순응하다	place an order	(물건 등을) 주문하다
concentrate on	~에 집중하다	put A back to B	A를 B에 다시 돌려놓다
conduct a survey	설문조사를 실시하다	reach an agreement	합의에 도달하다
enable A to B	A가 B를 할 수 있게 하다	recommend A to B	B에게 A를 추천하다
exceed a limit	허용치를 넘다	refer to	~을 참고하다
expect A to B	A가 B하도록 기대하다	refrain from	~하는 것을 삼가다
extend business hours	영업시간을 연장하다	replace A with B	A를 B로 교체하다
familiarize oneself with	~에 익숙해지다, ~을 숙지하다	specialize in	~을 전문으로 하다
fill prescriptions	처방약을 조제하다	submit A to B	B에 A를 제출하다
focus on	~에 초점을 맞추다	subscribe to	~을 구독하다
follow instructions	지시를 따르다	supply A to B	B에 A를 공급하다
hand A over	A를 넘기다	take A apart	A를 분해하다
lead to	~으로 이어지다	transfer A to B	A를 B로 옮기다
look for	~을 찾다	urge A to B	A가 B하도록 촉구하다
look into	~을 조사하다	use A up	A를 다 써버리다
negotiate a contract	계약을 협상하다	waive a fee	수수료를 면제하다

기출 공식 3 — 최신 빈출 형용사 어구

at full capacity	전면 가동 중인	be recognized as	~으로 인정되다
be accountable for	~에 대해 책임이 있다	be responsible for	~에 대한 책임이 있다
be aimed at	~을 목표로 삼다	be subject to	~의 대상이다
be aware of	~을 알다	budget flight	저가 항공편
be close to	~에 가깝다	commercial property	상업용 부동산
be dependent on	~에 의존하다	core value	핵심 가치
be eligible for/to do	~에 대한/할 자격이 있다	designated area	지정된 장소
be enthusiastic about	~에 열광하다	disposable umbrella	일회용 우산
be entitled to	~에 자격이 있다	extensive experience	폭넓은 경험
be exempt from	~이 면제되다	interpersonal skill	대인 관계 능력
be familiar with	~에 익숙하다	main entrance	정문
be famous for	~으로 유명하다	prestigious award	권위 있는 상
be impressed with	~에 감동받다, 감명받다	prior experience	사전 경험
be interested in	~에 관심이 있다	routine task	일상 업무
be likely to	~할 가능성이 크다	severe weather	험한 날씨
be pleased to	~해서 기쁘다	upward trend	상승추세, 오름세

기출 공식 4 — 최신 빈출 부사 어구

arrive punctually	시간에 맞춰 도착하다	officially open	공식적으로 문을 연
carefully review	주의 깊게 검토하다	partially covered	부분적으로 보장되는
commonly used	널리 사용되는, 관용의	periodically check	정기적으로 확인하다
consistently improve	지속적으로 향상하다	rapidly grow	급격하게 성장하다
conveniently located	편리한 위치에 있는	readily available	쉽게 구할 수 있는
cordially invite	정중하게 초대하다	take A seriously	A를 심각하게 생각하다
eagerly await	간절히 기다리다	shortly after	직후에
effective immediately	즉각 발효되는	significantly increase	상당히 증가하다
evenly requested	균등하게 요청되다	sincerely appreciate	진심으로 감사하다
fall sharply	급격하게 떨어지다	skillfully operate	능숙하게 조작하다
fully operational	완전히 가동하는	strictly prohibited	엄격히 금지된
highly qualified	충분히 자격을 갖춘	tentatively scheduled	잠정적으로 예정된
immediately after	직후에	thoroughly wash	철저히 세척하다
increasingly high	점점 더 높아지는	unanimously agree	만장일치로 동의하다
mutually acceptable	상호 수락할 수 있는	unusually high	대단히 높은
nearly all	거의 모든	work closely with	~와 긴밀히 협력하다

HACKERS TEST

DAY 09

01 ------- instructions carefully when operating heavy machinery to maintain workplace safety.

(A) Act (B) Chase
(C) Follow (D) Succeed

02 The economy of the island nation is mainly ------- on tourism.

(A) exclusive (B) dependent
(C) necessary (D) interested

03 Job applicants should make sure that their résumé contains accurate contact -------.

(A) delivery (B) information
(C) organization (D) emergency

04 During the economic recession, ------- all industries experienced substantial financial challenges.

(A) firmly (B) readily
(C) nearly (D) proudly

05 Students who wish to prepare for tomorrow's quiz should ------- to Chapter 9 of the textbook.

(A) refer (B) apply
(C) regard (D) assign

06 Those ------- in taking photography workshops don't necessarily need to bring professional cameras.

(A) skilled (B) concerned
(C) connected (D) interested

07 Corporate investors attentively analyzed the sales ------- to evaluate the company's growth potential.

(A) grounds (B) turnouts
(C) figures (D) viewpoints

08 The medical center is ------- located, providing easy access for patients from surrounding rural communities.

(A) collectively (B) conveniently
(C) cordially (D) considerably

09 Construction firms must ------- with regulations regarding worker safety and equipment standards.

(A) comply (B) mention
(C) suggest (D) compare

10 There is no minimum age ------- for virtual music lessons, so passionate learners can start at any time.

(A) desire (B) contribution
(C) impact (D) requirement

11 The flight was canceled because of ------- weather, so passengers waited six hours to depart.

(A) immense (B) striking
(C) nervous (D) severe

12 The loan officer has developed a strong ------- with the bank's regular clients.

(A) conversion (B) knowledge
(C) connection (D) agreement

13 Mr. Takahashi ------- his outdated smartphone with a newer model featuring a high-resolution screen.

(A) purchased (B) replaced
(C) questioned (D) publicized

14 The software can automate ------- tasks, allowing employees to focus on more complicated strategic planning.

(A) routine (B) tight
(C) neutral (D) genuine

15 Visitors should park their cars in the ------- area to avoid unnecessary parking fines.

(A) ongoing (B) designated
(C) objective (D) advanced

16 Historical buildings have a ------- to develop structural maintenance issues due to aging materials.

(A) trend (B) location
(C) tendency (D) movement

17 Fable & Leaf Bakery is ------- to announce partnerships with local organic farms for premium ingredient sourcing.

(A) successive (B) necessary
(C) attached (D) pleased

18 With rising environmental concerns, many organizations are ------- governments to implement stricter regulations.

(A) urging (B) reciting
(C) opting (D) addressing

19 The number of jobs fell ------- in the region after the major manufacturing plant closed last month.

(A) precisely (B) almost
(C) sharply (D) seldom

20 Orders should be ------- by 9 P.M. in order to guarantee delivery on the next business day.

(A) carried (B) placed
(C) estimated (D) distributed

21 To our manager's -------, all critical financial reports have been processed and submitted on time.

(A) ability (B) influence
(C) potential (D) knowledge

22 Participants must observe the rules of the contest at all times to remain ------- to win a prize.

(A) compatible (B) responsive
(C) eligible (D) privileged

23 As of March 10, our new Singapore branch located in the heart of the business district is ------- open.

(A) usually (B) officially
(C) extremely (D) accurately

24 Ms. Marino conducts comprehensive performance reviews for all department managers on an annual -------.

(A) basis (B) topic
(C) period (D) position

25 Readers who ------- to *Proseport* can gain access to exclusive interviews with contemporary authors.

(A) notify (B) receive
(C) describe (D) subscribe

26 To understand the complex legal document, the lawyer meticulously read the contract in its -------.

(A) pattern (B) supervision
(C) entirety (D) transparency

27 Bringing outside food is ------- prohibited in the museum's exhibition halls to prevent potential damage.

(A) strictly (B) severely
(C) closely (D) importantly

28 Visa applications from international students are ------- to review and thorough verification by immigration authorities.

(A) ideal (B) subject
(C) required (D) additional

실시간 토익시험 정답확인&해설강의

Hackers.co.kr

한 권으로 끝내는 해커스 토익 800+ LC+RC+VOCA

PART 6

DAY 10 문맥 파악 문제: 문법

DAY 11 문맥 파악 문제: 어휘

DAY 12 문맥 파악 문제: 문장

PART 6 소개   장문 빈칸 채우기 (16문제)

한 지문 내의 4개 빈칸에 알맞은 문법 사항, 어휘, 또는 문장을 4개의 보기 중에서 골라 채우는 파트이다. 16문제를 약 8분 내에 끝내야 PART 7에서 시간이 모자라지 않으므로, 각 문제를 25~30초 내에 풀어야 한다.

최신 예제 및 풀이 방법

Questions 131-134 refer to the following notice.

Attention Hotel Guests:

We recently completed renovations at our facility and are pleased to introduce the hotel's new features!

First, our swimming pool facilities ---131.--- and now include a new area for children. ---132.---. Furthermore, our reception desk was redecorated to have a tropical look. ---133.---, you can check out the artwork in our public areas and relax on the new sofas in the lobby.

When you're feeling hungry, try our newest restaurant located next to our reception desk! There you can have amazing ---134.--- along with a variety of beverages. The hours of operation are from 8 A.M. to 10 P.M., seven days a week.

---

131. (A) will be expanded
    (B) are expanding
    (C) have been expanded
    (D) to be expanded

132. (A) Keep such items out of the swimming areas.
    (B) You can request them from staff in the lobby.
    (C) The lessons were taught by a well-known instructor.
    (D) We also installed new changing rooms for your convenience.

133. (A) As a result
    (B) Best of all
    (C) To summarize
    (D) On the other hand

134. **(A) meals**
    (B) vacations
    (C) designs
    (D) gestures

Step 1   문제 유형 파악하기
보기를 먼저 보고 문법 문제, 어휘 문제, 문장 고르기 문제 중 어떤 유형의 문제인지 파악한다.

Step 2   빈칸 주변이나 문장의 구조 또는 문맥 파악하기
빈칸 주변이나 빈칸이 포함된 문장의 전체적인 구조 또는 문맥을 파악해서 정답을 고른다. 빈칸이 포함된 문장의 구조 및 문맥만으로 정답의 단서를 찾을 수 없는 경우, 앞뒤 문장이나 전체 지문의 문맥을 파악해서 정답을 골라야 한다.

최신 출제 경향

매회 총 4개의 지문이 출제되며, 16문제 중 문법 문제가 평균 7~8문제, 어휘 문제가 평균 4~5문제, 문장 고르기 문제가 4문제 출제된다. 문법 문제와 어휘 문제는 PART 5와 동일하게 출제되지만, 12문제 중 평균 6문제가 앞뒤 문장이나 전체 지문의 문맥 파악이 추가로 필요하다. 특히, 최근에 문맥 파악이 필요한 시제 문제와 접속부사 문제는 매회 최소 1문제씩 출제되고 있다.

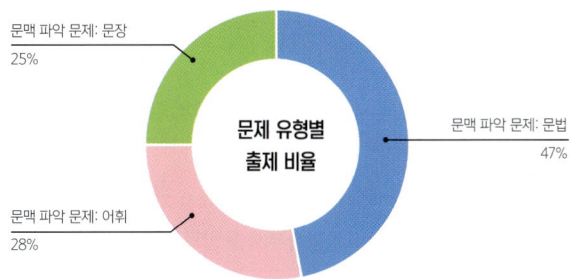

800+ 학습 전략

문맥 문제로만 출제되는 문법을 익힌다.
PART 6의 문법 문제 중 문맥 파악이 필요한 문제는 주로 시제, 대명사, 접속부사에서 출제되므로, 이들을 확실히 학습해 두면 문맥 문제 풀이가 쉬워진다. 특히, 최근에는 다양한 종류의 접속부사가 출제되고 있으므로, 최신 접속부사 리스트를 암기해 둔다.

자주 출제되는 어휘를 암기한다.
PART 6의 어휘 문제 중 문맥 파악이 필요한 문제는 어휘 자체의 난이도가 높지는 않으므로, 정답으로 자주 출제되는 어휘들을 알아 두면 실전 시험에서 더욱 빠르게 문제를 풀 수 있다.

문맥에 알맞은 문장을 고르는 방법을 익힌다.
빈칸 바로 앞뒤의 내용을 확인하는 전형적인 풀이 방법 외에도, 보기 안의 대명사 또는 연결어를 활용하여 문제를 풀이하는 방법을 익힌다. 특히, 난이도가 높은 문제에서는 앞뒤 문장과의 논리적 흐름이 자연스럽더라도 문장에서 지칭하는 대상이 앞뒤 문장과의 대상과 다른 오답이 출제되기도 하므로 주의한다.

문맥 파악 문제: 문법

출제 경향 매회 3~4문제
최근 3개년 오답률 20.8%

지문에서 빈칸이 있는 문장만으로는 알맞은 정답을 찾을 수 없으므로, 주변 또는 전체 문맥을 파악하여 알맞은 문법 사항을 고르는 문제이다.

출제 경향

문맥 파악이 필요한 문법 문제로는 주로 시제, 대명사, 접속부사가 출제된다.
▶ 시제와 대명사는 각각 PART 5 DAY 02(p.150)와 DAY 01(p.142)에서 자세히 다루고 있다.

800+ 공략

1. **시제 문제**: 빈칸 주변에 쓰인 동사의 시제를 확인하여 빈칸에 들어갈 동사의 시제를 예상한다. 만약 주변 문장에 날짜가 언급되어 있다면 지문 상단에 날짜가 언급되어 있는지도 함께 확인하여 시간의 흐름을 파악한다. PART 6에는 주로 미래 시제와 과거 시제가 정답으로 나오는 점을 알아 둔다.

2. **대명사 문제**: 빈칸이 가리키는 대상은 주로 빈칸 앞 문장에 있으므로 앞 문장의 명사들을 확인하여 가리키는 대상을 찾는다. 이때, 빈칸에서 가리키는 대상의 수와 인칭 등을 중점적으로 확인한다.

3. **접속부사 문제**: 빈칸이 있는 문장과 그 앞 문장의 의미 관계를 파악하여 내용을 자연스럽게 연결해 주는 접속부사를 고른다. PART 6에 정답으로 자주 출제되는 접속부사는 정해져 있으니 아래 접속부사를 반드시 알아 둔다.

역접	however 그러나 ☆최빈출 instead 대신에 ☆최빈출 on the other hand 반면에	regardless 그럼에도 불구하고 nevertheless 그럼에도 불구하고 nonetheless 그럼에도 불구하고	in contrast 그와 대조적으로 otherwise 그렇지 않으면 even so 그렇기는 하지만
인과	therefore 그러므로 ☆최빈출 thus 그러므로	accordingly 그러므로, 그에 따라 consequently 결과적으로	as a result 결과적으로 ☆최빈출 for that reason 그 이유로
예시	for example 예를 들어	for instance 예를 들어	
추가	in addition 게다가 ☆최빈출 besides 게다가, 뿐만 아니라	furthermore 더욱이 ☆최빈출 plus 또한	moreover 더욱이 additionally 게다가
기타	in particular 특히 namely 즉, 다시 말해 likewise 마찬가지로 similarly 비슷하게, 유사하게 in response 이에 대응하여 finally 마침내 alternatively 그 대신에 ☆최빈출 in this case 이 경우에는	at the same time 동시에 in short 간단히 말해서 above all 무엇보다도, 특히 to that end 그 목적을 위해 in the meantime 그동안 ☆최빈출 meanwhile 그동안 unfortunately 불행히도 ☆최빈출	in this way 이렇게 하면 in fact 실제로, 사실은 if so 만약 그렇다면 fortunately 다행히도 then 그러고 나서 in the end 결국 after all 결국에는

Example

Question 01 refers to the following e-mail.

Dear Mr. Winkle,

TG Metro would like to apologize for the inconvenience you experienced on March 14. We understand that even a short delay is enough to upset a busy schedule. Be assured that our goal is to make sure passengers always reach their destinations on time. Unfortunately, in this case, a tree branch ------- on one of our routes, causing the delay. We regret this incident, and we will work to improve passenger satisfaction.

01 (A) falls
(B) fell
(C) will fall
(D) has been falling

해설 올바른 시제의 동사 채우기 전체 문맥 파악 정답 (B)

문장에 주어(a tree branch)만 있고 동사가 없으므로 모든 보기가 정답의 후보이다. 빈칸이 있는 문장만으로 정답을 고를 수 없으므로 주변 문맥이나 전체 문맥을 파악한다. 앞부분에서 TG 지하철은 Mr. Winkle이 3월 14일에 겪었던 불편에 대해 사과하고 싶다고 했으므로 나뭇가지가 노선들 중 하나에 떨어져 문제가 발생한 시점이 과거임을 알 수 있다. 따라서 과거 시제 (B) fell이 정답이다.

토익실전문제

Questions 01-04 refer to the following memo.

TO: All staff
FROM: Olivia Cabral, Office Manager
SUBJECT: Photographer visit
DATE: August 26

As I informed you last week, a photographer ------- our office on August 30. He will bring professional equipment to ensure high-quality photos. All ------- should have their photos taken during this session. The photos taken on this day will replace the old ones in our online employee directory. They will also be used for press releases and other corporate materials as needed. -------, you are expected to wear formal business clothes for this occasion. You may have your picture taken anytime between 9 A.M. and 2 P.M. -------. It is expected to take less than 10 minutes per person.

시제 문제
01 (A) visit
(B) have visited
(C) will visit
(D) to visit

02 (A) neighbors
(B) clients
(C) employees
(D) applicants

전속부사 문제
03 (A) Therefore
(B) In contrast
(C) Regardless
(D) Similarly

04 (A) You can choose a day that suits your schedule.
(B) Another example is our employee identification badges.
(C) The photographer will not be available at that time.
(D) This will be done in the main conference room.

HACKERS TEST

Questions 01-04 refer to the following e-mail.

To: Dennis Craig <d.craig@quickmail.com>
From: Caroline Peel <c.peel@lbistro.com>
Date: February 21
Subject: Comment Card
Attachment: Voucher

Dear Mr. Craig,

I am writing in response to the comment card you ------- on February 19. I appreciate you taking the time to do this during your visit to our establishment. Although I am glad that you ------- your food, I regret that you found the service disappointing. Your meals should have been brought to you 20 minutes after you ordered -------.

-------. The next time you eat at Lochlane Bistro on a Friday night, there will be two more servers on duty.

To make up for your inconvenience, I have attached a voucher for $20 off your next dinner with us. We look forward to seeing you again.

Caroline Peel
Manager, Lochlane Bistro

01 (A) completed
(B) misplaced
(C) printed
(D) announced

02 (A) enjoy
(B) are enjoying
(C) enjoyed
(D) will enjoy

03 (A) either
(B) them
(C) it
(D) other

04 (A) Thanks to your feedback, we have adjusted our staff schedule.
(B) This is one of the reasons why reservations are required.
(C) We have a private dining room available for large parties.
(D) Our new branch will be just a couple of blocks away.

Questions 05-08 refer to the following article.

Hamlin International Airport Celebrates New Terminal

Hamlin International Airport has unveiled its second terminal ------- years of construction. The new terminal will open on May 2.
                                                               05

"The additional terminal has many amenities," stated airport spokesperson Kurt Vogel. -------. There
                                                                                        06
are dozens of comfortable sofas, and free drinks are provided.

-------, travelers arriving at one terminal and departing from the other may be inconvenienced due to
  07
the distance between the two. To address this issue, there will be a shuttle bus connecting the two terminals.

The new terminal is exclusively for SeaCrescent Air and Blue Fin Airlines. All other airlines will continue operating at the ------- terminal.
                              08

05 (A) beside
(B) since
(C) after
(D) into

06 (A) Maintenance problems have been reported in the terminal.
(B) Flight attendants have complained about the facilities.
(C) The cost of admission was discounted to mark the anniversary.
(D) Passengers will surely like the executive lounge.

07 (A) Once
(B) Consequently
(C) On the other hand
(D) Likewise

08 (A) original
(B) originate
(C) originally
(D) originality

Questions 09-12 refer to the following review.

STARLIGHT DREAM 2

We once called Campfire's original Starlight Dream "the best digital reader that money can buy." Many of you evidently agreed. Its large display, slim design, and long battery life made it highly -------09 upon release. The all-new Starlight Dream 2 goes further, but is it worth buying? Although cheaper overall than the initial -------10, the base unit still sells for 250 dollars. Let's look at the key features of the Starlight Dream 2. -------11. This new model is thinner and fits more comfortably in your hand. The slightly larger screen displays 30 percent more words. And the new -------12 exhibits a sturdy yet elegant aluminum body.

09 (A) popular
(B) predictable
(C) unavailable
(D) durable

10 (A) it
(B) that
(C) one
(D) all

11 (A) The previous model surpasses all others in every way.
(B) A premium version offers mobile Internet connectivity.
(C) There are a few subtle but important differences.
(D) Campfire is taking pre-orders ahead of the item's launch.

12 (A) device
(B) service
(C) order
(D) fund

Questions 13-16 refer to the following letter.

DOBRY YOGURT CO.
May 21

Amin Patel
CEO, Renowned Processed Foods
52 Sunder Lane
Mumbai, India 400070

Dear Mr. Patel,

Your company was selected as a candidate to be one of our future suppliers. We will now proceed with the -------. This assessment, which will be conducted by our designated contractor HDI International, is to ensure that your company meets our quality standards. -------. For now, I can only tell you that it will involve an evaluation of your production facility. The process will take two months. At the end, HDI ------- a report containing specific recommendations. We must confirm that you have complied with all recommendations before ------- you as a supplier. I can discuss this with you on my next visit to Mumbai.

Sincerely,

Stephanie Moravec
Regional Director for South Asia
Dobry Yogurt Co.

13 (A) registration
    (B) performance
    (C) invoice
    (D) inspection

14 (A) Exact details will be forthcoming.
    (B) The terms of our contract are clear.
    (C) I await further instructions from you.
    (D) Please describe the problem you are having.

15 (A) issued
    (B) will issue
    (C) had issued
    (D) would have issued

16 (A) approve
    (B) approved
    (C) approving
    (D) to approve

문맥 파악 문제: 어휘

출제 경향 매회 3~4문제
최근 3개년 오답률 21.6%

지문에서 빈칸이 있는 문장만으로는 알맞은 정답을 찾을 수 없으므로, 주변 또는 전체 문맥을 파악하여 알맞은 어휘를 고르는 문제이다.

출제 경향

문맥 파악이 필요한 어휘 문제로는 명사, 동사, 형용사, 부사가 출제되며, 특히 명사 어휘가 많이 출제된다.

800+ 공략

1. 주로 빈칸의 주변 문장에 단서가 되는 어휘나 표현이 포함되어 있으므로 빈칸 주변 문장을 반드시 확인한다.
2. 명사 어휘 문제에서 빈칸 앞에 정관사(the), 소유격(your, his/her, their 등), 지시대명사(this, those 등)가 있으면 가리키는 대상이 앞 문장에 언급되어 있으므로 빈칸 앞 문장을 먼저 확인한다.
3. 정답으로 자주 출제되는 어휘를 알아 둔다.

명사 어휘

appearance	등장, 외관	instrument	기구
business	사업체	item	물품
construction	공사	material	재료, 자료
conversation	대화	meal	식사
delivery	배달, 전달	patience	인내심
equipment	장비	property	건물, 부동산
goal	목표	space	자리, 공간

동사 어휘

acquire	얻다, 획득하다	choose	선택하다
approach	접근하다	discuss	논의하다
change	변경하다	expand	확장하다

형용사 어휘

extensive	광범위한	special	특별한
initial	처음의, 초기의	successful	성공적인
interactive	소통형의, 상호적인	updated	업데이트된

부사 어휘

also	또한	then	그때, 그다음에
as well	또한, 역시	there	그곳에(서)
soon	곧, 빨리	yet	아직

▶ PART 6에 출제되는 더 많은 어휘는 PART 5 DAY 08(p.188), 09(p.196)과 VOCA(시험장에도 들고 가는 토익 기출 VOCA) DAY 11~16에서 다루고 있다.

Example

Question 01 refers to the following e-mail.

Mr. Jurgens at the new branch called to say that the office equipment we ordered from Filepros arrived on October 9. He and the technicians are now busy installing the devices. Unfortunately, I have been notified that other ------- from Draper are experiencing shipping delays. The earliest the company can guarantee delivery is October 16, which will force us to delay the opening until October 20.

01 (A) items
   (B) people
   (C) proposals
   (D) images

해설 **명사 어휘 고르기** 주변 문맥 파악   정답 (A)

'Draper사의 다른 _____은 배송 지연을 겪고 있다는 사실을 통지받았다'라는 문맥이므로 모든 보기가 정답의 후보이다. 빈칸이 있는 문장만으로 정답을 고를 수 없으므로 주변 문맥이나 전체 문맥을 파악한다. 앞 문장에서 Filepros사에 주문한 사무 장비가 10월 9일에 도착했다고 했으므로 Draper사에서도 다른 물품들을 주문했지만 배송이 지연되고 있다는 것을 알 수 있다. 따라서 item(물품)의 복수형 (A) items가 정답이다. (B) people은 '사람', (C) proposals는 '제안', (D) images는 '이미지, 인상'이라는 의미이다.

토익실전문제

Questions 01-04 refer to the following announcement.

Gavin Hackett is coming to Waco!

The acclaimed entrepreneur Gavin Hackett ------- a talk at Waco's Evergrand Auditorium at 8 P.M. on Tuesday, September 13. In the first part of the talk, he will discuss the challenges he faced while building his profitable business. Next, Mr. Hackett will lead ------- sessions to share his entrepreneurial insights. By responding directly to participants' questions, he aims to create a dynamic learning environment.

Mr. Hackett's ------- here is part of a promotional tour for his upcoming book, *Rise to the Top*. He has authored several other titles over the past 20 years of his career.

An entry fee of $15 will be charged at the door. -------. Don't miss this exclusive opportunity!

01 (A) delivered
   (B) is delivered
   (C) will be delivering
   (D) has been delivered

02 (A) previous
   (B) interactive
   (C) identical
   (D) eventful

03 (A) acceptance
   (B) enrollment
   (C) appearance
   (D) donation

04 (A) Finally, Hackett's career will be recognized.
   (B) The winning entries will be announced after the event.
   (C) Visit whichever branch is most convenient for you.
   (D) The first 50 people to enter will receive a free book.

HACKERS TEST

Questions 01-04 refer to the following e-mail.

To: Amira Yaziri <amira72@goodtidings.tn>
From: Ernie Vollmer <e.vollmer@mahalsuites.com>
Date: December 9
Subject: Special arrangements

Dear Ms. Yaziri,

Firstly, thank you for ------- Mahal Suites for your stay in Jamesville. As you will be staying in one of our deluxe rooms, you are entitled to our free airport -------. Your reservation form indicates that your flight will be arriving at 1:26 A.M., but our shuttle runs only from 6 A.M. to 11 P.M. -------. We would be happy to contact a private pickup service for you. -------, the driver will meet you at your arrival gate.

Sincere regards,

Ernie Vollmer
Guest Services Agent
Mahal Suites

01 (A) acquiring
(B) choosing
(C) reviewing
(D) preparing

02 (A) access
(B) equipment
(C) entertainment
(D) transportation

03 (A) Do you need somewhere to park your car?
(B) The travel agency used to have an office in our lobby.
(C) So feel free to order room service at any time of the day.
(D) Therefore, we would like to offer you another option.

04 (A) Until then
(B) Elsewhere
(C) In this case
(D) Likewise

Questions 05-08 refer to the following article.

The travel agency Alexis Journeys recently announced that it would ------- its selection of tours. On August 1, Alexis Journeys will introduce trips to Colombia, El Salvador, and Mexico.

Alexis Journeys is known for its -------. Its new Mayan Discovery tour, for example, is only 1,050 dollars for one week, with all transportation and accommodations included. -------. Many customers noted that the tours exceeded their expectations.

"With our new packages, Alexis Journeys is attempting ------- travelers who have found trips to Latin America too expensive," said Marketing Director Hal Clive.

05 (A) combine
(B) expand
(C) move
(D) continue

06 (A) afford
(B) affordable
(C) affording
(D) affordability

07 (A) The tour schedule may change due to bad weather.
(B) It also has great reviews on all of its tour packages.
(C) This rumor has not yet been confirmed by the company.
(D) Guests may pay extra to take advantage of in-room Wi-Fi.

08 (A) target
(B) targeted
(C) will target
(D) to target

Questions 09-12 refer to the following advertisement.

Save Big at O'Toole's Gym!

Winter has arrived, but don't let that stop you from getting fit! O'Toole's Gym is offering special discounts that will last only for a month. So sign up ------- (09) at O'Toole's Gym to get up to 50 percent off the regular price. Customers ------- (10) register this month will be offered an additional 10 percent discount on all Pilates classes.

Our monthly and three-month passes are just $55 and $135, respectively, with the discount. In addition, you will receive even bigger discounts when you ------- (11) others.

All members will receive full access to our workout equipment. ------- (12). Fees must be paid for personal training and classes.

09 (A) regularly
(B) patiently
(C) immediately
(D) generally

10 (A) any
(B) which
(C) whose
(D) who

11 (A) invite
(B) invited
(C) will invite
(D) are invited

12 (A) Keep in mind that some services cost extra, though.
(B) Present the card to the front desk staff at any of our branches.
(C) You'd better act fast because we will be closing soon.
(D) Many people take advantage of these savings in the summer.

Questions 13-16 refer to the following information.

Important Registration Information

Ryder College requires payment of tuition by the first day of a semester. -------. Students may request a full refund for a course before it starts. ------- it has begun, they are eligible for an 80 percent refund if they withdraw within two weeks. After this, refunds are not available.

Course registration is generally done on a first-come, first-served basis. However, students in their senior year ------- those participating in special programs are given priority for upper-level courses. While we try to ensure there are ------- available for all interested students, this is not always possible. Therefore, students are encouraged to register early to secure a place.

13 (A) Instead, students can request financial aid.
   (B) A course calendar will be created.
   (C) Otherwise, a late fee will be applied.
   (D) Each semester lasts for four months.

14 (A) Once
   (B) Before
   (C) Until
   (D) So that

15 (A) despite
   (B) on behalf of
   (C) across from
   (D) along with

16 (A) books
   (B) spaces
   (C) supplies
   (D) funds

DAY 12 문맥 파악 문제: 문장

출제 경향 매회 4문제
최근 3개년 오답률 18.7%

지문에서 문맥상 빈칸에 들어갈 알맞은 문장을 고르는 문제이다.

출제 경향

1. 빈칸이 지문 처음에 제시되면 주로 지문의 주제나 목적을 나타내는 문장이 출제되며, 빈칸이 지문 중간이나 뒷부분에 제시되면 주로 빈칸 앞뒤 내용에 대한 요약, 강조, 첨가, 부연 설명, 이유, 결과와 관련된 문장이 출제된다.
2. 보기 안의 대명사나 연결어를 활용해서 풀이할 수 있는 문장도 종종 출제된다.
3. 지문의 주제에서 벗어나거나, 앞뒤 문장과의 논리적 흐름이 어색하거나, 문장에서 지칭하는 대상이 앞뒤 문장의 대상과 불일치하는 오답이 출제된다.

800+ 공략

1. 먼저 빈칸 바로 앞 문장과 뒤 문장을 확인해서 빈칸에 들어갈 내용을 예상하고, 주변 문맥만으로는 빈칸에 들어갈 내용을 예상하기 어려운 경우 지문의 주제나 목적을 확인한다.

| We have decided to hire Ms. Chen to join our team, as Nathan will soon be relocating to another city. <u>We assure you that the transition will be smooth.</u> Our goal is to maintain operational efficiency and minimize any potential disruption during this change. | Nathan이 곧 다른 도시로 이전할 것이기 때문에, 저희는 Ms. Chen을 저희 팀에 합류하도록 고용하기로 결정했습니다. 저희는 전환이 원활하게 진행될 것임을 장담합니다. 저희의 목표는 이 변화 동안 운영 효율성을 유지하고 어떠한 잠재적인 혼란도 최소화하는 것입니다. |

→ 앞 문장에서 Nathan이 다른 도시로 이전할 것이기 때문에 Ms. Chen을 고용할 것이라고 했고, 뒤 문장에서 우리의 목표는 이 변화 동안 운영 효율성을 유지하고 잠재적인 혼란을 최소화하는 것이라고 했다. 따라서, "저희는 전환이 원활하게 진행될 것임을 장담합니다."라는 내용이 들어가야 자연스럽다.

2. 보기 안에 대명사(it, them, these, that 등)가 있다면 빈칸 주변 문장에 언급된 명사와 일치하는지 확인한다.

| Could you please review this week's report while I'm away? Don't worry about the client e-mails that arrive today. <u>I'll reply to them when I return.</u> If anything requires immediate attention, please send a quick text message highlighting the key points. | 제가 자리를 비우는 동안 이번 주 보고서를 검토해 주실 수 있나요? 오늘 도착하는 고객 이메일에 대해서는 걱정하지 마세요. 제가 돌아오면 그것들에 답을 할 것입니다. 즉각적인 처리가 필요한 일이 있다면, 중요 포인트를 강조한 짧은 문자 메시지를 보내 주세요. |

→ 앞 문장의 client e-mails가 정답 문장의 인칭대명사 them이 가리키는 대상임을 알 수 있다. 따라서, "제가 돌아오면 그것들(client e-mails)에 답을 할 것입니다."라는 내용이 들어가야 자연스럽다.

3. 보기 안에 연결어(however, therefore, also 등)가 있다면 빈칸 앞뒤 문맥에 맞는 연결어인지 확인한다.

| GlideJet Airlines serves complimentary meals to its customers on all flights. <u>However, we will have to temporarily suspend the service.</u> This is due to ongoing supply chain issues and staff shortages. We anticipate resuming our full meal service within the next two to three months as our supply chain stabilizes. | GlideJet 항공사는 모든 항공편에서 고객들에게 무료 식사를 제공합니다. 그러나, 저희는 그 서비스를 일시적으로 중단해야 할 것입니다. 이는 지속적인 공급망 문제와 직원 부족 때문입니다. 저희는 공급망이 안정화됨에 따라 향후 2개월에서 3개월 이내에 전체 식사 서비스를 재개할 것으로 예상합니다. |

→ 앞 문장에서 GlideJet 항공사가 모든 비행에서 고객들에게 무료 식사를 제공한다고 했지만, 뒤 문장에서 공급망 문제와 직원 부족을 이유로 식사 서비스를 정상적으로 제공하기 어려운 상황임을 설명하고 있다. 따라서, 정답 문장에 접속부사 However가 쓰여 "그러나, 저희는 그 서비스를 일시적으로 중단해야 할 것입니다."라는 앞 문장과 대비되는 내용이 들어가야 자연스럽다.

Example

Question 01 refers to the following article.

Mr. Ward has received several distinguished awards for his contributions to the development of solar panel technology. ------. For these reasons, he was selected to be the new director of the Desmond Research Center. In a statement, Mr. Ward said, "I am truly honored to have been given the opportunity to lead such a prestigious institution."

01 (A) The company hopes to increase its share price.
   (B) He is also a well-respected figure in the field.
   (C) Other scientists question some of his findings.
   (D) His retirement announcement was expected.

해설 알맞은 문장 고르기   **정답** (B)

앞 문장 'Mr. Ward has received several distinguished awards for his contributions to the development of solar panel technology.'에서 Mr. Ward가 태양광 패널 기술 개발에 기여한 공로로 여러 권위 있는 상을 받았다고 했고, 뒤 문장 'For these reasons, he was selected to be the new director of the Desmond Research Center.'에서 이러한 이유로 그가 Desmond 연구소의 신임 소장으로 선출되었다고 했으므로, 빈칸에는 Mr. Ward 가 신임 소장으로 선출된 또 다른 이유와 관련된 내용이 들어가야 함을 알 수 있다. 따라서 (B)가 정답이다.

토익실전문제

Questions 01-04 refer to the following information.

Hong Kong Automotive Expo
How to receive your entrance pass

All ------ of this year's Hong Kong Automotive Expo must have a pass to enter the exhibition hall. Guests will receive their passes by mail during the last week of August. If yours has not arrived by August 31, please notify us. ------.
Regular registration for the event is now closed. ------, those who would like to register late will be required to pay a higher fee. In addition, their passes will not be mailed to them. These must be picked up at the venue's administration office ------ the start of the exposition.

01 (A) attendees
   (B) lecturers
   (C) reviewers
   (D) organizers

02 (A) We apologize for our late response to your inquiries.
   (B) A maximum of three guests can be brought along.
   (C) You can reach us by calling 555-2801.
   (D) We will then help you assemble your booth.

03 (A) Specifically
   (B) At that time
   (C) Overall
   (D) Accordingly

04 (A) about
   (B) between
   (C) without
   (D) before

HACKERS TEST

Questions 01-04 refer to the following letter.

November 19

Theodore Arum
99 West Wooley Road
California 93035

Dear Mr. Arum,

Thank you for visiting Silver Shore Community Center earlier this month to give a talk on 20th-century inventions. I especially appreciate that you went into a more detailed ------- compared to last time. Audience members actively contributed their perspectives, and there were a lot of meaningful exchanges. This made the event particularly enjoyable for those who ------- your presentation the year before.

------- you agreed to give your time to Silver Shore Community Center on a voluntary basis, we would like to offer you compensation. I am sending you a $50 gift voucher for the coffee chain Better Beans as a token of our appreciation. -------.

Best regards,

Valery Miranda
Event Coordinator, Silver Shore Community Center
Enclosure: Better Beans gift voucher

01
(A) procedure
(B) statement
(C) discussion
(D) variation

02
(A) had attended
(B) attending
(C) are attending
(D) have attended

03
(A) Likewise
(B) As if
(C) Indeed
(D) Although

04
(A) Complete your registration over the phone.
(B) We hope you return again for another speech.
(C) Once again, I apologize for the problem with the microphone.
(D) Your article is appearing in this month's issue.

Questions 05-08 refer to the following notice.

Notice to Shareholders

Orbitall Inc. has changed the venue of its planned shareholder meeting. It will ------- at the Rudalle Hotel instead of the JadeLink Center.
                                                                                                        05

In addition, we have made another change to the attendance policy. -------. You will receive an attendance reservation form shortly. Please fill it out and return it by October 31. Once your name has been added to the guest list, we will send an e-mail ------- your registration.
                                                                                                        07

We remind you ------- it is also possible to vote through Orbitall Inc.'s Web site, www.orbitall.com/vote.
                08

---

05 (A) hold
(B) holds
(C) be holding
(D) be held

06 (A) However, the meeting will certainly happen next year.
(B) The board has appointed a new company director.
(C) The announcements are usually made at press conferences.
(D) It now specifies that advance registration is required.

07 (A) confirm
(B) confirmed
(C) confirming
(D) confirmation

08 (A) which
(B) what
(C) that
(D) such as

Questions 09-12 refer to the following announcement.

Demair International Is Becoming Greener

Demair International recently joined the Green Stay Network (GSN), a group of hotels and guesthouses that work to engage in ------- sustainable practices. To fulfill its obligations as a GSN member, Demair International places ------- brochures in every suite. These explain in simple terms how to conserve water and energy while staying at our hotel. In addition, Demair International now requires that all staff ------- a training video on sustainable practices in the accommodation industry. Bigger improvements are planned as well. -------.

09 (A) environmental
(B) environmentally
(C) environment
(D) environmentalist

10 (A) controversial
(B) complicated
(C) instructional
(D) entertaining

11 (A) watch
(B) watching
(C) watches
(D) to watch

12 (A) For example, solar panels will be installed in the near future.
(B) To sign up for a tour, talk to the staff at the front desk.
(C) It will be filmed at various locations later this week.
(D) Reward points can be redeemed for room upgrades.

Questions 13-16 refer to the following job posting.

STAFF REQUIRED

Job Code: Y51633

A design agency that consists of creative, highly ------- staff is seeking individuals to join its team in Bangkok. The open positions involve developing original packaging ideas for clients.

-------. However, they must have relevant experience and knowledge of design software. Those with professional certifications are preferred.

Please apply ------- sending an e-mail to staff@bkrecruit.com. Attach your résumé and enclose a link to an online portfolio.

IMPORTANT: Enter the job code for this posting in the subject line of your e-mail. -------, we will send you a notification to let you know that your application was received.

---

13 (A) competitive
  (B) extensive
  (C) alternate
  (D) natural

14 (A) Computer software has advanced to a high degree.
  (B) The ability to drive a vehicle is crucial to the job.
  (C) Applicants do not need a degree in the relevant field.
  (D) You have been invited to an online interview.

15 (A) to
  (B) for
  (C) by
  (D) in

16 (A) Instead
  (B) Then
  (C) Even so
  (D) Nevertheless

실시간 토익시험 정답확인&해설강의

Hackers.co.kr

한 권으로 끝내는 해커스 토익 800+ LC+RC+VOCA

PART 7

DAY 13	주제/목적 및 육하원칙 문제
DAY 14	Not/True 및 추론 문제
DAY 15	의도 파악, 문장 위치 찾기, 동의어 문제
DAY 16	이메일/편지 및 메시지 대화문
DAY 17	양식 및 광고
DAY 18	기사 및 안내문
DAY 19	공고 및 회람
DAY 20	다중 지문

PART 7 소개
지문 읽고 문제 풀기 (54문제)

제시된 지문과 관련된 질문들에 대해 4개의 보기 중에서 적절한 답을 고르는 파트이다. 한 문제를 1분 내에 풀어야 모든 문제를 주어진 시간 내에 풀 수 있다.

최신 예제 및 풀이 방법

Questions 147-148 refer to the following e-mail.

To: Jonas Bianchi <jbianchi@adomosuits.com>
From: Valeria Lugo <vallugo@vsells.com>
Subject: Greetings
Date: August 10

Dear Mr. Bianchi,

I am a longtime follower of your company, and I really admire how you have built your brand into what it is today. I am an entrepreneur who hopes to be able to do the same one day, so I was wondering if you are able to point me in the right direction. If you are willing to visit the blog I use to market my products and let me know what you think of it, I would be very grateful. The address is www.icglyblog.com/V_sells.

Also, I was wondering if you ever purchased advertising space on social media Web sites to grow your customer base, and whether you found it effective. I'd be grateful if you could share any insights or suggestions.

Thank you so much for your time, and I hope to hear from you soon.

Valeria Lugo
Owner, V Sells

---

147. What is the purpose of the e-mail?
    (A) To inquire about a post on a blog
    (B) To seek feedback on a Web page
    (C) To apply for a position at a corporation
    (D) To express admiration for a product

148. What most likely is Ms. Lugo considering?
    (A) Launching a new Web site
    (B) Hiring a marketing assistant
    (C) Promoting goods online
    (D) Offering membership discounts

Step 1 지문의 내용 추측하기
지문의 종류나 글의 제목을 확인하여 지문이 어떤 내용을 담고 있을지 추측한다.

Step 2 질문의 핵심 어구와 관련된 정답의 단서 찾기
질문을 읽고 질문의 핵심 어구를 파악한 후, 지문에서 핵심 어구와 관련된 내용이 언급된 부분을 찾아 정답의 단서를 확인한다. 이중 지문이나 삼중 지문과 같은 연계 지문의 경우, 처음 확인한 단서만으로 정답을 선택할 수 없으면, 첫 번째 단서와 관련된 두 번째 단서를 다른 지문에서 찾는다.

Step 3 패러프레이징된 정답 고르기
정답의 단서가 패러프레이징된 보기를 골라야 하며, 정답의 단서를 그대로 언급한 정답도 종종 출제된다. 이중 지문이나 삼중 지문과 같은 연계 지문의 경우, 두 개의 지문에 언급된 각각의 단서를 종합하여 정답을 선택한다.

최신 출제 경향

매회 54문제가 출제되며, 단일 지문에서 29문제, 이중 지문에서 10문제, 삼중 지문에서 15문제가 출제된다. 비교적 빠르게 풀이할 수 있는 육하원칙 문제가 가장 높은 비율로 출제되지만, 풀이 시간이 오래 걸리는 Not/True 문제와 추론 문제가 그다음으로 많이 출제되므로 시간 분배를 잘 해야 한다. 지문은 이메일/편지가 가장 높은 비율로 출제되며, 특히 비즈니스와 관련된 내용이 최근까지도 가장 많이 출제되고 있다.

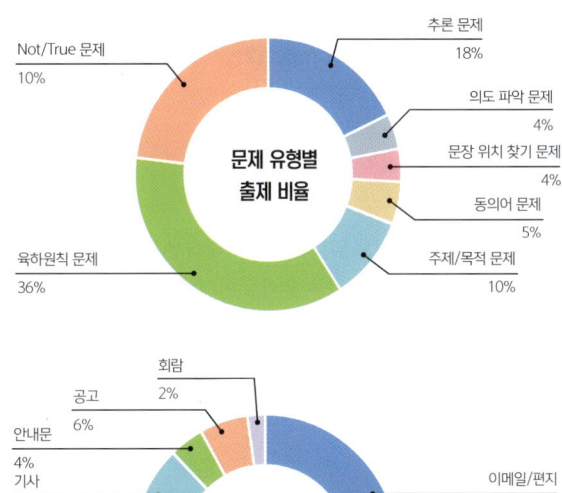

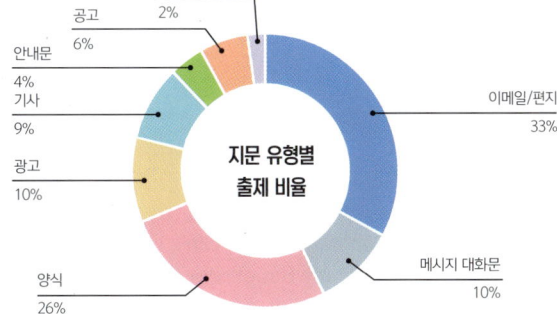

800+ 학습 전략

문제 유형별 풀이 공략을 익힌다.
　PART 7에 출제되는 문제들의 각 유형별 풀이 공략을 익혀 두면 실전 시험에서 문제 풀이를 하는 것이 쉬워진다. 예를 들어, 육하원칙 문제의 경우 질문에서 의문사와 핵심 어구를 확인하고 지문에서 핵심 어구와 관련된 정답의 단서를 빠르게 찾는 연습을 하면 시간을 많이 단축할 수 있다.

지문 유형별로 자주 등장하는 표현을 암기한다.
　PART 7에 지문 유형별로 자주 등장하는 표현을 암기해 두면 지문을 막힘없이 읽어 내용을 더욱 빠르게 파악할 수 있다. 특히, 기사와 같은 지문에서는 수준 높은 어휘가 많이 등장하므로, 이를 암기해 두면 실전 시험에서 당황하지 않고 문제를 정확하게 풀 수 있다.

주제/목적 및 육하원칙 문제

기출 유형 1 주제/목적 문제
최근 3개년 오답률 17.7%

글의 주제나 글을 쓴 목적이 무엇인지 묻는 문제로, 매회 5~6문제 출제된다.

출제 경향
1. 한 지문에 해당되는 문제들 중 첫 번째 문제로 출제된다.
2. 질문에 mainly about, main purpose, why ~ write 등을 사용하여 묻는다.

글의 주제	**What** is the article (**mainly**) **about**?	기사는 (주로) 무엇에 대한 것인가?
	What does the notice **mainly discuss**?	공고가 주로 논의하는 내용은 무엇인가?
글의 목적	**What** is the (**main**) **purpose** of the information?	안내문의 (주된) 목적은 무엇인가?
글을 쓴 이유	**Why** did Mr. Griffin **write** to Ms. Thompson?	Mr. Griffin은 왜 Ms. Thompson에게 글을 썼는가?
	Why was the letter **written**?	편지는 왜 쓰였는가?

800+ 공략
1. 글의 주제나 글을 쓴 목적은 주로 지문 초반에 언급되므로 앞부분을 주의해서 읽는다.
2. 주제가 글의 중후반에 있거나 글 전체에 흩어져 있는 경우, 다른 문제를 먼저 풀면서 지문의 전반적인 내용을 확인한 다음에 주제를 파악한다.
3. but(하지만), however(그러나), nevertheless(그럼에도 불구하고)와 같이 글의 내용이 반전이 되는 표현 뒤에 주제나 목적이 나오는 경우도 많다.

Example
해석 p.188

Question 01 refers to the following announcement.

> To Our Valued Patients:
> We regret to inform you that from January 15 to February 21, our clinic will be closed as we make the transition from our current space in Slate Tower to 6124 Gramercy Street. We apologize for any inconvenience this may cause. If you have an appointment booked during this period, a representative from the clinic will contact you to reschedule it. Thank you for your patience and understanding.

01 What is the purpose of the announcement?
(A) To explain a change in business ownership
(B) To announce a building renovation
(C) To introduce a service update
(D) To provide notice of a temporary closure

해설 목적 문제   정답 (D)

지문의 'We regret to inform you that from January 15 to February 21, our clinic will be closed as we make the transition from our current space ~ to 6124 Gramercy Street.'에서 병원이 현재의 장소에서 Gramercy가 6124번지로 이전함에 따라 1월 15일부터 2월 21일까지 문을 닫을 것이라고 했으므로 (D)가 정답이다.

목적 문제에 자주 나오는 필수 표현

목적 문제에는 정답에 자주 나오는 표현이 있으며, 아래는 해당 표현 및 정답의 단서가 패러프레이징된 예시이다.

자주 나오는 표현	정답의 단서	질문 및 정답
inform 알리다	Employees will now be allowed to work remotely up to three days per week. 직원들은 이제 최대 주 3일까지 재택근무를 할 수 있을 것입니다.	질문 What is the main purpose of the notice? 공지의 주된 목적은 무엇인가? 정답 To **inform** employees about changes to a work policy 직원들에게 근무 정책의 변경에 대해 알리기 위해
promote 홍보하다	Our recently launched AI-powered financial assistant helps you manage your finances with smart budgeting and automated spending analysis. 저희의 최근 출시된 AI 기반 금융 도우미는 스마트한 예산 관리와 자동화된 지출 분석 기능을 통해 재정을 관리하는 것을 돕습니다.	질문 What is the purpose of the Web page? 웹페이지의 목적은 무엇인가? 정답 To **promote** a new financial service 새로운 금융 서비스를 홍보하기 위해
request 요청하다	Our team needs the latest data for the project status meeting, so please send the report by tomorrow. 저희 팀은 프로젝트 진행 상황 관련 회의를 위해 최신 데이터가 필요하므로, 내일까지 보고서를 보내 주시기 바랍니다.	질문 Why did Ms. Chen write to Mr. Roberts? Ms. Chen은 왜 Mr. Roberts에게 글을 썼는가? 정답 To **request** a necessary document 필요한 문서를 요청하기 위해

토익실전문제

Questions 01-03 refer to the following information.

The City of Rochester is introducing the Corliss Gardens mobile application. Now, visitors can get convenient access to information about Corliss Gardens from any mobile device. Use it to explore the park's facilities, to plan a visit, or simply to obtain news on events and activities at Corliss Gardens.

Aside from having access to a detailed map of the park grounds, users can get directions to the nearest available parking spaces, receive notifications on the latest weather forecast, and even book any of the park's four event venues for a private function. Users who sign up on the application also become instantly eligible to receive special offers from local businesses.

For more information about Corliss Gardens, visit the City of Rochester's official Web site and click the "Municipal Parks" button.

01 What is the information mainly about?

(A) A new software program
(B) A change to a facility's policy
(C) Local business promotions
(D) Updates on park safety

02 How can people qualify for special offers?

(A) By completing a survey
(B) By visiting local businesses
(C) By registering on an application
(D) By making a donation

03 What can be concluded about Corliss Gardens?

(A) It recently expanded a parking area.
(B) It was chosen as the site for a trade event.
(C) It charges visitors an admission fee.
(D) It is managed by a city government.

정답·해석·해설 p.188

기출 유형 2   육하원칙 문제

최근 3개년 오답률 19.5%

무엇이, 언제, 왜, 어떻게 등과 관련된 글의 세부 내용을 묻는 문제로, 매회 20~21문제 출제된다.

출제 경향

1. 각 질문에는 질문에서 주요하게 묻는 대상인 핵심 어구가 존재하며, 주로 날짜나 고유명사를 포함한 어구로 이루어져 있다.
2. 질문에 What, When, Where, Why, Who, How 등의 의문사를 사용하여 묻는다.

무엇	**What** will happen on August 14?	8월 14일에 무슨 일이 일어날 것인가?
언제	**When** is the deadline for registration?	등록 마감 기한은 언제인가?
어디(에)서	**Where** will the new branch be located?	새로운 지사는 어디에 위치할 것인가?
왜	**Why** is the company relocating to New York?	회사는 왜 뉴욕으로 이전하는가?
누가	**Who** will receive the scholarship?	누가 장학금을 받을 것인가?
어떻게	**How** can people cancel their subscription?	사람들은 그들의 구독권을 어떻게 해지할 수 있는가?

800+ 공략

1. 질문에서 의문사와 핵심 어구를 확인한 뒤, 지문에서 핵심 어구가 언급된 곳을 찾아 주변 내용을 집중해서 읽는다. 이때, 핵심 어구가 지문 안에서 패러프레이징된 경우도 있으므로 주의한다.
2. 지문의 일부만 보고도 답을 빠르게 찾을 수 있기 때문에 풀이 시간을 절약할 수 있으며, 절약한 시간을 다른 문제 유형 풀이에 더 많이 쓰도록 한다.

Example

해석 p.188

Question 01 refers to the following article.

> Although the South African Art Festival was held in Johannesburg during previous years, the organizers have decided to make Cape Town the festival's new permanent site because it is more popular with tourists. "Being located along the coast means it attracts a large number of visitors each year, particularly during the summer," said organizer Joma Nkosi. As a result, attendance at the festival is expected to rise at its new Cape Town venue. Overseas visitors who have already made flight and hotel arrangements for the coming festival are advised to modify their reservations. Information about partner accommodations can be found at www.saaf.com.

01 What are some festivalgoers asked to do?
    (A) Make changes to a booking
    (B) Contact the festival's organizers
    (C) Call an event venue
    (D) Book a flight to Johannesburg

해설 육하원칙 문제   정답 (A)
지문의 'Overseas visitors who have already made flight and hotel arrangements for the coming festival are advised to modify their reservations.'에서 다가오는 축제를 위해 이미 항공편과 숙소를 마련한 해외 방문객들에게는 예약을 변경하도록 권고된다고 했으므로 (A)가 정답이다.

의문사별 빈출 핵심 어구

다음은 육하원칙 문제에 자주 출제되는 의문사별 핵심 어구이다.

What	[요청 사항] What are the guests **asked to do**? 손님들은 무엇을 하도록 요청받는가?
	[제품 특징] What are **the features of the new product**? 신제품의 특징은 무엇인가?
	[발생한 일] What **happened on May 3**? 5월 3일에 무슨 일이 일어났는가?
When	[회의 일정] When will **the meeting take place**? 회의는 언제 일어날 것인가?
	[마감 기한] When is **the deadline for applications**? 지원 마감일은 언제인가?
Where	[본사 위치] Where is **the headquarters located**? 본사는 어디에 위치해 있는가?
	[행사 장소] Where is **the event being held**? 행사는 어디에서 열리는가?
Why	[지연 원인] Why was **the flight delayed**? 비행편이 왜 지연되었는가?
Who	[담당 인물] Who is **in charge of budget allocation**? 누가 예산 분배를 담당하는가?
How	[할인 방법] How can customers **get discounts**? 고객들은 할인을 어떻게 받을 수 있는가?

토익실전문제

Questions 01-03 refer to the following e-mail.

To	Marcie Camden <mcamden@dawsoninc.com>
From	Christina Garcia <cgarcia@eshopping.com>
Date	November 10
Subject	Your order

Ms. Camden,

This is about the two Lucia Simonetti designer handbags you ordered from our Web site on November 8. Unfortunately, one of the handbags, Model #452, is currently out of stock. — [1] —. We placed an order with our supplier in Italy. — [2] —. The earliest we can expect the new item to arrive is two weeks from today.

We would like to know if you still wish to proceed with your order for Model #452. — [3] —. If not, we will issue a full refund for it and send the available item, Model #450, by overnight shipping at no extra cost. Or you can wait for Model #452 to arrive, and we will ship everything together. — [4] —. Kindly send us a reply e-mail to inform us of your decision. We apologize once more for the inconvenience.

Sincerely,
Christina Garcia
Sales representative
E-Shopping

01 Why did Ms. Garcia send the e-mail?

(A) To apologize for a billing error
(B) To promote a new handbag model
(C) To ask for a preference for an order
(D) To schedule a business trip

02 What does Ms. Garcia offer to provide at no additional charge?

(A) Expedited delivery of an item
(B) Repairs to a damaged product
(C) Help with handbag customization
(D) A replacement for an unavailable item

03 In which of the positions marked [1], [2], [3], and [4] does the following sentence best belong?

"However, they informed us there could be a delay due to a transport strike in Milan."

(A) [1]
(B) [2]
(C) [3]
(D) [4]

HACKERS TEST

DAY 13

Questions 01-02 refer to the following Web page.

---

www.canburyhospital.org/information

Canbury Hospital Intranet

Home >> Patient Management >> Dr. Michael Hatch >> Patient Information

Patient Name: Charlotte Reed
Phone Number: 555-4839

Medical History
Patient has experienced past symptoms of:

☐ chest pain	☑ stomach pain	☐ headaches
☑ earaches	☑ seasonal allergies	☑ skin irritation
☑ throat irritation	☐ back pain	☐ stress or anxiety

Appointment Details
Patient's next appointment with Dr. Hatch is scheduled for
Monday, April 22 at 11:30 A.M.

Click here to change the appointment time.

Notes
Dr. Hatch will be traveling to London to give a lecture on heart health from April 21 to 24, so Ms. Reed's checkup must be rescheduled.

---

01 What has Ms. Reed experienced in the past?

(A) Heart problems
(B) Back trouble
(C) Allergic reactions
(D) Work stress

02 Why does Ms. Reed's checkup have to be rescheduled?

(A) The hospital will be closing for a day.
(B) She did not submit her insurance details.
(C) Her physician is leaving on a trip.
(D) Some test results have not come in.

Questions 03-05 refer to the following e-mail.

TO	Evan Kensington <evkens44@nearmail.net>
FROM	Madison Gordon <m.gordon@fosteracademy.com>
SUBJECT	Business Writing Online Course
DATE	February 18

Dear Mr. Kensington,

Thank you for registering for the online business writing class with Foster Academy. This course will run for four weeks in total. Upon completion, you will know how to create important documents such as letters, reports, contracts, and more.

Before February 27—the first day of the class—there are a few tasks that you will need to complete. First and foremost, log on to your Foster Academy online account and click on "Assignments." You will see several reading assignments already listed at that link. Please be sure to look these over.

In addition, it's important that you download the TeachViewer software from www.fosteracademy.com/programs and check whether it works properly on your computer. Students will use the program to make posts on the class discussion forum.

Good luck as you get started, and please e-mail me with any questions or concerns.

Sincerely,

Madison Gordon, Instructor at Foster Academy

03 What is the main purpose of the e-mail?
(A) To prepare a student for a class
(B) To explain a registration process
(C) To request submission of some documents
(D) To provide a completion certificate

04 What is NOT mentioned about the business writing class?
(A) It will take place over several weeks.
(B) It will end with a graded writing assignment.
(C) It requires students to use an online account.
(D) It includes preliminary reading tasks.

05 Why must students download the specified software?
(A) To turn in assignments
(B) To track attendance
(C) To access course materials
(D) To interact with classmates

Not/True 및 추론 문제

기출 유형 1 Not/True 문제

최근 3개년 오답률 20.9%

4개의 보기 중 지문의 내용과 일치하지 않거나 일치하는 것을 고르는 문제로, 매회 12~13문제 출제된다.

출제 경향

1. 정답의 단서가 지문 전반에 걸쳐 등장한다.
2. 질문에 true, stated, mentioned, indicated 등을 사용하여 묻는다.

Not 문제	What is **NOT true** about Ridgeview Park? Ridgeview 공원에 대해 사실이 아닌 것은?
	What is **NOT stated/mentioned/indicated** in the article? 기사에서 언급되지 않은 것은?
True 문제	What is **indicated/true** about Ms. Romero? Ms. Romero에 대해 언급된/사실인 것은?
	What is **stated/mentioned/indicated** in the e-mail? 이메일에서 언급된 것은?

800+ 공략

1. Not 문제인지 True 문제인지 먼저 파악한 후 각 문제별로 필요한 정답의 단서를 찾는다. 지문의 내용과 일치하지 않거나 지문에 언급되지 않은 보기는 Not 문제의 정답, True 문제의 오답이다.
2. 질문에 핵심 어구가 있는 경우, 지문에서 핵심 어구와 관련된 정답의 단서를 찾은 후 보기의 내용과 대조한다.
3. 질문에 핵심 어구가 없는 경우, 각 보기의 핵심 어구를 먼저 확인한 후 지문 내용과 대조한다.

Example

해석 p.190

Question 01 refers to the following brochure.

> Our photographers specialize in capturing the magical moments of special occasions, such as weddings, anniversaries, and graduations. We are excited to announce a brand-new package:
>
> **Platinum Package ($2,000)**
> Two photographers will attend your event, and the pictures they take will be refined by a professional photo editor to ensure the best results. You will then be provided with digital copies of the final images. You may request up to 500 prints at no additional charge.

01 What is NOT mentioned about the Platinum Package?
   (A) Multiple photographers will be at an event.
   (B) Photographs will be edited by an expert.
   (C) A set number of free prints are available.
   (D) A custom photo album will be created.

해설 Not/True 문제　　　　　　　　　　　　　　　　　　　　　　　　　　　　　　　　정답 (D)

(D)는 지문에 언급되지 않은 내용이다. 따라서 (D)가 정답이다. (A)는 'Two photographers will attend your event'에서 두 명의 사진작가가 당신의 행사에 참석할 것이라고 했으므로 지문의 내용과 일치한다. (B)는 'the pictures ~ will be refined by a professional photo editor'에서 사진들은 전문 사진 편집자에 의해 보정될 것이라고 했으므로 지문의 내용과 일치한다. (C)는 'You may request up to 500 prints at no additional charge.'에서 추가 비용 없이 최대 500매의 인화본을 요청할 수 있다고 했으므로 지문의 내용과 일치한다.

빈출 패러프레이징

다음은 Not/True 문제에 자주 나오는 정답의 단서가 패러프레이징된 예시이다.

정답의 단서	질문 및 정답
Sam Wheeler and his colleagues are studying the effects of social media use on academic performance. Sam Wheeler와 그의 동료들은 소셜 미디어 사용이 학업 성적에 미치는 영향을 연구하고 있습니다.	**질문** What is indicated about Mr. Wheeler? Mr. Wheeler에 대해 언급된 것은? **정답** He is working on a project with associates. 동료들과 프로젝트를 진행하고 있다.
Westfield Public Library is open every day except Sundays. Members can borrow up to 10 books at a time for a period of two weeks. Overdue books incur a fine of $0.35 per day. Westfield 공립 도서관은 일요일을 제외하고 매일 운영합니다. 회원들은 한 번에 최대 10권까지 2주 동안 대출할 수 있습니다. 연체된 도서에는 하루당 0.35달러의 벌금이 부과됩니다.	**질문** What is NOT true about Westfield Public Library? Westfield 공립 도서관에 대해 사실이 아닌 것은? **정답** It operates all week long. 일주일 내내 운영한다. **오답** It charges a fee for late returns. 늦은 반납에 대해 연체료를 부과한다.

토익실전문제

Questions 01-03 refer to the following e-mail.

To: Lauren Bisson <laurenb@junomail.com>
From: Jaleela Attar <j_attar@geladatech.com>
Subject: RE: Questions
Date: February 8

Dear Ms. Bisson,

I understand that you may feel a bit nervous about starting work at Gelada Technologies, and I am glad that you want to be as prepared as possible. In response to your question about what to do once you get to our building, please stop at the front desk on the first floor. The staff there will assist you. Although your normal workday begins at 9:00 A.M., make sure to arrive at 8:00 A.M. on the first two days because you and some other new staff members will be participating in orientation sessions.

These sessions will cover your day-to-day responsibilities and the software applications you will be using. A laptop with these already installed will be issued to you. Please also note that lunch will be provided on both training days.

I hope this information addresses your questions. I'll see you next week.

Jaleela Attar
Human Resources Coordinator, Gelada Technologies

01 Why did Ms. Attar write the e-mail?
(A) To remind a trainee to submit some documents
(B) To reply to a question about a job interview
(C) To request feedback on an instructional workshop
(D) To prepare an employee for the first days of work

Not/True 문제
02 What is NOT true about the training session participants?
(A) They should come to a workplace early.
(B) They will learn about their daily duties.
(C) They should install a software program.
(D) They will be given an electronic device.

03 What is suggested about Gelada Technologies?
(A) It allows some employees to work from home.
(B) It updated the software used by workers.
(C) It will arrange two meals for some staff members.
(D) It recently relocated to a new office building.

기출 유형 2 추론 문제

최근 3개년 오답률 24.7%

지문에서 직접 언급되지 않은 사항을 지문의 내용을 바탕으로 추론하는 문제로, 매회 9~10문제 출제된다.

출제 경향

1. 글의 대상이나 글의 출처를 묻는 전체 정보 추론과 지문의 일부를 단서로 하여 특정 세부 사항을 추론하는 세부 정보 추론으로 나눌 수 있다.
2. 질문에 most likely, suggested, implied, indicated, probably, concluded 등을 사용하여 묻는다.

[전체 정보 추론]
글의 대상   **For whom** is the advertisement (**most likely**) intended? 광고는 누구를 대상으로 하는 (것 같은)가?
글의 출처   **Where** would this announcement **most likely** be found? 이 공고는 어디서 볼 수 있을 것 같은가?

[세부 정보 추론]
특정 세부 암시/추론   What is **suggested/implied/indicated** about the lecturer? 강사에 대해 암시/추론되는 것은?
                 What will **probably/most likely** take place on February 26? 2월 26일에 무슨 일이 일어날 것 같은가?
                 What can be **concluded** about Mr. Calloway? Mr. Calloway에 대해 결론지을 수 있는 것은?

800+ 공략

1. 전체 정보 추론 문제는 각 보기를 먼저 읽은 후 전반적인 지문의 내용을 파악해서 추론할 수 있는 정답을 고른다.
2. 세부 정보 추론 문제는 지문에서 질문의 핵심 어구와 관련된 정답의 단서를 찾은 후 추론할 수 있는 정답을 고른다.
3. 반드시 지문에 언급된 내용을 바탕으로 정답을 골라야 하며, 지문에서 언급되지 않은 일반 상식을 통해 추론할 수 있는 내용을 정답으로 고르지 않도록 주의한다.

Example

해석 p.191

Question 01 refers to the following notice.

> Be advised that Elevator 4, which is normally used as a service elevator to transport workers and equipment, will be unavailable from June 27 to 29 next week. Technicians will be performing routine maintenance. In the meantime, Elevator 3 will be used as a service elevator. Tenants' pass cards will not function in that elevator, so please use either Elevator 1 or 2.
>
> -Parker Residential Tower Management

01 For whom is the notice most likely intended?
   (A) Maintenance technicians
   (B) Security guards
   (C) Tour participants
   (D) Building residents

해설 추론 문제   정답 (D)

지문의 'Tenants' pass cards will not function in that elevator, so please use either Elevator 1 or 2.'에서 세입자들의 통행증은 그 승강기, 즉 3호 승강기에서 작동하지 않을 것이므로 1호 또는 2호 승강기 중 하나를 사용해 달라고 한 것을 통해, 이 공지가 건물 주민들을 대상으로 한다는 것을 추론할 수 있다. 따라서 (D)가 정답이다.

빈출 패러프레이징

다음은 추론 문제에 자주 나오는 정답의 단서가 패러프레이징된 예시이다.

정답의 단서	질문 및 정답
Should you forget something in the room you stayed in, check at the main reception desk. 당신이 묵었던 방에 무언가 두고 나온다면, 메인 프런트 데스크에서 확인하십시오.	질문 For whom is the notice most likely intended? 공고는 누구를 대상으로 하는 것 같은가? 정답 Guests at an accommodation facility 숙박시설에 있는 손님들
Ms. Wang, under the terms of your medical insurance, you are required to undergo this procedure every two years. You will see the same physician as last time, Dr. Kapur. Ms. Wang, 귀하의 의료 보험 약관에 따라, 귀하는 이 절차를 2년마다 받아야 합니다. 귀하는 지난번과 같은 의사인 Dr. Kapur를 만날 것입니다.	질문 What can be concluded about Ms. Wang? Ms. Wang에 대해 결론지을 수 있는 것은? 정답 She saw Dr. Kapur two years before. Dr. Kapur를 2년 전에 봤다.

토익실전문제

Questions 01-02 refer to the following e-mail.

To: Kendra Clark <kclark@zoommail.com>
From: George Adachi <g.adachi@npo_gov.com>
Subject: Earth Day Celebration
Date: June 3

Dear Ms. Clark,

The National Post Office has just released a stamp commemorating Earth Day. It features a painting of animals created by noted wildlife artist Carla Anderson. We believe your members will find this item particularly appealing.

The postal service has only produced 4,000 of this stamp. We are offering registered organizations such as yours the opportunity to purchase it directly from us. If any of your club members want to add this stamp to their collections, please reply to this e-mail by June 6.

All the best,

George Adachi
Retail director
National Post Office

01 What is the purpose of the e-mail?

(A) To show support for a fundraiser
(B) To schedule an organizational meeting
(C) To provide details about a product
(D) To announce a public holiday

02 Who most likely are the club members?

(A) Visual artists
(B) Stamp collectors
(C) Environmentalists
(D) Postal workers

HACKERS TEST

Questions 01-02 refer to the following text-message chain.

Agnes Beecroft [5:45 P.M.]
Bart, thanks for helping me with my accounting report. Would you be interested in going to a basketball game on Thursday night? Ms. Farrow from Hart Technologies gave me two tickets.

Bart Kreps [5:48 P.M.]
I can't make it. I have to participate in a conference call with a client that evening.

Agnes Beecroft [5:49 P.M.]
That's all right. Who else do you think I could ask?

Bart Kreps [5:51 P.M.]
What about Tina Rodriguez? I worked with her on the last advertising campaign we did for Hart Technologies. I always thought she did a great job and deserved some kind of reward.

Agnes Beecroft [5:54 P.M.]
OK, thanks! I'll ask Tina then.

---

01 At 5:48 P.M., what does Mr. Kreps mean when he writes, "I can't make it"?

(A) He is too busy to help with a task.
(B) He will not be able to attend an event.
(C) He has to leave work early on Thursday.
(D) He is not planning to speak at a conference.

02 What is indicated about Ms. Rodriguez?

(A) She was employed by Hart Technologies.
(B) She is being considered for a promotion.
(C) She worked with Mr. Kreps on a project.
(D) She belongs to the accounting team.

Questions 03-06 refer to the following memo.

BRONMAN HARDWARE

To: Store managers
From: Steven Tisdale, CEO
Subject: Future Plans
Date: September 6

As you know, I was at the 44th Annual Building Industries Trade Fair in Columbus, Ohio. I'd like to share a recent trend in construction materials that I observed during this event. — [1] —. It seems that there is a growing demand for locally sourced building supplies among homeowners.

In light of this news, I asked the marketing division to do some research. — [2] —. They drew up a list of local products that could do well in our stores. Next month, we will ask each store manager to hold a special promotion on all of these products. We will then look at the sales figures from each branch. — [3] —.

Naturally, these changes will affect our purchasing and transportation costs. — [4] —. However, the finance department has concluded that we will probably see substantial savings. Having suppliers nearby will allow us to reduce the number of items we keep in our warehouses.

03 Why did Mr. Tisdale write the memo?

(A) To describe how a company has been performing
(B) To explain a company's response to a new trend
(C) To confirm his attendance at an upcoming trade fair
(D) To remind supervisors about their responsibilities

04 What will store managers be expected to do?

(A) Promote products that are produced locally
(B) Conduct surveys to identify consumer trends
(C) Hire additional staff members to work in sales
(D) Prepare estimates of the costs of a new project

05 What is suggested about Bronman Hardware?

(A) It will reward stores that deliver the highest sales.
(B) It has been losing customers to competitors.
(C) It will open several new stores in the coming years.
(D) It spends a lot of money storing inventory.

06 In which of the positions marked [1], [2], [3], and [4] does the following sentence best belong?

"Based on this, we will decide which locally made items to begin offering regularly."

(A) [1]
(B) [2]
(C) [3]
(D) [4]

의도 파악, 문장 위치 찾기, 동의어 문제

기출 유형 1 의도 파악 문제
최근 3개년 오답률 16.5%

메시지 대화문에서 인용구가 어떤 의도로 쓰였는지를 파악하는 문제로, 매회 2문제 출제된다.

출제 경향

1. 메시지 대화문에서만 출제된다.
2. 질문에 At ~, what does ~ (most likely) mean when he/she writes, "~"?을 사용하여 묻는다.

   At 3:40 P.M., **what does** Mr. Norris **mean** when he writes, "Consider it done"?
   오후 3시 40분에, Mr. Norris가 "Consider it done"이라고 썼을 때, 그가 의도한 것은?

   At 10:13 A.M., **what does** Ms. Perez **most likely mean** when she writes, "Not at all"?
   오전 10시 13분에, Ms. Perez가 "Not at all"이라고 썼을 때, 그녀가 의도한 것 같은 것은?

800+ 공략

1. 지문에서 인용구의 주변 문장을 읽고 인용구의 문맥상 의미를 파악한다. 인용구의 주변 문장만 읽고 정답을 찾기 힘들 경우, 지문 전체의 흐름을 살펴본 후 주제를 확인하면 인용구의 의미를 파악할 수 있다.
2. 인용구 자체만으로는 여러 방향의 해석이 가능하므로, 반드시 지문의 내용에 근거하여 답을 선택한다.

Example
해석 p.193

Question 01 refers to the following text-message chain.

Joseph Donahue [10:46 A.M.]
Hi, Lesley. I received an assignment that requires me to compare data, so I was wondering if it would be possible to get a second computer monitor.

Lesley Roussell [10:47 A.M.]
I see. You can send a request to the IT department. It might take several days, though.

Joseph Donahue [10:48 A.M.]
That's not ideal. The assignment needs to be done by Friday.

---

01 At 10:48 A.M., what does Mr. Donahue mean when he writes, "That's not ideal"?
   (A) He requires more data to complete an assignment.
   (B) He cannot help new staff set up computers.
   (C) He wants to extend a project deadline.
   (D) He needs an immediate solution to a problem.

해설 의도 파악 문제   정답 (D)

지문의 'You can send a request to the IT department. It might take several days, though.'에서 Ms. Roussell이 당신, 즉 Mr. Donahue가 또 하나의 컴퓨터 모니터를 받기 위해 IT 부서에 요청서를 보낼 수 있지만 이것은 며칠이 걸릴 수도 있다고 하자, Mr. Donahue가 'That's not ideal'(그것은 이상적이지 않네요)이라고 한 후, 'The assignment needs to be done by Friday.'에서 업무가 금요일까지 완료되어야 한다고 한 것을 통해, Mr. Donahue가 문제에 대한 즉각적인 해결책이 필요하다는 것을 알 수 있다. 따라서 (D)가 정답이다.

빈출 인용구 표현

다음은 의도 파악 문제에 자주 출제되는 긍정과 부정의 인용구 표현이다.

긍정	Good idea. 좋은 생각이에요. Wise choice. 현명한 선택이에요. Makes sense. 일리가 있어요. What a relief. 다행이네요. Well done. 잘했어요. Got it. 알겠어요.	I can help you with that. 제가 그것을 도울 수 있어요. I'll take care of that. 제가 그것을 처리할게요. I can handle it. 제가 그것을 처리할 수 있어요. That should work. 그것은 괜찮겠어요. I'm convinced. 확신해요. Sounds great. 잘됐네요.
부정	Not yet. 아직이요. Not really. 그다지요. This is unusual. 일반적이지 않네요.	Too bad. 안됐네요. I've never heard of it. 저는 그것에 대해 들은 적이 없어요. It might be challenging. 어려울 수 있겠어요.

토익실전문제

토익 문제 이렇게 나온다!

Questions 01-04 refer to the following online chat discussion.

Fran Jenkins	[11:40 A.M.]	Hi, team. We need to figure out what to do for the office's social activity this summer. I'm considering a beach trip.
Harriet Tibbs	[11:43 A.M.]	Don't you think the water will be too cold? What about a picnic at a local park?
Fran Jenkins	[11:45 A.M.]	I like the idea of a picnic.
Gary Franklin	[11:47 A.M.]	Henderson Park has a nice picnic area.
Harriet Tibbs	[11:48 A.M.]	But it can get crowded. Gold Ridge Park might be better because it doesn't usually have as many people.
Fran Jenkins	[11:49 A.M.]	OK. I should also mention that our food budget is higher than it was last year. We can spend up to $1,200.
Gary Franklin	[11:50 A.M.]	Sounds great! We could even hire a caterer with that amount. I know a good one named Ruth Bernard. I could get an estimate from her.
Fran Jenkins	[11:52 A.M.]	Please do so. Find out how much she charges for about 40 people.

01 What does Ms. Jenkins want to discuss with her team?

(A) Finalizing a meeting agenda
(B) Confirming a travel itinerary
(C) Gathering volunteers for an event
(D) Developing ideas for an outing

02 What is indicated about Henderson Park?

(A) It is the nearest one to an office.
(B) It allows visitors to bring their pets.
(C) It tends to attract large crowds.
(D) It has indoor spaces for rent.

의도 파악 문제

03 At 11:50 A.M., what does Mr. Franklin mean when he writes, "Sounds great"?

(A) He is pleased that so many people are coming.
(B) The available funds are greater than he thought.
(C) He is surprised at the high quality of catering.
(D) A venue has a higher capacity than he expected.

04 What does Mr. Franklin recommend?

(A) Requesting employee feedback
(B) Changing an activity schedule
(C) Inviting additional guests
(D) Hiring a catering company

기출 유형 2　문장 위치 찾기 문제

최근 3개년 오답률 20.5%

지문의 흐름을 파악하여 주어진 문장이 들어갈 가장 적절한 위치를 고르는 문제로, 매회 2문제 출제된다.

출제 경향

1. 3~4문제가 나오는 지문에서 마지막 문제로 출제된다.
2. 질문에 In which of the positions ~ does the following sentence best belong?을 사용하여 묻는다.

   In which of the positions marked [1], [2], [3], and [4] **does the following sentence best belong**?
   [1], [2], [3], [4]로 표시된 위치 중, 다음 문장이 들어갈 곳으로 가장 적절한 것은?

800+ 공략

1. 주어진 문장 내의 단서를 이용해서 해당 문장이 들어갈 위치를 찾을 수 있으므로, 주어진 문장의 내용과 지문의 흐름을 정확하게 파악한 후 주어진 문장이 들어가기에 적절한 위치를 선택한다.
2. 주어진 문장에 단서가 없어, 앞뒤 문장과의 논리적 흐름으로만 정답을 골라야 하는 문제도 출제되므로 주의한다. 이때는 빈칸에 주어진 문장을 넣어보며 앞뒤 문장과 내용이 자연스럽게 연결되는 위치를 선택한다.

Example

해석 p.194

Question 01 refers to the following Web page.

> Harrison Home Furnishings has been in business for over 50 years, and its products are sold in fine furniture outlets around the world. — [1] —. Its factory in Ontario was expanded in 2010, and a warehouse and a shipping facility were added in 2015. — [2] —. Harrison Home Furnishings continues to receive honors for its original designs, and it often receives positive reviews from magazines such as *Modern Interiors Today* and *Inside Outside*. — [3] —. With a focus on sustainable materials and modern design, the company continues to attract design-conscious consumers. — [4] —.

01　In which of the positions marked [1], [2], [3], and [4] does the following sentence best belong?
　　"These changes significantly increased overall output."
　　(A) [1]
　　(B) [2]
　　(C) [3]
　　(D) [4]

해설　문장 위치 찾기 문제　　　　　　　　　　　　　　　　　　　　　　　　　　　　　　　　　　　정답 (B)

주어진 문장은 Harrison Home Furnishings사가 겪은 변화와 관련된 내용 주변에 나올 것임을 예상할 수 있다. [2]의 앞 문장인 'Its factory in Ontario was expanded in 2010, and a warehouse and a shipping facility were added in 2015.'에서 2010년에 온타리오주에 있는 공장이 확장되었으며, 2015년에는 창고와 운송 시설이 추가되었다고 했으므로, [2]에 주어진 문장이 들어가면 이러한 변화들이 전체 생산량을 크게 증가시켰다는 자연스러운 문맥이 된다는 것을 알 수 있다. 따라서 (B)가 정답이다.

빈출 정답의 단서와 풀이 방법

다음은 문장 위치 찾기 문제의 주어진 문장 안에 자주 나오는 정답의 단서와 각 풀이 방법이다.

인칭대명사(he/she, it, they 등)	앞 문장에 사람 이름, 직위·직책, 단체명, 회사명이 나오는지 확인한다. it의 경우 앞 문장 전체 내용을 가리키기도 한다.
지시대명사(this, that 등)	앞 문장에 지시대명사가 가리키는 대상이 나오는지 확인한다.
정관사(the)	정관사 뒤의 명사가 앞 문장에 나오는지 확인한다.
접속부사(however, thus 등)	접속부사의 의미를 파악하여 앞 문장과 자연스럽게 이어지는지 확인한다. ▶ 다양한 접속부사의 종류와 의미는 PART 5 DAY 10(p.204)에서 더 자세히 다루고 있다.

토익실전문제

Questions 01-03 refer to the following letter.

August 24

Leanna Murillo
111 Fort Street, Basseterre
St. Kitts & Nevis, 1201

Dear Ms. Murillo,

Carpenters United has begun planning its fifth annual symposium at a venue in Singapore from February 20 to 23. As with previous events, the aim will be to discuss the latest technological developments in our field. — [1] —. It will also be an opportunity for members to form connections.

This time, we will have the additional task of planning a publicity campaign about sustainable building materials. — [2] —. We will also need to decide whether to carry out this campaign through social media, public events, or traditional advertising. The symposium will conclude with a vote to determine the members of our leadership committee for the next three years. — [3] —.

We hope that, as a valued member of our association, you will be able to attend. — [4] —.

Danton Spritz
President, Carpenters United

01 What is the purpose of the letter?

(A) To confirm attendance at an event
(B) To report a change in leadership
(C) To announce a yearly gathering
(D) To introduce a set of rules

02 What is NOT mentioned about the symposium?

(A) It will feature a famous guest speaker.
(B) It will take place over several days.
(C) It will focus on advances in technology.
(D) It will provide networking opportunities.

03 In which of the positions marked [1], [2], [3], and [4] does the following sentence best belong?

"It will highlight the role of these materials in carpentry as well as the environmental benefits of using them."

(A) [1]
(B) [2]
(C) [3]
(D) [4]

기출 유형 3   동의어 문제

최근 3개년 오답률 23.1%

4개의 보기 중 지문에 언급된 단어와 가장 유사한 의미를 갖는 보기를 선택하는 문제로, 매회 2~3문제 출제된다.

출제 경향

1. 주로 한 가지 이상의 뜻을 가진 단어가 출제된 후, 그것의 동의어 여러 개가 보기에 출제된다.
2. 질문에 The word "~" is closest in meaning to를 사용하여 묻는다.

　단일 지문　**The word** "cover" in paragraph 2, line 6, **is closest in meaning to**
　　　　　　2문단 여섯 번째 줄의 단어 "cover"는 의미상 –와 가장 가깝다.

　다중 지문　In the letter, **the word** "lead" in paragraph 3, line 2, **is closest in meaning to**
　　　　　　편지에서, 3문단 두 번째 줄의 단어 "lead"는 의미상 –와 가장 가깝다.

800+ 공략

1. 지문에 언급된 단어가 사용된 문맥에 어울리는 보기가 정답이다.
2. 해당 단어의 사전적 동의어이지만 문맥에 어울리지 않는 단어가 오답 보기로 나오는 경우도 있으므로, 반드시 지문의 문맥을 통해 단어의 의미를 파악한다.

Example

해석 p.195

Question 01 refers to the following advertisement.

Keystone Interpretation

If you're an adult, becoming fluent in a second language can be a big challenge. Many experience day-to-day situations where communicating in a foreign language is difficult. This is where Keystone Interpretation comes in.

We offer a wide array of translation and interpretation services at competitive rates. Take a look at some of our services:
- Phone, video, or in-person interpretation is available.
- If you require written translation, we provide services in over 200 languages, including English, French, Chinese, and more.

Visit us at www.keyinterpretation.com, and get a quote based on your interpretation and translation needs. First-time customers are eligible for a 20 percent discount.

01 The word "quote" in paragraph 3, line 1, is closest in meaning to
   (A) reference
   (B) estimate
   (C) sample
   (D) demonstration

해설 동의어 문제　　　정답 (B)
quote를 포함하는 구절 'get a quote based on your interpretation and translation needs'에서 quote는 '견적'이라는 뜻으로 사용되었다. 따라서 (B)가 정답이다.

빈출 동의어

다음은 동의어 문제에 자주 출제되는 어휘이다.

appreciate	understand 이해하다 value 인정하다 give thanks for 감사하다
assume	suppose 생각하다, 추측하다 take on 책임을 지다
cover	include 포함하다 address/discuss 논의하다 pay for 지불하다 report on 보도하다 insure 보장하다 conceal 숨기다
draw	paint 그리다 attract 끌어들이다 gather 모으다
meet	satisfy 충족시키다 encounter 만나다
secure	obtain 얻다, 획득하다 protect 보호하다 fasten 고정시키다
facility	establishment/center 시설, 기관 ease 수월함
figure	amount 양 shape 모양 person 인물
term	condition 조건 period 기간
accessible	understandable 이해하기 쉬운 open 접근 가능한, 이용 가능한 available 이용 가능한
effective	efficient 효율적인 valid 유효한
original	first 처음의 unique 독창적인
quote	estimate 견적 reference 인용, 인용문

토익실전문제

토익 문제 이렇게 나온다!

Questions 01-04 refer to the following article.

Announcements Boost Tatkraft Share Price

June 13—The share price of German electric car manufacturer Tatkraft increased sharply following CEO Johannes Schneider's announcement of the company's performance. Last week, Mr. Schneider announced that Tatkraft made a profit of 212 million dollars the year before and expects to sell over half a million new cars this year. The company's stock price subsequently rose from 567 dollars to 601 dollars a share, securing investor confidence in the company's growth strategy.

Prior to last year, the company struggled to convince investors of its capacity for growth with production consistently failing to keep up with demand. Thanks to improvements implemented after the hiring of Elias Muller, an automotive industry veteran, the company simplified its manufacturing process and is now producing cars more efficiently. Today, Tatkraft is valued at over 100 billion dollars.

01 What did Mr. Schneider do last week?

(A) He purchased a commercial property.
(B) He appointed a new top executive.
(C) He provided information on anticipated sales.
(D) He performed an evaluation of a team.

02 What is implied about Tatkraft's investors?

(A) They placed orders for vehicles in the new year.
(B) They had doubts about the company's potential.
(C) They increased their investments two years before.
(D) They showed concern about product quality.

동의어 문제

03 The word "securing" in paragraph 1, line 4, is closest in meaning to

(A) fastening
(B) requiring
(C) obtaining
(D) supporting

04 What most likely is Mr. Muller responsible for?

(A) Meeting production goals
(B) Developing sales strategies
(C) Analyzing financial results
(D) Resolving customer complaints

정답·해석·해설 p.196

HACKERS TEST

토익 800+를 위한 실전 문제 정복

DAY 15

Questions 01-02 refer to the following online chat discussion.

Erika Raimond [10:46 A.M.] The custom pens we ordered last month were just delivered. Unfortunately, our firm's name is spelled incorrectly. I called the company that made them for us, but it will take at least three days for them to resolve this situation.

Jayce Vills [10:48 A.M.] That's too bad. We won't have anything to hand out at tomorrow's seminar.

Erika Raimond [10:50 A.M.] Actually, we have some notepads with our logo on them in storage. I don't think anyone will mind if we use them.

Jayce Vills [10:55 A.M.] You have a point. When the corrected pens are sent to us, we can save them for another event.

---

01 What did Ms. Raimond do this morning?

(A) Attended a seminar
(B) Made an appointment
(C) Mailed a package
(D) Contacted a supplier

02 At 10:55 A.M., what does Mr. Vills most likely mean when he writes, "You have a point"?

(A) An order needs to be refunded.
(B) An activity should be postponed.
(C) Some items may be used for an event.
(D) Some products should be placed in storage.

Questions 03-06 refer to the following article.

Electronics Monthly

SleekEffects Striving for Change

March 2—Electrical appliance manufacturer SleekEffects is making an attempt to recover from its poor sales last year. — [1] —. SleekEffects suffered a massive recall of its Cavalier line of electronic shavers last November. According to hundreds of complaints submitted by customers, the shavers had a tendency to overheat and posed a fire hazard. — [2] —.

To turn things around, SleekEffects CEO Leonard Martin announced major alterations to its production processes. — [3] —. In a press release, Mr. Martin said that the firm had addressed the shortcomings that resulted in the recall and was preparing to launch a new line of products designed to draw a wider range of customers. "The line of electronic foot, neck, and back massagers, called SleekSmooth, represents the company's first attempt to target female customers," he said. — [4] —.

03 What is the article mainly about?

(A) A company's efforts to improve
(B) The appointment of a new CEO
(C) A firm's overseas expansion
(D) A trend in personal care products

04 The word "draw" in paragraph 2, line 7, is closest in meaning to

(A) prepare
(B) paint
(C) preserve
(D) attract

05 What can be inferred about SleekEffects?

(A) It replaced some production equipment.
(B) It operates a chain of stores around the world.
(C) It provides incentives for customer feedback.
(D) It used to make items that were solely for men.

06 In which of the positions marked [1], [2], [3], and [4] does the following sentence best belong?

"As a result, nearly one million units of the products were removed from retailers' shelves."

(A) [1]
(B) [2]
(C) [3]
(D) [4]

DAY 16 이메일/편지 및 메시지 대화문

기출 유형 1 이메일/편지

비즈니스 또는 일상생활과 관련된 여러 정보를 전달하는 글로, 매회 7~8개의 지문이 출제된다.

출제 경향

1. 이메일/편지의 목적, 이메일/편지에 첨부 또는 동봉된 것, 수신자에게 요청하는 것, 이메일/편지에 언급된 사람이나 회사에 대한 세부 정보를 묻는 문제가 자주 출제된다.
2. 다음과 같은 주제가 자주 출제된다.

비즈니스	사내 또는 회사 간 직원들의 업무 논의, 구직자의 합격 소식 전달, 면접 일정 통보
일상생활	은행, 상점, 병원 등의 시설 담당자와 고객 간의 정보 전달 및 질의응답

800+ 공략

1. 이메일/편지의 수신자 및 발신자와 관련된 문제가 자주 출제되므로, 지문의 앞부분에서 이름을 정확하게 확인한다.
2. 이메일/편지에 자주 출제되는 비즈니스, 일상생활과 관련된 표현들을 알아 둔다.

Example

해석 p.198

Questions 01-02 refer to the following e-mail.

To: Gerald Browning <g.browning@heremail.com>
From: Clarissa Kim <c.kim@maximumbank.com>
Date: June 5

This e-mail is to confirm that the online request you made for a MaxJet credit card on June 2 has been approved. The card should arrive within the next three business days. You may use your card immediately to access numerous benefits, including:

- An annual $500 voucher valid for any SureSky Airlines flight
- 10 percent off all products at Maximum Bank's retail partner, BuySmart, every July

For more details about your benefits, download the Maximum Bank smartphone application.

01 What did Mr. Browning most likely do on June 2?
(A) He called a Maximum Bank branch.
(B) He set up a personal savings account.
(C) He turned in an application form.
(D) He made a credit card payment.

02 What can Mr. Browning do next month?
(A) Obtain a new credit card by mail
(B) Buy some items at a reduced price
(C) Attend an event sponsored by Maximum Bank
(D) Earn extra points by referring a friend

해설 **01 추론 문제**
정답 01 (C) 02 (B)
지문의 'the online request you made for a MaxJet credit card on June 2 has been approved'에서 당신, 즉 Mr. Browning이 6월 2일에 했던 MaxJet 신용카드에 대한 온라인 신청이 승인되었다고 했으므로 Mr. Browning이 6월 2일에 신용카드에 대한 신청서를 제출했다는 사실을 추론할 수 있다. 따라서 (C)가 정답이다.

02 육하원칙 문제
지문의 'Date: June 5'에서 이메일이 6월 5일에 작성되었다고 했고, '10 percent off all products at Maximum Bank's retail partner ~ every July'에서 매년 7월에 Maximum 은행의 제휴 소매업체에서 모든 제품들에 대한 10퍼센트 할인을 받을 수 있다고 했으므로 (B)가 정답이다.

이메일/편지에 자주 나오는 필수 표현

비즈니스

attach v. 첨부하다, 붙이다	expand v. 확장하다	revenue n. 수익, 매출
budget n. 예산, 예산안	initiative n. (새로운) 계획	résumé n. 이력서
contractor n. 계약자, 도급업자	inventory n. 재고, 재고품	specification n. (제품의) 사양, 세부 사항
credential n. 자격, 자격 증명서	promotion n. 승진, 홍보	substitute v. 대신하다, 교체되다
efficiency n. 효율(성), 능률	recommendation n. 추천, 권고	warehouse n. 창고

일상생활

anticipate v. 예상하다, 기대하다	faulty adj. 흠이 있는, 부적절한	retailer n. 소매상, 소매업체
appointment n. 약속, 예약	institution n. 기관	shipment n. 수송, 발송
auction n. 경매	overdue adj. (지불) 기한이 지난, 미불의	subscription n. 구독
authorization n. 공인, 허가	query n. 질문	voucher n. 상품권, 쿠폰

토익실전문제

Questions 01-04 refer to the following e-mail.

TO: Jason Briar <jbriar@postnet.com>
FROM: Jack Gray <grayjack@gilhoolytech.com>
SUBJECT: Application
DATE: April 27

Dear Mr. Briar,

Thank you for applying for Gilhooly Tech's summer student internship program. We received your résumé and application form a few days ago, and we will be scheduling interviews shortly. Should you meet our eligibility requirements, you will be contacted by phone at some point to set up an appointment at our office in Richmond.

Please note that this is a full-time, unpaid position that will last for a period of eight weeks. However, Gilhooly Tech will provide 3,000 dollars to your educational institution, Maryland Academy, to help pay for your tuition fees if you are selected. Gilhooly Tech is also prepared to offer a housing allowance of 500 dollars per month for interns who are from out of town.

Once again, thanks for taking an interest in our program, and we will contact you shortly.

Sincerely yours,

Jack Gray
Associate Recruitment Director, Gilhooly Tech

01 What has Mr. Briar recently done?

(A) Sent documents for a temporary position
(B) Completed a training program with a company
(C) Spoken to a recruiter on the telephone
(D) Requested information on his grades

02 The word "point" in paragraph 1, line 3, is closest in meaning to

(A) time
(B) location
(C) detail
(D) direction

03 What is implied about Mr. Briar?

(A) He is currently a resident of Richmond.
(B) He will have to do an online interview.
(C) He will not be paid directly for his work.
(D) He is currently attending a university on scholarship.

04 What is true about Gilhooly Tech?

(A) It is preparing to launch a new product.
(B) It provides a dormitory for regular staff.
(C) It offers support for housing expenses.
(D) It compensates employees based on performance.

기출 유형 2 　메시지 대화문

비즈니스 또는 일상생활과 관련된 여러 정보를 모바일이나 온라인 메신저상에서 2인 이상이 주고받는 글로, 매회 2개의 지문이 출제된다.

출제 경향

1. 대화문의 주제, 대화자의 요청 사항, 대화문에 언급된 사람이나 대화 내용에 대한 세부 정보, 대화문에서 특정 어구가 쓰인 의도를 묻는 문제가 자주 출제된다.
2. 다음과 같은 주제가 자주 출제된다.

비즈니스	회의, 일정, 회사 정책, 업무 세부 사항에 대한 사내 또는 회사 간 직원들의 논의
일상생활	행사 초대, 도움 요청 등에 대한 친구 또는 지인들의 논의

800+ 공략

1. 메시지 대화문에서는 지문에서 쓰인 특정 어구의 의도를 묻는 문제가 출제되므로, 대화문의 전체적인 흐름을 정확히 파악해야 한다.
2. 대화에 참여하는 사람이 여러 명이므로 각 메시지를 보낸 사람이 누구인지 정확하게 확인한다.
3. 메시지 대화문에 자주 출제되는 비즈니스, 일상생활과 관련된 표현들을 알아 둔다.

Example

해석 p.199

Questions 01-02 refer to the following text-message chain.

Pam Gordon　[9:10 A.M.]
I just e-mailed you the travel expense reimbursement form for your trip last week. Could you turn it in by the end of the month? Otherwise, your money won't be repaid to you with your next paycheck.

Hadassah Aboud　[9:12 A.M.]
Absolutely. I actually printed out the form from the intranet as soon as I got back and took it to the accounting department office right away.

Pam Gordon　[9:13 A.M.]
Great! I wasn't sure if you knew where to take it.

01　What is suggested about the form?
(A) It must specify a preferred payment method.
(B) It must be signed by a department supervisor.
(C) It must be submitted within a set amount of time.
(D) It must be filled out on a company Web site.

02　At 9:12 A.M., what does Ms. Aboud mean when she writes, "Absolutely"?
(A) She is able to give a coworker assistance.
(B) She has been repaid for the cost of a trip.
(C) She is on her way to hand in a form.
(D) She has completed a task already.

해설　**01 추론 문제**　　　　　　　　　　　　　　　　　　　　　　　　　　　　　　　　　　　　　**정답 01 (C)　02 (D)**
지문의 'Could you turn it in by the end of the month? Otherwise, your money won't be repaid ~ with your next paycheck.'에서 Ms. Gordon이 Ms. Aboud에게 이번 달 말까지 그것, 즉 출장 비용 환급 양식을 제출할 수 있는지 물은 후, 그러지 않으면 돈이 다음 급료와 함께 상환되지 않을 것이라고 했으므로, 양식이 정해진 시간 이내에 제출되어야 한다는 사실을 추론할 수 있다. 따라서 (C)가 정답이다.

02 의도 파악 문제
지문의 'Could you turn it in by the end of the month?'에서 Ms. Gordon이 이번 달 말까지 그것, 즉 출장 비용 환급 양식을 제출할 수 있는지 묻자, Ms. Aboud가 'Absolutely'(물론이죠)라고 한 후, 'I actually printed out the form ~ and took it to the ~ office right away.'에서 사실 양식을 출력해서 그것을 사무실로 바로 가져갔다고 한 것을 통해 Ms. Aboud가 이미 그 작업을 완료했다는 것을 알 수 있다. 따라서 (D)가 정답이다.

메시지 대화문에 자주 나오는 필수 표현

비즈니스

approval n. 승인	department n. 부, 부서	renovation n. 보수, 개조
branch n. 지점	exposition n. 전시회, 박람회	reimbursement n. 상환, 보상, 변제
compensation n. 보상, 보수	facility n. 시설, 기관	shift n. 교대 근무 (시간)
colleague n. 동료	instruct v. 지시하다, 알려 주다	sign up ~에 등록하다, 가입하다
conduct a seminar 세미나를 개최하다	office supply 사무용품	survey n. 조사, 설문조사
confirm v. 확인하다, 확정하다	overtime n. 초과 근무	timetable n. 일정표
coordinate v. 조정하다, 조직화하다	presentation n. 발표	trade fair 무역 박람회

일상생활

amenity n. 편의 시설	estimate n. 견적서; v. 추산하다	reasonable adj. 합리적인, 적정한
association n. 협회, 단체	handle v. 다루다, 처리하다	reception n. 접수처
availability n. 이용 가능성	parking lot 주차장	refund n. 환불; v. 환불하다
commute v. 통근하다; n. 통근	pick up ~을 구매하다	repair v. 수리하다, 고치다; n. 수리
equipment n. 장비, 장치	prepare v. 준비하다	reschedule v. 일정을 변경하다

토익실전문제

Questions 01-04 refer to the following online chat discussion.

Kevin Chase [1:50 P.M.]	Could someone recommend a supplier of office chairs? Mine broke earlier.
Miles Dunphy [1:52 P.M.]	Have you checked the stockroom? We might have some extra ones.
Kevin Chase [1:53 P.M.]	I already did, but it seems we're all out.
Megan Contreras [1:55 P.M.]	How much can you spend on a new one?
Kevin Chase [1:55 P.M.]	Less than $120.
Megan Contreras [1:56 P.M.]	I'm heading to Fastmax this afternoon for some printer ink. I can pick one up for you.
Kevin Chase [1:57 P.M.]	There's no hurry. I'm using a plastic chair for now.
Miles Dunphy [1:59 P.M.]	Every Office has one on sale for $97, which is 20 percent off the regular price. You can order it through their Web site. There's no charge for delivery.
Kevin Chase [2:00 P.M.]	Thanks, Miles! I'll check it out.
Miles Dunphy [2:01 P.M.]	No problem. I'd better get back to work. I have a report due in an hour.

01 What does Mr. Chase want to do?

(A) Conduct a customer survey
(B) Have an office computer repaired
(C) Replace a piece of furniture
(D) Count items in the stockroom

02 What is NOT true about Every Office?

(A) It has an overnight delivery service.
(B) It is offering a product at a discount.
(C) It sells some of its merchandise online.
(D) It provides free shipping to customers.

03 At 1:57 P.M., what does Mr. Chase mean when he writes, "There's no hurry"?

(A) He needs to wait for the manager's approval.
(B) He has found a temporary solution.
(C) He must request overtime hours.
(D) He has plenty of work to do in the meantime.

04 Why does Mr. Dunphy need to get back to work?

(A) He is preparing for a presentation.
(B) He has plans to assist a coworker.
(C) He has an imminent deadline to meet.
(D) He is heading to a store in the next hour.

정답·해석·해설 p.199

Questions 01-03 refer to the following letter.

Picica Insurance

Lavi Steinem
4304 Cordova Street
Vancouver, BC, V6B 1E1

February 2

Dear Mr. Steinem,

We have gone over the documents you submitted, and I regret to inform you that we cannot satisfy your claim for repairs to your automobile. As stated in your policy, you are required to notify Picica Insurance of an accident immediately. This would have allowed one of our agents to assess the damage and determine your coverage. Unfortunately, you did not notify us of the accident when it happened and instead contacted us after the repairs were completed. This makes it impossible for us to accurately verify the cause of the damage or its extent, even with the photo you provided of your car.

Please review your policy carefully. We kindly ask for your adherence to the agreement in the future. Should you require further clarification or wish to raise an objection, please visit your nearest Picica Insurance office or call 555-8899.

Regards,

Lou Mortimer

Lou Mortimer, Picica Insurance Agent

01 What is mentioned about Mr. Steinem?

(A) He had to pay a higher insurance fee.
(B) He did not report an accident right away.
(C) He failed to provide any supporting documents.
(D) He caused significant damage to his car.

02 The word "satisfy" in paragraph 1, line 1, is closest in meaning to

(A) convince
(B) reward
(C) please
(D) fulfill

03 What did Mr. Steinem send to Mr. Mortimer?

(A) A request for car repairs
(B) A photograph of a vehicle
(C) A record of a transaction
(D) A rejection of a compensation offer

Questions 04-07 refer to the following online chat discussion.

Jerry Miller [2:10 P.M.]		Are there any questions about Basket Burger's annual summertime promotion? I just sent each of your franchises new promotional materials.
Lois Denver [2:11 P.M.]		The seasonal menu will be the same as last year's, right? If so, I can start training my staff now.
Jerry Miller [2:13 P.M.]		That's right. However, we're discontinuing the frozen coffee beverages.
Kiel Bronson [2:14 P.M.]		Really? There have been many diners asking for them recently. I have leftover syrups for them as well. Can I sell the drinks until my supply runs out?
Jerry Miller [2:15 P.M.]		OK, but don't advertise them. Instead, promote our tornado pops and the half-off milkshake.
Lois Denver [2:18 P.M.]		Will the money from tornado pop sales go to charity again this year?
Jerry Miller [2:20 P.M.]		Yes. Is there anything else?
Kim Patton [2:21 P.M.]		I'm worried that my Beauville staff won't be able to handle this promotion. We just opened, and many are still training.
Jerry Miller [2:24 P.M.]		I see. I can send a couple of experienced employees to your facility during the promotion.

04 At 2:13 P.M., what does Mr. Miller mean when he writes, "That's right"?

(A) Extra funding will be provided for a promotion.
(B) Some supplies should be ordered before summertime.
(C) A chain's summer menu will remain largely unchanged.
(D) Seasonal items generate a significant percentage of profits.

05 Why does Mr. Bronson want to continue selling frozen coffee drinks?

(A) They produce more profits than other items.
(B) They require little time for staff to prepare.
(C) They are made with inexpensive ingredients.
(D) They are in high demand by customers.

06 What is NOT mentioned about Basket Burger?

(A) It plans to introduce a beverage soon.
(B) It holds a promotion on a yearly basis.
(C) It donates to a charitable organization.
(D) It has launched a new branch recently.

07 What does Mr. Miller offer to do?

(A) Send staff members to another location.
(B) Design an advertisement for a menu item
(C) Interview candidates for a manager role
(D) Distribute a copy of an employee manual

DAY 17 양식 및 광고

기출 유형 1 양식

초대장, 청구서, 쿠폰, 영수증, 웹페이지와 같이 다양한 형식을 갖춘 실용문으로, 매회 5~6개의 지문이 출제된다.

출제 경향

1. 양식에 언급된 행사의 목적, 추후 계획이나 일정, 양식에 언급된 사람이나 행사에 대한 세부 정보, 양식의 대상을 묻는 문제가 자주 출제된다.
2. 다음과 같은 지문이 자주 출제된다.

초대장	각종 행사나 모임에 초대하는 양식
청구서	송장이나 명세서 등의 지불 양식
쿠폰	제품이나 서비스, 시설을 홍보하는 광고지 및 할인 쿠폰
영수증	구매한 제품이나 서비스의 결제 내역과 금액을 보여주는 양식
웹페이지	인터넷상에서 회사의 제품 및 서비스를 소개하거나 신청하는 온라인 양식

800+ 공략

1. 초대장, 청구서·쿠폰·영수증, 웹페이지와 같이 다양한 양식과 관련된 표현들을 알아 둔다.

Example

해석 p.202

Questions 01-02 refer to the following invitation.

> You are cordially invited to the
> West Hobart Performing Arts Center
>
> Join us for the inauguration of the West Hobart Performing Arts Center on April 9 at 7:30 P.M. The evening will feature a 30-minute concert by the Hobart Symphony Orchestra at 8:30 P.M., followed by a stunning performance by renowned opera singer Kelly Tekanawa. This invitation admits you and one guest. Please confirm your attendance in advance.

01 Why is an event being held at the West Hobart Performing Arts Center?
(A) To introduce a group of musicians
(B) To celebrate a facility's opening
(C) To raise funds for a charity organization
(D) To honor a company's accomplishments

02 What is indicated about invited guests?
(A) They will be provided with a recording of a performance.
(B) They can purchase food and drinks at the event.
(C) They are members of an organization.
(D) They can bring an additional person.

해설 01 육하원칙 문제   정답 01 (B) 02 (D)

지문의 'Join us for the inauguration of the West Hobart Performing Arts Center'에서 West Hobart 공연예술 센터의 개관식에 함께해 달라고 했으므로 (B)가 정답이다.

02 Not/True 문제

(D)는 'This invitation admits you and one guest.'에서 이 초대장이 귀하와 다른 한 명의 입장을 허용한다고 했으므로 지문의 내용과 일치한다. 따라서 (D)가 정답이다. (A)는 'The evening will feature a 30-minute concert by the Hobart Symphony Orchestra'에서 저녁에는 Hobart 교향악단의 30분짜리 콘서트가 진행될 것이라고는 했으나 공연의 녹음본이 제공될 것인지는 언급되지 않았으므로 지문의 내용과 일치하지 않는다. (B)와 (C)는 지문에 언급되지 않은 내용이다.

양식에 자주 나오는 필수 표현

초대장

attendance n. 출석, 참석	beverage n. 음료	membership n. 회원, 회원권
banquet n. 연회, 축하연	commemorate v. 기념하다	reception n. 환영회, 환영

청구서·쿠폰·영수증

balance due 미불액, 잔금	exclusive adj. 독점적인, 한정된	redeem v. (쿠폰을) 사용하다, 교환하다
billing n. 청구, 청구서 (발행)	expiration n. 만료, 종료	subtotal n. 소계
charge n. 요금, 청구 금액; v. 청구하다	giveaway n. 경품, 무료 증정품	tax n. 세금; v. 과세하다
deal n. 거래, 특가	in-store adj. 매장 내의	transaction n. 거래, 매매
deposit n. 보증금, 예금; v. 입금하다, 맡기다	quantity n. 수량, 양	

웹페이지

cancellation n. 취소	registration n. 등록, 신청	scheme n. 설계, 계획
complete v. 작성하다, 완성하다	renew v. 갱신하다	submit v. 제출하다

토익실전문제

Questions 01-02 refer to the following online form.

Era Magazine
www.eramagazine.com

| Home | Sections | **Subscribe** | Contact Us | Help |

Subscribe to *Era* now for just $29 a year and save 10 percent off the regular price. Get 48 issues of the print edition as well as unrestricted access to our digital version and an online database of previous editions. To subscribe, complete the form below.

Personal Information:
First Name: Richard   Last Name: Stich
Address: 1455 Marcus Street
City: Huntsville   State: AL   ZIP: 35816
Please select your address type:
☐ Home   ☑ Office

Create your digital account:
E-mail: rich_stich@bamamail.com
Password: ********

Billing Information:
☐ Credit card   ☑ Debit card
Card number: 4376-XXXX-XXXX-XXXX

All subscriptions are automatically renewed until you cancel. You will be notified if there is a change in the price of your subscription. For international orders, please call 555-3590 or click here.

Submit Order

---

01 What is implied about the magazine subscription?

(A) It is valid for a period of six months.
(B) It only provides access to digital content.
(C) It is currently available at a reduced price.
(D) It requires payment on a weekly basis.

02 According to the online form, why might *Era Magazine* contact Mr. Stich?

(A) To report an issue with a credit card
(B) To notify him of a price change
(C) To ask questions for a survey
(D) To confirm an international order

기출 유형 2 광고

상품 또는 서비스를 홍보하거나 직원을 모집하는 글로, 매회 2~3개의 지문이 출제된다.

출제 경향

1. 광고되고 있는 것, 구매자가 얻을 수 있는 혜택, 혜택 신청 및 지원 자격, 상품이나 서비스에 대한 세부 정보, 광고의 대상이나 광고가 게재된 곳을 묻는 문제가 자주 출제된다.
2. 다음과 같은 주제가 자주 출제된다.

일반 광고	상품이나 서비스 이용 독려, 시설이나 행사 홍보
구인 광고	직원 모집

800+ 공략

1. 일반 광고는 제목 및 앞부분에서 광고되는 것을 우선 파악한 후 세부 내용을 확인한다.
2. 구인 광고는 주로 채용하려는 직급이 먼저 제시된 후 담당하게 될 업무, 지원 자격 등이 나오고 마지막에 지원 방법이 나온다는 점을 기억한다.
3. 일반 광고, 구인 광고와 관련된 표현들을 알아 둔다.

Example

해석 p.202

Questions 01-02 refer to the following advertisement.

Pixel Pro

Equipped with two offset presses, a high-speed copier, and three digital color printers, we can fulfill all of your needs quickly and reliably. Whether you need brochures, business cards, or party invitations, simply bring in your image or text, and we will produce a high-quality product. If you do not have materials ready, consult with our full-time graphic artists to come up with a custom design that works for you. Examples of their work can be found at www.pixelpro.com. We are open Monday through Saturday from 10:00 A.M. to 8:30 P.M.

01 What type of business is being advertised?
(A) An electronics manufacturer
(B) A delivery company
(C) A photography studio
(D) A print shop

02 According to the advertisement, why should customers visit a Web site?
(A) To download a price list
(B) To place an order
(C) To view samples
(D) To make appointments

해설 **01** 육하원칙 문제   정답 01 (D) 02 (C)

지문의 'Equipped with two offset presses, a high-speed copier, and three digital color printers'와 'Whether you need brochures, business cards, or party invitations, ~ we will produce a high-quality product.'에서 두 대의 오프셋 인쇄기, 한 대의 고속 복사기, 세 대의 디지털 컬러 인쇄기를 갖추고 있으며, 브로슈어, 명함, 혹은 파티 초대장 중 무엇이 필요하든 높은 품질의 상품을 제작할 것이라고 했으므로 인쇄소가 광고되고 있음을 알 수 있다. 따라서 (D)가 정답이다.

02 육하원칙 문제

지문의 'Examples of their work can be found at www.pixelpro.com.'에서 그들, 즉 정규직 그래픽 디자이너들의 작품 견본은 웹사이트인 www.pixelpro.com에서 확인할 수 있다고 했으므로 (C)가 정답이다.

광고에 자주 나오는 필수 표현

일반 광고

attraction n. 명소, 인기 있는 구경거리	housing n. 주거, 주택	promote v. 홍보하다, 승진시키다
bargain n. 특가품, 거래; v. 흥정하다	inhabitant n. 주민, 거주자	real estate 부동산, 부동산 중개업
bustling adj. 부산한, 붐비는	lease n. 임대차, 임대차 계약; v. 임대하다	showroom n. 전시실, 진열실
certified adj. 자격증을 소지한, 공인된	marketplace n. 시장, 장터	souvenir n. 기념품, 토산품
convenience n. 편의성, 편리함	on hand 준비된, 구할 수 있는	specialize in ~을 전문으로 하다
custom adj. 맞춤의, 주문한	patron n. 고객, 단골손님	tenure n. (부동산의) 보유, 거주권
enhance v. 향상시키다	personalize v. 맞춤화하다, 개인화하다	top-notch adj. 최고 수준의, 뛰어난
exhibit v. 전시하다, 보이다; n. 전시회, 전시품	premiere n. 초연, 개봉; v. 초연을 하다	unparalleled adj. 견줄 데 없는, 비할 바 없는
gourmet adj. 고급의	product line 제품군	warranty n. 보증서, 품질 보증

구인 광고

application n. 지원, 지원서	help-wanted n. 구인 광고	qualification n. 자격 요건
apprenticeship n. 실습 기간, 견습, 수습	internship n. 인턴사원 근무, 인턴직	recruit v. 모집하다; n. 신입 사원
candidate n. 지원자, 후보자	job opening (일자리) 공석	reference letter 추천서
certificate n. 자격증, 자격	oversee v. 감독하다	requirement n. 필요조건, 요건
corporation n. 기업, 회사	payroll n. 급여 대상자 명단, 급여 지급 총액	responsibility n. 책무, 책임
cover letter 자기소개서	pension n. 연금, 수당	senior adj. 상급의, 고위의
employment n. 고용, 채용	perk n. (급료 외의) 특전, 혜택	superintendent n. 관리자, 감독관
experience n. 업무 경력, 경험	professional adj. 전문적인	telecommuting n. 재택근무, 원격근무

토익실전문제

Questions 01-02 refer to the following advertisement.

Cine Clique Cinema

Cine Clique Cinema will launch its newest branch at 2993 Stanley Avenue on Monday, May 10. Guests can enjoy classic and critically acclaimed independent films from around the world. They can also choose from an array of snacks and beverages inside the theater.

Open daily from 9 A.M. through 11 P.M., the new theater is equipped with comfortable seating for up to 120 people as well as the latest in video projection equipment and sound systems. Patrons can also enjoy a meal at the adjacent Cine Café, where they can browse through a selection of movie-related magazines. All Cine Clique Cinemas offer free Wi-Fi service.

01 What is NOT mentioned about Cine Clique Cinema?
(A) It is planning to open a new location.
(B) It shows only the latest film releases.
(C) It closes at the same time each night.
(D) It provides free access to the Internet.

02 What can Cine Clique customers find at the Cine Café?
(A) An assortment of publications
(B) Free tickets to upcoming movies
(C) Coupons for a complimentary meal
(D) Souvenirs from classic movies

HACKERS TEST

토익 800+를 위한 실전 문제 정복   DAY 17

Questions 01-03 refer to the following receipt.

Silverpeak Mountain Resort

Thank you for choosing Silverpeak Resort. We are thrilled to have you join us for a memorable winter adventure!

Your Winter Ski Package Includes:
· Full access to all ski slopes
· Three two-hour lessons with a certified ski instructor
· Use of all necessary ski equipment

Reservation Details:
Name: Jennifer Matthews
Payment Date: December 15
Confirmation Code: ER9283474
Stay Period: January 22-24
Guests: 2
Total: $780.00
Payment method: Stanfield Credit Card (last four digits: 6824)

Check-in time is 3:00 P.M., and check-out time is 11:00 A.M. Late check-out requests are possible depending on room availability.

Note: You must notify us by e-mail of your intention to cancel this booking at least seven days prior to check-in to receive a full refund.

---

01 What is true about the package?

(A) It allows access only to beginner slopes.
(B) It includes multiple sessions of instruction.
(C) It requires additional payment for some equipment.
(D) It covers a period of four consecutive days.

02 What is suggested about Ms. Matthews?

(A) She is planning to travel with a companion.
(B) She will request permission to check out late.
(C) She has stayed at Silverpeak Resort before.
(D) She received a discount on a ski package.

03 How can Ms. Matthews get a refund?

(A) By calling the customer service center of a resort
(B) By e-mailing the organizers of a group tour
(C) By showing a transaction record to an employee
(D) By providing advance notice of a cancellation

Questions 04-07 refer to the following job advertisement.

Job Opening at Hamasaki Corporation

Hamasaki Corporation is a global corporation involved in the manufacture of automotive parts. We are currently seeking a warehouse supervisor to perform duties at our main production plant in Chicago, Illinois.

Primary duties:
- Coordinate shipment of finished goods to clients
- Maintain a safe and productive work environment
- Oversee the hiring, training, and terminating of employees
- Evaluate work processes and recommend improvements

Essential qualifications:
- Completion of at least a two-year college degree
- At least five years of experience in a related role, preferably in the automotive industry
- Ability to work with database programs
- Being highly organized and detail-oriented

This is a full-time role offering a competitive salary and benefits package. To apply, send your résumé to jobs@hamasakicorp.com. If you do not receive a confirmation e-mail, please contact our HR manager at 555-3090. Applications will not be accepted in person.

04 Which company posted the job advertisement?

(A) A car dealership
(B) A shipping provider
(C) A parts manufacturer
(D) A transport services firm

05 What is NOT mentioned about the position?

(A) It is offered by a multinational corporation.
(B) It includes the direct management of personnel.
(C) It requires involvement in product deliveries.
(D) It is available to part-time workers.

06 What is required of applicants for the position?

(A) Possession of a four-year university degree
(B) Recent participation in a company program
(C) Ability in more than one language
(D) Previous employment in a similar position

07 How should people apply?

(A) By sending an e-mail
(B) By mailing an application letter
(C) By contacting a manager
(D) By visiting the HR department

DAY 18 기사 및 안내문

기출 유형 1 기사

다양한 분야에 대한 사실이나 정보를 전달하기 위해 신문이나 잡지 등에 게재된 글로, 매회 2~3개의 지문이 출제된다.

출제 경향

1. 기사의 주제나 목적, 기사에 언급된 사람·회사·날짜·장소에 대한 세부 정보를 묻는 문제가 자주 출제된다.
2. 다음과 같은 주제가 자주 출제되며, 특히 비즈니스 관련 주제가 가장 많이 출제된다.

비즈니스	여러 산업에서의 동향, 지역 사업체 관련 소식
사회	교통, 문화 등의 다양한 사회적 이슈, 지역 행사 소식
환경	환경 관련 문제

800+ 공략

1. 기사의 앞부분이나 제목에서 주제를 정확히 파악하면 뒤따라오는 지문의 세부 내용을 파악하기 쉽다.
2. 비즈니스, 사회, 환경과 관련된 표현들을 알아 둔다. 기사의 경우 비교적 높은 수준의 어휘 능력이 요구되므로, 다양한 표현의 정확한 의미를 익히는 것이 도움이 된다.

Example

해석 p.205

Questions 01-02 refer to the following article.

OWENSBURG—German premium chocolate producer Hurlimann is opening its first international brick-and-mortar shop in Owensburg. It has scheduled a ribbon-cutting ceremony for January 8 at the Gilford Shopping Center.

According to store manager Joanne Lutz, the first 100 customers who purchase its chocolate will receive a free box of candy. Additionally, customers can get 50 percent off on selected merchandise for the first two weeks.

Founded over 100 years ago, Hurlimann has long exported its delicate chocolate products to vendors worldwide. "Now that we are finally opening our own branches overseas, we are excited to see what the future holds," said CEO David Carle.

01 How can customers receive a complimentary product?
(A) By answering some survey questions
(B) By being one of the first 100 buyers
(C) By purchasing specially selected items
(D) By returning within two weeks

02 What is true about Hurlimann?
(A) It will start to open shops abroad.
(B) It was founded in Owensburg a century ago.
(C) It has just appointed David Carle as a CEO.
(D) It is expanding its line of signature delicacies.

해설 01 육하원칙 문제

정답 01 (B) 02 (A)

지문의 'the first 100 customers who purchase its chocolate will receive a free box of candy'에서 그것, 즉 Hurlimann사의 초콜릿을 구매하는 첫 100명의 고객들은 무료 사탕 한 박스를 받을 것이라고 했으므로 (B)가 정답이다.

02 Not/True 문제

(A)는 'we are finally opening our own branches overseas'에서 저희, 즉 Hurlimann사는 마침내 해외에 자사 지점들을 여는 중이라고 했으므로 지문의 내용과 일치한다. 따라서 (A)가 정답이다. (B)는 'Founded over 100 years ago'에서 Hurlimann사가 100년 전에 설립되었다고는 했지만, 설립된 장소가 오웬즈버그라는 내용은 언급되지 않았으므로 지문의 내용과 일치하지 않는다. (C), (D)는 지문에 언급되지 않은 내용이다.

기사에 자주 나오는 필수 표현

비즈니스

brick-and-mortar adj. 오프라인의, 실제 매장의	industry n. 산업	privilege n. 혜택, 특권
finance n. 금융, 재정	market share 시장 점유율	producer n. 제조업체, 생산자
headquarters n. 본사	merchandise n. 상품, 물품	proposal n. 제안, 제안서
implement v. 시행하다, 이행하다	partnership n. 협력, 동업, 제휴	reliable adj. 믿을 수 있는, 신뢰할 수 있는

사회

charity n. 자선 단체, 자선	fundraising n. 모금 활동	proceeds n. 수익, 판매 대금
commercial adj. 상업적인	infrastructure n. 사회 기반 시설	public transportation 대중교통
community n. 지역 사회	local adj. 지역의, 현지의	residential adj. 주거의
contribute v. 기여하다, 기부하다	nonprofit adj. 비영리의	social welfare 사회 복지
donation n. 기부, 기증	outdated adj. 구식의, 시대에 뒤떨어진	

환경

conserve v. 보호하다, 보존하다	landfill n. 매립지	sustainable adj. 지속 가능한
contamination n. 오염	pollution n. 오염, 공해	temperature n. 기온, 온도
endangered adj. 멸종 위기에 처한	recyclable adj. 재활용 가능한	wildlife n. 야생 생물; adj. 야생 생물의
habitat n. 서식지, 자생지	renewable energy 재생 가능 에너지	wind power 풍력

토익실전문제

토익 문제 이렇게 나온다!

Questions 01-03 refer to the following article.

October 8—The finance corporation Bishop Advisors announced plans to sell its extensive collection of paintings and sculptures. The works were purchased by former CEO Aileen MacIntyre and are estimated to be worth over €3 million in total.

Current CEO Gavin Brodie admits that he is not interested in art, but this was not the main reason for his choice. "The company needs to raise funds, and there is not enough space for the collection in our new headquarters," Brodie commented.

Art collectors are excited by the news. "The collection includes paintings by Tessa Menzies and Bret Kennedy," said art expert Jennifer Harper, who plans to bid on some of the works. The sale, to be held on October 14, will be handled by Avidia Auctions.

01 What does the article mainly discuss?

(A) The appointment of a new executive
(B) A proposed set of financial regulations
(C) An upcoming sale of some artworks
(D) The discovery of a valuable piece of art

02 What is NOT mentioned as a reason for Mr. Brodie's decision?

(A) Lack of interest
(B) Financial necessities
(C) Space limitations
(D) Employee preferences

03 Who most likely will attend an event on October 14?

(A) Aileen MacIntyre
(B) Tessa Menzies
(C) Jennifer Harper
(D) Bret Kennedy

정답·해석·해설 p.205

기출 유형 2 　 안내문

일상에서 쉽게 접할 수 있는 다양한 정보를 제공하는 글로, 매회 1~2개의 지문이 출제된다.

출제 경향

1. 안내문의 주제나 목적, 안내문에서 얻을 수 있는 정보, 안내문에 언급된 업체나 상품에 대한 세부 정보, 안내문이 게재된 곳을 묻는 문제가 자주 출제된다.
2. 다음과 같은 주제가 자주 출제된다.

서비스/제품 안내	서비스 신청 방법 안내, 제품 사용 방법 설명
시설 안내	상점이나 호텔 등과 같은 시설 이용에 대한 설명
행사 안내	각종 행사에 대한 안내

800+ 공략

1. 지문 앞부분 또는 제목을 통해 먼저 주제를 파악한 후, 세부 내용을 읽어가면서 무엇에 대한 안내문인지 파악한다.
2. 서비스/제품 안내, 시설 안내, 행사 안내와 관련된 표현들을 알아 둔다.

Example

해석 p.206

Questions 01-02 refer to the following information.

We wish everyone a safe and pleasant visit to Lafayette County Park. To ensure that the park is kept fun and inviting for all, please observe the following rules:

- The park gates close at 10 P.M. and reopen at 6 A.M. Please do not enter the park when it is closed.
- Children should be supervised at all times. We accept no responsibility for any accidents occurring in the park.
- The basketball court and the soccer field next to the maintenance building are only available for use until 8 P.M.
- The speed limit is 20 miles per hour for all vehicles.
- We request that all visitors throw away trash only in designated trash bins.

Should a problem arise, contact the park supervisor at 555-6103.

01 What is NOT mentioned about Lafayette County Park?

(A) The hours of a maintenance office
(B) The location of sports facilities
(C) The speed limit for vehicles
(D) The contact information of a manager

02 According to the information, what are visitors urged to do?

(A) Pay an entrance fee
(B) Return rented equipment
(C) Dispose of trash properly
(D) Use designated parking areas

해설 01 Not/True 문제　　　　　　　　　　　　　　　　　　　　　　　　　　　　　　　　　　　　　　　정답 01 (A)　02 (C)

(A)는 지문에 언급되지 않은 내용이다. 따라서 (A)가 정답이다. (B)는 'The basketball court and the soccer field next to the maintenance building'에서 농구 코트와 축구장은 시설 관리 건물 옆에 위치해 있다고 했으므로 지문에 언급된 내용이다. (C)는 'The speed limit is 20 miles per hour for all vehicles.'에서 모든 차량의 제한 속도는 시속 20마일이라고 했으므로 지문에 언급된 내용이다. (D)는 'Should a problem arise, contact the park supervisor at 555-6103.'에서 문제가 발생하면 555-6103으로 공원 관리자에게 연락하라고 했으므로 지문에 언급된 내용이다.

02 육하원칙 문제

지문의 'We request that all visitors throw away trash only in designated trash bins.'에서 모든 방문객들이 쓰레기를 지정된 쓰레기통에만 버려 줄 것을 요청한다고 했으므로 (C)가 정답이다.

안내문에 자주 나오는 필수 표현

서비스/제품 안내

appliance n. 기구, 장치	component n. 구성 요소, 부품	return v. 반품하다; n. 반품
brand-new adj. 새로운, 신품의	launch v. 출시하다; n. 출시	shipping fee 배송비
bulk order 대량 주문	portable adj. 휴대용의, 휴대가 쉬운	up-to-date adj. 최신의, 첨단의
commodity n. 상품, 필수품	reserve v. (어떤 권한을) 갖다, 예약하다	user-friendly adj. 사용하기 쉬운

시설 안내

box office 매표소, 흥행 수익	grand opening 개장, 개점	premises n. 부지, 건물, 시설
complex n. 복합 건물, 단지	inaugural adj. 개시의, 취임의	premium adj. 고급의, 우수한
district n. 지구, 구역, 지역	maintenance n. 유지 관리, 보수	recreational adj. 여가의, 오락의
energy-efficient adj. 에너지 효율이 좋은	on-site adj. 현장의, 현지의	remodel v. 개조하다, 고치다

행사 안내

accommodate v. 수용하다, 편의를 제공하다	celebration n. 축하, 의식	participant n. 참가자
announce v. 발표하다	complimentary adj. 무료의	reveal v. 공개하다
anniversary n. 기념일	demonstration n. 시연	turn out 참석하다, 모이다
attendant n. 안내원, 종업원	entry n. 입장	venue n. 장소

토익실전문제

Questions 01-03 refer to the following information.

Seaver Department Store

Thank you for shopping at Seaver Department Store! We appreciate your business and always do our best to serve our valued customers.

If you make a purchase and, for any reason, would like to return it to the store for an exchange or refund, please read through the following up-to-date policies:

1. All exchange or refund requests must be made within 14 days of purchase.
2. All items must be accompanied by the original receipt.
3. We kindly ask that purchases be returned in the same condition as a brand-new product and with the original packaging.
4. Bathing suits and sportswear are not returnable.

Our staff reserves the right to reject a return request if any purchased item has been damaged by the customer.

01 What is the information about?

(A) Shipping processes
(B) Payment methods
(C) Retailer regulations
(D) Store promotions

02 What are customers asked to bring with an item being returned?

(A) The container the product came in
(B) An official return request form
(C) A valid piece of identification
(D) The credit card used to make a purchase

03 What is indicated about Seaver Department Store?

(A) It does not allow exchanges after one week.
(B) It sells some items that cannot be returned.
(C) It may refuse a refund request if an item was on sale.
(D) It does not offer repair services for damaged merchandise.

Questions 01-03 refer to the following information.

Astrapia Air—Using Reward Points for Seat Upgrades

To use your points to upgrade your seat when you reserve a ticket, select the "Reward Points Upgrade" option on our Web site. If you wish to do this after a ticket has been purchased, an upgrade can be requested in one of two ways: calling the Astrapia Air Call Center or modifying your booking on our Web site. Requests must be made at least 24 hours before your flight. The chart below indicates how many points are required to upgrade from one class to another within the various regions we fly to. Please note that upgrades may not be possible on some flights.

	From Economy Class to Premium Economy Class	From Premium Economy Class to Business Class	From Business Class to First Class
Europe	20,000 points	30,000 points	40,000 points
South America	20,000 points	30,000 points	
Central Asia	20,000 points	35,000 points	50,000 points
Southeast Asia	20,000 points		

01 The word "reserve" in paragraph 1, line 1, is closest in meaning to

(A) inquire
(B) operate
(C) restrict
(D) arrange

02 What is true about Astrapia Air?

(A) It prohibits upgrades within 24 hours of a flight.
(B) It maintains a partner program with other airlines.
(C) It does not accept calls for seat upgrades.
(D) It requires the most points for flights to Southeast Asia.

03 What can be inferred about flights to South America?

(A) Full ticket refunds are not possible.
(B) They can only be canceled on an airline Web site.
(C) They earn extra reward points for passengers.
(D) Upgrades are limited to certain seat classes.

Questions 04-06 refer to the following press release.

Zoet Foods Adapts to Changing Market Trends

March 21—Responding to current trends in the ice cream market, Switzerland's Zoet Foods has announced that it will be releasing new lines of products later this year. James Farnham, a marketing manager at Zoet, credits changing consumer tastes for this development. — [1] —. "Consumers are eating less ice cream and now prefer healthier alternatives like frozen yogurt," he said. The market has also been affected by demand for premium products like gelato and ice creams made with organic or non-dairy ingredients. — [2] —.

While Zoet has recently gained strength in China, Brazil, and India, the majority of its sales still come from Europe and the US. — [3] —. "We have plenty of room for growth," Farnham added, "but our biggest challenge is maintaining our leading position in Europe and the US." — [4] —. With Zoet's healthy new product lines, the company appears ready to take on this challenge.

04 What does the press release mainly discuss?

(A) Launch of new products in reaction to market conditions
(B) Innovations in a process for producing food items
(C) Global trends affecting the price of a product
(D) Strategies employed by some major food producers

05 How most likely does Zoet Foods plan to maintain its position in Europe and the US?

(A) By reducing the scale of its operations
(B) By utilizing lower-cost ingredients
(C) By introducing healthy products
(D) By reducing marketing efforts in Asia

06 In which of the positions marked [1], [2], [3], and [4] does the following sentence best belong?

"These categories are typically dominated by local specialty companies rather than global ones."

(A) [1]
(B) [2]
(C) [3]
(D) [4]

DAY 19 공고 및 회람

기출 유형 1 공고

변경된 규정이나 새로 시행되는 방침을 알리는 글로, 매회 1~2개의 지문이 출제된다.

출제 경향

1. 공고의 목적, 공고의 대상 및 그 대상에게 요청하는 것, 공고에 언급된 세부 정보를 묻는 문제가 자주 출제된다.
2. 다음과 같은 주제가 자주 출제된다.

일반 공고	지역 단체에서 시행하는 각종 행사 소개, 상점과 같은 시설의 안내 사항 전달
사내 공고	회사 내의 정책 변경 및 업무 관련 사항에 대한 알림

800+ 공략

1. 공고는 주로 목적이 먼저 명시된 후 추후 일정, 요청 사항, 관련된 사람 등이 뒤따라 나온다는 점을 기억한다.
2. 일반 공고, 사내 공고와 관련된 표현들을 알아 둔다.

Example

해석 p.208

Questions 01-02 refer to the following announcement.

The West University Writing Center offers all registered students assistance with editing their writing assignments for classes. Proofreading services are available Mondays through Fridays from 8:30 A.M. to 8:00 P.M.

For those seeking to improve their writing, we also arrange tutoring sessions via appointment at our main desk. Writing tutors are current graduate students in the colleges of education and liberal arts and are available to guide you through the writing process for any class assignment. Stop by the West University Writing Center at 450 Ernestine Hall for more information.

01 What is the purpose of the announcement?
 (A) To invite professional writers to a workshop
 (B) To publicize the opening of an educational center
 (C) To announce an upcoming change to a university service
 (D) To promote some services offered at a facility

02 What is NOT mentioned about the writing center?
 (A) It is accessible by anyone enrolled at the school.
 (B) It offers online classes for students with busy schedules.
 (C) It can arrange private instructional sessions.
 (D) It employs graduate students as tutors.

해설 01 목적 문제   정답 01 (D) 02 (B)

공고의 'The West University Writing Center offers all registered students assistance with editing their writing assignments for classes.'에서 West 대학의 글쓰기 센터는 모든 등록된 학생들에게 수업의 글쓰기 과제를 수정하는 데 도움을 제공한다고 한 후, 학생들이 이용 가능한 교정 서비스와 개인 교습에 대해 설명하고 있으므로 (D)가 정답이다.

02 Not/True 문제

(B)는 지문에 언급되지 않은 내용이다. 따라서 (B)가 정답이다. (A)는 'The West University Writing Center offers all registered students assistance with editing their writing assignments for classes.'에서 West 대학의 글쓰기 센터는 모든 등록된 학생들에게 수업의 글쓰기 과제를 수정하는 데 도움을 제공한다고 했으므로 지문의 내용과 일치한다. (C)는 'we ~ arrange tutoring sessions via appointment at our main desk'에서 메인 데스크에서 예약을 통해 개인 교습 시간을 마련해 준다고 했으므로 지문의 내용과 일치한다. (D)는 'Writing tutors are current graduate students'에서 글쓰기 개인 교사는 현재 대학원생이라고 했으므로 지문의 내용과 일치한다.

공고에 자주 나오는 필수 표현

일반 공고

city council 시의회	inform v. 알리다, 통지하다	postpone v. 연기하다, 미루다
description n. 설명, 묘사	installation n. 설치, 설비	prerequisite n. 필수 조건, 전제 조건
duration n. 지속 기간, 기간	investigate v. 살피다, 조사하다	quarterly adj. 분기별의
election n. 선거	municipal adj. 시립의, 지방 자치의	request v. 요청하다; n. 요청
host v. 주최하다; n. 주최자, 진행자	official adj. 공식적인; n. 관계자, 공무원	security n. 보안, 안전
in accordance with ~에 따라서	patronage n. 단골, 후원	storage n. 저장, 보관
incentive n. 장려책	place an order 주문하다	vacate v. 비우다, 떠나다

사내 공고

adhere v. 준수하다, 고수하다	distribute v. 분배하다, 나누어 주다	manager n. 관리자
auditorium n. 강당, 청중석	duty n. 의무, 직무	negotiate v. 교섭하다, 협상하다
board meeting 이사회 회의	gather v. 모이다, 집합하다	overview n. 개요, 개관
compromise n. 타협, 양보; v. 타협하다	inaccessible adj. 접근할 수 없는	persuade v. 설득하다, 납득시키다
consensus n. 합의, 의견 일치	instruction n. 지시, 설명	preliminary adj. 예비의, 준비의
disapprove v. 거절하다, 반대하다	keynote speaker 기조연설자	undertake v. (일·책임을) 맡다, 착수하다

토익실전문제

Questions 01-03 refer to the following notice.

Barnes Books is happy to announce that we will be moving to a larger location! Our current store at 449 Rooster Street will close on March 28. Our brand-new space, situated at 5983 Spencer Avenue, will be open to customers on April 16. Hours of operation will remain as they were before, from 10 A.M. through 8 P.M. Monday to Saturday.

Barnes Books is also pleased to announce that we will start offering a shipping service in the new store. Simply select the items you wish to purchase and fill out an address card. Your shipping fees will be calculated immediately, and all items will be sent within 24 hours.

So visit us at our new location on April 16 and receive 20 percent off any purchase to celebrate this special event for Barnes Books! Call us at 555-4059 for inquiries or further information. For a calendar of special events hosted by Barnes Books, go to www.barnesbooks.com/events or pick up a copy of our monthly newsletter.

01 What is NOT indicated about Barnes Books?

(A) It is open six days a week.
(B) It is selling off old inventory.
(C) It plans to close temporarily.
(D) It provides a regular publication.

02 The word "situated" in paragraph 1, line 2, is closest in meaning to

(A) positioned
(B) involved
(C) performed
(D) reached

03 What will Barnes Books do in April?

(A) It will extend its operating hours.
(B) It will hire additional employees.
(C) It will introduce a new service.
(D) It will increase the delivery fee.

기출 유형 2 회람

회사 내부에서 공지 사항 및 새로운 소식을 전달하는 글로, 매회 0~1개의 지문이 출제된다.

출제 경향

1. 회람의 주제나 목적, 회람에 언급된 업무나 사람에 대한 세부 정보, 수신자에게 요청하는 사항을 묻는 문제가 자주 출제된다.
2. 다음과 같은 주제가 자주 출제된다.

사내 방침	새로 시행되거나 변경되는 사내 방침 전달, 새로운 규정 공지
사내 시설	사내 시설 이용 관련 안내
업무 및 행사	업무 관련 공지, 회사 행사 개최 전달

800+ 공략

1. 회람은 주로 처음에 수신자(To ~)와 발신자(From ~)가 나오고, 'Subject ~' 뒤에 주제가 나오기도 하는 점을 기억한다.
2. 사내 방침, 사내 시설, 업무 및 행사와 관련된 표현들을 알아 둔다.

Example

해석 p.209

Questions 01-02 refer to the following memo.

MEMO

To: All staff
From: Amanda Robinson
Subject: Matthew Webb
Date: May 20

Please be informed that Matthew Webb will be replacing Daniel Rodgers as purchasing manager for Longview Holdings, effective June 1. Please address all purchase requests for office supplies and equipment to Mr. Webb from that date. As before, all request forms must be approved and signed by a departmental supervisor prior to submission. I appreciate your cooperation in making this transition smooth.

---

01 Why did Ms. Robinson write the memo?
(A) To provide instructions about a new office policy
(B) To request orders for office supplies
(C) To inform staff about an open position
(D) To notify employees about a change in personnel

02 How should employees at Longview Holdings request new office supplies?
(A) By filling out an online form
(B) By calling an office extension
(C) By submitting a signed document
(D) By going to a supplier's Web site

해설 01 글을 쓴 이유 문제 정답 01 (D)   02 (C)

지문의 'Please be informed that Matthew Webb will be replacing Daniel Rodgers as purchasing manager for Longview Holdings'에서 Matthew Webb이 Longview Holdings사의 구매 관리자로서 Daniel Rodgers를 대신하게 될 것임을 알아두라고 했으므로 (D)가 정답이다.

02 육하원칙 문제

지문의 'all request forms must be ~ signed by a departmental supervisor prior to submission'에서 모든 요청 양식은 제출 전에 부서 관리자에 의해 서명되어야 한다고 했으므로 (C)가 정답이다.

회람에 자주 나오는 필수 표현

사내 방침

abide by ~을 준수하다	expenditure n. 지출, 소비	policy n. 정책
address v. 제출하다, 다루다, 연설하다; n. 연설	merger n. 합병, 합동	profitable adj. 수익성이 있는, 유익한
cooperation n. 협조, 협력	ownership n. 소유, 소유권	shareholder n. 주주
division n. 부서, 부	personnel n. 인사, 직원	streamline v. 간소화하다, 능률적으로 하다

사내 시설

capacity n. 수용 인원, 용량	detour v. 우회하다, 돌아가다; n. 우회로, 우회	spacious adj. 넓은, 광대한
cater v. 음식을 조달하다	entrance n. 입장, 입구	stadium n. 경기장, 체육관
corridor n. 복도, 통로	locate v. (어떤 장소에) 위치하다, 배치하다	workspace n. 작업 공간

업무 및 행사

constructive adj. 건설적인, 발전적인	fulfill v. (의무 등을) 이행하다, 충족하다	reexamine v. 재검토하다, 다시 살펴보다
criticism n. 비판, 비평	liaison n. 연락 담당자, 연락	retreat n. (회사) 워크숍
employ v. 고용하다, 사용하다	procedure n. 절차, 과정	showcase v. 선보이다, 전시하다
follow-up n. 후속 조치; adj. 후속의	receptive adj. 수용적인, 받아들이는	transfer v. 옮기다, 이동하다; n. 전근, 이동

토익실전문제

Questions 01-03 refer to the following memo.

Organic Products Alliance

To: Administrative staff
From: Tom Williams, director
Date: August 10
Subject: Organic producers database

Our organization will be holding our Second Annual Organic Product Trade Show in Santa Cruz in October. We anticipate that nearly 2,000 exhibitors will participate in the show. At our last event, we had over 1,500 companies showcase their products. With more publicity, we are certain that the number will increase significantly this year.

In preparation for the upcoming event, the marketing team is going to create an accurate database of organic product companies. However, they need assistance from other departments since most of their members are busy organizing the event itself. Fortunately, Ms. Eliza Banks from the research division has volunteered to help. Therefore, I request that you work with Ms. Banks to complete this assignment. She will contact you to let you know when a meeting has been arranged. Please give her your full cooperation.

---

01 For whom is the memo intended?

(A) Employees assigned to do a specific task
(B) Producers of organic food items
(C) Leaders of event organization teams
(D) Businesses involved in the food service industry

02 What is indicated about Organic Products Alliance?

(A) It appointed a new administrative director.
(B) It moved its main office to Santa Cruz.
(C) It sponsored a fundraising event.
(D) It held a product exhibition.

03 Who will contact administrative staff about the meeting?

(A) A company president
(B) The head of the marketing team
(C) A member of the research department
(D) The event coordinator

Questions 01-03 refer to the following notice.

NOTICE

Attention: All Passengers Using Transit Passes

Passengers who have lost their transit pass cards can have their cards reissued for a three-dollar fee at any Madisonville Transit Authority ticket office. Any remaining credit will be transferred to the new one automatically. Passengers making a request must present one piece of identification containing a photograph. Corporate ID cards are not considered a valid form of identification. If you happen to find your old card after your card has been reissued, please discard it as it will no longer function.

Please note that these regulations do not apply to one-day or three-day tourist passes. Holders of such passes must purchase new cards. Tourist passes are available wherever regular transit cards are sold. If you require additional information about your transit pass, visit www.madisonvilletransit.org.

01 Why was the notice written?

(A) To announce fare adjustments
(B) To give updates on route changes
(C) To inform passengers of delays
(D) To offer information on travel cards

02 What is suggested about the Madisonville Transit Authority?

(A) It recently opened several new ticketing offices.
(B) It requires that travel cards have photographs.
(C) It deactivates cards that have been reported lost.
(D) It does not accept credit cards at stations.

03 What is true about the tourist passes?

(A) They can be purchased for three dollars each.
(B) They are not valid for longer than a single day.
(C) They must be returned once they have expired.
(D) They are sold at the same places as regular passes.

Questions 04-07 refer to the following memo.

Davenport Accounting

MEMO

TO: All Staff
FROM: Phillip Christensen

As most of you are already aware, we will soon be undergoing a complete update of our office hardware. — [1] —. Much of our old equipment will be replaced. We will be upgrading our server as well as providing new PCs to everyone who has not received one in the past five years. — [2] —. In addition, new printers will be stationed throughout the office.

If you are receiving a new computer, please make sure to copy all necessary files onto an external hard drive by Friday. This is important as the old equipment will be replaced over the weekend and will be inaccessible from Monday.

— [3] —. Should there be a delay, you will be notified. If you have any questions, call me at extension 115 or send me an e-mail at philchristensen@davenport.com. — [4] —.

---

04 What is the purpose of the memo?

(A) To remind employees about a planned activity
(B) To explain reasons for staff replacement
(C) To communicate a change in work hours
(D) To update workers on security procedures

05 What is NOT indicated in the memo?

(A) Some devices have been used for over five years.
(B) The office will receive some new printers.
(C) The equipment will be removed after Friday.
(D) Some staff will have to do overtime next week.

06 What does Mr. Christensen say employees are responsible for?

(A) Creating training materials for new equipment
(B) Scanning important documents for company records
(C) Transferring electronic files onto a backup device
(D) Rescheduling appointments due to an office closure

07 In which of the positions marked [1], [2], [3], and [4] does the following sentence best belong?

"The technicians aim to finish all the work by Sunday."

(A) [1]
(B) [2]
(C) [3]
(D) [4]

DAY 20 다중 지문

두 개의 지문이 한 세트로 구성된 이중 지문과 세 개의 지문이 한 세트로 구성된 삼중 지문이 있다. 이중 지문은 매회 2세트, 삼중 지문은 매회 3세트 출제된다.

출제 경향

1. 5개의 문제 중 1~2문제는 두 개 이상의 지문에서 각각 단서를 찾아 조합해야 정답을 찾을 수 있는 연계 문제로 출제된다.
2. 이중 지문은 다음과 같은 지문 조합이 자주 출제된다.

광고 & 이메일	업체 광고 & 이용 문의 이메일
광고 & 양식	제품 및 서비스에 대한 광고 & 고객의 이용 내역 및 후기
기사 & 이메일	비즈니스 업계 소식 관련 기사 & 해당 소식 관련 논의 이메일
양식 & 양식	제품 및 시설을 소개하는 웹페이지 & 고객의 주문 내역

3. 삼중 지문은 다음과 같은 지문 조합이 자주 출제된다.

양식 & 양식 & 이메일	제품 및 서비스에 대한 브로슈어 & 고객의 이용 후기 & 후기를 작성한 고객에게 직원이 보낸 이메일
이메일 & 양식 & 이메일	서비스 이용 관련 문의 이메일 & 서비스 이용 내역 & 문의에 대한 답변 이메일
이메일 & 광고 & 양식	제품 및 서비스 홍보 방안에 대한 세부 사항 & 제품 및 서비스에 대한 광고 & 고객의 이용 후기
공고 & 양식 & 기사	행사 공고 & 행사 참가 양식 & 행사 관련 기사
안내문 & 이메일 & 양식	서비스 신청 방법 안내문 & 고객의 서비스 신청 이메일 & 서비스 이용 영수증

800+ 공략

1. 시간 단축을 위해 주제/목적 문제처럼 초반부만 읽거나 동의어 문제처럼 지문의 일부분만 읽고 정답을 고를 수 있는 문제 유형을 먼저 풀이한다.
2. 육하원칙, Not/True, 추론 문제가 연계 문제로 가장 많이 출제되며, 이들은 풀이 시간이 비교적 오래 걸리므로 나중에 풀이한다.
3. 연계 문제는 지문에 나온 시간, 날짜, 가격, 수량 등의 숫자와 관련된 문제로 자주 출제되므로, 지문에 쓰인 숫자에 주목한다.

Example

Questions 01-02 refer to the following advertisement and booking confirmation.

Trans-Russia Railways

Trans-Russia Railways (TRR) is now offering special tourist passes, allowing unlimited travel to all TRR destinations within the country. Passes can be purchased at most train terminals or travel agencies in Russia, as well as at www.transrussiarailways.com.

Rail passes are valid for seven days. Simply present your pass to staff at any train station or terminal to gain access to trains. Rail passes cost $380 for adults, $320 for students, and $280 for children 12 and under.

For a flat fee of $100, food and beverage services will be offered for all trips. This will include all menu items available in dining cars.

Passes are nonrefundable and nontransferable.

Trans-Russia Railways Tourist Pass Confirmation

NAME	Fatima Khan	TRAVEL DATE	June 12
FEE	☐ $380 ■ $320 ☐ $280	MEALS	■ Yes ☐ No

Please note that tourist pass holders are permitted two pieces of luggage with a total weight of 50 kilograms. Travelers are recommended to arrive 30 minutes in advance of their scheduled departure.

---

01 What information is included in the advertisement?
(A) Requirements to receive a refund
(B) Ways to purchase a pass
(C) Cities connected by a railway
(D) Dishes served in a dining area

02 What is suggested about Ms. Khan?
(A) She has traveled to Russia before.
(B) She purchased an adult ticket.
(C) She paid an additional fee of $100.
(D) She is touring with a group.

해설 **01 육하원칙 문제**
정답 01 (B) 02 (C)

지문의 'Passes can be purchased at most train terminals or travel agencies in Russia, as well as at www.transrussiarailways.com.'에서 탑승권은 www.transrussiarailways.com뿐만 아니라 러시아 내의 대부분의 기차역이나 여행사에서 구매할 수 있다고 했으므로 (B)가 정답이다.

02 추론 문제 연계

질문의 핵심 어구인 Ms. Khan이 언급된 예약 확인서를 먼저 확인한다.

[단서 1] 예약 확인서의 'MEALS'와 '■ Yes'에서 Ms. Khan이 식사 서비스를 선택했다는 것을 확인할 수 있다. 그런데 식사 서비스에 대한 요금은 제시되지 않았으므로 광고에서 관련 내용을 확인한다.

[단서 2] 광고의 'For a flat fee of $100, food and beverage services will be offered'에서 100달러의 정액 요금으로 음식과 음료 서비스가 제공될 것이라고 했다.

두 단서를 종합할 때, Ms. Khan이 100달러의 추가 비용을 지불하여 식사 서비스를 이용할 것이라는 사실을 추론할 수 있다. 따라서 (C)가 정답이다.

Questions 01-05 refer to the following announcement, letter, and application form.

Soaring Skies Academy
Flight Attendant Training Program

Soaring Skies Academy offers comprehensive training to individuals wishing to become flight attendants. Our next program starts on June 1. It will cover a variety of topics, ranging from how to provide excellent customer service to what to do in situations that threaten the safety of our passengers.

Anyone interested in participating should fill out the application form on our Web site at www.soaringskies.com/trainingapp. The completed form must be submitted along with one letter of recommendation from a previous supervisor or teacher.

Upon completion of the training program, graduates will receive one-on-one counseling from our instructors regarding the most effective methods to obtain a flight attendant position.

Soaring Skies Academy
55 Westwood Avenue
San Francisco, CA 94125

April 28

Dear Sir or Madam,

I am pleased to provide my recommendation for Ms. Linda Sykes as a candidate for your flight attendant training program. During her time at the Harper Hotel, Ms. Sykes has proven herself to be a diligent and capable employee.

Additionally, Ms. Sykes has completed several flight attendant training courses at Redmond Online Vocational Academy. Thus, it is clear that her true passion lies in becoming a professional in the airline industry.

If you require further information or clarification regarding this reference, please feel free to contact me directly at 555-2329.

Sincerely,
Simon Chung

Soaring Skies Academy

Flight Attendant Training Program

Online Application Form

Full Name: Linda Sykes

Address: 120 Norwell Street, Sacramento, CA 94240

Phone Number: 555-1287

Have you attended any airline attendant training programs before?

☑ Yes   ☐ No

Attach a letter of recommendation by clicking here.

Application Fee Payment
Amount Due: $50
Payment Method: Credit card number XXXX-XXXX-7382-1281

*Tuition payment is due by June 9. A 10 percent discount will be applied if you have previous work experience at one of our academy's partner companies listed below:
- Graytown Rental Vehicles
- Pristine Travel Agency
- Harper Hotel

[SUBMIT]   [PRINT]

---

01 What is true about the program?

(A) It will take place over the course of a year.
(B) It is conducted entirely on the Internet.
(C) It will deal with emergency procedures.
(D) It is designed for current airline employees.

02 According to the announcement, what will happen at the end of the program?

(A) Trainees will participate in a social event.
(B) Instructors will administer a written test.
(C) Staff members will give advice to participants.
(D) Course graduates will attend a ceremony.

03 What can be concluded about Mr. Chung?

(A) He was Ms. Sykes's supervisor at a previous job.
(B) He is a long-term customer of Harper Hotel.
(C) He formed a business partnership with Ms. Sykes.
(D) He used to teach at the Soaring Skies Academy.

04 What does the application form ask about?

(A) Prior education experience
(B) Professional goals
(C) Financial details
(D) An e-mail address

05 What is Ms. Sykes eligible to receive?

(A) A guided tour of a training facility
(B) A free textbook for a course
(C) A membership in a rewards program
(D) A reduced rate on a tuition fee

Questions 01-05 refer to the following advertisement and e-mail.

Take a Vacation from Stress!

In today's fast-paced world, stress often impacts both mental and physical health. Yoga has been proven to alleviate stress, increase energy, and improve concentration.

For this month only, try out any of the yoga courses at the Tantra Meditation Center for free! Call 555-4994 to reserve your spot in one of the following sessions:

Beginners' Yoga	Instructor: Pradeep Rathnam	Monday 7 P.M.-8:30 P.M.
Intermediate Yoga	Instructor: Diana Koutsakis	Tuesday 7 P.M.-8:30 P.M.
Advanced Yoga	Instructor: Parvati Singh	Wednesday 7:30 P.M.-9:00 P.M.
Meditation and Yoga	Instructor: Dan Mathers	Thursday 6:30 P.M.-8:00 P.M.

Due to limited space, reservations must be made in advance for free classes. All classes are conducted at the Tantra Meditation Center at 3884 Bolton Way. Should you wish to continue a course, simply submit a registration form and pay the $120 monthly fee.

TO: Customer Service <cservice@tantracenter.com>
FROM: Leanne Allen <lallen@localmail.com>
DATE: January 11
SUBJECT: Yoga courses

My name is Leanne Allen, and I am currently enrolled in your center's complimentary yoga course trial. I am finding the session to be beneficial overall, so I would like to continue with the classes next month.

While I was at your center, I browsed through your selection of yoga-related accessories, and I am interested in purchasing a few things. One of your employees informed me that I am eligible for a discount of 15 percent if I am an enrolled member.

Could you possibly send me a registration form by e-mail? That way I can fill it out and drop it off at my next class.

Lastly, my husband Joel says he is interested in trying out Parvati Singh's class next week. Could you reserve a spot for him?

Thank you for your assistance.

Leanne Allen

01 What is the advertisement mainly about?

(A) Some specialized yoga equipment
(B) Complimentary instructional sessions
(C) A treatment for a medical condition
(D) A membership in an online program

02 What is mentioned about the Tantra Meditation Center?

(A) It accepts only cash payments.
(B) It opened a second branch.
(C) It offers private meditation sessions.
(D) It has limited class sizes.

03 What did Ms. Allen recently do at the Tantra Meditation Center?

(A) Checked out some fitness products
(B) Picked up an informational pamphlet
(C) Taught an intermediate yoga course
(D) Filled out an application form

04 What will Ms. Allen most likely be sent?

(A) A receipt for refund
(B) A schedule of classes
(C) An enrollment form
(D) A discount voucher

05 What does Ms. Allen indicate about her husband?

(A) He is interested in becoming an instructor.
(B) He has already paid for Ms. Singh's class.
(C) He wants to attend an advanced yoga class.
(D) He participated in a session on Wednesday.

Questions 06-10 refer to the following Web page and order form.

---

www.crawfordoffice.com

| Home | About | Shop | Accounts | Customer Service |

Crawford Office Supply

Find everything your office needs!

Crawford Office Supply has been meeting the needs of businesses in Dallas for over 30 years now. As a locally owned and operated company, we take pride in providing great customer service and low prices. And we are pleased to announce that we will be opening our second branch at 321 Victor Street on the south side of the city on June 15.

To celebrate, both of our stores will be offering customers a free tote bag for every purchase of office furniture from June 15 to 30. So whatever you need for your workspace, be sure to visit Crawford Office Supply. We are open from 9:00 A.M. until 10:00 P.M. seven days a week. See you soon!

Crawford Office Supply
Order Form

Customer Name: Yvonne Murphy   **Date:** June 20
Company: Stanford Accounting   **Phone Number:** 555-0396
Delivery Address: 789 Harbor Road, Dallas, TX 75001

Item #	Product	Quantity	Price
2837	EZ Write Pen	10	$15
5839	Harris Notebook	15	$60
6934	RX350 Printer Cartridge	2	$50
7135	Sylex Chair	4	$300

Notes:		
I would like my order to be delivered by June 23. Please call me back today to let me know if this is possible. Workers will be replacing the flooring in my office building's lobby from June 24 to 27, and no one will be allowed to use the main entryway during this period. Thank you.	Subtotal	$425
	Tax	$34
	Shipping	$48
	Total	$507

06 What is mentioned about Crawford Office Supply?

(A) It will open a new location in June.
(B) It will relocate staff to its Dallas store.
(C) It will establish branches in several cities.
(D) It will change its current operating hours.

07 What must customers do to take advantage of an offer?

(A) Select a certain brand
(B) Order within a specified period
(C) Make a minimum purchase
(D) Visit a particular branch

08 For which product did Ms. Murphy receive a free item?

(A) EZ Write Pen
(B) Harris Notebook
(C) RX350 Printer Cartridge
(D) Sylex Chair

09 What does Ms. Murphy ask for?

(A) Verification of a price
(B) Information about a location
(C) Confirmation regarding a request
(D) Cancellation of a purchase

10 What does Ms. Murphy mention about her office building?

(A) Windows will be replaced.
(B) A parking lot will be expanded.
(C) Elevators will be repaired.
(D) An entrance will be inaccessible.

Questions 11-15 refer to the following Web page and e-mails.

---

www.magnumcruises.com

Magnum Cruises

| HOME | ABOUT | PRESS | JOBS |

We are currently taking applicants for open positions on cruises operating in the following regions throughout the year.

Southern Africa
As a guest relations officer, work aboard the *Magnum Explorer* from October through March welcoming guests, organizing activities, and addressing customer concerns. See more

Australia & the Pacific
As an entertainment specialist, work aboard the *Magnum Endeavor* from November through February under the supervision of the entertainment director. See more

India & Sri Lanka
As a ship's nurse, work aboard the *Magnum Adventure* from April through July caring for passengers' health. See more

Southeast Asia
As an assistant restaurant manager, work aboard the *Magnum Pacifica* from May through September ensuring the smooth delivery of dining services. See more

To apply, send your résumé and cover letter to our head office at Suite 100, Capital Building, 65 Canal Road, Singapore 049513. Or you can send them by e-mail to hr@magnumcruises.com. We will contact applicants who pass the initial screening process. When applying, please state your desired position.

To	Human Resources <hr@magnumcruises.com>
From	Leo Manresa <l.manresa@hypemail.com>
Subject	Application
Date	October 22

Dear Sir or Madam,

I am interested in the assistant restaurant manager position. I hold a degree in food and beverage management, and I have previously worked on cruise ships. I also speak three languages, have a certificate of good health from a licensed physician, and have all necessary travel documents in order. I trust that my qualifications make me a strong candidate for this position with Magnum Cruises.

Sincerely,

Leo Manresa

To	Leo Manresa <l.manresa@hypemail.com>
From	Jessica Lewen <j.lewen@magnumcruises.com>
Subject	Interview
Date	November 11

Dear Mr. Manresa,

Thank you for applying for a position with Magnum Cruises. After reviewing your qualifications, we are pleased to invite you to an online interview on November 15 at 10:00 A.M. Detailed instructions will be provided once you have confirmed your availability. If successful, you will travel to our head office to undergo two months' training before officially starting your job at the beginning of the season.

Sincerely,

Jessica Lewen
Recruitment Manager
Magnum Cruises

11 What is true about Magnum Cruises?

(A) It has just introduced a new cruise itinerary.
(B) It has some openings at its head office.
(C) It provides services all year long.
(D) It sends ships to cities in North America.

12 According to the Web page, what is suggested about the hiring process?

(A) Some candidates will not receive replies.
(B) All interviews will be conducted in person.
(C) Language skills are required for all positions.
(D) Salaries will not be disclosed in advance.

13 On which ship is Mr. Manresa most likely applying to work?

(A) *Magnum Explorer*
(B) *Magnum Endeavor*
(C) *Magnum Adventure*
(D) *Magnum Pacifica*

14 What will Ms. Lewen be providing to Mr. Manresa?

(A) A list of job duties
(B) A training plan
(C) A plane ticket
(D) A set of instructions

15 What can be inferred about Mr. Manresa?

(A) He may be assigned to multiple regions.
(B) He might have to travel to Singapore.
(C) He is currently employed by another cruise company.
(D) He worked on a ship near India and Sri Lanka.

Questions 16-20 refer to the following e-mail, advertisement, and review.

To	All marketing staff <marketingteam@fizzlespark.com>
From	Irina Sokolov <i.sokolov@fizzlespark.com>
Date	April 4
Subject	Marketing Campaign

Hello all,

I want to thank everyone for their hard work finishing up our advertising campaign for the company's newly launched line of organic juices—Whole Renew. The CEO has reviewed the finalized ads and is delighted with the results.

As a reminder, details about our upcoming promotions will be posted on our homepage according to the following schedule:

May—Buy one, get one free offer
June—20 percent off promotion
July—Coupon for $5 off a future purchase

Finally, I encourage you to sample the line using your employee discount. Having tried them myself, I can guarantee that they are incredibly tasty!

Regards,

Irina Sokolov
Marketing Department Head, FizzleSpark National

FizzleSpark National
Whole Renew

Reach for a bottle of Whole Renew—a line of delicious juices made with 100 percent organic ingredients. Choose from a wide selection of drinks to suit your taste, from beet and apple to mango and ginger. Plus, all of these refreshing choices are two for the price of one this month.

The deals don't end there! Pick up a Whole Renew beverage at any Victoria Café location on June 10 and get a free organic snack. Download the Victoria Café smartphone application for additional details.

Victoria Café

Rating: ★★★★★ (5 stars)

While picking up some new clothes at the Shearmont Shopping Plaza on June 10, I decided to stop by this café. Overall, I was very impressed. The atmosphere was inviting, and the staff members were friendly. My server suggested that I try one of the Whole Renew juices as there was a promotion that day, and I'm glad I did. It was a delightful surprise—fresh and tasty! The next time you are in the Shearmont Shopping Plaza, I recommend visiting this café. You won't regret it.

-Sarah Klein

16 What type of company most likely is FizzleSpark National?

(A) A coffee shop
(B) A beverage producer
(C) An advertising agency
(D) A supermarket chain

17 According to the e-mail, what does Ms. Sokolov suggest?

(A) Contacting an executive about an evaluation
(B) Finishing a project ahead of schedule
(C) Making use of an employee benefit
(D) Changing the time of a client meeting

18 What is indicated about the deal discussed in the advertisement?

(A) It is only offered to customers enrolled in a membership program.
(B) It was rejected by the president of a corporation.
(C) It is limited to purchases made at one location.
(D) It was posted on a Web site in May.

19 What is one feature of Whole Renew?

(A) A variety of flavors
(B) A sugar-free ingredient
(C) Colorful packaging
(D) Ample vitamins

20 What did Ms. Klein most likely do at Victoria Café?

(A) Received a food item free of charge
(B) Signed up for a membership
(C) Spoke with a facility manager
(D) Picked up a limited-time coupon

Questions 21-25 refer to the e-mail, registration form, and schedule.

To: Marcus Dodd <mar_dodd@webbermail.com>
From: Keisha Joubert <kjoubert@seafairresort.com>
Date: July 24
Subject: Upcoming trip

Dear Mr. Dodd,

We are looking forward to your arrival at Seafair Resort on August 18. As you and the two other guests in your group will be staying for four days, you may want to take part in some of our offered activities. For instance, our tennis courts are available to anyone who wants to use them. We also have windsurfing equipment that can be used on a first-come, first-served basis. However, if you would like to join one of our popular hikes on Grand Soeur Island, you should register at our front desk or on our Web site at least one day in advance. This is also the case for kayaking trips to Petite Soeur Island and Reynolds Island, as well as snorkeling and scuba diving excursions to Coco Island. To join any of these activities, visit www.seafair.com/activities.

Sincerely,

Keisha Joubert
Activity Manager
Seafair Resort

Seafair Resort—Registration Form * Snorkeling

Name of Guest	Marcus Dodd
Room Number	723
Today's Date	August 19
Desired Date of Activity	August 20
Equipment Needed (Check All that Apply)	☐ Fins ☐ Mask ☐ Snorkel
Ability Level	☐ Inexperienced ☐ Competent ☑ Expert

Important Considerations
1. We are unable to rent or sell bathing suits. Participants must have their own.
2. This activity is limited to 15 people per day.
3. If fewer than five people have enrolled in the scuba diving excursion planned for the same day, they will join your group on the boat, the *Waveroller*.
4. If weather conditions are unsuitable, this activity will be canceled.
5. Participants with health conditions must provide relevant medical information to the guide.

Plan for August 20 Snorkeling Excursion Guide: Terry Haide, Bluewater License holder		
Activities	**Time**	**Notes**
Meet at Seafair Resort's Leisure Hut	9:00 A.M.	
Depart from Seafair Dock	9:10 A.M.	Scuba diving groups will take the same transport.
Arrive at Site 1	9:30 A.M.	
Attend a safety briefing	9:40 A.M.	
Receive instructions on using equipment	10:00 A.M.	
Snorkel around Ombre Reef	10:15 A.M.	Participants will be led on an underwater tour.
Take a break	11:00 A.M.	
Snorkel around Urchin Cove	11:30 A.M.	Participants will be able to explore on their own.
Have lunch	12:15 P.M.	Meals will be served at a picnic area.
Return to Seafair Resort	1:15 P.M.	

21 Why did Ms. Joubert contact Mr. Dodd?

(A) To inform him about leisure options
(B) To convince him to change a booking
(C) To ask about accommodation preferences
(D) To offer an incentive for joining a club

22 What is indicated about Mr. Dodd in the registration form?

(A) He signed up several days in advance.
(B) He will bring his own gear with him.
(C) He submitted a medical document.
(D) He will try snorkeling for the first time.

23 What is indicated about the scuba diving participants on August 20?

(A) They consist of fewer than five individuals.
(B) They are attempting to obtain the Bluewater License.
(C) They will have to pay extra fees upon checking out.
(D) They will return to Seafair Resort in the evening.

24 According to the schedule, when will an independent session take place?

(A) 9:10 A.M.
(B) 10:00 A.M.
(C) 10:15 A.M.
(D) 11:30 A.M.

25 Which island will the group led by Mr. Haide visit?

(A) Grand Soeur Island
(B) Petite Soeur Island
(C) Coco Island
(D) Reynolds Island

MEMO

한 권으로 끝내는
해커스 토익 800+plus

LC + RC + VOCA

정답·해석·해설
해설집

해커스 어학연구소

저작권자 ⓒ 2025, 해커스 어학연구소 이 책 및 음성파일의 모든 내용, 이미지, 디자인, 편집 형태에 대한 저작권은 저자에게 있습니다.
서면에 의한 저자와 출판사의 허락 없이 내용의 일부 혹은 전부를 인용, 발췌하거나 복제, 배포할 수 없습니다.

PART 1

DAY 01 사람 중심 사진

기출 유형 1 1인 사진

Example 캐나다 p.16

해석 (A) 그녀는 핸드백을 들여다보고 있다.
 (B) 그녀는 식료품 제품을 살펴보고 있다.
 (C) 그녀는 몇몇 상자를 들고 있다.
 (D) 그녀는 종이 파일을 분류하고 있다.

어휘 look in ~을 들여다보다   grocery n. 식료품   sort through ~을 분류하다

토익실전문제 p.17

| 01 (D) | 02 (C) | 03 (D) | 04 (B) |

01 1인 사진 미국

(A) He's reading a street sign.
(B) He's walking on a sidewalk.
(C) He's removing a bicycle helmet.
(D) He's riding a bicycle on a road.

sign n. 표지판, 간판   sidewalk n. 인도, 보도
remove v. 벗다, 제거하다   ride v. 타다

해석 (A) 그는 도로 표지판을 읽고 있다.
 (B) 그는 인도를 걷고 있다.
 (C) 그는 자전거 헬멧을 벗고 있다.
 (D) 그는 길에서 자전거를 타고 있다.

해설 (A) [x] 사진에 도로 표지판(street sign)이 없으므로 오답이다.
 (B) [x] walking(걷고 있다)은 남자의 동작과 무관하므로 오답이다.
 (C) [x] removing(벗고 있다)은 남자의 동작과 무관하므로 오답이다.
 (D) [o] 남자가 자전거를 타고 있는 모습을 가장 잘 묘사한 정답이다.

02 1인 사진 영국

(A) A man is putting a phone on a windowsill.
(B) A man is stacking cans of paint in a hallway.
(C) A man is painting a wall with a brush.
(D) A man is setting up a ladder in a room.

windowsill n. 창턱   stack v. 쌓다   set up ~을 설치하다   ladder n. 사다리

해석 (A) 한 남자가 창턱 위에 전화기를 놓고 있다.
 (B) 한 남자가 복도에 페인트 캔을 쌓고 있다.
 (C) 한 남자가 벽을 붓으로 페인트칠하고 있다.
 (D) 한 남자가 방에 사다리를 설치하고 있다.

해설 (A) [x] putting(놓고 있다)은 남자의 동작과 무관하므로 오답이다.
 (B) [x] stacking(쌓고 있다)은 남자의 동작과 무관하므로 오답이다.
 (C) [o] 남자가 벽을 붓으로 페인트칠하고 있는 모습을 가장 잘 묘사한 정답이다.
 (D) [x] setting up(설치하고 있다)은 남자의 동작과 무관하므로 오답이다.

03 1인 사진 호주

(A) She's installing a machine.
(B) She's reaching into a bucket.
(C) She's putting on gloves.
(D) She's using a tool.

install v. 설치하다   bucket n. 양동이   put on ~을 끼다, 입다
tool n. 공구, 도구

해석 (A) 그녀는 기계를 설치하고 있다.
 (B) 그녀는 양동이에 손을 뻗고 있다.
 (C) 그녀는 장갑을 끼고 있다.
 (D) 그녀는 공구를 사용하고 있다.

해설 (A) [x] installing(설치하고 있다)은 여자의 동작과 무관하므로 오답이다.
 (B) [x] 사진에 양동이(bucket)가 없으므로 오답이다.
 (C) [x] putting on(끼고 있다)은 여자의 동작과 무관하므로 오답이다.
 (D) [o] 여자가 공구를 사용하고 있는 모습을 가장 잘 묘사한 정답이다.

04 1인 사진 캐나다

(A) The woman is turning on a lamp.
(B) Some papers have been piled on a desk.
(C) The woman is pinning a notice on a board.
(D) A briefcase has been set on the floor.

turn on ~을 켜다   pile v. 쌓다   pin v. 고정하다

해석 (A) 여자가 전등을 켜고 있다.
 (B) 몇 장의 서류가 책상 위에 쌓여 있다.
 (C) 여자가 칠판에 메모를 고정하고 있다.
 (D) 서류 가방이 바닥에 놓여 있다.

해설 (A) [x] turning on(켜고 있다)은 여자의 동작과 무관하므로 오답이다.
 (B) [o] 책상 위에 서류가 쌓여 있는 모습을 가장 잘 묘사한 정답이다.
 (C) [x] pinning(고정하고 있다)은 여자의 동작과 무관하므로 오답이다.
 (D) [x] 사진에 서류 가방(briefcase)이 없으므로 오답이다.

기출 유형 2 2인 이상 사진

Example 호주 p.18

해석 (A) 몇몇 폴더가 의자 위에 남겨져 있다.
 (B) 몇몇 선반들이 방 벽을 따라 줄지어 있다.
 (C) 남자들 중 한 명이 컴퓨터 모니터 앞에 서 있다.
 (D) 여자들 중 한 명이 종이를 들고 있다.

어휘 line v. ~을 따라 줄지어 있다

토익실전문제 p.19

| 01 (A) | 02 (C) | 03 (B) | 04 (C) |

01 2인 이상 사진 🎧 캐나다

(A) They're carrying hiking poles.
(B) They're getting onto a bus.
(C) They're unpacking their backpacks.
(D) They're picking up branches off the ground.

carry v. 들다, 나르다   get onto ~에 타다   unpack v. (짐을) 풀다
pick up ~을 줍다   ground n. 땅

해석 (A) 그들은 등산용 스틱을 들고 있다.
(B) 그들은 버스에 타고 있다.
(C) 그들은 배낭을 풀고 있다.
(D) 그들은 땅에 떨어진 나뭇가지를 줍고 있다.

해설 (A) [o] 사람들이 등산용 스틱을 들고 있는 모습을 가장 잘 묘사한 정답이다.
(B) [x] getting onto(타고 있다)는 사람들의 동작과 무관하므로 오답이다.
(C) [x] unpacking(풀고 있다)은 사람들의 동작과 무관하므로 오답이다.
(D) [x] picking up(줍고 있다)은 사람들의 동작과 무관하므로 오답이다.

02 2인 이상 사진 🎧 영국

(A) Bicycles are lined up along a platform.
(B) There are signs posted in a parking area.
(C) Some people are walking next to a railroad track.
(D) Some people are waiting in line at a food stand.

along prep. ~을 따라   platform n. 플랫폼   railroad track 철로

해석 (A) 자전거가 플랫폼을 따라 줄지어 있다.
(B) 주차 구역에 표지판이 게시되어 있다.
(C) 몇몇 사람들이 철로 옆을 걷고 있다.
(D) 몇몇 사람들이 음식 가판대에서 줄을 서서 기다리고 있다.

해설 (A) [x] 사진에 플랫폼과 자전거는 보이지만, 자전거가 플랫폼을 따라 줄지어 있는(lined up) 모습은 아니므로 오답이다.
(B) [x] 사진에 표지판(signs)이 없으므로 오답이다.
(C) [o] 사람들이 철로 옆을 걷고 있는 모습을 가장 잘 묘사한 정답이다.
(D) [x] 사진에 음식 가판대(food stand)가 없으므로 오답이다.

03 2인 이상 사진 🎧 캐나다

(A) Some coffee cups have been placed on a table.
(B) The woman is resting her arm on a chair.
(C) Some office furniture is being moved.
(D) One of the men is standing in front of a door.

place v. 놓다, 두다   rest v. 얹혀[받쳐져] 있다, 기대다

해석 (A) 커피 잔 몇 개가 테이블 위에 놓여 있다.
(B) 여자가 의자에 팔을 얹고 있다.
(C) 몇몇 사무용 가구가 옮겨지고 있다.
(D) 남자들 중 한 명이 문 앞에 서 있다.

해설 (A) [x] 테이블 위에 커피 잔이 없으므로 오답이다.
(B) [o] 여자가 의자 위에 팔을 얹고 있는 모습을 가장 잘 묘사한 정답이다.
(C) [x] 사무용 가구가 옮겨지고(being moved) 있는 모습이 아니므로 오답이다.
(D) [x] 문 앞에 서 있는(standing) 남자가 없으므로 오답이다.

04 2인 이상 사진 🎧 미국

(A) Some people have gathered in a meeting room.
(B) An employee is mopping the floor.
(C) Some light fixtures have been hung from the ceiling.
(D) A suitcase has been put on a cart.

gather v. 모이다, 모으다   mop v. 대걸레로 닦다   light fixture 조명 기구
ceiling n. 천장

해석 (A) 몇몇 사람들이 회의실에 모여 있다.
(B) 한 직원이 바닥을 대걸레로 닦고 있다.
(C) 몇몇 조명 기구들이 천장에 매달려 있다.
(D) 여행 가방이 카트 위에 놓여 있다.

해설 (A) [x] 사진 속 장소가 회의실(meeting room)이 아니므로 오답이다.
(B) [x] 대걸레로 닦고 있는(mopping) 사람이 없으므로 오답이다.
(C) [o] 조명 기구들이 천장에 매달려 있는 모습을 가장 잘 묘사한 정답이다.
(D) [x] 사진에 여행 가방(suitcase)은 있지만 카트 위에 놓여 있는 모습이 아니므로 오답이다.

HACKERS TEST p.20

01 (B)	02 (C)	03 (D)	04 (A)	05 (D)
06 (B)	07 (C)	08 (C)	09 (A)	10 (D)
11 (A)	12 (C)			

01 1인 사진 🎧 캐나다

(A) He's loading some containers onto a truck.
(B) He's wearing a safety helmet.
(C) He's climbing down some stairs.
(D) He's looking behind a machine.

load v. 싣다   climb down ~을 내려가다   stairs n. 계단

해석 (A) 그는 트럭에 컨테이너를 싣고 있다.
(B) 그는 안전모를 쓰고 있다.
(C) 그는 계단을 내려가고 있다.
(D) 그는 기계 뒤를 보고 있다.

해설 (A) [x] 사진에 트럭(truck)이 없으므로 오답이다.
(B) [o] 남자가 안전모를 쓰고 있는 모습을 가장 잘 묘사한 정답이다.
(C) [x] climbing down(내려가고 있다)은 남자의 동작과 무관하므로 오답이다.
(D) [x] 사진에 기계(machine)가 없으므로 오답이다.

02 2인 이상 사진 🎧 영국

(A) Some people are stepping into an elevator.
(B) The boarding stairs are being inspected.
(C) Some people are standing in line to board an airplane.
(D) A passenger bus is exiting a parking garage.

step into ~에 들어가다   inspect v. 점검하다   board v. 탑승하다
exit v. 나가다, 퇴장하다   parking garage 주차장

해석 (A) 몇몇 사람들이 엘리베이터에 들어가고 있다.

(B) 탑승 계단이 점검되고 있다.
(C) 몇몇 사람들이 비행기에 탑승하기 위해 줄을 서 있다.
(D) 여객 버스가 주차장을 나가고 있다.

해설 (A) [×] 사진에 엘리베이터(elevator)가 없으므로 오답이다.
(B) [×] 사진에 탑승 계단(boarding stairs)은 있지만 점검되고 있는 (being inspected) 모습이 아니므로 오답이다.
(C) [○] 사람들이 비행기에 탑승하기 위해 줄을 서 있는 모습을 가장 잘 묘사한 정답이다.
(D) [×] 사진에 여객 버스(passenger bus)가 없으므로 오답이다.

03 1인 사진   호주

(A) A woman is holding a refrigerator door open.
(B) Artwork is being displayed on the walls of a kitchen.
(C) Some fruits and vegetables have been collected in a basket.
(D) **A woman is wiping a cupboard door with a cloth.**

artwork n. 예술 작품   display v. 전시하다   collect v. 모으다   wipe v. 닦다
cupboard n. 찬장   cloth n. 천

해석 (A) 여자가 냉장고 문을 연 채로 잡고 있다.
(B) 주방 벽에 예술 작품이 전시되어 있다.
(C) 과일과 채소가 바구니에 모아져 있다.
(D) 여자가 천으로 찬장 문을 닦고 있다.

해설 (A) [×] holding(잡고 있다)은 여자의 동작과 무관하므로 오답이다.
(B) [×] 사진에 예술 작품(artwork)이 없으므로 오답이다.
(C) [×] 사진에 과일과 채소(some fruits and vegetables)가 없으므로 오답이다.
(D) [○] 천으로 찬장 문을 닦고 있는 여자의 모습을 가장 잘 묘사한 정답이다.

04 2인 이상 사진   캐나다

(A) **Some tables are occupied by diners.**
(B) One of the people is handing a credit card to a cashier.
(C) A worker is sweeping a dining area.
(D) Some window curtains have been pulled shut.

occupy v. 사용하고 있다, 차지하다   diner n. 식사하는 사람   hand v. 건네다
sweep v. 빗자루로 쓸다

해석 (A) 몇몇 테이블은 식사하는 사람들에 의해 사용되고 있다.
(B) 사람들 중 한 명이 계산원에게 신용 카드를 건네고 있다.
(C) 한 직원이 식사 공간을 빗자루로 쓸고 있다.
(D) 일부 창문 커튼이 닫혀 있다.

해설 (A) [○] 몇몇 테이블에 식사하는 사람들이 있는 모습을 가장 잘 묘사한 정답이다.
(B) [×] 사진에 계산원(cashier)이 없으므로 오답이다.
(C) [×] 사진에 빗자루로 쓸고 있는(sweeping) 사람이 없으므로 오답이다.
(D) [×] 사진에 창문은 있지만 커튼이 닫혀 있는(curtains have been pulled shut) 모습은 아니므로 오답이다.

05 1인 사진   미국

(A) The woman is bending over to tie her shoelaces.
(B) Some flowers are being planted in a garden.

(C) The woman is installing a fence around a house.
(D) **Some leaves have been piled in a wheelbarrow.**

bend over 허리를 굽히다, 몸을 앞으로 숙이다   tie v. 묶다   fence n. 울타리
leaf n. (나뭇)잎   wheelbarrow n. 수레

해석 (A) 여자가 신발끈을 묶기 위해 허리를 굽히고 있다.
(B) 정원에 꽃이 심어지고 있다.
(C) 여자가 집 주위에 울타리를 설치하고 있다.
(D) 나뭇잎이 수레에 쌓여 있다.

해설 (A) [×] tie her shoelaces(신발끈을 묶다)는 여자의 동작과 무관하므로 오답이다.
(B) [×] 꽃이 심어지고 있는(flowers are being planted) 모습은 보이지 않으므로 오답이다.
(C) [×] installing(설치하다)은 여자의 동작과 무관하므로 오답이다.
(D) [○] 나뭇잎이 수레에 쌓여 있는 모습을 가장 잘 묘사한 정답이다.

06 2인 이상 사진   영국

(A) The workers are sitting at their desks.
(B) **The workers are moving a piece of furniture.**
(C) One of the workers is replacing a lightbulb.
(D) One of the workers is leaning against the back of a chair.

lightbulb n. 전구   lean against ~에 기대다

해석 (A) 작업자들이 책상에 앉아 있다.
(B) 작업자들이 가구를 옮기고 있다.
(C) 작업자들 중 한 명이 전구를 교체하고 있다.
(D) 작업자들 중 한 명이 의자 등받이에 기대고 있다.

해설 (A) [×] sitting(앉아 있다)은 작업자들의 동작과 무관하므로 오답이다.
(B) [○] 작업자들이 가구를 옮기고 있는 모습을 가장 잘 묘사한 정답이다.
(C) [×] 사진에 전구(lightbulb)가 없으므로 오답이다.
(D) [×] leaning against(~에 기대고 있다)는 작업자들의 동작과 무관하므로 오답이다.

07 1인 사진   미국

(A) Some food is being cut with a knife.
(B) The woman is grasping the handle of a shopping cart.
(C) **The woman is filling up a bag.**
(D) Some containers have been arranged on a dining table.

grasp v. 잡다, 쥐다   fill v. 채우다   container n. 용기, 그릇

해석 (A) 음식이 칼로 잘리고 있다.
(B) 여자가 쇼핑 카트의 손잡이를 잡고 있다.
(C) 여자가 봉투를 채우고 있다.
(D) 식탁 위에 몇 개의 용기가 놓여 있다.

해설 (A) [×] 잘리고 있는(being cut) 음식이 없으므로 오답이다.
(B) [×] 사진에 쇼핑 카트(shopping cart)가 없으므로 오답이다.
(C) [○] 여자가 봉투를 채우고 있는 모습을 가장 잘 묘사한 정답이다.
(D) [×] 사진에 식탁(dining table)이 없으므로 오답이다.

08 2인 이상 사진 호주

(A) Some train tracks are being fixed.
(B) They're hanging their bags on a railing.
(C) They're each pulling their suitcases.
(D) A train is traveling alongside a river.

railing n. 난간 pull v. 끌다, 당기다 alongside prep. ~의 옆에

해석 (A) 기차 선로가 수리되고 있다.
(B) 그들은 가방을 난간에 걸고 있다.
(C) 그들은 각자 여행 가방을 끌고 있다.
(D) 기차가 강 옆을 지나가고 있다.

해설 (A) [x] 사진에 선로가 수리되고 있는(being fixed) 모습은 보이지 않으므로 오답이다.
(B) [x] hanging(걸고 있다)은 사람들의 동작과 무관하므로 오답이다.
(C) [o] 사람들이 각자 여행 가방을 끌고 있는 모습을 가장 잘 묘사한 정답이다.
(D) [x] 사진에 강(river)이 없으므로 오답이다.

09 2인 이상 사진 캐나다

(A) A chart has been drawn on a whiteboard.
(B) Two of the people are setting a table.
(C) One of the men is typing on a laptop.
(D) One of the women is talking on a phone.

chart n. 차트, 그래프 set a table 식탁을 차리다

해석 (A) 화이트보드에 차트가 그려져 있다.
(B) 사람들 중 두 명이 식탁을 차리고 있다.
(C) 남자들 중 한 명이 노트북으로 타이핑을 하고 있다.
(D) 여자들 중 한 명이 전화로 통화하고 있다.

해설 (A) [o] 화이트보드에 차트가 그려져 있는 모습을 가장 잘 묘사한 정답이다.
(B) [x] 사진에 식탁을 차리고 있는(setting a table) 사람들이 없으므로 오답이다.
(C) [x] 사진에 타이핑하고 있는(typing) 남자가 없으므로 오답이다.
(D) [x] 사진에 전화로 통화하고 있는(talking on a phone) 여자가 없으므로 오답이다.

10 2인 이상 사진 미국

(A) Houses are facing a lake.
(B) People are gathered in a circle in a workspace.
(C) A musical instrument is displayed in a shop window.
(D) There are some musicians performing outside.

face v. 마주보다 workspace n. 작업 공간, 업무 공간
musical instrument 악기

해석 (A) 집들이 호수를 마주보고 있다.
(B) 사람들이 작업 공간에 둥글게 모여 있다.
(C) 상점 창문에 악기가 진열되어 있다.
(D) 밖에서 공연을 하고 있는 음악가들이 있다.

해설 (A) [x] 사진에 호수(lake)가 없으므로 오답이다.
(B) [x] 사람들이 둥글게(in a circle) 모여 있지 않고 사진 속 장소가 작업 공간(workspace)도 아니므로 오답이다.
(C) [x] 악기가 진열된(displayed) 모습이 아니므로 오답이다.
(D) [o] 밖에서 음악가들이 공연하고 있는 모습을 가장 잘 묘사한 정답이다.

11 1인 사진 호주

(A) Some bricks have been stacked in piles.
(B) The man is reaching for a bottle in a cabinet.
(C) The man is rolling up his sleeves.
(D) There is a folding chair propped against a stone wall.

brick n. 벽돌 reach for ~을 향해 손을 뻗다 sleeve n. 소매
prop against ~에 기대어 놓다, 받쳐 놓다

해석 (A) 몇몇 벽돌이 더미로 쌓여 있다.
(B) 남자가 캐비닛 안의 병에 손을 뻗고 있다.
(C) 남자가 소매를 걷어붙이고 있다.
(D) 돌담에 기대어 있는 접이식 의자가 있다.

해설 (A) [o] 몇몇 벽돌이 쌓여 있는 모습을 가장 잘 묘사한 정답이다.
(B) [x] 사진에 캐비닛(cabinet)이 없으므로 오답이다.
(C) [x] rolling up(걷어붙이고 있다)은 남자의 동작과 무관하므로 오답이다.
(D) [x] 사진에 접이식 의자(folding chair)가 없으므로 오답이다.

12 2인 이상 사진 미국

(A) One of the men is trimming some bushes.
(B) A truck is driving along a mountain road.
(C) Some crates are filled with items.
(D) The men are shaking hands with each other.

trim v. 손질하다, 다듬다 bush n. 덤불 crate n. 상자
shake hands 악수하다

해석 (A) 남자들 중 한 명이 덤불을 손질하고 있다.
(B) 트럭 한 대가 산길을 따라 달리고 있다.
(C) 몇몇 상자들이 물건으로 가득 차 있다.
(D) 남자들이 서로 악수를 하고 있다.

해설 (A) [x] trimming(손질하다)은 남자들의 동작과 무관하므로 오답이다.
(B) [x] 달리고 있는(driving) 트럭이 없으므로 오답이다.
(C) [o] 상자들이 물건으로 가득 차 있는 모습을 가장 잘 묘사한 정답이다.
(D) [x] shaking hands(악수를 하다)는 남자들의 동작과 무관하므로 오답이다.

DAY 02 사물/풍경 중심 사진

기출 유형 1 실내 사진

Example 호주   p.22

해석 (A) 안락의자 위에 쿠션이 놓여 있다.
(B) 벽에서 그림이 제거되고 있다.
(C) 몇몇 화분이 창문 위에 걸려 있다.
(D) 몇몇 책들이 바닥에 놓여 있다.

어휘 armchair n. 안락의자 hang v. 걸다, 매달다 lay v. 놓다, 두다

토익실전문제   p.23

| 01 (A) | 02 (C) | 03 (C) | 04 (B) |

01 실내 사진   🎧 미국

(A) Some flower arrangements are on a display stand.
(B) Some light fixtures have been left on the ground.
(C) A flower vase is being filled with water.
(D) An empty basket has been placed on a desk.

display stand 진열대   empty adj. 비어 있는, 빈

해석 (A) 진열대 위에 꽃꽂이들이 있다.
(B) 몇몇 조명 기구들이 땅바닥에 남겨져 있다.
(C) 꽃병에 물이 채워지고 있다.
(D) 빈 바구니가 책상 위에 놓여 있다.

해설 (A) [O] 진열대 위에 꽃꽂이가 놓여 있는 모습을 가장 잘 묘사한 정답이다.
(B) [×] 땅바닥에 조명 기구들이 없으므로 오답이다.
(C) [×] 꽃병에 물을 채우고 있는 사람이 없으므로 오답이다.
(D) [×] 사진에 빈 바구니(empty basket)가 없으므로 오답이다.

02 실내 사진   🎧 캐나다

(A) Dishes have been arranged on a display table.
(B) There is a row of chairs facing a podium.
(C) There are lamps lighting a seating area.
(D) Stools are being placed in front of a counter.

a row of 일렬로 줄지어   podium n. 연단, 연설대   seating n. 좌석, 자리
counter n. 계산대, 판매대

해석 (A) 접시들이 진열대 위에 정리되어 있다.
(B) 연단을 마주보고 있는 의자들이 줄지어 있다.
(C) 몇몇 좌석 공간을 비추는 전등이 있다.
(D) 스툴이 계산대 앞에 놓여지고 있다.

해설 (A) [×] 사진에 접시들(dishes)이 없으므로 오답이다.
(B) [×] 사진에 연단(podium)이 없으므로 오답이다.
(C) [O] 전등이 좌석 공간을 비추고 있는 모습을 가장 잘 묘사한 정답이다.
(D) [×] 스툴을 놓고 있는 사람이 없으므로 오답이다.

03 실내 사진   🎧 영국

(A) Some posters are being taken down.
(B) A computer monitor has been turned on.
(C) Several binders are being stored on shelves.
(D) Some books have been scattered on the floor.

take down (구조물을 해체하여) 치우다, 끌어내리다   store v. 보관하다
shelf n. 선반   scatter v. 흩어지다

해석 (A) 몇몇 포스터들이 치워지고 있다.
(B) 컴퓨터 모니터가 켜져 있다.
(C) 여러 개의 바인더가 선반에 보관되어 있다.
(D) 몇몇 책들이 바닥에 흩어져 있다.

해설 (A) [×] 사진에 포스터(posters)는 있지만 치워지고 있는(being taken down) 모습은 아니므로 오답이다.
(B) [×] 사진에 컴퓨터 모니터(computer monitor)는 있지만 켜져 있는 (turned on) 모습은 아니므로 오답이다.
(C) [O] 여러 개의 바인더가 선반에 보관되어 있는 모습을 가장 잘 묘사한 정답이다.
(D) [×] 사진에 바닥에 흩어져 있는(scattered) 책들은 없으므로 오답이다.

04 실내 사진   🎧 호주

(A) An appliance is plugged into an electrical outlet.
(B) Some boxes have been stacked on top of each other.
(C) Some wooden flooring is being replaced.
(D) A stepladder is leaning against a wall.

appliance n. 가전제품   electrical outlet 콘센트
wooden adj. 나무로 된, 목재의   replace v. 교체하다
stepladder n. 발판 사다리

해석 (A) 가전제품이 콘센트에 꽂혀 있다.
(B) 몇몇 상자들이 차곡차곡 쌓여 있다.
(C) 몇몇 나무 바닥재가 교체되고 있다.
(D) 발판 사다리가 벽에 기대어 있다.

해설 (A) [×] 사진에 가전제품(appliance)과 콘센트(electrical outlet)가 없으므로 오답이다.
(B) [O] 상자들이 차곡차곡 쌓여 있는 모습을 가장 잘 묘사한 정답이다.
(C) [×] 사진에 나무 바닥재(wooden flooring)는 있지만 교체되고 (being replaced) 있는 모습은 아니므로 오답이다.
(D) [×] 사진에 발판 사다리(stepladder)는 있지만 벽에 기대어 있는 (leaning against) 모습은 아니므로 오답이다.

기출 유형 2 야외 사진

Example 🎧 영국   p.24

해석 (A) 파라솔이 접히고 있다.
(B) 탁자들 위에 식탁보가 씌워져 있다.
(C) 안뜰에 그림자가 드리워지고 있다.
(D) 몇몇 의자들이 분수대 주변에 배치되어 있다.

어휘 fold v. 접다   tablecloth n. 식탁보   cast v. (그림자를) 드리우다
fountain n. 분수대

토익실전문제   p.25

| 01 (C) | 02 (C) | 03 (B) | 04 (D) |

01 야외 사진   🎧 캐나다

(A) Some trees are growing next to a road.
(B) A wooden fence is being installed around a body of water.
(C) There are benches positioned side by side.
(D) A picnic table has been set up near a trash bin.

grow v. 자라다   position v. 배치하다, 자리를 잡다   side by side 나란히
trash bin 쓰레기통

해석 (A) 도로 옆에 나무가 자라고 있다.
(B) 수역 주변에 나무로 된 울타리가 설치되고 있다.
(C) 벤치들이 나란히 배치되어 있다.
(D) 쓰레기통 근처에 피크닉 테이블이 설치되어 있다.

해설 (A) [x] 사진에 도로(road)가 없으므로 오답이다.
(B) [x] 사진에 울타리(fence)가 없으므로 오답이다.
(C) [o] 벤치들이 나란히 있는 모습을 가장 잘 묘사한 정답이다.
(D) [x] 사진에 피크닉 테이블(picnic table)이 없으므로 오답이다.

02 야외 사진   미국

(A) Some tires are being replaced.
(B) Some signs are attached to a brick building.
(C) Some vehicles are parked in front of houses.
(D) Some lane markings are being painted on a roadway.

attach v. 부착하다   lane marking 차선 표시   roadway n. 도로

해석 (A) 몇몇 타이어가 교체되고 있다.
(B) 몇몇 표지판이 벽돌 건물에 부착되어 있다.
(C) 몇몇 차량이 집 앞에 주차되어 있다.
(D) 도로에 몇몇 차선 표시가 칠해지고 있다.

해설 (A) [x] 사진에 타이어(tires)는 보이지만 교체되고 있는(being replaced) 모습은 아니므로 오답이다.
(B) [x] 사진에 표지판(signs)이 없으므로 오답이다.
(C) [o] 차량들이 집 앞에 주차되어 있는 모습을 가장 잘 묘사한 정답이다.
(D) [x] 차선 표시를 칠하고 있는 사람이 없으므로 오답이다.

03 야외 사진   호주

(A) A bridge has been built over a waterway.
(B) A canal flows between buildings.
(C) Several buildings overlook the city square.
(D) Boats are being paddled down a river.

waterway n. (강, 운하 등의) 수로   canal n. 운하   flow v. 흐르다

해석 (A) 수로 위에 다리가 건설되어 있다.
(B) 건물 사이로 운하가 흐른다.
(C) 여러 건물들이 도시 광장을 내려다보고 있다.
(D) 배들이 강을 따라 노를 저어 내려가고 있다.

해설 (A) [x] 사진에 다리(bridge)가 없으므로 오답이다.
(B) [o] 건물 사이로 운하가 흐르는 모습을 가장 잘 묘사한 정답이다.
(C) [x] 사진에 도시 광장(city square)이 없으므로 오답이다.
(D) [x] 사진에 노를 젓고 있는 사람이 없으므로 오답이다.

04 야외 사진   미국

(A) Some vehicles are being towed from a parking lot.
(B) Some tools have been left on the ground.
(C) Some workers are shoveling soil into a truck.
(D) Some cranes are erected at a construction site.

tow v. 견인하다   leave v. 남겨두다   shovel v. 삽질하다   soil n. 흙
erect v. (똑바로) 세우다

해석 (A) 몇몇 차량이 주차장에서 견인되고 있다.
(B) 몇몇 도구가 땅에 남겨져 있다.
(C) 몇몇 작업자들이 트럭으로 흙을 삽질하고 있다.
(D) 몇몇 크레인이 건설 현장에 세워져 있다.

해설 (A) [x] 사진에 견인되고 있는(being towed) 차량이 없으므로 오답이다.
(B) [x] 사진에 도구(tools)가 없으므로 오답이다.
(C) [x] 사진에 작업자들(workers)은 없으므로 오답이다.
(D) [o] 크레인이 건설 현장에 세워져 있는 모습을 가장 잘 묘사한 정답이다.

HACKERS TEST   p.26

01 (D)	02 (A)	03 (B)	04 (B)	05 (C)
06 (D)	07 (B)	08 (C)	09 (B)	10 (D)
11 (D)	12 (A)			

01 실내 사진   영국

(A) A hallway leads to a staircase.
(B) A bulletin board is being attached to a wall.
(C) There are some chairs blocking a door.
(D) There are doors on both sides of a corridor.

hallway n. 복도   block v. 막다   corridor n. 복도

해석 (A) 복도가 계단으로 연결된다.
(B) 게시판이 벽에 부착되고 있다.
(C) 문을 막고 있는 의자가 몇 개 있다.
(D) 복도 양쪽에 문이 있다.

해설 (A) [x] 사진에 계단(staircase)이 없으므로 오답이다.
(B) [x] 사진에 게시판(bulletin board)이 없으므로 오답이다.
(C) [x] 사진에 의자(chairs)가 있지만 문을 막고 있는(blocking) 모습은 아니므로 오답이다.
(D) [o] 복도 양쪽으로 문이 있는 모습을 가장 잘 묘사한 정답이다.

02 야외 사진   미국

(A) Some boats are lined up in a row.
(B) A person is boarding a ferry.
(C) Some water has pooled on a walkway.
(D) One of the boats is sailing out of a harbor.

pool v. 물웅덩이를 만들다   harbor n. 항구

해석 (A) 몇몇 배들이 일렬로 줄지어 있다.
(B) 한 사람이 페리에 탑승하고 있다.
(C) 산책로에 물이 고여 있다.
(D) 배 중 하나가 항구에서 나가고 있다.

해설 (A) [o] 배들이 일렬로 줄지어 있는 모습을 가장 잘 묘사한 정답이다.
(B) [x] 사진에 사람(person)이 없으므로 오답이다.
(C) [x] 사진에 산책로(walkway)가 없으므로 오답이다.
(D) [x] 사진에 항구에서 나가고 있는(sailing out) 배는 없으므로 오답이다.

03 야외 사진 　　　　　　　　　　　　　　🔊 호주

(A) A plant is being loaded onto the back of a truck.
(B) **A cart has been left near the vehicle.**
(C) A building has two rows of windows.
(D) A car is passing through an intersection.

load v. 싣다　row n. 열, 줄　intersection n. 교차로

해석 (A) 식물이 트럭 뒤에 실리고 있다.
　　 (B) 차량 근처에 카트가 남겨져 있다.
　　 (C) 건물에 두 줄의 창문이 있다.
　　 (D) 차가 교차로를 지나가고 있다.

해설 (A) [x] 사진에 트럭 뒤에 실리고 있는(being loaded) 식물이 없으므로 오답이다.
　　 (B) [o] 차량 근처에 카트가 남겨져 있는 모습을 가장 잘 묘사한 정답이다.
　　 (C) [x] 사진에 건물(building)이 없으므로 오답이다.
　　 (D) [x] 사진에 교차로(intersection)가 없으므로 오답이다.

04 야외 사진 　　　　　　　　　　　　　　🔊 캐나다

(A) A path is covered with fallen branches.
(B) **There is a product rack standing on a sidewalk.**
(C) Some lights are being installed above a garage door.
(D) Some umbrellas have been opened on a balcony.

path n. 길　fall v. 떨어지다　branch n. 나뭇가지　rack n. 선반, 받침대　garage n. 차고

해석 (A) 길이 떨어진 나뭇가지들로 덮여 있다.
　　 (B) 인도에 세워진 제품 선반이 있다.
　　 (C) 차고 문 위에 조명이 설치되고 있다.
　　 (D) 발코니에 몇몇 파라솔이 펼쳐져 있다.

해설 (A) [x] 사진에 나뭇가지들(branches)이 없으므로 오답이다.
　　 (B) [o] 인도에 제품 선반이 세워져 있는 모습을 가장 잘 묘사한 정답이다.
　　 (C) [x] 조명을 설치하고 있는 사람이 없으므로 오답이다.
　　 (D) [x] 사진에 파라솔(umbrellas)이 없으므로 오답이다.

05 야외 사진 　　　　　　　　　　　　　　🔊 영국

(A) A bicycle seat is being cleaned.
(B) Some scooters are going through a gate.
(C) **A bicycle is secured to a rack.**
(D) There is a water bottle hanging from a bicycle handlebar.

secure v. 고정하다　handlebar n. (자전거의) 핸들

해석 (A) 자전거 좌석이 청소되고 있다.
　　 (B) 몇몇 스쿠터가 문을 통과하고 있다.
　　 (C) 자전거가 거치대에 고정되어 있다.
　　 (D) 자전거 핸들에 물병이 걸려 있다.

해설 (A) [x] 자전거 좌석을 청소하고 있는 사람이 없으므로 오답이다.
　　 (B) [x] 사진에 스쿠터(scooters)가 없으므로 오답이다.
　　 (C) [o] 자전거가 거치대에 고정되어 있는 모습을 가장 잘 묘사한 정답이다.
　　 (D) [x] 사진에 물병(water bottle)이 없으므로 오답이다.

06 실내 사진 　　　　　　　　　　　　　　🔊 호주

(A) Some drawers have been left open.
(B) Some reading materials have been spread out on the carpet.
(C) A computer is being plugged in.
(D) **There is a trash bin under a desk.**

drawer n. 서랍　material n. 자료

해석 (A) 몇몇 서랍들이 열려 있다.
　　 (B) 몇몇 독서 자료가 카펫에 펼쳐져 있다.
　　 (C) 컴퓨터의 전원이 연결되고 있다.
　　 (D) 책상 아래에 쓰레기통이 있다.

해설 (A) [x] 사진에 서랍(drawers)은 있지만 열려 있지 않으므로 오답이다.
　　 (B) [x] 사진에 카펫(carpet)이 없으므로 오답이다.
　　 (C) [x] 컴퓨터의 전원을 연결하고 있는 사람이 없으므로 오답이다.
　　 (D) [o] 책상 아래에 있는 쓰레기통의 모습을 가장 잘 묘사한 정답이다.

07 실내 사진 　　　　　　　　　　　　　　🔊 영국

(A) A stool has fallen on its side.
(B) **Some clothes have been put on hangers.**
(C) A cash register has been connected to an outlet.
(D) A shelving unit is being assembled.

stool n. (등받이와 팔걸이가 없는) 의자, 스툴　hanger n. 옷걸이
cash register 금전 등록기　assemble v. 조립하다

해석 (A) 스툴이 옆으로 쓰러져 있다.
　　 (B) 몇몇 옷들이 옷걸이에 걸려 있다.
　　 (C) 금전 등록기가 콘센트에 연결되어 있다.
　　 (D) 선반 유닛이 조립되고 있다.

해설 (A) [x] 사진에 스툴(stool)이 없으므로 오답이다.
　　 (B) [o] 옷들이 옷걸이에 걸려 있는 모습을 가장 잘 묘사한 정답이다.
　　 (C) [x] 사진에 금전 등록기(cash register)가 없으므로 오답이다.
　　 (D) [x] 사진에 선반을 조립하고 있는 사람들이 없으므로 오답이다.

08 실내 사진 　　　　　　　　　　　　　　🔊 캐나다

(A) A laundry basket has been turned upside down.
(B) A rug has been rolled up on the floor.
(C) **Containers have been arranged on a shelf.**
(D) Some folded towels have been placed on top of a washing machine.

upside down 거꾸로　rug n. 깔개　washing machine 세탁기

해석 (A) 세탁 바구니가 거꾸로 뒤집혀 있다.
　　 (B) 깔개가 바닥에 둥글게 말려 있다.
　　 (C) 선반에 용기들이 정리되어 있다.
　　 (D) 몇몇 접힌 수건들이 세탁기 위에 놓여 있다.

해설 (A) [x] 사진에 세탁 바구니(laundry basket)는 있지만 거꾸로 뒤집혀 있는(turned upside down) 모습은 아니므로 오답이다.
　　 (B) [x] 사진에 깔개(rug)는 있지만 둥글게 말려 있는(rolled up) 모습은 아니므로 오답이다.
　　 (C) [o] 선반에 용기들이 정리되어 있는 모습을 가장 잘 묘사한 정답이다.
　　 (D) [x] 사진에 접힌 수건들(folded towels)이 없으므로 오답이다.

09 야외 사진 　　　　　　　　　　　영국

(A) Some clouds are scattered in the sky.
(B) Some wires are suspended over a road.
(C) A group of cyclists is going up a ramp.
(D) A truck is stopped at a pedestrian crossing.

wire n. 전선　suspend v. 매달다　cyclist n. 자전거 타는 사람
ramp n. 경사로　pedestrian crossing 횡단보도

해석　(A) 하늘에 구름이 흩어져 있다.
　　　(B) 전선이 도로 위에 매달려 있다.
　　　(C) 한 무리의 자전거 타는 사람들이 경사로를 올라가고 있다.
　　　(D) 트럭이 횡단보도에 멈춰 있다.

해설　(A) [×] 사진에 구름(clouds)이 없으므로 오답이다.
　　　(B) [○] 전선이 매달려 있는 모습을 가장 잘 묘사한 정답이다.
　　　(C) [×] 사진에 자전거 타는 사람들(cyclists)이 없으므로 오답이다.
　　　(D) [×] 사진에 트럭(truck)이 없으므로 오답이다.

10 야외 사진 　　　　　　　　　　　미국

(A) Streetlights stand in a row along a trail.
(B) Some trees are shading a parking lot.
(C) Tents have been set up in a park.
(D) There are handrails on either side of a walkway.

streetlight n. 가로등　shade v. 그늘을 드리우다　handrail n. 난간

해석　(A) 가로등이 오솔길을 따라 일렬로 서 있다.
　　　(B) 몇몇 나무들이 주차장에 그늘을 드리우고 있다.
　　　(C) 공원에 텐트들이 설치되어 있다.
　　　(D) 산책로 양쪽에 난간이 있다.

해설　(A) [×] 사진에 가로등(streetlights)이 없으므로 오답이다.
　　　(B) [×] 사진에 주차장(parking lot)이 없으므로 오답이다.
　　　(C) [×] 사진에 텐트(tents)가 없으므로 오답이다.
　　　(D) [○] 산책로 양쪽에 난간이 있는 모습을 가장 잘 묘사한 정답이다.

11 실내 사진 　　　　　　　　　　　호주

(A) Some window blinds are being lowered.
(B) Some magazines have been put on a countertop.
(C) Some cooking utensils are being washed in a sink.
(D) Some chairs are pushed in under a table.

lower v. 내리다　countertop n. 조리대　utensil n. 기구, 도구

해석　(A) 몇몇 창문 블라인드가 내려지고 있다.
　　　(B) 몇몇 잡지가 조리대 위에 놓여 있다.
　　　(C) 몇몇 조리 기구가 싱크대에서 세척되고 있다.
　　　(D) 몇몇 의자가 테이블 아래로 밀려 있다.

해설　(A) [×] 사진에 창문 블라인드를 내리고 있는 사람이 없으므로 오답이다.
　　　(B) [×] 사진에 잡지(magazines)가 없으므로 오답이다.
　　　(C) [×] 사진에 조리 기구를 세척하고 있는 사람이 없으므로 오답이다.
　　　(D) [○] 의자가 테이블 아래로 밀려 들어가 있는 모습을 가장 잘 묘사한 정답이다.

12 실내 사진 　　　　　　　　　　　영국

(A) A screen has been mounted on the wall.
(B) Some bedclothes are being dusted off.
(C) The floor is being vacuumed.
(D) Some bed linens are piled in the corner of a room.

mount v. 고정하다　bedclothes n. 이부자리, 침구　dust off 먼지를 털다
vacuum v. 진공 청소기로 청소하다

해석　(A) 스크린이 벽에 고정되어 있다.
　　　(B) 몇몇 침구류의 먼지가 털리고 있다.
　　　(C) 바닥이 진공 청소기로 청소되고 있다.
　　　(D) 침대보가 방 구석에 쌓여 있다.

해설　(A) [○] 스크린이 벽에 고정되어 있는 모습을 가장 잘 묘사한 정답이다.
　　　(B) [×] 침구류의 먼지를 털어내고 있는 사람이 없으므로 오답이다.
　　　(C) [×] 진공 청소기로 청소하고 있는 사람이 없으므로 오답이다.
　　　(D) [×] 사진에 침대보는 있지만 방 구석에 쌓여 있는(piled) 모습은 아니므로 오답이다.

PART 2

DAY 03 의문사 의문문: Who, What/Which

기출 유형 1 Who 의문문

Example 🎧 캐나다 → 영국 p.32
해석 누가 조립 공장을 위한 차량 부품 주문을 담당하고 있나요?
(A) Jonas가 그것을 관리해요.
(B) 연료 효율이 좋은 것이요.
(C) 조립을 마치기 위해서요.
어휘 **fuel efficient** 연료 효율이 좋은

토익실전문제 p.32

| 01 (B) | 02 (A) | 03 (C) | 04 (B) |

01 Who 의문문 🎧 미국 → 호주

Who has the most recent client feedback on product quality?
(A) For a client meeting.
(B) The sales department collected it.
(C) I've already been there.

recent adj. 최근의 **department** n. 부서 **collect** v. 수집하다

해석 누가 제품 품질에 대한 가장 최근의 고객 피드백을 가지고 있나요?
(A) 고객 미팅을 위해서요.
(B) 영업 부서에서 그것을 수집했어요.
(C) 저는 이미 그곳에 가봤어요.
해설 (A) [x] 질문의 client를 반복 사용하여 혼동을 준 오답이다.
(B) [o] 영업 부서에서 그것을 수집했다는 말로, 제품 품질에 대한 가장 최근의 고객 피드백을 가지고 있는 주체를 언급했으므로 정답이다.
(C) [x] 누가 가장 최근의 고객 피드백을 가지고 있는지 물었는데, 이와 관련이 없는 자신은 이미 그곳에 가봤다는 말로 응답했으므로 오답이다.

02 Who 의문문 🎧 캐나다 → 미국

Who can I talk to about getting a membership at this gym?
(A) Someone will help you in a few minutes.
(B) The shuttle is on its way.
(C) No, it's been rescheduled.

reschedule v. 일정을 변경하다

해석 이 체육관의 회원권 가입에 대해 누구와 이야기할 수 있나요?
(A) 누군가가 몇 분 내로 당신을 도와줄 거예요.
(B) 셔틀버스가 오는 중이에요.
(C) 아니요, 그것은 일정이 변경되었어요.
해설 (A) [o] 누군가가 몇 분 내로 도와줄 것이라는 말로, 회원권 가입에 대해 누구가 곧 도와줄 것임을 전달했으므로 정답이다.
(B) [x] 회원권 가입에 대해 누구와 이야기할 수 있는지 물었는데, 이와 관련이 없는 셔틀버스가 오는 중이라는 말로 응답했으므로 오답이다.
(C) [x] 의문사 의문문에 No로 응답했으므로 오답이다.

03 Who 의문문 🎧 영국 → 호주

Who's leading the sales presentation?
(A) Leadership strategies.
(B) Usually around 2 o'clock.
(C) I'm not involved in that.

lead v. 이끌다 **presentation** n. 발표, 설명 **strategy** n. 전략
involve v. 관여시키다, 수반하다

해석 누가 제품 발표를 이끌 것인가요?
(A) 리더십 전략이요.
(B) 보통 2시 경이요.
(C) 저는 그 일에 관여하지 않아요.
해설 (A) [x] leading - leadership의 유사 발음 어휘를 사용하여 혼동을 준 오답이다.
(B) [x] 누가 제품 소개를 이끌 것인지를 물었는데, 시간으로 응답했으므로 오답이다.
(C) [o] 그 일에 관여하지 않는다는 말로, 제품 발표를 이끌 사람이 누구인지 모른다는 것을 간접적으로 전달했으므로 정답이다.

04 Who 의문문 🎧 미국 → 영국

Who else is helping with the community garden?
(A) Only the flowers for indoor decoration.
(B) I'll check the list.
(C) Yes, it's windy outside.

community n. 지역 사회 **outside** adv. 밖에, 밖으로

해석 누가 또 그 지역 사회 정원에 대해 돕고 있나요?
(A) 실내 장식용 꽃들만이요.
(B) 제가 명단을 확인할게요.
(C) 네, 밖에 바람이 불어요.
해설 (A) [x] 질문의 garden(정원)과 관련 있는 flowers(꽃들)를 사용하여 혼동을 준 오답이다.
(B) [o] 명단을 확인하겠다는 말로, 지역 사회 정원에 대해 돕고 있는 또 다른 사람이 누구인지 모른다는 것을 간접적으로 전달했으므로 정답이다.
(C) [x] 의문사 의문문에 Yes로 응답했으므로 오답이다.

기출 유형 2 What/Which 의문문

Example 🎧 영국 → 호주 p.33
해석 곧 있을 워크숍의 주제는 무엇인가요?
(A) 아니요, 102호실에서요.
(B) 그것은 제가 가장 좋아하는 가게예요.
(C) 경영 기술이요.
어휘 **topic** n. 주제 **management** n. 경영, 관리 **skill** n. 기술

토익실전문제 p.33

| 01 (C) | 02 (B) | 03 (A) | 04 (C) |

01 Which 의문문

Which oven did you buy from the items in the catalog?
(A) An appliance repairperson is coming.
(B) Baking was a lot of fun.
(C) I ordered the cheapest one.

appliance n. 가전제품 order v. 주문하다

해석 카탈로그에 있는 물건들 중에서 어떤 오븐을 구매하셨나요?
(A) 가전제품 수리 기사가 오고 있어요.
(B) 베이킹은 아주 재미있었어요.
(C) 저는 가장 저렴한 것을 주문했어요.

해설 (A) [×] 카탈로그에 있는 물건들 중에서 어떤 오븐을 구매했는지를 물었는데 이와 관련이 없는 가전제품 수리 기사가 오고 있다고 응답했으므로 오답이다.
(B) [×] 질문의 oven(오븐)과 관련 있는 baking(베이킹)을 사용하여 혼동을 준 오답이다.
(C) [○] 가장 저렴한 것을 주문했다는 말로, 자신이 구매한 오븐이 어떤 것인지를 언급했으므로 정답이다.

02 What 의문문

What time does the pharmacy across the street open on weekdays?
(A) Yes, it's near the bank.
(B) At 10 o'clock.
(C) A doctor's prescription is required.

pharmacy n. 약국 prescription n. 처방(전)

해석 길 건너 약국은 평일에 몇 시에 문을 여나요?
(A) 네, 은행 근처에 있어요.
(B) 10시에요.
(C) 의사의 처방전은 필수예요.

해설 (A) [×] 의문사 의문문에 Yes로 응답했으므로 오답이다.
(B) [○] 10시에라는 말로, 약국이 문을 여는 시간을 언급했으므로 정답이다.
(C) [×] 질문의 pharmacy(약국)와 관련 있는 prescription(처방전)을 사용하여 혼동을 준 오답이다.

03 What 의문문

What do you think I should take to the job fair?
(A) Multiple copies of your résumé.
(B) No, it's on the third floor.
(C) I think that price is fair.

job fair 취업 박람회 multiple adj. 여럿의, 다수의 résumé n. 이력서

해석 취업 박람회에 제가 무엇을 가져가야 한다고 생각하세요?
(A) 여러 장의 이력서요.
(B) 아뇨, 3층에 있어요.
(C) 그 가격은 타당한 것 같아요.

해설 (A) [○] 여러 장의 이력서라는 말로, 취업 박람회에 무엇을 가져가야 할지를 언급했으므로 정답이다.
(B) [×] 의문사 의문문에 No로 응답했으므로 오답이다.
(C) [×] 질문의 fair(박람회)를 '타당한'이라는 의미의 형용사 fair로 반복 사용하여 혼동을 준 오답이다.

04 Which 의문문

Which local farmer's market has the freshest produce?
(A) Local businesses participated in the event.
(B) There are lots of organic vegetables.
(C) The Saturday market on Main Street.

local adj. 지역의, 현지의 produce n. 농산물, 생산품 organic adj. 유기농의

해석 어떤 지역 농산물 시장이 가장 신선한 농산물을 가지고 있나요?
(A) 지역 업체들이 그 행사에 참여했어요.
(B) 유기농 채소들이 많이 있어요.
(C) Main가의 토요일 시장이요.

해설 (A) [×] 질문의 local을 반복 사용하여 혼동을 준 오답이다.
(B) [×] 질문의 farmer's market(농산물 시장)과 관련 있는 vegetables(채소들)를 사용하여 혼동을 준 오답이다.
(C) [○] Main가의 토요일 시장이라는 말로, 신선한 농산물을 파는 시장을 언급했으므로 정답이다.

HACKERS TEST

p.34

01 (C)	02 (B)	03 (C)	04 (B)	05 (C)
06 (A)	07 (B)	08 (C)	09 (B)	10 (B)
11 (B)	12 (B)	13 (B)	14 (B)	15 (C)
16 (C)	17 (B)	18 (A)	19 (C)	20 (B)
21 (A)	22 (B)	23 (C)	24 (A)	25 (C)
26 (C)	27 (B)	28 (B)		

01 Who 의문문

Who conducted the job interview?
(A) On April 17.
(B) It might take an hour or so.
(C) The head of human resources.

conduct v. 진행하다, 수행하다 human resources 인사부, 인적 자원

해석 누가 취업 면접을 진행했나요?
(A) 4월 17일이에요.
(B) 한 시간 정도 걸릴 수도 있어요.
(C) 인사부장이요.

해설 (A) [×] 누가 취업 면접을 진행했는지를 물었는데, 날짜로 응답했으므로 오답이다.
(B) [×] 누가 취업 면접을 진행했는지를 물었는데, 시간으로 응답했으므로 오답이다.
(C) [○] 인사부장이라는 말로, 누가 취업 면접을 진행했는지를 언급했으므로 정답이다.

02 Which 의문문

Which store carries professional art supplies?
(A) Those are oil paintings.
(B) The one on Allen Street.
(C) OK, I'll go there now.

carry v. 보유하다, 들고 있다 professional adj. 전문적인 oil painting 유화

해석 어떤 가게가 전문적인 미술 용품을 보유하고 있나요?
(A) 그것들은 유화예요.
(B) Allen가에 있는 곳이요.
(C) 좋아요, 제가 지금 그곳으로 갈게요.

해설 (A) [×] 질문의 art(미술)에서 연상할 수 있는 그림과 관련된 oil paintings(유화)를 사용하여 혼동을 준 오답이다.
(B) [○] Allen가에 있는 곳이라는 말로, 어떤 가게가 전문적인 미술 용품을 보유하고 있는지를 언급했으므로 정답이다.

(C) [x] 질문의 store(가게)를 가리킬 때 쓸 수 있는 there(그곳으로)를 사용하여 혼동을 준 오답이다.

03 Who 의문문   미국 → 호주

Who will be speaking on stage tomorrow?
(A) In the auditorium.
(B) They want seats near the stage.
(C) Ms. Waldman will.

stage n. 무대   auditorium n. 강당

해석 누가 내일 무대 위에서 연설할 예정인가요?
(A) 강당에서요.
(B) 그들은 무대 근처의 좌석을 원해요.
(C) Ms. Waldman이 할 거예요.

해설 (A) [x] 누가 무대 위에서 연설할 예정인지를 물었는데, 장소로 응답했으므로 오답이다.
(B) [x] 질문의 stage를 반복 사용하여 혼동을 준 오답이다.
(C) [o] Ms. Waldman이 할 거라는 말로, 무대 위에서 연설할 사람의 이름을 언급했으므로 정답이다.

04 Which 의문문   영국 → 호주

Which file does Matilda need for her presentation?
(A) Yes, it will be ready by next Monday.
(B) The yellow one on the desk.
(C) I have 70 dollars to buy a present.

present n. 선물

해석 Matilda가 그녀의 발표를 위해 어떤 파일이 필요한가요?
(A) 네, 다음 주 월요일까지 준비될 거예요.
(B) 책상 위에 있는 노란색 파일이요.
(C) 저는 선물을 구매할 70달러를 가지고 있어요.

해설 (A) [x] 의문사 의문문에 Yes로 응답했으므로 오답이다. 질문의 file(파일)을 가리킬 때 쓸 수 있는 it(그것)을 사용하여 혼동을 주었다.
(B) [o] 책상 위에 있는 노란색 파일이라는 말로, 어떤 파일이 Matilda의 발표를 위해 필요한 것인지를 언급했으므로 정답이다.
(C) [x] presentation - present의 유사 발음 어휘를 사용하여 혼동을 준 오답이다.

05 Who 의문문   호주 → 영국

Who owns that minivan parked across the street?
(A) From the motor show last month.
(B) Parking is free here.
(C) It's mine.

own v. 소유하다

해석 길 건너편에 주차된 미니밴은 누가 소유하고 있나요?
(A) 지난달 자동차 전시회에서요.
(B) 이곳은 주차가 무료예요.
(C) 제 것이에요.

해설 (A) [x] 질문의 minivan(미니밴)과 관련 있는 motor show(자동차 전시회)를 사용하여 혼동을 준 오답이다.
(B) [x] parked - parking의 유사 발음 어휘를 사용하여 혼동을 준 오답이다.
(C) [o] 본인의 것이라는 말로, 미니밴을 누가 소유한 것인지를 언급했으므로 정답이다.

06 What 의문문   미국 → 영국

What were last month's sales numbers?
(A) Mr. Hans keeps track of that.
(B) That's the best option.
(C) There's a sale on electronics now.

sales n. 판매, 매출   keep track of ~에 대해 계속 파악하고 있다
electronics n. 전자제품

해석 지난달 판매 수치는 얼마였나요?
(A) Mr. Hans가 그것에 대해 계속 파악하고 있어요.
(B) 그게 최선의 선택지입니다.
(C) 지금 전자제품이 할인 중이에요.

해설 (A) [o] Mr. Hans가 그것에 대해 계속 파악하고 있다는 말로, Mr. Hans가 판매 수치를 알 거라고 간접적으로 전달했으므로 정답이다.
(B) [x] 지난달 판매 수치를 물었는데, 이와 관련이 없는 게 최선의 선택지라고 응답했으므로 오답이다.
(C) [x] 질문의 sales의 sale을 반복 사용하여 혼동을 준 오답이다.

07 Who 의문문   캐나다 → 호주

Who placed our lunch order with the restaurant?
(A) Sorry, we're not taking orders right now.
(B) I think Julie did about a half hour ago.
(C) By express mail.

place an order 주문을 넣다   express mail 속달 우편 서비스

해석 누가 식당에 우리의 점심 주문을 넣었나요?
(A) 죄송합니다, 저희는 지금 주문을 받지 않고 있어요.
(B) Julie가 약 30분 전에 주문한 것 같아요.
(C) 속달 우편으로요.

해설 (A) [x] 질문의 order를 orders로 반복 사용하여 혼동을 준 오답이다.
(B) [o] Julie가 약 30분 전에 주문한 것 같다는 말로, 식당에 점심 주문을 한 사람의 이름을 언급했으므로 정답이다.
(C) [x] 누가 식당에 점심 주문을 넣었는지를 물었는데, 이와 관련이 없는 우편 배송 방식으로 응답했으므로 오답이다.

08 What 의문문   호주 → 미국

What went wrong with the posters you printed?
(A) Her bill is incorrect.
(B) At a print shop on Chelsea Avenue.
(C) The font size is not large enough.

go wrong 잘못되다, 실수를 하다   incorrect adj. 맞지 않는, 부정확한
font n. 서체, 글꼴

해석 당신이 인쇄했던 포스터들에 무엇이 잘못됐나요?
(A) 그녀의 청구서가 맞지 않아요.
(B) Chelsea가에 있는 인쇄소에서요.
(C) 서체 크기가 충분히 크지 않아요.

해설 (A) [x] 질문의 wrong(잘못된)에서 연상할 수 있는 incorrect(맞지 않는)를 사용하여 혼동을 준 오답이다.
(B) [x] printed - print의 유사 발음 어휘를 사용하여 혼동을 준 오답이다.
(C) [o] 서체 크기가 충분히 크지 않다는 말로, 포스터들에 무엇이 잘못됐는지를 언급했으므로 정답이다.

09 Who 의문문   영국 → 미국

Who did Ms. Fleming meet with this afternoon?
(A) I'll greet the guests.

(B) Some board members.
(C) Please come in the morning.

greet v. 맞이하다, 환영하다   board member 이사회 임원

해석 Ms. Fleming은 오늘 오후에 누구와 만났나요?
(A) 제가 그 손님들을 맞이할게요.
(B) 몇몇 이사회 임원들이요.
(C) 오전에 오세요.

해설 (A) [x] 질문의 meet(만나다)과 관련 있는 greet(맞이하다)을 사용하여 혼동을 준 오답이다.
(B) [o] 몇몇 이사회 임원들이라는 말로, Ms. Fleming이 오늘 오후에 누구와 만났는지를 언급했으므로 정답이다.
(C) [x] 질문의 afternoon(오후)과 관련 있는 morning(오전)을 사용하여 혼동을 준 오답이다.

10 What 의문문   미국 → 호주

What time do you want a wake-up call?
(A) As long as we order room service.
(B) I'll just set the alarm on my phone.
(C) He hasn't called me back yet.

wake-up call 기상 전화, 모닝콜

해석 몇 시에 기상 전화를 받고 싶으신가요?
(A) 저희가 룸서비스를 주문하는 한이요.
(B) 그냥 제 휴대전화에 알람을 설정할게요.
(C) 그는 아직 제게 회신하지 않았어요.

해설 (A) [x] What time으로 물었는데, 조건으로 응답했으므로 오답이다.
(B) [o] 그냥 휴대전화 알람을 설정하겠다는 말로, 기상 전화 대신 알람을 사용하겠다는 간접적인 응답을 했으므로 정답이다.
(C) [x] 질문의 call(전화)을 '전화하다'라는 의미의 동사 called로 반복 사용하여 혼동을 준 오답이다.

11 Who 의문문   영국 → 캐나다

Who will bring refreshments to the office party?
(A) It should be a lot of fun.
(B) Patrick offered to.
(C) We are celebrating my promotion.

bring v. 가져오다   refreshment n. 다과, 간식   offer v. 하겠다고 하다
promotion n. 승진

해석 누가 사무실 파티에 다과를 가져올 건가요?
(A) 그것은 아주 재미있을 거예요.
(B) Patrick이 하겠다고 했어요.
(C) 우리는 제 승진을 축하할 거예요.

해설 (A) [x] 질문의 party에서 연상할 수 있는 fun(재미있는)을 사용하여 혼동을 준 오답이다.
(B) [o] Patrick이 하겠다고 했다는 말로, 사무실 파티에 다과를 가져올 사람을 언급했으므로 정답이다.
(C) [x] 질문의 office party(사무실 파티)에서 연상할 수 있는 파티의 목적과 관련된 promotion(승진)을 사용하여 혼동을 준 오답이다.

12 What 의문문   미국 → 영국

What made you decide to become a veterinarian?
(A) Let me check my wallet.
(B) I love being with animals.
(C) It took about eight years.

decide v. 결정하다   veterinarian n. 수의사

해석 무엇이 당신을 수의사가 되도록 결정하게 했나요?
(A) 제 지갑을 확인할게요.
(B) 저는 동물들과 함께 있는 것을 좋아해요.
(C) 약 8년이 걸렸어요.

해설 (A) [x] 무엇이 수의사가 되도록 결정하게 했는지를 물었는데, 이와 관련이 없는 지갑을 확인할 것이라고 응답했으므로 오답이다.
(B) [o] 동물들과 함께 있는 것을 좋아한다는 말로, 무엇이 수의사가 되도록 결정하게 했는지를 언급했으므로 정답이다.
(C) [x] 질문의 become a veterinarian(수의사가 되다)에서 연상할 수 있는 기간으로 응답하여 혼동을 준 오답이다.

13 Which 의문문   호주 → 미국

Which dessert are you going to order?
(A) A pastry chef.
(B) I'm still trying to decide.
(C) Sure, you can order business cards.

dessert n. 후식   pastry chef 제빵사   business card 명함

해석 어떤 후식을 주문할 건가요?
(A) 제빵사요.
(B) 저는 아직 결정하는 중이에요.
(C) 물론이죠, 당신은 명함을 주문할 수 있어요.

해설 (A) [x] 질문의 dessert(디저트)에서 연상할 수 있는 직업과 관련된 pastry chef(제빵사)를 사용하여 혼동을 준 오답이다.
(B) [o] 아직 결정하는 중이라는 말로, 어떤 후식을 주문할 것인지 곧 알려줄 것임을 간접적으로 전달했으므로 정답이다.
(C) [x] 질문의 order를 반복 사용하여 혼동을 준 오답이다.

14 Who 의문문   캐나다 → 미국

Who's available to give me a ride to the airport?
(A) A twelve-dollar fare.
(B) John has a flexible schedule today.
(C) We missed the connecting flight.

give a ride 태워주다   fare n. (교통) 요금   flexible adj. 유연한, 융통성 있는

해석 누가 저를 공항까지 태워줄 수 있나요?
(A) 12달러의 요금이요.
(B) John은 오늘 일정이 유연해요.
(C) 우리는 환승 비행기를 놓쳤어요.

해설 (A) [x] 질문의 ride(승차)에서 연상할 수 있는 교통비와 관련된 fare(요금)를 사용하여 혼동을 준 오답이다.
(B) [o] John은 오늘 일정이 유연하다는 말로, 공항까지 태워줄 수 있을 것임을 간접적으로 전달했으므로 정답이다.
(C) [x] 질문의 airport(공항)에서 연상할 수 있는 항공편과 관련된 connecting flight(환승 비행기)을 사용하여 혼동을 준 오답이다.

15 What 의문문   영국 → 캐나다

What benefits does your company offer employees?
(A) All staff need to prepare for the upcoming retreat.
(B) The office is on the first floor.
(C) We provide health insurance and a retirement plan.

benefit n. 혜택, 이득   retreat n. 야유회   insurance n. 보험

해석 당신의 회사는 직원들에게 무슨 혜택을 제공하나요?
(A) 모든 직원들이 다가오는 야유회를 준비해야 돼요.
(B) 그 사무실은 1층에 있어요.
(C) 저희는 건강보험과 퇴직 연금 제도를 제공해요.

해설 (A) [×] 질문의 company(회사)에서 연상할 수 있는 사내 행사와 관련된 retreat(야유회)을 사용하여 혼동을 준 오답이다.
(B) [×] 질문의 company(회사)와 관련된 office(사무실)를 사용하여 혼동을 준 오답이다.
(C) [o] 건강보험과 퇴직 연금 제도를 제공한다는 말로, 회사가 직원들에게 주는 혜택을 언급했으므로 정답이다.

16 Who 의문문
미국 → 영국

Who was told to write a draft of the proposal?
(A) It's on the left corner.
(B) We'll hold it in March.
(C) I thought Greg was supposed to do it.

draft n. 초안 proposal n. 제안서 be supposed to ~하기로 되어 있다

해설 누가 제안서의 초안을 작성하도록 지시받았나요?
(A) 그것은 왼쪽 모퉁이에 있어요.
(B) 저희는 3월에 그것을 개최할 거예요.
(C) Greg이 그것을 하기로 되어 있었던 것 같아요.

해설 (A) [×] 누가 제안서의 초안을 작성하도록 지시받았는지 물었는데, 위치로 응답했으므로 오답이다.
(B) [×] told - hold의 유사 발음 어휘를 사용하여 혼동을 준 오답이다.
(C) [o] Greg이 그것을 하기로 되어 있었던 것 같다는 말로, 제안서 초안을 작성하도록 지시받은 사람을 언급했으므로 정답이다.

17 Which 의문문
호주 → 캐나다

Which of these hiking trails is the easiest?
(A) Clear weather is expected.
(B) Maple Trail has gentle slopes.
(C) I prefer the white shirt.

hiking trail 등산로 slope n. 경사지

해설 이 등산로들 중 어느 것이 가장 쉽나요?
(A) 맑은 날씨가 예상돼요.
(B) Maple Trail이 완만한 경사지를 가지고 있어요.
(C) 저는 흰색 셔츠를 선호해요.

해설 (A) [×] 질문의 hiking(등산)에서 연상할 수 있는 날씨와 관련된 clear weather(맑은 날씨)를 사용하여 혼동을 준 오답이다.
(B) [o] Maple Trail이 완만한 경사지를 가지고 있다는 말로, Maple Trail이 등산로들 중 가장 쉽다는 것을 간접적으로 전달했으므로 정답이다.
(C) [×] 등산로들 중 어느 것이 가장 쉬운지를 물었는데, 이와 관련이 없는 흰색 셔츠를 선호한다고 응답했으므로 오답이다.

18 Who 의문문
영국 → 캐나다

Who did you hire to cater your birthday party?
(A) I went with your recommendation.
(B) The guest list was changed.
(C) No, we hired at least two.

cater v. (행사에) 요리를 제공하다 recommendation n. 추천

해설 당신의 생일 파티에 요리를 제공하기 위해 누구를 고용했나요?
(A) 당신의 추천대로 했어요.
(B) 손님 명단이 변경됐어요.
(C) 아니요, 우리는 최소 두 명을 고용했어요.

해설 (A) [o] 당신의 추천대로 했다는 말로, 생일 파티에 요리를 제공하기 위해 누구를 고용했는지 간접적으로 전달했으므로 정답이다.
(B) [×] 질문의 party(파티)와 관련 있는 guest list(손님 명단)를 사용하여 혼동을 준 오답이다.
(C) [×] 의문사 의문문에 No로 응답했으므로 오답이다. hire - hired의 유사 발음 어휘를 사용하여 혼동을 주었다.

19 Which 의문문
영국 → 미국

Which staff member do you want to add to your team?
(A) Thanks for organizing the meeting.
(B) The team has seven members.
(C) Do you have any suggestions?

add v. 추가하다 organize v. 마련하다, 준비하다 suggestion n. 제안

해설 어떤 직원을 당신의 팀에 추가하고 싶으신가요?
(A) 회의를 마련해줘서 고마워요.
(B) 그 팀은 7명의 구성원이 있어요.
(C) 제안이 있나요?

해설 (A) [×] 어떤 직원을 팀에 추가하고 싶은지를 물었는데, 이와 관련이 없는 회의를 마련해줘서 고맙다고 응답했으므로 오답이다.
(B) [×] 질문의 team을 반복 사용하여 혼동을 준 오답이다.
(C) [o] 제안이 있냐고 되물어, 팀에 추가할 직원에 대한 추가 정보를 요구하는 정답이다.

20 What 의문문
캐나다 → 호주

What type of printer do we need to order?
(A) This type of packaging, please.
(B) A color laser model.
(C) We can scan documents too.

packaging n. 포장(재) document n. 문서, 서류

해설 우리가 어떤 종류의 프린터를 주문해야 하나요?
(A) 이 유형의 포장재로 부탁해요.
(B) 컬러 레이저 모델이요.
(C) 우리는 문서도 스캔할 수 있어요.

해설 (A) [×] 질문의 type을 반복 사용하여 혼동을 준 오답이다.
(B) [o] 컬러 레이저 모델이라는 말로, 어떤 종류의 프린터를 주문해야 할지 언급했으므로 정답이다.
(C) [×] 질문의 printer(프린터)에서 연상할 수 있는 기능과 관련된 scan(스캔하다)을 사용하여 혼동을 준 오답이다.

21 Who 의문문
미국 → 캐나다

Who's finalizing the event details?
(A) Oh, I just e-mailed the file.
(B) Tomorrow is Saturday.
(C) A detailed agenda.

finalize v. 마무리짓다 detail n. 세부 사항

해설 누가 행사의 세부 사항들을 마무리지을 건가요?
(A) 아, 제가 방금 파일을 이메일로 보냈어요.
(B) 내일은 토요일이에요.
(C) 상세한 안건이요.

해설 (A) [o] 방금 파일을 이메일로 보냈다는 말로, 자신이 행사의 세부 사항을 마무리지었음을 간접적으로 전달했으므로 정답이다.
(B) [×] 누가 행사 세부 사항들을 마무리지을 것인지를 물었는데, 이와 관련이 없는 내일은 토요일이라고 응답했으므로 오답이다.
(C) [×] details - detailed의 유사 발음 어휘를 사용하여 혼동을 준 오답이다.

22 What 의문문 호주 → 미국

What date was set for the project deadline?
(A) Production line equipment.
(B) The last Friday of October.
(C) Did you set the table?

deadline n. 마감일   equipment n. 장비, 설비

해석 어떤 날짜가 프로젝트 마감일로 정해졌나요?
(A) 생산 라인 장비요.
(B) 10월의 마지막 금요일이요.
(C) 식탁을 차렸나요?

해설 (A) [x] deadline - line의 유사 발음 어휘를 사용하여 혼동을 준 오답이다.
(B) [o] 10월의 마지막 금요일이라는 말로, 어떤 날짜가 프로젝트 마감일로 정해졌는지를 언급했으므로 정답이다.
(C) [x] 질문의 set을 반복 사용하여 혼동을 준 오답이다.

23 Who 의문문 영국 → 캐나다

Who do I talk to about connecting flights?
(A) Your gate has changed to B12.
(B) Yes, it's closed.
(C) The airline representative.

connecting flight 환승 항공편   representative n. 직원

해석 환승 항공편에 대해 누구에게 말해야 하나요?
(A) 귀하의 탑승구는 B12로 변경되었습니다.
(B) 네, 그것은 폐쇄됐어요.
(C) 항공사 직원이요.

해설 (A) [x] 질문의 flights(항공편)에서 연상할 수 있는 gate(탑승구)를 사용하여 혼동을 준 오답이다.
(B) [x] 의문사 의문문에 Yes로 응답했으므로 오답이다.
(C) [o] 항공사 직원이라는 말로, 환승 항공편에 대해 누구에게 말해야 하는지를 언급했으므로 정답이다.

24 Which 의문문 캐나다 → 미국

Which firm was hired to redesign the company logo?
(A) That project was canceled.
(B) I really like the color too.
(C) Your reservation is confirmed.

firm n. 기업, 회사   cancel v. 취소하다   reservation n. 예약

해석 어떤 기업이 회사 로고를 다시 디자인하기 위해 고용되었나요?
(A) 그 프로젝트는 취소되었어요.
(B) 색상도 정말 좋아요.
(C) 귀하의 예약이 확정되었습니다.

해설 (A) [o] 그 프로젝트는 취소되었다는 말로, 회사 로고를 다시 디자인하기 위해 어떤 기업도 고용되지 않았음을 간접적으로 전달했으므로 정답이다.
(B) [x] 질문의 logo(로고)와 관련 있는 color(색상)를 사용하여 혼동을 준 오답이다.
(C) [x] firm - confirmed의 유사 발음 어휘를 사용하여 혼동을 준 오답이다.

25 What 의문문 미국 → 캐나다

What did Mr. Walker talk about at the convention?
(A) Because I have a question.
(B) Yes, it was extremely informative.
(C) I missed his speech.

convention n. 협회, 대표자 회의   informative adj. 유익한
speech n. 연설

해석 Mr. Walker는 그 협회에서 무엇에 대해 이야기했나요?
(A) 제가 질문이 있기 때문이에요.
(B) 네, 그것은 매우 유익했어요.
(C) 저는 그의 연설을 놓쳤어요.

해설 (A) [x] Mr. Walker가 협회에서 무엇에 대해 이야기했는지를 물었는데, 이와 관련이 없는 이유로 응답했으므로 오답이다.
(B) [x] 의문사 의문문에 Yes로 응답했으므로 오답이다. 질문의 convention(협회)에서 연상할 수 있는 informative(유익한)를 사용하여 혼동을 주었다.
(C) [o] 그의 연설을 놓쳤다는 말로, Mr. Walker가 협회에서 무엇에 대해 이야기했는지 모른다는 것을 간접적으로 전달했으므로 정답이다.

26 Who 의문문 호주 → 영국

Who has the performance review results?
(A) There's a great view of the ocean.
(B) Leave it at the front desk.
(C) Let's ask the manager.

performance n. 업무, 성과   result n. 결과   leave v. 놓고 가다, 남기고 가다

해석 누가 업무 평가 결과지를 가지고 있나요?
(A) 멋진 바다 풍경이 펼쳐져 있어요.
(B) 그것을 접수처에 놓고 가세요.
(C) 관리자에게 물어봅시다.

해설 (A) [x] review - view의 유사 발음 어휘를 사용하여 혼동을 준 오답이다.
(B) [x] 누가 업무 평가 결과지를 가지고 있는지를 물었는데, 이와 관련이 없는 그것을 접수처에 놓고 가라고 응답했으므로 오답이다.
(C) [o] 관리자에게 물어보자는 말로, 누가 업무 평가 결과지를 가지고 있는지 모른다는 것을 간접적으로 전달했으므로 정답이다.

27 Which 의문문 캐나다 → 미국

Which platform does the train to London leave from?
(A) About 10 minutes from now.
(B) Track number 2.
(C) Have you packed for your vacation?

platform n. 플랫폼   track n. 선로   pack v. (짐을) 싸다, 포장하다

해석 어떤 플랫폼에서 런던행 기차가 출발하나요?
(A) 지금부터 약 10분 후요.
(B) 2번 선로요.
(C) 휴가를 위한 짐을 쌌나요?

해설 (A) [x] 어떤 플랫폼에서 런던행 기차가 출발하는지를 물었는데, 시간으로 응답했으므로 오답이다.
(B) [o] 2번 선로라는 말로, 런던행 기차가 출발하는 플랫폼 번호를 언급했으므로 정답이다.
(C) [x] 질문의 train(기차)에서 연상할 수 있는 여행과 관련된 vacation(휴가)을 사용하여 혼동을 준 오답이다.

28 What 의문문 영국 → 호주

What did our focus group say about the new product design?
(A) They are 40 percent off.
(B) The marketing team is reviewing the feedback.

(C) No, the product was launched in May.

focus group 포커스 그룹(시장 조사를 위해 선출된 소수의 사람들)
launch v. 출시하다

해석 우리의 포커스 그룹은 그 신제품 디자인에 대해 뭐라고 말했나요?
(A) 그것들은 40퍼센트 할인돼요.
(B) 마케팅 팀이 의견을 검토하고 있어요.
(C) 아니요, 그 제품은 5월에 출시됐어요.

해석 (A) [x] 질문의 product(제품)에서 연상할 수 있는 할인 행사와 관련된 percent off(퍼센트 할인)를 사용하여 혼동을 준 오답이다.
(B) [o] 마케팅 팀이 의견을 검토하고 있다는 말로, 포커스 그룹이 신제품 디자인에 뭐라고 말했는지 모른다는 것을 간접적으로 전달했으므로 정답이다.
(C) [x] 의문사 의문문에 No로 응답했으므로 오답이다. 질문의 product를 반복 사용하여 혼동을 주었다.

DAY 04 의문사 의문문: Where, When

기출 유형 1 Where 의문문

Example 캐나다 → 미국 p.36
해석 제 주방에 둘 새 토스터를 어디에서 구입할 수 있을까요?
(A) Mina's 가전제품점에 한번 가보세요.
(B) 새로운 요리책이요.
(C) 저는 밀가루가 좀 필요해요.

어휘 appliance n. 가전제품 flour n. 밀가루

토익실전문제 p.36

| 01 (B) | 02 (B) | 03 (C) | 04 (A) |

01 Where 의문문 영국 → 호주

Where are the extra chairs stored?
(A) Several folding chairs.
(B) In the basement storage room.
(C) Because we need more seating.

store v. 보관하다, 저장하다 basement n. 지하(층) seating n. 좌석

해석 여분의 의자들은 어디에 보관되어 있나요?
(A) 여러 개의 접이식 의자들이요.
(B) 지하 창고 안에요.
(C) 우리는 더 많은 좌석이 필요하기 때문이에요.

해석 (A) [x] 질문의 chairs를 반복 사용하여 혼동을 준 오답이다.
(B) [o] 지하 창고 안에라는 말로, 여분의 의자들이 보관되어 있는 장소를 언급했으므로 정답이다.
(C) [x] 여분의 의자들이 어디에 보관되어 있는지 장소를 물었는데, 이유로 응답했으므로 오답이다.

02 Where 의문문 호주 → 미국

Where can I find good restaurants in this area?
(A) A table by the window, please.
(B) I use this restaurant app.
(C) That's a good plan.

area n. 지역, 구역

해석 이 지역 내 좋은 식당들을 어디에서 찾을 수 있나요?
(A) 창가 테이블로 주세요.
(B) 저는 이 식당 앱을 사용해요.
(C) 그거 좋은 계획이네요.

해석 (A) [x] 질문의 restaurants(식당들)와 관련 있는 table(테이블)을 사용하여 혼동을 준 오답이다.
(B) [o] 자신은 이 식당 앱을 사용한다는 말로, 좋은 식당들을 어디에서 찾을 수 있는지를 언급했으므로 정답이다.
(C) [x] 질문의 good을 반복 사용하여 혼동을 준 오답이다.

03 Where 의문문 영국 → 캐나다

Where should we install the new security cameras?
(A) To prevent theft.
(B) After next Wednesday.
(C) At all building entrances.

install v. 설치하다 prevent v. 예방하다, 막다 theft n. 훔침, 절도
entrance n. 입구

해석 새로운 보안 카메라들을 어디에 설치해야 하나요?
(A) 도난을 방지하기 위해서요.
(B) 다음 주 수요일 이후요.
(C) 모든 건물 입구요.

해석 (A) [x] 보안 카메라들을 어디에 설치해야 할지 위치를 물었는데, 목적으로 응답했으므로 오답이다.
(B) [x] 보안 카메라들을 어디에 설치해야 할지 위치를 물었는데, 시점으로 응답했으므로 오답이다. 질문의 Where를 When으로 혼동하여 이를 정답으로 선택하지 않도록 주의한다.
(C) [o] 모든 건물 입구에라는 말로, 보안 카메라들을 어디에 설치해야 할지를 언급했으므로 정답이다.

04 Where 의문문 미국 → 영국

Where are the conference materials for tomorrow?
(A) Andy had them this morning.
(B) Yes, that was a great conference.
(C) Thanks for your extra work on this.

material n. 자료, 재료

해석 내일의 학회 자료는 어디에 있나요?
(A) Andy가 오늘 아침에 그것들을 가지고 있었어요.
(B) 네, 그건 정말 좋은 학회였어요.
(C) 이 일에 대한 추가 작업에 감사드려요.

해석 (A) [o] Andy가 오늘 아침에 그것들을 가지고 있었다는 말로, 학회 자료를 가지고 있는 사람을 언급했으므로 정답이다.
(B) [x] 의문사 의문문에 Yes로 응답했으므로 오답이다. 질문의 conference를 반복 사용하여 혼동을 주었다.
(C) [x] 질문의 conference materials(학회 자료)와 관련 있는 work(작업)를 사용하여 혼동을 준 오답이다.

기출 유형 2 When 의문문

Example 호주 → 캐나다 p.37
해석 오늘 밤에 콘서트는 언제 시작하나요?
(A) Whitehead가에서요.
(B) 7시예요.
(C) 약 20,000명이요.

토익실전문제 p.37

| 01 (C) | 02 (B) | 03 (C) | 04 (A) |

01 When 의문문 　　　캐나다 → 미국

When does the summer discount promotion end?
(A) At all branch locations.
(B) Various payment methods.
(C) Next Friday.

branch location 지점　various adj. 다양한　method n. 방법

해석 여름 할인 행사는 언제 끝나나요?
　(A) 모든 지점들에서요.
　(B) 다양한 지불 방법들이요.
　(C) 다음 주 금요일이요.

해설 (A) [×] 여름 할인 행사가 언제 끝나는지 시점을 물었는데, 이과 관련이 없는 장소로 응답했으므로 오답이다. 질문의 When을 Where로 혼동하여 이를 정답으로 선택하지 않도록 주의한다.
　(B) [×] 질문의 discount(할인)와 관련 있는 payment(지불, 결제)를 사용하여 혼동을 준 오답이다.
　(C) [o] 다음 주 금요일이라는 말로, 여름 할인 행사가 끝날 시점을 언급했으므로 정답이다.

02 When 의문문 　　　영국 → 호주

When is the checkout time at this hotel?
(A) An inventory check.
(B) You have until noon tomorrow.
(C) The spa is on the fifth floor.

inventory n. 재고

해석 이 호텔의 체크아웃 시간은 언제인가요?
　(A) 재고 점검이요.
　(B) 내일 정오까지 시간이 있어요.
　(C) 스파는 5층에 있어요.

해설 (A) [×] checkout - check의 유사 발음 어휘를 사용하여 혼동을 준 오답이다.
　(B) [o] 내일 정오까지 시간이 있다는 말로, 시점을 언급했으므로 정답이다.
　(C) [×] 질문의 hotel(호텔)에서 연상할 수 있는 호텔 시설과 관련된 spa(스파)를 사용하여 혼동을 준 오답이다.

03 When 의문문 　　　미국 → 캐나다

When will the software update be available?
(A) Update the employee manual.
(B) No, I'm not available then.
(C) The development team is finalizing it.

available adj. 이용 가능한, 시간이 있는　finalize v. 마무리짓다

해석 소프트웨어 업데이트는 언제 이용 가능할까요?
　(A) 직원 매뉴얼을 업데이트하세요.
　(B) 아니요, 저는 그때 시간이 없어요.
　(C) 개발팀이 그것을 마무리짓는 중이에요.

해설 (A) [×] 질문의 update를 '업데이트하다'라는 의미의 동사로 반복 사용하여 혼동을 준 오답이다.
　(B) [×] 의문사 의문문에 No로 응답했으므로 오답이다. 질문의 available을 반복 사용하여 혼동을 주었다.
　(C) [o] 개발팀이 그것을 마무리짓는 중이라는 말로, 소프트웨어 업데이트가 곧 이용 가능할 것임을 간접적으로 전달했으므로 정답이다.

04 When 의문문 　　　호주 → 미국

When do we need to submit the quarterly reports?
(A) Probably at the end of this week.
(B) 25 pages long.
(C) This quarter's budget.

submit v. 제출하다　quarterly adj. 분기별의　budget n. 예산(안), 비용

해석 우리는 분기별 보고서를 언제 제출해야 하나요?
　(A) 아마도 이번 주 말에요.
　(B) 25페이지 분량이요.
　(C) 이번 분기의 예산이요.

해설 (A) [o] 이번 주 말이라는 말로, 분기별 보고서를 제출해야 할 시점을 언급했으므로 정답이다.
　(B) [×] 질문의 reports(보고서)에서 연상할 수 있는 분량과 관련된 25 pages long(25페이지 분량)을 사용하여 혼동을 준 오답이다.
　(C) [×] quarterly - quarter's의 유사 발음 어휘를 사용하여 혼동을 준 오답이다.

HACKERS TEST　　　p.38

01 (B)	02 (A)	03 (C)	04 (B)	05 (B)
06 (C)	07 (C)	08 (B)	09 (B)	10 (C)
11 (B)	12 (B)	13 (A)	14 (C)	15 (B)
16 (A)	17 (B)	18 (C)	19 (C)	20 (A)
21 (C)	22 (A)	23 (B)	24 (C)	25 (B)
26 (A)	27 (C)	28 (B)		

01 Where 의문문 　　　캐나다 → 미국

Where did you get your television repaired?
(A) I compared two models.
(B) The shop I bought it at.
(C) Last night.

repair v. 수리하다　compare v. 비교하다

해석 당신은 텔레비전을 어디에서 수리했나요?
　(A) 두 모델을 비교했어요.
　(B) 제가 그것을 구입했던 가게요.
　(C) 어젯밤이요.

해설 (A) [×] repaired - compared의 유사 발음 어휘를 사용하여 혼동을 준 오답이다.
　(B) [o] 자신이 그것을 구입했던 가게라는 말로, 텔레비전을 수리한 장소를 언급했으므로 정답이다.
　(C) [×] 텔레비전을 어디에서 수리했는지 장소를 물었는데, 시점으로 응답했으므로 오답이다. 질문의 Where를 When으로 혼동하여 이를 정답으로 선택하지 않도록 주의한다.

02 When 의문문 　　　영국 → 호주

When should we go over the marketing materials?
(A) This afternoon would be best.
(B) 15 dollars each.
(C) Write down the serial number.

go over ~을 검토하다, 거듭 살피다　serial number 일련번호, 제조 번호

해석 우리는 마케팅 자료들을 언제 검토해야 하나요?
　(A) 오늘 오후가 가장 좋을 거예요.

      (B) 각각 15달러요.
      (C) 일련번호를 적으세요.
해설 (A) [o] 오늘 오후가 가장 좋을 것이라는 말로, 마케팅 자료들을 검토해야 할 시점을 언급했으므로 정답이다.
    (B) [x] 마케팅 자료들을 언제 검토해야 할지 시점을 물었는데, 이와 관련이 없는 금액으로 응답했으므로 오답이다.
    (C) [x] 마케팅 자료들을 언제 검토해야 할지 시점을 물었는데, 이와 관련이 없는 일련번호를 적으라고 응답했으므로 오답이다.

03 Where 의문문   호주 → 미국

Where do we keep the first aid kit?
(A) I'll keep the key.
(B) Some bandages.
(C) In the bottom drawer.

first aid kit 구급상자   bandage n. 붕대   bottom adj. 맨 아래쪽의

해설 우리는 구급상자를 어디에 보관하나요?
      (A) 제가 열쇠를 보관할게요.
      (B) 몇 개의 붕대들이요.
      (C) 맨 아래쪽 서랍 안에요.
해설 (A) [x] 질문의 keep을 반복 사용하여 혼동을 준 오답이다.
    (B) [x] 질문의 first aid kit(구급상자)에서 연상할 수 있는 bandages(붕대들)를 사용하여 혼동을 준 오답이다.
    (C) [o] 맨 아래쪽 서랍 안이라는 말로, 구급상자를 보관하는 장소를 언급했으므로 정답이다.

04 Where 의문문   미국 → 캐나다

Where should I stay while in Paris?
(A) I'm flying there in July.
(B) I haven't been there.
(C) An overnight stay.

stay v. 머무르다   overnight stay 1박 숙박

해설 제가 파리에 있는 동안 어디에 머물러야 할까요?
      (A) 저는 7월에 그곳으로 비행할 거예요.
      (B) 저는 그곳에 가본 적이 없어요.
      (C) 1박 숙박이요.
해설 (A) [x] 파리에 있는 동안 어디에 머물러야 할지를 물었는데, 이와 관련이 없는 7월에 그곳으로 비행할 것이라고 응답했으므로 오답이다. 질문의 Where를 When으로 혼동하여 이를 정답으로 선택하지 않도록 주의한다.
    (B) [o] 자신은 그곳에 가본 적이 없다는 말로, 파리에 있는 동안 어디에 머물러야 할지 모른다는 것을 간접적으로 전달한 정답이다.
    (C) [x] 질문의 stay를 '숙박'이라는 의미의 명사로 반복 사용하여 혼동을 준 오답이다.

05 When 의문문   캐나다 → 호주

When can I expect to see the dentist?
(A) Yes, he's downstairs.
(B) At about 10 o'clock.
(C) Dr. Wilkins works at this clinic.

dentist n. 치과의사   clinic n. 진료소

해설 제가 치과의사를 언제 만날 수 있을까요?
      (A) 네, 그는 아래층에 있어요.
      (B) 10시경예요.
      (C) Dr. Wilkins는 이 진료소에서 근무해요.

해설 (A) [x] 의문사 의문문에 Yes로 응답했으므로 오답이다.
    (B) [o] 10시경이라는 말로, 치과의사를 만날 수 있는 시점을 언급했으므로 정답이다.
    (C) [x] 질문의 dentist(치과의사)와 관련 있는 Dr. Wilkins와 clinic(진료소)을 사용하여 혼동을 준 오답이다.

06 When 의문문   미국 → 캐나다

When's the press conference going to get underway?
(A) In the building's central lobby.
(B) An hour-long session.
(C) Once the mayor arrives.

press conference 기자 회견   get underway 시작하다
session n. (특정 활동의) 세션, 시간   mayor n. 시장, 구청장

해설 기자 회견은 언제 시작할 것인가요?
      (A) 건물의 중앙 로비에서요.
      (B) 한 시간 세션이요.
      (C) 시장이 도착하면요.
해설 (A) [x] 기자 회견이 언제 시작하는지 시점을 물었는데, 장소로 응답했으므로 오답이다. 질문의 When을 Where로 혼동하여 이를 정답으로 선택하지 않도록 주의한다.
    (B) [x] 기자 회견이 언제 시작하는지 시점을 물었는데, 이와 관련이 없는 한 시간 세션이라고 기간으로 응답했으므로 오답이다.
    (C) [o] 시장이 도착하면이라는 말로, 기자 회견이 시작할 시점을 언급했으므로 정답이다.

07 Where 의문문   영국 → 미국

Where can I find Ms. Lockwood's office?
(A) For the project manager.
(B) Some office supplies.
(C) Down the hall to the right.

office n. 사무실   hall n. 복도

해설 Ms. Lockwood의 사무실은 어디에서 찾을 수 있나요?
      (A) 프로젝트 관리자를 위해서요.
      (B) 몇몇 사무용품들이요.
      (C) 복도를 따라 내려가면 오른쪽에 있어요.
해설 (A) [x] Ms. Lockwood의 사무실이 어디 있는지를 물었는데, 이와 관련이 없는 프로젝트 관리자를 위해서라고 응답했으므로 오답이다.
    (B) [x] 질문의 office를 반복 사용하여 혼동을 준 오답이다.
    (C) [o] 복도를 따라 내려가면 오른쪽에 있다는 말로, Ms. Lockwood의 사무실을 어디에서 찾을 수 있는지 위치를 언급했으므로 정답이다.

08 When 의문문   미국 → 호주

When do you want me to help with moving those boxes?
(A) Several boxes with books.
(B) Let's do it now, thanks.
(C) No, it's not far from here.

move v. 옮기다   several adj. 여러, 몇몇의

해설 그 상자들을 옮기는 것을 제가 언제 돕기를 원하시나요?
      (A) 책이 들어 있는 여러 상자들이요.
      (B) 지금 합시다, 고마워요.
      (C) 아니요, 그것은 여기에서 멀지 않아요.
해설 (A) [x] 질문의 boxes를 반복 사용하여 혼동을 준 오답이다.
    (B) [o] 고맙다는 인사와 함께 지금 하자는 말로, 상자들을 옮기는 것을 도와주기를 원하는 시점을 언급했으므로 정답이다.

(C) [×] 의문사 의문문에 No로 응답했으므로 오답이다.

09 Where 의문문
호주 → 캐나다

Where is the invoice for this shipment?
(A) For the shipping address.
(B) In the filing cabinet.
(C) Sure, send me a reminder.

invoice n. 송장 address n. 주소
reminder n. (할 일 등을) 상기시켜 주는 메모, 상기시키는 것

해석 이 출하에 대한 송장은 어디에 있나요?
(A) 배송 주소를 위해서요.
(B) 서류함 안에요.
(C) 물론이죠, 상기시켜 주는 메모를 제게 보내세요.

해설 (A) [×] shipment - shipping의 유사 발음 어휘를 사용하여 혼동을 준 오답이다.
(B) [○] 서류함 안에라는 말로, 출하에 대한 송장이 있는 위치를 언급했으므로 정답이다.
(C) [×] 의문사 의문문에 Sure로 응답했으므로 오답이다.

10 When 의문문
캐나다 → 영국

When will the review of the application be posted?
(A) An online job posting.
(B) Yes, I use that application often.
(C) Right after lunch.

review n. 검토, 논평 job posting 채용 공고

해석 애플리케이션에 대한 검토 결과는 언제 게시될 것인가요?
(A) 온라인 채용 공고요.
(B) 네, 제가 그 애플리케이션을 자주 사용해요.
(C) 점심 직후요.

해설 (A) [×] posted - posting의 유사 발음 어휘를 사용하여 혼동을 준 오답이다.
(B) [×] 의문사 의문문에 Yes로 응답했으므로 오답이다. 질문의 application을 반복 사용하여 혼동을 주었다.
(C) [○] 점심 직후라는 말로, 검토 결과가 게시될 시점을 언급했으므로 정답이다.

11 When 의문문
미국 → 캐나다

When does the science museum open?
(A) In downtown Chicago.
(B) Not until 11 in the morning.
(C) The grand opening.

grand opening 개관식

해석 과학 박물관은 언제 문을 여나요?
(A) 시카고 시내에서요.
(B) 오전 11시가 돼서요.
(C) 개관식이요.

해설 (A) [×] 과학 박물관이 언제 문을 여는지 시점을 물었는데, 장소로 응답했으므로 오답이다. 질문의 When을 Where로 혼동하여 이를 정답으로 선택하지 않도록 주의한다.
(B) [○] 오전 11시가 돼서라는 말로, 과학 박물관이 문을 여는 시점을 언급했으므로 정답이다.
(C) [×] open - opening의 유사 발음 어휘를 사용하여 혼동을 준 오답이다.

12 Where 의문문
영국 → 호주

Where will you be traveling for work in March?
(A) Turn on the tablet.
(B) My team is going to Cape Town.
(C) He will return next week.

travel for work 출장 가다 turn on (전원을) 켜다

해석 당신은 3월에 어디로 출장 갈 예정인가요?
(A) 태블릿을 켜세요.
(B) 제 팀은 케이프타운으로 갈 거예요.
(C) 그는 다음 주에 돌아올 거예요.

해설 (A) [×] traveling - tablet의 유사 발음 어휘를 사용하여 혼동을 준 오답이다.
(B) [○] 자신의 팀이 케이프타운으로 갈 것이라는 말로, 3월 출장을 갈 장소를 언급했으므로 정답이다.
(C) [×] 3월에 어디로 출장을 갈 것인지를 물었는데, 이와 관련이 없는 그가 다음 주에 돌아온다고 응답했으므로 오답이다.

13 When 의문문
캐나다 → 호주

When do you expect your book to be published?
(A) Early next year.
(B) Yes, the same publisher.
(C) This is my favorite part of the book.

publish v. 출판하다 publisher n. 출판사 favorite adj. 가장 좋아하는

해석 당신의 책은 언제 출판될 것으로 예상하나요?
(A) 내년 초요.
(B) 네, 같은 출판사예요.
(C) 이 부분이 그 책에서 제가 가장 좋아하는 부분이에요.

해설 (A) [○] 내년 초라는 말로, 책이 출판될 것으로 예상되는 시점을 언급했으므로 정답이다.
(B) [×] 의문사 의문문에 Yes로 응답했으므로 오답이다. published - publisher의 유사 발음 어휘를 사용하여 혼동을 주었다.
(C) [×] 질문의 book을 반복 사용하여 혼동을 준 오답이다.

14 Where 의문문
캐나다 → 영국

Where's the nearest dry cleaner located?
(A) A few winter coats.
(B) I already cleaned the floor.
(C) There's one on Fifth Avenue.

be located 위치해 있다 floor n. 바닥

해석 가장 가까운 세탁소는 어디에 위치해 있나요?
(A) 몇 개의 겨울 코트들이요.
(B) 저는 이미 바닥을 청소했어요.
(C) 5번가에 하나 있어요.

해설 (A) [×] 질문의 dry cleaner(세탁소)에서 연상할 수 있는 옷과 관련된 coats(코트들)를 사용하여 혼동을 준 오답이다.
(B) [×] cleaner - cleaned의 유사 발음 어휘를 사용하여 혼동을 준 오답이다.
(C) [○] 5번가에 하나 있다는 말로, 가장 가까운 세탁소가 있는 위치를 언급했으므로 정답이다.

15 Where 의문문
호주 → 미국

Where should I put the completed surveys?
(A) It shouldn't take long.
(B) Give them to Miranda.

(C) She has already completed it.

complete v. 작성하다, 완료하다   survey n. (설문) 조사

해석 작성한 설문 조사는 어디에 둬야 하나요?
(A) 오래 걸리지 않을 거예요.
(B) 그것들을 Miranda에게 주세요.
(C) 그녀는 이미 그것을 완료했어요.

해설 (A) [×] 작성한 설문 조사를 어디에 둬야 할지를 물었는데, 이와 관련이 없는 오래 걸리지 않을 것이라고 응답했으므로 오답이다.
(B) [○] 그것들을 Miranda에게 주라는 말로, 완료된 설문 조사들을 전달할 사람을 언급했으므로 정답이다.
(C) [×] 질문의 completed를 반복 사용하여 혼동을 준 오답이다.

16 When 의문문   영국 → 미국

When are you going to leave for the airport?
(A) In about 30 minutes.
(B) To Terminal 3.
(C) No, we decided not to.

leave v. 떠나다

해석 당신은 공항으로 언제 떠날 예정인가요?
(A) 약 30분 후에요.
(B) 3번 터미널로요.
(C) 아니요, 우리는 안 가기로 결정했어요.

해설 (A) [○] 약 30분 후에 떠난다는 말로, 공항으로 떠날 시점을 언급했으므로 정답이다.
(B) [×] 공항으로 언제 떠날지를 물었는데, 이와 관련이 없는 장소로 응답했으므로 오답이다. 질문의 When을 Where로 혼동하여 이를 정답으로 선택하지 않도록 주의한다.
(C) [×] 의문사 의문문에 No로 응답했으므로 오답이다.

17 Where 의문문   호주 → 영국

Where are the spare microphones?
(A) Sound checks take time.
(B) In the supply cabinet.
(C) I saw a live performance there.

spare adj. 예비용의, 여분의   microphone n. 마이크

해석 예비용 마이크들은 어디에 있나요?
(A) 음향 점검은 시간이 걸려요.
(B) 비품 캐비닛 안에요.
(C) 저는 그곳에서 라이브 공연을 봤어요.

해설 (A) [×] 질문의 microphones(마이크들)와 관련 있는 sound checks(음향 점검)를 사용하여 혼동을 준 오답이다.
(B) [○] 비품 캐비닛 안이라는 말로, 예비용 마이크들이 있는 장소를 언급했으므로 정답이다.
(C) [×] 질문의 microphones(마이크들)에서 연상할 수 있는 live performance(라이브 공연)를 사용하여 혼동을 준 오답이다.

18 When 의문문   미국 → 호주

When's the final deadline for the spreadsheet revisions?
(A) Nobody has informed me.
(B) Sign on the dotted line.
(C) Because Mr. Downey is not satisfied.

revision n. 수정   inform v. 알려주다, 통지하다   dotted line 점선

해석 스프레드시트 수정의 최종 마감일은 언제인가요?
(A) 아무도 제게 알려주지 않았어요.
(B) 점선에 서명하세요.
(C) Mr. Downey가 만족하지 않았기 때문이에요.

해설 (A) [○] 아무도 자신에게 알려주지 않았다는 말로, 스프레드시트 수정의 최종 마감일이 언제인지 모른다는 것을 간접적으로 전달했으므로 정답이다.
(B) [×] deadline - dotted line의 유사 발음 어휘를 사용하여 혼동을 준 오답이다.
(C) [×] 스프레드시트 수정의 최종 마감일이 언제인지 시점을 물었는데, 이과 관련이 없는 이유로 응답했으므로 오답이다.

19 Where 의문문   캐나다 → 미국

Where did you last see the inventory checklist?
(A) I remember talking to him too.
(B) Actually, I have seen that movie.
(C) Doesn't Mr. Leeds have it?

inventory n. 재고(품), 물품 목록

해석 재고품 확인 목록을 마지막으로 어디에서 보셨나요?
(A) 저도 그에게 이야기했던 것을 기억해요.
(B) 사실, 저는 그 영화를 봤어요.
(C) Mr. Leeds가 그것을 가지고 있지 않나요?

해설 (A) [×] 재고품 확인 목록을 마지막으로 어디에서 봤는지를 물었는데, 이와 관련이 없는 자신도 그에게 이야기했던 것을 기억한다고 응답했으므로 오답이다.
(B) [×] see - seen의 유사 발음 어휘를 사용하여 혼동을 준 오답이다.
(C) [○] Mr. Leeds가 재고품 확인 목록을 가지고 있지 않냐고 되물어, 재고품 확인 목록이 Mr. Leeds에게 있음을 간접적으로 전달했으므로 정답이다.

20 When 의문문   미국 → 영국

When will the budget proposal be ready?
(A) I need a little more time.
(B) At the bank's downtown branch.
(C) Just take it over there.

downtown adj. 시내의, 도심의   take v. 가져가다

해석 예산안은 언제 준비될까요?
(A) 저는 조금 더 시간이 필요해요.
(B) 은행의 시내 지점에서요.
(C) 그냥 그것을 저기로 가져가세요.

해설 (A) [○] 조금 더 시간이 필요하다는 말로, 예산안이 언제 준비가 될지 불확실함을 간접적으로 전달한 정답이다.
(B) [×] 질문의 budget(예산)과 관련 있는 bank(은행)를 사용하여 혼동을 준 오답이다. 질문의 When을 Where로 혼동하여 이를 정답으로 선택하지 않도록 주의한다.
(C) [×] 예산안이 언제 준비될지를 물었는데, 이와 관련이 없는 그냥 그것을 저기로 가져가라고 응답했으므로 오답이다.

21 Where 의문문   호주 → 영국

Where can we find skilled freelance designers?
(A) Sorry, I don't have any extra tickets.
(B) I think that's a useful skill.
(C) I'll send you some portfolio links.

skilled adj. 숙련된, 전문적인   useful adj. 유용한   skill n. 기술, 기량

해석 숙련된 프리랜서 디자이너들을 어디에서 찾을 수 있을까요?

(A) 죄송해요, 저는 어떠한 여분의 표도 없어요.
(B) 그것은 유용한 기술인 것 같아요.
(C) 제가 몇몇 포트폴리오 링크들을 당신에게 보낼게요.

해설 (A) [x] 숙련된 프리랜서 디자이너들을 어디에서 찾을 수 있을지를 물었는데, 이와 관련이 없는 여분의 표가 없다고 응답했으므로 오답이다.
(B) [x] skilled - skill의 유사 발음 어휘를 사용하여 혼동을 준 오답이다.
(C) [o] 몇몇 포트폴리오 링크들을 보내겠다는 말로, 숙련된 프리랜서 디자이너들을 어디에서 찾을 수 있는지를 간접적으로 전달했으므로 정답이다.

22 Where 의문문 미국 → 캐나다

Where did you park your car?
(A) I took the bus today.
(B) The red sedan.
(C) About an hour ago.

park v. 주차하다 sedan n. 세단형 자동차

해설 당신의 차를 어디에 주차했나요?
(A) 저는 오늘 버스를 탔어요.
(B) 빨간색 세단이요.
(C) 약 한 시간 전에요.

해설 (A) [o] 오늘 버스를 탔다는 말로, 차를 어디에도 주차하지 않았음을 간접적으로 전달했으므로 정답이다.
(B) [x] 질문의 car(자동차)와 관련 있는 sedan(세단형 자동차)을 사용하여 혼동을 준 오답이다.
(C) [x] 차를 어디에 주차했는지 장소를 물었는데, 이와 관련이 없는 시점으로 응답했으므로 오답이다. 질문의 Where를 When으로 혼동하여 이를 정답으로 선택하지 않도록 주의한다.

23 When 의문문 캐나다 → 영국

When should we take the pizza out of the oven?
(A) Yes, that's the right size.
(B) We need to wait for another 15 minutes.
(C) He prefers vegetable pizza.

take ~ out ~을 꺼내다

해설 우리가 피자를 언제 오븐에서 꺼내야 할까요?
(A) 네, 그게 맞는 크기예요.
(B) 15분을 더 기다려야 돼요.
(C) 그는 야채 피자를 더 좋아해요.

해설 (A) [x] 의문사 의문문에 Yes로 응답했으므로 오답이다.
(B) [o] 15분을 더 기다려야 된다는 말로, 피자를 오븐에서 꺼내야 할 시점을 언급했으므로 정답이다.
(C) [x] 질문의 pizza를 반복 사용하여 혼동을 준 오답이다.

24 Where 의문문 캐나다 → 미국

Where's the best place to buy office supplies?
(A) Now would be best.
(B) My office is a block away.
(C) I usually order online.

office supplies 사무용품 order v. 주문하다

해설 사무용품을 구매하기 가장 좋은 장소는 어디인가요?
(A) 지금이 가장 좋을 거예요.
(B) 제 사무실은 한 블록 떨어져 있어요.
(C) 저는 보통 온라인으로 주문해요.

해설 (A) [x] 질문의 best를 반복 사용하여 혼동을 준 오답이다.

(B) [x] 질문의 office를 반복 사용하여 혼동을 준 오답이다.
(C) [o] 자신은 보통 온라인으로 주문한다는 말로, 사무용품을 구매하기 가장 좋은 장소가 어디인지를 간접적으로 전달했으므로 정답이다.

25 When 의문문 영국 → 호주

When can you meet me to plan the team-building event?
(A) Yes, I'm planning to go.
(B) How about tomorrow morning?
(C) At least five team members.

team-building n. 팀워크, 단합 at least 최소한, 적어도

해설 팀워크 행사를 계획하기 위해 저를 언제 만날 수 있으신가요?
(A) 네, 저는 가기로 계획 중이에요.
(B) 내일 아침은 어떨까요?
(C) 최소 5명의 팀원들이요.

해설 (A) [x] plan - planning의 유사 발음 어휘를 사용하여 혼동을 준 오답이다.
(B) [o] 내일 아침은 어떻냐고 되물어, 팀워크 행사를 계획하기 위해 내일 아침에 만날 수 있음을 간접적으로 전달했으므로 정답이다.
(C) [x] 질문의 team을 반복 사용하여 혼동을 준 오답이다.

26 When 의문문 호주 → 미국

When is the grand opening of the new shopping mall?
(A) They haven't announced it yet.
(B) I opened an account yesterday.
(C) Plenty of parking spaces.

announce v. 발표하다 account n. 계좌, 계정 plenty of 충분한, 많은

해설 새로운 쇼핑몰의 개관식은 언제인가요?
(A) 그들은 아직 그것을 발표하지 않았어요.
(B) 저는 어제 계좌를 개설했어요.
(C) 충분한 주차 공간이요.

해설 (A) [o] 그들이 아직 발표하지 않았다는 말로, 새로운 쇼핑몰의 개관식이 언제인지 모른다는 것을 간접적으로 전달했으므로 정답이다.
(B) [x] opening - opened의 유사 발음 어휘를 사용하여 혼동을 준 오답이다.
(C) [x] 질문의 shopping mall(쇼핑몰)에서 연상할 수 있는 부대시설과 관련된 parking spaces(주차 공간)를 사용하여 혼동을 준 오답이다.

27 Where 의문문 캐나다 → 영국

Where should we hang these employee group photographs from different years?
(A) Please pose for a photo.
(B) Let's introduce the new staff.
(C) Maybe in the main corridor?

hang v. 걸다 pose v. 자세를 취하다 corridor n. 복도

해설 각각 다른 연도에 찍은 이 직원 단체 사진들을 어디에 걸어야 할까요?
(A) 사진을 위한 자세를 취해 주세요.
(B) 신입 사원들을 소개합시다.
(C) 아마도 중앙 복도겠죠?

해설 (A) [x] photographs - photo의 유사 발음 어휘를 사용하여 혼동을 준 오답이다.
(B) [x] 질문의 employee(직원)와 관련 있는 new staff(신입 사원)를 사용하여 혼동을 준 오답이다.
(C) [o] 중앙 복도라는 말로, 직원 단체 사진들을 걸어야 할 장소를 언급했으므로 정답이다.

28 When 의문문   미국 → 호주

When will the maintenance team fix the elevator?
(A) The road is closed for maintenance.
(B) They're working on it right now.
(C) The third-floor button.

maintenance n. 유지보수   fix v. 고치다

해석 유지보수 팀은 엘리베이터를 언제 고칠 것인가요?
(A) 도로가 유지보수를 위해 폐쇄됐어요.
(B) 그들은 지금 그것을 작업하고 있어요.
(C) 3층 버튼이요.

해설 (A) [x] 질문의 maintenance를 반복 사용하여 혼동을 준 오답이다.
(B) [o] 그들이 지금 그것을 작업하고 있다는 말로, 유지보수 팀이 엘리베이터를 수리하는 시점을 언급했으므로 정답이다.
(C) [x] 질문의 elevator(엘리베이터)와 관련 있는 third-floor button (3층 버튼)을 사용하여 혼동을 준 오답이다.

DAY 05 의문사 의문문: Why, How

기출 유형 1 Why 의문문

Example   영국 → 호주   p.40

해석 당신은 왜 뉴욕시로 이사했나요?
(A) 제가 여기에서 일자리를 찾았기 때문이에요.
(B) 네, 몇 주 전에요.
(C) 더 조용한 장소로 이동합시다.

어휘 quiet adj. 조용한   location n. 장소, 위치

토익실전문제   p.40

| 01 (A) | 02 (B) | 03 (A) | 04 (C) |

01 Why 의문문   캐나다 → 미국

Why isn't the printer working?
(A) The paper tray is empty.
(B) I sent 10 copies to you.
(C) I'll be working from home.

paper tray 용지함   empty adj. 비어있는

해석 왜 프린터가 작동하지 않고 있나요?
(A) 용지함이 비어있어요.
(B) 제가 10부를 당신에게 보냈어요.
(C) 저는 집에서 일할 거예요.

해설 (A) [o] 용지함이 비어있다는 말로, 프린터가 작동하지 않는 이유를 언급했으므로 정답이다.
(B) [x] 질문의 printer(프린터)와 관련 있는 10 copies(10부)를 사용하여 혼동을 준 오답이다.
(C) [x] 왜 프린터가 작동하고 있지 않은지 이유를 물었는데, 이와 관련이 없는 집에서 일할 것이라고 응답했으므로 오답이다.

02 Why 의문문   호주 → 영국

Why are you returning these shoes?
(A) Yes, here's the receipt.
(B) Because they're not the right size for me.
(C) For a business trip.

return v. 반품하다   receipt n. 영수증   business trip 출장

해석 왜 이 신발들을 반품하시나요?
(A) 네, 여기 영수증이요.
(B) 제게 맞는 크기가 아니기 때문이에요.
(C) 출장을 위해서요.

해설 (A) [x] 의문사 의문문에 Yes로 응답했으므로 오답이다. 질문의 return (반품하다)과 관련 있는 receipt(영수증)를 사용하여 혼동을 주었다.
(B) [o] 자신에게 맞는 크기가 아니기 때문이라는 말로, 신발을 반품하는 이유를 언급했으므로 정답이다.
(C) [x] 왜 신발을 반품하는지 이유를 물었는데, 이와 관련이 없는 출장을 위해서라고 응답했으므로 오답이다.

03 Why 의문문   미국 → 캐나다

Why has the hotel increased its room rates?
(A) They completed major renovations recently.
(B) Check-in starts at 3 P.M.
(C) A double room with a balcony.

rate n. 요금   complete v. 완료하다, 작성하다
renovation n. 보수 공사, 수리 작업   recently adv. 최근에

해석 왜 그 호텔은 객실 요금을 인상했나요?
(A) 그들이 최근에 대대적인 보수 공사를 완료했어요.
(B) 체크인은 오후 3시에 시작해요.
(C) 발코니가 있는 2인실이요.

해설 (A) [o] 그들이 최근에 대대적인 보수 공사를 완료했다는 말로, 호텔이 객실 요금을 인상한 이유를 언급했으므로 정답이다.
(B) [x] 질문의 hotel(호텔)과 관련 있는 Check-in(체크인)을 사용하여 혼동을 준 오답이다.
(C) [x] 질문의 room을 반복 사용하여 혼동을 준 오답이다.

04 Why 의문문   영국 → 미국

Why are we switching to the new software system?
(A) No, I've just got this monitor.
(B) The new IT department head.
(C) Because our current one is outdated.

switch to ~으로 전환하다   current adj. 현재의, 지금의
outdated adj. 오래된, 구식의

해석 왜 우리는 새로운 소프트웨어 시스템으로 전환하려는 것인가요?
(A) 아니요, 저는 이 모니터를 방금 받았어요.
(B) 새로운 IT 부서장이요.
(C) 현재의 것이 오래됐기 때문이에요.

해설 (A) [x] 의문사 의문문에 No로 응답했으므로 오답이다.
(B) [x] 왜 새로운 소프트웨어 시스템으로 전환하려고 하는지 이유를 물었는데, 이와 관련이 없는 새로운 IT 부서장이라고 응답했으므로 오답이다.
(C) [o] 현재의 것이 오래됐기 때문이라는 말로, 새로운 소프트웨어 시스템으로 전환하려고 하는 이유를 언급했으므로 정답이다.

기출 유형 2 How 의문문

Example   호주 → 미국   p.41

해석 이 호텔에 대해 어떻게 알았나요?
(A) 12월 15일과 16일이요.
(B) 소셜 미디어에서 광고를 봤어요.
(C) 수영장에서요.

어휘 ad n. 광고

토익실전문제

p.41

| 01 (B) | 02 (C) | 03 (B) | 04 (A) |

01 How 의문문
미국 → 캐나다

How was your vacation in Thailand?
(A) I get one week of annual leave.
(B) It was absolutely amazing.
(C) Three times a month.

annual leave 연차 휴가 absolutely adv. 정말, 틀림없이

해석 태국에서의 당신의 휴가는 어땠어요?
(A) 저는 일주일의 연차 휴가를 받아요.
(B) 정말 굉장했어요.
(C) 한 달에 세 번이요.

해설 (A) [×] 질문의 vacation(휴가)과 관련 있는 annual leave(연차 휴가)를 사용하여 혼동을 준 오답이다.
(B) [o] 정말 굉장했다는 말로, 태국에서의 휴가가 어땠는지 의견을 언급했으므로 정답이다.
(C) [×] 태국에서의 휴가는 어땠는지 의견을 물었는데, 이와 관련이 없는 빈도로 응답했으므로 오답이다.

02 How 의문문
영국 → 호주

How much does the premium membership cost?
(A) Yes, I have a membership.
(B) It's valid for one full year.
(C) 299 dollars annually.

valid adj. 유효한, 타당한 annually adv. 연간, 해마다

해석 프리미엄 회원권은 얼마의 비용이 드나요?
(A) 네, 저는 회원권이 있어요.
(B) 1년 내내 유효해요.
(C) 연간 299달러요.

해설 (A) [×] 의문사 의문문에 Yes로 응답했으므로 오답이다. 질문의 membership을 반복 사용하여 혼동을 주었다.
(B) [×] 프리미엄 회원권이 얼마인지 가격을 물었는데, 이와 관련이 없는 기간으로 응답했으므로 오답이다.
(C) [o] 연간 299달러라는 말로, 프리미엄 회원권의 가격을 언급했으므로 정답이다.

03 How 의문문
캐나다 → 영국

How far is the nearest pharmacy from here?
(A) You need a prescription for that medication.
(B) It's about a 10-minute walk.
(C) To the nearest subway station.

pharmacy n. 약국 prescription n. 처방전 medication n. 약(물)

해석 가장 가까운 약국은 여기에서 얼마나 멀리 있나요?
(A) 당신은 그 약에 대한 처방전이 필요해요.
(B) 약 10분 도보 거리예요.
(C) 가장 가까운 지하철 역으로요.

해설 (A) [×] 질문의 pharmacy(약국)와 관련 있는 prescription(처방전)을 사용하여 혼동을 준 오답이다.
(B) [o] 약 10분 도보 거리라는 말로, 가장 가까운 약국이 얼마나 멀리 있는지 거리를 언급했으므로 정답이다.
(C) [×] 질문의 nearest를 반복 사용하여 혼동을 준 오답이다.

04 How 의문문
캐나다 → 호주

How do you feel about the new office layout?
(A) I think it improves collaboration.
(B) The moving company will arrive at 9 A.M.
(C) He's out of the office.

layout n. 배치 collaboration n. 협업, 공동 작업
moving company 이삿짐 센터

해석 새로운 사무실 배치에 대해 어떻게 생각하세요?
(A) 그것이 협업을 향상시킨다고 생각해요.
(B) 이삿짐 센터는 오전 9시에 도착할 거예요.
(C) 그는 사무실에 없어요.

해설 (A) [o] 그것이 협업을 향상시킨다고 생각한다는 말로, 새로운 사무실 배치에 대해 어떻게 생각하는지 의견을 언급했으므로 정답이다.
(B) [×] 질문의 new office layout(새로운 사무실 배치)에서 연상할 수 있는 이사와 관련된 moving company(이삿짐 센터)를 사용하여 혼동을 준 오답이다.
(C) [×] 질문의 office를 반복 사용하여 혼동을 준 오답이다.

HACKERS TEST
p.42

01 (C)	02 (A)	03 (B)	04 (A)	05 (C)
06 (A)	07 (B)	08 (B)	09 (C)	10 (A)
11 (B)	12 (A)	13 (C)	14 (A)	15 (B)
16 (C)	17 (B)	18 (A)	19 (C)	20 (A)
21 (A)	22 (C)	23 (B)	24 (C)	25 (B)
26 (B)	27 (A)	28 (C)		

01 Why 의문문
미국 → 캐나다

Why are the books still in the hallway?
(A) Next to the entrance.
(B) No, mostly sports news.
(C) I haven't had time to move them.

hallway n. 복도 entrance n. 입구

해석 왜 책들이 아직 복도에 있나요?
(A) 입구 옆에요.
(B) 아니요, 주로 스포츠 뉴스요.
(C) 제가 그것들을 옮길 시간이 없었어요.

해설 (A) [×] 질문의 hallway(복도)에서 연상할 수 있는 건물과 관련된 entrance(입구)를 사용하여 혼동을 준 오답이다.
(B) [×] 의문사 의문문에 No로 응답했으므로 오답이다.
(C) [o] 자신이 그것들을 옮길 시간이 없었다는 말로, 책들이 아직 복도에 있는 이유를 언급했으므로 정답이다.

02 How 의문문
영국 → 호주

How much does this sweater cost?
(A) 50 dollars.
(B) Two floors below.
(C) It's large enough.

cost v. (값이) ~이다, 비용이 들다 floor n. 층 enough adv. 충분히

해석 이 스웨터는 얼마인가요?
(A) 50달러요.
(B) 2층 아래요.
(C) 그것은 충분히 커요.

해설 (A) [o] 50달러라는 말로, 스웨터의 가격을 언급했으므로 정답이다.
(B) [x] 스웨터가 얼마인지 가격을 물었는데, 이와 관련이 없는 위치로 응답했으므로 오답이다. 숫자 표현을 사용하여 혼동을 주었다.
(C) [x] 스웨터가 얼마인지 가격을 물었는데, 크기로 응답했으므로 오답이다.

03 Why 의문문 호주 → 미국

Why have they blocked off Leister Square?
(A) About 3,000 square meters.
(B) For a holiday parade.
(C) It's two blocks farther.

block off (도로나 출입구를) 막다   square meter 제곱미터, 평방미터

해설 왜 그들은 Leister 광장을 막았나요?
(A) 약 3,000 제곱미터요.
(B) 휴일 퍼레이드 때문에요.
(C) 두 블록 더 멀리 있어요.

해설 (A) [x] Leister 광장을 막은 이유를 물었는데, 크기로 응답했으므로 오답이다.
(B) [o] 휴일 퍼레이드 때문이라는 말로, Leister 광장을 막은 이유를 언급했으므로 정답이다.
(C) [x] 질문의 block(막다)을 '블록, 구역'이라는 의미의 명사로 반복 사용하여 혼동을 준 오답이다.

04 How 의문문 캐나다 → 미국

How was the conference call with Mr. Horton?
(A) It was very productive.
(B) Yes, he has a lot of experience.
(C) In meeting room 203.

conference call 화상회의   productive adj. 생산적인, 결실 있는
experience n. 경험

해설 Mr. Horton과의 화상회의는 어땠어요?
(A) 그것은 매우 생산적이었어요.
(B) 네, 그는 많은 경험이 있어요.
(C) 203호 회의실에서요.

해설 (A) [o] 그것은 매우 생산적이었다는 말로, Mr. Horton과의 화상회의가 어땠는지 의견을 언급했으므로 정답이다.
(B) [x] 의문사 의문문에 Yes로 응답했으므로 오답이다. 질문의 Mr. Horton을 가리킬 때 쓸 수 있는 he(그)를 사용하여 혼동을 주었다.
(C) [x] 질문의 conference call(화상회의)과 관련 있는 meeting room(회의실)을 사용하여 혼동을 준 오답이다.

05 How 의문문 캐나다 → 영국

How many times have you visited Berlin?
(A) I didn't know he was visiting.
(B) Round trip by train.
(C) Several times.

round trip 왕복 여행

해설 당신은 베를린을 몇 번 방문하셨나요?
(A) 그가 방문할 줄은 몰랐어요.
(B) 기차로 한 왕복 여행이요.
(C) 여러 번이요.

해설 (A) [x] visited - visiting의 유사 발음 어휘를 사용하여 혼동을 준 오답이다.
(B) [x] 베를린을 몇 번 방문했는지를 물었는데, 이와 관련이 없는 기차로 한 왕복 여행이라고 응답했으므로 오답이다.
(C) [o] 여러 번이라는 말로, 베를린을 방문한 횟수를 언급했으므로 정답이다.

06 Why 의문문 영국 → 호주

Why are you working late tonight?
(A) Because my team is behind schedule.
(B) Actually, it is in the second-floor conference room.
(C) No, they didn't say when.

work late 야근하다   behind schedule 일정에 뒤처진

해설 당신은 왜 오늘 밤에 야근하시나요?
(A) 제 팀이 일정에 뒤처져 있기 때문이에요.
(B) 사실, 그것은 2층 회의실에 있어요.
(C) 아니요, 그들은 언제인지 말하지 않았어요.

해설 (A) [o] 자신의 팀이 일정에 뒤처져 있기 때문이라는 말로, 오늘 밤에 야근하는 이유를 언급했으므로 정답이다.
(B) [x] 왜 오늘 밤에 야근하는지를 물었는데, 이와 관련이 없는 2층 회의실에 있다고 응답했으므로 오답이다. Actually까지만 듣고 정답으로 고르지 않도록 주의한다.
(C) [x] 의문사 의문문에 No로 응답했으므로 오답이다.

07 Why 의문문 캐나다 → 영국

Why do we need four copies of the contract?
(A) Here is my contact information.
(B) Two are for Liam and Sadie.
(C) Join us for coffee.

contract n. 계약서

해설 우리는 왜 계약서 사본이 4부가 필요한가요?
(A) 여기 제 연락처예요.
(B) 두 개는 Liam과 Sadie를 위한 것이에요.
(C) 우리와 함께 커피를 마시러 가요.

해설 (A) [x] contract - contact의 유사 발음 어휘를 사용하여 혼동을 준 오답이다.
(B) [o] 두 개는 Liam과 Sadie를 위한 것이라는 말로, 계약서 사본이 4부가 필요한 이유를 언급했으므로 정답이다.
(C) [x] copies - coffee의 유사 발음 어휘를 사용하여 혼동을 준 오답이다.

08 How 의문문 미국 → 호주

How are you getting to the art festival on Saturday?
(A) She is planning to leave right after work.
(B) Maybe Brett will give me a ride.
(C) I wasn't able to make it.

give a ride (차로) 태워주다   make it 참석하다, 시간 맞춰 가다

해설 당신은 토요일 예술 축제에 어떻게 가실 건가요?
(A) 그녀는 퇴근 직후에 출발할 계획이에요.
(B) 아마도 Brett이 저를 태워줄 거예요.
(C) 저는 참석할 수 없었어요.

해설 (A) [x] 토요일 예술 축제에 어떻게 갈 것인지를 물었는데, 이와 관련이 없는 그녀는 퇴근 직후에 출발할 계획이라고 응답했으므로 오답이다.
(B) [o] 아마도 Brett이 자신을 태워줄 것이라는 말로, 토요일 예술 축제에 어떻게 갈 것인지 방법을 언급했으므로 정답이다.

(C) [×] 토요일 예술 축제에 어떻게 갈 것인지를 물었는데, 이와 관련이 없는 자신은 참석할 수 없었다고 응답했으므로 오답이다.

09 How 의문문 영국 → 미국

How will the delivery drivers get into the warehouse?
(A) It will be delivered by Thursday.
(B) Sure, it's really easy.
(C) They have an access code.

warehouse n. 창고   access code 접근 코드

해석 배달 기사들이 어떻게 창고로 들어갈 것인가요?
(A) 목요일까지 배달될 거예요.
(B) 물론이죠, 그건 정말 쉬워요.
(C) 그들은 접근 코드를 가지고 있어요.

해설 (A) [×] delivery - delivered의 유사 발음 어휘를 사용하여 혼동을 준 오답이다.
(B) [×] 배달 기사들이 어떻게 창고로 들어갈 것인지 방법을 물었는데, 이와 관련이 없는 정말 쉽다고 응답했으므로 오답이다.
(C) [○] 그들은 접근 코드를 가지고 있다는 말로, 배달 기사들이 어떻게 창고로 들어갈 것인지 방법을 언급했으므로 정답이다.

10 Why 의문문 미국 → 캐나다

Why wasn't our newsletter mailed to customers?
(A) Are you sure it wasn't?
(B) I heard about that discount.
(C) At the post office.

newsletter n. 소식지   mail v. 우편으로 보내다

해석 왜 우리의 소식지가 고객들에게 우편으로 발송되지 않았나요?
(A) 발송되지 않은 것이 확실한가요?
(B) 그 할인에 대해 들었어요.
(C) 우체국에서요.

해설 (A) [○] 발송되지 않은 것이 확실한 것인지 되물어, 왜 소식지가 고객들에게 우편으로 발송되지 않았는지 모른다는 것을 간접적으로 전달했으므로 정답이다.
(B) [×] 질문의 newsletter(소식지)에서 연상할 수 있는 discount(할인)를 사용하여 혼동을 준 오답이다.
(C) [×] 질문의 mail(우편으로 보내다)에서 연상할 수 있는 post office(우체국)를 사용하여 혼동을 준 오답이다.

11 Why 의문문 캐나다 → 호주

Why is the library closed?
(A) They're very close friends.
(B) Because it's being repainted.
(C) For a mobile phone only.

close v. (문을) 닫다; adj. 친한   repaint v. 다시 페인트칠하다

해석 왜 도서관이 문을 닫았나요?
(A) 그들은 매우 친한 친구들이에요.
(B) 다시 페인트칠이 되고 있기 때문이에요.
(C) 휴대폰만을 위해서요.

해설 (A) [×] closed - close의 유사 발음 어휘를 사용하여 혼동을 준 오답이다.
(B) [○] 다시 페인트칠이 되고 있기 때문이라는 말로, 도서관이 문을 닫은 이유를 언급했으므로 정답이다.
(C) [×] 도서관이 문을 닫은 이유를 물었는데, 이와 관련이 없는 휴대폰만을 위해서라고 응답했으므로 오답이다.

12 How 의문문 호주 → 미국

How soon can you finish the program outline?
(A) It shouldn't take more than three days.
(B) We are planning to host several programs.
(C) Your log-in information.

outline n. 개요, 윤곽   host v. 주최하다

해석 프로그램 개요를 얼마나 빨리 마무리할 수 있나요?
(A) 3일 이상은 걸리지 않을 거예요.
(B) 우리는 여러 프로그램을 주최할 계획이에요.
(C) 당신의 로그인 정보요.

해설 (A) [○] 3일 이상은 걸리지 않을 것이라는 말로, 프로그램 개요를 마무리할 수 있는 기간을 언급했으므로 정답이다.
(B) [×] 질문의 program을 반복 사용하여 혼동을 준 오답이다.
(C) [×] 질문의 program(프로그램)에서 연상할 수 있는 컴퓨터와 관련된 log-in information(로그인 정보)을 사용하여 혼동을 준 오답이다.

13 Why 의문문 미국 → 캐나다

Why was the repair request delayed?
(A) A pair of nice shoes.
(B) Sorry, I can't lend it to you.
(C) I think Patrick will know.

delay v. 지연시키다, 연기하다   lend v. 빌려주다

해석 왜 수리 요청이 지연되었나요?
(A) 멋진 한 켤레의 신발이요.
(B) 죄송합니다, 당신에게 그것을 빌려줄 수 없어요.
(C) Patrick이 알 것 같아요.

해설 (A) [×] repair - pair의 유사 발음 어휘를 사용하여 혼동을 준 오답이다.
(B) [×] 왜 수리 요청이 지연되었는지를 물었는데, 이와 관련이 없는 그것을 빌려줄 수 없다고 응답했으므로 오답이다.
(C) [○] Patrick이 알 것 같다는 말로, 왜 수리 요청이 지연됐는지 자신은 모른다는 것을 간접적으로 전달했으므로 정답이다.

14 Why 의문문 호주 → 영국

Why haven't you updated the list of suppliers?
(A) There aren't any changes.
(B) The updated blueprint.
(C) Please clean up the supply room.

supplier n. 공급업체   blueprint n. 청사진, 설계도

해석 왜 공급업체 목록을 업데이트하지 않았나요?
(A) 변경 사항이 없어요.
(B) 업데이트된 청사진이요.
(C) 비품실을 청소해주세요.

해설 (A) [○] 변경된 사항이 없다는 말로, 공급업체 목록을 업데이트하지 않은 이유를 언급했으므로 정답이다.
(B) [×] 질문의 updated를 반복 사용하여 혼동을 준 오답이다.
(C) [×] suppliers - supply의 유사 발음 어휘를 사용하여 혼동을 준 오답이다.

15 How 의문문 캐나다 → 호주

How should we arrange the desks for the seminar?
(A) Yes, this morning.
(B) Let's put them in a circle.

(C) From the Mason Furniture Store.

arrange v. 배치하다, 정렬하다 furniture n. 가구

해석 세미나를 위해 책상들을 어떻게 배치해야 할까요?
(A) 네, 오늘 아침이요.
(B) 원형으로 배치합시다.
(C) Mason 가구점에서요.

해설 (A) [x] 의문사 의문문에 Yes로 응답했으므로 오답이다.
(B) [o] 원형으로 배치하자는 말로, 세미나를 위해 책상을 어떻게 배치할지 방법을 언급했으므로 정답이다.
(C) [x] 질문의 desks(책상들)에서 연상할 수 있는 상점과 관련된 Furniture Store(가구점)를 사용하여 혼동을 준 오답이다.

16 Why 의문문 호주 → 미국

Why aren't there any snacks in the break room?
(A) No, I haven't received them.
(B) That would be helpful.
(C) I'll remind Jason later.

break room 휴게실 helpful adj. 도움이 되는 remind v. 상기시키다

해석 왜 휴게실에 간식이 하나도 없나요?
(A) 아니요, 저는 그것들을 받지 않았어요.
(B) 그건 도움이 될 거예요.
(C) 제가 Jason에게 나중에 상기시킬게요.

해설 (A) [x] 의문사 의문문에 No로 응답했으므로 오답이다.
(B) [x] 왜 휴게실에 간식이 없는지를 물었는데, 이와 관련이 없는 그것이 도움이 될 것이라고 응답했으므로 오답이다.
(C) [o] Jason에게 나중에 상기시킬 것이라는 말로, 담당자인 Jason에게 알려서 휴게실에 간식을 채우게 할 것임을 간접적으로 전달했으므로 정답이다.

17 How 의문문 미국 → 영국

How often does the shuttle come?
(A) Just across the street.
(B) Let me check the Web site.
(C) I'd like you to come into work early tomorrow.

shuttle n. 셔틀버스

해석 셔틀버스는 얼마나 자주 오나요?
(A) 바로 길 건너편이요.
(B) 제가 웹사이트를 확인할게요.
(C) 저는 당신이 내일 일찍 출근했으면 합니다.

해설 (A) [x] 셔틀버스가 얼마나 자주 오는지 빈도를 물었는데, 이와 관련이 없는 위치로 응답했으므로 오답이다.
(B) [o] 자신이 웹사이트를 확인하겠다는 말로, 셔틀버스가 얼마나 자주 오는지 모른다는 것을 간접적으로 전달한 정답이다.
(C) [x] 질문의 come을 반복 사용하여 혼동을 준 오답이다.

18 Why 의문문 미국 → 호주

Why didn't you make more copies of the brochure?
(A) I found an error on the cover.
(B) Ink for the copier.
(C) Sometime yesterday.

brochure n. 안내 책자 error n. 오류, 실수 copier n. 복사기

해석 왜 안내 책자의 사본을 더 많이 만들지 않았나요?
(A) 제가 표지에서 오류를 발견했어요.
(B) 복사기용 잉크요.
(C) 어제 어느 때쯤이었어요.

해설 (A) [o] 자신이 표지에서 오류를 발견했다는 말로, 안내 책자의 사본을 더 많이 만들지 않은 이유를 언급했으므로 정답이다.
(B) [x] copies - copier의 유사 발음 어휘를 사용하여 혼동을 준 오답이다.
(C) [x] 왜 안내 책자의 사본을 더 많이 만들지 않았는지 이유를 물었는데, 이와 관련이 없는 시점으로 응답했으므로 오답이다.

19 How 의문문 캐나다 → 영국

How are the new interns performing?
(A) Please review these job applications.
(B) The dance performance.
(C) Better than we expected.

perform v. (업무를) 수행하다 application n. 지원서, 신청서
expect v. 예상하다, 기대하다

해석 새로운 인턴들은 어떻게 업무를 수행하고 있나요?
(A) 이 구직 지원서들을 검토해 주세요.
(B) 춤 공연이요.
(C) 우리가 예상했던 것보다 더 잘 해요.

해설 (A) [x] 질문의 interns(인턴들)와 관련 있는 job applications(구직 지원서들)를 사용하여 혼동을 준 오답이다.
(B) [x] performing - performance의 유사 발음 어휘를 사용하여 혼동을 준 오답이다.
(C) [o] 예상보다 더 잘 한다는 말로, 새로운 인턴들이 어떻게 업무를 수행하고 있는지 의견을 전달했으므로 정답이다.

20 How 의문문 호주 → 영국

How many tables should be removed from the banquet room?
(A) I already took care of it.
(B) Your seat is just this way.
(C) I'll meet you in the lobby.

remove v. 치우다, 제거하다 banquet room 연회장
take care of ~을 처리하다, 책임지다 seat n. 좌석

해석 연회장에서 몇 개의 테이블이 치워져야 하나요?
(A) 제가 이미 그것을 처리했어요.
(B) 당신의 자리는 바로 이쪽이에요.
(C) 당신을 로비에서 뵐게요.

해설 (A) [o] 자신이 이미 그것을 처리했다는 말로, 연회장에서 치워야 할 테이블이 없음을 간접적으로 전달했으므로 정답이다.
(B) [x] 질문의 banquet room(연회장)과 관련 있는 seat(좌석)을 사용하여 혼동을 준 오답이다.
(C) [x] 연회장에서 치워야 할 테이블이 몇 개인지를 물었는데, 이와 관련이 없는 로비에서 뵐 것이라고 응답했으므로 오답이다.

21 Why 의문문 미국 → 캐나다

Why can't we access the shared document folder?
(A) I'll have to check with Hannah.
(B) By entering the code.
(C) Sure, I'll fold them.

access v. 접근하다, 이용하다 enter v. 입력하다 fold v. 접다

해석 왜 우리는 공유 문서 폴더에 접근할 수 없나요?
(A) 제가 Hannah에게 확인해 봐야겠어요.
(B) 코드를 입력함으로써요.

(C) 그럼요, 제가 그것들을 접을게요.

해설 (A) [o] 자신이 Hannah에게 확인해 봐야겠다는 말로, 공유 문서 폴더에 접근할 수 없는 이유를 모른다는 것을 간접적으로 전달했으므로 정답이다.
(B) [x] 질문의 access(접근하다)에서 연상할 수 있는 비밀번호와 관련된 code(코드)를 사용하여 혼동을 준 오답이다.
(C) [x] folder – fold의 유사 발음 어휘를 사용하여 혼동을 준 오답이다.

22 How 의문문   캐나다 → 영국

How do I adjust the settings on this device?
(A) The warranty expires next month.
(B) A new line of laptop computers.
(C) Press and hold the white button for three seconds.

device n. 기기, 장치 warranty n. 품질 보증서 expire v. 만료되다
press v. 누르다

해설 이 기기의 설정을 어떻게 조정하나요?
(A) 품질 보증서는 다음 달에 만료돼요.
(B) 새로운 노트북 컴퓨터 라인이요.
(C) 흰색 버튼을 3초 동안 누르고 있으세요.

해설 (A) [x] 질문의 device(기기)와 관련 있는 warranty(품질 보증서)를 사용하여 혼동을 준 오답이다.
(B) [x] 질문의 device(기기)와 관련 있는 laptop computers(노트북 컴퓨터)를 사용하여 혼동을 준 오답이다.
(C) [o] 흰색 버튼을 3초 동안 누르고 있으라는 말로, 기기의 설정을 어떻게 조정하는지 방법을 언급했으므로 정답이다.

23 Why 의문문   영국 → 미국

Why were you absent from the training session?
(A) The brown package you sent me.
(B) Didn't you get my text message?
(C) In the instruction manual.

absent adj. 결석한 instruction manual 사용 설명서

해설 당신은 왜 교육 과정에 결석했나요?
(A) 당신이 제게 보냈던 갈색 소포요.
(B) 제 문자 메시지 못 받았어요?
(C) 사용 설명서예요.

해설 (A) [x] absent – sent의 유사 발음 어휘를 사용하여 혼동을 준 오답이다.
(B) [o] 자신의 문자 메시지를 못 받았냐고 되물어, 교육 세션에 결석한 이유를 문자 메시지로 보냈음을 간접적으로 전달했으므로 정답이다.
(C) [x] 질문의 training session(교육 과정)에서 연상할 수 있는 교육 자료와 관련된 instruction manual(사용 설명서)을 사용하여 혼동을 준 오답이다.

24 How 의문문   영국 → 호주

How often do you recommend watering these indoor plants?
(A) These ceramic pots are on sale.
(B) Outdoors would be better.
(C) About twice a week should be sufficient.

water v. 물을 주다 indoor adj. 실내의 outdoors adv. 야외, 실외
sufficient adj. 충분한

해설 이 실내 식물에는 얼마나 자주 물을 줄 것을 권장하시나요?
(A) 이 도자기 화분들은 할인 중이에요.
(B) 야외가 더 좋을 거예요.
(C) 1주일에 2회 정도가 충분할 거예요.

해설 (A) [x] 질문의 plants(식물)와 관련 있는 pots(화분)를 사용하여 혼동을 준 오답이다.
(B) [x] indoor – Outdoors의 유사 발음 어휘를 사용하여 혼동을 준 오답이다.
(C) [o] 1주일에 2회 정도가 충분할 것이라는 말로, 실내 식물에 물을 줘야 하는 빈도를 언급했으므로 정답이다.

25 How 의문문   미국 → 캐나다

How soon can we expect delivery of the office supplies?
(A) The shipping cost is included.
(B) Within two business days.
(C) I didn't expect it.

shipping cost 배송비 include v. 포함하다

해설 사무용품의 배송을 얼마나 빨리 기대할 수 있나요?
(A) 배송비가 포함되어 있어요.
(B) 영업일 2일 이내요.
(C) 그것을 기대하지 않았어요.

해설 (A) [x] 질문의 delivery(배송)와 관련 있는 shipping cost(배송비)를 사용하여 혼동을 준 오답이다.
(B) [o] 영업일 2일 이내라는 말로, 사무용품의 배송 기간을 언급했으므로 정답이다.
(C) [x] 질문의 expect를 반복 사용하여 혼동을 준 오답이다.

26 Why 의문문   호주 → 영국

Why did you cancel your gym membership?
(A) For several months now.
(B) Because I've been too busy to go regularly.
(C) To recycle some aluminum cans.

regularly adv. 정기적으로 recycle v. 재활용하다

해설 당신은 왜 체육관 회원권을 취소했나요?
(A) 지금까지 몇 달 동안이요.
(B) 정기적으로 가기에 제가 너무 바쁘기 때문이에요.
(C) 몇 개의 알루미늄 캔을 재활용하기 위해서요.

해설 (A) [x] 왜 체육관 회원권을 취소했는지 이유를 물었는데, 이와 관련이 없는 기간으로 응답했으므로 오답이다.
(B) [o] 정기적으로 가기에 너무 바쁘기 때문이라는 말로, 체육관 회원권을 취소한 이유를 언급했으므로 정답이다.
(C) [x] cancel – cans의 유사 발음 어휘를 사용하여 혼동을 준 오답이다.

27 Why 의문문   캐나다 → 미국

Why hasn't the courier delivered our package yet?
(A) There was a traffic accident on the highway.
(B) I already packed my belongings.
(C) By express delivery?

courier n. 택배기사 package n. 소포 belongings n. 소지품, 재산

해설 왜 택배기사가 우리 소포를 아직 배달하지 않았나요?
(A) 고속도로에서 교통사고가 있었어요.
(B) 제 소지품을 이미 쌌어요.
(C) 특급 배송으로요?

해설 (A) [o] 고속도로에서 교통사고가 있었다는 말로, 택배기사가 소포를 아직 배달하지 않은 이유를 언급했으므로 정답이다.
(B) [x] package – packed의 유사 발음 어휘를 사용하여 혼동을 준 오답이다.

(C) [x] delivered - delivery의 유사 발음 어휘를 사용하여 혼동을 준 오답이다.

28 How 의문문
호주 → 캐나다

How many participants registered for the workshop?
(A) The registration desk is by the entrance.
(B) We need more chairs in Room B.
(C) I think Ms. Klein would have that information.

participant n. 참가자   registration n. 등록   information n. 정보

해석 워크숍에 몇 명의 참가자들이 등록했나요?
(A) 등록 데스크는 입구 옆에 있어요.
(B) 우리는 B실에 의자가 더 필요해요.
(C) Ms. Klein이 그 정보를 가지고 있을 것 같아요.

해설 (A) [x] registered - registration의 유사 발음 어휘를 사용하여 혼동을 준 오답이다.
(B) [x] 질문의 workshop(워크숍)에서 연상할 수 있는 교육 공간과 관련된 Room B(B실)를 사용하여 혼동을 준 오답이다.
(C) [o] Ms. Klein이 그 정보를 가지고 있을 것 같다는 말로, 워크숍에 몇 명의 참가자들이 등록했는지 자신은 모른다는 것을 간접적으로 전달했으므로 정답이다.

DAY 06 일반 의문문 및 부정 의문문

기출 유형 1 일반 의문문

Example 캐나다 → 미국   p.44
해석 디저트를 주문하시겠어요?
(A) 그것은 또 고장 났어요.
(B) 아니요, 저는 너무 배불러요.
(C) 11번 테이블에요.
어휘 out of order 고장 난

토익실전문제   p.44

| 01 (B) | 02 (A) | 03 (B) | 04 (C) |

01 일반 의문문
영국 → 호주

Was the issue with the accounting software resolved?
(A) In next month's issue.
(B) Daniel is still working on it.
(C) A savings account.

issue n. 문제, (간행물의) 호   resolve v. 해결하다
savings account 저축 계좌

해석 회계 소프트웨어의 문제가 해결됐나요?
(A) 다음 달 호에요.
(B) Daniel이 아직 그것을 작업하고 있어요.
(C) 저축 계좌요.

해설 (A) [x] 질문의 issue(문제)를 '(간행물의) 호'라는 의미의 명사로 반복 사용하여 혼동을 준 오답이다.
(B) [o] Daniel이 아직 그것을 작업하고 있다는 말로, 회계 소프트웨어의 문제가 해결되지 않았음을 간접적으로 전달했으므로 정답이다.
(C) [x] accounting - account의 유사 발음 어휘를 사용하여 혼동을 준 오답이다.

02 일반 의문문
미국 → 영국

Have you finished reviewing the sales report?
(A) I just need to check the final numbers.
(B) A news reporter.
(C) By 20 percent.

review v. 검토하다   sales report 매출 보고서

해석 매출 보고서 검토하는 것을 완료했나요?
(A) 최종 숫자들을 확인하기만 하면 돼요.
(B) 뉴스 기자요.
(C) 20퍼센트만큼요.

해설 (A) [o] 최종 숫자들을 확인하기만 하면 된다는 말로, 매출 보고서 검토하는 것을 아직 완료하지 않았음을 간접적으로 전달했으므로 정답이다.
(B) [x] report - reporter의 유사 발음 어휘를 사용하여 혼동을 준 오답이다.
(C) [x] 질문의 sales report(매출 보고서)에서 연상할 수 있는 매출 수치와 관련된 20 percent(20퍼센트)를 사용하여 혼동을 준 오답이다.

03 일반 의문문
호주 → 미국

Do you know where the new Italian restaurant is located?
(A) No, thanks. I'm not hungry.
(B) It's next to the movie theater downtown.
(C) That's our most popular menu item.

be located 위치해 있다   downtown adv. 시내에

해석 어디에 새로운 이탈리아 식당이 위치해 있는지 아시나요?
(A) 고맙지만, 사양할게요. 저는 배고프지 않아요.
(B) 시내 영화관 옆에 있어요.
(C) 그것이 우리의 가장 인기 있는 메뉴 항목이에요.

해설 (A) [x] 어디에 새로운 이탈리아 식당이 위치해 있는지 아냐고 물었는데, 이와 관련이 없는 고맙지만 사양한다며 배가 고프지 않다고 응답했으므로 오답이다.
(B) [o] 시내 영화관 옆에 있다는 말로, 어디에 새로운 이탈리아 식당이 위치해 있는지 전달했으므로 정답이다.
(C) [x] 질문의 restaurant(식당)과 관련 있는 menu item(메뉴 항목)을 사용하여 혼동을 준 오답이다.

04 일반 의문문
캐나다 → 영국

Do we still have time to submit our project proposal?
(A) With the project manager.
(B) I've been working here for three years.
(C) Yes. The deadline was extended until tomorrow.

proposal n. 제안서   extend v. 연장하다

해석 우리의 프로젝트 제안서를 제출할 시간이 아직 있나요?
(A) 프로젝트 매니저와 함께요.
(B) 저는 여기서 3년 동안 일해왔어요.
(C) 네. 마감일이 내일까지 연장됐어요.

해설 (A) [x] 질문의 project를 반복 사용하여 혼동을 준 오답이다.
(B) [x] 질문의 time(시간)과 관련 있는 three years(3년)를 사용하여 혼동을 준 오답이다.
(C) [o] Yes로 프로젝트 제안서를 제출할 시간이 아직 있음을 전달한 후, 마감일이 내일까지 연장됐다는 부연 설명을 했으므로 정답이다.

기출 유형 2 부정 의문문

Example 🔊 영국 → 호주　　　　　　　　　　　p.45

해석　당신은 오늘 발표하지 않나요?
(A) 매우 흥미로웠어요.
(B) 네. 점심 식사 직후에요.
(C) 당신에게 줄 선물을 준비했어요.

어휘　presentation n. 발표　present n. 선물

토익실전문제 p.45

| 01 (B) | 02 (C) | 03 (A) | 04 (B) |

---

01 부정 의문문　🔊 캐나다 → 미국

Aren't there any direct flights to the conference location?
(A) Send it directly to me.
(B) Unfortunately, all require a connection in Chicago.
(C) My presentation is on Thursday.

directly adv. 직접　connection n. 경유, 연결

해석　그 학회 장소로 가는 직항편이 전혀 없나요?
(A) 저에게 그것을 직접 보내세요.
(B) 안타깝게도, 모두 시카고에서의 경유를 필요로 해요.
(C) 제 발표는 목요일이에요.

해설　(A) [x] direct - directly의 유사 발음 어휘를 사용하여 혼동을 준 오답이다.
(B) [o] 안타깝게도, 모든 항공편이 시카고에서 경유해야 한다는 말로, 직항편이 없음을 간접적으로 전달했으므로 정답이다.
(C) [x] 질문의 conference(학회)와 관련 있는 presentation(발표)을 사용하여 혼동을 준 오답이다.

02 부정 의문문　🔊 영국 → 캐나다

Don't we need permits for the outdoor event?
(A) Event planning takes time.
(B) It was held in Belmont Hall.
(C) I already submitted the application to city hall.

permit n. 허가증　application n. 신청서, 지원서

해석　우리는 야외 행사를 위해서 허가증이 필요하지 않나요?
(A) 행사 기획에는 시간이 걸려요.
(B) 그것은 Belmont 홀에서 개최됐어요.
(C) 저는 이미 시청에 신청서를 제출했어요.

해설　(A) [x] 질문의 event를 반복 사용하여 혼동을 준 오답이다.
(B) [x] 질문의 event(행사)에서 연상할 수 있는 행사 장소와 관련된 Belmont Hall(Belmont 홀)을 사용하여 혼동을 준 오답이다.
(C) [o] 이미 시청에 신청서를 제출했다는 말로, 허가증에 대한 문제를 이미 해결했음을 간접적으로 전달했으므로 정답이다.

03 부정 의문문　🔊 미국 → 호주

Haven't you visited the national park during your stay?
(A) We're planning to go tomorrow.
(B) No, I told him to stay home.
(C) In the city park.

national park 국립공원　stay n. 체류, 머무름; v. 머무르다

해석　체류하는 동안 국립공원을 방문하지 않으셨나요?
(A) 저희는 내일 가려고 계획하고 있어요.
(B) 아니요, 그에게 집에서 머무르라고 말했어요.
(C) 도시 공원에서요.

해설　(A) [o] 내일 가려고 계획하고 있다는 말로, 아직 국립공원을 방문하지 않았음을 간접적으로 전달했으므로 정답이다.
(B) [x] 질문의 stay를 '머무르다'라는 의미의 동사로 반복 사용하여 혼동을 준 오답이다.
(C) [x] 질문의 park를 반복 사용하여 혼동을 준 오답이다.

04 부정 의문문　🔊 호주 → 캐나다

Wasn't the training session recorded for those who missed it?
(A) No, I'm still using them.
(B) We'll send everyone the video link.
(C) A new program.

training session 교육 과정　record v. 녹화하다

해석　그 교육 과정은 참석하지 못한 사람들을 위해 녹화되지 않았나요?
(A) 아니요, 제가 아직 그것들을 사용하고 있어요.
(B) 우리는 모든 사람들에게 영상 링크를 보낼 거예요.
(C) 새로운 프로그램이요.

해설　(A) [x] 참석하지 못한 사람들을 위해 교육 과정이 녹화되지 않았는지를 물었는데, 이와 관련이 없는 그것들을 사용하고 있다고 응답했으므로 오답이다.
(B) [o] 모든 사람들에게 영상 링크를 보낼 것이라는 말로, 교육 과정이 녹화되었음을 간접적으로 전달했으므로 정답이다.
(C) [x] 질문의 training session(교육 과정)과 관련 있는 program(프로그램)을 사용하여 혼동을 준 오답이다.

HACKERS TEST p.46

01 (B)	02 (C)	03 (A)	04 (B)	05 (C)
06 (C)	07 (C)	08 (B)	09 (B)	10 (A)
11 (B)	12 (A)	13 (C)	14 (B)	15 (A)
16 (A)	17 (B)	18 (C)	19 (B)	20 (C)
21 (A)	22 (B)	23 (B)	24 (C)	25 (B)
26 (B)	27 (A)	28 (C)		

---

01 일반 의문문　🔊 영국 → 호주

Can I take pictures in the art gallery?
(A) Only some of the sculptures were sold.
(B) Sorry, but that's prohibited.
(C) Everyone was waiting outside.

sculpture n. 조각품　prohibit v. 금지하다

해석　미술관에서 사진을 찍어도 될까요?
(A) 일부 조각품들만 팔렸어요.
(B) 죄송하지만, 그건 금지되어 있어요.
(C) 모두 밖에서 기다리고 있었어요.

해설　(A) [x] 질문의 art gallery(미술관)에서 연상할 수 있는 전시품과 관련된 sculptures(조각품들)를 사용하여 혼동을 준 오답이다.
(B) [o] 죄송하지만, 그건 금지되어 있다는 말로, 미술관에서 사진을 찍을 수 없음을 전달했으므로 정답이다.
(C) [x] 미술관에서 사진을 찍을 수 있는지를 물었는데, 이와 관련이 없는 모두 밖에서 기다리고 있었다고 응답했으므로 오답이다.

02 부정 의문문 캐나다 → 미국

Weren't there any errors in the expense form?
(A) The finance department.
(B) Yes, it's expensive.
(C) The information was correct.

expense n. 경비, 비용   expensive adj. 비싼   correct adj. 정확한, 맞는

해석 그 경비 명세서에 오류는 없었나요?
(A) 재무부요.
(B) 네, 그건 비싸요.
(C) 정보는 정확했어요.

해설 (A) [x] 질문의 expense form(경비 명세서)에서 연상할 수 있는 담당 부서와 관련된 finance department(재무부)를 사용하여 혼동을 준 오답이다.
(B) [x] expense - expensive의 유사 발음 어휘를 사용하여 혼동을 준 오답이다.
(C) [o] 정보는 정확했다는 말로, 경비 명세서에 오류가 없었음을 간접적으로 전달했으므로 정답이다.

03 일반 의문문 영국 → 미국

Is the Internet connection stable now?
(A) Yes. We fixed the issue.
(B) You can find it on our Web site.
(C) Our office has free Wi-Fi.

stable adj. 안정적인   fix v. 고치다, 수리하다

해석 지금 인터넷 연결이 안정적인가요?
(A) 네. 저희가 그 문제를 고쳤어요.
(B) 당신은 그것을 우리의 웹사이트에서 찾을 수 있어요.
(C) 우리 사무실은 무료 와이파이가 있어요.

해설 (A) [o] Yes로 지금 인터넷 연결이 안정적이라고 전달한 후, 그 문제를 고쳤다는 부연 설명을 했으므로 정답이다.
(B) [x] 질문의 Internet(인터넷)과 관련 있는 Web site(웹사이트)를 사용하여 혼동을 준 오답이다.
(C) [x] 질문의 Internet(인터넷)과 관련 있는 Wi-Fi(와이파이)를 사용하여 혼동을 준 오답이다.

04 부정 의문문 호주 → 캐나다

Can't we purchase a new projector for the conference room?
(A) She's on vacation this week.
(B) We'll have to check the budget.
(C) Because you need an adapter.

purchase v. 구매하다, 사다   budget n. 예산   adapter n. 어댑터, 확장 카드

해석 회의실을 위한 새 프로젝터를 구매할 수 없나요?
(A) 그녀는 이번 주에 휴가 중이에요.
(B) 우리는 예산을 확인해야 할 거예요.
(C) 어댑터가 필요하기 때문이에요.

해설 (A) [x] 회의실을 위한 새 프로젝터를 구매할 수 없는지 물었는데, 이와 관련 없는 그녀는 휴가 중이라고 응답했으므로 오답이다.
(B) [o] 예산을 확인해야 할 것이라는 말로, 회의실을 위한 새 프로젝터를 구매할 수 없을지 모른다는 것을 간접적으로 전달했으므로 정답이다.
(C) [x] 질문의 projector(프로젝터)와 관련 있는 adapter(어댑터)를 사용하여 혼동을 준 오답이다.

05 일반 의문문 캐나다 → 영국

Can I get a discount if I buy more than 30 products?
(A) A product demonstration.
(B) At least 20 years ago.
(C) Yes. Large orders are discounted.

discount n. 할인; v. 할인하다   demonstration n. 시연, 입증

해석 30개가 넘는 상품을 구매하면 할인을 받을 수 있나요?
(A) 제품 시연이요.
(B) 적어도 20년 전에요.
(C) 네. 대량 주문은 할인돼요.

해설 (A) [x] 질문의 product를 반복 사용하여 혼동을 준 오답이다.
(B) [x] 30개가 넘는 상품을 구매하면 할인을 받을 수 있는지 물었는데, 이와 관련이 없는 적어도 20년 전이라고 응답했으므로 오답이다.
(C) [o] Yes로 30개가 넘는 상품을 구매하면 할인을 받을 수 있음을 전달한 후, 대량 주문은 할인된다고 부연 설명을 했으므로 정답이다.

06 일반 의문문 미국 → 호주

Are these your keys on the desk?
(A) At the security desk.
(B) Directly to the client.
(C) No. They belong to Mike.

client n. 의뢰인, 고객   belong to ~의 것이다

해석 책상 위의 이 열쇠들이 당신의 것인가요?
(A) 보안 데스크에서요.
(B) 고객에게 직접이요.
(C) 아니요. 그것들은 Mike의 것이에요.

해설 (A) [x] 질문의 desk를 반복 사용하여 혼동을 준 오답이다.
(B) [x] 이 열쇠들이 당신의 것인지 물었는데, 이와 관련 없는 고객에게 직접이라고 응답했으므로 오답이다.
(C) [o] No로 열쇠들이 자신의 것이 아님을 전달한 후, Mike의 것이라는 부연 설명을 했으므로 정답이다.

07 부정 의문문 영국 → 호주

Isn't Alice transferring to the New Orleans branch?
(A) Yes. Our branch manager is on leave.
(B) She knows his extension number.
(C) That's what I've heard.

transfer v. 전근 가다, 이동하다   on leave 휴가 중인
extension number 내선 번호

해석 Alice는 뉴올리언스 지점으로 전근 가지 않나요?
(A) 네. 우리 지점장은 휴가 중이에요.
(B) 그녀는 그의 내선 번호를 알고 있어요.
(C) 그게 제가 들은 거예요.

해설 (A) [x] Alice는 뉴올리언스 지점으로 전근 가지 않는지 물었는데, 이와 관련이 없는 우리 지점장이 휴가 중이라고 응답했으므로 오답이다. Yes까지만 듣고 정답으로 고르지 않도록 주의한다.
(B) [x] Alice를 가리킬 때 쓸 수 있는 She(그녀)를 사용하여 혼동을 준 오답이다.
(C) [o] 그게 자신이 들은 것이라는 말로, Alice가 뉴올리언스 지점으로 전근을 갈 것임을 간접적으로 전달했으므로 정답이다.

08 부정 의문문 캐나다 → 미국

Didn't you schedule the client meeting?
(A) I've never been there.

(B) I'll set it up now.
(C) An updated concert schedule.

set ~ up ~을 준비하다, 설치하다

해석 당신이 고객 미팅 일정을 잡지 않았나요?
(A) 저는 그곳에 한 번도 가본 적이 없어요.
(B) 지금 바로 준비할게요.
(C) 업데이트된 콘서트 일정이요.

해설 (A) [x] 고객 미팅 일정을 잡지 않았는지 물었는데, 이와 관련이 없는 그곳에 한 번도 가본 적이 없다고 응답했으므로 오답이다.
(B) [o] 지금 바로 준비할 것이라는 말로, 고객 미팅 일정을 아직 잡지 않았음을 간접적으로 전달했으므로 정답이다.
(C) [x] 질문의 schedule을 '일정'이라는 의미의 명사로 반복 사용하여 혼동을 준 오답이다.

09 일반 의문문 🎧 호주 → 영국

Do you have your presentation notes with you?
(A) We don't have menus.
(B) Of course. Right inside this folder.
(C) It was successful.

successful adj. 성공적인

해석 당신의 프레젠테이션 메모를 가지고 계신가요?
(A) 우리는 메뉴를 가지고 있지 않아요.
(B) 물론이죠. 바로 이 폴더 안에요.
(C) 그것은 성공적이었어요.

해설 (A) [x] 질문의 have를 반복 사용하여 혼동을 준 오답이다.
(B) [o] Of course로 프레젠테이션 메모를 가지고 있음을 전달한 후, 폴더 안에 있다고 부연 설명을 했으므로 정답이다.
(C) [x] 질문의 presentation(프레젠테이션)에서 연상할 수 있는 successful(성공적인)을 사용하여 혼동을 준 오답이다.

10 부정 의문문 🎧 캐나다 → 호주

Shouldn't Ms. Fenwick check the shipping status?
(A) I'm meeting with her later today.
(B) Mostly, electronic goods.
(C) Yes, you did.

status n. 현황, 상태 electronic adj. 전자의, 전자적인 goods n. 제품, 상품

해석 Ms. Fenwick이 운송 현황을 확인해야 하지 않나요?
(A) 제가 오늘 늦게 그녀와 만날 거예요.
(B) 주로, 전자 제품이요.
(C) 네, 당신이 했어요.

해설 (A) [o] 오늘 늦게 그녀와 만날 것이라는 말로, Ms. Fenwick과 만나서 물어볼 것임을 간접적으로 전달했으므로 정답이다.
(B) [x] 질문의 shipping(운송)과 관련 있는 goods(제품)를 사용하여 혼동을 준 오답이다.
(C) [x] Ms. Fenwick이 운송 현황을 확인해야 하지 않는지 물었는데, 이와 관련이 없는 당신이 했다고 응답했으므로 오답이다. Yes까지만 듣고 정답으로 고르지 않도록 주의한다.

11 일반 의문문 🎧 호주 → 미국

Will many people attend the film festival this year?
(A) No. I already saw it.
(B) That's very likely.
(C) I thought the event was really fun.

attend v. 참석하다 likely adj. 그럴 가능성 있는, 그럴싸한

해석 올해 많은 사람들이 영화 축제에 참석할 것인가요?
(A) 아니요. 저는 이미 그것을 봤어요.
(B) 그럴 가능성이 아주 높아요.
(C) 그 행사는 정말 재미있었다고 생각했어요.

해설 (A) [x] 질문의 film(영화)과 관련 있는 saw(봤다)를 사용하여 혼동을 준 오답이다. No까지만 듣고 이를 정답으로 고르지 않도록 주의한다.
(B) [o] 그럴 가능성이 높다는 말로, 많은 사람들이 영화 축제에 참석할 것임을 간접적으로 전달했으므로 정답이다.
(C) [x] 질문의 festival(축제)과 관련 있는 event(행사)를 사용하여 혼동을 준 오답이다.

12 일반 의문문 🎧 캐나다 → 미국

Does the subway station have elevators?
(A) At both exits.
(B) It was crowded at the station.
(C) Yes, I usually walk home.

exit n. 출구 crowded adj. (사람들로) 붐비는, 복잡한

해석 그 지하철역에는 엘리베이터가 있나요?
(A) 양쪽 출구에요.
(B) 그 역은 붐볐어요.
(C) 네, 저는 보통 집에 걸어가요.

해설 (A) [o] 양쪽 출구라는 말로, 지하철역에 엘리베이터가 있음을 간접적으로 전달했으므로 정답이다.
(B) [x] 질문의 station을 반복 사용하여 혼동을 준 오답이다.
(C) [x] 질문의 subway(지하철)에서 연상할 수 있는 통근 방법과 관련된 walk(걸어가다)를 사용하여 혼동을 준 오답이다.

13 부정 의문문 🎧 미국 → 영국

Shouldn't we make another 10 copies of the pamphlet?
(A) Page 9, I think.
(B) Yes, that's a new coffee machine.
(C) The printer is out of ink.

pamphlet n. 팸플릿, 소책자

해석 우리는 팸플릿 10부를 추가로 만들어야 하지 않나요?
(A) 9쪽일 거예요.
(B) 네, 그건 새로운 커피 머신이에요.
(C) 프린터에 잉크가 떨어졌어요.

해설 (A) [x] 질문의 pamphlet(팸플릿)과 관련 있는 Page 9(9쪽)을 사용하여 혼동을 준 오답이다.
(B) [x] copies - coffee의 유사 발음 어휘를 사용하여 혼동을 준 오답이다.
(C) [o] 프린터에 잉크가 떨어졌다는 말로, 팸플릿 10부를 추가로 만들 수 없음을 간접적으로 전달했으므로 정답이다.

14 일반 의문문 🎧 호주 → 영국

Do you sell your products online?
(A) To discuss our newest product.
(B) No. Only in stores.
(C) You can pay by credit card.

product n. 제품 discuss v. 논의하다 pay v. 지불하다

해석 당신은 온라인으로 당신의 제품을 판매하나요?
(A) 우리의 최신 제품을 논의하기 위해서요.
(B) 아니요. 오직 매장에서만요.
(C) 신용카드로 결제하셔도 됩니다.

해설 (A) [×] 질문의 product를 반복 사용하여 혼동을 준 오답이다.
(B) [○] No로 자신의 제품을 온라인으로 판매하지 않음을 전달한 후, 오직 매장에서만 판매한다는 부연 설명을 했으므로 정답이다.
(C) [×] 질문의 sell(판매하다)에서 연상할 수 있는 결제 수단과 관련된 credit card(신용카드)를 사용하여 혼동을 준 오답이다.

15 부정 의문문
영국 → 호주

Won't we be late for the dentist appointment?
(A) What time is it now?
(B) The treatment wasn't painful.
(C) Thanks, that sounds great.

appointment n. 예약, 약속 painful adj. 아픈

해설 우리가 치과 진료 예약에 늦지 않을까요?
(A) 지금 몇 시인가요?
(B) 그 치료는 아프지 않았어요.
(C) 감사합니다, 그거 좋네요.

해설 (A) [○] 지금 몇 시인지 되물어, 치과 진료 예약에 늦지 않을지 모른다는 것을 간접적으로 전달했으므로 정답이다.
(B) [×] 질문의 dentist(치과)와 관련 있는 treatment(치료)를 사용하여 혼동을 준 오답이다.
(C) [×] 치과 진료 예약에 늦지 않을지 물었는데, 이와 관련이 없는 감사 인사로 응답했으므로 오답이다.

16 일반 의문문
미국 → 캐나다

Should we put out more beverages for the guests?
(A) Most people seem to be leaving.
(B) Yes, we recycle the paper boxes.
(C) I don't think he's here today.

beverage n. 음료 recycle v. 재활용하다

해설 손님들을 위해 더 많은 음료를 내놓아야 할까요?
(A) 대부분의 사람들이 떠나고 있는 것 같아요.
(B) 네, 우리는 종이 상자를 재활용해요.
(C) 제 생각에는 그가 오늘 여기 없는 것 같아요.

해설 (A) [○] 대부분의 사람들이 떠나고 있는 것 같다는 말로, 더 많은 음료를 내놓을 필요가 없음을 간접적으로 전달했으므로 정답이다.
(B) [×] 손님들을 위해 더 많은 음료를 내놓아야 할지를 물었는데, 이와 관련이 없는 종이 상자를 재활용한다고 응답했으므로 오답이다. Yes까지만 듣고 정답으로 고르지 않도록 주의한다.
(C) [×] 손님들을 위해 더 많은 음료를 내놓아야 할지를 물었는데, 이와 관련이 없는 그가 오늘 여기 없는 것 같다고 응답했으므로 오답이다.

17 일반 의문문
캐나다 → 영국

Did you see my latest memo?
(A) Just for the accounting staff.
(B) I was out of the office all day.
(C) No, I can't come tonight.

accounting staff 회계 직원

해설 저의 최신 회람을 보셨나요?
(A) 회계 직원들만을 위해서요.
(B) 저는 하루 종일 사무실 밖에 있었어요.
(C) 아니요, 저는 오늘 밤에 갈 수 없어요.

해설 (A) [×] 질문의 memo(회람)에서 연상할 수 있는 수신자와 관련된 for the accounting staff(회계 직원들을 위해)를 사용하여 혼동을 준 오답이다.

(B) [○] 하루 종일 사무실 밖에 있었다는 말로, 최신 회람을 보지 못했음을 간접적으로 전달했으므로 정답이다.
(C) [×] 자신의 최신 회람을 보았는지 물었는데, 이와 관련이 없는 오늘 밤에 갈 수 없다고 응답했으므로 오답이다. No까지만 듣고 정답으로 고르지 않도록 주의한다.

18 부정 의문문
미국 → 캐나다

Hasn't the cargo truck been loaded yet?
(A) The file is still uploading.
(B) Yes, a rental car.
(C) Some repairs are causing a delay.

load v. (짐을) 싣다, 적재하다 repair n. 수리 cause v. 야기하다, 일으키다

해설 화물 트럭이 아직 짐을 싣지 않았나요?
(A) 파일이 아직 업로드 중이에요.
(B) 네, 렌터카요.
(C) 일부 수리가 지연을 야기하고 있어요.

해설 (A) [×] loaded - uploading의 유사 발음 어휘를 사용하여 혼동을 준 오답이다.
(B) [×] 질문의 truck(트럭)과 관련 있는 car(자동차)를 사용하여 혼동을 준 오답이다.
(C) [○] 일부 수리가 지연을 야기하고 있다는 말로, 화물 트럭이 아직 짐을 싣지 않았음을 간접적으로 전달했으므로 정답이다.

19 일반 의문문
캐나다 → 미국

Do you know where Mr. Nakamura is?
(A) He has the skills to do it.
(B) All the department heads are at a meeting now.
(C) No, I don't think so.

skill n. 기술, 능력 department head 부서장

해설 Mr. Nakamura가 어디에 있는지 아시나요?
(A) 그는 그것을 할 수 있는 기술을 가지고 있어요.
(B) 모든 부서장들은 지금 회의 중이에요.
(C) 아니요, 저는 그렇게 생각하지 않아요.

해설 (A) [×] Mr. Nakamura를 가리킬 때 쓸 수 있는 He(그)를 사용하여 혼동을 준 오답이다.
(B) [○] 모든 부서장들은 지금 회의 중이라는 말로, Mr. Nakamura가 어디에 있는지 알고 있음을 간접적으로 전달했으므로 정답이다.
(C) [×] Mr. Nakamura가 어디에 있는지 아냐고 물었는데, 이와 관련이 없는 그렇게 생각하지 않는다고 응답했으므로 오답이다. No까지만 듣고 정답으로 고르지 않도록 주의한다.

20 일반 의문문
호주 → 영국

Has a new fitness machine been added recently?
(A) Follow the instructions carefully, please.
(B) It is a challenging routine.
(C) I just joined this gym.

follow v. 따르다 challenging adj. 도전적인, 어려운 routine n. 습관, 일상

해설 최근에 새로운 운동기구가 추가되었나요?
(A) 지시사항을 주의 깊게 따라주세요.
(B) 그것은 도전적인 습관이에요.
(C) 저는 이 헬스장에 방금 등록했어요.

해설 (A) [×] 질문의 fitness machine(운동기구)에서 연상할 수 있는 사용법과 관련된 instructions(지시사항)를 사용하여 혼동을 준 오답이다.
(B) [×] 최근에 새로운 운동기구가 추가되었는지를 물었는데, 이와 관련

이 없는 그것은 도전적인 습관이라고 응답했으므로 오답이다.
(C) [o] 자신이 이 헬스장에 방금 등록했다는 말로, 새로운 운동기구가 추가되었는지 모른다는 것을 간접적으로 전달했으므로 정답이다.

21 일반 의문문 영국 → 캐나다

Will there be enough parking for all attendees?
(A) The venue has reserved 200 spaces for us.
(B) Sure, we accept that coupon.
(C) She paid for a parking pass.

attendee n. 참석자   venue n. 개최지, 장소   reserve v. 예약하다

해석 모든 참석자들을 위해 충분한 주차 공간이 있을까요?
(A) 개최지에서 우리를 위해 200개의 주차 공간을 예약했어요.
(B) 물론이죠, 저희는 그 쿠폰을 받아요.
(C) 그녀는 주차권에 비용을 지불했어요.

해설 (A) [o] 개최지에서 우리를 위해 200개의 주차 공간을 예약했다는 말로, 모든 참석자들을 위한 충분한 주차 공간이 있음을 간접적으로 전달했으므로 정답이다.
(B) [x] 모든 참석자들을 위한 충분한 주차 공간이 있을지를 물었는데, 이와 관련이 없는 그 쿠폰을 받는다고 응답했으므로 오답이다. Sure까지만 듣고 정답으로 고르지 않도록 주의한다.
(C) [x] 질문의 parking을 반복 사용하여 혼동을 준 오답이다.

22 부정 의문문 미국 → 호주

Wasn't Devon assigned to handle the customer service inquiries?
(A) He's been transferred to the sales department.
(B) Yes, your name is on the list.
(C) Please complete this form.

inquiry n. 문의, 질문   complete v. 작성하다, 완료하다

해석 Devon이 고객 서비스 문의를 처리하도록 배정되지 않았나요?
(A) 그는 영업부로 이동했어요.
(B) 네, 당신의 이름이 그 목록에 있어요.
(C) 이 양식을 작성해 주세요.

해설 (A) [o] Devon이 영업부로 이동했다는 말로, 그가 고객 서비스 문의를 처리하도록 배정되지 않았음을 간접적으로 전달했으므로 정답이다.
(B) [x] Devon이 고객 서비스 문의를 처리하도록 배정되지 않았는지 물었는데, 이와 관련이 없는 당신의 이름이 목록에 있다고 응답했으므로 오답이다. Yes까지만 듣고 정답으로 고르지 않도록 주의한다.
(C) [x] 질문의 inquiries(문의)와 관련 있는 form(양식)을 사용하여 혼동을 준 오답이다.

23 일반 의문문 캐나다 → 영국

Are the concert tickets available at the box office?
(A) Our office assistant.
(B) You can also purchase them online.
(C) Yes, I enjoyed it.

box office 매표소   assistant n. 보조원

해석 매표소에서 콘서트 티켓을 구입할 수 있나요?
(A) 저희 사무실 보조원이요.
(B) 온라인으로도 그것들을 구매하실 수 있어요.
(C) 네, 저는 그것을 즐겼어요.

해설 (A) [x] 질문의 office를 반복 사용하여 혼동을 준 오답이다.
(B) [o] 온라인으로도 구매할 수 있다는 말로, 매표소에서 콘서트 티켓을 구입할 수 있음을 간접적으로 전달했으므로 정답이다.

(C) [x] 매표소에서 콘서트 티켓을 구입할 수 있는지를 물었는데, 이와 관련이 없는 그것을 즐겼다고 응답했으므로 오답이다. Yes까지만 듣고 정답으로 고르지 않도록 주의한다.

24 일반 의문문 미국 → 캐나다

Have you tried the new café in the shopping center?
(A) I need to pick up some groceries.
(B) Try this recipe.
(C) Their coffee is excellent.

grocery n. 식료품   recipe n. 조리법, 비결

해석 그 쇼핑 센터에 있는 새로운 카페를 가봤어요?
(A) 저는 식료품을 좀 사야 해요.
(B) 이 조리법을 시도해보세요.
(C) 그들의 커피는 훌륭해요.

해설 (A) [x] shopping center(쇼핑 센터)에서 연상할 수 있는 groceries(식료품)를 사용하여 혼동을 준 오답이다.
(B) [x] 질문의 tried의 try를 반복 사용하여 혼동을 준 오답이다.
(C) [o] 그들의 커피는 훌륭하다는 말로, 새로운 카페를 가봤음을 간접적으로 전달했으므로 정답이다.

25 일반 의문문 영국 → 호주

Should I forward the e-mail to the entire department?
(A) The latest mobile phone.
(B) Maybe just send it to the team leaders.
(C) Because he plans to retire next year.

forward v. 전달하다   entire adj. 전체의   retire v. 은퇴하다

해석 이메일을 전체 부서에 전달해야 할까요?
(A) 최신 휴대전화요.
(B) 그것을 팀장들에게만 보내셔도 될 것 같아요.
(C) 그가 내년에 은퇴할 계획이기 때문이에요.

해설 (A) [x] forward - phone의 유사 발음 어휘를 사용하여 혼동을 준 오답이다.
(B) [o] 팀장들에게만 보내도 될 것 같다는 말로, 이메일을 전체 부서에 전달할 필요가 없음을 간접적으로 전달했으므로 정답이다.
(C) [x] entire - retire의 유사 발음 어휘를 사용하여 혼동을 준 오답이다.

26 일반 의문문 호주 → 캐나다

Are we still meeting the clients at the airport tomorrow?
(A) He travels a lot for work.
(B) Yes. I've arranged transportation.
(C) This restaurant has good reviews.

transportation n. 교통수단   review n. 후기, 검토

해석 우리는 여전히 내일 공항에서 고객들을 만날 예정인가요?
(A) 그는 출장을 많이 가요.
(B) 네. 제가 교통수단을 마련했어요.
(C) 이 식당은 좋은 후기를 받았어요.

해설 (A) [x] 질문의 airport(공항)와 관련 있는 travel(여행가다)을 사용하여 혼동을 준 오답이다.
(B) [o] Yes로 내일 공항에서 고객들을 만날 예정이 맞음을 전달한 후, 자신이 교통수단을 마련했다는 부연 설명을 했으므로 정답이다.
(C) [x] 내일 공항에서 고객들을 만날 예정인지 물었는데, 이와 관련이 없는 식당이 좋은 후기를 받았다고 응답했으므로 오답이다.

27 부정 의문문 영국 → 미국

Don't we have an extra copy of the contract?
(A) I'll check the filing cabinet.
(B) The terms were negotiated last month.
(C) By sharing advice.

contract n. 계약서   terms n. 조건   negotiate v. 협상하다

해석 우리는 그 계약서의 여분 사본을 가지고 있지 않나요?
(A) 제가 서류함을 확인할게요.
(B) 조건은 지난달에 협상됐어요.
(C) 조언을 공유함으로써요.

해설 (A) [o] 서류함을 확인하겠다는 말로, 계약서의 여분 사본을 가지고 있는지 모른다는 것을 간접적으로 전달했으므로 정답이다.
(B) [x] 질문의 contract(계약서)와 관련 있는 terms(조건)를 사용하여 혼동을 준 오답이다.
(C) [x] 계약서의 여분 사본을 가지고 있지 않은지 물었는데, 이와 관련이 없는 방법으로 응답했으므로 오답이다.

28 일반 의문문 캐나다 → 영국

Do you know which customer asked for a napkin?
(A) I'll just have a sandwich.
(B) She works in customer service.
(C) The man at Table 4.

ask for ~을 요청하다

해석 어떤 고객이 냅킨을 요청했는지 아시나요?
(A) 저는 샌드위치만 먹을게요.
(B) 그녀는 고객 서비스에서 일해요.
(C) 4번 테이블의 남자요.

해설 (A) [x] 질문의 napkin(냅킨)에서 연상할 수 있는 음식과 관련된 sandwich(샌드위치)를 사용하여 혼동을 준 오답이다.
(B) [x] 질문의 customer를 반복 사용하여 혼동을 준 오답이다.
(C) [o] 4번 테이블의 남자라는 말로, 냅킨을 요청한 고객이 누구인지 알고 있음을 간접적으로 전달했으므로 정답이다.

DAY 07   선택 의문문 및 부가 의문문

기출 유형 1   선택 의문문

Example 호주 → 미국 p.48

해석 이 쿠폰을 온라인에서 사용할 수 있나요, 아니면 매장에서만 사용할 수 있나요?
(A) 저희 웹사이트에서 그것을 받아요.
(B) 5퍼센트 할인 쿠폰이요.
(C) 네트워크는 복구되었어요.

어휘 accept v. 받다, 인정하다   restore v. 복구하다

토익실전문제 p.48

| 01 (C) | 02 (B) | 03 (B) | 04 (C) |

01 선택 의문문 영국 → 캐나다

Should we take the train or rent a car for the business trip?
(A) She's away on a business trip.
(B) The hotel is fully booked.
(C) Let's rent a car.

rent v. 빌리다, 대여하다   business trip 출장   fully adv. 완전히, 철저히   book v. 예약하다

해석 출장을 위해서 기차를 타야 할까요, 아니면 차를 빌려야 할까요?
(A) 그녀는 출장으로 자리에 없어요.
(B) 호텔 예약이 완전히 찼어요.
(C) 차를 빌립시다.

해설 (A) [x] 질문의 business trip을 반복 사용하여 혼동을 준 오답이다.
(B) [x] 질문의 business trip(출장)에서 연상할 수 있는 숙박 시설과 관련된 hotel(호텔)을 사용하여 혼동을 준 오답이다.
(C) [o] 차를 빌리자는 말로, 차를 빌리는 것을 선택했으므로 정답이다.

02 선택 의문문 미국 → 캐나다

Are you joining us for dinner or heading home after the presentation?
(A) Yes, it's going to rain.
(B) I think I'll join everyone.
(C) The presentation went very well.

join v. 합류하다, 참여하다

해석 발표 후에 저희와 함께 저녁 식사에 합류하실 건가요, 아니면 집으로 가실 건가요?
(A) 네, 비가 올 거예요.
(B) 모두와 함께 할 것 같아요.
(C) 발표가 아주 잘 진행됐어요.

해설 (A) [x] 선택 의문문에 Yes로 응답했으므로 오답이다.
(B) [o] 모두와 함께 할 것 같다는 말로, 저녁 식사에 합류하는 것을 선택했으므로 정답이다.
(C) [x] 질문의 presentation을 반복 사용하여 혼동을 준 오답이다.

03 선택 의문문 영국 → 호주

Is the gym pass valid for weekdays only or weekends too?
(A) 50 dollars per month.
(B) I'm not sure.
(C) Probably only one.

gym pass 체육관 이용권   valid adj. 유효한   probably adv. 아마

해설 그 체육관 이용권은 주중에만 유효한가요, 아니면 주말도 유효한가요?
(A) 한 달에 50달러예요.
(B) 잘 모르겠어요.
(C) 아마 하나만요.

해설 (A) [x] 질문의 pass(이용권)에서 연상할 수 있는 비용과 관련된 50 dollars(50달러)를 사용하여 혼동을 준 오답이다.
(B) [o] 잘 모르겠다는 말로, 체육관 이용권이 주중에만 유효한지 아니면 주말도 유효한지 모른다고 응답했으므로 정답이다.
(C) [x] 질문의 only를 반복 사용하여 혼동을 준 오답이다.

04 선택 의문문 캐나다 → 호주

Do you water the plants daily or just once a week?
(A) A glass of water, please.
(B) Some new gardening tools.
(C) I give them water every three days.

daily adv. 매일   gardening tool 원예 도구

해석 당신은 식물에 매일 물을 주나요, 아니면 일주일에 한 번만 주나요?

(A) 물 한 잔 주세요.
(B) 몇몇 새로운 원예 도구들이요.
(C) 3일마다 그것들에 물을 줘요.

해설 (A) [x] 질문의 water를 '물'이라는 의미의 명사로 반복 사용하여 혼동을 준 오답이다.
(B) [x] 질문의 plants(식물)와 관련 있는 gardening tools(원예 도구)를 사용하여 혼동을 준 오답이다.
(C) [o] 3일마다 물을 준다는 말로, 매일 물을 주는 것과 일주일에 한 번만 주는 것 둘 다 선택하지 않은 정답이다.

기출 유형 2 부가 의문문

Example 미국 → 캐나다 p.49

해설 당신은 지난주에 새 아파트로 이사하셨죠, 그렇지 않나요?
(A) Mary의 집에서요.
(B) 네. 모든 것이 순조롭게 진행됐어요.
(C) 만약 모든 가구가 맞는다면요.

어휘 smoothly adv. 순조롭게   fit v. 맞다

토익실전문제 p.49

| 01 (C) | 02 (B) | 03 (A) | 04 (B) |

01 부가 의문문 호주 → 영국

The movie tickets sold out quickly, didn't they?
(A) That's fine with me.
(B) A famous actor.
(C) Yes. Within just two hours.

sell out 매진되다, 다 팔리다   famous adj. 유명한

해설 그 영화표는 빠르게 매진됐어요, 그렇지 않나요?
(A) 저는 괜찮아요.
(B) 유명한 배우요.
(C) 네, 단 두 시간 만에요.

해설 (A) [x] 영화표가 빠르게 매진된 것인지를 물었는데, 이와 관련이 없는 자신은 괜찮다고 응답했으므로 오답이다.
(B) [x] 질문의 movie(영화)와 관련 있는 actor(배우)를 사용하여 혼동을 준 오답이다.
(C) [o] Yes로 영화표가 빨리 매진되었음을 전달한 후, 단 두 시간 만에 매진됐다는 부연 설명을 했으므로 정답이다.

02 부가 의문문 캐나다 → 영국

This vacation package includes breakfast, doesn't it?
(A) That was enjoyable.
(B) Yes. And dinner on the first night too.
(C) Leave the package on my desk.

include v. 포함하다   enjoyable adj. 즐거운

해설 이 휴가 패키지 여행은 아침 식사를 포함하죠, 그렇지 않나요?
(A) 그것은 즐거웠어요.
(B) 네. 그리고 첫날 저녁 식사도요.
(C) 그 소포를 제 책상 위에 두세요.

해설 (A) [x] 질문의 vacation(휴가)에서 연상할 수 있는 enjoyable(즐거운)을 사용하여 혼동을 준 오답이다.
(B) [o] Yes로 휴가 패키지 여행은 아침 식사를 포함하고 있음을 전달한 후, 첫날 저녁 식사도 포함한다는 부연 설명을 했으므로 정답이다.
(C) [x] 질문의 package를 '소포, 포장물'이라는 의미의 명사로 반복 사용하여 혼동을 준 오답이다.

03 부가 의문문 미국 → 호주

The client wasn't satisfied with our initial proposal, was he?
(A) We need to revise it.
(B) The hiring initiative.
(C) Of course, I'll do it now.

initial adj. 처음의, 초기의   proposal n. 제안   revise v. 수정하다
initiative n. 계획

해설 고객이 우리의 첫 제안에 만족하지 않았어요, 그렇죠?
(A) 우리는 그것을 수정해야 해요.
(B) 채용 계획이요.
(C) 물론이죠, 지금 그것을 할게요.

해설 (A) [o] 우리가 그것을 수정해야 한다는 말로, 고객이 첫 제안에 만족하지 않았음을 간접적으로 전달했으므로 정답이다.
(B) [x] initial - initiative의 유사 발음 어휘를 사용하여 혼동을 준 오답이다.
(C) [x] 고객이 첫 제안에 만족하지 않았는지를 물었는데, 이와 관련이 없는 지금 그것을 하겠다고 응답했으므로 오답이다.

04 부가 의문문 영국 → 미국

The conference call with the Tokyo branch starts at 9 P.M. our time, right?
(A) No, I'm traveling alone.
(B) Actually, it's scheduled for 10 P.M.
(C) It is a lot of work.

conference call 전화 회의   alone adv. 혼자서

해설 도쿄 지사와의 전화 회의는 우리 시간으로 오후 9시에 시작하죠, 그렇죠?
(A) 아니요, 저는 혼자 여행 가요.
(B) 사실, 오후 10시로 예정되어 있어요.
(C) 그것은 많은 일이에요.

해설 (A) [x] 도쿄 지사와의 전화 회의가 우리 시간으로 오후 9시에 시작하는 것이 맞는지 물었는데, 이와 관련이 없는 혼자 여행 간다고 응답했으므로 오답이다. No까지만 듣고 정답으로 고르지 않도록 주의한다.
(B) [o] 사실 오후 10시로 예정되어 있다는 말로, 도쿄 지사와의 전화 회의가 오후 9시에 시작하는 것이 아님을 간접적으로 전달했으므로 정답이다.
(C) [x] 질문의 conference call(전화 회의)과 관련 있는 work(일)를 사용하여 혼동을 준 오답이다.

HACKERS TEST p.50

01 (B)	02 (C)	03 (B)	04 (B)	05 (A)
06 (B)	07 (B)	08 (A)	09 (C)	10 (C)
11 (B)	12 (B)	13 (A)	14 (C)	15 (C)
16 (B)	17 (B)	18 (A)	19 (B)	20 (A)
21 (B)	22 (A)	23 (C)	24 (A)	25 (C)
26 (C)	27 (B)	28 (B)		

01 선택 의문문 미국 → 캐나다

Would you rather go to the mall or the department store?
(A) In a product catalog.
(B) Let's visit the mall.
(C) That's what I meant.

mall n. 쇼핑몰　department store 백화점　mean v. 의미하다

해석 당신은 쇼핑몰에 가고 싶나요, 아니면 백화점에 가고 싶나요?
(A) 상품 카탈로그예요.
(B) 쇼핑몰을 방문합시다.
(C) 그것이 제가 의미했던 바예요.

해설 (A) [x] 질문의 mall(쇼핑몰), department store(백화점)과 관련 있는 product catalog(상품 카탈로그)를 사용하여 혼동을 준 오답이다.
(B) [o] 쇼핑몰에 가자는 말로, 쇼핑몰을 선택했으므로 정답이다.
(C) [x] 쇼핑몰에 가고 싶은지, 백화점에 가고 싶은지를 물었는데, 이와 관련이 없는 그것이 자신이 의미했던 바라고 응답했으므로 오답이다.

02 부가 의문문 　호주 → 미국

The book fair is being held in Atlanta, isn't it?
(A) I've been there several times.
(B) Ten dollars a copy.
(C) As far as I know.

hold v. 열다, 개최하다　as far as ~하는 한

해석 도서 박람회가 애틀랜타에서 개최될 것이죠, 그렇지 않나요?
(A) 저는 그곳에 여러 번 가봤어요.
(B) 한 부에 10달러예요.
(C) 제가 알기로는 그래요.

해설 (A) [x] 질문의 Atlanta를 가리킬 때 쓸 수 있는 there(그곳에)를 사용하여 혼동을 준 오답이다.
(B) [x] 질문의 book(책)과 관련 있는 copy(부, 사본)를 사용하여 혼동을 준 오답이다.
(C) [o] 자신이 알기로는 그렇다는 말로, 도서 박람회가 애틀랜타에서 개최될 것임을 간접적으로 전달했으므로 정답이다.

03 선택 의문문 　영국 → 호주

Are participants required to pay for the workshop now or when it ends?
(A) I know a great instructor.
(B) Not until after.
(C) She meets all the requirements.

participant n. 참가자　instructor n. 강사　requirement n. 요구사항

해석 참가자들은 워크숍 비용을 지금 지불해야 하나요, 아니면 그것이 끝났을 때 지불해야 하나요?
(A) 제가 좋은 강사를 알고 있어요.
(B) 끝난 후요.
(C) 그녀는 모든 요구사항을 충족해요.

해설 (A) [x] 질문의 workshop(워크숍)과 관련 있는 instructor(강사)를 사용하여 혼동을 준 오답이다.
(B) [o] 끝난 후라는 말로, 워크숍 비용을 끝났을 때 지불해야 하는 것을 선택했으므로 정답이다.
(C) [x] required - requirements의 유사 발음 어휘를 사용하여 혼동을 준 오답이다.

04 부가 의문문 　캐나다 → 미국

The flight attendant was nice, wasn't he?
(A) An aisle seat, please.
(B) I found him very helpful.
(C) Sorry to bother you.

aisle seat 통로 좌석　bother v. 성가시게 하다

해석 그 승무원은 친절했어요, 그렇지 않나요?
(A) 통로 좌석으로 주세요.
(B) 그가 매우 도움이 되었다고 생각해요.
(C) 당신을 성가시게 해서 죄송해요.

해설 (A) [x] 질문의 flight attendant(승무원)에서 연상할 수 있는 비행기와 관련된 aisle seat(통로 좌석)를 사용하여 혼동을 준 오답이다.
(B) [o] 그가 매우 도움이 되었다고 생각한다는 말로, 승무원이 친절했다는 말에 간접적으로 동의했으므로 정답이다.
(C) [x] 그 승무원이 도움이 되었는지 물었는데, 이와 관련이 없는 성가시게 해서 죄송하다고 응답했으므로 오답이다.

05 선택 의문문 　미국 → 호주

Are you managing the advertisement campaign, or is Lucy in charge of it?
(A) That's the director's job.
(B) Oh, the campaign was a success.
(C) Charge it to my credit card.

in charge of ~을 담당하는　director n. 관리자, 감독
success n. 성공작, 성공한 것

해석 당신이 광고 캠페인을 관리하고 있나요, 아니면 Lucy가 담당하고 있나요?
(A) 그것은 관리자의 일이에요.
(B) 아, 그 캠페인은 성공작이었어요.
(C) 제 신용카드에 청구하세요.

해설 (A) [o] 그것은 관리자의 일이라는 말로, 자신과 Lucy 둘 다 간접적으로 선택하지 않은 정답이다.
(B) [x] 질문의 campaign을 반복 사용하여 혼동을 준 오답이다.
(C) [x] 질문의 charge를 '비용을 청구하다'라는 의미의 동사로 반복 사용하여 혼동을 준 오답이다.

06 선택 의문문 　캐나다 → 영국

Would you rather go to the beach on Saturday or wait until Sunday?
(A) Sorry, I'm late.
(B) Neither day works for me.
(C) Esra forgot her towel at the beach.

beach n. 해변　neither adj. 어느 ~도 아니다

해석 토요일에 해변에 가고 싶나요, 아니면 일요일까지 기다리고 싶나요?
(A) 죄송합니다, 제가 늦었어요.
(B) 어느 날도 저에게는 안 돼요.
(C) Esra는 해변에서 그녀의 수건을 잊어버렸어요.

해설 (A) [x] wait - late의 유사 발음 어휘를 사용하여 혼동을 준 오답이다.
(B) [o] 어느 날도 자신에게는 안 된다는 말로, 토요일과 일요일 둘 다 간접적으로 선택하지 않은 정답이다.
(C) [x] 질문의 beach를 반복 사용하여 혼동을 준 오답이다.

07 부가 의문문 　호주 → 영국

The safety inspection is going to last for 30 minutes, right?
(A) No, it was delivered last week.
(B) Yes. It ends at noon.
(C) I submitted an application.

safety inspection 안전 점검　last v. 지속되다; adj. 지난　submit v. 제출하다

해석 안전 점검이 30분 동안 지속될 거예요, 그렇죠?
(A) 아니요, 그것은 지난주에 배송됐어요.

(B) 네, 정오에 끝나요.
(C) 저는 지원서를 제출했어요.

해설 (A) [x] 질문의 last를 '지난'이라는 의미의 형용사로 반복 사용하여 혼동을 준 오답이다. No까지만 듣고 정답으로 고르지 않도록 주의한다.
(B) [o] Yes로 안전 점검이 30분 동안 지속될 것임을 전달한 후, 정오에 끝난다는 부연 설명을 했으므로 정답이다.
(C) [x] inspection – application의 유사 발음 어휘를 사용하여 혼동을 준 오답이다.

08 부가 의문문 미국 → 캐나다

There's a bakery nearby, isn't there?
(A) Next to the bookstore across the street.
(B) A large assortment of pastries.
(C) I'll give them back to you soon.

nearby adv. 근처에 an assortment of 다양한, 여러 가지의

해설 근처에 제과점이 있죠, 그렇지 않나요?
(A) 길 건너편에 있는 서점 옆이에요.
(B) 매우 다양한 종류의 빵들이요.
(C) 제가 그것들을 곧 당신에게 돌려드릴게요.

해설 (A) [o] 길 건너편에 있는 서점 옆이라는 말로, 근처에 제과점이 있음을 간접적으로 전달했으므로 정답이다.
(B) [x] 질문의 bakery(제과점)와 관련 있는 pastries(빵들)를 사용하여 혼동을 준 오답이다.
(C) [x] 근처에 제과점이 있는지를 물었는데, 이와 관련이 없는 그것들을 곧 돌려주겠다고 응답했으므로 오답이다.

09 선택 의문문 영국 → 미국

Do we have enough paper, or should I purchase more?
(A) He's finishing that paperwork now.
(B) No, it's not available yet.
(C) There is plenty in the storage room.

plenty adj. 많은, 충분한 storage room 창고

해설 우리는 충분한 종이를 가지고 있나요, 아니면 제가 더 구매해야 하나요?
(A) 그는 지금 그 서류 작업을 마무리하고 있어요.
(B) 아니요, 그것은 아직 구매할 수 없어요.
(C) 창고에 많이 있어요.

해설 (A) [x] paper – paperwork의 유사 발음 어휘를 사용하여 혼동을 준 오답이다.
(B) [x] 질문의 purchase(구매하다)와 관련 있는 available(이용 가능한, 구할 수 있는)을 사용하여 혼동을 준 오답이다.
(C) [o] 창고에 많이 있다는 말로, 충분한 종이를 가지고 있음을 선택했으므로 정답이다.

10 부가 의문문 캐나다 → 미국

Seminar attendees will receive booklets to take home, won't they?
(A) Many people attended the dinner.
(B) The library is open until 10 P.M.
(C) They will be sent out by mail.

attendee n. 참석자 booklet n. 소책자

해설 세미나 참석자들은 집으로 가져갈 소책자들을 받을 거예요, 그렇지 않나요?
(A) 많은 사람들이 저녁 식사에 참석했어요.
(B) 그 도서관은 밤 10시까지 열려 있어요.
(C) 그것들은 우편으로 발송될 거예요.

해설 (A) [x] attendees – attended의 유사 발음 어휘를 사용하여 혼동을 준 오답이다.
(B) [x] 질문의 booklets(소책자들)에서 연상할 수 있는 library(도서관)를 사용하여 혼동을 준 오답이다.
(C) [o] 그것들은 우편으로 발송될 것이라는 말로, 세미나 참석자들이 소책자를 받을 것임을 간접적으로 전달했으므로 정답이다.

11 선택 의문문 캐나다 → 호주

Are you paying by credit card or cash?
(A) About 20 euros.
(B) I'll use my card.
(C) The receipt is missing.

cash n. 현금 missing adj. 없어진, 분실된

해설 신용카드로 지불할 건가요, 아니면 현금으로 지불할 건가요?
(A) 약 20 유로요.
(B) 제 카드를 사용할게요.
(C) 영수증이 없어졌어요.

해설 (A) [x] 질문의 paying(지불하다)과 관련 있는 euros(유로)를 사용하여 혼동을 준 오답이다.
(B) [o] 자신의 카드를 사용할 것이라는 말로, 신용카드로 지불할 것임을 선택했으므로 정답이다.
(C) [x] 신용카드로 지불할 것인지, 현금으로 지불할 것인지를 물었는데, 이와 관련이 없는 영수증이 없어졌다고 응답했으므로 오답이다.

12 부가 의문문 미국 → 영국

Lisa Stanly has been promoted to district manager, hasn't she?
(A) There are seven branches.
(B) Actually, she turned down the position.
(C) The store is holding a sales promotion.

promote v. 승진시키다 district n. 지역, 구역 turn down 거절하다 position n. 직책

해설 Lisa Stanly가 지역 관리자로 승진됐어요, 그렇지 않나요?
(A) 일곱 개의 지점이 있어요.
(B) 사실, 그녀는 그 직책을 거절했어요.
(C) 그 가게는 판매 촉진 행사를 열어요.

해설 (A) [x] 질문의 district manager(지역 관리자)와 관련 있는 branches(지점)를 사용하여 혼동을 준 오답이다.
(B) [o] 사실 그녀가 그 직책을 거절했다는 말로, Lisa Stanly가 지역 관리자로 승진하지 않았음을 간접적으로 전달했으므로 정답이다.
(C) [x] promoted – promotion의 유사 발음 어휘를 사용하여 혼동을 준 오답이다.

13 부가 의문문 영국 → 캐나다

Members get a 20 percent discount on their first purchase, right?
(A) That is no longer our policy.
(B) Almost 25 staff members.
(C) Yes, I'm working full-time.

purchase n. 구매 policy n. 정책

해설 회원들은 첫 구매에 20퍼센트 할인을 받아요, 그렇죠?
(A) 그것은 더 이상 우리의 정책이 아니에요.
(B) 거의 25명의 직원들이요.
(C) 네, 저는 전일제로 일하고 있어요.

해설 (A) [o] 그것은 더 이상 우리의 정책이 아니라는 말로, 회원들이 첫 구매에 20퍼센트 할인을 받지 않는다는 것을 간접적으로 전달했으므로 정답이다.
(B) [x] 질문의 members를 반복 사용하여 혼동을 준 오답이다.
(C) [x] 회원들이 첫 구매에 20퍼센트 할인을 받는지를 물었는데, 이와 관련이 없는 자신은 전일제로 일하고 있다고 응답했으므로 오답이다. Yes까지만 듣고 정답으로 고르지 않도록 주의한다.

14 선택 의문문
호주 → 영국

Will our client arrive at the airport on Wednesday or Thursday?
(A) Usually from London.
(B) She's flying on a different airline.
(C) Let me check her itinerary.

arrive v. 도착하다   itinerary n. 여행 일정

해설 우리 고객이 수요일에 공항에 도착할 건가요, 아니면 목요일에 도착할 건가요?
(A) 보통 런던으로부터요.
(B) 그녀는 다른 항공사를 이용할 거예요.
(C) 제가 그녀의 여행 일정을 확인할게요.

해설 (A) [x] 질문의 arrive(도착하다)에서 연상할 수 있는 from London(런던으로부터요)을 사용하여 혼동을 준 오답이다.
(B) [x] 질문의 airport(공항)와 관련 있는 airline(항공사)을 사용하여 혼동을 준 오답이다.
(C) [o] 그녀의 여행 일정을 확인할 것이라는 말로, 고객이 공항에 수요일에 도착할지, 아니면 목요일에 도착할지 모른다는 것을 간접적으로 전달했으므로 정답이다.

15 선택 의문문
캐나다 → 호주

Are you still searching for a gym, or have you found one you like?
(A) Both options sound great to me.
(B) That fitness equipment is expensive.
(C) Unfortunately, I'm still looking.

search for ~을 찾다   equipment n. 장비

해설 당신은 아직 체육관을 찾고 있나요, 아니면 마음에 드는 곳을 찾았나요?
(A) 두 가지 선택안 모두 저에게는 좋게 들려요.
(B) 그 운동 장비는 비싸요.
(C) 안타깝게도, 여전히 찾는 중이에요.

해설 (A) [x] 체육관을 찾고 있는지, 아니면 마음에 드는 곳을 찾았는지를 물었는데, 이와 관련이 없는 두 가지 선택안 모두 좋게 들린다고 응답했으므로 오답이다.
(B) [x] 질문의 gym(체육관)과 관련 있는 fitness equipment(운동 장비)를 사용하여 혼동을 준 오답이다.
(C) [o] 안타깝게도 여전히 찾는 중이라는 말로, 마음에 드는 체육관을 아직 찾고 있음을 선택했으므로 정답이다.

16 부가 의문문
영국 → 호주

This isn't the same route we took last time, is it?
(A) I don't think we've ever met.
(B) It doesn't seem familiar.
(C) Tyler took care of that.

route n. 경로   familiar adj. 익숙한   take care of ~을 처리하다

해설 이곳은 지난번에 우리가 갔던 동일한 경로가 아니에요, 그렇죠?
(A) 우리가 전에 만났다고 생각하지 않아요.
(B) 익숙하지 않은 것 같아요.
(C) Tyler가 그것을 처리했어요.

해설 (A) [x] 지난번에 갔던 동일한 경로가 아닌지 물었는데, 이와 관련이 없는 우리는 전에 만났다고 생각하지 않는다고 응답했으므로 오답이다.
(B) [o] 익숙하지 않은 것 같다는 말로, 지난번에 갔던 동일한 경로가 아님을 간접적으로 전달했으므로 정답이다.
(C) [x] 질문의 took을 반복 사용하여 혼동을 준 오답이다.

17 선택 의문문
캐나다 → 영국

Can you carry these boxes to the truck, or are they too heavy?
(A) There's heavy traffic on the highway.
(B) It would be easier with two people.
(C) No, I haven't seen them.

carry v. 운반하다   heavy adj. 무거운   traffic n. 교통

해설 당신은 이 상자들을 트럭까지 운반할 수 있나요, 아니면 그것들이 너무 무거울까요?
(A) 고속도로에 교통량이 많아요.
(B) 두 사람이 하면 더 쉬울 거예요.
(C) 아니요, 저는 그것들을 본 적이 없어요.

해설 (A) [x] 질문의 heavy를 반복 사용하여 혼동을 준 오답이다.
(B) [o] 두 사람이 하면 더 쉬울 거라는 말로, 상자들이 너무 무겁다는 것을 간접적으로 선택했으므로 정답이다.
(C) [x] 선택 의문문에 No로 응답했으므로 오답이다.

18 부가 의문문
미국 → 호주

Mr. Sanchez liked our investment proposal, didn't he?
(A) What did he specifically say?
(B) Let's revise it next week.
(C) A financial company in Berlin.

investment proposal 투자 제안서   specifically adv. 구체적으로
financial adj. 금융의, 재정의

해설 Mr. Sanchez가 우리의 투자 제안서를 좋아했어요, 그렇지 않나요?
(A) 그가 구체적으로 무엇이라고 말했나요?
(B) 그것을 다음 주에 수정합시다.
(C) 베를린에 있는 금융 회사요.

해설 (A) [o] 그가 구체적으로 무엇이라고 말했는지를 되물어, 투자 제안서에 대한 Mr. Sanchez의 반응이 어땠는지 모른다는 것을 간접적으로 전달했으므로 정답이다.
(B) [x] Mr. Sanchez가 투자 제안서를 좋아했는지를 물었는데, 이와 관련이 없는 그것을 수정하자고 응답했으므로 오답이다.
(C) [x] 질문의 investment proposal(투자 제안서)과 관련 있는 financial company(금융 회사)를 사용하여 혼동을 준 오답이다.

19 선택 의문문
영국 → 캐나다

Are you able to work evening or day shifts?
(A) The meeting was in the morning.
(B) I have to be home by 6 P.M.
(C) This Friday.

shift n. (교대) 근무

해설 당신은 야간에 근무가 가능한가요, 아니면 주간 근무가 가능한가요?
(A) 회의가 아침에 있었어요.
(B) 저는 오후 6시까지 집에 가야 돼요.
(C) 이번 주 금요일이요.

해설 (A) [x] 질문의 day shift(주간 근무)에서 연상할 수 있는 morning(아침)을 사용하여 혼동을 준 오답이다.
(B) [o] 자신은 오후 6시까지 집에 가야 된다는 말로, 주간 근무가 가능하다는 것을 간접적으로 선택했으므로 정답이다.
(C) [x] day - Friday의 유사 발음 어휘를 사용하여 혼동을 준 오답이다.

20 부가 의문문   호주 → 캐나다

You're coming to the trade show, aren't you?
(A) I just confirmed my registration.
(B) You should bring your passport.
(C) It was a fair trade.

trade show 무역 박람회   confirm v. 확인하다   fair adj. 공정한, 공평한

해설 당신은 무역 박람회에 올 거예요, 그렇지 않나요?
(A) 방금 제 등록을 확인했어요.
(B) 당신은 여권을 가져와야 돼요.
(C) 공정한 거래였어요.

해설 (A) [o] 방금 자신의 등록을 확인했다는 말로, 무역 박람회에 갈 것임을 간접적으로 전달했으므로 정답이다.
(B) [x] 무역 박람회에 올 것인지를 물었는데, 이와 관련이 없는 여권을 가져와야 된다고 응답했으므로 오답이다.
(C) [x] 질문의 trade를 반복 사용하여 혼동을 준 오답이다.

21 선택 의문문   영국 → 미국

Should we discuss the budget now or in tomorrow's meeting?
(A) Thanks for letting me know.
(B) Let's wait until everyone gets together.
(C) To discuss our newest product.

discuss v. 토론하다   budget n. 예산

해설 예산에 대해 지금 논의할까요, 아니면 내일 회의에서 논의할까요?
(A) 제게 알려주셔서 감사합니다.
(B) 모두 모일 때까지 기다립시다.
(C) 우리의 신제품을 논의하기 위해서요.

해설 (A) [x] 예산에 대해 지금 논의할지, 아니면 내일 회의에서 논의할지를 물었는데, 이와 관련이 없는 알려줘서 감사하다고 응답했으므로 오답이다.
(B) [o] 모두 모일 때까지 기다리자는 말로, 내일 회의에서 논의하는 것을 간접적으로 선택했으므로 정답이다.
(C) [x] 질문의 discuss를 반복 사용하여 혼동을 준 오답이다.

22 부가 의문문   캐나다 → 영국

You haven't booked the hotel yet, have you?
(A) I made the reservation last week.
(B) Every Wednesday.
(C) That was a great book.

reservation n. 예약

해설 그 호텔을 아직 예약하지 않았죠, 그렇죠?
(A) 지난주에 예약했어요.
(B) 매주 수요일이요.
(C) 그건 정말 좋은 책이었어요.

해설 (A) [o] 지난주에 예약했다는 말로, 호텔을 이미 예약했음을 간접적으로 전달했으므로 정답이다.
(B) [x] 호텔을 아직 예약하지 않았는지를 물었는데, 이와 관련이 없는 매주 수요일이라고 응답했으므로 오답이다.

(C) [x] 질문의 book(예약하다)을 '책'이라는 의미의 명사로 반복 사용하여 혼동을 준 오답이다.

23 부가 의문문   미국 → 호주

We've already paid the deposit for the event venue, correct?
(A) The second hall on the left.
(B) A bouquet of flowers.
(C) No. They're still waiting for our payment.

deposit n. 보증금   venue n. 장소, 현장   bouquet n. 꽃다발

해설 우리는 이미 행사장에 보증금을 지불했어요, 그렇죠?
(A) 왼쪽의 두 번째 홀이요.
(B) 꽃다발이요.
(C) 아뇨. 그들은 여전히 우리의 지불을 기다리고 있어요.

해설 (A) [x] 질문의 event venue(행사장)와 관련 있는 hall(홀)을 사용하여 혼동을 준 오답이다.
(B) [x] 질문의 event venue(행사장)에서 연상할 수 있는 장식품에 관련된 bouquet(꽃다발)을 사용하여 혼동을 준 오답이다.
(C) [o] No로 아직 행사장에 보증금을 지불하지 않았음을 전달한 후, 그들이 지불을 기다리고 있다는 부연 설명을 했으므로 정답이다.

24 선택 의문문   캐나다 → 호주

Would you like your item gift-wrapped or just put in a bag?
(A) I'll take it as it is.
(B) Andy might like the present.
(C) To get my backpack.

gift-wrap v. 선물용으로 포장하다   backpack n. 배낭

해설 당신의 물건이 선물용으로 포장되기를 원하시나요, 아니면 그냥 봉투에 넣기를 원하시나요?
(A) 저는 그것을 그대로 가져갈게요.
(B) Andy가 그 선물을 아마 좋아할 거예요.
(C) 제 배낭을 받기 위해서요.

해설 (A) [o] 그대로 가져갈 것이라는 말로, 선물용 포장이나 봉투에 넣는 것 둘 다 간접적으로 선택하지 않은 정답이다.
(B) [x] 질문의 gift-wrapped(선물용으로 포장된)와 관련 있는 present(선물)를 사용하여 혼동을 준 오답이다.
(C) [x] bag - backpack의 유사 발음 어휘를 사용하여 혼동을 준 오답이다.

25 부가 의문문   미국 → 캐나다

The museum closes early on Sundays, doesn't it?
(A) That's too early for me.
(B) Yes, I met him there.
(C) They extended their hours last month.

extend v. 연장하다

해설 박물관은 일요일마다 일찍 문을 닫아요, 그렇지 않나요?
(A) 그건 제게 너무 이른 시간이에요.
(B) 네, 그를 그곳에서 만났어요.
(C) 지난달에 운영 시간을 연장했어요.

해설 (A) [x] 질문의 early를 반복 사용하여 혼동을 준 오답이다.
(B) [x] 질문의 museum(박물관)을 가리킬 때 쓸 수 있는 there(그곳에서)를 사용하여 혼동을 준 오답이다.
(C) [o] 지난달에 운영 시간을 연장했다는 말로, 박물관이 일요일마다 일찍 문을 닫지 않는다는 것을 간접적으로 전달했으므로 정답이다.

26 부가 의문문   호주 → 영국

Ms. Kwon is starting her position here at the dental clinic tomorrow, isn't she?
(A) Press the start button.
(B) A dental appointment.
(C) No, not until next week.

position n. 직책, 자리   appointment n. 예약, 약속

해석 Ms. Kwon은 내일 여기 치과에서 그녀의 직책을 시작할 거예요, 그렇지 않나요?
(A) 시작 버튼을 누르세요.
(B) 치과 진료 예약이요.
(C) 아니요, 다음 주가 되어서요.

해설 (A) [×] 질문의 start를 '시작'이라는 의미의 명사로 반복 사용하여 혼동을 준 오답이다.
(B) [×] 질문의 dental을 반복 사용하여 혼동을 준 오답이다.
(C) [○] No로 Ms. Kwon이 내일 그녀의 직책을 시작하지 않을 것이라고 전달한 후, 다음 주가 되어서라는 부연 설명을 했으므로 정답이다.

27 선택 의문문   캐나다 → 미국

Can you fix the printer, or should we call a technician?
(A) He called me yesterday.
(B) It needs a new part that I don't have.
(C) Some black-and-white copies.

fix v. 수리하다   technician n. 기술자   part n. 부품

해석 당신이 그 프린터를 수리할 수 있나요, 아니면 우리가 기술자를 불러야 할까요?
(A) 그가 어제 제게 전화했어요.
(B) 제가 가지고 있지 않은 새 부품이 필요해요.
(C) 몇 장의 흑백 사본이요.

해설 (A) [×] call - called의 유사 발음 어휘를 사용하여 혼동을 준 오답이다.
(B) [○] 자신이 가지고 있지 않은 새 부품이 필요하다는 말로, 기술자를 부를 것을 간접적으로 선택했으므로 정답이다.
(C) [×] 질문의 printer(프린터)와 관련 있는 copies(사본들)을 사용하여 혼동을 준 오답이다.

28 선택 의문문   미국 → 호주

Have you purchased a new table, or are you still comparing options?
(A) Do you sell gift cards?
(B) I placed the order this morning.
(C) Put it on the table.

compare v. 비교하다   order n. 주문

해석 새 테이블을 구매했나요, 아니면 아직 선택지를 비교하고 있나요?
(A) 상품권을 판매하나요?
(B) 오늘 아침에 주문을 넣었어요.
(C) 그것을 그 테이블 위에 두세요.

해설 (A) [×] 새 테이블을 구매했는지, 아직 선택지를 비교하고 있는지를 물었는데, 이와 관련이 없는 상품권을 판매하냐고 물었으므로 오답이다.
(B) [○] 오늘 아침에 주문을 넣었다는 말로, 새 테이블을 구매했음을 간접적으로 선택했으므로 정답이다.
(C) [×] 질문의 table을 반복 사용하여 혼동을 준 오답이다.

DAY 08 제안/제공/요청 의문문 및 평서문

기출 유형 1 제안/제공/요청 의문문

Example   영국 → 호주   p.52
해석 제품 목록을 당신에게 보내드릴까요?
(A) 어제 그 물건을 반납했어요.
(B) 네, 그렇게 해주면 고맙겠습니다.
(C) 시설 견학이요.

어휘 return v. 반납하다, 돌려주다   appreciate v. 고마워하다, 인정하다
facility n. 시설, 기관

토익실전문제   p.52

01 (A)   02 (B)   03 (B)   04 (C)

01 요청 의문문   캐나다 → 미국

May I see your identification, please?
(A) Here's my driver's license.
(B) Yes, I enjoyed my stay.
(C) Actually, I usually wear a tie.

identification n. 신분증   driver's license 운전 면허증

해석 당신의 신분증을 좀 보여 주시겠어요?
(A) 여기 제 운전 면허증이에요.
(B) 네, 머무는 동안 즐거웠습니다.
(C) 사실, 저는 보통 넥타이를 매요.

해설 (A) [○] 여기 자신의 운전 면허증이라는 말로, 신분증을 보여 달라는 요청을 간접적으로 수락한 정답이다.
(B) [×] 신분증을 보여줄 수 있는지를 물었는데, 이와 관련이 없는 머무는 동안 즐거웠다고 응답했으므로 오답이다. Yes까지만 듣고 정답으로 고르지 않도록 주의한다.
(C) [×] 신분증을 보여줄 수 있는지를 물었는데, 이와 관련이 없는 자신은 보통 넥타이를 맨다고 응답했으므로 오답이다.

02 요청 의문문   미국 → 호주

Would you mind covering my shift this Saturday?
(A) Yes, as soon as possible.
(B) I can do that.
(C) For an updated schedule.

shift n. 교대 근무, 근무 시간대

해석 이번 주 토요일에 제 교대 근무를 맡아줄 수 있나요?
(A) 네, 최대한 빨리요.
(B) 제가 그렇게 할 수 있어요.
(C) 업데이트된 일정을 위해서요.

해설 (A) [×] 이번 주 토요일에 자신의 교대 근무를 맡아줄 수 있는지를 물었는데, 이와 관련이 없는 최대한 빨리라고 응답했으므로 오답이다. Yes까지만 듣고 정답으로 고르지 않도록 주의한다.
(B) [○] 자신이 그렇게 할 수 있다는 말로, 토요일 교대 근무를 맡아 달라는 요청을 수락했으므로 정답이다.
(C) [×] 질문의 shift(교대 근무)에서 연상할 수 있는 schedule(일정)을 사용하여 혼동을 준 오답이다.

03 요청 의문문   호주 → 영국

Could you turn down the music a little bit?
(A) I want to return this laptop computer.

(B) Sorry, I'll lower the volume.
(C) I did well. Thanks for asking.

turn down (소리·온도 등을) 낮추다   lower v. 내리다, 낮추다

해석 음악을 약간 낮춰 주시겠어요?
(A) 이 노트북 컴퓨터를 반품하고 싶어요.
(B) 죄송해요. 볼륨을 내릴게요.
(C) 저는 잘 했어요. 물어봐 주셔서 감사해요.

해설 (A) [x] turn - return의 유사 발음 어휘를 사용하여 혼동을 준 오답이다.
(B) [o] Sorry로 사과한 후 볼륨을 내리겠다는 말로, 음악을 낮춰 달라는 요청을 수락한 정답이다.
(C) [x] 음악을 낮춰 줄 수 있냐고 물었는데, 이와 관련이 없는 자신은 잘 했다며, 물어봐 줘서 고맙다고 응답했으므로 오답이다.

04 제안 의문문   영국 → 미국

Why don't we create an online survey to collect customer feedback?
(A) Some new advertising methods.
(B) More than 50 channels.
(C) That would give us more data than making phone calls.

survey n. 설문조사   method n. 방법   data n. 정보, 자료

해석 고객 피드백을 수집하기 위해 온라인 설문조사를 만드는 게 어떨까요?
(A) 몇 가지 새로운 광고 방법들이요.
(B) 50개가 넘는 채널들이요.
(C) 그렇게 하면 전화 통화를 하는 것보다 더 많은 정보를 얻을 수 있을 거예요.

해설 (A) [x] 고객 피드백을 수집하기 위한 온라인 설문조사를 만드는 게 어떻겠냐고 물었는데, 이와 관련이 없는 몇 가지 새로운 광고 방법들이라고 응답했으므로 오답이다.
(B) [x] 고객 피드백을 수집하기 위한 온라인 설문조사를 만드는 게 어떻겠냐고 물었는데, 이와 관련이 없는 50개가 넘는 채널들이라고 응답했으므로 오답이다.
(C) [o] 전화 통화를 하는 것보다 더 많은 데이터를 얻을 수 있을 거라는 말로, 제안을 간접적으로 수락한 정답이다.

기출 유형 2 평서문

Example 영국 → 호주   p.53

해석 다음 달에 자선 모금 행사를 개최합시다.
(A) 네, 지난달이었어요.
(B) 기꺼이 몇 개를 먹어볼게요.
(C) 좋아요, 몇 가지 아이디어를 생각해볼게요.

어휘 fundraiser n. 모금 행사   come up with ~을 생각해보다, 제시하다

토익실전문제   p.53

| 01 (B) | 02 (C) | 03 (C) | 04 (B) |

01 평서문   캐나다 → 미국

You can join our weekend hiking club.
(A) Patrick is helping me.
(B) That sounds fun.
(C) The weekly weather forecast.

weekly adj. 매주의, 주간의

해석 당신은 저희 주말 등산 클럽에 가입해도 돼요.
(A) Patrick이 저를 돕고 있어요.
(B) 그거 재미있을 것 같네요.
(C) 주간 일기 예보요.

해설 (A) [x] 주말 등산 클럽에 가입해도 된다는 말에, 이와 관련이 없는 Patrick이 자신을 돕고 있다고 응답했으므로 오답이다.
(B) [o] 재미있을 것 같다는 말로, 주말 등산 클럽에 가입해도 된다는 제안을 수락한 정답이다.
(C) [x] weekend - weekly의 유사 발음 어휘를 사용하여 혼동을 준 오답이다.

02 평서문   영국 → 캐나다

Please put the warning sign at the main entrance of the park.
(A) I'm sorry. I'll remove that sign.
(B) To the nearest park from the museum.
(C) I'll do that immediately.

warning sign 경고 표지판   remove v. 치우다, 제거하다
immediately adv. 바로, 즉시

해석 공원 정문에 경고 표지판을 설치해 주세요.
(A) 죄송해요. 그 표지판을 치울게요.
(B) 박물관에서 가장 가까운 공원으로요.
(C) 바로 그렇게 하겠습니다.

해설 (A) [x] 질문의 sign을 반복 사용하여 혼동을 준 오답이다.
(B) [x] 질문의 park를 반복 사용하여 혼동을 준 오답이다.
(C) [o] 바로 그렇게 하겠다는 말로, 공원 정문에 경고 표지판을 설치해 달라는 요청을 수락한 정답이다.

03 평서문   미국 → 호주

I heard the product launch had to be postponed again.
(A) Do you think we should?
(B) This is the latest edition.
(C) The marketing team must still be adjusting something.

launch n. 출시, 개시   postpone v. 연기하다, 미루다
adjust v. 조정하다

해석 제품 출시가 또 연기되어야 했다고 들었어요.
(A) 우리가 해야 된다고 생각하세요?
(B) 이것은 최신판이에요.
(C) 마케팅 팀이 여전히 무언가를 조정하고 있을 거예요.

해설 (A) [x] 제품 출시가 연기되어야 했다고 들었다고 했는데, 이와 관련이 없는 우리가 해야 된다고 생각하냐고 되물었으므로 오답이다.
(B) [x] 질문의 launch(출시)에서 연상할 수 있는 latest edition(최신판)을 사용하여 혼동을 준 오답이다.
(C) [o] 마케팅 팀이 여전히 무언가를 조정하고 있을 것이라는 말로, 제품 출시가 연기되어야 했던 이유를 제공했으므로 정답이다.

04 평서문   호주 → 캐나다

The door to the warehouse is locked.
(A) OK, how about another day?
(B) I think Jamie has the keys.
(C) It's the door at the end of the hallway.

warehouse n. 창고   lock v. 잠그다   hallway n. 복도

해석 창고 문이 잠겼어요.
(A) 그래요, 다른 날은 어떨까요?

(B) Jamie가 열쇠를 가지고 있는 것 같아요.
(C) 그것은 복도 끝에 있는 문이에요.

해설 (A) [x] 창고 문이 잠겼다고 말했는데, 이와 관련이 없는 다른 날은 어떻겠냐고 제안했으므로 오답이다. OK, how about까지만 듣고 정답으로 고르지 않도록 주의한다.
(B) [o] Jamie가 열쇠를 가지고 있는 것 같다는 말로, 창고 문이 잠긴 문제점에 대한 해결책을 제시했으므로 정답이다.
(C) [x] 질문의 door를 반복 사용하여 혼동을 준 오답이다.

HACKERS TEST p.54

01 (C)	02 (B)	03 (C)	04 (A)	05 (A)
06 (B)	07 (A)	08 (A)	09 (B)	10 (A)
11 (C)	12 (B)	13 (C)	14 (C)	15 (C)
16 (C)	17 (A)	18 (C)	19 (C)	20 (A)
21 (A)	22 (C)	23 (B)	24 (C)	25 (A)
26 (A)	27 (B)	28 (A)		

01 제안 의문문 영국 → 호주

Would you like to ride in the front seat of the car?
(A) Cash and credit cards.
(B) Because I'd like to sit by the window.
(C) No. The back is fine.

ride v. 타다, 승차하다 front seat 앞좌석

해설 차의 앞좌석에 타고 싶으신가요?
(A) 현금과 신용카드요.
(B) 저는 창가에 앉고 싶기 때문이에요.
(C) 아니요. 뒤쪽이 좋아요.

해설 (A) [x] car - cards의 유사 발음 어휘를 사용하여 혼동을 준 오답이다.
(B) [x] 차의 앞좌석에 타는 것을 제안하는 의문문에 이유로 응답했으므로 오답이다. seat - sit의 유사 발음 어휘를 사용하여 혼동을 주었다.
(C) [o] No로 제안을 거절한 후, 뒤쪽이 좋다는 말로 제안을 거절한 이유를 제시했으므로 정답이다.

02 평서문 캐나다 → 미국

Let's turn on the air conditioning in the office.
(A) A dimmable light switch.
(B) OK, it's a bit hot in here.
(C) In the conference room at two o'clock.

turn on 켜다 dimmable adj. 흐릿하게 할 수 있는

해설 사무실 안의 에어컨을 켭시다.
(A) 흐릿하게 할 수 있는 전등 스위치요.
(B) 좋아요, 여기 안이 조금 덥네요.
(C) 2시에 회의실에서요.

해설 (A) [x] 질문의 turn on(켜다)과 관련된 switch(스위치)를 사용하여 혼동을 준 오답이다.
(B) [o] OK로 제안을 수락한 후, 여기 안이 조금 덥다는 말로 제안을 수락한 이유를 제시했으므로 정답이다.
(C) [x] 질문의 office(사무실)와 관련 있는 conference room(회의실)을 사용하여 혼동을 준 오답이다.

03 요청 의문문 영국 → 미국

Could you review my résumé before I submit it?
(A) A different applicant.
(B) It will resume shortly.
(C) I'd be happy to do that.

résumé n. 이력서 resume v. 재개되다, 다시 시작하다

해설 제 이력서를 제출하기 전에 검토해 주시겠어요?
(A) 다른 지원자요.
(B) 그것은 곧 재개될 겁니다.
(C) 기꺼이 그렇게 할게요.

해설 (A) [x] 질문의 résumé(이력서)와 관련 있는 applicant(지원자)를 사용하여 혼동을 준 오답이다.
(B) [x] résumé - resume의 유사 발음 어휘를 사용하여 혼동을 준 오답이다.
(C) [o] 기꺼이 그렇게 하겠다는 말로, 이력서를 검토해 달라는 요청을 수락한 정답이다.

04 평서문 캐나다 → 미국

The sculptures in the lobby are quite impressive.
(A) Yes, I noticed them too.
(B) To hang on the wall.
(C) The reception desk in the lobby.

sculpture n. 조각품 quite adv. 꽤, 상당히 impressive adj. 인상적인

해설 로비에 있는 조각품들이 꽤 인상적이에요.
(A) 네, 저도 그것들을 알아챘어요.
(B) 벽에 걸기 위해서요.
(C) 로비의 접수 데스크요.

해설 (A) [o] Yes로 조각품들이 인상적이라는 말에 동의한다는 것을 전달한 후, 자신도 그것들을 알아챘다는 말로 부연 설명을 했으므로 정답이다.
(B) [x] 로비에 있는 조각품들이 꽤 인상적이라고 말했는데, 이와 관련이 없는 벽에 걸기 위해서라고 응답했으므로 오답이다.
(C) [x] 질문의 lobby를 반복 사용하여 혼동을 준 오답이다.

05 제공 의문문 영국 → 캐나다

Do you need me to distribute the handouts?
(A) On each desk, please.
(B) I already collected them yesterday.
(C) She is the first speaker.

distribute v. 나누어 주다, 배부하다 handout n. 유인물 collect v. 수집하다

해설 제가 유인물들을 나누어 줄까요?
(A) 각 책상 위에 부탁드려요.
(B) 제가 어제 이미 그것들을 수집했어요.
(C) 그녀가 첫 번째 연설자예요.

해설 (A) [o] 각 책상 위에 부탁드린다는 말로, 유인물들을 나누어 주겠다는 제공을 간접적으로 수락했으므로 정답이다.
(B) [x] 유인물들을 나누어 줄지를 물었는데, 이와 관련이 없는 자신이 이미 그것들을 수집했다고 응답했으므로 오답이다. 질문의 handouts을 가리킬 때 쓸 수 있는 them(그것들을)을 사용하여 혼동을 주었다.
(C) [x] 질문의 handouts(유인물들)에서 연상할 수 있는 발표와 관련된 speaker(연설자)를 사용하여 혼동을 준 오답이다.

06 평서문 호주 → 캐나다

I think the scanner was not installed properly.
(A) I'll purchase this model.
(B) Let me call the technical support team.
(C) Yes, it is cold outside.

install v. 설치하다 properly adv. 제대로, 적절하게

해석 그 스캐너가 제대로 설치되지 않았던 것 같아요.
(A) 이 모델을 살게요.
(B) 제가 기술 지원팀에 연락할게요.
(C) 네, 밖에 추워요.

해설 (A) [x] 질문의 scanner(스캐너)와 관련 있는 model(모델)을 사용하여 혼동을 준 오답이다.
(B) [o] 기술 지원팀에 연락하겠다는 말로, 스캐너가 제대로 설치되지 않았다는 문제점에 대한 해결책을 제시했으므로 정답이다.
(C) [x] 스캐너가 제대로 설치되지 않았던 것 같다고 말했는데, 이와 관련이 없는 밖에 춥다고 응답했으므로 오답이다. Yes까지만 듣고 정답으로 고르지 않도록 주의한다.

07 평서문 호주 → 영국

You should submit your project outline by next week.
(A) I'm finalizing the details now.
(B) The projector's not working correctly.
(C) Our quarterly goals.

submit v. 제출하다 correctly adv. 제대로, 올바르게 quarterly adj. 분기별의

해석 당신은 다음 주까지 프로젝트 개요를 제출해야 돼요.
(A) 지금 세부 사항을 마무리하고 있어요.
(B) 영사기가 제대로 작동하지 않아요.
(C) 우리의 분기별 목표요.

해설 (A) [o] 지금 세부 사항을 마무리하고 있다는 말로, 다음 주까지 프로젝트 개요를 제출하겠다고 전달했으므로 정답이다.
(B) [x] project - projector의 유사 발음 어휘를 사용하여 혼동을 준 오답이다.
(C) [x] 질문의 project outline(프로젝트 개요)과 관련 있는 quarterly goals(분기별 목표)를 사용하여 혼동을 준 오답이다.

08 제안 의문문 영국 → 호주

How about sharing a taxi downtown with me?
(A) No, thanks. I'm taking the bus.
(B) The fitness club downtown.
(C) OK, you can have some of mine.

share v. 함께 타다, 공유하다 downtown adv. 시내로

해석 저와 시내로 가는 택시를 함께 타는 게 어때요?
(A) 고맙지만 사양할게요. 저는 버스를 탈 거예요.
(B) 시내에 있는 헬스장이요.
(C) 좋아요, 제 것 중 일부를 가지셔도 돼요.

해설 (A) [o] No, thanks로 제안을 거절한 후, 자신은 버스를 탈 것이라는 부연 설명을 했으므로 정답이다.
(B) [x] 질문의 downtown을 반복 사용하여 혼동을 준 오답이다.
(C) [x] 시내로 가는 택시를 함께 타는 게 어떠냐고 물었는데, 이와 관련이 없는 자신의 것 중 일부를 가져도 된다고 응답했으므로 오답이다. OK까지만 듣고 정답으로 고르지 않도록 주의한다.

09 평서문 미국 → 영국

The retirement party for Mr. Lambros is going to take place on June 15.
(A) No, tomorrow is my last day.
(B) Should I bring anything?
(C) Oh, throughout the celebration.

retirement n. 은퇴 bring v. 가져오다 throughout prep. ~동안 쭉, 도처에 celebration n. 기념행사, 축하

해석 Mr. Lambros의 은퇴 파티가 6월 15일에 열릴 예정이에요.
(A) 아니요, 내일이 제 마지막 날이에요.
(B) 제가 무언가 가져가야 할까요?
(C) 아, 기념행사 동안 쭉이요.

해설 (A) [x] 질문의 retirement(은퇴)와 관련 있는 last day(마지막 날)를 사용하여 혼동을 준 오답이다.
(B) [o] 자신이 무언가 가져가야 할지 되물어, 은퇴 파티에 대한 추가 정보를 요구한 정답이다.
(C) [x] 질문의 party(파티)와 관련 있는 celebration(기념행사)을 사용하여 혼동을 준 오답이다.

10 제안 의문문 캐나다 → 호주

Would you like to try these cupcakes that I made?
(A) They look very delicious.
(B) Fifteen dollars.
(C) They are not for sale.

delicious adj. 맛있는 for sale 판매용의

해석 제가 만든 이 컵케이크들을 한번 먹어 볼래요?
(A) 그것들은 아주 맛있어 보여요.
(B) 15달러요.
(C) 그것들은 판매용이 아니에요.

해설 (A) [o] 그것들이 아주 맛있어 보인다는 말로, 컵케이크를 한번 먹어 보라는 제안을 간접적으로 수락한 정답이다.
(B) [x] 컵케이크를 한번 먹어 보겠냐고 제안하는 의문문에 비용으로 응답했으므로 오답이다.
(C) [x] 컵케이크를 한번 먹어 보겠냐고 물었는데, 이와 관련이 없는 판매용이 아니라고 응답했으므로 오답이다. 질문의 these cupcakes를 가리킬 때 쓸 수 있는 They(그것들)를 사용하여 혼동을 주었다.

11 평서문 호주 → 미국

Brentwood Interiors has a great team of designers.
(A) It would look better with another sofa.
(B) Once we make the request.
(C) I've never worked with them.

request n. 요청

해석 Brentwood 인테리어 회사는 훌륭한 디자이너 팀을 가지고 있어요.
(A) 다른 소파와 함께 있으면 더 좋아 보일 거예요.
(B) 일단 우리가 요청을 하면요.
(C) 저는 그들과 한 번도 일해본 적이 없어요.

해설 (A) [x] 질문의 Interiors(인테리어 회사)에서 연상할 수 있는 가구와 관련된 sofa(소파)를 사용하여 혼동을 준 오답이다.
(B) [x] Brentwood 인테리어 회사는 훌륭한 디자이너 팀을 가지고 있다고 말했는데, 이와 관련이 없는 일단 우리가 요청하면이라고 응답했으므로 오답이다.
(C) [o] 자신은 그들과 한 번도 일해본 적이 없다는 말로, Brentwood 인테리어 회사가 훌륭한 디자이너 팀을 가지고 있는지 모른다는 것

을 간접적으로 전달한 정답이다.

12 요청 의문문
🎧 캐나다 → 미국

Could you finish the product inventory by noon?
(A) Why did you finish it so soon?
(B) Sure. I'm almost done.
(C) We process the raw materials.

inventory n. 재고 목록, 재고품 process v. 가공하다, 처리하다
raw material 원자재

해석 제품 재고 목록을 정오까지 완료해 주시겠어요?
   (A) 왜 그렇게 빨리 끝냈어요?
   (B) 물론이죠. 거의 다 했어요.
   (C) 우리는 원자재를 가공해요.

해설 (A) [x] 질문의 finish를 반복 사용하여 혼동을 준 오답이다.
   (B) [o] Sure로 요청을 수락한 후, 거의 다 했다고 부연 설명을 했으므로 정답이다.
   (C) [x] 질문의 product(제품)에서 연상할 수 있는 재료와 관련된 raw materials(원자재)를 사용하여 혼동을 준 오답이다.

13 평서문
🎧 영국 → 호주

Berkshire Steel is one of the country's leading exporters.
(A) It has a great view of the city.
(B) This hallway leads to the parking area.
(C) It is a very successful company.

leading adj. 선두의, 가장 중요한 exporter n. 수출업체 lead to ~로 이어지다

해석 Berkshire 철강회사는 국내 선두 수출업체들 중 하나예요.
   (A) 도시의 멋진 전망을 가지고 있어요.
   (B) 이 복도는 주차장으로 이어져요.
   (C) 그곳은 매우 성공한 회사예요.

해설 (A) [x] Berkshire 철강회사는 국내 선두 수출업체들 중 하나라고 말했는데, 이와 관련이 없는 도시의 멋진 전망을 가지고 있다고 응답했으므로 오답이다.
   (B) [x] leading - leads의 유사 발음 어휘를 사용하여 혼동을 준 오답이다.
   (C) [o] 그곳은 매우 성공한 회사라는 말로, Berkshire 철강회사는 국내 선두 수출업체들 중 하나라는 말에 동의했으므로 정답이다.

14 평서문
🎧 호주 → 영국

The workshop will be held on Wednesday afternoon.
(A) That was very educational.
(B) A copy of the agenda.
(C) What time will it begin?

educational adj. 교육적인 agenda n. (회의의) 의제, 안건

해석 그 워크숍은 수요일 오후에 열릴 거예요.
   (A) 그것은 매우 교육적이었어요.
   (B) 회의 의제의 사본이요.
   (C) 몇 시에 시작할까요?

해설 (A) [x] 질문의 workshop(워크숍)과 관련 있는 educational(교육적인)을 사용하여 혼동을 준 오답이다.
   (B) [x] 워크숍은 수요일 오후에 열릴 것이라고 말했는데, 이와 관련 없는 회의 의제 사본이라고 응답했으므로 오답이다.
   (C) [o] 몇 시에 시작하는지 되물어, 워크숍에 대한 추가 정보를 요구하는 정답이다.

15 평서문
🎧 캐나다 → 영국

Please print the name tags for the attendees.
(A) They are being printed now.
(B) Her name was Natasha.
(C) On a weekly basis.

name tag 이름표 attendee n. 참석자

해석 참석자들을 위한 이름표를 출력해 주세요.
   (A) 그것들은 지금 출력되고 있어요.
   (B) 그녀의 이름은 Natasha였어요.
   (C) 일주일 단위로요.

해설 (A) [o] 지금 출력되고 있다는 말로, 참석자들을 위한 이름표를 출력해 달라는 요청을 간접적으로 수락한 정답이다.
   (B) [x] 질문의 name을 반복 사용하여 혼동을 준 오답이다.
   (C) [x] 참석자들을 위한 이름표를 출력해 달라고 말했는데, 이와 관련이 없는 일주일 단위라고 응답했으므로 오답이다.

16 평서문
🎧 영국 → 미국

The client is waiting in front of the office for a meeting.
(A) Would you like some coffee while you are waiting?
(B) It's a difficult decision.
(C) The manager is on her way.

client n. 고객 manager n. 관리자

해석 고객이 회의를 위해 사무실 앞에서 기다리고 있어요.
   (A) 기다리시는 동안 커피를 드시겠어요?
   (B) 어려운 결정이에요.
   (C) 관리자가 가는 중이에요.

해설 (A) [x] 질문의 waiting을 반복 사용하여 혼동을 준 오답이다.
   (B) [x] 고객이 회의를 위해 사무실 앞에서 기다리고 있다고 말했는데, 이와 관련이 없는 어려운 결정이라고 응답했으므로 오답이다.
   (C) [o] 관리자가 가는 중이라는 말로, 추가 정보를 제공했으므로 정답이다.

17 요청 의문문
🎧 캐나다 → 호주

Could you drop off these packages at the post office?
(A) I'm heading that way after lunch.
(B) They arrived this morning.
(C) The shipping costs are quite high.

head v. 가다, 향하다 shipping cost 배송 비용

해석 이 소포들을 우체국에 가져다 주시겠어요?
   (A) 저는 점심 후에 그쪽으로 갈 거예요.
   (B) 그것들은 오늘 아침에 도착했어요.
   (C) 배송 비용이 꽤 비싸요.

해설 (A) [o] 점심 후에 그쪽으로 갈 거라는 말로, 소포들을 우체국에 가져다 달라는 요청을 간접적으로 수락한 정답이다.
   (B) [x] 소포들을 우체국에 가져다 줄 수 있는지를 물었는데, 이와 관련이 없는 그것들이 오늘 아침에 도착했다고 응답했으므로 오답이다. these packages를 가리킬 때 쓸 수 있는 They(그것들은)를 사용하여 혼동을 주었다.
   (C) [x] 질문의 post office(우체국)에서 연상할 수 있는 배송과 관련된 shipping costs(배송 비용)를 사용하여 혼동을 준 오답이다.

18 제공 의문문
🎧 미국 → 캐나다

Do you want me to help you with packing the tools?
(A) A team of construction workers.

(B) He offered to drive me there.
(C) Thanks. That would be very helpful.

pack v. 포장하다, 꾸리다   tool n. 공구, 도구

해석 당신이 그 공구들을 싸는 것을 제가 돕기를 원하시나요?
(A) 건설 노동자들 한 팀이요.
(B) 그가 저를 그곳까지 태워주겠다고 제안했어요.
(C) 고마워요. 그러면 매우 도움이 될 것 같아요.

해설 (A) [x] 질문의 tools(공구)에서 연상할 수 있는 공사와 관련된 construction workers(건설 노동자들)를 사용하여 혼동을 준 오답이다.
(B) [x] 질문의 help(돕다)와 관련 있는 offered(제안했다)를 사용하여 혼동을 준 오답이다.
(C) [o] Thanks로 고맙다고 전달한 후, 그러면 매우 도움이 될 것 같다는 말로 도움 제공을 수락했으므로 정답이다.

19 평서문 🔊 캐나다 → 영국

The catering company wants to be paid by check.
(A) He works in marketing.
(B) Some guests arrived early.
(C) Mr. Kim takes care of the bills.

catering n. 음식 공급(업)   check n. 수표   bill n. 청구서

해석 그 음식 공급업체는 수표로 지급받기를 원해요.
(A) 그는 마케팅에서 일해요.
(B) 몇몇 손님들은 일찍 도착했어요.
(C) Mr. Kim이 청구서를 담당해요.

해설 (A) [x] 음식 공급업체가 수표로 지급받기를 원한다고 말했는데, 이와 관련이 없는 그는 마케팅에서 일한다고 응답했으므로 오답이다.
(B) [x] 질문의 catering(음식 공급업)에서 연상할 수 있는 guests(손님들)를 사용하여 혼동을 준 오답이다.
(C) [o] Mr. Kim이 청구서를 담당한다는 말로, 수표 지급 관련해서 자신은 모른다는 것을 간접적으로 전달했으므로 정답이다.

20 평서문 🔊 캐나다 → 미국

Including the case, this tablet weighs about 600 grams.
(A) I'm more concerned with the price.
(B) Both computers are expensive.
(C) Just in case I forget.

weigh v. 무게가 ~이다   price n. 가격

해석 케이스를 포함해서 이 태블릿의 무게는 약 600그램이에요.
(A) 저는 가격을 더 신경 써요.
(B) 두 컴퓨터들 모두 비싸요.
(C) 제가 잊어버릴 경우를 위해서요.

해설 (A) [o] 가격에 더 신경 쓴다는 말로, 제품 구매에 대한 추가 정보를 제공했으므로 정답이다.
(B) [x] 질문의 tablet(태블릿)과 관련 있는 computers(컴퓨터들)를 사용하여 혼동을 준 오답이다.
(C) [x] 질문의 case를 '경우'라는 의미의 명사로 반복 사용하여 혼동을 준 오답이다.

21 제안 의문문 🔊 호주 → 영국

Why don't we find a larger rug for our lobby?
(A) Do you have a particular style in mind?
(B) The images are too large.
(C) I'm scheduled for the 15th.

particular adj. 특정한, 특별한

해석 우리 로비를 위한 더 큰 러그를 찾아보는 게 어떨까요?
(A) 특정한 스타일을 생각하고 계시나요?
(B) 이미지들이 너무 커요.
(C) 15일로 일정이 잡혀 있어요.

해설 (A) [o] 특정한 스타일을 생각하고 있는지 되물어, 로비를 위한 더 큰 러그를 찾아보자는 제안을 간접적으로 수락한 정답이다.
(B) [x] larger - large의 유사 발음 어휘를 사용하여 혼동을 준 오답이다.
(C) [x] 로비를 위한 더 큰 러그를 찾아보는 게 어떠냐고 물었는데, 이와 관련이 없는 15일로 일정이 잡혀 있다고 응답했으므로 오답이다.

22 요청 의문문 🔊 미국 → 영국

May I borrow your presentation slides as a reference?
(A) No, he already bought a present.
(B) It's on Page 15.
(C) I'll e-mail them to you right away.

borrow v. 빌리다   reference n. 참고 자료

해석 당신의 발표 슬라이드를 제가 참고 자료로 빌려도 될까요?
(A) 아니요, 그는 이미 선물을 샀어요.
(B) 15페이지에 있어요.
(C) 제가 그것들을 바로 이메일로 보낼게요.

해설 (A) [x] presentation - present의 유사 발음 어휘를 사용하여 혼동을 준 오답이다. No까지만 듣고 정답을 고르지 않도록 주의한다.
(B) [x] 질문의 slides(슬라이드)와 관련 있는 Page(페이지)를 사용하여 혼동을 준 오답이다.
(C) [o] 그것들을 바로 이메일로 보내겠다는 말로, 발표 슬라이드를 참고 자료로 빌려 달라는 요청을 간접적으로 수락한 정답이다.

23 평서문 🔊 호주 → 캐나다

Let's begin planning the company retreat.
(A) No, at the beginning.
(B) I have some time after lunch.
(C) We need two sets of those.

company retreat 회사 야유회

해석 회사 야유회 계획을 짜는 것을 시작합시다.
(A) 아니요, 처음에요.
(B) 저는 점심 이후에 시간이 있어요.
(C) 우리는 그것들의 두 세트가 필요해요.

해설 (A) [x] begin - beginning의 유사 발음 어휘를 사용하여 혼동을 준 오답이다.
(B) [o] 점심 이후에 시간이 있다는 말로, 회사 야유회 계획을 짜는 것을 시작하자는 제안을 간접적으로 수락한 정답이다.
(C) [x] 회사 야유회 계획을 짜는 것을 시작하자고 말했는데, 이와 관련이 없는 그것들의 두 세트가 필요하다고 응답했으므로 오답이다.

24 제공 의문문 🔊 미국 → 캐나다

Would you like me to set up some extra chairs in the conference room?
(A) I have an extra pair in my car.
(B) You should reset your password.
(C) What time will you be able to do that?

set up 준비하다, 설치하다   extra adj. 추가의   reset v. 재설정하다

해설 당신은 회의실에 추가로 의자 몇 개를 제가 준비하기를 원하세요?
(A) 제 차에 추가로 한 쌍이 있어요.
(B) 당신의 비밀번호를 재설정해야 해요.
(C) 당신은 몇 시에 그렇게 할 수 있나요?

해설 (A) [x] 질문의 extra를 반복 사용하여 혼동을 준 오답이다.
(B) [x] set up - reset의 유사 발음 어휘를 사용하여 혼동을 준 오답이다.
(C) [o] 몇 시에 그렇게 할 수 있는지 되물어, 회의실에 추가로 의자 몇 개를 준비해 주겠다는 제공을 간접적으로 수락한 정답이다.

25 평서문   영국 → 호주

Our hotel is planning to employ temporary staff during the peak summer season.
(A) When do you need them to start?
(B) Our seasonal menu.
(C) The hotel increased its room rates last month.

employ v. 채용하다, 고용하다   temporary adj. 임시의, 일시적인
peak season 성수기

해설 우리 호텔은 여름 성수기 동안 임시 직원을 채용할 계획이에요.
(A) 그들은 언제 일을 시작해야 하나요?
(B) 우리의 계절 메뉴요.
(C) 그 호텔은 지난달에 객실 요금을 인상했어요.

해설 (A) [o] 그들이 언제 일을 시작해야 하는지 되물어, 호텔의 여름 성수기 동안의 임시 직원 채용에 대한 추가 정보를 요구한 정답이다.
(B) [x] season - seasonal의 유사 발음 어휘를 사용하여 혼동을 준 오답이다.
(C) [x] 질문의 hotel을 반복 사용하여 혼동을 준 오답이다.

26 요청 의문문   캐나다 → 호주

Would you mind if I use your office for a client call?
(A) Go ahead, I'll be in meetings all afternoon.
(B) The phones were just upgraded.
(C) A corporate e-mail account.

corporate adj. 회사의, 법인의

해설 제가 고객과의 통화를 위해 당신의 사무실을 사용해도 될까요?
(A) 쓰세요, 저는 오후 내내 회의에 있을 거예요.
(B) 전화기들이 방금 업그레이드됐어요.
(C) 회사 이메일 계정이요.

해설 (A) [o] Go ahead로 요청을 수락한 후, 자신은 오후 내내 회의에 있을 거라는 부연 설명을 했으므로 정답이다.
(B) [x] 질문의 call(전화)과 관련 있는 phones(전화기들)를 사용하여 혼동을 준 오답이다.
(C) [x] 질문의 office(사무실)와 관련 있는 corporate(회사의)을 사용하여 혼동을 준 오답이다.

27 평서문   영국 → 미국

The air conditioning units are taking a long time to install.
(A) A new sculpture installation.
(B) They require complex electrical wiring.
(C) The contract has several conditions.

require v. 필요로 하다, 요구하다   complex adj. 복잡한   wiring n. 배선
condition n. 조건, 상태

해설 에어컨 장치들은 설치하는 데 시간이 오래 걸리고 있어요.
(A) 새로운 조각품 설치요.
(B) 그것들은 복잡한 전기 배선을 필요로 해요.
(C) 그 계약은 여러 조건을 가지고 있어요.

해설 (A) [x] install - installation의 유사 발음 어휘를 사용하여 혼동을 준 오답이다.
(B) [o] 복잡한 전기 배선을 필요로 한다는 말로, 에어컨 장치들을 설치하는 데 시간이 오래 걸리는 것에 대한 이유를 제시했으므로 정답이다.
(C) [x] conditioning - conditions의 유사 발음 어휘를 사용하여 혼동을 준 오답이다.

28 요청 의문문   캐나다 → 영국

Could you proofread this training manual, please?
(A) Jin-su is more familiar with it.
(B) No, I'm pretty sure it wasn't.
(C) During the training session.

proofread v. 교정을 보다   familiar adj. 잘 아는, 익숙한

해설 이 교육 매뉴얼을 교정 봐 주실 수 있나요?
(A) Jin-su가 그것을 더 잘 알아요.
(B) 아니요, 그렇지 않았다고 매우 확신해요.
(C) 교육 과정 동안이요.

해설 (A) [o] Jin-su가 그것을 더 잘 안다는 말로, 교육 매뉴얼을 교정 봐 달라는 요청을 간접적으로 거절한 정답이다.
(B) [x] 교육 매뉴얼을 교정 봐 줄 수 있는지 물었는데, 이와 관련이 없는 그렇지 않았다고 확신한다고 응답했으므로 오답이다. No까지만 듣고 정답으로 고르지 않도록 주의한다.
(C) [x] 질문의 training을 반복 사용하여 혼동을 준 오답이다.

PART 3

DAY 09 주제/목적 및 화자/장소 문제

기출 유형 1 주제/목적 문제

Example 🎧 미국 → 캐나다　　　　　　　　　　p.60

해석
01번은 다음 대화에 관한 문제입니다.
여: Ryan, 다음 주 홍보 행사를 위한 물품을 정리하는 것을 끝냈나요?
남: 아직 완료하지 않았어요. 여전히 진열대를 정리하고 인하된 가격표를 부착하고 있어요.
여: 우리는 금요일 이전에 모든 것이 준비되도록 해야 해요. 제가 다른 직원에게 당신을 도우라고 해야겠어요.
남: 그럴 필요 없을 거예요. 제가 늦어도 내일 오후까지 모든 준비를 끝낼 수 있다고 저는 확신하니까요.

어휘　promotional　adj. 홍보의, 판촉의　organize　v. 정리하다, 조직하다
　　　reduced　adj. 인하된, 할인한

01
해석　대화는 주로 무엇에 관한 것인가?
　(A) 개업을 준비하는 것
　(B) 홍보 행사를 준비하는 것
　(C) 가격 견적을 확정하는 것
　(D) 사업장 위치를 선택하는 것

토익실전문제　　　　　　　　　　　　　　　　　p.61

| 01 (B) | 02 (D) | 03 (D) | 04 (C) | 05 (A) |
| 06 (C) | | | | |

[01-03] 🎧 미국 → 호주
Questions 01-03 refer to the following conversation.

W: Alex, ⁰¹did you see that the food critic Janice Walker posted about our restaurant on her social media page?
M: No. I missed that. What did she say?
W: She was happy with the service and atmosphere, and she thought the food was cooked well. ⁰²But she felt there weren't enough appetizer and entrée options. Maybe we should consider adding more to our menu.
M: Hmm . . . She has a point. ⁰³Why don't we have a meeting with our head chef to brainstorm some ideas for new dishes? Before that, I'll check what other restaurants are serving.

critic　n. 평론가　atmosphere　n. 분위기　add　v. 추가하다, 더하다
brainstorm　v. (아이디어를) 구상하다

해석
01-03번은 다음 대화에 관한 문제입니다.
여: Alex, ⁰¹음식 평론가 Janice Walker가 소셜 미디어에 우리 레스토랑에 대해 포스팅한 것을 봤어요?
남: 아뇨, 저는 그것을 못 봤어요. 그녀가 무엇이라고 말했나요?
여: 그녀는 서비스와 분위기에 만족했고, 음식이 잘 조리됐다고 생각했어요.

⁰²하지만 전채와 메인 요리 옵션이 충분하지 않다고 느꼈어요. 아마도 우리 메뉴에 더 많은 것을 추가하는 것을 고려해야 할 것 같아요.
남: 흠... 그녀의 말이 맞아요. ⁰³새로운 요리에 대한 아이디어를 구상하기 위해 우리의 수석 셰프와 회의를 갖는 게 어때요? 그 전에, 제가 다른 레스토랑에서 어떤 메뉴를 제공하는지 확인해 볼게요.

01 주제 문제
해석　화자들은 주로 무엇에 대해 이야기하고 있는가?
　(A) 예약
　(B) 후기
　(C) 개점
　(D) 광고

해설　대화의 주제를 묻는 문제이므로, 대화의 초반을 반드시 듣는다. 여자가 "did you see that the food critic Janice Walker posted about our restaurant on her social media page?"라며 음식 평론가 Janice Walker가 그녀의 소셜 미디어 페이지에 우리 레스토랑에 대해 포스팅한 것을 봤는지 물었고, 그 후기에 관한 내용으로 대화가 이어지고 있다. 따라서 (B)가 정답이다.

02 문제점 문제
해석　무슨 문제가 언급되는가?
　(A) 서비스가 형편없다.
　(B) 분위기가 매력적이지 않다.
　(C) 음식이 너무 익었다.
　(D) 메뉴가 제한되어 있다.

해설　대화에서 부정적인 표현이 언급된 주변을 주의 깊게 듣는다. 여자가 "But she felt there weren't enough appetizer and entrée options."라며 음식 평론가가 전채 요리와 메인 요리 옵션이 충분하지 않다고 했다고 하였다. 따라서 (D)가 정답이다.

어휘　poor　adj. 형편없는　uninviting　adj. 매력 없는, 마음을 끌지 못하는

03 제안 문제
해석　남자는 무엇을 할 것을 제안하는가?
　(A) 식사를 준비하는 것
　(B) 새로운 요리를 맛보는 것
　(C) 온라인 포스팅을 하는 것
　(D) 직원과 만나는 것

해설　남자의 말에서 제안과 관련된 표현이 언급된 다음을 주의 깊게 듣는다. 남자가 "Why don't we have a meeting with our head chef to brainstorm some ideas for new dishes?"라며 새로운 요리에 대한 아이디어를 구상하기 위해 우리의 수석 셰프와 회의를 가질 것을 제안하였다. 따라서 (D)가 정답이다.

어휘　prepare　v. 준비하다

[04-06] 🎧 캐나다 → 영국
Questions 04-06 refer to the following conversation.

M: Welcome to the Grossmont Community Garden.
W: Hello. ⁰⁴I heard that you are looking for volunteers. I'm interested in volunteering.
M: Great! ⁰⁵You need to complete this application form first. It's helpful to know how much gardening experience volunteers have.
W: Sure. Um . . . I have one question, though. Would I have to come on Saturdays or Sundays? ⁰⁶I'm not

available on weekends because of my part-time job.

M: As of right now, we have sufficient people on Saturdays and Sundays. So we'd be glad to have you here during the week.

volunteer n. 자원봉사자; v. 자원봉사하다　application form 지원서, 신청서
sufficient adj. 충분한

해석
04-06번은 다음 대화에 관한 문제입니다.
남: Grossmont 지역사회 정원에 오신 것을 환영합니다.
여: 안녕하세요. 04자원봉사자를 찾고 있다고 들었어요. 저는 자원봉사하는 것에 관심이 있습니다.
남: 좋아요! 05먼저 이 지원서를 작성하셔야 합니다. 자원봉사자들이 얼마나 많은 원예 경험을 가지고 있는지 아는 것이 도움이 됩니다.
여: 알겠습니다. 음... 그런데 한 가지 질문이 있어요. 제가 토요일이나 일요일에 와야 하나요? 06제 파트타임 일 때문에 주말에는 시간이 안 됩니다.
남: 현재로는 토요일과 일요일에 충분한 인원이 있어요. 그래서 주중에 오시면 좋겠습니다.

04 목적 문제
해석 여자가 방문한 목적은 무엇인가?
(A) 식물을 구매하기 위해
(B) 단체 견학의 일정을 잡기 위해
(C) 자원봉사 일자리에 지원하기 위해
(D) 원예 수업을 듣기 위해
해설 목적을 묻는 문제이므로 대화의 초반을 반드시 듣는다. 여자가 "I heard that you are looking for volunteers. I'm interested in volunteering."이라며 자원봉사자를 찾고 있다고 들었다며 자원봉사를 하는 것에 관심이 있다고 하였다. 따라서 (C)가 정답이다.
어휘 purchase v. 구매하다　apply for ~에 지원하다

05 언급 문제
해석 남자는 여자가 먼저 무엇을 해야 한다고 말하는가?
(A) 서류를 작성한다.
(B) 관리자와 이야기한다.
(C) 매뉴얼을 살펴본다.
(D) 신분증을 제시한다.
해설 남자의 말에서 질문의 핵심 어구(woman ~ do first)와 관련된 내용을 주의 깊게 듣는다. 남자가 "You need to complete this application form first."라며 여자에게 먼저 지원서를 작성해야 한다고 하였다. 따라서 (A)가 정답이다.
어휘 fill out ~을 작성하다　go through ~을 살펴보다, 검토하다
present v. 제시하다　identification n. 신분증

[Paraphrasing]
complete ~ application form 지원서를 작성하다 → Fill out a document 서류를 작성한다

06 이유 문제
해석 여자는 왜 주말에 시간이 안 되는가?
(A) 수업을 이끌어야 한다.
(B) 업무상 자주 출장을 간다.
(C) 파트타임 일이 있다.
(D) 워크숍에 참석해야 한다.
해설 여자의 말에서 질문의 핵심 어구(unavailable on weekends)와 관련된 내용을 주의 깊게 듣는다. 여자가 "I'm not available on weekends because of my part-time job."이라며 자신의 파트타임 일 때문에 주말에는 시간이 안 된다고 하였다. 따라서 (C)가 정답이다.
어휘 frequently adv. 자주

기출 유형 2 화자/장소 문제

Example　호주 → 미국　p.62

해석
01번은 다음 대화에 관한 문제입니다.
남: Bella 비스트로에 전화해 주셔서 감사합니다. 오늘 무엇을 도와드릴까요?
여: 저는 오후 7시로 예약하고 싶습니다. 그때 여섯 명이 앉을 수 있는 테이블이 있나요?
남: 확인해 보겠습니다... 7시에 예약이 꽉 찬 것 같아요. 하지만 7시 45분에 그 규모의 그룹을 수용할 수 있을 것 같습니다. 그게 괜찮을까요?
여: 괜찮을 것 같아요. Katherine Miller 이름으로 예약해 주세요.
어휘 appear v. ~인 것 같다　accommodate v. 수용하다

01
해석 남자는 누구인 것 같은가?
(A) 배달원
(B) 뉴스 기자
(C) 여행 가이드
(D) 레스토랑 직원

토익실전문제　p.63

| 01 (C) | 02 (B) | 03 (B) | 04 (A) | 05 (D) |
| 06 (C) | | | | |

[01-03]　캐나다 → 영국
Questions 01-03 refer to the following conversation.

M: 01You've reached the Hotel Flamingo's front desk. How can I help you today?
W: This is Nicole Branson in Room 713. I have an important video conference scheduled in an hour, but 03the Wi-Fi is not working. Whenever I try to use the Internet, there is no signal.
M: 02I apologize for the inconvenience. One of our staff will check on that now.
W: OK. And I need to print some documents for the meeting. 03Could you tell me where the printer is?
M: It is right next to the front desk on the first floor. If you need any assistance with printing, please feel free to ask us.

apologize v. 사과하다　inconvenience n. 불편　right adv. 바로
assistance n. 도움

해석
01-03번은 다음 대화에 관한 문제입니다.
남: 01Hotel Flamingo의 프론트 데스크입니다. 오늘 어떻게 도와드릴까요?
여: 저는 713호실의 Nicole Branson입니다. 한 시간 후에 중요한 화상 회의가 예정되어 있는데, 02와이파이가 작동하지 않아요. 제가 인터넷을 사용하려고 할 때마다 신호가 없어요.
남: 02불편을 드려 죄송합니다. 저희 직원 중 한 명이 지금 그것을 확인할 거예요.
여: 알겠어요. 그리고 제가 회의를 위해 몇 가지 문서를 인쇄해야 돼요. 03프린터가 어디 있는지 알려주실 수 있나요?
남: 1층 프론트 데스크 바로 옆에 있습니다. 인쇄하는 데 도움이 필요하시면 언제든지 저희에게 문의해 주세요.

01 화자 문제
해석 남자는 누구인 것 같은가?
(A) 기술자
(B) 판매원
(C) 접수원
(D) 건축가

해설 대화에서 신분 및 직업과 관련된 표현을 놓치지 않고 듣는다. 대화의 초반에서 남자가 "You've reached the Hotel Flamingo's front desk. How can I help you today?"라며 호텔 프론트 데스크라고 밝히고 어떻게 도와줄지 물었다. 따라서 (C)가 정답이다.

02 이유 문제
해석 남자는 왜 사과하는가?
(A) 회의가 지연되었다.
(B) 서비스를 이용할 수 없다.
(C) 도구가 잘못 놓여 있다.
(D) 잘못된 정보가 공유되었다.

해설 질문의 핵심 어구(apologize)와 관련된 내용을 주의 깊게 듣는다. 여자가 "the Wi-Fi is not working. Whenever I try to use the Internet, there is no signal."이라며 와이파이가 작동하지 않는다고 말하자, 남자가 "I apologize for the inconvenience."라며 불편을 드려 죄송하다고 하였다. 따라서 (B)가 정답이다.

어휘 misplace v. 제자리에 두지 않다   share v. 공유하다

Paraphrasing
the Wi-Fi is not working 와이파이가 작동하지 않는다 → A service is unavailable. 서비스를 이용할 수 없다.

03 특정 세부 사항 문제
해석 여자는 무엇에 대해 물어보는가?
(A) 할인된 가격
(B) 기기의 위치
(C) 식사 옵션
(D) 운영 시간

해설 여자의 말을 주의 깊게 듣는다. 여자가 "Could you tell me where the printer is?"라며 프린터가 어디 있는지 알려달라고 하였다. 따라서 (B)가 정답이다.

어휘 location n. 위치   meal n. 식사   operate v. 운영하다

Paraphrasing
where the printer is 프린터가 어디 있는지 → A device's location 기기의 위치

[04-06] 🇺🇸 → 🇬🇧 → 🇦🇺

Questions 04-06 refer to the following conversation with three speakers.

W1: Excuse me. ⁰⁴**When does the next bus to Lewisville depart?**

W2: ⁰⁴**I'm sorry, but there are no more tonight.** You'll have to wait for the one that leaves tomorrow at 6 A.M.

M: Oh, no. We should have checked the schedule beforehand.

W1: Yeah. We came here to represent our company at a trade show and just assumed we could catch a bus home once it was over. I guess we'll have to stay at a hotel.

W2: Well, ⁰⁵**I recommend the Belmont Inn. Its rooms are reasonably priced.** There's a brochure for it on the rack over there.

W1: I guess that's our best option.

M: Yeah. ⁰⁶**I'll call there now and book a couple of rooms.**

beforehand adv. 사전에, 미리   represent v. 대표하다
reasonably adv. 합리적으로

해석
04-06번은 다음 세 명의 대화에 관한 문제입니다.
여1: 실례합니다. ⁰⁴루이스빌로 가는 다음 버스는 언제 출발하나요?
여2: ⁰⁴죄송하지만 오늘 밤에는 더 이상 없습니다. 내일 오전 6시에 출발하는 버스를 기다리셔야 합니다.
남: 아, 이런. 우리가 미리 일정을 확인했어야 했어요.
여1: 네. 저희는 무역 박람회에서 회사를 대표하기 위해 여기 왔는데, 박람회가 끝나면 집으로 가는 버스를 잡을 수 있을 거라고 생각했어요. 우리가 호텔에서 묵어야 할 것 같네요.
여2: 음, ⁰⁵Belmont 호텔을 추천합니다. 그곳의 객실 가격이 합리적이에요. 저쪽 선반에 브로셔가 있습니다.
여1: 그게 우리의 최선의 선택인 것 같아요.
남: 네. ⁰⁶제가 지금 거기에 전화해서 방을 몇 개 예약할게요.

04 장소 문제
해석 대화는 어디에서 일어나고 있는 것 같은가?
(A) 버스 터미널에서
(B) 기차역에서
(C) 공항에서
(D) 택시 승강장에서

해설 대화에서 장소와 관련된 표현을 놓치지 않고 듣는다. 여자1이 "When does the next bus to Lewisville depart?"라며 루이스빌로 가는 다음 버스는 언제 출발하는지 묻자, 여자2가 "I'm sorry, but there are no more tonight."이라며 오늘 밤에는 더 이상 없다고 한 것을 통해, 대화가 버스 터미널에서 일어나고 있음을 알 수 있다. 따라서 (A)가 정답이다.

05 언급 문제
해석 Belmont 호텔에 대해 무엇이 언급되는가?
(A) 객실들을 개조했다.
(B) 무역 박람회를 개최할 것이다.
(C) 최근에 문을 열었다.
(D) 감당할 수 있는 가격이다.

해설 질문의 핵심 어구(Belmont Inn)가 언급된 주변을 주의 깊게 듣는다. 여자2가 "I recommend the Belmont Inn. Its rooms are reasonably priced."라며 Belmont 호텔을 추천한다며, 그곳의 객실 가격이 합리적이라고 하였다. 따라서 (D)가 정답이다.

어휘 affordable adj. 감당할 수 있는, 가격이 알맞은

06 다음에 할 일 문제
해석 남자는 다음에 무엇을 할 것인가?
(A) 환불을 요청한다.
(B) 행사에 참석한다.
(C) 예약을 한다.
(D) 티켓을 산다.

해설 남자의 말에서 질문의 핵심 어구(do next)와 관련된 내용을 주의 깊게 듣는다. 남자가 "I'll call there now and book a couple of rooms."라며 지금 호텔에 전화해서 방을 몇 개 예약하겠다고 하였다. 따라서 (C)가 정답이다.

Paraphrasing
book ~ rooms 방을 예약하다 → Make a reservation 예약을 한다

HACKERS TEST

p.64

01 (C)	02 (C)	03 (D)	04 (C)	05 (B)
06 (B)	07 (A)	08 (D)	09 (C)	10 (D)
11 (B)	12 (D)	13 (A)	14 (B)	15 (B)
16 (C)	17 (D)	18 (B)	19 (C)	20 (C)
21 (D)	22 (B)	23 (C)	24 (A)	

[01-03] 캐나다 → 미국

Questions 01-03 refer to the following conversation.

M: ⁰¹Diana, are the preparations for the awards ceremony going well?
W: ⁰¹Yes. I've selected the venue and made the reservation. Now we just need to send out the invitations. ⁰²How many invitations exactly do we need to print?
M: Uh, we'll need 85 invitations in total. Could you print them and put them on my desk? ⁰³I'm heading out for an important client meeting later this afternoon, so I'll send them out tomorrow morning.
W: No problem.

preparation n. 준비, 대비   select v. 선정하다   send out ~을 발송하다
invitation n. 초대장   exactly adv. 정확히

해석
01-03번은 다음 대화에 관한 문제입니다.

남: ⁰¹Diana, 시상식 준비는 잘 되어가고 있나요?
여: ⁰¹네. 장소를 선정하고 예약을 했어요. 이제 초대장을 발송하기만 하면 돼요. ⁰²정확히 몇 장의 초대장을 인쇄해야 하나요?
남: 아, 총 85장의 초대장이 필요할 거예요. 그것들을 인쇄해서 제 책상에 놓아주시겠어요? ⁰³저는 오늘 오후에 중요한 고객 미팅에 가야 해서, 내일 아침에 그것들을 발송할게요.
여: 알겠습니다.

01 주제 문제
해석 화자들은 주로 무엇에 대해 이야기하고 있는가?
(A) 여행 일정표
(B) 교육 프로그램
(C) 행사 준비
(D) 수상자들

해설 대화의 주제를 묻는 문제이므로, 대화의 초반을 반드시 듣는다. 남자가 "Diana, are the preparations for the awards ceremony going well?"이라며 시상식 준비가 잘 되어가는지 물었고, 여자가 "Yes. I've selected the venue and made the reservation."이라며 장소를 선정하고 예약했다고 하였다. 따라서 (C)가 정답이다.

어휘 recipient n. 수상자, 받는 사람

02 특정 세부 사항 문제
해석 여자는 무엇에 대해 묻는가?
(A) 제품 가격이 얼마인지
(B) 회의가 어디에서 열릴 것인지
(C) 얼마나 많은 초대장들이 인쇄되어야 하는지
(D) 관리자가 참석할 것인지

해설 대화에서 여자의 말을 주의 깊게 듣는다. 여자가 "How many invitations exactly do we need to print?"라며 정확히 몇 장의 초대장을 인쇄해야 하는지 물었다. 따라서 (C)가 정답이다.

어휘 cost v. (값, 비용이) ~이다

03 언급 문제
해석 남자는 오늘 오후에 무엇을 할 것이라고 말하는가?
(A) 보고서 초안을 작성한다.
(B) 몇몇 동료들에게 연락한다.
(C) 공지를 한다.
(D) 회의에 참석한다.

해설 남자의 말에서 질문의 핵심 어구(this afternoon)가 언급된 주변을 주의 깊게 듣는다. 남자가 "I'm heading out for an important client meeting later this afternoon"이라며 오늘 오후에 중요한 고객 미팅에 갈 것이라고 하였다. 따라서 (D)가 정답이다.

어휘 draft v. 초안을 작성하다   coworker n. 동료

[04-06] 영국 → 캐나다

Questions 04-06 refer to the following conversation.

W: This is Rainbow Carpets. How can I help you today?
M: Hello. ⁰⁴I'm planning to replace the carpet in my living room. So I'd like to arrange for someone from your company to visit my home later this week to discuss this.
W: Of course. What are you looking to replace it with?
M: I want something that is sturdy and won't wear out quickly.
W: ⁰⁵We only sell carpets that last for a long time. Why don't I visit your home on Saturday at around 2 P.M.?
M: Could you come on Thursday afternoon instead? ⁰⁶I'll be traveling to Portland this weekend to attend my cousin's wedding.
W: Hmm . . . Let me check my schedule.

replace v. 교체하다   sturdy adj. 튼튼한, 견고한   wear out 닳다
last v. 지속되다   attend v. 참석하다

해석
04-06번은 다음 대화에 관한 문제입니다.

여: 여기는 Rainbow Carpets입니다. 오늘 어떻게 도와드릴까요?
남: 안녕하세요. ⁰⁴저는 제 거실의 카펫을 교체하려고 계획하고 있어요. 그래서 이번 주 후반에 당신의 회사에서 누군가 저의 집에 와서 이에 대해 논의할 일정을 잡고 싶어요.
여: 물론이죠. 어떤 것으로 교체하길 원하시나요?
남: 튼튼하고 빨리 닳지 않는 것으로 원합니다.
여: ⁰⁵저희는 오래 지속되는 카펫만 판매합니다. 토요일 오후 2시경에 제가 댁으로 방문하는 것은 어떨까요?
남: 대신 목요일 오후에 오실 수 있을까요? ⁰⁶저는 사촌의 결혼식에 참석하기 위해 이번 주말에 포틀랜드에 갈 거예요.
여: 음... 제 일정을 확인해 보겠습니다.

04 목적 문제
해석 남자는 왜 전화하고 있는가?
(A) 주문을 취소하기 위해
(B) 회원권을 구매하기 위해
(C) 예약을 하기 위해
(D) 위치에 대해 묻기 위해

해설 전화의 목적을 묻는 문제이므로, 대화의 초반을 반드시 듣는다. 남자가 여자에게 "I'm planning to replace the carpet in my living room. So I'd like to arrange for someone from your company to visit my home later this week to discuss this."라며 거실의 카펫을 교체하려고 계획하고 있다며, 여자의 회사에서 누군가 남자의 집에 와서 이에 대해 논의할 일정을 잡고 싶다고 하였다. 따라서 (C)가 정답이다.

어휘 shipment n. 배송

05 언급 문제

해석 여자는 자신의 사업체에 대해 무엇이라고 말하는가?
(A) 최근에 개업했다.
(B) 내구성 있는 상품을 제공한다.
(C) 전국적으로 몇 개의 지점이 있다.
(D) 편리한 위치에 있다.

해설 여자의 말에서 질문의 핵심 어구(business)와 관련된 내용을 주의 깊게 듣는다. 여자가 "We only sell carpets that last for a long time."이라며 오래 지속되는 카펫만 판매한다고 했으므로 여자의 사업체는 내구성 있는 상품을 제공한다는 것을 알 수 있다. 따라서 (B)가 정답이다.

어휘 durable adj. 내구성 있는 nationwide adv. 전국적으로

Paraphrasing
last for a long time 오래 지속되다 → durable 내구성 있는

06 이유 문제

해석 남자는 왜 주말에 교외로 나갈 것인가?
(A) 비즈니스 박람회가 열릴 것이다.
(B) 사적인 행사가 예정되어 있다.
(C) 문화 축제가 열릴 것이다.
(D) 회사 워크숍이 계획되어 있다.

해설 남자의 말에서 질문의 핵심 어구(out of town on the weekend)와 관련된 내용을 주의 깊게 듣는다. 남자가 "I'll be traveling to Portland this weekend to attend my cousin's wedding."이라며 주말에 사촌의 결혼식이 있어서 포틀랜드로 갈 것이라고 하였다. 따라서 (B)가 정답이다.

어휘 exposition n. 박람회

Paraphrasing
cousin's wedding 사촌의 결혼식 → a private event 사적인 행사

[07-09] 호주 → 영국
Questions 07-09 refer to the following conversation.

M: This is Peter Romanov from ProTek Incorporated calling. ⁰⁷I'm following up on the e-mail I sent yesterday about installing the alarm system at your company.
W: Hello, Mr. Romanov. I was just looking through your estimate. Unfortunately, ⁰⁸the total cost of the installation will be higher than what we budgeted.
M: ⁰⁸Could we meet to discuss this in person? I'm sure we can come to an arrangement.
W: Well, I'm going to be away on a business trip for the next few days. But ⁰⁹my colleague, Mindy Davis, will be available to talk with you. Why don't you call her directly to set up a time?
M: Of course. ⁰⁹Please let me know her phone number.

alarm n. 경보(음)   estimate n. 견적(서)   budget v. 예산을 세우다
in person 직접

해석
07-09번은 다음 대화에 관한 문제입니다.

남: 저는 ProTek 사의 Peter Romanov입니다. ⁰⁷귀사에 경보 시스템을 설치하는 것에 관해 어제 보낸 이메일에 대한 후속 조치를 하고자 합니다.
여: 안녕하세요, Mr. Romanov. 저는 방금 귀하의 견적서를 살펴보고 있었어요. 유감스럽게도, ⁰⁸설치 총 비용이 저희가 예산을 세운 것보다 높네요.
남: ⁰⁸직접 만나서 이 문제에 대해 논의할 수 있을까요? 분명히 우리가 합의점을 찾을 수 있을 거예요.
여: 글쎄요, 저는 앞으로 며칠 동안 출장을 가 있을 거예요. 하지만 ⁰⁹제 동료인 Mindy Davis가 귀하와 이야기할 수 있을 거예요. 그녀에게 직접 전화하셔서 시간을 정하는 게 어떨까요?
남: 물론이죠. ⁰⁹그녀의 전화번호를 알려주세요.

07 화자 문제

해석 남자는 어떤 산업에서 일하는 것 같은가?
(A) 보안
(B) 건설
(C) 운송
(D) 교육

해설 대화에서 신분 및 직업과 관련된 표현을 놓치지 않고 듣는다. 남자가 "I'm following up on the e-mail I sent yesterday about installing the alarm system at your company."라며 여자의 회사에 경보 시스템을 설치하는 것에 관해 어제 보낸 이메일에 대한 후속 조치를 하고자 한다는 것을 통해 남자가 보안 업계에서 일한다는 것을 알 수 있다. 따라서 (A)가 정답이다.

08 이유 문제

해석 남자는 왜 여자를 만나고 싶어 하는가?
(A) 채용 공고에 대해 논의하기 위해
(B) 서비스를 설명하기 위해
(C) 계약을 설명하기 위해
(D) 가격을 협상하기 위해

해설 남자의 말에서 질문의 핵심 어구(want to meet with the woman)와 관련된 내용을 주의 깊게 듣는다. 여자가 "the total cost of the installation will be higher than what we budgeted"라며 설치 총 비용이 예산을 세운 것보다 높다고 하자, 남자가 "Could we meet to discuss this in person?"이라며 직접 만나서 이에 대해 논의하자고 하였다. 따라서 (D)가 정답이다.

어휘 describe v. 설명하다, 묘사하다   negotiate v. 협상하다

09 특정 세부 사항 문제

해석 여자는 다음에 어떤 정보를 제공할 것 같은가?
(A) 회사명
(B) 출발 시간
(C) 연락처
(D) 직원들의 이름

해설 대화의 마지막 부분을 주의 깊게 듣는다. 여자가 "my colleague, Mindy Davis, will be available to talk with you. Why don't you call her directly to set up a time?"이라며 동료인 Mindy Davis가 남자와 이야기할 수 있을 거며, 그녀에게 직접 전화해서 시간을 정하는 게 어떠냐고 제안하였다. 이어서 남자가 "Please let me know her phone number."라며 전화번호를 알려 달라고 한 것을 통해 여자는 다음에 Mindy Davis의 전화번호를 제공할 것임을 알 수 있다. 따라서 (C)가 정답이다.

어휘 departure n. 출발

[10-12] 미국 → 캐나다
Questions 10-12 refer to the following conversation.

W: ¹⁰Welcome to the Belleview Training Center. What can I help you with?
M: Hello. ¹⁰I'm interested in taking the software programming course you are offering in June. Can I sign up today?
W: There are still seats available. I can help you with the registration. Is this your first time signing up for classes with us?
M: Yes. My friend recommended this place to me.
W: Great! ¹¹We are offering a 30 percent discount on

the tuition fee for new students until the end of this week. ¹²Could you fill out this registration form? Make sure to provide your contact information and to mark the class you wish to take.

registration n. 등록　sign up for ~에 등록하다　tuition fee 수업료
fill out 작성하다

해석
10-12번은 다음 대화에 관한 문제입니다.
여: ¹⁰Belleview 교육 센터에 오신 것을 환영합니다. 무엇을 도와드릴까요?
남: 안녕하세요. ¹⁰저는 6월에 제공되는 소프트웨어 프로그래밍 과정을 수강하는 데 관심이 있어요. 오늘 등록할 수 있을까요?
여: 아직 자리가 남아있어요. 제가 등록을 도와드릴 수 있습니다. 저희와 수업을 처음 등록하시는 건가요?
남: 네. 제 친구가 이곳을 추천해 주었어요.
여: 좋습니다! ¹¹이번 주 말까지 신규 학생들에게 수업료의 30퍼센트 할인을 제공하고 있어요. ¹²이 등록 양식을 작성해 주시겠어요? 연락처 정보를 제공하시고 수강하고자 하는 수업에 표시하시기 바랍니다.

10 장소 문제
해석 대화는 어디에서 이루어지고 있는가?
(A) 철물점에서
(B) 회계 사무소에서
(C) 식료품점에서
(D) 교육 기관에서
해설 대화에서 장소와 관련된 표현을 놓치지 않고 듣는다. 여자가 "Welcome to the Belleview Training Center."라고 하였고 남자가 "I'm interested in taking the software programming course"라며 소프트웨어 프로그래밍 과정을 수강하는 데 관심이 있다고 하였다. 따라서 (D)가 정답이다.
어휘 institution n. 기관

11 언급 문제
해석 여자는 수수료에 대해 무엇이라고 말하는가?
(A) 일부 경우에는 환불될 수 있다.
(B) 제한된 기간 동안 할인된다.
(C) 한 달에 한 번 지불되어야 한다.
(D) 아주 최근에 도입되었다.
해설 여자의 말에서 질문의 핵심 어구(fee)가 언급된 주변을 주의 깊게 듣는다. 여자가 "We are offering a 30 percent discount on the tuition fee for new students until the end of this week."이라며 이번 주 말까지 신규 학생들에게 수업료의 30퍼센트 할인을 제공한다고 하였다. 따라서 (B)가 정답이다.
어휘 refund v. 환불하다　reduce v. 할인하다, 인하하다

[Paraphrasing]
are offering a 30 percent discount ~ until the end of this week 이번 주 말까지 30퍼센트 할인을 제공하다 → is reduced for a limited period 제한된 기간 동안 할인되다

12 다음에 할 일 문제
해석 남자는 다음에 무엇을 할 것 같은가?
(A) 달력을 확인한다.
(B) 소프트웨어를 설치한다.
(C) 결제를 취소한다.
(D) 서류 작업을 완료한다.
해설 대화의 마지막 부분을 주의 깊게 듣는다. 여자가 "Could you fill out this registration form?"이라며 등록 양식을 작성해달라고 하였다. 따라서 (D)가 정답이다.
어휘 payment n. 결제, 지불　paperwork n. 서류 작업

[13-15] 호주 → 미국 → 영국
Questions 13-15 refer to the following conversation with three speakers.

M: Look at how crowded it is! ¹³This year's charity event definitely has more people attending compared to last year's.
W1: Yeah. ¹⁴Rachel, is this your first time attending this charity event?
W2: Actually, ¹⁴I had the opportunity to attend with my boss last year. The keynote speaker was quite inspiring. He talked about the importance of education for underprivileged children.
M: I remember. That deeply moved me as well. I heard that a different speaker is coming this time.
W1: Yes. ¹⁵But I'm not sure about what topic will be discussed.
M: ¹⁵I'll pick up a brochure to find it out.

charity event 자선 행사　opportunity n. 기회
keynote speaker 기조 연설자　underprivileged adj. 저소득층의

해석
13-15번은 다음 세 명의 대화에 관한 문제입니다.
남: 얼마나 붐비는지 보세요! ¹³올해 자선 행사는 작년과 비교하면 확실히 더 많은 사람들이 참석하고 있네요.
여1: 네. ¹⁴Rachel, 당신은 이번이 이 자선 행사에 처음 참석하는 건가요?
여2: 사실, ¹⁴작년에 제 상사와 함께 참석할 기회가 있었어요. 기조 연설자가 꽤 인상적이었어요. 그는 저소득층 아이들을 위한 교육의 중요성에 대해 이야기했어요.
남: 기억나요. 저도 깊은 감동을 받았어요. 이번에는 다른 연설자가 온다고 들었어요.
여1: 네. ¹⁵하지만 어떤 주제가 논의될지는 잘 모르겠어요.
남: ¹⁵그것을 알아보기 위해 제가 책자를 가져올게요.

13 장소 문제
해석 화자들은 어디에 있는가?
(A) 자선 행사에
(B) 개업식에
(C) 무역 박람회에
(D) 시상식에
해설 대화에서 장소와 관련된 표현을 주의 깊게 듣는다. 남자가 "This year's charity event definitely has more people attending compared to last year's."라며 올해 자선 행사는 작년보다 많은 사람이 참석하고 있다고 하였다. 따라서 (A)가 정답이다.

14 특정 세부 사항 문제
해석 Rachel은 이전 행사에서 무엇이 가장 감동적이었다고 생각했는가?
(A) 영상
(B) 연설
(C) 공연
(D) 시연
해설 Rachel의 말에서 질문의 핵심 어구(inspiring about the previous event)와 관련된 내용을 주의 깊게 듣는다. 여자2[Rachel]가 "I had the opportunity to attend with my boss last year. The keynote speaker was quite inspiring."이라며 작년에 상사와 함께 참석했는데 기조 연설자가 꽤 인상적이었다고 하였다. 따라서 (B)가 정답이다.

15 특정 세부 사항 문제
해석 남자는 책자에서 어떤 정보를 찾고 싶어 하는가?
(A) 발표자의 이름

(B) 연설의 주제
(C) 발표 시간
(D) 행사장의 위치

해설 남자의 말에서 질문의 핵심 어구(find in a brochure)와 관련된 내용을 주의 깊게 듣는다. 여자1이 "But I'm not sure about what topic will be discussed."라며 어떤 주제가 논의될지 잘 모르겠다고 하자, 남자가 "I'll pick up a brochure to find it out."이라며 자신이 그것에 대해 알아보기 위해 책자를 가져오겠다고 하였다. 따라서 (B)가 정답이다.

어휘 presenter n. 발표자   venue n. 행사장, 장소

Paraphrasing
what topic ~ be discussed 어떤 주제가 논의될지 → topic of a talk 연설의 주제

[16-18] 미국 → 호주
Questions 16-18 refer to the following conversation.

W: Hello, Mr. Darbin. **¹⁶I'm a reporter from *The Heston Times*.** Thank you for organizing today's press conference. I'd like to ask you some questions about your firm's business plans.
M: Sure. What would you like to know?
W: **¹⁷You mentioned that your company intends to build a production plant here in Chicago.** I'm wondering how many people your firm plans to hire.
M: Our goal is to employ 200 people from the city. Actually, **¹⁸more details about our plans are outlined in an informational booklet that we created for today. You can find copies on the table near the door.**

firm n. 회사   production n. 제조   employ v. 고용하다
outline v. 개요를 서술하다, 나타내다   informational adj. 정보의

해석
16-18번은 다음 대화에 관한 문제입니다.
여: 안녕하세요, Mr. Darbin. ¹⁶저는 *The Heston Times*지의 기자입니다. 오늘 기자 회견을 열어 주셔서 감사합니다. 저는 귀사의 사업 계획에 대해 몇 가지 질문을 하고 싶어요.
남: 물론이죠. 무엇을 알고 싶으신가요?
여: ¹⁷귀사가 이곳 시카고에 제조 공장을 지으려고 하고 있다고 언급하셨는데요. 귀사에서 몇 명의 직원을 고용할 계획인지 궁금합니다.
남: 저희의 목표는 이 도시에서 200명을 고용하는 것입니다. 사실, ¹⁸저희의 계획에 대한 더 많은 세부 사항은 저희가 오늘을 위해 제작한 정보 안내서에 개요가 서술되어 있어요. 출입문 근처의 탁자에서 몇 부 찾으실 수 있을 거예요.

16 화자 문제
해석 여자는 누구인가?
   (A) 시 공무원
   (B) 상담가
   (C) 기자
   (D) 사업주

해설 대화에서 신분 및 직업과 관련된 표현을 놓치지 않고 듣는다. 여자가 "I'm a reporter from *The Heston Times*."라며 *The Heston Times*지의 기자라고 하였다. 따라서 (C)가 정답이다.

17 특정 세부 사항 문제
해석 여자에 따르면, 시카고에 무엇이 건설될 것인가?
   (A) 쇼핑 단지
   (B) 스포츠 시설
   (C) 지역 문화 회관
   (D) 제조 공장

해설 질문의 핵심 어구(Chicago)가 언급된 주변을 주의 깊게 듣는다. 여자가 "You mentioned that your company intends to build a production plant here in Chicago."라며 남자의 회사가 시카고에 제조 공장을 지으려고 한다고 하였다. 따라서 (D)가 정답이다.

Paraphrasing
production plant 제조 공장 → manufacturing plant 제조 공장

18 특정 세부 사항 문제
해석 탁자에는 무엇이 놓여 있는가?
   (A) 이름표들
   (B) 소책자들
   (C) 신청서들
   (D) 견본 제품들

해설 질문의 핵심 어구(table)가 언급된 주변을 주의 깊게 듣는다. 남자가 "more details ~ are outlined in an informational booklet ~. You can find copies on the table near the door"라며 출입문 근처의 탁자에서 정보 안내서를 몇 부 찾을 수 있을 거라고 하였다. 따라서 (B)가 정답이다.

Paraphrasing
booklet 안내서 → pamphlet 소책자

[19-21] 영국 → 캐나다
Questions 19-21 refer to the following conversation.

W: **¹⁹Welcome to the High Road Diner.** Do you have a reservation?
M: Yes. **¹⁹I booked a table** for six people under the name of Greg Jensen. And I requested the use of your private room.
W: Oh, **²⁰I'm very sorry Mr. Jensen. There was a mix-up, so another party is already using that room.** But we have a table by a window that will be large enough for your group.
M: Really? But I'm having lunch with some important international clients. That's why I requested the private room today.
W: Again, I apologize. **²¹To make up for our mistake, I'll have your waiter bring you a complimentary appetizer.**

book v. 예약하다   request v. 요청하다   international adj. 국제의
make up for ~에 대해 보상하다

해석
19-21번은 다음 대화에 관한 문제입니다.
여: ¹⁹High Road 식당에 오신 것을 환영합니다. 예약이 되어 있으신가요?
남: 네. Greg Jensen이라는 이름으로 6명을 위한 ¹⁹테이블을 예약했어요. 그리고 개인실 사용을 요청했습니다.
여: 아, ²⁰정말 죄송합니다, Mr. Jensen. 혼선이 있어서 다른 손님들이 이미 그 방을 사용 중입니다. 하지만 창가에 있는 테이블이 있는데, 이것이 손님 일행에게 충분히 클 것입니다.
남: 정말요? 하지만 저는 오늘 중요한 국제 고객들과 점심식사를 할 거예요. 그래서 오늘 개인실을 요청했던 겁니다.
여: 다시 한번 사과드립니다. ²¹저희의 실수에 대해 보상해 드리기 위해, 당신의 웨이터가 무료 전채 요리를 가져다 드리도록 하겠습니다.

19 장소 문제
해석 화자들은 어디에 있는 것 같은가?
   (A) 병원에
   (B) 호텔에
   (C) 레스토랑에

(D) 스파에

해설 장소와 관련된 표현을 놓치지 않고 듣는다. 여자가 "Welcome to the High Road Diner."라며 High Road 식당에 오신 것을 환영한다고 했고, 남자가 "I booked a table"이라며 테이블을 예약했다고 한 것을 통해 화자들이 레스토랑에 있음을 알 수 있다. 따라서 (C)가 정답이다.

20 문제점 문제
해석 여자는 무슨 문제를 언급하는가?
(A) 지불이 충분하지 않았다.
(B) 예약이 취소되었다.
(C) 공간이 현재 사용 중이다.
(D) 시설이 충분히 크지 않다.

해설 여자의 말에서 부정적인 표현이 언급된 주변을 주의 깊게 듣는다. 여자가 "I'm very sorry Mr. Jensen. There was a mix-up, so another party is already using that room."이라며 혼선이 있어서 다른 손님들이 이미 남자가 요청한 개인실을 사용 중이라고 하였다. 따라서 (C)가 정답이다.

어휘 sufficient adj. 충분한   in use 사용 중인

21 제안 문제
해석 여자는 무엇을 해주겠다고 제안하는가?
(A) 예약을 변경한다.
(B) 사진을 게시한다.
(C) 부분 환불을 해준다.
(D) 무료 품목을 제공한다.

해설 여자의 말에서 제안과 관련된 표현이 언급된 다음을 주의 깊게 듣는다. 여자가 "To make up for our mistake, I'll have your waiter bring you a complimentary appetizer."라며 실수에 대해 보상해 드리기 위해 웨이터에게 무료 전채 요리를 가져다주게 하겠다고 하였다. 따라서 (D)가 정답이다.

어휘 partial adj. 부분적인

Paraphrasing
complimentary appetizer 무료 전채 요리 → free item 무료 품목

[22-24] 🎧 미국 → 캐나다
Questions 22-24 refer to the following conversation.

W: MobileWave Service Center. How can I help you?
M: Hello. My name is Ken Withers. And [22]**I'm calling about last month's bill. I noticed an error in it.** I signed a three-year contract, not a one-year contract. So I should receive a 10 percent discount, but this was not applied to my bill.
W: Let me check your information . . . It appears that you changed the contract period through our mobile application. [23]**Due to a recent application upgrade, the change was not reflected in your bill.** [24]**I'll e-mail you the revised billing statement.**

bill n. 청구서   apply v. 적용하다   period n. 기간   reflect v. 반영하다

해설
22-24번은 다음 대화에 관한 문제입니다.
여: MobileWave 서비스 센터입니다. 어떻게 도와드릴까요?
남: 안녕하세요. 제 이름은 Ken Withers입니다. 그리고 [22]저는 지난달 청구서에 대해 전화드려요. 제가 그것에서 오류를 발견했거든요. 저는 1년 계약이 아닌 3년 계약에 서명했습니다. 그래서 저는 10퍼센트 할인을 받아야 하는데, 이것이 제 청구서에 적용되지 않았어요.
여: 고객님의 정보를 확인해 보겠습니다... 고객님께서 저희 모바일 애플리케이션을 통해 계약 기간을 변경하신 것으로 보이네요. [23]최근 애플리케이션 업그레이드로 인해 변경 사항이 청구서에 반영되지 않았습니다. [24]수정된 청구 명세서를 이메일로 보내드릴게요.

22 목적 문제
해석 남자는 왜 전화를 하고 있는가?
(A) 배송품을 추적하기 위해
(B) 실수를 바로잡기 위해
(C) 직원에 대해 불평하기 위해
(D) 업무 마감일을 확인하기 위해

해설 전화의 목적을 묻는 문제이므로, 대화의 초반을 반드시 듣는다. 남자가 "I'm calling about last month's bill. I noticed an error in it."이라며 지난달 청구서에 대해 전화했으며, 그 청구서에서 오류를 발견했다고 하였다. 따라서 (B)가 정답이다.

어휘 track v. 추적하다

23 언급 문제
해석 여자는 최근에 무슨 일이 있었다고 말하는가?
(A) 회사 합병이 마무리되었다.
(B) 점검이 수행되었다.
(C) 애플리케이션이 업데이트되었다.
(D) 온라인 주문이 취소되었다.

해설 여자의 말에서 질문의 핵심 어구(recently happened)와 관련된 내용을 주의 깊게 듣는다. 여자가 "Due to a recent application upgrade, the change was not reflected in your bill."이라며 최근 애플리케이션 업그레이드로 인해 변경 사항이 청구서에 반영되지 않았다고 하였다. 따라서 (C)가 정답이다.

어휘 merger n. 합병   conduct v. 수행하다

24 다음에 할 일 문제
해석 여자는 다음에 무엇을 할 것인가?
(A) 문서를 보낸다.
(B) 날짜를 변경한다.
(C) 기계를 확인한다.
(D) 계약을 협상한다.

해설 대화의 마지막 부분을 주의 깊게 듣는다. 여자가 "I'll e-mail you the revised billing statement."라며 수정된 청구 명세서를 이메일로 보내드리겠다고 하였다. 따라서 (A)가 정답이다.

어휘 machinery n. 기계   negotiate v. 협상하다

Paraphrasing
e-mail ~ the revised billing statement 수정된 청구 명세서를 이메일로 보내다 → Send a document 문서를 보낸다

DAY 10 요청/제안/언급 및 문제점 문제

기출 유형 1 요청/제안/언급 문제

Example 🎧 호주 → 영국   p.66
해설
01번은 다음 대화에 관한 문제입니다.
남: 안녕하세요. 저는 며칠 동안 이 리조트에 머물 예정인데, 토요일 활동을 계획하고 싶습니다.
여: 저희 리조트는 바다와 가까워서, 다양한 해양 활동을 제공하고 있어요.
남: 그것도 재미있겠지만, 저는 이곳의 문화와 관련된 활동을 해보고 싶어요.
여: 그렇다면, 이번 주말에 전통 춤 축제가 있어요. 현지인들과 함께 춤을 출 기회가 있을 거예요. 이 축제에 참석해 보시는 게 어떨까요?

어휘 close to ~에 가까운   related to ~과 관련된   local n. 현지인, 주민

01
해석 여자는 무엇을 할 것을 제안하는가?
(A) 시설 투어 예약하기
(B) 보트 타기 일정 잡기
(C) 문화 행사 참석하기
(D) 연극 공연 관람하기

토익실전문제
p.67

01 (C)	02 (D)	03 (A)	04 (B)	05 (C)
06 (C)				

[01-03] 영국 → 호주
Questions 01-03 refer to the following conversation.

W: Paul, ⁰¹did you contact media companies regarding our upcoming product launch?
M: Yes. I called several this morning, and five newspapers plan to send representatives.
W: Great. As you know, I'm preparing a presentation for the event. But the schedule is so tight that I can't do everything myself. ⁰²Could you help me make some slides?
M: Sure thing. I was involved in the last product launch, and our CEO was really impressed with my work. ⁰³I'll come up with some ideas for your presentation and then e-mail them to you tomorrow.

regarding prep. ~에 관하여   representative n. 직원, 대표자
be involved in ~에 참여하다

해석
01-03번은 다음 대화에 관한 문제입니다.
여: Paul, ⁰¹우리의 곧 있을 제품 출시에 관하여 언론사들에 연락했나요?
남: 네, 오늘 아침에 몇 군데 전화했고, 다섯 개의 신문사들이 대표자들을 보낼 계획이에요.
여: 좋아요. 아시다시피, 저는 행사를 위한 발표를 준비하고 있어요. 하지만 일정이 너무 빠듯해서 모든 것을 혼자서 할 수가 없어요. ⁰²슬라이드 몇 개 만드는 것을 도와주실 수 있으세요?
남: 물론이죠. 저는 지난번 제품 출시에 참여했었고, 우리 CEO가 제 작업에 정말 감명받았어요. ⁰³당신의 발표를 위한 몇 가지 아이디어를 생각해 내서 내일 이메일로 보내드릴게요.

01 화자 문제
해석 화자들은 어느 부서에서 일하는 것 같은가?
(A) 디자인
(B) 회계
(C) 홍보
(D) 인사

해설 대화에서 신분 및 직업과 관련된 표현을 놓치지 않고 듣는다. 여자가 "did you contact media companies regarding our upcoming product launch?"라며 곧 있을 제품 출시와 관련하여 언론사들에 연락했냐고 물은 것을 통해 화자들이 홍보 부서에서 일한다는 것을 알 수 있다. 따라서 (C)가 정답이다.

02 요청 문제
해석 여자는 남자에게 무엇을 도와달라고 요청하는가?
(A) 정책을 업데이트하는 것
(B) 신입 직원들을 교육하는 것
(C) 보고서를 편집하는 것
(D) 발표 슬라이드를 만드는 것

해설 여자의 말에서 요청과 관련된 표현이 언급된 다음을 주의 깊게 듣는다. 여자가 "Could you help me make some slides?"라며 슬라이드 몇 개 만드는 것을 도와달라고 요청하였다. 따라서 (D)가 정답이다.
어휘 policy n. 정책   edit v. 편집하다

03 다음에 할 일 문제
해석 남자는 내일 무엇을 할 것인가?
(A) 이메일을 보낸다.
(B) 송장을 가지고 온다.
(C) 서류에 서명한다.
(D) 학회를 위해 출장을 간다.

해설 대화의 마지막 부분을 주의 깊게 듣는다. 남자가 "I'll come up with some ideas for your presentation and then e-mail them to you tomorrow."라며 발표를 위한 아이디어를 생각해 내서 내일 이메일로 보내겠다고 하였다. 따라서 (A)가 정답이다.
어휘 invoice n. 송장

[04-06] 캐나다 → 미국
Questions 04-06 refer to the following conversation.

M: Ms. Choi, ⁰⁴have you finished planning the field trip for your students?
W: Yes. I'm taking them to the Museum of Natural History next Friday.
M: They should enjoy that. ⁰⁵I heard the museum just opened another exhibition hall.
W: Right. I booked a tour with the director of the museum, Mr. Willis. He will take us to areas that are off-limits to the general public.
M: I'd like to do something similar with my students.
W: ⁰⁶Why don't you call Mr. Willis to book a tour?

field trip 현장 학습   director n. 관장, 관리자   general adj. 일반의
off-limits adj. 출입금지의

해석
04-06번은 다음 대화에 관한 문제입니다.
남: Ms. Choi, ⁰⁴학생들을 위한 현장 학습을 계획하는 것을 마치셨나요?
여: 네. 저는 다음 주 금요일에 그들을 자연사 박물관으로 데려갈 예정이에요.
남: 그들이 좋아할 것 같네요. ⁰⁵저는 그 박물관이 또 다른 전시실을 막 열었다고 들었어요.
여: 맞아요. 저는 박물관 관장인 Mr. Willis와 투어를 예약했어요. 그가 일반인들에게는 출입금지인 구역으로 우리를 안내해 줄 거예요.
남: 저도 제 학생들과 비슷한 것을 해보고 싶네요.
여: ⁰⁶Mr. Willis에게 전화해서 투어를 예약하는 게 어때요?

04 주제 문제
해석 화자들은 주로 무엇에 대해 논의하고 있는가?
(A) 새로운 교과서
(B) 현장 학습
(C) 그룹 프로젝트
(D) 대학 정책

해설 대화의 주제를 묻는 문제이므로, 대화의 초반을 반드시 듣는다. 남자가 "have you finished planning the field trip for your students?"라며 학생들을 위한 현장 학습 계획을 마쳤는지 물었고 현장 학습에 대한 내용으로 대화가 이어지고 있다. 따라서 (B)가 정답이다.
어휘 textbook n. 교과서

05 언급 문제
해석 남자는 박물관에 대해 무엇이라고 말하는가?
(A) 여러 미술 수업을 제공한다.

(B) 인근에 있다.
(C) 새로운 시설을 포함한다.
(D) 이전될 것이다.

해설 남자의 말에서 질문의 핵심 어구(the museum)가 언급된 주변을 주의 깊게 듣는다. 남자가 "I heard the museum just opened another exhibition hall."이라며 박물관이 또 다른 전시실을 막 열었다고 들었다고 하였다. 따라서 (C)가 정답이다.

어휘 nearby adv. 인근에, 가까운 곳에

> Paraphrasing
> opened another exhibition hall 또 다른 전시실을 열었다 → includes a new facility 새로운 시설을 포함한다

06 제안 문제
해석 여자는 남자가 무엇을 할 것을 제안하는가?
(A) 자료를 인쇄한다.
(B) 교통편을 마련한다.
(C) 전화를 건다.
(D) 상세한 계획을 제출한다.

해설 여자의 말에서 제안과 관련된 표현이 언급된 다음을 주의 깊게 듣는다. 여자가 "Why don't you call Mr. Willis to book a tour?"라며 Mr. Willis에게 전화해서 투어를 예약하는 게 어떨지 제안하였다. 따라서 (C)가 정답이다.

어휘 submit v. 제출하다

기출 유형 2 문제점 문제

Example 캐나다 → 영국 p.68
해석
01번은 다음 대화에 관한 문제입니다.
남: 안녕하세요. 무엇을 도와드릴까요?
여: 안녕하세요. **저는 한 달 전에 이 스마트폰을 구입했는데, 오늘 아침에 작동을 멈추었어요.** 제가 몇 분 동안 사용하면 계속 꺼집니다. 그래서 이 서비스 센터에 가져왔어요.
남: 흠... 정확히 무엇이 문제인지 파악하는 데 며칠이 필요할 것 같아요. 문제를 파악하면 연락드리겠습니다. 이메일 주소를 남겨주시겠어요?
여: 물론이죠. 제가 적어드릴게요.

어휘 work v. 작동하다 determine v. 알아내다

01
해석 여자는 무슨 문제를 언급하는가?
(A) 기기가 오작동하고 있다.
(B) 웹사이트가 작동하지 않고 있다.
(C) 주차 구역이 문을 닫았다.
(D) 물품이 배송 중에 파손되었다.

토익실전문제
p.69

| 01 (B) | 02 (A) | 03 (B) | 04 (D) | 05 (B) |
| 06 (C) |

[01-03] 호주 → 미국
Questions 01-03 refer to the following conversation.

M: Hello, Ms. Patel? **⁰¹This is Harvey Miller from Hillside Legal Services.** We spoke last week about having your company cater our year-end party.
W: Of course. Have you had a chance to review the contract?
M: Yes. **⁰²But the contract seems to include a mistake.** It states that the party will be on December 22 rather than December 23.
W: My apologies. **⁰³I'll ask my assistant to revise the contract now.**

cater v. 음식을 제공하다 contract n. 계약서 state v. 명시하다
rather than ~ 대신에 assistant n. 비서

해석
01-03번은 다음 대화에 관한 문제입니다.
남: 안녕하세요, Ms. Patel? ⁰¹저는 Hillside 법률 서비스사의 Harvey Miller입니다. 당신의 회사에서 저희의 연말 파티에 음식을 제공하는 것에 관하여 지난주에 이야기했었어요.
여: 그럼요. 계약서를 검토해 보실 기회가 있으셨나요?
남: 네. ⁰²그런데 계약서에 실수가 있는 것 같아요. 계약서에는 파티가 12월 23일 대신에 12월 22일에 있을 것이라고 명시하고 있어요.
여: 죄송합니다. ⁰³제 비서에게 지금 계약서를 수정하라고 할게요.

01 화자 문제
해석 남자는 어디에서 일하는가?
(A) 백화점에서
(B) 법률 사무소에서
(C) 여행사에서
(D) 출판사에서

해설 대화에서 신분 및 직업과 관련된 표현을 놓치지 않고 듣는다. 남자가 "This is Harvey Miller from Hillside Legal Services."라고 하였다. 따라서 (B)가 정답이다.

어휘 publishing n. 출판

02 문제점 문제
해석 남자는 무슨 문제를 언급하는가?
(A) 문서가 오류를 포함하고 있다.
(B) 메시지가 수신되지 않았다.
(C) 행사가 지연되었다.
(D) 비서를 만날 수 없다.

해설 남자의 말에서 부정적인 표현이 언급된 다음을 주의 깊게 듣는다. 남자가 "But the contract seems to include a mistake."라며 계약서에 실수가 있는 것 같다고 하였다. 따라서 (A)가 정답이다.

어휘 include v. 포함하다 receive v. 수신하다, 받다

03 다음에 할 일 문제
해석 여자는 무엇을 할 것이라고 말하는가?
(A) 그녀의 사무실로 돌아간다.
(B) 직원에게 이야기한다.
(C) 보증서를 확인한다.
(D) 예약을 한다.

해설 대화의 마지막 부분을 주의 깊게 듣는다. 여자가 "I'll ask my assistant to revise the contract now."라며 비서에게 계약서를 수정하도록 지금 요청하겠다고 하였다. 따라서 (B)가 정답이다.

어휘 warranty n. 보증서

> Paraphrasing
> ask ~ assistant 비서에게 요청하다 → Speak to an employee 직원에게 이야기한다

[04-06] 영국 → 캐나다
Questions 04-06 refer to the following conversation.

W: I'm a bit worried about Friday. **⁰⁴It looks like we're not going to have enough people working at the water park then.** Since it's a holiday, we're expecting more guests than usual, so we'll need at least two extra lifeguards.

M: ⁰⁵**Doesn't Diana Harris usually take care of staffing issues?**

W: Actually, ⁰⁶**she called in sick today.** So we're going to have to figure something out ourselves.

M: Oh, I see. ⁰⁶**I'll make an announcement quickly to ask if anyone is willing to come in for an extra shift.** Hopefully, someone will be able to help out.

lifeguard n. 인명 구조원   call in sick 병가를 내다
be willing to ~할 의향이 있다   shift n. 근무(시간)

해석
04-06번은 다음 대화에 관한 문제입니다.

여: 저는 금요일이 조금 걱정돼요. ⁰⁴그때 워터파크에서 일할 충분한 사람이 없는 것으로 보여요. 그날이 휴일이기 때문에, 우리는 평소보다 더 많은 손님들을 예상하고 있어요. 그래서 우리는 최소한 두 명의 추가 인명 구조원이 필요할 거예요.

남: ⁰⁵Diana Harris가 보통 직원 문제를 다루지 않나요?

여: 사실, ⁰⁵그녀가 오늘 병가를 냈어요. 그래서 우리 스스로 해결해야 할 거예요.

남: 아, 그렇군요. ⁰⁶제가 추가 근무를 위해 올 의향이 있는 사람이 있는지 물어보기 위해서 얼른 공지를 할게요. 바라건대, 누군가가 도와줄 수 있을 거예요.

04 문제점 문제
해석 여자는 왜 걱정하는가?
(A) 인명 구조원이 훈련에 참석하지 않았다.
(B) 방문객이 부상을 입었다.
(C) 날씨가 좋지 않다.
(D) 시설에 더 많은 직원이 필요할 것이다.

해설 여자의 말에서 부정적인 표현이 언급된 주변을 주의 깊게 듣는다. 여자가 "It looks like we're not going to have enough people working at the water park then."이라며 금요일에 워터파크에서 일할 사람이 충분하지 않을 것 같다고 하였다. 따라서 (D)가 정답이다.

어휘 injure v. 부상을 입다

[Paraphrasing]
not going to have enough people working at the water park 워터파크에서 일할 충분한 사람이 없다 → A facility ~ need more staff 시설에 더 많은 직원이 필요하다

05 언급 문제
해석 Diana Harris에 대해서 무엇이 언급되는가?
(A) 제안에 동의하지 않는다.
(B) 오늘 직장에 있지 않다.
(C) 요청을 이행하지 않을 것이다.
(D) 양식을 작성했다.

해설 질문의 핵심 어구(Diana Harris)가 언급된 주변을 주의 깊게 듣는다. 남자가 "Doesn't Diana Harris usually take care of staffing issues?"라며 Diana Harris가 보통 직원 문제를 다루지 않냐고 묻자, 여자가 "she called in sick today"라며 그녀가 오늘 병가를 냈다고 하였다. 따라서 (B)가 정답이다.

어휘 disagree v. 동의하지 않다   fulfill v. 이행하다

06 이유 문제
해석 남자는 왜 공지를 할 것이라고 말하는가?
(A) 몇몇 직원들을 칭찬하기 위해
(B) 정책을 명백하게 설명하기 위해
(C) 지원자들을 요청하기 위해
(D) 실수를 사과하기 위해

해설 남자의 말에서 질문의 핵심 어구(make an announcement)가 언급된 주변을 주의 깊게 듣는다. 남자가 "I'll make an announcement quickly to ask if anyone is willing to come in for an extra shift."라며 추가 근무를 위해 올 의향이 있는 사람이 있는지 물어보기 위해서 공지를 하겠다고 하였다. 따라서 (C)가 정답이다.

어휘 praise v. 칭찬하다   clarify v. 명백하게 설명하다   volunteer n. 지원자

HACKERS TEST   p.70

01 (B)	02 (D)	03 (A)	04 (D)	05 (A)
06 (B)	07 (C)	08 (B)	09 (D)	10 (C)
11 (A)	12 (C)	13 (B)	14 (B)	15 (D)
16 (C)	17 (C)	18 (C)	19 (B)	20 (A)
21 (C)	22 (B)	23 (D)	24 (B)	

[01-03] 호주 → 미국
Questions 01-03 refer to the following conversation.

M: Good afternoon. This is Joshua Crawford from Sand Designs. ⁰¹**I'm calling about your recent order of company T-shirts. I just want to check that you'd like 30 T-shirts in blue and another 30 in dark green.**

W: Yes, that's right. ⁰²**And please make sure to use our updated logo.** The original order I placed mistakenly included an image of our old logo, but I sent you a follow-up e-mail with the correct one the following day.

M: I'll be sure to do that. ⁰³**We will ship the T-shirts next Monday**, so you will receive them by March 15.

recent adj. 최근의   original adj. 원래의   mistakenly adv. 실수로
following adj. 다음의   ship v. 배송하다

해석
01-03번은 다음 대화에 관한 문제입니다.

남: 안녕하세요. 저는 Sand 디자인사의 Joshua Crawford입니다. ⁰¹고객님의 최근 회사 티셔츠 주문에 관해 전화드렸습니다. 고객님께서 파란색 티셔츠 30장과 진한 녹색 티셔츠 30장을 원하시는지 확인하고 싶어서요.

여: 네, 맞습니다. ⁰²그리고 저희의 업데이트된 로고를 사용해 주세요. 제가 원래 주문했을 때 실수로 저희의 옛 로고 이미지를 포함시켰는데, 다음 날 맞는 것으로 후속 이미지를 보냈어요.

남: 반드시 그렇게 하겠습니다. ⁰³저희가 다음 주 월요일에 티셔츠를 배송할 예정이니, 3월 15일까지 받으실 수 있을 겁니다.

01 목적 문제
해석 남자는 왜 전화하고 있는가?
(A) 약속을 변경하기 위해
(B) 주문을 확인하기 위해
(C) 지불을 요청하기 위해
(D) 환불을 요청하기 위해

해설 전화를 건 목적을 묻는 문제이므로, 대화의 초반을 반드시 듣는다. 남자가 "I'm calling about your recent order of company T-shirts. I just want to check that you'd like 30 T-shirts in blue and another 30 in dark green."이라며 회사 티셔츠 주문에 관해 전화를 걸었고, 파란색 티셔츠 30장과 진한 녹색 티셔츠 30장을 원하는지 확인하고 싶다고 하였다. 따라서 (B)가 정답이다.

어휘 appointment n. 약속   payment n. 지불

02 언급 문제

해석 여자는 회사 로고에 대해 무엇이라고 말하는가?
(A) 웹사이트에 나타날 것이다.
(B) 현재 너무 작다.
(C) 여러 이미지를 포함한다.
(D) 변경되었다.

해설 여자의 말에서 질문의 핵심 어구(company's logo)와 관련된 내용을 주의 깊게 듣는다. 여자가 "And please make sure to use our updated logo."라며 업데이트된 로고를 사용해 달라고 하였으므로 회사 로고가 변경되었음을 알 수 있다. 따라서 (D)가 정답이다.

어휘 appear v. 나타나다, 보이게 되다 currently adv. 현재

Paraphrasing
updated 업데이트된 → changed 변경된

03 다음에 할 일 문제

해석 다음 주 월요일에 무슨 일이 일어날 것인가?
(A) 주문품이 배송될 것이다.
(B) 회의가 열릴 것이다.
(C) 지불이 이루어질 것이다.
(D) 청구서가 발송될 것이다.

해설 질문의 핵심 어구(next Monday)가 언급된 주변을 주의 깊게 듣는다. 남자가 "We will ship the T-shirts next Monday"라며 다음 주 월요일에 티셔츠를 배송할 것이라고 하였다. 따라서 (A)가 정답이다.

어휘 invoice n. 청구서

[04-06] 영국 → 캐나다

Questions 04-06 refer to the following conversation.

W: Excuse me, sir. 04**Are you the owner of the red sedan that was brought in to our shop this morning?**
M: Yes. Have you figured out why it wouldn't start?
W: As it turns out, the battery cables were disconnected. 05**Also, we noticed that the brake pads are old. I strongly encourage you to change them.**
M: How much will everything cost?
W: About 500 dollars. The repairs will take an hour.
M: OK, go ahead with the work. 06**I've written my phone number down on this form.** Please contact me when you are finished.

figure out ~을 알아내다 disconnect v. 끊다 strongly adv. 강력히 encourage v. 권장하다

해석
04-06번은 다음 대화에 관한 문제입니다.

여: 실례합니다, 손님. 04오늘 아침에 저희 정비소에 들어온 붉은색 세단을 소유한 분이신가요?
남: 네. 그것이 왜 시동이 걸리지 않는지 알아내셨나요?
여: 알고 보니, 배터리 선이 끊어져 있었어요. 05또한, 저희는 브레이크 패드가 낡은 것을 알아차렸어요. 저는 그것들을 교체하시기를 강력히 권장합니다.
남: 모두 비용이 얼마가 들까요?
여: 500달러 정도요. 수리는 한 시간 걸릴 거예요.
남: 좋아요, 작업을 진행해 주세요. 06저는 이 양식에 제 전화번호를 작성했어요. 당신이 완료되면 제게 연락해 주세요.

04 화자 문제

해석 여자는 어디에서 일하는 것 같은가?
(A) 주차 시설에서
(B) 대여 업체에서
(C) 차량 대리점에서
(D) 수리점에서

해설 대화에서 신분 및 직업과 관련된 표현을 놓치지 않고 듣는다. 여자가 "Are you the owner of the red sedan that was brought in to our shop this morning?"이라며 여자의 정비소에 들어온 붉은색 세단을 소유한 분인지 물은 것을 통해, 여자가 수리점에서 일하고 있음을 알 수 있다. 따라서 (D)가 정답이다.

어휘 agency n. 업체, 기관 dealership n. 대리점

05 제안 문제

해석 여자는 무엇을 권장하는가?
(A) 일부 부품을 교체하기
(B) 차를 견인시키기
(C) 다른 모델을 선택하기
(D) 몇몇 선택지를 비교하기

해설 여자의 말에서 제안과 관련된 표현이 언급된 다음을 주의 깊게 듣는다. 여자가 "Also, we noticed that the brake pads are old. I strongly encourage you to change them."이라며 브레이크 패드가 낡은 것을 알아차렸기 때문에 그것들을 교체하기를 강력히 권장한다고 하였다. 따라서 (A)가 정답이다.

Paraphrasing
change them[the brake pads] 그것들[브레이크 패드]을 교체하다 → Replacing some parts 일부 부품을 교체하기

06 특정 세부 사항 문제

해석 남자는 양식에 무엇을 작성했는가?
(A) 수령 시간
(B) 전화번호
(C) 이메일 주소
(D) 가격 견적

해설 질문의 핵심 어구(write on a form)와 관련된 내용을 주의 깊게 듣는다. 남자가 "I've written my phone number down on this form."이라며 이 양식에 전화번호를 작성했다고 하였다. 따라서 (B)가 정답이다.

어휘 estimate n. 견적(서)

[07-09] 미국 → 캐나다

Questions 07-09 refer to the following conversation.

W: Do you have a minute, Abed? I'm trying to prepare for my sales presentation this afternoon, 07**but the projector in the second-floor conference room keeps shutting down**. Do you have any idea what's wrong with it?
M: 08**You should ask David in tech support to look at it.** He usually handles these types of issues.
W: But my client will be arriving in about 30 minutes. I'm worried that there won't be enough time to fix it. 09**I'm going to check the schedule for the conference room on the first floor.** Hopefully, it's free.
M: Good idea. And if you need help moving your materials for the presentation, let me know.

prepare for ~을 준비하다 shut down 꺼지다 handle v. 다루다
issue n. 문제 material n. 자료, 재료

해석
07-09번은 다음 대화에 관한 문제입니다.

여: 잠시 시간 있나요, Abed? 오늘 오후에 있을 판매 발표를 준비하고 있는데, 072층 회의실의 프로젝터가 계속 꺼져요. 무엇이 문제인지 알고 계신가요?
남: 08기술 지원 부서의 David에게 그것을 확인해 달라고 요청하세요. 그는

보통 이런 유형의 문제들을 처리해요.
여: 하지만 제 고객이 약 30분 후에 도착할 예정이에요. 그것을 수리할 시간이 충분하지 않을까봐 걱정돼요. ⁰⁹저는 1층 회의실 일정을 확인해 볼게요. 비어있길 바라요.
남: 좋은 생각이에요. 그리고 발표를 위한 자료들을 옮기는 데 도움이 필요하시면 제게 알려주세요.

07 문제점 문제
해석 여자는 무슨 문제를 설명하는가?
(A) 발표가 취소되었다.
(B) 회의실이 사용 중이다.
(C) 장치가 오작동하고 있다.
(D) 요청이 거부되었다.

해설 여자의 말에서 부정적인 표현이 언급된 주변을 주의 깊게 듣는다. 여자가 "but the projector in the second-floor conference room keeps shutting down"이라며 2층 회의실의 프로젝터가 계속 꺼진다고 하였다. 따라서 (C)가 정답이다.

어휘 occupy v. 사용하다, 차지하다

Paraphrasing
projector ~ keeps shutting down 프로젝터가 계속 꺼진다 → A device is malfunctioning. 장치가 오작동하고 있다.

08 제안 문제
해석 남자는 무엇을 할 것을 제안하는가?
(A) 관리자에게 알리기
(B) 동료에게 연락하기
(C) 주문하기
(D) 장소 변경하기

해설 남자의 말에서 제안과 관련된 표현이 언급된 다음을 주의 깊게 듣는다. 남자가 "You should ask David in tech support to look at it."이라며 기술 지원 부서의 David에게 프로젝터를 확인해 달라고 요청하라고 하였다. 따라서 (B)가 정답이다.

어휘 notify v. 알리다

Paraphrasing
ask David in tech support 기술 지원 부서의 David에게 요청하다 → Contacting a coworker 동료에게 연락하기

09 다음에 할 일 문제
해석 여자는 다음에 무엇을 할 것 같은가?
(A) 관리자와 이야기한다.
(B) 자료를 검토한다.
(C) 웹사이트를 업데이트한다.
(D) 일정을 확인한다.

해설 대화의 마지막 부분을 주의 깊게 듣는다. 여자가 "I'm going to check the schedule for the conference room on the first floor"라며 1층 회의실 일정을 확인해 보겠다고 하였다. 따라서 (D)가 정답이다.

어휘 review v. 검토하다

[10-12] 🎧 호주 → 영국
Questions 10-12 refer to the following conversation.

M: ¹⁰**Welcome to Sunset Gardening. What can I do for you today?**
W: I want to decorate the patio behind my house. ¹¹**I saw your shop in an online advertisement and was impressed by the variety of flowers, so I came to take a look.**
M: Great. What kind of flowers are you looking for?
W: I want to create a cheerful atmosphere, so I'd like some bright, colorful flowers.
M: I have several types that might be suitable. ¹²**Could you show me a picture of your patio if you have one?**

decorate v. 장식하다   patio n. 파티오, 테라스   variety n. 품종, 다양성
cheerful adj. 밝은   suitable adj. 적합한

해석
10-12번은 다음 대화에 관한 문제입니다.
남: ¹⁰Sunset 정원 용품점에 오신 것을 환영합니다. 오늘 무엇을 도와드릴까요?
여: 제 집 뒤에 있는 파티오를 장식하고 싶어요. ¹¹온라인 광고에서 당신의 가게를 보았는데 꽃들의 품종이 인상 깊어서 둘러보러 왔어요.
남: 좋습니다. 어떤 종류의 꽃들을 찾고 계신가요?
여: 밝은 분위기를 만들고 싶어서, 밝고 화려한 색상의 꽃들을 원해요.
남: 적합할 것 같은 여러 종류를 보유하고 있습니다. ¹²혹시 파티오 사진이 있으시다면 보여주실 수 있을까요?

10 화자 문제
해석 남자는 어디에서 일하는가?
(A) 가구점에서
(B) 식료품점에서
(C) 정원 용품점에서
(D) 광고 회사에서

해설 대화에서 신분 및 직업과 관련된 표현을 놓치지 않고 듣는다. 남자가 "Welcome to Sunset Gardening. What can I do for you today?"라며 Sunset 정원 용품점에 오신 것을 환영한다며 무엇을 도와줄지를 묻고 있다. 따라서 (C)가 정답이다.

11 특정 세부 사항 문제
해석 여자가 사업체를 방문하게 동기부여한 것은 무엇인가?
(A) 온라인에서 광고를 보았다.
(B) 동료로부터 그것에 대해 들었다.
(C) 이전 구매에 만족했다.
(D) 신문에서 그것에 대해 읽었다.

해설 질문의 핵심 어구(motivated the woman to visit)와 관련된 내용을 주의 깊게 듣는다. 여자가 "I saw your shop in an online advertisement and was impressed by the variety of flowers, so I came to take a look."이라며 온라인 광고에서 남자의 가게를 보았고 꽃들의 품종이 인상 깊어서 둘러보러 왔다고 하였다. 따라서 (A)가 정답이다.

어휘 previous adj. 이전의

12 요청 문제
해석 남자는 여자에게 무엇을 하라고 요청하는가?
(A) 웹사이트를 방문한다.
(B) 추가 용품을 주문한다.
(C) 이미지를 제공한다.
(D) 치수를 잰다.

해설 남자의 말에서 요청과 관련된 표현이 언급된 다음을 주의 깊게 듣는다. 남자가 "Could you show me a picture of your patio if you have one?"이라며 파티오 사진이 있다면 보여달라고 하였다. 따라서 (C)가 정답이다.

Paraphrasing
show ~ a picture 사진을 보여주다 → Provide an image 이미지를 제공한다

[13-15] 🎧 미국 → 호주
Questions 13-15 refer to the following conversation.

W: Mr. Artigas. ¹³**The article you wrote for the last issue of our magazine was great.** I found your descriptions of local historic buildings to be very interesting.

M: Thank you. While writing that article, I learned a lot about architecture.
W: By the way, did you hear that Proto Construction has been selected to renovate the old post office on Elm Street?
M: Yes. I think it's a good choice. ¹⁴That company has successfully remodeled several other old buildings.
W: I plan to include an article about this project in the next issue. ¹⁵Proto Construction is holding a press conference tomorrow morning. Would you be able to attend?
M: Of course.

description n. 묘사 architecture n. 건축 renovate v. 개조하다
remodel v. 리모델링하다, 개조하다 issue n. (잡지의) 호

해석
13-15번은 다음 대화에 관한 문제입니다.

여: Mr. Artigas. ¹³당신이 우리 잡지의 지난 호에 쓴 기사는 훌륭했어요. 저는 지역의 역사적인 건물들에 대한 당신의 묘사가 매우 흥미롭다고 생각했어요.
남: 감사합니다. 그 기사를 쓰는 동안, 저는 건축에 관해 많은 것을 배웠어요.
여: 그런데, Proto 건설사가 Elm가에 있는 오래된 우체국을 개조하도록 선정되었다는 것을 들었어요?
남: 네, 좋은 선택이라고 생각합니다. ¹⁴그 회사는 다른 여러 오래된 건물들을 성공적으로 리모델링해 왔어요.
여: 저는 다음 호에 이 프로젝트에 관한 기사를 포함시킬 계획이에요. ¹⁵Proto 건설사가 내일 아침에 기자 회견을 열어요. 당신이 참석할 수 있을까요?
남: 물론이죠.

13 화자 문제
해석 화자들은 어떤 산업에서 일하는 것 같은가?
(A) 기술
(B) 출판
(C) 영화
(D) 관광

해설 대화에서 신분 및 직업과 관련된 표현을 놓치지 않고 듣는다. 여자가 남자에게 "The article you wrote for the last issue of our magazine were great."이라며 우리 잡지의 지난 호에 쓴 기사들이 훌륭했다고 한 것을 통해 화자들이 출판업에 종사하고 있음을 알 수 있다. 따라서 (B)가 정답이다.

14 언급 문제
해설 남자는 Proto 건설사에 대해 무엇이라고 말하는가?
(A) 명성 있는 상을 받았다.
(B) 많은 건물들을 성공적으로 개조해 왔다.
(C) 수십 년 동안 운영해 왔다.
(D) 해외에 여러 지점들이 있다.

해설 남자의 말에서 질문의 핵심 어구(Proto Construction)가 언급된 주변을 주의 깊게 듣는다. 남자가 "That company[Proto Construction] has successfully remodeled several other old buildings."라며 그 회사가 다른 여러 오래된 건물들을 성공적으로 리모델링해 왔다고 하였다. 따라서 (B)가 정답이다.

어휘 prestigious adj. 명성 있는 decade n. 10년

15 요청 문제
해설 여자는 남자에게 무엇을 하라고 요청하는가?
(A) 인터뷰를 실시한다.
(B) 기사 초안을 제출한다.
(C) 제안서를 다시 작성한다.
(D) 기자 회견에 참석한다.

해설 여자의 말에서 요청과 관련된 표현이 언급된 다음을 주의 깊게 듣는다. 여자가 "Proto Construction is holding a press conference tomorrow morning. Would you be able to attend?"라며 내일 아침에 Proto 건설사가 기자 회견을 열 예정인데 참석할 수 있는지 물었다. 따라서 (D)가 정답이다.

어휘 rewrite v. 다시 작성하다 proposal n. 제안서

[Paraphrasing]
attend 참석하다 → Participate in 참석하다

[16-18] 3# 미국 → 영국 → 호주
Questions 16-18 refer to the following conversation with three speakers.

W1: ¹⁶We're here to discuss your performance evaluation. How was your first three months as a nurse at our hospital?
W2: It was challenging but educational.
M: Your colleagues were very impressed with your caring attitude toward patients, ¹⁷Emily.
W2: That is something that was stressed by ¹⁷the nurse who trained me, Mr. Greer. I was sorry to hear that he will be retiring next month.
W1: Yeah, everyone will miss him. But we are happy to say that you have successfully completed your probationary period.
M: ¹⁸We will talk about your new contract on Monday. I'll send you a copy to review before the meeting.

evaluation n. 평가 caring adj. 배려 깊은 attitude n. 태도
patient n. 환자 train v. 교육하다 probationary period 수습 기간

해석
16-18번은 다음 세 명의 대화에 관한 문제입니다.

여1: ¹⁶우리는 당신의 업무 평가에 대해 논의하기 위해 이 자리에 모였어요. 우리 병원에서 간호사로서의 첫 3개월은 어땠나요?
여2: 도전적이었지만 교육적이었어요.
남: 당신의 동료들은 환자들을 향한 당신의 배려 깊은 태도에 매우 감명받았어요, ¹⁷Emily.
여2: 그것은 ¹⁷저를 교육해 준 간호사인 Patrick Greer가 강조했던 것이에요. 그가 다음 달에 은퇴한다는 소식을 들어서 유감이에요.
여1: 네, 모두가 그를 그리워할 거예요. 하지만 당신이 수습 기간을 성공적으로 마쳤다고 말할 수 있어서 기쁘네요.
남: ¹⁸우리는 월요일에 당신의 새 계약에 대해 이야기할 거예요. 회의 전에 검토할 수 있도록 사본을 보내드리겠습니다.

16 주제 문제
해설 대화는 주로 무엇에 관한 것인가?
(A) 의료 시설 설계
(B) 홍보 계획
(C) 업무 평가
(D) 다가오는 건강 박람회

해설 대화의 주제를 묻는 문제이므로, 대화의 초반을 반드시 듣는다. 여자1이 "We're here to discuss your performance evaluation."이라며 업무 평가에 대해 논의하기 위해 모였다고 말한 후, 평가 내용과 후속 절차에 대한 내용으로 대화가 이어지고 있다. 따라서 (C)가 정답이다.

어휘 initiative n. 계획

17 언급 문제
해설 Emily는 Mr. Greer에 대해 무엇이라고 말하는가?

(A) 최근에 승진했다.
(B) 고급 학위를 취득했다.
(C) 곧 은퇴한다.
(D) 파티를 준비하고 있다.

해설 Emily의 말에서 질문의 핵심 어구(Mr. Greer)가 언급된 주변을 주의 깊게 듣는다. 여자2[Emily]가 "the nurse who trained me, Mr. Greer. I was sorry to hear that he will be retiring next month."라며 본인을 교육해 준 Mr. Greer가 다음 달에 은퇴한다는 소식을 들어서 유감이라고 하였다. 따라서 (C)가 정답이다.

어휘 earn v. 취득하다, 얻다

18 다음에 할 일 문제
해설 화자들은 월요일에 무엇을 할 것 같은가?
(A) 직원들을 교육한다.
(B) 지원서를 검토한다.
(C) 새로운 계약을 협의한다.
(D) 단체 사진을 찍는다.

해설 질문의 핵심 어구(Monday)가 언급된 주변을 주의 깊게 듣는다. 남자가 "We will talk about your new contract on Monday."라며 월요일에 새 계약에 대해 이야기할 것이라고 하였다. 따라서 (C)가 정답이다.

어휘 application n. 지원서

[19-21] 캐나다 → 영국
Questions 19-21 refer to the following conversation.

M: Hello. This is Mark Lu. [19]I got your e-mail saying that there is an issue with my order.
W: Yes. The wood you want for the counter is not supplied domestically at the moment. So we need to order it from overseas. It will take about two weeks for the delivery to arrive at our workshop.
M: My café is scheduled to reopen around that time. Is there another option?
W: [20]Why don't you switch to a locally sourced wood? It is similar to the wood you originally selected.
M: Well . . . [21]I'd like to check a sample before making a decision.
W: Sure. I'll stop by your café to show it to you later this afternoon.

domestically adv. 국내에서   workshop n. 작업장
switch to ~으로 바꾸다, 변경하다   source v. 조달하다, 얻다

해설
19-21번은 다음 대화에 관한 문제입니다.
남: 안녕하세요. 저는 Mark Lu입니다. [19]제 주문에 문제가 있다는 당신의 이메일을 받았어요.
여: 네. 고객님이 원하시는 카운터용 목재가 현재 국내에서 공급되지 않고 있습니다. 그래서 저희가 해외에서 주문해야 돼요. 배송품이 저희 작업장에 도착하는 데 약 2주가 걸릴 거예요.
남: 제 카페가 그 시기쯤 다시 문을 열 예정입니다. 다른 선택지가 있을까요?
여: [20]국내에서 조달되는 목재로 바꾸시는 건 어떨까요? 원래 선택하신 목재와 비슷합니다.
남: 음... [21]결정하기 전에 샘플을 확인해 보고 싶어요.
여: 물론이죠. 오늘 오후 늦게 고객님의 카페에 들러서 보여드리겠습니다.

19 목적 문제
해설 남자는 왜 전화하고 있는가?
(A) 최근 요금에 대해 질문하기 위해
(B) 문제를 논의하기 위해
(C) 집 수리의 일정을 잡기 위해
(D) 우편 주소를 확인하기 위해

해설 전화의 목적을 묻는 문제이므로, 대화의 초반을 반드시 듣는다. 남자가 "I got your e-mail saying that there is an issue with my order."라며 자신의 주문에 문제가 있다는 이메일을 받았다고 말한 것으로 보아 남자는 주문 관련 문제를 논의하기 위해 전화했음을 알 수 있다. 따라서 (B)가 정답이다.

어휘 question v. 질문하다

20 제안 문제
해설 여자는 무엇을 할 것을 제안하는가?
(A) 재료를 교체하기
(B) 로고를 다시 디자인하기
(C) 전문가에게 조언 구하기
(D) 추가 지점을 열기

해설 여자의 말에서 제안과 관련된 표현이 언급된 다음을 주의 깊게 듣는다. 여자가 "Why don't you switch to a locally sourced wood?"라며 국내에서 조달되는 목재로 바꾸는 것이 어떨지 제안하였다. 따라서 (A)가 정답이다.

어휘 substitute v. 교체하다, 대신하다

Paraphrasing
switch to a locally sourced wood 국내에서 조달되는 목재로 바꾸다
→ Substituting a material 재료를 교체하기

21 특정 세부 사항 문제
해설 남자는 무엇을 하기를 원하는가?
(A) 조명 설비를 추가한다.
(B) 공장을 방문한다.
(C) 샘플을 검사한다.
(D) 주문을 취소한다.

해설 질문의 핵심 어구(man want to do)와 관련된 내용을 주의 깊게 듣는다. 남자가 "I'd like to check a sample before making a decision."이라며 결정하기 전에 샘플을 확인해 보고 싶다고 하였다. 따라서 (C)가 정답이다.

어휘 lighting fixture 조명 설비

Paraphrasing
check 확인하다 → Inspect 검사하다

[22-24] 영국 → 호주 → 캐나다
Questions 22-24 refer to the following conversation with three speakers.

W: [22]I went through all of the items in stock this morning. And [23]I noticed that sales of the Ranger remote-controlled car seem very low.
M1: [23]I think it is because of the new robot kits. They are getting more popular as gifts for children.
M2: That's right. The price of the Ranger remote-controlled car is also too high.
W: Since we have a lot of stock piled up, it would be good to dispose of it this quarter. Hmm . . . We should sell the car at a 15 percent discount.
M1: That's a good suggestion. [24]Lucas, would you be able to set up a display of the items with the discounted price?
M2: [24]Sure. I'll take care of that right away.

go through ~을 살펴보다   stock n. 재고   low adj. 저조한, 낮은
pile v. 쌓다   dispose of ~을 처분하다

해석
22-24번은 다음 세 명의 대화에 관한 문제입니다.
- 여: ²²제가 오늘 아침에 재고 물품들을 모두 살펴봤어요. 그리고 ²³Ranger 무선 조종 자동차의 판매가 매우 저조하다는 것을 알게 됐습니다.
- 남1: ²³새로운 로봇 키트 때문인 것 같아요. 그것들이 아이들을 위한 선물로 더 인기를 얻고 있어요.
- 남2: 맞아요. Ranger 무선 조종 자동차의 가격도 너무 높고요.
- 여: 재고가 많이 쌓여 있으니, 이번 분기에 그것을 처분하는 것이 좋겠어요. 음... 그 자동차를 15퍼센트 할인해서 판매해야겠어요.
- 남1: 좋은 제안이네요. ²⁴Lucas, 할인된 가격으로 그 상품들의 진열대를 설치해 줄 수 있을까요?
- 남2: ²⁴물론이죠. 지금 바로 처리하겠습니다.

22 특정 세부 사항 문제
해석 여자는 오늘 아침에 무엇을 했는가?
(A) 일정을 게시했다.
(B) 재고품 목록을 확인했다.
(C) 고객들에게 연락했다.
(D) 배송업체에 전화했다.
해설 질문의 핵심 어구(this morning)가 언급된 주변을 주의 깊게 듣는다. 여자가 "I went through all of the items in stock this morning."이라며 오늘 아침에 재고 물품들을 모두 확인했다고 하였다. 따라서 (B)가 정답이다.
어휘 examine v. 검토하다, 조사하다

[Paraphrasing]
went through ~ items in stock 재고 물품들을 살펴봤다 → checked some inventory 재고품 목록을 확인했다

23 문제점 문제
해석 화자들은 어떤 문제를 논의하고 있는가?
(A) 공급업체가 가격을 인상했다.
(B) 일부 부정적인 피드백이 제출되었다.
(C) 일부 장비가 작동하지 않는다.
(D) 제품의 성과가 저조하다.
해설 대화에서 부정적인 표현이 언급된 주변을 주의 깊게 듣는다. 여자가 "I noticed that sales of the Ranger remote-controlled car seem very low."라며 Ranger 무선 조종 자동차의 판매가 매우 저조하다고 했고, 남자1이 "I think it is because of the new robot kits. They are getting more popular as gifts for children."이라며 인기를 얻고 있는 새로운 로봇 키트 때문인 것 같다고 하였다. 따라서 (D)가 정답이다.
어휘 supplier n. 공급업체 underperform v. 성과가 저조하다, 기량 발휘를 못하다

24 다음에 할 일 문제
해석 Lucas는 다음에 무엇을 할 것인가?
(A) 상점 카탈로그를 수정한다.
(B) 제품 진열을 준비한다.
(C) 전자 기기를 구매한다.
(D) 시연을 한다.
해설 질문의 핵심 어구(Lucas)가 언급된 부분을 주의 깊게 듣는다. 남자1이 "Lucas, would you be able to set up a display of the items with the discounted price?"라며 할인된 가격으로 그 상품들의 진열대를 설치할 수 있는지 Lucas에게 물었고, 남자2[Lucas]가 "Sure. I'll take care of that right away."라며 지금 바로 그것을 처리하겠다고 하였다. 따라서 (B)가 정답이다.
어휘 demonstration n. 시연, 설명

DAY 11 이유/방법 및 특정 세부 사항 문제

기출 유형 1 이유/방법 문제

Example 영국 → 캐나다   p.72

해석
01번은 다음 대화에 관한 문제입니다.
- 여: Kendrick, 우리 회의를 지연시켜서 죄송해요... 예상치 못한 전화를 받았어요.
- 남: 괜찮아요. 음, 저는 우리 식료품점의 두 번째 지점에 대해 논의하기 위해 이 회의를 요청했어요. 그 지점은 개업을 축하하기 위해 우리가 제공해 오고 있는 할인에도 불구하고 실적이 좋지 않아요.
- 여: 알아요. 동네에 전단지를 배포하는 것에 대해 어떻게 생각하세요?
- 남: 한번 시도해 봅시다.

어휘 unexpected adj. 예상치 못한 poorly adv. 저조하게, 형편없이
   distribute v. 배포하다, 나누어 주다

01
해석 여자는 왜 사과하는가?
(A) 전화를 회신하지 않았다.
(B) 제품에 결함이 있다.
(C) 회의가 늦게 시작되었다.
(D) 할인이 유효하지 않다.
어휘 defective adj. 결함 있는

토익실전문제   p.73

| 01 (B) | 02 (B) | 03 (D) | 04 (C) | 05 (A) |
| 06 (B) |

[01-03] 호주 → 미국
Questions 01-03 refer to the following conversation.

M: Ms. Yoon. I heard you won the dessert competition that was held last week. Congratulations!
W: Thanks. ⁰¹**I was surprised by the large number of participants.** It made the contest really challenging. Um, what did you want to talk to me about today?
M: I'm interested in working with you on a project. ⁰²**My company is currently developing a new line of snacks.** We want to create healthy desserts targeting diet-conscious consumers. I think you're the ideal person for this project.
W: That sounds interesting. ⁰³**Could you send me an e-mail with details about your plan? I'll go over it tomorrow** and then get back to you.

competition n. 대회 develop v. 개발하다 target v. 대상으로 삼다
consumer n. 소비자 ideal adj. 가장 알맞은, 이상적인

해석
01-03번은 다음 대화에 관한 문제입니다.
- 남: Ms. Yoon. 지난주에 열렸던 디저트 대회에서 당신이 우승했다고 들었어요. 축하합니다!
- 여: 감사합니다. ⁰¹저는 많은 참가자 수에 놀랐어요. 그것이 대회를 정말 도전적으로 만들었죠. 음, 오늘 무엇에 관해 제게 이야기를 하고 싶으셨나요?
- 남: 저는 프로젝트에서 당신과 함께 일하는 데 관심이 있습니다. ⁰²저희 회사는 현재 새로운 스낵 라인을 개발하고 있어요. 저희는 식단에 신경 쓰는 소비자들을 대상으로 하는 건강한 디저트를 만들고 싶어요. 당신이 이 프로젝트에 가장 알맞은 사람이라고 생각해요.

여: 흥미롭게 들리네요. ⁰³당신의 계획에 대한 세부 사항이 담긴 이메일을 보내주시겠어요? 제가 내일 그것을 검토하고 연락드리겠습니다.

01 이유 문제
해석 여자는 왜 놀랐는가?
(A) 일정이 갑자기 변경되었다.
(B) 대회에 많은 참가자들이 있었다.
(C) 새로운 정책이 발표되었다.
(D) 사업체가 폐업했다.

해설 여자의 말에서 질문의 핵심 어구(surprised)와 관련된 내용을 주의 깊게 듣는다. 여자가 "I was surprised by the large number of participants."라며 많은 참가자 수에 놀랐다고 하였다. 따라서 (B)가 정답이다.

어휘 suddenly adv. 갑자기   close down 폐업하다

02 특정 세부 사항 문제
해석 남자의 회사는 무엇을 만드는가?
(A) 스포츠 용품
(B) 식품
(C) 주방 용품
(D) 요리책

해설 질문의 핵심 어구(man's company make)와 관련된 내용을 주의 깊게 듣는다. 남자가 "My company is currently developing a new line of snacks."라며 자신의 회사가 현재 새로운 스낵 라인을 개발하고 있다고 하였다. 따라서 (B)가 정답이다.

03 다음에 할 일 문제
해석 여자는 내일 무엇을 할 것인가?
(A) 새로운 디저트를 만들어낸다.
(B) 샘플을 보낸다.
(C) 지점을 방문한다.
(D) 제안서를 검토한다.

해설 질문의 핵심 어구(tomorrow)가 언급된 주변을 주의 깊게 듣는다. 여자가 "Could you send me an e-mail with details about your plan? I'll go over it tomorrow"라며 계획에 대한 세부 사항을 이메일로 보내주면 내일 검토하겠다고 하였다. 따라서 (D)가 정답이다.

Paraphrasing
details about your plan 당신의 계획에 대한 세부 사항 → proposal 제안서

[04-06] 🎧 캐나다 → 영국
Questions 04-06 refer to the following conversation.

M: Hello. I recently moved to this neighborhood, and ⁰⁴**I'd like to consult with you about some home renovations.**
W: Welcome. ⁰⁵**How did you find out about us?**
M: ⁰⁵**I compared reviews of various home renovation contractors on several Web sites.** From what I read, most people were pleased with your work.
W: Thanks. Is there any specific type of work that you're interested in?
M: Yes. I'm considering remodeling my bathroom. I want to replace the tiles with colorful ones and install a more modern bathtub and sink.
W: We're certainly able to provide those services. ⁰⁶**Let's sit together and look at some images of the bathrooms we recently renovated.**

neighborhood n. 동네   compare v. 비교하다
be pleased with ~에 만족하다   specific adj. 특정한

해석
04-06번은 다음 대화에 관한 문제입니다.

남: 안녕하세요. 저는 최근에 이 동네로 이사왔는데, ⁰⁴집 수리에 대해 당신과 상담하고 싶습니다.
여: 환영합니다. ⁰⁵저희에 대해 어떻게 알게 되셨나요?
남: ⁰⁵여러 웹사이트에서 다양한 집 수리 시공사들의 리뷰를 비교했어요. 제가 읽은 바로는, 대부분의 사람들이 당신의 작업에 만족했더군요.
여: 감사합니다. 관심 있는 특정 작업 유형이 있으신가요?
남: 네. 저는 욕실 리모델링을 고려하고 있어요. 타일을 화려한 것들로 교체하고 더 현대적인 욕조와 세면대를 설치하고 싶어요.
여: 저희는 확실히 그러한 서비스를 제공할 수 있습니다. ⁰⁶함께 앉아서 저희가 최근에 리모델링한 욕실들의 이미지를 몇 개 살펴봅시다.

04 목적 문제
해석 남자의 방문 목적은 무엇인가?
(A) 일자리에 지원하고 있다.
(B) 이사하는 것을 도움 받아야 한다.
(C) 상담을 원한다.
(D) 불만이 있다.

해설 방문 목적을 묻는 문제이므로, 대화의 초반을 반드시 듣는다. 남자가 여자에게 "I'd like to consult with you about some home renovations"라며 집 수리에 대해 여자와 상담하고 싶다고 하였다. 따라서 (C)가 정답이다.

어휘 apply for ~에 지원하다

Paraphrasing
I'd like to consult 상담하고 싶다 → wants a consultation 상담을 원한다

05 방법 문제
해석 남자는 여자의 회사에 대해 어떻게 알게 되었는가?
(A) 웹사이트를 통해
(B) 출판물을 통해
(C) TV 광고를 통해
(D) 현지 사업장 주인을 통해

해설 남자의 말에서 질문의 핵심 어구(learn about the woman's company)와 관련된 내용을 주의 깊게 듣는다. 여자가 "How did you find out about us?"라며 자신의 사업체를 어떻게 알게 되었냐고 묻자, 남자가 "I compared reviews of various home renovation contractors on several Web sites."라며 웹사이트에서 다양한 집 수리 시공사들의 리뷰를 비교했다고 하였다. 따라서 (A)가 정답이다.

어휘 publication n. 출판물

06 특정 세부 사항 문제
해석 여자는 남자에게 무엇을 보여줄 것인가?
(A) 평면도
(B) 사진
(C) 3D 모델
(D) 비용 견적

해설 질문의 핵심 어구(woman show the man)와 관련된 내용을 주의 깊게 듣는다. 여자가 "Let's sit together and look at some images of the bathrooms we recently renovated."라며 최근에 자신이 리모델링한 욕실들의 이미지를 함께 살펴보자고 하였다. 따라서 (B)가 정답이다.

기출 유형 2 특정 세부 사항 문제

Example 🎧 영국 → 캐나다   p.74

해석
01번은 다음 대화에 관한 문제입니다.

여: Mr. Choi, 당신은 이제 우리 회사에 한 달 정도 있었네요. 어떻게 지내

DAY 11 이유/방법 및 특정 세부 사항 문제 63

고 있나요?
남: 좋습니다. 저는 특히 사무실 배치가 마음에 들어요. 제 일에 집중하기 쉽게 해줘요.
여: 그 말을 들으니 기쁘네요. **우리는 작년 여름에 이 사무실로 이사했어요.** 많은 직원들이 그 이후로 생산성이 향상되었다고 말했어요.
남: 흥미롭네요. 그나저나, 선임 매니저들과의 점심 미팅이 여전히 오늘인가요?
여: 네, 낮 12시까지 로비로 오시면 돼요.

어휘 layout n. 배치 productivity n. 생산성

01
해석 작년 여름에 무슨 일이 일어났는가?
(A) 기업 합병이 마무리되었다.
(B) 새로운 지점이 문을 열었다.
(C) 작업 공간이 이전되었다.
(D) 추가 직원들이 고용되었다.

토익실전문제   p.75

01 (C)   02 (B)   03 (A)   04 (C)   05 (C)
06 (A)

[01-03] 미국 → 호주
Questions 01-03 refer to the following conversation.

W: Hello, Oliver. This is Karen. ⁰¹**As you already know, Jim Bates is stepping down as head copywriter at the end of this month. That means we'll have to move someone into his position. Who do you think would be a good candidate?**
M: ⁰²**What about Richard Hammel?** He's been a dedicated employee for 10 years. ⁰²**He's written the text for a variety of advertisements** and understands all aspects of the job.
W: Actually, I have several candidates in mind, and Mr. Hammel is one of them. ⁰³**I'd like to talk about this matter further. Can you meet me in the conference room in an hour?**
M: Sure thing. See you then.

step down 물러나다, 퇴직하다 candidate n. 후보자
dedicated adj. 헌신적인, 전념하는 aspect n. 측면 matter n. 사안

해석
01-03번은 다음 대화에 관한 문제입니다.
여: 안녕하세요, Oliver. 저는 Karen이에요. ⁰¹이미 알고 계시겠지만, Jim Bates가 이번 달 말에 수석 카피라이터직에서 물러나요. 그것은 우리가 누군가를 그의 자리로 이동시켜야 한다는 것을 의미합니다. 누가 좋은 후보자가 될 것 같으세요?
남: ⁰²Richard Hammel은 어떨까요? 그는 10년 동안 헌신적인 직원이었습니다. ⁰²그는 다양한 광고의 본문을 작성했고 업무의 모든 측면을 이해하고 있어요.
여: 사실, 저는 마음속에 몇 명의 후보자가 있고 Mr. Hammel도 그들 중 한 명이에요. ⁰³저는 이 사안에 대해 더 이야기하고 싶어요. 한 시간 후에 회의실에서 저를 만나실 수 있나요?
남: 물론이죠. 그때 뵙겠습니다.

01 목적 문제
해석 여자는 왜 전화하고 있는가?
(A) 일자리를 제안하기 위해
(B) 약속 일정을 변경하기 위해
(C) 후임자에 대해 논의하기 위해
(D) 면접 날짜를 변경하기 위해

해설 전화를 거는 목적을 묻는 문제이므로, 대화의 초반을 반드시 듣는다. 여자가 "As you already know, Jim Bates is stepping down as head copywriter at the end of this month. That means we'll have to move someone into his position. Who do you think would be a good candidate?"라며 Jim Bates가 이번 달 말에 수석 카피라이터직에서 물러나서 누군가를 그 자리로 이동시켜야 한다고 말한 후, 좋은 후보자가 누구일지에 대해 묻고 있다. 따라서 (C)가 정답이다.

어휘 replacement n. 후임자

02 특정 세부 사항 문제
해석 Richard Hammel은 누구인 것 같은가?
(A) 정치인
(B) 카피라이터
(C) 학회 조직자
(D) 잡지 편집자

해설 질문의 핵심 어구(Richard Hammel)가 언급된 주변을 주의 깊게 듣는다. 남자가 "What about Richard Hammel?"이라며 Richard Hammel은 어떠냐고 한 뒤, "He's written the text for a variety of advertisements"라며 그가 다양한 광고의 본문을 작성했다고 한 것을 통해 그가 광고 카피라이터임을 알 수 있다. 따라서 (B)가 정답이다.

03 요청 문제
해석 여자는 남자에게 무엇을 하라고 요청하는가?
(A) 회의에 참석한다.
(B) 서류를 제출한다.
(C) 지원서를 살펴본다.
(D) 잠재적 후보자에게 전화한다.

해설 여자의 말에서 요청과 관련된 표현이 언급된 다음을 주의 깊게 듣는다. 여자가 "I'd like to talk about this matter further. Can you meet me in the conference room in an hour?"라며 후보자들에 대해 이야기하기 위해 한 시간 후에 회의실에서 만나자고 하였다. 따라서 (A)가 정답이다.

Paraphrasing
meet ~ in the conference room 회의실에서 만나다 → Attend a meeting 회의에 참석한다

[04-06] 캐나다 → 영국
Questions 04-06 refer to the following conversation.

M: ⁰⁴**I see that you're looking at our store's newest collection of speakers.** If you have any questions, I'd be happy to answer them.
W: Well, I'm interested in buying a speaker for my friend as a gift. He wants a portable one to connect to his cell phone.
M: Then, I recommend the Tide EX. ⁰⁵**It was recently developed by Echo Incorporated** and is designed specifically for cell phones. It's lightweight and has wireless capabilities.
W: Um, ⁰⁶**are you still giving away a free set of earphones to anyone who buys a product at your store?**
M: Yes. If you post a review of your purchase on our Web site, we'll have it delivered to your home.

portable adj. 휴대용의 connect v. 연결하다 lightweight adj. 가벼운
capability n. 기능

해석
04-06번은 다음 대화에 관한 문제입니다.

남: ⁰⁴저희 매장의 최신 스피커 컬렉션을 보고 계시는군요. 질문이 있으시면 기꺼이 답해 드리겠습니다.
여: 네, 제 친구에게 선물로 스피커를 사 주고 싶어요. 그는 휴대폰에 연결할 수 있는 휴대용 스피커를 원해요.
남: 그렇다면, 저는 Tide EX를 추천합니다. ⁰⁵그것은 최근에 Echo사에서 개발했으며 특별히 휴대폰용으로 설계되었어요. 가볍고 무선 기능이 있습니다.
여: 음, ⁰⁶이 매장에서 제품을 구매하는 사람에게 여전히 이어폰 세트를 무료로 제공하고 있나요?
남: 네. 저희 웹사이트에 구매 후기를 게시하시면, 집으로 배송해 드리겠습니다.

04 장소 문제
해석 대화는 어디에서 일어나고 있는 것 같은가?
(A) 서비스 센터에서
(B) 연구소에서
(C) 전자제품 상점에서
(D) 비즈니스 박람회에서
해설 대화에서 장소와 관련된 표현을 놓치지 않고 듣는다. 남자가 "I see that you're looking at our store's newest collection of speakers."라며 여자에게 매장의 최신 스피커 컬렉션을 보고 있다고 한 것을 통해 대화가 전자제품을 파는 상점에서 이루어지고 있음을 알 수 있다. 따라서 (C)가 정답이다.
어휘 exposition n. 박람회

05 특정 세부 사항 문제
해석 Echo사는 최근에 무엇을 했는가?
(A) 업계 상을 받았다.
(B) 더 많은 직원들을 고용했다.
(C) 신제품을 개발했다.
(D) 해외로 확장했다.
해설 질문의 핵심 어구(Echo Incorporated)가 언급된 주변을 주의 깊게 듣는다. 남자가 "It was recently developed by Echo Incorporated"라며 Tide EX가 최근에 Echo사에서 개발되었다고 하였다. 따라서 (C)가 정답이다.
어휘 expand v. 확장하다

06 특정 세부 사항 문제
해석 여자는 무엇에 대해 묻는가?
(A) 무료 제품
(B) 할인된 가격
(C) 업체 위치
(D) 배송 날짜
해설 질문의 핵심 어구(woman ask about)와 관련된 내용을 주의 깊게 듣는다. 여자가 "are you still giving away a free set of earphones to anyone who buys a product at your store?"라며 이 매장에서 제품을 구매하는 사람에게 여전히 이어폰 세트를 무료로 제공하고 있는지 물었다. 따라서 (A)가 정답이다.

HACKERS TEST — p.76

01 (B)	02 (C)	03 (B)	04 (A)	05 (B)
06 (D)	07 (D)	08 (A)	09 (B)	10 (D)
11 (C)	12 (C)	13 (B)	14 (D)	15 (A)
16 (D)	17 (A)	18 (B)	19 (B)	20 (B)
21 (C)	22 (B)	23 (C)	24 (A)	

[01-03] 영국 → 캐나다
Questions 01-03 refer to the following conversation.

W: Liam, ⁰¹we should seriously think about making upgrades to the plant. It's been a decade since we replaced the equipment here.
M: ⁰¹I agree. However, the process will force us to shut down the plant temporarily. ⁰²I'm worried that we won't meet our production target for this month.
W: Well, ⁰³I'll speak with the factory supervisor this afternoon and ask him how long it would take to set up new equipment. Maybe it can be done faster than we expect.

seriously adv. 진지하게, 심각하게   plant n. 공장
temporarily adv. 일시적으로   target n. 목표

해석
01-03번은 다음 대화에 관한 문제입니다.
여: Liam, ⁰¹우리 공장에 업그레이드를 하는 것에 대해 진지하게 생각해야 해요. 우리가 여기 장비를 교체한 후로 10년이 지났어요.
남: ⁰¹동의합니다. 하지만, 그 과정으로 인해 공장을 일시적으로 폐쇄해야 할 거예요. ⁰²우리가 이번 달 생산 목표를 달성하지 못할까 봐 걱정됩니다.
여: 음, ⁰³제가 오늘 오후에 공장 감독관과 얘기해서 새 장비를 설치하는 데 얼마나 시간이 걸릴지 물어볼게요. 아마도 우리가 예상하는 것보다 더 빨리 될 수도 있어요.

01 주제 문제
해석 화자들은 주로 무엇에 대해 논의하고 있는가?
(A) 새 감독관을 선정하는 것
(B) 장비를 교체하는 것
(C) 자선 경매를 계획하는 것
(D) 보상을 인상하는 것
해설 대화의 주제를 묻는 문제이므로, 대화의 초반을 반드시 듣는다. 여자가 "we should seriously think about making upgrades to the plant. After all, it's been a decade since we replaced the equipment here."라며 공장에 업그레이드를 하는 것에 대해 진지하게 생각해야 하며 교체한 후로 10년이 지났다고 했다. 이에 대해 남자가 "I agree."라며 동의한다고 한 후 공장의 장비를 교체하는 내용으로 대화가 이어지고 있다. 따라서 (B)가 정답이다.
어휘 compensation n. 보상

02 문제점 문제
해석 남자는 왜 걱정하는가?
(A) 일부 팀원들이 시간이 안 된다.
(B) 교육 매뉴얼이 구식이다.
(C) 생산 목표가 달성되지 않을 수 있다.
(D) 구역이 너무 좁다.
해설 남자의 말에서 부정적인 표현이 언급된 주변을 주의 깊게 듣는다. 남자가 "I'm worried that we won't meet our production target for this month."라며 이번 달 생산 목표를 달성하지 못할까 봐 걱정된다고 하였다. 따라서 (C)가 정답이다.
어휘 outdated adj. 구식인

Paraphrasing
won't meet ~ production target 생산 목표를 달성하지 못할 것이다 → prduction goal might not be met 목표가 달성되지 않을 수 있다

03 이유 문제
해석 여자는 왜 감독관에게 연락할 것인가?
(A) 더 많은 직원들을 요청하기 위해
(B) 설치 일정에 대해 이야기하기 위해

(C) 보고서가 언제까지 하기로 예정된 것인지 물어보기 위해
(D) 변경이 이루어진 이유를 설명하기 위해

해설 여자의 말에서 질문의 핵심 어구(contact the supervisor)와 관련된 내용을 주의 깊게 듣는다. 여자가 "I'll speak with the factory supervisor this afternoon and ask him how long it would take to set up new equipment."라며 오늘 오후에 공장 감독관과 얘기해서 새 장비를 설치하는 데 얼마나 시간이 걸릴지 물어볼 것이라고 하였다. 따라서 (B)가 정답이다.

어휘 due adj. ~하기로 예정된

[04-06] 호주 → 미국
Questions 04-06 refer to the following conversation.

M: ⁰⁴Welcome to Tanya Coffee Shop. May I take your order?
W: I'd like some drinks and food for my company's morning meeting. Do you offer delivery service?
M: Yes. We provide free delivery for orders over 30 dollars.
W: OK. I'd like coffee and an assortment of pastries for about 15 people. And please ensure that the pastries are nut-free as ⁰⁵some of our team members have nut allergies.
M: No problem. Do you think you will be placing similar orders in the future?
W: Yes. We are planning to have a meeting like this each month.
M: ⁰⁶If you order through our mobile app, you can get a 20 percent discount on all your repeat orders. I suggest downloading it.

an assortment of 다양한 종류의, 여러 가지의 ensure v. 반드시 ~이게 하다
similar adj. 비슷한, 유사한

해석
04-06번은 다음 대화에 관한 문제입니다.
남: ⁰⁴Tanya 커피숍에 오신 것을 환영합니다. 주문하시겠습니까?
여: 회사 아침 회의를 위한 음료와 음식을 주문하고 싶어요. 배달 서비스를 제공하나요?
남: 네. 30달러 이상 주문하시면 무료로 배달해 드립니다.
여: 알겠습니다. 약 15명을 위한 커피와 다양한 종류의 페이스트리를 주문하고 싶어요. 그리고 ⁰⁵일부 팀원들이 견과류 알레르기가 있으니 페이스트리에 견과류가 없도록 해주세요.
남: 문제 없습니다. 앞으로도 이와 비슷한 주문을 하실 계획인가요?
여: 네. 매달 이런 회의를 열 계획입니다.
남: ⁰⁶모바일 앱으로 주문하시면 모든 재주문에 대해 20퍼센트 할인을 받으실 수 있어요. 앱을 다운로드하시는 것을 추천합니다.

04 장소 문제
해설 대화는 어디에서 일어나고 있는 것 같은가?
(A) 카페에서
(B) 슈퍼마켓에서
(C) 문구점에서
(D) 배송 회사에서

해설 대화에서 장소와 관련된 표현을 놓치지 않고 듣는다. 남자가 "Welcome to Tanya Coffee Shop. May I take your order?"라고 한 것을 통해 대화가 커피숍에서 일어나고 있음을 알 수 있다. 따라서 (A)가 정답이다.

05 언급 문제
해설 여자는 일부 직원들에 대해 무엇이라고 말하는가?
(A) 최근에 고용되었다.
(B) 식품 알레르기가 있다.
(C) 오전 근무만 한다.
(D) 해외로 파견될 것이다.

해설 여자의 말에서 질문의 핵심 어구(some staff)와 관련된 내용을 주의 깊게 듣는다. 여자가 "some of our team members have nut allergies"라며 일부 팀원들이 견과류 알레르기가 있다고 하였다. 따라서 (B)가 정답이다.

어휘 dispatch v. 파견하다

06 방법 문제
해설 여자는 추후의 주문에 대해 어떻게 할인을 받을 수 있는가?
(A) 회원 가입을 함으로써
(B) 특정 날짜에 방문함으로써
(C) 쿠폰 코드를 제시함으로써
(D) 모바일 애플리케이션을 사용함으로써

해설 질문의 핵심 어구(discount)가 언급된 주변을 주의 깊게 듣는다. 남자가 "If you order through our mobile app, you can get a 20 percent discount on all your repeat orders."라며 모바일 앱으로 주문하면 모든 재주문에 대해 20퍼센트 할인을 받을 수 있다고 하였다. 따라서 (D)가 정답이다.

[07-09] 영국 → 호주
Questions 07-09 refer to the following conversation.

W: Good morning. This is Casey Taylor calling. ⁰⁷You were supposed to come to my house to fix my broken air conditioner at 10 o'clock today. But it's already 10:15.
M: Ms. Taylor, hello. Unfortunately, my truck got a flat tire. ⁰⁸I'm very sorry for not calling to let you know I'd be late.
W: Oh, I see. What time do you think you'll get here?
M: I should arrive at 11. ⁰⁹I'm just waiting for someone from the service center I called to arrive and fix my tire. After that, I'll go directly to your house.

fix v. 고치다, 수리하다 broken adj. 고장 난 flat adj. 바람이 빠진, 펑크 난
directly adv. 바로, 곧장

해석
07-09번은 다음 대화에 관한 문제입니다.
여: 안녕하세요. 저는 Casey Taylor입니다. ⁰⁷당신은 오늘 10시에 고장 난 에어컨을 고치기 위해 저의 집에 오시기로 되어 있었어요. 그런데, 이미 10시 15분이에요.
남: Ms. Taylor, 안녕하세요. 안타깝게도, 제 트럭의 타이어가 바람이 빠졌어요. ⁰⁸제가 늦을 것이라고 알리기 위해 전화드리지 못해 정말 죄송해요.
여: 아, 알겠어요. 여기에 몇 시에 도착하실 것 같나요?
남: 11시에 도착할 것 같아요. ⁰⁹저는 와서 타이어를 고쳐줄 서비스 센터의 직원을 기다리고 있어요. 그 후에, 당신의 집으로 바로 가겠습니다.

07 목적 문제
해설 여자는 왜 전화를 하고 있는가?
(A) 약속 일정이 변경되어야 한다.
(B) 영수증이 수정되어야 한다.
(C) 배송품이 일찍 도착했다.
(D) 직원이 늦는다.

해설 전화의 목적을 묻는 문제이므로, 대화의 초반을 반드시 듣는다. 여자가 "You were supposed to come to my house to fix my broken air conditioner at 10 o'clock today. But it's already 10:15."이라며 남자가 오늘 10시에 고장 난 에어컨을 고치기 위해 여자의 집에 오기로 했는데 이미 10시 15분이라고 한 것을 통해, 여자가 직원이 늦어서 전화를 하고 있음을 알 수 있다. 따라서 (D)가 정답이다.

어휘 receipt n. 영수증

08 특정 세부 사항 문제
해석 남자는 무엇에 대해 사과하는가?
(A) 고객에게 연락하지 않았다.
(B) 주문을 취소하지 않았다.
(C) 잘못된 금액을 청구했다.
(D) 도구를 가져오는 것을 잊었다.

해설 질문의 핵심 어구(apologize)와 관련된 내용을 주의 깊게 듣는다. 남자가 "I'm very sorry for not calling to let you know I'd be late."라며 늦을 것이라고 알리기 위해 전화드리지 못해 정말 죄송하다고 하였다. 따라서 (A)가 정답이다.

어휘 charge v. 청구하다 amount n. 금액

09 특정 세부 사항 문제
해석 남자는 누구를 기다리고 있는 것 같은가?
(A) 트럭 운전사
(B) 수리공
(C) 점원
(D) 배달원

해설 질문의 핵심 어구(man ~ waiting for)와 관련된 내용을 주의 깊게 듣는다. 남자가 "I'm just waiting for someone from the service center I called to arrive and fix my tire."라며 타이어를 고쳐줄 서비스 센터의 직원을 기다리고 있다고 하였다. 따라서 (B)가 정답이다.

[10-12] 캐나다 → 영국
Questions 10-12 refer to the following conversation.

> M: Emma, **¹⁰how are the preparations for the training sessions going?**
> W: I'm feeling a little overwhelmed. We hired so many new employees this quarter that I'm spending a lot of time on this project. I'm not sure if I will be able to get everything done.
> M: Hmm . . . **¹¹It sounds like you are overworked. Maybe we should change the plan to address this. I think online training sessions might work better.** The instructors could stream their workshops, and the employees could participate at their desks.
> W: That would be great. **¹²Could you suggest a software program that we can use for these online sessions?**

overwhelmed adj. 압도된 quarter n. 분기 overwork v. 과로하다
address v. 해결하다 stream v. 스트리밍하다

해석
10-12번은 다음 대화에 관한 문제입니다.
남: Emma, ¹⁰교육 세션을 위한 준비는 어떻게 진행되고 있나요?
여: 좀 부담감을 느끼고 있어요. 이번 분기에 너무 많은 신입 직원들을 고용해서 이 프로젝트에 많은 시간을 쓰고 있어요. 모든 일을 다 끝낼 수 있을지 모르겠어요.
남: 음... ¹¹당신이 과로하고 있는 것 같군요. 이를 해결하기 위해 계획을 바꿔야 할 것 같아요. 저는 온라인 교육 세션이 더 괜찮을 것 같아요. 강사들은 자신들의 워크숍을 스트리밍할 수 있고, 직원들은 자신의 책상에서 참여할 수 있을 거예요.
여: 그거 좋겠네요. ¹²이러한 온라인 세션에 사용할 만한 소프트웨어 프로그램을 추천해 주실 수 있나요?

10 주제 문제
해석 대화는 주로 무엇에 관한 것인가?
(A) 건설 프로젝트
(B) 인력 변경
(C) 기자 회견
(D) 교육 계획

해설 대화의 주제를 묻는 문제이므로, 대화의 초반을 반드시 듣는다. 남자가 "how are the preparations for the training sessions going?"이라며 교육 세션을 위한 준비가 어떻게 진행되고 있는지 물었고, 교육 방식 변경 계획에 대한 내용으로 대화가 이어지고 있다. 따라서 (D)가 정답이다.

어휘 initiative n. 계획

11 이유 문제
해석 남자는 왜 계획을 바꾸는 것을 제안하는가?
(A) 특별한 혜택을 받기 위해
(B) 고객의 불만을 해결하기 위해
(C) 업무 부담을 덜어 주기 위해
(D) 현재 추세에 맞추기 위해

해설 남자의 말에서 질문의 핵심 어구(changing a plan)와 관련된 내용을 주의 깊게 듣는다. 남자가 "It sounds like you are overworked. Maybe we should change the plan to address this. I think online training sessions might work better."라며 여자가 과로하고 있는 것 같다며 이를 해결하기 위해 온라인 교육 세션이 더 괜찮을 것 같다고 하였다. 따라서 (C)가 정답이다.

어휘 ease v. 덜어 주다 burden n. 부담, 짐

12 요청 문제
해석 여자는 남자에게 무엇을 하라고 요청하는가?
(A) 예약을 한다.
(B) 직원에게 연락한다.
(C) 애플리케이션을 추천한다.
(D) 계정을 만든다.

해설 여자의 말에서 요청과 관련된 표현이 언급된 다음을 주의 깊게 듣는다. 여자가 "Could you suggest a software program that we can use for these online sessions?"라며 온라인 세션에 사용할 수 있는 소프트웨어 프로그램을 추천해 달라고 하였다. 따라서 (C)가 정답이다.

Paraphrasing
suggest a software program 소프트웨어 프로그램을 추천하다 →
Recommend an application 애플리케이션을 추천한다

[13-15] 호주 → 미국 → 캐나다
Questions 13-15 refer to the following conversation with three speakers.

> M1: Hello. **¹³We recently opened a gym on Green Street.** We're looking for a laundry service provider for our gym.
> W: Welcome. We provide laundry services for various establishments.
> M2: Yeah. **¹⁴We were listening to the radio the other day and heard about this place.** We need to have our towels washed, dried, and folded on a weekly basis.
> W: We can do that. One of our staff will collect the laundry from your establishment and deliver it back the following day.
> M2: Sounds perfect. What are your rates?
> W: **¹⁵I'll give you a brochure that explains the fees we charge.**

provider n. 제공업체 establishment n. 업체 fold v. 접다 rate n. 요금
charge v. 청구하다

해석
13-15번은 다음 세 명의 대화에 관한 문제입니다.
남1: 안녕하세요. ¹³저희는 최근에 Green가에 체육관을 열었어요. 저희 체육관을 위한 세탁 서비스 제공업체를 찾고 있습니다.
여: 어서 오세요. 저희는 다양한 업체에 세탁 서비스를 제공합니다.
남2: 네. ¹⁴저희는 지난번에 라디오를 듣다가 이곳에 대해 알게 되었어요. 저희는 매주 수건을 세탁하고, 건조하고, 접어야 돼요.
여: 그렇게 해드릴 수 있습니다. 저희 직원 중 한 명이 귀하의 업체에서 세탁물을 수거하여 다음 날 다시 배달해 드릴 것입니다.
남2: 완벽하네요. 요금은 어떻게 되나요?
여: ¹⁵저희가 청구하는 요금을 설명하는 책자를 드리겠습니다.

13 특정 세부 사항 문제
해석 남자들은 어떤 사업체를 열었는가?
(A) 가사 서비스
(B) 피트니스 센터
(C) 사무용품 상점
(D) 출장 요리 회사

해설 질문의 핵심 어구(the men open)와 관련된 내용을 주의 깊게 듣는다. 남자1이 "We recently opened a gym on Green Street."이라며 최근에 Green가에 체육관을 열었다고 하였다. 따라서 (B)가 정답이다.

Paraphrasing
gym 체육관 → fitness center 피트니스 센터

14 방법 문제
해석 남자들은 어떻게 여자의 사업체에 대해 알게 되었는가?
(A) 책자를 통해
(B) 온라인 광고를 통해
(C) 이전 동료를 통해
(D) 라디오 광고를 통해

해설 질문의 핵심 어구(learn about the woman's business)와 관련된 내용을 주의 깊게 듣는다. 남자2가 "We were listening to the radio the other day and heard about this place."라며 지난번에 라디오를 듣다가 이곳에 대해 알게 되었다고 하였다. 따라서 (D)가 정답이다.

어휘 former adj. 이전의

15 특정 세부 사항 문제
해석 여자는 다음에 어떤 정보를 제공할 것인가?
(A) 가격 세부 정보
(B) 지점 위치
(C) 서비스 기간
(D) 직원 이름

해설 대화의 마지막 부분을 주의 깊게 듣는다. 여자가 "I'll give you a brochure that explains the fees we charge."라며 요금을 설명하는 책자를 주겠다고 하였다. 따라서 (A)가 정답이다.

Paraphrasing
brochure that explains the fees 요금을 설명하는 책자 → Pricing details 가격 세부 정보

[16-18] 미국 → 캐나다
Questions 16-18 refer to the following conversation.

W: ¹⁶**The patient waiting room is now full.** We are pretty busy in here today.
M: Yes. The clinic is fully booked, probably because the flu is going around.
W: By the way, are you attending the medical conference next month?
M: Well . . . ¹⁷**I'm afraid I can't make it. I have a surgery scheduled on the same day.**
W: That's too bad. It'll be a great opportunity to learn about the latest surgical techniques.¹⁸ **I can write down the key points of each presentation for you to look over.**

fully adv. 완전히 make it 참석하다, 가다 opportunity n. 기회
surgical adj. 수술의

해석
16-18번은 다음 대화에 관한 문제입니다.
여: ¹⁶환자 대기실이 이제 꽉 찼어요. 우리 오늘 꽤 바쁘네요.
남: 네. 병원이 완전히 예약이 찼어요. 아마도 독감이 유행하고 있기 때문인 것 같아요.
여: 그런데, 다음 달 의학 학회에 참석하실 건가요?
남: 음... ¹⁷참석할 수 없을 것 같아요. 같은 날 예정된 수술이 있어요.
여: 그거 유감이네요. 최신 수술 기법에 대해 배울 수 있는 좋은 기회가 될 텐데요. ¹⁸제가 각 발표의 핵심 내용을 당신이 볼 수 있게 필기해 드릴게요.

16 장소 문제
해석 대화는 어디에서 일어나는 것 같은가?
(A) 기술 회사에서
(B) 컨벤션 센터에서
(C) 창고에서
(D) 의료 시설에서

해설 대화에서 장소와 관련된 표현을 놓치지 않고 듣는다. 여자가 "The patient waiting room is now full."이라며 환자 대기실이 꽉 찼다고 한 것을 통해 대화가 의료 시설에서 이루어지고 있음을 알 수 있다. 따라서 (D)가 정답이다.

17 이유 문제
해석 남자는 왜 학회에 참석할 수 없을 것인가?
(A) 일정이 겹친다.
(B) 사전에 등록하지 못했다.
(C) 초대받지 않았다.
(D) 교통편을 마련할 수 없다.

해설 질문의 핵심 어구(man be unable to attend)와 관련된 내용을 주의 깊게 듣는다. 남자가 "I'm afraid I can't make it. I have a surgery scheduled on the same day."라며 같은 날 예정된 수술이 있어서 학회에 참석할 수 없다고 하였다. 따라서 (A)가 정답이다.

어휘 fail to ~하지 못하다 in advance 사전에, 미리

18 제안 문제
해석 여자는 무엇을 해주겠다고 제안하는가?
(A) 목록을 수정한다.
(B) 양식을 작성한다.
(C) 상사에게 전화한다.
(D) 메모한다.

해설 여자의 말에서 제안과 관련된 표현이 언급된 다음을 주의 깊게 듣는다. 여자가 "I can write down the key points of each presentation for you to look over."라며 각 발표의 핵심 내용을 남자가 볼 수 있게 필기해 주겠다고 하였다. 따라서 (D)가 정답이다.

어휘 modify v. 수정하다

Paraphrasing
write down the key points 핵심 내용을 필기하다 → Take some notes 메모한다

[19-21] 호주 → 영국
Questions 19-21 refer to the following conversation.

M: Welcome to the Redwoods Shopping Mall. How can I help you today?
W: ¹⁹**I want to exchange this sweater I bought at a**

shop here called Dove Fit, but it's closed. I thought all the stores in the mall were open today.

M: [20]**Dove Fit is being remodeled right now.** It will reopen in two weeks.

W: I can't wait two weeks. Is there another branch near here?

M: There's one on Alfredo Street. [21]**You can get there easily by subway.** Just get off at Forest Hill Station, and you will see the store across the street.

exchange v. 교환하다　reopen v. 다시 문을 열다　easily adv. 쉽게
get off 내리다

해석

19-21번은 다음 대화에 관한 문제입니다.

남: Redwoods 쇼핑몰에 오신 것을 환영합니다. 오늘 어떻게 도와드릴까요?

여: [19]제가 이곳에 있는 Dove Fit이라는 상점에서 구입한 이 스웨터를 교환하고 싶은데, 문을 닫았네요. 오늘 쇼핑몰 안의 모든 상점이 열려 있을 것이라고 생각했어요.

남: [20]Dove Fit은 현재 리모델링 중이에요. 2주 후에 다시 문을 열 것입니다.

여: 저는 2주를 기다릴 수 없어요. 이 근처에 다른 지점이 있나요?

남: Alfredo가에 한 곳이 있어요. [21]지하철을 타고 쉽게 가실 수 있어요. Forest Hill 역에서 내리시면 길 건너편에 그 상점이 보일 거예요.

19 목적 문제

해석 여자의 방문 목적은 무엇인가?
(A) 선물을 구매해야 한다.
(B) 물건을 교환하고 싶다.
(C) 특정 직원을 찾고 있다.
(D) 건물을 견학하고 있다.

해설 대화의 목적을 묻는 문제이므로, 대화의 초반을 반드시 듣는다. 여자가 "I want to exchange this sweater I bought at a shop here called Dove Fit"이며 Dove Fit이라는 상점에서 구입한 스웨터를 교환하고 싶다고 하였다. 따라서 (B)가 정답이다.

20 언급 문제

해석 남자는 Dove Fit에 관해 무엇이라고 말하는가?
(A) 할인을 하고 있다.
(B) 보수되고 있다.
(C) 이전되었다.
(D) 정책을 변경했다.

해설 남자의 말에서 질문의 핵심 어구(Dove Fit)가 언급된 내용을 주의 깊게 듣는다. 남자가 "Dove Fit is being remodeled right now."라며 Dove Fit이 현재 리모델링 중이라고 하였다. 따라서 (B)가 정답이다.

Paraphrasing
being remodeled 리모델링 중인 → being renovated 보수되고 있는

21 특정 세부 사항 문제

해석 여자는 어디로 향할 것 같은가?
(A) 주차장으로
(B) 탈의실로
(C) 지하철역으로
(D) 안내 데스크로

해설 질문의 핵심 어구(woman ~ head)와 관련된 내용을 주의 깊게 듣는다. 남자가 "You can get there easily by subway."라며 지하철을 타고 쉽게 갈 수 있다고 했으므로 여자는 다른 지점으로 가기 위해 지하철역으로 향할 것임을 알 수 있다. 따라서 (C)가 정답이다.

어휘 head v. 향하다

[22-24] 🔊 미국 → 호주

Questions 22-24 refer to the following conversation.

W: Martin, [22]**do you know when the next quarter's budget will be finalized?**

M: [22]**My team is working on it now**, and we should be done by early next week.

W: I see. I want to have some additional funds allotted for a marketing campaign. [23]**The one for the tablet our company is launching this spring.**

M: Hmm . . . Adjustments are still possible. But [24]**the head of the marketing department will need to fill out this request form and then get it back to us by tomorrow afternoon.**

W: Got it. I'll speak to my manager about this now. Thank you for your help.

budget n. 예산　finalize v. 최종적으로 승인하다, 마무리짓다　allot v. 할당하다
adjustment n. 조정

해석

22-24번은 다음 대화에 관한 문제입니다.

여: Martin, [22]다음 분기 예산이 언제 최종적으로 승인될지 알고 있나요?

남: [22]제 팀이 지금 그것에 대해 작업 중이고, 다음 주 초까지는 끝낼 것 같아요.

여: 알겠어요. 마케팅 캠페인을 위한 추가 자금을 할당받고 싶어요. [23]우리 회사가 이번 봄에 출시하는 태블릿을 위한 것이요.

남: 음... 조정은 여전히 가능해요. 하지만 [24]마케팅 부서의 책임자가 이 요청 양식을 작성한 후에 내일 오후까지 저희에게 돌려주셔야 할 거예요.

여: 알겠어요. 지금 제 관리자에게 이것에 대해 말씀드릴게요. 도움 주셔서 감사해요.

22 화자 문제

해석 남자는 어느 부서에서 일하는 것 같은가?
(A) 마케팅
(B) 회계
(C) 엔지니어링
(D) 정보 통신 기술

해설 대화에서 신분 및 직업과 관련된 표현을 놓치지 않고 듣는다. 여자가 "do you know when the next quarter's budget will be finalized?"라며 다음 분기 예산이 언제 최종적으로 승인될지 아냐고 물었고, 남자가 "My team is working on it now"라며 본인의 팀이 그것에 대해 작업 중이라고 한 것을 통해 남자가 회계 부서에서 일하는 것임을 알 수 있다. 따라서 (B)가 정답이다.

23 특정 세부 사항 문제

해석 화자들의 회사는 봄에 무엇을 할 것인가?
(A) 해외 지사를 연다.
(B) 부서장을 교체한다.
(C) 새 제품을 출시한다.
(D) 온라인 서비스를 시작한다.

해설 대화에서 질문의 핵심 어구(company ~ spring)와 관련된 내용을 주의 깊게 듣는다. 여자가 "The one for the tablet our company is launching this spring."이며 회사가 봄에 태블릿을 출시할 것이라고 하였다. 따라서 (C)가 정답이다.

Paraphrasing
is launching 출시할 것이다 → Release 출시하다

24 언급 문제

해석 남자는 내일 오후까지 무엇이 제공되어야 한다고 말하는가?
(A) 양식
(B) 설명서

(C) 일정표
(D) 사진

해설 남자의 말에서 질문의 핵심 어구(by tomorrow afternoon)가 언급된 주변을 주의 깊게 듣는다. 남자가 "the head of the marketing department will need to fill out this request form and then get it back to us by tomorrow afternoon"이라며 내일 오후까지 작성 완료된 요청 양식을 제출해야 한다고 하였다. 따라서 (A)가 정답이다.

DAY 12 다음에 할 일 및 의도 파악 문제

기출 유형 1 다음에 할 일 문제

Example 영국 → 캐나다 p.78

해설
01번은 다음 대화에 관한 문제입니다.
여: Erik, Fosh 타워에 임대할 아파트가 아직 있나요? 저는 Sylvia Miller라는 잠재 고객과 이야기를 나누었는데, 그녀가 그 단지로 이사하는 것에 관심이 있어요.
남: 확인해보겠습니다... 음, 현재 그 단지에 세 개의 아파트가 이용 가능해요.
여: 현재 입주자가 있나요?
남: 아니요. 비어 있어서, 언제든지 그녀에게 보여줄 수 있습니다.
여: 완벽하네요. Ms. Miller와 연락해서 그녀가 아파트들을 볼 수 있는 시간을 정하도록 할게요.

어휘 potential adj. 잠재적인 occupy v. 점유하다, 차지하다

01
해설 여자는 다음에 무엇을 할 것인가?
(A) 동료와 이야기한다.
(B) 공지를 게시한다.
(C) 임대 계약을 체결한다.
(D) 약속을 잡는다.

어휘 agreement n. 계약

토익실전문제 p.79

| 01 (B) | 02 (D) | 03 (A) | 04 (D) | 05 (C) |
| 06 (D) |

[01-03] 미국 → 호주
Questions 01-03 refer to the following conversation.

W: Thank you for calling Sports World. How can I help you?
M: I bought some soccer gear through your Web site a couple of days ago. ⁰¹I was billed twice for the purchase. Can you check the charge on my billing statement?
W: Of course. ⁰²Could you give me the order number? It should be at the top of your purchase confirmation e-mail.
M: Let me check my e-mail . . . Uh, it's 6457.
W: Thank you. It looks like the double payment was due to a system error. I'll cancel the extra charge. ⁰³The refund will take about 24 hours to process, so please check your account tomorrow.

어휘 gear n. 장비 bill v. 청구하다 billing statement 청구서
process v. 처리하다 account n. 계좌, 계정

해석
01-03번은 다음 대화에 관한 문제입니다.
여: Sports World에 전화해 주셔서 감사합니다. 어떻게 도와드릴까요?
남: 제가 며칠 전에 귀사 웹사이트를 통해 축구 장비를 구매했는데요. ⁰¹그 구매에 대해 요금이 두 번 청구됐어요. 제 청구 명세서에서 요금을 확인해 주실 수 있나요?
여: 물론이죠. ⁰²주문 번호를 말씀해 주시겠어요? 구매 확인 이메일의 맨 위에 있을 거예요.
남: 제 이메일을 확인해 볼게요... 아, 6457이에요.
여: 감사합니다. 이중 결제는 시스템 오류로 인한 것으로 보이네요. 추가 요금을 취소해 드리겠습니다. ⁰³환불은 처리하는 데 약 24시간이 걸리니, 내일 계좌를 확인해 주세요.

01 목적 문제
해설 남자는 왜 전화하고 있는가?
(A) 기술적 지원을 요청하기 위해
(B) 청구서의 요금에 대해 문의하기 위해
(C) 온라인 주문을 취소하기 위해
(D) 늦은 배송에 대해 불평하기 위해

해설 전화의 목적을 묻는 문제이므로, 대화의 초반을 반드시 듣는다. 남자가 "I was billed twice for the purchase. Can you check the charge on my billing statement?"라며 구매에 대해 요금이 두 번 청구되었으니 청구 명세서에서 요금을 확인해 달라고 하였다. 따라서 (B)가 정답이다.

어휘 question v. 문의하다 complain v. 불평하다

02 요청 문제
해설 여자는 무엇을 요청하는가?
(A) 계정 번호
(B) 우편 주소
(C) 회사명
(D) 주문 번호

해설 여자의 말에서 요청과 관련된 표현이 언급된 다음을 주의 깊게 듣는다. 여자가 "Could you give me the order number?"라며 주문 번호를 알려 달라고 하였다. 따라서 (D)가 정답이다.

03 다음에 할 일 문제
해설 내일 무슨 일이 일어날 것인가?
(A) 지불금이 환불될 것이다.
(B) 배송품이 배달될 것이다.
(C) 유지보수가 수행될 것이다.
(D) 운영 시간이 연장될 것이다.

해설 질문의 핵심 어구(tomorrow)가 언급된 주변을 주의 깊게 듣는다. 여자가 "The refund will take about 24 hours to process, so please check your account tomorrow."라며 환불은 처리하는 데 약 24시간이 걸리니 내일 계좌를 확인하라고 하였다. 따라서 (A)가 정답이다.

어휘 perform v. 수행하다 extend v. 연장하다

[04-06] 영국 → 호주 → 캐나다
Questions 04-06 refer to the following conversation with three speakers.

W: Ron and Michael, ⁰⁴I heard you two are in charge of editing the new cookbook.
M1: Yes. The deadline is less than two weeks away, and we're worried about meeting it.
M2: Right. Especially since the CEO wants us to completely reorganize several chapters.
W: ⁰⁵I think you should request that additional staff be assigned to your project. Maybe some members

of teams that are not busy right now can help you out.
M1: That's a good idea. ⁰⁶**Michael, why don't you call the department head to ask about this?**
M2: ⁰⁶**Sure.** We can't extend the deadline, so this seems like our only option.

in charge of ~을 담당하는 deadline n. 마감일 reorganize v. 재구성하다
additional adj. 추가의 assign v. 배정하다

해석
04-06번은 다음 세 명의 대화에 관한 문제입니다.
여: Ron 그리고 Michael, ⁰⁴두 분이 새 요리책 편집을 맡고 있다고 들었어요.
남1: 네. 마감일이 2주도 채 남지 않았고, 저희는 그것을 맞출 수 있을지 걱정이에요.
남2: 맞아요. 특히 CEO는 저희가 몇 개의 장들을 완전히 재구성할 것을 원하기 때문이죠.
여: ⁰⁵추가 인력이 당신들의 프로젝트에 배정되도록 요청해야 할 것 같아요. 아마 지금 바쁘지 않은 팀들의 몇몇 구성원들이 당신들을 도울 수 있을 거예요.
남1: 좋은 생각이에요. ⁰⁶Michael, 이것에 대해 물어보기 위해 당신이 부서장에게 전화해 보는 게 어때요?
남2: ⁰⁶물론이죠. 우리는 마감일을 연장할 수 없으니, 이것이 우리의 유일한 선택지인 것 같네요.

04 화자 문제
해석 화자들은 어디에서 일하는 것 같은가?
(A) 서점에서
(B) 법률 사무소에서
(C) 채용 대행사에서
(D) 출판사에서

해설 대화에서 신분 및 직업과 관련된 표현을 놓치지 않고 듣는다. 여자가 "I heard you two are in charge of editing the new cookbook."이라며 두 남자가 새 요리책 편집을 맡고 있다고 한 것을 통해 화자들이 출판사에서 일한다는 것을 알 수 있다. 따라서 (D)가 정답이다.

05 제안 문제
해석 여자는 무슨 제안을 하는가?
(A) 일정 수정하기
(B) 주말 동안 일하기
(C) 추가 인력 요청하기
(D) 더 많은 용품 주문하기

해설 여자의 말에서 제안과 관련된 표현이 언급된 다음을 주의 깊게 듣는다. 여자가 "I think you should request that additional staff be assigned to your project."라며 추가 인력이 프로젝트에 배정되도록 요청해야 할 것 같다고 하였다. 따라서 (C)가 정답이다.

06 다음에 할 일 문제
해석 Michael은 다음에 무엇을 할 것 같은가?
(A) 행사에 참여한다.
(B) 회의를 확정한다.
(C) 책을 홍보한다.
(D) 관리자에게 연락한다.

해설 대화의 마지막 부분을 주의 깊게 듣는다. 남자1[Ron]이 "Michael, why don't you call the department head to ask about this?"라며 Michael에게 부서장에게 전화해서 추가 인력 배정에 대해 물어보라고 하자, 남자2[Michael]가 "Sure."라고 했으므로 Michael이 관리자에게 전화할 것임을 알 수 있다. 따라서 (D)가 정답이다.

Paraphrasing
department head 부서장 → manager 관리자

기출 유형 2 의도 파악 문제

Example 🎧 캐나다 → 미국   p.80

해석
01번은 다음 대화에 관한 문제입니다.
남: 당신 팀의 다가오는 홍콩 출장에 대한 예산을 논의하고 싶어요. 어제 제출하신 자금 지원 요청서를 검토했는데요. **당신은 지난번에는 직원을 단 세 명만 보냈어요.**
여: 몇몇 신입 직원들이 교육 목적으로 이번 출장에 동행할 예정이에요. 그것이 문제가 될까요?
남: 당신의 예산이 출장에 허용된 **최대 금액**을 초과합니다. 비용을 줄일 방법을 찾으셔야 돼요.
여: 음... Doyle 호텔이 이번 달에 30퍼센트 할인을 제공하고 있어요. 아마도 제가 거기에서 객실을 예약할 수 있을 것 같아요.

어휘 budget n. 예산 accompany v. 동행하다, 동반하다 exceed v. 초과하다
amount n. 금액, 양

01
해석 남자는 왜 "당신은 지난번에는 직원을 단 세 명만 보냈어요"라고 말하는가?
(A) 팀을 칭찬하기 위해
(B) 결정에 의문을 제기하기 위해
(C) 격려를 하기 위해
(D) 도움을 요청하기 위해

어휘 compliment v. 칭찬하다 encouragement n. 격려

토익실전문제   p.81

| 01 (B) | 02 (D) | 03 (C) | 04 (B) | 05 (C) |
| 06 (A) |

[01-03] 🎧 호주 → 영국
Questions 01-03 refer to the following conversation.

M: Ms. Beyer. ⁰¹**We've run into one problem with your remodeling project.** The chandelier you want for your boutique will cost more than I thought. ⁰²**There are some additional shipping fees since we have to order it from overseas.**
W: Well, I like the distinctive appearance of the chandelier. ⁰²**It perfectly matches my store's concept.**
M: OK. Then, I'll place the order right away. It should arrive within three days.
W: Thanks. ⁰³**Could you e-mail me the final cost estimate reflecting this expense?**
M: Sure. ⁰³**I'll send it tomorrow morning.**

run into 부딪히다, 맞닥뜨리다 distinctive adj. 독특한
appearance n. 외관 match v. 어울리다 expense n. 비용

해석
01-03번은 다음 대화에 관한 문제입니다.
남: Ms. Beyer. ⁰¹저희가 당신의 리모델링 프로젝트에서 한 가지 문제에 부딪혔습니다. 당신이 부티크를 위해 원하는 상들리에가 제가 생각했던 것보다 더 비쌀 것 같아요. ⁰²해외에서 주문해야 하기 때문에 추가 배송료가 있습니다.
여: 음, 저는 상들리에의 독특한 외관이 마음에 들어요. ⁰²그것은 제 상점 컨셉과 완벽하게 어울려요.
남: 알겠습니다. 그럼, 바로 주문을 넣을게요. 3일 내에 도착할 겁니다.
여: 감사합니다. ⁰³이 비용이 반영된 최종 비용 견적서를 제게 이메일로 보내

주실 수 있나요?
남: 물론이죠. ⁰³내일 아침에 보내드리겠습니다.

01 이유 문제
해석 여자는 왜 남자의 회사를 고용했는가?
(A) 건물을 점검하기 위해
(B) 개조를 하기 위해
(C) 사진을 찍기 위해
(D) 회사 야유회를 준비하기 위해

해설 질문의 핵심 어구(woman hire the man's company)와 관련된 내용을 주의 깊게 듣는다. 남자가 여자에게 "We've run into one problem with your remodeling project."라며 여자의 리모델링 프로젝트에 문제가 생겼다고 한 것을 통해 여자가 리모델링 공사를 위해 남자의 회사를 고용했음을 알 수 있다. 따라서 (B)가 정답이다.

어휘 inspect v. 점검하다

02 의도 파악 문제
해석 여자가 "저는 샹들리에의 독특한 외관이 마음에 들어요"라고 말할 때 무엇을 의도하는가?
(A) 그녀의 결정을 바꾸고 싶다.
(B) 의견을 받을 필요가 있다.
(C) 일부 진행 상황에 깊은 인상을 받았다.
(D) 추가 비용을 지불할 의향이 있다.

해설 질문의 인용어구(I like the distinctive appearance of the chandelier)가 언급된 주변을 주의 깊게 듣는다. 남자가 "There are some additional shipping fees since we have to order it from overseas."라며 샹들리에를 해외에서 주문해야 하기 때문에 추가 배송료가 있을 것이라고 하자, 여자가 "It perfectly matches my store's concept."이라며 샹들리에가 자신의 상점 컨셉과 완벽하게 잘 어울린다고 하였다. 이는 추가 배송료를 내더라도 그 샹들리에를 원한다는 것이므로, 추가 비용을 지불할 의향이 있음을 알 수 있다. 따라서 (D)가 정답이다.

어휘 willing to ~할 의향이 있는

03 특정 세부 사항 문제
해석 남자는 내일 아침에 여자에게 무엇을 보낼 것인가?
(A) 수정된 일정
(B) 디자인 샘플
(C) 비용 견적서
(D) 연락처

해설 질문의 핵심 어구(send ~ tomorrow morning)가 언급된 주변을 주의 깊게 듣는다. 여자가 "Could you e-mail me the final cost estimate reflecting this expense?"라며 최종 비용 견적서를 이메일로 보내달라고 요청하자, 남자가 "I'll send it tomorrow morning."이라며 내일 아침에 보내겠다고 하였다. 따라서 (C)가 정답이다.

[04-06] 미국 → 캐나다
Questions 04-06 refer to the following conversation.

W: Hello. I'm a guest here at the Winston Hotel, and ⁰⁴I'm attending the conference at Pearson University this afternoon. The organizers mentioned that a shuttle service had been set up.
M: That's right. ⁰⁵The bus arrives here at 2 P.M.
W: Hmm . . . ⁰⁵I'm one of the speakers, so I need to get there earlier than that.
M: In that case, we partner with a taxi company. Guests receive a 50 percent discount.
W: Wonderful. ⁰⁶Can you arrange a ride for me?
M: Sure. ⁰⁶If you stand near the entrance, a taxi will arrive shortly.

partner with ~와 제휴를 맺다 arrange v. 마련하다, 처리하다
shortly adv. 곧

해석
04-06번은 다음 대화에 관한 문제입니다.
여: 안녕하세요. 저는 여기 Winston 호텔의 손님인데요, ⁰⁴오늘 오후에 Pearson 대학교에서 열리는 학회에 참석할 것입니다. 주최 측에서 셔틀 서비스가 마련되어 있다고 말해서요.
남: 맞습니다. ⁰⁵버스는 여기에 오후 2시에 도착합니다.
여: 음... 저는 발표자 중 한 명이라서, 그보다 더 일찍 그곳에 가야 돼요.
남: 그런 경우라면, 저희가 택시 회사와 제휴를 맺고 있습니다. 손님들은 50퍼센트 할인을 받으실 수 있어요.
여: 좋네요. ⁰⁶제게 차량을 마련해 주실 수 있으신가요?
남: 물론이죠. ⁰⁶입구 근처에 서 계시면, 택시가 곧 도착할 겁니다.

04 특정 세부 사항 문제
해석 여자에 따르면, 오늘 무엇이 열리는가?
(A) 축제
(B) 학회
(C) 기금 모금 만찬
(D) 시상식

해설 여자의 말에서 질문의 핵심 어구(taking place today)와 관련된 내용을 주의 깊게 듣는다. 여자가 "I'm attending the conference at Pearson University this afternoon."이라며 오늘 오후에 Pearson 대학교에서 열리는 학회에 참석할 것이라고 하였다. 따라서 (B)가 정답이다.

어휘 banquet n. 만찬

05 의도 파악 문제
해석 남자는 왜 "저희가 택시 회사와 제휴를 맺고 있습니다"라고 말하는가?
(A) 변경 사항을 알리기 위해
(B) 결정을 정당화하기 위해
(C) 제안을 하기 위해
(D) 오해를 바로잡기 위해

해설 질문의 인용어구(we partner with a taxi company)가 언급된 주변을 주의 깊게 듣는다. 남자가 "The bus arrives here at 2 P.M."이라며 버스가 오후 2시에 도착한다고 하자, 여자가 "I'm one of the speakers, so I need to get there earlier than that."이라며 그것보다 더 일찍 도착해야 한다고 하였다. 남자가 이에 대해 그럴 경우 택시 회사와 제휴를 맺고 있다고 한 것은 셔틀버스의 대안으로 택시를 이용하라고 제안하는 것임을 알 수 있다. 따라서 (C)가 정답이다.

어휘 announce v. 알리다

06 다음에 할 일 문제
해석 여자는 다음에 무엇을 할 것 같은가?
(A) 입구 근처에서 기다린다.
(B) 방으로 돌아간다.
(C) 업체에 연락한다.
(D) 보고서를 평가한다.

해설 대화의 마지막 부분을 주의 깊게 듣는다. 여자가 "Can you arrange a ride for me?"라며 택시를 준비해줄 것을 부탁하자, 남자가 "If you stand near the entrance, a taxi will arrive shortly."라며 입구에서 기다리면 곧 택시가 도착할 것이라고 하였다. 따라서 (A)가 정답이다.

HACKERS TEST

p.82

01 (A)	02 (A)	03 (D)	04 (B)	05 (D)
06 (D)	07 (A)	08 (D)	09 (C)	10 (C)
11 (B)	12 (B)	13 (A)	14 (B)	15 (C)
16 (D)	17 (C)	18 (A)	19 (D)	20 (A)
21 (C)	22 (C)	23 (B)	24 (A)	

[01-03] 영국 → 캐나다

Questions 01-03 refer to the following conversation.

W: Ventura Home Goods. How can I help you?
M: Hello. I received the mirror that I ordered from your Web site. ⁰¹But when I opened the box, I discovered a large crack on the mirror's surface.
W: I apologize for that. Maybe it got damaged during shipment. ⁰²Could you please provide me with your name?
M: Derek Anderson.
W: Let me see . . . You ordered a white standing mirror. We have the item in stock, so we can send a new one right away. ⁰³Please put the damaged one by your door. A delivery driver in your area will pick it up this afternoon.

crack n. 균열, 금 surface n. 표면 damage v. 손상시키다
shipment n. 수송, 배송

해석

01-03번은 다음 대화에 관한 문제입니다.

여: Ventura 가정 용품점입니다. 어떻게 도와드릴까요?
남: 안녕하세요. 귀사의 웹사이트에서 주문한 거울을 받았어요. ⁰¹그런데 상자를 열었을 때, 거울 표면에 큰 균열이 있는 것을 발견했어요.
여: 그것에 대해 사과드립니다. 아마도 배송 중에 손상된 것 같네요. ⁰²성함을 알려주시겠어요?
남: Derek Anderson입니다.
여: 확인해 볼게요... 흰색 스탠딩 거울을 주문하셨네요. 저희가 그 상품을 재고로 보유하고 있어서 새 것을 바로 보내드릴 수 있어요. ⁰³손상된 것은 문 옆에 놓아주세요. 오늘 오후에 귀하 지역의 배송 기사가 수거해 갈 것입니다.

01 문제점 문제

해석 남자는 어떤 문제를 언급하는가?
(A) 상품이 손상되었다.
(B) 웹사이트가 작동하지 않는다.
(C) 주문품이 도착하지 않았다.
(D) 청구 명세서가 부정확하다.

해설 남자의 말에서 부정적인 표현이 언급된 주변을 주의 깊게 듣는다. 남자가 "But when I opened the box, I discovered a large crack on the mirror's surface."라며 상자를 열었을 때 거울 표면에 큰 균열이 있는 것을 발견했다고 하였다. 따라서 (A)가 정답이다.

[Paraphrasing]
a large crack on the mirror's surface 거울 표면에 큰 균열 → An item is damaged. 상품이 손상되었다.

02 특정 세부 사항 문제

해석 여자는 무엇에 대해 묻는가?
(A) 고객 이름
(B) 주문 번호
(C) 지불 방법

(D) 구매 날짜

해설 여자의 말에서 질문의 핵심 어구(ask about)와 관련된 내용을 주의 깊게 듣는다. 여자가 "Could you please provide me with your name?"이라며 남자에게 이름을 알려 달라고 하였다. 따라서 (A)가 정답이다.

어휘 method n. 방법

03 다음에 할 일 문제

해석 남자는 다음에 무엇을 할 것 같은가?
(A) 주문서를 다운로드한다.
(B) 교환 정책을 확인한다.
(C) 배송 담당자에게 전화한다.
(D) 지정된 장소에 물건을 둔다.

해설 대화의 마지막 부분을 주의 깊게 듣는다. 여자가 "Please put the damaged one by your door. A delivery driver in your area will pick it up this afternoon."이라며 손상된 거울을 문 옆에 두면 오늘 오후에 가져갈 것이라고 하였다. 따라서 (D)가 정답이다.

어휘 designated adj. 지정된

[04-06] 호주 → 미국

Questions 04-06 refer to the following conversation.

M: Good morning, Ms. Sanders. This is Carter from Gold Realtors. ⁰⁴I'm calling to let you know about a newly listed three-bedroom apartment in the San Lucas neighborhood.
W: Thank you for calling. Um, ⁰⁵are there many buses in that area? As I mentioned before, I want to live in a building with easy access to public transportation.
M: It's close to a metro station. ⁰⁵So you will be able to get around easily.
W: Great. Could you show me that apartment on Saturday morning?
M: I have appointments with several other clients before lunch. How about 2 P.M.?
W: OK. ⁰⁶Please text me the address, and I'll make sure to arrive on time.

realtor n. 공인중개사 newly adv. 새로, 최근에 close to ~에 가까운
get around 돌아다니다 on time 정시에

해석

04-06번은 다음 대화에 관한 문제입니다.

남: 안녕하세요, Ms. Sanders. Gold 공인중개사 사무소의 Carter입니다. ⁰⁴샌 루카스 지역에 새로 매물로 나온 침실 세 개짜리 아파트에 대해 알려드리려고 전화드립니다.
여: 전화해 주셔서 감사해요. ⁰⁵음, 그 지역에 버스가 많이 다니나요? 제가 전에 언급했듯이, 대중교통에 쉽게 접근할 수 있는 건물에서 살고 싶어요.
남: 지하철역 가까이에 있어요. ⁰⁵그래서 쉽게 돌아다니실 수 있을 거예요.
여: 좋네요. 토요일 오전에 그 아파트를 보여주실 수 있나요?
남: 제가 점심 전에 다른 여러 고객들과 약속이 있어요. 오후 2시는 어떨까요?
여: 알겠습니다. ⁰⁶주소를 문자로 보내주세요, 그러면 제가 정시에 도착할 수 있도록 하겠습니다.

04 목적 문제

해석 남자는 왜 전화하고 있는가?
(A) 첫 면접 일정을 잡기 위해
(B) 아파트에 대한 정보를 제공하기 위해
(C) 요구 사항에 대해 물어보기 위해
(D) 집수리 일정을 잡기 위해

해설 전화의 목적을 묻는 문제이므로, 대화의 초반을 반드시 듣는다. 남

DAY 12 다음에 할 일 및 의도 파악 문제 **73**

자가 "I'm calling to let you know about a newly listed three-bedroom apartment in the San Lucas neighborhood."라며 샌 루카스 지역에 새로 매물로 나온 침실 세 개짜리 아파트에 대해 알려주려고 전화했다고 하였다. 따라서 (B)가 정답이다.

어휘 requirement n. 요구 사항

05 의도 파악 문제
해석 남자는 왜 "지하철역 가까이에 있어요"라고 말하는가?
(A) 도움을 요청하기 위해
(B) 시스템 개선을 칭찬하기 위해
(C) 잘못된 추측을 바로잡기 위해
(D) 안심시키기 위해

해설 질문의 인용어구(It's close to a metro station)가 언급된 주변을 주의 깊게 듣는다. 여자가 "are there many buses in that area? As I mentioned before, I want to live in a building with easy access to public transportation."이라며 그 지역에 버스가 많이 다니는지 물으면서 대중교통에 쉽게 접근할 수 있는 건물에 살고 싶다고 하였다. 이에 대해 남자가 "It's close to a metro station. So you will be able to get around easily."라며 지하철역에 가까이 있으니 쉽게 돌아다닐 수 있을 거라고 하였다. 따라서 (D)가 정답이다.

어휘 assumption n. 추측, 가정 reassurance n. 안심시키는 말

06 요청 문제
해석 여자는 남자에게 무엇을 보내달라고 요청하는가?
(A) 행사 초대장
(B) 추적 번호
(C) 고용 계약서
(D) 주택의 주소

해설 여자의 말에서 요청과 관련된 표현이 언급된 다음을 주의 깊게 듣는다. 여자가 "Please text me the address"라며 아파트 주소를 문자로 보내달라고 하였다. 따라서 (D)가 정답이다.

어휘 residential adj. 주택의

[07-09] 🎧 캐나다 → 미국 → 호주
Questions 07-09 refer to the following conversation with three speakers.

M1: Before we wrap up our meeting today, ⁰⁷**I'd like to get an update on our company's year-end party**.
W: Unfortunately, Madras Hall, the venue we used last year, is already fully booked. So I asked Peter to look for some alternatives. ⁰⁸**Have you found any, Peter?**
M2: Yes. West Hotel's event hall could be a suitable option. However, ⁰⁸**I'm worried that the dishes served there are too expensive**. Providing a meal for attendees may cost more than we anticipated.
M1: I see. ⁰⁹**Why don't we review the event budget at our meeting next week?**
M2: OK. ⁰⁹**I'll prepare a report before then** comparing the West Hotel's costs with those of other potential venues.

wrap up ~을 마치다, 끝내다 alternative n. 대안 serve v. 제공하다
potential adj. 잠재적인

해석
07-09번은 다음 세 명의 대화에 관한 문제입니다.

남1: 오늘 회의를 마치기 전에, ⁰⁷우리 회사의 연말 파티에 관한 업데이트를 듣고 싶습니다.
여: 안타깝게도, 작년에 우리가 사용했던 장소인 Madras 홀은 이미 완전히 예약이 찼어요. 그래서 Peter에게 대안을 찾아보라고 부탁했어요. ⁰⁸찾은 것이 있나요, Peter?
남2: 네. West 호텔의 행사장이 적절한 선택이 될 수 있을 것 같아요. ⁰⁸하지만, 저는 그곳에서 제공되는 음식이 너무 비싸다는 것이 걱정됩니다. 참석자들에게 식사를 제공하는 것이 우리가 예상했던 것보다 비용이 더 들 수 있어요.
남1: 알겠습니다. ⁰⁹다음 주 회의 때 행사 예산을 검토하는 것이 어떨까요?
남2: 좋습니다. 제가 그때까지 West 호텔의 비용과 다른 잠재적 장소들의 비용을 비교하는 ⁰⁹보고서를 준비하겠습니다.

07 주제 문제
해석 화자들은 주로 무엇에 관해 논의하고 있는가?
(A) 기업 행사
(B) 호텔 개업
(C) 출장
(D) 교육 워크숍

해설 대화의 주제를 묻는 문제이므로, 대화의 초반을 반드시 듣는다. 남자1이 "I'd like to get an update on our company's year-end party"라며 회사의 연말 파티에 관한 업데이트를 듣고 싶다고 했고, 연말 파티를 열기 위한 행사장에 대한 내용으로 대화가 이어지고 있다. 따라서 (A)가 정답이다.

Paraphrasing
company's year-end party 회사의 연말 파티 → A corporate event 기업 행사

08 문제점 문제
해석 Peter는 어떤 우려를 지적하는가?
(A) 일부 메뉴 옵션을 이용할 수 없다.
(B) 프로젝트는 인력이 부족할 수 있다.
(C) 공간이 청소돼야 한다.
(D) 일부 음식이 비싸다.

해설 Peter의 말에서 부정적인 표현이 언급된 주변을 주의 깊게 듣는다. 여자가 남자2에게 "Have you found any, Peter?"라며 대안이 될 수 있는 행사장을 찾아보았냐고 물었고, 이에 대해 남자2[Peter]가 "I'm worried that the dishes served there are too expensive"라며 대안이 될 수 있는 West 호텔에서 제공되는 음식이 너무 비싸서 걱정이라고 하였다. 따라서 (D)가 정답이다.

어휘 understaffed adj. 인력이 부족한

Paraphrasing
dishes 요리 → food 음식

09 다음에 할 일 문제
해석 다음 주에 무슨 일이 일어날 것인가?
(A) 상이 수여될 것이다.
(B) 회사가 새로운 장소로 이전할 것이다.
(C) 보고서가 검토될 것이다.
(D) 기자 회견이 열릴 것이다.

해설 질문의 핵심 어구(next week)가 언급된 주변을 주의 깊게 듣는다. 남자1이 "Why don't we review the event budget at our meeting next week?"이라며 다음 주 회의 때 행사 예산을 검토하자고 하였고, 이에 남자2가 "I'll prepare a report before then"이라며 그때까지 비교 보고서를 준비하겠다고 하였다. 따라서 (C)가 정답이다.

[10-12] 🎧 호주 → 영국
Questions 10-12 refer to the following conversation.

M: ¹⁰**Welcome to Dalton International Airport.** What can I do for you?
W: Hi. Um, ¹¹**I tried to use the self check-in machine, and it doesn't seem to be working.** No matter what I do, it won't scan my passport.

M: Actually, there's an issue with the system, and it will likely take about an hour to resolve. You're going to have to check in at the airline's counter.
W: I don't have a lot of time until my flight departs. ¹²I hope the line is not too long.
M: Well, today is less crowded than usual.

issue n. 문제   resolve v. 해결하다   depart v. 출발하다
crowded adj. 혼잡한, 붐비는

해석
10-12번은 다음 대화에 관한 문제입니다.
남: ¹⁰Dalton 국제공항에 오신 것을 환영합니다. 무엇을 도와드릴까요?
여: 안녕하세요. 음, ¹¹저는 방금 셀프 체크인 기계를 사용하려고 했는데, 그것이 작동하지 않는 것 같네요. 제가 무엇을 해도 제 여권을 스캔하지 못하네요.
남: 사실, 시스템에 문제가 있어서 해결하는 데 약 한 시간 정도 걸릴 것 같아요. 항공사 카운터에서 체크인하셔야 할 거예요.
여: 제 비행기가 출발하기까지 시간이 많이 없어요. ¹²줄이 너무 길지 않기를 바랍니다.
남: 음, 오늘은 평소보다 덜 혼잡해요.

10 장소 문제
해석 대화는 어디에서 이루어지고 있는가?
(A) 기념품 가게에서
(B) 수퍼마켓에서
(C) 공항에서
(D) 레스토랑에서
해설 장소와 관련된 표현을 놓치지 않고 듣는다. 남자가 "Welcome to Dalton International Airport."라며 Dalton 국제공항에 오신 것을 환영한다고 하였다. 따라서 (C)가 정답이다.

11 언급 문제
해석 여자는 방금 무엇을 하려고 했다고 말하는가?
(A) 주문을 한다.
(B) 기기를 사용한다.
(C) 서류를 찾는다.
(D) 지불을 한다.
해설 여자의 말에서 질문의 핵심 어구(tried to do)와 관련된 내용을 주의 깊게 듣는다. 여자가 "I tried to use the self check-in machine, and it doesn't seem to be working."이라며 셀프 체크인 기계를 사용하려고 했는데 작동하지 않는 것 같다고 하였다. 따라서 (B)가 정답이다.
[Paraphrasing]
self check-in machine 셀프 체크인 기계 → device 기기

12 의도 파악 문제
해석 남자가 "오늘은 평소보다 덜 혼잡해요"라고 말할 때 무엇을 의도하는가?
(A) 문제가 해결되었다.
(B) 여자의 우려는 타당하지 않다.
(C) 추정치가 업데이트되었다.
(D) 여자의 요청이 합리적이지 않다.
해설 질문의 인용어구(today is less crowded than usual)가 언급된 주변을 주의 깊게 듣는다. 여자가 "I hope the line is not too long."이라며 줄이 너무 길지 않기를 바란다고 하자, 남자가 "Well, today is less crowded than usual."이라며 오늘은 평소보다 덜 혼잡하다고 하였다. 이는 여자가 줄이 길까 봐 걱정할 필요가 없다는 것이므로, 여자의 우려가 타당하지 않음을 알 수 있다. 따라서 (B)가 정답이다.
어휘 valid adj. 타당한, 유효한   reasonable adj. 합리적인

[13-15] 미국 → 캐나다
Questions 13-15 refer to the following conversation.

W: Look at the departure board, Max. ¹³Our train to Chicago has been delayed for an hour because of engine problems.
M: Hmm . . . So we'll arrive at 1:15 P.M.? That won't give us enough time to get to Mr. Tanaka's office.
W: ¹⁴He's one of our most important clients. I don't want to cancel the meeting with him.
M: I'm sure he will understand that this situation is not our fault. Why don't we check if he can see us later in the afternoon?
W: ¹⁵I'll text Mr. Tanaka and ask him to postpone the meeting. If he is available at 3 P.M., we should be able to make it.

departure board 출발 안내판   delay v. 지연시키다   situation n. 상황
fault n. 잘못   postpone v. 미루다

해석
13-15번은 다음 대화에 관한 문제입니다.
여: 출발 안내판을 봐요, Max. ¹³우리의 시카고행 열차가 엔진 문제로 한 시간 지연되었어요.
남: 음… 그러면 우리가 오후 1시 15분에 도착하겠네요? 그러면 Mr. Tanaka의 사무실에 가기에 충분한 시간이 없을 거예요.
여: ¹⁴그는 우리의 가장 중요한 고객들 중 한 명이에요. 저는 그와의 회의를 취소하고 싶지 않아요.
남: 이 상황이 우리의 잘못이 아니라는 것을 그가 이해할 거라고 확신해요. 그가 오후 늦게 우리를 만날 수 있는지 확인해 보는 게 어떨까요?
여: ¹⁵제가 Mr. Tanaka에게 문자메시지를 보내서 회의를 연기해 달라고 요청할게요. 그가 오후 3시에 시간이 된다면, 우리는 갈 수 있을 거예요.

13 이유 문제
해석 지연의 이유는 무엇인가?
(A) 기계적 문제가 발생했다.
(B) 기상 상태가 좋지 않다.
(C) 여러 직원들이 결근했다.
(D) 일부 정보가 부정확했다.
해설 질문의 핵심 어구(reason for a delay)와 관련된 내용을 주의 깊게 듣는다. 여자가 "Our train to Chicago has been delayed for an hour because of engine problems."라며 열차가 엔진 문제로 지연되었다고 하였다. 따라서 (A)가 정답이다.
어휘 occur v. 발생하다   absent adj. 결근한, 부재 중인
[Paraphrasing]
engine problems 엔진 문제 → Mechanical issues 기계적 문제

14 특정 세부 사항 문제
해석 화자들은 누구와 만나기로 예정되어 있는가?
(A) 검사관
(B) 고객
(C) 이전 동료
(D) 가족 구성원
해설 대화에서 질문의 핵심 어구(scheduled to meet with)와 관련된 내용을 주의 깊게 듣는다. 여자가 "He's one of our most important clients. I don't want to cancel the meeting with him."이라며 그는 중요한 고객이라서 그와의 회의를 취소하고 싶지 않다고 한 것을 통해 고객을 만날 예정임을 알 수 있다. 따라서 (B)가 정답이다.

15 다음에 할 일 문제

해설 여자는 자신이 무엇을 할 것이라고 말하는가?
(A) 애플리케이션을 다운로드한다.
(B) 표를 구매한다.
(C) 메시지를 보낸다.
(D) 링크를 제공한다.

해설 여자의 말에서 질문의 핵심 어구(she will do)와 관련된 내용을 주의 깊게 듣는다. 여자가 "I'll text Mr. Tanaka and ask him to postpone the meeting."이라며 Mr. Tanaka에게 문자메시지를 보내겠다고 하였다. 따라서 (C)가 정답이다.

어휘 purchase v. 구매하다

[16-18] 영국 → 호주
Questions 16-18 refer to the following conversation.

W: ¹⁶Kyle, we've got a problem with the projector in Cinema 5. It turns on, but no image is projected onto the screen.
M: ¹⁷Maybe we should have a technician come before the movie starts.
W: That is in just half an hour. ¹⁷We won't have enough time to get the projector repaired.
M: Then, let's show the movie in Cinema 3 instead. It isn't being used right now.
W: OK. I'll get everything ready in Cinema 3. ¹⁸Could you make an announcement for the ticketholders?

turn on ~을 켜다 project v. 투사하다, 보여주다 instead adv. 대신에
ticketholder n. 티켓 소지자

해설
16-18번은 다음 대화에 관한 문제입니다.
여: ¹⁶Kyle, 영화관 5관의 프로젝터에 문제가 있어요. 켜지긴 하는데, 화면에 이미지가 투사되지 않아요.
남: ¹⁷영화가 시작하기 전에 기술자를 불러야 할 것 같아요.
여: 그건 불과 30분 후에 있어요. ¹⁷프로젝터를 수리할 만한 충분한 시간이 없을 거예요.
남: 그러면, 대신 영화를 3관에서 상영합시다. 지금 사용되지 않고 있어요.
여: 좋아요. 제가 3관에 모든 것을 준비할게요. ¹⁸당신이 티켓 소지자들에게 안내 방송을 해 주시겠어요?

16 화자 문제

해설 화자들은 어디에서 일하는 것 같은가?
(A) 소매점에서
(B) 전자제품 상점에서
(C) 사진 스튜디오에서
(D) 영화관에서

해설 대화에서 신분 및 직업과 관련된 표현을 놓치지 않고 듣는다. 여자가 "Kyle, we've got a problem with the projector in Cinema 5."라며 영화관 5관의 프로젝터에 문제가 있다고 하였다. 따라서 (D)가 정답이다.

17 의도 파악 문제

해설 여자가 "그건 불과 30분 후에 있어요"라고 말할 때 무엇을 의도하는가?
(A) 그녀는 더 많은 세부 사항을 요청하고 있다.
(B) 그녀는 좌석 요청을 변경하고 싶어한다.
(C) 그녀는 제안에 대해 의구심을 표현하고 있다.
(D) 그녀는 그녀의 일정을 조정할 수 있다.

해설 질문의 인용어구(That is in just half an hour)가 언급된 주변을 주의 깊게 듣는다. 남자가 "Maybe we should have a technician come before the movie starts."라며 영화가 시작하기 전에 기술자를 불러야 할 것 같다고 제안하자, 여자가 "We won't have enough time to get the projector repaired."라며 프로젝터를 수리할 만한 충분한 시간이 없을 것이라고 한 것을 통해 남자의 제안에 대해 의구심을 표현하고 있는 것임을 알 수 있다. 따라서 (C)가 정답이다.

18 요청 문제

해설 여자는 남자에게 무엇을 하라고 요청하는가?
(A) 변경 사항을 공지한다.
(B) 장소를 예약한다.
(C) 점검을 수행한다.
(D) 동료를 돕는다.

해설 여자의 말에서 요청과 관련된 표현이 언급된 다음을 주의 깊게 듣는다. 여자가 "Could you make an announcement for the ticketholders?"라며 티켓 소지자들에게 안내 방송을 해 달라고 하였다. 따라서 (A)가 정답이다.

어휘 reserve v. 예약하다 assist v. 돕다

[19-21] 호주 → 영국
Questions 19-21 refer to the following conversation.

M: Did you hear the news, Stacy? ¹⁹Star Café decided to buy our commercial coffee machines.
W: Yeah. The equipment will be used at 15 locations. As an added benefit, I'm thinking of holding a workshop for its staff. ²⁰Do you know of any venues that I could use for that? I estimate there'll be 200 participants.
M: The Richfield Hotel has a fully equipped conference room. You'd better book it soon, though. It's fairly popular.
W: ²¹I'll call the human resources manager of Star Café now to find out a convenient date for the training. After I speak to her, I'll make a reservation at the hotel.

commercial adj. 상업용의 add v. 추가하다 benefit n. 혜택
equip v. 장비를 갖추다 convenient adj. 편리한

해설
19-21번은 다음 대화에 관한 문제입니다.
남: 소식 들었어요, Stacy? ¹⁹Star 카페가 우리의 상업용 커피 기계들을 사기로 결정했어요.
여: 네. 그 장비는 15개 지점에서 사용될 거예요. 추가적인 혜택으로, 저는 그곳의 직원들에게 워크숍을 열어 주는 것을 생각하고 있어요. ²⁰제가 그것을 위해 사용할 만한 장소들을 알고 계신가요? 저는 200명의 참석자가 있을 것으로 예상해요.
남: Richfield 호텔에 장비를 완전히 갖춘 회의실이 있어요. 하지만, 빨리 예약하시는 것이 좋을 거예요. 그곳은 꽤 인기 있어요.
여: 교육을 위해 편리한 날짜를 알아보기 위해 ²¹지금 Star 카페의 인사 관리자에게 전화해 볼게요. 그녀와 이야기하고 나서, 그 호텔에 예약해야겠어요.

19 특정 세부 사항 문제

해설 화자들의 회사는 어떤 종류의 제품을 만드는가?
(A) 의류
(B) 사무용 가구
(C) 스포츠 용품
(D) 가전제품

해설 질문의 핵심 어구(speaker's company make)와 관련된 내용을 주의 깊게 듣는다. 남자가 "Star Café decided to buy our commercial coffee machines."라며 Star 카페가 화자들의 상업용 커피 머신을 사기로 결정했다고 하였다. 따라서 (D)가 정답이다.

Paraphrasing
coffee machines 커피 머신 → Appliances 가전제품

20 특정 세부 사항 문제
해석 여자는 무엇에 대해 문의하는가?
(A) 행사 장소
(B) 손님 목록
(C) 제품 견본
(D) 사용 설명서

해설 여자의 말에서 질문의 핵심 어구(ask about)와 관련된 내용을 주의 깊게 듣는다. 여자가 "Do you know of any venues that I could use for that?"이라며 워크숍을 위해 사용할 만한 장소들을 아는지 물었다. 따라서 (A)가 정답이다.

21 다음에 할 일 문제
해석 여자는 다음에 무엇을 할 것 같은가?
(A) 안내서를 읽는다.
(B) 계획을 발표한다.
(C) 관리자에게 연락한다.
(D) 웹사이트를 업데이트한다.

해설 대화의 마지막 부분을 주의 깊게 듣는다. 여자가 "I'll call the human resources manager of Star Café now"라며 지금 Star 카페의 인사 관리자에게 전화하겠다고 하였다. 따라서 (C)가 정답이다.

Paraphrasing
call 전화하다 → Contact 연락하다

[22-24] 캐나다 → 미국
Questions 22-24 refer to the following conversation.

M: Anita, ²²**I want to discuss productivity at our shoe factory**. It's been low lately. We're barely meeting our monthly quotas.
W: What do you think is causing this decline?
M: ²³**I think the issue is the staff members we recruited last year.**
W: What do you mean?
M: They aren't meeting our performance expectations. ²⁴**It is likely because they did not receive proper training.**
W: But they went through our normal orientation process.
M: Actually, they only got two days of training instead of the usual four.
W: Hmm . . . Maybe we should organize some additional workshops.

productivity n. 생산성 lately adv. 최근에 barely adv. 간신히, 가까스로 cause v. 야기하다 recruit v. 채용하다 expectation n. 기대(치)

해석
22-24번은 다음 대화에 관한 문제입니다.
남: Anita, ²²저는 우리 신발 공장의 생산성에 대해 논의하고 싶어요. 최근에 생산성이 낮아졌어요. 우리는 간신히 월별 할당량을 맞추고 있어요.
여: 이러한 하락을 야기하는 원인이 무엇이라고 생각하세요?
남: ²³저는 문제가 작년에 우리가 채용한 직원들이라고 생각해요.
여: 무슨 말씀이신가요?
남: 그들은 우리의 업무 성과 기대치를 충족시키지 못하고 있어요. ²⁴아마도 적절한 교육을 받지 못했기 때문일 거예요.
여: 하지만 그들은 정상적인 오리엔테이션 과정을 거쳤어요.
남: 사실, 그들은 보통의 4일 대신 2일간의 교육만 받았어요.
여: 흠... 아마도 우리가 추가 워크숍을 준비해야 할 것 같네요.

22 화자 문제
해석 화자들은 어디에서 일하는 것 같은가?
(A) 식당에서
(B) 백화점에서
(C) 제조 시설에서
(D) 컨설팅 회사에서

해설 대화에서 신분 및 직업과 관련된 표현을 놓치지 않고 듣는다. 남자가 "I want to discuss productivity at our shoe factory"라며 우리 신발 공장의 생산성에 대해 논의하고 싶다고 하였다. 따라서 (C)가 정답이다.

Paraphrasing
shoe factory 신발 공장 → manufacturing facility 제조 시설

23 특정 세부 사항 문제
해석 화자들의 회사는 작년에 무엇을 했는가?
(A) 온라인 교육을 실시했다.
(B) 직원들을 고용했다.
(C) 일부 직원들을 전근시켰다.
(D) 광고 워크숍을 개최했다.

해설 질문의 핵심 어구(last year)가 언급된 주변을 주의 깊게 듣는다. 남자가 "I think the issue is the staff members we recruited last year."라며 작년에 화자들이 채용한 직원들이 문제인 것 같다고 하였다. 따라서 (B)가 정답이다.

어휘 transfer v. 전근시키다

24 의도 파악 문제
해석 여자는 왜 "그들은 정상적인 오리엔테이션 과정을 거쳤어요"라고 말하는가?
(A) 이견을 보이기 위해
(B) 만족감을 표시하기 위해
(C) 과정에 대해 문의하기 위해
(D) 확인을 제공하기 위해

해설 질문의 인용어구(they went through our normal orientation process)가 언급된 주변을 주의 깊게 듣는다. 남자가 "It is likely because they did not receive proper training."이라며 신입 직원들이 적절한 교육을 받지 못했다고 말한 것에 대해 여자가 "But they went through the normal orientation process."라며 그들은 정상적인 오리엔테이션 과정을 거쳤다고 한 것을 통해 남자의 말에 반대하는 의견을 보이기 위함임을 알 수 있다. 따라서 (A)가 정답이다.

DAY 13 시각 자료 문제

기출 유형 1 표 및 그래프

Example 미국 → 호주   p.84

01번은 다음 대화와 제품 목록에 관한 문제입니다.
여: Steve, 우리 회사가 저를 다음 주에 마케팅 컨벤션에 참석하도록 방콕으로 보낼 거예요. 저는 며칠 더 묵으면서 몇몇 해변에 방문할 예정이라서, 햇빛 차단용 모자에 대한 당신의 의견이 필요해요.
남: 어느 모자를 고려하고 있나요?
여: 이것들이 온라인에서 구매 가능한 것들이에요. Bongo Fashion사의 모자가 보기 좋은데, 그것은 너무 비싸요.
남: **저는 25달러짜리를 사야 한다고 생각해요.** 그것이 굉장히 멋져요.
여: 네, 저도 그게 좋아요. 이제, 주문을 할 수 있도록 이 온라인 쇼핑 사이트에서 계정을 만들기만 하면 돼요.

SAVALL MOTORS사 팀 빌딩 워크숍	
연설자	주제
Logan Jenkins	직원 의사소통
02Betty Graham	직장에서의 신뢰
Aubrey Hammond	신입 직원 교육
Carson Filby	팀 효율성

어휘 consider v. 고려하다 account n. 계정

01
해석 시각 자료를 보아라. 여자는 어떤 브랜드를 살 것 같은가?
(A) Bongo Fashion
(B) West Coast Apparel
(C) Luna Beachwear
(D) Sunny Clothes

토익실전문제   p.85

| 01 (D) | 02 (B) | 03 (A) | 04 (B) | 05 (B) |
| 06 (A) | | | | |

[01-03]   영국 → 캐나다
Questions 01-03 refer to the following conversation and program.

W: Hey, Stan. How did everything go at the teambuilding event yesterday? 01**I couldn't attend it because I had to complete a report.**
M: It was great. I really enjoyed getting to know our colleagues who work in other departments.
W: Good for you. 02**Which workshop did you attend?**
M: 02**The one about building trust in the workplace.** It was pretty interesting.
W: I was hoping to go to that one, too.
M: 03**For those who couldn't attend, videos of all the lectures are going to be posted on our company Web site.** You can watch them later today.

complete v. 완료하다 colleague n. 동료 build v. 쌓다
workplace n. 직장 lecture n. 강연

해석
01-03번은 다음 대화와 프로그램에 관한 문제입니다.
여: 안녕하세요, Stan. 어제 팀 빌딩 행사가 어떻게 진행되었나요? 01저는 보고서를 완료해야 해서 그것에 참석할 수가 없었어요.
남: 좋았어요. 다른 부서에서 일하는 우리 동료들을 알게 되어 정말 즐거웠어요.
여: 잘 됐네요. 02어느 워크숍에 참석했나요?
남: 02직장에서 신뢰를 쌓는 것에 관한 것이요. 꽤 흥미로웠어요.
여: 저도 그것을 듣고 싶었어요.
남: 03참석할 수 없었던 사람들을 위해, 모든 강연의 영상은 우리 회사 웹사이트에 게시될 거예요. 오늘 오후에 그것들을 볼 수 있을 거예요.

01 이유 문제
해석 여자는 왜 행사에 참여할 수 없었는가?
(A) 관리자를 도와야 했다.
(B) 출장을 가야 있었다.
(C) 중요한 고객과 만나야 했다.
(D) 업무를 완료해야 했다.

해설 질문의 핵심 어구(unable to attend)와 관련된 내용을 주의 깊게 듣는다. 여자가 "I couldn't attend it because I had to complete a report."라며 보고서를 완료해야 해서 팀 빌딩 행사에 참석할 수 없었다고 하였다. 따라서 (D)가 정답이다.

어휘 assist v. 돕다 assignment n. 업무

Paraphrasing
report 보고서 → assignment 업무

02 시각 자료 문제
해석 시각 자료를 보아라. 남자가 참석한 워크숍을 누가 진행했는가?
(A) Logan Jenkins
(B) Betty Graham
(C) Aubrey Hammond
(D) Carson Filby

해설 프로그램의 정보를 확인한 후 질문의 핵심 어구(workshop ~ man participated in)와 관련된 내용을 주의 깊게 듣는다. 여자가 "Which workshop did you attend?"라며 어떤 워크숍에 참석했는지 묻자, 남자가 "The one about building trust in the workplace."라며 직장에서 신뢰를 쌓는 것에 관한 것이라고 하였다. 프로그램에서 직장에서 신뢰를 쌓는 것에 대한 워크숍은 Betty Graham이 진행했음을 알 수 있다. 따라서 (B)가 정답이다.

03 특정 세부 사항 문제
해석 무엇이 온라인에 게시될 것인가?
(A) 영상
(B) 대본
(C) 지도
(D) 일정

해설 질문의 핵심 어구(posted online)와 관련된 내용을 주의 깊게 듣는다. 남자가 "For those who couldn't attend, videos of all the lectures are going to be posted on our company Web site."라며 참석하지 못한 사람들을 위해 모든 강연의 영상이 우리 회사 웹사이트에 게시될 것이라고 하였다. 따라서 (A)가 정답이다.

[04-06]   호주 → 미국
Questions 04-06 refer to the following conversation and graph.

M: 04**Mindy, is the customer survey for our store going well?**
W: Yes. About 300 customers have responded. 05**I'll send you the survey results next Wednesday.**
M: Good. And I reviewed the quarterly sales report this morning. Sales have significantly increased compared to last quarter.
W: I think that's because of the ads we posted on

various social media platforms.
M: Right. But ⁰⁶I'm concerned about the brand with the second-lowest sales. It hasn't sold well for several months now. Hmm . . . We should probably offer a discount.
W: ⁰⁶I agree. Why don't we mark it down by 15 percent?

survey n. 설문조사   respond v. 응답하다   compared to ~와 비교하여

해석
04-06번은 다음 대화와 그래프에 관한 문제입니다.
남: ⁰⁴Mindy, 우리 매장에 대한 고객 설문조사가 잘 진행되고 있나요?
여: 네, 대략 300명의 고객들이 응답했어요. ⁰⁵다음 주 수요일에 설문조사 결과를 보내드릴게요.
남: 좋아요. 그리고 오늘 아침에 분기별 판매 보고서를 검토했어요. 지난 분기와 비교해서 판매가 크게 증가했어요.
여: 그것은 우리가 다양한 소셜 미디어 플랫폼에 게시한 광고 덕분이라고 생각해요.
남: 맞아요. 하지만 ⁰⁶저는 두 번째로 낮은 판매량을 가진 브랜드가 걱정돼요. 몇 개월 동안 잘 팔리지 않았어요. 흠... 아마도 우리는 할인을 제공해야 할 것 같아요.
여: ⁰⁶동의해요. 15퍼센트 정도 할인하는 건 어떨까요?

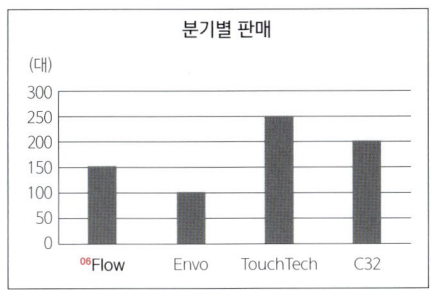

04 화자 문제
해석 화자들은 어디에서 일하는 것 같은가?
(A) 제조 공장에서
(B) 소매점에서
(C) 광고 회사에서
(D) 텔레비전 스튜디오에서

해설 대화에서 신분 및 직업과 관련된 표현을 놓치지 않고 듣는다. 남자가 "Mindy, is the customer survey for our store going well?"이라며 우리 매장에 대한 고객 설문조사가 잘 진행되고 있냐고 물은 것을 통해 화자들이 소매점에서 일한다는 것을 알 수 있다. 따라서 (B)가 정답이다.

[Paraphrasing]
store 매장 → retail shop 소매점

05 특정 세부 사항 문제
해석 여자는 남자에게 무엇을 보낼 것인가?
(A) 연간 판매 보고서
(B) 고객 설문조사 결과
(C) 분기별 지출 보고서
(D) 제품 개발 계획

해설 여자의 말에서 질문의 핵심 어구(send the man)와 관련된 내용을 주의 깊게 듣는다. 여자가 남자에게 "I'll send you the survey results next Wednesday."라며 다음 주 수요일에 설문조사 결과를 보내겠다고 하였다. 따라서 (B)가 정답이다.

06 시각 자료 문제
해석 시각 자료를 보아라. 어떤 브랜드가 할인될 것인가?
(A) Flow
(B) Envo
(C) TouchTech
(D) C32

해설 제시된 그래프의 정보를 확인한 후 질문의 핵심 어구(going to be discounted)와 관련된 내용을 주의 깊게 듣는다. 남자가 "I'm concerned about the brand with the second-lowest sales. It hasn't sold well for several months now. Hmm . . . We should probably offer a discount."라며 두 번째로 낮은 판매량을 가진 브랜드가 걱정된다며 몇 개월 동안 잘 팔리지 않으니 아마도 할인을 제공해야 할 것 같다고 하자, 여자가 "I agree."라며 동의한다고 하였다. 그래프에서 두 번째로 낮은 판매량의 브랜드는 Flow임을 알 수 있다. 따라서 (A)가 정답이다.

기출 유형 2 약도 및 기타 시각 자료

Example 호주 → 영국   p.86
01번은 다음 대화와 요리법에 관한 문제입니다.
남: 좋아요, 우리는 요리 수업을 위한 도구를 준비하는 것을 마쳤어요. 우리는 요리법을 검토해 봐야 해요. 학생들이 45분 후에 도착하기 시작할 거예요.
여: 네, 여기 우리가 사용할 팬케이크 요리법이에요. 그런데 요리법 단계 중 하나를 약간 변경해야 해요. 몇몇 학생들은 유제품을 먹지 않아서, 팬에 버터 대신 기름을 사용해야 해요.
남: 아, 그렇네요. 제가 보관실에서 필요한 재료들을 가져올게요.

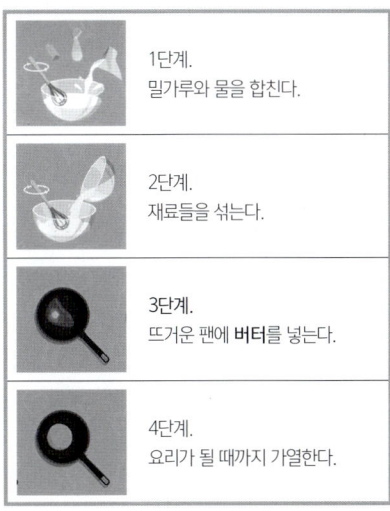

어휘 recipe n. 요리법   slightly adv. 약간   dairy n. 유제품

01
해석 시각 자료를 보아라. 어느 단계가 변경돼야 하는가?
(A) 1단계
(B) 2단계
(C) 3단계
(D) 4단계

토익실전문제   p.87

| 01 (A) | 02 (D) | 03 (C) | 04 (B) | 05 (B) |
| 06 (D) | | | | |

[01-03] 영국 → 캐나다

Questions 01-03 refer to the following conversation and floor plan.

W: Hello. My name is Sandra Wilkins, and ⁰¹**I'm supposed to interview Mr. Garcia for the *Newfield Times*.** My appointment is in a few minutes.
M: Oh, he's expecting you, Ms. Wilkins. Just take the elevator on your left, and go up to the second floor. ⁰²**You'll see his office right next to the conference room.**
W: Thank you. Do I need a visitor's badge to move around the building?
M: I was just going to mention that. I'll give you one with a temporary access card. ⁰³**Please write down your name and phone number here.**

appointment n. 약속   mention v. 말하다, 언급하다   temporary adj. 임시의

해석
01-03번은 다음 대화와 평면도에 관한 문제입니다.
여: 안녕하세요. 제 이름은 Sandra Wilkins이고, ⁰¹저는 *Newfield Times*를 위해 Mr. Garcia와 인터뷰를 하기로 되어 있어요. 제 약속은 몇 분 후에 있습니다.
남: 아, 그는 당신을 기다리고 있습니다, Ms. Wilkins. 왼쪽에 있는 엘리베이터를 타고 2층으로 올라가세요. ⁰²회의실 바로 옆에 그의 사무실이 보일 겁니다.
여: 감사합니다. 건물 내에서 이동하기 위해 방문자 배지가 필요한가요?
남: 제가 그것에 대해 말하려던 참이었습니다. 임시 출입 카드가 있는 배지를 드리겠습니다. ⁰³여기에 이름과 전화번호를 적어주세요.

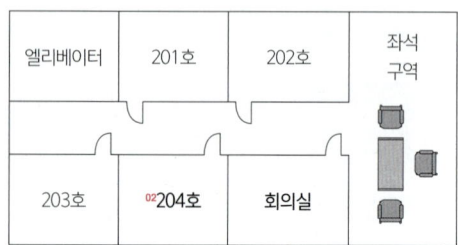

01 목적 문제
해석 여자가 방문한 목적은 무엇인가?
(A) 인터뷰를 진행할 것이다.
(B) 건물을 둘러볼 것이다.
(C) 작업 공간을 점검할 것이다.
(D) 일자리에 지원할 것이다.

해설 대화의 초반을 주의 깊게 듣는다. 여자가 "I'm supposed to interview Mr. Garcia for the *Newfield Times*"라며 *Newfield Times*에서 Mr. Garcia와 인터뷰를 하기 위해 방문했다고 하였다. 따라서 (A)가 정답이다.

어휘 property n. 건물, 소유물

02 시각 자료 문제
해석 시각 자료를 보아라. 여자는 어디를 방문할 것인가?
(A) 201호
(B) 202호
(C) 203호
(D) 204호

해설 제시된 평면도의 정보를 확인한 후 질문의 핵심 어구(woman going to visit)와 관련된 내용을 주의 깊게 듣는다. 남자가 여자에게 "You'll see his office right next to the conference room."이라며 회의실 바로 옆에 그의 사무실이 있을 것이라고 하였다. 평면도에서 회의실 (Conference Room) 바로 옆에 있는 방은 204호임을 알 수 있다. 따라서 (D)가 정답이다.

03 요청 문제
해석 남자는 여자에게 무엇을 하라고 요청하는가?
(A) 소지품을 보관한다.
(B) 관리자에게 연락한다.
(C) 연락처 정보를 제공한다.
(D) 평가 양식을 작성한다.

해설 남자의 말에서 요청과 관련된 표현이 언급된 다음을 주의 깊게 듣는다. 대화의 마지막 부분에서 남자가 "Please write down your name and phone number here."라며 여자에게 이름과 전화번호를 적어달라고 하였다. 따라서 (C)가 정답이다.

어휘 secure v. 보관하다

[04-06] 캐나다 → 미국

Questions 04-06 refer to the following conversation and boarding pass.

M: ⁰⁴**I'm glad we were both invited to the technology exhibition in Sydney.** There will be a lot of innovative products revealed at this year's event.
W: I'm especially excited because this is my first time attending. Um, I heard you'll be speaking as a presenter.
M: Right. ⁰⁵**I'll be giving a presentation about the new features of our company's photo-editing application.** I'm going to focus on the various ways in which we have incorporated AI into the program.
W: I'm looking forward to it. Oh, look at the display board. ⁰⁶**Our gate has been changed.**
M: Well, that's quite far from here. We should hurry.

invite v. 초대하다   innovative adj. 혁신적인   reveal v. 공개하다
feature n. 특징   display board 전광판

해석
04-06번은 다음 대화와 탑승권에 관한 문제입니다.
남: ⁰⁴우리 둘 다 시드니에서 열리는 기술 전시회에 초대받게 되어 기뻐요. 올해 행사에서는 많은 혁신적인 제품들이 공개될 것입니다.
여: 저는 특히 이번이 제 첫 참석이라서 매우 기대돼요. 음, 당신이 발표자로서 연설한다고 들었어요.
남: 맞아요. ⁰⁵저는 우리 회사의 사진 편집 애플리케이션의 새로운 특징들에 대해 발표할 거예요. 저는 우리가 인공지능을 프로그램에 통합한 다양한 방법들에 중점을 둘 겁니다.
여: 기대가 되네요. 아, 전광판을 보세요. ⁰⁶우리 탑승구가 변경되었어요.
남: 음, 여기서 꽤 멀리 있네요. 서둘러야겠어요.

탑승권	
	비즈니스 클래스
목적지: 시드니	좌석: B-07
출발 날짜: 5월 24일 오후 6:30	⁰⁶탑승구: C42

04 특정 세부 사항 문제
해석 화자들은 어떤 유형의 행사에 초대되었는가?
(A) 미술 전시회
(B) 무역 박람회
(C) 주주 총회
(D) 기자 회견

해설 질문의 핵심 어구(type of event)와 관련된 내용을 주의 깊게 듣는다. 남자가 "I'm glad we were both invited to the technology exhibition in Sydney."라며 화자들 둘 다 시드니에서 열리는 기술 전시회에 초대되어 기쁘다고 하였다. 따라서 (B)가 정답이다.

Paraphrasing
technology exhibition 기술 전시회 → trade show 무역 박람회

05 언급 문제

해석 남자는 어떤 주제에 대해 논의할 것이라고 말하는가?
(A) 시설 개조
(B) 제품 개선
(C) 정부 프로그램
(D) 회사 정책

해설 남자의 말에서 질문의 핵심 어구(he will discuss)와 관련된 내용을 주의 깊게 듣는다. 남자가 "I'll be giving a presentation about the new features of our company's photo-editing application."이라며 회사의 사진 편집 애플리케이션의 새로운 특징들에 대해 발표를 할 것이라고 하였다. 따라서 (B)가 정답이다.

어휘 modification n. 개조, 수정

06 시각 자료 문제

해석 시각 자료를 보아라. 어떤 정보가 변경되었는가?
(A) 비즈니스 클래스
(B) 5월 24일
(C) B-07
(D) C42

해설 제시된 탑승권의 정보를 확인한 후 질문의 핵심 어구(information ~ changed)와 관련된 내용을 주의 깊게 듣는다. 여자가 "Our gate has been changed."라며 탑승구가 변경되었다고 하였다. 탑승권에서 탑승구의 번호는 C42이므로 이 정보가 변경되었음을 알 수 있다. 따라서 (D)가 정답이다.

HACKERS TEST   p.88

01 (D)	02 (A)	03 (D)	04 (B)	05 (C)
06 (B)	07 (A)	08 (C)	09 (A)	10 (C)
11 (B)	12 (C)

[01-03] 호주 → 미국

Questions 01-03 refer to the following conversation and list.

M: Welcome to Swift Auto Rentals. Are you interested in a rental today?
W: 01My coworkers and I just arrived here in Seattle to represent our company at an international book fair. But I forgot to book a vehicle in advance.
M: No worries. We have a variety of cars available. What specific requirements do you have?
W: We need a car that can comfortably seat five people and has enough space for our luggage, as we're traveling with quite a bit of equipment.
M: In that case, 02I recommend our largest vehicle, which can hold 10 people.
W: Sounds good. Also, 03I'd like to pay extra for damage insurance. What are my options?

represent v. 대표하다   requirement n. 요구사항   hold v. 수용하다
insurance n. 보험

해석
01-03번은 다음 대화와 목록에 관한 문제입니다.

남: Swift 자동차 렌트 업체에 오신 것을 환영합니다. 오늘 렌트에 관심이 있으신가요?
여: 01저와 동료들이 우리 회사를 대표해서 국제 도서 박람회에 참석하기 위해 방금 시애틀에 도착했어요. 하지만 제가 미리 차량을 예약하는 것을 잊었어요.
남: 걱정하지 마세요. 다양한 차량이 이용 가능합니다. 어떤 특별한 요구사항이 있으신가요?
여: 저희는 다섯 명이 편안하게 앉을 수 있고 짐을 위한 충분한 공간이 있는 차가 필요해요. 꽤 많은 장비를 가지고 이동 중이거든요.
남: 그런 경우라면, 02저는 저희의 가장 큰 차량을 추천하는데, 그 차는 10명을 수용할 수 있습니다.
여: 좋아요. 또한, 03손해 보험을 위해 추가 비용을 지불하고 싶어요. 어떤 선택지가 있나요?

Swift 자동차 렌트 업체

02옵션 1   옵션 2
10명까지   5명까지

옵션 3   옵션 4
2명까지   4명까지

01 이유 문제

해석 여자는 왜 시애틀을 방문하고 있는가?
(A) 지사를 개설하기 위해
(B) 몇몇 부동산을 점검하기 위해
(C) 고객들을 만나기 위해
(D) 산업 행사에 참석하기 위해

해설 질문의 핵심 어구(woman visiting Seattle)와 관련된 내용을 주의 깊게 듣는다. 여자가 "My coworkers and I just arrived here in Seattle to represent our company at an international book fair."라며 국제 도서 박람회에 회사를 대표하여 참석하기 위해 시애틀을 방문했다고 하였다. 따라서 (D)가 정답이다.

Paraphrasing
an international book fair 국제 도서 박람회 → an industry event 산업 행사

02 시각 자료 문제

해석 시각 자료를 보아라. 남자는 어느 옵션을 제안하는가?
(A) 옵션 1
(B) 옵션 2
(C) 옵션 3
(D) 옵션 4

해설 목록의 정보를 확인한 후 질문의 핵심 어구(option ~ man recommend)와 관련된 내용을 주의 깊게 듣는다. 남자가 "I recommend our largest vehicle, which can hold 10 people"이라며 10명까지 수용할 수 있는 가장 큰 차량을 추천한다고 하였다. 목록에서 10명까지 수용할 수 있는 차량은 옵션 1임을 알 수 있다. 따라서 (A)가 정답이다.

03 특정 세부 사항 문제

해석 여자는 무엇을 위해 추가로 비용을 지불하고 싶어 하는가?
(A) 호텔 픽업
(B) 차량 수리
(C) 내비게이션 시스템
(D) 보험

해설 질문의 핵심 어구(pay extra)가 언급된 주변을 주의 깊게 듣는다. 여자가 "I'd like to pay extra for damage insurance"라며 손해 보험을 위해 추가 비용을 지불하고 싶다고 하였다. 따라서 (D)가 정답이다.

[04-06] 캐나다 → 영국
Questions 04-06 refer to the following conversation and delivery schedule.

M: Good morning. This is Mitch Han calling from Nolan Beverage Company. I want to let you know that I am on the way with your soft drinks.
W: I was just planning to contact your company. As it turns out, ⁰⁴the order we placed is wrong. We need two additional boxes. Is that going to be an issue?
M: Hmm . . . I don't have any extra with me at the moment. However, ⁰⁵I'm still close to our warehouse, so I can go back quickly to get a couple more.
W: That would be wonderful. Um, ⁰⁶what time should I expect you to arrive?
M: ⁰⁶I'll be there at 9:45 A.M. as scheduled.
W: Great. Thank you so much!

contact v. 연락하다 additional adj. 추가의 warehouse n. 창고
expect v. 예상하다

해석
04-06번은 다음 대화와 배달 일정표에 관한 문제입니다.
남: 안녕하세요. Nolan 음료 회사에서 전화드리는 Mitch Han입니다. 귀사의 음료를 배달하는 중이라는 것을 알려드리고 싶어서요.
여: 저는 방금 당신의 회사에 연락할 계획이었어요. 알고 보니, ⁰⁴저희가 한 주문이 잘못되었어요. 저희는 추가로 두 상자가 필요해요. 이것이 문제가 될까요?
남: 흠… 지금은 저에게 여분이 없어요. 하지만, ⁰⁵저는 저희 창고와 여전히 가까워서, 두 상자 더 가지러 빨리 돌아갈 수 있습니다.
여: 그럼 정말 좋을 것 같아요. 음, ⁰⁶당신이 몇 시에 도착하는 것으로 제가 예상해야 할까요?
남: ⁰⁶저는 예정대로 그곳에 오전 9시 45분에 도착할 거예요.
여: 좋아요. 정말 감사합니다!

고객	배달 시간
Gibbs 마켓	오전 9시
⁰⁶Star 주유소	오전 9시 45분
Black Bird 카페	오전 10시 30분
Weston 식료품점	오전 11시 15분

04 문제점 문제
해설 여자는 무슨 문제를 언급하는가?
(A) 청구서가 지불되지 않았다.
(B) 주문이 맞지 않다.
(C) 가게를 일찍 닫아야 한다.
(D) 배송품이 도착하지 않았다.

해설 대화에서 부정적인 표현이 언급된 주변을 주의 깊게 듣는다. 여자가 "the order we placed is wrong. We need two additional boxes."라며 주문이 잘못되었고 추가로 두 상자가 필요하다고 하였다. 따라서 (B)가 정답이다.

어휘 incorrect adj. 맞지 않은, 부정확한

05 제안 문제
해설 남자는 무엇을 해주겠다고 제안하는가?
(A) 몇몇 제품 견본을 제공한다.
(B) 마감일을 연장한다.
(C) 보관 시설로 돌아간다.
(D) 할인을 제공한다.

해설 남자의 말에서 제안과 관련된 표현이 언급된 다음을 주의 깊게 듣는다. 남자가 "I'm still close to our warehouse, so I can go back quickly to get a couple more."라며 본인이 창고와 여전히 가까워서, 두 상자 더 가지러 빨리 돌아갈 수 있다고 하였다. 따라서 (C)가 정답이다.

어휘 due date 마감일 storage n. 보관, 저장

Paraphrasing
warehouse 창고 → storage facility 보관 시설

06 시각 자료 문제
해설 시각 자료를 보아라. 여자는 어디에서 일하는가?
(A) Gibbs 마켓
(B) Star 주유소
(C) Black Bird 카페
(D) Weston 식료품점

해설 배달 일정표의 정보를 확인한 후 질문의 핵심 어구(woman work)와 관련된 내용을 주의 깊게 듣는다. 여자가 "what time should I expect you to arrive?"라며 남자가 몇 시에 도착하는 것으로 예상해야 할지 묻자, 남자가 "I'll be there at 9:45 A.M. as scheduled."라며 예정대로 그곳에 오전 9시 45분에 도착할 것이라고 하였다. 배달 일정표에서 배달 시간이 오전 9시 45분인 곳은 Star 주유소이므로 여자가 Star 주유소에서 일한다는 것을 알 수 있다. 따라서 (B)가 정답이다.

[07-09] 미국 → 캐나다
Questions 07-09 refer to the following conversation and Web site.

W: Kyle, I'd like your opinion on the Web site for the technology conference that we are holding in May. Take a look at my screen. ⁰⁷Where do you think I should put the registration button?
M: Hmm . . . ⁰⁷I think it should be directly below the conference name. That way, it'll be easy to see.
W: Thanks. Um, how are your preparations for the event going?
M: Good. In fact, ⁰⁸I created the invitations this morning. ⁰⁹I was planning to send them out now.
W: ⁰⁹Could you send them later? There may be a few more companies that I want to add to the list.

opinion n. 의견 registration n. 등록 directly adv. 바로
below prep. 아래에

해석
07-09번은 다음 대화와 웹사이트에 관한 문제입니다.
여: Kyle, 우리가 5월에 개최할 기술 학회 웹사이트에 대한 당신의 의견을 듣고 싶어요. 제 화면을 보세요. ⁰⁷등록 버튼을 어디에 두는 게 좋을까요?
남: 음… ⁰⁷학회 이름 바로 아래에 두는 것이 좋을 것 같아요. 그렇게 하면 보기 쉬울 거예요.
여: 고마워요. 음, 행사 준비는 어떻게 되어가고 있나요?
남: 잘 되고 있어요. 사실, ⁰⁸오늘 아침에 초대장을 만들었어요. ⁰⁹지금 그것들을 발송하려고 했어요.
여: ⁰⁹그것을 나중에 보내주실 수 있나요? 제가 목록에 추가하고 싶은 회사가 몇 개 더 있을 수도 있어요.

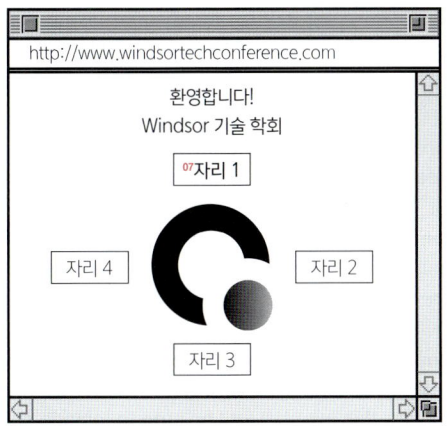

07 시각 자료 문제

해석 시각 자료를 보아라. 남자는 어디에 등록 버튼을 두기를 원하는가?
(A) 자리 1
(B) 자리 2
(C) 자리 3
(D) 자리 4

해설 웹사이트의 정보를 확인한 후 질문의 핵심 어구(registration button)가 언급된 주변을 주의 깊게 듣는다. 여자가 "Where do you think I should put the registration button?"이라며 등록 버튼을 어디에 두어야 한다고 생각하는지 묻자, 남자가 "I think it should be directly below the conference name."이라며 그것이 학회 이름 바로 밑에 있어야 한다고 하였다. 웹사이트에서 학회 이름 바로 밑은 자리 1임을 알 수 있다. 따라서 (A)가 정답이다.

어휘 place v. 두다, 놓다

08 특정 세부 사항 문제

해석 남자는 오늘 아침에 무엇을 만들었는가?
(A) 설명서들
(B) 설문지들
(C) 초대장들
(D) 이름표들

해설 질문의 핵심 어구(this morning)가 언급된 주변을 주의 깊게 듣는다. 남자가 "I created invitations this morning"이라며 오늘 아침에 초대장들을 만들었다고 하였다. 따라서 (C)가 정답이다.

어휘 questionnaire n. 설문지

09 요청 문제

해석 여자는 무엇을 요청하는가?
(A) 업무를 연기하기
(B) 행사를 확장하기
(C) 계약서를 준비하기
(D) 파일을 다운로드하기

해설 여자의 말에서 요청과 관련된 표현이 언급된 주변을 주의 깊게 듣는다. 남자가 "I was planning to send them out now."라며 지금 초대장을 발송하려고 했다고 하자, 여자가 "Could you send them later?"이라며 초대장을 나중에 보내줄 수 있냐고 하였다. 따라서 (A)가 정답이다.

어휘 expand v. 확장하다, 확대하다

[10-12] 〔호주 → 영국〕
Questions 10-12 refer to the following conversation and building directory.

M: Evelyn, do you want to go to the Finley Department Store with me on Saturday? I bought a sweater there yesterday, but it's a bit tight. ¹⁰**I'm going to take it back and get a larger size.**
W: Sure. ¹¹**I'll drive. I can pick you up at 11 A.M.**
M: Great. Is there anything you want to get while we're at the department store?
W: Well, I do need a new pair of computer speakers.
M: Actually, ¹²**the electronics section is closed this weekend.** Apparently, the entire floor is being repainted.
W: Hmm . . . That's unfortunate. Still, I will join you on Saturday.

tight adj. 꽉 끼는   apparently adv. 듣자 하니   entire adj. 전체의
repaint v. 다시 칠하다

해석
10-12번은 다음 대화와 건물 안내판에 관한 문제입니다.
남: Evelyn, 토요일에 저와 함께 Finley 백화점에 가실래요? 어제 거기에서 스웨터를 샀는데, 좀 꽉 끼어요. ¹⁰그것을 다시 가져가서 더 큰 사이즈로 가져오려고요.
여: 물론이죠. ¹¹제가 운전할게요. 당신을 오전 11시에 픽업할 수 있어요.
남: 좋아요. 우리가 백화점에 있는 동안 사고 싶은 게 있나요?
여: 음, 새 컴퓨터 스피커가 필요하긴 해요.
남: 사실, ¹²전자제품 구역은 이번 주말에 문을 닫아요. 듣자 하니, 전체 층이 다시 칠해지고 있어요.
여: 흠... 유감스럽네요. 그래도, 토요일에 같이 갈게요.

Finley 백화점 매장 안내판	
1층	화장품
2층	의류
¹²3층	전자제품
4층	스포츠 용품

10 이유 문제

해석 남자는 왜 백화점을 방문하고 싶어 하는가?
(A) 제품을 구매하기 위해
(B) 환불을 요청하기 위해
(C) 물건을 교환하기 위해
(D) 주문품을 수령하기 위해

해설 질문의 핵심 어구(man ~ visit a department store)와 관련된 내용을 주의 깊게 듣는다. 남자가 "I'm going to take it[sweater] back and get a larger size."라며 스웨터를 다시 가져가서 더 큰 사이즈로 가져올 것이라고 하였다. 이를 통해, 남자가 물건을 교환하기 위해 백화점을 방문하고 싶어함을 알 수 있다. 따라서 (C)가 정답이다.

어휘 exchange v. 교환하다   order n. 주문품

[Paraphrasing]
take ~ back and get a larger size 다시 가져가서 더 큰 사이즈로 가져오다
→ exchange 교환하다

11 제안 문제

해석 여자는 무엇을 해주겠다고 제안하는가?
(A) 예약을 한다.
(B) 교통편을 제공한다.
(C) 식사 값을 지불한다.
(D) 온라인에서 정보를 찾는다.

해설 여자의 말에서 제안과 관련된 표현이 언급된 다음을 주의 깊게 듣는다. 여자가 "I'll drive. I can pick you up at 11 A.M."이라며 본인이 운전할

것이고 오전 11시에 남자를 픽업할 수 있다고 하였다. 따라서 (B)가 정답이다.

12 시각 자료 문제
해석 시각 자료를 보아라. 어떤 층이 이번 주말에 닫는가?
(A) 1층
(B) 2층
(C) 3층
(D) 4층

해설 건물 안내판의 정보를 확인한 후 질문의 핵심 어구(closed this weekend)가 언급된 주변을 주의 깊게 듣는다. 남자가 "the electronics section is closed this weekend"라며 전자제품 구역은 이번 주말에 문을 닫는다고 하였다. 건물 안내판에서 전자제품 구역은 3층임을 알 수 있다. 따라서 (C)가 정답이다.

DAY 14 대화 상황

기출 유형 1 회사 생활

Example 미국 → 호주   p.90
해석
01-03번은 다음 대화에 관한 문제입니다.
여: Paul, 01사무실 복사기에 무슨 문제가 있는지 아세요? 02저는 오후 2시까지 이 보고서 사본을 저의 관리자에게 제출해야 하는데, 기계가 작동하지 않아요.
남: 음... 만약 당신이 컬러 복사를 하려고 한다면, 잉크가 떨어졌을 수 있어요. 제가 마지막으로 프린터를 사용했을 때, 컬러 잉크 카트리지를 곧 교체해야 할 것이라는 메시지가 있었어요.
여: 저는 컬러 복사를 해야 해요. 잉크 카트리지를 교체해 본 적이 있나요?
남: 네. 03비품실에 새 잉크 카트리지가 있을 거예요. 당신이 그것을 가져오면, 제가 복사기에 있는 것을 교체하는 것을 도와드릴게요.

어휘 photocopier n. 복사기   run out 다 떨어지다   supply room 비품실

01
해설 대화는 주로 무엇에 관한 것인가?
(A) 사업 보고서
(B) 사무용 기계
(C) 새로운 관리자
(D) 정책 변경

02
해설 여자는 왜 보고서를 복사하고 싶어 하는가?
(A) 관리자에게 제출하기 위해
(B) 고객에게 보내기 위해
(C) 회의에서 논의하기 위해
(D) 발표를 준비하기 위해

03
해설 여자는 다음에 무엇을 할 것 같은가?
(A) 비품을 주문한다.
(B) 물품을 반품한다.
(C) 문서를 검토한다.
(D) 보관 장소로 간다.

토익실전문제   p.91
01 (D)   02 (D)   03 (C)   04 (A)   05 (D)
06 (C)

[01-03] 캐나다 → 영국
Questions 01-03 refer to the following conversation.

M: Have you started working on the product display for the trade fair in May? I was wondering if you could also highlight 01**the new laptop model that our company released last January.**
W: Yes. I'm working on it now. I've also begun making a promotional video to show at our booth. It will include content on the new laptop and our line of televisions. Everything should be finished before the final week of April.
M: 02**I'm relieved that you have chosen to concentrate on those products. They are the most appropriate ones for this event.** 03**Just be sure to include specific information on what distinguishes our laptop and televisions from those of our competitors.**

trade fair 무역 박람회   highlight v. 강조하다   relieved adj. 안심이 되는
concentrate v. 집중하다   distinguish v. 구별짓다

해석
01-03번은 다음 대화에 관한 문제입니다.
남: 5월에 있을 무역 박람회를 위한 제품 전시 작업을 시작했나요? 01지난 1월에 우리 회사가 출시한 새로운 노트북 모델을 강조할 수 있나 궁금했어요.
여: 네. 지금 그것을 작업하고 있어요. 저는 또한 우리 부스에서 상영할 홍보 영상을 만들기 시작했어요. 그것은 새로운 노트북과 우리의 텔레비전 제품들에 대한 내용을 포함할 거예요. 모든 것이 아마 4월 마지막 주 전에 끝날 거예요.
남: 02그 제품들에 집중하기로 결정했다니 안심이 되네요. 그것들이 이 행사를 위한 가장 적합한 제품들이에요. 03무엇이 우리 노트북과 텔레비전을 경쟁업체의 것들과 구별짓는지에 대한 구체적인 정보를 반드시 포함시키세요.

01 화자 문제
해설 화자들은 어디에서 일하는 것 같은가?
(A) 컨벤션 센터에서
(B) 마케팅 회사에서
(C) 전화 서비스 공급업체에서
(D) 전자기기 제조업체에서

해설 대화에서 신분 및 직업과 관련된 표현을 놓치지 않고 듣는다. 남자가 "the new computer model that our company released last January"라며 우리 회사가 지난 1월에 출시한 새로운 노트북 모델이라고 하였다. 이를 통해 화자들의 회사가 노트북을 만드는 전자기기 제조업체임을 알 수 있다. 따라서 (D)가 정답이다.

02 특정 세부 사항 문제
해설 남자는 무엇에 대해 안심을 표하는가?
(A) 잘 교육된 직원들이 업무 가능하다.
(B) 여자가 프로젝트 마감기한을 지켰다.
(C) 고객 후기들이 대개 긍정적이다.
(D) 여자가 적절한 선택을 했다.

해설 남자의 말에서 질문의 핵심 어구(express relief about)와 관련된 내용을 주의 깊게 듣는다. 남자가 "I'm relieved that you have chosen to concentrate on those products. They are the most appropriate ones for this event."라며 여자가 홍보 영상에 새로운 노트북과 텔레비전 제품들에 집중하기로 한 것에 안심이 되고 그것들이 가장 적절한 제품들이라고 하였다. 따라서 (D)가 정답이다.

어휘 generally adv. 대개, 일반적으로

03 요청 문제

해석 남자는 여자에게 어떤 정보를 포함하라고 요청하는가?
(A) 판촉용 가격
(B) 모델 번호
(C) 제품들의 특징
(D) 환불 지침

해설 남자의 말에서 요청과 관련된 표현이 언급된 다음을 주의 깊게 듣는다. 남자가 여자에게 "Just be sure to include specific information on what distinguishes our laptop and televisions from those of our competitors."라며 무엇이 우리 노트북과 텔레비전을 경쟁업체들의 것과 구별시키는지에 대한 구체적인 정보를 포함시키라고 하였다. 따라서 (C)가 정답이다.

어휘 feature n. 특징

[Paraphrasing]
specific information on what distinguishes our laptop and televisions from those of our competitors 무엇이 우리 노트북과 텔레비전을 경쟁업체들의 것과 구별시키는지에 대한 구체적인 정보 → Features of products 제품들의 특징

[04-06] 🎧 미국 → 호주
Questions 04-06 refer to the following conversation.

W: Hi, Alberto. As you requested, ⁰⁴I read through the transcript of the speech you plan to give at the Glendale Investors Conference next week. Your analysis of the investment strategies is really thorough. But there is one issue . . . It will be almost an hour long.

M: ⁰⁵Yeah, I guess I got carried away. I'll go through it this afternoon and make some cuts. Would you mind reading it once more when I am finished?

W: Of course. ⁰⁶I'll be leaving the office early today because I have to get my annual health exam. But I can read it again first thing tomorrow morning for you.

analysis n. 분석 investment n. 투자 thorough adj. 빈틈없는, 철저한 health exam 건강 검진

해석
04-06번은 다음 대화에 관한 문제입니다.

여: 안녕하세요, Alberto. 요청하신 대로, ⁰⁴다음 주에 당신이 Glendale 투자자 학회에서 할 예정인 연설문을 읽어봤어요. 투자 전략에 대한 당신의 분석은 정말 빈틈없더군요. 하지만 한 가지 문제가 있어요... 거의 한 시간이 될 거예요.

남: ⁰⁵네, 제가 좀 도취되었나봐요. 오늘 오후에 다시 검토해서 몇 군데를 줄여볼게요. 제가 완성하면 한 번 더 읽어보실 수 있나요?

여: 물론이죠. ⁰⁶오늘은 제가 연례 건강 검진을 받아야 해서 일찍 퇴근할 거예요. 하지만 내일 아침 첫 일정으로 다시 읽어볼게요.

04 화자 문제

해석 화자들은 어느 분야에서 일하는 것 같은가?
(A) 금융
(B) 교통
(C) 법률
(D) 의료

해설 대화에서 신분 및 직업과 관련된 표현을 놓치지 않고 듣는다. 여자가 "I read through the transcript of the speech you plan to give at the Glendale Investors Conference next week. Your analysis of the investment strategies is really thorough."라며 남자가 Glendale 투자자 학회에서 연설을 할 연설문을 읽어봤고 투자 전략이 빈틈없었다고 한 것을 통해 화자들이 금융 분야에 일하고 있음을 알 수 있다. 따라서 (A)가 정답이다.

05 의도 파악 문제

해석 여자가 "거의 한 시간이 될 거예요"라고 말할 때 무엇을 의도하는가?
(A) 연설이 유익할 것이다.
(B) 몇 가지 문제들이 다뤄졌다.
(C) 학회가 연장되었다.
(D) 몇 가지 수정이 필요하다.

해설 질문의 인용어구(It will be almost an hour long)가 언급된 주변을 주의 깊게 듣는다. 여자가 "It will be almost an hour long."이라고 하자, 이에 대해 남자가 "Yeah, I guess I got carried away. I'll go through it this afternoon and make some cuts."라며 연설문을 쓰다가 좀 도취된 것 같다며 길이를 줄이겠다고 하였다. 따라서 여자는 연설문이 너무 길어서 수정이 필요하다는 것을 의도하고 있음을 알 수 있다. 따라서 (D)가 정답이다.

어휘 informative adj. 유익한 address v. 다루다, 처리하다

06 이유 문제

해석 여자는 왜 오늘 사무실을 일찍 떠날 것인가?
(A) 서비스 센터를 방문하기 위해
(B) 자격증 시험을 치르기 위해
(C) 건강 검진을 받기 위해
(D) 업계 행사에 참석하기 위해

해설 질문의 핵심 어구(woman leave the office early)와 관련된 내용을 주의 깊게 듣는다. 여자가 "I'll be leaving the office early today because I have to get my annual health exam."이라며 연례 건강 검진을 받기 위해 오늘 일찍 퇴근할 것이라고 하였다. 따라서 (C)가 정답이다.

[Paraphrasing]
health exam 건강 검진 → medical checkup 건강 검진

기출 유형 2 일상 생활

Example 🎧 호주 → 미국   p.92
해석
01-03번은 다음 대화에 관한 문제입니다.

남: Ms. Parker, 안녕하세요. ⁰¹제가 약속 시간에 늦어서 정말 죄송합니다. 오늘 아침에 제가 어떤 집을 보여주어야 하는지 혼동해서 다른 집에 갔습니다.

여: 괜찮아요. 저도 몇 분 전에 도착했어요. 음, ⁰²이 집은 3월 1일에 임대가 가능한 거죠, 그렇죠? 제 현재 임대차 계약이 2월 28일에 끝나거든요.

남: 맞습니다. 원하신다면 더 일찍 입주하실 수도 있어요. 현재 비어 있거든요.

여: 알려주셔서 감사합니다. 아, ⁰³당신이 저를 안내하는 동안 집 내부를 사진 찍으려고 계획하고 있어요. 그것이 문제가 되지 않을 것으로 생각해요.

남: 물론 그렇지 않습니다. 그럼, 투어를 시작하시죠.

어휘 confuse v. 혼동하다 current adj. 현재의 agreement n. 계약
vacant adj. 비어 있는 assume v. (사실이라고) 생각하다, 추정하다

01

해석 남자는 왜 약속에 늦었는가?
(A) 그는 잘못된 건물로 갔다.
(B) 그는 교통 체증에 막혔다.
(C) 그는 서류를 가지고 올 것을 잊어버렸다.
(D) 그는 날짜에 대해 혼동했다.

02

해석 여자는 무엇에 대해 문의하는가?
(A) 임대 기간
(B) 월 임대료
(C) 이용 가능 날짜

(D) 계약 조건

03
해석 여자는 무엇을 할 것이라고 말하는가?
(A) 투어 일정을 다시 잡는다.
(B) 사진을 찍는다.
(C) 몇몇 부동산을 비교한다.
(D) 세입자를 만난다.

토익실전문제   p.93

01 (D)	02 (C)	03 (A)	04 (B)	05 (D)
06 (B)				

[01-03] 3ɯ 호주 → 영국
Questions 01-03 refer to the following conversation.

M: Welcome to *Urban Spaces*. For today's episode, ⁰¹my guest is Zhao Ni. She designed the new branch of the Chicago Public Library in the Sherwood neighborhood. It's quite beautiful. Welcome, Ms. Ni.

W: Thank you. I'm glad you like my work. ⁰²That project was particularly challenging. Many residents of the area had strong opinions about their new library, and it was hard to satisfy everyone.

M: Well, I think your efforts paid off. I drove by the library last week, and it's really impressive. ⁰³When will it officially open?

W: ⁰³On June 17. And I encourage everyone to come that day. There will be a special ceremony to mark the occasion.

particularly adv. 특히   resident n. 주민   satisfy v. 만족시키다
effort n. 노력   mark v. 기념하다   occasion n. 행사

해석
01-03번은 다음 대화에 관한 문제입니다.

남: *Urban Spaces*에 오신 것을 환영합니다. 오늘 방송에서 ⁰¹제 게스트는 Zhao Ni입니다. 그녀는 Sherwood 지역에 새로운 시카고 공공 도서관 분관을 설계했습니다. 그것은 정말 아름답습니다. 어서 오세요, Ms. Ni.

여: 감사합니다. 제 작품이 마음에 드신다니 기쁩니다. ⁰²그 프로젝트는 특히 도전적이었어요. 그 지역의 많은 주민들이 새 도서관에 대해 강한 의견을 가지고 있었고, 모든 사람을 만족시키는 것은 어려웠어요.

남: 음, 당신의 노력이 결실을 맺은 것 같습니다. 저는 지난주에 그 도서관을 차를 타고 지나갔는데, 정말 인상적이더군요. ⁰³언제 공식적으로 개관하나요?

여: ⁰³6월 17일이에요. 그리고 그날 모든 분들이 오시길 권장합니다. 그 행사를 기념하는 특별한 식이 있을 예정이에요.

01 화자 문제
해석 여자는 누구인 것 같은가?
(A) 작가
(B) 정치인
(C) 사서
(D) 건축가

해설 대화에서 신분 및 직업과 관련된 표현을 놓치지 않고 듣는다. 남자가 "my guest is Zhao Ni. She designed the new branch of the Chicago Public Library in the Sherwood neighborhood."라며 오늘의 게스트인 Zhao Ni를 소개하면서 그녀가 시카고 공공 도서관의 Sherwood 지역 분관을 설계했다고 하였다. 따라서 (D)가 정답이다.

02 언급 문제
해석 여자는 프로젝트에 대해 무엇이 어려웠다고 말하는가?
(A) 촉박한 기한을 맞추는 것
(B) 적합한 동업자를 찾는 것
(C) 대중의 기대를 충족시키는 것
(D) 충분한 자금을 모으는 것

해설 여자의 말에서 질문의 핵심 어구(difficult about a project)와 관련된 내용을 주의 깊게 듣는다. 여자가 "That project was particularly challenging. Many residents of the area had strong opinions about their new library, and it was hard to satisfy everyone."이라며 지역 주민들이 새 도서관에 대해 강한 의견을 가지고 있었고, 모든 사람을 만족시키는 것은 어려웠다고 하였다. 따라서 (C)가 정답이다.

어휘 public adj. 대중의, 공공의   raise v. 모으다   adequate adj. 충분한

03 특정 세부 사항 문제
해석 6월 17일에 무슨 일이 일어날 것인가?
(A) 시설이 개장할 것이다.
(B) 발표가 있을 것이다.
(C) 축제가 열릴 것이다.
(D) 규정이 변경될 것이다.

해설 질문의 핵심 어구(June 17)가 언급된 부분을 주의 깊게 듣는다. 남자가 "When will it[the library] officially open?"이라며 도서관이 언제 개관하는지 묻자, 여자가 "On June 17."이라며 6월 17일이라고 하였다. 따라서 (A)가 정답이다.

어휘 regulation n. 규정

[04-06] 3ɯ 캐나다 → 미국
Questions 04-06 refer to the following conversation.

M: Hi, Ms. Choi. This is Evan from Dale Air Conditioning Services. ⁰⁴I'm calling to reschedule the installation of your air conditioner.

W: Really? But you told me that it would be done tomorrow morning.

M: ⁰⁵The problem is that the model you ordered, the Coolmax 78, is in high demand. So we won't get another shipment until next week.

W: I see. What's the earliest that I can expect the installation to be done?

M: We can send someone to your home on Wednesday morning or Thursday afternoon.

W: I'm busy in the mornings, so Thursday would be best.

M: Thank you for understanding. And ⁰⁶I'll text you the technician's phone number later this week in case you need it.

reschedule v. 일정을 변경하다   installation n. 설치   demand n. 수요
in case ~할 경우에 대비해서

해석
04-06번은 다음 대화에 관한 문제입니다.

남: 안녕하세요, Ms. Choi. 저는 Dale 에어컨 서비스의 Evan입니다. ⁰⁴고객님의 에어컨 설치 일정을 변경하기 위해 전화 드렸습니다.

여: 정말요? 하지만 내일 아침에 설치될 것이라고 말씀하셨잖아요.

남: ⁰⁵문제는 고객님이 주문하신 모델인 Coolmax 78이 수요가 많다는 것입니다. 그래서 다음 주가 되어서야 추가 배송을 받을 것 같습니다.

여: 알겠어요. 제가 설치를 가장 빨리 기대할 수 있는 시기는 언제인가요?

남: 수요일 아침이나 목요일 오후에 저희가 누군가를 댁으로 보내드릴 수 있습니다.

여: 저는 아침에 바빠서요, 목요일이 가장 좋겠네요.

남: 이해해 주셔서 감사합니다. 그리고 ⁰⁶필요하실 경우에 대비해서 기술자의 전화번호를 이번 주 후반에 문자로 보내드리겠습니다.

04 목적 문제
해석 남자는 왜 여자에게 전화하는가?
(A) 새로운 회사 정책을 설명하기 위해
(B) 약속을 변경하기 위해
(C) 집 수리 일정을 잡기 위해
(D) 출장 요리에 대해 문의하기 위해
해설 전화의 목적을 묻는 문제이므로, 대화의 초반을 반드시 듣는다. 남자가 "I'm calling to reschedule the installation of your air conditioner."라며 에어컨 설치 일정을 변경하기 위해 전화했다고 하였다. 따라서 (B)가 정답이다.
어휘 describe v. 설명하다

05 언급 문제
해석 남자는 Coolmax 78에 대해 무엇이라고 말하는가?
(A) 최근에 출시된 모델이다.
(B) 에너지 효율적이다.
(C) 할인된 가격으로 제공된다.
(D) 상당한 인기를 얻고 있다.
해설 남자의 말에서 질문의 핵심 어구(Coolmax 78)가 언급된 주변을 주의 깊게 듣는다. 남자가 "The problem is that the model you ordered, the Coolmax 78, is in high demand."라며 Coolmax 78이 수요가 많다고 하였다. 따라서 (D)가 정답이다.
어휘 energy-efficient adj. 에너지 효율적인 gain v. 얻다

Paraphrasing
in high demand 수요가 많은 → gaining significant popularity 상당한 인기를 얻고 있는

06 특정 세부 사항 문제
해석 여자는 나중에 무엇을 받을 것인가?
(A) 물품 목록
(B) 연락처
(C) 계정 접근 권한
(D) 설문조사 링크
해설 대화의 마지막 부분을 주의 깊게 듣는다. 남자가 "I'll text you the technician's phone number later this week in case you need it"이라며 여자에게 이번 주 후반에 기술자의 전화번호를 문자로 보내주겠다고 하였다. 따라서 (B)가 정답이다.

Paraphrasing
phone number 전화번호 → Contact information 연락처

HACKERS TEST p.94
01 (C)	02 (B)	03 (C)	04 (D)	05 (B)
06 (D)	07 (C)	08 (C)	09 (B)	10 (D)
11 (B)	12 (A)	13 (C)	14 (B)	15 (C)
16 (C)	17 (B)	18 (D)		

[01-03] 호주 → 미국
Questions 01-03 refer to the following conversation.

M: Miranda, ⁰¹are you coming to the company's annual picnic this Saturday? A soccer match will be held as a teambuilding exercise. ⁰²The members of the winning team will receive a voucher for a free lunch at a local restaurant.

W: I'd like to come, but I'll be out of town that day.
M: Oh, that's too bad. Where will you be traveling to?
W: ⁰³I'm going to Boston this weekend to spend time with my brother, as I haven't seen him since he moved last winter. I really wanted to attend this picnic. Please take lots of pictures for me.

annual adj. 연례의 match n. 경기 receive v. 받다
voucher n. 상품권, 쿠폰 attend v. 참석하다

해석
01-03번은 다음 대화에 관한 문제입니다.
남: Miranda, ⁰¹이번 토요일에 회사의 연례 소풍에 오실 건가요? 팀워크 활동으로 축구 경기가 열릴 거예요. ⁰²우승 팀의 구성원들은 지역 식당에서 무료 점심 식사를 할 수 있는 상품권을 받을 거예요.
여: 가고 싶지만, 그날 저는 타지에 있을 거예요.
남: 아, 안타깝네요. 어디로 여행할 예정인가요?
여: 제 남동생이 지난 겨울에 이사한 이후로 보지 못했기 때문에 ⁰³남동생과 시간을 보내기 위해 보스턴에 갈 거예요. 저는 정말 이 소풍에 참석하고 싶었어요. 저를 위해 사진을 많이 찍어 주세요.

01 주제 문제
해석 화자들은 어떤 종류의 행사에 대해 주로 이야기하고 있는가?
(A) 개점
(B) 도시 축제
(C) 회사 야유회
(D) 제품 출시
해설 대화의 주제를 묻는 문제이므로, 대화의 초반을 반드시 듣는다. 남자가 "are you coming to the company's annual picnic this Saturday?"라며 여자에게 회사의 연례 소풍에 참석할 것인지 물은 후, 회사 소풍에 대한 내용으로 대화가 이어지고 있다. 따라서 (C)가 정답이다.
어휘 outing n. 야유회, 견학

Paraphrasing
company's annual picnic 회사의 연례 소풍 → company outing 회사 야유회

02 특정 세부 사항 문제
해석 남자에 따르면, 몇몇 참석자들은 무엇을 받을 것인가?
(A) 사진
(B) 식사 상품권
(C) 의류 품목
(D) 멤버십 카드
해설 남자의 말에서 질문의 핵심 어구(some attendees receive)와 관련된 내용을 주의 깊게 듣는다. 남자가 "The members of the winning team will receive a voucher for a free lunch at a local restaurant."라며 우승한 팀의 구성원들은 지역 식당에서 무료 점심 식사를 할 수 있는 상품권을 받을 것이라고 하였다. 따라서 (B)가 정답이다.

03 이유 문제
해석 여자는 왜 보스턴으로 여행할 예정인가?
(A) 연설하기 위해
(B) 회의에 참석하기 위해
(C) 가족을 방문하기 위해
(D) 일자리를 위한 면접을 보기 위해
해설 질문의 핵심 어구(woman ~ travel to Boston)와 관련된 내용을 주의 깊게 듣는다. 여자가 "I'm going to Boston this weekend to spend time with my brother"라며 이번 주말에 남동생과 시간을 보내기 위해 보스턴에 간다고 하였다. 따라서 (C)가 정답이다.

Paraphrasing
brother 남동생 → family member 가족

[04-06] 🎧 미국 → 캐나다 → 영국
Questions 04-06 refer to the following conversation with three speakers.

> W1: Jacob, ⁰⁴I've just inspected the site of the building project you're supervising. I'm relieved to see that everything is progressing smoothly.
> M: Yes, everything is coming along as planned. In fact, ⁰⁵we might even finish a few days ahead of schedule if we continue to work at our current pace.
> W1: That's good to hear. ⁰⁶Ms. Lowery will be here soon to discuss the material expenses. Oh, there she is.
> W2: Hello. ⁰⁶I wanted to review the recent material cost breakdown and confirm we're staying within the project budget. Have you prepared the detailed report?
> M: Yes. I've got the details ready for you to review.

supervise v. 감독하다 progress v. 진행되다 smoothly adv. 순조롭게
pace n. 속도 material n. 자재 breakdown n. 내역, 명세

해석
04-06번은 다음 세 명의 대화에 관한 문제입니다.
여1: Jacob, ⁰⁴당신이 감독하고 있는 건축 프로젝트의 현장을 방금 점검했어요. 모든 것이 순조롭게 진행되고 있는 것을 보니 안심이 되네요.
남: 네, 모든 것이 계획한 대로 진행되고 있어요. 사실, ⁰⁵현재 속도로 계속 일하면 예정보다 며칠 일찍 끝낼 수도 있을 것 같아요.
여1: 그 말을 들으니 좋네요. ⁰⁶Ms. Lowery가 자재 비용 내역에 대해 논의하기 위해 곧 여기에 올 거예요. 아, 저기 오고 계시네요.
여2: 안녕하세요. ⁰⁶저는 최근 자재 비용 내역을 검토하고 우리가 프로젝트 예산 내에서 진행되고 있는지 확인하고 싶었어요. 상세 보고서를 준비하셨나요?
남: 네. 검토하실 수 있도록 세부 사항을 준비해 두었습니다.

04 화자 문제
해석 화자들은 어떤 종류의 사업체에서 일하는가?
(A) 정원용품점
(B) 이사 회사
(C) 조경 서비스
(D) 건설 회사

해설 대화에서 신분 및 직업과 관련된 표현을 놓치지 않고 듣는다. 여자1이 "I've just inspected the site of the building project you're supervising"이라며 남자가 감독하는 건축 프로젝트의 현장을 점검했다고 말한 것과 자재 비용에 대한 논의가 이루어지고 있는 것을 통해 화자들이 건설 회사에서 일한다는 것을 알 수 있다. 따라서 (D)가 정답이다.

05 언급 문제
해석 남자는 프로젝트에 대해 무엇이라고 말하는가?
(A) 며칠 후에 시작할 것이다.
(B) 예상보다 일찍 끝날 수 있다.
(C) 추가 작업자가 필요하다.
(D) 악천후로 중단되었다.

해설 남자의 말에서 질문의 핵심 어구(the project)와 관련된 내용을 주의 깊게 듣는다. 남자가 "we might even finish a few days ahead of schedule if we continue to work at our current pace"라며 현재 속도로 계속 일하면 예정보다 며칠 일찍 끝낼 수도 있을 것이라고 하였다. 따라서 (B)가 정답이다.

어휘 interrupt v. 중단시키다
Paraphrasing
a few days ahead of schedule 예정보다 며칠 일찍 → earlier than expected 예상보다 일찍

06 요청 문제
해석 Ms. Lowery는 무엇을 요청하는가?
(A) 업데이트된 일정
(B) 현장 설계도
(C) 물품 목록
(D) 예산 보고서

해설 Ms. Lowery의 말에서 요청과 관련된 표현이 언급된 내용을 주의 깊게 듣는다. 여자 1이 "Ms. Lowery will be here soon ~. Oh, there she is."라며 Ms. Lowery가 여기 왔다고 했고, 여자2[Ms. Lowery]가 남자에게 "I wanted to review the recent material cost breakdown and confirm we're staying within the project budget. Have you prepared the detailed report?"라며 최근 자재 비용 내역을 검토하고 프로젝트 예산 내에서 진행되고 있는지 확인하기 위한 상세 보고서를 준비했는지 물었다. 따라서 (D)가 정답이다.

어휘 blueprint n. 설계도, 청사진

[07-09] 🎧 영국 → 호주
Questions 07-09 refer to the following conversation.

> W: ⁰⁷I've been trying to call you this morning. Where have you been?
> M: Sorry. ⁰⁷My car kept having trouble, so I was at the repair shop.
> W: That's too bad. Um, ⁰⁸did you hear about the art fair happening this weekend?
> M: No. ⁰⁸How did you find out about it?
> W: ⁰⁸I saw an advertisement in the newspaper. Apparently, over 100 local artists will be showing their work. Why don't we check it out together this Saturday?
> M: Sure. Do you want me to pick you up? My car will be ready by Friday.
> W: Let's just take the subway. ⁰⁹The fair is held at Greener Park, which is just a five-minute walk from the station.

repair shop 정비소 fair n. 박람회 happen v. (일이) 있다, 발생하다
apparently adv. 듣자 하니, 보아 하니

해석
07-09번은 다음 대화에 관한 문제입니다.
여: ⁰⁷오늘 아침에 당신에게 계속 전화하려고 했어요. 어디 있었어요?
남: 죄송해요. ⁰⁷제 차가 계속 문제가 있어서 정비소에 있었어요.
여: 안됐네요. 음, ⁰⁸이번 주말에 열리는 미술 박람회에 대해 들었나요?
남: 아니요. ⁰⁸그것에 대해 어떻게 알게 되었나요?
여: ⁰⁸신문에서 광고를 봤어요. 듣자 하니, 100명이 넘는 지역 예술가들이 그들의 작품을 전시할 거래요. 이번 토요일에 함께 가 보는 게 어때요?
남: 좋아요. 제가 당신을 데리러 갈까요? 제 차는 금요일까지 준비될 거예요.
여: 그냥 지하철을 타죠. ⁰⁹그 박람회는 Greener 공원에서 열리는데, 역에서 단 5분 거리예요.

07 특정 세부 사항 문제
해석 남자는 오늘 아침에 무엇을 했는가?
(A) 휴대폰을 수리했다.
(B) 고객과 만났다.
(C) 정비소에 갔다.
(D) 업무 전화를 했다.

해설 질문의 핵심 어구(this morning)가 언급된 주변을 주의 깊게 듣는다. 여자가 "I've been trying to call you this morning. Where have you been?"이라며 남자에게 오늘 아침에 어디 있었냐고 묻자, 남자가 "My car kept having trouble, so I was at the repair shop."이라며 차에 문제가 있어서 정비소에 있었다고 하였다. 따라서 (C)가 정답이다.

Paraphrasing
repair shop 정비소 → service center 정비소

08 방법 문제
해석 여자는 어떻게 미술 박람회에 대해 알게 되었는가?
(A) 동료로부터
(B) 온라인 후기로부터
(C) 신문 광고로부터
(D) 현지 업주로부터

해설 질문의 핵심 어구(woman learn about the art fair)와 관련된 내용을 주의 깊게 듣는다. 여자가 "did you hear about the art fair happening this weekend?"라며 이번 주에 열리는 미술 박람회에 대해 들었는지 남자에게 물었고, 남자가 "How did you find out about it[art fair]?"이라며 여자에게 되물었다. 이에 대해 여자가 "I saw an advertisement in the newspaper."라며 신문에서 광고를 봤다고 하였다. 따라서 (C)가 정답이다.

09 언급 문제
해석 여자는 Greener 공원에 대해 무엇이라고 말하는가?
(A) 주차장이 작다.
(B) 대중교통으로 접근하기 편리하다.
(C) 여러 축제들을 개최해 왔다.
(D) 시설들이 보수 공사 중이다.

해설 여자의 말에서 질문의 핵심 어구(Greener Park)가 언급된 주변을 주의 깊게 듣는다. 여자가 "The fair is held at Greener Park, which is just a five-minute walk from the station."이라며 Greener 공원은 역에서 단 5분 거리에 있다고 하였다. 따라서 (B)가 정답이다.

어휘 host v. 개최하다

[10-12] 캐나다 → 영국
Questions 10-12 refer to the following conversation.

M: Ms. Meyers, ¹⁰have you reviewed the office renovation schedule I e-mailed you yesterday?
W: Yes. We plan to hire new employees next month. Please make sure that the renovation work is completed before the interviews start.
M: Of course. ¹¹But I've heard nothing from headquarters about the funds we asked for.
W: Hmm . . . we submitted our request three weeks ago.
M: I'm getting concerned. If we don't receive the funds soon, we might have to postpone the entire renovation project.
W: I know. ¹²I'll call the head of the finance department to see if she can expedite the approval process.

headquarters n. 본사 fund n. 자금 expedite v. 신속히 처리하다
approval n. 승인 process n. 절차

해석
10-12번은 다음 대화에 관한 문제입니다.
남: Ms. Meyers, ¹⁰제가 어제 이메일로 보낸 사무실 개조 일정을 검토하셨나요?
여: 네. 저희는 다음 달에 새 직원을 고용할 계획이에요. 인터뷰가 시작되기 전에 개조 작업이 완료되도록 확실히 해 주세요.
남: 물론이죠. ¹¹하지만 저희가 요청한 자금에 대해 본사로부터 아무 소식도 듣지 못했어요.
여: 음... 저희가 3주 전에 요청서를 제출했는데요.
남: 저는 점점 우려가 돼요. 만약 우리가 곧 자금을 받지 못하면, 개조 프로젝트 전체를 연기해야 할 수도 있어요.
여: 알아요. ¹²제가 재무 부서장에게 전화해서 그녀가 승인 절차를 신속히 처리할 수 있는지 확인해 볼게요.

10 주제 문제
해석 대화는 주로 무엇에 대한 것인가?
(A) 공장 이전 계획
(B) 리모델링 프로젝트
(C) 채용 계획
(D) 기자 회견

해설 대화의 주제를 묻는 문제이므로, 대화의 초반을 반드시 듣는다. 남자가 "have you reviewed the office renovation schedule I e-mailed you yesterday?"라며 사무실 개조 일정을 검토했는지 물었고, 뒤이어 개조 프로젝트에 관한 내용으로 이어지고 있다. 따라서 (B)가 정답이다.

11 의도 파악 문제
해설 여자가 "저희가 3주 전에 요청서를 제출했는데요"라고 말할 때 무엇을 의도하는가?
(A) 채용 공고가 곧 게시될 것이다.
(B) 결정이 예상보다 오래 걸리고 있다.
(C) 프로젝트가 원래 계획대로 진행될 수 있다.
(D) 업무 일정이 이미 변경되었다.

해설 질문의 인용어구(we submitted our request three weeks ago)가 언급된 주변을 주의 깊게 듣는다. 남자가 "But I've heard nothing from headquarters about the funds we asked for."라며 요청한 자금에 대해 본사로부터 아무 소식이 없다고 말하자, 여자가 "we submitted our request three weeks ago"라고 답했다. 이는 3주 전에 이미 요청을 했는데도 아직 본사에서 답변이 없다는 것으로, 결정(자금 승인)이 예상보다 오래 걸리고 있다는 것을 의도한 것이다. 따라서 (B)가 정답이다.

어휘 carry on 진행되다

12 다음에 할 일 문제
해석 여자는 다음에 무엇을 할 것 같은가?
(A) 관리자에게 연락한다.
(B) 계약을 협상한다.
(C) 사무실 예산을 검토한다.
(D) 교육 매뉴얼 초안을 작성한다.

해설 대화의 마지막 부분을 주의 깊게 듣는다. 여자가 "I'll call the head of the finance department"라며 재무 부서장에게 전화하겠다고 하였다. 따라서 (A)가 정답이다.

Paraphrasing
head of the finance department 재무 부서장 → manager 관리자

[13-15] 영국 → 캐나다
Questions 13-15 refer to the following conversation and schedule.

W: ¹³Jim Bartley's lecture is almost over, and it's your turn next. Is there anything you need me to do in preparation for your talk?
M: Just one thing. I'm planning to show a video. ¹⁴Could you check if the projector in the hall is working properly?
W: Of course. I'll do that right after Mr. Bartley's lecture. It should take about 10 minutes.

M: Thank you. And where can I find the participant list for my seminar?
W: I expect some people might not attend today. So ¹⁵I'll give you the final list of attendees after the seminar concludes.

lecture n. 강연　preparation n. 준비　properly adv. 제대로
conclude v. 끝나다　attendee n. 참석자

해석
13-15번은 다음 대화와 일정표에 관한 문제입니다.
여: ¹³Jim Bartley의 강연은 거의 끝나가고 있고, 다음은 당신의 차례입니다. 발표 준비를 위해 제가 해드릴 일이 있나요?
남: 한 가지만요. 제가 영상을 보여줄 계획이에요. ¹⁴홀에 있는 프로젝터가 제대로 작동하는지 확인해 주시겠어요?
여: 물론이죠. Mr. Bartley의 강연이 끝나고 바로 확인하겠습니다. 약 10분 정도 걸릴 것 같아요.
남: 감사합니다. 그리고 제 세미나 참가자 명단은 어디서 찾을 수 있을까요?
여: 오늘 참석하지 않는 사람들이 있을 수 있을 것 같아요. 그래서 ¹⁵세미나가 끝난 후에 최종 참석자 명단을 드리겠습니다.

지역사회 건강 세미나 일정		
연설자	주제	시간
Jim Bartley	예방적 심장 관리	오전 8시-오전 9시
Adrian Smith	¹³균형 잡힌 식단 전략	오전 10시-오전 11시
Carlos Fernandez	노인을 위한 운동 재활	오전 11시 30분 - 오후 12시 30분
Yi Lang	스트레스 대처	오후 2시-오후 3시

13 시각 자료 문제
해석 시각 자료를 보아라. 남자는 어떤 주제를 다룰 것인가?
(A) 예방적 심장 관리
(B) 균형 잡힌 식단 전략
(C) 노인을 위한 운동 재활
(D) 스트레스 대처
해설 제시된 일정표의 정보를 확인한 후 질문의 핵심 어구(man going to cover)와 관련된 내용을 주의 깊게 듣는다. 여자가 남자에게 "Jim Bartley's lecture is almost over, and it's your turn next."라며 Jim Bartley의 강연은 거의 끝나가고 있으며 다음은 남자의 차례라고 하였고, 일정표에서 Jim Bartley 다음 연설자는 Adrian Smith이고, 그가 다룰 주제는 '균형 잡힌 식단 전략'임을 알 수 있다. 따라서 (B)가 정답이다.

14 요청 문제
해석 남자는 여자에게 무엇을 하라고 요청하는가?
(A) 자료를 배부한다.
(B) 장비를 테스트한다.
(C) 문서를 인쇄한다.
(D) 안전 검사를 준비한다.
해설 남자의 말에서 요청과 관련된 표현이 언급된 다음을 주의 깊게 듣는다. 남자가 "Could you check if the projector in the hall is working properly?"라며 홀에 있는 프로젝터가 제대로 작동하는지 확인해 달라고 하였다. 따라서 (B)가 정답이다.
어휘 distribute v. 배부하다, 나누어 주다

Paraphrasing
projector 프로젝터 → equipment 장비

15 특정 세부 사항 문제
해석 여자는 나중에 어떤 정보를 제공할 것 같은가?

(A) 행사 장소
(B) 업체 주소
(C) 참가자 명단
(D) 시간 예상치
해설 질문의 핵심 어구(woman ~ provide later)와 관련된 내용을 주의 깊게 듣는다. 여자가 "I'll give you the final list of attendees after the seminar concludes."라며 세미나가 끝난 후에 최종 참석자 명단을 남자에게 제공하겠다고 하였다. 따라서 (C)가 정답이다.

Paraphrasing
list of attendees 참석자 명단 → Names of participants 참가자 명단

[16-18] 호주 → 미국
Questions 16-18 refer to the following conversation and menu.

M: I have a reservation under the name of Chris Harris for 12:30. ¹⁶I'm sorry for being late. A road was closed because of construction work, so I had to take a longer route than usual.
W: Not a problem, Mr. Harris. Here's your table. Just so you know, ¹⁷the daily special is the beef lasagna. This dish was just added to our menu last week, but it is already popular with our customers.
M: Actually, I don't eat red meat, so I'll pass on that. Can you suggest anything else?
W: In that case, ¹⁸why don't you try the seafood spaghetti? It's quite delicious.
M: ¹⁸OK, I'll take that.

reservation n. 예약　construction n. 공사　dish n. 요리
popular adj. 인기 많은　suggest v. 제안하다

해석
16-18번은 다음 대화와 메뉴에 관한 문제입니다.
남: 저는 Chris Harris의 이름으로 12시 30분에 예약되어 있어요. ¹⁶늦어서 죄송합니다. 공사 작업 때문에 도로가 폐쇄되어 있어서, 평소보다 더 오래 걸리는 경로를 타야 했어요.
여: 문제없습니다, Mr. Harris. 여기가 당신의 테이블입니다. 참고로 말씀드리자면, ¹⁷비프 라자냐가 오늘의 특선이에요. 이 요리는 지난주에 저희 메뉴에 추가되었는데, 이미 저희 고객들에게 인기가 많습니다.
남: 사실, 저는 붉은 고기를 먹지 않아서, 그건 사양할게요. 다른 것을 제안해 주실 수 있나요?
여: 그런 경우라면, ¹⁸해물 스파게티를 드셔 보시는 건 어떤가요? 그건 꽤 맛있습니다.
남: ¹⁸좋아요, 그걸로 할게요.

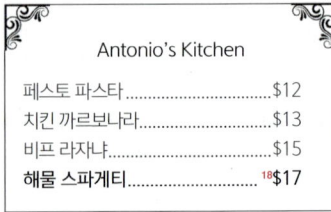

Antonio's Kitchen	
페스토 파스타	$12
치킨 까르보나라	$13
비프 라자냐	$15
해물 스파게티	¹⁸$17

16 이유 문제
해석 남자는 왜 늦었는가?
(A) 주차 공간을 이용할 수 없었다.
(B) 회의가 지연되었다.
(C) 도로가 접근 불가능했다.
(D) 식당이 찾기 어려웠다.
해설 질문의 핵심 어구(late)가 언급된 내용을 주의 깊게 듣는다. 대화 초

반부에서 남자가 "I'm sorry for being late. A road was closed because of construction work"라고 한 것을 통해, 도로가 접근 불가능했음을 알 수 있다. 따라서 (C)가 정답이다.

어휘 **parking spot** 주차 공간 **inaccessible** adj. 접근 불가능한

Paraphrasing
closed 폐쇄된 → **inaccessible** 접근 불가능한

17 언급 문제

해석 여자는 오늘의 특선에 대해 무엇을 말하는가?
(A) 무료 음료와 함께 제공된다.
(B) 새로 도입된 요리이다.
(C) 가족 요리법에 기반한다.
(D) 평일에만 가능하다.

해설 여자의 말에서 질문의 핵심 어구(daily special)가 언급된 주변을 주의 깊게 듣는다. 여자가 "the daily special is the beef lasagna. This dish was just added to our menu last week"이라며 비프 라자냐가 오늘의 특선인데 이 요리는 지난주에 메뉴에 추가되었다고 하였다. 따라서 (B)가 정답이다.

Paraphrasing
just added ~ last week 지난주에 추가된 → **newly introduced** 새로 도입된

18 시각 자료 문제

해석 시각 자료를 보아라. 남자의 식사 비용은 얼마일 것인가?
(A) 12달러
(B) 13달러
(C) 15달러
(D) 17달러

해설 메뉴의 정보를 확인한 후 질문의 핵심 어구(meal cost)와 관련된 내용을 주의 깊게 듣는다. 여자가 "why don't you try the seafood spaghetti?"라며 해물 스파게티를 먹어 보는 건 어떤지 묻자, 남자가 "OK, I'll take that."이라며 그걸로 하겠다고 하였고, 메뉴에서 해물 스파게티의 비용이 17달러임을 알 수 있다. 따라서 (D)가 정답이다.

PART 4

DAY 15 문제 유형

기출 유형 1 전체 지문 관련 문제

Example 🔊 캐나다   p.100

해석
01번은 다음 회의 발췌에 관한 문제입니다.
아시다시피, 우리 레스토랑에서는 최근에 새로운 직원들을 채용했습니다. 그에 따라, 제가 방금 직원 휴게실의 게시판에 업데이트된 근무 일정을 게시했어요. 한 가지 더 말씀드리자면... 주방장이 우리의 점심 메뉴에 치킨 누들 수프와 버섯 파니니 샌드위치를 포함하여 새로운 요리를 추가했습니다. 고객들에게 이 메뉴들을 추천하는 것을 잊지 마세요. 좋습니다, 모두 일하러 돌아가세요.

어휘 recently adv. 최근에   accordingly adv. 그에 따라, 그래서
bulletin board 게시판   add v. 추가하다

01
해석 청자들은 어디에서 일하는가?
(A) 식료품점에서
(B) 식당에서
(C) 요리 학교에서
(D) 주방용품점에서

토익실전문제   p.101

01 (C)	02 (B)	03 (D)	04 (D)	05 (D)
06 (B)				

[01-03] 🔊 미국
Questions 01-03 refer to the following advertisement.

> ⁰¹Spring has arrived, which means it's time to make your way down to Evergreen's! We've got a huge selection of gardening equipment and supplies. Plus, ⁰²during the city government's annual award ceremony in February, we won the Best Small Business category. ⁰³Make sure to sign up for our newsletter so you can be the first to hear about our special offers. We hope to see you soon!

equipment n. 장비   supplies n. 용품   sign up for ~을 신청하다
special adj. 특별한   offer n. 제안

해석
01-03번은 다음 광고에 관한 문제입니다.
⁰¹봄이 왔습니다, 바로 Evergreen's를 방문하실 때라는 뜻이죠! 저희는 대량의 원예 장비와 용품을 보유하고 있습니다. 게다가, ⁰²2월에 시 정부의 연례 시상식에서, 저희는 베스트 소규모 사업체 부문에서 상을 받았습니다. ⁰³저희의 특별 제안에 대해 가장 먼저 들으실 수 있도록 저희 소식지를 꼭 신청하세요. 여러분을 곧 만나 뵙기를 바랍니다!

01 주제 문제
해석 어떤 사업체가 광고되고 있는가?
(A) 슈퍼마켓
(B) 수리점
(C) 원예 상점
(D) 배관 회사

해설 광고의 주제를 묻는 문제이므로, 지문의 초반을 반드시 듣는다. "Spring has arrived, which means it's time to make your way down to Evergreen's! We've got a huge selection of gardening equipment and supplies."라며 봄이 왔으니 Evergreen's를 방문할 때라며, 대량의 원예 장비와 용품을 보유하고 있다고 한 후, 상점 홍보로 내용이 이어지고 있다. 따라서 (C)가 정답이다.

어휘 repair n. 수리, 수선   plumbing n. 배관, 수도 시설

02 특정 세부 사항 문제
해석 2월에 무슨 일이 일어났는가?
(A) 계절 세일이 끝났다.
(B) 회사가 상을 받았다.
(C) 상점이 추가 지점을 열었다.
(D) 정부 프로그램이 시작되었다.

해설 질문의 핵심 어구(February)가 언급된 주변을 주의 깊게 듣는다. "during the city government's annual award ceremony in February, we won the Best Small Business category"라며 2월에 시 정부의 연례 시상식에서 베스트 소규모 사업체 부문에서 상을 받았다고 하였다. 따라서 (B)가 정답이다.

어휘 seasonal adj. 계절의   conclude v. 끝나다, 결론을 내리다
launch v. 출간하다, 시작하다

03 제안 문제
해석 화자는 무엇을 하라고 제안하는가?
(A) 대회 참여하기
(B) 후기 작성하기
(C) 채널 구독하기
(D) 간행물 신청하기

해설 지문에서 제안과 관련된 표현이 언급된 다음을 주의 깊게 듣는다. "Make sure to sign up for our newsletter so you can be the first to hear about our special offers."라며 특별 제안에 대해 가장 먼저 들을 수 있도록 소식지를 신청하라고 하였다. 따라서 (D)가 정답이다.

어휘 subscribe to ~을 구독하다

[Paraphrasing]
newsletter 소식지 → publication 간행물

[04-06] 🔊 영국
Questions 04-06 refer to the following telephone message.

> Good afternoon, Mr. Renauld. ⁰⁴This is Zoey Frank, the head of the human resources department at Rochester Corporation. I'm calling about your recent interview. I'm delighted to tell you that ⁰⁵we are very impressed with your extensive work history. Accordingly, we'd like to offer you the position of investment manager at our firm. ⁰⁶I'm sending you an e-mail with a detailed job description. If you're interested, please call me back. Thanks.

human resources 인사부, 인적 자원   delighted adj. 기쁜
extensive adj. 폭넓은, 대규모의   position n. 직책, 위치
detailed adj. 상세한   job description 직무 설명서

해석
04-06번은 다음 전화 메시지에 관한 문제입니다.
안녕하세요, Mr. Renauld. 저는 Rochester사의 ⁰⁴인사부장인 Zoey Frank

입니다. 최근 귀하의 면접과 관련해 연락드려요. ⁰⁵귀하의 폭넓은 업무 경력에 깊은 인상을 받았다는 것을 말씀드릴 수 있어 기쁩니다. 그에 따라, 저희 회사의 투자 관리자 직위를 제안드리고 싶습니다. ⁰⁶상세한 직무 설명서가 포함된 이메일을 귀하께 보낼 것입니다. 관심이 있으시다면, 저에게 다시 연락 주시기 바랍니다. 감사합니다.

04 화자 문제
해석 화자는 누구인가?
(A) 회사 대표
(B) 언론인
(C) 접수 담당자
(D) 부서 관리자

해설 지문에서 신분 및 직업과 관련된 표현을 주의 깊게 듣는다. "This is ~ the head of the human resources department"라며 자신은 인사부장이라고 하였다. 따라서 (D)가 정답이다.

[Paraphrasing]
the head of the human resources department 인사부장
→ department manager 부서 관리자

05 특정 세부 사항 문제
해석 화자에 따르면, 청자의 어떤 점이 인상적인가?
(A) 정직하다.
(B) 유능한 지도자이다.
(C) 좋은 소통 능력을 보유하고 있다.
(D) 많은 업무 경력을 가지고 있다.

해설 질문의 핵심 어구(impressive)가 언급된 주변을 주의 깊게 듣는다. "we are very impressed with your extensive work history"라며 청자의 폭넓은 업무 경력에 깊은 인상을 받았다고 하였다. 따라서 (D)가 정답이다.

어휘 honest adj. 정직한   effective adj. 유능한

[Paraphrasing]
extensive work history 폭넓은 업무 경력 → a lot of work experience 많은 업무 경력

06 특정 세부 사항 문제
해석 이메일에는 무엇이 포함되어 있는가?
(A) 회사 소개
(B) 직무 세부 사항
(C) 회의 시간
(D) 배송 주소

해설 질문의 핵심 어구(e-mail)가 언급된 주변을 주의 깊게 듣는다. "I'm sending you an e-mail with a detailed job description."이라며 상세한 직무 설명서가 포함된 이메일을 보낼 것이라고 하였다. 따라서 (B)가 정답이다.

기출 유형 2 세부 사항 관련 문제

Example 〔호주〕 p.102
해석
01번은 다음 회의 발췌에 관한 문제입니다.

회의를 마치기 전에, 저는 모든 생산 라인 직원들에게 중요한 공지를 하겠습니다. 우리에게 운동화 제작을 의뢰한 Senica Shoes사에서 처음에 합의했던 날짜보다 일주일 일찍 이 제품들이 필요하다고 알렸습니다. 이 상황에 대처하기 위해, 모든 직원들이 다음 주에 매일 추가로 2시간씩 일할 것을 요청하고자 합니다. 물론, 여러분들은 그 추가 근무 시간에 대해 추가 급여를 받으실 것입니다.

어휘 announcement n. 공지   assembly line 생산 라인   inform v. 알리다
product n. 제품   originally adv. 처음에, 원래
deal with ~에 대처하다, 처리하다   additional adj. 추가의

01
해석 화자는 청자들에게 무엇을 하라고 요청하는가?
(A) 문서를 업데이트한다.
(B) 추가 시간을 일한다.
(C) 보호 장비를 착용한다.
(D) 매뉴얼을 검토한다.

어휘 protective adj. 보호용의   review v. 검토하다

토익실전문제 p.103

| 01 (B) | 02 (C) | 03 (D) | 04 (A) | 05 (C) |
| 06 (A) |

[01-03] 〔미국〕
Questions 01-03 refer to the following telephone message.

Hi, James. This is Cheryl from the marketing department. I'm calling because ⁰¹the projector in Conference Room C isn't working properly. When I push the power button, the projector switches on for just a few minutes, but then it turns off after that. ⁰²I really need to get this fixed quickly because I have to do an important client presentation at 3 P.M. today. Could you please come up to the 10th floor and take a look at it? ⁰³I'll text you the projector model number right away.

properly adv. 제대로, 올바로   turn off 꺼지다   fix v. 수리하다, 고치다
quickly adv. 빨리

해석
01-03번은 다음 전화 메시지에 관한 문제입니다.

안녕하세요, James. 저는 마케팅 부서의 Cheryl입니다. ⁰¹회의실 C에 있는 프로젝터가 제대로 작동하지 않아서 전화드려요. 제가 전원 버튼을 누르면 프로젝터가 몇 분 동안만 켜지고, 그 후에는 꺼집니다. ⁰²오늘 오후 3시에 중요한 고객 프레젠테이션을 해야 해서 이것을 정말로 빨리 수리해야 돼요. 10층으로 올라와서 그것을 한번 봐주실 수 있을까요? ⁰³프로젝터 모델 번호를 곧바로 문자로 보내드리겠습니다.

01 문제점 문제
해석 화자에 따르면, 무엇이 문제인가?
(A) 방이 현재 잠겨 있다.
(B) 기기가 제대로 작동하지 않고 있다.
(C) 이미지에 편집이 필요하다.
(D) 문서에 접근할 수 없다.

해설 질문의 핵심 어구(problem)와 관련된 내용을 주의 깊게 듣는다. "the projector in Conference Room C isn't working properly"라며 회의실 C에 있는 프로젝터가 제대로 작동하지 않는다고 하였다. 따라서 (B)가 정답이다.

어휘 currently adv. 현재   malfunction v. 제대로 작동하지 않다
inaccessible adj. 접근할 수 없는

[Paraphrasing]
projector ~ isn't working properly 프로젝터가 제대로 작동하지 않는다
→ device is malfunctioning 기기가 제대로 작동하지 않고 있다

02 이유 문제
해석 화자는 왜 작업이 빨리 완료되기를 원하는가?
(A) 보고서를 마무리해야 한다.
(B) 문서를 인쇄하고 싶다.
(C) 프레젠테이션을 해야 한다.
(D) 예산을 확정해야 한다.

해설 질문의 핵심 어구(work ~ done quickly)와 관련된 내용을 주의 깊게

듣는다. "I really need to get this fixed quickly because I have to do an important client presentation at 3 P.M. today."라며 오늘 오후 3시에 중요한 고객 프레젠테이션을 해야 해서 프로젝터를 빨리 수리해야 한다고 하였다. 따라서 (C)가 정답이다.

어휘 confirm v. 확정하다, 확인해 주다 budget n. 예산

03 특정 세부 사항 문제

해석 화자는 청자에게 무엇을 보낼 것인가?
(A) 비밀번호
(B) 이메일 주소
(C) 계약서 사본
(D) 모델 번호

해설 질문의 핵심 어구(send)와 관련된 내용을 주의 깊게 듣는다. "I'll text you the projector model number right away."라며 프로젝터 모델 번호를 곧바로 문자로 보내주겠다고 하였다. 따라서 (D)가 정답이다.

[04-06] 🎧 영국

Questions 04-06 refer to the following excerpt from a meeting.

> [04]I'm glad to have members of our software development team here today. I want to talk about the upcoming release of our mobile banking application. [05]I strongly recommend that you focus on adding some new features, like real-time transaction tracking. And [06]several new team members will be joining us tomorrow. But, um . . . they'll be trained over the next two weeks. OK, those are the essentials for now. We'll discuss this matter further during Friday's meeting.

upcoming adj. 곧 있을, 다가오는 release n. 출시, 공개
strongly adv. 강력히 focus on ~에 집중하다 feature n. 기능
transaction n. 거래, 처리 essential n. 핵심 사항, 필수적인 것
further adv. 더 (나아가)

해석
04-06번은 다음 회의 발췌에 관한 문제입니다.

[04]오늘 이 자리에 저희 소프트웨어 개발팀 구성원들이 참석해 주셔서 기쁩니다. 저는 우리의 모바일 뱅킹 애플리케이션의 곧 있을 출시에 대해 이야기하고 싶습니다. 실시간 거래 추적과 같은 [05]몇 가지 새로운 기능을 추가하는 데 집중하시길 강력히 권장합니다. 그리고 [06]몇몇 신입 팀원들이 내일 저희와 합류할 예정입니다. 하지만, 음... 그들은 앞으로 2주 동안 교육을 받을 것입니다. 좋아요, 지금으로서는 그것들이 핵심 사항입니다. 금요일 회의에서 이 문제에 대해 더 논의하겠습니다.

04 청자 문제

해석 청자들은 누구인 것 같은가?
(A) 소프트웨어 개발자들
(B) 호텔 접수원들
(C) 기계 엔지니어들
(D) 영업 사원들

해설 지문에서 신분 및 직업과 관련된 표현을 놓치지 않고 듣는다. "I'm glad to have members of our software development team here today."라며 오늘 이 자리에 소프트웨어 개발팀 구성원들이 참석해 주셔서 기쁘다고 한 것을 통해 청자들은 소프트웨어 기술자들임을 알 수 있다. 따라서 (A)가 정답이다.

어휘 mechanical adj. 기계의, 기계적인 associate n. 사원

05 제안 문제

해석 화자는 무엇을 제안하는가?
(A) 예산 줄이기
(B) 광고 수 줄이기
(C) 새로운 기능 추가하기
(D) 다른 애플리케이션 사용하기

해설 지문의 중후반에서 제안과 관련된 표현을 주의 깊게 듣는다. "I strongly recommend that you focus on adding some new features"라며 몇 가지 새로운 기능을 추가하는 데 집중하기를 강력히 권장한다고 하였다. 따라서 (C)가 정답이다.

어휘 decrease v. 줄이다

06 의도 파악 문제

해석 화자는 "그들은 앞으로 2주 동안 교육을 받을 것입니다"라고 말할 때 무엇을 의도하는가?
(A) 도움을 바로 줄 수는 없을 것이다.
(B) 회사 정책이 업데이트되었다.
(C) 회의가 연기될 것이다.
(D) 장소가 이용될 준비가 되어 있지 않다.

해설 질문의 인용어구(they'll be trained over the next two weeks)가 언급된 주변을 주의 깊게 듣는다. "several new team members will be joining us tomorrow"라며 몇몇 신입 팀원들이 내일 합류하는데, 2주 동안 교육을 받을 것이라고 한 것을 통해, 신입 팀원들이 도움을 바로 줄 수는 없을 것임을 알 수 있다. 따라서 (A)가 정답이다.

어휘 assistance n. 도움, 지원 immediately adv. 바로, 즉시
postpone v. 연기하다, 미루다 venue n. 장소

HACKERS TEST   p.104

01 (A)	02 (D)	03 (D)	04 (C)	05 (B)
06 (D)	07 (B)	08 (A)	09 (D)	10 (D)
11 (C)	12 (A)	13 (B)	14 (D)	15 (C)
16 (B)	17 (A)	18 (B)	19 (D)	20 (D)
21 (B)				

[01-03] 🎧 미국

Questions 01-03 refer to the following broadcast.

> [01]This is Katie Jackson with the morning traffic update. Drivers heading downtown should be aware of heavy traffic on the Bayport Bridge. A three-car collision at the south entrance of the bridge has resulted in the closure of two of the northbound lanes. Additionally, [02]emergency repair work on the Harborview Expressway is causing delays of up to 40 minutes. It will likely be about two hours before the situation improves. So [03]it would be best to commute by subway this morning.

head v. 향하다 be aware of ~을 주의하다, ~을 알다 traffic n. 교통
collision n. 충돌 entrance n. 입구 result in ~을 발생시키다
closure n. 폐쇄 northbound adj. 북쪽 방향의 delay n. 지연, 연기
commute v. 통근하다

해석
01-03번은 다음 방송에 관한 문제입니다.

[01]아침 교통 상황 업데이트를 전하는 Katie Jackson입니다. 시내로 향하는 운전자들은 Bayport 다리의 심한 교통 정체를 주의하셔야 합니다. 다리의 남쪽 입구에서 발생한 세 대의 차량 충돌로 인해 북쪽 방향 차선 두 개가 폐쇄되었습니다. 또한, [02]Harborview 고속도로에서의 긴급 보수 작업으로 인해 최대 40분까지의 지연이 발생하고 있습니다. 상황이 개선되기까지는 약 두 시간이 걸릴 것 같습니다. 그러므로 [03]오늘 아침에는 지하철로 통근하는 것이 가장 좋을 것 같습니다.

01 주제 문제

해석 방송은 주로 무엇에 관한 것인가?
(A) 교통 정체
(B) 정부 프로그램
(C) 고속도로 공사
(D) 건물 보수

해설 방송의 주제를 묻는 문제이므로, 지문의 초반을 주의 깊게 듣는다. "This is Katie Jackson with the morning traffic update."라며 아침 교통 상황 업데이트를 전하는 Katie Jackson이라고 한 것을 통해, 교통 상황에 대한 내용임을 알 수 있고, 뒤이어 "Drivers heading downtown should be aware of heavy traffic on the Bayport Bridge."라며 시내로 향하는 운전자들이 Bayport 다리의 심한 교통 정체를 주의해야 한다고 했으므로 교통 정체에 관한 것임을 알 수 있다. 따라서 (A)가 정답이다.

어휘 congestion n. 정체, 혼잡 construction n. 공사, 건설

02 언급 문제

해석 화자는 Harborview 고속도로에 대해 무엇을 말하는가?
(A) Bayport 다리와 연결되어 있다.
(B) 지역 사회 행사를 위해 폐쇄되었다.
(C) 사용하기 위해 통행료를 지불해야 한다.
(D) 예정되지 않은 보수 작업을 진행 중이다.

해설 질문의 핵심 어구(Harborview Expressway)와 관련된 내용을 주의 깊게 듣는다. "emergency repair work on the Harborview Expressway is causing delays of up to 40 minutes"라며 Harborview 고속도로에서의 긴급 보수 작업으로 인해 최대 40분까지의 지연이 발생하고 있다고 한 것을 통해, 예정되지 않은 보수 작업을 진행하고 있음을 알 수 있다. 따라서 (D)가 정답이다.

어휘 community n. 지역 사회 payment n. 지불, 결제
undergo v. 진행하다, 경험하다 unscheduled adj. 예정되지 않은

> [Paraphrasing]
> emergency repair work 긴급 보수 작업 → unscheduled repairs 예정되지 않은 보수 작업

03 제안 문제

해석 화자는 청자들에게 무엇을 하라고 제안하는가?
(A) 상담 서비스에 전화한다.
(B) 대체 경로를 이용한다.
(C) 시내 지역을 피한다.
(D) 대중교통을 이용한다.

해설 지문의 후반부에서 제안과 관련된 표현이 언급된 다음을 주의 깊게 듣는다. "it would be best to commute by subway this morning"이라며 오늘 아침에는 지하철로 통근하는 것이 가장 좋을 것이라고 하였다. 따라서 (D)가 정답이다.

어휘 hotline n. 상담 서비스 전화, 직통 전화 alternative adj. 대체의, 대안적인
avoid v. 피하다

> [Paraphrasing]
> subway 지하철 → public transportation 대중교통

[04-06] 🎧 호주

Questions 04-06 refer to the following announcement.

> Welcome, everyone, to this orientation session for our institute's certification course for Web software developers. **04I'll be leading the course for the next few weeks.** Before we begin, I'd like to share some information with you. When your course is completed, **05you'll have the chance to meet with a professional career consultant free of charge**. It'll be of great benefit to you, so I hope you make the most of it. Now, let's go ahead and start our first session. **06Please log on to our training system by entering your username and password.**

institute n. 기관, 협회 certification n. 자격증, 증명서 교부
share v. 공유하다 professional adj. 전문가의 free of charge 무료로
benefit n. 이득, 혜택

해석
04-06번은 다음 공고에 관한 문제입니다.

여러분, 저희 기관의 웹 소프트웨어 개발자를 위한 자격증 과정 오리엔테이션에 오신 것을 환영합니다. 04저는 앞으로 몇 주 동안 이 과정을 이끌 것입니다. 시작하기 전에, 여러분과 몇 가지 정보를 공유하고 싶습니다. 여러분의 과정이 완료되면, 05여러분은 전문 진로 상담사와 무료로 상담할 기회를 갖게 될 것입니다. 이것은 여러분에게 큰 이득이 될 것이니, 최대한 활용하시기 바랍니다. 자, 이제 첫 번째 세션을 시작하겠습니다. 사용자 이름과 비밀번호를 입력하여 06저희 교육 시스템에 로그인해 주세요.

04 화자 문제

해석 화자는 누구인 것 같은가?
(A) 사무 보조원
(B) 컴퓨터 수리 기술자
(C) 수업 강사
(D) 보안 요원

해설 지문에서 신분 및 직업과 관련된 표현을 놓치지 않고 듣는다. "I'll be leading the course for the next few weeks."라며 화자가 앞으로 몇 주 동안 이 과정을 이끌 것이라고 한 것을 통해, 화자는 수업을 이끄는 강사임을 알 수 있다. 따라서 (C)가 정답이다.

어휘 assistant n. 보조원, 조수 repairperson n. 수리 기술자 instructor n. 강사

05 특정 세부 사항 문제

해석 화자에 따르면, 무엇이 무료로 제공될 것인가?
(A) 교육용 도서
(B) 진로 상담
(C) 온라인 멤버십
(D) 소프트웨어 프로그램

해설 질문의 핵심 어구(free of charge)가 언급된 주변을 주의 깊게 듣는다. "you'll each have the chance to meet with a professional career consultant free of charge"라며 각자 전문 진로 상담사와 무료로 상담할 기회를 갖게 될 것이라고 하였다. 따라서 (B)가 정답이다.

어휘 educational adj. 교육용의 career n. 진로, 경력 consultation n. 상담

06 요청 문제

해석 화자는 청자들에게 무엇을 하라고 요청하는가?
(A) 비밀번호를 변경한다.
(B) 시스템 계정을 생성한다.
(C) 몇몇 일자리에 지원한다.
(D) 시스템에 로그인한다.

해설 지문의 후반부에서 요청과 관련된 표현이 언급된 다음을 주의 깊게 듣는다. "Please log on to our training system"이라며 교육 시스템에 로그인해 달라고 하였다. 따라서 (D)가 정답이다.

> [Paraphrasing]
> log on to 로그인하다 → Sign in to 로그인하다

[07-09] 🎧 캐나다

Questions 07-09 refer to the following excerpt from a meeting.

> As you all know, **07we're doing a catering job this Thursday for a new client, Ledman Industries**. **08It will be challenging because there will be about 400 people, which is more than we have ever handled.** But if we do well, this client will likely hire us for future events. We're

going to get together tomorrow morning to go over the necessary details. ⁰⁹**Erica, could you create a list of the equipment and other items we will need for this job? We will go through it together during our meeting tomorrow.**

catering n. 출장 연회, 음식 공급업 **challenging** adj. 어려운
handle v. 다루다, 처리하다 **go over** 검토하다 **necessary** adj. 필요한
equipment n. 장비 **go through** 검토하다

해석
07-09번은 다음 회의 발췌에 관한 문제입니다.

여러분 모두 알다시피, ⁰⁷우리는 이번 주 목요일에 신규 고객인 Ledman 산업사를 위해 출장 연회 일을 할 것입니다. ⁰⁸약 400명의 사람들이 있을 것인데, 이는 우리가 이제까지 다뤘던 것보다 더 많은 인원이기 때문에 어려울 것입니다. 하지만 우리가 잘한다면, 이 고객사는 앞으로 있을 행사에 우리를 고용할 가능성이 있습니다. 우리는 내일 아침에 필요한 세부 사항들을 검토하기 위해 모일 것입니다. ⁰⁹Erica, 이 일에 필요한 장비와 기타 물품들의 목록을 작성해 주시겠어요? 우리가 내일 회의 동안 함께 그것을 검토할 것입니다.

07 청자 문제
해석 청자들은 어떤 종류의 업체에서 일하는 것 같은가?
(A) 호텔 체인
(B) 출장 연회 서비스
(C) 시장 조사 기관
(D) 이삿짐 센터

해설 지문에서 신분 및 직업과 관련된 표현을 놓치지 않고 듣는다. "we're doing a catering job this Thursday for a new client, Ledman Industries"라며 목요일에 신규 고객인 Ledman 산업사를 위해 출장 연회 일을 할 것이라고 한 것을 통해, 청자들은 출장 연회 서비스 업체에서 일한다는 것을 알 수 있다. 따라서 (B)가 정답이다.

어휘 **agency** n. 기관, 대리점

08 이유 문제
해석 화자는 왜 그 일이 어려울 것이라고 말하는가?
(A) 행사에 참석자들이 많을 것이다.
(B) 행사가 낯선 장소에서 열릴 것이다.
(C) 회사는 인력이 부족하다.
(D) 준비 시간이 충분하지 않다.

해설 질문의 핵심 어구(work will be difficult)와 관련된 내용을 주의 깊게 듣는다. "It will be challenging because there will be about 400 people, which is more than we have ever handled."라며 약 400명의 사람들이 있을 것인데, 이는 이제까지 다뤘던 것보다 더 많은 인원이기 때문에 어려울 것이라고 하였다. 따라서 (A)가 정답이다.

어휘 **unfamiliar** adj. 낯선, 익숙지 않은 **understaffed** adj. 인력이 부족한
insufficient adj. 불충분한

09 다음에 할 일 문제
해석 Erica는 내일 회의 전에 무엇을 할 것인가?
(A) 물품을 주문한다.
(B) 고객에게 연락한다.
(C) 설문 조사를 한다.
(D) 목록을 준비한다.

해설 질문의 핵심 어구(Erica ~ before the meeting tomorrow)와 관련된 내용을 주의 깊게 듣는다. "Erica, could you create a list of the equipment and other items we will need for this job? We will go through it together during our meeting tomorrow."라며 Erica에게 필요한 장비와 기타 물품들의 목록을 작성해 달라고 요청한 후, 내일 회의에서 그것을 검토할 예정이라고 한 것을 통해, Erica가 내일 회의 전에 목록을 준비할 것임을 알 수 있다. 따라서 (D)가 정답이다.

어휘 **conduct** v. (특정 활동을) 하다

[10-12] 영국

Questions 10-12 refer to the following telephone message.

Hello, Mr. Hwang. My name is Claire Walter, and I'm the curator at the Chroma Gallery. ¹⁰**I'm calling because I would like to feature your photographs in an upcoming exhibit.** It will run for two months, from November 1 to December 31, and ¹¹**the focus will be on wilderness scenes.** You have captured many images of mountains, and ¹¹**they are quite stunning.** ¹²**If you would like the names of the other photographers who will display their work, please e-mail me and I will send them to you.** Otherwise, you can reach me at 555-3957 to discuss this matter further.

feature v. 특별히 포함하다, 특징으로 삼다 **upcoming** adj. 다가오는, 곧 있을
capture v. 기록하다, 붙잡다 **quite** adv. 상당히, 꽤
stunning adj. 멋진, 깜짝 놀랄 **display** v. 전시하다 **further** adv. 더, 더 멀리

해석
10-12번은 다음 전화 메시지에 관한 문제입니다.

안녕하세요, Mr. Hwang. 제 이름은 Claire Walter이고, 저는 Chroma 갤러리의 전시 책임자입니다. ¹⁰다가오는 전시회에 귀하의 사진을 특별히 포함하고 싶어서 연락드립니다. 전시회는 11월 1일부터 12월 31일까지 2개월간 진행될 예정이고, ¹¹중심 주제는 야생 풍경입니다. 귀하께서는 산의 많은 이미지를 기록해 오셨고, ¹¹그것들은 상당히 멋집니다. ¹²전시회에 작품을 전시할 다른 사진작가들의 이름을 원하신다면, 저에게 이메일을 보내주시면 그것들을 보내드리겠습니다. 아니면, 이 사안에 대해 더 논의하기 위해 555-3957로 저에게 연락하셔도 됩니다.

10 목적 문제
해석 화자는 왜 전화하고 있는가?
(A) 과제에 도움을 제공하기 위해
(B) 서비스에 관한 정보를 제공하기 위해
(C) 물품 구매에 관해 문의하기 위해
(D) 행사 참여를 요청하기 위해

해설 전화 메시지의 목적을 묻는 문제이므로, 지문의 초반을 반드시 듣는다. "I'm calling because I would like to feature your photographs in an upcoming exhibit."이라며 다가오는 전시회에 청자의 사진을 특별히 포함하고 싶어서 연락한다고 하였다. 따라서 (D)가 정답이다.

어휘 **assignment** n. 과제, 임무 **inquire** v. 문의하다 **involvement** n. 참여, 관여

11 의도 파악 문제
해석 화자가 "귀하께서는 산의 많은 이미지를 기록해 오셨고"라고 말할 때 무엇을 의도하는가?
(A) 그녀는 프로젝트가 승인되기를 기대한다.
(B) 그녀는 이미지 중 하나를 사고 싶어 한다.
(C) 그녀는 청자의 작품이 적합하다고 생각한다.
(D) 그녀는 청자가 다른 무언가의 사진을 찍기를 원한다.

해설 질문의 인용어구(You have captured many images of mountains)가 언급된 주변을 주의 깊게 듣는다. "the focus will be on wilderness scenes"라며 중심 주제는 야생 풍경이라고 한 후, "You have captured many images of mountains, and they are quite stunning."이라며 청자가 산의 많은 이미지를 기록해 왔고, 그것들이 상당히 멋지다고 한 것을 통해 청자의 작품이 전시회의 주제에 적합하다고 생각한다는 것을 알 수 있다. 따라서 (C)가 정답이다.

어휘 **approve** v. 승인하다, 찬성하다 **suitable** adj. 적합한, 알맞은

12 특정 세부 사항 문제

해석 화자에 따르면, 무엇이 이메일로 요청될 수 있는가?
(A) 참가자 목록
(B) 장소 지도
(C) 제품 샘플
(D) 비용 견적서

해설 질문의 핵심 어구(requested by e-mail)와 관련된 내용을 주의 깊게 듣는다. "If you would like the names of the other photographers who will display their work, please e-mail me and I will send them to you."라며 전시회에 작품을 전시할 다른 사진작가들의 이름을 원할 경우, 이메일을 보내면 그것들을 청자에게 보내주겠다고 하였다. 따라서 (A)가 정답이다.

어휘 participant n. 참가자 venue n. 장소 estimate n. 견적서, 추정치

[Paraphrasing]
names of the other photographers 다른 사진작가들의 이름 → list of participants 참가자 목록

[13-15] 🎧 호주
Questions 13-15 refer to the following excerpt from a meeting.

> Good morning. I'm pleased to say that revenues are up this quarter. ¹³**We have a lot of new clients wanting to make use of our graphic design services.** But ¹⁴**I'm a bit concerned because company expenditures have increased recently.** This is mainly because of the rise in electricity usage. ¹⁵**So in order to reduce this cost, please set your computers to sleep mode before you go to lunch or a meeting. Also, if you're the last person to leave the office, make sure to turn off the lights.** This will become part of our daily routine.

revenue n. 수익, 수입 quarter n. 분기, 4분의 1
make use of ~을 이용하다 expenditure n. 비용 rise n. 증가, 인상
usage n. 사용량, 사용 routine n. 일상

해석
13-15번은 다음 회의 발췌에 관한 문제입니다.

안녕하세요. 이번 분기에 수익이 증가했다고 말씀드리게 되어 기쁩니다. ¹³우리의 그래픽 디자인 서비스를 이용하고자 하는 새로운 고객들이 많습니다. 하지만, ¹⁴최근에 회사 지출이 증가했기 때문에 다소 걱정입니다. 이는 주로 전기 사용량 증가 때문입니다. ¹⁵따라서 이 비용을 줄이기 위해, 점심 식사나 회의에 가기 전에 컴퓨터를 절전 모드로 설정해 주세요. 또한, 사무실을 마지막으로 나가는 사람이라면, 불을 꺼주세요. 이것은 매일 행해지는 우리의 일상이 될 것입니다.

13 청자 문제

해석 청자들은 어디에서 일하는 것 같은가?
(A) 은행에서
(B) 그래픽 디자인 회사에서
(C) 법률 사무소에서
(D) 전자제품 판매점에서

해설 지문에서 신분 및 직업과 관련된 표현을 놓치지 않고 듣는다. "We have a lot of new clients wanting to make use of our graphic design services."라며 우리의 그래픽 디자인 서비스를 이용하고자 하는 새로운 고객들이 많다고 한 것을 통해, 청자들이 그래픽 디자인 회사에서 일하는 것을 알 수 있다. 따라서 (B)가 정답이다.

어휘 electronics n. 전자제품, 전자 기술

14 문제점 문제

해석 화자는 어떤 문제점을 언급하는가?
(A) 요청이 거부되었다.
(B) 배송이 지연되었다.
(C) 고객이 불평했다.
(D) 비용이 증가했다.

해설 질문의 핵심 어구(problem)와 관련된 내용을 주의 깊게 듣는다. "I'm a bit concerned because company expenditures have increased recently"라며 회사 지출이 최근에 증가했기 때문에 다소 걱정이라고 하였다. 따라서 (D)가 정답이다.

어휘 deny v. 거부하다, 부인하다

[Paraphrasing]
company expenditures ~ increased 회사 지출이 증가했다 → cost ~ increased 비용이 증가했다

15 의도 파악 문제

해석 화자는 왜 "이것은 매일 행해지는 우리의 일상이 될 것입니다"라고 말하는가?
(A) 다른 사람들에게 일부 행사에 참석하도록 격려하기 위해
(B) 업무 일정의 변경을 설명하기 위해
(C) 일부 변화의 중요성을 강조하기 위해
(D) 건강한 생활 방식을 촉진하기 위해

해설 질문의 인용어구(This will become part of our daily routine)가 언급된 주변을 주의 깊게 듣는다. "So in order to reduce this cost, please set your computers to sleep mode ~ make sure to turn off the lights."라며 비용을 줄이기 위해 점심 식사나 회의에 가기 전에 컴퓨터를 절전 모드로 설정하고, 사무실을 마지막으로 나가는 사람은 불을 꺼 달라고 요청한 것을 통해, 비용을 절약하기 위한 새로운 방침들의 중요성을 강조하기 위함임을 알 수 있다. 따라서 (C)가 정답이다.

어휘 stress v. 강조하다 importance n. 중요성 promote v. 촉진하다

[16-18] 🎧 미국
Questions 16-18 refer to the following announcement.

> ¹⁶**Thank you all for attending the annual Mechanical Engineering Expo.** As you walk around the convention center, ¹⁷**you'll notice booths set up by participating firms from many different countries**. The representatives will be more than happy to tell you about the goods that their companies manufacture. Also, ¹⁸**I suggest taking a few minutes to view the short video that's being shown in the lobby**. It provides an interesting summary of the history of this particular event, and it is only about 10 minutes long.

attend v. 참석하다 annual adj. 연례의, 해마다의 goods n. 상품, 제품
manufacture v. 제조하다, 생산하다 view v. 보다 summary n. 개요, 요약
particular adj. 특별한, 특정한

해석
16-18번은 다음 공고에 관한 문제입니다.

¹⁶연례 기계공학 박람회에 참석해 주셔서 감사합니다. 여러분이 컨벤션 센터를 돌아다니시면서, ¹⁷다양한 국가에서 참여한 업체들에 의해 설치된 부스들을 보시게 될 것입니다. 직원들은 자신들의 회사가 제조하는 제품에 대해 여러분에게 기꺼이 설명해 줄 것입니다. 또한, ¹⁸로비에서 상영 중인 짧은 영상을 보기 위해 몇 분의 시간을 내어 주시기를 제안합니다. 그것은 이 특별한 행사의 역사에 관한 흥미로운 개요를 제공하며, 단 10분 정도의 분량입니다.

16 장소 문제

해석 공지는 어디에서 이뤄지는 것 같은가?
(A) 미술관에서
(B) 산업 박람회에서
(C) 쇼핑몰에서
(D) 스포츠 행사에서

해설 지문에서 장소와 관련된 표현을 놓치지 않고 듣는다. "Thank you all for attending the annual Mechanical Engineering Expo."라며 연례 기계공학 박람회에 참석해 줘서 감사하다고 한 것을 통해, 공지는 산업 박람회에서 이뤄지고 있음을 알 수 있다. 따라서 (B)가 정답이다.

Paraphrasing
Mechanical Engineering Expo 기계공학 박람회 → trade show 산업 박람회

17 언급 문제
해설 화자는 행사 참가자들에 대해 무엇이라고 말하는가?
(A) 그들은 다양한 국가에서 온다.
(B) 그들은 현장에서 상품을 판매하고 있다.
(C) 그들은 자원봉사자들로부터 도움을 받았다.
(D) 그들은 입장료를 지불해야 했다.

해설 질문의 핵심 어구(event participants)와 관련된 내용을 주의 깊게 듣는다. "you'll notice booths set up by participating firms from many different countries"라며 다양한 국가에서 참여한 업체들이 설치한 부스들을 보게 될 것이라고 하였다. 따라서 (A)가 정답이다.

어휘 various adj. 다양한   merchandise n. 상품   on-site adv. 현장에서
volunteer n. 자원봉사자   admission fee 입장료

18 제안 문제
해설 화자는 무엇을 할 것을 제안하는가?
(A) 예약하기
(B) 영상 시청하기
(C) 명찰 착용하기
(D) 강의 듣기

해설 지문의 중후반에서 제안과 관련된 표현이 언급된 주변을 주의 깊게 듣는다. "I suggest taking a few minutes to view the short video that's being shown in the lobby"라며 로비에서 상영 중인 짧은 영상 클립을 시청하기 위해 몇 분의 시간을 내어 주기를 제안한다고 하였다. 따라서 (B)가 정답이다.

어휘 reservation n. 예약   lecture n. 강의

Paraphrasing
view the short video 짧은 영상을 보다 → Watching a video 영상 시청하기

[19-21] 🎧 캐나다
Questions 19-21 refer to the following talk and map.

> [19]Welcome to Fairwood Park. Our park includes over 90 square miles of rainforest. It's also home to many rare wild animals. I'm going to give you some information about the different hiking routes. The Stonehill Route, which passes through the Twin Peak Mountains, is the toughest. I only recommend it for experienced hikers. For first-time visitors, [20]I suggest taking the route that runs along the lake. It's the easiest one and offers incredible views. Oh . . . And, [21]remember to download our park's application to get access to trail maps.

include v. 포함하다   rainforest n. 열대 우림   rare adj. 희귀한
route n. 경로   tough adj. 힘든, 어려운   experienced adj. 경험 많은, 능숙한

해석
19-21번은 다음 담화와 지도에 관한 문제입니다.

[19]Fairwood 공원에 오신 것을 환영합니다. 저희 공원은 90제곱 마일이 넘는 열대 우림을 포함하고 있습니다. 또한 많은 희귀 야생 동물들의 서식지이기도 합니다. 저는 다양한 하이킹 경로에 대한 정보를 알려드리려 합니다. Twin Peak 산맥을 지나가는 Stonehill 경로가 가장 어렵습니다. 저는 경험 많은 하이커들에게만 이것을 추천합니다. 처음 방문하시는 분들에게는, [20]호수를 따라 이어지는 경로를 추천해 드립니다. 그것이 가장 쉬운 경로이고 놀라운 경치를

제공합니다. 아... 그리고 [21]산책로 지도를 이용하기 위해서 저희 공원의 애플리케이션을 다운로드하실 것을 기억하세요.

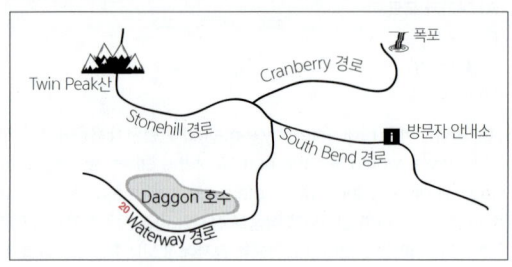

19 언급 문제
해설 화자는 Fairwood 공원에 대해 무엇이라고 말하는가?
(A) 주요 도시 근처에 있다.
(B) 복원 프로젝트를 홍보하고 있다.
(C) 최근에 확장되었다.
(D) 많은 흔치 않은 동물들이 있다.

해설 질문의 핵심 어구(Fairwood Park)가 언급된 주변을 주의 깊게 듣는다. "Welcome to Fairwood Park. Our park ~ also home to many rare wild animals."라며 Fairwood 공원에 온 것을 환영한다고 한 뒤, 공원은 많은 희귀 야생 동물들의 서식지라고 하였다. 따라서 (D)가 정답이다.

어휘 promote v. 홍보하다, 촉진하다   restoration n. 복원, 복구
expand v. 확장시키다   uncommon adj. 흔치 않은

Paraphrasing
home to ~ rare wild animals 희귀 야생 동물들의 서식지 → has ~ uncommon animals 흔치 않은 동물들이 있다

20 시각 자료 문제
해설 시각 자료를 보아라. 어느 것이 가장 쉬운 경로인가?
(A) Stonehill 경로
(B) Cranberry 경로
(C) South Bend 경로
(D) Waterway 경로

해설 제시된 지도의 정보를 확인한 후 질문의 핵심 어구(easiest route)와 관련된 내용을 주의 깊게 듣는다. "I suggest taking the route that runs along the lake. It's the easiest one"이라며 호수를 따라 이어지는 경로가 가장 쉬운 경로라고 했고, 지도에서 호수를 따라 이어지는 경로는 Waterway 경로임을 알 수 있다. 따라서 (D)가 정답이다.

21 특정 세부 사항 문제
해설 애플리케이션에서 무엇을 이용할 수 있는가?
(A) 주차권
(B) 산책로 정보
(C) 공원 야생 동물 사진
(D) 셔틀버스 서비스 일정

해설 질문의 핵심 어구(application)가 언급된 주변을 주의 깊게 듣는다. "remember to download our park's application to get access to trail maps"라며 산책로 지도를 이용하기 위해 공원의 애플리케이션을 다운로드할 것을 기억하라고 하였다. 따라서 (B)가 정답이다.

DAY 16 음성 메시지 및 회의 발췌

기출 유형 1 음성 메시지

Example 영국   p.106

해석
01-03번은 다음 전화 메시지에 관한 문제입니다.
저는 Leroy's 정장 전문점의 Amanda입니다. 01지난주에 요청하신 고객님의 정장 수선이 이제 완료되었음을 알려드리기 위해 전화드립니다. 02매장에 오셔서 정장을 입어보시고 그것이 맞는지 확인해 주시면 좋겠습니다. 그렇게 해야, 저희 재단사가 필요한 경우 수정을 할 수 있습니다. 최종 수정이 완료되면, 정장을 찾으러 다시 오시거나 귀하의 자택으로 배송해 드릴 수 있습니다. 03배송에는 추가로 15달러가 부과된다는 점 참고해 주세요. 감사합니다.

어휘 alteration n. 수선, 변경   fit v. 맞다   tailor n. 재단사   necessary adj. 필요한   adjustment n. 수정, 조정   residence n. 자택, 거주지   charge v. 비용이 부과되다, 청구하다

01
해석 화자는 왜 전화하고 있는가?
(A) 다가오는 홍보 행사에 대해 논의하기 위해
(B) 업체 위치에 대해 정보를 제공하기 위해
(C) 완료된 일에 대해 고객에게 알리기 위해
(D) 청구 실수에 대한 이유를 제공하기 위해

어휘 notify v. 알리다   task n. 일, 과제

02
해석 화자는 청자에게 무엇을 하라고 요청하는가?
(A) 사업체를 방문한다.
(B) 잔액을 지불한다.
(C) 치수를 보낸다.
(D) 관리자와 만난다.

어휘 balance n. 잔액, 균형   measurement n. 치수, 측정

03
해석 화자는 추가 비용으로 무엇을 제공하는가?
(A) 개인 상담
(B) 제품 업그레이드
(C) 연장된 보증
(D) 배송 서비스

어휘 private adj. 개인의, 사적인   extended adj. 연장된, 늘어난

토익실전문제   p.107

| 01 (B) | 02 (A) | 03 (C) | 04 (A) | 05 (D) |
| 06 (B) | | | | |

[01-03] 호주

Questions 01-03 refer to the following recorded message.

> 01**You have reached Bretford Auto Services.** If you would like to schedule an appointment with a mechanic, call back during our regular hours of operation . . . Monday through Sunday from 8 A.M. to 7 P.M. Please note that 02**our shop will be closed on Friday, May 17 so that we can count the replacement parts we have in stock.** 03**We are also pleased to announce a special benefit for our customers. Starting June 1, our warranty period will be extended** from six months to eight months. We hope to hear from you soon.

> mechanic n. 정비공, 기술자   operation n. 운영, 작업
> count v. 총 수를 확인하다, 계산하다   replacement n. 교체(물), 후임자
> warranty n. 품질 보증서   extend v. 연장하다, 확장하다

해석
01-03번은 다음 녹음된 메시지에 관한 문제입니다.
01Bretford 자동차 서비스에 연락하셨습니다. 정비공과의 약속 일정을 잡기 원하신다면, 저희의 정규 영업시간 중에 다시 전화해 주세요... 월요일부터 일요일까지 오전 8시부터 오후 7시까지입니다. 025월 17일 금요일에는 저희 매장이 재고로 가지고 있는 교체 부품들의 총 수를 확인하기 위해 문을 닫을 예정이니 참고해 주세요. 03또한 저희는 고객 여러분을 위한 특별한 혜택을 알려드리게 되어 기쁩니다. 6월 1일부터 당사의 품질 보증서 기간이 6개월에서 8개월로 연장될 것입니다. 곧 연락 주시기를 바랍니다.

01 특정 세부 사항 문제
해석 업체는 어떤 종류의 제품을 수리하는가?
(A) 컴퓨터
(B) 차량
(C) 가전제품
(D) 악기

해설 지문에서 업체의 종류와 관련된 표현을 주의 깊게 듣는다. "You have reached Bretford Auto Services."라며 Bretford 자동차 서비스에 연락했다고 한 것을 통해, 이 업체가 차량을 수리하는 곳임을 알 수 있다. 따라서 (B)가 정답이다.

02 이유 문제
해석 금요일에 업체는 왜 문을 닫는가?
(A) 재고 확인을 위해
(B) 지점 이전을 위해
(C) 교육 세션을 위해
(D) 장비 설치를 위해

해설 질문의 핵심 어구(closed on Friday)가 언급된 주변을 주의 깊게 듣는다. "our shop will be closed on Friday, May 17 so that we can count the replacement parts we have in stock"이라며 5월 17일 금요일에 업체에서 재고로 가지고 있는 교체 부품의 총 수를 확인하기 위해 문을 닫을 예정이라고 하였다. 따라서 (A)가 정답이다.

어휘 inventory n. 재고(품), 물품 목록   relocation n. 이전   installation n. 설치

[Paraphrasing]
count ~ parts we have in stock 재고로 가지고 있는 부품들의 총 수를 확인하다 → inventory count 재고 확인

03 특정 세부 사항 문제
해석 화자가 언급하는 특별한 혜택은 무엇인가?
(A) 상품권
(B) 무료 서비스
(C) 연장된 보증
(D) 가격 인하

해설 질문의 핵심 어구(special benefit)가 언급된 주변을 주의 깊게 듣는다. "We are also pleased to announce a special benefit ~ our warranty period will be extended"라며 특별한 혜택을 알려드리게 되어 기쁘다고 한 뒤, 6월 1일부터 보증 기간이 연장될 것이라고 하였다. 따라서 (C)가 정답이다.

어휘 complimentary adj. 무료의   reduction n. 인하, 감소

[04-06] 미국

Questions 04-06 refer to the following telephone message.

> Hi. My name is Ronda Rhodes, and I'm interested in becoming a member at Exercise Central. 04**A friend of mine recommended your gym to me, and he told me**

about some of your yoga classes. He mentioned that you offer classes at four different difficulty levels. [05]I've been doing yoga for six months. [05]I'm not sure which level this corresponds to. So [06]it'd be great if you would contact me to set up a consultation.

mention v. 말하다, 언급하다   offer v. 제공하다
correspond to ~에 해당하다, ~과 일치하다   consultation n. 상담

해석
04-06번은 다음 전화 메시지에 관한 문제입니다.
안녕하세요. 제 이름은 Ronda Rhodes이고, Exercise Central의 회원이 되는 것에 관심이 있습니다. [04]제 친구가 귀하의 체육관을 추천해 주었고, 몇몇 요가 수업에 대해 알려주었습니다. 그는 귀사가 네 가지 다른 난이도 레벨의 수업을 제공한다고 말해주었어요. 저는 요가를 6개월 동안 해왔습니다. [05]이것이 어느 레벨에 해당하는지 확실하지 않습니다. 그래서 [06]상담을 예약하기 위해 저에게 연락해 주시면 좋을 것 같습니다.

04 특정 세부 사항 문제
해석 친구가 화자에게 무엇에 관한 정보를 말해주었는가?
(A) 이용 가능한 강좌
(B) 회원 요금
(C) 시설의 운영시간
(D) 강사의 일정

해설 질문의 핵심 어구(friend tell ~ about)와 관련된 내용을 주의 깊게 듣는다. "A friend of mine recommended your gym to me, and he told me about some of your yoga classes."라며 자신의 친구가 체육관을 추천해 주었고, 요가 수업에 대해 말해주었다고 하였다. 따라서 (A)가 정답이다.

05 의도 파악 문제
해석 화자는 왜 "저는 요가를 6개월 동안 해왔습니다"라고 말하는가?
(A) 자신의 헌신을 보여주기 위해
(B) 업적을 강조하기 위해
(C) 결정을 설명하기 위해
(D) 자신의 불확실함을 나타내기 위해

해설 질문의 인용어구(I've been doing yoga for six months)가 언급된 주변을 주의 깊게 듣는다. "I'm not sure which level this corresponds to."라며 자신이 6개월 동안 요가를 한 것이 어느 레벨에 해당하는지 확실하지 않다고 한 것을 통해, 어떤 레벨의 수업에 적합한지에 대한 불확실함을 나타내기 위함임을 알 수 있다. 따라서 (D)가 정답이다.

어휘 dedication n. 헌신   highlight v. 강조하다   achievement n. 업적, 성취
uncertainty n. 불확실함

06 이유 문제
해석 청자는 왜 화자에게 연락하도록 요청받는가?
(A) 지불을 확인하기 위해
(B) 만남을 주선하기 위해
(C) 건물 출입권을 얻기 위해
(D) 행사에 대한 업데이트를 제공하기 위해

해설 질문의 핵심 어구(asked to contact the speaker)와 관련된 내용을 주의 깊게 듣는다. "it'd be great if you would contact me to set up a consultation"이라며 상담을 예약하기 위해 자신에게 연락을 주면 좋을 것 같다고 하였다. 따라서 (B)가 정답이다.

어휘 payment n. 지불(금)   access n. 출입권, 접근

[Paraphrasing]
set up a consultation 상담을 예약하다 → arrange a meeting 만남을 주선하다

기출 유형 2 회의 발췌

Example 캐나다   p.108

해석
01-03번은 다음 회의 발췌에 관한 문제입니다.
[01]다음 주에 있을 우리의 최신 태블릿 컴퓨터 출시 파티에 대해 논의해 봅시다. 좋은 소식이 있어요. [02]우리 광고에 출연하는 인기 있는 음악가인 Darrell Bedford가 행사에 참석할 것입니다. 이것은 틀림없이 많은 참석자들을 끌어 모을 것입니다. 따라서, [03]모든 것이 확실히 원활하게 진행되도록 하기 위해 추가 보안 요원들을 고용할 필요가 있습니다. Haley, 이 업무를 맡아 주시고, 오늘이 끝나기 전에 진척 상황에 대해 저에게 알려주세요.

어휘 commercial n. 광고   definitely adv. 틀림없이   attract v. 끌어 모으다
attendee n. 참석자   security guard 보안 요원
take charge of ~을 맡다, ~의 책임을 지다   status n. 상황, 상태

01
해석 화자는 어디에서 일하는 것 같은가?
(A) 가구점에서
(B) 운동 경기장에서
(C) 전자제품 회사에서
(D) 보험 회사에서

어휘 insurance n. 보험

02
해석 Darrell Bedford는 누구인가?
(A) 운동선수
(B) 음악가
(C) 작가
(D) 모델

03
해석 화자는 Haley에게 무엇을 할 것을 요청하는가?
(A) 인력을 모집한다.
(B) 서류에 서명한다.
(C) 행사 공간을 예약한다.
(D) 보안 장치를 설치한다.

어휘 recruit v. 모집하다   personnel n. 인력, 인사과   book v. 예약하다

토익실전문제   p.109

| 01 (B) | 02 (C) | 03 (D) | 04 (D) | 05 (C) |
| 06 (B) | | | | |

[01-03] 영국
Questions 01-03 refer to the following excerpt from a meeting.

Before we wrap up the meeting, [01]I want to provide an update on the two-day Newark Hip-Hop Show our company has been hired to organize. Everything is going smoothly, with one exception . . . [02]we don't have enough seats for the VIP section directly in front of the stage. There are 40 people to be seated in this area but only 25 chairs. So we should purchase more. [03]This afternoon, Tanya will determine whether the budget will cover this added expense. If not, I'll ask our client for additional funds before placing an order.

wrap up 마무리 짓다   organize v. 준비하다, 조직하다   exception n. 예외
directly adv. 바로, 곧장   determine v. 알아내다, 결정하다
expense n. 비용   fund n. 자금

해석
01-03번은 다음 회의 발췌에 관한 문제입니다.

회의를 마무리 짓기 전에, ⁰¹우리 회사가 준비하도록 채용된 2일간의 Newark 힙합 쇼에 대한 최신 소식을 제공하고 싶습니다. 모든 것이 순조롭게 진행되고 있습니다, 한 가지 예외를 제외하고 말이죠... ⁰²무대 바로 앞의 VIP 구역에 좌석이 충분하지 않습니다. 이 구역에 40명을 앉혀야 하는데 의자는 25개뿐입니다. 그래서 더 많은 의자를 구매해야 합니다. ⁰³오늘 오후에 Tanya가 예산이 이 추가 비용을 충당할 수 있을지 알아낼 것입니다. 그렇지 않다면, 주문하기 전에 고객사에 추가 자금을 요청하겠습니다.

01 특정 세부 사항 문제
해석 어떤 종류의 행사가 계획되고 있는가?
(A) 스포츠 대회
(B) 음악 축제
(C) 연극 공연
(D) 회사 야유회
해설 질문의 핵심 어구(event ~ planned)와 관련된 표현을 주의 깊게 듣는다. "I want to provide an update on the two-day Newark Hip-Hop Show our company has been hired to organize"라며 회사가 준비하도록 채용된 2일간의 Newark 힙합 쇼에 대한 최신 소식을 제공하고 싶다고 한 것을 통해, 음악 축제가 계획되고 있음을 알 수 있다. 따라서 (B)가 정답이다.
어휘 competition n. 대회, 경쟁 performance n. 공연, 성과

02 문제점 문제
해석 화자는 어떤 문제를 언급하는가?
(A) 무대가 다시 칠해져야 한다.
(B) 보안이 적절하지 않다.
(C) 좌석이 충분하지 않다.
(D) 입장료가 너무 비싸다.
해설 질문의 핵심 어구(problem)와 관련된 내용을 주의 깊게 듣는다. "we don't have enough seats for the VIP section directly in front of the stage"라며 무대 바로 앞의 VIP 구역에 좌석이 충분하지 않다고 하였다. 따라서 (C)가 정답이다.
어휘 inadequate adj. 적절하지 않은 insufficient adj. 충분하지 않은 entrance n. 입장, 입구

Paraphrasing
don't have enough seats 좌석이 충분하지 않다 → insufficient seating 충분하지 않은 좌석

03 특정 세부 사항 문제
해석 Tanya는 오늘 무엇을 할 것 같은가?
(A) 고객과 만난다.
(B) 물품을 구매한다.
(C) 시작 시간을 확정한다.
(D) 예산을 확인한다.
해설 질문의 핵심 어구(Tanya ~ today)와 관련된 내용을 주의 깊게 듣는다. "This afternoon, Tanya will determine whether the budget will cover this added expense."라며 오늘 오후에 Tanya가 예산이 이 추가 비용을 충당할 수 있을지 알아낼 것이라고 하였다. 따라서 (D)가 정답이다.

Paraphrasing
determine whether the budget will cover ~ 예산이 ~을 충당할 수 있을지 알아내다 → Check a budget 예산을 확인한다

[04-06] 호주
Questions 04-06 refer to the following excerpt from a meeting.

As you know, ⁰⁴our company officially released the Motive luxury sedan on August 1. ⁰⁵We predicted that it would be our top-selling vehicle, but so far it hasn't met our expectations. It seems there are many new products on the market. Therefore, we need to develop an effective marketing campaign to differentiate our product from those of our competitors. Of course, this means that the advertising budget will need to be increased. ⁰⁶I am planning to meet with our CEO this afternoon to discuss this matter.

officially adv. 공식적으로 release v. 출시하다 predict v. 예상하다
vehicle n. 차량, 수단 expectation n. 기대, 예상 effective adj. 효과적인
differentiate v. 차별화하다, 구별하다 competitor n. 경쟁사

해석
04-06번은 다음 회의 발췌에 관한 문제입니다.

아시다시피, ⁰⁴우리 회사는 8월 1일에 Motive 고급 세단을 공식적으로 출시했습니다. ⁰⁵우리는 그것이 최고 판매 차량이 될 것으로 예상했지만, 지금까지는 우리의 기대에 미치지 못했습니다. 시장에는 신제품들이 많이 있는 것 같습니다. 따라서, 우리 제품을 경쟁사의 제품들과 차별화하기 위해 효과적인 마케팅 캠페인을 개발할 필요가 있습니다. 물론, 이것은 광고 예산이 증가되어야 함을 의미합니다. ⁰⁶저는 오늘 오후에 이 사안에 대해 논의하기 위해 CEO와 만날 계획입니다.

04 청자 문제
해석 청자들은 어디에서 일하는 것 같은가?
(A) 가전제품 판매점에서
(B) 자동차 정비소에서
(C) 마케팅 회사에서
(D) 자동차 제조업체에서
해설 지문에서 신분 및 직업과 관련된 표현을 주의 깊게 듣는다. "our company officially released the Motive luxury sedan on August 1"라며 회사가 8월 1일에 Motive 고급 세단을 공식적으로 출시했다고 한 것을 통해, 청자들은 자동차 제조업체에서 일하는 것을 알 수 있다. 따라서 (D)가 정답이다.
어휘 appliance n. 가전제품 manufacturer n. 제조업체

05 의도 파악 문제
해석 화자는 왜 "시장에는 신제품들이 많이 있는 것 같습니다"라고 말하는가?
(A) 경쟁사들의 목록을 요청하기 위해
(B) 제품을 제안하기 위해
(C) 낮은 판매량을 설명하기 위해
(D) 피드백을 요청하기 위해
해설 질문의 인용어구(It seems there are many new products on the market)가 언급된 주변을 주의 깊게 듣는다. "We predicted that it would be our top-selling vehicle, but so far it hasn't met our expectations."라며 그들의 신규 차량이 최고 판매 차량이 될 것으로 예상했지만, 지금까지는 기대에 미치지 못했다고 한 것을 통해, 판매량이 낮은 이유에 대해 설명하기 위함임을 알 수 있다. 따라서 (C)가 정답이다.
어휘 low adj. 낮은 ask for ~을 요청하다

06 다음에 할 일 문제
해석 화자는 자신이 무엇을 할 것이라고 말하는가?
(A) 문서를 편집한다.
(B) 임원과 얘기한다.
(C) 제품 디자인을 공개한다.
(D) 광고를 승인한다.
해설 질문의 핵심 어구(the speaker ~ he will do)와 관련된 내용을 주의 깊게 듣는다. "I am planning to meet with our CEO this afternoon to discuss this matter."라며 오늘 오후에 이 사안에 대해 논의하기 위해 CEO와 만날 계획이라고 하였다. 따라서 (B)가 정답이다.

어휘 edit v. 편집하다   executive n. 임원, 경영진   approve v. 승인하다

> Paraphrasing
> meet with our CEO ~ to discuss 논의하기 위해 CEO와 만나다 → Talk to an executive 임원과 얘기한다

HACKERS TEST   p.110

01 (A)	02 (B)	03 (B)	04 (D)	05 (B)
06 (D)	07 (A)	08 (D)	09 (C)	10 (C)
11 (B)	12 (D)	13 (B)	14 (A)	15 (C)
16 (B)	17 (D)	18 (D)	19 (A)	20 (B)
21 (D)				

[01-03] 🎧 미국

Questions 01-03 refer to the following telephone message.

Good afternoon, Mr. Bryant. This is Jasmin Chung from Real Interiors. ⁰¹**I'm calling to let you know that my firm has decided to offer you a position as an interior decorator.** If you decide to take the job, I would like you to start on Monday, May 3. While I know you have extensive experience in the industry, ⁰²**I still want you to take part in our standard two-day orientation.** ⁰³**I have sent you a copy of the employment contract by e-mail.** Once you have reviewed it, please let me know if you have any questions or concerns. I look forward to hearing back from you.

firm n. 회사   decorator n. 장식가   extensive adj. 폭넓은, 광범위한   standard adj. 일반적인, 표준의   contract n. 계약서   concern n. 우려 사항

해석
01-03번은 다음 전화 메시지에 관한 문제입니다.

안녕하세요, Mr. Bryant. 저는 Real 인테리어사의 Jasmin Chung입니다. ⁰¹실내 장식가로서 귀하를 채용하기로 제 회사가 결정했음을 알려드리기 위해 전화드립니다. 이 직책을 수락하기로 결정하신다면, 5월 3일 월요일부터 시작하셨으면 합니다. 귀하가 업계에 폭넓은 경험을 가지고 있다는 것을 알고 있지만, ⁰²저는 여전히 귀하가 저희의 일반적인 이틀간의 오리엔테이션에 참여하시기를 바랍니다. ⁰³제가 이메일로 고용 계약서 사본을 보내드렸습니다. 그것을 검토하신 후, 질문이나 우려 사항이 있으시면 알려주시기 바랍니다. 귀하에게 답변을 들을 수 있기를 기대합니다.

01 목적 문제
해석 화자는 왜 전화하고 있는가?
  (A) 채용을 제안하기 위해
  (B) 거래를 주선하기 위해
  (C) 서비스를 홍보하기 위해
  (D) 면접 일정을 잡기 위해

해설 전화 메시지의 목적을 묻는 문제이므로, 지문의 초반을 반드시 듣는다. "I'm calling to let you know that my firm has decided to offer you a position as an interior decorator."라며 실내 장식가로서의 직책을 제안하기로 회사가 결정했음을 알리기 위해 전화한다고 하였다. 따라서 (A)가 정답이다.

어휘 employment n. 채용, 고용   transaction n. 거래, 매매   publicize v. 홍보하다, 알리다

02 특정 세부 사항 문제
해석 화자는 청자가 무엇을 하기를 원하는가?
  (A) 직원을 교육한다.
  (B) 오리엔테이션에 참석한다.
  (C) 발표를 한다.
  (D) 디자인 팀을 이끈다.

해설 질문의 핵심 어구(wants the listener to do)와 관련된 내용을 주의 깊게 듣는다. "I still want you to take part in our standard two-day orientation"이라며 일반적인 이틀 간의 오리엔테이션에 참여하기를 원한다고 하였다. 따라서 (B)가 정답이다.

어휘 train v. 교육하다   attend v. 참석하다   head v. 이끌다, 책임지다

> Paraphrasing
> take part in 참여하다 → Attend 참석한다

03 특정 세부 사항 문제
해석 화자는 청자에게 무엇을 보냈는가?
  (A) 직원 안내서
  (B) 법률 합의서
  (C) 진행 보고서
  (D) 비용 견적서

해설 질문의 핵심 어구(send to the listener)와 관련된 내용을 주의 깊게 듣는다. "I have sent you a copy of the employment contract by e-mail."이라며 청자에게 이메일로 고용 계약서 사본을 보냈다고 하였다. 따라서 (B)가 정답이다.

어휘 manual n. 안내서, 설명서   legal adj. 법률의, 합법적인   agreement n. 합의서, 동의

> Paraphrasing
> a copy of the employment contract 고용 계약서 사본 → A legal agreement 법률 합의서

[04-06] 🎧 캐나다

Questions 04-06 refer to the following excerpt from a meeting.

⁰⁴**The advertising campaign we created for Whitewave Snowboards is doing very well.** Whitewave's sales figures are far higher than anticipated, and its CEO believes that this success is largely due to us. Because of the strong response from consumers, ⁰⁵**we've been asked to create another campaign.** The project will be for one of Whitewave's upcoming lines of recreational equipment, which is going to be released this September. ⁰⁶**I'll start researching our target market this week.**

sales figures 매출액   anticipate v. 예상하다   response n. 반응   consumer n. 소비자   equipment n. 장비   release v. 출시하다   research v. 조사하다

해석
04-06번은 다음 회의 발췌에 관한 문제입니다.

⁰⁴Whitewave 스노보드사를 위해 우리가 만든 광고 캠페인이 매우 잘 진행되고 있습니다. Whitewave의 매출액이 예상한 것보다 훨씬 높으며, 그 회사의 CEO는 이 성취를 크게 우리 덕분이라고 생각합니다. 소비자들의 열렬한 반응 때문에, ⁰⁵우리는 또 다른 캠페인을 만들어 달라는 요청을 받았습니다. 그 프로젝트는 Whitewave의 다가오는 레크리에이션 장비 라인을 위한 것인데, 이는 올해 9월에 출시될 예정입니다. ⁰⁶저는 이번 주에 저희의 목표 고객층에 대한 조사를 시작할 것입니다.

04 화자 문제
해석 화자는 어떤 유형의 업체에서 일하는가?
  (A) 건설 회사
  (B) 스포츠 용품점
  (C) 레크리에이션 센터
  (D) 마케팅 회사

해설 지문에서 신분 및 직업과 관련된 표현을 놓치지 않고 듣는다. "The advertising campaign we created for Whitewave Snowboards is doing very well."이라며 Whitewave 스노보드사를 위해 만든 광고 캠페인이 매우 잘 진행되고 있다고 한 것을 통해, 화자가 광고 캠페인을 제작하는 마케팅 회사에서 일하고 있음을 알 수 있다. 따라서 (D)가 정답이다.

어휘 recreational adj. 레크리에이션의, 오락의

05 특정 세부 사항 문제

해석 화자의 회사는 무엇을 해달라는 요청을 받았는가?
(A) 설문 조사를 한다.
(B) 프로젝트를 한다.
(C) 제품을 테스트한다.
(D) 시설을 점검한다.

해설 질문의 핵심 어구(company been asked to do)와 관련된 내용을 주의 깊게 듣는다. "we've been asked to create another campaign"이라며 다른 캠페인을 만들어 달라는 요청을 받았다고 하였다. 따라서 (B)가 정답이다.

어휘 conduct v. (특정 활동을) 하다 inspect v. 점검하다 facility n. 시설, 기관

06 다음에 할 일 문제

해석 화자는 자신이 무엇을 할 것이라고 말하는가?
(A) 일부 정보를 정정한다.
(B) 도표를 업데이트한다.
(C) 고객에게 연락한다.
(D) 조사를 수행한다.

해설 지문의 마지막 부분을 주의 깊게 듣는다. "I'll start researching our target market this week."이라며 이번 주에 목표 고객층에 대한 조사를 시작할 것이라고 하였다. 따라서 (D)가 정답이다.

어휘 correct v. 정정하다, 바로잡다 chart n. 도표 research n. 조사, 연구

Paraphrasing
start researching 조사를 시작하다 → Perform some research 조사를 수행하다

[07-09] 영국
Questions 07-09 refer to the following excerpt from a meeting.

I'd like to begin today by sharing some important news. ⁰⁷Welkin's Sportswear bought the building across the street from our clothing shop last week. It plans to open a branch there. ⁰⁷/⁰⁸That chain has become really famous recently. And you know, people like to shop at well-known stores. ⁰⁸We need to find a way to avoid losing customers. ⁰⁹I will send out an e-mail this afternoon with tasks for each of you related to this goal.

share v. 공유하다 chain n. 체인점 well-known adj. 잘 알려진
avoid v. 막다, 피하다 related to ~과 관련된

해석
07-09번은 다음 회의 발췌에 관한 문제입니다.

오늘은 몇 가지 중요한 소식을 공유하며 시작하고 싶습니다. ⁰⁷Welkin's 스포츠 의류사가 지난주에 우리 의류 매장 맞은편 건물을 매입했습니다. 그곳에 지점을 열 계획입니다. ⁰⁷/⁰⁸그 체인점은 최근에 정말 유명해졌습니다. 그리고 아시다시피, 사람들은 잘 알려진 상점에서 쇼핑하기를 좋아합니다. ⁰⁸우리는 고객을 잃는 것을 막을 방법을 찾아야 합니다. ⁰⁹저는 오늘 오후에 이 목표와 관련된 여러분 각자의 업무가 포함된 이메일을 보낼 것입니다.

07 주제 문제

해석 회의는 주로 무엇에 관한 것인가?
(A) 경쟁사
(B) 합병
(C) 매출액
(D) 지점 폐쇄

해설 회의의 주제를 묻는 문제이므로, 지문의 초반을 반드시 듣는다. "Welkin's Sportswear bought the building across the street from our clothing shop last week."이라며 Welkin's 스포츠 의류사가 당사의 의류 매장 맞은편 건물을 매입했다고 한 뒤, "That chain has become really famous recently."라며 그 체인점은 최근에 정말 유명해졌다고 한 것을 통해, 회의는 경쟁사에 관한 것임을 알 수 있다. 따라서 (A)가 정답이다.

08 의도 파악 문제

해석 화자가 "사람들은 잘 알려진 상점에서 쇼핑하기를 좋아합니다"라고 말할 때 무엇을 의도하는가?
(A) 고객이 피드백을 제공했다.
(B) 직원들은 제안을 할 것을 요청받을 것이다.
(C) 마케팅 활동이 성공적이었다.
(D) 난제가 예상되어야 한다.

해설 질문의 인용어구(people like to shop at well-known stores)가 언급된 주변을 주의 깊게 듣는다. "That chain has become really famous recently."라며 그 체인점은 최근에 정말 유명해졌다고 한 뒤, "We need to find a way to avoid losing customers."라며 고객을 잃는 것을 막을 방법을 찾아야 한다고 한 것을 통해, 경쟁사에 고객을 뺏길 수 있는 난제를 예상해야 한다는 것임을 알 수 있다. 따라서 (D)가 정답이다.

어휘 effort n. 활동, 노력 challenge n. 난제, 도전

09 특정 세부 사항 문제

해석 오후에 무엇이 보내질 것인가?
(A) 여행 일정표
(B) 성과 평가서
(C) 업무 할당
(D) 급여 명세서

해설 질문의 핵심 어구(the afternoon)가 언급된 주변을 주의 깊게 듣는다. "I will send out an e-mail this afternoon with tasks for each of you related to this goal."이라며 오늘 오후에 목표와 관련된 직원들 각자의 업무가 포함된 이메일을 보낼 것이라고 하였다. 따라서 (C)가 정답이다.

어휘 itinerary n. 일정표 evaluation n. 평가(서) assignment n. 업무, 배정 statement n. 명세서, 진술서

Paraphrasing
an e-mail ~ with tasks 업무가 포함된 이메일 → Work assignments 업무 할당

[10-12] 호주
Questions 10-12 refer to the following telephone message.

My name is Jamal Watts. ¹⁰I hired your landscaping company for the first time after noticing your advertisement in the local newspaper. ¹¹I chose your company because the ad guaranteed customer satisfaction. But the crew you sent to trim my trees just left, and there are leaves all over my backyard. Please call me back as soon as possible to address the issue. Just note that ¹²I'll be in a videoconference with a customer between 1 P.M. and 3 P.M., so I won't be available then.

landscaping n. 조경 notice v. ~을 보다, 주목하다
guarantee v. 보장하다, 약속하다 customer satisfaction 고객 만족
crew n. 직원 trim v. (나무 등을) 다듬다 address v. 해결하다

해석
10-12번은 다음 전화 메시지에 관한 문제입니다.
제 이름은 Jamal Watts입니다. ¹⁰저는 지역 신문에 게재된 광고를 보고 당신의 조경 회사를 처음으로 고용했습니다. 광고에서 고객 만족을 보장한다고 했기 때문에 귀사의 회사를 선택했습니다. 하지만 ¹¹제 나무를 다듬기 위해 보내주신 작업팀이 방금 떠났는데, 제 뒷마당에는 나뭇잎이 여기저기 흩어져 있습니다. 이 문제를 해결하기 위해 가능한 한 빨리 저에게 다시 전화해 주세요. 단, ¹²저는 오후 1시부터 3시 사이에 고객과 화상 회의가 있어 그 시간에는 연락이 안 된다는 점 참고해 주세요.

10 방법 문제
해설 화자는 업체에 대해 어떻게 알게 되었는가?
(A) 친구와 대화함으로써
(B) 텔레비전을 시청함으로써
(C) 신문을 읽음으로써
(D) 이메일을 확인함으로써

해설 질문의 핵심 어구(learn about a business)와 관련된 내용을 주의 깊게 듣는다. "I hired your landscaping company for the first time after noticing your advertisement in the local newspaper."라며 지역 신문에 게재된 광고를 보고 청자의 조경 회사를 처음으로 고용했다고 하였다. 따라서 (C)가 정답이다.

11 의도 파악 문제
해설 화자가 "제 뒷마당에는 나뭇잎이 여기저기 흩어져 있습니다"라고 말할 때 무엇을 의도하는가?
(A) 업무를 할 것을 잊어버렸다.
(B) 서비스에 만족하지 않는다.
(C) 할인에 관심이 있다.
(D) 제안에 대해 의심하고 있다.

해설 질문의 인용어구(there are leaves all over my backyard)가 언급된 주변을 주의 깊게 듣는다. "I chose your company because the ad guaranteed customer satisfaction. But the crew you sent to trim my trees just left"라며 광고에서 고객 만족을 보장한다고 해서 청자의 회사를 선택했지만, 나무를 다듬으러 온 작업팀이 방금 떠났다고 한 뒤, "there are leaves all over my backyard"라며 자신의 뒷마당에는 나뭇잎이 여기저기 흩어져 있다고 한 것을 통해, 회사의 조경 서비스에 만족하지 않는다는 것을 알 수 있다. 따라서 (B)가 정답이다.

어휘 doubtful adj. 의심하는

12 이유 문제
해설 화자는 왜 오늘 오후에 연락이 안 되는가?
(A) 출장 중일 것이다.
(B) 의사를 만나야 한다.
(C) 그의 가족을 방문할 것이다.
(D) 고객과 이야기해야 한다.

해설 질문의 핵심 어구(unavailable this afternoon)와 관련된 내용을 주의 깊게 듣는다. "I'll be in a videoconference with a customer between 1 P.M. and 3 P.M., so I won't be available then"이라며 오후 1시부터 3시 사이에 고객과 화상 회의가 있어서 그 시간에는 연락이 안 된다고 하였다. 따라서 (D)가 정답이다.

[Paraphrasing]
be in a videoconference with a customer 고객과 화상 회의를 하다
→ talk to a customer 고객과 이야기하다

[13-15] 🎧 미국
Questions 13-15 refer to the following excerpt from a meeting.

¹³Our art center is planning to display some works by Oscar Juan in October. I expect the show will attract many potential buyers as well as some media attention. ¹⁴This exhibit will be unlike any of our previous ones. Visitors will be able to use QR codes to leave comments on our social media page about individual works. And the artist will respond to these in real-time. It is crucial that everything goes smoothly. ¹⁵Our curator will now show us some slides of the paintings we will be displaying and provide some background information on each.

display v. 전시하다   potential adj. 잠재적인, 가능성이 있는
previous adj. 이전의   comment n. 의견, 논평
individual adj. 개별적인, 개인의   crucial adj. 중요한, 결정적인

해석
13-15번은 다음 회의 발췌에 관한 문제입니다.
¹³저희 아트 센터는 10월에 Oscar Juan의 작품 몇 점을 전시할 계획입니다. 저는 이 전시회가 언론의 관심뿐만 아니라 많은 잠재적 구매자들을 끌어 모을 것으로 기대합니다. ¹⁴이 전시회는 이전의 어떤 전시회들과도 다를 것입니다. 방문객들은 QR 코드를 사용하여 저희 소셜 미디어 페이지에 개별 작품에 대한 의견을 남길 수 있을 것입니다. 그리고 작가는 이러한 의견에 실시간으로 응답할 것입니다. 모든 것이 원활하게 진행되는 것이 중요합니다. ¹⁵이제 전시 책임자가 우리가 전시할 그림들의 몇몇 슬라이드를 보여줄 것이고, 각각에 대한 배경 정보를 제공할 것입니다.

13 특정 세부 사항 문제
해설 Oscar Juan은 누구일 것 같은가?
(A) 전시 책임자
(B) 예술가
(C) 비평가
(D) 잡지 편집자

해설 질문의 핵심 어구(Oscar Juan)가 언급된 주변을 주의 깊게 듣는다. "Our art center is planning to display some works by Oscar Juan in October."라며 아트 센터가 10월에 Oscar Juan의 작품을 전시할 계획이라고 한 것을 통해, Oscar Juan은 예술가임을 알 수 있다. 따라서 (B)가 정답이다.

어휘 curator n. 전시 책임자   editor n. 편집자

14 언급 문제
해설 화자는 전시회에 대해 무엇이 특별할 것이라고 말하는가?
(A) 온라인 소통을 포함할 것이다.
(B) 디지털 예술 작품을 특징으로 삼을 것이다.
(C) 전문가의 강연을 포함할 것이다.
(D) 값비싼 물품들을 전시할 것이다.

해설 질문의 핵심 어구(special about an exhibit)와 관련된 내용을 주의 깊게 듣는다. "This exhibit will be unlike any of our previous ones."라며 이 전시회는 이전의 어떤 전시회들과도 다를 것이라고 한 뒤, "Visitors will be able to use QR codes to leave comments ~. And the artist will respond to these in real-time."이라며 방문객들이 QR 코드를 사용하여 의견을 남기고, 작가는 이러한 의견에 실시간으로 응답할 것이라고 하였다. 따라서 (A)가 정답이다.

어휘 interaction n. 소통, 상호작용   feature v. 특징으로 삼다
showcase v. 전시하다   valuable adj. 값비싼, 귀중한

[Paraphrasing]
be unlike ~과 다르다 → be special 특별하다

15 다음에 할 일 문제
해설 청자들은 다음에 무엇을 할 것 같은가?
(A) 활동들을 계획한다.
(B) 치수를 잰다.
(C) 프레젠테이션을 본다.

(D) 다른 센터에 방문한다.

해설 지문의 마지막 부분을 주의 깊게 듣는다. "Our curator will now show us some slides of the paintings ~ and provide some background information on each."라며 이제 전시 책임자가 전시할 그림들의 슬라이드와 각 그림에 대한 배경 정보를 제공할 것이라고 한 것을 통해, 청자들은 전시 책임자의 프레젠테이션을 볼 것임을 알 수 있다. 따라서 (C)가 정답이다.

어휘 measurement n. 치수, 측정

[16-18] 영국

Questions 16-18 refer to the following recorded message.

> ¹⁶You have reached Branford Legal Services. We specialize in all matters related to residential and commercial property law. ¹⁷To arrange a free consultation, please leave your name and a phone number after the beep. One of our employees will call you back during our regular office hours to schedule an appointment. ¹⁸If you are interested in the accountant position that we recently advertised, please visit our Web site. There, you will find information on the role and instructions on how to apply. Thank you.

specialize in ~을 전문으로 하다   related to ~과 관련된
residential adj. 주택의, 거주하기 좋은   commercial adj. 상업용의, 상업적인
property n. 부동산, 건물   beep n. 삐 소리   accountant n. 회계사
instruction n. 설명, 지시   apply v. 지원하다

해설
16-18번은 다음 녹음된 메시지에 관한 문제입니다.

¹⁶Branford 법률 서비스에 연락하셨습니다. 저희는 주택 및 상업용 부동산에 관련된 모든 법률 문제를 전문으로 합니다. ¹⁷무료 상담을 주선하기 위해서는, 삐 소리 후에 성함과 전화번호를 남겨 주세요. 저희 직원 중 한 명이 약속을 잡기 위해 정규 근무 시간 중에 전화드릴 것입니다. ¹⁸최근에 저희가 광고한 회계사 직책에 관심이 있으시다면, 저희 웹사이트를 방문해 주세요. 거기에서 직무에 대한 정보와 지원 방법에 대한 설명을 찾으실 것입니다. 감사합니다.

16 화자 문제

해설 화자는 어디에서 일하는가?
(A) 부동산 중개 사무실에서
(B) 법률 사무소에서
(C) 출판사에서
(D) 회계 법인에서

해설 지문에서 신분 및 직업과 관련된 표현을 놓치지 않고 듣는다. "You have reached Branford Legal Services. We specialize in all matters related to residential and commercial property law."라며 Branford 법률 서비스에 연락했으며, 주택 및 상업용 부동산에 관련된 법률 문제를 전문으로 한다고 한 것을 통해, 화자는 법률 사무소에서 일하고 있음을 알 수 있다. 따라서 (B)가 정답이다.

어휘 real estate n. 부동산 중개업   firm n. 회사   accounting n. 회계

17 특정 세부 사항 문제

해설 화자는 청자들에게 무엇을 남기라고 요청하는가?
(A) 청구서 번호
(B) 연락처 정보
(C) 약속 시간
(D) 사용자 후기

해설 질문의 핵심 어구(ask listeners to leave)와 관련된 내용을 주의 깊게 듣는다. "To arrange a free consultation, please leave your name and a phone number after the beep."이라며 무료 상담을 주선하기 위해서는 삐 소리 후에 성함과 전화번호를 남겨 달라고 요청하였다. 따라서 (B)가 정답이다.

Paraphrasing
name and a phone number 성함과 전화번호 → Contact information 연락처 정보

18 특정 세부 사항 문제

해설 화자의 회사는 최근에 무엇을 했는가?
(A) 운영시간을 변경했다.
(B) 새로운 서비스를 시작했다.
(C) 근로 방침을 업데이트했다.
(D) 구인 광고를 게재했다.

해설 질문의 핵심 어구(company recently do)와 관련된 내용을 주의 깊게 듣는다. "If you are interested in the accountant position that we recently advertised, please visit our Web site."라며 최근에 광고한 회계사 직책에 관심이 있다면 웹사이트를 방문해 달라고 하였다. 따라서 (D)가 정답이다.

어휘 launch v. 시작하다, 착수하다

[19-21] 캐나다

Questions 19-21 refer to the following excerpt from a meeting and map.

> As you know, ¹⁹our company will be moving into a building on the corner of Oak Street and Center Avenue next week. I'd like to go over a couple of things related to this. First, ²⁰please remember that all staff members will need a new employee ID card to enter the building. So don't forget to pick one up at our reception desk tomorrow morning. Second, many of you have asked about parking. ²¹There is a large parking garage that you will be able to use. I'll send all of you an e-mail that includes the rules for this facility later today.

related to ~과 관련된   reception desk 접수처   include v. 포함하다
rule n. 규정, 규칙   facility n. 시설, 기관

해설
19-21번은 다음 회의 발췌와 지도에 관한 문제입니다.

아시다시피, ¹⁹우리 회사는 다음 주에 Oak가와 Center가 모퉁이에 있는 건물로 이사할 예정입니다. 이와 관련된 몇 가지 사항을 살펴보고자 합니다. 첫째, ²⁰모든 직원들은 그 건물에 출입하기 위해 새로운 사원증이 필요하다는 것을 기억해 주세요. 따라서 내일 아침 접수처에서 하나를 받아가는 것을 잊지 마세요. 둘째, 많은 분들이 주차에 대해 문의하셨습니다. ²¹그곳에는 여러분들이 사용할 수 있는 대형 주차장이 있습니다. 오늘 중으로 이 시설에 대한 규정들이 포함된 이메일을 모두에게 발송할 것입니다.

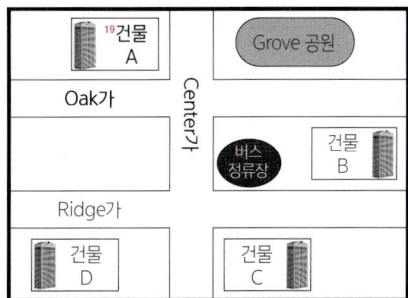

19 시각 자료 문제

해설 시각 자료를 보아라. 회사의 새 사무실은 어디에 위치할 것인가?
(A) A 건물에

(B) B 건물에
(C) C 건물에
(D) D 건물에

해설 제시된 지도의 정보를 확인한 후 질문의 핵심 어구(company's new office)와 관련된 내용을 주의 깊게 듣는다. "our company will be moving into a building on the corner of Oak Street and Center Avenue next week"이라며 회사가 다음 주에 Oak가와 Center가 모퉁이에 있는 건물로 이사할 예정이라고 하였고, 지도에서 Oak가와 Center가의 모퉁이에 위치한 건물이 A 건물임을 알 수 있다. 따라서 (A)가 정답이다.

20 특정 세부 사항 문제
해석 청자들은 내일 아침에 무엇을 하도록 상기되는가?
(A) 몇몇 가구를 설치한다.
(B) 신분 카드를 획득한다.
(C) 일부 가격을 확인한다.
(D) 몇몇 장비를 옮긴다.

해설 질문의 핵심 어구(tomorrow morning)가 언급된 주변을 주의 깊게 듣는다. "please remember that all staff members will need a new employee ID card ~. So don't forget to pick one[a new employee ID card] up ~ tomorrow morning."이라며 건물을 들어가려면 새로운 사원증이 필요하므로, 내일 아침에 새 카드를 받아가는 것을 잊지 말라고 하였다. 따라서 (B)가 정답이다.

어휘 furniture n. 가구 equipment n. 장비

[Paraphrasing]
employee ID card 사원증 → identification card 신분 카드

21 특정 세부 사항 문제
해석 회의 후에 무엇이 공유될 것인가?
(A) 사무실 안내도
(B) 제품 디자인
(C) 건물 주소
(D) 주차 규정

해설 질문의 핵심 어구(shared after the meeting)와 관련된 내용을 주의 깊게 듣는다. "There is a large parking garage ~. I'll send all of you an e-mail that includes the rules for this facility later today."라며 건물에 대형 주차장이 있으며, 오늘 중으로 해당 시설에 대한 규정이 포함된 이메일을 발송할 것이라고 하였다. 따라서 (D)가 정답이다.

[Paraphrasing]
rules 규정들 → regulations 규정

DAY 17 공지 및 관광 안내

기출 유형 1 공지

Example 호주 p.112
해석
01-03번은 다음 공지에 관한 문제입니다.
주목해 주시겠습니까? 01오늘 저녁 공연은 오후 8시에 시작될 예정이었습니다. 02안타깝게도, 저희가 조명 시스템에 기술적인 문제를 겪고 있어서 약간의 지연이 있을 것입니다. 03연극은 이제 8시 30분에 시작될 것으로 예상됩니다. 불편을 드려 진심으로 사과드립니다. 그 동안에, 03저희 로비에 있는 이 공연에 관한 특별 전시를 자유롭게 둘러보시기 바랍니다. 여러분들의 인내에 감사드립니다.

어휘 performance n. 공연 experience v. 겪다, 경험하다
technical adj. 기술적인 issue n. 문제 delay n. 지연, 지체

sincerely adv. 진심으로 inconvenience n. 불편 display n. 전시

01
해석 공지는 어디에서 이뤄지고 있는 것 같은가?
(A) 연회장에서
(B) 극장에서
(C) 박물관에서
(D) 컨벤션 센터에서

02
해석 왜 행사가 지연되었는가?
(A) 일부 손님들이 오지 않았다.
(B) 기술적인 문제가 있다.
(C) 일부 공연자들이 준비가 되지 않았다.
(D) 좌석이 부족하다.

어휘 present adj. 있는, 참석한 shortage n. 부족, 결핍

03
해석 화자는 무엇을 할 것을 제안하는가?
(A) 전시물을 보는 것
(B) 예약하는 것
(C) 프로그램을 살펴보는 것
(D) 향후 공연에 대해 문의하는 것

어휘 reservation n. 예약 read through ~을 살펴보다 inquire v. 문의하다

토익실전문제 p.113

01 (B)	02 (C)	03 (A)	04 (C)	05 (D)
06 (B)				

[01-03] 미국
Questions 01-03 refer to the following announcement.

May I have everyone's attention, please? Next Monday, 01a new conveyor system will be installed in our warehouse. The work is expected to take several hours to complete, and the main area of our facility will be off-limits while it is in progress. During that time, 02I plan to conduct some training. My goal is to reduce the number of workplace accidents and injuries. 03I'll now give each of you a manual that covers the topics we will be discussing during the workshop. Please be sure to go through it carefully before we meet on Monday.

conveyor system 반송 설비 시스템 install v. 설치하다
warehouse n. 창고 off-limits adj. 출입이 금지된 in progress 진행 중인
conduct v. 실시하다 injury n. 부상 manual n. 설명서
go through ~을 살펴보다, 검토하다 carefully adv. 주의 깊게

해석
01-03번은 다음 공지에 관한 문제입니다.
모두 주목해 주시겠어요? 다음 주 월요일, 01새로운 반송 설비 시스템이 우리 창고에 설치될 예정입니다. 작업이 완료되기까지 몇 시간이 걸릴 것으로 예상되며, 진행되는 동안 시설의 주요 구역은 출입이 금지될 것입니다. 그 시간 동안, 02저는 교육을 실시할 계획입니다. 제 목표는 작업장 사고와 부상의 수를 줄이는 것입니다. 03이제 워크숍 중에 논의할 주제를 다루고 있는 설명서를 여러분 각자에게 나눠 드리겠습니다. 월요일에 만나기 전에 꼭 그것을 주의 깊게 살펴봐 주세요.

01 청자 문제
해석 청자들은 어디에서 일하는 것 같은가?
(A) 약국에서

(B) 창고에서
(C) 서비스 센터에서
(D) 소매점에서

해설 지문에서 신분 및 직업과 관련된 표현을 놓치지 않고 듣는다. "a new conveyor system will be installed in our warehouse"라며 창고에 새로운 반송 설비 시스템이 설치될 예정이라고 한 것을 통해, 청자들은 창고에서 일하고 있음을 알 수 있다. 따라서 (B)가 정답이다.

02 특정 세부 사항 문제

해설 교육 시간의 목표는 무엇인가?
(A) 낭비를 줄이는 것
(B) 생산성을 높이는 것
(C) 안전을 개선하는 것
(D) 팀워크를 장려하는 것

해설 질문의 핵심 어구(goal of the training)와 관련된 내용을 주의 깊게 듣는다. "I plan to conduct some training. My goal is to reduce the number of workplace accidents and injuries."라며 교육을 실시할 계획인데, 목표는 작업장 사고와 부상의 수를 줄이는 것이라고 하였다. 따라서 (C)가 정답이다.

Paraphrasing
reduce the number of workplace accidents and injuries 작업장 사고와 부상의 수를 줄이다 → improve safety 안전을 개선하다

03 요청 문제

해설 화자는 청자들에게 무엇을 하라고 요청하는가?
(A) 설명서를 읽는다.
(B) 주제를 제안한다.
(C) 작업장을 점검한다.
(D) 사고를 보고한다.

해설 지문의 중후반에서 요청과 관련된 표현이 포함된 문장을 주의 깊게 듣는다. "I'll now give each of you a manual ~. Please be sure to go through it carefully"라며 설명서를 나눠줄 테니, 그것을 주의 깊게 살펴보라고 하였다. 따라서 (A)가 정답이다.

어휘 inspect v. 점검하다   worksite n. 작업장

[04-06] 🎧 캐나다
Questions 04-06 refer to the following announcement.

Attention, everyone. This is your captain speaking. On behalf of Regina Air, ⁰⁴**I apologize for the delay. I just want to inform you that the cargo door has now been fixed**, and ⁰⁵**we will take off shortly. At this time, please return to your seats and fasten your seatbelts.** Also, those travelers who have connecting flights will disembark first upon arrival in Winnipeg. If this is your final destination, please remain seated until instructed otherwise. ⁰⁶**We will have several staff members at the arrivals gate to assist passengers with connections.** Thank you again for your patience and understanding.

on behalf of ~를 대표하여, ~을 대신하여   inform v. 알리다, 통지하다
take off 이륙하다   shortly adv. 곧   fasten v. 매다, 고정시키다
disembark v. (비행기에서) 내리다   assist v. 돕다

해설
04-06번은 다음 공지에 관한 문제입니다.

여러분 주목해 주십시오. 기장입니다. Regina 항공을 대표하여, ⁰⁴지연에 대해 사과드립니다. 화물칸 문이 이제 수리되었음을 알려드리고자 하며, ⁰⁵곧 이륙할 것입니다. 지금 좌석으로 돌아가 안전벨트를 매주시기 바랍니다. 또한, 연결 항공편이 있는 여행객들은 위니펙에 도착하면 먼저 내리실 것입니다. 이곳이 최종 목적지인 경우, 별도로 지시가 있을 때까지 착석해 계시기 바랍니다. ⁰⁶저희는 연결 항공편이 있는 승객들을 돕기 위해 도착 게이트에 여러 직원을 배치할 예정입니다. 여러분들의 인내와 양해에 다시 한번 감사드립니다.

04 특정 세부 사항

해설 무엇이 지연을 야기했는가?
(A) 기상 문제
(B) 예약 오류
(C) 기계적 문제
(D) 예기치 않은 중단

해설 질문의 핵심 어구(delay)가 언급된 주변을 주의 깊게 듣는다. "I apologize for the delay. I just want to inform you that the cargo door has now been fixed"라며 지연에 대해 사과드리며, 화물칸 문이 이제 수리됐음을 알려드리고자 한다고 한 것을 통해, 기계적 문제로 인해 지연됐음을 알 수 있다. 따라서 (C)가 정답이다.

어휘 complication n. 문제   mechanical adj. 기계적인, 기계의

05 장소 문제

해설 청자들은 어디에 있는 것 같은가?
(A) 공항 터미널에
(B) 통근 열차에
(C) 매표소에
(D) 여객기에

해설 지문에서 장소와 관련된 표현을 놓치지 않고 듣는다. "we will take off shortly. At this time, please return to your seats and fasten your seatbelts."라며 곧 이륙할 것이고, 지금 좌석으로 돌아가 안전벨트를 매주시기 바란다고 한 것을 통해, 청자들이 여객기에 있음을 알 수 있다. 따라서 (D)가 정답이다.

06 특정 세부 사항 문제

해설 화자는 직원들이 무엇을 할 것이라고 말하는가?
(A) 다과를 제공한다.
(B) 연결 항공편 승객들을 돕는다.
(C) 양식을 나눠준다.
(D) 부분 환불을 제공한다.

해설 질문의 핵심 어구(staff will do)와 관련된 내용을 주의 깊게 듣는다. "We will have several staff members at the arrivals gate to assist passengers with connections."라며 연결 항공편이 있는 승객들을 돕기 위해 도착 게이트에 여러 직원들을 배치할 예정이라고 하였다. 따라서 (B)가 정답이다.

어휘 refreshment n. 다과   pass out ~을 나눠주다, 배포하다
partial adj. 부분적인

기출 유형 2 관광 안내

Example 🎧 호주   p.114

해설
01-03번은 다음 관광 안내에 관한 문제입니다.

Grandview 협곡에 오신 것을 환영합니다. ⁰¹이 장소는 수천 년 전에 바위에 새겨진 동물들의 멋진 이미지로 유명합니다. 우리가 산책로를 따라 하이킹할 때, ⁰²여러분에게 주어진 보호용 머리 장비를 착용하세요. 그렇게 하지 않으면, 떨어지는 돌에 다칠 수도 있습니다. 또한 제가 말씀드려야 할 것은, 음... 오늘 여러 다른 투어 그룹들이 이곳에 있다는 것입니다. ⁰³저희가 천천히 이동하는 그룹 뒤에서 막히게 되면 인내심을 가져 주시기 바랍니다. 좋아요, 시작합시다.

01

해설 이 장소는 무엇으로 유명한가?
(A) 어려운 산책로
(B) 열대 식물
(C) 야생 동물

(D) 바위 조각술

어휘 challenging adj. 어려운, 도전적인 carving n. 조각술, 조각품

02
해석 화자는 청자들에게 무엇을 착용하라고 말하는가?
(A) 이름표
(B) 헬멧
(C) 배낭
(D) 재킷

Paraphrasing
protective headgear 보호용 머리 장비 → helmet 헬멧

03
해석 화자가 "오늘 여러 다른 투어 그룹들이 이곳에 있다는 것입니다"라고 말할 때 무엇을 의도하는가?
(A) 일부 장비를 이용할 수 없다.
(B) 한 구역에 접근이 제한되어 있다.
(C) 경로가 변경될 것이다.
(D) 지체될 수도 있다.

어휘 unavailable adj. 이용할 수 없는 restrict v. 제한하다, 통제하다

토익실전문제
p.115

| 01 (C) | 02 (B) | 03 (D) | 04 (A) | 05 (B) |
| 06 (D) | | | | |

[01-03] 🎧 미국
Questions 01-03 refer to the following talk.

⁰¹**To begin our tour of the Hampton Historical Center, I am going to lead you through our largest exhibit.** Entitled *The Beginnings*, the exhibit focuses on the founding of our city. There are over 100 historical items and photographs, and ⁰²**you can find more information about this event in our most recent museum newsletter.** ⁰³**Please be reminded that many of the artifacts on display are old and fragile. They are for your viewing pleasure only and not to be handled in any way.** OK, let's start the tour.

entitle v. 제목을 붙이다 focus on ~에 초점을 맞추다 founding n. 설립
historical adj. 역사적인 artifact n. 유물 fragile adj. 손상되기 쉬운, 취약한
handle v. (손으로) 만지다, 다루다

해석
01-03번은 다음 담화에 관한 문제입니다.

⁰¹Hampton 역사 센터의 투어를 시작하기 위해, 저는 여러분을 저희의 가장 큰 전시관으로 안내하겠습니다. *The Beginnings*라는 제목의 이 전시는 우리 도시의 설립에 초점을 맞추고 있습니다. 100개 이상의 역사적 물품과 사진들이 있으며, ⁰²이 행사에 대한 더 많은 정보를 저희의 가장 최근 박물관 소식지에서 찾아보실 수 있습니다. ⁰³전시 중인 많은 유물들이 오래되었고 손상되기 쉽다는 것을 다시 한번 숙지해 주십시오. 그것들은 단지 여러분의 감상의 즐거움을 위함일 뿐이며, 어떤 식으로든 만져서는 안 됩니다. 자, 투어를 시작합시다.

01 장소 문제
해석 청자들은 어디에 있을 것 같은가?
(A) 시청에
(B) 스포츠 경기장에
(C) 역사 박물관에
(D) 공공 도서관에
해설 지문에서 장소와 관련된 표현을 놓치지 않고 듣는다. "To begin our tour of the Hampton Historical Center, I am going to lead you through our largest exhibit."이라며 Hampton 역사 센터의 투어를 시작하기 위해 청자들을 가장 큰 전시관으로 안내하겠다고 한 말을 통해, 청자들이 역사 박물관에 있음을 알 수 있다. 따라서 (C)가 정답이다.

02 방법 문제
해석 화자에 따르면, 청자들은 어떻게 주제에 대해 더 많이 배울 수 있는가?
(A) 녹음된 것을 들음으로써
(B) 출판물을 읽음으로써
(C) 강의에 참석함으로써
(D) 웹사이트를 방문함으로써
해설 질문의 핵심 어구(learn more about a topic)와 관련된 내용을 주의 깊게 듣는다. "you can find more information about this event in our most recent museum newsletter"라며 이 행사에 대한 더 많은 정보를 가장 최근의 박물관 소식지에서 찾을 수 있다고 하였다. 따라서 (B)가 정답이다.

Paraphrasing
museum newsletter 박물관 소식지 → publication 출판물

03 특정 세부 사항 문제
해석 청자들은 무엇을 하도록 상기되는가?
(A) 설문조사를 완료한다.
(B) 음료를 밖에 둔다.
(C) 몇몇 사진을 게시한다.
(D) 물품을 만지지 않는다.
해설 질문의 핵심 어구(reminded to do)와 관련된 내용을 주의 깊게 듣는다. "Please be reminded that many of the artifacts on display are old and fragile. ~ and not to be handled in any way."라며 전시 중인 많은 유물들이 오래되었고 손상되기 쉽다며, 어떤 식으로든 만져서는 안 된다고 하였다. 따라서 (D)가 정답이다.

어휘 beverage n. 음료

Paraphrasing
not to be handled 만져서는 안 되는 → Avoid touching 만지지 않는다

[04-06] 🎧 영국
Questions 04-06 refer to the following tour information.

During our three-hour boat tour along the River Seine, ⁰⁴**you'll see many historic structures, including a few castles.** I'll answer any questions you might have about these. And if you get hungry, ⁰⁵**there are soft drinks, chips, and other snacks available.** Just ask me or one of the other guides. We are now ready to begin. ⁰⁶**Please put on the life vest you will find under your seat.** This must be worn at all times during the tour.

historic adj. 역사적으로 중요한, 역사적인 structure n. 건축물, 구조(물)
castle n. 성 available adj. 이용 가능한

해석
04-06번은 다음 관광 안내에 관한 문제입니다.

센 강을 따라 3시간 동안 진행되는 저희 보트 투어 동안, ⁰⁴여러분은 몇몇 성을 포함한 역사적으로 중요한 많은 건축물들을 보게 될 것입니다. 이것들에 관해 여러분이 가질 수 있는 질문에 제가 답변해 드리겠습니다. 그리고 배가 고프시면, ⁰⁵이용 가능한 청량음료, 과자, 그리고 다른 간식들이 있습니다. 저나 다른 가이드 중 한 명에게 요청해 주세요. 이제 시작할 준비가 되었습니다. ⁰⁶좌석 아래에서 구명조끼를 찾아 착용해 주세요. 이것은 투어 내내 항상 착용하셔야 합니다.

04 특정 세부 사항 문제
해석 화자에 따르면, 청자들은 무엇을 볼 것인가?

(A) 건물들
(B) 동상들
(C) 차량들
(D) 식물들

해설 질문의 핵심 어구(listeners see)와 관련된 내용을 주의 깊게 듣는다. "you'll see many historic structures, including a few castles"라며 청자들이 몇몇 성을 포함한 역사적으로 중요한 많은 건축물들을 보게 될 것이라고 하였다. 따라서 (A)가 정답이다.

Paraphrasing
structures, including ~ castles 성을 포함한 건축물들 → Buildings 건물들

05 특정 세부 사항 문제
해설 보트에서 무엇이 이용 가능한가?
(A) 지역 지도
(B) 다과
(C) 배터리 충전기
(D) 가이드북

해설 질문의 핵심 어구(available on the boat)와 관련된 내용을 주의 깊게 듣는다. "there are soft drinks, chips, and other snacks available"이라며 이용 가능한 청량음료, 과자, 그리고 다른 간식들이 있다고 하였다. 따라서 (B)가 정답이다.

Paraphrasing
soft drinks, chips, and other snacks 청량음료, 과자, 그리고 다른 간식들 → Refreshments 다과

06 요청 문제
해설 화자는 청자들에게 무엇을 하라고 요청하는가?
(A) 자리에 계속 앉아 있는다.
(B) 짐을 보관한다.
(C) 티켓을 보여준다.
(D) 안전 장비를 착용한다.

해설 지문의 중후반에서 요청과 관련된 표현이 포함된 문장을 주의 깊게 듣는다. "Please put on the life vest you will find under your seat."이라며 좌석 아래에서 구명조끼를 찾아 착용해 달라고 하였다. 따라서 (D)가 정답이다.

Paraphrasing
life vest 구명조끼 → safety gear 안전 장비

HACKERS TEST   p.116

01 (C)	02 (D)	03 (C)	04 (B)	05 (A)
06 (C)	07 (A)	08 (B)	09 (D)	10 (C)
11 (B)	12 (C)	13 (A)	14 (C)	15 (B)
16 (C)	17 (B)	18 (A)	19 (B)	20 (D)
21 (A)				

[01-03] 캐나다
Questions 01-03 refer to the following announcement.

⁰¹This is an announcement for all tenants of Westfield Apartments. ⁰²Tomorrow afternoon, our building's fire alarm system will be tested. You may hear a loud siren during the system check. ⁰³Please read the pamphlet that was placed in front of the entrance to each apartment unit. It contains the standard evacuation guidelines and other emergency information. Thank you for your patience during the emergency test.

tenant n. 세입자 test v. 점검하다, 시험하다 place v. 놓다, 두다
contain v. 포함하다 standard adj. 표준의, 일반적인
evacuation n. 대피, 철수 emergency n. 비상(사태)

해석
01-03번은 다음 공지에 관한 문제입니다.
⁰¹이것은 Westfield 아파트의 모든 세입자들을 위한 공지입니다. ⁰²내일 오후에, 우리 건물의 화재 경보 시스템이 점검될 예정입니다. 시스템 점검 동안 큰 사이렌 소리가 들릴 수 있습니다. ⁰³각 아파트 세대의 출입문 앞에 놓인 팸플릿을 읽어보시기 바랍니다. 그것에는 표준 대피 지침과 기타 비상 정보가 포함되어 있습니다. 긴급 점검 동안 여러분의 인내에 감사드립니다.

01 장소 문제
해설 공지는 어디에서 이뤄지고 있는가?
(A) 지하철역에서
(B) 부동산 사무실에서
(C) 아파트 단지에서
(D) 연구소에서

해설 지문에서 장소와 관련된 표현을 놓치지 않고 듣는다. "This is an announcement for all tenants of Westfield Apartments."라며 Westfield 아파트의 모든 세입자들을 위한 공지라고 한 것을 통해, 아파트 단지에서 이뤄지고 있음을 알 수 있다. 따라서 (C)가 정답이다.

02 다음에 할 일 문제
해설 화자에 따르면, 내일 오후에 무슨 일이 일어날 것인가?
(A) 일부 기계가 교체될 것이다.
(B) 주차장이 폐쇄될 것이다.
(C) 일부 지침이 배포될 것이다.
(D) 시스템 점검이 수행될 것이다.

해설 질문의 핵심 어구(tomorrow afternoon)가 언급된 주변을 주의 깊게 듣는다. "Tomorrow afternoon, our building's fire alarm system will be tested."라며 내일 오후에 건물 화재 경보 시스템이 점검될 것이라고 하였다. 따라서 (D)가 정답이다.

어휘 machinery n. 기계 replace v. 교체하다 distribute v. 배포하다

Paraphrasing
fire alarm system will be tested 화재 경보 시스템이 점검될 것이다 → system test will be performed 시스템 점검이 수행될 것이다

03 제안 문제
해설 화자는 무엇을 하기를 권장하는가?
(A) 사무실 방문하기
(B) 프로그램에 등록하기
(C) 팸플릿 확인하기
(D) 몇몇 컴퓨터 끄기

해설 지문의 중후반에서 제안과 관련된 표현이 포함된 문장을 주의 깊게 듣는다. "Please read the pamphlet that was placed in front of the entrance to each apartment unit."이라며 각 아파트 세대의 출입문 앞에 놓인 팸플릿을 읽어 달라고 하였다. 따라서 (C)가 정답이다.

어휘 register in ~에 등록하다 turn off ~을 끄다

[04-06] 영국
Questions 04-06 refer to the following tour information.

My name is Mindy, and today ⁰⁴I'm going to show you around the Wellmont Wildlife Park. The park was opened 30 years ago to house animals from around the world. With an area of 4.2 square kilometers, ⁰⁵this facility stands out as the largest wildlife park in England. Moreover, the park just unveiled a new lion exhibit last Thursday, so you'll get to see that as well. Now, as we tour the facility, ⁰⁶I'd like to remind everyone to please remain with the group. I don't want anyone to wander off and get lost.

house v. 수용하다, 보관하다   stand out 두각을 나타내다, 눈에 띄다
unveil v. 공개하다, 발표하다   wander off 혼자 떨어져 다니다, 떠돌아 다니다

Now, the fabric is stored in the back cabinet.

sewing n. 재봉   basic adj. 기본적인   technique n. 기술, 기법
afterward adv. 그런 다음, 나중에   previously adv. 이전에   fabric n. 천, 직물
storage n. 보관   store v. 보관하다

해석
04-06번은 다음 관광 안내에 관한 문제입니다.

제 이름은 Mindy이고, 오늘 ⁰⁴저는 Wellmont 야생 동물 공원을 안내해 드리겠습니다. 이 공원은 전 세계의 동물들을 수용하기 위해 30년 전에 개장했습니다. 면적이 4.2제곱킬로미터인 ⁰⁵이 시설은 영국에서 가장 큰 야생 동물 공원으로 두각을 나타냅니다. 게다가, 공원은 지난주 목요일에 새로운 사자 전시관을 공개했기 때문에, 여러분은 그것도 관람하실 것입니다. 이제, 우리가 시설을 둘러보는 동안, ⁰⁶모든 분들께서는 그룹과 함께 계속 있어 주시기를 상기시켜 드립니다. 누구든 혼자 떨어져 다니다가 길을 잃지 않기를 바랍니다.

04 화자 문제
해석 화자는 누구인 것 같은가?
(A) 교수
(B) 관광 가이드
(C) 부동산 중개인
(D) 팟캐스트 진행자

해설 지문에서 신분 및 직업과 관련된 표현을 놓치지 않고 듣는다. "I'm going to show you around the Wellmont Wildlife Park"라며 Wellmont 야생 동물 공원을 안내할 것이라고 한 것을 통해, 화자가 관광 가이드임을 알 수 있다. 따라서 (B)가 정답이다.

05 언급 문제
해석 화자는 시설에 대해 무엇이 독특하다고 말하는가?
(A) 그것의 크기
(B) 그것의 디자인
(C) 그것의 역사
(D) 그것의 기능

해설 질문의 핵심 어구(unique about a facility)와 관련된 내용을 주의 깊게 듣는다. "this facility stands out as the largest wildlife park in England"라며 이 시설은 영국에서 가장 큰 야생 동물 공원으로서 두각을 나타낸다고 하였다. 따라서 (A)가 정답이다.

06 특정 세부 사항 문제
해석 화자는 청자들에게 무엇을 하라고 상기시키는가?
(A) 소지품을 관리한다.
(B) 공연에 참석한다.
(C) 그룹과 함께 있는다.
(D) 기념품을 구매한다.

해설 질문의 핵심 어구(remind the listeners to do)와 관련된 내용을 주의 깊게 듣는다. "I'd like to remind everyone to please remain with the group"이라며 그룹과 함께 계속 있어 주기를 상기시킨다고 하였다. 따라서 (C)가 정답이다.

어휘 belongings n. 소지품, 재산   souvenir n. 기념품

[07-09] 미국
Questions 07-09 refer to the following talk.

Welcome to the sewing class at the Desmond Community Center. First, ⁰⁷let me apologize for not showing up on time. I left my class notes at my house, so I had to go get them. I promise that won't happen again. ⁰⁸I will now show you some basic sewing techniques. Afterward, you will have the chance to try them. Oh . . . And ⁰⁹we previously kept fabric in the small closet near the door. But that storage space was too small to hold everything.

해석
07-09번은 다음 담화에 관한 문제입니다.

Desmond 커뮤니티 센터의 재봉 수업에 오신 것을 환영합니다. 우선, ⁰⁷제가 제시간에 나타나지 않은 것에 대해 사과드립니다. 수업 자료를 집에 두고 오는 바람에, 그것들을 가지러 가야 했습니다. 다시는 그런 일이 없을 것을 약속드립니다. ⁰⁸이제 기본적인 재봉 기술을 몇 가지 보여드리겠습니다. 그런 다음, 여러분이 그것들을 시도해볼 기회가 있을 것입니다. 아... 그리고 ⁰⁹우리는 이전에 문 근처의 작은 벽장에 천을 보관했습니다. 하지만, 그 보관 공간은 모든 것을 수용하기에 너무 작았습니다. 이제, 천은 뒤쪽 캐비닛에 보관되어 있습니다.

07 이유 문제
해석 화자는 왜 사과하는가?
(A) 그녀가 늦게 도착했다.
(B) 그녀가 공지를 보내는 것을 잊었다.
(C) 방이 너무 작다.
(D) 수업이 예상보다 일찍 끝날 것이다.

해설 질문의 핵심 어구(apologize)가 언급된 주변을 주의 깊게 듣는다. "let me apologize for not showing up on time"이라며 제시간에 나타나지 않은 것에 대해 사과한다고 하였다. 따라서 (A)가 정답이다.

어휘 send out ~을 보내다, 발송하다

[Paraphrasing]
not showing up on time 제시간에 나타나지 않은 것 → arrived late 늦게 도착했다

08 다음에 할 일 문제
해석 화자는 다음에 무엇을 할 것인가?
(A) 영상을 보여준다.
(B) 시범을 보여준다.
(C) 설명서를 나누어 준다.
(D) 기계를 설치한다.

해설 질문의 핵심 어구(do next)와 관련된 내용을 주의 깊게 듣는다. "I will now show you some basic sewing techniques."라며 기본적인 재봉 기술을 몇 가지 보여줄 것이라고 하였다. 따라서 (B)가 정답이다.

어휘 demonstration n. 시범, 시연   distribute v. 나누어 주다, 배부하다
manual n. 설명서

09 의도 파악 문제
해석 화자가 "천은 뒤쪽 캐비닛에 보관되어 있습니다"라고 말할 때 무엇을 의도하는가?
(A) 주문품이 제시간에 도착했다.
(B) 한 조직이 기증을 받아들였다.
(C) 제안이 적용되었다.
(D) 문제가 해결되었다.

해설 질문의 인용어구(the fabric is stored in the back cabinet)가 언급된 주변을 주의 깊게 듣는다. "we previously kept fabric in the small closet near the door. But that storage space was too small to hold everything."이라며 이전에는 문 근처의 작은 벽장에 천을 보관했는데, 그 보관 공간은 모든 것을 수용하기에 너무 작았다고 한 것을 통해, 천을 뒤쪽 캐비닛에 둠으로써 보관 공간이 너무 작았던 문제가 해결되었음을 알 수 있다. 따라서 (D)가 정답이다.

어휘 organization n. 조직, 단체   accept v. 받아들이다, 수락하다
donation n. 기증, 기부   apply v. 적용하다, 신청하다   address v. 해결하다

[10-12] 호주
Questions 10-12 refer to the following tour information.

> Thank you all for visiting the Gladesdale Mansion. **¹⁰While I show you around this landmark, I will share with you its long history.** It was built in 1905 by the renowned Italian architect Alfonso Vento. Mr. Vento spent five years overseeing the work. But it was worth the effort to create such a beautiful building. **¹¹I should mention that you can pick up some free photographs of this structure in the lobby.** OK, let's begin the tour. **¹²We will now proceed to the library for a brief introductory speech by one of the caretakers of this building.**
>
> 어휘 landmark n. 명소, 획기적 사건 renowned adj. 유명한 architect n. 건축가
> oversee v. 감독하다 proceed to ~로 이동하다, ~에 이르다
> brief adj. 짧은, 간단한 introductory adj. 소개의, 도입부의
> caretaker n. 관리인, 경비원

해석 10-12번은 다음 관광 안내에 관한 문제입니다.

Gladesdale 대저택에 방문해 주셔서 모두 감사드립니다. ¹⁰제가 이 명소를 안내하면서, 여러분들과 그것의 긴 역사를 공유할 것입니다. 그것은 1905년에 유명한 이탈리아 건축가인 Alfonso Vento에 의해 지어졌습니다. Mr. Vento는 5년 동안 그 작업을 감독했습니다. 하지만 이런 아름다운 건물을 만들기 위한 노력은 가치가 있었습니다. ¹¹로비에서 이 건축물의 무료 사진을 받아가실 수 있다는 점을 언급해야겠습니다. 자, 투어를 시작합시다. ¹²이제 우리는 이 건물의 관리인 중 한 명의 짧은 소개 연설을 위해 도서관으로 이동하겠습니다.

10 주제 문제
해석 투어의 중점은 무엇인가?
(A) 농업
(B) 사업
(C) 역사
(D) 과학

해설 투어의 주제를 묻는 문제이므로, 지문의 초반을 반드시 듣는다. "While I show you around this landmark, I will share with you its long history."라며 이 명소를 안내하면서 그것의 긴 역사를 공유할 것이라고 한 뒤, 건물의 역사에 대해 설명하고 있다. 따라서 (C)가 정답이다.

11 언급 문제
해석 화자는 로비에서 무엇을 이용할 수 있다고 말하는가?
(A) 안내 책자
(B) 사진
(C) 다과
(D) 지도

해설 질문의 핵심 어구(available in the lobby)와 관련된 내용을 주의 깊게 듣는다. "I should mention that you can pick up some free photographs of this structure in the lobby."라며 로비에서 건축물의 무료 사진을 가져갈 수 있다고 하였다. 따라서 (B)가 정답이다.

Paraphrasing
photographs 사진 → Pictures 사진

12 다음에 할 일 문제
해석 청자들은 다음에 무엇을 할 것 같은가?
(A) 식사를 한다.
(B) 차량에 탑승한다.
(C) 강연을 듣는다.
(D) 건축가를 만난다.

해설 지문의 마지막 부분을 주의 깊게 듣는다. "We will now proceed to the library for a brief introductory speech by one of the caretakers of this building."이라며 이제 건물의 관리인 중 한 명의 짧은 소개 연설을 위해 도서관으로 이동할 것이라고 하였다. 따라서 (C)가 정답이다.

어휘 board v. 탑승하다 vehicle n. 차량

[13-15] 캐나다
Questions 13-15 refer to the following announcement.

> May I have your attention, please? Thank you for your patience. **¹³Please take your seats for today's soccer match.** **¹⁴The visiting team arrived a bit late, so the game was delayed.** But everyone is ready to play now. Also, **¹⁵a special ceremony will take place after the game.** Mick Tomley, the former coach of the Missouri Wildcats, will receive an award to commemorate his years of work. Everyone is welcome to stay and celebrate with us.
>
> 어휘 match n. 경기 visiting team 원정팀 ceremony n. 행사, 의식
> former adj. 이전의 commemorate v. 기념하다
> celebrate v. 축하하다, 기념하다

해석 13-15번은 다음 공지에 관한 문제입니다.

주목해 주시겠습니까? 기다려 주셔서 감사합니다. ¹³오늘의 축구 경기를 위해 자리에 착석해 주세요. ¹⁴원정팀이 약간 늦게 도착해서 경기가 지연되었습니다. 하지만 이제 모두 경기를 할 준비가 되었습니다. 또한, ¹⁵경기 후에 특별한 행사가 개최될 것입니다. Missouri Wildcats의 이전 감독인 Mick Tomley가 그의 오랜 업적을 기념하기 위한 상을 받을 것입니다. 모든 분들이 함께 남아서 축하해 주시기를 바랍니다.

13 장소 문제
해석 공지는 어디에서 이뤄지고 있는 것 같은가?
(A) 스포츠 경기장에서
(B) 피트니스 센터에서
(C) 기차역에서
(D) 의료 클리닉에서

해설 지문에서 장소와 관련된 표현을 놓치지 않고 듣는다. "Please take your seats for today's soccer match."라며 오늘의 축구 경기를 위해 자리에 착석해 달라고 한 것을 통해, 공지가 스포츠 경기장에서 이뤄지고 있음을 알 수 있다. 따라서 (A)가 정답이다.

14 특정 세부 사항 문제
해석 화자에 따르면, 무엇이 지연을 야기했는가?
(A) 기술적 오작동
(B) 심한 폭풍
(C) 늦은 도착
(D) 교통사고

해설 질문의 핵심 어구(caused a delay)와 관련된 내용을 주의 깊게 듣는다. "The visiting team arrived a bit late, so the game was delayed."라며 원정팀이 약간 늦게 도착해서 경기가 지연되었다고 하였다. 따라서 (C)가 정답이다.

어휘 malfunction n. 오작동, 고장 storm n. 폭풍 arrival n. 도착

15 다음에 할 일 문제
해석 화자는 나중에 무슨 일이 일어날 것이라고 말하는가?
(A) 사인회가 열릴 것이다.
(B) 행사가 열릴 것이다.
(C) 질문이 답변될 것이다.
(D) 인터뷰가 진행될 것이다.

해설 지문의 중후반부를 주의 깊게 듣는다. "a special ceremony will take place after the game"이라며, 경기 후에 특별한 행사가 개최될 것이라고 하였다. 따라서 (B)가 정답이다.

Paraphrasing
take place 개최되다 → be held 열리다

[16-18] 미국
Questions 16-18 refer to the following tour information.

Welcome to the Atwood Museum of Contemporary Art. My name is Lorraine East, and I'll be your tour guide today. ¹⁶**We'll go to our photography hall first**, where you will see the works of hundreds of world-famous photographers. After that, ¹⁷**we'll look at the Gonzalo Ruiz displays in the sculpture room upstairs**. Then, at 11:30 A.M., we'll stop for a 30-minute lunch break. ¹⁸**Please make sure to be in the lobby by noon** so that we can continue the tour. Thank you.

contemporary adj. 현대의, 동시대의   display n. 전시   sculpture n. 조각품
continue v. 계속하다

해설
16-18번은 다음 관광 안내에 관한 문제입니다.

Atwood 현대 미술관에 오신 것을 환영합니다. 제 이름은 Lorraine East이고, 오늘 여러분의 투어 가이드가 될 것입니다. ¹⁶우리는 먼저 사진관으로 가볼 것인데, 그곳에서 세계적으로 유명한 수백 명의 사진작가들의 작품을 볼 것입니다. 그 후에, ¹⁷우리는 위층 조각품 실에 있는 Gonzalo Ruiz 전시를 볼 것입니다. 그런 다음, 오전 11시 30분에는 30분간의 점심 시간을 가질 것입니다. 투어를 계속할 수 있도록 ¹⁸정오까지 로비에 모여 있어 주시기 바랍니다. 감사합니다.

16 특정 세부 사항 문제
해설 청자들은 가장 먼저 어디로 갈 것인가?
(A) 매표소로
(B) 방문자 센터로
(C) 사진관으로
(D) 건물 로비로

해설 질문의 핵심 어구(go first)와 관련된 내용을 주의 깊게 듣는다. "We'll go to our photography hall first"라며 먼저 사진관으로 갈 것이라고 하였다. 따라서 (C)가 정답이다.

17 특정 세부 사항 문제
해설 Gonzalo Ruiz는 누구인 것 같은가?
(A) 음식 제공자
(B) 조각가
(C) 전시 책임자
(D) 가이드

해설 질문의 핵심 어구(Gonzalo Ruiz)가 언급된 주변을 주의 깊게 듣는다. "we'll look at the Gonzalo Ruiz displays in the sculpture room upstairs"라며 위층의 조각품 실에 있는 Gonzalo Ruiz 전시를 볼 것이라고 한 것을 통해, Gonzalo Ruiz가 조각가임을 알 수 있다. 따라서 (B)가 정답이다.

18 요청 문제
해설 청자들은 무엇을 하라고 요청받는가?
(A) 한 장소에 모인다.
(B) 줄을 선다.
(C) 시간표를 확인한다.
(D) 입장권을 구매한다.

해설 지문의 중후반에서 요청과 관련된 표현이 포함된 문장을 주의 깊게 듣는다. "Please make sure to be in the lobby by noon"이라며 정오까지 로비에 모여 달라고 하였다. 따라서 (A)가 정답이다.

어휘 gather v. 모이다, 모으다   timetable n. 시간표

[19-21] 캐나다
Questions 19-21 refer to the following talk and schedule.

¹⁹**I hope you all have a wonderful time at the Pittsburgh Planetarium today. We have a number of attractions for all of you to enjoy.** On the second floor, you can stop by our newly opened exhibit about the formation of our galaxy. Also, there are several shows playing at our theater today. However, ²⁰**please note that the afternoon show has been canceled**. To make up for this, ²¹**we've decided to give away some free items, including a poster, key chain, and hat. Stop by the gift shop to pick up your gifts.**

planetarium n. 천문관   a number of 많은   attraction n. 볼거리, 명소
stop by ~에 방문하다   formation n. 형성   galaxy n. 은하
make up for ~에 대해 보상하다, ~을 만회하다   give away ~을 나누어 주다
pick up ~을 받다, 줍다

해설
19-21번은 다음 담화와 일정표에 관한 문제입니다.

¹⁹여러분 모두가 오늘 피츠버그 천문관에서 멋진 시간을 보내시길 바랍니다. 저희는 여러분 모두가 즐길 수 있는 많은 볼거리를 준비했습니다. 2층에서는 우리 은하의 형성에 관한 새로 개장한 전시회에 들르실 수 있습니다. 또한, 오늘 저희 극장에서는 여러 공연이 상영되고 있습니다. 그러나 ²⁰오후 공연이 취소되었음을 참고해 주세요. 이에 대해 보상하기 위해서, ²¹저희는 포스터, 열쇠고리, 모자를 포함한 무료 상품을 나눠 드리기로 했습니다. 선물을 받으시려면 선물 가게를 방문하세요.

피츠버그 천문관 극장 상영 - 8월 9일	
공연 이름	시간
Stars and Planets	오전 9시 - 오전 10시
The Northern Lights	오전 10시 - 오전 11시
Traveling Through Space	오전 11시 - 오후 12시
²⁰Views of Earth	오후 1시 - 오후 3시

19 청자 문제
해설 청자들은 누구인 것 같은가?
(A) 자원봉사자들
(B) 시설 방문객들
(C) 수업 참가자들
(D) 교육생들

해설 지문에서 신분 및 직업과 관련된 표현을 놓치지 않고 듣는다. "I hope you all have a wonderful time at the Pittsburgh Planetarium today. We have a number of attractions for all of you to enjoy."라며 청자들 모두 피츠버그 천문관에서 멋진 시간을 보내기를 바란다며, 청자들이 즐길 수 있는 많은 볼거리를 준비했다고 한 것을 통해, 청자들은 천문관을 방문한 방문객들임을 알 수 있다. 따라서 (B)가 정답이다.

20 시각 자료 문제
해설 시각 자료를 보아라. 어느 공연이 취소되었는가?
(A) Stars and Planets
(B) The Northern Lights
(C) Traveling Through Space

(D) *Views of Earth*

해설 제시된 일정표의 정보를 확인한 후 질문의 핵심 어구(show was canceled)와 관련된 내용을 주의 깊게 듣는다. "please note that the afternoon show has been canceled"라며 오후 공연이 취소되었음을 참고해 달라고 하였고, 오후에 상영 예정이었던 공연은 *Views of Earth*임을 일정표에서 알 수 있다. 따라서 (D)가 정답이다.

21 특정 세부 사항 문제

해설 청자들은 어디에서 무료 상품을 받을 수 있는가?
(A) 선물 가게에서
(B) 정원에서
(C) 안내 데스크에서
(D) 정문에서

해설 질문의 핵심 어구(free items)가 언급된 주변을 주의 깊게 듣는다. "we've decided to give away some free items, ~. Stop by the gift shop to pick up your gifts."라며 무료 상품을 제공하기로 했고, 선물을 받으려면 선물 가게를 방문하라고 하였다. 따라서 (A)가 정답이다.

DAY 18 연설 및 강연

기출 유형 1 연설

Example 🎧 캐나다 p.118

01-03번은 다음 연설에 관한 문제입니다.

우리는 오늘 밤 요크빌 의료 시설의 기념일을 축하하기 위해 이곳에 왔습니다. ⁰¹이사회의 일원으로서, 여러분 모두 앞에서 연설을 하게 된 것은 저의 영광입니다. 정확히 100년 전 이 병원은 처음 대중에게 문을 열었습니다. ⁰²초기에는, 이 시설에 겨우 10명의 의사만 있었습니다. 그러나 현재는 75명이 훨씬 넘으며, 그에 더해 많은 간호사들이 있습니다. 시간이 지나면서, 요크빌 지역 사회는 저희의 높은 퀄리티의 치료의 진가를 알아보게 되었습니다. 저녁 식사가 곧 제공될 예정이나, ⁰³먼저 Dr. Lily Driver께서 요크빌 의료 시설의 역사에 대한 **짧은 연설**을 해주시겠습니다. ⁰³무대로 모실 그녀를 환영해주십시오.

어휘 celebrate v. 축하하다 anniversary n. 기념일
trustee n. 이사, 신탁 관리자 numerous adj. 많은
appreciate v. 진가를 알아보다

01

해설 화자는 누구인가?
(A) 이사회 일원
(B) 지역 관리자
(C) 수석 의사
(D) 보안 요원

02

해설 화자는 요크빌 의료 시설에 대해 무엇을 언급하는가?
(A) 지역 기부자들에 의해 자금을 받았다.
(B) 최근 이전되었다.
(C) 건설 공사는 예상보다 오래 걸렸다.
(D) 직원들은 해가 지남에 따라 늘어났다.

03

해설 다음에 무슨 일이 일어날 것 같은가?
(A) 노래가 라이브로 공연될 것이다.
(B) 연사가 무대에 오를 것이다.
(C) 짧은 영화가 상영될 것이다.
(D) 퍼레이드가 열릴 것이다.

토익실전문제 p.119

| 01 (B) | 02 (A) | 03 (C) | 04 (C) | 05 (D) |
| 06 (B) |

[01-03] 🎧 영국

Questions 01-03 refer to the following speech.

⁰¹**Thank you all for coming to the fifth annual British Publishers Convention.** This event is an opportunity for the nation's leading publishing houses to showcase their works. As you walk around the venue, ⁰²**be sure to stop at each booth and pick up a pamphlet that describes the books the firm plans to release this year**. Also, ⁰³**I encourage everyone to head to Edwards Hall at 5 P.M., where you will be able to listen to a story** written by the distinguished author Susan Holmes.

leading adj. 선도적인 publishing house 출판사 describe v. 설명하다
head v. 향하다 distinguished adj. 저명한 author n. 작가

해설
01-03번은 다음 연설에 관한 문제입니다.

⁰¹제5회 영국 출판사 컨벤션에 참석해 주셔서 감사합니다. 이 행사는 국내의 선도적인 출판사들이 그들의 작품들을 보여줄 기회입니다. 현장을 돌아다니시면서, ⁰²각 부스에 들러 회사들이 올해 발간할 계획인 책들에 대해 설명하는 책자를 꼭 챙기시기 바랍니다. 또한, ⁰³저는 모두가 오후 5시에 Edwards 홀로 향하시기를 권하는데, 그곳에서 저명한 작가 Susan Holmes가 쓴 이야기를 들으실 수 있습니다.

01 장소 문제

해설 화자는 어디에 있는 것 같은가?
(A) 미술관에
(B) 컨벤션 센터에
(C) 도서관에
(D) 쇼핑몰에

해설 장소와 관련된 표현을 놓치지 않고 듣는다. "Thank you all for coming to the fifth annual British Publishers Convention."이라며 출판사 컨벤션에 참석해 주셔서 감사하다고 했으므로 화자가 컨벤션 센터에 있음을 알 수 있다. 따라서 (B)가 정답이다.

02 특정 세부 사항 문제

해설 화자에 따르면, 책자는 무엇을 포함하는가?
(A) 다음 출판물들
(B) 디자이너들의 목록
(C) 발표자들의 명단
(D) 워크숍 세부사항

해설 질문의 핵심 어구(pamphlet)와 관련된 내용을 주의 깊게 듣는다. "be sure to ~ pick up a pamphlet that describes the books the firm plans to release this year"라며 회사들이 올해 발간할 계획인 책들에 대해 설명하는 책자를 꼭 챙기라고 하였다. 따라서 (A)가 정답이다.

어휘 presenter n. 발표자

Paraphrasing
books 책들 → publications 출판물

03 특정 세부 사항 문제

해설 청자들은 Edwards 홀에서 무엇을 할 수 있는가?
(A) 책을 구매한다.
(B) 학회 배지를 가져간다.
(C) 이야기를 듣는다.

(D) 다큐멘터리를 본다.

해설 질문의 핵심 어구(Edwards Hall)가 언급된 주변을 주의 깊게 듣는다. "I encourage everyone to head to Edwards Hall at 5 P.M., where you can listen to a story"라며 모두가 오후 5시에 Edwards 홀로 향하시기를 권하며 그곳에서 이야기를 들을 수 있을 거라고 하였다. 따라서 (C)가 정답이다.

[04-06] 🎧 호주
Questions 04-06 refer to the following talk.

> We are gathered here tonight to honor Daryl Meyers from Pioneer Architecture. 04**Mr. Meyers has been selected to receive the Designer of the Year Prize** for his work on the Lower Town Theater. While Mr. Meyers has long been a respected architect, 05**the groundbreaking design of the Lower Town Theater deserves special praise.** In recognition of his work, 04**Mr. Meyers will be given a medal as well as a cash prize** of 10,000 dollars. But first, 06**Mr. Meyers would like to say a few words to thank some of his colleagues** who helped on the project. Let's all give him a very generous round of applause.
>
> groundbreaking adj. 획기적인 deserve v. ~할 만하다
> praise n. 찬사; v. 칭찬하다

해설
04-06번은 다음 담화에 관한 문제입니다.

우리는 Pioneer 건축 사무소의 Daryl Meyers에게 존경을 표하기 위해 오늘 밤 이곳에 모였습니다. 04Mr. Meyers는 그의 Lower Town 극장 작업으로 올해의 디자이너 상을 받도록 선정되었습니다. Mr. Meyers가 오래 전부터 존경받는 건축가였기는 하지만, 05Lower Town 극장에 사용한 그의 획기적인 설계 방식은 특별한 찬사를 받을 만합니다. 그의 업적을 인정하여, 04Mr. Meyers는 10,000 달러의 상금은 물론이고 훈장도 받을 것입니다. 하지만 먼저, 06Mr. Meyers가 프로젝트에 도움을 준 동료들에게 감사를 표하기 위해 짧은 연설을 하고자 합니다. 그에게 큰 박수를 보내줍시다.

04 주제 문제
해설 어떤 종류의 행사가 진행되고 있는가?
(A) 무역 박람회
(B) 은퇴 축하연
(C) 시상식
(D) 극장 개장식

해설 진행되고 있는 행사의 종류를 묻는 문제이므로, 지문의 초반을 반드시 듣는다. "Mr. Meyers has been selected to receive the Designer of the Year Prize"라며 Mr. Meyers가 올해의 디자이너 상을 받도록 선정되었다고 한 뒤, "Mr. Meyers will be given a medal as well as a cash prize"라며 그는 훈장과 상금을 받을 것이라고 하였다. 이를 통해 시상식이 열리고 있음을 알 수 있다. 따라서 (C)가 정답이다.

05 특정 세부 사항 문제
해설 화자는 Daryl Meyers에 대해 무엇을 칭찬하는가?
(A) 유명한 건물 디자인을 연구한 것
(B) 인기 있는 장치를 발명한 것
(C) 새로운 소재로 실험한 것
(D) 혁신적인 디자인을 만들어낸 것

해설 질문의 핵심 어구(praise Daryl Meyers)와 관련된 내용을 주의 깊게 듣는다. "the groundbreaking design of the Lower Town Theater deserves special praise"라며 Daryl Meyers의 획기적인 설계 방식은 특별한 찬사를 받을 만하다고 하였다. 따라서 (D)가 정답이다.

어휘 experiment v. 실험하다

06 이유 문제
해설 Daryl Meyers는 왜 연설을 할 것인가?
(A) 그의 경력에 대해 설명하기 위해
(B) 그의 동료들에게 감사를 표하기 위해
(C) 건축 회사를 칭찬하기 위해
(D) 향후 프로젝트를 논의하기 위해

해설 질문의 핵심 어구(give a talk)와 관련된 내용을 주의 깊게 듣는다. "Mr. Meyers would like to say a few words to thank some of his colleagues"라며 Mr. Meyers가 동료들에게 감사를 표하기 위해 짧은 연설을 하고자 한다고 하였다. 따라서 (B)가 정답이다.

어휘 acknowledge v. 감사를 표하다, 인정하다

> Paraphrasing
> thank ~ colleagues 동료들에게 감사를 표하다
> → acknowledge ~ coworkers 동료들에게 감사를 표하다

기출 유형 2 강연

Example 🎧 미국   p.120
해설
01-03번은 다음 설명에 관한 문제입니다.

모두 환영합니다. 제 이름은 Lana이고, 01저는 오늘 저녁에 자연 풍경을 그리는 법을 가르쳐 드릴 것입니다. 여러분 중 많은 분들이 그림에 처음이시기 때문에, 제가 그 과정의 각 단계를 안내해드리겠습니다. 수업은 약 2시간 동안 진행될 것이며, 다 하시면 02여러분의 그림을 집으로 가져가셔도 됩니다. 음... 03나가시기 전에 앞치마들과 도구들을 교실 문 근처의 탁자 위에 반드시 올려놓으세요. 지금까지 질문 있으신가요?

어휘 scene n. 풍경 approximately adv. 약, 대략 process n. 과정
apron n. 앞치마 head out 나가다, 향하다

01
해설 화자는 누구인 것 같은가?
(A) 사진가
(B) 미술관 주인
(C) 강사
(D) 기계 조작자

02
해설 청자들은 무엇을 집으로 가져갈 수 있는가?
(A) 미술품
(B) 소책자
(C) 자격증
(D) 사진

03
해설 화자는 청자들에게 무엇을 하라고 상기시키는가?
(A) 도구들을 조심스럽게 사용한다.
(B) 기념품들을 구매한다.
(C) 탁자들을 재배열한다.
(D) 물건들을 두고 간다.

토익실전문제   p.121

| 01 (C) | 02 (A) | 03 (B) | 04 (B) | 05 (D) |
| 06 (B) |

[01-03] 🎧 영국
Questions 01-03 refer to the following talk.

> 01**In today's class, we're going to focus on taking pictures of the dishes that you order in restaurants.**

It seems like social media is flooded with these types of images. So for yours to stand out, they must be perfect. ⁰²**The most important thing to consider is the lighting. Whether the dish is illuminated by soft candlelight, the harsh glare from fluorescent bulbs, or something in-between determines the filter you should use.** I'll now show you several pictures that illustrate my point. ⁰³**Just give me a minute to get the overhead projector in position on the table and turn it on.**

flood v. 넘치다, 가득 차게 하다 stand out 돋보이다
illuminate v. 비추다, 밝히다 fluorescent bulb 형광등
determine v. 결정하다 illustrate v. 설명하다

해석
01-03번은 다음 담화에 관한 문제입니다.
⁰¹오늘 수업에서는 여러분이 식당에서 주문하는 음식의 사진을 찍는 것에 중점을 두겠습니다. 소셜 미디어가 이런 종류의 이미지로 넘쳐나는 것 같습니다. 그래서 여러분의 사진이 돋보이려면 완벽해야 합니다. ⁰²가장 중요하게 고려해야 할 것은 조명입니다. 요리가 은은한 촛불로 비쳐지는지, 형광등의 강한 빛으로 비쳐지는지, 아니면 그 중간 정도인지에 따라 사용해야 할 필터가 결정됩니다. 이제 제 요점을 설명하는 몇 가지 사진을 보여드리겠습니다. ⁰³제가 오버헤드 프로젝터를 탁자 위 제 위치에 설치하고 켜기 위해 잠시만 시간을 주세요.

01 특정 세부 사항 문제
해석 화자가 논의할 사진 촬영의 종류는 무엇인가?
(A) 꽃
(B) 패션
(C) 음식
(D) 여행

해설 질문의 핵심 어구(photography ~ discuss)와 관련된 내용을 주의 깊게 듣는다. "In today's class, we're going to focus on taking pictures of the dishes that you order in restaurants."라며 오늘 수업에서는 식당에서 주문하는 음식의 사진을 찍는 것에 중점을 두겠다고 하였다. 이를 통해 화자가 음식 사진 촬영에 대해 논의할 것을 알 수 있다. 따라서 (C)가 정답이다.

02 언급 문제
해석 화자는 무엇이 가장 중요한 고려 사항이라고 말하는가?
(A) 광원의 종류
(B) 물체의 위치
(C) 색상의 밝기
(D) 배경 품목의 개수

해설 질문의 핵심 어구(most important consideration)와 관련된 내용을 주의 깊게 듣는다. "The most important thing to consider is the lighting. Whether ~ by soft candlelight, the harsh glare from fluorescent bulbs, or something in-between determines the filter you should use."라며 가장 중요하게 고려해야 할 것은 조명이라고 한 후, 요리가 은은한 촛불로 비쳐지는지, 형광등의 강한 빛으로 비쳐지는지, 아니면 그 중간 정도인지에 따라 사용해야 할 필터가 결정된다고 하였다. 이를 통해 광원의 종류가 가장 중요한 고려 사항임을 알 수 있다. 따라서 (A)가 정답이다.

어휘 brightness n. 밝기

03 다음에 할 일 문제
해석 화자는 다음에 무엇을 할 것인가?
(A) 유인물을 배부한다.
(B) 장치를 설치한다.
(C) 탁자를 옮긴다.
(D) 이미지를 인쇄한다.

해설 지문의 마지막 부분을 주의 깊게 듣는다. "Just give me a minute to get the overhead projector in position on the table and turn it on."이라며 오버헤드 프로젝터를 탁자 위 제 위치에 설치하고 켜기 위해 잠시 시간을 달라고 하였다. 따라서 (B)가 정답이다.

Paraphrasing
overhead projector 오버헤드 프로젝터 → device 장치

[04-06] 캐나다
Questions 04-06 refer to the following instructions.

Welcome to the Madison Community Center's weekend gardening workshop. ⁰⁴**Today, I'll be explaining how to get rid of harmful insects that can destroy your plants.** We'll look at a variety of effective pesticides, including organic ones that don't harm the environment. And I'll explain how to apply these to get the best results. ⁰⁵**After our lunch break, we'll head out to the center's garden so that you can have the chance to try the method you will learn today.** Of course, ⁰⁶**I'll provide you with rubber gloves and a face mask to protect you from the pesticides.** OK, let's get started.

get rid of ~을 제거하다 harmful adj. 해로운 destroy v. 파괴하다
pesticide n. 살충제 rubber n. 고무

해석
04-06번은 다음 설명에 관한 문제입니다.
Madison 커뮤니티 센터의 주말 원예 워크숍에 오신 것을 환영합니다. ⁰⁴오늘은 여러분의 식물을 파괴할 수 있는 해충을 제거하는 방법에 대해 설명해 드리겠습니다. 환경에 해를 끼치지 않는 유기농 제품을 포함하여 다양한 효과적인 살충제를 살펴볼 것입니다. 그리고 최상의 결과를 얻기 위해 이것들을 적용하는 방법을 설명해 드리겠습니다. ⁰⁵점심 식사 후에는 센터의 정원으로 나가서 오늘 배우실 방법을 시도해 볼 기회를 갖게 될 것입니다. 물론, ⁰⁶살충제로부터 여러분을 보호하기 위해 고무장갑과 마스크를 제공해 드리겠습니다. 좋아요, 시작합시다.

04 주제 문제
해석 워크숍의 주제는 무엇인가?
(A) 토양 품질
(B) 해충 방제
(C) 정원 설계
(D) 꽃 선택

해설 담화의 주제를 묻는 문제이므로, 지문의 초반을 반드시 듣는다. "Today, I'll be explaining how to get rid of harmful insects that can destroy your plants."라며 오늘은 식물을 파괴할 수 있는 해충을 제거하는 방법에 대해 설명하겠다고 하였다. 따라서 (B)가 정답이다.

05 특정 세부 사항 문제
해석 청자들은 점심 식사 후에 무엇을 할 것인가?
(A) 영상을 시청한다.
(B) 시험을 본다.
(C) 장소를 둘러본다.
(D) 기법을 시도한다.

해설 질문의 핵심 어구(after lunch)와 관련된 내용을 주의 깊게 듣는다. "After our lunch break, we'll head out to the center's garden so that you can have the chance to try the method you will learn today."라며 점심 식사 후에 센터의 정원으로 나가서 오늘 배울 방법을 시도해 볼 기회를 갖게 될 것이라고 하였다. 따라서 (D)가 정답이다.

06 특정 세부 사항 문제
해석 화자에 따르면, 청자들은 무엇을 받을 것인가?
(A) 원예 도구
(B) 보호 장비
(C) 하이킹 장비
(D) 보관 용기

해설 질문의 핵심 어구(receive)와 관련된 내용을 주의 깊게 듣는다. "I'll provide you with rubber gloves and a face mask to protect you from the pesticides."라며 살충제로부터 보호하기 위해 고무장갑과 마스크를 제공할 것이라고 하였다. 따라서 (B)가 정답이다.

어휘 **storage** n. 보관, 저장

HACKERS TEST p.122

01 (C)	02 (A)	03 (B)	04 (C)	05 (A)
06 (A)	07 (B)	08 (D)	09 (B)	10 (A)
11 (D)	12 (B)	13 (B)	14 (D)	15 (C)
16 (A)	17 (D)	18 (A)	19 (B)	20 (B)
21 (C)				

[01-03] 미국

Questions 01-03 refer to the following talk.

⁰¹**Welcome to our workshop on merchandising displays.** My name is Rebecca Chambers, and I'm a merchandising consultant at the National Retailer Association. Our workshop will last for one day, and ⁰²**my hope is that it will help you all come up with successful ways of showcasing products in your own small businesses.** This morning, we will begin by studying some successful merchandise displays. ⁰³**In the afternoon, we will separate into small groups to think of ways to attractively arrange products.** Does anyone have any questions so far?

merchandising n. 판매 **showcase** v. 전시하다, 진열하다
attractively adv. 매력적으로 **arrange** v. 배치하다

해석
01-03번은 다음 담화에 관한 문제입니다.
⁰¹판매 진열에 관한 저희 워크숍에 오신 것을 환영합니다. 제 이름은 Rebecca Chambers이며, 저는 전국 소매업 협회의 상품 컨설턴트입니다. 저희 워크숍은 하루 동안 진행될 것이며, ⁰²이 워크숍이 여러분 모두가 여러분의 소규모 사업체에서 제품을 전시하는 성공적인 방법들을 찾는 데 도움이 되기를 바랍니다. 오늘 아침에는, 성공적인 제품 전시의 몇몇 사례들을 살펴보는 것으로 시작할 것입니다. ⁰³오후에는 소규모 그룹으로 나누어서 제품들을 매력적으로 배치하는 방법을 생각해 볼 것입니다. 지금까지 질문 있으신 분 계신가요?

01 목적 문제
해석 담화의 주된 목적은 무엇인가?
(A) 초청 연설자를 소개하기 위해
(B) 참가자들에게 일정 변경을 알리기 위해
(C) 워크숍의 개요를 제공하기 위해
(D) 새로운 가게 컨셉을 설명하기 위해

해설 담화의 목적을 묻는 문제이므로, 지문의 초반을 반드시 듣는다. "Welcome to our workshop on merchandising displays."라며 판매 진열에 관한 워크숍에 온 것을 환영한다고 한 뒤, 워크숍이 어떻게 진행될지 소개하는 내용으로 이어지고 있다. 따라서 (C)가 정답이다.

어휘 **inform** v. 알리다 **overview** n. 개요

02 청자 문제
해석 청자들은 누구인 것 같은가?
(A) 사업주들
(B) 일자리 지원자들
(C) 실내 장식가들
(D) 광고 회사 임원들

해설 지문에서 신분 및 직업과 관련된 표현을 놓치지 않고 듣는다. "my hope is that it will help ~ in your own small businesses"라며 워크숍이 청자들의 소규모 사업체에 도움이 되기를 바란다고 하였으므로 청자들이 사업주들임을 알 수 있다. 따라서 (A)가 정답이다.

03 다음에 할 일 문제
해석 청자들은 오후에 무엇을 할 것인가?
(A) 초청 연설자에게 질문을 한다.
(B) 그룹 활동에 참여한다.
(C) 지난 전시들의 사례들을 살펴본다.
(D) 백화점을 견학한다.

해설 질문의 핵심 어구(in the afternoon)가 언급된 주변을 주의 깊게 듣는다. "In the afternoon, we will separate into small groups to think of ways to attractively arrange products."라며 오후에는 소규모 그룹으로 나누어서 가게의 제품들을 매력적으로 배치하는 방법을 생각해 볼 것이라고 하였다. 따라서 (B)가 정답이다.

어휘 **take part in** ~에 참여하다

[04-06] 캐나다

Questions 04-06 refer to the following talk.

I'm pleased to give Greiss Corporation's Employee of the Year Award to Dianne Littleton. ⁰⁴**Ms. Littleton, the current manager of our public relations department**, has been working at Greiss for 20 years. She's being recognized for the successful publicity campaign she organized for us this year. ⁰⁵**It has attracted a lot of media coverage and increased product sales.** ⁰⁶**Ms. Littleton, please come up and say a few words.**

current adj. 현재의 **public relations** 홍보 **publicity** n. 홍보
organize v. 준비하다 **attract** v. 불러일으키다 **coverage** n. 보도

해석
04-06번은 다음 담화에 관한 문제입니다.
저는 Dianne Littleton에게 Greiss사의 올해의 직원상을 수여하게 되어 기쁩니다. ⁰⁴현재 저희 홍보 부서 관리자인 Ms. Littleton은 Greiss사에서 20년 동안 일해 왔습니다. 그녀는 올해 우리를 위해 준비했던 성공적인 홍보 캠페인으로 상을 받게 되었습니다. ⁰⁵그것은 많은 언론 보도를 불러일으켰고, 제품 판매도 증가시켰습니다. ⁰⁶Ms. Littleton, 올라오셔서 몇 마디 말씀해 주세요.

04 특정 세부 사항 문제
해석 Ms. Littleton은 누구인 것 같은가?
(A) 마케팅 컨설턴트
(B) 금융 고문
(C) 부서장
(D) 개인 비서

해설 질문의 핵심 어구(Ms. Littleton)가 언급된 주변을 주의 깊게 듣는다. "Ms. Littleton, the current manager of our public relations department"라며 현재 홍보 부서 관리자인 Ms. Littleton이라고 하였다. 따라서 (C)가 정답이다.

어휘 **advisor** n. 고문, 조언자 **personal assistant** 개인 비서

05 언급 문제
해석 홍보 캠페인에 대해 화자는 무엇을 말하는가?
(A) 영업 실적을 늘렸다.
(B) 회사가 상을 받게 했다.
(C) 예산을 초과했다.
(D) 소셜 미디어에서 시행되었다.

해설 질문의 핵심 어구(publicity campaign)가 언급된 주변을 주의 깊게 듣는다. "It[publicity campaign] has attracted a lot of media coverage and increased product sales."라며 홍보 캠페인이 많은 언론 보도를 불러일으켰고, 제품 판매도 증가시켰다고 하였다. 이를 통해, 홍보 캠페인이 영업 실적을 늘렸음을 알 수 있다. 따라서 (A)가 정답이다.

어휘 exceed v. 초과하다

06 다음에 할 일 문제
해석 다음에 무슨 일이 일어날 것 같은가?
(A) 연설이 제공될 것이다.
(B) 사진이 찍힐 것이다.
(C) 소개가 진행될 것이다.
(D) 수상자가 발표될 것이다.

해설 지문의 마지막 부분을 주의 깊게 듣는다. "Ms. Littleton, please come up and say a few words."라며 Ms. Littleton에게 올라와서 몇 마디 말해 달라고 하였다. 따라서 (A)가 정답이다.

[07-09] 🎧 미국
Questions 07-09 refer to the following instructions.

> ⁰⁷**I'm pleased to welcome all of you to Coral Software. In today's session, you will be introduced to the company's policies as well as your duties here.** To begin with, there are some forms on the table in front of me. ⁰⁸**You must provide all of the information requested.** After that, a member of the human resources department will explain each section of the employee manual. ⁰⁹**Please note that although the e-mail I sent you earlier stated that the head of HR, Jenna Coyle, would give this presentation, she is unfortunately ill today. Instead, her assistant will handle this.**
>
> duty n. 직무   explain v. 설명하다   ill adj. 아픈   instead adv. 대신
> assistant n. 조수, 보조원

해석
07-09번은 다음 설명에 관한 문제입니다.
⁰⁷여러분 모두를 Coral 소프트웨어사에 맞이하게 되어 기쁩니다. 오늘 세션에서는 여러분의 여기서의 직무뿐만 아니라 회사의 정책에 대해 소개받으실 것입니다. 우선, 제 앞에 있는 탁자에 몇 가지 양식이 있습니다. ⁰⁸여러분은 요청된 모든 정보를 제공하셔야 합니다. 그 후에, 인사부 직원이 직원 매뉴얼의 각 섹션을 설명해 줄 것입니다. ⁰⁹제가 앞서 보낸 이메일에는 인사부장 Jenna Coyle이 이 발표를 맡을 것이라고 했지만, 그녀가 안타깝게도 오늘 아프다는 점을 참고해 주세요. 대신, 그녀의 조수가 이것을 맡을 것입니다.

07 청자 문제
해석 청자들은 누구인 것 같은가?
(A) 포커스 그룹 일원들
(B) 오리엔테이션 참석자들
(C) 구직자들
(D) 회사 주주들

해설 지문에서 신분 및 직업과 관련된 표현을 놓치지 않고 듣는다. "I'm pleased to welcome all of you to Coral Software."라며 여러분 모두를 Coral 소프트웨어사에 맞이하게 되어 기쁘다고 한 후, "In today's session, you will be introduced to the company's policies as well as your duties here."라며 오늘 세션에서는 회사 정책과 직무에 대해 소개할 것이라고 한 것을 통해, 청자들이 오리엔테이션에 참석한 신입 직원들임을 알 수 있다. 따라서 (B)가 정답이다.

어휘 shareholder n. 주주

08 의도 파악 문제
해석 화자는 "제 앞에 있는 탁자에 몇 가지 양식이 있습니다"라고 말할 때 무엇을 의미하는가?
(A) 연구가 실시될 것이다.
(B) 청자들은 파일을 인쇄해야 한다.
(C) 청자들은 시험을 봐야 한다.
(D) 서류 작업이 완료되어야 한다.

해설 질문의 인용어구(there are some forms on the table in front of me)가 언급된 주변을 주의 깊게 듣는다. "You must provide all of the information requested."라며 청자들은 요청된 모든 정보를 제공해야 한다고 하였다. 이는 청자들이 양식에 정보를 기입해야 한다는 것이므로, 서류 작업이 완료되어야 한다는 것임을 알 수 있다. 따라서 (D)가 정답이다.

09 특정 세부 사항 문제
해석 화자에 따르면, 무엇이 변경되었는가?
(A) 장소
(B) 발표자
(C) 주제
(D) 일정표

해설 질문의 핵심 어구(changed)와 관련된 내용을 주의 깊게 듣는다. "Please note that although the e-mail I sent you earlier stated that the head of HR, Jenna Coyle, would give this presentation, ~. Instead, her assistant will handle this."라며 이메일에는 인사부장 Jenna Coyle이 발표를 맡을 것이라고 했지만, 그녀가 아파서 대신 그녀의 조수가 맡을 것이라고 하였다. 따라서 (B)가 정답이다.

[10-12] 🎧 호주
Questions 10-12 refer to the following lecture.

> ¹⁰**Today, our lesson will be about plants that are native to our region.** ¹¹**I originally planned for us to visit Lansdowne Park, where several of these species grow. But unfortunately, we will have to remain inside** today because of the heavy rain. Don't worry, though . . . I have an extensive collection of photographs for you to look at. They show many specimens in the various stages of their life cycles. ¹²**Just give me a minute to shut off the overhead lights**, and then we will begin.
>
> region n. 지역   species n. 종   extensive adj. 광범위한
> specimen n. 표본   various adj. 다양한   shut off ~을 끄다

해석
10-12번은 다음 강의에 관한 문제입니다.
¹⁰오늘 우리의 수업은 우리 지역에 자생하는 식물에 관한 것이 될 것입니다. ¹¹원래 저는 이러한 종들이 자라는 Lansdowne 공원을 방문하는 것을 계획했습니다. 하지만 안타깝게도, 오늘은 폭우 때문에 실내에 머물러야 할 것입니다. 하지만 걱정하지 마세요... 여러분이 볼 수 있는 광범위한 사진 모음집이 있습니다. 그것들은 여러 생애 주기의 다양한 단계에 있는 많은 표본들을 보여줍니다. ¹²제가 천장 조명을 끄는 데 잠시만 시간을 주세요, 그런 다음 우리는 시작하겠습니다.

10 주제 문제
해석 수업은 주로 무엇에 관한 것인가?
(A) 자생 식물
(B) 농업 방법

(C) 지역 생태계
(D) 환경적 위험

해설 강의의 주제를 묻는 문제이므로, 지문의 초반을 반드시 듣는다. "Today, our lesson will be about plants that are native to our region."이라며 오늘 수업은 우리 지역에 자생하는 식물에 관한 것이 될 것이라고 하였다. 따라서 (A)가 정답이다.

어휘 **agricultural** adj. 농업의 **ecosystem** n. 생태계

11 특정 세부 사항 문제
해설 오늘 수업은 강사가 계획했던 것과 어떻게 다른가?
(A) 초청 연사가 특별히 포함될 것이다.
(B) 더 많은 학생들이 참여할 것이다.
(C) 더 일찍 끝날 것이다.
(D) 실내에서 진행될 것이다.

해설 질문의 핵심 어구(different from what the instructor planned)와 관련된 내용을 주의 깊게 듣는다. "I originally planned for us to visit Lansdowne Park, where several of these species grow. But unfortunately, we will have to remain inside"라며 원래는 이러한 종들이 자라는 Lansdowne 공원을 방문하는 것을 계획했지만, 안타깝게도 실내에 머물러야 할 것이라고 하였다. 따라서 (D)가 정답이다.

Paraphrasing
inside 실내에 → indoors 실내에서

12 다음에 할 일 문제
해설 화자는 다음에 무엇을 할 것인가?
(A) 애플리케이션을 설치한다.
(B) 불을 끈다.
(C) 사진을 배부한다.
(D) 과제를 수집한다.

해설 지문의 마지막 부분을 주의 깊게 듣는다. "Just give me a minute to shut off the overhead lights"라며 천장 조명을 끄는 데 잠시만 시간을 달라고 하였다. 따라서 (B)가 정답이다.

[13-15] 🎧 영국
Questions 13-15 refer to the following instructions.

¹³It has come to my attention that some of you are not properly following the procedures to be reimbursed for travel expenses. So I want to briefly review the steps. Everyone is required to record travel costs in an expense report. ¹⁴The report must include details on your method of travel, where you stayed, and whether you rented a vehicle. However, you don't need to include the cost of meals, as you will have a fixed daily budget. ¹⁵A manual with further information about the procedures can be found on the company's Web site, so please download a copy.

properly adv. 정확히, 적당히   **procedure** n. 절차   **reimburse** v. 상환하다
briefly adv. 간단하게   **expense** n. 경비   **fixed** adj. 고정된

해설
13-15번은 다음 설명에 관한 문제입니다.

¹³여러분 일부가 출장 경비 상환을 위한 절차를 정확히 따르지 않는다는 점이 저의 주의를 끌었습니다. 그래서 저는 그 단계들을 간단하게 되새기고자 합니다. 모두 출장 경비를 경비 보고서에 기록할 것을 요구받습니다. ¹⁴보고서에는 이동 수단, 어디에 묵었는지, 그리고 차량을 빌렸는지에 대한 세부 사항이 포함되어야 합니다. 하지만, 식사 비용은 포함할 필요가 없는데, 그것들은 고정된 일일 예산으로 정해져 있기 때문입니다. ¹⁵절차에 대한 더 많은 정보가 담긴 안내서는 회사 웹사이트에서 찾을 수 있으므로, 사본을 다운로드 하시기 바랍니다.

13 주제 문제
해설 화자는 주로 무엇에 관해 논의하고 있는가?
(A) 발표를 위한 지침
(B) 경비 상환을 위한 규정
(C) 행사 장소로 가는 길
(D) 고객의 요청 사항

해설 설명의 주제를 묻는 문제이므로, 지문의 초반을 반드시 듣는다. "It has come to my attention that some of you are not properly following our procedure to be reimbursed for travel expenses. So I want to briefly review the steps."라며 여러분 일부가 출장 경비 상환을 위한 절차를 적절하게 따르지 않고 있으니, 그 단계들을 되새기고자 한다고 하였다. 따라서 (B)가 정답이다.

14 특정 세부 사항 문제
해설 화자에 따르면, 보고서에는 무엇이 포함되어야 하는가?
(A) 분기별 예산
(B) 판매 예측
(C) 식사 비용
(D) 출장 세부 사항

해설 질문의 핵심 어구(included in a report)와 관련된 내용을 주의 깊게 듣는다. "The report must include details on your method of travel, where you stayed, and whether you rented a vehicle."이라며 보고서에는 이동 수단, 어디에 묵었는지, 그리고 차량을 빌렸는지에 대한 세부 사항이 포함되어야 한다고 하였다. 따라서 (D)가 정답이다.

어휘 **quarterly** adj. 분기별의   **forecast** n. 예측, 예상

15 이유 문제
해설 청자들은 왜 웹사이트에 방문할 것인가?
(A) 관리자들을 위한 제안을 남기기 위해
(B) 워크숍에 등록하기 위해
(C) 문서의 사본을 얻기 위해
(D) 직원 복지 혜택에 등록하기 위해

해설 질문의 핵심 어구(visit a Web site)와 관련된 내용을 주의 깊게 듣는다. "A manual with further information about the procedures can be found on the company's Web site, so please download a copy."라며 절차에 대한 더 많은 정보가 담긴 안내서는 회사 웹사이트에서 찾을 수 있으므로, 사본을 다운로드하라고 하였다. 따라서 (C)가 정답이다.

[16-18] 🎧 캐나다
Questions 16-18 refer to the following talk.

I'm pleased to see all of you at the third annual 3D Printer Expo. ¹⁶I was shocked to hear that over 900 people came to this year's event. That's almost double last year's number! This shows that interest in these amazing devices is rising. Our first presentation today will be by Mike Roberts of Neo Technologies. ¹⁷In a few minutes, he will give you the chance to see his company's newest product in action. But before he takes the stage, I have a brief announcement. ¹⁸Some of you were not given a gift bag when you entered. Please stop by the information desk in the lobby.

double v. 두 배이다   **rise** v. 증가하다   **in action** 작동하는
brief adj. 간단한, 짧은

해설
16-18번은 다음 담화에 관한 문제입니다.

여러분 모두를 제3회 연례 3D 프린터 박람회에서 뵙게 되어 기쁩니다. ¹⁶저는 올해 행사에 900명이 넘는 사람들이 왔다는 소식을 듣고 충격을 받았습니다

다. 그것은 작년 인원수의 거의 두 배입니다! 이것은 이 놀라운 기기에 대한 관심이 증가하고 있다는 것을 보여줍니다. 오늘의 첫 번째 발표는 Neo 기술사의 Mike Roberts가 맡을 것입니다. ¹⁷그는 몇 분 후 여러분들에게 그의 회사의 최신 제품이 작동하는 것을 볼 기회를 제공할 것입니다. 하지만 그가 무대에 오르기 전에, 간단한 공지가 있습니다. ¹⁸여러분들 중 몇몇은 입장할 때 기념품 가방을 받지 못했습니다. 로비에 있는 안내 데스크에 들러주시기 바랍니다.

16 특정 세부 사항 문제
해석 화자는 무엇에 놀랐는가?
  (A) 참가자 수
  (B) 장소의 크기
  (C) 행사의 기간
  (D) 표의 이용 가능성

해설 질문의 핵심 어구(surprised about)와 관련된 내용을 주의 깊게 듣는다. "I was shocked to hear that over 900 people came to this year's event. That's almost double last year's number!"라며 올해 행사에 900명이 넘는 사람들이 왔다는 소식을 듣고 충격을 받았으며, 그것은 작년 인원수의 거의 두 배라고 하였다. 따라서 (A)가 정답이다.

17 다음에 할 일 문제
해석 몇 분 후에 무슨 일이 일어날 것인가?
  (A) 주최자가 소개될 것이다.
  (B) 상이 수여될 것이다.
  (C) 투어가 시작될 것이다.
  (D) 시연이 시작될 것이다.

해설 질문의 핵심 어구(in a few minutes)와 관련된 내용을 주의 깊게 듣는다. "In a few minutes, he will give you the chance to see his company's newest product in action."이라며 몇 분 후에 회사의 최신 제품이 작동하는 것을 볼 기회를 제공할 것이라고 하였다. 따라서 (D)가 정답이다.

어휘 commence v. 시작되다

18 의도 파악 문제
해석 화자는 왜 "로비에 있는 안내 데스크에 들러주시기 바랍니다"라고 말하는가?
  (A) 품목을 이용할 수 있음을 나타내기 위해
  (B) 도움을 받는 방법을 설명하기 위해
  (C) 표를 구매할 수 있는 장소를 명시하기 위해
  (D) 직원의 위치를 명시하기 위해

해설 질문의 인용어구(Please stop by the information desk in the lobby)가 언급된 주변을 주의 깊게 듣는다. "Some of you were not given a gift bag when you entered. Please stop by the information desk in the lobby."라며 여러분들 중 몇몇은 입장할 때 기념품 가방을 받지 못했으니 로비에 있는 안내 데스크에 들러달라고 한 것을 통해, 못 받은 기념품 가방이 안내 데스크에서 이용 가능하다는 것임을 알 수 있다. 따라서 (A)가 정답이다.

[19-21] 🎧 미국

Questions 19-21 refer to the following speech and award nominees.

¹⁹**I'm honored to have been selected as the winner of the Carter Award for Best Novel. As *Fallen Leaves* was my first novel**, writing and editing it seemed like an impossible task. ²⁰**But one of my former university professors, Elaine Morris, told me that this feeling was normal and that I should just focus on my goal. Her advice gave me the motivation I needed to finish.** I also have some great news to share. ²¹**There are now French, Spanish, and Italian versions of my book.** I just can't believe that people all over the world will be reading what I wrote. Thank you.

select v. 선정하다 **former** adj. 이전의 **focus on** ~에 집중하다
goal n. 목표 **motivation** n. 동기

해석
19-21번은 다음 연설과 수상 후보에 관한 문제입니다.

¹⁹저는 카터상 최우수 소설 부문 수상자로 선정된 것을 영광으로 생각합니다. *Fallen Leaves*는 제 첫 소설이었기 때문에, 그것을 쓰고 편집하는 것이 불가능한 일처럼 보였습니다. ²⁰하지만 제 이전 대학 교수님 중 한 분이신 Elaine Morris 교수님께서 이러한 감정은 정상적인 것이며 제 목표에만 집중해야 한다고 말씀해 주셨습니다. 그분의 조언이 제가 완성하는 데 필요한 동기를 주었습니다. 또한 나눌 좋은 소식이 있습니다. ²¹이제 제 책의 프랑스어, 스페인어, 이탈리아어 버전이 나왔습니다. 전 세계 사람들이 제가 쓴 것을 읽게 된다는 것이 믿기지 않습니다. 감사합니다.

카터상 최우수 소설 부문 수상 후보자	
Kevin Peterson *This Old Life*	Jose Gomez *Win It All*
¹⁹Beth Anderson *Fallen Leaves*	Tara Choi *Away from Home*

19 시각 자료 문제
해석 시각 자료를 보아라. 누가 최우수 소설 부문 상을 받았는가?
  (A) Kevin Peterson
  (B) Beth Anderson
  (C) Jose Gomez
  (D) Tara Choi

해설 제시된 수상 후보의 정보를 확인한 후 질문의 핵심 어구(won the award for best novel)와 관련된 내용을 주의 깊게 듣는다. "I'm honored to have been selected as the winner of the Carter Award for Best Novel. As *Fallen Leaves* was my first novel"이라며 화자가 최우수 소설 부문 수상자로 선정되었는데 *Fallen Leaves*가 자신의 첫 소설이라고 하였다. 수상 후보에서 *Fallen Leaves*를 쓴 사람은 Beth Anderson임을 알 수 있다. 따라서 (B)가 정답이다.

20 특정 세부 사항 문제
해석 화자에게 동기를 부여한 것은 무엇인가?
  (A) 편집자의 피드백
  (B) 지도자의 조언
  (C) 친구의 지원
  (D) 동료의 모범

해설 질문의 핵심 어구(motivated the speaker)와 관련된 내용을 주의 깊게 듣는다. "But one of my former university professors, Elaine Morris, told me that ~. Her advice gave me the motivation I needed to finish."라며 목표에만 집중해야 한다고 말해준 대학 교수님의 조언이 소설을 완성하는 데 필요한 동기를 주었다고 하였다. 따라서 (B)가 정답이다.

어휘 support n. 지원

[Paraphrasing]
one of ~ professors 교수님 중 한 분 → instructor 지도자

21 언급 문제

해석 화자의 책에 대해 무엇이 언급되는가?
(A) 기사에서 다루어졌다.
(B) 삽화를 포함한다.
(C) 번역되었다.
(D) 실화에 기반한다.

해설 질문의 핵심 어구(speaker's book)와 관련된 내용을 주의 깊게 듣는다. "There are now French, Spanish, and Italian versions of my book."이라며 이제 자신의 책의 프랑스어, 스페인어, 이탈리아어 버전이 나왔다고 한 것을 통해, 책이 다른 언어로 번역되었다는 것을 알 수 있다. 따라서 (C)가 정답이다.

어휘 translate v. 번역하다　based on ~에 기반하는

DAY 19 방송 및 보도

기출 유형 1 방송

Example 호주　　　　　　　　　　　　　　p.124
해석
01-03번은 다음 방송에 관한 문제입니다.

여러분께서는 *Our Society*를 듣고 계십니다. 저는 여러분의 진행자인 James Ash입니다. 01오늘 방송에서는, 일반적인 미국인 식습관의 건강상 효과에 중점을 둘 것입니다. 저는 이 주제에 대해 영양 전문가인 Omani Khan과 이야기를 나눌 것입니다. 02Dr. Khan은 최근 *Health Today*지에 게재된 그녀의 기사에 관해 이야기할 것입니다. 03저희 웹사이트에서, 여러분은 성인들을 위한 그녀의 이상적인 주간 식단을 찾아보실 수 있습니다. 자유롭게 확인해 보세요.

어휘 host n. 진행자　health effect 건강상 효과　typical adj. 일반적인　diet n. 식습관　nutrition n. 영양　specialist n. 전문가　ideal adj. 이상적인　meal plan 식단

01
해석 방송은 주로 무엇에 관한 것인가?
(A) 여행
(B) 예술
(C) 건강
(D) 운동

02
해석 화자에 따르면, Dr. Khan은 최근에 무엇을 했는가?
(A) 기사를 썼다.
(B) 회의에 참석했다.
(C) 라디오 쇼를 시작했다.
(D) 학위를 수여받았다.

03
해석 청자들은 웹사이트에서 무엇을 찾을 수 있는가?
(A) 요리 영상
(B) 담화 대본
(C) 식단
(D) 행사 일정

토익실전문제　　　　　　　　　　　　　　p.125

| 01 (D) | 02 (A) | 03 (D) | 04 (B) | 05 (C) |
| 06 (B) |

[01-03] 영국
Questions 01-03 refer to the following podcast.

Welcome to the *Frequent Traveler* podcast. 01**Today, I'll be discussing Eastern Airline's recent decision to compensate passengers for delays of 30 minutes or more.** This policy change will be implemented on October 14. 02**According to Eastern Airline CEO Jacob Wilkins, it is a response to criticism by customers.** And there is now a growing demand for other airlines to develop similar regulations because passengers often do not reach their destinations on time. If you are interested in learning more, 03**the government has released a report comparing the performance of all airlines**. You can download a copy from my blog.

compensate v. 보상하다　implement v. 시행하다　criticism n. 비판
growing adj. 증가하는　reach v. 도착하다　on time 제시간에

해석
01-03번은 다음 팟캐스트에 관한 문제입니다.

Frequent Traveler 팟캐스트에 오신 것을 환영합니다. 01오늘 저는 Eastern 항공이 30분 이상 지연되는 경우 승객들에게 보상하기로 한 최근 결정에 대해 논의할 것입니다. 이 정책 변경은 10월 14일에 시행될 것입니다. 02Eastern 항공의 CEO인 Jacob Wilkins에 따르면, 이는 고객들의 비판에 대한 대응입니다. 그리고 승객들이 종종 제시간에 목적지에 도착하지 못하기 때문에 다른 항공사들도 비슷한 규정을 마련하려는 요구가 증가하고 있습니다. 더 알아보고 싶으시다면, 03정부에서 모든 항공사들의 성과를 비교한 보고서를 발표했습니다. 제 블로그에서 사본을 다운로드하실 수 있습니다.

01 주제 문제
해석 팟캐스트는 어떤 산업에 관한 것인가?
(A) 농업
(B) 건설
(C) 에너지
(D) 항공

해설 팟캐스트의 주제를 묻는 문제이므로, 지문의 초반을 반드시 듣는다. "Today, I'll be discussing Eastern Airline's recent decision to compensate passengers for delays of 30 minutes or more."라며 Eastern 항공이 30분 이상 지연되는 경우 승객들에게 보상하기로 한 최근 결정에 대해 논의할 것이라고 하였다. 이를 통해 팟캐스트가 항공 산업에 관한 것임을 알 수 있다. 따라서 (D)가 정답이다.

02 이유 문제
해석 왜 정책이 변경되었는가?
(A) 고객 불만을 처리하기 위해
(B) 운영 비용을 줄이기 위해
(C) 안전 기준을 충족하기 위해
(D) 시설 폐쇄를 방지하기 위해

해설 질문의 핵심 어구(policy been changed)와 관련된 내용을 주의 깊게 듣는다. "According to Eastern Airline CEO Jacob Wilkins, it is a response to criticism by customers."라며 Eastern 항공의 CEO Jacob Wilkins에 따르면, 정책 변경은 고객들의 비판에 대한 대응이라고 하였다. 따라서 (A)가 정답이다.

어휘 reduce v. 줄이다　meet v. 충족하다　prevent v. 방지하다　closure n. 폐쇄

[Paraphrasing]
response to criticism 비판에 대한 대응 → address ~ complaints 불만을 처리하다

03 특정 세부 사항 문제

해석 보고서에는 무엇이 포함되어 있는가?
(A) 혜택 요약
(B) 비용 계산
(C) 규정에 대한 개요
(D) 회사들의 비교

해설 질문의 핵심 어구(included in the report)와 관련된 내용을 주의 깊게 듣는다. "the government has released a report comparing the performance of all airlines"라며 정부에서 모든 항공사의 성과를 비교한 보고서를 발표했다고 하였다. 따라서 (D)가 정답이다.

어휘 summary n. 요약 calculation n. 계산 comparison n. 비교

[04-06] 캐나다
Questions 04-06 refer to the following broadcast.

In regional news, ⁰⁴the city of Townsend has experienced a dramatic increase in tourism because it served as the setting for the hit film *Crossing the River*. While this development is welcomed by local businesses, many residents are not pleased. ⁰⁵The main problem is that the city's streets are heavily congested by traffic, making it difficult for people to get around. Mayor Collins acknowledged the issue and said that the city government is gathering feedback before making a plan. ⁰⁶If you want to share your opinion, visit the Townsend city hall Web site. There is a questionnaire posted for residents to complete.

regional adj. 지역의 development n. 발전, 개발 pleased adj. 기쁜
heavily adv. 심하게 congested adj. 혼잡한 acknowledge v. 인정하다
questionnaire n. 설문지

해석
04-06번은 다음 방송에 관한 문제입니다.
지역 뉴스에서, ⁰⁴타운센드시는 히트작인 *Crossing the River*의 배경으로 사용되면서 관광객이 급격히 증가했습니다. 이러한 발전은 지역 사업체들에게는 환영받지만, 많은 주민들은 기쁘지 않습니다. ⁰⁵주요 문제는 도시의 거리가 교통으로 심하게 혼잡해져서 사람들이 돌아다니기 어렵다는 것입니다. Collins 시장은 이 문제를 인정하고 계획을 세우기 전에 시 정부가 의견을 모으고 있다고 말했습니다. ⁰⁶여러분의 의견을 공유하고 싶으시다면, 타운센드 시청 웹사이트를 방문하세요. 주민들이 작성할 설문지가 게시되어 있습니다.

04 이유 문제

해석 타운센드는 최근에 왜 유명해졌는가?
(A) 관광 명소를 열었다.
(B) 영화에 등장했다.
(C) 국제적인 행사를 개최했다.
(D) 마케팅 캠페인을 시작했다.

해설 질문의 핵심 어구(Townsend become famous)와 관련된 내용을 주의 깊게 듣는다. "the city of Townsend has experienced a dramatic increase in tourism because it served as the setting for the hit film"이라며 타운센드시는 히트작의 배경으로 사용되면서 관광객이 급격히 증가했다고 하였다. 따라서 (B)가 정답이다.

05 특정 세부 사항 문제

해석 주민들은 무엇에 대해 불만족스러워하는가?
(A) 높은 가격
(B) 과도한 소음
(C) 교통 체증
(D) 대기 오염

해설 질문의 핵심 어구(residents unhappy)와 관련된 내용을 주의 깊게 듣는다. "The main problem is that the city's streets are heavily congested by traffic, making it difficult for people to get around."라며 주요 문제는 도시의 거리가 교통으로 심하게 혼잡해져서 사람들이 돌아다니기 어렵다는 것이라고 하였다. 따라서 (C)가 정답이다.

어휘 excessive adj. 과도한

Paraphrasing
heavily congested by traffic 교통으로 심하게 혼잡한 → Traffic jams 교통 체증

06 특정 세부 사항 문제

해석 화자에 따르면, 청자들은 웹사이트에서 무엇을 할 수 있는가?
(A) 앱을 다운로드한다.
(B) 설문조사를 작성한다.
(C) 보고서를 읽는다.
(D) 지도를 확인한다.

해설 질문의 핵심 어구(Web site)가 언급된 주변을 주의 깊게 듣는다. "If you want to share your opinion, visit the Townsend city hall Web site. There is a questionnaire ~ to complete."이라며 의견을 공유하고 싶으면 웹사이트에 방문하면 되는데, 그곳에 주민들이 작성할 설문지가 게시되어 있다고 하였다. 따라서 (B)가 정답이다.

기출 유형 2 보도

Example 미국   p.126

해석
01-03번은 다음 뉴스 보도에 관한 문제입니다.

⁰¹이제 시에서 최근 발표한 전동 스쿠터에 대한 정책 변경에 관한 보도입니다. 벨뷰의 많은 사람들이 이 전동 스쿠터를 타기 시작했습니다. 하지만, 지난 몇 주 동안 몇 명의 운전자들이 부상을 입은 후, ⁰²/⁰³어제 시의회는 운전자들이 반드시 헬멧을 쓰고 자전거 전용도로만 이용해야 한다고 결정했습니다. 의회는 또한 이 기기들에 대해 시속 15킬로미터의 속도 제한을 정했습니다. ⁰³이 모든 것에도 불구하고, 그 제품을 파는 가게들 밖에는 여전히 긴 줄이 있습니다.

어휘 motorized adj. 전동의, 엔진이 달린 adjustment n. 변경, 수정
injure v. 부상을 입다 city council 시의회

01

해석 뉴스 보도의 주요 주제는 무엇인가?
(A) 지역 사회 축제
(B) 도로 폐쇄
(C) 교통 혼잡
(D) 정책 변경

02

해석 화자에 따르면, 운전자들은 무엇을 하도록 요청받는가?
(A) 안전 장비를 착용한다.
(B) 도시 보도에 머무른다.
(C) 어두워진 후 타는 것을 피한다.
(D) 그들의 기기들을 등록한다.

03

해석 화자는 "그 제품을 파는 가게들 밖에는 여전히 긴 줄이 있습니다"라고 말할 때 무엇을 의도하는가?
(A) 소비자들이 환불을 요구했다.
(B) 몇몇 지시들이 따라지지 않았다.
(C) 행사가 연기되었다.
(D) 규제들이 판매에 영향을 주지 않았다.

토익실전문제

p.127

01 (C)	02 (B)	03 (A)	04 (D)	05 (B)
06 (C)				

[01-03] 호주

Questions 01-03 refer to the following news report.

In a press conference on Monday, city council member Justin Faulk confirmed that Wheaton Avenue will reopen on June 17 as scheduled. ⁰¹This thoroughfare, which connects the suburb of Langford with the city center, is being converted from two lanes to four. ⁰²However, Mr. Faulk also revealed an unexpected problem. The $12 million set aside for the project is insufficient, and an additional $8 million is required. To reassure the public, Mr. Faulk promised that additional taxes would not be imposed to pay for the work. And he stated that ⁰³the city council will host an open session on May 25 to address questions from residents.

thoroughfare n. 간선 도로   suburb n. 교외 지역   convert v. 전환하다
reveal v. 밝히다   insufficient adj. 불충분한   impose v. 부과하다

해석
01-03번은 다음 뉴스 보도에 관한 문제입니다.
월요일 기자 회견에서, 시의회 의원 Justin Faulk는 Wheaton가가 예정대로 6월 17일에 재개통될 것이라고 확인했습니다. ⁰¹이 간선 도로는 랭포드 교외 지역과 도심을 연결하는 도로로, 2차선에서 4차선으로 전환될 것입니다. ⁰²그러나 Mr. Faulk는 또한 예상치 못한 문제를 밝혔습니다. 이 프로젝트를 위해 배정된 1,200만 달러가 불충분하며, 800만 달러가 추가로 필요합니다. 대중을 안심시키기 위해, Mr. Faulk는 이 작업에 비용을 지불하기 위한 추가 세금이 부과되지 않을 것이라고 약속했습니다. 그리고 그는 ⁰³시의회가 5월 25일에 주민들의 질문에 답하기 위한 공개 세션을 개최할 것이라고 말했습니다.

01 주제 문제
해석 뉴스 보도는 주로 무엇에 관한 것인가?
(A) 교외 지역의 개발
(B) 통행료 시행
(C) 도로 확장
(D) 다리 건설

해설 뉴스 보도의 주제를 묻는 문제이므로, 지문의 초반을 반드시 듣는다. "This thoroughfare, which connects the suburb of Langford with the city center, is being converted from two lanes to four."라며 간선 도로는 랭포드 교외 지역과 도심을 연결하는 도로로, 2차선에서 4차선으로 전환될 것이라고 한 후, 도로 공사 프로젝트에 대한 내용으로 지문이 이어지고 있다. 따라서 (C)가 정답이다.

어휘 toll n. 통행료

02 문제점 문제
해석 화자는 무슨 문제를 언급하는가?
(A) 일정이 변경될 것이다.
(B) 예산이 초과될 것이다.
(C) 세금이 인상될 것이다.
(D) 프로젝트가 취소될 것이다.

해설 질문의 핵심 어구(problem)와 관련된 내용을 주의 깊게 듣는다. "However, Mr. Faulk also revealed an unexpected problem. The $12 million set aside for the project is insufficient, and an additional $8 million is required."라며 Mr. Faulk가 예상치 못한 문제를 밝혔는데, 프로젝트를 위해 배정된 1,200만 달러가 불충분하며 800만 달러가 추가로 필요하다고 하였다. 따라서 (B)가 정답이다.

어휘 alter v. 변경하다   exceed v. 초과하다

03 다음에 할 일 문제
해석 5월 25일에 무슨 일이 일어날 것인가?
(A) 공개 회의
(B) 시 선거
(C) 개막식
(D) 자선 기금 모금 행사

해설 질문의 핵심 어구(May 25)가 언급된 주변을 주의 깊게 듣는다. "the city council will host an open session on May 25 to address questions from residents"라며 시의회가 5월 25일에 주민들의 질문에 답하기 위한 공개 세션을 개최할 것이라고 하였다. 따라서 (A)가 정답이다.

[04-06] 영국

Questions 04-06 refer to the following news report.

⁰⁴In business news, just-walk-out technology may soon replace traditional cashiers. In a store that utilizes this system, whatever merchandise customers leave with is detected by scanners and charged to their credit card. ⁰⁵Up until last year, this technology was not widely utilized. But over the past few months, it has attracted a lot of interest. Now, around 20 major retail chains use it. And there is the potential for more businesses to make the switch. ⁰⁶A report published by Anna Lewis of the National Retailer Association last month predicts that over 60 percent of stores will adopt just-walk-out technology in the coming year.

cashier n. 계산원   utilize v. 활용하다   detect v. 감지하다   switch n. 변화
predict v. 예측하다   adopt v. 채택하다

해석
04-06번은 다음 뉴스 보도에 관한 문제입니다.
⁰⁴비즈니스 뉴스에서는, 걸어 나가기만 하면 결제되는 기술이 곧 전통적인 계산원을 대체할지도 모릅니다. 이 시스템을 활용하는 매장에서는, 고객이 가져가는 어떠한 상품이라도, 스캐너에 의해 감지되어 신용카드에 청구됩니다. ⁰⁵작년까지만 해도 이 기술은 널리 활용되지 않았습니다. 하지만 지난 몇 달 동안, 이것은 많은 관심을 끌었습니다. 현재, 약 20개의 주요 소매 체인점들이 그것을 사용합니다. 그리고 더 많은 기업들이 변화할 가능성이 있습니다. ⁰⁶지난달 전국 소매 협회의 Anna Lewis가 발표한 보고서는 내년에 60퍼센트 이상 매장이 걸어 나가기만 하면 결제되는 기술을 채택할 것이라고 예측합니다.

04 주제 문제
해석 뉴스 보도는 주로 무엇에 관한 것인가?
(A) 기업 합병
(B) 사업 확장
(C) 보안 조치
(D) 결제 과정

해설 뉴스 보도의 주제를 묻는 문제이므로, 지문의 초반을 반드시 듣는다. "In business news, just-walk-out technology may soon replace traditional cashiers."라며 걸어 나가기만 하면 결제되는 기술이 곧 전통적인 계산원을 대체할지도 모른다고 한 후, 이 결제 기술에 대한 내용으로 지문이 이어지고 있다. 따라서 (D)가 정답이다.

05 의도 파악 문제
해석 화자는 왜 "현재, 약 20개의 주요 소매 체인점들이 그것을 사용합니다"라고 말하는가?

(A) 문제에 대한 해결책을 제안하기 위해
(B) 트렌드의 성장을 보여주기 위해
(C) 기술의 출처를 식별하기 위해
(D) 변화의 이유를 나타내기 위해

해설 질문의 인용어구(Now, around 20 major retail chains use it)가 언급된 주변을 주의 깊게 듣는다. "Up until last year, this technology was not widely utilized. But over the past few months, it has attracted a lot of interest."라며 작년까지만 해도 이 기술은 널리 활용되지 않았지만, 지난 몇 달 동안 많은 관심을 끌었다고 했으므로 이 기술에 대한 트렌드가 성장하고 있음을 보여주기 위해 현재 약 20개의 주요 소매 체인점들이 그것을 사용한다고 말했음을 알 수 있다. 따라서 (B)가 정답이다.

어휘 growth n. 성장 identify v. 식별하다

06 특정 세부 사항 문제
해석 Ms. Lewis는 지난달에 무엇을 했는가?
(A) 책을 출판했다.
(B) 연설을 했다.
(C) 보고서를 발표했다.
(D) 행사를 조직했다.

해설 질문의 핵심 어구(Ms. Lewis)가 언급된 주변을 주의 깊게 듣는다. "A report published by Anna Lewis of the National Retailer Association last month"라며 지난달 전국 소매 협회의 Anna Lewis가 발표한 보고서라고 하였다. 따라서 (C)가 정답이다.

HACKERS TEST   p.128

01 (C)	02 (C)	03 (A)	04 (C)	05 (B)
06 (C)	07 (D)	08 (A)	09 (B)	10 (B)
11 (A)	12 (C)	13 (C)	14 (D)	15 (A)
16 (D)	17 (A)	18 (C)	19 (A)	20 (B)
21 (B)				

[01-03] 호주
Questions 01-03 refer to the following podcast.

You're listening to *Classical Alive*. I'm your host, Liam Murphy, and ⁰¹**I'm interviewing renowned violinist Marcia Gray**. Ms. Gray is recognized across the globe for the many exceptional performances she has given as a member of the Harrisburg Symphony. ⁰²**If you visit her blog, you can watch short clips of her performances.** ⁰³**But today, we'll be discussing the music school Ms. Gray recently opened.** She hopes to teach the region's youth to appreciate and perform classical music. Welcome, Ms. Gray.

renowned adj. 유명한 recognize v. 인정하다 exceptional adj. 뛰어난
youth n. 청소년 appreciate v. 감상하다

해석
01-03번은 다음 팟캐스트에 관한 문제입니다.

여러분은 *Classical Alive*를 듣고 계십니다. 저는 진행자 Liam Murphy이며, ⁰¹저는 유명한 바이올리니스트인 Marcia Gray를 인터뷰할 것입니다. Ms. Gray는 Harrisburg 심포니의 일원으로서 많은 뛰어난 공연을 선보인 것으로 전 세계적으로 인정받고 있습니다. ⁰²그녀의 블로그를 방문하시면, 그녀의 공연들의 짧은 영상 클립들을 보실 수 있습니다. ⁰³하지만 오늘은 Ms. Gray가 최근에 개설한 음악 학교에 대해 이야기할 것입니다. 그녀는 이 지역의 청소년들이 클래식 음악을 감상하고 연주하는 법을 가르치기를 희망합니다. 환영합니다, Ms. Gray.

01 특정 세부 사항 문제
해석 Marcia Gray는 누구인가?
(A) 배우
(B) 안무가
(C) 음악가
(D) 운동선수

해설 질문의 핵심 어구(Marcia Gray)가 언급된 주변을 주의 깊게 듣는다. "I'm interviewing renowned violinist Marcia Gray"라며 유명한 바이올리니스트인 Marcia Gray를 인터뷰할 것이라고 하였다. 따라서 (C)가 정답이다.

Paraphrasing
violinist 바이올리니스트 → musician 음악가

02 이유 문제
해석 왜 청자들은 웹사이트를 방문하겠는가?
(A) 메시지를 읽기 위해
(B) 후기를 게시하기 위해
(C) 동영상을 시청하기 위해
(D) 수업에 등록하기 위해

해설 질문의 핵심 어구(visit a Web site)와 관련된 내용을 주의 깊게 듣는다. "If you visit her blog, you can watch short clips of her performances."라며 Ms. Gray의 블로그를 방문하면 그녀의 공연들의 짧은 영상 클립들을 볼 수 있다고 하였다. 따라서 (C)가 정답이다.

03 특정 세부 사항 문제
해석 화자에 따르면, Ms. Gray는 최근에 무엇을 했는가?
(A) 교육기관을 열었다.
(B) 상을 받았다.
(C) 텔레비전에 출연했다.
(D) 회고록을 출판했다.

해설 질문의 핵심 어구(recently do)와 관련된 내용을 주의 깊게 듣는다. "But today, we'll be discussing the music school Ms. Gray recently opened."라며 오늘은 Ms. Gray가 최근에 개설한 음악 학교에 대해 이야기할 것이라고 하였다. 따라서 (A)가 정답이다.

어휘 appear v. 출연하다, 나타나다 memoir n. 회고록, 전기

Paraphrasing
the music school ~ opened 개설한 음악 학교 → opened an academy 교육기관을 열었다

[04-06] 영국
Questions 04-06 refer to the following news report.

The Hearthside Orchestra announced today that ⁰⁴**it is going to postpone the start of its upcoming season. The decision comes as a result of months of contract negotiations** between the musicians and management. However, the news has relieved ⁰⁵**some fans, who were worried that the entire season would be called off**. The orchestra is scheduled to return to the stage in late fall. Its first show will be on November 11, and the orchestra will perform weekly until May 21. As there is much interest in this season, ⁰⁶**we recommend purchasing tickets well in advance of the show.**

negotiation n. 협상 management n. 경영진 relieve v. 안심시키다
call off 취소하다 recommend v. 권장하다

해석
04-06번은 다음 뉴스 보도에 관한 문제입니다.

Hearthside 교향악단은 오늘 ⁰⁴다가오는 공연의 시작을 연기할 것이라고 발표했습니다. 그 결정은 음악가들과 경영진 사이에 수개월 동안의 계약 협상의 결과로 내려진 것입니다. 하지만, 그 소식은 ⁰⁵시즌 전체가 취소될 것을 걱정했던 몇몇 팬들을 안심시켰습니다. 교향악단은 늦가을에 무대로 돌아올 예정입니다. 첫 번째 공연은 11월 11일이며, 5월 21일까지 매주 공연할 것입니다. 이번 시즌에 대한 관심이 크기 때문에, ⁰⁶티켓을 공연 전에 훨씬 미리 구입할 것을 권장합니다.

04 특정 세부 사항 문제
해석 무엇이 지연을 야기했는가?
(A) 일정의 겹침
(B) 부족한 자금
(C) 계약 문제
(D) 장소 보수

해설 질문의 핵심 어구(caused the delay)와 관련된 내용을 주의 깊게 듣는다. "it is going to postpone the start of its upcoming season. The decision comes as a result of months of contract negotiations"라며 다가오는 공연의 시작을 연기할 것이며, 이는 수개월 동안의 계약 협상의 결과로 인한 것이라고 하였다. 따라서 (C)가 정답이다.

05 이유 문제
해석 화자에 따르면, 몇몇 팬들은 왜 걱정했는가?
(A) 그들은 새로운 지휘자에 대해 확신이 없었다.
(B) 그들은 공연들이 취소될 것이라 예상했다.
(C) 그들은 부정확한 정보를 받았다.
(D) 그들은 주문하는 데 문제를 겪었다.

해설 질문의 핵심 어구(some fans concerned)와 관련된 내용을 주의 깊게 듣는다. "some fans, who were worried that the entire season would be called off"라며 몇몇 팬들이 시즌 전체가 취소될 것을 걱정했다고 하였다. 따라서 (B)가 정답이다.

어휘 uncertain adj. 불확실한   conductor n. 지휘자

Paraphrasing
be called off 취소되다 → be canceled 취소되다

06 제안 문제
해석 청자들은 무엇을 하도록 권유받는가?
(A) 앨범을 듣는다.
(B) 경영진에게 연락한다.
(C) 일찍 티켓을 산다.
(D) 애플리케이션을 다운로드한다.

해설 지문에서 제안과 관련된 표현이 포함된 문장을 주의 깊게 듣는다. "we recommend purchasing tickets well in advance of the show"라며 티켓을 공연 전에 훨씬 미리 구입할 것을 권장한다고 하였다. 따라서 (C)가 정답이다.

Paraphrasing
purchasing ~ well in advance 훨씬 미리 구입할 것 → Buy ~ early 일찍 사다

[07-09] 🎧 캐나다
Questions 07-09 refer to the following broadcast.

This is Manuel Larroga reporting from Central Park in Cebu City. ⁰⁷**Right now, the city is preparing for a major storm.** It's calm at the moment, but severe wind and rain are expected just two hours from now. The local government has asked residents to stay indoors until the storm ends. For public safety, ⁰⁸**the coastal highway and all beaches are closed. While this storm is expected to be rather strong**, it will probably last a short amount of time. ⁰⁹**Stay tuned for more updates after a quick commercial break.**

calm adj. 고요한, 잔잔한   severe adj. 극심한   coastal adj. 해안의
rather adv. 다소   commercial break 광고

해석
07-09번은 다음 방송에 관한 문제입니다.

세부시의 중앙 공원에서 전해드리고 있는 저는 Manuel Larroga입니다. ⁰⁷바로 지금, 도시는 큰 폭풍우를 대비하고 있습니다. 현재는 고요하지만, 지금으로부터 단지 2시간 후에는 극심한 바람과 비가 예상됩니다. 지역 정부는 주민들에게 폭풍우가 끝날 때까지 실내에 머물도록 요청했습니다. 공공 안전을 위해, ⁰⁸해안 고속도로와 모든 해변은 폐쇄되었습니다. 이 폭풍우는 다소 강할 것으로 예상되지만, 그것은 아마 짧은 시간만 지속될 것입니다. ⁰⁹잠깐의 광고 이후에 더 많은 세부 사항을 위해 채널을 고정해 주세요.

07 주제 문제
해석 방송은 주로 무엇에 관한 것인가?
(A) 경제 예측
(B) 시 선거
(C) 성공적인 소기업들
(D) 안 좋은 날씨

해설 방송의 주제를 묻는 문제이므로, 지문의 초반을 주의 깊게 듣는다. "Right now, the city is preparing for a major storm."이라며 지금 도시는 큰 폭풍우를 대비하고 있다고 한 후, 앞으로의 기상 상황에 대한 내용으로 지문이 이어지고 있다. 따라서 (D)가 정답이다.

어휘 election n. 선거

08 의도 파악 문제
해석 화자는 왜 "그것은 아마 짧은 시간만 지속될 것입니다"라고 말하는가?
(A) 안심시키는 말을 하기 위해
(B) 도움을 요청하기 위해
(C) 실망을 표현하기 위해
(D) 계획을 마무리하기 위해

해설 질문의 인용어구(it will probably last a short amount of time)가 언급된 주변을 주의 깊게 듣는다. "the coastal highway and all beaches are closed. While this storm is expected to be rather strong"이라며 해안 고속도로와 모든 해변은 폐쇄되었으며, 이 폭풍우는 다소 강할 것으로 예상되지만 아마 짧은 시간만 지속될 것이라고 하였으므로 안심시키는 말을 하기 위함을 알 수 있다. 따라서 (A)가 정답이다.

어휘 reassurance n. 안심시키는 말

09 다음에 할 일 문제
해석 청자들은 다음에 무엇을 들을 것인가?
(A) 인터뷰
(B) 광고
(C) 스포츠 소식 업데이트
(D) 비즈니스 뉴스

해설 지문의 후반부를 주의 깊게 듣는다. "Stay tuned for more updates after a quick commercial break."라며 광고 이후에 더 많은 세부 사항을 위해 채널을 고정해 달라고 했으므로 청자들은 다음에 광고를 들을 것임을 알 수 있다. 따라서 (B)가 정답이다.

Paraphrasing
commercial break 광고 → advertisement 광고

[10-12] 미국

Questions 10-12 refer to the following podcast.

> In this week's episode of the *City Life* podcast, ¹⁰**I will be speaking with Diego Franco. He has acquired a reputation for being incredibly effective at fundraising for local charity groups.** For example, he just raised 20,000 dollars for an organization that provides free tutoring to underprivileged children. ¹¹**I have several questions for Mr. Franco about his latest project, a three-hour-long concert in Mason Park.** The proceeds from this event will be given to the Broad Street Homeless Shelter. ¹²**I urge all of you to check out Mr. Franco's social media feed for more details.**

acquire v. 얻다 reputation n. 명성 effective adj. 유능한, 효과적인
proceeds n. 수익금 urge v. 강력히 권고하다

해석
10-12번은 다음 팟캐스트에 관한 문제입니다.

이번 주 *City Life* 팟캐스트 에피소드에서, ¹⁰저는 Diego Franco와 이야기를 나눌 것입니다. 그는 지역 자선 단체를 위한 모금 활동에 있어 매우 유능하다는 평판을 얻었습니다. 예를 들어, 그는 최근에 소외 계층 아이들에게 무료 과외를 제공하는 단체를 위해 2만 달러를 모금했습니다. ¹¹저는 Mason 공원에서 열리는 3시간 동안의 콘서트인 그의 최신 프로젝트에 관해 Mr. Franco에게 몇 가지 질문이 있습니다. 이 행사의 수익금은 Broad가의 노숙자 쉼터에 기부될 것입니다. ¹²저는 여러분 모두가 더 자세한 정보를 위해 Mr. Franco의 소셜 미디어 피드를 확인해 보시기를 권고합니다.

10 특정 세부 사항 문제

해석 Diego Franco는 무엇으로 알려져 있는가?
(A) 학생들을 가르치는 것
(B) 기부금을 모금하는 것
(C) 투자를 하는 것
(D) 사업체를 홍보하는 것

해설 질문의 핵심 어구(Diego Franco)가 언급된 주변을 주의 깊게 듣는다. "I will be speaking with Diego Franco. He has acquired a reputation for being incredibly effective at fundraising for local charity groups."라며 Diego Franco와 이야기를 나눌 것인데, 그는 지역 자선 단체를 위한 모금 활동에 있어 매우 유능하다는 평판을 얻었다고 하였다. 이를 통해 그가 기부금을 모금하는 것으로 알려져 있음을 알 수 있다. 따라서 (B)가 정답이다.

11 특정 세부 사항 문제

해석 화자는 Mr. Franco에게 무엇에 관해 질문할 것인가?
(A) 음악 공연
(B) 패션쇼
(C) 박물관 전시회
(D) 스포츠 경기

해설 질문의 핵심 어구(ask Mr. Franco about)와 관련된 내용을 주의 깊게 듣는다. "I have several questions for Mr. Franco about his latest project, a three-hour-long concert in Mason Park."라며 Mason 공원에서 열리는 3시간 동안의 콘서트인 그의 최신 프로젝트에 관해 질문할 예정이라고 하였다. 따라서 (A)가 정답이다.

Paraphrasing
concert 콘서트 → musical performance 음악 공연

12 제안 문제

해석 화자는 청자들에게 무엇을 하도록 권장하는가?
(A) 소셜 미디어 계정을 만든다.
(B) 장비 설치를 돕는다.
(C) 온라인에서 정보를 찾는다.
(D) 행사 주최자에게 연락한다.

해설 지문의 중후반에서 제안과 관련된 표현을 주의 깊게 듣는다. "I urge all of you to check out Mr. Franco's social media feed for more details."라며 더 자세한 정보를 위해 Mr. Franco의 소셜 미디어 피드를 확인해 보기를 권고한다고 하였다. 따라서 (C)가 정답이다.

[13-15] 영국

Questions 13-15 refer to the following news report.

> Hello. I'm Alice Parsons, and I'm here on Thorpe Avenue. For drivers who use this street regularly, I have some great news. ¹³**The road expansion that has lasted for 10 months is about to wrap up.** ¹⁴**The road had significant traffic problems before the project began, and these became worse once the work was underway.** But this is about to change. When all parts of the avenue reopen next Monday, there will be three lanes going in each direction. ¹⁵**Now, I'll speak with one of the residents**, Dennis Bowes. He'll give us his thoughts on the project.

expansion n. 확장 wrap up 마무리짓다 reopen v. 재개통하다, 다시 열다
lane n. 차선 resident n. 주민 thought n. 생각

해석
13-15번은 다음 뉴스 보도에 관한 문제입니다.

안녕하세요, 저는 Alice Parsons이며, 여기 Thorpe가에 있습니다. 이 도로를 정기적으로 이용하는 운전자들을 위해, 저는 몇 가지 좋은 소식이 있습니다. ¹³10개월 동안 지속된 도로 확장이 거의 마무리되고 있습니다. ¹⁴도로는 이 사업이 시작되기 전에 상당한 교통 문제가 있었고, 공사가 진행되자 이것은 더 심각해졌습니다. 하지만 이것은 이제 바뀔 것입니다. 도로의 모든 부분이 다음 주 월요일에 재개통되면, 양쪽에 세 개의 차선이 생길 것입니다. ¹⁵이제, 주민 중 한 분인 Dennis Bowes와 이야기를 나눠 보겠습니다. 그는 우리에게 프로젝트에 대한 그의 생각을 말해줄 것입니다.

13 특정 세부 사항 문제

해석 화자에 따르면, 무엇이 곧 끝날 것인가?
(A) 공원 청소
(B) 가게 확장
(C) 공사 프로젝트
(D) 도시 축제

해설 질문의 핵심 어구(finish soon)와 관련된 내용을 주의 깊게 듣는다. "The road expansion that has lasted for 10 months is about to wrap up."이라며 10개월 동안 지속된 도로 확장이 거의 마무리되고 있다고 하였다. 따라서 (C)가 정답이다.

Paraphrasing
wrap up 마무리되다 → finish 끝나다

14 의도 파악 문제

해석 화자는 "하지만 이것은 이제 바뀔 것입니다"라고 말할 때 무엇을 의도하는가?
(A) 더 많은 버스 정류소가 있기를 바란다.
(B) 도로가 자전거 이용자들에게 더 안전해지기를 원한다.
(C) 운전자들이 그 도로를 거의 사용하지 않을 것이라고 예측한다.
(D) 교통량이 덜 할 것이라고 생각한다.

해설 질문의 인용어구(But this is about to change)가 언급된 주변을 주의 깊게 듣는다. "The road had significant traffic problems ~ these became worse once the work was underway."라며 도로는 상당한 교통 문제가 있었고 더 심각해졌다고 한 뒤, "But this is about to change"라며 하지만 이것이 바뀔 것이라고 한 것은 도로 확장 완료 후에 교통이 덜 혼잡해질 것이라고 생각한다는 것임을 알 수 있다. 따라서

(D)가 정답이다.

어휘 predict v. 예측하다

15 다음에 할 일 문제
해석 화자는 다음에 무엇을 할 것인가?
(A) 주민을 인터뷰한다.
(B) 부지를 점검한다.
(C) 공무원과 이야기한다.
(D) 준공식에 참여한다.

해설 지문의 마지막 부분을 주의 깊게 듣는다. "Now, I'll speak with one of the residents"라며 이제 주민 중 한 분과 이야기를 나눠보겠다고 하였다. 따라서 (A)가 정답이다.

어휘 site n. 부지, 현장

Paraphrasing
speak with 이야기를 나누다 → Interview 인터뷰하다

[16-18] 호주
Questions 16-18 refer to the following radio broadcast.

¹⁶In business news, AltCore, a major food company, plans to purchase another industry giant, Swenson Foods. A spokesperson for AltCore made the announcement this morning and stated that the acquisition would cost the firm around one billion dollars. Once AltCore absorbs Swenson Foods, many of Swenson Foods' minor brands will be discontinued. However, ¹⁷its major cereal brands, such as the popular Health Bites breakfast cereal, will continue to be produced. AltCore plans to retain most of the staff from Swenson Foods. ¹⁸Additional details on the deal are expected to be released later this week.

spokesperson n. 대변인 acquisition n. 인수
absorb v. 통합하다, 흡수하다 discontinue v. 중지하다, 중단하다
retain v. 확보하다, 유지하다

해석
16-18번은 다음 라디오 방송에 관한 문제입니다.
¹⁶산업 뉴스에서는, 주요 식품 생산 회사인 AltCore사가 다른 거대 사업체인 Swenson Foods사를 매입할 계획입니다. AltCore사의 대변인은 오늘 아침에 발표를 했으며 인수에 회사가 약 10억 달러의 비용이 들 것이라고 말했습니다. 일단 AltCore사가 Swenson Foods사와 통합하면, Swenson Foods사의 많은 작은 브랜드들의 생산이 중지될 것입니다. 하지만, ¹⁷인기 있는 Health Bites 아침 식사용 시리얼 같은 주요 시리얼 브랜드들은 계속 생산될 것입니다. AltCore사는 또한 Swenson Foods사의 직원 대부분을 확보할 계획입니다. ¹⁸거래에 관한 추가적인 세부 사항들은 이번 주 후반에 발표될 것으로 예상됩니다.

16 주제 문제
해석 방송은 주로 무엇에 관한 것인가?
(A) 공장의 수리
(B) 컨벤션을 위한 준비
(C) 제조 협상
(D) 기업 합병

해설 방송의 주제를 묻는 문제이므로, 지문의 초반을 반드시 듣는다. "In business news, AltCore, the major food production company, plans to purchase another industry giant, Swenson Foods."라며 주요 식품 생산 회사인 AltCore사가 다른 거대 사업체인 Swenson Foods사를 매입할 것이라고 한 후, 합병에 대한 내용으로 지문이 이어지고 있다. 따라서 (D)가 정답이다.

17 언급 문제
해석 화자는 Health Bites에 대해 무엇을 말하는가?
(A) 계속 생산될 것이다.
(B) 가격이 오를 것이다.
(C) 다른 재료를 사용할 것이다.
(D) 포장이 바뀔 것이다.

해설 질문의 핵심 어구(Health Bites)가 언급된 주변을 주의 깊게 듣는다. "its major cereal brands, such as the popular Health Bites breakfast cereal, will continue to be produced"라며 Health Bites 아침 식사용 시리얼 같은 주요 시리얼 브랜드들은 계속 생산될 예정이라고 하였다. 따라서 (A)가 정답이다.

Paraphrasing
continue to be produced 계속 생산되다 → remain in production 계속 생산되다

18 다음에 할 일 문제
해석 화자에 따르면, 이번 주 후반에 무슨 일이 일어날 것인가?
(A) 기자 회견이 열릴 것이다.
(B) 새 공장이 문을 열 것이다.
(C) 정보를 구할 수 있게 될 것이다.
(D) 직원들이 새로운 직책을 위해 교육받을 것이다.

해설 질문의 핵심 어구(later this week)가 언급된 주변을 주의 깊게 듣는다. "Additional details on the deal are expected to be released later this week."이라며 거래에 관한 추가적인 세부 사항들은 이번 주 후반에 발표될 것이라고 하였다. 따라서 (C)가 정답이다.

[19-21] 캐나다
Questions 19-21 refer to the following broadcast and weather forecast.

You're listening to Channel Four Radio, and we have some great news for you. ¹⁹The band Karma Birds will be performing at the Concerts in the Garden festival for the first time. The show starts at 5 P.M. Tickets are already on sale and are 20 dollars per person. However, ²⁰there has been a change in venue. Instead of performing at the south garden stage, the band will play in the Nora Concert Hall. This is because ²¹rain is expected the day before the show, and the outdoor arena will be too muddy. Stay tuned for more updates.

perform v. 공연하다 venue n. 장소 outdoor adj. 야외의
arena n. 공연장 muddy adj. 질퍽한, 진흙투성이인

해석
19-21번은 다음 방송과 일기 예보에 관한 문제입니다.
여러분은 채널4 라디오를 듣고 계시며, 여러분을 위한 몇 가지 좋은 소식이 있습니다. ¹⁹밴드 Karma Birds가 Concerts in the Garden 축제에서 처음으로 공연할 것입니다. 이 공연은 오후 5시에 시작합니다. 입장권은 이미 판매 중이며 인당 20달러입니다. 하지만, ²⁰장소에 변경 사항이 있습니다. 남쪽 정원 무대에서 공연하는 대신, 그 밴드는 Nora 콘서트홀에서 공연할 것입니다. 이것은 ²¹행사 전날에 비가 예상되어서 야외 공연장이 지나치게 질퍽거리게 될 것이기 때문입니다. 소식 업데이트를 위해 채널 고정해 주세요.

일기 예보			
목요일	²¹금요일	토요일	일요일

19 언급 문제

해석 화자는 Karma Birds에 대해 무엇을 말하는가?
(A) 행사에서 처음으로 공연할 것이다.
(B) 오전에 연주할 것이다.
(C) 무대 중 하나를 사용하는 것을 거절했다.
(D) 가장 유명한 밴드이다.

해설 질문의 핵심 어구(Karma Birds)가 언급된 주변을 주의 깊게 듣는다. "The band Karma Birds will be performing at the Concerts in the Garden festival for the first time."이라며 밴드인 Karma Birds가 Concerts in the Garden 축제에서 처음으로 공연할 것이라고 하였다. 따라서 (A)가 정답이다.

어휘 decline v. 거절하다, 감소하다

20 특정 세부 사항 문제

해석 화자에 따르면, 무엇이 변경되었는가?
(A) 공연자
(B) 장소
(C) 시작 시간
(D) 입장료

해설 질문의 핵심 어구(changed)와 관련된 내용을 주의 깊게 듣는다. "there has been a change in venue. Instead of performing at the south garden stage, the band will play in the Nora Concert Hall."이라며 장소에 변경 사항이 있는데 남쪽 정원 무대에서 공연하는 대신, Nora 콘서트홀에서 공연할 것이라고 하였다. 따라서 (B)가 정답이다.

Paraphrasing
venue 장소 → location 장소

21 시각 자료 문제

해석 시각 자료를 보아라. 어느 요일에 행사가 열릴 것인가?
(A) 목요일
(B) 금요일
(C) 토요일
(D) 일요일

해설 일기 예보의 정보를 확인한 후 질문의 핵심 어구(event ~ held)와 관련된 내용을 주의 깊게 듣는다. "rain is expected the day before the show"라며 행사 전날에 비가 예상된다고 하였고, 비가 온 다음날은 금요일임을 일기 예보에서 알 수 있다. 따라서 (B)가 정답이다.

DAY 20 광고 및 소개

기출 유형 1 광고

Example 영국 p.130

해석
01-03번은 다음 광고에 관한 문제입니다.

Stinson Woodworking사는 주에서 가장 훌륭한 핸드메이드 탁자와 의자를 제공하게 되어 자랑스럽습니다. 01저희의 개별 매장은 주문 제작에 대한 명성이 있으며, 모든 제품들이 특별합니다. 게다가, 02저희는 저희가 생산하는 모든 것에 대한 10년의 보증 기간을 제공함으로써 고객 만족을 보장합니다. Stinson Woodworking사에 대한 추가 세부 사항을 위해, 03저희 웹사이트를 방문하실 수 있습니다. 그곳에서 저희가 과거에 제작했던 몇몇 의자와 테이블의 사진들을 보게 되실 것입니다.

어휘 independent adj. 개별의, 독자적인 reputation n. 명성
custom adj. 주문한, 맞춤의 one of a kind 특별한 것
warranty n. 보증, 보증서 produce v. 생산하다

01
해석 Stinson Woodworking사는 무엇으로 알려져 있는가?
(A) 현대적인 스타일을 사용하는 것
(B) 경쟁력 있는 가격을 제공하는 것
(C) 빠른 배송을 제공하는 것
(D) 맞춤 주문을 이행하는 것

02
해석 화자에 따르면, Stinson Woodworking사는 고객들에게 무엇을 제공하는가?
(A) 무료 제품
(B) 제품 보증서
(C) 신속한 배송
(D) 할인된 가격

03
해석 청자들은 온라인에서 무엇을 찾을 수 있는가?
(A) 제품의 사진
(B) 가격의 목록
(C) 지점으로 가는 경로
(D) 매장의 영업시간

토익실전문제 p.131

| 01 (B) | 02 (D) | 03 (B) | 04 (A) | 05 (B) |
| 06 (B) |

[01-03] 미국
Questions 01-03 refer to the following advertisement.

01Here at the Mason Vista Institute, we pride ourselves on teaching students to drive safely. Most of our students pass the truck driving test on the first try. 02Our comprehensive training program includes driving practice with the latest trucks. Also, 02we have a proven track record, with 95 percent of our students passing the test on their first attempt. 03After you graduate from our course, we'll help you find a job with a commercial trucking company.

comprehensive adj. 포괄적인 latest adj. 최신의 attempt n. 시도
graduate v. 졸업하다 commercial adj. 상업용의

해석
01-03번은 다음 광고에 관한 문제입니다.

01이곳 Mason Vista 기관에서 우리는 학생들에게 안전하게 운전하는 법을 가르치는 것을 자랑스럽게 생각합니다. 우리 학생들 대부분은 트럭 운전 시험에 첫 번째 응시에서 합격합니다. 02우리의 포괄적인 교육 프로그램은 최신 트럭으로 운전 연습하는 것을 포함합니다. 또한, 02우리는 95퍼센트의 학생들이 첫 시도에서 시험에 합격한다는 입증된 실적을 가지고 있습니다. 03우리 과정을 졸업한 후에는, 상업용 트럭 운송 회사에서의 일자리를 찾도록 도와드리겠습니다.

01 특정 세부 사항 문제
해석 Mason Vista 기관은 무엇을 가르치는가?
(A) 고객 서비스
(B) 운전
(C) 판매 기법
(D) 프로그래밍

해설 질문의 핵심 어구(Mason Vista Institute teach)와 관련된 내용을 주의 깊게 듣는다. "Here at the Mason Vista Institute, we pride ourselves on teaching students to drive safely."라며 Mason

Vista 기관에서는 학생들에게 안전하게 운전하는 법을 가르치는 것을 자랑스럽게 생각한다고 하였다. 따라서 (B)가 정답이다.

02 언급 문제

해석 프로그램에 관해 무엇이 언급되는가?
(A) 입학 시험을 포함한다.
(B) 저녁 시간에 진행된다.
(C) 수업 규모가 제한적이다.
(D) 성공률이 매우 높다.

해설 질문의 핵심 어구(program)와 관련된 내용을 주의 깊게 듣는다. "Our comprehensive training program ~ the latest trucks."라며 그들의 포괄적인 교육 프로그램은 최신 트럭으로 운전 연습하는 것을 포함한다고 한 뒤, "we have a proven track record, with 95 percent of our students passing the test on their first attempt"라며 95퍼센트의 학생들이 첫 시도에서 시험에 합격한다는 입증된 실적을 가지고 있다고 하였다. 따라서 (D)가 정답이다.

03 특정 세부 사항 문제

해석 졸업생들에게 무엇이 제공되는가?
(A) 사진 촬영
(B) 취업 지원
(C) 온라인 워크숍
(D) 교육 시설 이용

해설 질문의 핵심 어구(offered to graduates)와 관련된 내용을 주의 깊게 듣는다. "After you graduate from our course, we'll help you find a job with a commercial trucking company."라며 과정을 졸업한 후에는 상업용 트럭 운송 회사에서의 일자리를 찾도록 도와준다고 하였다. 따라서 (B)가 정답이다.

어휘 **assistance** n. 지원, 도움 **access** n. 이용, 접근

[04-06] 🎧 캐나다

Questions 04-06 refer to the following advertisement.

04If you are planning your next family holiday, consider the Shady Hills Resort. Located on beautiful Lake Madden, our 50 acre property includes 35 cabins. Each is equipped with comfortable furniture, air conditioning, and a full kitchen. And if you want to explore the many tourist attractions in the area, 05we run a shuttle bus for our guests. It departs every hour from 8 A.M. to 7 P.M. daily. Visit our Web site to book your cabin today. 06If you make a reservation before the end of the month, we'll take 15 percent off your total price. Don't miss out!

be equipped with ~을 갖추고 있다 **explore** v. 탐험하다
run v. 운행하다, 운영하다 **depart** v. 출발하다

해석
04-06번은 다음 광고에 관한 문제입니다.

04다음 가족 휴가를 계획하고 계시다면, Shady Hills 리조트를 고려해 보세요. 아름다운 Madden 호수에 위치한 저희의 50 에이커 부지에는 35채의 통나무집을 가지고 있습니다. 각각 편안한 가구, 에어컨, 그리고 완비된 주방을 갖추고 있습니다. 그리고 지역의 많은 관광 명소를 탐험하고 싶으시다면, 05저희는 투숙객을 위한 셔틀버스를 운행합니다. 매일 오전 8시부터 오후 7시까지 매시간 출발합니다. 오늘 저희 웹사이트를 방문하여 통나무집을 예약하세요. 06이번 달 말 이전에 예약하시면, 총 가격에서 15퍼센트를 할인해 드립니다. 놓치지 마세요!

04 주제 문제

해석 무엇이 광고되고 있는가?
(A) 숙박 시설
(B) 행사 장소
(C) 여행사
(D) 식당

해설 광고의 주제를 묻는 문제이므로, 지문의 초반을 반드시 듣는다. "If you are planning your next family holiday, consider the Shady Hills Resort."라며 다음 가족 휴가를 계획하고 있다면 Shady Hills 리조트를 고려해 보라고 한 후, 리조트의 장점에 대한 내용으로 지문이 이어지고 있다. 따라서 (A)가 정답이다.

Paraphrasing
Resort 리조트 → **accommodation facility** 숙박 시설

05 특정 세부 사항 문제

해석 화자는 버스에 관해 무엇을 강조하는가?
(A) 크기
(B) 일정
(C) 비용
(D) 편안함

해설 질문의 핵심 어구(bus)와 관련된 내용을 주의 깊게 듣는다. "we run a shuttle bus for our guests. It departs every hour from 8 A.M. to 7 P.M. daily"라며 투숙객을 위한 셔틀버스를 운행하는데, 매일 오전 8시부터 오후 7시까지 매시간 출발한다고 하였다. 따라서 (B)가 정답이다.

06 이유 문제

해석 화자에 따르면, 청자들은 왜 이번 달에 예약을 해야 하는가?
(A) 선물을 받기 위해
(B) 할인을 받기 위해
(C) 혼잡을 피하기 위해
(D) 업그레이드를 받기 위해

해설 질문의 핵심 어구(make a booking this month)와 관련된 내용을 주의 깊게 듣는다. "If you make a reservation before the end of the month, we'll take 15 percent off your total price."라며 이번 달 말 이전에 예약하면 총 가격에서 15퍼센트를 할인해 준다고 하였다. 따라서 (B)가 정답이다.

어휘 **obtain** v. 받다, 획득하다

기출 유형 2 소개

Example 🎧 호주   p.132

해석
01-03번은 다음 소개에 관한 문제입니다.

01저는 우리 학교의 생물학 부서를 이끌도록 선발된 Jenna MacArthur를 소개하고 싶습니다. 그녀는 Raymount 대학교의 생물학 교수였고, 그녀가 우리 학교에 합류하기로 결정한 것을 기쁘게 생각합니다. 몇 분 후에, 02Ms. MacArthur가 우리 부서에 만들 몇몇 조정 사항에 대해 말씀하실 겁니다. 03하지만 먼저, Mr. Dryson에게 주목해주세요. 그는 다음 주 워크숍의 일정을 가지고 있습니다.

어휘 **select** v. 선발하다 **biology** n. 생물학 **adjustment** n. 조정

01

해석 Jenna MacArthur는 왜 고용되었는가?
(A) 비서로 근무하기 위해
(B) 학생들을 상담하기 위해
(C) 대학을 홍보하기 위해
(D) 학과를 이끌기 위해

02

해석 Ms. MacArthur는 무엇에 대해 이야기할 것인가?
(A) 인기 있는 과목

(B) 몇몇 시험 세부사항
(C) 몇몇 계획된 변화
(D) 행정적 의무

03
해석 화자는 "그는 다음 주 워크숍의 일정을 가지고 있습니다"라고 말할 때 무엇을 의도하는가?
(A) 시작하는 새로운 연구 프로젝트가 있다.
(B) 공유될 정보가 더 있다.
(C) 수업이 연기될 것이다.
(D) 몇몇 지원 연설자가 필요하다.

토익실전문제 p.133

01 (B)	02 (D)	03 (A)	04 (A)	05 (B)
06 (B)				

[01-03] 영국

Questions 01-03 refer to the following introduction.

I'm pleased to welcome everyone to the *Musical Alley* podcast. I have a very special guest today. ⁰¹**Elena Park is a local singer and songwriter whose amazing performances at regional festivals have attracted a lot of attention.** In fact, she is now so popular that she has started booking solo concerts around the country and beyond. Today, ⁰²**she is going to talk about her planned tour of the western United States and Canada this summer.** ⁰³**And make sure to stick around once the interview is over . . . I have a copy of her latest album, and I'll play a song off it for your enjoyment.**

regional adj. 지역의   attention n. 관심   beyond adv. 그 너머까지
enjoyment n. 즐거움

해석
01-03번은 다음 소개에 관한 문제입니다.

Musical Alley 팟캐스트에 오신 모든 분들을 환영합니다. 오늘은 아주 특별한 손님이 함께하고 있습니다. ⁰¹Elena Park은 지역 축제에서의 놀라운 공연으로 많은 관심을 받아온 지역 가수이자 작곡가입니다. 사실, 그녀는 이제 너무 인기가 많아서 전국과 그 너머까지 솔로 콘서트 예약을 시작했습니다. 오늘, ⁰²그녀는 올여름 미국 서부와 캐나다에서의 계획된 투어에 관해 이야기할 것입니다. ⁰³그리고 인터뷰가 끝난 후에도 계속 들어주세요... 저는 그녀의 최신 앨범을 가지고 있으며, 여러분의 즐거움을 위해 그 중 한 곡을 틀어드리겠습니다.

01 특정 세부 사항 문제
해석 Ms. Park은 무엇으로 알려져 있는가?
(A) 외국 음악가들과 협업하는 것
(B) 긍정적인 평가를 받은 것
(C) 학생들에게 수업을 제공하는 것
(D) 자선 콘서트에서 공연하는 것

해설 질문의 핵심 어구(Ms. Park known for)와 관련된 내용을 주의 깊게 듣는다. "Elena Park is a local singer and songwriter whose amazing performances at regional festivals have attracted a lot of attention."이라며 Elena Park은 지역 축제에서의 놀라운 공연으로 많은 관심을 받아온 지역 가수이자 작곡가라고 하였다. 따라서 (B)가 정답이다.

어휘 charity n. 자선

02 특정 세부 사항 문제
해석 Ms. Park은 무엇에 대해 이야기할 것 같은가?

(A) 그녀의 최근 앨범
(B) 그녀의 새로운 책
(C) 그녀의 경력 변화
(D) 그녀의 다가오는 투어

해설 질문의 핵심 어구(Mr. Park ~ talk about)와 관련된 내용을 주의 깊게 듣는다. "she is going to talk about her planned tour ~ this summer."라며 그녀는 올여름에 계획된 투어에 관해 이야기할 것이라고 하였다. 따라서 (D)가 정답이다.

03 특정 세부 사항 문제
해석 화자는 인터뷰 후에 무엇을 하려고 계획하고 있는가?
(A) 녹음된 것을 재생한다.
(B) 노래를 공연한다.
(C) 티켓을 나눠준다.
(D) 손님을 소개한다.

해설 질문의 핵심 어구(after the interview)와 관련된 내용을 주의 깊게 듣는다. "And make sure to stick around once the interview is over... I have a copy of her latest album, and I'll play a song off it for your enjoyment."라며 인터뷰가 끝난 후에도 계속 들어달라고 한 후, 그녀의 최신 앨범을 가지고 있으며 그 중 한 곡을 틀어주겠다고 하였다. 따라서 (A)가 정답이다.

Paraphrasing
play a song 한 곡을 틀다 → Play a recording 녹음된 것을 재생한다

[04-06] 호주

Questions 04-06 refer to the following introduction.

⁰⁴**I'd like to introduce Mark Lee, who will be leading today's workshop on how to avoid cyber threats while using the Internet at work.** ⁰⁵**As administrative clerks at this hospital, it is especially important that you understand how to do this** because you regularly deal with confidential patient information. If our databases were breached by hackers, it would be a disaster. ⁰⁶**We created a manual that you should refer to throughout the workshop.** It includes the various steps you must take to protect our data. **I will now hand one out to each of you**, and then Mark will begin his presentation.

administrative adj. 행정의   confidential adj. 기밀의   breach v. 침해하다
refer to ~을 참조하다   protect v. 보호하다

해석
04-06번은 다음 소개에 관한 문제입니다.

⁰⁴직장에서 인터넷을 사용하는 동안 사이버 위협을 피하는 방법에 대한 오늘의 워크숍을 이끌어 주실 Mark Lee를 소개해 드리고 싶습니다. ⁰⁵이 병원의 행정 사무원으로서, 여러분이 정기적으로 환자의 기밀 정보를 다루기 때문에 이 방법을 이해하는 것은 특히 중요합니다. 저희 데이터베이스가 해커들에 의해 침해된다면, 그것은 재앙이 될 것입니다. ⁰⁶저희는 워크숍 전반에 걸쳐 참조하셔야 할 매뉴얼을 만들었습니다. 여기에는 데이터를 보호하기 위해 여러분이 취해야 하는 다양한 단계가 포함되어 있습니다. 지금 여러분 각자에게 하나씩 나눠드릴 것이고, 그런 다음 Mark가 발표를 시작할 것입니다.

04 특정 세부 사항 문제
해석 Mr. Lee는 무엇에 대해 이야기할 것인가?
(A) 온라인 보안
(B) 소프트웨어 업데이트
(C) 고객 충성도
(D) 훈련 기법

해설 질문의 핵심 어구(Mr. Lee talk about)와 관련된 내용을 주의 깊게 듣는다. "I'd like to introduce Mark Lee, who will be leading today's workshop on how to avoid cyber threats while using the Internet at work."라며 Mark Lee는 직장에서 인터넷을 사용하는 동안 사이버 위협을 피하는 방법에 대한 워크숍을 이끌 것이라고 하였다. 따라서 (A)가 정답이다.

05 청자 문제
해석 청자들은 어디에서 일하는 것 같은가?
(A) 금융 기관에서
(B) 의료 시설에서
(C) 법률 사무소에서
(D) 보험 회사에서

해설 지문에서 신분 및 직업과 관련된 표현을 놓치지 않고 듣는다. "As administrative clerks at this hospital, it is especially important that you understand how to do this"라며 이 병원의 행정 사무원으로서, 이 방법을 이해하는 것이 특히 중요하다고 하였다. 따라서 (B)가 정답이다.

06 다음에 할 일 문제
해석 화자는 다음에 무엇을 할 것인가?
(A) 발표를 한다.
(B) 문서를 배포한다.
(C) 과정을 설명한다.
(D) 목록을 확인한다.

해설 지문의 후반부를 주의 깊게 듣는다. "We created a manual that you should refer to throughout the workshop."이라며 워크숍 전반에 걸쳐 참조해야 할 매뉴얼을 만들었다고 한 뒤, "I will now hand one out to each of you"라며 지금 그것을 각자에게 하나씩 나누어 주겠다고 하였다. 따라서 (B)가 정답이다.

어휘 process n. 과정

[Paraphrasing]
hand one[manual] out 매뉴얼을 나눠 주다 → Distribute a document 문서를 배포한다

HACKERS TEST   p.134

01 (B)	02 (B)	03 (A)	04 (B)	05 (B)
06 (D)	07 (A)	08 (D)	09 (C)	10 (D)
11 (A)	12 (C)	13 (B)	14 (B)	15 (D)
16 (C)	17 (D)	18 (A)	19 (D)	20 (B)
21 (B)				

[01-03] 캐나다
Questions 01-03 refer to the following advertisement.

⁰¹**Are you tired of exercising at home? Then, head over to SilverPlus Gym!** ⁰²**We've recently updated our class schedule to include new yoga and Pilates sessions.** We have also hired additional trainers to help our members achieve their fitness goals. Plus, ⁰³**if you register by the end of this month, you will receive a yoga mat or a foam roller as a gift.** Join SilverPlus Gym today.

include v. 포함하다   additional adj. 추가의   achieve v. 달성하다
register v. 등록하다   receive v. 받다

해석
01-03번은 다음 광고에 관한 문제입니다.
⁰¹집에서 운동하는 것에 싫증 나셨나요? 그럼, SilverPlus 체육관으로 오세요! ⁰²저희는 최근에 새로운 요가 및 필라테스 수업을 포함하도록 운동 수업 일정을 업데이트했습니다. 또한, 저희 회원들이 운동 목표를 달성하는 데 도움이 되도록 추가 트레이너들을 고용하였습니다. 게다가, ⁰³이번 달 말까지 등록하시면, 요가 매트 또는 폼롤러를 선물로 받으실 것입니다. 오늘 SilverPlus 체육관에 가입하세요.

01 주제 문제
해석 무엇이 광고되고 있는가?
(A) 운동 용품점
(B) 체육관
(C) 도자기 공방
(D) 지역 대학

해설 광고의 주제를 묻는 문제이므로, 지문의 초반을 주의 깊게 듣는다. "Are you tired of exercising at home? Then, head over to SilverPlus Gym!"이라며 집에서 운동하는 것에 싫증 났다면, SilverPlus 체육관으로 오라고 한 것을 통해 체육관이 광고되고 있음을 알 수 있다. 따라서 (B)가 정답이다.

02 특정 세부 사항 문제
해석 화자에 따르면, 최근에 무엇이 업데이트되었는가?
(A) 가격 목록
(B) 수업 일정
(C) 환불 정책
(D) 회사 규정

해설 질문의 핵심 어구(recently ~ updated)가 언급된 주변을 주의 깊게 듣는다. "We've recently updated our class schedule to include new yoga and Pilates sessions."라며 최근에 요가와 필라테스 수업을 포함하도록 운동 수업 일정을 업데이트했다고 하였다. 따라서 (B)가 정답이다.

어휘 regulation n. 규정

03 방법 문제
해석 청자들은 어떻게 무료 물품을 받을 수 있는가?
(A) 마감 일자까지 등록함으로써
(B) 행사에 참석함으로써
(C) 쿠폰을 가져옴으로써
(D) 온라인에 사진을 게시함으로써

해설 질문의 핵심 어구(get a free item)와 관련된 내용을 주의 깊게 듣는다. "if you register by the end of this month, you will receive a yoga mat or a foam roller as a gift."라며 이번 달 말까지 등록하면, 요가 매트 또는 폼롤러를 선물로 받을 것이라고 하였다. 따라서 (A)가 정답이다.

[04-06] 미국
Questions 04-06 refer to the following introduction.

Good morning. ⁰⁴**My name is Serena Martinez, and I'm the organizer of the Grantville Chamber of Commerce's annual conference for entrepreneurs.** In a few minutes, our keynote speaker, Matthew Nolan, will take the stage. ⁰⁵**Mr. Nolan owns several successful companies and was the winner of the Businessperson of the Year award.** He will be sharing tips on how to overcome the common challenges people face when starting a company. But before Mr. Nolan comes out, ⁰⁶**I would like to remind you that my organization's new mobile application includes details about all of the activities planned for this year's event.** So be sure to download it. Now, please welcome Mr. Nolan!

entrepreneur n. 기업가   own v. 소유하다   overcome v. 극복하다
common adj. 흔한, 일반적인   remind v. 상기시키다, 다시 알려 주다

해석
04-06번은 다음 소개에 관한 문제입니다.

안녕하세요. ⁰⁴제 이름은 Serena Martinez이고, 저는 Grantville 상공회의소의 연례 기업가 학회의 주최자입니다. 몇 분 후에, 우리의 기조연설자인 Matthew Nolan이 무대에 오를 것입니다. ⁰⁵Mr. Nolan은 여러 성공적인 회사들을 소유하고 있으며 올해의 기업인상을 수상했습니다. 그는 사람들이 회사를 시작할 때 직면하는 흔한 도전들을 극복하는 방법에 대한 조언을 공유할 예정입니다. 하지만 Mr. Nolan이 나오기 전에, ⁰⁶저는 제 기관의 새로운 모바일 애플리케이션에 올해 행사를 위해 계획된 모든 활동에 대한 세부 정보가 포함되어 있다는 점을 상기시켜 드리고 싶습니다. 그러니 그것을 꼭 다운로드 하세요. 이제, Mr. Nolan을 환영해 주세요!

04 화자 문제
해석 화자는 누구인 것 같은가?
(A) 사업주
(B) 행사 주최자
(C) 기조연설자
(D) 대회 심사위원

해설 지문에서 신분 및 직업과 관련된 표현을 놓치지 않고 듣는다. "My name is Serena Martinez, and I'm the organizer of the Grantville Chamber of Commerce's annual conference for entrepreneurs."라며 자신이 Grantville 상공회의소의 연례 기업가 학회의 주최자라고 하였다. 따라서 (B)가 정답이다.

어휘 judge n. 심사위원

05 특정 세부 사항 문제
해석 Mr. Nolan은 무엇을 받았는가?
(A) 추천장
(B) 기업상
(C) 정부 대출
(D) 일자리 제안

해설 질문의 핵심 어구(Mr. Nolan receive)와 관련된 내용을 주의 깊게 듣는다. "Mr. Nolan owns several successful companies and was the winner of the Businessperson of the Year award."라며 Mr. Nolan은 여러 성공적인 회사들을 소유하고 있으며 올해의 기업인상을 수상했다고 하였다. 따라서 (B)가 정답이다.

06 이유 문제
해석 청자들은 왜 애플리케이션을 다운로드해야 하는가?
(A) 다른 참석자들과 소통하기 위해
(B) 행사장 지도를 이용하기 위해
(C) 연설 원고를 읽기 위해
(D) 활동에 관한 정보를 찾기 위해

해설 질문의 핵심 어구(download an application)와 관련된 내용을 주의 깊게 듣는다. "I would like to remind you that my organization's new mobile application includes details about all of the activities planned for this year's event."라며 기관의 새로운 모바일 애플리케이션에 올해 행사를 위해 계획된 모든 활동에 대한 세부 정보가 포함되어 있다고 하였다. 따라서 (D)가 정답이다.

[07-09] 영국
Questions 07-09 refer to the following advertisement.

⁰⁷Do you want your home to look as appealing as possible? If so, contact Niles Interiors. Our interior decorators offer a range of services at unbeatable prices, including wall color and furniture suggestions. ⁰⁸And unlike our competitors, we do not charge for the first meeting with one of our designers. Moreover, ⁰⁹we're running a special promotion for the rest of this month. **Customers can get 10 percent off their total price** when they enter the promotional code on our Web site. So what are you waiting for?

appealing adj. 매력적인   a range of 다양한
unbeatable adj. 훌륭한, 더이상 좋을 수 없는   competitor n. 경쟁사
charge v. 비용을 청구하다

해석
07-09번은 다음 광고에 관한 문제입니다.

⁰⁷당신의 집이 가능한 한 매력적으로 보이기를 원하시나요? 그렇다면, Niles 인테리어사에 연락하세요. 저희 실내 장식가들은 벽색과 가구 제안을 포함한 다양한 서비스를 훌륭한 가격에 제공합니다. 그리고 ⁰⁸저희의 경쟁사들과 달리, 저희는 디자이너 중 한 사람과의 첫 만남에는 비용을 청구하지 않습니다. 게다가, ⁰⁹이번 달 나머지 기간 동안 특별 행사를 진행하고 있습니다. 고객들은 저희 웹사이트에 할인 코드를 입력하시면 총액에서 10퍼센트 할인을 받으실 수 있습니다. 자, 무엇을 기다리고 계신가요?

07 주제 문제
해석 어떤 종류의 업체가 광고되고 있는가?
(A) 실내 장식 회사
(B) 보험 회사
(C) 주택 청소 서비스
(D) 부동산 중개소

해설 광고의 주제를 묻는 문제이므로, 광고의 초반을 주의 깊게 듣는다. "Do you want your home to look as appealing as possible? If so, contact Niles Interiors."라며 Niles 인테리어사를 소개한 후, 주요 혜택에 대한 내용으로 지문이 이어지고 있다. 따라서 (A)가 정답이다.

어휘 insurance n. 보험

08 특정 세부 사항 문제
해석 화자의 회사는 그곳의 경쟁사들과 어떻게 다른가?
(A) 여러 지점들이 있다.
(B) 모바일 애플리케이션이 있다.
(C) 배달 서비스를 제공한다.
(D) 무료 첫 상담을 제공한다.

해설 질문의 핵심 어구(different from ~ competitors)와 관련된 내용을 주의 깊게 듣는다. "And unlike our competitors, we do not charge for the first meeting with one of our designers."라며 경쟁사들과 달리, 디자이너와의 첫 만남에는 비용을 청구하지 않는다고 하였다. 따라서 (D)가 정답이다.

어휘 initial adj. 처음의   consultation n. 상담

Paraphrasing
first meeting 첫 만남 → initial consultations 첫 상담

09 특정 세부 사항 문제
해석 무엇이 이달의 나머지 기간 동안 이용 가능한가?
(A) 빠른 배송
(B) 무료 회원권
(C) 판촉 할인
(D) 상품권

해설 질문의 핵심 어구(the rest of ~ month)가 언급된 주변을 주의 깊게 듣는다. "we're running a special promotion for the rest of this month. Customers can get 10 percent off their total price"라며 이번 달 나머지 기간 동안 특별 행사를 진행하고 있는데 고객들은 총액에서 10퍼센트 할인을 받을 수 있다고 하였다. 따라서 (C)가 정답이다.

Paraphrasing
10 percent off ~ total price 총액에서 10퍼센트 할인 → promotional discount 판촉 할인

[10-12] 호주
Questions 10-12 refer to the following introduction.

I'd like everyone to meet Andrew Larson. ¹⁰**Mr. Larson has been hired to be the head designer of our clothing company.** He comes to us after working for Borderline, one of the top companies in the men's fashion industry. ¹¹**Mr. Larson's first project here will be to design a new clothing line for our winter collection**, and he will work on this over the next three months. But ¹²**for today, Mr. Larson will meet with each team to develop an understanding of our current projects**. Please provide him with any information he requests.

industry n. 업계, 사업   understanding n. 이해(도), 합의
provide v. 제공하다   request v. 요청하다

해석
10-12번은 다음 소개에 관한 문제입니다.

여러분 모두 Andrew Larson을 만나보시길 바랍니다. ¹⁰Mr. Larson은 우리 의류 회사의 수석 디자이너로 고용되었습니다. 그는 남성 패션 업계의 최고 회사들 중 하나인 Borderline사에서 근무한 뒤 우리에게 왔습니다. ¹¹이곳에서 Mr. Larson의 첫 프로젝트는 겨울 컬렉션을 위한 새 의류 라인을 디자인하는 일이 될 것이며, 그는 앞으로 세 달 동안 이 작업을 할 것입니다. 하지만, ¹²오늘은 Mr. Larson이 우리의 현 프로젝트들에 대한 이해도를 높이기 위해 각 팀과 만날 것입니다. 그가 요청하는 어떠한 정보라도 그에게 제공해주세요.

10 청자 문제
해석 청자들은 어디에서 일하는 것 같은가?
(A) 유통 센터에서
(B) 컨설팅 회사에서
(C) 소매 상점에서
(D) 패션 회사에서
해설 지문에서 신분 및 직업과 관련된 표현을 놓치지 않고 듣는다. "Mr. Larson has been hired to be the head designer for our clothing company."라며 Mr. Larson이 우리 의류 회사의 수석 디자이너로 고용되었다고 하였다. 따라서 (D)가 정답이다.
어휘 distribution n. 유통

11 특정 세부 사항 문제
해석 Mr. Larson은 무슨 업무를 맡을 것인가?
(A) 제품 제작하기
(B) 기계 수리하기
(C) 직원 교육시키기
(D) 시설 유지 보수하기
해설 질문의 핵심 어구(task ~ Mr. Larson)와 관련된 내용을 주의 깊게 듣는다. "Mr. Larson's first project here will be to design a new clothing line for our winter collection"이라며 Mr. Larson의 첫 프로젝트는 겨울 컬렉션을 위한 새 의류 라인을 디자인하는 일이 될 것이라고 하였다. 따라서 (A)가 정답이다.

Paraphrasing
design ~ clothing line 의류 라인 디자인하기 → Creating ~ products 제품 제작하기

12 특정 세부 사항 문제
해석 Mr. Larson은 오늘 무엇을 할 예정인가?
(A) 기록을 검토한다.
(B) 평가를 수행한다.
(C) 직원들을 만난다.
(D) 발표를 한다.
해설 질문의 핵심 어구(Mr. Larson scheduled to do today)와 관련된 내용을 주의 깊게 듣는다. "for today, Mr. Larson will meet with each team to develop an understanding of our current projects"라며 오늘 Mr. Larson은 현 프로젝트들에 대한 이해도를 높이기 위해 각 팀과 만날 것이라고 하였다. 따라서 (C)가 정답이다.

[13-15] 미국
Questions 13-15 refer to the following introduction.

Well, ¹³**now that everyone has gathered here in the laboratory**, let's begin. ¹⁴**This meeting has been arranged to introduce Scott Bailey**, who will be working with us from today. ¹⁴**His main responsibility will be equipment maintenance and repairs.** I'm going to give him a brief tour of our facility. Afterwards, ¹⁵**please take a few minutes to tell him of any equipment you regularly use that is having problems**. He can focus his attention on these devices first.

gather v. 모이다   arrange v. 마련하다, 주선하다
responsibility n. 임무, 책임   brief adj. 잠시 동안의, 간략한
regularly adv. 정기적으로

해석
13-15번은 다음 소개에 관한 문제입니다.

자, ¹³이제 모두들 이곳 연구실에 모였으니 시작합시다. ¹⁴이 모임은 Scott Bailey를 소개하기 위해 마련되었고, 그는 오늘부터 저희와 함께 일하게 될 것입니다. ¹⁴그의 주요 임무는 장비 유지 보수와 수리가 될 것입니다. 제가 그와 우리 시설을 잠시 동안 둘러볼 예정입니다. 그 후에, ¹⁵여러분이 정기적으로 사용하는 장비 중 문제가 있는 것이 있다면 그에게 몇 분 정도 시간을 내어 알려주세요. 그가 이러한 장비들에 우선적으로 집중할 수 있을 것입니다.

13 장소 문제
해석 소개는 어디에서 이뤄지고 있는가?
(A) 사무실에서
(B) 실험실에서
(C) 창고에서
(D) 전시장에서
해설 지문에서 장소와 관련된 표현을 놓치지 않고 듣는다. "now that everyone has gathered here in the laboratory"라며 모두들 연구실에 모였다고 한 것을 통해, 소개는 연구실에서 이뤄지고 있음을 알 수 있다. 따라서 (B)가 정답이다.

14 특정 세부 사항 문제
해석 Scott Bailey는 누구인가?
(A) 영업사원
(B) 기술자
(C) 연구원
(D) 디자이너
해설 질문의 핵심 어구(Scott Bailey)가 언급된 주변을 주의 깊게 듣는다. "This meeting has been arranged to introduce Scott Bailey"라며 모임은 Scott Bailey를 소개하기 위해 마련되었다고 한 뒤, "His main responsibility will be equipment maintenance and repairs."라며 그의 주요 임무는 장비 유지 보수와 수리가 될 것이라고 한 것을 통해, 그가 기술자임을 알 수 있다. 따라서 (B)가 정답이다.

15 요청 문제
해석 청자들은 무엇을 해달라는 요청을 받았는가?
(A) 장비를 구매한다.
(B) 서류를 제출한다.
(C) 기구를 청소한다.
(D) 정보를 공유한다.

해설 지문에서 요청과 관련된 표현이 언급된 부분을 주의 깊게 듣는다. "please take a few minutes to tell him of any equipment you regularly use that is having problems"라며 청자들에게 정기적으로 사용하는 장비 중 문제가 있는 것들에 대해 Scott Bailey에게 알려 달라고 하였다. 따라서 (D)가 정답이다.

[16-18] 호주

Questions 16-18 refer to the following advertisement.

> Do you want the latest sports equipment at unbeatable prices? [16]**If so, come to Flynn Recreation, where we carry Edmonton's widest selection of athletic merchandise!** No matter what activity you're interested in, we have what you need. [17]**And if you sign up for our Flynn Loyalty Club, you will qualify for special discounts of up to 20 percent.** These are only available to members. We are also pleased to announce that [18]**we will begin offering equipment rentals. Starting next month, customers can rent gear for activities such as skiing, cycling, and camping at reasonable rates.** Visit us at 51 Baker Avenue to learn more!

unbeatable adj. 더 이상 좋을 수 없는 carry v. 취급하다
athletic adj. 운동의 qualify v. 자격을 갖추다 gear n. 장비
reasonable adj. 합리적인 rate n. 가격

해석
16-18번은 다음 광고에 관한 문제입니다.

최신 더 이상 좋을 수 없는 가격의 스포츠 장비를 원하시나요? [16]그렇다면, 에드먼턴에서 가장 다양한 운동 용품을 취급하는 Flynn Recreation으로 오세요! 어떤 활동에 관심이 있으시든, 저희는 여러분이 필요한 것을 갖추고 있습니다. [17]그리고 저희 Flynn 로열티 클럽에 가입하시면, 최대 20퍼센트의 특별 할인을 받을 자격을 갖추게 됩니다. 이러한 할인은 회원들에게만 제공됩니다. 저희는 또한 [18]장비 대여 서비스를 시작할 것을 기쁘게 알려드립니다. 다음 달부터, 고객들은 스키, 자전거, 캠핑과 같은 활동을 위한 장비를 합리적인 가격으로 대여할 수 있습니다. 더 자세히 알아보려면 Baker가 51번지로 저희를 방문해 주세요!

16 주제 문제
해설 무엇이 광고되고 있는가?
(A) 보관 시설
(B) 수리점
(C) 소매점
(D) 여행사

해설 광고의 주제를 묻는 문제이므로, 지문의 초반을 반드시 듣는다. "If so, come to Flynn Recreation, where we carry Edmonton's widest selection of athletic merchandise!"라며 에드먼턴에서 가장 다양한 운동 용품을 취급하는 Flynn Recreation으로 오라고 하였다. 이를 통해 Flynn Recreation은 운동 용품을 판매하는 소매점임을 알 수 있다. 따라서 (C)가 정답이다.

17 의도 파악 문제
해설 화자는 왜 "이러한 할인은 회원들에게만 제공됩니다"라고 말하는가?
(A) 만족을 표현하기 위해
(B) 과정을 설명하기 위해
(C) 결정을 정당화하기 위해
(D) 동기를 부여하기 위해

해설 질문의 인용어구(These are only available to members)가 언급된 주변을 주의 깊게 듣는다. "And if you sign up for our Flynn Loyalty Club, you will qualify for special discounts of up to 20 percent. These are only available to members."라며 Flynn 로열티 클럽에 가입하면 최대 20퍼센트의 특별 할인을 받을 자격이 생긴다고 한 후, 이러한 할인은 회원들에게만 제공된다고 하였다. 이를 통해 화자는 청자들에게 회원 가입을 하도록 동기를 부여하고 있음을 알 수 있다. 따라서 (D)가 정답이다.

18 다음에 할 일 문제
해설 화자는 다음 달에 무슨 일이 일어날 것이라고 말하는가?
(A) 새로운 서비스가 출시될 것이다.
(B) 해외 지점이 개점할 것이다.
(C) 연례 할인 행사가 열릴 것이다.
(D) 사업체가 이전할 것이다.

해설 질문의 핵심 어구(next month)와 관련된 내용을 주의 깊게 듣는다. "we will begin offering equipment rentals. Starting next month, customers can rent gear for activities ~ at reasonable rates."라며 장비 대여 서비스를 시작할 것이며, 다음 달부터 고객들이 활동을 위한 장비를 합리적인 가격으로 대여할 수 있다고 하였다. 따라서 (A)가 정답이다.

Paraphrasing
will begin offering equipment rentals 장비 대여 서비스를 시작할 것이다 → new service will be launched 새로운 서비스가 출시될 것이다

[19-21] 영국

Questions 19-21 refer to the following advertisement and sales report.

> [19]**The next time you are feeling hungry, look for Razzle— the nation's favorite brand of potato chips!** With over 10 delicious flavors and natural ingredients, this crunchy snack is perfect for almost any occasion. [20]**And we are thrilled to announce that our product now comes in eco-friendly bags that are completely recyclable.** So they won't harm the environment. This change was implemented in response to feedback from [21]**our fastest-growing age group of customers, who bought $6 billion worth of our chips** last year alone. So head to the nearest store, and get yourself some Razzle.

ingredient n. 재료 occasion n. 상황, 경우 recyclable adj. 재활용 가능한
harm v. 해를 끼치다 implement v. 시행하다 in response to ~에 대응하여

해석
19-21번은 다음 광고와 판매 보고서에 관한 문제입니다.

[19]다음번에 배고픔을 느끼실 때는, Razzle을 찾아보세요—국내에서 가장 인기 있는 감자칩 브랜드입니다! 10가지가 넘는 맛있는 맛과 천연 재료로, 이 바삭한 간식은 거의 모든 상황에 완벽합니다. [20]그리고 저희는 이제 제품이 완전히 재활용 가능한 친환경 봉지에 담겨 나온다는 것을 기쁘게 알려드립니다. 따라서 환경에 해를 끼치지 않을 것입니다. 이러한 변화는 작년에만 [21]60억 달러어치의 칩을 구매한, 저희의 가장 빠르게 성장하는 연령대 고객들의 의견에 대응하여 시행되었습니다. 그러니 가장 가까운 상점으로 가셔서, Razzle을 구매해 보세요.

연령대	연간 매출
16-25	80억 달러
[21]26-35	60억 달러
36-55	40억 달러
56-65	20억 달러

19 주제 문제
해설 어떤 종류의 제품이 광고되고 있는가?
(A) 보드 게임
(B) 음식 보관 봉투
(C) 음료

(D) 간식

해설 광고의 주제를 묻는 문제이므로, 지문의 초반을 반드시 듣는다. "The next time you are feeling hungry, look for Razzle—the nation's favorite brand of potato chips!"라며 다음번에 배고픔을 느끼실 때는, 국내에서 가장 인기 있는 감자칩 브랜드인 Razzle을 찾아보라고 하였다. 따라서 (D)가 정답이다.

20 특정 세부 사항 문제

해석 화자에 따르면, 최근에 무엇이 변경되었는가?
(A) 회사 로고
(B) 포장
(C) 향미
(D) 브랜드명

해설 질문의 핵심 어구(recently changed)와 관련된 내용을 주의 깊게 듣는다. "And we are thrilled to announce that our product now comes in eco-friendly bags that are completely recyclable."이라며 제품이 이제 완전히 재활용 가능한 친환경 봉지에 담겨 나온다고 하였다. 따라서 (B)가 정답이다.

[Paraphrasing]
eco-friendly bags 친환경 봉지 → Packaging 포장

21 시각 자료 문제

해석 시각 자료를 보아라. 어떤 것이 가장 빠르게 성장하는 고객 연령대인가?
(A) 16-25
(B) 26-35
(C) 36-55
(D) 56-65

해설 제시된 판매 보고서의 정보를 확인한 후 질문의 핵심 어구(fastest-growing age group)와 관련된 내용을 주의 깊게 듣는다. "our fastest-growing age group of customers, who bought $6 billion worth of our chips"라며 60억 달러어치의 칩을 구매한, 저희의 가장 빠르게 성장하는 연령대 고객이라고 하였고, 판매 보고서에서 60억 달러어치를 구매한 연령대는 26-35세임을 알 수 있다. 따라서 (B)가 정답이다.

PART 5

DAY 01 명사와 대명사

기출 공식 1~3

토익실전문제 p.140

| 01 (C) | 02 (D) | 03 (B) | 04 (A) |

01 명사 자리 채우기
해석 인사부의 가장 큰 우려는 자격을 갖춘 지원자들의 부족이다.
해설 부정관사(a) 다음에 올 수 있고 빈칸 뒤의 전치사구(of qualified candidates)의 꾸밈을 받을 수 있는 것은 명사이므로 명사 (C) shortage(부족)가 정답이다. 형용사 (A), 동사 (B), 부사 (D)는 명사 자리에 올 수 없다.
어휘 concern n. 우려 qualified adj. 자격을 갖춘 shorten v. 짧게 하다 shortly adv. 곧

02 명사 자리 채우기
해석 Opticore Financial사는 새 사무실을 위한 적합한 위치를 찾아오고 있다.
해설 빈칸은 동사(searching for)의 목적어이면서 형용사(suitable)의 꾸밈을 받는 명사 자리이므로 명사 (D) location(위치)이 정답이다. 동사 (A), 형용사 (B), 동사 또는 과거분사 (C)는 명사 자리에 올 수 없다.
어휘 locate v. 두다, 설치하다 locatable adj. 찾아낼 수 있는

03 가산 명사와 불가산 명사 구별하여 채우기
해석 싱가포르에서 전근을 오는 직원은 취업 비자 신청에 관해 필요한 서류를 준비해 달라는 요청을 받았다.
해설 빈칸은 동사(prepare)의 목적어이면서 형용사(necessary)의 꾸밈을 받는 명사 자리이므로 명사 (A)와 (B)가 정답의 후보이다. document (서류)는 반드시 앞에 한정사가 오거나 복수형으로 쓰이는 가산 명사이므로 복수형 (B) documents가 정답이다. 과거분사 (C)와 to 부정사 (D)는 형용사의 꾸밈을 받을 수 없다.
어휘 transfer v. 전근하다, 이동하다 necessary adj. 필요한 regarding prep. ~에 관하여

04 가산 명사와 불가산 명사 구별하여 채우기
해석 프로젝트 매니저는 마침내 세 명의 선임 소프트웨어 개발자를 고용할 승인을 받았다.
해설 빈칸은 동사(got)의 목적어이면서 to 부정사구(to hire ~ developers)의 꾸밈을 받는 명사 자리이므로 명사 (A)와 (B)가 정답의 후보이다. approval(승인)은 앞에 부정관사가 올 수 없고 복수형으로 쓰일 수 없는 불가산 명사이므로 (A) approval이 정답이다. 동사 (C)와 (D)는 명사 자리에 올 수 없다.
어휘 finally adv. 마침내 approve v. 승인하다

기출 공식 4~5

토익실전문제 p.141

| 01 (B) | 02 (A) | 03 (B) | 04 (C) |

01 사람명사와 사물/추상명사 구별하여 채우기
해석 참석자들은 지장을 주지 않기 위해 발표 중에 그들의 휴대폰을 꺼야 할 것이다.
해설 빈칸은 동사(will have to turn off)의 주어 자리이므로 명사 (B)와 (D), 동명사 (C)가 정답의 후보이다. '참석자들은 그들의 휴대폰을 꺼야 할 것이다'라는 의미가 되어야 하므로 사람명사 (B) Attendees(참석자)가 정답이다. 동명사 (C) Attending(참석하는 것)과 사물/추상명사 (D) Attendances(출석)를 쓸 경우 '참석하는 것/출석이 그들의 휴대폰을 꺼야 할 것이다'라는 어색한 의미를 만들기 때문에 답이 될 수 없다. 동사 (A)는 명사 자리에 올 수 없다.
어휘 disruption n. 지장, 방해 attend v. 참석하다

02 명사 자리 채우기
해석 Maison Luxe사의 새로운 제품 라인은 환경 과학자들과 함께 개발된 지속 가능한 소재를 특징으로 한다.
해설 빈칸은 소유격(Maison Luxe's) 뒤에 있고 형용사(new)의 꾸밈을 받고 있으므로, 빈칸 앞 명사 product와 함께 '제품 라인'이라는 의미의 복합 명사 product line을 만드는 명사 (A) line이 정답이다. 동사 또는 과거분사 (B), to 부정사 (C), 동명사 (D)는 product와 함께 복합 명사를 만들 수 없다.
어휘 feature v. 특징으로 하다 sustainable adj. 지속 가능한

03 사람명사와 사물/추상명사 구별하여 채우기
해석 대학교는 연구 역량을 강화하기 위해 실험실 장비에 투자를 하기로 결정했다.
해설 빈칸은 동사(make)의 목적어인 명사 자리이므로 명사 (B)와 (C)가 정답의 후보이다. '실험실 장비에 투자를 하다'라는 의미가 되어야 하므로 사물/추상명사 (B) investment(투자)가 정답이다. 사람명사 (C) investor(투자자)를 쓸 경우 '실험실 장비에 투자자를 만들다'라는 어색한 의미를 만들기 때문에 답이 될 수 없다. 동사 (A)와 (D)는 명사 자리에 올 수 없다. 참고로, make an investment는 '투자를 하다'라는 의미로 쓰인다.
어휘 substantial adj. 상당한 enhance v. 강화하다 capability n. 역량 invest v. 투자하다

04 명사 자리 채우기
해석 그 식물원은 3,000종 이상의 식물을 수용하는데, 연구 센터와 관광 명소 둘 다로서 역할을 한다.
해설 빈칸은 전치사(as)의 목적어 자리이므로, 빈칸 앞 명사 tourist와 함께 '관광 명소'라는 의미의 복합 명사 tourist attraction을 만드는 명사 (C) attraction이 정답이다. 동사 (A), 형용사 (B), 동명사 (D)는 tourist와 함께 복합 명사를 만들 수 없다.
어휘 botanical garden 식물원 house v. 수용하다, 보관하다 attract v. 마음을 끌다 attractive adj. 매력적인

기출 공식 6~8

토익실전문제 p.142

| 01 (C) | 02 (A) | 03 (B) | 04 (B) |

01 재귀대명사 채우기
해석 부동산 세미나에서 그들 자신을 소개한 사람들은 모두 그들의 분야에서 전문가였다.

해설 빈칸은 동사(introduced)의 목적어 자리이므로 목적어 자리에 올 수 있는 재귀대명사 (C) themselves가 정답이다. 주격 인칭대명사 (A)와 소유격 인칭대명사 (B)는 목적어 자리에 올 수 없다. (D) their own은 '그들만의'라는 의미로 소유격의 역할을 하므로 목적어 자리에 올 수 없고, on their own(스스로, 저절로)이라는 관용 표현으로 주로 쓰인다.

02 지시대명사 that 채우기
해설 새로운 에어컨 모델의 디자인은 이전 버전의 것보다 더 세련되었다.

해설 빈칸은 전치사(than)의 목적어이면서 전치사구(of the previous version)의 꾸밈을 받는 명사 자리이므로 지시대명사 (A)와 (C), 목적격 인칭대명사 (D)가 정답의 후보이다. '새로운 모델의 디자인은 이전 버전의 것보다 더 세련되었다'라는 의미가 되어야 하므로 앞에 나온 단수 명사 (design)를 대신하는 지시대명사 (A) that이 정답이다. 지시대명사 (C)와 목적격 인칭대명사 (D)는 앞에 나온 복수 명사를 대신해서 사용한다. 명사절 접속사 (B)는 뒤에 전치사구가 아닌 절이 와야 한다.

어휘 sophisticated adj. 세련된 previous adj. 이전의

03 지시대명사 those 채우기
해설 목요일에 있을 워크숍은 IT 업계에서 경력을 쌓는 것에 관심이 있는 사람들을 위한 것이다.

해설 빈칸은 전치사(for)의 목적어이면서 과거분사구(interested ~ industry)의 꾸밈을 받는 명사 자리이므로 지시대명사 (A)와 (B)가 정답의 후보이다. '경력을 쌓는 것에 관심이 있는 사람들'이라는 의미가 되어야 하므로 분사구의 꾸밈을 받아 '~한 사람들'이라는 의미로 쓰이는 지시대명사 (B) those가 정답이다. 지시대명사 (A)는 '~한 사람들'이라는 의미로 쓰일 수 없다. 명사절 접속사 (C)와 (D)는 뒤에 전치사구가 아닌 절이 와야 한다.

04 격에 맞는 인칭대명사 채우기
해설 우리는 이 프로그램을 성공적으로 만든 그녀의 기여를 인정하고 싶다.

해설 명사(contribution) 앞에서 형용사처럼 명사를 꾸밀 수 있는 인칭대명사는 소유격이므로 소유격 인칭대명사 (B) her가 정답이다. 주격 인칭대명사 (A), 소유대명사 (C), 재귀대명사 (D)는 명사를 꾸밀 수 없다.

기출 공식 9

토익실전문제 p.143

| 01 (A) | 02 (D) | 03 (B) | 04 (C) |

01 부정대명사 채우기
해설 그래픽 디자인을 위한 모니터를 선정할 때, 높은 색상 정확도와 해상도를 가진 하나를 골라라.

해설 '모니터를 선정할 때 높은 색상 정확도와 해상도를 가진 하나를 골라라'라는 의미가 되어야 하므로, 정해지지 않은 단수 가산 명사를 대신하는 부정대명사 (A) one(하나)이 정답이다. 참고로, one은 앞에 있는 monitor(모니터)를 지칭하고 있음을 알아 둔다. (B) ones는 복수 가산 명사를 대신한다. (C) other는 형용사로만 쓰이므로 동사(select)의 목적어 자리에 올 수 없다. (D) none은 '아무도, 아무것도'라는 의미이므로 문맥상 어색하다.

어휘 accuracy n. 정확도 resolution n. 해상도

02 부정대명사 채우기
해설 비록 Mr. Evans와 Mr. Ivanov는 경험이 풍부하지만, 둘 다 압박감 아래에서 잘 수행하지 않는다.

해설 빈칸은 주절의 주어 자리이므로, 주어 자리에 올 수 있는 모든 보기가 정답의 후보이다. '둘 다 압박감 아래에서 잘 수행하지 않는다'라는 의미가 되어야 하므로 부정대명사 (D) neither(둘 다 아닌 것)가 정답이다. (A) any는 '몇몇', (C) many는 '다수'라는 의미이므로 문맥상 어색하다. (B) nobody는 뒤에 'of the + 명사'가 올 수 없다.

어휘 experienced adj. 경험이 풍부한 under pressure 압박감 아래에서

03 부정대명사 채우기
해설 어떤 경우는 즉각적인 조치를 요구하는 반면에, 대부분은 숙고를 위한 시간을 허용한다.

해설 '어떤 경우는 즉각적인 조치를 요구하는 반면에, 대부분은 숙고를 위한 시간을 허용한다'라는 의미가 되어야 하므로 '대부분'이라는 의미를 나타내는 (B) most가 정답이다. (A) one, (C) another, (D) the other는 단수 취급하는데, 뒤에 복수 동사(allow)가 있으므로 답이 될 수 없다.

어휘 occasion n. 경우 demand v. 요구하다 immediate adj. 즉각적인 consideration n. 숙고, 고려

04 부정대명사 채우기
해설 전력 시스템 중 몇몇이라도 가동이 중단된다면, 시설 운영자들은 비상 규약을 따라야 한다.

해설 빈칸은 If절의 주어 자리이므로, 주어 자리에 올 수 있는 (A), (C), (D)가 정답의 후보이다. '전력 시스템 중 몇몇이라도 가동이 중단된다면'이라는 의미가 되어야 하므로 주로 조건문에 쓰이는 부정대명사 (C) any(몇몇)가 정답이다. (A) anything은 뒤에 'of the + 명사'가 올 수 없다. (D) each는 뒤에 'of the + 복수 명사 + 단수 동사'가 와야 하는데, 복수 동사(shut)가 있으므로 답이 될 수 없다. 형용사 또는 부사 (B) only는 주어 자리에 올 수 없다.

어휘 shut down 가동이 중단되다 facility n. 시설 operator n. 운영자 emergency protocol 비상 규약

HACKERS TEST p.144

01 (B)	02 (B)	03 (D)	04 (C)	05 (C)
06 (A)	07 (D)	08 (D)	09 (A)	10 (D)
11 (C)	12 (A)	13 (B)	14 (D)	15 (C)
16 (B)	17 (C)	18 (D)	19 (B)	20 (A)
21 (C)	22 (D)	23 (B)	24 (C)	25 (C)
26 (B)	27 (C)	28 (B)		

01 격에 맞는 인칭대명사 채우기
해설 Mr. Claiborne은 마케팅 컨설턴트로서 소비자들이 무엇을 원하는지 알아내는 것이 그의 일이라고 생각한다.

해설 명사(job) 앞에서 형용사처럼 명사를 꾸밀 수 있는 인칭대명사는 소유격이므로 소유격 인칭대명사 (B) his가 정답이다. 주격 인칭대명사 (A), 목적격 인칭대명사 (C), 재귀대명사 (D)는 명사를 꾸밀 수 없다.

어휘 find out ~을 알아내다, 알게 되다 consumer n. 소비자

02 부정형용사 채우기
해설 몇몇 중대한 문제가 해결되지 않은 상태였기 때문에 이사회 회의가 연장되어야 했다.

해설 빈칸 뒤의 명사(issues)를 꾸밀 수 있는 부정형용사 (A), (B), (C)가 정답의 후보이다. '몇몇 문제가 해결되지 않은 상태이다'라는 의미가 되어야 하므로 주로 긍정문에 쓰이는 부정형용사 (B) some(몇몇)이 정답이다. (A) any는 주로 부정문, 의문문, 조건문에 쓰인다. 부정형용사 (C)는 뒤에 단수 명사가 오므로 답이 될 수 없다. 대명사 (D) everybody는 형용사 자리에 올 수 없다.

어휘 board meeting 이사회 회의 extend v. 연장하다 critical adj. 중대한 unresolved adj. 해결되지 않은

03 명사 자리 채우기
해설 새로운 행사 담당자로서, Ms. Adrian은 다가오는 자선 경매를 위한 연회를 준비할 것이다.

해설 타동사(organize)의 목적어 자리에 올 수 있는 것은 명사이므로 명사 (D) entertainment(연회, 환대)가 정답이다. 동사 (A)와 (C), 동사 또는 과거분사 (B)는 명사 자리에 올 수 없다.

어휘 event coordinator 행사 담당자 organize v. 준비하다, 조직하다
upcoming adj. 다가오는 charity auction 자선 경매
entertain v. 즐겁게 해주다, 접대하다

04 가산 명사와 불가산 명사 구별하여 채우기

해석 사무실 보수 기간 동안, 직원들은 일시적으로 재택근무를 해야 했다.

해설 빈칸은 동사(had to work)의 주어 자리이므로 명사 (B)와 (C)가 정답의 후보이다. employee(직원)는 반드시 앞에 한정사가 오거나 복수형으로 쓰이는 가산 명사이므로 복수형 (C) employees가 정답이다. 동사 (A)와 (D)는 명사 자리에 올 수 없다.

어휘 renovation n. 보수 temporarily adv. 일시적으로 employ v. 고용하다

05 격에 맞는 인칭대명사 채우기

해석 오래된 책들을 버리는 대신, Inkwell 서점은 지역 도서관에 그것들을 기증하기로 결정했다.

해설 빈칸은 to 부정사(to donate)의 목적어 자리이므로 목적어 자리에 올 수 있는 인칭대명사 (A)와 (C), 재귀대명사 (D)가 정답의 후보이다. '오래된 책들을 버리는 대신 그것들을 기증하기로 결정했다'라는 의미가 되어야 하므로 복수 명사를 대신하는 목적격 인칭대명사 (C) them이 정답이다. 인칭대명사 (A)는 단수 명사를 대신한다. 재귀대명사 (D)는 '오래된 책들을 버리는 대신 그것 자신들을 기증하기로 결정했다'라는 어색한 의미를 만들기 때문에 답이 될 수 없다. 소유격 인칭대명사 (B)는 목적어 자리에 올 수 없다.

06 명사 자리 채우기

해석 교체 가구 주문품의 도착일은 다음 주 월요일이다.

해설 빈칸은 동사(is)의 주어 자리이고 전치사구(for ~ order)의 꾸밈을 받고 있으므로, 빈칸 앞 명사 arrival과 함께 '도착일'이라는 의미의 복합 명사 arrival date를 만드는 명사 (A)와 (C)가 정답의 후보이다. 뒤에 단수 동사(is)가 쓰였으므로 단수 명사 (A) date가 정답이다. 동사 또는 과거분사 (B), 동명사 (D)는 arrival과 함께 복합 명사를 만들 수 없다.

어휘 replacement n. 교체

07 사람명사와 사물/추상명사 구별하여 채우기

해석 훈련된 영업 보조원은 성수기 동안 장시간을 근무함에도 불구하고 능숙함을 유지했다.

해설 빈칸은 과거분사(trained)의 꾸밈을 받으며, 동사(remained)의 주어 자리이므로 명사 (B)와 (D)가 정답의 후보이다. '훈련된 영업 보조원은 장시간을 근무함에도 불구하고 능숙함을 유지했다'라는 의미가 되어야 하므로 사람명사 (D) assistant(보조원)가 정답이다. 사물/추상명사 (B) assistance(원조)를 쓸 경우 '훈련된 영업 원조는 장시간을 근무함에도 불구하고 능숙함을 유지했다'라는 어색한 의미를 만들기 때문에 답이 될 수 없다. 동사 (A)와 동사 또는 과거분사 (C)는 명사 자리에 올 수 없다.

어휘 professional adj. 능숙한, 전문적인 peak season 성수기

08 명사 자리 채우기

해석 많은 주민들은 고속도로를 폐쇄하겠다는 시의 결정에 대해 만족하지 않는다.

해설 소유격(the city's) 다음에 올 수 있는 것은 명사이므로 명사 (D) decision(결정)이 정답이다. 동사 (A), 형용사 (B), 동사 또는 과거분사 (C)는 명사 자리에 올 수 없다.

어휘 resident n. 주민, 거주자 highway n. 고속도로

09 격에 맞는 인칭대명사 채우기

해석 만약 당신이 예약을 해야 한다면, 저희 병원의 온라인 예약 시스템을 통해 등록해 주십시오.

해설 If절에 동사(need)만 있고, 주어가 없으므로 주어 역할을 할 수 있는 소유대명사 (A)와 주격 인칭대명사 (B)가 정답의 후보이다. '만약 당신이 예약을 해야 한다면'이라는 의미가 되어야 하므로 주격 인칭대명사 (A) you가 정답이다. 소유대명사 (B)를 쓸 경우 '만약 당신의 것이 예약을 해야 한다면'이라는 어색한 문맥을 만든다. 소유격 인칭대명사 (C)는 주어 역할을 할 수 없다. 재귀대명사 (D)는 목적어가 주어와 같은 사람이나 사물을 지칭할 때나, 주어나 목적어를 강조할 때 쓰인다.

어휘 make an appointment 예약을 하다, 약속을 잡다 register v. 등록하다

10 재귀대명사 채우기

해석 Data Pulse Solutions사는 그것 자신을 선도적인 인공지능 분석 회사로 변모시켰다.

해설 빈칸은 동사(transformed)의 목적어 자리이므로 목적어 자리에 올 수 있는 재귀대명사 (D) itself가 정답이다. 소유격 관계대명사 (A) whose는 뒤에 꾸밈을 받는 명사가 와야 하므로 답이 될 수 없다. 복합관계부사 (B) wherever는 뒤에 완전한 절이 와야 한다. (C) its own은 '그것만의'라는 소유격의 역할을 하므로 목적어 자리에 올 수 없고, on its own (스스로, 저절로)이라는 관용 표현으로 주로 쓰인다.

어휘 transform v. 변모시키다 leading adj. 선도적인

11 명사 자리 채우기

해석 Dr. Cruz는 회의에서 연설하도록 요청받았을 때 약간의 망설임을 보였지만, 결국 동의했다.

해설 타동사(showed)의 목적어 자리에 올 수 있으면서 빈칸 앞의 한정사(some)의 꾸밈을 받을 수 있는 것은 명사이므로 명사 (C) hesitation (망설임)이 정답이다. 동사 (A), 형용사 (B), 동사 또는 과거분사 (D)는 명사 자리에 올 수 없다.

어휘 ultimately adv. 결국, 궁극적으로 consent v. 동의하다
hesitate v. 망설이다, 주저하다 hesitant adj. 망설이는, 주저하는

12 부정대명사 채우기

해석 마을의 레스토랑 중에서, 최대 300명의 손님을 수용할 수 있는 유일한 한 곳이 Grand Palace이다.

해설 '마을의 레스토랑 중에서, 최대 300명의 손님을 수용할 수 있는 유일한 한 곳은 Grand Palace이다'라는 의미가 되어야 하므로, 정해지지 않은 단수 가산 명사를 대신하는 부정대명사 (A) one(하나)이 정답이다. 참고로, one은 앞에 있는 restaurant(식당)를 지칭하고 있음을 알아 둔다. (B) none(아무도, 아무것도)과 (C) most(대부분)는 어색한 문맥을 만든다. (D) others는 복수를 나타내므로 단수 동사(is)와 함께 쓸 수 없다.

어휘 accommodate v. 수용하다

13 사람명사와 사물/추상명사 구별하여 채우기

해석 Mr. Hawthorne은 회사에 대한 그의 기여에 대해 상여금을 받았다.

해설 빈칸은 소유격(his)과 전치사구(to the company)의 꾸밈을 받는 명사 자리이므로 명사 (B)와 (C)가 정답의 후보이다. '회사에 대한 그의 기여에 대해 상여금을 받았다'라는 의미가 되어야 하므로 사물/추상명사 (B) contribution(기여, 공헌)이 정답이다. 사람명사 (C) contributor(공헌자)를 쓸 경우 '회사에 대한 그의 공헌자에 대해 상여금을 받았다'라는 어색한 의미를 만들기 때문에 답이 될 수 없다. 동사 (A)와 동사 또는 과거분사 (D)는 명사 자리에 올 수 없다.

어휘 award v. 주다, 수여하다 bonus n. 상여금 contribution n. 기여

14 지시대명사 those 채우기

해석 휴가 패키지를 3개월 전에 예약하는 사람들에게 특별 할인이 제공된다.

해설 빈칸은 전치사(for)의 목적어이면서 관계절(who ~ advance)의 꾸밈을 받는 명사 자리이므로 목적격 인칭대명사 (A), 지시대명사 (B), 부정대명사 (D)가 정답의 후보이다. '3개월 전에 예약하는 사람들'이라는 의미가 되어야 하므로 관계절의 꾸밈을 받아 '~한 사람들'이라는 의미로 쓰이는 지시대명사 (B) those가 정답이다. 목적격 인칭대명사 (A)와 부정대명사 (D)는 '~한 사람들'이라는 의미로 쓰일 수 없다. 관계대명사 (C) 뒤에는 관계대명사(who)로 시작하는 관계절이 올 수 없다.

15 명사 자리 채우기

해석 Gasmark International사는 추가로 5년 연장 가능성이 있는 5년짜리 계약에 동의했다.

해설 부정관사(a) 다음에 오면서 빈칸 앞의 형용사(possible)의 꾸밈을 받을 수 있는 것은 명사이므로 명사 (C) extension(연장)이 정답이다. 동사 (A), 형용사 (B), 동사 또는 과거분사 (D)는 명사 자리에 올 수 없다.

어휘 extend v. 연장하다   extensive adj. 대규모의, 광범위한

16 명사 자리 채우기

해석 그 대형 소매업체는 증가하는 고객 수요를 충족하기 위해 그것의 가장 큰 규모의 물류 센터를 이전할 것이다.

해설 빈칸은 형용사(largest)의 꾸밈을 받는 명사 자리이므로, 빈칸 뒤 명사 center와 함께 '물류 센터'라는 의미의 복합 명사 distribution center를 만드는 명사 (B) distribution이 정답이다. 동사 (A)와 동사 또는 과거분사 (C)는 명사 자리에 올 수 없다. 과거분사 (C)와 형용사 (D)를 빈칸 뒤의 center를 꾸미는 것으로 본다 해도, '분배된/분배할 수 있는 센터'라는 어색한 의미를 만들기 때문에 답이 될 수 없다.

어휘 retail giant 대형 소매업체   relocate v. 이전하다   meet v. 충족하다, 만나다
demand n. 수요

17 부정대명사 채우기

해석 한 후보자는 선거 지출을 줄이기로 약속했지만, 다른 후보자들은 지출을 제한하는 것을 거부했다.

해설 빈칸은 동사(declined)의 주어 자리이고, '한 후보자는 선거 지출을 줄이기로 약속했지만, 다른 후보자들은 지출을 제한하는 것을 거부했다'라는 의미가 되어야 하므로 '이미 언급한 것 이외의 것들 중 몇몇'이라는 의미의 부정대명사 (C) others가 정답이다. 참고로, others는 앞에 있는 candidate(후보자)를 지칭하고 있음을 알아 둔다. 복합관계대명사 (A)는 뒤에 절이 와야 하고, 부정형용사 (B)와 재귀대명사 (D)는 주어 자리에 올 수 없다.

어휘 pledge v. 약속하다   decline v. 거절하다   limit v. 제한하다

18 사람명사와 사물/추상명사 구별하여 채우기

해석 연례 차량 검사는 대부분의 주에서 의무적이어서, 운전자들은 그들의 차가 요구되는 기준을 반드시 충족하도록 해야 한다.

해설 빈칸은 동사(are)의 주어 자리이므로 명사 (B)와 (D)가 정답의 후보이다. '연례 차량 검사는 의무적이다'라는 의미가 되어야 하므로 사물/추상 명사 (D) inspections(검사)가 정답이다. 사람명사 (B) inspectors(검사자)를 쓸 경우 '연례 차량 검사자는 의무적이다'라는 어색한 의미를 만들기 때문에 답이 될 수 없다. 동사 (A)와 동사 또는 과거분사 (C)는 명사 자리에 올 수 없다. 과거분사 (C)를 빈칸 앞의 vehicle을 꾸미는 과거분사로 본다 해도, 구를 이루지 않고 명사를 뒤에서 꾸밀 수 없으므로 답이 될 수 없다.

어휘 annual adj. 연례의   mandatory adj. 의무적인
ensure v. 반드시 ~하도록 하다   required adj. 요구되는
inspect v. 점검하다

19 부정대명사 채우기

해석 권장된 변경 사항 중 아무것도 최종 버전에 시행되지 않았다.

해설 '권장된 변경 사항 중 아무것도 시행되지 않았다'라는 의미가 되어야 하므로 부정대명사 (B) None(아무것도)이 정답이다. (A) One과 (C) No one은 단수 명사를 대신하는데, 뒤에 복수 동사(were implemented)가 있으므로 답이 될 수 없다. 참고로, no one은 주로 사람명사를 지칭한다는 점을 알아 둔다. (D) Nothing은 뒤에 'of the + 명사'가 올 수 없다.

어휘 implement v. 시행하다

20 명사 자리 채우기

해석 그 수석 건축가는 Greene 재단의 프로젝트들 중 하나를 감독하기 위한 권한을 부여받았다.

해설 빈칸 앞에 목적어를 두 개 가지는 4형식 동사 give(~에게 -을 주다)가 수동태로 쓰여 간접 목적어(The senior architect)가 주어 자리에 왔으므로, 빈칸은 직접 목적어 자리이다. 따라서 목적어 자리에 올 수 있는 명사 (A) authority(권한)가 정답이다. 동사 (B), 형용사 (C), 부사 (D)는 명사 자리에 올 수 없다. 동사 give를 목적어를 한 개만 갖는 3형식 동사로 보고 부사 (D)가 동사(was given)를 꾸미는 것으로 본다 해도, '수석 건축가가 위압적으로 주어졌다'라는 어색한 문맥을 만들기 때문에 답이 될 수 없다.

어휘 oversee v. 감독하다   authorize v. 권한을 부여하다
authoritative adj. 권위적인   authoritatively adv. 위압적으로

21 지시대명사 that 채우기

해석 폭염 동안의 실제 기온은 기상 예측 모델의 것과 달랐다.

해설 빈칸은 전치사(from)의 목적어이면서 전치사구(in ~ model)의 꾸밈을 받는 명사 자리이므로 지시대명사 (B)와 (C)가 정답의 후보이다. '실제 기온은 기상 예측 모델의 것과 달랐다'라는 의미가 되어야 하므로 앞에 나온 단수 명사(temperature)를 대신하는 지시대명사 (C) that이 정답이다. 지시대명사 (B)는 앞에 나온 복수 명사를 대신해서 사용한다. 형용사 또는 부사 (A)와 전치사 (D)는 명사 자리에 올 수 없다.

어휘 heatwave n. 폭염   differ v. 다르다   prediction n. 예측

22 재귀대명사 채우기

해석 Ms. Wynn은 24년간의 교육 경험을 바탕으로 고급 과정을 위한 커리큘럼을 직접 개발했다.

해설 이 문장은 주어(Ms. Wynn), 동사(developed), 목적어(the curriculum ~ courses)를 갖춘 완전한 절이므로 빈칸은 수식어 거품으로 보아야 한다. 'Ms. Wynn은 커리큘럼을 직접 개발했다'라는 의미가 되어야 하므로 강조 용법의 재귀대명사 (D) herself가 정답이다. 참고로, 강조 용법의 재귀대명사는 부사 역할을 하여 강조하고자 하는 말 바로 뒤나 문장 맨 뒤에 올 수 있다. 주격 인칭대명사 (A), 소유격 또는 목적격 인칭대명사 (B), 소유대명사 (C)는 수식어 거품 자리에 올 수 없다.

어휘 advanced adj. 고급의

23 명사 자리 채우기

해석 회사 웹사이트의 오해의 소지가 있는 제품 설명서는 수많은 고객 불만을 야기했다.

해설 빈칸은 형용사(misleading)의 꾸밈을 받는 명사 자리이므로, 빈칸 앞 명사 product와 함께 '제품 설명서'라는 의미의 복합 명사 product description을 만드는 명사 (B) description이 정답이다. 동사 (A)와 형용사 (C)는 명사 자리에 올 수 없다. 동명사 (D)는 명사 자리에는 올 수 있지만, product와 함께 복합 명사를 만들 수 없다.

어휘 misleading adj. 오해의 소지가 있는   result in ~을 야기하다
numerous adj. 수많은   complaint n. 불만   describe v. 묘사하다
descriptive adj. 서술하는

24 가산 명사와 불가산 명사 구별하여 채우기

해석 그 환경 기관은 대기질 수준이 상당히 개선되었다는 정보를 공유했다.

해설 빈칸은 동사(shared)의 목적어 자리이므로 명사 (C)와 (D)가 정답의 후보이다. information(정보)은 앞에 부정관사가 올 수 없고 복수형으로 쓰일 수 없는 불가산 명사이므로 (C) information이 정답이다. 동사 (A)와 동사 또는 과거분사 (B)는 명사 자리에 올 수 없다.

어휘 air quality 대기질   significantly adv. 상당히   inform v. 알리다

25 명사 자리 채우기

해석 유전자 변형 기술로 실험을 수행한 연구팀은 유망한 결과를 보였다.

해설 빈칸은 동명사(conducting)의 목적어 자리이므로 명사 (C) experiments(실험)가 정답이다. 참고로, 동명사는 명사의 성질을 가지므로 목적어를 가질 수 있다는 점을 알아 둔다. 동사 또는 과거분사 (A), 형용사 (B), 부사 (D)는 명사 자리에 올 수 없다.

어휘 conduct v. (실험 등을) 수행하다   genetic modification 유전자 변형

promising adj. 유망한 experiment v. 실험하다; n. 실험
experimental adj. 실험적인 experimentally adv. 실험적으로

26 사람명사와 사물/추상명사 구별하여 채우기
해석 Quantum Analytics사에서 근무하는 금융 상담가들은 회사가 투자 전략을 탐색하는 데 도움을 주고 있다.

해설 빈칸은 동사(are helping)의 주어 자리이며 현재분사구(working at Quantum Analytics)의 꾸밈을 받는 자리이므로 명사 (B), (C), (D)가 정답의 후보이다. 'Quantum Analytics사에서 근무하는 금융 상담가들'이라는 의미가 되어야 하므로 사람명사 (B) consultants(상담가)가 정답이다. 사물/추상명사 (C) consultations(상담)와 (D) consultancies(컨설팅사)를 쓸 경우 'Quantum Analytics사에서 근무하는 금융 상담들/컨설팅사들'이라는 어색한 의미를 만들기 때문에 답이 될 수 없다. 동사 (A)는 명사 자리에 올 수 없다.

어휘 financial adj. 금융의 navigate v. 탐색하다 consult v. 상담하다

27 명사 자리 채우기
해석 정부는 그것이 Habro Chemical사와의 합의에서 받았던 돈을 오염된 수로를 복구하기 위해 사용했다.

해설 전치사(from)의 목적어 역할을 하면서 부정관사(a) 다음에 올 수 있는 것은 명사이므로 명사 (C) settlement(합의, 해결)가 정답이다. 동사 (A), 동사 또는 과거분사 (B), 형용사 (D)는 명사 자리에 올 수 없다.

어휘 government n. 정부 restore v. 복구하다, 회복시키다
polluted adj. 오염된, 더럽혀진 waterway n. 수로
settle v. 해결하다, 합의를 보다 settleable adj. 자리 잡을 수 있는

28 부정대명사 채우기
해석 Kenneth 출판사는 운영 비용을 줄이는 효과적인 방법을 제안하는 회사의 누구에게든 상여금을 줄 것이다.

해설 빈칸은 주격 관계절(who suggests ~ costs)의 선행사 자리인데, 선행사와 수 일치하는 관계절의 동사(suggests)가 단수 동사이므로 단수 취급되는 부정대명사 (D) anyone(누구나)이 정답이다. 지시대명사 (A)는 '~한 사람들'이라는 의미로, 복수 취급되므로 복수 동사와 쓰여야 한다. 부정형용사 (B)는 명사 자리에 올 수 없다. 부정대명사 (C)를 쓸 경우 '효과적인 방법을 제안하는 회사의 누구에게도 상여금을 제공하지 않을 것이다'라는 어색한 문맥이 된다.

어휘 effective adj. 효과적인, 시행되는, 유효한 reduce v. 줄이다
operating cost 운영 비용, 경영 비용

DAY 02 동사

기출 공식 1~3

토익실전문제 p.146

01 (A)   02 (D)   03 (D)   04 (C)

01 조동사 다음에 동사원형 채우기
해석 VisionTech 프로그램의 개발자는 필요한 개선을 하기 위해 사용자의 피드백을 수집해야 한다.

해설 조동사(should) 다음에 올 수 있는 것은 동사원형이므로 동사원형 (A) gather(수집하다)가 정답이다. 동사의 3인칭 단수형 (B), 동사의 과거형 또는 과거분사 (C), 동명사 또는 현재분사 (C)는 조동사 다음의 동사원형 자리에 올 수 없다.

어휘 necessary adj. 필요한 improvement n. 개선

02 제안·요청·의무의 주절을 뒤따르는 that절에 동사원형 채우기
해석 Ms. Paige의 조언은 마케팅 전략에 소셜 미디어 요소가 포함되어야 한다는 것이었다.

해설 that절(that ~ component)에 동사가 없고 주절(Ms. Paige's advice was)에 제안·요청·의무를 나타내는 명사(advice)가 왔으므로 that절의 동사 자리에는 동사원형이 와야 한다. 따라서 동사원형 (D) include (포함하다)가 정답이다. 동명사 또는 현재분사 (A), 동사의 과거형 또는 과거분사 (B), 동사의 3인칭 단수형 (C)는 동사원형 자리에 올 수 없다.

어휘 advice n. 충고 component n. 요소

03 제안·요청·의무의 주절을 뒤따르는 that절에 동사원형 채우기
해석 항상 신뢰할 수 있는 결과를 보장하기 위해 데이터가 정확하게 분석되는 것은 필수적이다.

해설 that절(that ~ time)에 동사가 없고 주절(It is imperative)에 제안·요청·의무를 나타내는 형용사(imperative)가 왔으므로 that절의 동사 자리에는 동사원형이 와야 한다. 따라서 동사원형을 포함하는 (D) be analyzed(분석되다)가 정답이다. 동사의 3인칭 단수형 (A), 동사의 3인칭 단수형을 포함하는 (B), 명사 (C)는 동사원형 자리에 올 수 없다.

어휘 imperative adj. 필수적인 accurately adv. 정확하게 ensure v. 보장하다
reliable adj. 신뢰할 수 있는 all the time 항상

04 동사 자리 채우기
해석 신제품 포장을 디자인하기 위해, 브랜드 정체성에 맞는 색상 구성표를 선택하세요.

해설 이 문장은 주어가 없는 명령문이므로, 명령문의 동사 자리에 올 수 있는 동사원형 (C) choose(선택하다)가 정답이다. 동사의 과거형 (A), 과거분사 (B), 명사 (D)는 명령문의 동사 자리에 올 수 없다.

어휘 color scheme 색상 구성표 match v. (색, 스타일 등이 서로) 맞다
identity n. 정체성

기출 공식 4~5

토익실전문제 p.147

01 (A)   02 (B)   03 (A)   04 (C)

01 주어와 수일치하는 동사 채우기
해석 등록금을 줄이는 것은 교육을 더 접근성 있게 만들기 위한 중요한 단계이다.

해설 문장에 주어(Reducing tuition fees)만 있고 동사가 없으므로 동사 (A), (B), (C)가 정답의 후보이다. 동명사구 주어는 단수 취급하므로 단수 동사 (A) is가 정답이다. 복수 동사 (B)와 (C)는 복수 주어와 함께 써야 한다. 동명사 또는 현재분사 (D)는 동사 자리에 올 수 없다.

어휘 tuition fee 등록금 critical adj. 중요한 accessible adj. 접근성 있는

02 주어와 수일치하는 동사 채우기
해석 각 자동차 엔진은 특히 가속하거나 고속으로 달릴 때 제작사와 모델에 따라 소리가 다르게 들린다.

해설 문장에 주어(Each car engine)만 있고 동사가 없으므로 동사 (A)와 (B)가 정답의 후보이다. 'each + 명사'는 단수 취급하므로 단수 동사 (B) sounds(들리다)가 정답이다. 복수 동사 (A)는 복수 주어와 함께 써야 한다. 동명사 또는 현재분사 (C)와 부사 (D)는 동사 자리에 올 수 없다.

어휘 depending on ~에 따라 make n. 제작사 especially adv. 특히
accelerate v. 가속하다 soundly adv. 깊이, 타당하게

03 주어와 수일치하는 동사 채우기
해석 인사 통계에 따르면, 직원 중 20퍼센트만이 회사의 건강 프로그램을 이용한다.

해설 문장에 주어(only 20 percent of employees)만 있고 동사가 없으므로 동사 (A), (B), (C)가 정답의 후보이다. percent는 of 뒤의 명사에 동

04 주어와 수일치하는 동사 채우기
해석 사용자가 그들의 재정을 관리할 수 있도록 하는 새로운 앱은 이제 다운로드가 가능하다.
해설 빈칸은 명사(The new app)를 꾸미는 주격 관계절(that ~ finances)의 동사 자리이므로 동사 (A)와 (C)가 정답의 후보이다. 주격 관계절의 동사는 선행사(The new app)와 수일치하므로 단수 동사 (C) allows(~하게 하다)가 정답이다. 복수 동사 (A)는 복수 선행사와 함께 써야 한다. 동명사 또는 현재분사 (B)와 명사 (D)는 동사 자리에 올 수 없다.
어휘 manage v. 관리하다 finance n. 재정 available adj. 가능한 allowance n. 용돈, 비용

기출 공식 6~7

토익실전문제　　　　　　　　　　　　　　　　　p.148

01 (B)　**02** (A)　**03** (C)　**04** (B)

01 자동사와 타동사 구별하여 채우기
해석 부서장은 예상치 못한 비용 증가에 대해 설명하라는 요청을 받았다.
해설 '예상치 못한 비용 증가에 대해 설명하라는 요청을 받았다'라는 문맥이므로 (B) account(설명하다)가 정답이다. (A) explain(설명하다)과 (C) address(말하다)도 해석상 그럴듯해 보이지만 타동사이므로 빈칸 뒤의 전치사(for)와 함께 쓰일 수 없다. (D) await는 '기다리다'라는 의미이다.
어휘 department head 부서장 unexpected adj. 예상치 못한 expense n. 비용

02 자동사와 타동사 구별하여 채우기
해석 Mr. Taylor의 상사는 보고서의 연장된 기한에 대한 요청을 승인했다.
해설 '보고서의 연장된 기한에 대한 요청을 승인했다'라는 문맥이므로 (A) approved(승인하다)가 정답이다. (B) agreed(동의하다), (C) objected(반대하다), (D) reacted(반응하다)도 해석상 그럴듯해 보이지만 자동사이므로 목적어(his request)와 함께 쓰이기 위해서는 전치사가 필요하다.
어휘 extended adj. 연장된 deadline n. 기한

03 3형식 동사와 4형식 동사 구별하여 채우기
해석 항공사는 폭풍으로 인해 항공편이 지연되었다는 것을 승객들에게 알렸다.
해설 '항공사는 항공편이 지연되었다는 것을 승객들에게 알렸다'라는 문맥이고, 빈칸 뒤에 간접 목적어(the passengers)와 직접 목적어(that ~ storm)가 둘 다 있으므로 4형식 동사 (C) notified(알리다)가 정답이다. (A) said(말하다), (B) described(설명하다), (D) mentioned(말하다)도 해석상 그럴듯해 보이지만 3형식 동사이므로 뒤에 목적어가 두 개 나올 수 없다.

04 자동사와 타동사 구별하여 채우기
해석 저희의 고객 서비스 팀은 24시간 이내에 귀하의 문의에 답변하겠습니다.
해설 '24시간 이내에 귀하의 문의에 답변하겠습니다'라는 문맥이므로 (B) respond(답변하다)가 정답이다. (A) answer(대답하다)도 해석상 그럴듯해 보이지만 타동사이므로 빈칸 뒤의 전치사(to)와 함께 쓰일 수 없다. (C) obey는 '따르다', (D) instruct는 '지시하다'라는 의미의 타동사이다.
어휘 inquiry n. 문의 within prep. ~ 이내에

기출 공식 8~9

토익실전문제　　　　　　　　　　　　　　　　　p.149

01 (B)　**02** (C)　**03** (A)　**04** (C)

01 태에 맞는 동사 채우기
해석 대학교는 그것의 학업 프로그램을 강화하기 위해 다양한 분야의 전문가들을 모집했다.
해설 문장에 주어(The university)만 있고 동사가 없으므로 동사 (A), (B), (C)가 정답의 후보이다. 빈칸 뒤에 목적어(experts)가 있고 '전문가들을 모집하다'라는 능동의 의미가 되어야 하므로 능동태 동사 (B) recruited(모집하다)가 정답이다. 주어가 단수이므로 복수 동사 (A)는 답이 될 수 없다. 동명사 또는 현재분사 (D)는 동사 자리에 올 수 없다.
어휘 expert n. 전문가 various adj. 다양한 field n. 분야 strengthen v. 강화하다

02 태에 맞는 동사 채우기
해석 생산성을 평가하기 위해 직원들의 성과는 정기적으로 감독되어야 한다.
해설 문장에 주어(Employee's performance)만 있고 동사가 없으므로 be동사(be)와 함께 동사를 만드는 현재분사 (B)와 과거분사 (C)가 정답의 후보이다. 목적어가 없고 '성과는 감독되어야 한다'라는 수동의 의미가 되어야 하므로 수동태를 만드는 과거분사 (C) monitored(감독하다)가 정답이다. 동사원형 (A)와 to 부정사 (D)는 be동사와 함께 동사를 만들 수 없다.
어휘 performance n. 성과 regularly adv. 정기적으로 assess v. 평가하다 productivity n. 생산성

03 수동태 관용 표현 채우기
해석 사무실 전체가 회사의 창립 50주년 기념 행사에 참석할 것을 요청받았다.
해설 문장에 주어(The entire office)만 있고 동사가 없으므로 동사 (A)와 (B)가 정답의 후보이다. '기념 행사에 참석할 것을 요청받았다'라는 의미가 되어야 하므로 '~할 것을 요청받다'라는 표현을 만드는 (A) is invited가 정답이다. 명사 (C)와 동명사 또는 현재분사 (D)는 동사 자리에 올 수 없다.
어휘 entire adj. 전체의 attend v. 참석하다 invitation n. 초대, 초대장

04 수동태 관용 표현 채우기
해석 Ms. Bianchi는 최근에 그녀가 온라인에서 구매한 제품의 낮은 품질에 실망했다.
해설 '제품의 낮은 품질에 실망했다'라는 의미가 되어야 하므로 '~에 실망하다'라는 표현을 만드는 (C) disappointed가 정답이다. 동사원형 (A)와 부사 (D)는 be동사 뒤에 올 수 없다.
어휘 poor adj. (품질 등이) 낮은 recently adv. 최근에

기출 공식 10~11

토익실전문제　　　　　　　　　　　　　　　　　p.150

01 (D)　**02** (D)　**03** (C)　**04** (D)

01 올바른 시제의 동사 채우기
해석 Urban Thread사는 곧 출시될 재킷과 코트 컬렉션을 선보이기 위해 다음 주에 팝업 스토어를 열 것이다.
해설 문장에 주어(Urban Thread)만 있고 동사가 없으므로 동사 (A), (C), (D)가 정답의 후보이다. 미래를 나타내는 표현인 next week(다음 주)가 있으므로 미래 시제 (D) will open(열다)이 정답이다. 현재 시제 (A)도 미래에 예정된 일을 나타낼 수 있지만, 주어가 단수이므로 복수 동사는 답이 될 수 없다. to 부정사 (B)는 동사 자리에 올 수 없다.

02 올바른 시제의 동사 채우기

해석 만약 우리의 새로운 700Q 헤드폰이 성공적으로 출시된다면, 우리의 시장 점유율은 상당히 증가할 것이다.

해설 If절에 주어(our new 700Q headphone)만 있고 동사가 없으므로 동사 (A)와 (D)가 정답의 후보이다. 조건을 나타내는 종속절에서는 미래 시제 대신 현재 시제를 쓰므로 현재 시제 (D) launches(출시되다)가 정답이다. 동명사 또는 현재분사 (B)와 to 부정사 (C)는 동사 자리에 올 수 없다.

어휘 successfully adv. 성공적으로   market share 시장 점유율
significantly adv. 상당히

03 올바른 시제의 동사 채우기

해석 마이크가 작동을 멈췄을 때 그 발표자는 주요한 개념을 설명하고 있었다.

해설 주절에 주어(The speaker)만 있고 동사가 없으므로 모든 보기가 정답의 후보이다. 주절은 when이 이끄는 종속절과 같은 시점에 일어났고, 종속절(when ~ working)에 과거 시제 동사(stopped)가 쓰였으므로 과거진행 시제 (C) was explaining(설명하다)이 정답이다. 빈칸 뒤에 목적어(key concepts)가 있으므로 과거 시제 수동태 (D)는 답이 될 수 없다.

어휘 key adj. 주요한   concept n. 개념   work v. 작동하다

04 올바른 시제의 동사 채우기

해석 안전을 강화하기 위해 건물에 선진 보안 시스템이 설치되고 있다.

해설 be동사(is) 뒤에 올 수 있는 명사 (B)와 (C), 현재진행 시제를 만드는 (D)가 정답의 후보이다. '선진 보안 시스템이 설치되고 있다'라는 의미가 되어야 하므로 빈칸 앞의 be동사(is)와 함께 현재진행 시제를 만드는 (D)가 정답이다. (B) installation(설치)과 (C) installment(할부금)를 쓸 경우 '선진 보안 시스템이 설치/할부금이다'라는 어색한 의미를 만들기 때문에 답이 될 수 없다. 동사원형 (A)는 be동사 뒤에 올 수 없다.

어휘 advanced adj. 선진의   security system 보안 시스템
enhance v. 강화하다

기출 공식 12

토익실전문제   p.151

01 (B)   02 (C)   03 (D)   04 (C)

01 올바른 시제의 동사 채우기

해석 Local Lift 재단은 지난 30년 동안 지역 사업체들에 재정적인 지원을 제공해 왔다.

해설 문장에 주어(The Local Lift Foundation)만 있고 동사가 없으므로 동사 (B)와 (C)가 정답의 후보이다. 현재완료를 나타내는 표현인 'over the last + 기간'(지난 ~ 동안)이 있으므로 현재완료 시제 (B) has provided(제공하다)가 정답이다. 명사 (A)와 to 부정사 (D)는 동사 자리에 올 수 없다.

어휘 financial adj. 재정적인   support n. 지원   provision n. 공급, 제공

02 올바른 시제의 동사 채우기

해석 인사부는 최종 후보자를 선발하기 전에 수백 명의 지원자를 가려냈다.

해설 주절에 주어(The HR department)만 있고 동사가 없으므로 동사 (A), (C), (D)가 정답의 후보이다. 주절(The HR department ~ applicants)에서 나타내는 사건, 즉 인사부가 지원자를 가려낸 시점은 before가 이끄는 절(they ~ candidates)에서 나타내는 사건, 즉 인사부가 최종 후보자를 선발한 것보다 먼저 일어난 일이다. before가 이끄는 절에 과거 시제 동사(selected)가 쓰였으므로 과거의 특정 시점 이전에 발생한 일을 나타내는 과거완료 시제 (C) had screened(가려내다)가 정답이다. 동명사 또는 현재분사 (B)는 동사 자리에 올 수 없다.

어휘 applicant n. 지원자   select v. 선발하다   candidate n. 후보자

03 올바른 시제의 동사 채우기

해석 엔지니어링팀이 중대한 결함을 발견한 이후로 그 전자 기기는 교체를 위해 제조업체에 반환되어 왔다.

해설 주절에 주어(The electronic devices)만 있고 동사가 없으므로 동사 (B), (C), (D)가 정답의 후보이다. 현재완료를 나타내는 표현인 'since + 주어 + 과거 시제'(~한 이후로)가 있고 '반환되어 왔다'라는 수동의 의미가 되어야 하므로 현재완료 시제 수동태 (D) have been returned (반환하다)가 정답이다. to 부정사 (A)는 동사 자리에 올 수 없다.

어휘 electronic device 전자 기기   manufacturer n. 제조업체
replacement n. 교체   identify v. 발견하다   flaw n. 결함

04 올바른 시제의 동사 채우기

해석 다수의 국제 디자인 수상자인 David Chen은 20년 동안 혁신적인 건축물을 설계해 왔다.

해설 문장에 주어(David Chen)만 있고 동사가 없으므로 모든 보기가 정답의 후보이다. 현재완료를 나타내는 표현인 'for + 기간'(~ 동안)이 있으므로 현재완료진행 시제 (C) has been designing(설계하다)이 정답이다. '건축물을 설계해 왔다'라는 능동의 의미가 되어야 하므로 수동태 (A)와 (D)는 답이 될 수 없고, 주어가 단수이므로 복수 동사 (B)는 답이 될 수 없다.

어휘 multiple adj. 다수의   innovative adj. 혁신적인   architecture n. 건축물

HACKERS TEST   p.152

01 (A)	02 (D)	03 (B)	04 (A)	05 (D)
06 (B)	07 (B)	08 (C)	09 (A)	10 (B)
11 (D)	12 (C)	13 (C)	14 (D)	15 (B)
16 (A)	17 (B)	18 (D)	19 (D)	20 (C)
21 (B)	22 (A)	23 (B)	24 (D)	25 (C)
26 (C)	27 (B)	28 (B)		

01 동사 자리 채우기

해석 필요한 모든 영수증을 첨부하여 여러분의 지출 보고서를 제출해 주세요.

해설 이 문장은 주어가 없는 명령문이므로, 명령문의 동사 자리에 올 수 있는 동사원형 (A) submit(제출하다)이 정답이다. 동사의 과거형 또는 과거분사 (B), 3인칭 단수형 (C), 명사 (D)는 명령문의 동사 자리에 올 수 없다.

어휘 expense report 지출 보고서   receipt n. 영수증   attach v. 첨부하다

02 주어와 수일치하는 동사 채우기

해석 봉사자들 중 다수가 지역 자선단체와 비영리 기구를 위한 기금을 마련하는 것을 돕는다.

해설 문장에 주어(Many of the volunteers)만 있고 동사가 없으므로 동사 (A), (C), (D)가 정답의 후보이다. 'many of the + 명사'는 복수 취급하므로 복수 동사 (D) help(돕다)가 정답이다. 단수 동사 (A)와 (C)는 단수 주어와 함께 써야 한다. 형용사 (B)는 동사 자리에 올 수 없다.

어휘 volunteer n. 봉사자   raise fund 기금을 마련하다   charity n. 자선단체
non-profit organization 비영리 기구   helpful adj. 도움이 되는

03 자동사와 타동사 구별하여 채우기

해석 Apex Gas사는 Fairfax시 의회의 요청에 따라 그것의 요금 인상을 연기하는 것에 동의했다.

해설 '요금 인상을 연기하는 것에 동의했다'라는 문맥이므로 (B) agreed (동의하다)가 정답이다. (D) approved(승인하다)도 해석상 그럴듯해 보이지만 타동사이므로 빈칸 뒤의 전치사(to)와 함께 쓰일 수 없다. (A) reached는 '도착하다', (C) reminded는 '상기시키다'라는 의미이다.

어휘 rate n. 요금

04 태에 맞는 동사 채우기

해석 그 정책은 설탕이 함유된 음료들에 더 높은 세금을 부과함으로써 설탕 소비를 줄일 것이다.

해설 문장에 주어(The measure)만 있고 동사가 없으므로 동사 (A), (B), (D)가 정답의 후보이다. 빈칸 뒤에 목적어(sugar consumption)가 있고 '설탕 소비를 줄일 것이다'라는 능동의 의미가 되어야 하므로 능동태 동사 (A) will reduce(줄이다)가 정답이다. 동명사 또는 현재분사 (C)는 동사 자리에 올 수 없다.

어휘 measure n. 정책 consumption n. 소비 sweetened adj. 설탕이 함유된

05 올바른 시제의 동사 채우기

해석 Ms. Ko는 작년에 신입 사원을 위한 종합 교육 프로그램을 개발했다.

해설 문장에 주어(Ms. Ko)만 있고 동사가 없으므로 동사 (A), (C), (D)가 정답의 후보이다. 과거를 나타내는 표현인 last year(작년)가 있으므로 과거 시제 (D) developed(개발하다)가 정답이다. 명사 (B)는 동사 자리에 올 수 없다.

어휘 comprehensive adj. 종합의

06 주어와 수일치하는 동사 채우기

해석 Sandy 주방장이 만들 메뉴는 채식 선택지를 포함할 것이다.

해설 문장에 주어(The menus)만 있고 동사가 없으므로 동사 (A), (B), (D)가 정답의 후보이다. 주어(The menus)가 복수이므로 복수 동사 (B) are가 정답이다. 단수 동사 (A)와 (D)는 단수 주어와 함께 써야 한다. to 부정사 (C)는 동사 자리에 올 수 없다. 참고로, 주어와 동사 사이에 있는 수식어 거품(that Chef Sandy will create)은 동사의 수 결정에 아무런 영향을 주지 않는다.

어휘 create v. 만들다 include v. 포함하다 option n. 선택지

07 수동태 관용 표현 채우기

해석 그 사업주는 규정 준수 문제에 대해 변호사와 상담할 것을 권고받았다.

해설 '변호사와 상담할 것을 권고받았다'라는 의미가 되어야 하므로 '~할 것을 권고받다'라는 표현인 'be advised + to 부정사'를 만드는 동사원형 (B) consult(상담하다)가 정답이다.

어휘 lawyer n. 변호사 compliance n. 규정 준수 consultant n. 상담가 consultation n. 상담

08 태에 맞는 동사 채우기

해석 모든 고객 서비스 통화는 품질 관리를 보장하고 서비스 기준을 유지하기 위해 기록된다.

해설 문장에 주어(All customer service calls)만 있고 동사가 없으므로 be동사(are)와 함께 동사를 만드는 과거분사 (C)와 현재분사 (D)가 정답의 후보이다. 목적어가 없고 '모든 고객 서비스 통화는 기록된다'라는 수동의 의미가 되어야 하므로 수동태를 만드는 과거분사 (C) recorded(기록하다)가 정답이다. 동사원형 (A)와 명사 (B)는 be동사와 함께 동사를 만들 수 없다. 명사 (B)를 be동사의 보어로 본다 해도 '모든 고객 서비스 통화는 녹음기이다'라는 어색한 의미를 만들기 때문에 답이 될 수 없다.

어휘 ensure v. 보장하다 quality control 품질 관리 maintain v. 유지하다 standard n. 기준

09 주어와 수일치하는 동사 채우기

해석 Samir Patel은 전국 곳곳에 생동감 넘치는 벽화를 그리는 열정적인 거리 예술가이다.

해설 빈칸은 명사(street artist)를 꾸미는 주격 관계절(who ~ country)의 동사 자리이므로 동사 (A)와 (C)가 정답의 후보이다. 주격 관계절의 동사는 선행사(street artist)와 수일치하므로 단수 동사 (A) paints(그리다)가 정답이다. 복수 동사 (C)는 복수 선행사와 함께 써야 한다. 명사 (B)와 동명사 또는 현재분사 (D)는 동사 자리에 올 수 없다.

어휘 passionate adj. 열정적인 vibrant adj. 생동감 넘치는 mural n. 벽화

10 올바른 시제의 동사 채우기

해석 회의 센터에 도착하면, 안내 데스크에서 체크인하는데, 그곳에서 저희 직원이 당신의 회의실의 위치를 찾는 것을 도울 것입니다.

해설 When절에 주어(you)만 있고 동사가 없으므로 동사 (B)와 (C)가 정답의 후보이다. 시간을 나타내는 종속절에서는 미래 시제 대신 현재 시제를 쓰므로 현재 시제 (B) arrive(도착하다)가 정답이다. 명사 (A)와 to 부정사 (D)는 동사 자리에 올 수 없다.

어휘 locate v. 위치를 찾다

11 태에 맞는 동사 채우기

해석 새로운 액션 영화의 개봉은 몇몇 편집 수정으로 인해 지연될 것이다.

해설 문장에 주어(The release of the new action film)만 있고 조동사(will) 뒤에 동사가 없으므로 조동사 뒤에 올 수 있는 동사원형을 포함하는 (A), (C), (D)가 정답의 후보이다. 목적어가 없고 '영화의 개봉이 지연될 것이다'라는 수동의 의미가 되어야 하므로 수동태 (D) be delayed(지연되다)가 정답이다. 동명사 또는 현재분사 (B)는 조동사 뒤에 올 수 없다.

어휘 release n. 개봉 due to ~로 인해 adjustment n. 수정

12 올바른 시제의 동사 채우기

해석 두 주요 회사 간의 제휴 계약이 한 달 전에 갱신되었다.

해설 문장에 주어(The partnership)만 있고 동사가 없으므로 동사 (B), (C), (D)가 정답의 후보이다. 과거를 나타내는 표현인 a month ago(한 달 전에)가 있으므로 과거 시제 (C) was renewed(갱신하다)가 정답이다. 명사 (A)는 동사 자리에 올 수 없다.

어휘 partnership n. 제휴 계약, 동업 major adj. 주요한 renewal n. 갱신, 재개

13 조동사 다음에 동사원형 채우기

해석 새로운 직원들은 그들의 정규 업무를 시작하기 전에 오리엔테이션 프로그램을 완료해야 한다.

해설 조동사처럼 쓰이는 표현(ought to) 다음에 올 수 있는 것은 동사원형이므로 동사원형 (C) complete(완료하다)가 정답이다. 명사 (A), 동명사 또는 현재분사 (B), 동사의 과거형 또는 과거분사 (D)는 조동사 다음의 동사원형 자리에 올 수 없다.

어휘 regular adj. 정규의

14 올바른 시제의 동사 채우기

해석 최근 보도에 따르면, Nine East 쇼핑몰은 다음 달까지 새로운 장소로 이전할 것이다.

해설 문장에 주어(Nine East Mall)만 있고 동사가 없으므로 동사 (A), (C), (D)가 정답의 후보이다. 미래를 나타내는 표현인 next month(다음 달)가 있으므로 미래 시제 (D) will move(이전하다)가 정답이다. 동명사 또는 현재분사 (B)는 동사 자리에 올 수 없다.

어휘 report n. 보도; v. 알리다

15 주어와 수일치하는 동사 채우기

해석 역사적인 마을 광장에서 열리는 몇 가지 행사는 민속춤 공연으로 지역 전통을 기념한다.

해설 문장에 주어(A couple of events)만 있고 동사가 없으므로 동사 (B), (C), (D)가 정답의 후보이다. 'a couple of + 복수 명사'는 복수 취급하므로 복수 동사 (B) celebrate(기념하다)가 정답이다. 단수 동사 (C)와 (D)는 단수 주어와 함께 써야 한다. 명사 (A)는 동사 자리에 올 수 없다. 참고로, 주어와 동사 사이에 있는 수식어 거품(taking place in the historic town square)은 동사의 수 결정에 아무런 영향을 주지 않는다.

어휘 take place 열리다 square n. 광장 tradition n. 전통 folk adj. 민속의

16 동사 자리 채우기

해석 이메일로 전송된 인증 링크를 클릭함으로써 당신의 계정을 활성화하세요.

해설 이 문장은 주어가 없는 명령문이므로, 명령문의 동사 자리에 올 수 있는

동사원형 (A) Activate(활성화하다)가 정답이다. 명사 (B), 동사의 과거형 또는 과거분사 (C), 부사 (D)는 명령문의 동사 자리에 올 수 없다.

어휘 account n. 계정 verification n. 인증 activation n. 활성화
actively adv. 적극적으로

17 태, 시제에 맞는 동사 채우기

해석 조직 위원회는 곧 있을 세미나의 마지막에 모든 참가자들에게 간식을 제공할 것이다.

해설 문장에 동사가 없으므로 동사인 모든 보기가 정답의 후보이다. 주어(The organizing committee)와 동사(serve)가 '조직 위원회는 간식을 제공할 것이다'라는 능동의 의미가 되어야 하고 미래를 나타내는 표현인 upcoming(곧 있을)이 있으므로 미래 시제 능동태 (B) will be serving이 정답이다. 수동태 (C)와 (D)는 각각 '조직 위원회는 모든 참가자들에게 간식을 제공받을 것이다/받고 있었다'라는 어색한 문맥을 만들고, 'A에게 B를 제공하다'라는 의미의 serve B to A가 수동태로 바뀌면 B be served to A가 되어 served 바로 뒤에 목적어가 없어야 하므로 빈칸 뒤의 명사(refreshments)를 목적어로 취할 수 없다. 과거 시제 (A)는 미래를 나타낼 수 없다.

어휘 committee n. 위원회 refreshment n. 간식 attendee n. 참석자

18 올바른 시제의 동사 채우기

해석 국립 과학 박물관은 작년 12월 이후로 로봇 공학에 초점을 맞춘 상호작용 워크숍을 개최해 오고 있다.

해설 문장에 주어(The national science museum)만 있고 동사가 없으므로 동사 (C)와 (D)가 정답의 후보이다. 현재완료를 나타내는 표현인 'since + 과거 시간 표현'(~ 이후로)이 있으므로 현재완료진행 시제 (D) has been hosting(개최하다)이 정답이다. 동명사 또는 현재분사 (A)와 to 부정사 (B)는 동사 자리에 올 수 없다.

어휘 interactive adj. 상호적인 robotics n. 로봇 공학

19 수, 태에 맞는 동사 채우기

해석 Era 은행의 이용자들은 그들의 정보가 해커들에 의해 접근된 후에 그들의 암호를 변경하도록 지시받고 있다.

해설 주어(Users of Era Bank)가 복수이고, 동사 instruct가 '지시하다'라는 의미의 타동사인데 빈칸 뒤에 목적어가 없으므로 복수 동사이면서 수동태인 현재진행 시제 수동태 (D) are being instructed가 정답이다. 능동태 (A)와 (B)는 각각 '은행 이용자들이 그들의 암호를 변경하도록 지시한다/지시할 것이다'라는 어색한 문맥을 만든다. 단수 동사 (C)는 단수 주어와 함께 써야 한다.

어휘 access v. 접근하다

20 제안·요청·의무의 주절을 뒤따르는 that절에 동사원형 채우기

해석 대학교는 방문객들이 특정 캠퍼스 건물에 들어가기 위해 신분증을 제시할 것을 요청한다.

해설 that절(that ~ buildings)에 동사가 없고 주절(The university requests)에 제안·요청·의무를 나타내는 동사(requests)가 왔으므로 that절의 동사 자리에는 동사원형이 와야 한다. 따라서 동사원형 (C) present(제시하다)가 정답이다. 동사의 과거형 또는 과거분사 (A), 동명사 또는 현재분사 (B), 명사 (D)는 동사원형 자리에 올 수 없다.

어휘 visitor n. 방문객 identification card 신분증 certain adj. 특정한, 확실한

21 올바른 시제의 동사 채우기

해석 기자는 다음 주 환경 정상회담에서 기후 변화 연구자들과 인터뷰를 진행할 것이다.

해설 문장에 주어(The reporter)만 있고 동사가 없으므로 동사 (B), (C), (D)가 정답의 후보이다. 미래를 나타내는 표현인 next week(다음 주)가 있으므로 미래진행 시제 (B) will be conducting(진행하다)이 정답이다. to 부정사 (A)는 동사 자리에 올 수 없다.

어휘 climate change 기후 변화 environmental adj. 환경의 summit n. 정상회담

22 3형식 동사와 4형식 동사 구별하여 채우기

해석 Biomira Cosmetics사는 민감한 피부 타입을 위한 새로운 비건 스킨케어 라인을 출시할 것이라고 발표했다.

해설 '새로운 스킨케어 라인을 출시할 것이라고 발표했다'라는 문맥이고, 빈칸 뒤에 that절(that ~ types)이 바로 나왔으므로 3형식 동사 (A) announced(발표하다)가 정답이다. (B) told(말하다)와 (D) convinced(확신시키다)도 해석상 그럴듯해 보이지만 4형식 동사이므로 뒤에 간접 목적어와 직접 목적어가 와야 한다. (C) continued는 '계속하다'라는 의미이다.

어휘 sensitive adj. 민감한

23 올바른 시제의 동사 채우기

해석 Mr. Martinez는 내일 열리는 기술 박람회에서 Integra Systems사를 대표할 것이다.

해설 문장에 주어(Mr. Martinez)만 있고 동사가 없으므로 동사 (A), (B), (D)가 정답의 후보이다. 미래를 나타내는 표현인 tomorrow(내일)가 있으므로 미래 시제를 나타낼 수 있는 현재진행 시제 (B) is representing(대표하다)이 정답이다. 참고로, 현재진행 시제는 예정된 일이나 곧 일어나려고 하는 일을 표현하여 미래를 나타낼 수 있다는 점을 알아 둔다. 현재 시제 (A)도 미래에 예정된 일을 나타낼 수 있지만, 주어가 단수이므로 복수 동사는 답이 될 수 없다. 명사 (C)는 동사 자리에 올 수 없다.

어휘 exposition n. 박람회 representation n. 묘사, 표현

24 동사의 수에 맞는 명사 채우기

해석 새로 공개된 사무실 보수 디자인은 현대적이면서도 실용적이며, 최신 업무 현장의 트렌드를 반영한다.

해설 빈칸 앞의 과거분사(unveiled)와 빈칸 뒤의 전치사구(for the office renovation)의 꾸밈을 받을 수 있는 것은 명사이므로 명사 (A), (B), (D)가 정답의 후보이다. '사무실 보수 디자인은 현대적이면서도 실용적이다'라는 의미가 되어야 하고 복수 동사(are)가 왔으므로 복수 사물/추상명사 (D) designs(디자인)가 정답이다. 사람명사 (A) designer(디자이너)를 쓸 경우 '사무실 보수 디자이너는 현대적이면서도 실용적이다'라는 어색한 의미를 만들고, 단수 명사이므로 복수 동사(are)와 함께 쓸 수 없다. 과거형 동사 또는 과거분사 (C)는 명사 자리에 올 수 없다.

어휘 unveiled adj. 공개된 modern adj. 현대적인 functional adj. 실용적인
reflect v. 반영하다 current adj. 최신의, 현재의

25 태에 맞는 동사 채우기

해석 Vitaro Organic 식료품점의 신규 고객은 30달러 이상의 첫 구매에서 할인 혜택을 제공받는다.

해설 문장에 주어(First-time customers)만 있고 동사가 없으므로 동사 (A), (C), (D)가 정답의 후보이다. '신규 고객은 할인 혜택을 제공받는다'라는 수동의 의미가 되어야 하므로 수동태 (C) are offered(제공하다)가 정답이다. 참고로, 4형식 동사 offer의 수동태 뒤에는 목적어 중 한 개(discounts)가 남으므로, discounts를 보고 바로 능동태를 고르지 않도록 주의한다. 동명사 또는 현재분사 (B)는 동사 자리에 올 수 없다.

어휘 discount n. 할인 purchase n. 구매

26 올바른 시제의 동사 채우기

해석 Sparks Entertainment사의 사장은 지난주에 주요 조직 변화를 공개했다.

해설 문장에 주어(The president)만 있고 동사가 없으므로 동사 (A), (C), (D)가 정답의 후보이다. 과거를 나타내는 표현인 last week(지난주)가 있으므로 과거 시제 (C) revealed(공개하다)가 정답이다. 동명사 또는 현재분사 (B)는 동사 자리에 올 수 없다. 참고로, 현재완료 시제는 과거를 나타내는 표현과 함께 쓸 수 없다는 점을 알아 둔다.

어휘 organizational adj. 조직적인

27 수동태 관용 표현 채우기

해석 고층 건물에서 작업하는 도급업자는 안전 교육을 받고 보호 장비를 착용하도록 요구받는다.

해설 '안전 교육을 받고 보호 장비를 착용하도록 요구받는다'라는 의미가 되어야 하므로 '~하도록 요구받다'라는 표현인 'be required + to 부정사'를 만드는 (A) required가 정답이다. 동명사 또는 현재분사 (B)와 명사 (D)는 동사 자리에 올 수 없다.

어휘 contractor n. 도급업자 high-rise building 고층 건물
undergo v. 받다, 겪다 protective gear 보호 장비

28 올바른 시제의 동사 채우기

해석 저자는 그녀의 원고를 편집자에게 보내는 것을 시작하기 전에 원고를 세 번 이상 수정했다.

해설 주절에 주어(The author)만 있고 동사가 없으므로 모든 보기가 정답의 후보이다. 주절(The author ~ times)에서 나타내는 사건, 즉 저자가 원고를 세 번 이상 수정한 시점은 before가 이끄는 절(she ~ editors)에서 나타내는 사건, 즉 원고를 편집자에게 보내기 시작한 것보다 먼저 일어난 일이다. before가 이끄는 절에 과거 시제 동사(started)가 쓰였으므로 과거의 특정 시점 이전에 발생한 일을 나타내는 과거완료 시제 (B) had revised(수정하다)가 정답이다. '저자는 원고를 세 번 이상 수정했다'라는 능동의 의미가 되어야 하므로 과거 시제 수동태 (A)는 답이 될 수 없다.

어휘 manuscript n. 원고 editor n. 편집자

DAY 03 to 부정사, 동명사, 분사

기출 공식 1~2

토익실전문제 p.154

01 (C)   02 (B)   03 (A)   04 (D)

01 to 부정사 채우기

해석 교육 개혁 계획의 목표는 학생들에게 평등한 학습 기회를 제공하는 것이다.

해설 be동사(is)의 보어 자리에 올 수 있는 과거분사 (B)와 to 부정사 (C)가 정답의 후보이다. '교육 개혁 계획의 목표는 평등한 기회를 제공하는 것이다'라는 의미가 되어야 하므로 to 부정사 (C) to provide가 정답이다. 과거분사 (B)를 쓸 경우 be동사(is)와 함께 수동태를 만들어 '교육 개혁 계획의 목표는 평등한 기회를 제공된다'라는 어색한 의미가 되고, 3형식 동사 provide가 수동태로 쓰이면 뒤에 목적어가 없어야 하므로 빈칸 뒤의 명사(equal learning opportunities)를 목적어로 취할 수 없다. 동사 (A)와 '전치사 + 동명사' (D)는 보어 자리에 올 수 없다.

어휘 reform n. 개혁 initiative n. 계획 equal adj. 평등한 provide v. 제공하다

02 to 부정사의 in order to 채우기

해석 Nexus Enterprises사는 직원들의 일과 삶의 균형을 촉진하기 위해 유연 근무제를 도입했다.

해설 이 문장은 주어(Nexus Enterprises), 동사(introduced), 목적어(flexible working hours)를 갖춘 완전한 절이므로, ___ ~ employees는 수식어 거품으로 보아야 한다. 따라서 수식어 거품을 이끌 수 있는 모든 보기가 정답의 후보이다. 이 수식어 거품은 동사 (promote)만 있고 주어가 없으며 '일과 삶의 균형을 촉진하기 위해'라는 의미가 되어야 하므로, 목적을 나타내는 to 부정사를 만들기 위해 동사원형(promote) 앞에 to가 와야 한다. 따라서 목적을 나타내는 to 부정사 대신 쓰일 수 있는 (B) in order to가 정답이다. 전치사 (A), (C), (D)는 뒤에 명사가 와야 한다. 참고로, to 부정사가 목적을 나타낼 때는 to 대신

in order to를 쓸 수 있음을 알아 둔다.

어휘 introduce v. 도입하다 flexible adj. 유연한 promote v. 촉진하다
work-life balance 일과 삶의 균형

03 to 부정사 채우기

해석 중소기업들은 더 큰 기업들과 경쟁하기 위해 그들의 디지털 마케팅 전략을 확대하고 있다.

해설 이 문장은 주어(Small businesses), 동사(are expanding), 목적어(their digital marketing strategies)를 갖춘 완전한 절이므로, ___ ~ corporations는 수식어 거품으로 보아야 한다. 이 수식어 거품은 동사가 없는 거품구이므로, 거품구를 이끌며 '더 큰 기업들과 경쟁하기 위해'라는 의미의 목적을 나타내는 to 부정사 (A) to compete가 정답이다. 형용사 (B)는 뒤에 있는 명사를 꾸미거나 보어로 쓰여야 하므로 답이 될 수 없다. 동사 (C)와 명사 (D)는 수식어 거품을 이끌 수 없다.

어휘 expand v. 확대하다 corporation n. 기업 compete v. 경쟁하다
competitive adj. 경쟁력 있는 competition n. 경쟁, 대회

04 to 부정사와 동명사 구별하여 채우기

해석 Dr. Laurent는 세계 건강 혁신에 대한 국제 회담을 조직하고 싶어 한다.

해설 동사 would like의 목적어 자리에 올 수 있는 to 부정사 (D) to organize가 정답이다. 동사 (A)와 (C), 동명사 또는 현재분사 (B)는 would like의 목적어 자리에 올 수 없다.

어휘 innovation n. 혁신 organize v. 조직하다

기출 공식 3~5

토익실전문제 p.155

01 (D)   02 (B)   03 (B)   04 (C)

01 to 부정사 채우기

해석 무료 셔틀 서비스는 관광객들이 해안선을 따라 아름다운 해변을 탐험할 수 있게 해준다.

해설 동사 enable(enables)의 목적격 보어 자리에 올 수 있는 to 부정사 (D) to explore가 정답이다. 동사 (A)와 (C), 명사 (B)는 enable의 목적격 보어 자리에 올 수 없다.

어휘 complimentary adj. 무료의 enable v. ~할 수 있게 하다
coastline n. 해안선 explore v. 탐험하다 exploration n. 탐험

02 to 부정사 채우기

해석 World Bridge 항공사는 새로운 국제노선을 추가할 계획을 발표했다.

해설 이 문장은 주어(World Bridge Airways), 동사(has announced), 목적어(the plan)를 갖춘 완전한 절이므로, ___ ~ routes는 수식어 거품으로 보아야 한다. 이 수식어 거품은 동사가 없는 거품구이므로, 거품구를 이끌며 명사 plan 뒤에서 명사를 꾸미는 형용사 역할을 하는 to 부정사 (B) to add가 정답이다. 동사 (A)와 (C), 부사 (D)는 형용사 자리에 올 수 없다.

어휘 route n. 노선 add v. 추가하다 additionally adv. 추가로

03 to 부정사 채우기

해석 경험 많은 그 코치는 젊은 운동선수들이 그들의 잠재력을 개발하도록 도왔다.

해설 동사 help(helped)의 목적격 보어 자리에는 원형 부정사나 to 부정사가 올 수 있으므로 to 부정사 (B) to develop이 정답이다. 동사 (A)와 (C), 명사 (D)는 help의 목적격 보어 자리에 올 수 없다. (C)를 과거분사로 본다 해도, '젊은 운동선수들이 잠재력을 개발되도록'이라는 어색한 문맥이 되고 수동태 뒤에 목적어(their potential)가 오게 되므로 답이 될 수 없다.

어휘 experienced adj. 경험 많은 athlete n. 운동선수

potential n. 잠재력; adj. 잠재적인　develop v. 개발하다
development n. 발전, 개발

04 분사 채우기
해석　박물관은 모든 고대 유물을 연대순으로 전시했는데, 이를 방문객들이 흥미롭게 여겼다.
해설　사역동사 have(had)의 목적격 보어 자리에 올 수 있는 과거분사 (C) displayed가 정답이다. 참고로, '목적어가 목적격 보어 되다'라는 수동의 의미로 해석되면 목적격 보어 자리에 과거분사가 오는 점을 알아 둔다. 동사 (A), to 부정사 (B)와 (D)는 have의 목적격 보어 자리에 올 수 없다.
어휘　ancient adj. 고대의　artifact n. 유물　in chronological order 연대순으로　display v. 전시하다

기출 공식 6~8

토익실전문제　p.156

| 01 (A) | 02 (C) | 03 (D) | 04 (D) |

01 동명사 채우기
해석　첨단 보안 시스템을 설치하는 것은 기업 네트워크를 잠재적 사이버 위협으로부터 방어하는 데 도움을 준다.
해설　빈칸은 동사(helps)의 주어 자리이므로 동명사 (A)와 (B)가 정답의 후보이다. '첨단 보안 시스템을 설치하는 것'이라는 능동의 의미가 되어야 하므로 동명사의 능동형 (A) Installing이 정답이다. 동명사의 수동형 (B)를 쓸 경우 '첨단 보안 시스템을 설치되는 것'이라는 어색한 의미를 만들기 때문에 답이 될 수 없다. 동사 (C)와 (D)는 주어 자리에 올 수 없다.
어휘　advanced adj. 첨단의　security system 보안 시스템　defend v. 방어하다　corporate adj. 기업의　threat n. 위협　install v. 설치하다

02 동명사 채우기
해석　환경 보존 팀들은 추적 기술을 이용하여 멸종 위기종을 보호하는 혁신적인 방법을 시행하고 있다.
해설　전치사(of)의 목적어 자리에 올 수 있는 동명사 (C) protecting이 정답이다. 동사 (A)와 (B), 형용사 (D)는 전치사의 목적어 자리에 올 수 없다.
어휘　conservation n. 보존　implement v. 시행하다　innovative adj. 혁신적인　endangered species 멸종 위기종　tracking n. 추적　protect v. 보호하다　protective adj. 보호하는, 방어적인

03 to 부정사와 동명사 구별하여 채우기
해석　Mr. Lee는 팀 생산성과 협업을 개선하기 위해 현재 프로젝트 관리 접근법을 재구성하는 것을 고려하고 있다.
해설　동사 consider(is considering)의 목적어 자리에 올 수 있는 동명사 (D) restructuring이 정답이다. to 부정사 (B)는 consider의 목적어 자리에 올 수 없고, 동사 (A)와 동사 또는 과거분사 (C)는 목적어 자리에 올 수 없다.
어휘　consider v. 고려하다　current adj. 현재의　approach n. 접근법　collaboration n. 협업　restructure v. 재구성하다

04 동명사 채우기
해석　BioGenix사는 주요 제약 투자자들에 의해 핵심 연구 자금이 철회되었을 때 재정적 문제를 겪기 시작했다.
해설　동사 start(started)의 목적어 자리에 올 수 있는 동명사 (D) having이 정답이다. 동사 (A), (B), (C)는 목적어 자리에 올 수 없다. 참고로, start는 동명사와 to 부정사를 모두 목적어로 가지는 동사임을 알아 둔다.
어휘　withdraw v. 철회하다　major adj. 주요한　pharmaceutical adj. 제약의　investor n. 투자자

기출 공식 9~10

토익실전문제　p.157

| 01 (C) | 02 (B) | 03 (C) | 04 (D) |

01 동명사와 명사 구별하여 채우기
해석　의사는 적당량의 다크 초콜릿을 섭취하는 것이 심혈관 질환의 위험을 줄이는 데 도움을 줄 수도 있다고 언급했다.
해설　that절(that ~ diseases) 안에 주어가 없으므로 주어 자리에 올 수 있는 동명사 (C)와 명사 (D)가 정답의 후보이다. 빈칸 뒤에 목적어 (moderate amounts of dark chocolate)가 있으므로 목적어를 가질 수 있는 동명사 (C) consuming이 정답이다. 명사 (D) consumption은 목적어를 가질 수 없으므로 답이 될 수 없다. 동사 (A)와 동사 또는 과거분사 (B)는 주어 자리에 올 수 없다.
어휘　mention v. 언급하다　moderate adj. 적당한　risk n. 위험　cardiovascular adj. 심혈관의　consume v. 섭취하다　consumption n. 섭취, 소비

02 동명사와 명사 구별하여 채우기
해석　교육 혁신가들은 각 학생이 필요한 것에 교육을 맞추는 적응형 학습 시스템을 만들 것을 제안한다.
해설　동사(suggest)의 목적어 자리에 올 수 있는 동명사 (B)와 명사 (C)가 정답의 후보이다. 빈칸 뒤에 목적어(an adaptive learning system)가 있으므로 목적어를 가질 수 있는 동명사 (B) creating이 정답이다. 명사 (C) creation은 목적어를 가질 수 없으므로 답이 될 수 없다. 동사 (A)와 형용사 (D)는 목적어 자리에 올 수 없다.
어휘　educational adj. 교육의　innovator n. 혁신가　adaptive adj. 적응형의　personalize v. (개인에게) 맞추다　create v. 만들다　creation n. 창조, 창작　creative adj. 창의적인

03 동명사 관용 표현 채우기
해석　지역 창업 재단은 신흥 기술 벤처에 창업 자본을 지원하는 데 전념한다.
해설　빈칸 앞 is committed와 함께 'be committed to + 동명사'(~에 전념하다) 표현을 만드는 (C) to granting이 정답이다. 동사 (A), (B), (D)는 is committed 뒤에 올 수 없다.
어휘　entrepreneurship n. 창업　foundation n. 재단　capital n. 자본　emerging adj. 신흥의　grant v. 지원하다, 주다; n. 보조금

04 동명사 관용 표현 채우기
해석　Mr. Alvarez는 시차로 인해 해외팀과 협업하는 데 어려움을 겪고 있다.
해설　전치사(in)의 목적어 자리에 오면서 'have difficulty in + 동명사'(~하는 데 어려움을 겪다) 표현을 만드는 동명사 (D) coordinating이 정답이다. 동사 (A)와 (C), to 부정사 (B)는 전치사의 목적어 자리에 올 수 없다.
어휘　overseas adj. 해외의　coordinate v. 협업하다

기출 공식 11~12

토익실전문제　p.158

| 01 (D) | 02 (B) | 03 (C) | 04 (C) |

01 분사 채우기
해석　회사 정책은 훈련받은 직원들만이 위험한 물질을 다루도록 규정한다.
해설　빈칸 뒤의 명사(employees)를 꾸밀 수 있는 것은 형용사이므로 분사 (D) trained가 정답이다. 동사 (A)와 (B)는 형용사 자리에 올 수 없다. to 부정사 (C)는 명사를 뒤에서 꾸며주므로 답이 될 수 없다.
어휘　mandate v. 규정하다　handle v. 다루다　hazardous adj. 위험한　material n. 물질

02 분사 채우기

해석 젊은 전문가들은 국제 회의를 매우 흥미롭다고 생각했으며, 신흥 산업 동향에 대한 새로운 통찰력을 얻었다.

해설 동사(found)의 목적격 보어 자리에 올 수 있는 현재분사 (B)와 명사 (D)가 정답의 후보이다. '흥미롭다고 생각했다'라는 의미가 되어야 하므로 현재분사 (B) engaging이 정답이다. 명사 (D) engagement를 쓸 경우 '약속으로 생각했다'라는 어색한 문맥이 된다. 참고로, find는 주로 형용사나 분사를 목적격 보어로 가지는 점을 알아 둔다. 동사 (A)와 (C)는 목적격 보어 자리에 올 수 없다.

어휘 quite adv. 매우, 꽤 gain v. 얻다 insight n. 통찰력

03 분사구문 채우기

해석 마케팅에 대한 광범위한 경험을 가지고 있기 때문에, Ms. Petrov는 성공적인 제품 출시 캠페인을 이끌 수 있었다.

해설 이 문장은 주어(Ms. Petrov), 동사(was able to lead), 목적어(successful product launch campaigns)를 갖춘 완전한 절이므로, ____ ~ marketing은 수식어 거품으로 보아야 한다. 따라서 보기 중 수식어 거품이 될 수 있는 분사구문을 만드는 현재분사 (C) Having이 정답이다. 동사 (A), (B), (D)는 수식어 거품을 이끌 수 없다. (B)를 과거분사로 본다 해도, '마케팅에 대한 경험을 가지고 있다'라는 능동의 의미가 되어야 하므로 답이 될 수 없다.

어휘 extensive adj. 광범위한 lead v. 이끌다 launch n. 출시

04 분사구문 채우기

해석 새로운 전략을 실행한 이후로, Innova Logistics사는 운영 효율성을 상당히 개선했다.

해설 이 문장은 주어(Innova Logistics), 동사(has ~ improved), 목적어(its operational efficiency)를 갖춘 완전한 절이므로, Since ____ the new strategy는 수식어 거품으로 보아야 한다. 따라서 보기 중 수식어 거품이 될 수 있는 분사구문을 만드는 현재분사 (C) implementing이 정답이다. 동사 (A)와 명사 (D)는 수식어 거품을 이끌 수 없다. 형용사 (B)는 목적어(the new strategy)를 가질 수 없다. 참고로, 분사구문의 뜻을 분명하게 하기 위해 부사절 접속사(Since)가 분사구문 앞에 온 점을 알아 둔다.

어휘 strategy n. 전략 significantly adv. 상당히 operational adj. 운영의 efficiency n. 효율성 implement v. 시행하다 implemental adj. 도구의, 도움이 되는 implementation n. 시행

기출 공식 13~14

토익실전문제 p.159

01 (B)	02 (A)	03 (D)	04 (B)

01 현재분사와 과거분사 구별하여 채우기

해석 그 군사 시설은 산맥의 고립된 지역에 전략적으로 배치되었다.

해설 빈칸 뒤의 명사(area)를 꾸밀 수 있는 것은 형용사이므로 과거분사 (B)와 현재분사 (C)가 정답의 후보이다. 꾸밈을 받는 명사(area)와 분사가 '고립된 지역'이라는 의미의 수동 관계이므로 과거분사 (B) secluded가 정답이다. 현재분사 (C) secluding을 쓸 경우 '고립하는 지역'이라는 어색한 문맥이 된다. 동사 (A)와 명사 (D)는 형용사 자리에 올 수 없다.

어휘 military facility 군사 시설 strategically adv. 전략적으로 position v. 배치하다 mountain range 산맥 seclude v. 고립시키다 seclusion n. 은둔

02 현재분사와 과거분사 구별하여 채우기

해석 세계 보건 기구에 의해 승인되어서, 그 백신은 저렴한 비용으로 대중에게 배포될 것이다.

해설 이 문장은 주어(the vaccine)와 동사(will be distributed)를 갖춘 완전한 절이므로, ____ ~ Organization은 수식어 거품으로 보아야 한다. 따라서 수식어 거품이 될 수 있는 분사구문을 만드는 과거분사 (A)와 현재분사 (C)가 정답의 후보이다. '세계 보건 기구에 의해 승인된 백신'이라는 수동의 의미가 되어야 하므로 과거분사 (A) Approved가 정답이다. 현재분사 (C) Approving을 쓸 경우 '세계 보건 기구에 의해 승인하는 백신'이라는 어색한 문맥이 된다. 명사 (B)와 동사 (D)는 수식어 거품을 이끌 수 없다.

어휘 vaccine n. 백신 distribute v. 배포하다 cost n. 비용 approve v. 승인하다 approval n. 승인

03 현재분사와 과거분사 구별하여 채우기

해석 Pearl Marina 리조트는 평화로운 해변가 휴양지를 찾는 가족들에게 즐거운 경험을 제공한다.

해설 빈칸 뒤의 명사(experience)를 꾸밀 수 있는 것은 형용사이므로 형용사 역할을 하는 과거분사 (C)와 현재분사 (D)가 정답의 후보이다. 꾸밈을 받는 명사(experience)가 감정의 원인이므로 현재분사 (D) pleasing이 정답이다. 동사 (A)와 명사 (B)는 형용사 자리에 올 수 없다.

어휘 peaceful adj. 평화로운 beachfront n. 해변가 getaway n. 휴양지, 휴양 pleasure n. 기쁨

04 현재분사와 과거분사 구별하여 채우기

해석 그녀의 자신감 있는 발표로, 지원자는 최종 면접에서 오래 지속되는 인상을 남겼다.

해설 빈칸 뒤의 명사(impression)를 꾸밀 수 있는 것은 형용사이므로 과거분사 (A), 현재분사 (B), 형용사 (D)가 정답의 후보이다. '오래 지속되는 인상'이라는 의미가 되어야 하므로 현재분사 (B) lasting이 정답이다. 참고로, lasting impression은 '오래 지속되는 인상'이라는 의미의 표현으로 자주 쓰이는 점을 알아 둔다. 형용사의 비교급 (D) later를 쓸 경우 '더 뒤의 인상'이라는 어색한 문맥이 된다. 부사 (C)는 형용사 자리에 올 수 없다.

어휘 confident adj. 자신감 있는 candidate n. 지원자, 후보자 last v. 지속하다 lastly adv. 마지막으로

HACKERS TEST p.160

01 (B)	02 (A)	03 (C)	04 (D)	05 (D)
06 (C)	07 (B)	08 (A)	09 (D)	10 (D)
11 (B)	12 (C)	13 (B)	14 (C)	15 (D)
16 (A)	17 (C)	18 (D)	19 (C)	20 (B)
21 (D)	22 (A)	23 (C)	24 (B)	25 (C)
26 (A)	27 (B)	28 (D)		

01 to 부정사 채우기

해석 Green Bite는 영양가가 높은 육류 대체품으로 그것의 식물성 제품 범위를 넓힐 것을 목표로 한다.

해설 동사 aim(aims)의 목적어 자리에 올 수 있는 to 부정사 (B) to broaden이 정답이다. 동사원형 (A), 3인칭 단수 동사 (C), 동사 또는 과거분사 (D)는 동사의 목적어 자리에 올 수 없다.

어휘 aim v. 목표로 하다 nutritious adj. 영양가가 높은 alternative n. 대체품; adv. 대체의 broaden v. 넓히다

02 분사 채우기

해석 그 호화로운 호텔은 등록된 투숙객에게 고급 스파 시설에 대한 독점적 이용권과 환영 간식을 제공한다.

해설 빈칸 뒤의 명사(guests)를 꾸밀 수 있는 것은 형용사이므로 과거분사 (A) registered가 정답이다. 3인칭 단수 동사 (B), 명사 (C), 동사원형 (D)는 형용사 자리에 올 수 없다.

어휘 exclusive adj. 독점적인 access n. 이용권, 접근 register v. 등록하다

registration n. 등록

03 to 부정사와 동명사 구별하여 채우기
해석 그 재단은 장학금과 멘토링 기회를 제공함으로써 소외된 학생들을 돕는다.
해설 전치사(by)의 목적어 자리에 올 수 있고 명사구(scholarships and mentorship opportunities)를 목적어로 가질 수 있는 동명사 (C) providing이 정답이다. 동사 (A), 동사 또는 과거분사 (B), to 부정사 (D)는 전치사의 목적어 자리에 올 수 없다.
어휘 underprivileged adj. 소외된 mentorship n. 멘토링 provide v. 제공하다

04 현재분사와 과거분사 구별하여 채우기
해석 대대적인 마케팅에도 불구하고, 겨울 컬렉션의 실망스러운 판매는 Nordic Edge사가 가격을 인하하게 만들었다.
해설 빈칸 뒤의 명사(sales)를 꾸밀 수 있는 것은 형용사이므로 과거분사 (C)와 현재분사 (D)가 정답의 후보이다. 꾸밈을 받는 명사(sales)가 감정의 원인이므로 현재분사 (D) disappointing이 정답이다. 동사 (A)와 부사 (B)는 형용사 자리에 올 수 없다.
어휘 force v. ~하게 만들다

05 to 부정사의 in order to 채우기
해석 Ms. Angler는 선도적인 투자 은행에서 일하기 위해 그녀의 컨설팅 회사를 떠났다.
해설 이 문장은 주어(Ms. Angler), 동사(left), 목적어(her consulting firm)를 갖춘 완전한 절이므로, ___ ~ bank는 수식어 거품으로 보아야 한다. 따라서 수식어 거품을 이끌 수 있는 (A), (B), (D)가 정답의 후보이다. 이 수식어 거품은 동사(take)만 있고 주어가 없으며 '선도적인 투자 은행에서 일하기 위해'라는 의미가 되어야 하므로, 목적을 나타내는 to 부정사를 만들기 위해 동사원형(take) 앞에 to가 와야 한다. 따라서 목적을 나타내는 to 부정사 대신 쓸 수 있는 (D) in order to가 정답이다. 전치사 (A)는 뒤에 명사가 와야 한다. 부사절 접속사 (B)는 뒤에 주어와 동사를 갖춘 완전한 절이 와야 한다. 접속부사 (C)는 수식어 거품을 이끌 수 없다. 참고로, to 부정사가 목적을 나타낼 때는 to 대신 in order to를 쓸 수 있음을 알아 둔다.
어휘 firm n. 회사 leading adj. 선도적인 as long as ~하는 한 for instance 예를 들어

06 분사구문 채우기
해석 8월 1일에 시작해서, 국립공원은 야생동물 서식지에 대한 새로운 보존 조치를 시행할 예정이다.
해설 이 문장은 주어(the national park), 동사(will implement), 목적어(new conservation measures)를 갖춘 완전한 절이므로, ____ August 1은 수식어 거품으로 보아야 한다. 따라서 보기 중 수식어 거품이 될 수 있는 분사구문을 만드는 현재분사 (C) Beginning이 정답이다. 동사원형 (A), 3인칭 단수 동사 (B), 명사 (D)는 수식어 거품을 이끌 수 없다.
어휘 national park 국립공원 conservation n. 보존 measure n. 조치 wildlife habitat 야생동물 서식지

07 현재분사와 과거분사 구별하여 채우기
해석 즉각적인 도움을 받기 위해 우리의 고객 서비스팀에 연락하기 전에 손상된 가전을 촬영해 주세요.
해설 빈칸 뒤의 명사(appliance)를 꾸밀 수 있는 것은 형용사이므로 과거분사 (B)와 현재분사 (C)가 정답의 후보이다. 꾸밈을 받는 명사(appliance)와 분사가 '손상된 가전'이라는 의미의 수동 관계이므로 과거분사 (B) damaged가 정답이다. 현재분사 (C) damaging을 쓸 경우 '손상하는 가전'이라는 어색한 의미가 된다. 동사 (A)와 동사 또는 명사 (D)는 형용사 자리에 올 수 없다.
어휘 photograph v. 촬영하다; n. 사진 immediate adj. 즉각적인 assistance n. 도움 damage v. 손상시키다; n. 피해, 손상

08 to 부정사 채우기
해석 공원 경비원은 등산객들에게 표시된 길에 머물면서 지역 환경을 존중하라고 요청한다.
해설 동사 ask(asks)의 목적격 보어 자리에 올 수 있는 to 부정사 (A) to respect가 정답이다. 동사 (B), (C), (D)는 목적격 보어 자리에 올 수 없다.
어휘 park ranger 공원 경비원 marked adj. 표시된 trail n. 길 respect v. 존중하다

09 현재분사와 과거분사 구별하여 채우기
해석 해양 생물학의 선도적인 전문가인 Mr. Shimizu는 산호초 생태계를 연구하는 데 20년을 보냈다.
해설 빈칸 뒤의 명사(expert)를 꾸밀 수 있는 것은 형용사이므로 과거분사 (A)와 현재분사 (B)가 정답의 후보이다. 꾸밈을 받는 명사(expert)와 분사가 '선도적인 전문가'라는 의미의 능동 관계이므로 현재분사 (B) leading이 정답이다. 과거분사 (A) led를 쓸 경우 '선도되는 전문가'라는 어색한 의미가 된다. 동사 (C)와 명사 (D)는 형용사 자리에 올 수 없다.
어휘 expert n. 전문가 marine biology 해양 생물학 coral reef 산호초 ecosystem n. 생태계 lead v. 선도하다, 이끌다 leader n. 지도자

10 분사 채우기
해석 건물 관리자는 LED 조명을 설치한 후에 에너지 비용이 상당히 감소한 것에 놀랐다.
해설 be동사(was)의 보어 자리에 올 수 있는 명사 (A)와 과거분사 (D)가 정답의 후보이다. '건물 관리자는 놀랐다'라는 의미가 되어야 하므로 과거분사 (D) surprised가 정답이다. 명사 (A) surprise를 쓸 경우 '건물 관리자는 놀라움이었다'라는 어색한 의미가 된다. 부사 (B)와 동사 (C)는 보어 자리에 올 수 없다. 참고로, The building manager(건물 관리자)가 감정을 느끼는 주체이므로 과거분사가 왔다.
어휘 cost n. 비용 drop v. 감소하다 considerably adv. 상당히

11 동명사 관용 표현 채우기
해석 Urban Bridge Canvas는 젊은 예술가들을 잠재적인 구매자 및 갤러리와 연결함으로써 그들을 지원하는 데 헌신적이다.
해설 be dedicated to(is dedicated to)의 to는 전치사이므로 전치사 뒤에 올 수 있는 동명사 (B) supporting이 정답이다. 동사 (A), 형용사 (C), 동사 또는 과거분사 (D)는 전치사의 목적어 자리에 올 수 없다.
어휘 dedicated adj. 헌신적인 connect v. 연결하다 support v. 지원하다 supportive adj. 지원하는, 힘을 주는

12 to 부정사 채우기
해석 Sage & Spice는 배달을 통해 수익을 높이기 위해 온라인 주문 서비스를 도입할 것이다.
해설 이 문장은 주어(Sage & Spice), 동사(is going to introduce), 목적어(online ordering services)를 갖춘 완전한 절이므로, ___ ~ deliveries는 수식어 거품으로 보아야 한다. 이 수식어 거품은 동사가 없는 거품이므로, 거품구를 이끌며 '수익을 높이기 위해'라는 의미의 목적을 나타내는 to 부정사 (C) to increase가 정답이다. 동사 (A)와 (B)는 수식어 거품을 이끌 수 없다. 부사 (D)는 목적어(revenues)를 가질 수 없다.
어휘 introduce v. 도입하다 revenue n. 수익 delivery n. 배달 increase v. 높이다 increasingly adv. 점점 더

13 현재분사와 과거분사 구별하여 채우기
해석 Mr. Marchetti는 어제 아침에 완료된 대출 서류를 은행에 제출했다.
해설 빈칸 뒤의 명사구(loan documents)를 꾸밀 수 있는 것은 형용사이므로 과거분사 (B)와 현재분사 (C)가 정답의 후보이다. 꾸밈을 받는 명사구(loan documents)와 분사가 '완료된 대출 서류'라는 의미의 수동 관계이므로 과거분사 (B) completed가 정답이다. 현재분사 (C)

completing을 쓸 경우 '완료하는 대출 서류'라는 어색한 문맥이 된다. 동사 (A)와 명사 (D)는 형용사 자리에 올 수 없다.

어휘 turn in 제출하다 complete v. 완료하다 completion n. 완료, 완성

14 원형 부정사 채우기

해석 그 진단 도구는 분해의 필요 없이 정비공이 엔진 문제를 식별하는 것을 돕는다.

해설 동사 help(helps)의 목적격 보어 자리에는 원형 부정사나 to 부정사가 올 수 있으므로 원형 부정사 (C) identify가 정답이다. 동사 (A), 동명사 또는 현재분사 (B), 명사 (D)는 help의 목적격 보어 자리에 올 수 없다. (A)를 과거분사로 본다 해도, '정비공이 식별되는 것을 돕는다'라는 어색한 문맥이 되므로 답이 될 수 없다.

어휘 diagnostic adj. 진단의 mechanic n. 정비공 disassembly n. 분해 identify v. 식별하다 identification n. 신원 확인, 인지

15 to 부정사와 동명사 구별하여 채우기

해석 투자자들은 특히 불확실한 시장 상황에서 포트폴리오를 다각화하는 것을 고려하는 것을 원할 수도 있다.

해설 동사 want의 목적어 자리에 올 수 있는 to 부정사 (B)와 (D)가 정답의 후보이다. to 부정사의 행위자(Investors)와 to 부정사가 '투자자들이 고려하는 것을 원하다'라는 의미의 능동 관계이므로 to 부정사의 능동형 (D) to consider가 정답이다. to 부정사의 수동형 (B)는 빈칸 뒤에 to 부정사의 목적어(diversifying their portfolios)가 있으므로 답이 될 수 없다. 동명사 (A)는 want의 목적어 자리에 올 수 없고, 형용사 (C)는 목적어 자리에 올 수 없다.

어휘 diversify v. 다각화하다 especially adv. 특히 uncertain adj. 불확실한 consider v. 고려하다 considerable adj. 상당한

16 현재분사와 과거분사 구별하여 채우기

해석 허리케인 시즌 동안 주민들은 대피 절차에 대해 잘 알고 있는 상태로 있도록 요구받는다.

해설 stay의 보어 자리에 올 수 있는 과거분사 (A)와 현재분사 (B)가 정답의 후보이다. '주민들은 대피 절차에 대해 잘 알고 있는 상태로 있도록 요구받는다'라는 의미가 되어야 하므로 과거분사 (A) informed가 정답이다. 현재분사 (B) informing은 정보를 알리는 대상이 있어야 하므로 답이 될 수 없다. 명사 (C)는 '주민들은 정보인 상태로 있도록 요구받는다'라는 어색한 의미를 만들므로 답이 될 수 없고, 부사 (D)는 보어 자리에 올 수 없다. 참고로, inform은 inform A(정보를 알리는 대상) of B(정보)의 형태로 자주 쓰인다는 것을 알아 둔다.

어휘 urge v. 요구하다 evacuation n. 대피 procedure n. 절차 inform v. 알리다 information n. 정보 informatively adv. 유익하게

17 to 부정사 채우기

해석 그 앱은 개인 맞춤형 추천을 제공함으로써 사용자가 어떤 보험 상품을 구매할지 결정하는 것을 안내한다.

해설 명사구(insurance plan) 뒤에서 명사를 꾸미는 형용사 역할을 하는 현재분사 (B)와 to 부정사 (C)가 정답의 후보이다. '사용자가 어떤 보험 상품을 구매할지'라는 의미가 되어야 하므로 to 부정사 (C) to buy가 정답이다. 현재분사 (B) buying을 쓸 경우 '어떤 보험 상품이 구매할지'라는 어색한 의미가 된다. 참고로, 현재분사는 꾸미는 대상이 현재분사가 나타내는 행위의 주체인 점을 알아 둔다. 동사 (A)와 명사 (D)는 형용사 자리에 올 수 없다.

어휘 insurance plan 보험 상품 personalized adj. 개인 맞춤형의 recommendation n. 추천

18 현재분사와 과거분사 구별하여 채우기

해석 많은 통근자들은 그들의 업무 일정에 영향을 미치는 잦은 열차 지연에 대해 불평했다.

해설 빈칸 앞의 명사(delays)를 꾸밀 수 있는 것은 형용사이고 빈칸 뒤에 목적어(their work schedules)가 있으므로 현재분사 (B) affecting이 정답이다. 동사 (A)와 명사 (C)는 형용사 자리에 올 수 없다. 빈칸 뒤에 목적어가 있고 '업무 일정에 영향을 미치는 지연'이라는 능동의 의미가 되어야 하므로 과거분사 (D)는 답이 될 수 없다.

어휘 commuter n. 통근자 complain v. 불평하다 frequent adj. 잦은 affect v. 영향을 미치다 affection n. 애착

19 to 부정사 채우기

해석 Klein 교수는 대학원생들이 그들의 연구 프로젝트를 위해 실험실 장비를 빌릴 수 있도록 허가했다.

해설 동사 permit(permitted)의 목적격 보어 자리에 올 수 있는 to 부정사 (C) to borrow가 정답이다. 원형 부정사 (A)는 permit의 목적격 보어 자리에 올 수 없고, 동사 (B), (D)는 목적격 보어 자리에 올 수 없다.

어휘 permit v. 허가하다 graduate student 대학원생 laboratory n. 실험실

20 현재분사와 과거분사 구별하여 채우기

해석 전시회를 위해 작품을 제출하기를 소망하는 사람들은 지정된 크기 요건을 따라야 한다.

해설 빈칸 앞의 명사(Those)를 꾸밀 수 있는 것은 형용사이고 빈칸 뒤에 목적어(to submit ~ exhibition)가 있으므로 현재분사 (B) wishing이 정답이다. 동사 또는 명사 (A)와 (D)는 형용사 자리에 올 수 없다. 빈칸 뒤에 목적어가 있고 '작품을 제출하기를 소망하는 사람들'이라는 능동의 의미가 되어야 하므로 과거분사 (C)는 답이 될 수 없다. 참고로, those는 관계절, 분사, 전치사구의 꾸밈을 받아 '~한 사람들'이라는 의미로 쓰인다.

어휘 submit v. 제출하다 specified adj. 지정된 requirement n. 요건

21 분사 채우기

해석 국제 투어에 보내기 전에 박물관 큐레이터는 몇몇 고대 유물들이 전문가들에 의해 조심스럽게 복원되도록 했다.

해설 사역동사 have(had)의 목적격 보어 자리에 올 수 있는 원형 부정사 (C)와 과거분사 (D)가 정답의 후보이다. '몇몇 고대 유물들이 전문가들에 의해 복원되도록 했다'라는 수동의 의미를 만드는 과거분사 (D) restored가 정답이다. 원형 부정사 (C) restore를 쓸 경우 '몇몇 고대 유물들이 전문가들에 의해 복원하도록 했다'라는 어색한 문맥이 된다. 명사 (A)와 to 부정사 (B)는 have의 목적격 보어 자리에 올 수 없다.

어휘 ancient adj. 고대의 relic n. 유물 carefully adv. 조심스럽게 restoration n. 복구 restore v. 복원하다

22 현재분사와 과거분사 구별하여 채우기

해석 지난주에 회계 부서에서 민감한 재무 기록을 담고 있는 폴더가 사라졌다.

해설 빈칸 앞의 명사(folder)를 꾸밀 수 있는 것은 형용사이고 빈칸 뒤에 목적어(sensitive financial records)가 있으므로 현재분사 (D) containing이 정답이다. 동사 (A)는 형용사 자리에 올 수 없다. 형용사 (B)는 목적어를 가질 수 없으므로 답이 될 수 없다. 빈칸 뒤에 목적어가 있고 '민감한 재무 기록을 담고 있는 폴더'라는 능동의 의미가 되어야 하므로 과거분사 (C)는 답이 될 수 없다.

어휘 sensitive adj. 민감한 financial adj. 재무의 disappear v. 사라지다 accounting department 회계 부서 contain v. 담다, 들어 있다 containable adj. 들어갈 수 있는

23 to 부정사 채우기

해석 Wellness World 체육관은 소중한 회원들에게 다음 분기부터 회비가 조정될 것임을 알려드리게 되어 유감입니다.

해설 동사 regret(regrets)의 목적어 자리에 올 수 있는 to 부정사 (C)와 명사 (D)가 정답의 후보이다. 빈칸 뒤에 목적어(valued members)가 있으므로 목적어를 가질 수 있는 to 부정사 (C) to notify가 정답이다. 명사 (D) notification은 목적어를 가질 수 없으므로 답이 될 수 없다. 동사 (A)와 형용사 (B)는 동사의 목적어 자리에 올 수 없다.

어휘 regret v. ~하게 되어 유감이다, 후회하다 valued adj. 소중한 membership fee 회비 adjust v. 조정하다 quarter n. 분기 notify v. 알리다 notifiable adj. 신고해야 하는 notification n. 알림, 통지

24 분사 채우기
해석 Verdure Rentals사는 전기 자전거 대여와 친환경 투어를 전문으로 하는 새롭고 혁신적인 사업체이다.

해설 빈칸 앞의 명사(business)를 꾸밀 수 있는 것은 형용사이므로 분사 (B) specializing이 정답이다. 동사 (A)와 (C), 명사 (D)는 형용사 자리에 올 수 없다.

어휘 innovative adj. 혁신적인 electric bike 전기 자전거 rental n. 대여
eco-friendly adj. 친환경적인 specialize v. 전문으로 하다
specialization n. 전문화

25 현재분사와 과거분사 구별하여 채우기
해석 모바일 기기에서 구매된 티켓은 게이트에서의 원활한 체크인을 위해 당신의 디지털 지갑에 자동으로 추가됩니다.

해설 빈칸 앞의 명사(Tickets)를 꾸밀 수 있는 것은 형용사이므로 과거분사 (C)와 현재분사 (D)가 정답의 후보이다. 꾸밈을 받는 명사(Tickets)와 분사가 '구매된 티켓'이라는 의미의 수동 관계이므로 과거분사 (C) purchased가 정답이다. 현재분사 (D) purchasing을 쓸 경우 '구매하는 티켓'이라는 어색한 문맥이 된다. 동사 또는 명사 (A)와 명사 (B)는 형용사 자리에 올 수 없다.

어휘 mobile device 모바일 기기 automatically adv. 자동으로
seamless adj. 원활한

26 동명사와 명사 구별하여 채우기
해석 경험이 풍부한 프로젝트 리더는 팀의 사기를 꾸준히 높게 유지하면서 빠듯한 마감일을 관리하는 것에 뛰어나다.

해설 전치사(at)의 목적어 자리에 올 수 있는 동명사 (A)와 명사 (C)가 정답의 후보이다. 빈칸 뒤에 목적어(tight deadlines)가 있으므로 목적어를 가질 수 있는 동명사 (A) managing이 정답이다. 명사 (C) management는 목적어를 가질 수 없으므로 답이 될 수 없다. 동사 또는 과거분사 (B)와 동사 (D)는 목적어 자리에 올 수 없다.

어휘 excel at ~에 뛰어나다 tight adj. 빠듯한 deadline n. 마감일
morale n. 사기 consistently adv. 꾸준히 manage v. 관리하다
management n. 경영, 관리

27 to 부정사 채우기
해석 Jeff Blackwell은 지금까지 지역 체스 토너먼트에서 세 번 연속으로 우승한 최초의 사람이었다.

해설 명사(one) 뒤에서 명사를 꾸미는 형용사 역할을 하는 to 부정사 (B)와 과거분사 (C)가 정답의 후보이다. '우승한 최초의 사람이다'라는 의미가 되어야 하므로 to 부정사 (B) to win이 정답이다. 과거분사 (C) won은 목적어(three consecutive championships)를 가질 수 없으므로 답이 될 수 없다. 동사 (A)와 명사 (D)는 형용사 자리에 올 수 없다. 참고로, ever는 '지금까지'라는 의미로 서수나 비교급 뒤에서 그 말을 강조한다.

어휘 consecutive adj. 연속의 regional adj. 지역의

28 분사구문 채우기
해석 제조 시스템을 업그레이드한 이후로, 그 자동차 공장은 생산 효율성을 두 배로 높였다.

해설 이 문장은 주어(the automobile factory), 동사(has doubled), 목적어(its production efficiency)를 갖춘 완전한 절이므로, Since ___ its manufacturing systems는 수식어 거품으로 보아야 한다. 따라서 보기 중 수식어 거품이 될 수 있는 분사구문을 만드는 과거분사 (B)와 현재분사 (D)가 정답의 후보이다. 빈칸 뒤에 목적어(its manufacturing systems)가 있고 '제조 시스템을 업그레이드하다'라는 능동의 의미가 되어야 하므로 현재분사 (D) upgrading이 정답이다. 과거분사 (B)는 목적어를 가질 수 없으므로 답이 될 수 없다. 동사 또는 명사 (A)와 (C)는 수식어 거품을 이끌 수 없다. 참고로, 분사구문의 뜻을 분명하게 해주기 위해 부사절 접속사(Since)가 분사구문 앞에 온 점을 알아 둔다.

어휘 manufacturing system 제조 시스템 automobile n. 자동차
factory n. 공장 double v. 두 배로 높이다 efficiency n. 효율성

DAY 04 형용사, 부사, 비교 구문

기출 공식 1~2

토익실전문제 p.162

01 (B)　　**02** (C)　　**03** (D)　　**04** (B)

01 형용사 자리 채우기
해석 지역 자선 단체에는 매주 자원봉사를 하는 적극적인 지지자들이 있다.

해설 빈칸 뒤의 명사(supporters)를 꾸밀 수 있는 것은 형용사이므로 형용사 (B) active(적극적인)가 정답이다. 동사 (A), 부사 (C), 명사 (D)는 형용사 자리에 올 수 없다.

어휘 charity organization 자선 단체 supporter n. 지지자
on a weekly basis 매주 act v. 행동하다 actively adv. 적극적으로
action n. 행동

02 형용사 자리 채우기
해석 Pixel Matrix는 사진을 편집하는 것뿐만 아니라 그래픽 디자인을 개발하는 것에도 유용하다.

해설 빈칸이 be동사(is) 다음에 왔으므로 진행형을 만드는 현재분사 (B)와 보어 자리에 오는 형용사 (C)가 정답의 후보이다. 'Pixel Matrix는 유용하다'라는 의미가 되어야 하므로 형용사 (C) useful(유용한)이 정답이다. 현재분사 (B)를 쓸 경우 'Pixel Matrix는 사용하고 있다'라는 어색한 문맥이 된다. 동사 (A)와 부사 (D)는 보어 자리에 올 수 없다.

어휘 edit v. 편집하다 use v. 사용하다 usefully adv. 유용하게

03 수량 형용사 채우기
해석 전시된 여러 물품은 100년이 더 되어서, 특별한 보존 방법이 필요하다.

해설 빈칸 뒤의 복수 가산 명사 items를 꾸밀 수 있는 수량 형용사가 와야 하므로 수량 형용사 (D) Several(여러 개의)이 정답이다. 수량 형용사 (A)와 (B)는 단수 가산 명사를 꾸미고, 수량 형용사 (C)는 불가산 명사를 꾸민다.

어휘 on display 전시된 preservation n. 보존 method n. 방법

04 수량 형용사 채우기
해석 각각의 부서가 회사의 전체 목표에 부합하는 것이 극히 중요하다.

해설 빈칸 뒤의 단수 가산 명사 department를 꾸밀 수 있는 수량 형용사가 와야 하므로 수량 형용사 (B) each(각각의)가 정답이다. 수량 형용사 (A), (C), (D)는 복수 가산 명사를 꾸민다.

어휘 essential adj. 극히 중요한, 필수적인 align with ~에 부합하다, ~와 일치하다
overall adj. 전체의 objective n. 목표

기출 공식 3~4

토익실전문제 p.163

01 (C)　　**02** (B)　　**03** (D)　　**04** (C)

01 형태가 비슷하지만 의미가 다른 형용사 자리 채우기
해석 재생 에너지 법안은 국가 전역의 탄소 배출 감소에 상당한 영향을 미친다.

해설 빈칸 뒤의 명사(effect)를 꾸밀 수 있는 것은 형용사이므로 형용사 (B)와 (C)가 정답의 후보이다. '법안은 탄소 배출 감소에 상당한 영향을 미친다'라는 의미가 되어야 하므로 형용사 (C) considerable(상당한, 중요한)이 정답이다. 형용사 (B)를 쓸 경우 '법안은 탄소 배출 감소에 사려 깊은 영향을 미친다'라는 어색한 의미가 된다. 동사 (A)와 명사 (D)는 형용사 자리에 올 수 없다.

어휘 renewable energy 재생 에너지 legislation n. 법안 effect n. 영향

carbon emission 탄소 배출   consider v. 고려하다
consideration n. 사려, 고려 사항

02 형태가 비슷하지만 의미가 다른 형용사 자리 채우기
해석 Gentle Giant사의 전문 이사팀은 귀하의 개인적인 소지품을 신중하게 포장하고 새 거주지로 운반할 것입니다.

해설 빈칸 뒤의 명사(belongings)를 꾸밀 수 있는 것은 형용사이므로 형용사 (B)와 (C)가 정답의 후보이다. '귀하의 개인적인 소지품'이라는 의미가 되어야 하므로 형용사 (B) personal(개인적인)이 정답이다. 형용사 (C)를 쓸 경우 '귀하의 매력적인 소지품'이라는 어색한 의미가 된다. 명사 (A)와 부사 (D)는 형용사 자리에 올 수 없다.

어휘 professional adj. 전문적인   carefully adv. 신중하게, 주의 깊게
pack v. 포장하다   transport v. 운반하다   belonging n. 소지품
residence n. 거주지   person n. 사람   personally adv. 개인적으로

03 형용사 자리 채우기
해석 새로운 친환경 선크림은 환경적으로 의식이 높은 소비자들에게 수용 가능할 것으로 예상된다.

해설 '환경적으로 의식이 높은 소비자들에게 수용 가능할 것으로 예상된다'라는 의미가 되어야 하므로 빈칸 앞의 be동사(be)와 뒤의 전치사 to와 함께 '~에게 수용 가능하다'라는 의미의 어구 'be acceptable to + 명사'를 만드는 형용사 (D) acceptable이 정답이다. 명사 (C)를 be의 보어로 본다 해도, '환경적으로 의식이 높은 소비자들에게 수락일 것으로 예상된다'라는 어색한 의미를 만든다. 동사 (A)와 to 부정사 (B)는 be동사와 함께 해당 표현을 만들 수 없다.

어휘 eco-friendly adj. 친환경의   expect v. 예상하다
environmentally adv. 환경적으로   conscious adj. 의식이 높은
consumer n. 소비자   accept v. 수락하다

04 형용사 자리 채우기
해석 재무 분석가는 비용 절감 조치에 관한 회사의 최근 경영 결정에 대해 비판적이다.

해설 '결정에 대해 비판적이다'라는 의미가 되어야 하므로 빈칸 앞의 be동사 (is)와 뒤의 전치사 of와 함께 '~에 대해 비판적이다'라는 의미의 어구 be critical of를 만드는 형용사 (C) critical이 정답이다. 명사 (A)는 is의 보어로 본다 해도, 단수 주어(The financial analyst)와 수일치가 되지 않으므로 답이 될 수 없다. 동사 (B)와 부사 (D)는 be동사 뒤에 올 수 없다.

어휘 financial analyst 재무 분석가   recent adj. 최근의
regarding prep. ~에 관한   cost-cutting n. 비용 절감   measure n. 조치
critic n. 비평가   criticize v. 비판하다   critically adv. 비판적으로

기출 공식 5~7

토익실전문제
p.164

| 01 (D) | 02 (C) | 03 (B) | 04 (A) |

01 부사 자리 채우기
해석 회사의 CollabFlow라는 새 애플리케이션은 원격 근무 환경에서 생산성을 향상시키기 위해 특별히 설계되었다.

해설 동사(is ~ designed)를 꾸밀 수 있는 것은 부사이므로 부사 (D) specifically(특별히)가 정답이다. 동사 (A), 형용사 (B), 명사 (C)는 동사를 꾸밀 수 없다. 명사 (C)를 be동사(is)의 보어로 본다 해도, '새 애플리케이션은 특수함이다'라는 어색한 문맥을 만든다.

어휘 enhance v. 향상시키다   productivity n. 생산성   remote adj. 원격의
specify v. 명시하다   specific adj. 구체적인

02 부사 자리 채우기
해석 재정적으로 책임감 있는 개인들은 조기에 은퇴 저축을 시작하고 일관된 장기 투자를 한다.

해설 빈칸 뒤의 형용사(responsible)를 꾸밀 수 있는 것은 부사이므로 부사 (C) Financially(재정적으로)가 정답이다. 명사 (A)와 (D), 형용사 (B)는 형용사를 꾸밀 수 없다.

어휘 responsible adj. 책임감 있는   individual n. 개인
retirement saving 은퇴 저축   consistent adj. 일관된
investment n. 투자   finance n. 재정   financial adj. 재정의

03 형태가 비슷하지만 의미가 다른 부사 자리 채우기
해석 Prism Solutions사는 직원의 혁신과 창의적인 문제 해결 접근법을 매우 중요하게 여긴다.

해설 동사(values)를 꾸밀 수 있는 것은 부사이므로 모든 보기가 정답의 후보이다. '매우 중요하게 여긴다'라는 의미가 되어야 하므로 부사 (B) highly(매우)가 정답이다. 부사 (A) high(높게), (C) higher(더 높게), (D) highest(가장 높은)를 쓸 경우 물리적인 높이가 높다는 것을 의미하기 때문에 어색한 문맥이 된다.

어휘 value v. 중요하게 여기다   innovation n. 혁신   creative adj. 창의적인
approach n. 접근법

04 빈도 부사 자리 채우기
해석 Dr. Erikson은 주제가 그의 전문 분야와 직접적으로 관련된 경우를 제외하고는 회의에서 거의 말하지 않는다.

해설 동사(speaks)를 꾸밀 수 있는 것은 부사이므로 모든 보기가 정답의 후보이다. 빈칸이 일반동사 앞에 있고 '그의 전문 분야와 직접적으로 관련된 경우를 제외하고는 거의 말하지 않는다'라는 의미가 되어야 하므로 빈도 부사 (A) seldom(거의 ~않다)이 정답이다. 부사 (B) almost는 '거의'라는 의미이다. 부사 (C) yet은 부정문에서 '아직', 의문문에서 '이미, 벌써'라는 의미로 쓰인다. 부사 (D) well은 '잘'이라는 의미이다. 참고로, well은 주로 동사의 뒤에서 동사를 꾸민다는 점을 알아 둔다.

어휘 directly adv. 직접적으로   involve v. ~와 관련되다
field of expertise 전문 분야

기출 공식 8~9

토익실전문제
p.165

| 01 (C) | 02 (A) | 03 (C) | 04 (D) |

01 강조 부사 자리 채우기
해석 전설적인 예술가의 개인 컬렉션은 도시에서 가장 명망 있는 박물관에서 오직 하루 동안만 전시될 것이다.

해설 빈칸 뒤의 전치사구(for a day)를 강조할 수 있는 강조 부사 (C) only (오직)가 정답이다. 강조 부사 (A) quite(꽤, 굉장한)는 주로 형용사, 부사, 또는 'a/an + 명사'를 앞에서 강조할 때 쓴다. 강조 부사 (B) very (매우)는 원급을 강조한다. 강조 부사 (D) far(훨씬)는 비교급을 강조한다.

어휘 legendary adj. 전설적인   private adj. 개인의   prestigious adj. 명망 있는

02 강조 부사 자리 채우기
해석 그 스마트 주방 가전은 초보 요리사조차도 정교한 고급 요리를 준비할 수 있을 만큼 충분히 자동화되어 있다.

해설 빈칸 뒤의 구(a novice chef)를 강조하면서 '초보 요리사조차도 정교한 고급 요리를 준비할 수 있다'라는 의미를 만드는 강조 부사 (A) even(~조차도, ~까지도)이 정답이다. 강조 부사 (B) right(바로)는 before나 after를 강조한다. 부사 (C) well은 '잘'이라는 의미이며, 강조 부사로 쓰일 때는 '훨씬'이라는 의미로 전치사구를 강조한다. 부사 (D) soon은 '곧'이라는 의미이다.

어휘 appliance n. 가전   automated adj. 자동화된   novice n. 초보
elaborate adj. 정교한   gourmet adj. 고급의

03 부사 자리 채우기

해석 고객 서비스 담당자들은 높은 고객 만족을 보장하기 위해 즉각적으로 대응하도록 훈련받는다.

해설 빈칸 앞의 동사(respond)를 꾸밀 수 있는 것은 부사이므로 부사 (C) promptly(즉각적으로)가 정답이다. 형용사 또는 동사 (A), 동사 (B), 동명사 또는 현재분사 (D)는 동사를 꾸밀 수 없다. 참고로, promptly는 respond와 함께 쓰여 '즉각적으로 대응하다'라는 의미로 자주 쓰인다는 점을 알아 둔다.

어휘 representative n. 담당자, 대표 ensure v. 보장하다 client n. 고객 prompt adj. 즉각적인; v. 촉발하다

04 부사 자리 채우기

해석 Solar Drive사의 최신 전기차는 지속 가능한 교통을 위해 친환경적일 뿐만 아니라 합리적으로 가격이 매겨졌다.

해설 빈칸 뒤의 분사(priced)를 꾸밀 수 있는 것은 부사이므로 부사 (D) reasonably(합리적으로)가 정답이다. 명사 또는 동사 (A), 동사 또는 과거분사 (B), 형용사 (C)는 분사를 꾸밀 수 없다.

어휘 electric vehicle 전기차 sustainable adj. 지속 가능한 transportation n. 교통 reason n. 이유; v. 판단하다 reasonable adj. 합리적인

기출 공식 10~11

토익실전문제   p.166

| 01 (A) | 02 (C) | 03 (C) | 04 (B) |

01 원급 표현 채우기

해석 은행은 추가 ATM을 설치함으로써 고객의 대기 시간을 가능한 한 짧게 유지하려고 노력했다.

해설 keep(to keep)의 목적격 보어 자리에 올 수 있고 빈칸 뒤의 as(~만큼)와 함께 원급 표현을 만드는 형용사의 원급 (A) short(짧은)가 정답이다. 형용사의 비교급 (C)와 최상급 (D)는 원급 표현과 함께 쓰일 수 없다. 부사 (B)는 keep의 목적격 보어 자리에 올 수 없다. 참고로, 'as + 원급 + as + possible'은 '가능한 한 ~한'이라는 의미로 쓰인다는 것을 알아 둔다.

어휘 additional adj. 추가의 shortly adv. 곧

02 비교급 표현 채우기

해석 저렴한 모바일 기술 덕분에, 전 세계의 스마트폰 사용자 수는 그 어느 때보다도 더 높다.

해설 be동사(is)의 보어 자리에 올 수 있고 빈칸 뒤의 than(~보다)과 함께 비교급 표현을 만드는 형용사의 비교급 (C) higher(높은)가 정답이다. 형용사의 원급 (A)와 최상급 (D)는 비교급 표현과 함께 쓰일 수 없다. 부사 (B)는 be동사의 보어 자리에 올 수 없다.

어휘 thanks to ~ 덕분에 affordable adj. 저렴한

03 비교급 표현 채우기

해석 Flex Factory는 인근의 다른 어떤 피트니스 센터보다 더 나은 회원 혜택을 제공한다.

해설 빈칸 앞에 비교급(better)이 있으므로 비교급 표현을 만드는 (C) than(~보다)이 정답이다. (A) as(~만큼)는 원급 표현을 만든다. 강조 부사 (B) even(훨씬)은 비교급 형용사나 부사 바로 앞에서 '훨씬'이라는 의미로 강조한다. 부사절 접속사 (D)는 뒤에 절이 와야 한다.

어휘 benefit n. 혜택 neighborhood n. 인근, 동네 so that ~할 수 있도록

04 비교급 표현 채우기

해석 종종 숙박과 교통을 포함하는 단체 여행 패키지는 개별 예약보다 덜 비싼 경향이 있다.

해설 빈칸 뒤에 원급 형용사(expensive)와 비교급 표현을 만드는 than이 있으므로 '~보다 덜 -한'이라는 표현을 만드는 (B) less가 정답이다. 강조 부사 (A) a lot(훨씬)은 비교급 형용사나 부사를 바로 앞에서 강조한다. (C) rather(꽤, 약간)도 해석상 그럴듯해 보이지만 비교급 표현을 만드는 than이 있으므로 원급인 expensive만 단독으로 쓸 수 없다. 수량 형용사 (D) few는 뒤에 복수 가산 명사가 온다.

어휘 group travel 단체 여행 accommodation n. 숙박 transportation n. 교통 individual adj. 개별의 booking n. 예약

기출 공식 12~13

토익실전문제   p.167

| 01 (D) | 02 (B) | 03 (C) | 04 (B) |

01 최상급 표현 채우기

해석 좋은 건강을 유지하는 데 있어, 가장 중요한 요인은 건강한 생활 방식 선택에 대한 일관성이다.

해설 빈칸 뒤의 명사(factor)를 꾸밀 수 있는 것은 형용사이므로 형용사 important(중요한)의 최상급 (D) most important가 정답이다. 부사 (A)와 (B), 명사 (C)는 명사를 꾸밀 수 없다.

어휘 maintain v. 유지하다 factor n. 요인 consistency n. 일관성 importantly adv. 중요하게 importance n. 중요성

02 최상급 표현 채우기

해석 모든 고객 서비스 문제 중, 배송 지연이 전자상거래 사업에서 가장 일반적인 불만 사항이다.

해설 '가장 일반적인 불만 사항'이라는 의미가 되어야 하고, 빈칸 앞에 최상급과 함께 쓰이는 the가 있으므로 최상급을 만드는 (B) most가 정답이다. 부사 (A) both는 긍정문에서 '~도', (C) either는 부정문에서 '~도'라는 의미이다. 부사 (D) between은 '그 사이에'라는 의미이다.

어휘 shipping delay 배송 지연 common adj. 일반적인 e-commerce n. 전자상거래

03 비교급 표현 채우기

해석 현대 독자들은 편리성과 수천 권의 서적에 대한 즉각적인 접근성 때문에 인쇄된 버전보다는 전자책을 점점 더 선택한다.

해설 '인쇄된 버전보다는 전자책을 선택한다'라는 의미가 되어야 하므로 비교급 표현 (C) rather than(~보다는)이 정답이다. 전치사 (A) upon(~ 위에)과 강조 부사 (B) even(~조차도, ~까지도)은 어색한 문맥을 만든다. 접속부사 (D) at any rate(어쨌든, 적어도)는 문장과 문장을 의미적으로 연결해야 하므로 답이 될 수 없다.

어휘 modern adj. 현대의 increasingly adv. 점점 더 convenience n. 편리성 instant adj. 즉각적인 access n. 접근성 title n. 서적

04 비교급 표현 채우기

해석 공항으로 가는 급행열차는 가장 혼잡한 시간에도 길어야 30분이 걸릴 것이다.

해설 빈칸 앞의 no와 빈칸 뒤의 than과 함께 '길어야 ~이다'라는 의미를 만드는 (B) longer가 정답이다. 형용사의 원급 (A), 명사 또는 형용사 (C), 형용사의 최상급 (D)는 no, than과 함께 표현을 만들 수 없다.

어휘 express train 급행열차 peak hour 가장 혼잡한 시간

HACKERS TEST

p.168

01 (B)	02 (B)	03 (C)	04 (B)	05 (A)
06 (A)	07 (D)	08 (B)	09 (D)	10 (C)
11 (A)	12 (B)	13 (C)	14 (C)	15 (D)
16 (A)	17 (B)	18 (C)	19 (D)	20 (C)
21 (A)	22 (C)	23 (B)	24 (B)	25 (C)
26 (A)	27 (C)	28 (B)		

01 부사 자리 채우기

해석 Velocic International사는 고객의 문의에 항상 빠르게 대응한다.

해설 동사(responds)를 꾸밀 수 있는 것은 부사이고 '고객의 문의에 빠르게 대응하다'라는 의미가 되어야 하므로 부사 (B) quickly(빠르게)가 정답이다. 강조 부사 (A)와 (D)는 동사를 꾸밀 수 없고, 형용사나 부사를 꾸며 그 정도를 강조한다. 시간 부사 (C) ago(전에)는 시간 표현 바로 다음에 와서 현재를 기준으로 그 시간 이전에 일어난 일을 나타낸다.

어휘 respond v. 대응하다, 반응하다 inquiry n. 문의, 연구 very adv. 매우
so adv. 너무나, 대단히

02 수량 형용사 채우기

해석 기름 유출에 관한 뉴스는 그것에 관한 영상이 인터넷에서 퍼지기 전에는 거의 주목을 얻지 못했다.

해설 빈칸 뒤의 '주목, 주의'라는 의미의 불가산 명사 attention을 꾸밀 수 있는 수량 형용사가 와야 하므로 수량 형용사 (B) little(거의 없는)이 정답이다. 수량 형용사 (A)와 (C)는 복수 가산 명사를 꾸미고, 수량 형용사 (D)는 단수 가산 명사를 꾸민다. 참고로, attention은 주로 '주목, 주의, 관심, 보살핌' 등의 의미의 불가산 명사로 쓰이지만, '(관심을 끌기 위한) 행동, 배려'라는 의미일 때는 가산 명사로 쓰인다는 것을 알아 둔다.

어휘 oil spill 기름 유출 spread v. 퍼지다, 확산하다 few adj. 거의 없는
many adj. 많은 a single 하나의

03 형용사 자리 채우기

해석 Garnet 통신사의 신규 고객들을 위한 특별 할인은 첫 3개월의 서비스에 대해 30퍼센트 할인을 약속한다.

해설 빈칸 뒤의 명사(offer)를 꾸밀 수 있는 것은 형용사이므로 현재분사 (A)와 형용사 (C)가 정답의 후보이다. '신규 고객들을 위한 특별 할인'이라는 의미가 되어야 하므로 형용사 (C) special(특별한)이 정답이다. 현재분사 (A)를 쓸 경우 '신규 고객들을 위해 전문으로 하는 할인'이라는 어색한 문맥을 만든다. 동사 (B)와 부사 (D)는 명사를 꾸밀 수 없다.

어휘 offer n. 할인, 제공; v. 제공하다, 제안하다
specialize v. ~을 전문으로 하다, 전공하다 specially adv. 특히, 특별히

04 부사 자리 채우기

해석 건축 현장에서, 노동자들은 현장 안전 감독관에 의해 정기적으로 관리될 것이다.

해설 동사(will be ~ monitored)를 꾸밀 수 있는 것은 부사이므로 부사 (B) regularly(정기적으로)가 정답이다. 형용사 또는 명사 (A), 명사 (C)와 (D)는 동사를 꾸밀 수 없다. 명사 (A), (C), (D)를 be동사(will be)의 보어로 본다 해도, 각각 '노동자들은 감독관에 의해 관리되는 단골손님/규칙적임/규정이다'라는 어색한 문맥을 만든다.

어휘 construction site 건축 현장 monitor v. 관리하다, 감시하다
on-site adj. 현장의 inspector n. 감독관

05 원급 표현 채우기

해석 창고 직원들은 성수기 동안 들어오는 화물을 할 수 있는 한 효율적으로 정리한다.

해설 동사(organize)를 꾸밀 수 있고 빈칸 뒤의 as(~만큼)와 함께 원급 표현을 만드는 부사의 원급 (A) efficiently(효율적으로)가 정답이다. 부사의 최상급 (D)는 원급 표현과 함께 쓰일 수 없다. 형용사 (B)와 명사 (C)는 동사를 꾸밀 수 없다. 참고로, 'as + 원급 + as + 주어 + can'은 '주어가 ~할 수 있는 한'이라는 의미로 쓰인다는 것을 알아 둔다.

어휘 warehouse n. 창고 incoming adj. 들어오는 shipment n. 화물
peak season 성수기 efficient adj. 효율적인 efficiency n. 효율성

06 형용사 자리 채우기

해석 실내 장식가는 비용을 줄이기 위해 흰색 페인트의 광범위한 사용을 추천한다.

해설 동명사(making)의 목적어 자리에 온 명사(use)를 꾸밀 수 있는 것은 형용사이므로 형용사 (A) extensive(광범위한, 아주 많은)가 정답이다. 명사 (B), 부사 (C), 동사 (D)는 명사를 꾸밀 수 없다.

어휘 decorator n. 실내 장식가 recommend v. 추천하다
make use of ~을 사용하다 lower v. 줄이다 cost n. 비용
extension n. 확대 extensively adv. 광범위하게, 널리 extend v. 확대하다

07 빈도 부사 자리 채우기

해석 Blue Scale Industries사는 항상 혁신적인 사고와 적응력을 기반으로 신입 사원을 채용한다.

해설 동사(hires)를 꾸밀 수 있는 것은 부사이므로 모든 보기가 정답의 후보이다. 빈칸이 일반동사 앞에 있고 '항상 혁신적인 사고와 적응력을 기반으로 신입 사원을 채용한다'라는 의미가 되어야 하므로 빈도 부사 (D) always(항상)가 정답이다. 부사 (A) once(한때)는 막연한 과거의 시점을 나타낸다. 부사 (B) enough(충분히)는 형용사 또는 부사를 뒤에서 꾸민다. 부사 (C) most(가장)는 형용사 또는 부사 앞에서 최상급을 나타낸다.

어휘 based on ~을 기반으로 innovative adj. 혁신적인 thinking n. 사고
adaptability n. 적응력

08 형용사 자리 채우기

해석 식당에 더하여, Aviato 카드에 적립된 포인트들은 특정 소매업체에서 교환할 수 있다.

해설 빈칸이 be동사(are) 다음에 왔으므로 진행형을 만드는 현재분사 (A)와 be동사의 보어 자리에 올 수 있는 형용사 (B)가 정답의 후보이다. '적립된 포인트들은 특정 소매업체에서 교환할 수 있다'라는 의미가 되어야 하므로 형용사 (B) redeemable(교환할 수 있는)이 정답이다. 현재분사 (A)를 쓸 경우 '포인트들은 교환하는 중이다'라는 어색한 문맥이 된다. 동사 (C)와 (D)는 be동사 다음에 올 수 없다.

어휘 retail establishment 소매업체 redeem v. 교환하다, 보완하다

09 부사 자리 채우기

해석 Relivium Pro는 다른 브랜드들보다 두통 증상을 감소시키는 데 훨씬 더 효과적이다.

해설 빈칸 뒤의 형용사(more effective)를 꾸밀 수 있는 것은 부사이므로 부사 (D) significantly(훨씬, 매우)가 정답이다. 동사 (A), 명사 (B), 형용사 (C)는 형용사를 꾸밀 수 없다.

어휘 effective adj. 효과적인 headache n. 두통 symptom n. 증상
signify v. 의미하다, 나타내다 signifier n. 기표 significant adj. 상당한

10 비교급 표현 채우기

해석 그 회사는 즉각적인 이익을 추구하기보다는 장기적인 관계 구축에 중점을 둔다.

해설 동명사구(pursuing immediate profits) 앞에 올 수 있고, '즉각적인 이익을 추구하기보다는 장기적인 관계 구축에 중점을 둔다'라는 의미가 되어야 하므로 비교급 표현 (C) rather than(~보다는)이 정답이다. 명사절 접속사 (A), 부사절 접속사 (B)와 (D)는 뒤에 동명사구가 아닌 절이 와야 한다.

어휘 relationship n. 관계 pursue v. 추구하다 profit n. 이익

11 시간 부사 자리 채우기

해석 Mr. Weiss가 이미 Sandro's Italian에 자리를 예약했기 때문에, 파티 장소를 더 찾아볼 필요가 없다.

해설 빈칸은 동사(has ~ booked)를 꾸미는 부사 자리이고, 'Mr. Weiss가 이미 자리를 예약했다'라는 의미가 되어야 하므로 시간 부사 (A) already(이미, 벌써)가 정답이다. (B) still(여전히)을 쓸 경우 'Mr. Weiss가 여전히 자리를 예약했다'라는 어색한 문맥이 된다. (C) later(그 시간 이후에)는 시간 표현 바로 다음에 와야 하므로 답이 될 수 없다. (D) forward(앞으로)를 쓸 경우 'Mr. Weiss가 앞으로 자리를 예약했다'라는 어색한 문맥이 된다.

어휘 book a table 자리를 예약하다 venue n. 장소

12 비교급 표현 채우기

해석 Stratedge Advertising사는 모바일 광고 업계에서 경쟁사들보다 더 큰 인정을 받았다.

해설 명사(recognition)를 꾸밀 수 있고 빈칸 뒤의 than(~보다)과 함께 비교급 표현을 만드는 형용사의 비교급 (B) greater(큰)가 정답이다. 형용사의 원급 (A)와 최상급 (D)는 비교급 표현과 함께 쓰일 수 없다. 부사 (C)는 명사를 꾸미는 형용사 자리에 올 수 없다.

어휘 gain v. 받다, 얻다 recognition n. 인정, 인식 competitor n. 경쟁사, 경쟁자 greatly adv. 대단히, 크게

13 형용사 자리 채우기

해석 Sparta 재단의 멘토링 프로그램은 학생들에게 유익하다고 판명되었다.

해설 빈칸은 be동사(be) 다음에 온 보어 자리이므로 형용사 (C)와 명사 (D)가 정답의 후보이다. 'Sparta 재단의 멘토링 프로그램은 유익하다고 판명되었다'라는 의미로, 보어가 주어(Sparta Foundation's mentoring program)의 상태를 설명하고 있으므로 형용사 (C) informative(유익한)가 정답이다. 명사 (D)를 쓸 경우 주어와 동격이 되어 'Sparta 재단의 멘토링 프로그램은 정보라고 판명되었다'라는 어색한 문맥이 된다. 동사 (A)와 (B)는 보어 자리에 올 수 없다.

어휘 foundation n. 재단 prove v. 판명되다, 입증하다 inform v. 알리다

14 부사 자리 채우기

해석 그 책장은 특수 나사 세트로 안전하게 벽에 붙어 있도록 설계되었다.

해설 동사(be ~ attached)를 꾸밀 수 있는 것은 부사이므로 부사 (C) securely(안전하게, 튼튼하게)가 정답이다. 형용사 또는 동사 (A), 명사 (B), 동사 또는 과거분사 (D)는 동사를 꾸밀 수 없다. 명사 (B)를 be동사(be)의 보어로 보고 빈칸 뒤의 분사(attached)가 명사를 수식하는 것으로 본다 해도, '그 책장은 벽에 붙여진 안정성으로 설계되었다'라는 어색한 의미를 만든다.

어휘 attach v. 붙이다, 연결하다 screw n. 나사 secure adj. 안심하는, 안전한; v. 확보하다 security n. 안정성, 경비

15 강조 부사 자리 채우기

해석 그 보수 프로젝트는 인근 도시에서 완료된 비슷한 프로젝트보다 훨씬 더 적은 자금을 필요로 했다.

해설 형용사(less)를 꾸밀 수 있는 것은 부사이므로 모든 보기가 정답의 후보이다. 빈칸 뒤에 비교급 형용사(less)가 있으므로 비교급을 강조하는 강조 부사 (D) much(훨씬)가 정답이다. (A) right(바로)는 주로 before, after를 강조하고, (B) very(매우)는 원급을 강조한다. (C) further(더욱이)는 정도가 더 하다는 것을 나타내며, 이미 비교급이므로 비교급 앞에 올 수 없다.

어휘 renovation n. 보수 funding n. 자금 similar adj. 비슷한 neighboring adj. 인근의

16 형용사 자리 채우기

해석 소규모 자영업자는 경제 회복 기간 동안 정부 보조금에 대한 자격이 있다.

해설 '소규모 자영업자는 정부 보조금에 대한 자격이 있다'라는 의미가 되어야 하므로 빈칸 앞의 be동사(are)와 뒤의 전치사 for와 함께 '~에 대한 자격이 있다'라는 의미의 어구 be eligible for를 만드는 형용사 (A) eligible이 정답이다. 명사 (B)와 (D)를 be동사(are)의 보어로 본다 해도, 각각 '소규모 자영업자는 정부 보조금을 위한 적격/바람직함이다'라는 어색한 문맥을 만든다. 부사 (C)는 be동사, 전치사 for와 함께 어구를 만들 수 없다.

어휘 government grant 정부 보조금 recovery n. 회복 period n. 기간 eligibly adv. 적임으로, 적당하게

17 최상급 표현 채우기

해석 고객 피드백은 제품 개발 및 개선에서 가장 필수적인 부분이다.

해설 빈칸 뒤의 명사(part)를 꾸밀 수 있는 것은 형용사이므로 형용사 essential(필수적인)의 최상급 (B) most essential이 정답이다. 명사 (A), 부사 (C)와 (D)는 형용사 자리에 올 수 없다.

어휘 essence n. 본질 essentially adv. 근본적으로

18 부사 자리 채우기

해석 전국적으로 인정받는 건축가들이 그 국가에서 성장하는 도시 공동체를 위해 지속 가능한 주택을 설계할 것이다.

해설 빈칸 뒤의 분사(recognized)를 꾸밀 수 있는 것은 부사이므로 부사 (C) Nationally(전국적으로)가 정답이다. 명사 (A)와 (D), 형용사 (B)는 분사를 꾸밀 수 없다.

어휘 recognized adj. 인정받는 architect n. 건축가 housing n. 주택 urban adj. 도시의 nation n. 국가 national adj. 국가의, 전국적인 nationality n. 국적, 민족

19 형용사 자리 채우기

해석 그 워크숍은 실습을 통해 참가자들의 관리하는 능력을 효과적으로 향상시키는 것을 목표로 한다.

해설 빈칸 뒤의 명사(skills)를 꾸밀 수 있는 것은 형용사이므로 형용사 역할을 하는 과거분사 (C)와 형용사 (D)가 정답의 후보이다. '참가자들의 관리하는 능력을 향상시킨다'라는 의미가 되어야 하므로 형용사 (D) supervisory(관리하는, 감독하는)가 정답이다. 과거분사 (C) supervised(관리되는)를 쓸 경우 '참가자들의 관리되는 능력을 향상시킨다'라는 어색한 문맥이 된다. 동사 (A)와 (B)는 명사를 꾸밀 수 없다.

어휘 aim v. 목표로 하다 effectively adv. 효과적으로 practical exercise 실습 supervise v. 감독하다

20 부사 자리 채우기

해석 Dr. Sharma는 화합물을 정확하게 측정했고 그녀의 실험을 여러 번 반복했다.

해설 동사(measured)를 꾸밀 수 있는 것은 부사이므로 부사 (C) accurately(정확하게)가 정답이다. 형용사 (A)와 (D), 명사 (B)는 동사를 꾸밀 수 없다.

어휘 measure v. 측정하다 chemical compound 화합물 repeat v. 반복하다 multiple adj. 여러, 많은 accurate adj. 정확한 accuracy n. 정확도

21 수량 형용사 채우기

해석 모든 세션의 시작에, 그 요가 강사는 학생들에게 부드러운 호흡 운동을 안내한다.

해설 빈칸 뒤의 단수 가산 명사 session을 꾸밀 수 있는 수량 형용사가 와야 하므로 수량 형용사 (A) every(모든)가 정답이다. 수량 형용사 (B)와 (C)는 가산 명사를 꾸밀 때 복수 명사 앞에만 올 수 있다. 수량 형용사 (D)는 불가산 명사를 꾸민다.

어휘 instructor n. 강사 gentle adj. 부드러운 breathing n. 호흡

22 형태가 비슷하지만 의미가 다른 부사 자리 채우기

해석 Paramount Legal Solutions사의 법률 사무소 직원인 Ms. Valdez는 변호사들 및 고객들과 긴밀하게 일한다.

해설 동사(works)를 꾸밀 수 있는 것은 부사이므로 부사 (A), (B), (C)가 정

답의 후보이다. '변호사들 및 고객들과 긴밀하게 일한다'라는 의미가 되어야 하므로 부사 (C) closely(긴밀하게, 밀접하게)가 정답이다. 부사 (A) close(가까이)와 (B) closer(더 가까이)를 쓸 경우 물리적인 거리의 가까움을 의미하기 때문에 어색한 문맥이 되며, '~와 가깝게'라는 의미를 가지기 위해서는 전치사 with가 아닌 to와 함께 쓰여야 한다. 명사 (D)는 동사를 꾸밀 수 없다. 동사 work를 '~을 작동시키다, ~을 일으키다'라는 의미의 타동사로 보고 명사 (D)를 목적어로 본다 해도, '변호사들 및 고객들과의 폐쇄를 작동시킨다/일으킨다'라는 어색한 문맥을 만든다.

어휘 **legal assistant** 법률 사무소 직원 **closure** n. 폐쇄

23 비교급 표현 채우기

해석 그 추적 장치는 반려동물 관찰이라는 주요 기능 이외에도 야생동물 보호에 쓰인다.

해설 명사구(its ~ monitor) 앞에 올 수 있고, '반려동물 관찰이라는 주요 기능 이외에도 야생동물 보호에 쓰인다'라는 의미가 되어야 하므로 비교급 표현 (B) other than(~ 이외에도)이 정답이다. 전치사 (A) since(~ 이후로)도 뒤에 명사구가 올 수 있지만, 시점 표현이 와야 하므로 답이 될 수 없다. 접속부사 (C)는 명사구 앞에 올 수 없다. 목적을 나타내는 (D) in order to 뒤에는 동사원형이 와서 '~하기 위해'라는 의미를 나타낸다.

어휘 **tracking device** 추적 장치 **have uses in** ~에 쓰이다
conservation n. 보호 **primary** adj. 주요한 **function** n. 기능
moreover adv. 게다가, 더욱이

24 형용사 자리 채우기

해석 그 최고경영자는 다수의 주주들이 현재 재정 상태에 대해 계속 많이 알고 있도록 하기 위해 노력했다.

해설 동사 keep은 목적어와 목적격 보어를 가지는 동사이며, 동사(keep) 뒤에 목적어(the ~ shareholders)가 있으므로 빈칸은 목적격 보어 자리이다. 따라서 동사 keep의 목적격 보어 자리에 올 수 있는 형용사 (B)와 과거분사 (D)가 정답의 후보이다. '다수의 주주들이 현재 재정 상태에 대해 계속 많이 알고 있도록 하다'라는 의미가 되어야 하므로 형용사 (B) knowledgeable(많이 알고 있는, 아는 것이 많은)이 정답이다. 과거분사 (D) known(알려진)을 쓸 경우 '현재 재정 상태로 알려진 다수의 주주들'이라는 어색한 의미가 된다. 명사 (A) knowledge(지식)를 쓸 경우 목적어를 2개 갖는 4형식 동사 keep(~을 위해 -을 남겨 두다)이 되어 '다수의 주주들을 위해 현재 재정 상태에 대한 지식을 남겨 두다'라는 어색한 문맥이 된다. 동사 (C)는 보어 자리에 올 수 없다.

어휘 **majority** n. 다수 **shareholder** n. 주주 **current** adj. 현재의
financial situation 재정 상태

25 부사 자리 채우기

해석 대규모 화재로 인해, 몇몇 농산물들은 식료품점에서 비교적 찾기 어려워졌다.

해설 빈칸 뒤의 형용사(hard)를 꾸밀 수 있는 것은 부사이므로 부사 (C) relatively(비교적)가 정답이다. 동사 (A), 형용사 또는 명사 (B), 명사 (D)는 형용사를 꾸밀 수 없다.

어휘 **massive** adj. 대규모의 **agricultural product** 농산물 **relate** v. 관련시키다
relative adj. 관련된; n. 친척 **relativity** n. 상대성

26 강조 부사 자리 채우기

해석 Aether 항공사는 국제적 확장의 초기 단계에서 오직 세 곳의 목적지만 취항하고 있다.

해설 동사(is serving)의 목적어 자리에 온 명사구(three destinations)를 꾸밀 수 있는 강조 부사 (A)와 수량 형용사 (C)가 정답의 후보이다. '오직 세 곳의 목적지만 취항하고 있다'라는 의미가 되어야 하므로 강조 부사 (A) only(오직)가 정답이다. 수량 형용사 (C) many(많은)는 기수 (three)와 함께 쓸 수 없다. 강조 부사 (B) quite(꽤, 굉장한)는 주로 형용사, 부사 또는 'a/an + 명사'를 앞에서 강조할 때 쓴다. 전치사 (D)는 동사의 목적어가 되는 명사구를 이끌 수 없다.

어휘 **destination** n. 목적지 **initial** adj. 초기의 **phase** n. 단계

expansion n. 확장 **including** prep. ~을 포함하여

27 부사 자리 채우기

해석 Queensland Holdings사는 지난 십 년 동안 지속적으로 긍정적인 수익을 창출함으로써 투자자들을 만족시켰다.

해설 빈칸은 동명사(generating)를 꾸미는 부사 자리이므로 부사 (C) consistently(지속적으로)가 정답이다. 형용사 (A), 명사 (B), 동사 (D)는 동명사를 꾸밀 수 없다.

어휘 **generate** v. 창출하다, 발생시키다 **return** n. 수익
consistent adj. 지속적인 **consistency** n. 일관성
consist v. (요소로) 되어 있다

28 형태가 비슷하지만 의미가 다른 형용사 자리 채우기

해석 현대의 얼굴 인식 소프트웨어는 많은 군중 속에서 개인을 식별하는 데 있어 인간의 기억보다 더 신뢰할 수 있다.

해설 빈칸이 be동사(is) 다음에 왔으므로 진행형을 만드는 현재분사 (A), 형용사 (B)와 (C)가 정답의 후보이다. '소프트웨어는 인간의 기억보다 더 신뢰할 수 있다'라는 의미가 되어야 하므로 형용사 (B) reliable(신뢰할 수 있는)이 정답이다. 현재분사 (A)와 형용사 (C)를 쓸 경우 각각 '소프트웨어는 더 신뢰하고 있다/의지한다'라는 어색한 문맥이 된다. 동사 (D)는 be동사 다음에 올 수 없다.

어휘 **facial recognition** 얼굴 인식 **crowd** n. 군중 **rely** v. 의지하다

DAY 05 전치사

기출 공식 1~2

토익실전문제   p.170

| 01 (B) | 02 (B) | 03 (D) | 04 (A) |

01 in/on/at 구별하여 채우기

해석 Terra Motors사의 수입이 지난 분기에 5천만 달러를 초과하며, 연간 성장에 대한 새로운 기록을 세웠다.

해설 분기(the last quarter) 앞에는 전치사 in을 쓰므로 전치사 (B) in(~에)이 정답이다. (A) at은 '~에'라는 의미이지만 분기 앞에 쓰일 수 없고, (C) to는 '~로, ~ 쪽으로', (C) up은 '~ 위로'라는 의미이다.

어휘 **revenue** n. 수입 **exceed** v. 초과하다 **annual** adj. 연간의

02 in/on/at 구별하여 채우기

해석 최신 기기를 제공하는 전자 제품 가게는 Lakeline 쇼핑몰의 3층에서 찾을 수 있다.

해설 층(the third floor) 앞에는 전치사 on을 쓰므로 전치사 (B) on(~에)이 정답이다. (A) for는 '~을 위해, ~ 동안', (C) off는 '벗어나서', (D) onto는 '~ 위에, ~ 위로'라는 의미이다.

어휘 **gadget** n. 기기

03 전치사 채우기

해석 구매자는 계약을 체결한 후 7일 이내에 철저한 부동산 검사를 수행할 수 있다.

해설 이 문장은 주어(Buyers), 동사(can conduct), 목적어(a ~ property inspection)를 모두 갖춘 완전한 절이므로, ___ ~ contract는 수식어 거품으로 보아야 한다. 이 수식어 거품은 동사가 없는 거품구이므로 거품구를 이끌 수 있는 전치사 (B)와 (D)가 정답의 후보이다. '계약을 체결한 후 7일 이내에'라는 의미가 되어야 하므로 전치사 (D) within(~ 이내에)이 정답이다. 전치사 (B) since(~ 이후로)는 뒤에 시점 표현이 와야 한다. 부사절 접속사 (A) while(~하는 동안)은 거품구가 아닌 거품절을 이끈다. 강조 부사 (C) even은 '~조차도, ~까지도'라는 의미이다.

어휘 conduct v. 수행하다　thorough adj. 철저한　property n. 부동산
inspection n. 검사　contract n. 계약

04 전치사 채우기

해석 기조연설자인 Mr. Sealey는 회의를 위해 오전 10시까지 도착할 것으로 예상된다.

해설 빈칸은 명사구(10 A.M.)를 목적어로 가지는 전치사 자리이므로 모든 보기가 정답의 후보이다. '오전 10시까지 도착할 것으로 예상된다'라는 의미가 되어야 하므로 특정 시점까지 행동이 완료되는 것을 의미하는 전치사 (A) by(~까지)가 정답이다. (C) until도 '~까지'라는 의미이지만, 특정 시점까지 상황이나 상태가 계속되는 것을 의미하므로 답이 될 수 없다. (B) on은 시각(10 A.M.) 앞에 올 수 없다. (D) into는 '~ 안으로'라는 의미이다.

어휘 keynote speaker 기조연설자　expect v. 예상하다　conference n. 회의

기출 공식 3~4

토익실전문제 p.171

| 01 (D) | 02 (B) | 03 (A) | 04 (C) |

01 전치사 채우기

해석 그 회사와 공급업체 사이의 계약 분쟁은 중재를 통해 성공적으로 해결되었다.

해설 빈칸은 명사구(the company and its supplier)를 목적어로 가지는 전치사 자리이므로 모든 보기가 정답의 후보이다. '그 회사와 공급업체 사이의 계약 분쟁'이라는 의미가 되어야 하므로 전치사 (D) between(~ 사이에)이 정답이다. 참고로, between은 주로 두 개의 대상 사이를 나타내는 점을 알아 둔다. (A) after는 '~ 후에', (B) along은 '~을 따라서', (C) until은 '~까지'라는 의미이다.

어휘 dispute n. 분쟁　successfully adv. 성공적으로　resolve v. 해결하다
mediation n. 중재

02 전치사 채우기

해석 극찬 받은 그 연극 공연은 Ms. Kennedy의 지시에 따라 공연되었다.

해설 빈칸은 명사(the direction)를 목적어로 가지는 전치사 자리이므로 모든 보기가 정답의 후보이다. 'Ms. Kennedy의 지시에 따라'라는 의미가 되어야 하므로 (B) under(~ 아래에)가 정답이다. 참고로, under the direction of는 '~의 지시에 따라'라는 의미의 관용 표현으로 쓰이는 점을 알아 둔다. (A) among은 '~ 사이에'라는 뜻으로, 셋 이상의 사람이나 사물 사이를 나타낼 때 쓰인다. (C) behind는 '~ 뒤에', (D) opposite는 '~ 건너편에, ~ 맞은 편에'라는 의미이다.

어휘 critically acclaimed 극찬 받은　stage v. 공연하다

03 전치사 채우기

해석 Modern Living Designs는 계절 재고 재구성을 위해 11월 20일부터 11월 25일까지 휴업할 것이다.

해설 빈칸은 명사구(November 20)를 목적어로 가지는 전치사 자리이므로 모든 보기가 정답의 후보이다. 빈칸 뒤에 시점 표현(November 20)이 있고 '11월 20일부터 11월 25일까지'라는 의미가 되어야 하므로 (A) from(~로부터)이 정답이다. 참고로, from A to B는 'A부터 B까지'라는 의미의 관용 표현으로 쓰이는 점을 알아 둔다. (B) outside는 '~ 밖에', (C) near는 '~ 가까이, ~ 근처에', (D) under는 '~ 아래에'라는 의미이다.

어휘 seasonal adj. 계절의　inventory n. 재고　reconfiguration n. 재구성

04 전치사 채우기

해석 백신 프로그램은 전국적인 유행병에 대응하기 위해 전역에 걸쳐 체계적으로 실행되었다.

해설 빈칸은 명사구(the entire nation)를 목적어로 가지는 전치사 자리이므로 모든 보기가 정답의 후보이다. '전역에 걸쳐 실행되었다'라는 의미가 되어야 하므로 (C) across(~의 전역에 걸쳐)가 정답이다. 참고로, across the nation은 '전역에 걸쳐, 전국에'라는 의미의 관용 표현으로 쓰이는 점을 알아 둔다. (A) beside는 '~ 옆에', (B) out of는 '~ 밖으로', (D) beneath는 '~ 아래에'라는 의미이다.

어휘 vaccination n. 백신　systematically adv. 체계적으로
implement v. 실행하다　combat v. ~에 대응하다　pandemic n. 유행병

기출 공식 5~6

토익실전문제 p.172

| 01 (B) | 02 (C) | 03 (D) | 04 (B) |

01 전치사 채우기

해석 악천후 때문에 야구 선수권 대회가 다음 주말로 일정이 변경되었다.

해설 빈칸은 명사구(inclement weather)를 목적어로 가지는 전치사 자리이므로 전치사 (B), (C), (D)가 정답의 후보이다. '악천후 때문에 선수권 대회가 일정이 변경되었다'라는 의미가 되어야 하므로 전치사 (B) Because of(~ 때문에)가 정답이다. (C) In spite of는 '~ 에도 불구하고', (D) Except for는 '~을 제외하고'라는 의미이다. 부사절 접속사 (A)는 명사구를 목적어로 가질 수 없다.

어휘 inclement weather 악천후, 궂은 날씨　reschedule v. 일정을 변경하다
although conj. 비록 ~이지만

02 전치사 채우기

해석 첨단 VR 게임 시스템은 높은 비용에도 불구하고 최신 기술에 능한 소비자들 사이에서 계속해서 인기를 얻고 있다.

해설 빈칸은 명사구(the high cost)를 목적어로 가지는 전치사 자리이므로 모든 보기가 정답의 후보이다. '높은 비용에도 불구하고 계속해서 인기를 얻고 있다'라는 의미가 되어야 하므로 전치사 (C) despite(~에도 불구하고)가 정답이다. (A) until은 '~까지', (B) against는 '~에 반대하여, ~에 기대어', (D) owing to는 '~ 때문에'라는 의미이다.

어휘 cutting-edge adj. 첨단의　popularity n. 인기
tech-savvy adj. 최신 기술에 능한

03 전치사 채우기

해석 대화형 요소를 추가함으로써, 교사들은 온라인 학습 플랫폼에서 학생들의 참여도를 높일 수 있다.

해설 빈칸은 동명사구(adding interactive elements)를 목적어로 가지는 전치사 자리이므로 모든 보기가 정답의 후보이다. '대화형 요소를 추가함으로써, 교사들은 학생들의 참여도를 높일 수 있다'라는 의미가 되어야 하므로 전치사 (D) By(~함으로써)가 정답이다. (A) Within은 '~ 이내에', (B) Under는 '~ 아래에', (C) Of는 '~의'라는 의미이다.

어휘 add v. 추가하다　interactive adj. 대화형의, 상호적인　element n. 요소
engagement n. 참여도

04 전치사 채우기

해석 화물 회사들은 개별 소포와 총 적하물의 무게를 기준으로 차량 적재를 전략적으로 계획한다.

해설 빈칸은 명사(individual packages and the total shipment)를 목적어로 가지는 전치사 자리이므로 모든 보기가 정답의 후보이다. '개별 소포와 총 적하물의 무게'라는 의미가 되어야 하므로 전치사 (B) of(~의)가 정답이다. (A) as는 '~로서', (C) about은 '~에 관하여', (D) among은 '~ 사이에'라는 의미이다.

어휘 freight n. 화물　strategically adv. 전략적으로　loading n. 적재
total adj. 총　shipment n. 적하물

기출 공식 7~8

토익실전문제 p.173

| 01 (C) | 02 (B) | 03 (D) | 04 (C) |

HACKERS TEST p.174

01 (D)	02 (A)	03 (C)	04 (D)	05 (C)
06 (B)	07 (B)	08 (A)	09 (C)	10 (D)
11 (B)	12 (D)	13 (A)	14 (C)	15 (A)
16 (C)	17 (B)	18 (B)	19 (B)	20 (A)
21 (C)	22 (D)	23 (A)	24 (D)	25 (B)
26 (C)	27 (C)	28 (B)		

01 전치사 채우기

해석 설문 조사 결과에 따르면, 유연한 근무 시간은 직원의 만족도와 생산성을 크게 높인다.

해설 빈칸은 명사구(the survey results)를 목적어로 가지는 전치사 자리이므로 전치사 (B), (C), (D)가 정답의 후보이다. '설문 조사 결과에 따르면'이라는 의미가 되어야 하므로 전치사 (C) According to(~에 따르면)가 정답이다. (B) In addition to는 '~에 더해서', (D) In place of는 '~을 대신하여'라는 의미이다. 부사절 접속사 (A)는 명사구를 목적어로 가질 수 없다.

어휘 survey n. 설문 조사   result n. 결과   flexible adj. 유연한
significantly adv. 크게, 상당히   because conj. ~하기 때문에

02 전치사 채우기

해석 화재가 발생할 경우에 모든 입주자는 지정된 비상구를 사용하여 즉시 건물에서 대피해야 한다.

해설 빈칸은 명사(fire)를 목적어로 가지는 전치사 자리이므로 전치사 (A), (B), (D)가 정답의 후보이다. '화재가 발생할 경우에 즉시 건물에서 대피해야 한다'라는 의미가 되어야 하므로 전치사 (B) in the event of(~할 경우에)가 정답이다. (A) contrary to는 '~에 반해', (D) in exchange for는 '~의 대신으로'라는 의미이다. 부사절 접속사 (C)는 명사를 목적어로 가질 수 없다.

어휘 occupant n. 입주자   evacuate v. 대피하다   designated adj. 지정된
emergency exit 비상구   in order that ~할 수 있도록

03 전치사 표현 채우기

해석 컨설팅 회사는 고객들이 정보에 입각한 투자 결정을 내리는 데 도움을 주기 위해 그들에게 상세한 시장 분석 보고서를 제공한다.

해설 빈칸은 명사구(detailed market analysis reports)를 목적어로 가지는 전치사 자리이므로 모든 보기가 정답의 후보이다. '고객들에게 상세한 시장 분석 보고서를 제공한다'라는 의미가 되어야 하므로, 빈칸 앞의 동사 provides와 함께 'A에게 B를 제공하다'라는 의미의 어구인 provide A with B를 만드는 전치사 (D) with가 정답이다. (B) for(~를 위해서)를 쓰면 '고객들을 상세한 시장 분석 보고서에 제공한다'라는 어색한 의미가 되므로 답이 될 수 없다. (A) at은 '~에', (C) to는 '~로, ~ 쪽으로'라는 의미이다.

어휘 client n. 고객   detailed adj. 상세한   analysis n. 분석

04 전치사 표현 채우기

해석 첫 주택 구매자들은 더 낮은 이자율을 가진 특별 대출 프로그램에 대한 자격이 있다.

해설 빈칸은 명사구(special loan programs)를 목적어로 가지는 전치사 자리이므로 모든 보기가 정답의 후보이다. '특별 대출 프로그램에 대한 자격이 있다'라는 의미가 되어야 하므로 빈칸 앞의 형용사 eligible과 함께 '~에 대한 자격이 있다'라는 의미의 어구인 eligible for를 만드는 전치사 (C) for가 정답이다. (A) on, (B) by, (D) from은 eligible on/by/from의 형태로 쓰일 수 없다.

어휘 homebuyer n. 주택 구매자   loan n. 대출   interest rate 이자율

01 전치사 채우기

해석 그 CEO는 회사 창립 25주년 기념일을 축하하는 행사 동안 영감을 주는 연설을 했다.

해설 이 문장은 주어(The CEO), 동사(delivered), 목적어(an inspiring speech)를 모두 갖춘 완전한 절이므로, ___ ~ anniversary는 수식어 거품으로 보아야 한다. 이 수식어 거품은 동사가 없는 거품구이므로 거품구를 이끌 수 있는 모든 보기가 정답의 후보이다. '행사 동안 영감을 주는 연설을 했다'라는 의미가 되어야 하고, the ceremony라는 명사가 와서 '언제 일어나는지'를 나타내고 있으므로 전치사 (D) during(~ 동안)이 정답이다. (A) above는 '~ 위에', (B) beside는 '~ 옆에', (C) between은 '~ 사이에'라는 의미로 위치를 나타낸다.

어휘 inspiring adj. 영감을 주는   mark v. 축하하다, 기념하다
anniversary n. 기념일

02 in/on/at 구별하여 채우기

해석 약 5시 정각에 시내로 들어가는 주요 고속도로에서 교통 체증이 증가하기 시작한다.

해설 시각(approximately five o'clock) 앞에는 전치사 at을 쓰므로 (A) at(~에)이 정답이다. (B) on은 '~에'라는 의미이지만 시각 앞에 쓰일 수 없고, (C) for는 '~ 동안', (D) up은 '~ 위로'라는 의미이다.

어휘 build up 증가하다   approximately adv. 약

03 전치사 채우기

해석 배달 서비스에 대한 증가하는 수요 때문에, Swift Go사는 전국적으로 1,000명 이상의 새로운 운전기사를 고용했다.

해설 이 문장은 주어(Swift Go), 동사(has hired), 목적어(over ~ drivers)를 모두 갖춘 완전한 절이므로, ___ ~ services는 수식어 거품으로 보아야 한다. 이 수식어 거품은 동사가 없는 거품구이므로 거품구를 이끌 수 있는 전치사 (A)와 (C)가 정답의 후보이다. '배달 서비스에 대한 증가하는 수요 때문에 새로운 운전기사를 고용했다'라는 의미가 되어야 하므로 전치사 (C) Owing to(~ 때문에)가 정답이다. (A) Toward는 '~ 쪽으로, ~을 향하여'라는 의미로 방향을 나타낸다. 부사절 접속사 (B) Although(비록 ~이지만)와 (D) Now that(~이니까)은 거품구가 아닌 거품절을 이끈다.

04 전치사 채우기

해석 Mr. Kazuka의 Starlight Fractals가 Barton에서 Fort Bend까지 모든 주요 서점들에 배부될 것이다.

해설 이 문장은 주어(Starlight Fractals)와 동사(will be distributed)를 갖춘 완전한 절이므로, ___ ~ Fort Bend는 수식어 거품으로 보아야 한다. 이 수식어 거품은 동사가 없는 거품구이므로 거품구를 이끌 수 있는 전치사 (A), (C), (D)가 정답의 후보이다. 'Starlight Fractals가 Barton에서 Fort Bend까지 주요 서점들에 배부될 것이다'라는 의미가 되어야 하므로 빈칸 뒤의 to와 함께 from A to B(A에서 B까지)를 만드는 (D) from(~부터)이 정답이다. 전치사 (A) among(~ 사이에)과 (C) between(~ 사이에)도 해석상 그럴듯해 보이지만, (A)는 셋 이상의 사람이나 사물 사이에를 나타내고, (C)는 두 개의 대상 사이의 관계나 위치, 또는 시간을 나타내며 보통 between A and B(A와 B 사이에)의 형태로 쓰이기 때문에 답이 될 수 없다. 부사절 접속사 (B) when(~할 때)은 거품

구가 아닌 거품절을 이끈다.

어휘 distribute v. 배부하다 major adj. 주요한

05 전치사 채우기

해석 태양광 패널 설치 비용에도 불구하고, 주택 소유자들은 그것을 재생 에너지의 해결책으로서 수용하려고 노력하고 있다.

해설 이 문장은 주어(homeowners), 동사(are trying), 목적어(to embrace ~ solution)를 갖춘 완전한 절이므로, ___ ~ installation은 수식어 거품으로 보아야 한다. 이 수식어 거품은 동사가 없는 거품구이므로 거품구를 이끌 수 있는 전치사 (A), (B), (C)가 정답의 후보이다. '태양광 패널 설치 비용에도 불구하고 재생 에너지의 해결책으로서 수용하려고 노력하다'라는 의미가 되어야 하므로 전치사 (C) Despite(~에도 불구하고)가 정답이다. (A) Before는 '~ 전에'라는 의미로, (B) During은 '~ 동안'이라는 의미로 시간을 나타낸다. 부사절 접속사 (D) Though(비록 ~이지만)는 거품구가 아닌 거품절을 이끈다.

어휘 solar panel 태양광 패널 installation n. 설치 embrace v. 수용하다
renewable energy 재생 에너지 solution n. 해결책

06 전치사 채우기

해석 Ms. Potter는 Wallace's 중고 서점에서 일요일을 제외하고 매일 일한다.

해설 빈칸은 명사(Sunday)를 목적어로 가지는 전치사 자리이므로 모든 보기가 정답의 후보이다. 'Ms. Potter는 일요일을 제외하고 매일 일한다'라는 의미가 되어야 하므로 제외를 나타내는 전치사 (B) except(~을 제외하고)가 정답이다. (A) around는 '~ 주위에', (C) across는 '~을 가로질러', (D) within은 '~ 이내에, ~ 내에'라는 의미이다.

07 전치사 채우기

해석 Mr. Robertson은 어떤 주식을 구매할 것인지 선택하기 전에 재정 전문가들의 조언을 구했다.

해설 빈칸은 동명사(choosing)를 목적어로 가지는 전치사 자리이므로 모든 보기가 정답의 후보이다. '어떤 주식을 구매할 것인지 선택하기 전에 재정 전문가들의 조언을 구했다'라는 의미가 되어야 하므로 전치사 (B) before(~전에)가 정답이다. (A) according to는 '~에 따르면', (C) through는 '~을 통해서', (D) far from은 '전혀 ~이 아닌'이라는 의미이다.

어휘 seek v. 구하다, 찾다 financial expert 재정 전문가 stock n. 주식

08 전치사 채우기

해석 디지털 결제 수단은 젊은 소비자들 사이에 기본 거래 옵션이 되었다.

해설 빈칸은 명사(young consumers)를 목적어로 가지는 전치사 자리이므로 모든 보기가 정답의 후보이다. '젊은 소비자들 사이에 기본 거래 옵션이 되었다'라는 의미가 되어야 하므로 전치사 (A) among(~ 사이에)이 정답이다. (B) against는 '~에 반대하여, ~에 기대어', (C) onto는 '~ 위에, ~ 위로', (D) beneath는 '~ 아래에'라는 의미이다.

어휘 method n. 수단, 방법 default n. 기본, 디폴트 transaction n. 거래
consumer n. 소비자

09 전치사 채우기

해석 Metro Vista 쇼핑몰 방문객들은 실내 게임과 가상 현실 체험과 같은 다양한 활동을 즐길 수 있다.

해설 이 문장은 주어(Metro Vista Mall visitors), 동사(can enjoy), 목적어(various activities)를 갖춘 완전한 절이므로, ___ ~ experiences는 수식어 거품으로 보아야 한다. 이 수식어 거품은 동사가 없는 거품구이므로 거품구를 이끌 수 있는 전치사 (B)와 (C)가 정답의 후보이다. '실내 게임과 가상 현실 체험과 같은 다양한 활동'이라는 의미가 되어야 하므로 전치사 (C) such as(~와 같은)가 정답이다. (B) about은 '~에 관하여'라는 의미이다. 부사절 접속사 (A) whereas(~한 반면에)와 접속부사 (D) likewise(마찬가지로)는 거품구를 이끌 수 없다.

어휘 various adj. 다양한 activity n. 활동 indoor adj. 실내의
virtual reality 가상 현실

10 전치사 채우기

해석 정규 근무 시간을 연장하는 것에 더해서, 그 어린이집은 이제 편리하게도 주말 돌봄 서비스를 제공한다.

해설 이 문장은 주어(the childcare center), 동사(provides), 목적어(weekend care services)를 갖춘 완전한 절이므로, ___ ~ hours는 수식어 거품으로 보아야 한다. 이 수식어 거품은 동사가 없는 거품구이므로 거품구를 이끌 수 있는 전치사 (C)와 (D)가 정답의 후보이다. '정규 근무 시간을 연장하는 것에 더해서 주말 돌봄 서비스를 제공한다'라는 의미가 되어야 하므로 전치사 (D) In addition to(~에 더해서)가 정답이다. (C) Except for는 '~을 제외하고'라는 의미이다. 명사절 접속사 (A) Whether(~인지 아닌지)는 거품구를 이끌 수 없다. 목적을 나타내는 (B) In order to 뒤에는 동사원형이 와서 '~하기 위해서'라는 의미를 나타낸다.

어휘 expand v. 연장하다 childcare center 어린이집
conveniently adv. 편리하게

11 전치사 표현 채우기

해석 복사기에 인접한 사무용품 보관장 안에 여분의 종이와 토너 카트리지가 들어 있다.

해설 빈칸은 명사구(the copy machine)를 목적어로 가지는 전치사 자리이므로 모든 보기가 정답의 후보이다. '복사기에 인접한 사무용품 보관장'이라는 의미가 되어야 하므로 빈칸 앞의 형용사 adjacent와 함께 '~에 인접한'이라는 의미의 어구인 adjacent to를 만드는 전치사 (B) to가 정답이다. (A) as, (C) off, (D) into는 adjacent as/off/into의 형태로 쓰일 수 없다.

어휘 cabinet n. 보관장 extra adj. 여분의

12 전치사 채우기

해석 Techspire Dynamics사는 10년 전 그것의 설립 이후로 50개가 넘는 혁신적인 소프트웨어 프로그램을 개발해 왔다.

해설 이 문장은 주어(Techspire Dynamics), 동사(has developed), 목적어(more than 50 innovative software programs)를 갖춘 완전한 절이므로, ___ ~ ago는 수식어 거품으로 보아야 한다. 이 수식어 거품은 동사가 없는 거품구이므로 거품구를 이끌 수 있는 전치사 (A), (B), (C)가 정답의 후보이다. '설립 이후로 소프트웨어 프로그램을 개발해 왔다'라는 의미가 되어야 하므로 전치사 (A) since(~ 이후로)가 정답이다. (B) throughout(~ 동안, ~ 내내)은 기간을 나타내므로 빈칸 뒤에 특정 시점이 아닌 기간을 나타내는 표현이 와야 한다. (C) except for(~을 제외하고)도 설립 당시에는 소프트웨어 프로그램을 개발하지 않았다는 의미로 해석상 그럴듯해 보이지만, 특정한 하나를 제외하고 나머지는 다 그러하다는 의미를 나타내므로 이 문장의 경우에는 빈칸 뒤에 개발하지 않은 특정 소프트웨어 프로그램을 언급해야 한다. 부사절 접속사 (D) even though(비록 ~이지만)는 거품구가 아닌 거품절을 이끈다.

어휘 promote v. 홍보하다 numerous adj. 수많은 founding n. 설립

13 전치사 채우기

해석 유지보수팀은 내일 아침까지 엘리베이터를 수리할 수 없을 것이다.

해설 빈칸은 명사구(tomorrow morning)를 목적어로 가지는 전치사 자리이므로 전치사 (A)와 (D)가 정답의 후보이다. '내일 아침까지 수리할 수 없을 것이다'라는 의미가 되어야 하므로 시점 표현과 함께 쓰이는 전치사 (A) until(~까지)이 정답이다. (D) without은 '~ 없이'라는 의미이다. 부사절 접속사 (B) while(~하는 동안)과 부사 (C) lately(최근에)는 명사구를 목적어로 가질 수 없다.

어휘 maintenance team 유지보수팀

14 전치사 채우기

해석 웹사이트 또는 모바일 앱 중 하나에서 상호작용이 가능한 안내도를 이용함으로써 당신 근처에 있는 저희의 모든 매장을 찾으세요.

해설 빈칸은 명사(you)를 목적어로 가지는 전치사 자리이므로 전치사 (A), (B), (C)가 정답의 후보이다. '당신 근처에 있는 모든 매장'이라는 의미

가 되어야 하므로 전치사 (C) near(~ 근처에, ~ 가까이)가 정답이다. (A) out of는 '~ 밖으로', (B) along은 '~을 따라서'라는 의미이다. 부사 (D) next(그다음에는)는 명사를 목적어로 가질 수 없고, 전치사로 쓰이기 위해서는 next to(~ 옆에)의 형태로 쓰여야 한다.

어휘 interactive adj. 상호작용이 가능한 location map 안내도

15 전치사 채우기

해석 Mr. Cory는 업무 시간과 관련하여 변경된 정책에 관한 직원들의 우려를 해결하기 위해 회의를 소집했다.

해설 빈칸은 뒤에 명사구(the revised policy on work hours)를 목적어로 가지는 전치사 자리이므로 모든 보기가 정답의 후보이다. '변경된 정책에 관한 직원들의 우려'라는 의미가 되어야 하므로 전치사 (A) regarding(~에 관하여)이 정답이다. (B) around은 '~ 주위에', (C) among은 '~ 사이에', (D) throughout은 '~ 동안, ~ 내내'라는 의미이다.

어휘 call a meeting 회의를 소집하다 address v. 해결하다, 다루다
concern n. 우려, 걱정 revised adj. 변경된, 수정된

16 전치사 채우기

해석 소포들을 발송하기 전에, 위험 물질은 적절히 분류되고 인증되어야 한다.

해설 빈칸은 동명사(sending out)를 목적어로 가지는 전치사 자리이므로 전치사 (B), (C), (D)가 정답의 후보이다. '소포들을 발송하기 전에 위험 물질은 분류되고 인증되어야 한다'라는 의미가 되어야 하므로 전치사 (C) Prior to(~ 전에)가 정답이다. (B) Past는 '~을 지나서', (D) Aside from은 '~ 외에는'이라는 의미이다. 부사절 접속사 (A) By the time(~할 때 쯤이면, ~할 때까지)은 동명사를 목적어로 가질 수 없다.

어휘 hazardous adj. 위험한 material n. 물질 properly adv. 적절히
label v. 분류하다 certify v. 인증하다

17 전치사 채우기

해석 Mirado 제과점은 재료들의 가격 상승 때문에 몇몇 제품들의 가격을 인상해야 했다.

해설 빈칸은 명사구(an increase ~ ingredients)를 목적어로 가지는 전치사 자리이므로 모든 보기가 정답의 후보이다. '재료들의 가격 상승 때문에 제품들의 가격을 인상해야 했다'라는 의미가 되어야 하므로 이유를 나타내는 전치사 (B) due to(~ 때문에)가 정답이다. (A) as of는 '~부터, ~로', (C) such as는 '~와 같은', (D) besides는 '~에 더해서'라는 의미이다.

18 전치사 표현 채우기

해석 Fasheng International사의 직원들은 온라인 중국어 강좌에 대한 할인을 받을 자격이 있다.

해설 빈칸은 명사구(online ~ courses)를 목적어로 가지는 전치사 자리이다. '온라인 강좌에 대한 할인'이라는 의미가 되어야 하므로 빈칸 앞의 명사 discounts(할인)와 함께 '~에 대한 할인'이라는 의미의 어구인 discounts on을 만드는 전치사 (B) on(~에 대한)이 정답이다. (A) of(~의)도 해석상 그럴듯해 보이지만, discount of 다음에는 할인되는 금액이 와야 한다. (C) into와 (D) like는 discounts into/like의 형태로 쓰일 수 없다.

어휘 be entitled to ~을 받을 자격이 있다 discount n. 할인

19 전치사 채우기

해석 홍보 기간 동안 쇼핑객들은 모든 구매 건에 대해 두 배의 보상 포인트를 받을 수 있다.

해설 빈칸은 명사구(the promotional period)를 목적어로 가지는 전치사 자리이므로 모든 보기가 정답의 후보이다. '홍보 기간 동안 쇼핑객들은 모든 구매 건에 대해 보상 포인트를 받을 수 있다'라는 의미가 되어야 하므로 기간을 나타내는 전치사 (B) throughout(~ 동안, ~ 내내)이 정답이다. 전치사 (A) among과 (C) between도 '~ 사이에'라는 의미로 해석상 그럴듯해 보이지만, (A)는 세 개 이상, (C)는 두 개의 대상 사이에 나타내고, 뒤에 복수 명사 또는 between A and B의 형태가 와야 한다. (D) to는 '~로, ~ 쪽으로'라는 의미이다.

어휘 promotional adj. 홍보의, 판촉의

20 전치사 표현 채우기

해석 Ms. Brooks는 까다로운 고객 불만을 다룰 수 있는 것으로 임원에게 인정받았다.

해설 빈칸은 동명사구(being ~ complaints)를 목적어로 가지는 전치사 자리이므로 모든 보기가 정답의 후보이다. '까다로운 고객 불만을 다룰 수 있는 것으로 인정받다'라는 의미가 되어야 하므로 빈칸 앞의 동사 was recognized와 함께 '~으로 인정받다'라는 의미의 어구인 be recognized for를 만드는 전치사 (A) for(~으로)가 정답이다. (B) about(~에 관하여)도 해석상 그럴듯해 보이지만, be recognized about의 형태로 쓰일 수 없다. (C) within은 '~ 내에', (D) outside는 '~ 밖에'라는 의미이다.

어휘 recognize v. 인정하다 handle v. 다루다

21 전치사 채우기

해석 초기 예측에 반해, 그 열대성 폭풍은 방향을 바꾸어 해안 지역 사회를 완전히 피하게 해줬다.

해설 빈칸은 명사구(the initial forecast)를 목적어로 가지는 전치사 자리이므로 (A)와 (C)가 정답의 후보이다. '초기 예측에 반해 그 폭풍은 방향을 바꿨다'라는 의미가 되어야 하므로 전치사 (C) Contrary to(~에 반해)가 정답이다. (A) On behalf of는 '~을 대신하여'라는 의미로 어색한 문맥을 만든다. 부사절 접속사 (B) Provided that(오직 ~하는 경우에만)과 (D) As soon as(~하자마자)는 명사구를 목적어로 가질 수 없다.

어휘 initial adj. 초기의 forecast n. 예측; v. 예측하다 shift v. 바꾸다
spare v. 피하게 해주다 coastal adj. 해안의 entirely adv. 완전히

22 전치사 채우기

해석 그 고대 사원은 건조한 사막 기후와 최소한의 인간 개입 때문에 잘 보존되어 있다.

해설 빈칸은 명사구(the dry ~ interference)를 목적어로 가지는 전치사 자리이므로 (C)와 (D)가 정답의 후보이다. '건조한 사막 기후와 최소한의 인간 개입 때문에 잘 보존되어 있다'라는 의미가 되어야 하므로 전치사 (D) because of(~ 때문에)가 정답이다. (C) out of는 '~ 밖으로'라는 의미이다. 접속부사 (B) for example(예를 들어)과 부사절 접속사 (A) so that(~할 수 있도록)은 명사구를 목적어로 가질 수 없다.

어휘 ancient adj. 고대의 temple n. 사원 well-preserved adj. 잘 보존된
climate n. 기후 minimal adj. 최소한의 interference n. 개입, 간섭

23 전치사 채우기

해석 제작자 Joel Manning이 Harper Studios사에서 사임했다는 소식은 연예계 전역에 걸쳐 퍼졌다.

해설 빈칸은 명사구(the entertainment industry)를 목적어로 가지는 전치사 자리이므로 모든 보기가 정답의 후보이다. '소식은 연예계 전역에 걸쳐 퍼졌다'라는 의미가 되어야 하므로 전치사 (A) across(~ 전역에 걸쳐)가 정답이다. (D) between(~ 사이에)도 해석상 그럴듯해 보이지만, 두 개의 대상 사이의 위치나 관계, 또는 시간을 나타내며, 주로 between A and B의 형태로 쓰이므로 답이 될 수 없다. (B) above는 '~ 위에', (C) onto는 '~ 위에, ~ 위로'라는 의미이다.

어휘 resign v. 사임하다, 퇴직하다 spread v. 퍼지다, 확산되다

24 전치사 채우기

해석 모든 참가자들은 4일간의 무역 박람회의 마지막에 반환될 50달러의 보증금을 지불해야 한다.

해설 빈칸은 명사구(the four-day trade show)를 목적어로 가지는 전치사 자리이므로 모든 보기가 정답의 후보이다. 빈칸 앞의 명사(the end)가 the four-day trade show의 한 부분이므로, 부분을 나타내는 전치사 (D) of(~의)가 정답이다. (A) into는 '~ 안으로', (B) in은 '~에, ~ 안에',

(C) for는 '~을 위해서, ~ 동안'이라는 의미이다.

어휘 deposit n. 보증금   return v. 반환하다, 돌려주다

25 전치사 채우기

해석 몇몇 기술적인 어려움에도 불구하고, 그 우주 임무는 모든 주요 목표를 예정보다 일찍 달성했다.

해설 빈칸은 명사구(some technical difficulties)를 목적어로 가지는 전치사 자리이므로 (A), (B), (C)가 정답의 후보이다. '기술적인 어려움에도 불구하고 모든 주요 목표를 예정보다 일찍 달성했다'라는 의미가 되어야 하므로 전치사 (B) In spite of(~에도 불구하고)가 정답이다. (A) During은 '~ 동안', (C) In favor of는 '~에 찬성하여'라는 의미이다. 접속부사 (D) Nevertheless(그럼에도 불구하고)는 명사구를 목적어로 가질 수 없다.

어휘 technical adj. 기술적인   achieve v. 달성하다   primary adj. 주요의   objective n. 목표   ahead of ~보다 일찍

26 전치사 채우기

해석 인공지능 적용은 지난 몇 년 동안 의료 진단에 혁명을 일으켜 왔다.

해설 빈칸은 명사구(the last few years)를 목적어로 가지는 전치사 자리이므로 (A), (B), (C)가 정답의 후보이다. the last few years는 기간을 나타내는 표현이고 '지난 몇 년 동안 혁명을 일으켜 왔다'라는 의미가 되어야 하므로 전치사 (C) over(~ 동안)가 정답이다. (A) since(~ 이후로)와 (B) until(~까지)은 시점을 나타내므로 빈칸 뒤에 기간이 아닌 특정 시점을 나타내는 표현이 와야 한다. 부사 (D) nearly(거의)는 명사구를 목적어로 가질 수 없다.

어휘 artificial intelligence 인공지능   application n. 적용   revolutionize v. 혁명을 일으키다   diagnosis n. 진단

27 전치사 채우기

해석 지역 물류 센터의 폐쇄를 고려하여, 우리는 새로운 물류 파트너를 찾고 있다.

해설 이 문장은 주어(we), 동사(are looking for), 목적어(a new logistics partner)를 모두 갖춘 완전한 절이므로, ___ ~ center는 수식어 거품으로 보아야 한다. 이 수식어 거품은 동사가 없는 거품구이므로 거품구를 이끌 수 있는 전치사 (A), (C), (D)가 정답의 후보이다. '지역 물류 센터의 폐쇄를 고려하여 새로운 물류 파트너를 찾고 있다'라는 의미가 되어야 하므로 전치사 (C) In light of(~을 고려하여)가 정답이다. (A) According to(~에 따르면)도 해석상 그럴듯해 보이지만, 정보의 출처나 근거를 인용할 때 사용하므로 답이 될 수 없다. (D) In spite of는 '~에도 불구하고'라는 의미이다. 부사절 접속사 (B) In case(~에 대비하여, ~의 경우)는 거품구가 아닌 거품절을 이끈다.

어휘 closure n. 폐쇄   regional adj. 지역의   distribution center 물류 센터   logistics n. 물류

28 전치사 채우기

해석 지역 사회의 항의 때문에 폐기물 처리 시설의 건설이 중단되었다.

해설 빈칸은 명사구(local community protests)를 목적어로 가지는 전치사 자리이므로 (A), (B), (C)가 정답의 후보이다. '항의 때문에 폐기물 처리 시설의 건설이 중단되었다'라는 의미가 되어야 하므로 (B) on account of(~ 때문에)가 정답이다. (A) such as는 '~와 같은', (C) opposite는 '~ 건너편에, ~ 맞은 편에'라는 의미이다. 부사절 접속사 (D) in order that(~할 수 있도록)은 명사구를 목적어로 가질 수 없다.

어휘 construction n. 건설   waste treatment facility 폐기물 처리 시설   pause v. 중단하다   protest n. 항의

DAY 06 접속사

기출 공식 1~3

토익실전문제 p.176

| 01 (C) | 02 (A) | 03 (D) | 04 (A) |

01 등위접속사 채우기

해석 Dr. Sanchez는 6월 30일에 은퇴하지만, 그의 후임자는 8월까지 도착하지 않을 것이다.

해설 절(Dr. Sanchez ~ June 30)과 절(his replacement ~ August)을 대등하게 연결해 주는 등위접속사가 필요하고 'Dr. Sanchez는 6월 30일에 은퇴하지만 그의 후임자는 8월까지 도착하지 않을 것이다'라는 의미가 되어야 하므로 등위접속사 (C) but(하지만)이 정답이다. (A) or는 '또는', (B) nor는 '~도 아니다', (D) for는 '왜냐하면'이라는 의미이다. 참고로, nor는 주로 neither A nor B(A도 B도 아닌) 형태의 상관접속사로 쓰이는 점을 알아 둔다.

어휘 retire v. 은퇴하다   replacement n. 후임자

02 등위접속사 채우기

해석 Sophia Anderson은 유명한 해양 생물학자이고 Ocean Guard Initiative의 설립자이다.

해설 동사(is)의 보어인 명사구(a renowned marine biologist)와 명사구(a founder of Ocean Guard Initiative)를 대등하게 연결해 주는 등위접속사가 필요하고 '유명한 해양 생물학자이고 Ocean Guard Initiative의 설립자이다'라는 의미가 되어야 하므로 등위접속사 (A) and(그리고)가 정답이다. (B) but은 '하지만, 그러나', (D) nor는 '~도 아니다'라는 의미이다. (C) so(그래서)는 절과 절만 연결할 수 있으며, 단어나 구는 연결할 수 없다.

어휘 renowned adj. 유명한   marine biologist 해양 생물학자   founder n. 설립자

03 상관접속사 채우기

해석 편의를 위해, 참가자들은 비즈니스 회의에 온라인 또는 현장 중 하나에서 등록할 수 있다.

해설 등위접속사 or와 맞는 짝인 (D) either(둘 중 하나의)가 정답이다. (A)는 and와 함께 상관접속사 both A and B(A와 B 둘 다)의 형태로 쓰이며, (B)는 nor와 함께 상관접속사 neither A nor B(A도 B도 아닌)의 형태로 쓰인다. (C)는 B as well as A의 형태로 쓰여 'A뿐 아니라 B도'라는 의미를 나타낸다.

어휘 convenience n. 편의   at the venue 현장에서

04 주어와 수일치하는 동사 채우기

해석 감독과 배우는 촬영이 시작되기 전에 대본이 수정이 필요하다는 것에 동의한다.

해설 문장에 주어(The director and the actor)만 있고 동사가 없으므로 동사 (A)와 (B)가 정답의 후보이다. A and B는 항상 복수 동사를 쓰므로 복수 동사 (A) agree(동의하다)가 정답이다. 단수 동사 (B)는 단수 주어와 함께 써야 한다. 동명사 또는 현재분사 (C)와 명사 (D)는 동사 자리에 올 수 없다.

기출 공식 4~5

토익실전문제 p.177

| 01 (B) | 02 (C) | 03 (A) | 04 (C) |

01 명사절 접속사 채우기

해석 Work Flow Hub의 가장 혁신적인 특징은 화상 통화 중 배경 소음을 자동으로 제거한다는 것이다.

해설 빈칸은 동사(is)의 보어 역할을 하는 명사절(___ it ~ calls)을 이끄는 명사절 접속사 자리이므로 명사절 접속사 (B)와 (D)가 정답의 후보이다. '가장 혁신적인 특징은 소음을 자동으로 제거한다는 것이다'라는 의미가 되어야 하므로 (B) that(~라는 것)이 정답이다. (D) whether는 '~인지 아닌지'라는 의미이다. 부사절 접속사 또는 전치사 (A), 접속부사 (C)는 명사절을 이끌 수 없다.

어휘 innovative adj. 혁신적인   feature n. 특징   automatically adv. 자동으로   eliminate v. 제거하다   background noise 배경 소음   thus adv. 따라서

02 명사절 접속사 채우기

해석 작물이 번성하는지 아닌지는 토양 조건, 기상 패턴, 그리고 적절한 관개 방법에 달려있다.

해설 빈칸은 동사(depends on)의 주어 역할을 하는 명사절(___ crops thrive)을 이끄는 명사절 접속사 자리이므로 명사절 접속사 (C) Whether(~인지 아닌지)가 정답이다. (A) If도 명사절 접속사로 쓰일 수 있지만, 주어 자리에는 올 수 없다. 대명사 또는 부사 (B), 빈도 부사 (D)는 명사절을 이끌 수 없다.

어휘 crop n. 작물   thrive v. 번성하다   soil n. 토양   proper adj. 적절한   irrigation n. 관개   often adv. 종종

03 명사절 접속사 채우기

해석 최근 시장 분석은 AI 기술을 도입하는 소기업들이 운영 효율성에서 30퍼센트의 증가를 보였다고 제안했다.

해설 빈칸은 동사(suggested)의 목적어 역할을 하는 명사절(___ small businesses ~ efficiency)을 이끄는 명사절 접속사 자리이므로 명사절 접속사 (A) that(~라고)이 정답이다. 지시대명사 (B), 부사 (C)와 (D)는 명사절을 이끌 수 없다. (B)를 지시형용사로 보고 목적어로 쓰인 명사절 접속사 that이 생략되어 빈칸 뒤의 명사(small businesses)를 꾸미는 것으로 본다 해도, this 뒤에는 단수 명사가 와야 하므로 답이 될 수 없다.

어휘 analysis n. 분석   adopt v. 도입하다   operational adj. 운영의

04 명사절 접속사 채우기

해석 당신의 비행편에서 창가 좌석이나 통로 측 좌석 중 어느 쪽을 선호하는지 여행 코디네이터에게 알려주세요.

해설 빈칸은 원형 부정사(know)의 목적어 역할을 하는 명사절(___ you ~ flight)을 이끄는 명사절 접속사 자리이므로 명사절 접속사 (C) whether(~인지 아닌지)가 정답이다. 부사절 접속사 (A)와 (D)는 명사절을 이끌 수 없다. 의문대명사 또는 의문형용사 (B)는 뒤에 불완전한 절이 와야 하므로 답이 될 수 없다.

어휘 prefer v. 선호하다   aisle n. 통로

기출 공식 6~8

토익실전문제   p.178

| 01 (C) | 02 (C) | 03 (A) | 04 (B) |

01 의문사 채우기

해석 진행자는 후보들이 TV로 방영되는 토론에서 어느 주제에 대해 논의할지 발표했다.

해설 빈칸은 동사(announced)의 목적어 역할을 하는 명사절(___ topics ~ debate)을 이끌면서 뒤에 나온 명사(topics)를 꾸밀 수 있는 의문형용사 자리이므로 의문형용사 (C) which가 정답이다. 부사절 접속사 또는 전치사 (A)는 명사절을 이끌 수 없다. 의문대명사 (B)는 뒤에 명사가 올 수 없으므로 답이 될 수 없다. 명사절 접속사 (D)는 뒤에 완전한 절이 와야 하므로 답이 될 수 없다.

어휘 moderator n. 진행자   candidate n. 후보   televised adj. TV로 방영되는

02 의문사 채우기

해석 그 관리자는 모든 부서장과 상담한 후 언제 예산안 회의가 열릴지 확정했다.

해설 빈칸은 동사(confirmed)의 목적어 역할을 하는 명사절(___ the budget meeting would be held)을 이끄는 명사절 접속사 자리이므로 모든 보기가 정답의 후보이다. 빈칸 뒤에 완전한 절이 왔으므로 의문부사 (C) when이 정답이다. 의문대명사 (A), (B), (D) 뒤에는 불완전한 절이 와야 하므로 답이 될 수 없다.

어휘 confirm v. 확정하다   budget n. 예산안   consult v. 상담하다   department head 부서장

03 의문사 채우기

해석 인증된 산업 안전 강사인 Vince Scott는 새 장비를 어떻게 안전하게 작동할지 설명할 것이다.

해설 빈칸은 동사(will explain)의 목적어 역할을 하는 '의문사 + to 부정사'의 의문사 자리이므로 (A), (C), (D)가 정답의 후보이다. '새 장비를 어떻게 안전하게 작동할지 설명할 것이다'라는 의미가 되어야 하므로 의문부사 (A) how가 정답이다. 의문대명사 (C)와 (D)를 쓸 경우 각각 '새 장비를 무엇을/누구를 안전하게 작동할지 설명할 것이다'라는 어색한 문맥이 된다. 의문부사 (B) why는 '의문사 + to 부정사'의 형태로 쓰일 수 없다.

어휘 certified adj. 인증된   industrial adj. 산업의

04 복합관계대명사 채우기

해석 오리엔테이션을 진행하는 누구든 간에 신입 직원들이 명확하고 실용적인 지침을 필요로 한다는 점을 명심해야 한다.

해설 동사(should keep in mind)의 주어 역할을 하는 절(___ ~ orientation)의 맨 앞에 올 수 있는 것은 명사절 접속사이므로 복합관계대명사 (A)와 (B), 의문형용사 (C)가 정답의 후보이다. '오리엔테이션을 진행하는 누구든 간에'라는 의미가 되어야 하므로 복합관계대명사 (B) Whoever(누구든 간에)가 정답이다. 복합관계대명사 (A) Whatever(무엇이든 간에)는 사물을 지칭할 때 쓰이므로 답이 될 수 없다. 의문형용사 (C) Whose는 '누구의'라는 의미로 뒤에 명사가 와야 한다. 대명사 (D)는 절을 이끌 수 없다.

어휘 conduct v. 진행하다   keep in mind ~을 명심하다   practical adj. 실용적인   guidance n. 지침

기출 공식 9~11

토익실전문제   p.179

| 01 (B) | 02 (D) | 03 (A) | 04 (B) |

01 부사절 접속사 채우기

해석 Pure Origins사는 겨울이 오기 전에 보온성이 좋은 새로운 프리미엄 터틀넥을 출시할 계획이다.

해설 빈칸은 동사(arrives)가 있는 거품절(___ winter arrives)을 이끄는 부사절 접속사 자리이고, '겨울이 오기 전에 새로운 터틀넥을 출시할 계획이다'라는 의미가 되어야 하므로 시간을 나타내는 부사절 접속사 (B) before(~하기 전에)가 정답이다. (C) whereas는 '~한 반면에', (D) even though는 '비록 ~이지만'이라는 의미이다. 전치사 (A)는 거품절을 이끌 수 없다.

어휘 release v. 출시하다   thermal adj. 보온성이 좋은

02 부사절 접속사 채우기

해석 구독은 활성화된 후에 초기 24시간 체험 기간이 지나면 더 이상 환불될 수 없다.

해설 빈칸은 동사(is activated, has elapsed)가 있는 거품절(____ it ~ elapsed)을 이끄는 부사절 접속사 자리이므로 부사절 접속사 (B)와 (D)가 정답의 후보이다. '구독은 활성화된 후에 초기 24시간 체험 기간이 지나면 더 이상 환불될 수 없다'라는 의미가 되어야 하므로 시간을 나타내는 부사절 접속사 (D) once(~한 후에, ~하자마자)가 정답이다. (B) unless는 '만약 ~이 아니라면'이라는 의미이다. 등위접속사 (A)와 의문사 (C)는 거품절을 이끌 수 없다.

어휘 subscription n. 구독   refund v. 환불하다; n. 환불   activate v. 활성화하다
trial adj. 체험의   elapse v. (시간이) 지나다

03 부사절 접속사 채우기

해석 만약 정오 이전에 청소용품을 주문하시면, 그것들은 다음 영업일에 배송될 것입니다.

해설 빈칸은 동사(order)가 있는 거품절(____ you ~ noon)을 이끄는 부사절 접속사 자리이고, '만약 정오 이전에 주문하면 다음 영업일에 배송될 것이다'라는 의미가 되어야 하므로 조건을 나타내는 부사절 접속사 (A) If(만약 ~라면)가 정답이다. 참고로, 조건을 나타내는 부사절에서 미래를 나타내기 위해 미래 시제 대신 현재 시제(order)가 쓰였음을 알아 둔다. 목적을 나타내는 to 부정사 대신 쓰일 수 있는 (B) In order to(~하기 위해)는 뒤에 동사원형이 와야 하므로 답이 될 수 없다. 부사 (C)와 상관접속사 (D)는 거품절을 이끌 수 없다.

04 부사절 접속사 채우기

해석 비록 개발자들이 새로운 방법을 시도하고 광범위한 테스트 절차를 수행했지만, 결과는 미미한 개선을 보여줬다.

해설 빈칸은 동사(tried, conducted)가 있는 거품절(____ the developers ~ procedures)을 이끄는 부사절 접속사 자리이고, '비록 새로운 방법을 시도하고 광범위한 테스트 절차를 수행했지만, 결과는 미미한 개선을 보여줬다'라는 의미가 되어야 하므로 양보를 나타내는 부사절 접속사 (B) Although(비록 ~이지만)가 정답이다. (A) Unless는 '만약 ~이 아니라면', (C) So that은 '~할 수 있도록', (D) Since는 '~이기 때문에'라는 의미이다.

어휘 method n. 방법   extensive adj. 광범위한   procedure n. 절차
minimal adj. 미미한, 최소의

기출 공식 12~13

토익실전문제
p.180

| 01 (C) | 02 (D) | 03 (D) | 04 (B) |

01 부사절 접속사 채우기

해석 Main가의 주차가 제한될 것이기 때문에 새로운 고속도로 프로젝트는 도심 사업체들에 영향을 미칠 것으로 예상된다.

해설 빈칸은 동사(will be limited)가 있는 거품절(____ parking ~ limited)을 이끄는 부사절 접속사 자리이고, '주차가 제한될 것이기 때문에 새로운 고속도로 프로젝트는 도심 사업체들에 영향을 미칠 것으로 예상된다'라는 의미가 되어야 하므로 이유를 나타내는 부사절 접속사 (C) because(~이기 때문에)가 정답이다. (B) though는 '비록 ~이지만', (D) in order that은 '~할 수 있도록'이라는 의미이다. 전치사 또는 접속부사 (A)는 거품절을 이끌 수 없다.

어휘 highway n. 고속도로   impact v. 영향을 미치다
downtown adj. 도심의, 시내의   parking n. 주차 (공간)

02 부사절 접속사 채우기

해석 저희의 IT팀이 문제를 진단할 수 있도록 시스템 오류 문제를 상세히 설명해 주세요.

해설 빈칸은 동사(can diagnose)가 있는 거품절(____ our ~ problem)을 이끄는 부사절 접속사 자리이고, '문제를 진단할 수 있도록 시스템 오류 문제를 상세히 설명해 주세요'라는 의미가 되어야 하므로 목적을 나타내는 부사절 접속사 (D) so that(~할 수 있도록)이 정답이다. (B) whatever는 '무엇을 ~하더라도', (C) given that은 '~을 고려했을 때'라는 의미이다. 접속부사 (A)는 거품절을 이끌 수 없다.

어휘 describe v. 설명하다   in detail 상세히   diagnose v. 진단하다
instead adv. 대신에

03 부사절 접속사 채우기

해석 모든 지역 사무실에 걸쳐 네트워크 개선이 완료되었으므로, 팀들은 원격으로 일할 수 있게 될 것이다.

해설 빈칸은 동사(have been done)가 있는 거품절(____ the network ~ done)을 이끄는 부사절 접속사 자리이므로 부사절 접속사 (A)와 (D)가 정답의 후보이다. '네트워크 개선이 완료되었으므로 원격으로 일할 수 있게 될 것이다'라는 의미가 되어야 하므로 이유를 나타내는 부사절 접속사 (D) Now that(~이므로)이 정답이다. (A) As if는 '마치 ~처럼'이라는 의미이다. 접속부사 (B)와 전치사 (C)는 거품절을 이끌 수 없다.

어휘 enhancement n. 개선   remotely adv. 원격으로   in fact 사실
in case of ~의 경우에

04 복합관계부사 채우기

해석 학생들이 언제 강좌에 참여하더라도, 모든 이전 콘텐츠에 접근할 수 있어서, 늦은 등록자들도 과거 자료를 검토할 수 있게 한다.

해설 빈칸은 동사(join)가 있는 거품절(____ students join the course)을 이끄는 부사절 접속사 자리이므로 복합관계대명사 (A)와 복합관계부사 (B)가 정답의 후보이다. '학생들이 언제 강좌에 참여하더라도'라는 의미가 되어야 하므로 복합관계부사 (B) Whenever(언제 ~하더라도)가 정답이다. 복합관계대명사 (A) Whoever는 뒤에 불완전한 절이 와야 하므로 답이 될 수 없다. 전치사 (C)와 접속부사 (D)는 거품절을 이끌 수 없다.

어휘 course n. 강좌   previous adj. 이전의   enrollee n. 등록자
material n. 자료   regarding prep. ~에 관하여   moreover adv. 더욱이

기출 공식 14

토익실전문제
p.181

| 01 (A) | 02 (C) | 03 (D) | 04 (C) |

01 부사절 접속사 채우기

해석 12월 내내 폭설이 예상되기 때문에 그 도시는 추가 제설 장비를 준비했다.

해설 빈칸은 동사(is expected)가 있는 거품절(____ heavy ~ December)을 이끄는 부사절 접속사 자리이므로 부사절 접속사 (A)와 (D)가 정답의 후보이다. '폭설이 예상되기 때문에 추가 제설 장비를 준비했다'라는 의미가 되어야 하므로 이유를 나타내는 부사절 접속사 (A) because(~이기 때문에)가 정답이다. (D) except that은 '~을 제외하고는'이라는 의미이다. 전치사 (B)와 (C)는 거품절을 이끌 수 없다.

어휘 additional adj. 추가의   snow removal equipment 제설 장비
because of ~ 때문에   instead of ~ 대신에

02 전치사 채우기

해석 그 패밀리 레스토랑은 현대 식사 트렌드의 몇몇 변화에도 불구하고 전통 레시피를 계속 제공한다.

해설 빈칸은 명사구(some changes ~ trends)를 목적어로 가지는 전치사 자리이므로 전치사 (C) in spite of(~에도 불구하고)가 정답이다. 부사절 접속사 (A)와 (D), 접속부사 (B)는 명사구를 목적어로 가질 수 없다. (A) since를 '~ 이후로'라는 의미의 전치사로 본다 해도, 뒤에 특정 과거 시점이 와야 하므로 답이 될 수 없다.

어휘 traditional adj. 전통의   modern adj. 현대의, 현대적인   dietary adj. 식사의

03 부사절 접속사 채우기

해석 Mr. Matthews는 이사회 회의를 준비할 수 있도록 1시간 일찍 사무실에 도착했다.

해설 빈칸은 동사(could prepare)가 있는 거품절(___ he ~ meeting)을 이끄는 부사절 접속사 자리이므로 부사절 접속사 (A)와 (D)가 정답의 후보이다. '회의를 준비할 수 있도록 일찍 사무실에 도착했다'라는 의미가 되어야 하므로 부사절 접속사 (D) in order that(~할 수 있도록)이 정답이다. (A) unless는 '만약 ~이 아니라면'이라는 의미이다. 전치사 (B)는 거품절을 이끌 수 없고, (C)는 뒤에 동사원형이 와야 한다.

04 전치사 채우기

해석 Nexusphere사의 클라우드 서비스는 사용자의 지리적 위치에 상관없이 일관된 성능을 제공해서, 세계적인 기업 운영을 지원한다.

해설 빈칸은 명사구(users' geographic location)를 목적어로 가지는 전치사 자리이므로 전치사 (B)와 (C)가 정답의 후보이다. '지리적 위치에 상관없이 일관된 성능을 제공한다'라는 의미가 되어야 하므로 전치사 (C) regardless of(~에 상관없이)가 정답이다. (B) due to는 '~ 때문에'라는 의미이다. 부사절 접속사 또는 명사절 접속사 (A), 부사절 접속사 (D)는 명사구를 목적어로 가질 수 없다.

어휘 consistent adj. 일관된 performance n. 성능 geographic adj. 지리적인 location n. 위치 support v. 지원하다 except that ~을 제외하고는

HACKERS TEST p.182

01 (A)	02 (D)	03 (A)	04 (C)	05 (C)
06 (D)	07 (C)	08 (B)	09 (B)	10 (D)
11 (A)	12 (B)	13 (C)	14 (C)	15 (D)
16 (A)	17 (B)	18 (C)	19 (D)	20 (D)
21 (C)	22 (B)	23 (D)	24 (A)	25 (C)
26 (C)	27 (B)	28 (D)		

01 부사절 접속사 채우기

해석 쇼가 시작될 때 모든 전자기기를 끄고 대화하는 것을 삼가세요.

해설 빈칸은 동사(begins)가 있는 거품절(___ the show begins)을 이끄는 부사절 접속사 자리이고, '쇼가 시작될 때'라는 의미가 되어야 하므로 시간을 나타내는 부사절 접속사 (A) when(~할 때)이 정답이다. 부사 (B), 의문사 (C)와 (D)는 거품절을 이끌 수 없다.

어휘 electronic device 전자기기 refrain from ~하는 것을 삼가다

02 부사절 접속사 채우기

해석 새로운 가방에 대한 수요가 높았기 때문에, 대부분의 소매상들은 곧 재고가 없을 수도 있다.

해설 빈칸은 동사(has been)가 있는 거품절(___ demand ~ high)을 이끄는 부사절 접속사 자리이고, '수요가 높았기 때문에, 대부분의 소매상들은 곧 재고가 없을 수도 있다'라는 의미가 되어야 하므로 이유를 나타내는 부사절 접속사 (D) Because(~이기 때문에)가 정답이다. (A) Even if는 '비록 ~일지라도', (B) Unless는 '만약 ~이 아니라면', (C) Although는 '비록 ~이지만'이라는 의미이다.

어휘 demand n. 수요, 요구; v. 요구하다 retailer n. 소매상, 소매업자 run out of 재고가 없다, (~이) 없어지다

03 상관접속사 채우기

해석 설문조사 응답자들은 출근길에 오디오북 또는 팟캐스트들 중 하나를 듣는 것을 선호한다고 말했다.

해설 등위접속사 or과 맞는 짝인 (A) either(둘 중 하나의)가 정답이다. 참고로, either A or B가 명사(audiobooks)와 명사(podcasts)를 연결하고 있음을 알아 둔다. (B)는 and와 함께 상관접속사 both A and B(A와 B 둘 다)의 형태로 쓰이며, (D)는 nor과 함께 상관접속사 neither A nor B(A도 B도 아닌)의 형태로 쓰인다. 수량 형용사 (C)는 두 단어를 연결할 수 없고, 복수 명사가 아닌 단수 명사 앞에 와야 한다.

어휘 respondent n. 응답자 prefer v. 선호하다 way to work 출근길

04 명사절 접속사 채우기

해석 뉴스는 시의회가 새로운 공원을 위한 계획을 마침내 승인했다고 보도했다.

해설 빈칸은 동사(reported)의 목적어 역할을 하는 명사절(___ the city ~ park)을 이끄는 명사절 접속사 자리이므로 의문사 (B)와 명사절 접속사 (C)가 정답의 후보이다. '계획을 마침내 승인했다고 보도했다'라는 의미가 되어야 하고, 빈칸 뒤에 완전한 절이 왔으므로 명사절 접속사 (C) that(~라고)이 정답이다. 의문사 (B) what 뒤에는 불완전한 절이 와야 하므로 답이 될 수 없다. 지시대명사 (A)와 부사 (D)는 명사절을 이끌 수 없다.

어휘 report v. 보도하다 city council 시의회 finally adv. 마침내 approve v. 승인하다

05 부사절 접속사 채우기

해석 만약 제품이 원래 포장 상태로 반환되지 않는다면 환불이 되지 않을 것이다.

해설 빈칸은 동사(is returned)가 있는 거품절(___ the product ~ packaging)을 이끄는 부사절 접속사 자리이고, '만약 제품이 원래 포장 상태로 반환되지 않는다면 환불이 되지 않을 것이다'라는 의미가 되어야 하므로 조건을 나타내는 부사절 접속사 (C) unless(만약 ~이 아니라면)가 정답이다. (D) since는 '~한 이후로, ~이기 때문에'라는 의미이다. 부사 (A)와 접속부사 (B)는 거품절을 이끌 수 없다.

어휘 original adj. 원래의 even adv. ~ 조차도 therefore adv. 그러므로

06 부사절 접속사 채우기

해석 비록 건설 비용이 치솟고 있었지만 Eterna Motors사는 새 공장을 건설하기로 결정했다.

해설 빈칸은 동사(were soaring)가 있는 거품절(___ construction costs were soaring)을 이끄는 부사절 접속사 자리이고, '비록 건설 비용이 치솟고 있었지만 새 공장을 건설하기로 결정했다'라는 의미가 되어야 하므로 양보를 나타내는 부사절 접속사 (D) even though(비록 ~이지만)가 정답이다. (C) as though는 '마치 ~처럼'이라는 의미이다. 전치사 (A)와 (B)는 거품절을 이끌 수 없다.

어휘 construction n. 건설 soar v. 치솟다 such as ~와 같은 notwithstanding prep. ~에도 불구하고

07 등위접속사 채우기

해석 Branson 영화사는 몇몇 저예산이지만 성공적인 영화들을 제작하는 것으로 유명하다.

해설 명사(films)를 꾸미는 형용사(low-budget)와 형용사(successful)를 대등하게 연결해 주는 등위접속사가 필요하고 '저예산이지만 성공적인 영화들'이라는 의미가 되어야 하므로 등위접속사 (C) but(하지만)이 정답이다. (A)는 neither와 함께 neither A nor B(A도 B도 아닌)의 상관접속사 형태로 쓰인다. 부사절 접속사 또는 전치사 (B) as는 단어와 단어를 대등하게 연결할 수 없다. (D) for는 '왜냐하면'이라는 의미의 등위접속사로 쓰일 수 있지만 오직 절과 절을 연결할 수 있으며, 단어나 구는 연결할 수 없다.

어휘 produce v. 제작하다 low-budget adj. 저예산의

08 부사절 접속사 채우기

해석 Greg Larson이 그의 미지불된 요금을 지불할 때까지, 그의 전화 서비스는 다시 연결될 수 없다.

해설 빈칸은 동사(pays)가 있는 거품절(___ Greg ~ charges)을 이끄는 부사절 접속사 자리이고, 'Greg Larson이 그의 미지불된 요금을 지불할 때까지, 그의 전화 서비스는 다시 연결될 수 없다'라는 의미가 되어야 하므로 시간을 나타내는 부사절 접속사 (B) Until(~할 때까지)이 정답이다. (D) Because(~이기 때문에)를 쓸 경우 'Greg Larson이 그의 미지불된 요금을 지불하기 때문에, 그의 전화 서비스는 다시 연결될 수 없다'라는 어색한 문맥이 된다. 전치사 (A)와 (C)는 거품절을 이끌 수 없다.

어휘 unpaid adj. 미지불된 charge n. 요금; v. 청구하다, 부과하다

despite prep. ~에도 불구하고 from prep. ~에서부터

09 명사절 접속사 채우기
해석 감사는 그 회사가 지난 회계 연도에 재무 규정을 준수했는지 아닌지를 판단할 것이다.

해설 빈칸은 동사(will determine)의 목적어 역할을 하는 명사절(___ the company ~ year)을 이끄는 명사절 접속사 자리이므로 명사절 접속사 (B) whether(~인지 아닌지)가 정답이다. 부사절 접속사 (A)와 (D), 부사 (C)는 명사절을 이끌 수 없다.

어휘 audit n. 감사 comply with ~을 준수하다 regulation n. 규정 fiscal year 회계 연도 until conj. ~할 때까지 even adv. ~조차도 though conj. 비록 ~이지만

10 부사절 접속사 채우기
해석 Saffron Ember가 확장된 주방이 있는 더 큰 장소로 옮겼으므로, 그곳은 두 배 더 많은 고객들에게 식사를 제공할 수 있다.

해설 빈칸은 동사(has moved)가 있는 거품절(___ Saffron Ember ~ kitchen)을 이끄는 부사절 접속사 자리이고, '더 큰 장소로 옮겼으므로 더 많은 고객들에게 식사를 제공할 수 있다'라는 의미가 되어야 하므로 이유를 나타내는 부사절 접속사 (D) Now that(~이므로)이 정답이다. 접속부사 (A), 전치사 (B)와 (D)는 거품절을 이끌 수 없다.

어휘 expanded adj. 확장된 in fact 사실 in case of ~의 경우에 despite prep. ~에도 불구하고

11 부사절 접속사 채우기
해석 Ms. Piquet는 복잡한 데이터가 더 명확하게 시각화될 수 있도록 프레젠테이션 형식을 수정했다.

해설 빈칸은 동사(could be visualized)가 있는 거품절(___ the complex ~ clearly)을 이끄는 부사절 접속사 자리이고, '복잡한 데이터가 더 명확하게 시각화될 수 있도록 프레젠테이션 형식을 수정했다'라는 의미가 되어야 하므로 목적을 나타내는 부사절 접속사 (A) so that(~할 수 있도록)이 정답이다. (C) as if는 '마치 ~처럼'이라는 의미이다. 전치사 (B)와 접속부사 (D)는 거품절을 이끌 수 없다.

어휘 revise v. 수정하다 format n. 형식 complex adj. 복잡한 visualize v. 시각화하다 instead of ~ 대신에 in contrast 그에 반해서

12 등위접속사 채우기
해석 시스템 업그레이드로 인해, 고객들은 그들의 온라인 계정 또는 거래 내역에 접근할 수 없다.

해설 동사(access)의 목적어인 명사(their online accounts)와 명사(transaction histories)를 대등하게 연결해 주는 등위접속사가 필요하고 '온라인 계정 또는 거래 내역에 접근할 수 없다'라는 의미가 되어야 하므로 등위접속사 (B) or(또는)가 정답이다. 등위접속사 (A)는 '하지만'이라는 의미이고, (C)는 오직 절과 절을 연결할 수 있으며, 단어나 구는 연결할 수 없다. (D)는 and와 함께 both A and B(A와 B 모두)의 상관접속사 형태로 쓰인다.

어휘 account n. 계정 transaction history 거래 내역

13 전치사 채우기
해석 부동산 관리인은 세입자의 서면 동의 없이 주거 공간에 들어가면 안 된다.

해설 빈칸은 명사구(written consent from tenants)를 목적어로 가지는 전치사 자리이므로 전치사 (A), (C), (D)가 정답의 후보이다. '세입자의 서면 동의 없이 주거 공간에 들어가면 안 된다'라는 의미가 되어야 하므로 전치사 (C) without(~ 없이)이 정답이다. (A) about은 '~에 관하여', (D) against는 '~에 반대하여'라는 의미이다. 부사절 접속사 (B)는 명사구를 목적어로 가질 수 없다.

어휘 residential unit 주거 공간 written consent 서면 동의 tenant n. 세입자 unless conj. 만약 ~아니라면

14 부사절 접속사 채우기
해석 당신의 결제가 처리되는 동안, 이 브라우저 창을 새로고침하거나 닫지 마세요.

해설 빈칸은 동사(is being processed)가 있는 거품절(___ your ~ processed)을 이끄는 부사절 접속사 자리이고, '결제가 처리되는 동안'이라는 의미가 되어야 하므로 시간을 나타내는 부사절 접속사 (C) While(~하는 동안)이 정답이다. 부사 (A), 전치사 (B)와 (D)는 거품절을 이끌 수 없다.

어휘 payment n. 결제 process v. 처리하다; n. 과정, 절차 refresh v. 새로고침하다 still adv. 여전히 during prep. ~ 동안 regarding prep. ~에 관하여

15 부사절 접속사 채우기
해석 비록 일부 사람들은 보안 조치가 불필요하다고 여기지만, 그것들은 직원과 회사 자산을 보호한다.

해설 빈칸은 동사(might regard)가 있는 거품절(___ some ~ unnecessary)을 이끄는 부사절 접속사 자리이고, '비록 일부 사람들은 보안 조치가 불필요하다고 여기지만, 그것들은 직원과 회사 자산을 보호한다'라는 의미가 되어야 하므로 양보를 나타내는 부사절 접속사 (D) Though(비록 ~이지만)가 정답이다. (A) After는 '~한 이후에', (B) Because는 '~이기 때문에'라는 의미이다. 전치사 (C)는 거품절을 이끌 수 없다.

어휘 regard v. 여기다 security measure 보안 조치 unnecessary adj. 불필요한 asset n. 자산 except for ~을 제외하고

16 주어와 수일치하는 동사 채우기
해석 최고경영자뿐만 아니라 이사회 멤버들도 연례 주주 총회에 참석한다.

해설 문장에 주어(Not only the CEO but also board members)만 있고 동사가 없으므로 동사 (A)와 (B)가 정답의 후보이다. not only A but also B는 B(board members)에 동사의 수를 일치시키므로 복수 동사 (A) participate(참석하다)가 정답이다. 단수 동사 (B)는 단수 주어와 함께 써야 한다. 명사 (C)와 (D)는 동사 자리에 올 수 없다.

어휘 annual adj. 연례의 participant n. 참가자 participation n. 참가, 참여

17 부사절 접속사 채우기
해석 런던과 맨체스터 사이의 기차 서비스는 손상된 철로가 교체되자마자 재개될 것이다.

해설 빈칸은 동사(are replaced)가 있는 거품절(___ the damaged ~ replaced)을 이끄는 부사절 접속사 자리이고, '기차 서비스는 손상된 철로가 교체되자마자 재개될 것이다'라는 의미가 되어야 하므로 시간을 나타내는 부사절 접속사 (B) as soon as(~하자마자)가 정답이다. (C) unless는 '만약 ~이 아니라면'이라는 의미이다. 전치사 (A)는 거품절을 이끌 수 없고, (D)는 뒤에 동사원형이 와야 한다.

어휘 resume v. 재개하다 damaged adj. 손상된 replace v. 교체하다 due to ~ 때문에

18 의문사 채우기
해석 소방관들은 무엇이 지난밤 대규모 창고 폭발을 야기했는지 파악하려고 노력하고 있다.

해설 빈칸은 to 부정사(to figure out)의 목적어 역할을 하는 명사절(___ caused ~ last night)을 이끄는 명사절 접속사 자리이므로 명사절 접속사 (B), 의문사 (C)와 (D)가 정답의 후보이다. '무엇이 폭발을 야기했는지 파악하려고 노력하다'라는 의미가 되어야 하고 빈칸 뒤에 불완전한 절이 왔으므로 의문대명사 (C) what이 정답이다. 명사절 접속사 (B)와 의문부사 (D)는 뒤에 완전한 절이 와야 하므로 답이 될 수 없다. 인칭대명사 (A)는 명사절을 이끌 수 없다.

어휘 figure out ~을 파악하다 cause v. 야기하다 massive adj. 대규모의 warehouse n. 창고 explosion n. 폭발

19 부사절 접속사 채우기

해석 Mr. Davis는 오직 예산이 허락하는 경우에만 화장실과 발코니 리모델링 모두를 고려할 것이다.

해설 빈칸은 동사(allows)가 있는 거품절(___ the budget allows it)을 이끄는 부사절 접속사 자리이고, '오직 예산이 허락하는 경우에만 화장실과 발코니 리모델링 모두를 고려할 것이다'라는 의미가 되어야 하므로 조건을 나타내는 부사절 접속사 (D) only if(오직 ~하는 경우에만)가 정답이다. 전치사 (A)와 (C)는 거품절을 이끌 수 없다. 목적을 나타내는 (B)는 뒤에 동사원형이 와야 하므로 답이 될 수 없다.

어휘 budget n. 예산   allow v. 허락하다   in case of ~의 경우에
so as to ~하기 위해   up to ~까지

20 전치사 채우기

해석 그 시내 아파트는 대중교통 근처의 좋은 위치를 고려하면 놀랍도록 비싸지 않았다.

해설 빈칸은 명사구(its prime location)를 목적어로 가지는 전치사 자리이므로 전치사 (D) considering(~을 고려하면)이 정답이다. 부사절 접속사 (A), (B), (C)는 명사구를 목적어로 가질 수 없다. (C) since를 '~ 이후로'라는 의미의 전치사로 본다 해도, 뒤에 특정 과거 시점이 와야 하므로 답이 될 수 없다.

어휘 surprisingly adv. 놀랍도록   inexpensive adj. 비싸지 않은
prime adj. 좋은, 주요한   public transportation 대중교통
while conj. ~하는 동안   given that ~을 고려했을 때
since conj. ~이기 때문에

21 등위접속사 채우기

해석 상점이 20퍼센트 가격 인하를 시행해서, 더 많은 고객들이 그곳에서 쇼핑하기 시작했다.

해설 절(The store ~ reduction)과 절(more customers ~ there)을 연결하면서 콤마 바로 뒤에 올 수 있는 접속사가 필요하므로 등위접속사 (C) so(그래서)가 정답이다. 전치사 (A)와 (B)는 절과 절을 연결할 수 없다. 관계대명사 또는 명사절 접속사 (D)는 콤마 바로 뒤에 올 수 없다.

어휘 implement v. 시행하다   reduction n. 인하, 감소

22 부사절 접속사 채우기

해석 Union Apex 은행은 디지털 뱅킹 서비스가 더 안전하게 접근될 수 있도록 인증 절차를 강화했다.

해설 빈칸은 동사(could be accessed)가 있는 거품절(___ its ~ securely)을 이끄는 부사절 접속사 자리이고, '디지털 뱅킹 서비스가 더 안전하게 접근될 수 있도록 인증 절차를 강화했다'라는 의미가 되어야 하므로 목적을 나타내는 부사절 접속사 (B) in order that(~할 수 있도록)이 정답이다. (C) as though는 '마치 ~처럼'이라는 의미이다. 전치사 (A)와 (D)는 거품절을 이끌 수 없다.

어휘 enhance v. 강화하다   verification n. 인증   securely adv. 안전하게
based on ~에 기반하여   according to ~에 따르면

23 복합관계부사 채우기

해석 그 전기 회사는 중대한 문제가 보고될 때마다 즉시 수리 직원을 보낸다.

해설 빈칸은 동사(is reported)가 있는 거품절(___ ~ reported)을 이끄는 부사절 접속사 자리이므로 부사절 접속사 (A)와 (B), 복합관계부사 (D)가 정답의 후보이다. '그 회사는 중대한 문제가 보고될 때마다 즉시 수리 직원을 보낸다'라는 의미가 되어야 하므로 복합관계부사 (D) whenever(~할 때마다)가 정답이다. 부사절 접속사 (A)와 (B)를 쓸 경우 각각 '그 회사는 마치 중대한 문제가 보고된 것처럼/보고되는 반면에 즉시 수리 직원을 보낸다'라는 어색한 문맥이 된다. 전치사 (C)는 거품절을 이끌 수 없다.

어휘 send out ~를 보내다   repair n. 수리; v. 수리하다   crew n. 직원, 팀

24 부사절 접속사 채우기

해석 제품 품질에 대한 고객 피드백은 긍정적이었던 반면에 가격에 대한 후기는 부정적이었다.

해설 빈칸은 동사(were)가 있는 거품절(___ reviews ~ pricing)을 이끄는 부사절 접속사 자리이고, '제품 품질에 대한 고객 피드백은 긍정적이었던 반면에 가격에 대한 후기는 부정적이었다'라는 의미가 되어야 하므로 양보를 나타내는 부사절 접속사 (A) whereas(~한 반면에)가 정답이다. (B) unless는 '만약 ~이 아니라면'이라는 의미이다. 접속부사 (C)와 복합관계대명사 (D)는 거품절을 이끌 수 없다.

어휘 positive adj. 긍정적인   quality n. 품질   negative adj. 부정적인
pricing n. 가격   likewise adv. 마찬가지로

25 상관접속사 채우기

해석 방콕의 요리 투어는 길거리 음식 모험뿐 아니라 현지 시장 방문으로도 구성되어 있다.

해설 동사(consists of)의 목적어인 명사구(local market visits)와 명사구(street food adventures)를 대등하게 연결해 주는 등위접속사 또는 상관접속사가 필요하고 '길거리 음식 모험뿐 아니라 현지 시장 방문으로도 구성되어 있다'라는 의미가 되어야 하므로 상관접속사 (C) as well as(~뿐 아니라 –도)가 정답이다. 접속부사 (A)와 (D), 부사절 접속사 (B)는 명사구와 명사구를 대등하게 연결할 수 없다.

어휘 culinary adj. 요리의   adventure n. 모험   for example 예를 들어
in case ~에 대비하여   thus adv. 그러므로

26 전치사 채우기

해석 Lumeo Enterprises사는 시장 상황이 어려웠다는 사실에도 불구하고 수익성을 유지했다.

해설 빈칸은 명사(the fact)를 목적어로 가지는 전치사 자리이고, '시장 상황이 어려웠다는 사실에도 불구하고 수익성을 유지했다'라는 의미가 되어야 하므로 전치사 (C) in spite of(~에도 불구하고)가 정답이다. (D) as a result of는 '~의 결과로'라는 의미이므로, '시장 상황이 어려웠다는 사실의 결과로 수익성을 유지했다'라는 어색한 문맥을 만든다. 부사절 접속사 (A)와 접속부사 (B)는 명사를 목적어로 가질 수 없다.

어휘 profitable adj. 수익성이 있는   fact n. 사실   challenging adj. 어려운
although conj. 비록 ~이지만   nevertheless adv. 그럼에도 불구하고

27 부사절 접속사 채우기

해석 메인 서버가 고장 나는 경우에 대비하여 회사는 기록의 사본을 포함하는 예비 서버를 가지고 있다.

해설 빈칸은 동사(should ~ fail)가 있는 거품절(___ the main ~ fail)을 이끄는 부사절 접속사 자리이므로 부사절 접속사 (B), (C), (D)가 정답의 후보이다. '메인 서버가 고장 나는 경우에 대비하여 예비 서버를 가지고 있다'라는 문맥이므로 부사절 접속사 (B) in the event that(~에 대비하여)이 정답이다. (C) as long as는 '오직 ~하는 경우에만', (D) now that은 '~이므로'라는 의미이다. 전치사구 (A)는 거품절을 이끌 수 없다.

어휘 backup adj. 예비의   contain v. 포함하다   duplicate adj. 사본의
records n. 기록   fail v. 고장 나다   because of ~ 때문에

28 복합관계대명사 채우기

해석 교과서는 디지털 또는 인쇄 버전으로 제공되어서, 학습자들은 자신이 원하는 어느 형식이든 간에 선택할 수 있다.

해설 동사(can choose)의 목적어 자리에 온 명사절(___ format they like)의 명사(format)를 꾸미면서, '학습자들은 자신이 원하는 어느 형식이든 간에 선택할 수 있다'라는 의미를 만드는 복합관계형용사 (D) whichever(어느 것이든 간에)가 정답이다. 상관접속사를 만드는 (A), 의문대명사 (B), 접속부사 (C)는 명사절을 이끌면서 뒤에 나온 명사를 꾸밀 수 없다. (A)를 '둘 다'라는 의미의 수량 형용사로 본다 해도, 뒤에 복수 명사가 와야 하므로 답이 될 수 없다.

어휘 textbook n. 교과서   format n. 형식   however adv. 그러나

DAY 07 관계사

기출 공식 1~2

토익실전문제   p.184

| 01 (A) | 02 (B) | 03 (C) | 04 (B) |

01 관계대명사 채우기
해석 Ms. Sharma는 회사의 전 세계적 확장 프로젝트를 이끄는 데 가장 적합한 후보이다.
해설 이 문장은 주어(Ms. Sharma), 동사(is), 보어(the candidate)를 갖춘 완전한 절이므로, ___ ~ project는 수식어 거품으로 보아야 한다. 이 수식어 거품은 빈칸 앞의 명사(candidate)를 선행사로 갖는 관계절이므로 관계대명사 (A), (B), (D)가 정답의 후보이다. 선행사가 사람이고 빈칸 뒤에 주어가 없는 불완전한 절이 왔으므로 주격 관계대명사 (A) who가 정답이다. (B) which는 사람을 선행사로 가질 수 없고, (D) whose는 뒤에 선행사가 소유하는 명사가 와야 한다. 관계부사 (C) 뒤에는 완전한 절이 와야 한다.
어휘 candidate n. 후보자 suited adj. 적합한 expansion n. 확장

02 관계대명사 채우기
해석 작년에 폭풍에 의해 손상된 100년 된 벽돌 건물은 완전히 복구되었다.
해설 이 문장은 주어(The century-old brick building)와 동사(has been ~ restored)를 갖춘 완전한 절이므로, ___ ~ last year는 수식어 거품으로 보아야 한다. 이 수식어 거품은 빈칸 앞의 명사(building)를 선행사로 갖는 관계절이므로 관계대명사 (B) that이 정답이다. 목적격 인칭대명사 (A), 의문대명사 (C), 복합관계대명사(D)는 수식어 거품을 이끌 수 없다.
어휘 century-old adj. 100년 된 fully adv. 완전히 restore v. 복구하다

03 관계대명사 채우기
해석 그림이 깊은 인간의 감정을 탐구하는 신진 예술가 Marcus Stormfield는 국제적인 인정을 받고 있다.
해설 빈칸은 삽입구문(a rising artist ~ emotions) 안의 명사(a rising artist)를 선행사로 갖는 관계절을 이끌므로, 관계대명사 (A), (B), (C)가 정답의 후보이다. 빈칸 뒤에 선행사가 소유하는 명사(paintings)가 있으므로 소유격 관계대명사 (C) whose가 정답이다. (A) that과 (B) whom은 뒤에 불완전한 절이 와야 한다. 관계부사 (D)는 사람을 선행사로 가질 수 없다.
어휘 rising adj. 신진의 explore v. 탐구하다 emotion n. 감정 recognition n. 인정

04 '수량 표현 + 관계대명사' 채우기
해석 Grotto Haven은 지하 동굴 객실로 유명한데, 그들 모두는 일 년 내내 자연적으로 시원한 온도를 유지한다.
해설 빈칸 앞에 수량 표현 all of가 있고, 빈칸이 이끄는 절은 앞의 명사(rooms)를 선행사로 갖는 관계절이므로 관계대명사 (A)와 (B)가 정답의 후보이다. 선행사가 사물이므로 관계대명사 (B) which가 정답이다. (A) whom은 사물을 선행사로 가질 수 없다. (C) that은 전치사 뒤에 올 수 없다. 소유격 인칭대명사 (D)는 관계절을 이끌 수 없다.
어휘 underground adj. 지하의 cave n. 동굴 maintain v. 유지하다 naturally adv. 자연적으로 temperature n. 온도

기출 공식 3

토익실전문제   p.185

| 01 (B) | 02 (D) | 03 (C) | 04 (D) |

01 관계부사 채우기
해석 금요일은 대부분의 쇼핑몰이 늦은 밤 쇼핑객들을 위해 그들의 영업시간을 연장하는 날이다.
해설 이 문장은 주어(Friday), 동사(is), 보어(the day)를 갖춘 완전한 절이므로, ___ ~ shoppers는 수식어 거품으로 보아야 한다. 이 수식어 거품은 완전한 절이고, 빈칸 앞의 명사(day)를 선행사로 갖는 관계절이므로 시간을 나타내는 선행사와 함께 쓰이는 관계부사 (B) when이 정답이다. 관계부사 (A)는 이유를 나타내는 선행사와 함께 쓰인다. 의문대명사 (C)와 관계대명사 (D) 뒤에는 불완전한 절이 와야 한다.
어휘 extend v. 연장하다 opening hours 영업시간 late-night adj. 늦은 밤의

02 관계부사 채우기
해석 성공적인 브로드웨이의 제작자인 Ms. Roberts는 그녀가 성장한 교외 마을의 오래된 극장을 개조했다.
해설 이 문장은 주어(Ms. Roberts), 동사(renovated), 목적어(the old theater in the suburban town)를 갖춘 완전한 절이므로, ___ she grew up은 수식어 거품으로 보아야 한다. 이 수식어 거품은 완전한 절이고, 빈칸 앞의 명사(town)를 선행사로 갖는 관계절이므로 장소를 나타내는 선행사와 함께 쓰이는 관계부사 (D) where가 정답이다. 관계대명사 (A)와 의문대명사 (B) 뒤에는 불완전한 절이 와야 한다. 관계부사 (C)는 시간을 나타내는 선행사와 함께 쓰인다.
어휘 successful adj. 성공적인 renovate v. 개조하다, 보수하다 suburban adj. 교외의

03 관계부사 채우기
해석 열악한 인터넷 연결은 온라인 회의가 기술적 어려움을 겪은 이유였다.
해설 이 문장은 주어(A poor Internet connection), 동사(was), 보어(the reason)를 갖춘 완전한 절이므로, ___ ~ difficulties는 수식어 거품으로 보아야 한다. 이 수식어 거품은 완전한 절이고, 빈칸 앞의 명사(the reason)를 선행사로 갖는 관계절이므로 이유를 나타내는 선행사와 함께 쓰이는 관계부사 (C) why가 정답이다. 관계대명사 (A)와 (B) 뒤에는 불완전한 절이 와야 한다. 관계부사 (D)는 방법을 나타낸다.
어휘 poor adj. 열악한 connection n. 연결 technical adj. 기술적인 difficulty n. 어려움

04 '전치사 + 관계대명사' 채우기
해석 영양사는 사람들이 해외여행 중에 건강한 식습관을 유지할 수 있는 몇몇 방법을 제안했다.
해설 이 문장은 주어(The nutritionist), 동사(suggested), 목적어(some ways)를 갖춘 완전한 절이므로, ___ ~ abroad는 수식어 거품으로 보아야 한다. 이 수식어 거품은 완전한 절이고, 빈칸 앞의 명사(some ways)를 선행사로 갖는 관계절이므로 방법을 나타내는 선행사와 함께 쓰이는 (D) in which가 정답이다. 관계대명사 (A)와 의문대명사 (C) 뒤에는 불완전한 절이 와야 한다. 관계부사 (B)는 선행사 some ways와 함께 쓸 수 없다.
어휘 nutritionist n. 영양사 eating habit 식습관

HACKERS TEST   p.186

01 (A)	02 (B)	03 (D)	04 (B)	05 (C)
06 (D)	07 (A)	08 (D)	09 (A)	10 (B)
11 (C)	12 (A)	13 (C)	14 (B)	15 (D)
16 (B)	17 (C)	18 (D)	19 (B)	20 (B)
21 (D)	22 (C)	23 (B)	24 (B)	25 (C)
26 (D)	27 (A)	28 (D)		

01 관계대명사 채우기

해석 Willow Cove 리조트는 일주일 이상 머무르는 투숙객들에게 특별 할인을 제공한다.

해설 이 문장은 주어(Willow Cove Resort), 동사(offers), 목적어(special discounts)를 갖춘 완전한 절이므로, ___ ~ week는 수식어 거품으로 보아야 한다. 이 수식어 거품은 빈칸 앞의 명사(guests)를 선행사로 갖는 관계절이므로 관계대명사 (A)와 (D)가 정답의 후보이다. 선행사가 사람이고 빈칸 뒤에 주어가 없는 불완전한 절이 왔으므로 주격 관계대명사 (A) who가 정답이다. (D) which는 사람을 선행사로 가질 수 없다. 부정대명사 (B)는 관계절을 이끌 수 없다. 관계부사 (C) 뒤에는 완전한 절이 와야 한다.

02 관계부사 채우기

해석 임원들이 주간 회의를 여는 회의실은 최첨단 프레젠테이션 기술을 갖추고 있다.

해설 이 문장은 주어(The conference room), 동사(features), 목적어(state-of-the-art presentation technology)를 갖춘 완전한 절이므로, ___ ~ meetings는 수식어 거품으로 보아야 한다. 이 수식어 거품은 완전한 절이고, 빈칸 앞의 명사(conference room)를 선행사로 갖는 관계절이므로 장소를 나타내는 선행사와 함께 쓰이는 관계부사 (B) where가 정답이다. 관계대명사 (A) 뒤에는 불완전한 절이 와야 한다. 전치사 (C)와 (D)는 관계절을 이끌 수 없다.

어휘 executive n. 임원 feature v. 갖추고 있다, 특징으로 하다
state-of-the-art adj. 최첨단의

03 관계대명사 채우기

해석 경영진이 지난 분기에 시행한 정책은 전반적인 업무 현장 생산성을 상당히 개선했다.

해설 이 문장은 주어(The policy), 동사(has ~ improved), 목적어(overall workplace productivity)를 갖춘 완전한 절이므로, ___ ~ quarter는 수식어 거품으로 보아야 한다. 이 수식어 거품은 빈칸 앞의 명사(policy)를 선행사로 갖는 관계절이므로 관계대명사 (A)와 (D)가 정답의 후보이다. 선행사가 사물이므로 관계대명사 (D) that이 정답이다. (A) who는 사물을 선행사로 가질 수 없다. 의문대명사 (B)와 인칭대명사 (C)는 수식어 거품을 이끌 수 없다.

어휘 policy n. 정책 implement v. 시행하다 quarter n. 분기
overall adj. 전반적인 productivity n. 생산성

04 관계대명사 채우기

해석 Cloud Guard Elite는 사이버 위협으로부터 민감한 사업 정보를 보호하는 소프트웨어 프로그램이다.

해설 이 문장은 주어(Cloud Guard Elite), 동사(is), 보어(a software program)를 갖춘 완전한 절이므로, ___ ~ threats는 수식어 거품으로 보아야 한다. 이 수식어 거품은 빈칸 앞의 명사(software program)를 선행사로 갖는 관계절이므로 관계대명사 (A)와 (B)가 정답의 후보이다. 빈칸 뒤에 동사가 있으므로 주격 관계대명사 (B) which가 정답이다. (A) whose는 뒤에 선행사가 소유하는 명사가 와야 한다. 복합관계대명사 (C)와 부정대명사 (D)는 관계절을 이끌 수 없다.

어휘 protect v. 보호하다 sensitive adj. 민감한 threat n. 위협

05 관계부사 채우기

해석 9월은 Sunnyvale 과수원이 그것의 대표적인 유기농 사과를 수확하는 달이다.

해설 이 문장은 주어(September), 동사(is), 보어(the month)를 갖춘 완전한 절이므로, ___ ~ apples는 수식어 거품으로 보아야 한다. 이 수식어 거품은 완전한 절이고, 빈칸 앞의 명사(month)를 선행사로 갖는 관계절이므로 시간을 나타내는 선행사와 함께 쓰이는 관계부사 (C) when이 정답이다. 관계대명사 (A)와 (D) 뒤에는 불완전한 절이 와야 한다. 관계부사 (B)는 이유를 나타내는 선행사와 함께 쓰인다.

어휘 orchard n. 과수원 harvest v. 수확하다; n. 수확 signature adj. 대표적인
organic adj. 유기농의

06 관계대명사 채우기

해석 주차 허가증이 차량 등록과 일치하지 않는 방문객은 기록을 업데이트하도록 권장된다.

해설 이 문장은 주어(Visitors)와 동사(are advised)를 갖춘 완전한 절이므로, ___ ~ registration은 수식어 거품으로 보아야 한다. 빈칸 뒤에 선행사(Visitors)가 소유하는 명사(parking permit)가 있으므로 소유격 관계대명사 (D) whose가 정답이다. 관계대명사 (A), (B), (C)는 뒤에 불완전한 절이 와야 한다.

어휘 visitor n. 방문객 parking permit 주차 허가증 match v. 일치하다
vehicle registration 차량 등록 advise v. 권장하다, 충고하다

07 주어와 수일치하는 동사 채우기

해석 지역사회 봉사 오리엔테이션에 참석하는 자원봉사자에게 무료 식사 쿠폰이 제공된다.

해설 빈칸은 명사(volunteers)를 꾸미는 주격 관계절(who ~ orientation)의 동사 자리이므로 동사 (A)와 (C)가 정답의 후보이다. 주격 관계절의 동사는 선행사(volunteers)와 수일치하므로 복수 동사 (A) attend(참석하다)가 정답이다. 단수 동사 (C)는 단수 선행사와 함께 써야 한다. 동명사 또는 현재분사 (B)와 명사 (D)는 동사 자리에 올 수 없다.

어휘 complimentary adj. 무료의 voucher n. 쿠폰
community service 지역사회 봉사 attendance n. 출석, 참석

08 명사 자리 채우기

해석 정부는 새로운 여행 제한을 도입했는데, 그것은 국제 항공편에 즉각 영향을 미쳤다.

해설 빈칸은 동사(imposed)의 목적어이면서 형용사(new)의 꾸밈을 받는 명사 자리이므로 명사 (D) restrictions(제한)이 정답이다. 참고로, restriction은 명사 travel과 함께 복합 명사 형태로 쓰여 '여행 제한'이라는 의미를 나타내는 점을 알아 둔다. 동사 (A), 동사 또는 과거분사 (B), 형용사 (C)는 명사 자리에 올 수 없다.

어휘 government n. 정부 impose v. 도입하다, 부과하다
affect v. 영향을 미치다 restrict v. 제한하다 restrictive adj. 제한하는

09 관계부사 채우기

해석 워크숍은 전략적 키워드가 어떻게 당신의 이력서를 돋보이게 할 수 있는지 시연할 것입니다.

해설 빈칸은 동사(will demonstrate)의 목적어 역할을 하는 완전한 절(strategic ~ stand out)을 이끄는 자리이고, '전략적 키워드가 어떻게 당신의 이력서를 돋보이게 할 수 있는지'라는 의미가 되어야 하므로 관계부사 (A) how가 정답이다. 참고로, 관계부사 how 앞에는 선행사(the way)가 오지 않는 점을 알아 둔다. 부정대명사 (B)는 절을 이끌 수 없다. 관계대명사 (C)는 앞에 선행사가 오고 뒤에 불완전한 절이 와야 한다. 복합관계부사 (D)는 목적어 역할을 하는 절을 이끌 수 없다.

어휘 demonstrate v. 시연하다 strategic adj. 전략적인 stand out 돋보이다

10 '수량 표현 + 관계대명사' 채우기

해석 그 실험은 두 과학자에 의해 주도될 것인데, 그들 둘 다 해당 분야에서 수십 년의 경험을 가지고 있다.

해설 빈칸 앞에 수량 표현 both of가 있고, 빈칸이 이끄는 절은 앞의 명사(scientists)를 선행사로 갖는 관계절이므로 관계대명사 (B) whom이 정답이다. 목적격 인칭대명사 (A)는 관계절을 이끌 수 없다. (C) whose는 뒤에 선행사가 소유하는 명사가 와야 한다. (D) which는 사람을 선행사로 가질 수 없다.

어휘 experiment n. 실험 lead v. 주도하다 decade n. 10년 field n. 분야

11 관계대명사 채우기

해석 직장인 부모에게, 그들의 직장과 가까운 어린이집이 있다는 것은 엄청나

해설 이 문장은 주어(having a daycare center), 동사(is), 보어(beneficial)를 갖춘 완전한 절이므로, ___ ~ workplace는 수식어 거품으로 보아야 한다. 이 수식어 거품은 빈칸 앞의 명사(daycare center)를 선행사로 갖는 관계절이므로 관계대명사 (A)와 (C)가 정답의 후보이다. 선행사가 사물이고 빈칸 뒤에 주어가 없는 불완전한 절이 왔으므로 주격 관계대명사 (C) that이 정답이다. (A) who는 사물을 선행사로 가질 수 없다. 재귀대명사 (B)와 목적격 인칭대명사 (D)는 관계절을 이끌 수 없다.

어휘 daycare center 어린이집 incredibly adv. 엄청나게
beneficial adj. 유용한

12 부사절 접속사 채우기

해석 여행자들은 바르셀로나의 거리를 탐험할 때 놀라운 건축물과 역사적 장소를 발견할 수 있다.

해설 빈칸은 동사(explore)가 있는 거품절(___ they ~ Barcelona)을 이끄는 부사절 접속사 자리이고, '바르셀로나의 거리를 탐험할 때 놀라운 건축물과 역사적 장소를 발견할 수 있다'라는 의미가 되어야 하므로 시간을 나타내는 부사절 접속사 (A) as(~할 때)가 정답이다. (B) unless는 '만약 ~이 아니라면'이라는 의미이다. 관계대명사 (C)는 뒤에 불완전한 절이 와야 한다. 전치사 (D)는 거품절을 이끌 수 없다.

어휘 discover v. 발견하다 stunning adj. 놀라운 during prep. ~ 동안

13 지시대명사 those 채우기

해석 Hincey Skincare의 메이크업 리무버는 민감한 피부를 가진 사람들에게 자극을 유발하지 않고 화장품을 제거한다.

해설 빈칸은 전치사(for)의 목적어이면서 전치사구(with sensitive skin)의 꾸밈을 받는 명사 자리이므로 지시대명사 (B)와 (C)가 정답의 후보이다. '민감한 피부를 가진 사람들'이라는 의미가 되어야 하므로 전치사구의 꾸밈을 받아 '~한 사람들'이라는 의미로 쓰이는 지시대명사 (C) those가 정답이다. 지시대명사 (B)는 '~한 사람들'이라는 의미로 쓰일 수 없다. 관계대명사 (A)와 (D)는 뒤에 전치사구가 아닌 절이 와야 한다.

어휘 wipe away ~을 제거하다 cosmetics n. 화장품 irritation n. 자극
sensitive adj. 민감한

14 분사 채우기

해석 주 터미널과 국제 게이트를 연결하는 보행로는 거의 800미터에 걸쳐 있다.

해설 빈칸 앞의 명사(walkway)를 꾸밀 수 있는 것은 형용사이고 빈칸 뒤에 목적어(the main terminal and the international gates)가 있으므로 현재분사 (B) connecting이 정답이다. 동사 (A), 명사 (C)와 (D)는 형용사 자리에 올 수 없다. 참고로, 해당 문장의 동사는 stretches임을 알아 둔다.

어휘 walkway n. 보행로 stretch v. 걸쳐 있다 nearly adv. 거의
connect v. 연결하다 connection n. 관련성, 접속 connectivity n. 연결

15 관계대명사 채우기

해석 상을 받은 건축가는 두 대륙에 걸쳐 지속 가능한 건물을 설계했다.

해설 이 문장은 주어(The architect), 동사(designed), 목적어(sustainable buildings)를 갖춘 완전한 절이므로, to ___ the award was given은 수식어 거품으로 보아야 한다. 이 수식어 거품은 빈칸 앞의 명사(architect)를 선행사로 갖는 관계절이고, 빈칸 바로 앞에 전치사(to)가 있으므로 관계대명사 (D) whom이 정답이다. 관계대명사 (A) that은 전치사 뒤에 올 수 없고, (B) which는 사람을 선행사로 가질 수 없다. 의문대명사 (C)는 관계절을 이끌 수 없다.

어휘 architect n. 건축가 sustainable adj. 지속 가능한 continent n. 대륙

16 전치사 표현 채우기

해석 전략적 마케팅 캠페인을 개발하는 것은 Ms. Lemoine이 책임이 있는 중요한 업무들 중 하나이다.

해설 빈칸은 명사(tasks)를 꾸미는 관계절(which ~ responsible) 앞에 있고, 선행사(tasks)가 관계절의 꾸밈을 받기 위해서는 선행사를 목적어로 취하는 전치사가 필요하므로 전치사 (A), (B), (C)가 정답의 후보이다. 관계절 안의 responsible과 함께 '~에 책임이 있는'이라는 의미의 어구인 responsible for를 만드는 전치사 (B) for가 정답이다. (A) on과 (C) from은 responsible on/from의 형태로 쓰일 수 없다. 부사절 접속사 (D)는 명사를 목적어로 가질 수 없다.

어휘 strategic adj. 전략적인 critical adj. 중요한 because conj. ~이기 때문에

17 '전치사 + 관계대명사' 채우기

해석 그 연구는 문화적 차이가 어떻게 소비자 선호도와 소비 행동을 형성하는지 보여주었다.

해설 이 문장은 주어(The research), 동사(showed), 목적어(the way)를 갖춘 완전한 절이므로, ___ ~ behaviors는 수식어 거품으로 보아야 한다. 이 수식어 거품은 완전한 절이고, 빈칸 앞의 명사(the way)를 선행사로 갖는 관계절이므로 방법을 나타내는 선행사와 함께 쓰이는 (C) in which가 정답이다. 관계부사 (A)는 선행사 way와 함께 쓸 수 없다. 부사절 접속사 (B) in that은 '~라는 점에서'라는 의미이다. 참고로, that이 관계대명사로 쓰인 경우 전치사 in 뒤에 올 수 없다는 점을 알아 둔다. 복합관계대명사 (D)는 관계절을 이끌 수 없다.

어휘 cultural adj. 문화적인 difference n. 차이 shape v. 형성하다
preference n. 선호도 purchasing behavior 소비 행동

18 태에 맞는 동사 채우기

해석 늦게 배송되는 모든 소포는 자동으로 배송비의 50퍼센트를 환불받는다.

해설 관계절(that ___ late)에 동사가 없으므로 동사 (A)와 (D)가 정답의 후보이다. 빈칸 뒤에 목적어가 없고 '늦게 배송되는 소포'라는 수동의 의미가 되어야 하므로 수동태 동사 (D) is delivered(배송되다)가 정답이다. 동명사 또는 현재분사 (B)와 명사 (C)는 동사 자리에 올 수 없다.

어휘 automatically adv. 자동으로 receive v. 받다 shipping cost 배송비

19 관계대명사 채우기

해석 Revone 의원은 물리치료가 필요한 환자들을 맞춤형 재활 프로그램으로 돕는다.

해설 이 문장은 주어(Revone Clinic), 동사(assists), 목적어(patients)를 갖춘 완전한 절이므로, ___ ~ therapy는 수식어 거품으로 보아야 한다. 이 수식어 거품은 빈칸 앞의 명사(patients)를 선행사로 갖는 관계절이므로 관계대명사 (B)와 (C)가 정답의 후보이다. 선행사가 사람이고 빈칸 뒤에 주어가 없는 불완전한 절이 왔으므로 주격 관계대명사 (B) who가 정답이다. (C) which는 사람을 선행사로 가질 수 없다. 부정대명사 (A)와 복합관계대명사 (D)는 관계절을 이끌 수 없다.

어휘 assist v. 돕다 patient n. 환자 physical therapy 물리치료
customized adj. 맞춤형의 rehabilitation n. 재활

20 사람명사와 사물/추상명사 구별하여 채우기

해석 Mr. Kowalski는 공동 텃밭 관리를 정기적으로 돕는 4B 아파트의 입주자이다.

해설 빈칸은 동사(is)의 보어 자리이므로 명사 (B), (C), (D)가 정답의 후보이다. 'Mr. Kowalski는 4B 아파트의 입주자이다'라는 의미가 되어야 하므로 사람명사 (B) occupant(입주자)가 정답이다. 사물/추상명사 (C) occupation(직업)과 (D) occupancy(점유)를 쓸 경우 'Mr. Kowalski는 4B 아파트의 직업/점유이다'라는 어색한 의미를 만들기 때문에 답이 될 수 없다. 동사 (A)는 명사 자리에 올 수 없다.

어휘 regularly adv. 정기적으로 occupy v. 거주하다, 차지하다

21 '수량 표현 + 관계대명사' 채우기

해석 Ms. Benson은 세 개의 투자 회사로부터 일자리 제안을 받았는데, 그들 중 어느 곳도 그녀의 거주지 근처에 위치하지 않았다.

해설 빈칸 앞에 수량 표현 none of가 있고, 빈칸이 이끄는 절은 앞의 명사(investment companies)를 선행사로 갖는 관계절이므로 관계대명사

(D) which가 정답이다. (A) who와 (C) that은 전치사 뒤에 올 수 없다. 관계부사 (B)는 뒤에 완전한 절이 와야 한다.

어휘 offer n. 일자리 제안 locate v. 위치시키다 residence n. 거주지

22 부사 자리 채우기

해석 ReTouch Studio 2.0의 사용자들은 대용량 이미지 파일을 처리하는 동안 자주 발생하는 오류를 보고하고 있다.

해설 동사(occurs)를 꾸밀 수 있는 것은 부사이므로 부사 (C) frequently(자주)가 정답이다. 형용사 또는 동사 (A), 동사 (B), 명사 (D)는 동사를 꾸밀 수 없다. 참고로, occurs는 명사 error를 꾸미는 주격 관계절(that ~ files) 안의 동사임을 알아 둔다.

어휘 occur v. 발생하다 process v. 처리하다 frequent adj. 잦은; v. 자주 다니다 frequency n. 빈도

23 관계대명사 채우기

해석 새로운 소프트웨어 시스템을 도입하는 것을 계획하는 관리자들은 직원들에게 충분한 교육을 제공해야 한다.

해설 이 문장은 주어(Managers), 동사(should provide), 목적어(adequate training)를 갖춘 완전한 절이므로, ___ ~ systems는 수식어 거품으로 보아야 한다. 이 수식어 거품은 빈칸 앞의 명사(Managers)를 선행사로 갖는 관계절이므로 관계대명사 (B), (C), (D)가 정답의 후보이다. 선행사가 사람이고 빈칸 뒤에 주어가 없는 불완전한 절이 왔으므로 주격 관계대명사 (B) who가 정답이다. (C) which는 사람을 선행사로 가질 수 없고, (D) whose는 뒤에 선행사가 소유하는 명사가 와야 한다. 부정대명사 (A)는 관계절을 이끌 수 없다.

어휘 adequate adj. 충분한 training n. 교육

24 명사절 접속사 채우기

해석 마케팅 책임자는 회사의 새로운 무선 이어폰인 WavePods가 젊은 소비자들을 유인할 것이라고 확신한다.

해설 빈칸은 형용사(sure)와 함께 쓰이는 명사절(___ the company's ~ consumers)을 이끄는 명사절 접속사 자리이므로 명사절 접속사 (B) that이 정답이다. 참고로, be sure는 명사절 접속사 that과 함께 쓰여 '~라고 확신하다'라는 의미를 나타내는 점을 알아 둔다. 전치사 (A), 지시대명사 (C), 관계대명사 (D)는 명사절을 이끌 수 없다.

어휘 wireless adj. 무선의 attract v. 유인하다, 끌어들이다

25 관계대명사 채우기

해석 인사팀은 신입사원들이 회사 정책에 대해 배울 교육 세션을 편성할 것이다.

해설 이 문장은 주어(The HR team), 동사(will coordinate), 목적어(a training session)를 갖춘 완전한 절이므로, ___ ~ policies는 수식어 거품으로 보아야 한다. 이 수식어 거품은 빈칸 앞의 명사(training session)를 선행사로 갖는 관계절이고, 빈칸 바로 앞에 전치사(during)가 있으므로 관계대명사 (C) which가 정답이다. 관계대명사 (A) who와 (B) that은 전치사 뒤에 올 수 없다. 전치사 (D)는 관계절을 이끌 수 없다.

어휘 coordinate v. 편성하다, 조정하다 new hire 신입사원 policy n. 정책

26 현재분사와 과거분사 구별하여 채우기

해석 제조사는 즉각적인 안전 점검을 위해 결함 있는 에어백 센서가 장착된 많은 차량을 회수했다.

해설 빈칸 앞의 명사(cars)를 꾸밀 수 있는 것은 형용사이므로 현재분사 (C)와 과거분사 (D)가 정답의 후보이다. 꾸밈을 받는 명사(cars)와 분사가 '센서가 장착된 차량'이라는 의미의 수동 관계이므로 과거분사 (D) equipped가 정답이다. 현재분사 (C) equipping을 쓸 경우 '센서가 장착하는 차량'이라는 어색한 의미가 된다. 참고로, equip은 equip A with B의 형태로 쓰여 'A에 B를 장착하다'라는 의미를 나타내는 점을 알아 둔다. 동사 (A)와 명사 (B)는 형용사 자리에 올 수 없다.

어휘 manufacturer n. 제조사 recall v. 회수하다 faulty adj. 결함 있는

inspection n. 점검 equipment n. 장비

27 관계대명사 채우기

해석 회사는 직원들이 중복되는 책임과 업무를 가지는 여러 부서들을 통합했다.

해설 이 문장은 주어(The company), 동사(merged), 목적어(several departments)를 갖춘 완전한 절이므로, ___ ~ duties는 수식어 거품으로 보아야 한다. 빈칸 뒤에 선행사(several departments)가 소유하는 명사(staff members)가 있으므로 소유격 관계대명사 (A) whose가 정답이다. 관계대명사 (B)와 (D)는 뒤에 불완전한 절이 와야 한다. 의문대명사 (C)는 수식어 거품을 이끌 수 없다.

어휘 merge v. 통합하다 department n. 부서 overlapping adj. 중복되는 responsibility n. 책임 duty n. 업무

28 '전치사 + 관계대명사' 채우기

해석 많은 오페라 가수들이 공연하는 그 콘서트홀은 음향 시스템을 개선하기 위해 보수 중이다.

해설 이 문장은 주어(The concert hall), 동사(is undergoing), 목적어(renovation)를 갖춘 완전한 절이므로, ___ ~ perform은 수식어 거품으로 보아야 한다. 이 수식어 거품은 완전한 절이고, 빈칸 앞의 명사(concert hall)를 선행사로 갖는 관계절이므로 장소를 나타내는 선행사와 함께 쓰이는 (D) at which가 정답이다. 참고로, 장소를 나타내는 관계부사 where가 '전치사 + 관계대명사' 형태인 at which로 바뀐 점을 알아 둔다. 관계부사 (A)는 시간을 나타내는 선행사와 함께 쓰인다. 관계대명사 (B) 뒤에는 불완전한 절이 와야 하며, (C)는 뒤에 선행사가 소유하는 명사가 와야 한다.

어휘 perform v. 공연하다 acoustic adj. 음향의

DAY 08 최신 빈출 어휘

HACKERS TEST   p.190

01 (C)	02 (D)	03 (B)	04 (B)	05 (B)
06 (A)	07 (A)	08 (C)	09 (B)	10 (C)
11 (B)	12 (B)	13 (A)	14 (D)	15 (A)
16 (C)	17 (D)	18 (B)	19 (B)	20 (D)
21 (C)	22 (A)	23 (C)	24 (D)	25 (A)
26 (B)	27 (D)	28 (D)	29 (D)	30 (D)
31 (B)	32 (D)	33 (D)	34 (A)	35 (B)
36 (C)	37 (B)	38 (C)	39 (B)	40 (A)
41 (B)	42 (B)	43 (D)	44 (C)	45 (B)
46 (B)	47 (A)	48 (C)	49 (D)	50 (B)
51 (D)	52 (A)	53 (C)	54 (C)	55 (C)
56 (A)	57 (A)	58 (D)	59 (B)	60 (D)
61 (C)	62 (C)	63 (C)	64 (D)	65 (A)
66 (B)	67 (C)	68 (C)	69 (B)	70 (C)
71 (A)	72 (B)	73 (B)	74 (B)	75 (D)
76 (D)	77 (A)	78 (C)	79 (D)	80 (A)
81 (C)	82 (C)	83 (D)	84 (B)	

01 명사 어휘 고르기

해석 5월 25일은 여름 음악 페스티벌의 얼리버드 티켓의 구매 기한이다.

해설 '5월 25일은 얼리버드 티켓의 구매 기한이다'라는 문맥이므로 명사 (C) deadline(기한)이 정답이다. (A) attitude는 '태도', (B) comment는

'논평, 언급', (D) description은 '묘사, 표현'이라는 의미이다.

02 부사 어휘 고르기
해석 Hillside 지역의 주민들은 대부분 근처 Morgan 대학의 학생들로 구성되어 있다.

해설 '주민들은 대부분 근처 Morgan 대학의 학생들로 구성되어 있다'라는 문맥이므로 부사 (D) mostly(대부분)가 정답이다. (A) namely는 '즉, 다시 말해', (B) frequently는 '자주', (C) publicly는 '공개적으로'라는 의미이다.

어휘 resident n. 주민, 거주민 consist of ~으로 구성되다

03 형용사 어휘 고르기
해석 Mr. Mattson은 그의 발표 주제에 대한 간단한 개요를 나누어줌으로써 발표를 시작했다.

해설 '발표 주제에 대한 간단한 개요를 나누어줌으로써 발표를 시작했다'라는 문맥이므로 (B) brief(간단한)가 정답이다. (A) constant는 '끊임없는, 거듭되는', (C) talented는 '재능이 있는', (D) potential은 '가능성 있는, 잠재적인'이라는 의미이다.

어휘 pass out ~을 나누어 주다 outline n. 개요

04 명사 어휘 고르기
해석 자동차 구매자들은 전기차 시장에서 선택할 수 있는 다양한 선택권이 있다.

해설 '자동차 구매자들은 선택할 수 있는 다양한 선택권이 있다'라는 문맥이므로 (B) options(선택권)가 정답이다. (A) abilities는 '능력', (C) incomes는 '수입', (D) exchanges는 '교환, 맞바꿈'이라는 의미이다.

어휘 a vast array of 다양한 electric vehicle 전기차

05 동사 어휘 고르기
해석 그 연구 기관은 현재 생명공학을 전문으로 하는 과학자들을 모집하고 있다.

해설 '그 연구 기관은 과학자들을 모집하고 있다'라는 문맥이므로 (B) recruiting(모집하다)이 정답이다. (D) earning(얻다)도 해석상 그럴듯해 보이지만, 평판 등을 얻거나 돈을 버는 것을 의미한다. (A) rising은 '오르다, 올라가다', (C) realizing은 '깨닫다, 알아차리다'라는 의미이다.

어휘 institute n. 기관 currently adv. 현재 specialize in ~을 전문으로 하다 biotechnology n. 생명공학

06 형용사 어휘 고르기
해석 다가오는 회의의 등록은 이제 공식 행사 웹사이트에서 가능하다.

해설 '회의의 등록은 웹사이트에서 가능하다'라는 문맥이므로 (A) available(가능한)이 정답이다. (B) capable(~을 할 수 있는)도 해석상 그럴듯해 보이지만, 사람이 능력이나 자격 면에서 무언가를 할 수 있다는 것을 의미한다. (C) decisive는 '결정적인, 결단력 있는', (D) comparable은 '비슷한, 비교할 만한'이라는 의미이다.

어휘 registration n. 등록 upcoming adj. 다가오는 official adj. 공식적인

07 명사 어휘 고르기
해석 동남아시아 내의 전략적인 아웃소싱 위치 덕분에 Alpine Solutions사의 인건비용은 낮다.

해설 '동남아시아 내의 전략적 아웃소싱 위치 덕분에 인건비용이 낮다'라는 문맥이므로 (A) costs(비용)가 정답이다. 참고로, costs가 명사 labor와 함께 복합 명사 형태로 쓰여 '인건비용'이라는 의미를 나타내고 있음을 알아 둔다. (B) tickets는 '표', (C) schedules는 '일정', (D) inputs는 '투입, 조언'이라는 의미이다.

어휘 strategic adj. 전략적인 outsourcing n. 아웃소싱 location n. 위치

08 부사 어휘 고르기
해석 비록 주연 배우들은 그들의 배역을 완벽하게 연기했지만, 음악가들은 잘하지 못했다.

해설 '주연 배우들은 그들의 배역을 완벽하게 연기했지만, 음악가들은 잘하지 못했다'라는 문맥이므로 (C) perfectly(완벽하게)가 정답이다. (A) equally는 '동일하게', (B) occasionally는 '가끔', (D) simply는 '간단히'라는 의미이다.

어휘 perform v. 연기하다, 공연하다 role n. 배역

09 동사 어휘 고르기
해석 사용 설명서는 복사기를 작동하는 방법을 몇 가지 언어로 설명한다.

해설 '사용 설명서는 복사기를 작동하는 방법을 설명한다'라는 문맥이므로 (B) operate(작동하다)가 정답이다. (A) print는 '인쇄하다', (C) reveal은 '드러내다, 밝히다', (D) overlook은 '간과하다'라는 의미이다.

어휘 instruction manual 사용 설명서 photocopier n. 복사기

10 명사 어휘 고르기
해석 오래된 호텔의 보수공사는 성공적이었으며, 그것은 이제 꽤 현대적으로 보인다.

해설 '오래된 호텔의 보수공사는 성공적이었으며, 그것은 이제 꽤 현대적으로 보인다'라는 문맥이므로 (C) renovations(보수공사)가 정답이다. (D) productions(생산, 제조)도 무언가를 만든다는 의미로 해석상 그럴듯해 보이지만, 식품, 상품, 자재 등을 대량으로 생산하는 것을 의미한다. (A) locations는 '위치', (B) advantages는 '이점, 장점'이라는 의미이다.

어휘 quite adv. 꽤 modern adj. 현대적인

11 형용사 어휘 고르기
해석 Primordial Technologies사는 넉 달 동안 50,000달러를 사용했는데, 이는 그것의 그해 전체 광고 예산의 절반이었다.

해설 '이는 그해 전체 광고 예산의 절반이었다'라는 문맥이므로 (B) entire(전체의)가 정답이다. (A) eager는 '열렬한, 열망하는', (C) reliant는 '의존하는, 의지하는', (D) adjacent는 '인접한'이라는 의미이다.

어휘 advertising n. 광고

12 부사 어휘 고르기
해석 예전에 컴퓨팅 혁신에서의 선두 주자로 여겨졌던 Frye Systems사는 몇 년 동안 신제품을 출시하지 않았다.

해설 '예전에 선두 주자로 여겨졌던 Frye Systems사는 몇 년 동안 신제품을 출시하지 않았다'라는 문맥이므로 (B) Formerly(예전에)가 정답이다. (A) Necessarily는 '필연적으로', (C) Eventually는 '결국', (D) Wisely는 '현명하게'라는 의미이다.

어휘 consider v. 여기다 computing n. 컴퓨팅(컴퓨터를 사용하는 행위) innovation n. 혁신

13 명사 어휘 고르기
해석 소비자 지출의 급격한 감소는 많은 소매점들이 전국적으로 문을 닫도록 했다.

해설 '소비자 지출의 급격한 감소는 많은 소매점들이 문을 닫도록 했다'라는 문맥이므로 (A) decline(감소)이 정답이다. (B) merger는 '합병', (C) replacement는 '교체, 대체', (D) commitment는 '약속, 헌신'이라는 의미이다.

어휘 sharp adj. 급격한 spending n. 지출 force v. ~하도록 하다 retail store 소매점 nationwide adv. 전국적으로

14 동사 어휘 고르기
해석 그 건축가는 주거용 타워의 수정된 청사진을 도시 계획 부서에 제출했다.

해설 '수정된 청사진을 도시 계획 부서에 제출했다'라는 문맥이므로 (D) submitted(제출하다)가 정답이다. (A) taught는 '가르치다', (B) invented는 '발명하다', (C) replaced는 '교체하다'라는 의미이다. 참고로, submit은 submit A to B(B에 A를 제출하다)라는 형태로 자주 쓰임을 알아 둔다.

어휘 **architect** n. 건축가　**revised** adj. 수정된　**blueprint** n. 청사진
　　　residential adj. 주거용의

15 형용사 어휘 고르기
해석 특별 쿠폰은 쇼핑객이 주문 시 30달러 이상을 지출할 때만 유효하다.
해설 '특별 쿠폰은 주문 시 30달러 이상을 지출할 때만 유효하다'라는 문맥이므로 (A) valid(유효한)가 정답이다. (B) accurate는 '정확한', (C) efficient는 '효율적인', (D) significant는 '중요한'이라는 의미이다.
어휘 **order** n. 주문; v. 주문하다

16 명사 어휘 고르기
해석 공중보건 관계자는 바이러스의 확산을 막기 위해 공공장소에서 마스크를 착용하는 것을 권장한다.
해설 '바이러스의 확산을 막기 위해 공공장소에서 마스크를 착용하는 것을 권장한다'라는 문맥이므로 (C) spread(확산)가 정답이다. (A) break는 '휴식, 중단', (B) interior는 '내부', (D) location은 '장소'라는 의미이다.
어휘 **official** n. 관계자, 공무원　**recommend** v. 권장하다　**wear** v. 착용하다, 입다
　　　public space 공공장소

17 동사 어휘 고르기
해석 그들의 문제에 신속한 답변이 필요한 고객들은 인공지능 도우미와의 온라인 채팅을 시작할 수 있다.
해설 '신속한 답변이 필요한 고객들은 온라인 채팅을 시작할 수 있다'라는 문맥이므로 (D) require(필요하다)가 정답이다. (A) constrain(강요하다, 억제하다)도 해석상 그럴듯해 보이지만, 복종 등을 강요하거나 무언가를 억지로 하게 하는 것을 의미한다. (B) release는 '출시하다', (C) provide는 '제공하다'라는 의미이다.
어휘 **prompt** adj. 신속한　**assistant** n. 도우미, 보조

18 형용사 어휘 고르기
해석 비록 이사회는 생산성도 높이기를 바라지만, 그 프로젝트의 주된 목표는 제조 비용을 줄이는 것이다.
해설 '생산성도 높이기를 바라지만, 그 프로젝트의 주된 목표는 제조 비용을 줄이는 것이다'라는 문맥이므로 (B) primary(주된)가 정답이다. (A) adverse는 '부정적인, 불리한', (C) fluent는 '능숙한, 유창한', (D) neutral은 '중립의'라는 의미이다.
어휘 **lower** v. 줄이다　**manufacturing cost** 제조 비용　**board** n. 이사회, 위원회
　　　productivity n. 생산성

19 명사 어휘 고르기
해석 Veran Tech사는 해킹을 예방하는 컴퓨터 소프트웨어의 새로운 발전을 발표했다.
해설 '해킹을 예방하는 컴퓨터 소프트웨어의 새로운 발전을 발표했다'라는 문맥이므로 (B) advancement(발전)가 정답이다. (A) destination은 '(여행의) 목적지, 도착지', (C) moderation은 '적당함', (D) qualification은 '자질, 자격'이라는 의미이다.
어휘 **prevent** v. 예방하다, 막다

20 부사 어휘 고르기
해석 정보가 유출되는 것을 방지하기 위해 신제품에 대한 모든 세부 사항들이 철저히 숨겨졌다.
해설 '정보가 유출되는 것을 방지하기 위해 세부 사항들이 철저히 숨겨졌다'라는 문맥이므로 (D) thoroughly(철저히)가 정답이다. (A) lastly는 '마지막으로', (B) hopefully는 '바라건대', (C) remotely는 '원격으로, 멀리서'라는 의미이다.
어휘 **detail** n. 세부 사항　**conceal** v. 숨기다, 감추다　**prevent** v. 방지하다, 막다
　　　leak v. 유출되다

21 형용사 어휘 고르기
해석 BioPharmin사에 의해 만들어진 항생제는 전염병에 효과적인 치료제임이 드러났다.
해설 '항생제가 전염병에 효과적인 치료제임이 드러났다'라는 문맥이므로 (C) effective(효과적인)가 정답이다. (A) assembled는 '모인, 집합된', (B) impartial은 '공정한', (D) intimate는 '친밀한'이라는 의미이다.
어휘 **antibiotic** n. 항생제　**prove** v. ~임이 드러나다, 판명되다
　　　treatment n. 치료제　**infectious** adj. 전염성의

22 동사 어휘 고르기
해석 Lumeva Apparel사는 유럽 선두 패션 디자이너들과의 사업 제휴를 발표할 것이다.
해설 '유럽 선두 패션 디자이너들과의 사업 제휴를 발표할 것이다'라는 문맥이므로 (A) announce(발표하다)가 정답이다. (B) issue(발행하다, 발표하다)도 해석상 그럴듯해 보이지만, 잡지나 글 등을 발행하거나 성명 등을 발표하는 것을 의미한다. (C) consist는 '이루어져 있다', (D) reduce는 '줄이다, 낮추다'라는 의미이다.
어휘 **partnership** n. 동업　**leading** adj. 선두의

23 명사 어휘 고르기
해석 Dr. Abalkin은 최근 발표된 그의 연구 논문에 있는 자료의 출처를 밝히도록 요청받았다.
해설 '연구 논문에 있는 자료의 출처를 밝히도록 요청받았다'라는 문맥이므로 (C) source(출처)가 정답이다. (A) plan은 '계획', (B) reply는 '대답', (D) trade는 '거래, 무역'이라는 의미이다.
어휘 **cite** v. (출처를) 밝히다, 인용하다　**recently** adv. 최근에

24 형용사 어휘 고르기
해석 의료 전문가들은 진단이 정확한지 확실하게 하기 위해 각 환자의 기록을 재확인한다.
해설 '진단이 정확한지 확실하게 하기 위해 각 환자의 기록을 재확인한다'라는 문맥이므로 (B) accurate(정확한)이 정답이다. (A) probable은 '사실일 것 같은', (C) remarkable은 '놀라운', (D) fortunate은 '운 좋은'이라는 의미이다.
어휘 **medical professional** 의료 전문가　**double-check** v. 재확인하다
　　　diagnosis n. 진단

25 부사 어휘 고르기
해석 현대 디지털 플랫폼에서 사생활이 거의 보장되지 않기 때문에, 사용자들은 그들의 개인 정보를 적극적으로 보호해야 한다.
해설 '사생활이 거의 보장되지 않기 때문에, 사용자들은 그들의 개인 정보를 적극적으로 보호해야 한다'라는 문맥이므로 (A) rarely(거의 ~않다)가 정답이다. (B) widely는 '널리', (C) readily는 '손쉽게, 선뜻', (D) publicly는 '공개적으로'라는 의미이다.
어휘 **privacy** n. 사생활　**guarantee** v. 보장하다　**proactively** adv. 적극적으로

26 명사 어휘 고르기
해석 Harvina Alliance는 비어 있는 도시 부지를 생산적인 공동체 정원과 농지로 변화시키는 기구이다.
해설 'Harvina Alliance는 도시 부지를 공동체 정원과 농지로 변화시키는 기구이다'라는 문맥이므로 (B) organization(기구)이 정답이다. (A) adjustment는 '조정, 적응', (C) leadership은 '대표직, 지도력', (D) neighborhood는 '이웃, 주민'이라는 의미이다.
어휘 **transform** v. 변화시키다　**vacant** adj. 비어 있는　**lot** n. 부지
　　　productive adj. 생산적인

27 동사 어휘 고르기
해석 추가적인 토양 검사는 멸종 위기종을 심기에 가장 적절한 위치를 결정하는 데 도움을 줄 것이다.

해설 '멸종 위기종을 심기에 가장 적절한 위치를 결정하다'라는 문맥이므로 (C) determine(결정하다)이 정답이다. (A) overcome은 '극복하다', (B) deserve는 '~을 받을 만하다', (D) combine은 '결합하다'라는 의미이다.

어휘 additional adj. 추가적인 soil n. 토양 appropriate adj. 적절한 endangered adj. 멸종 위기의

28 부사 어휘 고르기

해석 Beemz Cable사는 그들의 청구서 지불 기한이 지난 모든 고객들의 서비스를 즉시 중단할 것이다.

해설 '청구서 지불 기한이 지난 모든 고객들의 서비스를 즉시 중단할 것이다'라는 문맥이 되어야 하므로 (D) immediately(즉시)가 정답이다. (A) instinctively는 '본능적으로', (B) positively는 '긍정적으로', (C) mutually는 '서로'라는 의미이다.

어휘 bill n. 청구서 overdue adj. (지불) 기한이 지난

29 형용사 어휘 고르기

해석 정부의 군사 전략은 엄격히 기밀이며 허가받지 않은 인원과 공유되지 않을 것이다.

해설 '군사 전략은 엄격히 기밀이며 허가받지 않은 인원과 공유되지 않을 것이다'라는 문맥이므로 (D) confidential(기밀의)이 정답이다. (A) different는 '다른', (B) frequent는 '잦은, 빈번한', (C) dominant는 '우세한, 지배적인'이라는 의미이다.

어휘 military adj. 군사의 strictly adv. 엄격히 unauthorized adj. 허가받지 않은 personnel n. 인원, 직원

30 부사 어휘 고르기

해석 스타트업 창업자들은 경험 있는 산업 전문가들로부터 멘토링을 적극적으로 요청해야 한다.

해설 '스타트업 창업자들은 멘토링을 적극적으로 요청해야 한다'라는 문맥이므로 (D) actively(적극적으로)가 정답이다. (A) extremely는 '극도로', (B) lightly는 '가볍게', (C) densely는 '빽빽하게'라는 의미이다.

어휘 founder n. 창업자 solicit v. 요청하다 experienced adj. 경험 있는

31 명사 어휘 고르기

해석 무료 코딩 워크숍은 단 12개의 자리만 있기 때문에 신속한 등록이 필요하다.

해설 '무료 코딩 워크숍은 신속한 등록이 필요하다'라는 문맥이므로 (B) registration(등록)이 정답이다. (A) payment(지불)도 해석상 그럴듯해 보이지만, 워크숍이 무료라고 했으므로 답이 될 수 없다. (C) submission은 '제출', (D) certification은 '증명'이라는 의미이다.

어휘 prompt adj. 신속한; v. 촉발하다

32 동사 어휘 고르기

해석 뛰어난 품질을 보장하기 위해, Royal Carat의 모든 다이아몬드는 공인된 보석학자들에 의해 검사된다.

해설 '뛰어난 품질을 보장하기 위해, 모든 다이아몬드는 공인된 보석학자들에 의해 검사된다'라는 문맥이므로 (C) ensure(보장하다)가 정답이다. (A) conclude는 '결론짓다, 끝내다', (B) arrange는 '마련하다, 정리하다', (D) foresee는 '예견하다'라는 의미이다.

어휘 outstanding adj. 뛰어난 quality n. 품질 examine v. 검사하다 certified adj. 공인된 gemologist n. 보석학자

33 형용사 어휘 고르기

해석 경제적 어려움에 대응하여, Aviara 항공사는 운영 비용 관리에 상당한 변화를 줄 것이다.

해설 '운영 비용 관리에 상당한 변화를 줄 것이다'라는 문맥이므로 (D) substantial(상당한)이 정답이다. (A) chaotic은 '혼란스러운', (B) inaccessible은 '접근할 수 없는', (C) exclusive는 '독점적인, 전용의'라는 의미이다.

어휘 in response to ~에 대응하여 operational adj. 운영의 cost n. 비용 management n. 관리

34 명사 어휘 고르기

해석 만약 보험 정책에 특별히 추가되지 않는다면 주택 보험은 홍수 피해와 관련된 비용을 보장하지 않을 수도 있다.

해설 '주택 보험은 홍수 피해와 관련된 비용을 보장하지 않을 수도 있다'라는 문맥이므로 (A) expenses(비용)가 정답이다. (B) challenges는 '도전', (C) displays는 '전시', (D) reports는 '보고, 보도'라는 의미이다.

어휘 cover v. 보장하다 related to ~과 관련된 flood n. 홍수 specifically adv. 특별히, 구체적으로

35 부사 어휘 고르기

해석 행사 주최자는 공연자들이 관객에게 또렷하게 보이도록 무대 단상을 높였다.

해설 '공연자들이 관객에게 또렷하게 보이도록 무대 단상을 높였다'라는 문맥이므로 (B) clearly(또렷하게)가 정답이다. (A) tightly는 '단단히', (C) eagerly는 '간절히', (D) commonly는 '흔히, 보통'이라는 의미이다.

어휘 organizer n. 주최자 raise v. 높이다, 올리다 performer n. 공연자 visible adj. 보이는 audience n. 관객

36 동사 어휘 고르기

해석 최고경영자를 교체하기로 한 Howell사의 결정은 많은 투자자들에게 긍정적인 변화의 신호로 여겨진다.

해설 'Howell사의 결정은 많은 투자자들에게 긍정적인 변화의 신호로 여겨진다'라는 문맥이므로 (C) perceived(~라고 여기다)가 정답이다. (A) charged는 '청구하다', (B) determined는 '결정하다, 알아내다', (D) instructed는 '지시하다'라는 의미이다.

어휘 replace v. 교체하다 positive adj. 긍정적인 investor n. 투자자

37 형용사 어휘 고르기

해석 영업팀은 특정 요구사항을 이해하기 위해 잠재적 고객들과 개인화된 상담을 진행했다.

해설 '영업팀은 잠재적 고객들과 상담을 진행했다'라는 문맥이므로 (C) potential(잠재적인)이 정답이다. (A) paid는 '보수가 주어지는', (B) secure는 '안심하는, 안전한', (D) profitable은 '수익성이 있는'이라는 의미이다.

어휘 conduct v. 진행하다 personalized adj. 개인화된 consultation n. 상담 specific adj. 특정한 requirement n. 요구사항

38 부사 어휘 고르기

해석 관리자가 보통 모든 구매를 승인하지만, 50달러 이하의 물품들에는 예외가 적용될 수 있다.

해설 '관리자가 보통 모든 구매를 승인하지만, 50달러 이하의 물품들에는 예외가 적용될 수 있다'라는 문맥이므로 (C) normally(보통)가 정답이다. (A) relatively는 '비교적', (B) greatly는 '대단히, 크게', (D) patiently는 '끈기 있게, 참을성 있게'라는 의미이다.

어휘 approve v. 승인하다 exception n. 예외, 이례

39 명사 어휘 고르기

해석 보안 요원들은 공항의 버려진 저장실에서 분실된 소포를 발견했다.

해설 '저장실에서 분실된 소포를 발견했다'라는 문맥이므로 (B) packages(소포)가 정답이다. (A) worries는 '걱정, 우려', (C) locations는 '장소', (D) responsibilities는 '책임, 책무'라는 의미이다.

어휘 security personnel 보안 요원 missing adj. 분실된 abandoned adj. 버려진 storage room 저장실

40 동사 어휘 고르기

해석 그 아파트는 바닥에서 천장까지 뻗은 창문을 특별히 포함하고 있어서, 숨이 멎을 듯한 도시 전망을 제공한다.

해설 '그 아파트는 바닥에서 천장까지 뻗은 창문을 특별히 포함하고 있다'라는 문맥이므로 (A) features(특별히 포함하다)가 정답이다. (B) designs는 '설계하다', (C) sounds는 '~처럼 들리다', (D) establishes는 '설립하다'라는 의미이다.

어휘 stretch v. 뻗다 floor n. 바닥 ceiling n. 천장
breathtaking adj. 숨이 멎을 듯한

41 부사 어휘 고르기
해설 창고 직원들은 환불을 처리하고 재고 기록을 갱신하기 위해 반품된 물품을 주의 깊게 세었다.

해설 '창고 직원들은 반품된 물품을 주의 깊게 세었다'라는 문맥이므로 (B) carefully(주의 깊게)가 정답이다. (A) politely는 '공손히', (C) arguably는 '주장하건대', (D) spaciously는 '넓게, 거대하게'라는 의미이다.

어휘 warehouse n. 창고 count v. 세다 process v. 처리하다
inventory n. 재고

42 명사 어휘 고르기
해설 이사회는 제조 시설에서의 작업장 안전 기준을 개선하는 것에 대한 Ms. Russell의 헌신을 칭찬했다.

해설 '이사회는 작업장 안전 기준을 개선하는 것에 대한 Ms. Russell의 헌신을 칭찬했다'라는 문맥이므로 (C) dedication(헌신)이 정답이다. (A) adaptation은 '각색, 적응', (B) distribution은 '분배, 분포', (D) deduction은 '추론, 추정'이라는 의미이다.

어휘 board n. 이사회 praise v. 칭찬하다 facility n. 시설

43 형용사 어휘 고르기
해설 혁신적인 제품 설계는 Artisan 가구점의 최근 몇 년간 인상적인 성장에 기여했다.

해설 '혁신적인 제품 설계는 인상적인 성장에 기여했다'라는 문맥이므로 (D) impressive(인상적인)가 정답이다. (A) involved는 '관여하는, 몰두하는', (B) favorite은 '가장 좋아하는', (C) assembled는 '모인, 결집한'이라는 의미이다.

어휘 innovative adj. 혁신적인 contribute v. 기여하다 growth n. 성장

44 동사 어휘 고르기
해설 운전자들은 해외에서 렌터카를 대여하기 위해 여권과 국제 운전 면허증을 제시해야 한다.

해설 '렌터카를 대여하기 위해 여권과 국제 운전 면허증을 제시해야 한다'라는 문맥이므로 (C) lease(대여하다)가 정답이다. (A) fulfill은 '이행하다, 달성하다', (B) qualify는 '자격이 있다', (D) place는 '놓다, 설치하다'라는 의미이다.

어휘 passport n. 여권 driving permit 운전 면허증 rental car 렌터카
abroad adv. 해외에서

45 부사 어휘 고르기
해설 Ms. Alunga가 자주 가는 레스토랑은 완전히 예약되어 있어서, 그녀가 대체 식사 옵션을 선택하도록 했다.

해설 '레스토랑은 완전히 예약되어 있어서, 그녀가 대체 식사 옵션을 선택하도록 했다'라는 문맥이므로 (B) completely(완전히)가 정답이다. (A) broadly는 '대략', (C) kindly는 '친절하게', (D) annually는 '일 년에 한 번'이라는 의미이다.

어휘 frequently adv. 자주 book v. 예약하다 alternative adj. 대체

46 명사 어휘 고르기
해설 Sophus Industries사에서는, 지속 가능한 생산이 전 세계 모든 기술 센터에 걸쳐 최고 우선 사항이다.

해설 '지속 가능한 생산이 전 세계 모든 기술 센터에 걸쳐 최고 우선 사항이다'라는 문맥이므로 (B) priority(우선 사항)가 정답이다. (A) honor는 '존경, 공경', (C) revenue는 '수익, 수입', (D) position은 '위치, 일자리'라는 의미이다.

어휘 sustainable adj. 지속 가능한 across prep. ~에 걸쳐
technological adj. 기술의

47 형용사 어휘 고르기
해설 모든 신입 직원들은 회사의 핵심 윤리 가치를 이해하기 위해 의무적인 교육 프로그램을 받아야 한다.

해설 '모든 신입 직원들은 의무적인 교육 프로그램을 받아야 한다'라는 문맥이므로 (A) mandatory(의무적인)가 정답이다. (B) curious는 '호기심 있는', (C) lacking은 '결핍된', (D) strong은 '강한'이라는 의미이다.

어휘 core adj. 핵심의 ethical adj. 윤리적인 value n. 가치

48 부사 어휘 고르기
해설 그 명문 대학은 다가오는 여름 연구 프로그램에 대한 지원을 현재 받고 있다.

해설 '다가오는 여름 연구 프로그램에 대한 지원을 현재 받고 있다'라는 문맥이므로 (C) currently(현재)가 정답이다. (A) vividly는 '생생하게', (B) recently는 '최근에', (D) exactly는 '정확하게'라는 의미이다. 참고로, recently는 주로 현재완료 시제와 함께 쓰이는 점을 알아 둔다.

어휘 prestigious adj. 명문의 application n. 지원 upcoming adj. 다가오는

49 동사 어휘 고르기
해설 시의회가 최종 건축 허가를 승인하자마자 건설은 시작될 수 있다.

해설 '최종 건축 허가를 승인하자마자 건설은 시작될 수 있다'라는 문맥이므로 (D) commence(시작하다)가 정답이다. (A) originate는 '기원하다, 발생하다', (B) maximize는 '최대화하다', (C) acknowledge는 '인정하다, 승인하다'라는 의미이다.

어휘 once conj. ~하자마자 grant v. 승인하다 permit n. 허가; v. 허용하다

50 명사 어휘 고르기
해설 Mr. Kumar는 제조 공정에 인공지능을 통합하기 위한 상세한 제안서를 개발했다.

해설 '제조 공정에 인공지능을 통합하기 위한 상세한 제안서를 개발했다'라는 문맥이므로 (B) proposal(제안서)이 정답이다. (A) question은 '질문', (C) merger는 '합병', (D) line은 '조립 공정, 선'이라는 의미이다.

어휘 detailed adj. 상세한 integrate v. 통합하다 process n. 공정

51 부사 어휘 고르기
해설 현대 농업 방식은 지하수 저장을 활용하여 물 소비를 상당히 줄일 수 있다.

해설 '지하수 저장을 활용하여 물 소비를 상당히 줄일 수 있다'라는 문맥이므로 (D) considerably(상당히)가 정답이다. (A) richly(풍부하게, 후하게)도 해석상 그럴듯해 보이지만, 색깔, 맛, 향이 진하고 풍부하다는 것을 의미한다. (B) adversely는 '부정적으로', (C) previously는 '이전에'라는 의미이다.

어휘 agricultural adj. 농업의 practice n. 방식, 관행 consumption n. 소비
utilize v. 활용하다 underground water 지하수 storage n. 저장

52 동사 어휘 고르기
해설 확장된 도서관은 대학생들에게 충분한 학습 공간을 제공할 것이다.

해설 '확장된 도서관은 충분한 학습 공간을 제공할 것이다'라는 문맥이므로 (A) provide(제공하다)가 정답이다. (B) propose는 '제안하다', (C) reach는 '도달하다, 닿다', (D) accept는 '받아들이다'라는 의미이다. 참고로, provide A for B는 'B에게 A를 제공하다'라는 의미로 쓰인다는 점을 알아 둔다.

어휘 expand v. 확장하다 abundant adj. 충분한 space n. 공간

53 형용사 어휘 고르기
해설 지역 관광 명소와의 근접성과 합리적인 가격은 Elysian 호텔을 관광객들에게 이상적인 숙박시설로 만든다.

해설 '지역 관광 명소와의 근접성과 합리적인 가격은 Elysian 호텔을 이상적인 숙박시설로 만든다'라는 문맥이므로 (C) ideal(이상적인)이 정답이다. (A) abstract는 '추상적인', (B) indifferent는 '무관심한', (D) excessive는 '과도한'이라는 의미이다.

어휘 proximity n. 근접성 attraction n. 관광 명소
affordable adj. 합리적인, 감당할 수 있는 accommodation n. 숙박시설

54 명사 어휘 고르기
해설 재정 위원회는 각 부서에 예산의 일부를 배분한다.
해설 '각 부서에 예산의 일부를 배분한다'라는 문맥이므로 (C) portions(일부)가 정답이다. (A) objects는 '물건, 목표', (B) salaries는 '급여', (D) patterns는 '패턴'이라는 의미이다.

어휘 finance committee 재정 위원회 allocate v. 배분하다, 할당하다

55 동사 어휘 고르기
해설 그 소식지는 구독자들에게 매주 발송되며, 미디어 산업의 최신 동향을 요약한다.
해설 '그 소식지는 미디어 산업의 최신 동향을 요약한다'라는 문맥이므로 (D) summarizing(요약하다)이 정답이다. (A) admitting(인정하다, 시인하다)도 해석상 그럴듯해 보이지만, 무언가를 사실이라고 마지못해 인정하는 것을 나타낸다. (B) implementing은 '실행하다', (C) relieving은 '안도하게 하다, 경감하다'라는 의미이다.

어휘 newsletter n. 소식지, 회보 subscriber n. 구독자, 가입자

56 형용사 어휘 고르기
해설 장학금 지원 시스템은 너무 복잡해서 학생들을 위해 단순화될 필요가 있다.
해설 '장학금 지원 시스템은 너무 복잡해서 단순화될 필요가 있다'라는 문맥이므로 (A) complex(복잡한)가 정답이다. (B) successive는 '연속적인', (C) considerate은 '사려 깊은', (D) favorable은 '호의적인'이라는 의미이다.

어휘 scholarship n. 장학금 simplify v. 단순화하다

57 명사 어휘 고르기
해설 Seculen Digital사의 야외 보안 카메라는 어떤 날씨 조건에도 견딜 수 있도록 내구성을 고려하여 설계되었다.
해설 '야외 보안 카메라는 어떤 날씨 조건에도 견딜 수 있도록 내구성을 고려하여 설계되었다'라는 문맥이므로 (A) durability(내구성)가 정답이다. (B) enthusiasm은 '열정', (C) freshness는 '신선함', (D) proximity는 '근접성'이라는 의미이다.

어휘 outdoor adj. 야외의 security camera 보안 카메라 withstand v. 견디다 condition n. 조건

58 부사 어휘 고르기
해설 자원봉사자들은 자연재해로 영향받은 지역사회에 필수 자원을 제공하기 위해 열심히 일했다.
해설 '자원봉사자들은 지역사회에 필수 자원을 제공하기 위해 열심히 일했다'라는 문맥이므로 (D) diligently(열심히)가 정답이다. (A) completely는 '완전히', (B) extremely는 '극도로', (C) previously는 '이전에'라는 의미이다. 참고로, extremely는 동사보다는 주로 형용사나 부사를 꾸미는 점을 알아 둔다.

어휘 volunteer n. 자원봉사자; v. 자원하다 essential adj. 필수적인
resource n. 자원 natural disaster 자연재해

59 동사 어휘 고르기
해설 이사회는 후임자가 찾아질 때까지 임시 이사로서 일하도록 Mr. Salman을 임명했다.
해설 '후임자가 찾아질 때까지 임시 이사로서 일하도록 임명했다'라는 문맥이므로 (B) serve(일하다)가 정답이다. (A) hire는 '고용하다', (C) drive는 '운전하다', (D) describe는 '설명하다, 묘사하다'라는 의미이다.

어휘 appoint v. 임명하다 temporary adj. 임시의 replacement n. 후임자, 교체

60 형용사 어휘 고르기
해설 Meadowfire Grill은 수십 년의 요리 경험을 가진 주방장들이 준비한 우수한 요리를 자랑한다.
해설 '수십 년의 요리 경험을 가진 주방장들이 준비한 우수한 요리'라는 문맥이므로 (D) exceptional(우수한)이 정답이다. (A) severe는 '극심한, 심각한', (B) productive는 '생산적인', (C) estimated는 '견적의, 추측의'라는 의미이다.

어휘 boast v. 자랑하다 decade n. 10년 culinary adj. 요리의

61 부사 어휘 고르기
해설 소음 공해와 알맞은 가격의 주택의 부족은 인구 밀도가 높은 도시들의 몇 가지 문제들이다.
해설 '소음 공해와 주택의 부족은 인구 밀도가 높은 도시들의 문제들이다'라는 문맥이므로 (C) heavily(심하게, 아주 많이)가 정답이다. 참고로, heavily[densely] populated(인구 밀도가 높은)를 관용구로 알아 둔다. (A) solely는 '단독으로, 오로지', (B) evenly는 '균등하게', (D) nearly는 '거의'라는 의미이다.

어휘 noise pollution 소음 공해 affordable adj. 알맞은 가격의 housing n. 주택

62 동사 어휘 고르기
해설 모델 번호를 제공하는 것에 더하여, 환불을 요구하는 고객들은 구매 날짜를 반드시 명시해야 한다.
해설 '환불을 요구하는 고객들은 구매 날짜를 반드시 명시해야 한다'라는 문맥이므로 (C) specify(명시하다)가 정답이다. (B) propose(제시하다, 제안하다)도 해석상 그럴듯해 보이지만, 제안이나 의견 등을 제시하는 것을 의미한다. (A) accept는 '받아들이다, 수락하다', (D) insist는 '주장하다'라는 의미이다.

어휘 in addition to ~에 더하여 request v. 요구하다, 요청하다

63 형용사 어휘 고르기
해설 그 사업체가 연말까지 수익성을 향상시킬 것이라는 점이 분명해졌다.
해설 '수익성을 향상시킬 것이라는 점이 분명해졌다'라는 문맥이므로 (C) obvious(분명한)가 정답이다. (A) attractive는 '매력적인, 멋진', (B) honest는 '정직한, 솔직한', (D) inclusive는 '포함된, 포괄적인'이라는 의미이다.

어휘 profitability n. 수익성, 수익

64 명사 어휘 고르기
해설 안전 규정은 실험실에서 화학 실험을 하는 연구자들에 의해 따라져야 한다.
해설 '안전 규정은 연구자들에 의해 따라져야 한다'라는 문맥이므로 (D) regulations(규정)가 정답이다. 참고로, regulations가 명사 Safety와 함께 복합 명사 형태로 쓰여 '안전 규정'이라는 의미를 나타내고 있음을 알아 둔다. (A) ceremonies는 '의식', (B) departments는 '부서', (C) constructions는 '건설, 공사'라는 의미이다.

어휘 researcher n. 연구자 chemical adj. 화학의 laboratory n. 실험실

65 동사 어휘 고르기
해설 Ms. Wright는 서비스 팀장들과의 회의에서 반복되는 고객 불만 사항을 다룰 것이다.
해설 'Ms. Wright는 회의에서 반복되는 고객 불만 사항을 다룰 것이다'라는 문맥이므로 (A) address(다루다)가 정답이다. (B) respond(답변하다)도 해석상 그럴듯해 보이지만, 구두로 대답하거나 동작으로 반응하는 것을 의미하며, 보통 전치사 to와 함께 쓰인다. (C) function은 '기능하다', (D) complete는 '완성하다'라는 의미이다.

어휘 recurring adj. 반복되는 complaint n. 불만 사항

66 형용사 어휘 고르기

해석 기기는 기본 설명서에서 다루지 않는 고급 기능을 설명하는 보충 설명서와 함께 제공된다.

해설 '기본 설명서에서 다루지 않는 고급 기능을 설명하는 보충 설명서'라는 문맥이므로 (B) supplemental(보충의)이 정답이다. (A) eager는 '열렬한, 열망하는', (C) promising은 '유망한', (D) temporary는 '임시의'라는 의미이다.

어휘 device n. 장비 explain v. 설명하다 advanced adj. 고급의
feature n. 기능 cover v. 다루다

67 부사 어휘 고르기

해석 직원 안내서는 연장된 휴가를 요청하는 과정을 구체적으로 설명한다.

해설 '직원 안내서는 과정을 구체적으로 설명한다'라는 문맥이므로 (C) specifically(구체적으로)가 정답이다. (A) consequently는 '그 결과, 따라서', (B) immediately는 '즉시', (D) accidentally는 '우연히'라는 의미이다.

어휘 manual n. 안내서 extended adj. 연장된 leave of absence 휴가

68 명사 어휘 고르기

해석 지역 예술가들은 미술 박람회가 있는 주말을 더 많은 그림을 판매할 수 있는 기회로 활용할 수 있다.

해설 '미술 박람회가 있는 주말을 더 많은 그림을 판매할 수 있는 기회로 활용하다'라는 문맥이므로 (D) opportunity(기회)가 정답이다. (A) candidate는 '후보자, 지원자', (B) preference는 '선호', (C) impression은 '인상'이라는 의미이다.

어휘 take advantage of ~을 활용하다

69 동사 어휘 고르기

해석 수개월간의 협상 후, Alpha Core Systems사는 9억 7,500만 달러에 Digency Networks사를 인수했다.

해설 'Alpha Core Systems사는 9억 7,500만 달러에 Digency Networks사를 인수했다'라는 문맥이므로 (B) acquired(인수하다)가 정답이다. (C) achieved(얻다, 이루다)도 해석상 그럴듯해 보이지만, 명성을 얻거나 일, 목적 등을 이루는 것을 의미한다. (A) divided는 '나누다', (D) reacted는 '반응하다'라는 의미이다.

어휘 negotiation n. 협상

70 부사 어휘 고르기

해석 배송 회사들은 투명한 소포 추적을 위해 고객들에게 추적 정보를 직접 보내야 한다.

해설 '투명한 소포 추적을 위해 고객들에게 추적 정보를 직접 보내다'라는 문맥이므로 (C) directly(직접)가 정답이다. (A) distinctly는 '또렷하게, 분명하게', (B) basically는 '기본적으로', (D) reasonably는 '합리적으로'라는 의미이다. 참고로, distinctly는 발음, 소리, 기억 등이 또렷하고 분명하다는 것을 나타내는 점을 알아 둔다.

어휘 shipping company 배송 회사 tracking information 추적 정보
transparent adj. 투명한 monitoring n. 추적

71 부사 어휘 고르기

해석 수년간 인쇄본 책을 출판한 후, Inkspire 출판사는 디지털 형식으로 완전히 전환할 계획이다.

해설 '수년간 인쇄본 책을 출판한 후, 디지털 형식으로 완전히 전환할 계획이다'라는 문맥이므로 (A) entirely(완전히)가 정답이다. (B) famously는 '유명하게', (C) commonly는 '일반적으로', (D) internationally는 '국제적으로'라는 의미이다.

어휘 print book 인쇄본 책 shift v. 전환하다

72 형용사 어휘 고르기

해석 Mr. Thorne은 잠재적 이점들에 관해 설득력 있는 주장을 함으로써 그의 전략을 채택하도록 위원회를 납득시켰다.

해설 'Mr. Thorne은 설득력 있는 주장을 함으로써 위원회를 납득시켰다'라는 문맥이므로 (B) compelling(설득력 있는)이 정답이다. (D) talented(재능 있는)도 해석상 그럴듯해 보이지만, 주로 사람을 대상으로 꾸미기 때문에 답이 될 수 없다. (A) fortunate은 '운 좋은', (C) reputable은 '평판이 좋은'이라는 의미이다.

어휘 convince v. 납득시키다, 확신시키다 adopt v. 채택하다
argument n. 주장, 논점 potential adj. 잠재적인, 가능성이 있는

73 동사 어휘 고르기

해석 발표를 할 때, 연구원들은 주제에 대한 철저한 이해를 보여주어야 한다.

해설 '발표를 할 때, 연구원들은 철저한 이해를 보여주어야 한다'라는 문맥이므로 (B) demonstrate(보여주다)가 정답이다. (A) arrange는 '준비하다, 배치하다', (C) initiate는 '시작하다', (D) substitute는 '대체하다'라는 의미이다.

어휘 presentation n. 발표 thorough adj. 철저한 subject matter 주제

74 형용사 어휘 고르기

해석 면접은 지원자들이 자격과 경력을 충분히 표현할 수 있는 충분한 시간을 허용해야 한다.

해설 '지원자들이 자격과 경력을 충분히 표현할 수 있는 충분한 시간'이라는 문맥이므로 (B) adequate(충분한)이 정답이다. (A) constant는 '지속적인', (C) receptive는 '수용적인', (D) perpetual은 '영원한'이라는 의미이다.

어휘 allow v. 허용하다 candidate n. 지원자 fully adv. 충분히, 완전히
express v. 표현하다 qualification n. 자격

75 명사 어휘 고르기

해석 Biblio 서점은 최근 출시된 전자책 컬렉션의 판매를 장려하기 위해 온라인 홍보를 시작했다.

해설 '최근 출시된 전자책 컬렉션의 판매를 장려하기 위해 온라인 홍보를 시작했다'라는 문맥이므로 (D) promotion(홍보)이 정답이다. (A) contact는 '연락처', (B) information은 '정보', (C) volume은 '용량, 권'이라는 의미이다.

어휘 encourage v. 장려하다 launch v. 출시하다

76 부사 어휘 고르기

해석 프리랜서 작가들은 직접적인 편집 감독 없이 독립적으로 일하기 위한 강력한 기술이 필요하다.

해설 '프리랜서 작가들은 직접적인 편집 감독 없이 독립적으로 일하기 위한 기술이 필요하다'라는 문맥이므로 (D) independently(독립적으로)가 정답이다. (A) shortly는 '곧, 잠깐', (B) particularly는 '특히', (C) certainly는 '확실히'라는 의미이다.

어휘 immediate adj. 직접적인 editorial adj. 편집의 supervision n. 감독

77 명사 어휘 고르기

해석 앱 개발자들은 다음 업데이트를 출시하기 전에 사용자 의견을 적극적으로 구하고 있다.

해설 '앱 개발자들은 사용자 의견을 적극적으로 구하고 있다'라는 문맥이므로 (A) feedback(의견)이 정답이다. (B) access는 '접근', (C) conclusion은 '결론', (D) quality는 '품질'이라는 의미이다.

어휘 actively adv. 적극적으로 seek v. 구하다 release v. 출시하다

78 부사 어휘 고르기

해석 로켓 발사는 임무 통제관들이 모든 순간을 모니터링하는 상태로, 정확히 오후 2시 37분에 예정되어 있다.

해설 '로켓 발사는 정확히 오후 2시 37분에 예정되어 있다'라는 문맥이므로 (C) precisely(정확히)가 정답이다. (A) infinitely는 '무한히', (B) hourly는 '매시간', (D) absently는 '멍하니, 무심코'라는 의미이다.

어휘 launch n. 발사 controller n. 통제관

79 형용사 어휘 고르기
해석 미술관은 유명 작품에 대한 지속적인 접근을 제공하기 위해 종종 유명 예술가의 영구적인 전시를 유지한다.
해설 '미술관은 종종 유명 예술가의 영구적인 전시를 유지한다'라는 문맥이므로 (D) permanent(영구적인)가 정답이다. (A) complex는 '복잡한', (B) succinct는 '간결한', (C) hesitant는 '주저하는'이라는 의미이다.
어휘 exhibition n. 전시 renowned adj. 유명한 consistent adj. 지속적인 access n. 접근

80 동사 어휘 고르기
해석 관광 도시의 시장으로서, Mr. Venturi는 주민들과 방문객들의 요구 사이에서 균형을 맞춰야 한다.
해설 '주민들과 방문객들의 요구 사이에서 균형을 맞춰야 한다'라는 의미가 되어야 하므로 (A) balance(균형을 맞추다)가 정답이다. (B) waive는 '포기하다', (C) overcome은 '극복하다', (D) expose는 '노출하다, 드러내다'라는 의미이다.
어휘 mayor n. 시장 need n. 요구, 필요 local n. 주민, 거주자; adj. 지역의

81 형용사 어휘 고르기
해석 Astralis Technologies사는 다른 어떤 회사도 성공적으로 모방할 수 없는 독특한 사이버보안 솔루션을 개발했다.
해설 '다른 어떤 회사도 성공적으로 모방할 수 없는 독특한 사이버보안 솔루션'이라는 문맥이므로 (C) distinct(독특한)가 정답이다. (A) chronic은 '만성적인', (B) cautious는 '신중한', (D) determined는 '결심한, 단호한'이라는 의미이다.
어휘 cybersecurity solution 사이버보안 솔루션 successfully adv. 성공적으로 imitate v. 모방하다

82 명사 어휘 고르기
해석 도시의 물 보존 계획은 2년 이내에 주거용 물 소비를 30퍼센트 줄이는 것을 목표로 한다.
해설 '물 보존 계획은 주거용 물 소비를 30퍼센트 줄이는 것을 목표로 한다'라는 문맥이므로 (C) initiative(계획)가 정답이다. (A) permission은 '허가', (B) alternative는 '대안', (D) allocation은 '할당'이라는 의미이다.
어휘 conservation n. 보존 aim v. 목표로 하다 residential adj. 주거용의 consumption n. 소비 within prep. ~ 이내에

83 부사 어휘 고르기
해석 온라인 뱅킹 서비스는 중요한 시스템 유지보수 및 보안 업데이트 때문에 일시적으로 중단될 것이다.
해설 '온라인 뱅킹 서비스는 일시적으로 중단될 것이다'라는 문맥이므로 (D) temporarily(일시적으로)가 정답이다. (A) greatly는 '크게', (B) carelessly는 '부주의하게', (C) fairly는 '꽤, 공정하게'라는 의미이다.
어휘 shut down 중단되다 critical adj. 중요한

84 동사 어휘 고르기
해석 기업가들이 소규모 사업을 시작하도록 장려될 수 있게 시의회는 상업 지구를 확대하는 것에 찬성한다.
해설 '소규모 사업을 시작하도록 장려될 수 있게 상업 지구를 확대하는 것에 찬성한다'라는 문맥이므로 (B) enlarging(확대하다)이 정답이다. (A) enveloping은 '동봉하다', (C) relieving은 '줄이다, 경감하다', (D) constraining은 '제한하다'라는 의미이다.
어휘 city council 시의회 favor v. 찬성하다 entrepreneur n. 기업가 encourage v. 장려하다

DAY 09 최신 빈출 어구

HACKERS TEST p.198

01 (C)	02 (B)	03 (B)	04 (C)	05 (A)
06 (D)	07 (C)	08 (B)	09 (A)	10 (D)
11 (D)	12 (C)	13 (B)	14 (A)	15 (B)
16 (C)	17 (D)	18 (A)	19 (C)	20 (B)
21 (D)	22 (C)	23 (B)	24 (A)	25 (D)
26 (C)	27 (A)	28 (B)		

01 동사 관련 어구 완성하기
해석 작업장 안전을 유지하기 위해 중장비를 작동할 때 지시를 주의 깊게 따르세요.
해설 '중장비를 작동할 때 지시를 주의 깊게 따르다'라는 문맥이므로 빈칸 뒤의 instructions와 함께 '지시를 따르다'라는 의미의 어구인 follow instructions를 만드는 (C) Follow(따르다)가 정답이다. (A) Act(행동하다), (B) Chase(추적하다), (D) Succeed(성공하다)는 '지시를 따르다'라는 의미의 어구를 만들 수 없다.
어휘 carefully adv. 주의 깊게 operate v. 작동하다 heavy machinery 중장비 maintain v. 유지하다

02 형용사 관련 어구 완성하기
해석 그 섬나라의 경제는 주로 관광업에 의존한다.
해설 '경제는 관광업에 의존한다'라는 문맥이므로 빈칸 뒤의 on과 함께 '~에 의존하다'라는 의미의 어구인 be dependent on을 만드는 (B) dependent(의존하는, 의지하는)가 정답이다. (A) exclusive(독점적인, 배타적인)도 해석상 그럴듯해 보이지만, 전치사 to와 함께 쓰여야 한다. (C) necessary(필수의, 필요한), (D) interested(관심이 있는)는 '~에 의존하다'라는 의미의 어구를 만들 수 없다.
어휘 tourism n. 관광업

03 명사 관련 어구 완성하기
해석 구직자들은 자신의 이력서에 정확한 연락처가 포함되어 있는지 확실하게 해야 한다.
해설 '정확한 연락처'라는 문맥이므로 빈칸 앞의 contact와 함께 '연락처'라는 의미의 어구인 contact information을 만드는 (B) information(정보)이 정답이다. (A) delivery(배송), (C) organization(기구, 단체), (D) emergency(비상)는 '연락처'라는 의미의 어구를 만들 수 없다.
어휘 job applicant 구직자 make sure ~을 확실하게 하다 contain v. 포함하다 accurate adj. 정확한

04 부사 관련 어구 완성하기
해석 경제 침체 기간 동안, 거의 모든 산업이 상당한 재정적 어려움을 겪었다.
해설 '거의 모든 산업이 재정적 어려움을 겪었다'라는 문맥이므로 빈칸 뒤의 all과 함께 '거의 모든'이라는 의미의 어구인 nearly all을 만드는 (C) nearly(거의)가 정답이다. (A) firmly(단호히, 확고히), (B) readily(기꺼이), (D) proudly(자랑스럽게)는 '거의 모든'이라는 의미의 어구를 만들 수 없다.
어휘 economic recession 경제 침체 substantial adj. 상당한 financial adj. 재정적인 challenge n. 어려움

05 동사 관련 어구 완성하기
해석 내일 있을 시험을 준비하고자 하는 학생들은 교과서의 챕터 9를 참고해야 한다.
해설 '학생들은 교과서를 참고해야 한다'라는 문맥이므로 빈칸 뒤의 to와 함께 '~을 참고하다'라는 의미의 어구인 refer to를 만드는 (A) refer(참고하

다)가 정답이다. (B) apply(지원하다, 적용하다), (C) regard(~으로 여기다, 간주하다), (D) assign(배정하다, 맡기다)은 '~을 참고하다'라는 의미의 어구를 만들 수 없다.

06 형용사 관련 어구 완성하기

해석 사진 워크숍을 듣는 것에 관심이 있는 사람들은 반드시 전문 카메라를 가져올 필요는 없다.

해설 '워크숍을 듣는 것에 관심이 있는 사람들'이라는 문맥이므로 빈칸 뒤의 in과 함께 '~에 관심이 있다'라는 의미의 어구인 be interested in을 만드는 (D) interested(관심이 있는)가 정답이다. (C) connected(관련이 있는)도 해석상 그럴듯해 보이지만, 전치사 to와 함께 쓰여야 한다. (A) skilled(숙련된, 노련한), (B) concerned(걱정하는, 염려하는)는 '~에 관심이 있다'라는 의미의 어구를 만들 수 없다.

어휘 necessarily adv. 반드시 professional adj. 전문의

07 명사 관련 어구 완성하기

해석 기업 투자자들은 회사의 성장 잠재력을 평가하기 위해 매출액을 주의 깊게 분석했다.

해설 '매출액을 주의 깊게 분석했다'라는 문맥이므로 빈칸 앞의 sales와 함께 '매출액'이라는 의미의 어구인 sales figures를 만드는 (C) figures(수치, 통계)가 정답이다. (A) grounds(근거), (B) turnouts(참석자 수), (D) viewpoints(관점)는 '매출액'이라는 의미의 어구를 만들 수 없다.

어휘 corporate adj. 기업의 investor n. 투자자 attentively adv. 주의 깊게
analyze v. 분석하다 evaluate v. 평가하다
potential n. 잠재력; adj. 잠재적인

08 부사 관련 어구 완성하기

해석 그 의료 센터는 편리한 위치에 있어서, 주변 시골 지역 환자들에게 쉬운 접근성을 제공한다.

해설 '그 의료 센터는 편리한 위치에 있어서 쉬운 접근성을 제공한다'라는 문맥이므로 빈칸 뒤의 located와 함께 '편리한 위치에 있는'이라는 의미의 어구인 conveniently located를 만드는 (B) conveniently(편리하게)가 정답이다. (A) collectively(집단적으로), (C) cordially(다정하게, 진심으로), (D) considerably(상당히)는 '편리한 위치에 있는'이라는 의미의 어구를 만들 수 없다.

어휘 medical center 의료 센터 access n. 접근성 patient n. 환자
surrounding adj. 주변의 rural adj. 시골의

09 동사 관련 어구 완성하기

해석 건설 회사들은 작업자 안전 및 장비 표준에 관한 규정을 지켜야 한다.

해설 '작업자 안전 및 장비 표준에 관한 규정을 지키다'라는 문맥이므로 빈칸 뒤의 with와 함께 '~을 지키다'라는 의미의 어구인 comply with를 만드는 (A) comply(지키다, 준수하다)가 정답이다. (B) mention(언급하다), (C) suggest(제안하다), (D) compare(비교하다)는 '~을 지키다'라는 의미의 어구를 만들 수 없다.

어휘 construction firm 건설 회사 regulation n. 규정
regarding prep. ~에 관한 equipment n. 장비 standard n. 표준, 기준

10 명사 관련 어구 완성하기

해석 온라인 음악 레슨은 최소 나이 제한이 없어서, 열정적인 학습자들은 언제든 시작할 수 있다.

해설 '최소 나이 제한이 없어서 학습자들은 언제든 시작할 수 있다'라는 문맥이므로 빈칸 앞의 age와 함께 '나이 제한'이라는 의미의 어구인 age requirement를 만드는 (D) requirement(필요조건)가 정답이다. (A) desire(욕구), (B) contribution(기여), (C) impact(영향)는 '나이 제한'이라는 의미의 어구를 만들 수 없다.

어휘 minimum adj. 최소한의 virtual adj. 온라인상의, 가상의
passionate adj. 열정적인

11 형용사 관련 어구 완성하기

해석 험한 날씨 때문에 항공편이 취소되어서, 승객들은 출발하기 위해 6시간을 기다렸다.

해설 '험한 날씨 때문에 항공편이 취소되었다'라는 문맥이므로 빈칸 뒤의 weather와 함께 '험한 날씨'라는 의미의 어구인 severe weather를 만드는 (D) severe(험한, 심각한)가 정답이다. (A) immense(엄청난, 거대한)도 해석상 그럴듯해 보이지만, 수, 양, 크기가 엄청난 것을 의미한다. (B) striking(눈에 띄는, 치는)도 해석상 그럴듯해 보이지만, 시선을 끄는 방식에 있어서 특이하거나 정도가 심한 것을 의미한다. (C) nervous(초조한)는 '험한 날씨'라는 의미의 어구를 만들 수 없다.

어휘 flight n. 항공편 passenger n. 승객 depart v. 출발하다

12 명사 관련 어구 완성하기

해석 대출 담당 직원은 은행의 단골 고객들과의 견고한 관계를 발전시켰다.

해설 '단골 고객들과의 견고한 관계를 발전시켰다'라는 문맥이므로 빈칸 앞의 strong과 빈칸 뒤의 with와 함께 '~과의 견고한 관계'라는 의미의 어구인 strong connection with를 만드는 (C) connection(관계)이 정답이다. (D) agreement(동의)도 해석상 그럴듯해 보이지만, agreement는 주로 conclude(체결하다, 끝내다), reach(이르다, 도달하다) 등의 동사와 함께 쓰인다. (A) conversion(전환), (B) knowledge(지식)는 '~과의 견고한 관계'라는 의미의 어구를 만들 수 없다.

어휘 loan officer 대출 담당 직원 regular client 단골 고객

13 동사 관련 어구 완성하기

해석 Mr. Takahashi는 그의 구식 스마트폰을 고해상도 화면을 갖춘 새로운 모델로 교체했다.

해설 '구식 스마트폰을 새로운 모델로 교체했다'라는 문맥이므로 빈칸 뒤의 with와 함께 'A를 B로 교체하다'라는 의미의 어구인 replace A with B를 만드는 (B) replaced(교체하다)가 정답이다. (A) purchased(구매하다), (C) questioned(질문하다, 의문을 제기하다), (D) publicized(알리다, 홍보하다)는 'A를 B로 교체하다'라는 의미의 어구를 만들 수 없다.

어휘 outdated adj. 구식의 feature v. ~을 갖추다, ~을 특징으로 하다
high-resolution adj. 고해상도의

14 형용사 관련 어구 완성하기

해석 그 소프트웨어는 일상 업무를 자동화할 수 있어서, 직원들이 더 복잡한 전략적 계획에 집중할 수 있게 한다.

해설 '소프트웨어는 일상 업무를 자동화할 수 있다'라는 문맥이므로 빈칸 뒤의 tasks와 함께 '일상 업무'라는 의미의 어구인 routine task를 만드는 (A) routine(일상적인, 반복적인)이 정답이다. (B) tight(단단한, 긴밀한), (C) neutral(중립적인), (D) genuine(진정한)은 '일상 업무'라는 의미의 어구를 만들 수 없다.

어휘 automate v. 자동화하다 focus on ~에 집중하다 complicated adj. 복잡한

15 부사 관련 어구 완성하기

해석 방문객들은 불필요한 주차 위반 벌금을 피하기 위해 지정된 장소에 차를 주차해야 한다.

해설 '지정된 장소에 차를 주차해야 한다'라는 문맥이므로 빈칸 뒤의 area와 함께 '지정된 장소'라는 의미의 어구인 designated area를 만드는 (B) designated(지정된)가 정답이다. (A) ongoing(진행 중인), (C) objective(객관적인), (D) advanced(고급의)는 '지정된 장소'라는 의미의 어구를 만들 수 없다.

어휘 visitor n. 방문객 avoid v. 피하다 unnecessary adj. 불필요한
parking fine 주차 위반 벌금

16 명사 관련 어구 완성하기

해석 역사적 건물들은 노후한 재료로 인해 구조적 유지보수 문제가 생기는 경향이 있다.

해설 '역사적 건물들은 구조적 유지보수 문제가 생기는 경향이 있다'라

는 문맥이므로 빈칸 뒤의 to와 함께 '~하는 경향'이라는 의미의 어구인 a tendency to를 만드는 (C) tendency(경향)가 정답이다. (D) movement(움직임)도 해석상 그럴듯해 보이지만, 주로 물리적 이동이나 사회적 변화를 의미한다. (A) trend(유행, 동향), (B) location(위치)은 '~하는 경향'이라는 의미의 어구를 만들 수 없다.

어휘 structural adj. 구조적인 maintenance n. 유지보수 due to ~로 인해
aging adj. 노후한 material n. 재료

17 형용사 관련 어구 완성하기

해석 Fable & Leaf 제과점은 고급 재료 조달을 위해 현지 유기농 농장과의 동업을 발표하게 되어 기쁘다.

해설 '동업을 발표하게 되어 기쁘다'라는 문맥이므로 빈칸 뒤의 to와 함께 '~해서 기쁘다'라는 의미의 어구인 be pleased to를 만드는 (D) pleased(기쁜)가 정답이다. (A) successive(연속적인), (B) necessary(필요한), (C) attached(붙어 있는)는 '~해서 기쁘다'라는 의미의 어구를 만들 수 없다.

어휘 announce v. 발표하다 partnership n. 동업, 제휴 local adj. 현지의
premium adj. 고급의 ingredient n. 재료 sourcing n. 조달

18 동사 관련 어구 완성하기

해석 환경에 대한 우려가 커지면서, 많은 기구들은 정부가 더 엄격한 규제를 시행하도록 촉구하고 있다.

해설 '많은 기구들은 정부가 더 엄격한 규제를 시행하도록 촉구하고 있다'라는 문맥이므로 빈칸 뒤의 to와 함께 'A가 B하도록 촉구하다'라는 의미의 어구인 urge A to B를 만드는 (A) urging(촉구하다)이 정답이다. (B) reciting(암송하다), (C) opting(선택하다), (D) addressing(다루다)은 'A가 B하도록 촉구하다'라는 의미의 어구를 만들 수 없다.

어휘 concern n. 우려 government n. 정부 implement v. 시행하다
strict adj. 엄격한

19 부사 관련 어구 완성하기

해석 주요 제조 공장이 지난달 폐쇄된 후에 그 지역의 일자리 수는 급격하게 떨어졌다.

해설 '일자리 수는 급격하게 떨어졌다'라는 문맥이므로 빈칸 앞의 fell과 함께 '급격하게 떨어지다'라는 의미의 어구인 fall sharply를 만드는 (C) sharply(급격하게, 크게)가 정답이다. (A) precisely(정확하게), (B) almost(거의), (D) seldom(거의 ~않는)은 '급격하게 떨어지다'라는 의미의 어구를 만들 수 없다. 참고로, almost와 seldom은 주로 일반동사의 앞에서 쓰이는 점을 알아 둔다.

어휘 region n. 지역 major adj. 주요의 manufacturing plant 제조 공장

20 동사 관련 어구 완성하기

해석 다음 영업일 배송을 보장하기 위해 오후 9시까지 주문되어야 한다.

해설 '오후 9시까지 주문되어야 한다'라는 문맥이므로 빈칸 앞의 Orders와 함께 '주문하다'라는 의미의 어구인 place an order를 만드는 (B) placed(주문하다)가 정답이다. 참고로, Orders가 주어가 되면서 수동태 동사 be placed가 쓰였다. (A) carried(운반하다), (C) estimated(추정하다), (D) distributed(배포하다)는 '주문하다'라는 의미의 어구를 만들 수 없다.

어휘 guarantee v. 보장하다 business day 영업일

21 명사 관련 어구 완성하기

해석 관리자가 알고 있는 바로는, 모든 중요한 재무 보고서가 제때 처리되고 제출되었다.

해설 '관리자가 알고 있는 바로는'이라는 문맥이므로 빈칸 앞의 To our manager's와 함께 '~가 알고 있는 바로는'이라는 의미의 어구인 to one's knowledge를 만드는 (D) knowledge(지식, 인식)가 정답이다. (A) ability(능력), (B) influence(영향력), (C) potential(잠재성)은 '~가 알고 있는 바로는'이라는 의미의 어구를 만들 수 없다.

어휘 financial adj. 재무의 process v. 처리하다 submit v. 제출하다
on time 제때

22 형용사 관련 어구 완성하기

해석 참가자들은 계속 상을 탈 자격이 있기 위해 항상 대회의 규칙을 준수해야 한다.

해설 '계속 상을 탈 자격이 있기 위해 대회의 규칙을 준수해야 한다'라는 문맥이므로 빈칸 뒤의 to win과 함께 '~할 자격이 있다'라는 의미의 어구인 be eligible to do를 만드는 (C) eligible(자격이 있는)이 정답이다. (A) compatible(양립될 수 있는), (B) responsive(즉각 반응하는), (D) privileged(특권을 가진)는 '~할 자격이 있다'라는 의미의 어구를 만들 수 없다.

어휘 participant n. 참가자 observe v. (법률·규칙 등을) 준수하다, 관찰하다
remain v. 계속 ~이다

23 부사 관련 어구 완성하기

해석 3월 10일 자로, 상업지구 중심부에 위치한 우리의 새로운 싱가포르 지사는 공식적으로 문을 연다.

해설 '새로운 지사는 공식적으로 문을 연다'라는 문맥이므로 빈칸 뒤의 open과 함께 '공식적으로 문을 연'이라는 의미의 어구인 officially open을 만드는 (B) officially(공식적으로)가 정답이다. (A) usually(보통), (C) extremely(극도로), (D) accurately(정확하게)는 '공식적으로 문을 연'이라는 의미의 어구를 만들 수 없다.

어휘 as of ~일자로 branch n. 지사 heart n. 중심부 district n. 지구, 구역

24 명사 관련 어구 완성하기

해석 Ms. Marino는 모든 부서 관리자에 대한 종합적인 성과 검토를 해마다 수행한다.

해설 '종합적인 성과 검토를 해마다 수행한다'라는 문맥이므로 빈칸 앞의 on an annual과 함께 '해마다'라는 의미의 어구인 on an annual basis를 만드는 (A) basis(기준, 근거)가 정답이다. (B) topic(주제), (C) period(기간), (D) position(위치)은 '해마다'라는 의미의 어구를 만들 수 없다.

어휘 comprehensive adj. 종합적인

25 동사 관련 어구 완성하기

해석 *Proseport*를 구독하는 독자들은 현대 작가들과의 독점 인터뷰에 대한 접근권을 얻을 수 있다.

해설 '*Proseport*를 구독하는 독자'라는 문맥이므로 빈칸 뒤의 to와 함께 '~을 구독하다'라는 의미의 어구인 subscribe to를 만드는 (D) subscribe(구독하다)가 정답이다. (B) receive(받다)도 해석상 그럴듯해 보이지만, 타동사이므로 전치사 없이 바로 뒤에 목적어가 와야 한다. (A) notify(알리다), (C) describe(설명하다)는 '~을 구독하다'라는 의미의 어구를 만들 수 없다.

어휘 gain v. 얻다 exclusive adj. 독점적인 contemporary adj. 현대의

26 명사 관련 어구 완성하기

해석 복잡한 법적 문서를 이해하기 위해, 그 변호사는 계약서 전부를 꼼꼼하게 읽었다.

해설 '계약서 전부를 꼼꼼하게 읽었다'라는 문맥이므로 빈칸 앞의 in its와 함께 '전부'라는 의미의 어구인 in its entirety를 만드는 (C) entirety(전체)가 정답이다. (A) pattern(패턴), (B) supervision(감독), (D) transparency(투명성)는 '전부'라는 의미의 어구를 만들 수 없다.

어휘 complex adj. 복잡한 legal adj. 법적인 meticulously adv. 꼼꼼하게
contract n. 계약서

27 부사 관련 어구 완성하기

해석 박물관 전시관으로 외부 음식을 가져오는 것은 잠재적 손상을 방지하기 위해 엄격히 금지된다.

해설 '박물관 전시관으로 외부 음식을 가져오는 것은 엄격히 금지된다'라는 문맥이므로 빈칸 뒤의 prohibited와 함께 '엄격히 금지된'이라는 의미의

어구인 strictly prohibited를 만드는 (A) strictly(엄격히)가 정답이다. (B) severely(심하게)도 해석상 그럴듯해 보이지만, 행위나 상황의 강도를 나타낸다. (C) closely(면밀히, 밀접하게), (D) importantly(중요하게)는 '엄격히 금지된'이라는 의미의 어구를 만들 수 없다.

어휘 **exhibition hall** 전시관   **prevent** v. 방지하다   **damage** n. 손상

28 형용사 관련 어구 완성하기

해석 국제 학생들의 비자 신청은 이민 당국의 검토와 철저한 확인의 대상이다.

해설 '비자 신청은 검토와 철저한 확인의 대상이다'라는 문맥이므로 빈칸 뒤의 to와 함께 '~의 대상이다'라는 의미의 어구인 be subject to를 만드는 (B) subject(~될 수 있는)가 정답이다. (A) ideal(이상적인), (C) required(필수의), (D) additional(추가의)은 '~의 대상이다'라는 의미의 어구를 만들 수 없다. 참고로, be required to(~하도록 요구받다)도 자주 쓰이는 표현이지만, to 뒤에 동사원형이 오는 점을 알아 둔다.

어휘 **application** n. 신청   **international** adj. 국제적인   **thorough** adj. 철저한   **verification** n. 확인   **immigration authority** 이민 당국

PART 6

DAY 10 문맥 파악 문제: 문법

Example p.205
01번은 다음 이메일에 관한 문제입니다.

Mr. Winkle께,
TG 지하철은 귀하가 3월 14일에 겪었던 불편에 대해 사과드리고 싶습니다. 저희는 아주 짧은 지연조차도 바쁜 일정을 충분히 틀어지게 만들 수 있다는 점을 이해합니다. 저희의 목표는 승객들이 항상 제시간에 목적지에 도착하도록 하는 것임을 보장드립니다. 유감스럽게도, 이번 경우에는, 나뭇가지가 저희의 노선들 중 하나에 떨어졌고, 이는 지연을 일으켰습니다. 저희는 이 사건에 대해 유감스럽게 생각하며, 승객 만족도를 개선하기 위해 노력할 것입니다.

apologize v. 사과하다 delay n. 지연; v. 지연시키다, 미루다
upset v. (계획·상황 등을) 틀어지게 만들다 assure v. 보장하다, 확신하다
passenger n. 승객 destination n. 목적지, 도착지 on time 제시간에
regret v. 유감스럽게 생각하다, 후회하다 incident n. 사건

토익실전문제 p.205

| 01 (C) | 02 (C) | 03 (A) | 04 (D) |

01-04번은 다음 회람에 관한 문제입니다.

수신: 전 직원
발신: Olivia Cabral, 사무장
제목: 사진작가 방문
날짜: 8월 26일

⁰¹지난주에 안내해 드린 바와 같이, 사진작가가 8월 30일에 우리 사무실을 방문할 것입니다. 그는 고품질 사진을 보장하기 위해 전문 장비를 가져올 것입니다. ⁰²이번 촬영 시간 동안 모든 직원들은 사진을 촬영해야 합니다. 이날 촬영된 사진들은 우리의 온라인 직원 주소 성명록에 있는 오래된 사진들을 대체할 것입니다. 그것들은 또한 필요에 따라 보도 자료와 다른 회사 자료들에 사용될 것입니다. ⁰³그러므로, 이때를 위해 여러분은 격식을 차린 정장을 입어야 합니다. 여러분은 오전 9시부터 오후 2시 사이에 언제든 사진을 찍으실 수 있습니다. ⁰⁴이것은 주 회의실에서 이루어질 것입니다. 그것은 한 사람당 10분이 채 걸리지 않을 것으로 예상됩니다.

directory n. 주소 성명록, (이름 등이 나열된) 안내 책자
press release 보도 자료, 공식 발표 corporate adj. 회사의, 기업의
as needed 필요에 따라 formal adj. 격식을 차린, 공식적인
business clothes 정장 occasion n. (어떠한 일이 일어나는) 때, 경우

01 올바른 시제의 동사 채우기 주변 문맥 파악
해설 문장에 주어(a photographer)만 있고 동사가 없으므로 동사 (A), (B), (D)가 정답의 후보이다. 빈칸이 있는 문장만으로 정답을 고를 수 없으므로 주변 문맥이나 전체 문맥을 파악한다. 뒤 문장에서 미래 시제(will bring)를 사용해서 그가 고품질 사진을 보장하기 위해 전문 장비를 가져올 것이라고 했으므로, 사진작가가 방문하는 시점이 미래임을 알 수 있다. 따라서 미래 시제 (C) will visit가 정답이다.

02 명사 어휘 고르기 주변 문맥 파악
해설 '모든 ___은 사진을 촬영해야 한다'라는 문장이므로 모든 보기가 정답의 후보이다. 빈칸이 있는 문장만으로 정답을 고를 수 없으므로 주변 문맥이나 전체 문맥을 파악한다. 뒤 문장에서 이날 촬영된 사진들은 온라인 직원 주소 성명록에 있는 오래된 사진들을 대체할 것이라고 했으므로 직원들이 사진을 촬영해야 한다는 것을 알 수 있다. 따라서 (C) employees (직원들)가 정답이다. (A) neighbors는 '이웃', (B) clients는 '고객', (D) applicants는 '지원자'라는 의미이다.

03 접속부사 채우기 주변 문맥 파악
해설 빈칸이 콤마와 함께 문장의 맨 앞에 온 접속부사 자리이므로, 앞 문장과 빈칸이 있는 문장의 의미 관계를 파악하여 정답을 선택한다. 앞 문장에서 그것들, 즉 이날 촬영된 사진들은 필요에 따라 보도 자료들과 다른 회사 자료들에 사용될 것이라고 했고, 빈칸이 있는 문장에서는 이때를 위해 직원들은 격식을 차린 정장을 입어야 한다고 했으므로, 원인에 대한 결과를 나타낼 때 사용되는 (A) Therefore(그러므로)가 정답이다.
어휘 in contrast 그와 대조적으로 regardless adv. 그럼에도 불구하고
similarly adv. 비슷하게, 유사하게

04 알맞은 문장 고르기
해석 (A) 여러분은 여러분의 일정에 맞는 날을 선택할 수 있습니다.
(B) 또 다른 예시는 우리의 직원 신분 확인 명찰입니다.
(C) 사진작가는 그때 시간이 안 될 것입니다.
(D) 이것은 주 회의실에서 이루어질 것입니다.
해설 앞 문장 'You may have your picture taken anytime between 9 A.M. and 2 P.M.'에서 오전 9시부터 오후 2시 사이에 언제든 사진을 찍을 수 있다고 하며 사진 촬영 시간에 관해 설명했으므로, 빈칸에는 사진 촬영에 대한 추가적인 정보, 즉 사진 촬영이 이루어질 장소에 관한 내용이 들어가야 함을 알 수 있다. 따라서 (D)가 정답이다.
어휘 suit v. 맞다, 어울리다 identification badge 신분 확인 명찰

HACKERS TEST p.206

01 (A)	02 (C)	03 (B)	04 (B)	05 (C)
06 (D)	07 (C)	08 (A)	09 (C)	10 (C)
11 (C)	12 (A)	13 (D)	14 (A)	15 (B)
16 (C)				

01-04번은 다음 이메일에 관한 문제입니다.

수신: Dennis Craig <d.craig@quickmail.com>
발신: Caroline Peel <c.peel@lbistro.com>
날짜: 2월 21일
제목: 의견 카드
첨부: 상품권

Mr. Craig께,

⁰¹저는 당신이 2월 19일에 작성한 의견 카드에 대한 응답으로 이메일을 씁니다. 당신이 저희 점포를 방문하신 동안에 시간을 내어 이것을 해 주신 것에 감사드립니다. ⁰²저는 당신이 당신의 음식을 즐기셨다니 기쁘지만, 서비스는 실망스럽다고 느끼셨던 것에 대해 유감스럽게 생각합니다. ⁰³당신의 식사들은 당신이 그것들을 주문하고 20분 후에 제공되었어야 했습니다.

⁰⁴당신의 의견 덕분에, 저희는 직원 일정을 조정했습니다. 다음번에 당신이 금요일 밤에 Lochlane Bistro에서 식사하실 때는, 두 명 더 많은 종업원들이 근무 중일 것입니다.

당신의 불편에 대해 보상하기 위해, 저는 당신이 저희 식당에서 다음 저녁 식사 시 20달러 할인을 받으실 수 있는 상품권을 첨부했습니다. 저희는 당신을 다시 만나기를 기대합니다.

Caroline Peel 드림
관리자, Lochlane Bistro

in response to ~에 대한 응답으로   establishment n. 점포, 설립
on duty 근무 중인, 당번인   inconvenience n. 불편, 애로
voucher n. 상품권, 할인권   make up for ~에 대해 보상하다, 만회하다
look forward to ~을 기대하다

01 동사 어휘 고르기 전체 문맥 파악
해설 '당신이 2월 19일에 ___한 의견 카드에 대한 응답으로 이메일을 쓴다'라는 문맥이므로 모든 보기가 정답의 후보이다. 빈칸이 있는 문장만으로 정답을 고를 수 없으므로 주변 문맥이나 전체 문맥을 파악한다. 뒤 문장에서 당신, 즉 Mr. Craig가 점포를 방문한 동안에 시간을 내어 이것을 해 준 것에 감사하다고 한 후, 뒷부분에서 Mr. Craig가 음식과 서비스에 대해 남긴 의견에 대해 답변하고 있으므로 Mr. Craig가 2월 19일에 의견 카드를 작성했다는 것을 알 수 있다. 따라서 동사 complete(작성하다, 완료하다)의 과거형 (A) completed가 정답이다. (B) misplaced는 '잘못 두다', (C) printed는 '인쇄하다', (D) announced는 '발표하다, 알리다'라는 의미이다.

02 올바른 시제의 동사 채우기 주변 문맥 파악
해설 that절(that ~ food)에 주어(you)만 있고 동사가 없으므로 모든 보기가 정답의 후보이다. 빈칸이 있는 문장만으로 정답을 고를 수 없으므로 주변 문맥이나 전체 문맥을 파악한다. 앞 문장에서 점포를 방문한 동안에 시간을 내어 이렇게 해 준 것, 즉 의견 카드를 작성해 준 것에 감사하다고 했으므로, 점포에 방문하여 음식을 즐긴 것 또한 과거에 일어난 일임을 알 수 있다. 따라서 과거 시제 (C) enjoyed가 정답이다.

03 인칭대명사 채우기
해설 동사(ordered)의 목적어 자리에 올 수 있는 것은 명사이므로 (A), (B), (C)가 정답의 후보이다. '당신의 식사들은 당신이 ___을 주문하고 20분 후에 제공되었어야 했다'라는 의미가 되어야 하므로 빈칸에 들어갈 대명사가 가리키는 것은 Your meals(당신의 식사들)이다. 따라서 복수 사물 명사(Your meals)를 가리키는 목적격 인칭대명사 (B) them(그들을)이 정답이다. 부정대명사 또는 부사 (A) either는 부정대명사로 쓰일 경우 '어느 하나'라는 의미로 어색한 문맥을 만들고, 부사로 쓰일 경우 명사 자리에 올 수 없다. 인칭대명사 (C) it은 단수 명사를 가리킨다. 부정형용사 (D) other는 명사 자리에 올 수 없다.

04 알맞은 문장 고르기
해설 (A) 당신의 의견 덕분에, 저희는 직원 일정을 조정했습니다.
(B) 이것이 예약이 필요한 이유 중 하나입니다.
(C) 저희는 대규모 파티에 이용 가능한 개인 식사 공간을 보유하고 있습니다.
(D) 저희의 새로운 지점은 불과 몇 블록 떨어져 있을 것입니다.
해설 뒤 문장 'The next time you eat at Lochlane Bistro on a Friday night, there will be two more servers on duty.'에서 다음번에 당신이 금요일 밤에 Lochlane Bistro에서 식사할 때는 두 명 더 많은 종업원들이 근무 중일 것이라고 했으므로, 빈칸에는 변경된 직원 근무 일정과 관련된 내용이 들어가야 함을 알 수 있다. 따라서 (A)가 정답이다.
어휘 feedback n. 의견, 피드백   adjust v. 조정하다, 적응하다

05-08번은 다음 기사에 관한 문제입니다.

Hamlin 국제 공항이 새로운 터미널 개장을 축하하다
⁰⁵Hamlin 국제 공항이 몇 년 동안의 공사 후에 두 번째 터미널을 공개했다. 새로운 터미널은 5월 2일에 개장할 것이다.
"추가 터미널에는 많은 편의 시설들이 있습니다."라고 공항 대변인 Kurt Vogel이 말했다. ⁰⁶승객들은 분명히 고급 라운지를 좋아할 것이다. 그곳에는 많은 편한 소파들이 있으며, 무료 음료들이 제공된다.
⁰⁷반면에, 한 터미널에 도착한 뒤 다른 터미널에서 출발하는 여행객들

은 두 곳 사이의 거리로 인해 불편을 겪을 수도 있다. 이 문제를 해결하기 위해, 두 터미널을 연결하는 셔틀버스가 운행될 것이다.
새로운 터미널은 오로지 SeaCrescent 항공사와 Blue Fin 항공사만을 위한 것이다. ⁰⁸모든 다른 항공사들은 계속해서 기존 터미널에서 운영될 것이다.

celebrate v. 축하하다, 기념하다   unveil v. 공개하다, 발표하다
amenity n. 편의 시설   spokesperson n. 대변인   dozens of 많은
inconvenience v. 불편을 겪게 하다; n. 불편
exclusively adv. 오로지 ~만, 독점적으로

05 전치사 채우기
해설 'Hamlin 국제 공항이 몇 년 동안의 공사 후에 두 번째 터미널을 공개했다'라는 의미가 되어야 하므로 시점을 나타내는 전치사 (C) after(~ 후에)가 정답이다. (B) since(~ 이후로)도 해석상 그럴듯해 보이지만, 특정 시점 이후 계속되는 일을 나타내어 'Hamlin 국제 공항이 몇 년 동안의 공사 이후로 계속해서 두 번째 터미널을 공개했다'라는 어색한 문장을 만든다. (A) beside는 '~ 옆에', (D) into는 '~ 안으로'라는 의미이다.

06 알맞은 문장 고르기
해석 (A) 터미널에서 유지보수 문제들이 보고되었다.
(B) 승무원들은 시설들에 대해 불평해 왔다.
(C) 기념일을 축하하기 위해 입장 요금이 할인되었다.
(D) 승객들은 분명히 고급 라운지를 좋아할 것이다.
해설 앞 문장 'The additional terminal has many amenities'에서 추가 터미널에는 많은 편의 시설들이 있다고 했고, 뒤 문장 'There are dozens of comfortable sofas and free drinks are provided.'에서 그곳에는 많은 편한 소파들이 있으며 무료 음료들이 제공된다고 했으므로, 빈칸에는 편의 시설들 중 하나이면서 소파가 있고 무료 음료가 제공되는 고급 라운지에 관한 내용이 들어가야 함을 알 수 있다. 따라서 (D)가 정답이다.
어휘 flight attendant 승무원   admission n. 입장   mark v. 축하하다, 기념하다
surely adv. 분명히   executive adj. 고급의

07 접속부사 채우기 주변 문맥 파악
해설 빈칸이 콤마와 함께 문장의 맨 앞에 온 접속부사 자리이므로, 앞 문장과 빈칸이 있는 문장의 의미 관계를 파악하여 정답을 선택한다. 앞 문장에서 고급 라운지에는 많은 편한 소파들이 있으며 무료 음료들이 제공된다고 했고, 빈칸이 있는 문장에서는 한 터미널에 도착한 뒤 다른 터미널에서 출발하는 여행객들은 두 곳 사이의 거리로 인해 불편을 겪을 수도 있다고 했으므로, 앞에서 말한 내용과 다른 내용으로 전환되는 문장을 언급할 때 사용되는 (C) On the other hand(반면에)가 정답이다.
어휘 once adv. 한때, 언젠가   consequently adv. 결과적으로
likewise adv. 마찬가지로

08 형용사 자리 채우기
해설 빈칸 뒤의 명사(terminal)를 꾸밀 수 있는 것은 형용사이므로 형용사 (A) original(기존의, 초기의)이 정답이다. 동사 (B), 부사 (C), 명사 (D)는 형용사 자리에 올 수 없다.
어휘 originate v. 기원하다, 유래하다   originally adv. 원래
originality n. 독창성, 참신함

09-12번은 다음 후기에 관한 문제입니다.

STARLIGHT DREAM 2
우리는 한때 Campfire사의 초기 Starlight Dream을 '돈으로 구매할 수 있는 최고의 디지털 리더기'라고 불렀습니다. 여러분들 중 많은 이들이 분명히 동의했습니다. ⁰⁹그것의 큰 화면, 날렵한 디자인, 그리고 긴 배터리 수명은 이것이 출시되자마자 매우 인기 있게 만들었습니다. 완전히 새로운 Starlight Dream 2는 더 발전했지만, 그것을 구매할 가치가 있을까요?
¹⁰비록 전반적으로 처음의 것보다는 저렴하지만, 기본 장치는 여전히

250달러에 팔립니다. Starlight Dream 2의 핵심 기능들을 살펴봅시다. ¹¹몇 개의 미묘하지만 중요한 차이들이 있습니다. 이 새로운 모델은 더 얇고 당신의 손에 더 편안하게 맞습니다. 약간 더 큰 화면은 30퍼센트 더 많은 단어들을 보여줍니다. ¹²또한 그 새로운 장치는 견고하면서도 우아한 알루미늄 본체를 드러냅니다.

evidently adv. 분명히, 눈에 띄게 display n. 화면; v. 보여주다
upon prep. ~하자마자 release n. 출시; v. 출시하다
all-new adj. 완전히 새로운 overall adv. 전반적으로 initial adj. 처음의
unit n. 장치 feature n. 기능, 특징 exhibit v. 드러내다, 전시하다
sturdy adj. 견고한 elegant adj. 우아한

09 형용사 어휘 고르기 전체 문맥 파악

해설 '그것의 큰 화면, 날렵한 디자인, 그리고 긴 배터리 수명은 이것[초기 Starlight Dream]이 출시되자마자 매우 ____ 만들었다'라는 문맥이므로 모든 보기가 정답의 후보이다. 빈칸이 있는 문장만으로 정답을 고를 수 없으므로 주변 문맥이나 전체 문맥을 파악한다. 앞부분에서 초기 Starlight Dream을 '돈으로 구매할 수 있는 최고의 디지털 리더기'라고 불렀다고 했으며, 많은 이들이 이에 동의했다고 했으므로 출시되자마자 매우 인기가 있었음을 알 수 있다. 따라서 (A) popular(인기 있는)가 정답이다. (B) predictable은 '예상할 수 있는', (C) unavailable은 '이용할 수 없는', (D) durable은 '내구성 있는'이라는 의미이다.

10 부정대명사 채우기

해설 '비록 전반적으로 처음의 것보다는 저렴하지만'이라는 의미가 되어야 하므로, 정해지지 않은 단수 가산 명사를 대신하는 부정대명사 (C) one(~것)이 정답이다. 참고로, one은 앞에서 언급된 Starlight Dream을 지칭하고 있음을 알아둔다. 인칭대명사 (A)와 지시대명사 (B)는 형용사의 꾸밈을 받을 수 없다. 한정사 또는 부정대명사 (D)도 형용사의 꾸밈을 받을 수 없다.

11 알맞은 문장 고르기

해석 (A) 이전의 모델은 다른 모든 것들을 모든 면에서 능가합니다.
(B) 프리미엄 버전은 모바일 인터넷 연결 기능을 제공합니다.
(C) 몇 개의 미묘하지만 중요한 차이들이 있습니다.
(D) Campfire사는 제품 출시에 앞서 선주문을 받고 있습니다.

해설 앞 문장 'Let's look at the key features of the Starlight Dream 2.'에서 Starlight Dream 2의 핵심 기능들을 살펴보자고 했고, 뒤 문장 'This new model is thinner and fits more comfortably in your hand.'에서 이 새로운 모델, 즉 Starlight Dream 2는 더 얇고 당신의 손에 더 편안하게 맞다고 했으므로, 빈칸에는 Starlight Dream 2와 초기 Starlight Dream의 차이에 관한 내용이 들어가야 함을 알 수 있다. 따라서 (C)가 정답이다.

어휘 surpass v. 능가하다 connectivity n. 연결 subtle adj. 미묘한
pre-order n. 선주문

12 명사 어휘 고르기

해설 '새로운 장치는 견고하면서도 우아한 알루미늄 본체를 드러낸다'라는 문맥이므로 (A) device(장치)가 정답이다. (B) service는 '서비스', (C) order는 '주문', (D) fund는 '기금, 자금'이라는 의미이다.

13-16번은 다음 편지에 관한 문제입니다.

DOBRY YOGURT사
5월 21일

Amin Patel
최고경영자, Renowned 가공식품회사
52번지 Sunder로
뭄바이시, 인도 400070

Mr. Patel께,

귀사는 저희의 미래 공급업체 후보 중 하나로 선정되었습니다. ¹³저희는 이제 점검을 진행할 것입니다. 저희의 지정 계약업체인 HDI International사에 의해 실시될 이 평가는 귀사가 저희의 품질 기준을 충족한다는 것을 확실하게 하기 위한 것입니다. ¹⁴정확한 세부 사항은 곧 나올 것입니다. 현재로서는, 저는 당신에게 이것이 귀사의 생산 시설에 대한 평가를 포함할 것이라는 점만 말씀드릴 수 있습니다. 이 과정은 2개월이 걸릴 것입니다. ¹⁵마지막에, HDI사가 구체적인 권장 사항들을 포함한 보고서를 발표할 것입니다. ¹⁶저희는 귀사를 공급업체로 승인하기 전에 귀사가 모든 권장 사항들을 준수했음을 확인해야 합니다. 제가 다음에 뭄바이를 방문할 때 당신과 이것에 대해 논의할 수 있을 것입니다.

Stephanie Moravec 드림
남아시아 지역 지사장
Dobry Yogurt사

supplier n. 공급업체, 공급자 proceed with ~을 진행하다
assessment n. 평가 conduct v. 실시하다, 지휘하다; n. 행동
designated adj. 지정된, 임명된 contractor n. 계약업체, 도급업체
ensure v. 확실하게 하다, 보장하다 standard n. 기준, 표준
involve v. 포함하다, 수반하다 recommendation n. 권장 사항, 추천
comply with ~을 준수하다, 따르다 regional director 지사장

13 명사 어휘 고르기 주변 문맥 파악

해설 '우리는 이제 ____을 진행할 것이다'라는 문맥이므로 모든 보기가 정답의 후보이다. 빈칸이 있는 문장만으로 정답을 고를 수 없으므로 주변 문맥이나 전체 문맥을 파악하여 정답을 고른다. 뒤 문장에서 이 평가는 귀사, 즉 Dobry Yogurt사의 품질 기준을 충족한다는 것을 확실하게 하기 위한 것이라고 했으므로, Dobry Yogurt사가 Renowned 가공식품회사를 대상으로 점검을 진행할 것임을 알 수 있다. 따라서 (D) inspection(점검, 검사)이 정답이다. (A) registration은 '등록, 신고', (B) performance는 '실적, 공연', (C) invoice는 '송장, 청구서'라는 의미이다.

14 알맞은 문장 고르기

해석 (A) 정확한 세부 사항은 곧 나올 것입니다.
(B) 저희 계약서의 조건들은 명확합니다.
(C) 저는 당신으로부터의 추가적인 지시를 기다립니다.
(D) 당신이 겪고 있는 문제를 설명해 주십시오.

해설 뒤 문장 'For now, I can only tell you that it will involve an evaluation of your production facility.'에서 현재로서는, 이것, 즉 점검이 생산 시설에 대한 평가를 포함할 것이라는 점만 말해 줄 수 있다고 하며 제한적인 정보만을 제공했으므로, 빈칸에는 점검에 대한 정확한 세부 사항이 곧 나올 것이라는 내용이 들어가야 함을 알 수 있다. 따라서 (A)가 정답이다.

어휘 exact adj. 정확한, 꼼꼼한 forthcoming adj. 곧 나오는, 다가오는
await v. 기다리고 있다, 기대하다 instruction n. 지시
describe v. 설명하다, 묘사하다

15 올바른 시제의 동사 채우기 주변 문맥 파악

해설 문장에 주어(HDI)만 있고 동사가 없으므로 모든 보기가 정답의 후보이다. 빈칸이 있는 문장만으로 정답을 고를 수 없으므로 주변 문맥이나 전체 문맥을 파악한다. 앞 문장에서 미래 시제(will take)를 사용해서 점검 과정이 2개월이 걸릴 것이라고 했으므로, 점검 마지막에 HDI사가 보고서를 발표하는 시점 또한 미래임을 알 수 있다. 따라서 미래 시제 (B) will issue가 정답이다.

어휘 issue v. 발표하다, 발행하다

16 동명사 채우기

해설 전치사(before)의 목적어 자리에 올 수 있고 명사(you)를 목적어로 취할 수 있는 동명사 (C) approving(승인하는 것)이 정답이다. 동사 (A), 동사 또는 과거분사 (B), to 부정사 (D)는 전치사의 목적어 자리에 올 수 없다.

DAY 11 문맥 파악 문제: 어휘

Example
p.211

01번은 다음 이메일에 관한 문제입니다.

> 새로운 지사의 Mr. Jurgens가 전화하여 우리가 Filepros사에 주문한 사무장비가 10월 9일에 도착했다고 말했습니다. 그와 기술자들은 현재 그 장비를 설치하느라 바쁩니다. 유감스럽게도, 저는 Draper사의 다른 물품들은 배송 지연을 겪고 있다는 사실을 통지받았습니다. 그 회사가 배송을 보장할 수 있는 가장 이른 날짜는 10월 16일이며, 이는 우리가 개점을 10월 20일로 연기할 수밖에 없게 만들 것입니다.
>
> equipment n. 장비, 설비　install v. 설치하다　device n. 장비, 장치
> guarantee v. 보장하다　force v. ~할 수밖에 없게 만들다, 강요하다

토익실전문제
p.211

| 01 (C) | 02 (B) | 03 (C) | 04 (D) |

01-04번은 다음 공고에 관한 문제입니다.

> **Gavin Hackett가 Waco시에 옵니다!**
>
> 01호평을 받는 기업가 Gavin Hackett가 9월 13일 화요일 오후 8시에 Waco시의 Evergrand 강당에서 강연을 할 것입니다. 강연의 첫 부분에서, 그는 그의 성공적인 비즈니스를 구축하는 동안 직면했던 어려움들에 대해 이야기할 것입니다. 02다음으로, Mr. Hackett는 그의 기업가적 통찰력을 공유하기 위해 소통형 세션을 이끌 것입니다. 참가자들의 질문에 직접 응답함으로써, 그는 역동적인 학습 환경을 조성하는 것을 목표로 합니다.
>
> 03이곳에서의 Mr. Hackett의 등장은 그의 곧 출간될 책 Rise to the Top에 대한 홍보 투어의 일환입니다. 그는 지난 20년의 경력 동안 여러 다른 책들을 썼습니다.
>
> 출입구에서 입장료 15달러가 부과될 것입니다. 04처음 입장하는 50명은 무료 책을 받을 것입니다. 이 특별한 기회를 놓치지 마세요!
>
> acclaimed adj. 호평을 받는　entrepreneur n. 기업가
> profitable adj. 성공적인, 수익성 있는　session n. 세션, 강의 시간
> insight n. 통찰력　dynamic adj. 역동적인　promotional adj. 홍보의
> upcoming adj. 곧 출간될, 다가오는　author n. (책을) 쓰다, 저술하다
> title n. 책, 제목　entry fee 입장료　exclusive adj. 특별한, 단독의
> opportunity n. 기회

01 올바른 시제의 동사 채우기　주변 문맥 파악

해설 문장에 주어(The acclaimed entrepreneur Gavin Hackett)만 있고 동사가 없으므로 빈칸 뒤의 목적어(a talk)를 가질 수 있는 능동태 동사 (A)와 (C)가 정답의 후보이다. 빈칸이 있는 문장만으로 정답을 고를 수 없으므로 주변 문맥이나 전체 문맥을 파악한다. 뒤 문장에서 Mr. Hackett는 강연의 첫 부분에서 그의 성공적인 비즈니스를 구축하는 동안 직면했던 어려움들에 대해 이야기할 것이라며 미래 시제(will discuss)를 사용했으므로, 그가 강연을 하는 시점이 미래임을 알 수 있다. 따라서 특정한 미래 시점에 진행되고 있을 일을 표현하는 미래진행 시제 (C) will be delivering이 정답이다. 참고로, 현재 시제 수동태 (B)와 현재완료 시제 수동태 (D)는 뒤에 목적어를 취할 수 없음을 알아 둔다.

어휘 deliver v. (강연을) 하다, 배달하다

02 형용사 어휘 고르기　주변 문맥 파악

해설 '그의 기업가적 통찰력을 공유하기 위해 ___ 세션을 이끌 것이다'라는 문맥이므로 (B), (C), (D)가 정답의 후보이다. 빈칸이 있는 문장만으로 정답을 고를 수 없으므로 주변 문맥이나 전체 문맥을 파악한다. 뒤 문장에서 참가자들의 질문에 직접 응답함으로써 그[Mr. Hackett]는 역동적인 학습 환경을 조성하는 것을 목표로 한다고 했으므로, Mr. Hackett가 참가자들로부터 질문을 받고 직접 응답하는 소통형 세션을 이끌 것임을

알 수 있다. 따라서 (B) interactive(소통형의, 상호적인)가 정답이다. (A) previous는 '이전의', (C) identical은 '동일한', (D) eventful은 '다사다난한'이라는 의미이다.

03 명사 어휘 고르기　전체 문맥 파악

해설 '이곳에서의 Mr. Hackett의 ___은 그의 곧 출간될 책 Rise to the Top에 대한 홍보 투어의 일환이다'라는 문맥이므로 모든 보기가 정답의 후보이다. 빈칸이 있는 문장만으로 정답을 고를 수 없으므로 주변 문맥이나 전체 문맥을 파악한다. 앞부분에서 Mr. Hackett가 Waco시의 Evergrand 강당에서 강연을 할 것이라고 했으므로 Mr. Hackett가 이곳, 즉 Evergrand 강당에 등장할 것임을 알 수 있다. 따라서 (C) appearance(등장)가 정답이다. (A) acceptance는 '수락, 승인', (B) enrollment는 '등록, 입학', (D) donation은 '기부, 기증'이라는 의미이다.

04 알맞은 문장 고르기

해석 (A) 마침내, Hackett의 경력이 인정받을 것입니다.
(B) 수상작들은 행사 이후에 발표될 것입니다.
(C) 당신에게 가장 편리한 지점을 방문하세요.
(D) 처음 입장하는 50명은 무료 책을 받을 것입니다.

해설 뒤 문장 'Don't miss this exclusive opportunity!'에서 이 특별한 기회를 놓치지 말라고 했으므로, 빈칸에는 강연에 참석한 사람들이 누릴 수 있는 특별한 혜택과 관련된 내용이 들어가야 함을 알 수 있다. 따라서 (D)가 정답이다.

어휘 recognize v. 인정하다, 알아보다　winning entry 수상작
enter v. 입장하다, 들어가다

HACKERS TEST
p.212

01 (B)	02 (D)	03 (D)	04 (C)	05 (B)
06 (D)	07 (B)	08 (D)	09 (C)	10 (D)
11 (A)	12 (A)	13 (C)	14 (A)	15 (D)
16 (B)

01-04번은 다음 이메일에 관한 문제입니다.

> 수신: Amira Yaziri <amira72@goodtidings.tn>
> 발신: Ernie Vollmer <e.vollmer@mahalsuites.com>
> 날짜: 12월 9일
> 제목: 특별한 준비
>
> Ms. Yaziri께,
>
> 01첫째로, Jamesville에서의 숙박을 위해 Mahal Suites를 선택해 주신 것에 감사드립니다. 02귀하는 저희의 디럭스 객실 중 하나에 묵으실 것이므로, 귀하는 저희의 무료 공항 교통편을 제공받을 자격이 있습니다. 귀하의 예약 신청서는 귀하의 항공편이 오전 1시 26분에 도착할 것이라고 나타내는데, 저희 셔틀버스는 오전 6시부터 오후 11시까지만 운행합니다. 03따라서, 저희는 귀하께 다른 선택지를 제공해 드리고 싶습니다. 저희는 귀하를 위해 개인 픽업 서비스에 기꺼이 연락해 드릴 수 있습니다. 04이 경우에는, 운전기사가 귀하의 도착 게이트에서 귀하를 맞이할 것입니다.
>
> Ernie Vollmer 드림
> 고객 서비스 직원
> Mahal Suites
>
> arrangement n. 준비, 계획, 마련　be entitled to ~받을 자격이 있다
> contact v. 연락하다; n. 연락　arrival n. 도착

01 동사 어휘 고르기　주변 문맥 파악

해설 '숙박을 위해 Mahal Suites를 ___해 준 것에 감사하다'라는 문맥이므로 모든 보기가 정답의 후보이다. 빈칸이 있는 문장만으로 정답을 고를 수 없으므로 주변 문맥이나 전체 문맥을 파악한다. 뒤 문장에서 귀하가 우

리, 즉 Mahal Suites의 디럭스 객실 중 하나에 묵을 것이라고 했으므로, Mahal Suites를 숙소로 선택했음을 알 수 있다. 따라서 동사 choose (선택하다)의 동명사형 (B) choosing이 정답이다. (A) acquiring은 '인수하다, 얻다', (C) reviewing은 '검토하다, 논평하다', (D) preparing은 '준비하다'라는 의미이다.

02 명사 어휘 고르기 주변 문맥 파악

해설 '무료 공항 ___을 제공받을 자격이 있다'라는 문맥이므로 (A), (B), (D)가 정답의 후보이다. 빈칸이 있는 문장만으로 정답을 고를 수 없으므로 주변 문맥이나 전체 문맥을 파악한다. 뒤 문장에서 우리, 즉 Mahal Suites의 셔틀버스가 오전 6시부터 오후 11시까지 운행한다고 했으므로 Mahal Suites가 공항과 숙소 간의 교통편을 제공한다는 것을 알 수 있다. 따라서 (D) transportation(교통편, 교통)이 정답이다. (A) access는 '접근', (B) equipment는 '장비', (C) entertainment는 '오락, 오락물'이라는 의미이다.

03 알맞은 문장 고르기

해석 (A) 귀하의 차를 주차할 곳이 필요하신가요?
(B) 여행사는 저희 로비에 사무실이 있었습니다.
(C) 그러니 하루 중 어느 때에나 자유롭게 룸서비스를 주문해 주십시오.
(D) 따라서, 저희는 귀하께 다른 선택지를 제공해 드리고 싶습니다.

해설 앞 문장 'Your reservation form indicates that your flight will be arriving at 1:26 A.M., but our shuttle runs only from 6 A.M. to 11 P.M.'에서 귀하의 예약 신청서는 항공편이 오전 1시 26분에 도착할 것이라고 나타내는데, 숙소 측 셔틀버스는 오전 6시부터 오후 11시까지만 운행한다고 했고, 뒤 문장 'We would be happy to contact a private pickup service for you.'에서 귀하를 위해 개인 픽업 서비스에 기꺼이 연락해 줄 수 있다고 했으므로 빈칸에는 숙소 측에서 교통편에 대한 다른 선택지를 제공하는 것과 관련된 내용이 들어가야 함을 알 수 있다. 따라서 (D)가 정답이다.

어휘 offer v. 제공하다; n. 제의, 제안 option n. 선택지

04 접속부사 채우기 주변 문맥 파악

해설 빈칸이 콤마와 함께 문장의 맨 앞에 온 접속부사 자리이므로, 앞 문장과 빈칸이 있는 문장의 의미 관계를 파악하여 정답을 선택한다. 앞 문장에서 귀하를 위해 개인 픽업 서비스에 기꺼이 연락해 줄 수 있다고 했고, 빈칸이 있는 문장에서는 운전기사가 도착 게이트에서 귀하를 맞이할 것이라고 했으므로, 앞 문장에서 특정 상황을 언급한 후 이와 관련하여 추가적인 내용을 나타낼 때 사용되는 접속부사 (C) In this case(이 경우에는)가 정답이다.

어휘 until then 그때까지 elsewhere adv. 다른 곳으로 likewise adv. 마찬가지로

05-08번은 다음 기사에 관한 문제입니다.

> ⁰⁵여행사 Alexis Journeys사는 최근에 투어 종류를 확장할 것이라고 발표했다. 8월 1일에, Alexis Journeys사는 콜롬비아, 엘살바도르, 그리고 멕시코로의 여행들을 소개할 것이다.
>
> ⁰⁶Alexis Journeys사는 경제적인 가격으로 알려져 있다. 예를 들어, 새로운 Mayan Discovery 투어는 모든 교통과 숙박을 포함하여 일주일에 단 1,050달러이다. ⁰⁷그것은 또한 모든 투어 패키지들에 좋은 후기를 보유하고 있다. 많은 고객들은 그 투어들이 그들의 기대를 넘어섰다고 언급했다.
>
> ⁰⁸"저희의 새로운 패키지들과 함께, Alexis Journeys사는 라틴 아메리카로의 여행이 너무 비싸다고 생각했던 여행자들을 공략하려고 시도하고 있습니다."라고 마케팅 담당자 Hal Clive가 말했다.

be known for ~으로 알려져 있다 accommodation n. 숙박, 적응
note v. 언급하다, 주목하다 exceed v. 넘어서다, 초월하다
expectation n. 기대 attempt v. 시도하다; n. 시도

05 동사 어휘 고르기 주변 문맥 파악

해설 '여행사 Alexis Journeys사는 최근에 투어 종류를 ___할 것이라고 발표했다'라는 문맥이므로 모든 보기가 정답의 후보이다. 빈칸이 있는 문장만으로 정답을 고를 수 없으므로 주변 문맥이나 전체 문맥을 파악한다. 뒤 문장에서 Alexis Journeys사는 콜롬비아, 엘살바도르, 그리고 멕시코로의 여행들을 소개할 것이라고 했으므로 최근에 투어 종류를 확장할 것이라고 발표했음을 알 수 있다. 따라서 (B) expand(확장하다)가 정답이다. (A) combine은 '결합하다', (C) move는 '옮기다, 움직이다', (D) continue는 '계속하다'라는 의미이다.

06 명사 자리 채우기

해설 빈칸은 소유격(its)의 꾸밈을 받는 명사 자리이므로 명사 역할을 하는 동명사 (C)와 명사 (D)가 정답의 후보이다. '경제적인 가격으로 알려져 있다'라는 문맥이므로 (D) affordability(경제적인 가격)가 정답이다. 동명사 (C)는 '(금전적·시간적으로) ~할 여유가 되는 것'이라는 의미로 어색한 문맥을 만들기 때문에 답이 될 수 없다. 동사 (A)와 형용사 (B)는 명사 자리에 올 수 없다.

어휘 afford v. (금전적·시간적으로) 여유가 되다 affordable adj. 감당할 수 있는

07 알맞은 문장 고르기

해석 (A) 궂은 날씨 때문에 투어 일정이 변경될 수도 있다.
(B) 그것은 또한 모든 투어 패키지들에 좋은 후기를 보유하고 있다.
(C) 이 소문은 아직 회사에 의해 확인되지 않았다.
(D) 손님들은 객실 내 와이파이를 이용하기 위해 추가로 요금을 낼 수도 있다.

해설 뒤 문장 'Many customers noted that the tours exceeded their expectations.'에서 많은 고객들은 투어들이 그들의 기대를 넘어섰다고 언급했다고 했으므로, 빈칸에는 투어 패키지들이 좋은 후기를 보유하고 있다는 것에 관한 내용이 들어가야 함을 알 수 있다. 따라서 (B)가 정답이다.

어휘 take advantage of ~을 이용하다 in-room adj. 객실 내의

08 to 부정사 채우기

해설 빈칸 앞에 to 부정사를 목적어로 취하는 동사 attempt가 있으므로 to 부정사 (D) to target이 정답이다. 동사 (A)와 (C), 동사 또는 과거분사 (B)는 to 부정사 자리에 올 수 없다. (A)를 '목표'라는 의미의 명사로 본다 해도, 명사는 목적어(travelers)를 가질 수 없으므로 답이 될 수 없다.

어휘 target v. 공략하다, 목표하다; n. 목표(물)

09-12번은 다음 광고에 관한 문제입니다.

> **O'Toole's 체육관에서 크게 절약하세요!**
>
> 겨울이 왔지만, 그것이 당신이 건강해지는 것을 막도록 두지 마세요! O'Toole's 체육관에서 한 달 동안만 진행되는 특별 할인을 제공합니다. ⁰⁹그러므로 정가의 50퍼센트까지 할인받기 위해 O'Toole's 체육관에 즉시 등록하세요. ¹⁰이번 달에 등록하는 고객들은 모든 필라테스 수업에서 추가 10퍼센트 할인을 받을 것입니다.
>
> 저희의 1개월과 3개월 정기권은 할인된 가격으로 각각 단 55달러와 135달러입니다. ¹¹게다가, 다른 사람들을 초대하면 당신은 더 큰 할인을 받을 것입니다.
>
> 모든 회원들은 저희의 운동 기구에 대한 전체 이용 권한을 받을 것입니다. ¹²그러나, 몇몇 서비스들은 추가 비용이 든다는 것을 명심하세요. 개인 지도와 수업들에 대해서는 요금이 지불되어야 합니다.

fit adj. 건강한 up to ~까지 regular price 정가 respectively adv. 각각
access n. 이용 권한, 접근 workout n. 운동

09 부사 어휘 고르기 주변 문맥 파악

해설 '정가의 50퍼센트까지 할인받기 위해 O'Toole's 체육관에 ___ 등록하세요'라는 문맥이므로 (A), (B), (C)가 정답의 후보이다. 빈칸이 있는 문장만으로 정답을 고를 수 없으므로 주변 문맥이나 전체 문맥을 파악한다. 앞 문장에서 O'Toole's 체육관에서 한 달 동안만 진행되는 특별 할인을 제공한다고 했으므로 할인 혜택을 누리려면 즉시 체육관에 등록해야 한

다는 것을 알 수 있다. 따라서 (C) immediately(즉시)가 정답이다. (A) regularly는 '규칙적으로, 정기적으로', (B) patiently는 '인내심을 가지고', (D) generally는 '일반적으로, 대체로'라는 의미이다.

10 관계대명사 채우기
해설 이 문장은 필수성분(Customers ~ discount)을 갖춘 완전한 절이므로, ___ ~ this month는 수식어 거품으로 보아야 한다. 이 수식어 거품은 빈칸 앞의 명사(Customers)를 선행사로 갖는 관계절이므로, 관계대명사 (B), (C), (D)가 정답의 후보이다. 관계절(___ ~ this month) 내에 주어가 없고 선행사 Customers가 사람이므로, 사람을 나타내는 주격 관계대명사 (D) who가 정답이다. 관계대명사 (B) which는 선행사가 사물일 때 올 수 있으며, 소유격 관계대명사 (C) whose는 뒤에 선행사가 소유하는 명사가 와야 하므로 답이 될 수 없다. 부정대명사 또는 부정형용사 (A) any(어느, 어떤)는 관계절을 이끌 수 없다.

11 올바른 시제의 동사 채우기
해설 when으로 시작하는 종속절에 주어(you)만 있고 동사가 없으므로 빈칸 뒤의 목적어(others)를 가질 수 있는 능동태 동사 (A), (B), (C)가 정답의 후보이다. 주절(you will receive ~ discounts)에서 미래 시제(will receive)를 사용하여 할인을 받을 것이라고 했으므로, when으로 시작하는 종속절도 미래를 나타내야 하는데, 시간을 나타내는 종속절에서는 미래 시제 대신 현재 시제를 쓰므로 현재 시제 (A) invite(초대하다)가 정답이다.

12 알맞은 문장 고르기
해설 (A) 그러나, 몇몇 서비스들은 추가 비용이 든다는 것을 명심하세요.
(B) 저희의 어느 지점에서든 프런트 데스크 직원에게 카드를 제시하세요.
(C) 저희는 곧 문을 닫을 예정이니 서두르시는 것이 좋습니다.
(D) 많은 사람들이 여름에 이러한 할인 혜택을 이용합니다.
해설 앞 문장 'All members will receive full access to our workout equipment.'에서 모든 회원들은 운동 기구에 대한 전체 이용 권한을 받을 것이라고 했고, 뒤 문장 'Fees must be paid for personal training and classes.'에서 개인 지도와 수업에 대해서는 요금이 지불되어야 한다고 했으므로, 빈칸에는 몇몇 서비스들은 추가 비용이 든다는 내용이 들어가야 함을 알 수 있다. 따라서 (A)가 정답이다.
어휘 keep in mind ~을 명심하다 present v. 제시하다, 보여주다
saving n. 할인 혜택, 절약

13-16번은 다음 안내문에 관한 문제입니다.

> 중요 등록 안내문
> Ryder 대학은 학기 첫날까지 등록금을 납부할 것을 요구합니다. ¹³그렇지 않으면, 연체료가 부과될 것입니다. 학생들은 강좌가 시작되기 전에 그것에 대해 전액 환불을 요청할 수 있습니다. ¹⁴강좌가 시작된 후에는, 그들이 2주 이내에 취소하면 80퍼센트를 환불받을 수 있습니다. 그 이후에는, 환불이 불가능합니다.
> 수강 신청은 일반적으로 선착순으로 이루어집니다. ¹⁵하지만, 특별 프로그램에 참여하는 학생들과 마찬가지로 졸업반 학생들에게는 심화 과정 강좌에 대한 우선권이 부여됩니다. ¹⁶저희는 관심 있어 하는 모든 학생들에게 자리가 마련될 수 있도록 노력하지만, 이것이 항상 가능한 것은 아닙니다. 따라서, 학생들은 자리를 확보하기 위해 조기에 신청하는 것이 권장됩니다.

payment n. 납부, 지불, 지불금 tuition n. 등록금, 수업료
eligible adj. ~할 수 있는, 자격이 있는 withdraw v. 취소하다, 철회하다
first-come, first-served basis 선착순 priority n. 우선권, 우선순위
upper-level adj. 심화 과정의, 상급의 register v. 신청하다
secure v. 확보하다; adj. 안전한

13 알맞은 문장 고르기
해설 (A) 대신에, 학생들은 재정 지원을 요청할 수 있습니다.
(B) 강좌 일정표가 제작될 것입니다.
(C) 그렇지 않으면, 연체료가 부과될 것입니다.
(D) 각 학기는 4개월 동안 지속됩니다.
해설 앞 문장 'Ryder College requires payment of tuition by the first day of a semester.'에서 Ryder 대학은 학기 첫날까지 등록금을 납부할 것을 요구한다고 했으므로, 빈칸에는 첫날까지 등록금을 납부하지 않을 경우 발생할 일에 관한 내용이 들어가야 함을 알 수 있다. 따라서 (C)가 정답이다.
어휘 financial adj. 재정의, 금융의 late fee 연체료

14 부사절 접속사 채우기
해설 이 문장은 주어(they), 동사(are), 보어(eligible)를 갖춘 완전한 문장이므로, ___ ~ begun은 수식어 거품으로 보아야 한다. 이 수식어 거품은 주어(it)와 동사(has begun)를 갖춘 완전한 절이므로 부사절 접속사인 모든 보기가 정답의 후보이다. '강좌가 시작된 후에는, 2주 이내에 취소하면 80퍼센트를 환불받을 수 있다'라는 의미가 되어야 하므로 (A) Once(~한 후에)가 정답이다. (B) Before는 '~하기 전에', (C) Until은 '~할 때까지', (D) So that은 '~할 수 있도록'이라는 의미이다.

15 전치사 채우기
해설 '특별 프로그램에 참여하는 학생들과 마찬가지로 졸업반 학생들에게는 심화 과정 강좌에 대한 우선권이 부여된다'라는 의미가 되어야 하므로, 전치사 (D) along with(~와 마찬가지로)가 정답이다. (A) despite는 '~에도 불구하고', (B) on behalf of는 '~를 대신하여', (C) across from은 '~의 바로 맞은편에'라는 의미이다.

16 명사 어휘 고르기 주변 문맥 파악
해설 '저희는 관심 있어 하는 모든 학생들에게 ___가 마련될 수 있도록 노력하지만, 이것이 항상 가능한 것은 아니다'라는 문맥이므로 모든 보기가 정답의 후보이다. 빈칸이 있는 문장만으로 정답을 고를 수 없으므로 주변 문맥이나 전체 문맥을 파악한다. 뒤 문장에서 학생들은 자리를 확보하기 위해 조기에 신청하는 것이 권장된다고 했으므로, Ryder College는 관심 있어 하는 모든 학생들에게 강좌 자리가 마련될 수 있도록 노력하지만 이것이 항상 가능하지는 않다는 것을 알 수 있다. 따라서 (B) spaces(자리)가 정답이다. (A) books는 '책', (C) supplies는 '공급품, 공급', (D) funds는 '자금'이라는 의미이다.

DAY 12 문맥 파악 문제: 문장

Example
01번은 다음 기사에 관한 문제입니다.

> Mr. Ward는 태양광 패널 기술 개발에 기여한 공로로 여러 권위 있는 상을 받았다. 그는 또한 해당 분야에서 매우 존경받는 인물이다. 이러한 이유로, 그는 Desmond 연구소의 신임 소장으로 선출되었다. 성명에서, Mr. Ward는 "이렇게 명망 있는 기관을 이끌 기회를 받게 되어 진심으로 영광입니다."라고 말했다.

distinguished adj. 권위 있는, 성공한 contribution n. 공헌, 기여
prestigious adj. 명망 높은 institution n. 기관

해석 (A) 회사는 이것의 주가를 올리기를 희망한다.
(B) 그는 또한 해당 분야에서 매우 존경받는 인물이다.
(C) 다른 과학자들이 그의 일부 연구 결과에 의문을 제기한다.
(D) 그의 은퇴 발표는 예견된 일이었다.
어휘 share price 주가 well-respected adj. 매우 존경받는 retirement n. 은퇴

토익실전문제

| 01 (A) | 02 (C) | 03 (D) | 04 (D) |

01-04번은 다음 안내문에 관한 문제입니다.

> 홍콩 자동차 박람회
> 입장권을 수령하는 방법
>
> ⁰¹올해 홍콩 자동차 박람회의 모든 참석자들은 전시회장에 입장하기 위해 입장권을 가지고 있어야 합니다. 손님들은 8월의 마지막 주에 우편으로 그들의 입장권을 받을 것입니다. 만약 당신의 것이 8월 31일까지 도착하지 않는다면, 저희에게 알려주십시오. ⁰²555-2801로 전화하여 저희에게 연락하실 수 있습니다.
>
> 행사의 정규 등록은 현재 마감되었습니다. ⁰³따라서, 추가로 등록하고자 하는 사람들은 더 많은 요금을 내야 할 것입니다. 게다가, 입장권은 그들에게 우편으로 발송되지 않을 것입니다. ⁰⁴이것들은 박람회 시작 전에 행사장 행정실에서 수령되어야 합니다.

automotive adj. 자동차의 **pass** n. 입장권 **exhibition hall** 전시회장
subject to ~해야 한다, ~의 대상이다 **venue** n. 행사장, 장소
administration office 행정실 **exposition** n. 박람회

01 명사 어휘 고르기 전체 문맥 파악

해설 '자동차 박람회의 모든 ___은 전시회장에 입장하기 위해 입장권을 가지고 있어야 한다'라는 문맥이므로 모든 보기가 정답의 후보이다. 빈칸이 있는 문장만으로 정답을 고를 수 없으므로 주변 문맥이나 전체 문맥을 파악하여 정답을 고른다. 뒤 문장에서 손님들은 우편으로 입장권을 받을 것이라고 했고, 뒷부분에서 추가로 등록하고자 하는 사람들은 더 많은 요금을 내야 할 것이라고 했으므로 박람회의 참석자들이 입장권을 가지고 있어야 함을 알 수 있다. 따라서 (A) attendees(참석자)가 정답이다. (B) lecturers는 '강연자', (C) reviewers는 '비평가', (D) organizers는 '주최자'라는 의미이다.

02 알맞은 문장 고르기

해설 (A) 귀하의 문의에 답변이 늦어진 점 사과드립니다.
(B) 최대 3명의 손님들을 데려올 수 있습니다.
(C) 555-2801로 전화하여 저희에게 연락하실 수 있습니다.
(D) 그럼 저희가 당신의 부스 조립을 도와드릴 것입니다.

해설 앞 문장 'If yours has not arrived by August 31, please notify us.'에서 만약 당신의 것, 즉 입장권이 8월 31일까지 도착하지 않는다면 알려달라고 했으므로, 빈칸에는 555-2801로 전화하여 연락할 수 있다는 내용이 들어가야 함을 알 수 있다. 따라서 (C)가 정답이다.

어휘 **response** n. 답변, 응답 **inquiry** n. 문의, 질문 **maximum** n. 최대
reach v. 연락하다, 도달하다 **assemble** v. 조립하다, 모이다

03 접속부사 채우기 주변 문맥 파악

해설 빈칸이 콤마와 함께 문장의 맨 앞에 온 접속부사 자리이므로, 앞 문장과 빈칸이 있는 문장의 의미 관계를 파악하여 정답을 선택한다. 앞 문장에서 행사의 정규 등록은 현재 마감되었다고 했고, 빈칸이 있는 문장에서는 추가로 등록하고자 하는 사람들은 더 많은 요금을 내야 한다고 했으므로, 앞 문장의 내용에 대한 결과를 언급할 때 사용되는 접속부사 (D) Accordingly(따라서)가 정답이다. (B) At that time(그때)도 해석상 그럴듯해 보이지만, 앞서 언급된 특정한 시간을 의미하므로 답이 될 수 없다.

어휘 **specifically** adv. 분명히, 구체적으로 **overall** adv. 종합적으로, 전반적인

04 전치사 채우기

해설 '이것들[입장권]은 박람회 시작 전에 행사장 행정실에서 수령되어야 한다'라는 의미가 되어야 하므로 전치사 (D) before(~ 전에)가 정답이다. (A) about은 '~에 대해', (B) between은 '~ 사이에', (C) without은 '~ 없이'라는 의미이다.

HACKERS TEST p.218

01 (C)	02 (A)	03 (D)	04 (B)	05 (D)
06 (D)	07 (C)	08 (C)	09 (B)	10 (C)
11 (A)	12 (A)	13 (A)	14 (C)	15 (C)
16 (B)				

01-04번은 다음 편지에 관한 문제입니다.

> 11월 19일
>
> Theodore Arum
> 99번지 West Wooley로
> 캘리포니아주 93035
>
> Mr. Arum께,
>
> 이번 달 초에 20세기의 발명품들에 대한 강연을 하기 위해 Silver Shore 시민 문화회관을 방문해 주셔서 감사합니다. ⁰¹저는 당신이 지난번과 비교하여 더욱 상세한 논의를 해 주신 것에 대해 특히 감사드립니다. 청중들이 적극적으로 자신의 견해를 제시했고, 의미 있는 대화가 많이 오갔습니다. ⁰²이것은 지난해에 당신의 강연에 참석했던 사람들에게 행사를 특히 즐겁게 만들어 주었습니다.
>
> ⁰³비록 당신이 자원봉사로 Silver Shore 시민 문화회관에 시간을 내주시는 것에 동의하셨지만, 저희는 당신에게 보상을 제공해 드리고 싶습니다. 저는 감사의 표시로 당신에게 커피 체인점 Better Beans의 50달러 상품권을 보냅니다. ⁰⁴당신이 또 다른 강연을 위해 다시 방문해 주시기를 바랍니다.
>
> Valery Miranda 드림
> 행사 진행자, Silver Shore 시민 문화회관
> 동봉물: Better Beans 상품권

give a talk 강연을 하다 **invention** n. 발명품 **appreciate** v. 감사하다
detailed adj. 상세한 **audience member** 청중
contribute v. (의견을) 제시하다, 기여하다 **perspective** n. 견해, 관점
particularly adv. 특히 **voluntary** adj. 자원봉사로 하는, 자발적인
compensation n. 보상 **gift voucher** 상품권 **token** n. 표시, 징표
coordinator n. 진행자 **enclosure** n. 동봉물

01 명사 어휘 고르기 주변 문맥 파악

해설 '지난번과 비교하여 더욱 상세한 ___를 해 준 것에 대해 특히 감사드린다'라는 문맥이므로 모든 보기가 정답의 후보이다. 빈칸이 있는 문장만으로 정답을 고를 수 없으므로 주변 문맥이나 전체 문맥을 파악하여 정답을 고른다. 뒤 문장에서 청중들이 적극적으로 자신의 견해를 제시했고 의미 있는 대화가 많이 오갔다고 했으므로 (C) discussion(논의)이 정답이다. (B) statement(성명, 진술, 발표)도 해석상 그럴듯해 보이지만, 주로 공식적인 성명, 진술, 발표를 의미하므로 답이 될 수 없다. (A) procedure는 '절차', (D) variation은 '변형, 변화'라는 의미이다.

02 올바른 시제의 동사 채우기

해설 빈칸은 주격 관계절(who ~ before)의 동사 자리이므로 동사 (A), (C), (D)가 정답의 후보이다. 관계절(who ~ before)에서 나타내는 사건, 즉 지난해에 사람들이 Mr. Arum의 강연에 참석했던 일은 주절(This ~ those)에서 나타내는 사건, 즉 이번 달 초 강연 때 청중들이 적극적으로 자신의 견해를 제시하고 의미 있는 대화가 많이 오감으로써 행사를 특히 즐겁게 만든 시점보다 먼저 일어난 일이다. 따라서, 과거의 특정 시점 이전에 발생한 일을 표현할 수 있는 과거완료 시제 (A) had attended가 정답이다. 현재진행 시제 (C)와 현재 완료 시제 (D)는 과거의 특정 시점 이전에 발생한 일을 표현할 수 없다. 동명사 또는 현재분사 (B)는 동사 자리에 올 수 없다.

어휘 **attend** v. 참석하다

03 부사절 접속사 채우기

해설 이 문장은 필수성분(we would like to offer you compensation)을 갖춘 완전한 절이므로, ___ ~ a voluntary basis는 수식어 거품으로 보아야 한다. 이 수식어 거품은 동사(agreed)가 있는 거품절이므로, 거품절을 이끌 수 있는 부사절 접속사 (B)와 (D)가 정답의 후보이다. '비록 당신이 자원봉사로 시간을 내주는 것에 동의했지만, 당신에게 보상을 제공하고 싶다'라는 의미가 되어야 하므로 (D) Although(비록 ~이지만)가 정답이다. (B) As if(마치 ~처럼)를 쓰면 '마치 당신이 자원봉사로 시간을 내주는 것에 동의한 것처럼'이라는 어색한 문맥이 된다. 부사 (A) Likewise(마찬가지로)와 (C) Indeed(정말, 확실히)는 거품절을 이끌 수 없다.

04 알맞은 문장 고르기

해석 (A) 전화 통화를 통해 당신의 등록을 완료해 주십시오.
(B) 당신이 또 다른 강연을 위해 다시 방문해 주시기를 바랍니다.
(C) 다시 한번, 저는 마이크 문제에 대해 사과드립니다.
(D) 당신의 기사가 이번 달 호에 나올 것입니다.

해설 앞 문장 'I am sending you a $50 gift voucher for the coffee chain Better Beans as a token of our appreciation.'에서 감사의 표시로 커피 체인점 Better Beans의 50달러 상품권을 보낸다고 했으므로, 빈칸에는 감사를 표한 후 앞으로 또 다른 강연을 위해 다시 방문해 주기를 희망하는 내용이 들어가야 함을 알 수 있다. 따라서 (B)가 정답이다.

어휘 complete v. 완료하다 appear v. 나오다, 등장하다

05-08번은 다음 공고에 관한 문제입니다.

주주들을 위한 공지

Orbital사는 예정된 주주총회의 장소를 변경했습니다. ⁰⁵그것은 JadeLink 센터 대신 Rudalle 호텔에서 열릴 것입니다.

또한, 저희는 참석 규정에 또 다른 변경 사항을 적용했습니다. ⁰⁶그것은 이제 사전 등록이 필요하다는 것을 명시하고 있습니다. 여러분은 참석 예약 양식을 곧 받아보시게 될 것입니다. 그것을 작성하여 10월 31일까지 다시 보내주십시오. ⁰⁷여러분의 이름이 참석자 명단에 추가되면, 등록을 확정하는 이메일을 저희가 발송해 드릴 것입니다.

⁰⁸저희는 Orbital사의 웹사이트 www.orbitall.com/vote를 통해 투표하는 것 또한 가능하다는 것을 알려 드립니다.

shareholder n. 주주 attendance n. 참석 policy n. 규정, 정책
vote v. 투표하다; n. 투표

05 태에 맞는 동사 채우기

해설 빈칸 앞에 조동사(will)가 있으므로 조동사 뒤에 올 수 있는 동사원형 (A), (C), (D)가 정답의 후보이다. 주어(It)와 동사(hold)가 '그것[주주총회]이 열리다'라는 수동의 의미가 되어야 하므로 수동태 동사 (D) be held가 정답이다.

어휘 hold v. 열다, 개최하다

06 알맞은 문장 고르기

해석 (A) 그러나, 그 회의는 다음 해에 틀림없이 열릴 것입니다.
(B) 이사회는 새로운 대표 이사를 임명했습니다.
(C) 발표는 보통 기자 회견에서 이뤄집니다.
(D) 그것은 이제 사전 등록이 필요하다는 것을 명시하고 있습니다.

해설 앞 문장 'In addition, we have made another change to the attendance policy.'에서 참석 규정에 또 다른 변경 사항을 적용했다고 했으므로, 빈칸에는 참석 규정의 변경 사항에 대한 세부 내용이 들어가야 함을 알 수 있다. 따라서 (D)가 정답이다. 참고로, (D)의 It은 the attendance policy(참석 규정)를 가리킨다.

어휘 board n. 이사회 appoint v. 임명하다 press conference 기자 회견
advance adj. 사전의

07 현재분사와 과거분사 구별하여 채우기

해설 이 문장은 주어(we), 동사(will send), 목적어(an e-mail)를 갖춘 완전한 절이므로, ___ your registration은 수식어 거품으로 보아야 한다. 보기 중 수식어 거품이 될 수 있는 것은 과거분사 (B)와 현재분사 (C)이고, 빈칸 앞의 명사(e-mail)를 '등록을 확정하는 이메일'이라는 능동의 의미로 수식하는 현재분사 (C) confirming이 정답이다. 동사 (A)와 명사 (D)는 수식어 거품을 이끌 수 없다.

어휘 confirm v. 확정하다, 확인하다 confirmation n. 확정, 확인

08 명사절 접속사 채우기

해설 빈칸 이하(___ it is also possible to ~)는 동사(remind)의 직접 목적어 역할을 하고 있으므로, 동사의 목적어 자리에 올 수 있고 명사절을 이끌 수 있는 (A), (B), (C)가 정답의 후보이다. 빈칸이 포함된 절이 주어(it), 동사(is), 보어(possible)가 있는 완전한 절이므로 명사절 접속사 (C) that이 정답이다. 의문사 (A)와 (B)는 뒤에 불완전한 절이 와야 한다. 전치사 (D)는 명사절을 이끌 수 없다.

09-12번은 다음 공고에 관한 문제입니다.

Demair International사는 더 친환경적으로 변화하고 있습니다

⁰⁹Demair International사는 최근 Green Stay Network(GSN)에 가입했는데, 이는 환경적으로 지속 가능한 활동들에 참여하기 위해 노력하는 호텔과 게스트 하우스의 단체입니다. ¹⁰GSN의 회원으로서 그것의 의무들을 이행하기 위해, Demair International사는 모든 스위트룸에 교육용 책자를 비치합니다. 이것들에는 저희 호텔에 머무는 동안 물과 에너지를 절약하는 방법이 간단한 용어들로 설명되어 있습니다. ¹¹게다가, Demair International사는 이제 모든 직원들이 숙박 산업에서의 지속 가능한 활동들에 대한 교육용 영상을 볼 것을 요구합니다. 또한 더 큰 개선이 계획되어 있습니다. ¹²예를 들어, 가까운 미래에 태양광 패널이 설치될 것입니다.

join v. 가입하다 engage in ~에 참여하다 sustainable adj. 지속 가능한
practice n. 활동, 실천 fulfill v. 이행하다, 달성하다 obligation n. 의무
brochure n. 책자 suite n. 스위트룸 conserve v. 절약하다, 보존하다
as well 또한, 역시

09 부사 자리 채우기

해설 빈칸 뒤의 형용사(sustainable)를 꾸밀 수 있는 것은 부사이므로 부사 (B) environmentally(환경적으로)가 정답이다. 형용사 (A), 명사 (C)와 (D)는 형용사를 꾸밀 수 없다.

어휘 environmental adj. 환경의 environment n. 환경
environmentalist n. 환경운동가

10 형용사 어휘 고르기 주변 문맥 파악

해설 '모든 스위트룸에 ___ 책자를 비치한다'라는 문맥이므로, 모든 보기가 정답의 후보이다. 빈칸이 있는 문장만으로 정답을 고를 수 없으므로 주변 문맥이나 전체 문맥을 파악하여 정답을 고른다. 뒤 문장에서 이것들[책자]에는 호텔에 머무는 동안 물과 에너지를 절약하는 방법이 간단한 용어로 설명되어 있다고 했으므로 물과 에너지를 절약할 수 있는 방법에 관한 교육용 책자를 비치한다는 것을 알 수 있다. 따라서 (C) instructional(교육용의)이 정답이다. (A) controversial은 '논란의, 논란이 많은', (B) complicated는 '복잡한', (D) entertaining은 '재미있는, 즐거움을 주는'이라는 의미이다.

11 제안·요청·의무의 주절을 뒤따르는 that절에 동사원형 채우기

해설 that절(that ~ industry)에 동사가 없고 주절(Demair International ~ requires)에 요청을 나타내는 동사(requires)가 왔으므로 that절의 동사 자리에는 동사원형이 와야 한다. 따라서 동사원형 (A) watch가 정답이다. 동명사 또는 현재분사 (B), 3인칭 단수 동사 (C), to 부정사 (D)는 동사원형 자리에 올 수 없다.

12 알맞은 문장 고르기

해석 (A) 예를 들어, 가까운 미래에 태양광 패널이 설치될 것입니다.

(B) 투어를 신청하시려면, 안내 데스크의 직원에게 이야기하십시오.
(C) 그것은 이번 주 후반에 다양한 장소에서 촬영될 것입니다.
(D) 보상 포인트는 객실 업그레이드를 위해 사용될 수 있습니다.

해설 앞 문장 'Bigger improvements are planned as well.'에서 또한 더 큰 개선이 계획되어 있다고 했으므로 빈칸에는 계획되어 있는 개선의 예시가 들어가야 함을 알 수 있다. 따라서 (A)가 정답이다.

어휘 **reward point** 보상 포인트   **redeem** v. (상품권 등을) 사용하다, 교환하다

13-16번은 다음 채용 공고에 관한 문제입니다.

> 직원 모집
> 채용 코드: Y51633
>
> **13**창의적이고, 매우 경쟁력 있는 직원들로 구성된 디자인 대행사가 방콕에 있는 팀에 합류할 사람들을 찾고 있습니다. 이 공석은 고객들을 위한 독창적인 포장 아이디어를 개발하는 것과 관련된 직무입니다.
>
> **14**지원자는 관련 분야의 학위를 소지할 필요는 없습니다. 그러나, 그들은 디자인 소프트웨어 관련 경험과 지식을 보유해야 합니다. 전문 자격증을 보유한 사람이 선호됩니다.
>
> **15**staff@bkrecruit.com으로 이메일을 보냄으로써 지원하십시오. 귀하의 이력서를 첨부하고 온라인 포트폴리오 링크를 첨부하십시오.
>
> 중요: 귀하의 이메일 제목란에 이 게시글의 채용 코드를 입력하십시오. **16**그러고 나서, 저희는 귀하의 지원서가 접수되었음을 알려드리기 위해 알림을 보내드릴 것입니다.

consist of ~로 구성되다   **creative** adj. 창의적인   **individual** n. 사람, 개인
open position 공석   **original** adj. 독창적인   **relevant** adj. 관련된
professional certification 전문 자격증   **enclose** v. 첨부하다, 동봉하다
posting n. 게시글   **subject line** 제목란   **notification** n. 알림

13 형용사 어휘 고르기
해설 '창의적이고, 매우 경쟁력 있는 직원들로 구성된 디자인 대행사'라는 문맥이므로 (A) competitive(경쟁력 있는)가 정답이다. (B) extensive는 '광범위한, 폭넓은', (C) alternate는 '교대의, 번갈아 하는', (D) natural은 '자연스러운'이라는 의미이다.

14 알맞은 문장 고르기
해석 (A) 컴퓨터 소프트웨어가 고도로 발전했습니다.
(B) 자동차를 운전하는 능력이 이 직무에 매우 중요합니다.
(C) 지원자는 관련 분야의 학위를 소지할 필요는 없습니다.
(D) 귀하는 온라인 면접에 초청받았습니다.

해설 뒤 문장 'However, they must have relevant experience and knowledge of design software.'에서 그러나 그들, 즉 지원자들은 디자인 소프트웨어 관련 경험과 지식을 보유해야 한다고 했으므로, 빈칸에는 지원자의 자격 요건과 관련된 내용이 들어가야 함을 알 수 있다. 따라서 (C)가 정답이다. (B)도 지원자의 자격 요건과 관련이 있지만, 뒤 문장이 However(그러나)로 시작하므로 흐름이 어색하다.

어휘 **vehicle** n. 자동차   **crucial** adj. 매우 중요한

15 전치사 채우기
해설 빈칸은 동명사구(sending an e-mail)를 목적어로 취하는 전치사 자리이므로 모든 보기가 정답의 후보이다. '이메일을 보냄으로써 지원하라'라는 의미가 되어야 하므로 전치사 (C) by(~함으로써)가 정답이다. 전치사 (A) to, (B) for, (D) in을 쓸 경우 각각 '이메일을 보내는 것에 적용하라/이메일을 보내는 것에 지원하라/이메일을 보내다가 지원하라'라는 어색한 문맥이 되므로 답이 될 수 없다.

16 접속부사 채우기 주변 문맥 파악
해설 빈칸이 콤마와 함께 문장의 맨 앞에 온 접속부사 자리이므로, 앞 문장과 빈칸이 있는 문장의 의미 관계를 파악하여 정답을 선택한다. 앞 문장에서 귀하의 이메일 제목란에 게시글의 채용 코드를 입력하라고 했고, 빈칸이 있는 문장에서는 귀하의 지원서가 접수되었음을 알리기 위해 알림을 보낼 것이라고 했으므로, 앞 문장의 내용에 이어질 다음 과정을 설명할 때 사용되는 (B) Then(그러고 나서)이 정답이다.

어휘 **instead** adv. 대신에   **even so** 그렇기는 하지만
nevertheless adv. 그럼에도 불구하고

PART 7

DAY 13 주제/목적 및 육하원칙 문제

기출 유형 1 주제/목적 문제

Example p.226

01번은 다음 공고에 관한 문제입니다.

> 저희의 소중한 환자분들께:
>
> 저희 병원이 Slate Tower에 위치한 현재의 장소에서 Gramercy가 6124번지로 이전함에 따라 1월 15일부터 2월 21일까지 문을 닫을 것임을 알려드리게 되어 유감입니다. 이것이 초래할 수 있는 모든 불편에 대해 사과드립니다. 해당 기간 동안 예약이 되어 있으시다면, 병원 직원이 일정을 변경하기 위해 연락드릴 것입니다. 여러분의 인내와 이해에 감사드립니다.

regret v. 유감스럽게 생각하다, 후회하다 transition n. 이전, 변화
inconvenience n. 불편 appointment n. 예약, 약속 book v. 예약하다
representative n. 직원, 대표 reschedule v. 일정을 변경하다
patience n. 인내

01

해석 공고의 목적은 무엇인가?
(A) 사업 소유권 변경에 관해 설명하기 위해
(B) 건물의 보수 공사를 발표하기 위해
(C) 서비스 업데이트를 소개하기 위해
(D) 일시적인 휴업을 알리기 위해

어휘 ownership n. 소유권 renovation n. 보수 공사 temporary adj. 일시적인
closure n. 휴업, 폐쇄

토익실전문제 p.227

| 01 (A) | 02 (C) | 03 (D) |

01-03번은 다음 안내문에 관한 문제입니다.

> ⁰¹로체스터시는 Corliss Gardens 모바일 애플리케이션을 소개합니다. 이제, 방문객들은 어떤 모바일 기기에서든지 Corliss Gardens에 대한 정보에 편리하게 접근하실 수 있습니다. 공원의 시설들을 살펴보거나, 방문을 계획하거나, 또는 그저 Corliss Gardens에서의 행사 및 활동에 관한 소식을 얻기 위해 이것을 사용해 보세요.
>
> 공원 부지의 상세 지도에 접근할 수 있는 것 이외에도, 사용자들은 가장 가까운 이용 가능한 주차 공간까지 가는 길을 안내받고, 최신 기상 예보에 대한 알림을 받으며, 심지어 개인 행사를 위해 공원의 네 개 행사 장소들 중 어디든 예약할 수 있습니다. 또한 ⁰²애플리케이션에서 가입하는 사용자들은 지역 사업체들로부터 특별 할인을 받을 자격을 즉시 얻습니다.
>
> Corliss Gardens에 대한 더 많은 정보를 위해서는, ⁰³로체스터시 공식 웹사이트를 방문하여 "시립 공원" 버튼을 클릭하세요.

explore v. 살펴보다, 탐험하다 facility n. 시설, 기관 obtain v. 얻다, 획득하다
aside from ~ 이외에도, ~을 제외하고 notification n. 알림
weather forecast 기상 예보 function n. 행사, 기능; v. 기능하다
instantly adv. 즉시 municipal adj. 시의, 지방 자치제의

01 주제 문제

해석 안내문은 주로 무엇에 대한 것인가?
(A) 새로운 소프트웨어 프로그램
(B) 시설의 정책 변경
(C) 지역 사업체 홍보
(D) 공원 안전 관련 최신 정보

해설 지문의 'The City of Rochester is introducing the Corliss Gardens mobile application.'에서 로체스터시는 Corliss Gardens 모바일 애플리케이션을 소개한다고 한 후, 애플리케이션의 다양한 기능들을 설명하고 있으므로 (A)가 정답이다.

어휘 promotion n. 홍보, 승진

Paraphrasing
mobile application 모바일 애플리케이션 → software program 소프트웨어 프로그램

02 육하원칙 문제

해석 사람들은 어떻게 특별 할인에 대한 자격을 얻을 수 있는가?
(A) 설문조사를 완료함으로써
(B) 지역 사업체를 방문함으로써
(C) 애플리케이션에서 등록함으로써
(D) 기부를 함으로써

해설 지문의 'Users who sign up on the application ~ become instantly eligible to receive special offers'에서 애플리케이션에서 가입하는 사용자들은 특별 할인을 받을 자격을 즉시 얻는다고 했으므로 (C)가 정답이다.

어휘 qualify for ~에 대한 자격을 얻다 donation n. 기부

Paraphrasing
become ~ eligible to receive special offers 특별 할인을 받을 자격을 얻다 → qualify for special offers 특별 할인에 대한 자격을 얻다
sign up 가입하다 → register 등록하다

03 추론 문제

해석 Corliss Gardens에 대해 결론지을 수 있는 것은?
(A) 최근에 주차 공간을 확장했다.
(B) 무역 행사를 위한 장소로 선정되었다.
(C) 방문객들에게 입장료를 청구한다.
(D) 시 정부에 의해 관리된다.

해설 지문의 'The City of Rochester is introducing the Corliss Gardens mobile application.'에서 로체스터시는 Corliss Gardens 모바일 애플리케이션을 소개한다고 했고, 'visit the City of Rochester's official Web site and click the "Municipal Parks" button'에서 로체스터시 공식 웹사이트를 방문하여 "시립 공원" 버튼을 클릭하라고 했으므로 Corliss Gardens가 로체스터시에 의해 관리된다는 사실을 추론할 수 있다. 따라서 (D)가 정답이다.

어휘 expand v. 확장하다 admission fee 입장료

기출 유형 2 육하원칙 문제

Example p.228

01번은 다음 기사에 관한 문제입니다.

> 남아프리카 예술 축제는 예전에는 요하네스버그에서 열렸지만, 주최자들은 케이프타운을 이 축제의 새로운 영구적인 개최지로 선정하기로 결정했는데 이는 그곳이 관광객들에게 더 인기가 많기 때문이다. "해안을 따라 위치해 있다는 것은 이곳이 매년, 특히 여름에 많은 수의 방문객들을 끌어들인다는 것을 의미합니다."라고 주최자 Joma Nkosi가 말했다. 이에 따라, 케이프타운의 새로운 개최지에서 축제의 참석자 수가 증가할 것으로 예상된다. 다가오는 축제를 위해 이미 항공편과 숙소를 마련한 해외 방문객들에게는

예약을 변경하도록 권고된다. 제휴 숙소에 관한 정보는 www.saaf.com 에서 확인할 수 있다.

permanent adj. 영구적인, 불변의 **coast** n. 해안
attract v. 끌어들이다, 유치하다 **particularly** adv. 특히
attendance n. 참석자 수, 참석 **overseas** adj. 해외의
arrangement n. 마련, 준비 **modify** v. 변경하다, 수정하다

01
해석 축제에 가는 몇몇 사람들은 무엇을 하도록 요청받는가?
(A) 예약을 변경한다.
(B) 축제 주최자에게 연락한다.
(C) 행사 장소에 전화한다.
(D) 요하네스버그로 가는 항공편을 예매한다.

어휘 **festivalgoer** n. 축제에 가는 사람

토익실전문제   p.229

| 01 (C) | 02 (A) | 03 (B) |

01-03번은 다음 이메일에 관한 문제입니다.

수신: Marcie Camden <mcamden@dawsoninc.com>
발신: Christina Garcia <cgarcia@eshopping.com>
날짜: 11월 10일
제목: 귀하의 주문

Ms. Camden께,

이 이메일은 귀하께서 11월 8일에 저희 웹사이트에서 주문하신 두 개의 Lucia Simonetti 디자이너 핸드백에 관한 것입니다. 안타깝게도, ⁰¹핸드백 중 하나인 모델 번호 452는 현재 재고가 없습니다. — [1] —. ⁰³저희는 이탈리아에 있는 저희 공급업체에 주문을 넣었습니다. — [2] —. ⁰³새 제품이 도착할 것으로 예상할 수 있는 가장 이른 날짜는 오늘로부터 2주 후입니다.

⁰¹저희는 귀하께서 여전히 모델 번호 452에 대한 주문을 진행하고 싶으신지 알고 싶습니다. — [3] —. 만약 아니라면, 저희는 그것에 대해 전액 환불해 드리고 ⁰²구매 가능한 물품인 모델 번호 450을 추가 비용 없이 익일 배송으로 보내드릴 것입니다. 아니면 귀하께서는 모델 번호 452가 도착하길 기다리셔도 되는데, 그럴 경우 저희가 모든 것을 함께 보내드릴 것입니다. — [4] —. 귀하의 결정을 저희에게 알려주시기 위해 회신 이메일을 보내주시기 바랍니다. 불편을 끼쳐드려 다시 한번 사과드립니다.

Christina Garcia 드림
판매 담당자
E-Shopping사

currently adv. 현재, 지금 **out of stock** 재고가 없는
proceed with ~을 진행하다, 계속하다 **overnight** adj. 익일 배달의, 밤사이의
ship v. 보내다, 수송하다

01 글을 쓴 이유 문제
해석 Ms. Garcia는 왜 이메일을 보냈는가?
(A) 청구 오류에 대해 사과하기 위해
(B) 새로운 핸드백 모델을 홍보하기 위해
(C) 주문에 대한 선호 사항을 묻기 위해
(D) 출장 일정을 잡기 위해

해설 지문의 'one of the handbags, Model #452, is currently out of stock'에서 Ms. Garcia가 핸드백 중 하나인 모델 번호 452가 현재 재고가 없다고 한 후, 'We would like to know if you still wish to proceed with your order for Model #452.'에서 귀하가 여전히 모델 번호 452에 대한 주문을 진행하고 싶은지 알고 싶다고 했으므로 (C)가 정답이다.

어휘 **preference** n. 선호, 애호

02 육하원칙 문제
해석 Ms. Garcia는 추가 비용 없이 무엇을 제공하겠다고 제안하는가?
(A) 물품의 신속한 배송
(B) 손상된 제품의 수리
(C) 핸드백 맞춤 제작 지원
(D) 구할 수 없는 상품의 대체품

해설 지문의 'we will ~ send the available item, Model #450, by overnight shipping at no extra cost'에서 구매 가능한 물품인 모델 번호 450을 추가 비용 없이 익일 배송으로 보내줄 것이라고 했으므로 (A)가 정답이다.

어휘 **expedited** adj. 신속한, 촉진된 **customization** n. 맞춤 제작

03 문장 위치 찾기 문제
해석 [1], [2], [3], [4]로 표시된 위치 중, 다음 문장이 들어갈 곳으로 가장 적절한 것은?

"그러나, 그들은 밀라노에서의 수송 파업 때문에 지연이 발생할 수 있다고 알렸습니다."

(A) [1]
(B) [2]
(C) [3]
(D) [4]

해설 주어진 문장은 지연과 관련된 내용이 나오는 부분에 들어가야 함을 알 수 있다. [2]의 앞 문장인 'We placed an order with our supplier in Italy.'에서 이탈리아에 있는 공급업체에 주문을 넣었다고 했고, 뒤 문장인 'The earliest we can expect the new item to arrive is two weeks from today.'에서는 새 제품이 도착할 것으로 예상할 수 있는 가장 이른 날짜가 오늘로부터 2주 후라고 했다. 따라서 [2]에 제시된 문장이 들어가면 이탈리아에 있는 공급업체에 주문을 넣었으나 그들, 즉 공급업체가 밀라노에서 발생한 수송 파업으로 인해 지연이 발생할 수 있다고 알렸고, 빨라도 2주 후에야 새 제품이 도착할 것이라는 자연스러운 문맥이 된다는 것을 알 수 있다. 따라서 (B)가 정답이다.

어휘 **due to** ~ 때문에 **strike** n. 파업, 공습

HACKERS TEST   p.230

| 01 (C) | 02 (C) | 03 (A) | 04 (B) | 05 (D) |

01-02번은 다음 웹페이지에 관한 문제입니다.

www.canburyhospital.org/information
Canbury 병원 인트라넷

홈 >> 환자 관리 >> Dr. Michael Hatch >> 환자 정보
⁰¹환자 이름: Charlotte Reed
전화번호: 555-4839

의료 기록
⁰¹환자는 다음의 과거 증상들을 경험했습니다:

☐ 흉통	☑ 복통	☐ 두통
☑ 귀통증	⁰¹☑ 계절성 알레르기	☑ 피부 염증
☑ 목 염증	☐ 허리 통증	☐ 스트레스 또는 불안

예약 세부 사항
환자의 Dr. Hatch와의 다음 예약은
4월 22일 월요일, 오전 11시 30분으로 예정되어 있습니다.

예약 시간을 변경하시려면 여기를 클릭하십시오.

참고
⁰²Dr. Hatch는 심장 건강에 대한 강연을 하기 위해 4월 21일부터 24일까지 런던에 출장을 갈 것이므로, Ms. Reed의 건강 검진 일정이 변경되어야 합니다.

어휘 patient n. 환자   symptom n. 증상, 징후   irritation n. 염증, 자극
　　 seasonal adj. 계절성의, 계절의   anxiety n. 불안, 염려
　　 checkup n. 건강 검진

01 육하원칙 문제
해석 Ms. Reed는 과거에 무엇을 경험했는가?
　　(A) 심장 문제
　　(B) 허리 통증
　　(C) 알레르기 반응
　　(D) 업무 스트레스

해설 지문의 'Patient Name: Charlotte Reed', 'Patient has experienced past symptoms of:', '☑ seasonal allergies'에서 Ms. Reed가 과거에 계절성 알레르기 증상을 경험했다고 했으므로 (C)가 정답이다.

어휘 trouble n. 통증, 병, 문제   reaction n. 반응, 반작용

02 육하원칙 문제
해석 Ms. Reed의 건강 검진 일정은 왜 변경되어야 하는가?
　　(A) 병원이 하루 동안 문을 닫을 것이다.
　　(B) 그녀의 보험 관련 정보를 제출하지 않았다.
　　(C) 그녀의 의사가 출장을 갈 예정이다.
　　(D) 몇몇 검사 결과들이 나오지 않았다.

해설 지문의 'Dr. Hatch will be traveling to London ~, so Ms. Reed's checkup must be rescheduled.'에서 Dr. Hatch가 런던에 출장을 갈 것이므로 Ms. Reed의 건강 검진 일정이 변경되어야 한다고 했으므로 (C)가 정답이다.

어휘 physician n. 의사

03-05번은 다음 이메일에 관한 문제입니다.

수신: Evan Kensington <evkens44@nearmail.net>
발신: Madison Gordon <m.gordon@fosteracademy.com>
제목: 비즈니스 작문 온라인 강좌
날짜: 2월 18일

Mr. Kensington께,

Foster 학원의 온라인 비즈니스 작문 수업에 등록해 주셔서 감사합니다. 04-(A)이 강좌는 총 4주 동안 진행될 것입니다. 수료하고 나면, 당신은 편지, 보고서, 계약서 등과 같은 중요한 문서들을 어떻게 작성하는지 알게 될 것입니다.

03수업의 첫날인 2월 27일 전에, 당신이 완료해야 할 몇 가지 작업이 있습니다. 무엇보다 먼저, 04-(C)당신의 Foster 학원 온라인 계정에 로그인하여 "과제"를 클릭하세요. 04-(D)당신은 그 링크에 이미 올려져 있는 몇 가지 읽기 과제를 발견할 것입니다. 이것들을 꼭 살펴보십시오.

또한, 당신이 www.fosteracademy.com/programs에서 TeachViewer 소프트웨어를 다운받고 그것이 당신의 컴퓨터에서 제대로 작동하는지 확인하는 것이 매우 중요합니다. 05학생들은 수업 토론 포럼에 게시글을 작성하기 위해 이 프로그램을 사용할 것입니다.

시작하시는 데 행운을 빌며, 질문이나 우려 사항이 있다면 제게 이메일을 보내주십시오.

Foster 학원의 강사 Madison Gordon 드림

어휘 register v. 등록하다   run v. 진행되다   in total 총, 통틀어
　　 completion n. 수료, 완료   first and foremost 무엇보다 먼저
　　 account n. 계정   assignment n. 과제   discussion n. 토론

03 목적 문제
해석 이메일의 주된 목적은 무엇인가?
　　(A) 학생을 수업에 준비시키기 위해
　　(B) 등록 과정을 설명하기 위해
　　(C) 몇몇 서류들의 제출을 요청하기 위해
　　(D) 수료 증서를 제공하기 위해

해설 지문의 'Before ~ the first day of the class—there are a few tasks ~ to complete.'에서 수업의 첫날 전에 완료해야 할 몇 가지 작업이 있다고 한 후, 수업 전 준비해야 할 사항들을 설명하고 있으므로 (A)가 정답이다.

어휘 certificate n. 증서

04 Not/True 문제
해석 비즈니스 작문 수업에 대해 언급되지 않은 것은?
　　(A) 몇 주에 걸쳐 진행될 것이다.
　　(B) 성적이 매겨지는 글쓰기 과제와 함께 끝날 것이다.
　　(C) 학생들이 온라인 계정을 사용할 것을 요구한다.
　　(D) 사전 읽기 과제가 포함되어 있다.

해설 (B)는 지문에 언급되지 않은 내용이다. 따라서 (B)가 정답이다. (A)는 'This course will run for four weeks in total.'에서 이 강좌는 총 4주 동안 진행될 것이라고 했으므로 지문의 내용과 일치한다. (C)는 'log on to your Foster Academy online account and click on "Assignments"'에서 Foster 학원 온라인 계정에 로그인하여 "과제"를 클릭하라고 했으므로 지문의 내용과 일치한다. (D)는 'You will see several reading assignments already listed at that link. Please be sure to look these over.'에서 당신이 링크에 이미 올려져 있는 몇 가지 읽기 과제들을 발견할 것이며, 이것들을 꼭 살펴보라고 했으므로 지문의 내용과 일치한다.

어휘 grade v. 성적을 매기다   preliminary adj. 사전의

05 육하원칙 문제
해석 학생들은 왜 지정된 소프트웨어를 다운로드해야 하는가?
　　(A) 과제를 제출하기 위해
　　(B) 출석 현황을 관리하기 위해
　　(C) 수업 자료에 접근하기 위해
　　(D) 같은 반 학생들과 소통하기 위해

해설 지문의 'Students will use the program to make posts on the class discussion forum.'에서 학생들은 수업 토론 포럼에 게시글을 작성하기 위해 이 프로그램, 즉 TeachViewer 소프트웨어를 사용할 것이라고 했으므로 (D)가 정답이다.

어휘 specified adj. 지정된   track v. (추적하여) 관리하다
　　 interact v. 소통하다, 상호작용하다

DAY 14 Not/True 및 추론 문제

기출 유형 1 Not/True 문제

Example　　　　　　　　　　　　　　　　　　　　p.232
01번은 다음 브로슈어에 관한 문제입니다.

저희의 사진작가들은 결혼식, 기념일, 그리고 졸업식과 같은 특별한 행사들의 마법 같은 순간들을 포착하는 것을 전문으로 합니다. 저희는 새로운 패키지를 발표하게 되어 기쁩니다:

플래티넘 패키지 (2,000달러)
(A)두 명의 사진작가가 당신의 행사에 참석할 것이며, 최상의 결과를 보장하기 위해 (B)그들이 촬영한 사진들은 전문 사진 편집자에 의해 보정될 것입니다. 그러고 나서 당신은 최종 사진의 디지털 사본을 제공받을 것입니다. (C)당신은 추가 비용 없이 최대 500매의 인화본을 요청하실 수 있습니다.

specialize in ~을 전문으로 하다   capture v. 포착하다
anniversary n. 기념일   refine v. 보정하다, 개선하다

01

해설 플래티넘 패키지에 대해 언급되지 않은 것은?
(A) 여러 명의 사진작가가 행사에 참석할 것이다.
(B) 사진이 전문가에 의해 편집될 것이다.
(C) 일정 수량의 무료 인화본을 받을 수 있다.
(D) 맞춤형 사진 앨범이 제작될 것이다.

어휘 expert n. 전문가; adj. 전문가의

[Paraphrasing]
Two photographers 두 명의 사진작가 → Multiple photographers 여러 명의 사진작가
be refined by a professional photo editor 전문 사진 편집자에 의해 보정되다 → be edited by an expert 전문가에 의해 편집되다
up to 500 prints at no additional charge 추가 비용 없이 최대 500매의 인화본 → A set number of free prints 일정 수량의 무료 인화본

토익실전문제 p.233

| 01 | (D) | 02 | (C) | 03 | (C) |

01-03번은 다음 이메일에 관한 문제입니다.

수신: Lauren Bisson <laurenb@junomail.com>
발신: Jaleela Attar <j_attar@geladatech.com>
제목: 회신: 질문
날짜: 2월 8일

Ms. Bisson께,

⁰¹저는 당신이 Gelada Technologies사에서 일을 시작하는 것에 대해 조금 긴장감을 느낄 수도 있다는 것을 이해하며, 당신이 최대한 철저히 준비하고 싶어 한다는 사실이 기쁩니다. 저희 건물에 도착하면 무엇을 해야 하는지에 대한 당신의 질문에 답변드리자면, 일 층의 안내 데스크에 들러 주세요. 그곳의 직원이 당신을 도와줄 것입니다. ⁰²⁻⁽ᴬ⁾비록 당신의 정규 근무는 오전 9시에 시작되지만, 당신과 다른 몇몇 ⁰³신입 직원들은 오리엔테이션 세션에 참여할 것이므로 ⁰²⁻⁽ᴬ⁾처음 이틀 동안은 반드시 오전 8시에 도착하십시오.

⁰²⁻⁽ᴮ⁾이 세션들은 당신의 일상 업무와 당신이 사용하게 될 소프트웨어 애플리케이션을 다룰 것입니다. ⁰²⁻⁽ᶜ⁾⁽ᴰ⁾이것들이 이미 설치된 노트북이 당신에게 지급될 것입니다. ⁰³교육이 진행되는 이틀 모두 점심이 제공된다는 것 또한 알고 계시기 바랍니다.

저는 이 정보가 당신의 궁금증을 해결해 주기를 바랍니다. 다음 주에 뵙겠습니다.

Jaleela Attar 드림
인사부 관리자, Gelada Technologies사

participate v. 참여하다, 참석하다   cover v. 다루다
day-to-day adj. 일상의, 그날그날의   issue v. 지급하다
address v. 해결하다, 다루다

01 글을 쓴 이유 문제

해설 Ms. Attar는 왜 이메일을 썼는가?
(A) 수습 직원에게 몇 가지 문서들을 제출할 것을 상기시키기 위해
(B) 구직 면접에 대한 질문에 답하기 위해
(C) 교육 워크숍에 대한 의견을 요청하기 위해
(D) 출근 첫날에 대해 직원을 준비시키기 위해

해설 지문의 'I understand that you may feel ~ nervous about starting work ~, and I am glad that you want to be as prepared as possible.'에서 저, 즉 Ms. Attar는 당신이 일을 시작하는 것에 대해 긴장감을 느낄 수 있다는 것을 이해하며 당신이 최대한 철저히 준비하고 싶어 한다는 사실이 기쁘다고 한 후, 출근 첫날에 진행될 일과 유의 사항을 안내하고 있으므로 (D)가 정답이다.

어휘 trainee n. 수습 직원   instructional adj. 교육의

02 Not/True 문제

해설 교육 세션 참가자들에 대해 사실이 아닌 것은?
(A) 직장에 일찍 와야 한다.
(B) 일상 업무에 대해 배울 것이다.
(C) 소프트웨어 프로그램을 설치해야 한다.
(D) 전자기기를 받을 것이다.

해설 (C)는 'A laptop with these already installed will be issued to you.'에서 이것들, 즉 소프트웨어 프로그램이 이미 설치된 노트북이 지급될 것이라고 했으므로 지문의 내용과 일치하지 않는다. 따라서 (C)가 정답이다. (A)는 'Although your normal workday begins at 9:00 A.M., make sure to arrive at 8:00 A.M. on the first two days'에서 비록 정규 근무는 오전 9시에 시작되지만 처음 이틀 동안은 반드시 오전 8시에 도착하라고 했으므로 지문의 내용과 일치한다. (B)는 'These sessions will cover your day-to-day responsibilities'에서 오리엔테이션 세션들은 일상 업무를 다룰 것이라고 했으므로 지문의 내용과 일치한다. (D)는 'A laptop ~ will be issued to you.'에서 노트북이 지급될 것이라고 했으므로 지문의 내용과 일치한다.

어휘 workplace n. 직장   electronic device 전자기기   duty n. 업무, 의무

[Paraphrasing]
day-to-day responsibilities 일상 업무 → daily duties 일상 업무
laptop 노트북 → electronic device 전자기기

03 추론 문제

해설 Gelada Technologies사에 대해 암시되는 것은?
(A) 몇몇 직원들이 재택근무를 하도록 허용한다.
(B) 직원들에 의해 사용되는 소프트웨어를 업데이트했다.
(C) 몇몇 직원들을 위해 두 끼의 식사를 준비할 것이다.
(D) 최근에 새로운 사무실 건물로 이전했다.

해설 지문의 'new staff members will be participating in orientation sessions'에서 신입 직원들은 오리엔테이션 세션에 참여할 것이라고 했고, 'lunch will be provided on both training days'에서 교육이 진행되는 이틀 모두 점심이 제공될 것이라고 했으므로 Gelada Technologies사가 몇몇 직원들을 위해 이틀 동안 점심, 즉 총 두 끼의 식사를 준비할 것이라는 사실을 추론할 수 있다. 따라서 (C)가 정답이다.

어휘 arrange v. 준비하다

[Paraphrasing]
lunch 점심 → meals 식사

기출 유형 2 추론 문제

Example p.234

01번은 다음 공고에 관한 문제입니다.

직원들과 장비를 이동시키기 위해 보통 업무용 승강기로 이용되는 4호 승강기가 다음 주 6월 27일부터 29일까지 이용할 수 없을 것이라는 점을 알아 두시기 바랍니다. 기술자들이 정기 보수를 시행할 것입니다. 그동안에, 3호 승강기가 업무용 승강기로 사용될 것입니다. 세입자들의 통행증은 그 승강기에서 작동하지 않을 것이므로, 1호 또는 2호 승강기 중 하나를 사용해 주십시오.

-Parker 주거 타워 관리진

transport v. 이동시키다, 옮기다   equipment n. 장비
unavailable adj. 이용할 수 없는   technician n. 기술자
routine maintenance 정기 보수   in the meantime 그동안에
tenant n. 세입자   pass card 통행증   residential adj. 주거의

01

해설 공고는 누구를 대상으로 하는 것 같은가?
(A) 유지보수 기술자들
(B) 보안 요원들

(C) 투어 참가자들
(D) 건물 주민들

어휘 **resident** n. 주민, 거주자

토익실전문제 p.235

01 (C)   **02** (B)

01-02번은 다음 이메일에 관한 문제입니다.

수신: Kendra Clark <kclark@zoommail.com>
발신: George Adachi <g.adachi@npo_gov.com>
제목: 지구의 날 기념
날짜: 6월 3일

Ms. Clark께,

⁰¹국립 우체국에서 지구의 날을 기념하는 우표를 막 발행했습니다. 이것은 유명한 야생 동물 화가인 Carla Anderson이 그린 동물들의 그림을 담고 있습니다. ⁰²저희는 당신의 회원들이 이 상품을 특히 매력적으로 느낄 것이라 생각합니다.

우체국에서는 이 우표를 단 4,000장만 제작했습니다. 저희는 당신의 동호회와 같이 등록된 단체들에 저희로부터 그것을 직접 구매할 수 있는 기회를 제공해 드리고 있습니다. ⁰²당신의 동호회 회원 중 이 우표를 수집품에 추가하고 싶어 하는 분이 계신다면, 6월 6일까지 이 이메일에 회신해 주시기 바랍니다.

George Adachi 드림
소매 거래 관리자
국립 우체국

release v. 발행하다, 공개하다   **stamp** n. 우표
commemorate v. 기념하다, 축하하다   **noted** adj. 유명한, 저명한
appealing adj. 매력적인   **registered** adj. (공식적으로) 등록된
purchase v. 구매하다   **directly** adv. 직접   **collection** n. 수집품, 수집

01 목적 문제
해석 이메일의 목적은 무엇인가?
(A) 모금 행사에 대한 지지를 보여주기 위해
(B) 조직 회의 일정을 잡기 위해
(C) 제품에 대한 세부 정보를 제공하기 위해
(D) 공휴일을 공지하기 위해

해설 'The National Post Office has just released a stamp commemorating Earth Day.'에서 국립 우체국에서 지구의 날을 기념하는 우표를 막 발행했다고 한 후, 기념우표에 관한 세부 정보와 구매 방법에 대해 설명하고 있으므로 (C)가 정답이다.

어휘 **fundraiser** n. 모금 행사

02 추론 문제
해석 동호회의 회원은 누구일 것 같은가?
(A) 시각 예술가
(B) 우표 수집가
(C) 환경론자
(D) 우체국 직원

해설 이메일의 'We believe your members will find this item particularly appealing.'에서 당신의 회원들이 이 상품, 즉 지구의 날을 기념하여 새로 발행된 우표를 특히 매력적으로 느낄 것이라 생각한다고 했고, 'If any of your club members want to add this stamp to their collections'에서 동호회 회원 중 우표를 수집품에 추가하고 싶어 하는 사람이 있을 경우에 대해 이야기하고 있으므로, 동호회의 회원은 우표 수집가들이라는 사실을 추론할 수 있다. 따라서 (B)가 정답이다.

어휘 **visual** adj. 시각의   **environmentalist** n. 환경론자

HACKERS TEST p.236

01 (B)   **02** (C)   **03** (B)   **04** (A)   **05** (D)
06 (C)

01-02번은 다음 문자 메시지 대화문에 관한 문제입니다.

Agnes Beecroft [오후 5시 45분]
Bart, 저의 회계 보고서와 관련해 저를 도와줘서 고마워요. ⁰¹당신은 목요일 밤 농구 경기를 보러 가는 것에 관심이 있나요? Hart Technologies사의 Ms. Farrow가 저에게 티켓 두 장을 줬어요.

Bart Kreps [오후 5시 48분]
저는 참석할 수 없어요. ⁰¹그날 저녁에 고객과의 전화 회의에 참여해야 해요.

Agnes Beecroft [오후 5시 49분]
괜찮아요. 당신이 생각하기에 제가 물어볼 수 있는 다른 사람은 누구인가요?

Bart Kreps [오후 5시 51분]
Tina Rodriguez는 어때요? ⁰²⁻⁽ᶜ⁾우리가 Hart Technologies사를 위해 진행했던 지난 광고 캠페인에서 저는 그녀와 같이 일했어요. 저는 항상 그녀가 잘 해냈고 어떤 종류의 보상을 받을 자격이 있다고 생각했어요.

Agnes Beecroft [오후 5시 54분]
알겠어요, 고마워요! 그럼 제가 Tina에게 물어볼게요.

accounting n. 회계   **make it** (모임 등에) 참석하다
deserve v. ~을 받을 자격이 있다   **reward** n. 보상; v. 보상하다

01 의도 파악 문제
해석 오후 5시 48분에, Mr. Kreps가 "I can't make it"이라고 썼을 때 그가 의도한 것은?
(A) 업무를 돕기에는 너무 바쁘다.
(B) 행사에 참석할 수 없을 것이다.
(C) 목요일에 일찍 퇴근해야 한다.
(D) 회의에서 발표할 계획이 없다.

해설 지문의 'Would you be interested in going to a basketball game on Thursday night?'에서 Ms. Beecroft가 목요일 밤 농구 경기를 보러 가는 것에 관심이 있는지 묻자, Mr. Kreps가 'I can't make it' (저는 참석할 수 없어요)이라고 한 후, 'I have to participate in a conference call with a client that evening.'에서 그날 저녁에 고객과의 전화 회의에 참여해야 한다고 한 것을 통해, Mr. Kreps는 농구 경기에 참석할 수 없을 것이라는 것을 알 수 있다. 따라서 (B)가 정답이다.

어휘 **task** n. 업무, 과제

02 Not/True 문제
해석 Ms. Rodriguez에 대해 언급된 것은?
(A) Hart Technologies사에 의해 고용되었다.
(B) 승진이 고려되고 있다.
(C) 프로젝트에서 Mr. Kreps와 함께 일했다.
(D) 회계팀에 속해 있다.

해설 (C)는 'I worked with her on the last advertising campaign we did for Hart Technologies.'에서 저, 즉 Mr. Kreps가 Hart Technologies사를 위해 진행했던 지난 광고 캠페인에서 그녀, 즉 Ms. Rodriguez와 같이 일했다고 했으므로 지문의 내용과 일치한다. 따라서 (C)가 정답이다. (A), (B), (D)는 지문에 언급되지 않은 내용이다.

어휘 **employ** v. 고용하다, 사용하다   **consider** v. 고려하다
belong to ~에 속하다, ~의 소유물이다

03-06번은 다음 회람에 관한 문제입니다.

BRONMAN HARDWARE사

수신: 매장 관리자들
발신: Steven Tisdale, 최고경영자
제목: 향후 계획
날짜: 9월 6일

여러분도 아시다시피, 저는 오하이오주 콜럼버스에서 열린 제44회 연례 건축 산업 무역 박람회에 참석했습니다. ⁰³제가 이 행사에서 관찰한 건축 자재들 관련 최신 트렌드를 여러분에게 공유하고자 합니다. — [1] —. 주택 소유주들 사이에서 현지에서 조달되는 건축 물자에 대한 수요가 증가하고 있는 것으로 보입니다.

이 소식을 고려하여, 저는 마케팅 부서에 조사를 할 것을 요청했습니다. — [2] —. 그들은 우리 매장에서 잘 팔릴 수 있는 현지 제품들의 목록을 작성했습니다. ^{04/06}다음 달에, 우리는 각 매장 관리자에게 이 모든 제품들에 대해 특별 판촉 활동을 할 것을 요청할 것입니다. ⁰⁶우리는 그다음에 각 지점의 매출액을 살펴볼 것입니다. — [3] —.

물론, 이 변화들은 우리의 구매 및 운송 비용에 영향을 줄 것입니다. — [4] —. 하지만, ⁰⁵재무 부서는 우리에게 아마도 상당한 수준의 비용 절감이 있을 것이라고 결론 내렸습니다. 근처에 공급업체들이 있는 것은 우리가 창고에 보관하는 물품의 수를 줄이는 것을 가능하게 할 것입니다.

industry n. 산업, 업계   construction n. 건축
observe v. 관찰하다, 준수하다   demand n. 수요, 요구; v. 요구하다
source v. 조달하다, 얻다; n. 근원   supply n. 물자, 용품; v. 공급하다
in light of ~을 고려하여, ~에 비추어   division n. 부서, 분할
draw up ~을 작성하다, 만들다   sales figure 매출액
naturally adv. 물론, 자연스럽게   conclude v. 결론 내리다
substantial adj. 상당한   saving n. 비용 절감, 절약
nearby adv. 근처에; adj. 인근의   warehouse n. 창고

03 글을 쓴 이유 문제

해석 Mr. Tisdale은 왜 회람을 썼는가?
(A) 회사가 어떻게 성과를 내고 있는지 설명하기 위해
(B) 새로운 트렌드에 대한 회사의 대응을 설명하기 위해
(C) 다가오는 무역 박람회에 대한 그의 참석을 확정하기 위해
(D) 관리자들에게 그들의 책임에 대해 상기시키기 위해

해설 지문의 'I'd like to share a recent trend in construction materials that I observed during this event.'에서 이 행사, 즉 건축 산업 무역 박람회에서 관찰한 건축 자재들 관련 최신 트렌드를 공유하고자 한다고 한 후, 현지에서 조달되는 건축 물자에 대한 수요가 증가하고 있는 것으로 보이며 회사가 이에 대해 어떤 조치를 취할 것인지에 대해 설명하고 있으므로 (B)가 정답이다.

어휘 supervisor n. 관리자, 감독관

04 육하원칙 문제

해석 매장 관리자들은 무엇을 하도록 요구받을 것인가?
(A) 현지에서 생산되는 제품들을 홍보한다.
(B) 소비자 트렌드를 파악하기 위해 설문조사를 실시한다.
(C) 영업 부서에서 근무할 추가 직원을 고용한다.
(D) 새로운 프로젝트의 비용 견적을 준비한다.

해설 지문의 'Next month, we will ask each store manager to hold a special promotion on all of these products.'에서 다음 달에 각 매장 관리자에게 이 모든 제품들, 즉 잘 팔릴 수 있는 현지 제품들에 대해 특별 판촉 활동을 할 것을 요청할 것이라고 했으므로 (A)가 정답이다.

어휘 conduct v. 실시하다   identify v. 파악하다, 확인하다   sales n. 영업 부서
estimate n. 견적, 견적서

Paraphrasing
hold a ~ promotion 판촉 활동을 하다 → promote 홍보하다

05 추론 문제

해석 Bronman Hardware사에 대해 암시되는 것은?
(A) 가장 높은 매출을 올린 매장에 보상을 제공할 것이다.
(B) 경쟁사에 고객들을 빼앗아왔다.
(C) 앞으로 몇 년 동안 여러 신규 매장을 열 것이다.
(D) 재고를 보관하는 데 큰 비용을 지출한다.

해설 지문의 'the finance department has concluded that we will probably see substantial savings. Having suppliers nearby will allow us to reduce the number of items we keep in our warehouses.'에서 재무 부서는 우리에게 아마도 상당한 수준의 비용 절감이 있을 것이라고 결론 내렸으며, 근처에 공급업체들이 있는 것은 창고에 보관하는 물품의 수를 줄이는 것을 가능하게 할 것이라고 했으므로, 현재 창고에 많은 물품을 보관하고 있어서 재고 보관에 큰 비용을 지출하고 있다는 사실을 추론할 수 있다. 따라서 (D)가 정답이다.

어휘 competitor n. 경쟁사, 경쟁 상대   inventory n. 재고, 물품

Paraphrasing
items we keep in ~ warehouses 창고에 보관하는 물품 → inventory 재고

06 문장 위치 찾기 문제

해석 [1], [2], [3], [4]로 표시된 위치 중, 다음 문장이 들어갈 곳으로 가장 적절한 것은?

"이에 근거하여, 우리는 어떤 현지 생산 제품들을 정기적으로 제공하기 시작할지 결정할 것입니다."

(A) [1]
(B) [2]
(C) [3]
(D) [4]

해설 주어진 문장은 정기적으로 제공할 현지 생산 제품들을 선정하는 근거와 관련된 내용이 나오는 부분에 들어가야 함을 알 수 있다. [3]의 앞부분인 'Next month, we will ask each store manager to hold a special promotion on all of these products.'에서 다음 달에 각 매장 관리자에게 이 모든 제품들, 즉 잘 팔릴 수 있는 현지 제품들에 대해 특별 판촉 활동을 할 것을 요청할 것이라고 했으며, 앞 문장인 'We will then look at the sales figures from each branch.'에서 그다음에 각 지점의 매출액을 살펴볼 것이라고 했으므로, [3]에 제시된 문장이 들어가면 각 매장 관리자에게 잘 팔릴 수 있는 현지 제품들의 특별 판촉 활동을 요청하고, 그다음에 각 지점의 매출액을 살펴본 후, 이에 근거하여 어떤 현지 생산 제품들을 정기적으로 제공하기 시작할지 결정할 것이라는 자연스러운 문맥이 된다는 것을 알 수 있다. 따라서 (C)가 정답이다.

어휘 based on ~에 근거하여   regularly adv. 정기적으로

DAY 15 의도 파악, 문장 위치 찾기, 동의어 문제

기출 유형 1 의도 파악 문제

Example   p.238

01번은 다음 문자 메시지 대화문에 관한 문제입니다.

Joseph Donahue [오전 10시 46분]
안녕하세요, Lesley. 저는 자료를 비교하도록 요구하는 업무를 받아서, 또 하나의 컴퓨터 모니터를 받는 것이 가능할지 궁금해요.

Lesley Roussell [오전 10시 47분]
그렇군요. 당신은 IT 부서에 요청서를 보낼 수 있어요. 하지만, 이것은 며칠이 걸릴 수도 있어요.

Joseph Donahue [오전 10시 48분]
그것은 이상적이지 않네요. 이 업무는 금요일까지 완료되어야 해요.

assignment n. 업무   wonder v. 궁금하다; n. 경이   ideal adj. 이상적인

01

해석 오전 10시 48분에, Mr. Donahue가 "That's not ideal"이라고 썼을 때, 그가 의도한 것은?
(A) 업무를 완료하기 위해 더 많은 자료가 필요하다.
(B) 새로운 직원이 컴퓨터를 설치하는 것을 도울 수 없다.
(C) 프로젝트 마감일을 연장하고 싶어 한다.
(D) 문제에 대한 즉각적인 해결책이 필요하다.

어휘 extend v. 연장하다   immediate adj. 즉각적인   solution n. 해결책

토익실전문제   p.239

01 (D)   **02** (C)   **03** (B)   **04** (D)

01-04번은 다음 온라인 채팅 대화문에 관한 문제입니다.

Fran Jenkins [오전 11시 40분]
안녕하세요, 팀원들. 01우리는 이번 여름 사무실의 친목 활동으로 무엇을 할지 생각해 내야 해요. 저는 해변 여행을 고려하고 있어요.

Harriet Tibbs [오전 11시 43분]
물이 너무 차가울 것이라고 생각하지 않나요? 동네 공원으로 소풍을 가는 것은 어떤가요?

Fran Jenkins [오전 11시 45분]
소풍에 대한 아이디어가 마음에 들어요.

Gary Franklin [오전 11시 47분]
02-(C)Henderson 공원에 좋은 소풍 장소가 있어요.

Harriet Tibbs [오전 11시 48분]
02-(C)하지만 그곳은 혼잡해질 수 있어요. Gold Ridge 공원은 보통 그만큼 많은 사람들이 있지는 않아서 그곳이 더 좋은 선택일 수도 있어요.

Fran Jenkins [오전 11시 49분]
좋아요. 03작년보다 식비 예산이 더 많다는 점도 말씀드려야겠네요. 저희는 최대 1,200달러까지 쓸 수 있어요.

Gary Franklin [오전 11시 50분]
잘됐네요! 03/04그 정도 금액이면 출장 요식업자도 고용할 수 있겠네요. 저는 Ruth Bernard라는 괜찮은 사람을 알아요. 제가 그녀로부터 견적서를 받을 수 있어요.

Fran Jenkins [오전 11시 52분]
그렇게 해 주세요. 대략 40명의 사람들에 대해서 그녀가 얼마를 청구하는 지 알아봐 주세요.

---

figure out ~을 생각해 내다   social adj. 친목의, 사교적인
crowded adj. 혼잡한   budget n. 예산   caterer n. 출장 요식업자
estimate n. 견적서   charge v. 청구하다

01 육하원칙 문제

해석 Ms. Jenkins는 그녀의 팀과 무엇을 논의하고 싶어 하는가?
(A) 회의 안건을 마무리 짓는 것
(B) 여행 일정표를 확정하는 것
(C) 행사를 위한 자원봉사자를 모으는 것
(D) 야유회에 대한 아이디어들을 발전시키는 것

해설 지문의 'We need to figure out what to do for the office's social activity'에서 Ms. Jenkins가 사무실의 친목 활동으로 무엇을 할지 생각해 내야 한다고 했으므로 (D)가 정답이다.

어휘 agenda n. 안건   travel itinerary 여행 일정표   gather v. 모으다
volunteer n. 자원봉사자; v. 자원하다   develop v. 발전시키다, 개발하다
outing n. 야유회

02 Not/True 문제

해석 Henderson 공원에 대해 언급된 것은?

(A) 사무실에 가장 가까운 곳이다.
(B) 방문객들이 반려동물을 데려오는 것을 허용한다.
(C) 많은 인파를 끌어들이는 경향이 있다.
(D) 대여할 수 있는 실내 공간이 있다.

해설 (C)는 'Henderson Park has a nice picnic area.'에서 Mr. Franklin이 Henderson 공원에 좋은 소풍 장소가 있다고 하자, 'But it can get crowded.'에서 Ms. Tibbs가 하지만 그곳, 즉 Henderson 공원은 혼잡해질 수 있다고 했으므로 지문의 내용과 일치한다. 따라서 (C)가 정답이다. (A), (B), (D)는 지문에 언급되지 않은 내용이다.

어휘 attract v. 끌어들이다   indoor adj. 실내의

[Paraphrasing]
get crowded 혼잡해지다 → attract large crowds 많은 인파를 끌어들이다

03 의도 파악 문제

해석 오전 11시 50분에, Mr. Franklin이 "Sounds great"이라고 썼을 때, 그가 의도한 것은?
(A) 그는 매우 많은 사람이 온다는 것에 기쁘다.
(B) 사용 가능한 자금이 그가 생각했던 것보다 많다.
(C) 그는 출장 음식 서비스의 높은 품질에 놀랐다.
(D) 한 장소의 수용 인원이 그가 예상했던 것보다 많다.

해설 지문의 'I should ~ mention that our food budget is higher than it was last year. We can spend up to $1,200.'에서 Ms. Jenkins가 작년보다 식비 예산이 더 많다고 하며, 최대 1,200달러까지 쓸 수 있다고 하자, Mr. Franklin이 'Sounds great'(잘됐네요)이라고 한 후, 'We could even hire a caterer with that amount.'에서 그 정도 금액이면 출장 요식업자도 고용할 수 있겠다고 한 것을 통해, 사용 가능한 자금이 Mr. Franklin이 생각했던 것보다 많음을 알 수 있다. 따라서 (B)가 정답이다.

어휘 pleased adj. 기쁜   capacity n. 수용 인원

04 육하원칙 문제

해석 Mr. Franklin은 무엇을 추천하는가?
(A) 직원들의 의견을 요청하는 것
(B) 활동 일정을 변경하는 것
(C) 추가 손님을 초대하는 것
(D) 출장 요식업체를 고용하는 것

해설 지문의 'We could even hire a caterer ~. I know a good one named Ruth Bernard.'에서 Mr. Franklin이 출장 요식업자도 고용할 수 있겠다며 그가 Ruth Bernard라는 괜찮은 사람을 안다고 했으므로 (D)가 정답이다.

어휘 request v. 요청하다; n. 요청   additional adj. 추가의

기출 유형 2 문장 위치 찾기 문제

Example   p.240

01번은 다음 웹페이지에 관한 문제입니다.

Harrison Home Furnishings사는 50년 이상 사업을 운영해 왔으며, 제품들은 전 세계의 고급 가구 할인점에서 판매됩니다. ─ [1] ─. 2010년에 온타리오주에 있는 공장이 확장되었으며, 2015년에는 창고와 운송 시설이 추가되었습니다. ─ [2] ─. Harrison Home Furnishings사는 독창적인 디자인으로 계속해서 찬사를 받고 있으며, 종종 *Modern Interiors Today*지와 *Inside Outside*지와 같은 잡지로부터 긍정적인 평가를 받습니다. ─ [3] ─. 지속 가능한 소재와 현대적인 디자인에 중점을 두고, 이 회사는 디자인에 민감한 소비자들을 계속해서 유치합니다. ─ [4] ─.

fine adj. 고급의, 질 높은   outlet n. 할인점, 아울렛   warehouse n. 창고
shipping facility 운송 시설   original adj. 독창적인, 원래의
sustainable adj. (환경 파괴 없이) 지속 가능한
design-conscious adj. 디자인에 민감한

01

해석 [1], [2], [3], [4]로 표시된 위치 중, 다음 문장이 들어갈 곳으로 가장 적절한 것은?

"이러한 변화들은 전체 생산량을 크게 증가시켰습니다."

(A) [1]
(B) [2]
(C) [3]
(D) [4]

어휘 significantly adv. 크게, 상당히   output n. 생산량, 산출량

토익실전문제   p.241

01 (C)	02 (A)	03 (B)

01-03번은 다음 편지에 관한 문제입니다.

> 8월 24일
>
> Leanna Murillo
> 111번지 Fort가, 바스테르
> 세인트 키츠 네비스, 1201
>
> Ms. Murillo께,
>
> ⁰¹Carpenters United는 ⁰²⁻⁽ᴮ⁾2월 20일부터 23일까지 싱가포르의 한 장소에서 열릴 ⁰¹제5회 연례 학술 토론회를 계획하기 시작했습니다. 이전의 행사들처럼, ⁰²⁻⁽ᶜ⁾목표는 우리 분야의 최신 기술 발전을 논의하는 것이 될 것입니다. ─ [1] ─. ⁰²⁻⁽ᴰ⁾그것은 또한 회원들이 인맥을 형성할 기회가 될 것입니다.
>
> 이번에, ⁰³우리는 지속 가능한 건축 자재에 대한 홍보 캠페인을 기획하는 추가적인 과제를 수행해야 할 것입니다. ─ [2] ─. 우리는 또한 이 캠페인을 소셜 미디어, 공개 행사, 혹은 전통적인 광고 중 어느 것을 통해 진행할지 결정해야 할 것입니다. 학술 토론회는 향후 3년 동안의 우리 대표직 위원회의 위원들을 결정하는 투표로 마무리될 것입니다. ─ [3] ─.
>
> 우리는 당신이 우리 협회의 소중한 회원으로서 참석할 수 있기를 바랍니다. ─ [4] ─.
>
> Danton Spritz
> 회장, Carpenters United

annual adj. 연례의   symposium n. 학술 토론회   venue n. 장소
as with ~처럼   aim n. 목표; v. 목표하다   discuss v. 논의하다
connection n. 인맥, 연결   publicity campaign 홍보 캠페인
material n. 자재, 자료   carry out ~을 진행하다, 수행하다
determine v. 결정하다   leadership n. 대표직   committee n. 위원회
association n. 협회

01 목적 문제

해석 편지의 목적은 무엇인가?
(A) 행사의 참석을 확정하기 위해
(B) 대표직의 변화를 알리기 위해
(C) 연례 모임에 대해 알리기 위해
(D) 일련의 규칙들을 소개하기 위해

해설 지문의 'Carpenters United has begun planning its fifth annual symposium'에서 Carpenters United가 제5회 연례 학술 토론회를 계획하기 시작했다고 한 후, 학술 토론회에 대한 정보를 제공하고 있으므로 (C)가 정답이다.

어휘 gathering n. 모임   a set of 일련의

> [Paraphrasing]
> fifth annual symposium 제5회 연례 학술 토론회 → a yearly gathering 연례 모임

02 Not/True 문제

해설 학술 토론회에 대해 언급되지 않은 것은?

(A) 유명한 초청 연사가 참석할 것이다.
(B) 여러 날에 걸쳐 진행될 것이다.
(C) 기술 발전에 초점을 맞출 것이다.
(D) 관계 형성 기회를 제공할 것이다.

해설 (A)는 지문에 언급되지 않은 내용이다. 따라서 (A)가 정답이다. (B)는 'from February 20 to 23'에서 학술 토론회가 2월 20일부터 23일까지 열릴 것이라고 했으므로 지문의 내용과 일치한다. (C)는 'the aim will be to discuss the latest technological developments in our field'에서 목표는 우리 분야의 최신 기술 발전을 논의하는 것이 될 것이라고 했으므로 지문의 내용과 일치한다. (D)는 'It will ~ be an opportunity for members to form connections.'에서 그것, 즉 학술 토론회는 회원들이 인맥을 형성할 기회가 될 것이라고 했으므로 지문의 내용과 일치한다.

어휘 advance n. 발전, 전진; v. 진행하다, 다가가다

> [Paraphrasing]
> from February 20 to 23 2월 20일부터 23일까지 → over several days 여러 날에 걸쳐
> technological developments 기술 발전 → advances in technology 기술 발전
> opportunity for members to form connections 회원들이 인맥을 형성할 기회 → networking opportunities 관계 형성 기회

03 문장 위치 찾기 문제

해설 [1], [2], [3], [4]로 표시된 위치 중, 다음 문장이 들어갈 곳으로 가장 적절한 것은?

"이것은 이러한 자재들을 사용하는 것의 환경적 이점뿐만 아니라 그것들의 목공에서의 역할도 강조할 것입니다."

(A) [1]
(B) [2]
(C) [3]
(D) [4]

해설 주어진 문장은 환경적 이점이 있는 자재들과 관련된 내용 주변에 나와야 함을 예상할 수 있다. [2]의 앞 문장인 'we will have the additional task of planning a publicity campaign about sustainable building materials'에서 지속 가능한 건축 자재에 대한 홍보 캠페인을 기획하는 추가적인 과제를 수행해야 할 것이라고 했으므로, [2]에 주어진 문장이 들어가면 이것, 즉 지속 가능한 건축 자재에 대한 홍보 캠페인은 이러한 자재들을 사용하는 것의 환경적 이점뿐만 아니라 그것들의 목공에서의 역할도 강조할 것이라는 자연스러운 문맥이 된다는 것을 알 수 있다. 따라서 (B)가 정답이다.

어휘 highlight v. 강조하다   carpentry n. 목공

기출 유형 3 동의어 문제

Example   p.242

01번은 다음 광고에 관한 문제입니다.

> **Keystone 통역사**
>
> 만약 당신이 성인이라면, 제2외국어에 유창해지는 것은 아주 어려운 일일 수 있습니다. 많은 사람들이 외국어로 의사소통하는 것이 어려운 일상 상황을 경험합니다. 이때가 Keystone 통역사가 관여하는 지점입니다.
>
> 저희는 다수의 번역 및 통역 서비스를 경쟁력 있는 가격에 제공합니다. 저희의 몇 가지 서비스를 살펴보세요:
> · 전화, 화상, 또는 대면 통역이 가능합니다.
> · 문서 번역이 필요한 경우, 영어, 프랑스어, 중국어 등을 포함하여 200개 이상의 언어로 서비스를 제공합니다.
>
> www.keyinterpretation.com을 방문하여, **당신의 통역 및 번역 요구사항에 따라 견적을 받아보세요.** 처음 이용하시는 고객은 20퍼센트 할인을 받을 수 있습니다.

interpretation n. 통역 fluent adj. 유창한, 능통한
a wide array of 다양한, 다수의 translation n. 번역
competitive adj. 경쟁력 있는 rate n. 가격, 요금
in-person adj. 대면의, 직접 하는

01
해석 3문단 첫 번째 줄의 단어 "quote"는 의미상 -와 가장 가깝다.
(A) 인용문
(B) 견적
(C) 견본
(D) 시연

토익실전문제
p.243

| 01 (C) | 02 (B) | 03 (C) | 04 (A) |

01-04번은 다음 기사에 관한 문제입니다.

발표가 Tatkraft사의 주가를 증가시키다

6월 13일—독일의 전기차 제조회사인 Tatkraft사의 주가가 최고경영자 Johannes Schneider의 회사 실적 발표 후에 급격히 상승했다. 01지난주, Mr. Schneider는 Tatkraft사가 지난해 2억 1천2백만 달러의 수익을 냈으며 올해 50만 대 이상의 새로운 자동차를 판매할 것으로 예상한다고 발표했다. 회사의 주가는 그 후에 주당 567달러에서 601달러로 상승했으며, 03이를 통해 회사의 성장 전략에 대한 투자자들의 신뢰를 얻었다.

02/04작년 이전에는, 생산량이 수요를 따라가는 것을 계속해서 실패함에 따라 그 회사는 투자자들에게 그것이 성장할 역량이 있다는 것을 확신시키는 데 어려움을 겪었다. 04자동차 산업 전문가 Elias Muller를 고용한 후 시행된 개선들 덕분에, 회사는 제조 과정을 간소화하여 이제는 자동차를 더욱 효율적으로 생산하고 있다. 현재, Tatkraft사는 1천억 달러 이상의 가치가 있는 것으로 평가된다.

share price 주가 manufacturer n. 제조회사 profit n. 수익
stock price 주가 subsequently adv. 그 후에, 나중에 prior to ~ 이전에
struggle v. 어려움을 겪다 convince v. 확신시키다, 설득하다
capacity n. 역량, 능력 consistently adv. 지속적으로
keep up with ~을 따라가다 improvement n. 개선 implement v. 시행하다
automotive adj. 자동차의 veteran n. 전문가 simplify v. 간소화하다
efficiently adv. 효율적으로

01 육하원칙 문제
해석 Mr. Schneider는 지난주에 무엇을 했는가?
(A) 상업용 부지를 매입했다.
(B) 새로운 고위 간부를 임명했다.
(C) 예상되는 판매량에 대한 정보를 제공했다.
(D) 팀에 대한 평가를 수행했다.

해설 지문의 'Last week, Mr. Schneider announced that Tatkraft ~ expects to sell over half a million new cars this year.'에서 지난주, Mr. Schneider는 Tatkraft사가 올해 50만 대 이상의 새로운 자동차를 판매할 것으로 예상한다고 발표했다고 했으므로 (C)가 정답이다.

어휘 commercial adj. 상업용의 property n. 부지 appoint v. 임명하다
top executive 고위 간부 anticipated adj. 예상되는

[Paraphrasing]
expects to sell over half a million ~ cars 50만 대 이상의 자동차를 판매할 것으로 예상하다 → anticipated sales 예상되는 판매량

02 추론 문제
해석 Tatkraft사의 투자자들에 대해 암시되는 것은?
(A) 새해에 차량을 주문했다.
(B) 회사의 잠재력에 대해 의심을 품었다.
(C) 2년 전에 그들의 투자를 늘렸다.
(D) 제품 품질에 대해 우려를 나타냈다.

해설 지문의 'Prior to last year, the company struggled to convince investors of its capacity for growth'에서 작년 이전에는, 그 회사, 즉 Tatkraft사가 투자자들에게 회사가 성장할 역량이 있다는 것을 확신시키는 데 어려움을 겪었다고 했으므로 투자자들이 회사의 잠재력에 대해 의심을 품었다는 사실을 추론할 수 있다. 따라서 (B)가 정답이다.

어휘 place an order 주문하다 doubt n. 의심; v. 의심하다

[Paraphrasing]
capacity for growth 성장할 역량 → potential 잠재력

03 동의어 문제
해석 1문단 네 번째 줄의 단어 "securing"은 의미상 -와 가장 가깝다.
(A) 고정하는
(B) 요구하는
(C) 얻는
(D) 지지하는

해설 securing을 포함한 구절 'securing investor confidence in the company's growth strategy'에서 securing은 '얻는'이라는 뜻으로 사용되었다. 따라서 (C)가 정답이다.

04 추론 문제
해석 Mr. Muller는 무엇을 담당하는 것 같은가?
(A) 생산 목표를 달성하는 것
(B) 판매 전략을 개발하는 것
(C) 재정 결과를 분석하는 것
(D) 고객 불만 사항을 해결하는 것

해설 지문의 'Prior to last year, the company struggled to convince investors of its capacity for growth with production consistently failing to keep up with demand.'에서 작년 이전에는, 생산량이 수요를 따라가는 것을 계속해서 실패함에 따라 그 회사는 투자자들에게 회사가 성장할 역량이 있다는 것을 확신시키는 데 어려움을 겪었다고 하며 생산량이 부족했다는 것을 언급한 후, 'after the hiring of Elias Muller, ~ the company simplified its manufacturing process and is now producing cars more efficiently'에서 Elias Muller를 고용한 후 회사는 제조 과정을 간소화하여 이제는 자동차를 더욱 효율적으로 생산하고 있다고 했으므로 Mr. Muller가 주로 생산 목표를 달성하는 것을 담당한다는 사실을 추론할 수 있다. 따라서 (A)가 정답이다.

어휘 meet v. 달성하다 analyze v. 분석하다 resolve v. 해결하다

HACKERS TEST
p.244

| 01 (D) | 02 (C) | 03 (A) | 04 (D) | 05 (D) |
| 06 (B) | | | | |

01-02번은 다음 온라인 채팅 대화문에 관한 문제입니다.

Erika Raimond [오전 10시 46분]
우리가 지난달 주문했던 주문 제작 펜들이 방금 배달되었어요. 안타깝게도, 우리 회사의 이름이 철자가 잘못 쓰여 있어요. 01제가 우리에게 그것들을 만들어 준 회사에 전화했지만, 그들이 이 상황을 해결하는 데 최소 3일이 걸릴 거예요.

Jayce Vills [오전 10시 48분]
그것참 안됐네요. 02우리는 내일 세미나에서 나누어 줄 것이 아무것도 없을 거예요.

Erika Raimond [오전 10시 50분]
02사실, 우리는 우리의 로고가 새겨져 있는 몇 개의 메모지를 창고에 보관 중이에요. 저는 우리가 그것들을 사용해도 아무도 신경 쓸 것 같지 않아요.

Jayce Vills [오전 10시 55분]
당신 말이 맞아요. 재제작된 펜이 도착하면, 그것들을 다른 행사에서 사용할 수 있도록 보관하면 되겠어요.

custom adj. 주문 제작의 at least 최소한 resolve v. 해결하다
hand out ~을 나누어 주다 in storage 창고에 보관 중인
mind v. 신경 쓰다, 꺼리다

01 육하원칙 문제
해석 Ms. Raimond는 오늘 아침에 무엇을 했는가?
(A) 세미나에 참석했다.
(B) 약속을 잡았다.
(C) 소포를 부쳤다.
(D) 공급회사에 연락했다.

해설 지문의 'I called the company that made them for us'에서 Ms. Raimond가 우리에게 그것들, 즉 주문 제작 펜들을 만들어 준 회사에 전화했다고 했으므로 (D)가 정답이다.

어휘 mail v. 부치다, 보내다 package n. 소포 supplier n. 공급회사, 공급자

Paraphrasing
called the company that made them 그것들을 만들어 준 회사에 전화했다
→ Contacted a supplier 공급회사에 연락했다

02 의도 파악 문제
해석 오전 10시 55분에, Mr. Vills가 "You have a point"라고 썼을 때, 그가 의도한 것 같은 것은?
(A) 주문이 환불되어야 한다.
(B) 활동이 연기되어야 한다.
(C) 몇몇 물품들이 행사에 사용될 수 있다.
(D) 몇몇 상품들이 창고에 보관되어야 한다.

해설 지문의 'We won't have anything to hand out at tomorrow's seminar.'에서 Mr. Vills가 내일 세미나에서 나누어 줄 것이 아무것도 없을 것이라고 했고, 'Actually, we have some notepads ~ in storage. I don't think anyone will mind if we use them.'에서 Ms. Raimond가 사실, 우리는 몇 개의 메모지를 창고에 보관 중이며 그것들을 사용해도 아무도 신경 쓸 것 같지 않다고 하자, Mr. Vills가 'You have a point'(당신 말이 맞아요)라고 한 것을 통해, 몇몇 물품들, 즉 메모지가 세미나에 사용될 수 있음을 알 수 있다. 따라서 (C)가 정답이다.

어휘 postpone v. 연기하다

Paraphrasing
notepads 메모지들 → items 물품
seminar 세미나 → event 행사

03-06번은 다음 기사에 관한 문제입니다.

*Electronics Monthly*지
03변화를 위해 노력하는 SleekEffects사

3월 2일―전기 기기 제조업체 03SleekEffects사가 지난해 좋지 못한 영업 실적에서 회복하려고 시도하고 있다. ― [1] ―. SleekEffects사는 지난 11월에 전기면도기 Cavalier 라인의 대규모 제품 회수를 겪었다. 06고객들이 제출한 수백 개의 불만에 따르면, 면도기가 과열되는 경향이 있었으며 화재 위험을 야기했다. ― [2] ―.

상황을 호전시키기 위해, SleekEffects사 최고경영자 Leonard Martin은 그것의 생산 과정에 중대한 변화를 발표했다. ― [3] ―. 보도 자료에서, Mr. Martin은 제품 회수를 야기했던 결점들을 회사가 해결했으며 04더 넓은 범위의 고객들을 끌어들이기 위해 설계된 새로운 라인의 제품들을 출시하려 준비하고 있다고 말했다. 05"SleekSmooth라는 이름의 전자식 발, 목, 등 마사지기 라인은 회사가 여성 고객을 겨냥하려는 첫 시도를 나타냅니다." 라고 그는 말했다. ― [4] ―.

strive v. 노력하다, 힘쓰다 appliance n. 기기 make an attempt 시도하다
recover v. 회복하다, 되찾다 suffer v. 겪다, 고통받다
massive adj. 대규모의 recall n. (결함이 발견된 제품의) 회수, 리콜
tendency n. 경향, 성향 overheat v. 과열되다 pose v. 야기하다

hazard n. 위험 turn around ~을 호전시키다 alteration n. 변화, 교체
address v. 해결하다, 다루다 shortcoming n. 결점, 단점
represent v. 나타내다, 대표하다

03 주제 문제
해석 기사는 주로 무엇에 대한 것인가?
(A) 회사의 개선하려는 노력
(B) 새로운 최고경영자의 임명
(C) 회사의 해외 진출
(D) 개인 관리 제품들의 트렌드

해설 지문의 'SleekEffects Striving for Change'와 'SleekEffects is making an attempt to recover from its poor sales last year'에서 SleekEffects사가 변화를 위해 노력하고 있으며 지난해 좋지 못한 영업 실적에서 회복하려고 시도하고 있다고 한 후, 상황을 개선하려는 회사의 노력과 관련된 세부 내용을 전달하고 있으므로 (A)가 정답이다.

어휘 appointment n. 임명 overseas adj. 해외의; adv. 해외로
expansion n. 진출, 확장

04 동의어 문제
해석 2문단 일곱 번째 줄의 단어 "draw"는 의미상 -와 가장 가깝다.
(A) 준비하다
(B) 그리다
(C) 보호하다
(D) 끌어들이다

해설 draw를 포함한 구절 'designed to draw a wider range of customers'에서 draw는 '끌어들이다'라는 뜻으로 사용되었다. 따라서 (D)가 정답이다.

05 추론 문제
해석 SleekEffects사에 대해 추론될 수 있는 것은?
(A) 일부 생산 장비를 교체했다.
(B) 전 세계에 체인점을 운영한다.
(C) 고객 의견을 받기 위해 장려책을 제공한다.
(D) 이전에는 오로지 남성만을 위한 제품을 만들었다.

해설 지문의 'The line of electronic ~ massagers, called SleekSmooth, represents the company's first attempt to target female customers'에서 SleekSmooth라는 이름의 전자식 마사지기 라인은 회사가 여성 고객을 겨냥하려는 첫 시도를 나타낸다고 했으므로, SleekEffects사가 이전에는 오로지 남성만을 위한 제품을 만들었다는 사실을 추론할 수 있다. 따라서 (D)가 정답이다.

어휘 incentive n. 장려책, 보상 solely adv. 오로지, 단독으로

06 문장 위치 찾기 문제
해석 [1], [2], [3], [4]로 표시된 위치 중, 다음 문장이 들어갈 곳으로 가장 적절한 것은?
"그 결과, 거의 100만 개에 달하는 제품들이 소매업체들의 진열대에서 철수되었다."
(A) [1]
(B) [2]
(C) [3]
(D) [4]

해설 주어진 문장은 제품들이 소매업체들의 진열대에서 철수되게 된 배경과 관련된 내용 주변에 나올 것임을 예상할 수 있다. [2]의 앞 문장인 'According to ~ complaints submitted by customers, the shavers had a tendency to overheat and posed a fire hazard.'에서 고객들이 제출한 불만에 따르면, 면도기가 과열되는 경향이 있었으며 화재 위험을 야기했다고 했으므로, [2]에 제시된 문장이 들어가면 면도기가 과열되는 경향이 있고 화재 위험을 야기했기 때문에 거의 100만 개에 달하는 제품들이 소매업체들의 진열대에서 철수되었다는 자연스러운 문맥이 된다는 것을 알 수 있다. 따라서 (B)가 정답이다

어휘 retailer n. 소매업체, 소매상

DAY 16 이메일/편지 및 메시지 대화문

기출 유형 1 이메일/편지

Example p.246

01-02번은 다음 이메일에 관한 문제입니다.

수신: Gerald Browning <g.browning@heremail.net>
발신: Clarissa Kim <c.kim@maximumbank.com>
02날짜: 6월 5일

Mr. Browning께,

이 이메일은 01귀하가 6월 2일에 했던 MaxJet 신용카드에 대한 온라인 신청이 승인되었다는 것을 확정하기 위한 것입니다. 카드는 영업일 기준 3일 이내에 귀하의 우편 주소로 도착할 것입니다. 귀하는 카드를 즉시 사용하여 다음과 같은 다양한 혜택을 이용하실 수 있습니다:

- SureSky 항공사의 어떤 항공편에든지 사용할 수 있는 연간 500달러 상품권
- 02매년 7월 Maximum 은행의 제휴 소매업체 BuySmart에서 모든 제품들에 대한 10퍼센트 할인

혜택에 대한 더 많은 정보를 위해서는, Maximum 은행의 스마트폰 애플리케이션을 다운로드하세요.

confirm v. 확정하다, 확인하다 business day 영업일
voucher n. 상품권, 할인권 valid adj. 사용할 수 있는, 유효한

01
해석 Mr. Browning은 6월 2일에 무엇을 했을 것 같은가?
(A) Maximum 은행의 지점에 전화했다.
(B) 개인 저축 계좌를 만들었다.
(C) 신청서를 제출했다.
(D) 신용 카드 결제를 했다.
어휘 set up ~을 만들다, 준비하다 account n. 계좌, 계정 turn in ~을 제출하다 credit card 신용카드 payment n. 결제

02
해석 Mr. Browning은 다음 달에 무엇을 할 수 있는가?
(A) 우편으로 새로운 신용카드를 받는다.
(B) 할인된 가격으로 몇몇 상품을 구매한다.
(C) Maximum 은행에 의해 후원되는 행사에 참석한다.
(D) 친구를 소개함으로써 추가 포인트를 얻는다.
어휘 sponsor v. 후원하다 refer v. 소개하다, 참조하다

Paraphrasing
10 percent off ~ products 제품들에 대한 10퍼센트 할인 → items at a reduced price 할인된 가격의 상품들

토익실전문제 p.247

| 01 (A) | 02 (A) | 03 (C) | 04 (C) |

01-04번은 다음 이메일에 관한 문제입니다.

수신: Jason Briar <jbriar@postnet.com>
발신: Jack Gray <grayjack@gilhoolytech.com>
제목: 지원
날짜: 4월 27일

Mr. Briar께,

01Gilhooly Tech사의 여름 학생 인턴십 프로그램에 지원해 주셔서

감사드립니다. 저희는 며칠 전에 당신의 이력서와 지원서를 받았고, 곧 면접 일정을 잡을 것입니다. 만약 당신이 저희의 적격 요건을 충족한다면, 당신은 리치먼드에 있는 저희의 사무실에서 만날 약속을 잡기 위해 02어느 시점에 전화로 연락받을 것입니다.

03이것이 8주 동안 지속될 풀타임, 무보수 일자리라는 점에 유의해 주시기 바랍니다. 03하지만, 당신이 선정된다면 당신의 등록금 지불을 돕기 위해 Gilhooly Tech사는 당신의 교육 기관인 Maryland 학교에 3,000달러를 제공할 것입니다. 04-(C)Gilhooly Tech사는 또한 시외에서 온 인턴들에게 매달 500달러의 주거 수당을 제공할 준비가 되어 있습니다.

다시 한번, 저희의 프로그램에 관심을 가져주셔서 감사드리며, 곧 연락드리겠습니다.

Jack Gray 드림
직원 채용 관리자, Gilhooly Tech사

résumé n. 이력서 eligibility n. 적격, 적격성 requirement n. 요건
position n. 일자리, 위치 institution n. 기관 tuition n. 등록금, 수업료
housing n. 주거, 주택 공급 allowance n. 수당, 비용
associate n. 직원, 동료 recruitment n. 채용, 모집

01 육하원칙 문제
해석 Mr. Briar는 최근에 무엇을 했는가?
(A) 임시직을 위해 서류를 보냈다.
(B) 회사에서 교육 프로그램을 수료했다.
(C) 채용 담당자와 전화로 이야기했다.
(D) 그의 성적에 대한 정보를 요청했다.
해설 지문의 'Thank you for applying for Gilhooly Tech's summer student internship program. We received your résumé and application form a few days ago'에서 Gilhooly Tech사의 여름 학생 인턴십 프로그램에 지원해 주어서 감사하다고 하며, 며칠 전에 당신, 즉 Mr. Briar의 이력서와 지원서를 받았다고 했으므로 (A)가 정답이다.
어휘 temporary adj. 임시의, 일시적인 recruiter n. 채용 담당자, 모집자 grade n. 성적, 품질

Paraphrasing
a few days ago 며칠 전에 → recently 최근에

02 동의어 문제
해석 1문단 세 번째 줄의 단어 "point"는 의미상 -와 가장 가깝다.
(A) 시점
(B) 장소
(C) 세부 사항
(D) 방향
해설 point를 포함한 구절 'you will be contacted by phone at some point'에서 당신, 즉 Mr. Briar는 어느 시점에 전화로 연락받을 것이라고 했으므로 point는 '시점'이라는 뜻으로 사용되었다. 따라서 (A)가 정답이다.

03 추론 문제
해석 Mr. Briar에 대해 암시되는 것은?
(A) 현재 리치먼드의 거주자이다.
(B) 온라인 면접을 봐야 할 것이다.
(C) 그의 업무에 대해 직접적으로 급여를 받지 못할 것이다.
(D) 현재 장학금을 받으며 대학에 다니고 있다.
해설 지문의 'Please note that this is a full-time, unpaid position'과 'However, Gilhooly Tech will provide 3,000 dollars to your educational institution ~ if you are selected.'에서 이것, 즉 Mr. Briar가 지원한 일자리가 풀타임, 무보수 일자리라는 점에 유의해 달라고 한 후, 하지만 그가 선정된다면 Gilhooly Tech사가 그의 교육 기관에 3,000달러를 제공할 것이라고 했으므로 Mr. Briar가 업무에 대해 직접적으로 급여를 받지 못할 것이라는 사실을 추론할 수 있다. 따라서 (C)

가 정답이다.

어휘 resident n. 거주자   scholarship n. 장학금

04 Not/True 문제

해석 Gilhooly Tech사에 대해 사실인 것은?
(A) 새로운 제품을 출시하려고 준비하고 있다.
(B) 정규 직원에게 기숙사를 제공한다.
(C) 주거비에 대한 지원을 제공한다.
(D) 직원들에게 성과에 따라 보수를 지급한다.

해설 (C)는 'Gilhooly Tech is ~ prepared to offer a housing allowance ~ for interns who are from out of town.'에서 Gilhooly Tech사는 시외에서 온 인턴들에게 주거 수당을 제공할 준비가 되어 있다고 했으므로 지문의 내용과 일치한다. 따라서 (C)가 정답이다. (A), (B), (D)는 지문에 언급되지 않은 내용이다.

어휘 launch v. 출시하다, 시작하다   dormitory n. 기숙사
expense n. 비용, 경비   compensate v. 보수를 지급하다, 보상하다

> Paraphrasing
> housing allowance 주거 수당 → support for housing expenses 주거비에 대한 지원

기출 유형 2 메시지 대화문

Example   p.248

01-02번은 다음 문자 메시지 대화문에 관한 문제입니다.

> Pam Gordon [오전 9시 10분]
> 저는 방금 당신의 지난주 출장에 대한 출장 비용 환급 양식을 당신에게 이메일로 보냈어요. 01/02이번 달 말까지 그것을 제출하실 수 있나요? 01그러지 않으면, 당신의 돈은 당신의 다음 급료와 함께 상환되지 않을 거예요.
>
> Hadassah Aboud [오전 9시 12분]
> 물론이죠. 02저는 사실 돌아오자마자 인트라넷에서 양식을 출력해서 그것을 회계 부서 사무실로 바로 가져갔어요.
>
> Pam Gordon [오전 9시 13분]
> 좋아요! 저는 당신이 그것을 어디로 가져가야 하는지 알고 있는지 확실하지 않았어요.

expense n. 비용   reimbursement n. 환급, 상환
turn in ~을 제출하다, 반납하다   repay v. 상환하다, 되돌려주다

01

해설 양식에 대해 암시되는 것은?
(A) 선호하는 결제 방법을 명시해야 한다.
(B) 부서장에 의해 서명되어야 한다.
(C) 정해진 시간 내에 제출되어야 한다.
(D) 회사 웹사이트에서 작성되어야 한다.

어휘 specify v. 명시하다   supervisor n. 상사, 관리자

> Paraphrasing
> turn ~ in by the end of the month 이번 달 말까지 제출하다 → be submitted within a set amount of time 정해진 시간 내에 제출되다

02

해설 오전 9시 12분에, Ms. Aboud가 "Absolutely"라고 썼을 때, 그녀가 의도한 것은?
(A) 동료에게 도움을 줄 수 있다.
(B) 출장 비용에 대해 돈을 되돌려 받았다.
(C) 양식을 제출하러 가는 중이다.
(D) 이미 업무를 완료했다.

어휘 assistance n. 도움   on one's way 가는 중인   hand in ~을 제출하다

토익실전문제   p.249

| 01 (C) | 02 (A) | 03 (B) | 04 (C) |

01-04번은 다음 온라인 채팅 대화문에 관한 문제입니다.

> Kevin Chase [오후 1시 50분]
> 01누군가 사무실 의자 공급업체를 추천해 줄 수 있나요? 제 것이 아까 고장 났어요.
>
> Miles Dunphy [오후 1시 52분]
> 창고를 확인해 봤나요? 우리는 몇몇 여분의 것들을 가지고 있을 수도 있어요.
>
> Kevin Chase [오후 1시 53분]
> 이미 확인했는데, 다 떨어진 것 같아요.
>
> Megan Contreras [오후 1시 55분]
> 당신은 새로운 것에 얼마를 쓸 수 있나요?
>
> Kevin Chase [오후 1시 55분]
> 120달러보다 적게요.
>
> Megan Contreras [오후 1시 56분]
> 저는 오늘 오후에 프린터 잉크를 사러 Fastmax로 향할 예정이에요. 03제가 당신을 위해 하나 구매해 올 수 있어요.
>
> Kevin Chase [오후 1시 57분]
> 서두르지 않으셔도 돼요. 03저는 우선은 플라스틱 의자를 사용하고 있어요.
>
> Miles Dunphy [오후 1시 59분]
> 02-(B)Every Office에서 하나를 97달러에 판매 중인데, 이것은 정가에서 20퍼센트 할인된 가격이에요. 02-(C)웹사이트를 통해 그것을 주문하실 수 있어요. 02-(D)배송에는 요금이 부과되지 않아요.
>
> Kevin Chase [오후 2시]
> 고마워요, Miles! 제가 확인해 볼게요.
>
> Miles Dunphy [오후 2시 1분]
> 별말씀을요. 04저는 다시 일하러 가야겠어요. 한 시간 후에 마감인 보고서가 있거든요.

recommend v. 추천하다   supplier n. 공급업체, 공급자   stockroom n. 창고
head v. ~로 향하다   delivery n. 배송   due adj. 마감의, 예정된

01 육하원칙 문제

해석 Mr. Chase는 무엇을 하기를 원하는가?
(A) 고객 설문조사를 실시한다.
(B) 사무실 컴퓨터를 수리받는다.
(C) 가구 한 점을 교체한다.
(D) 창고에 있는 물품들의 수를 센다.

해설 지문의 'Could someone recommend a supplier of office chairs? Mine broke earlier.'에서 Mr. Chase가 사무실 의자 공급업체를 추천해 달라고 하며 본인의 것이 아까 고장 났다고 했으므로 (C)가 정답이다.

어휘 repair v. 수리하다

> Paraphrasing
> chairs 의자 → furniture 가구

02 Not/True 문제

해석 Every Office에 대해 사실이 아닌 것은?
(A) 익일 배송 서비스를 제공한다.
(B) 할인된 가격에 제품을 제공하고 있다.
(C) 일부 상품을 온라인으로 판매한다.
(D) 고객들에게 무료 배송을 해 준다.

해설 (A)는 지문에 언급되지 않은 내용이다. 따라서 (A)가 정답이다. (B)는 'Every Office has one on sale for $97, which is 20 percent off the regular price.'에서 Every Office에서 의자 하나를 97달러에 판

DAY 16 이메일/편지 및 메시지 대화문   199

매 중인데, 이것은 정가에서 20퍼센트 할인된 가격이라고 했으므로 지문의 내용과 일치한다. (C)는 'You can order it through their Web site.'에서 웹사이트를 통해 그것, 즉 의자를 주문할 수 있다고 했으므로 지문의 내용과 일치한다. (D)는 'There's no charge for delivery.'에서 배송에는 요금이 부과되지 않는다고 했으므로 지문의 내용과 일치한다.

어휘 overnight adj. 익일의, 하룻밤 사이의 merchandise n. 상품
free shipping 무료 배송

Paraphrasing
20 percent off the regular price 정가에서 20퍼센트 할인된 가격 → at a discount 할인된 가격에
through ~ Web site 웹사이트를 통해 → online 온라인으로
There's no charge for delivery 배송에는 요금이 부과되지 않는다 → provides free shipping 무료 배송을 해 주다

03 의도 파악 문제
해석 오후 1시 57분에, Mr. Chase가 "There's no hurry"라고 썼을 때, 그가 의도한 것은?
(A) 관리자의 승인을 기다려야 한다.
(B) 임시 해결책을 찾았다.
(C) 초과 근무 시간을 신청해야 한다.
(D) 그사이에 해야 할 많은 일이 있다.

해설 지문의 'I can pick one up for you.'에서 Ms. Contreras가 의자 하나를 당신, 즉 Mr. Chase를 위해 구매해 올 수 있다고 하자, Mr. Chase가 'There's no hurry'(서두르지 않으셔도 돼요)라고 한 후, 'I'm using a plastic chair for now.'에서 우선은 플라스틱 의자를 사용하고 있다고 한 것을 통해, Mr. Chase가 임시 해결책을 찾았다는 것을 알 수 있다. 따라서 (B)가 정답이다.

어휘 overtime n. 초과 근무 in the meantime 그사이에

04 육하원칙 문제
해석 Mr. Dunphy는 왜 다시 일하러 가야 하는가?
(A) 발표를 준비하고 있다.
(B) 동료를 도울 계획이 있다.
(C) 지켜야 할 임박한 마감 기한이 있다.
(D) 한 시간 후에 가게로 향할 것이다.

해설 지문의 'I'd better get back to work. I have a report due in an hour.'에서 Mr. Dunphy가 한 시간 후에 마감인 보고서가 있어서 다시 일하러 가야겠다고 했으므로 (C)가 정답이다.

어휘 presentation n. 발표 coworker n. 동료, 협력자
imminent adj. 임박한, 촉박한 deadline n. 마감 기한

Paraphrasing
due in an hour 한 시간 후에 마감인 → an imminent deadline 임박한 마감 기한

HACKERS TEST   p.250

| 01 (B) | 02 (D) | 03 (B) | 04 (C) | 05 (D) |
| 06 (A) | 07 (A) | | | |

01-03번은 다음 편지에 관한 문제입니다.

Picica 보험사
Lavi Steinem
4304번지 Cordova가
밴쿠버시, 브리티시 컬럼비아주, V6B 1E1
2월 2일
Mr. Steinem께,
저희는 귀하가 제출하신 서류들을 검토했으며, 02저희가 귀하의 자동차

수리에 대한 청구를 이행할 수 없음을 알려드리게 되어 유감입니다. 01-(B)귀하의 보험 약관에 명시된 바와 같이, 귀하는 사고에 대해 즉시 Picica 보험사에 알리셔야 합니다. 그렇게 하셨다면 우리 직원들 중 한 명이 손상 상태를 평가하고 귀하의 보상 범위를 결정할 수 있었을 것입니다. 안타깝게도, 01-(B)귀하는 사고가 발생했을 때 저희에게 알리지 않았고 대신에 수리가 완료된 후에 연락을 주셨습니다. 이것은 03귀하가 제공한 귀하의 차량 사진을 가지고도, 저희가 손상의 원인이나 정도를 정확하게 확인하는 것을 불가능하게 합니다.

귀하의 보험 약관을 꼼꼼하게 검토해 주십시오. 앞으로는 약관을 준수해 주시기를 부탁드립니다. 만약 추가 설명이 필요하시거나 이의를 제기하시고자 하신다면, 가장 가까운 Picica 보험사 사무실을 방문하시거나 555-8899로 연락해 주시기 바랍니다.

Lou Mortimer 드림
Picica 보험사 직원

go over ~을 검토하다 claim n. 청구, 요구 state v. 명시하다
policy n. 보험 약관, 정책 agent n. 직원 assess v. 평가하다
accurately adv. 정확하게 verify v. 확인하다, 입증하다 extent n. 정도
adherence n. 준수, 고수 agreement n. 약관, 계약 clarification n. 설명
raise an objection 이의를 제기하다

01 Not/True 문제
해석 Mr. Steinem에 대해 언급된 것은?
(A) 더 높은 보험료를 지불해야 했다.
(B) 사고를 즉시 알리지 않았다.
(C) 어떤 증빙 서류도 제출하지 않았다.
(D) 자신의 차에 큰 손상을 입혔다.

해설 (B)는 'As stated in your policy, you are required to notify Picica Insurance of an accident immediately.'에서 보험 약관에 명시된 바와 같이 귀하, 즉 Mr. Steinem은 사고에 대해 즉시 Picica 보험사에 알려야 한다고 했고, 'you did not notify us of the accident when it happened and instead contacted us after the repairs were completed'에서 귀하는 사고가 발생했을 때 저희, 즉 보험사에 알리지 않았고 대신에 수리가 완료된 후에 연락을 줬다고 했으므로 지문의 내용과 일치한다. 따라서 (B)가 정답이다. (A), (C), (D)는 지문에 언급되지 않은 내용이다.

어휘 insurance fee 보험료 significant adj. 큰, 상당한

Paraphrasing
did not notify ~ of the accident when it happened 사고가 발생했을 때 알리지 않았다 → did not report an accident right away 사고를 즉시 알리지 않았다

02 동의어 문제
해석 1문단 첫 번째 줄의 단어 "satisfy"는 의미상 -와 가장 가깝다.
(A) 설득하다
(B) 보상하다
(C) 만족시키다
(D) 이행하다

해설 satisfy를 포함한 구절 'we cannot satisfy your claim for repairs to your automobile'에서 satisfy는 '이행하다'라는 뜻으로 사용되었다. 따라서 (D)가 정답이다.

03 육하원칙 문제
해석 Mr. Steinem은 Mr. Mortimer에게 무엇을 보냈는가?
(A) 자동차 수리에 대한 요청서
(B) 차량 사진
(C) 거래 기록
(D) 보상 제공에 대한 거절

해설 지문의 'the photo you provided of your car'에서 귀하, 즉 Mr. Steinem이 차량 사진을 제공했다고 했으므로 (B)가 정답이다.

어휘 transaction n. 거래   rejection n. 거절   compensation n. 보상

[Paraphrasing]
the photo ~ of ~ car 차량 사진 → A photograph of a vehicle 차량 사진

04-07번은 다음 온라인 채팅 대화문에 관한 문제입니다.

> **Jerry Miller** [오후 2시 10분]
> 06-(B)Basket Burger의 연례 여름철 판촉 행사에 대해 질문이 있나요? 저는 방금 새로운 홍보 자료들을 여러분의 각 체인점으로 발송했습니다.
>
> **Lois Denver** [오후 2시 11분]
> 04계절 메뉴는 작년의 것과 같을 거예요, 그렇죠? 만약 그렇다면, 저는 지금부터 제 직원들을 교육하기 시작할 수 있겠어요.
>
> **Jerry Miller** [오후 2시 13분]
> 맞아요. 04하지만, 05얼린 커피 음료는 중단할 거예요.
>
> **Kiel Bronson** [오후 2시 14분]
> 정말요? 05최근에 그것들을 요청하는 손님들이 많았어요. 또한 저는 그것들을 위한 남은 시럽도 있어요. 05제 재고가 떨어질 때까지 그 음료를 팔아도 될까요?
>
> **Jerry Miller** [오후 2시 15분]
> 알겠어요, 하지만 그것들을 광고하지는 마세요. 대신에, 우리의 토네이도 막대 아이스크림과 반값 밀크셰이크를 홍보하세요.
>
> **Lois Denver** [오후 2시 18분]
> 06-(C)토네이도 막대 아이스크림에서 나오는 수익금은 올해에도 자선 단체에 전달될 것인가요?
>
> **Jerry Miller** [오후 2시 20분]
> 06-(C)맞아요. 다른 질문이 더 있나요?
>
> **Kim Patton** [오후 2시 21분]
> 07저는 저의 Beauville 지점 직원들이 이 판촉 행사를 감당하지 못할까 봐 걱정돼요. 07/06-(D)저희는 막 개점해서, 많은 사람들이 아직 교육을 받고 있어요.
>
> **Jerry Miller** [오후 2시 24분]
> 그렇군요. 07제가 판촉 행사 기간 동안 두어 명의 숙련된 직원들을 당신의 매장으로 보낼 수 있어요.

promotion n. 판촉 행사, 홍보   discontinue v. 중단하다, 그만두다
beverage n. 음료   diner n. (식사하는) 손님   leftover adj. 남은; n. 남은 음식
run out (공급품이) 다 떨어지다   half-off adj. 반값의   charity n. 자선 단체
experienced adj. 숙련된

04 의도 파악 문제
해설 오후 2시 13분에, Mr. Miller가 "That's right"이라고 썼을 때, 그가 의도한 것은?
(A) 판촉 행사를 위해 추가 자금이 제공될 것이다.
(B) 여름 전에 일부 재고가 주문되어야 한다.
(C) 체인점의 여름 메뉴는 대체로 바뀌지 않을 것이다.
(D) 계절 제품들은 상당한 비율의 수익을 창출한다.

해설 지문의 'The seasonal menu will be the same as last year's, right?'에서 Ms. Denver가 계절 메뉴는 작년의 것과 같을 것인지 묻자, Mr. Miller가 'That's right'(맞아요)이라고 한 후, 'However, we're discontinuing the frozen coffee beverages.'에서 하지만 얼린 커피 음료는 중단한다고 한 것을 통해 얼린 커피 음료를 제외한 체인점의 여름 메뉴는 대체로 바뀌지 않을 것임을 알 수 있다. 따라서 (C)가 정답이다.

어휘 largely adv. 대체로, 주로   generate v. 창출하다, 만들어 내다
profit n. 수익, 이윤

05 육하원칙 문제
해설 Mr. Bronson은 왜 얼린 커피 음료를 계속해서 팔고 싶어 하는가?
(A) 다른 상품들보다 더 많은 수익을 낸다.
(B) 직원들이 준비하는 데 적은 시간을 필요로 한다.
(C) 저렴한 재료들로 만들어진다.
(D) 고객들의 수요가 많다.

해설 지문의 'we're discontinuing the frozen coffee beverages'에서 Mr. Miller가 얼린 커피 음료는 중단한다고 하자, 'There have been many diners asking for them recently.'에서 Mr. Bronson이 최근에 그것들, 즉 얼린 커피 음료를 요청하는 손님들이 많았다고 했고, 'Can I sell the drinks until my supply runs out?'에서 재고가 떨어질 때까지 해당 음료를 팔아도 되는지 물었으므로 (D)가 정답이다.

어휘 inexpensive adj. 저렴한, 비싸지 않은   ingredient n. 재료

06 Not/True 문제
해설 Basket Burger에 대해 언급되지 않은 것은?
(A) 곧 음료를 새롭게 선보일 계획이다.
(B) 매년 판촉 행사를 진행한다.
(C) 자선 단체에 기부한다.
(D) 최근에 새로운 지점을 개점했다.

해설 (A)는 지문에 언급되지 않은 내용이다. 따라서 (A)가 정답이다. (B)는 'Are there any questions about ~ annual summertime promotion?'에서 Mr. Miller가 연례 여름철 판촉 행사에 대해 질문이 있는지 물었으므로 지문의 내용과 일치한다. (C)는 'Will the money from tornado pop sales go to charity again this year?'에서 Ms. Denver가 토네이도 막대 아이스크림에서 나오는 수익금이 올해에도 자선 단체에 전달될 것인지 묻자, 'Yes.'에서 Mr. Miller가 맞다고 했으므로 지문의 내용과 일치한다. (D)는 'We just opened, and many are still training.'에서 Ms. Patton이 우리는 막 개점해서, 많은 사람들이 아직 교육을 받고 있다고 했으므로 지문의 내용과 일치한다.

어휘 introduce v. 새롭게 선보이다, 소개하다   charitable adj. 자선의

[Paraphrasing]
annual 연례의 → on a yearly basis 매년
the money ~ go to charity 수익금이 자선 단체에 전달되다 → donates to a charitable organization 자선 단체에 기부하다
just opened 막 개점했다 → has launched a new branch recently 최근에 새로운 지점을 개점했다

07 육하원칙 문제
해설 Mr. Miller는 무엇을 하겠다고 제안하는가?
(A) 직원들을 다른 지점으로 보낸다.
(B) 한 메뉴 항목에 대한 광고를 디자인한다.
(C) 관리자 직책 지원자들을 면접한다.
(D) 직원 지침서의 사본을 나눠준다.

해설 지문의 'I'm worried that my Beauville staff won't be able to handle this promotion. We just opened, and many are still training.'에서 Ms. Patton이 그녀의 Beauville 지점 직원들이 이 판촉 행사를 감당하지 못할까 봐 걱정된다고 하며, 그들은 막 개점해서 많은 사람들이 아직 교육을 받고 있다고 하자, 'I can send a couple of experienced employees to your facility during the promotion.'에서 Mr. Miller가 판촉 행사 기간 동안 두어 명의 숙련된 직원들을 그녀의 매장으로 보낼 수 있다고 했으므로 (A)가 정답이다.

어휘 advertisement n. 광고   distribute v. 나눠주다, 배부하다
manual n. 지침서, 안내서

DAY 17 양식 및 광고

기출 유형 1 양식

Example p.252

01-02번은 다음 초대장에 관한 문제입니다.

> West Hobart 공연예술 센터에
> 여러분을 정중히 초대합니다
>
> 4월 9일 오후 7시 30분 ⁰¹West Hobart 공연예술 센터의 개관식에 함께 해 주세요. ⁰²⁻⁽ᴬ⁾저녁에는 8시 30분에 Hobart 교향악단의 30분짜리 콘서트가 진행되고, 유명 오페라 가수 Kelly Tekanawa의 멋진 공연이 이어질 것입니다. ⁰²⁻⁽ᴰ⁾이 초대장은 귀하와 다른 한 명의 입장을 허용합니다. 귀하의 참석 여부를 사전에 확정해 주시기 바랍니다.
>
> cordially adv. 정중히, 다정하게 inauguration n. 개관식, 취임식
> stunning adj. 멋진 renowned adj. 유명한 admit v. 허용하다
> in advance 사전에

01
해석 왜 West Hobart 공연예술 센터에서 행사가 열리는가?
(A) 한 무리의 음악가들을 소개하기 위해
(B) 시설의 개관식을 축하하기 위해
(C) 자선 단체를 위한 기금을 모금하기 위해
(D) 회사의 성과를 기리기 위해

어휘 celebrate v. 축하하다 opening n. 개관식 raise v. 모금하다
fund n. 기금 honor v. 기리다 accomplishment n. 성과, 성취

[Paraphrasing]
inauguration 개관식 → opening 개관식

02
해석 초대된 손님들에 대해 언급된 것은?
(A) 공연의 녹음본을 제공받을 것이다.
(B) 행사에서 음식과 음료를 구매할 수 있다.
(C) 한 단체의 구성원들이다.
(D) 추가 인원을 데려올 수 있다.

어휘 additional adj. 추가의

토익실전문제 p.253

01 (C)   02 (B)

01-02번은 다음 온라인 양식에 관한 문제입니다.

```
                        Era지
                   www.eramagazine.com
        홈  |  분야  |  구독  |  연락처  |  도움말

⁰¹Era지를 1년에 단 29달러로 지금 구독하고 정가에서 10퍼센트를 절약하십시오. 우리 잡지의 디지털 버전과 지난 호들의 온라인 데이터베이스에 대한 무제한 접근뿐 아니라 48부의 인쇄본을 받으십시오. 구독하시려면, 아래 양식을 작성해 주세요.

개인 정보:
이름: [Richard]        성: [Stich]
주소: [1455번지 Marcus가]
도시: [헌츠빌]   주: [앨라배마주]   우편 번호: [35816]
배송지 유형을 선택해 주십시오:
☐ 자택   ☑ 직장

디지털 계정을 생성하십시오:
이메일: [rich_stich@bamamail.com]
```

비밀번호: [********]
청구 정보:
☐ 신용카드   ☑ 직불카드
카드 번호: [4376-XXXX-XXXX-XXXX]

모든 구독은 귀하께서 취소하실 때까지 자동으로 갱신됩니다. ⁰²구독료에 변동이 있을 경우 귀하는 통지받으실 것입니다. 해외 주문을 위해서는, 555-3590으로 전화하시거나 여기를 클릭하십시오.

[주문하기]

subscribe v. 구독하다, 서명하다 issue n. 부(발행 부수), 호, 간행물
unrestricted adj. 무제한의 previous adj. 지난, 이전의
edition n. (간행물의) 호 account n. 계정, 계좌
billing n. 청구, 청구서 (발행) automatically adv. 자동으로
renew v. 갱신하다 international adj. 해외의

01 추론 문제
해석 잡지 구독에 대해 암시되는 것은?
(A) 6개월 동안 유효하다.
(B) 디지털 콘텐츠에 대한 접근을 제공한다.
(C) 현재 할인된 가격에 이용 가능하다.
(D) 매주 결제가 요구된다.

해설 지문의 'Subscribe to *Era* now for just $29 a year and save 10 percent off the regular price.'에서 *Era*지를 1년에 단 29달러로 지금 구독하고 정가에서 10퍼센트를 절약하라고 했으므로 할인된 가격에 잡지 구독 서비스를 이용 가능하다는 사실을 추론할 수 있다. 따라서 (C)가 정답이다.

어휘 currently adv. 현재

02 육하원칙 문제
해석 온라인 양식에 따르면, *Era*지는 왜 Mr. Stich에게 연락할 수도 있는가?
(A) 신용카드 관련 문제를 알리기 위해
(B) 가격 변경을 알리기 위해
(C) 설문 조사를 위한 질문을 하기 위해
(D) 해외 주문을 확인하기 위해

해설 지문의 'You will be notified if there is a change in the price of your subscription.'에서 구독료에 변동이 있을 경우 귀하, 즉 Mr. Stich는 통지받을 것이라고 했으므로 (B)가 정답이다.

기출 유형 2 광고

Example p.254

01-02번은 다음 광고에 관한 문제입니다.

> **Pixel Pro**
>
> ⁰¹두 대의 오프셋 인쇄기, 한 대의 고속 복사기, 세 대의 디지털 컬러 인쇄기를 갖추고 있는 저희는 당신의 요구를 빠르고 확실하게 만족시킬 수 있습니다. ⁰¹당신이 브로슈어, 명함, 혹은 파티 초대장 중 무엇이 필요하든, 당신의 이미지 또는 글을 가져오시기만 하세요, 그러면 저희는 높은 품질의 상품을 제작할 것입니다. 만약 자료가 준비되지 않았다면, 당신에게 적합한 맞춤형 디자인을 생각해 내기 위해 저희의 정규직 그래픽 디자이너들과 상의하세요. ⁰²그들의 작품 견본은 www.pixelpro.com에서 확인하실 수 있습니다. 저희는 월요일부터 토요일에 오전 10시부터 오후 8시 30분까지 영업합니다.
>
> equip with ~을 갖추다 offset press 오프셋 인쇄기
> fulfill v. 만족시키다, 실현하다 reliably adv. 확실하게, 믿을 수 있게
> consult v. 상의하다, 참고하다 full-time adj. 정규직의
> come up with ~을 생각해 내다, 떠올리다

01
해석 어떤 종류의 사업체가 광고되고 있는가?

(A) 전자 기기 제조업체
(B) 배달 업체
(C) 사진 스튜디오
(D) 인쇄소

어휘 electronics n. 전자 기기, 전자 기술

02

해석 광고에 따르면, 고객들은 왜 웹사이트를 방문해야 하는가?
(A) 가격표를 다운로드하기 위해
(B) 주문하기 위해
(C) 견본을 보기 위해
(D) 약속을 잡기 위해

어휘 place an order 주문하다

Paraphrasing
Examples 견본 → samples 견본

토익실전문제   p.255

01 (B)   02 (A)

01-02번은 다음 광고에 관한 문제입니다.

Cine Clique 영화관
01-(A)Cine Clique 영화관은 5월 10일 월요일에 Stanley가 2993번지에 최신 지점을 열 것입니다. 방문객들은 고전적이고 비평가들의 극찬을 받은 전 세계 독립 영화들을 감상하실 수 있습니다. 그들은 또한 영화관 안에서 다양한 간식과 음료 중에서 선택하실 수 있습니다.
01-(C)매일 오전 9시부터 오후 11시까지 영업하는 새로운 영화관은 최신 비디오 영사 장치 및 음향 시스템뿐만 아니라 120명까지 앉을 수 있는 편안한 좌석을 갖추고 있습니다. 02고객들은 또한 근처 Cine 카페에서 식사를 즐길 수 있는데, 이곳에서 다양한 영화 관련 잡지를 살펴볼 수 있습니다.
01-(D)모든 Cine Clique 영화관은 무료 와이파이 서비스를 제공합니다.

launch v. (상점 등을) 열다, 개시하다 branch n. 지점, 지사
critically acclaimed 비평가들의 극찬을 받은
independent film 독립 영화 projection n. 영사, 영상
patron n. 고객, 후원자 adjacent adj. 근처의, 인접한
browse v. 살펴보다, 둘러보다 a selection of 다양한

01 Not/True 문제
해석 Cine Clique 영화관에 대해 언급되지 않은 것은?
(A) 새로운 지점을 개장할 계획이다.
(B) 최신 개봉 영화만 상영한다.
(C) 매일 밤 같은 시간에 문을 닫는다.
(D) 무료 인터넷 접속을 제공한다.

해설 (B)는 지문에 언급되지 않은 내용이다. 따라서 (B)가 정답이다. (A)는 'Cine Clique Cinema will launch its newest branch ~ on Monday, May 10.'에서 Cine Clique 영화관은 5월 10일 월요일에 최신 지점을 열 것이라고 했으므로 지문에 언급된 내용이다. (C)는 'Open daily from 9 A.M. through 11 P.M.'에서 매일 오전 9시부터 오후 11시까지 영업한다고 했으므로 지문에 언급된 내용이다. (D)는 'All Cine Clique Cinemas offer free Wi-Fi service.'에서 모든 Cine Clique 영화관은 무료 와이파이 서비스를 제공한다고 했으므로 지문에 언급된 내용이다.

어휘 release n. (영화 등의) 개봉, 출시; v. 출시하다, 풀어 주다

Paraphrasing
will launch ~ newest branch 최신 지점을 열 것이다 → is planning to open a new location 새로운 지점을 개장할 계획이다
free Wi-Fi service 무료 와이파이 서비스 → free access to the Internet 무료 인터넷 접속

02 육하원칙 문제
해석 Cine Clique 고객들은 Cine 카페에서 무엇을 찾을 수 있는가?
(A) 여러 가지 출판물
(B) 곧 개봉할 영화들에 대한 무료 표
(C) 무료 식사 쿠폰
(D) 고전 영화 기념품

해설 지문의 'Patrons can ~ enjoy a meal at the adjacent Cine Café, where they can browse through a selection of movie-related magazines.'에서 고객들은 근처 Cine 카페에서 식사를 즐길 수 있는데, 이곳에서 다양한 영화 관련 잡지를 살펴볼 수 있다고 했으므로 (A)가 정답이다.

어휘 an assortment of 여러 가지의 publication n. 출판물
complimentary adj. 무료의 souvenir n. 기념품

Paraphrasing
a selection of ~ magazines 다양한 잡지 → An assortment of publications 여러 가지 출판물

HACKERS TEST   p.256

01 (B)   02 (A)   03 (D)   04 (C)   05 (D)
06 (D)   07 (A)

01-03번은 다음 영수증에 관한 문제입니다.

Silverpeak Mountain 리조트
Silverpeak 리조트를 선택해 주셔서 감사합니다. 잊지 못할 겨울 모험에 귀하가 저희와 함께하게 되어 매우 기쁩니다!

겨울 스키 패키지 포함 사항:
· 01-(A)모든 스키 슬로프에 대한 전면 이용 권한
· 01-(B)자격증을 소지한 스키 강사와 함께하는 2시간짜리 강습 3회
· 01-(C)모든 필수 스키 장비 사용 권한

예약 세부 사항:
02이름: Jennifer Matthews
결제일: 12월 15일
예약 확인 코드: ER9283474
숙박 기간: 1월 22일–24일
02투숙 인원: 2명
총 결제 금액: 780달러
결제 방법: Stanfield 신용카드 (마지막 네 자리: 6824)

체크인 시간은 오후 3시이며, 체크아웃 시간은 오전 11시입니다. 해당 객실의 이용 가능 여부에 따라 늦은 체크아웃 요청이 가능합니다.

참고: 03전액 환불을 받기 위해서는 체크인 최소 7일 전까지 저희에게 이메일로 예약 취소 의사를 알려주셔야 합니다.

thrilled adj. 매우 기쁜, 신이 난 memorable adj. 잊지 못할, 기억에 남을 만한
adventure n. 모험 slope n. 슬로프(스키장에서 스키를 탈 수 있는 경사진 곳)
certified adj. 자격증을 소지한, 공인된 instructor n. 강사
reservation n. 예약 payment method 결제 방법 intention n. 의사, 의도
cancel v. 취소하다 prior to ~보다 이전에

01 Not/True 문제
해석 패키지에 대해 사실인 것은?
(A) 초급자용 슬로프에만 접근을 허용한다.
(B) 여러 강습 세션이 포함되어 있다.
(C) 몇몇 장비에 대해 추가 비용을 요구한다.
(D) 연속된 4일 동안 이용할 수 있다.

해설 (B)는 'Three two-hour lessons with a certified ski instructor'에서 자격증을 소지한 스키 강사와 함께하는 2시간짜리 강습 3회가 겨울 스키 패키지에 포함된다고 했으므로 지문의 내용과 일치한다. 따라서 (B)

가 정답이다. (A)는 'Full access to all ski slopes'에서 모든 스키 슬로프에 대한 전면 이용 권한이 패키지에 포함된다고 했으므로 지문의 내용과 일치하지 않는다. (C)는 'Use of all necessary ski equipment'에서 모든 필수 스키 장비 사용 권한이 패키지에 포함된다고 했으므로 지문의 내용과 일치하지 않는다. (D)는 지문에 언급되지 않은 내용이다.

어휘 beginner n. 초급자, 초보자 instruction n. 강습 consecutive adj. 연속의

[Paraphrasing]
Three ~ lessons 강습 3회 → multiple sessions of instruction 여러 강습 세션

02 추론 문제
해석 Ms. Matthews에 대해 암시되는 것은?
(A) 일행과 함께 여행할 계획이다.
(B) 늦은 체크아웃에 대한 허가를 요청할 것이다.
(C) 예전에 Silverpeak 리조트에 묵은 적 있다.
(D) 스키 패키지에 대해 할인을 받았다.

해설 지문의 'Name: Jennifer Matthews'와 'Guests: 2'에서 Ms. Matthews가 Silverpeak 리조트에 방문할 때 2명의 인원이 투숙할 것이라고 했으므로, Ms. Matthews가 일행과 함께 여행할 것임을 추론할 수 있다. 따라서 (A)가 정답이다.

어휘 companion n. 일행, 동반자 permission n. 허가, 승인

03 육하원칙 문제
해석 Ms. Matthews는 어떻게 환불받을 수 있는가?
(A) 리조트의 고객 서비스 센터에 전화함으로써
(B) 단체 투어 주최자에게 이메일을 보냄으로써
(C) 직원에게 거래 내역을 보여줌으로써
(D) 예약 취소에 대해 사전에 통보함으로써

해설 지문의 'You must notify us ~ of your intention to cancel this booking at least seven days prior to check-in to receive a full refund.'에서 전액 환불을 받기 위해서는 Ms. Matthews가 체크인 최소 7일 전까지 예약 취소 의사를 알려주어야 한다고 했다. 따라서 (D)가 정답이다.

어휘 transaction n. 거래, 처리 advance adj. 사전의

04-07번은 다음 구인 광고에 관한 문제입니다.

Hamasaki사의 채용 공고

04/05-(A)Hamasaki사는 자동차 부품들의 제조와 관련된 글로벌 기업입니다. 저희는 현재 일리노이주 시카고에 있는 저희의 주요 생산 공장에서 직무를 수행할 창고 관리자를 찾고 있습니다.

05-(B)/(C)주된 업무:
- 05-(C)고객들에게 보낼 완제품의 배송을 조정한다
- 안전하고 생산적인 작업 환경을 유지한다
- 05-(B)직원들의 채용, 교육, 그리고 해고 절차를 감독한다
- 작업 절차를 평가하고 개선을 제안한다

06필수 자격 요건:
- 최소 2년제 대학 학위 수료
- 되도록이면 자동차 산업에서의 06최소 5년의 관련 업무 경력
- 데이터베이스 프로그램 작업 능력
- 매우 체계적이며 꼼꼼한 성격

05-(D)이것은 경쟁력 있는 임금과 복리후생제도를 제공하는 정규직입니다. 07지원하기 위해서는, 당신의 이력서를 jobs@hamasakicorp.com으로 보내 주십시오. 만약 당신이 확인 이메일을 받지 못하신다면, 저희의 인사 담당자에게 555-3090으로 연락해 주십시오. 지원서를 직접 받지 않을 것입니다.

---

automotive adj. 자동차의 warehouse n. 창고 supervisor n. 관리자
primary adj. 주된, 주요한 coordinate v. 조정하다
finished goods 완제품 productive adj. 생산적인
terminating n. 해고 절차, 종료 evaluate v. 평가하다
improvement n. 개선 essential adj. 필수의 qualification n. 자격 요건
preferably adv. 되도록이면 organized adj. 체계적인
detail-oriented adj. 꼼꼼한 salary n. 임금, 급여
benefits package 복리후생제도 in person 직접, 몸소

04 육하원칙 문제
해석 어떤 회사가 구인 광고를 게시했는가?
(A) 자동차 대리점
(B) 배송 업체
(C) 부품 제조사
(D) 운송 서비스 회사

해설 지문의 'Hamasaki Corporation is a ~ corporation involved in the manufacture of automotive parts.'에서 Hamasaki사는 자동차 부품들의 제조와 관련된 기업이라고 했으므로 (C)가 정답이다.

어휘 dealership n. 대리점 firm n. 회사

[Paraphrasing]
a ~ corporation involved in the manufacture of automotive parts 자동차 부품들의 제조와 관련된 기업 → A parts manufacturer 부품 제조사

05 Not/True 문제
해석 일자리에 대해 언급되지 않은 것은?
(A) 다국적 기업에 의해 제공된다.
(B) 직원들을 직접 관리하는 업무를 포함한다.
(C) 제품 배송에 관여할 것을 요구한다.
(D) 시간제 근로자에게 주어질 수 있다.

해설 (D)는 'This is a full-time role'에서 이것, 즉 Hamasaki사가 채용하는 일자리는 정규직이라고 했으므로 지문의 내용과 일치하지 않는다. 따라서 (D)가 정답이다. (A)는 'Hamasaki Corporation is a global corporation'에서 Hamasaki사가 글로벌 기업이라고 했으므로 지문의 내용과 일치한다. (B)는 'Primary duties:'와 'Oversee the hiring, training, and terminating of employees'에서 직원들의 채용, 교육, 그리고 해고 절차를 감독하는 것이 주된 업무 중 하나라고 했으므로 지문의 내용과 일치한다. (C)는 'Primary duties:'와 'Coordinate shipment of finished goods to clients'에서 고객들에게 보낼 완제품의 배송을 조정하는 것이 주된 업무 중 하나라고 했으므로 지문의 내용과 일치한다.

어휘 multinational adj. 다국적의 personnel n. 직원, 인사
part-time worker 시간제 근로자

[Paraphrasing]
global corporation 글로벌 기업 → multinational corporation 다국적 기업
Oversee the hiring, training, and terminating of employees 직원들의 채용, 교육, 그리고 해고 절차를 감독하다 → direct management of personnel 직원들을 직접 관리하는 업무
Coordinate shipment of finished goods 완제품의 배송을 조정하다 → involvement in product deliveries 제품 배송에 관여

06 육하원칙 문제
해석 일자리의 지원자들에게 무엇이 요구되는가?
(A) 4년제 대학 학위 소유
(B) 최근에 회사 프로그램에 참여한 경험
(C) 한 개보다 많은 언어를 구사하는 능력
(D) 유사한 직책에서의 이전 근무 이력

해설 지문의 'Essential qualifications:'와 'At least five years of experience in a related role'에서 최소 5년의 관련 업무 경력이 필수 자격 요건이라고 했으므로 (D)가 정답이다.

어휘 possession n. 소유 employment n. 근무 이력, 고용

[Paraphrasing]
experience in a related role 관련 업무 경력 → Previous employment in a similar position 유사한 직책에서의 이전 근무 이력

07 육하원칙 문제

해석 사람들은 어떻게 지원해야 하는가?
(A) 이메일을 보냄으로써
(B) 지원서를 우편 발송함으로써
(C) 관리자에게 연락함으로써
(D) 인사팀에 방문함으로써

해설 지문의 'To apply, send your résumé to jobs@hamasakicorp. com.'에서 지원하기 위해서는, 당신의 이력서를 jobs@hamasakicorp.com으로 보내라고 했으므로 (A)가 정답이다.

어휘 application letter 지원서

> [Paraphrasing]
> send ~ résumé to jobs@hamasakicorp.com 이력서를 jobs@hamasakicorp.com으로 보내다 → sending an e-mail 이메일을 보내는 것

DAY 18 기사 및 안내문

기출 유형 1 기사

Example p.258

01-02번은 다음 기사에 관한 문제입니다.

> 오웬즈버그—독일의 고급 초콜릿 제조업체 Hurlimann사가 오웬즈버그에 첫 번째 국제 오프라인 매장을 연다. 그것은 1월 8일 Gilford 쇼핑센터에 개관식 일정을 잡아두었다.
>
> 매장 관리자 Joanne Lutz에 따르면, ⁰¹그것의 초콜릿을 구매하는 첫 100명의 고객들은 무료 사탕 한 박스를 받을 것이다. 게다가, 처음 2주 동안 고객들은 선정된 상품에 50퍼센트 할인을 받을 수 있다.
>
> ⁰²⁻⁽ᴮ⁾100년 전에 설립된 Hurlimann사는 오랫동안 맛있는 초콜릿 제품들을 전 세계의 판매업자들에게 수출해 왔다. "⁰²⁻⁽ᴬ⁾저희는 마침내 해외에 자사 지점들을 여는 중이기 때문에, 미래가 어떻게 될지 기대됩니다."라고 최고경영자 David Carle이 말했다.

brick-and-mortar adj. 오프라인의, 실제 매장의
ribbon-cutting ceremony 개관식, 준공식　merchandise n. 상품, 제품
found v. 설립하다　export v. 수출하다　delicate adj. 맛있는, 섬세한
vendor n. 판매업자, 판매 회사

01

해석 고객들은 어떻게 무료 상품을 받을 수 있는가?
(A) 몇 가지 설문조사 질문에 답함으로써
(B) 가게의 첫 100명의 구매자들 중 한 명이 됨으로써
(C) 특별히 선정된 물품들을 구매함으로써
(D) 2주 내로 재방문함으로써

> [Paraphrasing]
> a free box of candy 무료 사탕 한 박스 → a complimentary product 무료 상품
> customers who purchase 구매하는 고객들 → buyers 구매자들

02

해석 Hurlimann사에 대해 사실인 것은?
(A) 해외에 매장들을 열기 시작할 것이다.
(B) 100년 전에 오웬즈버그에 설립되었다.
(C) David Carle을 최고경영자로 막 임명했다.
(D) 대표적인 별미 제품 라인을 확장하고 있다.

어휘 century n. 100년, 세기　appoint v. 임명하다, 정하다
delicacy n. 별미, 맛있는 것

> [Paraphrasing]
> are ~ opening ~ branches overseas 해외에 지점들을 여는 중이다 → open shops abroad 해외에 매장들을 열다

토익실전문제 p.259

01 (C)　**02** (D)　**03** (C)

01-03번은 다음 기사에 관한 문제입니다.

> ⁰¹10월 8일—금융 회사 Bishop Advisors사는 자사의 방대한 그림 및 조각품 컬렉션을 매각할 계획을 발표했다. 이 작품들은 이전 최고경영자 Aileen MacIntyre에 의해 구매되었으며 총 3백만 유로 이상의 가치가 있다고 추산된다.
>
> 현재의 최고경영자 ⁰²⁻⁽ᴬ⁾Gavin Brodie는 자신이 예술에 관심이 없다고 인정했지만, 이것이 그의 선택의 주요한 이유는 아니었다. "⁰²⁻⁽ᴮ⁾회사는 자금을 모아야 하며, ⁰²⁻⁽ᶜ⁾우리의 새로운 본사에는 컬렉션을 보관할 충분한 공간이 없습니다."라고 Brodie는 언급했다.
>
> 미술품 수집가들은 이 소식에 들떠 있다. "이 컬렉션에는 Tessa Menzies와 Bret Kennedy의 그림이 포함되어 있습니다."라고 ⁰³예술 전문가 Jennifer Harper는 말했는데, 그녀는 몇몇 작품에 입찰할 계획이다. ⁰¹10월 14일에 열리는 이 경매는 Avidia Auctions사에 의해 진행될 것이다.

extensive adj. 방대한, 아주 많은　sculpture n. 조각품　former adj. 이전의
estimate v. 추산하다　worth adj. ~의 가치가 있는　admit v. 인정하다
raise v. (자금을) 모으다, 들어 올리다　fund n. 자금　headquarters n. 본사
comment v. 언급하다　bid on ~에 입찰하다　sale n. 경매, 판매

01 주제 문제

해석 기사가 주로 논의하는 내용은 무엇인가?
(A) 새로운 경영진의 임명
(B) 제안된 일련의 재무 규정
(C) 곧 있을 예술 작품 판매
(D) 가치 있는 예술 작품의 발견

해설 지문의 'October 8— ~ Bishop Advisors announced plans to sell its extensive collection of paintings and sculptures.'에서 10월 8일에 기사가 쓰였으며 Bishop Advisors사가 자사의 방대한 그림 및 조각품 컬렉션을 매각할 계획을 발표했다고 했고, 'The sale, to be held on October 14'에서 경매가 10월 14일에 열릴 것이라고 했으므로 (C)가 정답이다.

어휘 executive n. 경영진　regulation n. 규정　valuable adj. 가치 있는

02 Not/True 문제

해석 Mr. Brodie의 결정에 대한 이유로 언급되지 않은 것은?
(A) 흥미의 부족
(B) 재정적 필요
(C) 공간 제약
(D) 직원의 기호

해설 (D)는 지문에 언급되지 않은 내용이다. 따라서 (D)가 정답이다. (A)는 'Gavin Brodie ~ is not interested in art'에서 Gavin Brodie는 예술에 관심이 없다고 했으므로 지문의 내용과 일치한다. (B)는 'The company needs to raise funds'에서 회사, 즉 Bishop Advisors사는 자금을 모아야 한다고 했으므로 지문의 내용과 일치한다. (C)는 'there is not enough space for the collection in our new headquarters'에서 새로운 본사에는 컬렉션을 보관할 충분한 공간이 없다고 했으므로 지문의 내용과 일치한다.

어휘 limitation n. 제약　preference n. 기호, 선호

> [Paraphrasing]
> is not interested 관심이 없다 → Lack of interest 흥미의 부족
> needs to raise funds 자금을 모아야 한다 → Financial necessities 재정적 필요
> is not enough space 충분한 공간이 없다 → Space limitations 공간 제약

03 추론 문제

해석 누가 10월 14일 행사에 참석할 것 같은가?
(A) Aileen MacIntyre
(B) Tessa Menzies
(C) Jennifer Harper
(D) Bret Kennedy

해설 지문의 'art expert Jennifer Harper ~ plans to bid on some of the works'에서 예술 전문가 Jennifer Harper가 몇몇 작품에 입찰할 계획이라고 했으므로 그녀가 경매에 참석할 것이라는 사실을 추론할 수 있다. 따라서 (C)가 정답이다.

기출 유형 2 안내문

Example p.260

01-02번은 다음 안내문에 관한 문제입니다.

> 저희는 모두가 Lafayette 군립 공원에 안전하고 즐거운 방문을 할 수 있기를 희망합니다. 공원이 모두에게 재미있고 매력적인 상태로 유지되도록 하기 위해, 아래 규칙들을 준수해 주시기 바랍니다:
> - 공원 출입문은 오후 10시에 닫고 오전 6시에 다시 엽니다. 문을 닫았을 때 공원에 들어가지 마시기 바랍니다.
> - 아이들은 항상 감독하에 있어야 합니다. 공원 내 발생하는 어떠한 사고에 대해서도 저희는 책임을 지지 않습니다.
> - 01-(B)시설 관리 건물 옆에 위치한 농구 코트와 축구장은 오후 8시까지만 이용 가능합니다.
> - 01-(C)모든 차량의 제한 속도는 시속 20마일입니다.
> - 02저희는 모든 방문객들이 쓰레기를 지정된 쓰레기통에만 버려 주실 것을 요청드립니다.
>
> 01-(D)문제가 발생하면, 555-6103으로 공원 관리자에게 연락해 주시기 바랍니다.

pleasant adj. 즐거운, 기쁜 inviting adj. 매력적인, 솔깃한
observe v. 준수하다, 관찰하다 supervise v. 감독하다, 지도하다
limit n. 제한, 한계; v. 제한하다 designated adj. 지정된
supervisor n. 관리자

01

해석 Lafayette 군립 공원에 대해 언급되지 않은 것은?
(A) 관리 사무소의 운영 시간
(B) 스포츠 시설의 위치
(C) 차량 제한 속도
(D) 관리자의 연락처

어휘 facility n. 시설

02

해석 안내문에 따르면, 방문객들은 무엇을 하도록 권고되는가?
(A) 입장료를 지불한다.
(B) 대여한 장비를 반납한다.
(C) 쓰레기를 제대로 버린다.
(D) 지정된 주차장을 이용한다.

어휘 dispose of ~을 버리다, 처리하다

Paraphrasing
throw away trash ~ in designated trash bins 쓰레기를 지정된 쓰레기통에 버리다 → Dispose of trash properly 쓰레기를 제대로 버리다

토익실전문제 p.261

01 (C)   02 (A)   03 (B)

01-03번은 다음 안내문에 관한 문제입니다.

> **Seaver 백화점**
>
> Seaver 백화점에서 쇼핑해 주셔서 감사합니다! 여러분의 이용에 감사드리며 저희는 소중한 고객분들께 항상 최선을 다해 서비스를 제공합니다.
> 01물건을 구매하신 후에 어떤 이유로든 교환 또는 환불을 위해 매장으로 반품하시고 싶으시면, 다음의 최신 규정들을 읽어 보십시오:
> 1. 03-(A)모든 교환 또는 환불 요청은 구매일로부터 14일 이내에 이루어져야 합니다.
> 2. 모든 상품들은 원본 영수증이 지참되어야 합니다.
> 3. 02구매하신 제품을 새 제품과 동일한 상태로, 원래의 포장과 함께 반품해 주시기를 정중히 요청드립니다.
> 4. 03-(B)수영복과 운동복은 반품이 불가합니다.
>
> 03-(C)저희 직원은 어떤 구매 제품이든 고객에 의해 파손된 경우 반품 요청을 거부할 권리가 있습니다.

appreciate v. 감사하다, 인정하다 valued adj. 소중한, 귀중한
make a purchase 물건을 구매하다 return v. 반품하다, 반환하다; n. 반품
exchange n. 교환; v. 교환하다 refund n. 환불; v. 환불하다
up-to-date adj. 최신의, 첨단의 accompany v. 지참하다, 동반하다
receipt n. 영수증 brand-new adj. 새로운, 신품의
packaging n. 포장, 포장재 bathing suit 수영복 sportswear n. 운동복
reserve v. (어떤 권한을) 갖다, 예약하다 right n. 권리, 정당한 요구
reject v. 거부하다, 거절하다 damage v. 파손하다, 손상을 입히다

01 주제 문제

해석 안내문은 무엇에 대한 것인가?
(A) 배송 절차
(B) 결제 방법
(C) 소매점의 규정
(D) 매장의 판촉 행사

해설 지문의 'If you make a purchase and ~ would like to return it ~, please read through the following up-to-date policies:'에서 물건을 구매한 후에 반품하고 싶다면 다음의 최신 규정들을 읽어 보라고 한 후, 반품 규정에 대한 세부 사항을 설명하고 있으므로 (C)가 정답이다.

Paraphrasing
policies 규정 → regulations 규정

02 육하원칙 문제

해석 고객은 반품되는 물건과 함께 무엇을 가져오도록 요청되는가?
(A) 제품이 담겨 있던 용기
(B) 공식 반품 요청서
(C) 유효한 신분증
(D) 구매 시 사용한 신용카드

해설 지문의 'We kindly ask that purchases be returned ~ with the original packaging.'에서 구매한 제품을 원래의 포장과 함께 반품해 주기를 요청한다고 했으므로 (A)가 정답이다.

어휘 container n. 용기, 그릇

Paraphrasing
original packaging 원래의 포장 → container the product came in 제품이 담겨 있던 용기

03 Not/True 문제

해석 Seaver 백화점에 대해 언급된 것은?
(A) 일주일 후에는 교환을 허용하지 않는다.
(B) 반품될 수 없는 몇몇 상품을 판매한다.
(C) 할인되었던 상품에 대해서는 환불 요청을 거부할 수 있다.
(D) 파손된 상품에 대해 수리 서비스를 제공하지 않는다.

해설 (B)는 'Bathing suits and sportswear are not returnable.'에서 수영복과 운동복은 반품이 불가하다고 했으므로 지문의 내용과 일치한

다. 따라서 (B)가 정답이다. (A)는 'All exchange ~ requests must be made within 14 days of purchase.'에서 모든 교환 요청은 구매일로부터 14일 이내에 이루어져야 한다고 했으므로 지문의 내용과 일치하지 않는다. (C)는 'Our staff reserves the right to reject a return request if any purchased item has been damaged by the customer.'에서 어떤 구매 제품이든 고객에 의해 파손된 경우 직원이 반품 요청을 거부할 권리가 있다고 했지, 할인되었던 상품에 대해서 반품 요청을 거부할 수 있다고 한 것은 아니므로 지문의 내용과 일치하지 않는다. (D)는 지문에 언급되지 않은 내용이다.

어휘 repair n. 수리, 수선; v. 수리하다

Paraphrasing
are not returnable 반품이 불가하다 → cannot be returned 반품될 수 없다

HACKERS TEST   p.262

01 (D)   02 (A)   03 (D)   04 (A)   05 (C)
06 (B)

01-03번은 다음 안내문에 관한 문제입니다.

Astrapia 항공사—보상 포인트를 좌석 업그레이드에 이용하기

⁰¹당신이 티켓을 예약할 때 좌석을 업그레이드하기 위해 포인트를 사용하시려면, 당사 웹사이트의 '보상 포인트 업그레이드' 옵션을 선택하세요. ⁰²⁻⁽ᶜ⁾만약 티켓을 구매한 후에 이렇게 하기를 원하신다면, 두 가지 방법 중 하나를 통해 업그레이드를 요청하실 수 있는데, Astrapia 항공사 콜센터에 전화하시거나 당사 웹사이트에서 귀하의 예약 내역을 수정하시면 됩니다. ⁰²⁻⁽ᴬ⁾요청은 비행 최소 24시간 전까지 완료되어야 합니다. 아래의 표는 저희가 비행하는 다양한 지역들 내에서 하나의 등급에서 다른 등급으로 업그레이드하기 위해 포인트가 얼마나 필요한지를 나타냅니다. ⁰³몇몇 항공편에서는 업그레이드가 가능하지 않을 수도 있다는 점을 유의해 주십시오.

	⁰²⁻⁽ᴰ⁾이코노미석에서 프리미엄 이코노미석으로	프리미엄 이코노미석에서 비즈니스석으로	⁰³비즈니스석에서 일등석으로
유럽	20,000포인트	30,000포인트	40,000포인트
⁰³남아메리카	20,000포인트	30,000포인트	
중앙아시아	20,000포인트	35,000포인트	50,000포인트
⁰²⁻⁽ᴰ⁾동남아시아	⁰²⁻⁽ᴰ⁾20,000포인트		

domestic adj. 국내의, 국산의   reserve v. 예약하다   modify v. 수정하다
indicate v. 나타내다   region n. 지역

01 동의어 문제

해석 1문단 첫 번째 줄의 단어 "reserve"는 의미상 -와 가장 가깝다.
(A) 문의하다
(B) 운영하다
(C) 제한하다
(D) 마련하다

해설 reserve를 포함한 구절 'when you reserve a ticket'에서 reserve는 '예약하다'라는 뜻으로 사용되었다. 따라서 (D)가 정답이다.

02 Not/True 문제

해석 Astrapia 항공사에 대해 사실인 것은?
(A) 비행 직전 24시간 이내에는 업그레이드를 금지한다.
(B) 다른 항공사들과의 제휴 프로그램을 유지한다.
(C) 좌석 업그레이드를 위한 전화를 받지 않는다.
(D) 동남아시아행 항공편에 가장 많은 포인트를 필요로 한다.

해설 (A)는 'Requests must be made at least 24 hours before your flight.'에서 업그레이드 요청은 비행 최소 24시간 전까지 완료되어야 한다고 했으므로 지문의 내용과 일치한다. 따라서 (A)가 정답이다. (B)는 지문에 언급되지 않은 내용이다. (C)는 'If you wish to do this after a ticket has been purchased, an upgrade can be requested in one of two ways: calling the Astrapia Air Call Center'에서 만약 티켓을 구매한 후에 이렇게, 즉 좌석 업그레이드를 하기를 원한다면 두 가지 방법 중 하나를 통해 업그레이드를 요청할 수 있는데, Astrapia 항공사 콜센터에 전화하면 된다고 했으므로 지문의 내용과 일치하지 않는다. (D)는 'Southeast Asia', 'From Economy Class to Premium Economy Class', '20,000 points'에서 동남아시아 항공편의 이코노미석에서 프리미엄 이코노미석으로 업그레이드할 때 20,000포인트가 필요한데, 유럽과 남아메리카, 중앙아시아 항공편 또한 이코노미석에서 프리미엄 이코노미석으로 업그레이드할 때 동일하게 20,000포인트를 필요로 하는 것을 알 수 있으므로 지문의 내용과 일치하지 않는다.

어휘 prohibit v. 금지하다   maintain v. 유지하다
partner program 제휴 프로그램

03 추론 문제

해석 남아메리카행 항공편에 대해 추론될 수 있는 것은?
(A) 티켓 전액 환불이 불가능하다.
(B) 항공사 웹사이트에서만 취소될 수 있다.
(C) 승객에게 추가 보상 포인트를 적립해 준다.
(D) 업그레이드는 특정 좌석 등급으로 제한되어 있다.

해설 지문의 'Please note that upgrades may not be possible on some flights.'에서 몇몇 항공편에서는 업그레이드가 가능하지 않을 수도 있다는 점을 유의해 달라고 했고, 'South America', 'From Business Class to First Class'에서 남아메리카 항공편의 경우 비즈니스석에서 일등석으로 업그레이드를 할 때 필요한 포인트가 나와 있지 않으므로 남아메리카행 항공편에서는 특정 좌석 등급만 업그레이드가 가능하다는 사실을 추론할 수 있다. 따라서 (D)가 정답이다.

어휘 earn v. 적립해 주다, 얻다

04-06번은 다음 보도 자료에 관한 문제입니다.

Zoet 식품사가 변화하는 시장추세에 적응하다

3월 21일—⁰⁴아이스크림 시장의 최근 동향에 대응하여, 스위스의 Zoet 식품사는 올해 말에 새로운 제품 라인을 출시할 것이라고 밝혔다. Zoet사의 마케팅 관리자 James Farnham은 고객들의 변화하는 입맛을 이러한 개발에 대한 원인으로 돌렸다. — [1] —. "소비자들은 아이스크림을 덜 먹고 있으며 이제 얼린 요거트 같은 더 건강한 대체재들을 선호합니다."라고 그는 말했다. ⁰⁶시장은 또한 유기농 또는 비유제품 재료로 만들어진 젤라토와 아이스크림 같은 고급 제품들에 대한 수요의 영향을 받았다. — [2] —. Zoet사가 최근 중국, 브라질, 그리고 인도에서 영향력을 늘리긴 했지만, 매출의 대부분은 여전히 유럽과 미국에서 나온다. — [3] —. Farnham은 "우리는 많은 성장의 여지를 가지고 있지만, ⁰⁵우리의 가장 큰 도전은 유럽과 미국에서 우리의 선두적인 입지를 유지하는 것입니다."라고 덧붙였다. — [4] —. ⁰⁵Zoet사의 건강한 신규 제품 라인과 함께, 회사는 이러한 도전을 받아들일 준비가 된 것으로 보인다.

respond v. 대응하다   credit v. 원인으로 돌리다
alternative n. 대체재; adj. 대체 가능한   premium adj. 고급의, 우수한
organic adj. 유기농의   non-dairy adj. 비유제품의   ingredient n. 재료
majority n. 대부분   plenty of 많은   room n. 여지, 공간
challenge n. 도전, 어려움   leading adj. 선두적인
take on ~을 받아들이다, 떠맡다

04 주제 문제

해석 보도 자료가 주로 논의하는 내용은 무엇인가?
(A) 시장 상황에 반응한 신제품의 출시
(B) 식품을 생산하는 과정에서의 혁신
(C) 제품의 가격에 영향을 미치는 세계적 동향

(D) 몇몇 주요 음식 생산업체에 의해 이용되는 전략

해설 지문의 'Responding to current trends in the ice cream market, ~ Zoet Foods has announced that it will be releasing a new line of products'에서 아이스크림 시장의 최근 동향에 대응하여 Zoet 식품사는 새로운 제품 라인을 출시할 것이라고 밝혔다고 했으므로 (A)가 정답이다.

어휘 innovation n. 혁신 strategy n. 전략

05 추론 문제

해설 Zoet 식품사는 유럽과 미국에서 어떻게 입지를 유지할 계획인 것 같은가?
(A) 운영 규모를 감소시킴으로써
(B) 더 낮은 가격의 재료를 사용함으로써
(C) 건강한 제품들을 소개함으로써
(D) 아시아에서의 마케팅 활동을 줄임으로써

해설 지문의 'our biggest challenge is maintaining our leading position in Europe and the US'에서 우리, 즉 Zoet 식품사의 가장 큰 도전은 유럽과 미국에서 선두적인 입지를 유지하는 것이라고 했고, 'With Zoet's healthy new product lines, the company appears ready to take on this challenge.'에서 Zoet사의 건강한 신규 제품 라인과 함께, 회사는 이러한 도전, 즉 유럽과 미국에서 선두적인 입지를 유지하기 위한 도전을 받아들일 준비가 된 것으로 보인다고 했으므로 유럽과 미국에 건강한 제품들을 소개함으로써 입지를 유지할 계획이라는 사실을 추론할 수 있다. 따라서 (C)가 정답이다.

어휘 scale n. 규모 operation n. 운영 utilize v. 사용하다

06 문장 위치 찾기 문제

해설 [1], [2], [3], [4]로 표시된 위치 중, 다음 문장이 들어갈 곳으로 가장 적절한 것은?
"이러한 종류들은 일반적으로 세계적인 회사들보다 지역 전문 회사들에 의해 주도된다."
(A) [1]
(B) [2]
(C) [3]
(D) [4]

해설 주어진 문장은 특정 종류의 제품이 언급된 내용 주변에 나올 것임을 예상할 수 있다. [2]의 앞 문장인 'The market has ~ been affected by demand for premium products like gelato and ice creams made with organic or non-dairy ingredients.'에서 시장은 유기농 또는 비유제품 재료로 만들어진 젤라토와 아이스크림 같은 고급 제품들에 대한 수요의 영향을 받았다고 했으므로, [2]에 주어진 문장이 들어가면 이러한 종류의 고급 제품들은 일반적으로 세계적인 회사들보다 지역 전문 회사들에 의해 주도된다는 자연스러운 문맥이 된다는 것을 알 수 있다. 따라서 (B)가 정답이다.

어휘 category n. 종류 typically adv. 일반적으로
dominate v. 주도하다, 지배하다 specialty n. 전문, 본업

DAY 19 공고 및 회람

기출 유형 1 공고

Example   p.264

01-02번은 다음 공고에 관한 문제입니다.

01/02-(A)West 대학의 글쓰기 센터는 모든 등록된 학생들에게 수업의 글쓰기 과제를 수정하는 데 도움을 제공합니다. 교정 서비스는 월요일부터 금요일 오전 8시 30분부터 오후 8시까지 이용 가능합니다.

글쓰기 능력을 더 발전시키려고 하는 사람들을 위해, 02-(C)저희는 메인 데스크에서 예약을 통해 개인 교습 시간 또한 마련해 드립니다. 02-(D)글쓰기 개인 교사는 현재 교육대학원과 인문과학대학원에 재학 중인 대학원생이고 어떠한 수업 과제로도 글쓰기 과정 내내 여러분을 지도하는 것이 가능합니다. 더 많은 정보를 위해 Ernestine홀 450호에 있는 West 대학 글쓰기 센터에 방문하십시오.

registered adj. 등록된 proofreading n. 교정 graduate student 대학원생
liberal arts 인문과학, 교양 과목

01

해설 공고의 목적은 무엇인가?
(A) 전문 작가들을 워크숍에 초대하기 위해
(B) 교육 센터의 개장을 홍보하기 위해
(C) 대학교 서비스의 다가오는 변경을 알리기 위해
(D) 시설에서 제공되는 몇몇 서비스들을 홍보하기 위해

어휘 publicize v. 홍보하다

02

해설 글쓰기 센터에 대해 언급되지 않은 것은?
(A) 학교에 등록된 누구나 이용 가능하다.
(B) 바쁜 일정을 가진 학생들에게 온라인 수업을 제공한다.
(C) 개인 교습 시간을 마련해 줄 수 있다.
(D) 대학원생을 개인 교사로 고용한다.

어휘 accessible adj. 이용 가능한 enroll v. 등록하다

토익실전문제   p.265

| 01 (B) | 02 (A) | 03 (C) |

01-03번은 다음 공고에 관한 문제입니다.

Barnes 서점은 더 큰 곳으로 이전하게 될 것을 알리게 되어 기쁩니다! Rooster가 449번지에 있는 01-(C)현재의 매장은 3월 28일에 문을 닫을 것입니다. 01-(C)/02Spencer가 5983번지에 위치한 저희의 새로운 매장은 4월 16일에 고객들에게 문을 열 것입니다. 01-(A)영업시간은 월요일부터 토요일 오전 10시부터 오후 8시까지로 이전과 같이 유지될 것입니다.

Barnes 서점은 또한 03새로운 매장에서 배송 서비스 제공을 시작할 것임을 알리게 되어 기쁩니다. 당신이 구매하고 싶은 품목을 고르고 주소 카드를 작성하시기만 하면 됩니다. 배송비는 즉시 계산될 것이며, 모든 품목들이 24시간 이내로 발송될 것입니다.

그러니 4월 16일에 저희의 새로운 지점에 방문하시고 Barnes 서점의 이 특별한 행사를 기념하여 모든 구매에 대해 20퍼센트 할인을 받으세요! 문의 사항이나 추가 정보를 위해서는 555-4059로 전화주세요. Barnes 서점에 의해 주최되는 특별 행사의 일정표를 보시려면, www.barnesbooks.com/events를 방문하시거나 01-(D)저희 월간 소식지 한 부를 받아보세요.

brand-new adj. 새로운 situate v. 위치시키다, (어떤 위치에) 두다
hours of operation 영업시간 fill out ~을 작성하다, 기입하다
pick up ~을 받다, 얻다

01 Not/True 문제

해설 Barnes 서점에 대해 언급되지 않은 것은?
(A) 일주일에 6일 연다.
(B) 오래된 재고품을 싸게 팔아 치우고 있다.
(C) 일시적으로 문을 닫을 계획이다.
(D) 정기 출판물을 제공한다.

해설 (B)는 지문에 언급되지 않은 내용이다. 따라서 (B)가 정답이다. (A)는 'Hours of operation will remain as they were before, from 10 A.M. through 8 P.M. Monday to Saturday.'에서 영업시간은 월요일부터 토요일 오전 10시부터 오후 8시까지로 이전과 같이 유지될 것이라고 했으므로 지문의 내용과 일치한다. (C)는 'Our current store ~ will close on March 28.'에서 현재의 매장은 3월 28일에 문을

닫을 것이라고 했고, 'Our brand-new space ~ will be open to customers on April 16.'에서 새로운 매장은 4월 16일에 고객들에게 문을 열 것이라고 했으므로 지문의 내용과 일치한다. (D)는 'pick up a copy of our monthly newsletter'에서 자신들의 월간 소식지 한 부를 받아보라고 했으므로 지문의 내용과 일치한다.

어휘 sell off ~을 싸게 팔아 치우다 temporarily adv. 일시적으로
regular adj. 정기적인

02 동의어 문제

해석 1문단 두 번째 줄의 단어 "situated"는 의미상 -와 가장 가깝다.
(A) 위치한
(B) 관련된
(C) 수행된
(D) 도달한

해설 situated를 포함한 구절 'Our brand-new space, situated at 5983 Spencer Avenue, will be open'에서 situated는 '위치한'이라는 뜻으로 사용되었다. 따라서 (A)가 정답이다.

03 육하원칙 문제

해석 Barnes 서점은 4월에 무엇을 할 것인가?
(A) 영업시간을 연장할 것이다.
(B) 추가 직원을 고용할 것이다.
(C) 새로운 서비스를 도입할 것이다.
(D) 배송비를 올릴 것이다.

해설 지문의 앞부분에서 Barnes 서점의 새로운 매장은 4월 16일에 고객들에게 문을 열 것이라고 했고, 'we will start offering a shipping service in the new store'에서 새로운 매장에서 배송 서비스를 제공하기 시작할 것이라고 했으므로 (C)가 정답이다.

어휘 extend v. 연장하다 introduce v. 도입하다

기출 유형 2 회람

Example p.266

01-02번은 다음 회람에 관한 문제입니다.

> 회람
> 수신: 모든 직원들
> 발신: Amanda Robinson
> 제목: Matthew Webb
> 날짜: 5월 20일
>
> 6월 1일을 기하여, 01Matthew Webb이 Longview Holdings사의 구매 관리자로서 Daniel Rodgers를 대신하게 될 것임을 알아두시기 바랍니다. 사무용품 및 장비에 대한 모든 구매 요청서는 그날부터 Mr. Webb에게 제출해 주십시오. 이전과 같이, 02모든 요청 양식은 제출 전에 부서 관리자에 의해 허가되고 서명되어야 합니다. 이 전환이 원활하게 이루어질 수 있도록 협조해 주셔서 감사합니다.

replace v. 대신하다, 대체하다 effective adj. (특정한 일시를) 기하여, 효과적인
address v. 제출하다, 다루다, 연설하다 n. 연설 departmental adj. 부서의
supervisor n. 관리자, 감독 transition n. 전환

01
해석 Ms. Robinson은 왜 회람을 썼는가?
(A) 새로운 회사 정책에 대한 설명을 제공하기 위해
(B) 사무용품에 대한 주문을 요청하기 위해
(C) 공석에 대해 직원들에게 알리기 위해
(D) 인사 변경에 대해 직원들에게 공지하기 위해

02
해석 Longview Holdings사의 직원들은 어떻게 새로운 사무용품을 요청해야 하는가?

(A) 온라인 양식을 작성함으로써
(B) 사무실 내선으로 전화함으로써
(C) 서명된 문서를 제출함으로써
(D) 공급업체의 웹사이트를 방문함으로써

어휘 extension n. 내선, 구내전화

토익실전문제 p.267

01 (A) **02** (D) **03** (C)

01-03번은 다음 회람에 관한 문제입니다.

> 02-(D)유기농 제품 연합
>
> 수신: 행정 직원
> 02-(D)발신: Tom Williams, 이사
> 날짜: 8월 10일
> 제목: 유기농 생산업체 데이터베이스
>
> 우리 단체는 10월에 산타크루스에서 제2회 연례 유기농 제품 무역 박람회를 열 것입니다. 우리는 약 2천 명의 출품자가 박람회에 참가할 것으로 예상합니다. 02-(D)지난번 행사에서, 1,500개 이상의 기업들이 제품을 선보였습니다. 더 많은 홍보에 따라, 저희는 이 숫자가 올해 크게 증가할 것이라고 확신합니다.
>
> 다가오는 행사의 준비를 위해, 01마케팅팀에서는 유기농 제품 회사들에 대한 정확한 데이터베이스를 만들 것입니다. 그러나, 그들 구성원 대부분이 행사 자체를 기획하는 것만으로도 바쁘기 때문에 다른 부서의 도움이 필요합니다. 다행히도, 03연구부서의 Ms. Eliza Banks가 돕기로 자원했습니다. 따라서, 01저는 여러분이 이 작업을 완료하기 위해 Ms. Banks와 함께 일할 것을 요청드립니다. 03그녀는 회의가 준비되었을 때 여러분에게 알려주기 위해 연락할 것입니다. 그녀에게 전적으로 협조해 주시기를 바랍니다.

anticipate v. 예상하다 exhibitor n. 출품자
showcase v. 선보이다, 전시하다 publicity n. 홍보
certain adj. 확신하는 accurate adj. 정확한 assistance n. 도움

01 추론 문제
해석 회람은 누구를 대상으로 하는가?
(A) 특정한 업무를 하도록 배정받은 직원들
(B) 유기농 식품 생산업체들
(C) 행사 기획팀들의 팀장들
(D) 음식 서비스 산업과 관련된 사업체들

해설 지문의 'the marketing team is going to create an accurate database'에서 마케팅팀에서는 정확한 데이터베이스를 만들 것이라고 한 후, 'I request that you work ~ to complete this assignment'에서 여러분이 이 작업을 완료하기 위해 일할 것을 요청한다고 했으므로 데이터베이스를 만드는 업무를 하도록 배정받은 직원들을 대상으로 하는 회람이라는 사실을 추론할 수 있다. 따라서 (A)가 정답이다.

어휘 specific adj. 특정한 industry n. 산업

02 Not/True 문제
해석 유기농 제품 연합에 대해 언급된 것은?
(A) 새로운 행정 이사를 임명했다.
(B) 산타크루스로 본사를 옮겼다.
(C) 모금 행사를 후원했다.
(D) 제품 박람회를 개최했다.

해설 (D)는 'Organic Products Alliance', 'From: Tom Williams, director', 'At our last event, we had over 1,500 companies showcase their products.'에서 유기농 제품 연합의 이사 Tom Williams에 따르면 지난번 행사에서 1,500개 이상의 기업들이 제품을 선보였다고 했으므로 지문의 내용과 일치한다. 따라서 (D)가 정답이다. (A), (B), (C)는 지문에 언급되지 않은 내용이다.

어휘 sponsor v. 후원하다

03 육하원칙 문제
해석 누가 행정 직원들에게 회의에 대해 연락할 것인가?
(A) 기업 회장
(B) 마케팅팀의 팀장
(C) 연구부서의 직원
(D) 행사 진행자

해설 지문의 'Ms. Eliza Banks from the research division has volunteered to help'에서 연구부서의 Ms. Eliza Banks가 돕기로 자원했다고 한 뒤, 'She will contact you to let you know when a meeting has been arranged.'에서 그녀는 회의가 준비되었을 때 여러분, 즉 행정 직원들에게 알려 주기 위해 연락할 것이라고 했으므로 연구부서의 직원인 Ms. Banks가 행정 직원들에게 회의에 대해 연락할 것임을 알 수 있다. 따라서 (C)가 정답이다.

HACKERS TEST   p.268

| 01 (D) | 02 (C) | 03 (D) | 04 (A) | 05 (D) |
| 06 (C) | 07 (C) | | | |

01-03번은 다음 공고에 관한 문제입니다.

공고
알림: 교통 카드를 사용하시는 모든 승객들께

⁰¹교통 카드를 잃어버린 승객들은 어느 Madisonville 교통 당국의 매표소에서나 3달러의 요금으로 카드를 재발급받을 수 있습니다. 잔액은 자동으로 새로운 카드로 옮겨질 것입니다. 요청을 하는 승객들은 사진을 포함한 신분증 한 개를 제시해야 합니다. 회사 신분증은 유효한 형태의 신분증으로 간주되지 않습니다. ⁰²만약 여러분의 카드가 발급된 후에 이전 카드를 찾으시면, 그것은 더 이상 작동하지 않을 것이므로 폐기하시기 바랍니다.
이 규정은 ⁰³⁻⁽ᴮ⁾1일권 또는 3일권 관광객 카드에는 적용되지 않음을 유의하시기 바랍니다. 이러한 카드의 소지자들은 새로운 카드를 구매하셔야 합니다. ⁰³⁻⁽ᴰ⁾관광객 카드는 일반 교통 카드가 판매되는 어느 곳에서나 구매하실 수 있습니다. 교통 카드에 대한 추가 정보가 필요하시면, www.madisonvilletransit.org를 방문하십시오.

reissue v. 재발급하다   transfer v. 옮기다   automatically adv. 자동으로
identification n. 신분증   consider v. 간주하다, 여기다
discard v. 폐기하다, 버리다   regulation n. 규정

01 글을 쓴 이유 문제
해석 공고는 왜 쓰였는가?
(A) 요금 조정을 알리기 위해
(B) 노선 변경에 대한 최신 정보를 제공하기 위해
(C) 승객들에게 지연에 대해 알리기 위해
(D) 교통 카드에 대한 정보를 제공하기 위해

해설 지문의 'Passengers who have lost their transit pass cards can have their cards reissued ~ at any Madisonville Transit Authority ticket office.'에서 교통 카드를 잃어버린 승객들은 어느 Madisonville 교통 당국의 매표소에서나 카드를 재발급받을 수 있다고 한 후, 교통 카드 재발급 방법을 알려 주고 있으므로 (D)가 정답이다.

어휘 fare n. 요금, 운임   adjustment n. 조정, 조절   route n. 노선, 항로

02 추론 문제
해석 Madisonville 교통 당국에 대해 암시되는 것은?
(A) 최근에 몇 개의 새로운 매표소를 열었다.
(B) 교통 카드에 사진이 포함되도록 요구한다.
(C) 분실 신고된 카드를 정지시킨다.
(D) 역에서 신용카드를 받지 않는다.

해설 지문의 'If you happen to find your old card after your card has been reissued, please discard it as it will no longer function.'에서 카드가 발급된 후에 이전 카드를 찾으면, 그것은 더 이상 작동하지 않을 것이므로 폐기하라고 했으므로, Madisonville 교통 당국이 분실된 이전 카드를 정지시킨다는 사실을 추론할 수 있다. 따라서 (C)가 정답이다.

어휘 deactivate v. 정지시키다, 비활성화시키다

03 Not/True 문제
해석 관광객 카드에 대해 사실인 것은?
(A) 각각 3달러에 구매될 수 있다.
(B) 하루 이상 유효하지 않다.
(C) 만료되면 반드시 반환되어야 한다.
(D) 일반 카드와 같은 장소에서 판매된다.

해설 (D)는 'Tourist passes are available wherever regular transit cards are sold.'에서 관광객 카드는 일반 교통 카드가 판매되는 어느 곳에서나 구매할 수 있다고 했으므로 지문의 내용과 일치한다. 따라서 (D)가 정답이다. (A)와 (C)는 지문에 언급되지 않은 내용이다. (B)는 'one-day or three-day tourist passes'에서 1일권 또는 3일권 관광객 카드가 있다고 했으므로 지문의 내용과 일치하지 않는다.

어휘 expire v. 만료되다

04-07번은 다음 회람에 관한 문제입니다.

Davenport 회계 회사

회람

수신: 전 직원
발신: Phillip Christensen

⁰⁴여러분 중 대부분이 이미 알고 있듯이, 우리는 곧 사무실 장비의 전체적인 업데이트를 받을 것입니다. — [1] —. 우리의 많은 오래된 장비가 교체될 것입니다. ⁰⁵⁻⁽ᴬ⁾우리는 지난 5년간 새 컴퓨터를 받지 못했던 모든 사람에게 하나를 제공할 뿐 아니라 서버를 개선할 것입니다. — [2] —. 추가로, ⁰⁵⁻⁽ᴮ⁾새 프린터기가 사무실 곳곳에 배치될 것입니다.

당신이 새 컴퓨터를 받을 것이라면, 금요일까지 ⁰⁶필요한 파일들을 외장 하드 드라이브에 반드시 복사하십시오. ⁰⁵⁻⁽ᶜ⁾오래된 장비들이 주말 동안 교체되어 월요일부터는 접근할 수 없게 될 것이기 때문에 이것은 중요합니다. — [3] —. ⁰⁷만약 지연이 발생한다면, 여러분은 공지받으실 것입니다. 질문이 있으시다면, 저에게 내선 번호 115로 전화 주시거나 philchristensen@davenport.com으로 이메일을 보내 주시기 바랍니다. — [4] —.

aware adj. ~을 알고 있는, ~에 정통한   complete adj. 전체적인, 완전한
station v. 배치하다   external hard drive 외장 하드 드라이브
inaccessible adj. 접근할 수 없는   notify v. 공지하다

04 목적 문제
해석 회람의 목적은 무엇인가?
(A) 직원들에게 예정된 작업을 상기시키기 위해
(B) 직원 교체의 이유를 설명하기 위해
(C) 근무 시간 변경을 전달하기 위해
(D) 직원들에게 보안 절차를 새롭게 알려주기 위해

해설 지문의 'As most of you are already aware, we will soon be undergoing a complete update of our office hardware.'에서 대부분이 이미 알고 있듯이 곧 사무실 장비의 전체적인 업데이트를 받을 것이라고 한 후, 업데이트 관련 세부 사항 및 요청 사항에 대해 설명하고 있으므로 (A)가 정답이다.

어휘 procedure n. 절차, 순서   communicate v. 전달하다, 의사소통하다

05 Not/True 문제
해석 회람에서 언급되지 않은 것은?
(A) 몇몇 장비들은 5년 넘게 사용되었다.

(B) 사무실은 몇몇 새 프린터기를 받을 것이다.
(C) 장비는 금요일 이후에 치워질 것이다.
(D) 몇몇 직원들은 다음 주에 추가 근무를 해야 할 것이다.

해설 (D)는 지문에 언급되지 않은 내용이다. 따라서 (D)가 정답이다. (A)는 'We will be ~ providing new PCs to everyone who has not received one in the past five years.'에서 지난 5년간 새 컴퓨터를 받지 못했던 모든 사람들에게 하나를 제공할 것이라고 했으므로 지문의 내용과 일치한다. (B)는 'new printers will be stationed throughout the office'에서 새 프린터기가 사무실 곳곳에 배치될 것이라고 했으므로 지문의 내용과 일치한다. (C)는 'the old equipment will be replaced over the weekend and will be inaccessible'에서 오래된 장비들이 주말 동안 교체되어 접근할 수 없게 될 것이라고 했으므로 지문의 내용과 일치한다.

[Paraphrasing]
will be replaced ~ and will be inaccessible 교체되어 접근 불가능하게 될 것이다 → will be removed 치워질 것이다

06 육하원칙 문제

해설 Mr. Christensen은 직원들이 무엇에 책임이 있다고 말하는가?
(A) 새로운 장비를 위한 교육 자료를 만드는 것
(B) 회사 기록용의 중요한 문서를 스캔하는 것
(C) 전자 파일을 백업 장치로 옮기는 것
(D) 사무실 폐쇄로 인해 약속 일정을 변경하는 것

해설 지문의 'please make sure to copy all necessary files onto an external hard drive'에서 필요한 파일들을 외장 하드 드라이브에 반드시 복사하라고 했으므로 (C)가 정답이다.

어휘 training material 교육 자료 transfer v. 옮기다 appointment n. 약속

[Paraphrasing]
copy ~ files onto an external hard drive 파일들을 외장 하드 드라이브에 복사하다 → Transferring electronic files onto a backup device 전자 파일을 백업 장치로 옮기는 것

07 문장 위치 찾기 문제

해설 [1], [2], [3], [4]로 표시된 위치 중, 다음 문장이 들어갈 곳으로 가장 적절한 것은?

"기술자들은 모든 작업을 일요일까지 마치는 것을 목표로 합니다."

(A) [1]
(B) [2]
(C) [3]
(D) [4]

해설 주어진 문장은 작업 일정과 관련된 내용 주변에 들어가야 함을 알 수 있다. [3]의 뒤 문장인 'Should there be a delay, you will be notified.'에서 만약 지연이 발생한다면 공지받을 것이라고 했으므로, [3]에 제시된 문장이 들어가면 작업을 일요일까지 마치는 것이 목표인데, 만약 지연이 발생한다면 공지받을 것이라는 자연스러운 문맥이 된다는 것을 알 수 있다. 따라서 (C)가 정답이다.

DAY 20 다중 지문

Example
p.271

01-02번은 다음 광고와 예약 확인서에 관한 문제입니다.

러시아 횡단 철도

러시아 횡단 철도(TRR)가 현재 특별한 여행자 탑승권을 제공하고 있는데, 이는 국내의 모든 TRR 정차역으로의 무제한 여행을 허용합니다. **01**탑승권은 www.transrussiarailways.com뿐만 아니라 러시아 내의 대부분의 기차역이나 여행사에서 구매할 수 있습니다.

철도 탑승권은 7일 동안 유효합니다. 기차를 이용하기 위해서는 탑승권을 아무 기차역이나 터미널에 있는 직원에게 보여주세요. 철도 탑승권 가격은 성인 380달러, 학생 320달러, 12세 이하의 아동 280달러입니다.

02100달러의 정액 요금으로, 모든 여행에 음식과 음료 서비스가 제공될 것입니다. 이것은 식당차에서 이용 가능한 모든 메뉴를 포함할 것입니다.

탑승권은 환불이 불가능하며 양도할 수 없습니다.

railway n. 철도, 철로 pass n. 탑승권, 통과; v. 지나가다, 통과하다
destination n. 목적지 travel agency 여행사 valid adj. 유효한, 정당한
present v. 보여주다, 제시하다; adj. 현재의 flat fee 정액 요금, 균일 요금
dining car (기차의) 식당차 nonrefundable adj. 환불이 불가능한
nontransferable adj. 양도할 수 없는

러시아 횡단 철도 여행자 탑승권 확인서			
이름	Fatima Khan	여행 일자	6월 12일
요금	☐ 380달러 ■ 320달러 ☐ 280달러	**02**식사	**02**■ 예 ☐ 아니오

여행자 탑승권 소지자들은 총 무게가 50킬로그램인 수하물 두 개가 허용된다는 점을 알아 두시기 바랍니다. 여행객들은 예정된 출발 30분 전에 미리 도착하는 것이 권장됩니다.

confirmation n. 확인서, 확인 holder n. 소지자, 보유자 permit v. 허용하다
weight n. 무게, 체중 in advance ~ 전에, 사전에 departure n. 출발, 떠남

01
해설 어떤 정보가 광고에 포함되어 있는가?
(A) 환불을 받기 위한 필요조건들
(B) 승차권을 구매하는 방법들
(C) 철도로 이어진 도시들
(D) 식당에서 제공되는 요리들

어휘 requirement n. 필요조건, 요건

02
해설 Ms. Khan에 대해 암시되는 것은?
(A) 이전에 러시아에 여행을 간 적이 있다.
(B) 성인 티켓을 구입했다.
(C) 100달러의 추가 비용을 지불했다.
(D) 단체와 함께 여행하고 있다.

토익실전문제
p.272

| 01 (C) | 02 (C) | 03 (A) | 04 (A) | 05 (D) |

01-05번은 다음 공고, 편지, 신청서에 관한 문제입니다.

Soaring Skies 아카데미
승무원 교육 프로그램

01-(D) Soaring Skies 아카데미는 승무원이 되기를 원하는 사람들에게 종합적인 교육을 제공합니다. 저희의 다음 프로그램은 6월 1일에 시작합니다. **01-(C)**이것은 다양한 주제들을 다룰 것인데, 이는 훌륭한 고객 서비스를 제공하는 방법에서부터 승객들의 안전을 위협하는 상황에서 무엇을 해야 하는지까지를 포함합니다.

참여에 관심이 있는 분들은 저희의 웹사이트 www.soaringskies.com/trainingapp에서 신청서를 작성해야 합니다. **03**작성된 양식은 이전 상사 또는 선생님의 추천서 한 장과 함께 제출되어야 합니다.

02교육 프로그램 종료와 동시에, 수료자들은 승무원 직책을 얻기 위한 가장 효과적인 방법에 관해 저희 강사들로부터 일대일 상담을 받을 것입니다.

flight attendant 승무원 comprehensive adj. 종합적인, 포괄적인
threaten v. 위협하다, 협박하다 submit v. 제출하다, 항복하다
recommendation n. 추천, 권고 supervisor n. 상사, 감독관

graduate n. 수료자, 졸업생; v. 졸업하다 one-on-one adj. 일대일의
counseling n. 상담, 조언

Soaring Skies 아카데미
55번지 Westwood가
샌프란시스코, 캘리포니아주 94125

4월 28일

관계자분께,

03저는 귀사의 승무원 교육 프로그램의 후보로 Ms. Linda Sykes를 추천하게 되어 기쁩니다. 03/05Harper 호텔에서 근무하는 동안, Ms. Sykes는 자신이 성실하고 유능한 직원임을 입증했습니다.

또한, Ms. Sykes는 Redmond 온라인 직업 교육 아카데미에서 여러 승무원 교육 강좌들을 수료했습니다. 따라서, 그녀의 진정한 열정이 항공 업계에서 전문가가 되는 것에 있다는 것은 확실합니다.

이 추천서와 관련하여 추가 정보나 설명이 필요하시다면, 언제든지 555-2329로 저에게 직접 연락해 주시기 바랍니다.

Simon Chung 드림

candidate n. 후보, 지원자 diligent adj. 성실한, 근면한
capable adj. 유능한 vocational adj. 직업 교육의, 직업상의
passion n. 열정, 흥미 professional n. 전문가; adj. 전문적인, 직업의
clarification n. 설명, 해명 reference n. 추천서, 참고

Soaring Skies 아카데미
승무원 교육 프로그램
온라인 신청서

성명: Linda Sykes
주소: 120번지 Norwell가, 새크라멘토, 캘리포니아주 94240
전화번호: 555-1287

04당신은 이전에 항공사 승무원 교육 프로그램에 참석한 적이 있습니까?
☑ 네   ☐ 아니요

여기를 클릭하여 추천서를 첨부하십시오.

신청비 지불
지불 금액: 50달러
지불 방법: 신용카드 번호 XXXX-XXXX-7382-1281

*수업료 지불은 6월 9일까지입니다. 05만약 아래 나열된 저희 아카데미의 제휴 회사들 중 한 곳에서 과거 근무 경험이 있다면 10퍼센트 할인이 적용될 것입니다.
· Graytown Rental Vehicles사
· Pristine 여행 대행사
· 05Harper 호텔

[제출] [인쇄]

attend v. 참석하다 tuition n. 수업료, 등록금

01 Not/True 문제

해설 프로그램에 대해 사실인 것은?
(A) 일 년에 걸쳐 이루어질 것이다.
(B) 전적으로 인터넷을 통해 실시된다.
(C) 위급 상황 조치 절차를 다룰 것이다.
(D) 현직 항공사 직원들을 위해 설계되었다.

해설 (C)는 공고의 'It will cover ~ what to do in situations that threaten the safety of our passengers.'에서 이것, 즉 승무원 교육 프로그램은 승객들의 안전을 위협하는 상황에서 무엇을 해야 하는지를 다룰 것이라고 했으므로 지문의 내용과 일치한다. 따라서 (C)가 정답이다. (A)와 (B)는 지문에 언급되지 않은 내용이다. (D)는 'Soaring Skies Academy offers comprehensive training to individuals wishing to become flight attendants.'에서 Soaring Skies 아카데미는 승무원이 되기를 원하는 사람들에게 종합적인 교육을 제공한다고 했으므로 지문의 내용과 일치하지 않는다.

어휘 deal with ~을 다루다, 처리하다

02 육하원칙 문제

해설 공고에 따르면, 프로그램이 끝날 때 무슨 일이 일어날 것인가?
(A) 교육생들은 사교 행사에 참여할 것이다.
(B) 강사들이 필기시험을 실시할 것이다.
(C) 직원들이 참가자들에게 조언을 해줄 것이다.
(D) 교육 수료자들이 기념식에 참석할 것이다.

해설 공고의 'Upon completion of the training program, graduates will receive one-on-one counseling from our instructors'에서 교육 프로그램 종료와 동시에, 수료자들은 저희, 즉 Soaring Skies 아카데미의 강사들로부터 일대일 상담을 받을 것이라고 했으므로 (C)가 정답이다.

어휘 trainee n. 교육생, 훈련생 administer v. 실시하다, 관리하다

[Paraphrasing]
Upon completion of the ~ program 프로그램 종료와 동시에 → at the end of the program 프로그램이 끝날 때

03 추론 문제 연계

해설 Mr. Chung에 대해 결론지을 수 있는 것은?
(A) 이전 직장에서 Ms. Sykes의 상사였다.
(B) Harper 호텔의 오랜 고객이다.
(C) Ms. Sykes와 사업 제휴를 맺었다.
(D) 과거에 Soaring Skies 아카데미에서 강의했었다.

해설 Mr. Chung이 작성한 편지를 먼저 확인한다.
[단서 1] 편지의 'I am pleased to provide my recommendation for Ms. Linda Sykes'에서 Ms. Linda Sykes를 추천하게 되어 기쁘다고 했고, 'During her time at the Harper Hotel, Ms. Sykes has proven herself to be a diligent and capable employee.'에서 Ms. Sykes가 Harper 호텔에서 근무하는 동안 자신이 성실하고 유능한 직원임을 입증했다고 했다. 그런데 Mr. Chung과 Ms. Sykes가 무슨 관계인지 제시되지 않았으므로 공고에서 관련 내용을 확인한다.
[단서 2] 공고의 'The completed form must be submitted along with one letter of recommendation from a previous supervisor or teacher.'에서 작성된 양식, 즉 신청서는 이전 상사 또는 선생님의 추천서 한 장과 함께 제출되어야 한다고 했다.
두 단서를 종합할 때, 추천서를 작성한 Mr. Chung은 Harper 호텔에서 Ms. Sykes의 이전 상사였음을 추론할 수 있다. 따라서 (A)가 정답이다.

어휘 long-term adj. 오랜, 장기적인

04 육하원칙 문제

해설 신청서는 어떤 정보에 대해 묻는가?
(A) 이전의 교육 경험
(B) 직업적 목표
(C) 재정 관련 정보
(D) 이메일 주소

해설 신청서의 'Have you attended any airline attendant training programs before?'에서 이전에 항공사 승무원 교육 프로그램에 참석한 적이 있는지 물었으므로 (A)가 정답이다.

어휘 prior adj. 이전의, 과거의

[Paraphrasing]
attended ~ training programs before 이전에 교육 프로그램에 참석했다 → Prior education experience 이전의 교육 경험

05 육하원칙 문제 연계

해설 Ms. Sykes는 무엇을 받을 자격이 있는가?
(A) 교육 시설의 가이드 투어
(B) 수업을 위한 무료 교과서

(C) 보상 프로그램의 회원권
(D) 수업료에 대한 할인된 금액

해설 Ms. Sykes가 작성한 신청서를 먼저 확인한다.

단서 1 신청서의 'A 10 percent discount will be applied if you have previous work experience at one of our academy's partner companies listed below:'와 'Harper Hotel'에서 만약 아래 나열된 아카데미의 제휴 회사들 중 한 곳에서 과거 근무 경험이 있다면 10퍼센트 할인이 적용될 것이라고 했고, 이 제휴 회사들에 Harper 호텔이 포함된다고 했다. 그런데 Ms. Sykes가 이 할인을 받을 수 있는지 제시되지 않았으므로 편지에서 관련 내용을 확인한다.

단서 2 편지의 'During her time at the Harper Hotel, Ms. Sykes has proven herself to be a diligent and capable employee.'에서 Ms. Sykes가 Harper 호텔에서 근무하는 동안 자신이 성실하고 유능한 직원임을 입증했다고 했으므로 Ms. Sykes가 Harper 호텔에서 근무했다는 사실을 확인할 수 있다.

두 단서를 종합할 때, Ms. Sykes는 Harper 호텔에서 과거에 근무한 경험이 있으므로 수업료의 10퍼센트 할인을 받을 자격이 있다는 것을 알 수 있다. 따라서 (D)가 정답이다.

어휘 eligible adj. ~할 자격이 있는, 적격의

HACKERS TEST   p.274

01 (B)	02 (D)	03 (A)	04 (C)	05 (C)
06 (A)	07 (B)	08 (D)	09 (C)	10 (D)
11 (C)	12 (A)	13 (D)	14 (D)	15 (B)
16 (B)	17 (C)	18 (D)	19 (D)	20 (A)
21 (A)	22 (B)	23 (A)	24 (D)	25 (C)

01-05번은 다음 광고와 이메일에 관한 문제입니다.

스트레스로부터 휴식을 취하세요!

오늘날 빠르게 돌아가는 세상에서, 스트레스는 종종 정신 건강과 육체 건강에 영향을 미칩니다. 요가는 스트레스를 줄이고, 에너지를 높이며, 집중력을 개선한다고 입증된 바 있습니다.

이번 달에만, [01]Tantra 명상 센터에서 어떤 요가 수업이든 무료로 체험해 보세요! 다음 세션 중 하나에 당신의 자리를 예약하기 위해 555-4994로 전화하세요:

초급 요가	강사: Pradeep Rathnam	월요일 오후 7시-8시 30분
중급 요가	강사: Diana Koutsakis	화요일 오후 7시-8시 30분
[05]상급 요가	[05]강사: Parvati Singh	수요일 오후 7시 30분-9시
명상과 요가	강사: Dan Mathers	목요일 오후 6시 30분-8시

[02-(D)]한정된 자리 때문에, 무료 수업을 위해서는 사전에 예약이 되어야 합니다. 모든 수업은 Bolton로 3884번지에 있는 Tantra 명상 센터에서 진행됩니다. 수업을 계속 듣고 싶으시면, 신청서를 제출하고 한 달 수업료 120달러를 내시기만 하면 됩니다.

fast-paced adj. 빠르게 돌아가는   mental adj. 정신의, 마음의
physical adj. 육체의   prove v. 입증하다, 드러나다   alleviate v. 완화하다
concentration n. 집중, 농도   try out ~을 체험해 보다, 시험하다
meditation n. 명상   spot n. 자리, 점   beginner n. 초급자, 초보자
intermediate adj. 중급의, 중간의; n. 중급자   advanced adj. 상급의, 고급의

수신: 고객 서비스 <cservice@tantracenter.com>
발신: Leanne Allen <lallen@localmail.com>
날짜: 1월 11일
제목: 요가 수업

제 이름은 Leanne Allen이고, 현재 당신의 센터의 무료 요가 체험 수업에 등록되어 있습니다. 저는 그 세션이 전반적으로 유익하다고 느끼고 있어서, 다음 달에도 계속 수업을 듣고 싶습니다.

[03]제가 당신의 센터에 있었을 때, 저는 여러 가지 요가 관련 부대용품을 둘러봤고, 몇 가지를 구매하는 데 관심이 있습니다. 당신의 직원들 중 한 명이 제가 등록된 회원이면 15퍼센트 할인을 받을 수 있다고 알려 주었습니다.

[04]가능하다면 이메일로 신청서를 보내 주실 수 있나요? 그러면 제가 작성해서 다음 수업 때 가져다드릴 수 있습니다.

마지막으로, [05]제 남편 Joel이 다음 주에 Parvati Singh의 수업을 체험하는 데 관심이 있다고 말합니다. 그를 위해서 자리를 예약해 주실 수 있나요? 도와주셔서 감사합니다.

Leanne Allen

beneficial adj. 유익한, 이로운   browse v. 둘러보다, 훑어보다
drop off ~을 가져다주다, 내려 주다   assistance n. 도움, 지원

01 주제 문제

해설 광고는 주로 무엇에 대한 것인가?
(A) 전문 요가 장비
(B) 무료 강습 세션
(C) 질병에 대한 치료
(D) 온라인 프로그램 멤버십

해설 광고의 'try out any of the yoga courses at the Tantra Meditation Center for free'에서 Tantra 명상 센터에서 어떤 요가 수업이든 무료로 체험해 보라고 한 뒤, 여러 요가 수업에 대해 설명하고 있으므로 (B)가 정답이다.

어휘 specialized adj. 전문의, 전문화된   treatment n. 치료, 대우
medical condition 질병

Paraphrasing
yoga courses ~ for free 무료 요가 수업 → Complimentary instructional sessions 무료 강습 세션

02 Not/True 문제

해설 Tantra 명상 센터에 대해 언급된 것은?
(A) 현금 결제만 받는다.
(B) 두 번째 지점을 열었다.
(C) 개인 명상 세션을 제공한다.
(D) 한정된 수업 규모를 가지고 있다.

해설 (D)는 광고의 'Due to limited space, reservations must be made in advance'에서 한정된 자리 때문에 사전에 예약이 되어야 한다고 했으므로 지문의 내용과 일치한다. 따라서 (D)가 정답이다. (A), (B), (C)는 지문에 언급되지 않은 내용이다.

Paraphrasing
limited space 한정된 자리 → limited class sizes 한정된 수업 규모

03 육하원칙 문제

해설 Ms. Allen은 최근 Tantra 명상 센터에서 무엇을 했는가?
(A) 몇몇 운동 제품을 살펴봤다.
(B) 안내 책자를 가져갔다.
(C) 중급 요가 수업을 가르쳤다.
(D) 신청서를 작성했다.

해설 이메일의 'While I was at your center, I browsed through your selection of yoga-related accessories'에서 Ms. Allen이 Tantra 명상 센터에서 요가 관련 부대용품을 둘러봤다고 했으므로 (A)가 정답이다.

어휘 fitness n. 운동, 건강   informational adj. 안내의, 정보의   pamphlet n. 책자

Paraphrasing
browsed through ~ yoga-related accessories 요가 관련 부대용품을 둘러봤다 → Checked out ~ fitness products 운동 제품을 살펴봤다

04 추론 문제

해석 Ms. Allen에게 무엇이 보내질 것 같은가?
(A) 환불 영수증
(B) 수업 시간표
(C) 등록 양식
(D) 할인 상품권

해설 이메일의 'Could you possibly send me a registration form by e-mail?'에서 Ms. Allen이 가능하다면 이메일로 신청서를 보내 줄 수 있는지 물었으므로 Ms. Allen에게 등록 양식이 보내질 것이라는 사실을 추론할 수 있다. 따라서 (C)가 정답이다.

Paraphrasing
a registration form 신청서 → An enrollment form 등록 양식

05 추론 문제 연계

해석 Ms. Allen이 그녀의 남편에 대해 암시하는 것은?
(A) 강사가 되는 것에 관심이 있다.
(B) Ms. Singh의 수업에 대해 이미 결제를 했다.
(C) 상급 요가 수업에 참석하고 싶어 한다.
(D) 수요일 세션에 참석했다.

해설 질문의 핵심 어구인 Ms. Allen의 남편과 관련된 내용이 언급된 이메일을 먼저 확인한다.
단서 1 이메일의 'my husband ~ is interested in trying out Parvati Singh's class'에서 Ms. Allen의 남편이 Parvati Singh의 수업을 체험하는 데 관심이 있다는 것을 알 수 있다. 그런데 Parvati Singh의 수업이 어떤 수업인지 제시되지 않았으므로 광고에서 관련 내용을 확인한다.
단서 2 광고의 'Advanced Yoga'와 'Instructor: Parvati Singh'에서 Parvati Singh이 가르치는 수업은 상급 요가 수업이라는 것을 알 수 있다.
두 단서를 종합할 때, Ms. Allen의 남편은 Parvati Singh이 가르치는 상급 요가 수업에 참석하고 싶어 한다는 사실을 추론할 수 있다. 따라서 (C)가 정답이다.

Paraphrasing
is interested in trying out ~ class 수업을 체험하는 데 관심이 있다 → wants to attend ~ class 수업에 참석하고 싶어 하다

06-10번은 다음 웹페이지와 주문 양식에 관한 문제입니다.

www.crawfordoffice.com

| 홈 | 소개 | 가게 | 계정 | 고객 서비스 |

Crawford Office Supply사
당신의 사무실에 필요한 모든 것들을 찾아보세요!

Crawford Office Supply사는 댈러스시에서 현재 30년 이상 동안 사업체들의 요구를 충족시켜 오고 있습니다. 지역적으로 소유되고 운영되는 회사로서, 저희는 훌륭한 고객 서비스와 낮은 가격을 제공하는 것에 자부심이 있습니다. 그리고 06-(A)⁶월 15일에 저희의 두 번째 지점을 도시 남쪽 지역의 Victor가 321번지에 개점할 것임을 알리게 되어 저희는 기쁩니다.

기념하기 위해, ⁰⁷/⁰⁸저희 두 가게 모두가 6월 15일부터 30일까지의 모든 사무용 가구 구매 건에 대해 고객들에게 무료 손가방을 제공할 것입니다. 그러므로 당신의 사무실에 무엇이 필요하든, 꼭 Crawford Office Supply사를 방문해 보세요. 저희는 일주일 내내 오전 9시부터 오후 10시까지 영업합니다. 곧 뵙겠습니다!

locally adv. 지역적으로   own v. 소유하다   operate v. 운영하다
take pride in ~에 자부심이 있다   offer v. 제공하다; n. 혜택, 특가
workspace n. 사무실

Crawford Office Supply사
주문 양식

⁰⁸고객명: Yvonne Murphy   ⁰⁸날짜: 6월 20일
회사: Stanford Accounting사   전화번호: 555-0396
배송 주소: 789번지 Harbor로, 댈러스시, 텍사스주 98250

품목 번호	제품	수량	가격
2837	EZ Write 펜	10	15달러
5839	Harris 공책	15	60달러
6934	RX350 프린터 카트리지	2	50달러
7135	⁰⁸Sylex 의자	4	300달러

참고:		
⁰⁹저는 제 주문품이 6월 23일까지 배송되기를 원합니다. 이것이 가능한지 알려주기 위해 오늘 저에게 전화 주시기 바랍니다. ¹⁰작업자들이 6월 24일부터 27일까지 제 사무실 건물 로비의 바닥재를 교체하고 있을 것이어서, 이 기간 동안 아무도 주요 출입구를 사용할 수 없을 것입니다. 감사합니다.	소계	425달러
	세금	34달러
	배송	48달러
	합계	507달러

replace v. 교체하다   flooring n. 바닥재   entryway n. 출입구

06 Not/True 문제

해석 Crawford Office Supply사에 대해 언급된 것은?
(A) 6월에 새로운 지점을 열 것이다.
(B) 직원들을 댈러스시 매장으로 이동시킬 것이다.
(C) 여러 도시에 지점을 설립할 것이다.
(D) 현재의 영업시간을 변경할 것이다.

해설 (A)는 웹페이지의 'we will be opening our second branch ~ on June 15'에서 저희, 즉 Crawford Office Supply사가 6월 15일에 두 번째 지점을 개점할 것이라고 했으므로 지문의 내용과 일치한다. 따라서 (A)가 정답이다. (B)와 (D)는 지문에 언급되지 않은 내용이다. (C)는 'we will be opening our second branch ~ on the south side of the city'에서 두 번째 지점을 도시 남쪽 지역에 개점한다고 했으므로 지문의 내용과 일치하지 않는다.

어휘 location n. 지점, 장소   relocate v. 이동시키다

Paraphrasing
will be opening ~ second branch 두 번째 지점을 개점할 것이다 → will open a new location 새로운 지점을 열 것이다

07 육하원칙 문제

해석 고객들은 혜택을 누리기 위해 무엇을 해야 하는가?
(A) 특정 브랜드를 선택한다.
(B) 지정된 기간 내에 주문한다.
(C) 최소 구매를 한다.
(D) 특정 지점을 방문한다.

해설 웹페이지의 'both of our stores will be offering customers a free tote bag for every purchase of office furniture from June 15 to 30'에서 Crawford Office Supply사의 두 가게 모두가 6월 15일부터 30일까지의 모든 사무용 가구 구매 건에 대해 고객들에게 무료 손가방을 제공할 것이라고 했으므로 (B)가 정답이다.

어휘 specified adj. 지정된, 명시된   particular adj. 특정한

Paraphrasing
purchase ~ from June 15 to 30 6월 15일부터 30일까지의 구매 건 → Order within a specified period 지정된 기간 내에 주문하다

08 육하원칙 문제 연계

해석 Ms. Murphy는 어떤 제품 때문에 무료 물품을 받았는가?
(A) EZ Write 펜
(B) Harris 공책

(C) RX350 프린터 카트리지
(D) Sylex 의자

해설 무료 물품을 제공하는 조건을 설명하는 웹페이지를 먼저 확인한다.

[단서 1] 웹페이지의 'both of our stores will be offering customers a free tote bag for every purchase of office furniture from June 15 to 30'에서 두 가게 모두가 6월 15일부터 30일까지의 모든 사무용 가구 구매 건에 대해 고객들에게 무료 손가방을 제공할 것이라고 한 사실을 확인할 수 있다. 그런데 Ms. Murphy가 어떤 사무용 가구를 구매했는지 제시되지 않았으므로 주문 양식에서 관련 내용을 확인한다.

[단서 2] 주문 양식의 'Customer Name: Yvonne Murphy', 'Date: June 20', 'Sylex Chair'에서 Ms. Murphy가 6월 20일에 Sylex 의자를 구매했음을 알 수 있다.

두 단서를 종합할 때, Ms. Murphy는 사무용 가구인 Sylex 의자를 구매하여 손가방, 즉 무료 물품을 받았다는 것을 알 수 있다. 따라서 (D)가 정답이다.

[Paraphrasing]
a free tote bag 무료 손가방 → a free item 무료 물품

09 육하원칙 문제

해설 Ms. Murphy는 무엇을 요청하는가?
(A) 가격 확인
(B) 위치에 대한 정보
(C) 요청에 대한 확인
(D) 구매 건의 취소

해설 주문 양식의 'I would like my order to be delivered by June 23. Please call me back today to let me know if this is possible.'에서 저, 즉 Ms. Murphy가 주문품이 6월 23일까지 배송되기를 원하며, 이것이 가능한지 알려주기 위해 오늘 자신에게 전화 달라고 했으므로 (C)가 정답이다.

어휘 verification n. 확인, 조회 confirmation n. 확인

10 Not/True 문제

해설 Ms. Murphy가 그녀의 사무실 건물에 대해 언급하는 것은?
(A) 창문이 교체될 것이다.
(B) 주차장이 확장될 것이다.
(C) 엘리베이터가 수리될 것이다.
(D) 출입구가 이용 불가능할 것이다.

해설 (D)는 주문 양식의 'Workers will be replacing the flooring in my office building's lobby ~, and no one will be allowed to use the main entryway during this period.'에서 작업자들이 그녀의 사무실 건물 로비의 바닥재를 교체하고 있을 것이어서, 이 기간 동안 아무도 주요 출입구를 사용할 수 없을 것이라고 했으므로 지문의 내용과 일치한다. 따라서 (D)가 정답이다. (A), (B), (C)는 지문에 언급되지 않은 내용이다.

[Paraphrasing]
no one will be allowed to use the ~ entryway 아무도 출입구를 사용할 수 없을 것이다 → entrance will be inaccessible 출입구가 이용 불가능할 것이다.

11-15번은 다음 웹페이지와 두 이메일에 관한 문제입니다.

---

www.magnumcruises.com
Magnum 크루즈사

홈	소개	보도	일자리

저희는 현재 다음 지역에서 11-(C)일 년 내내 운영하는 크루즈들에서의 일자리들에 대한 지원자들을 모집하고 있습니다.

11-(D)남아프리카
고객 관리 담당자로서, 10월부터 3월까지 Magnum Explorer에 탑승하여 일하며 손님들을 맞이하고, 활동을 준비하고, 고객의 불편 사항을 처리하십시오. 더 보기

11-(D)호주 & 태평양 국가
오락 전문가로서, 11월부터 2월까지 Magnum Explorer에 탑승하여 오락 책임자의 감독 아래에서 일하십시오. 더 보기

11-(D)인도 & 스리랑카
선상 간호사로서, 4월부터 7월까지 Magnum Adventure에 탑승하여 일하며 승객들의 건강을 보살피십시오. 더 보기

11-(D)동남아시아
13레스토랑 보조 매니저로서, 5월부터 9월까지 Magnum Pacifica에 탑승하여 일하며 식사 서비스의 원활한 전달을 보장하십시오. 더 보기

지원하시려면, 당신의 자기소개서와 이력서를 15Capital 빌딩 100호, Canal로 65번지, 싱가포르 049513에 있는 저희의 본사로 보내십시오. 또는 hr@magnumcruises.com으로 이메일을 통해 그것들을 보내주셔도 됩니다. 12저희는 초기 심사 과정을 통과한 지원자들에게 연락을 드릴 것입니다. 지원하실 때, 당신의 희망 직책을 명시해 주십시오.

region n. 지역, 지방 aboard prep. 탑승한 address v. 처리하다, 다루다
specialist n. 전문가, 전공자 supervision n. 감독, 관리
cover letter 자기소개서 initial adj. 초기의, 처음의 screening n. 심사
state v. 명시하다, 언급하다 desired adj. 희망하는

수신: 인사팀 <hr@magnumcruises.com>
발신: Leo Manresa <l.manresa@hypemail.com>
제목: 지원서
날짜: 10월 22일

관계자분께,

13저는 레스토랑 보조 매니저 자리에 관심이 있습니다. 저는 식음료 관리 학위를 가지고 있으며, 이전에 크루즈선에서 일한 적이 있습니다. 저는 또한 3개 국어를 할 수 있고, 면허증을 소지한 의사로부터 발급받은 양호한 건강을 나타내는 증명서를 가지고 있으며, 필요한 모든 여행 서류들이 준비되어 있습니다. 제 자격 요건들은 저를 Magnum 크루즈사의 해당 직책에 적합한 후보로 만들어 준다고 생각합니다.

Leo Manresa 드림

certificate n. 증명서, 증명 licensed adj. 면허증을 소지한, 허가받은
physician n. 의사 in order 준비된 qualification n. 자격 요건, 조건

14수신: Leo Manresa <l.manresa@hypemail.com>
14발신: Jessica Lewen <j.lewen@magnumcruises.com>
제목: 면접
날짜: 11월 11일

Mr. Manresa께,

Magnum 크루즈사의 일자리에 지원해 주셔서 감사합니다. 당신의 자격 요건을 검토한 후, 저희는 11월 15일 오전 10시에 진행되는 온라인 면접에 당신을 초청하게 되어 기쁩니다. 당신이 참석 가능 여부를 확정하신 후에 14세부적인 안내 사항이 제공될 것입니다. 15만약 합격하신다면, 당신은 시즌 초 업무를 공식적으로 시작하기 전에 2개월간의 교육을 받기 위해 저희의 본사로 출장을 갈 것입니다.

Jessica Lewen 드림
채용 담당자
Magnum 크루즈사

detailed adj. 세부적인 head office 본사, 본점 undergo v. 받다, 겪다
officially adv. 공식적으로

11 Not/True 문제

해설 Magnum 크루즈사에 대해 사실인 것은?
(A) 새로운 크루즈 여행 일정표를 막 소개했다.
(B) 본사에 몇몇 빈자리가 있다.
(C) 서비스를 일 년 내내 제공한다.
(D) 북아메리카의 도시들로 배를 보낸다.

해설 (C)는 웹페이지의 'cruises operating ~ throughout the year'에서 Magnum 크루즈사의 크루즈들이 일 년 내내 운영한다고 했으므로 지문의 내용과 일치한다. 따라서 (C)가 정답이다. (A)와 (B)는 지문에 언급되지 않은 내용이다. (D)는 'Southern Africa', 'Australia & the Pacific', 'India & Sri Lanka', 'Southeast Asia'에서 남아프리카, 호주, 태평양 국가, 인도, 스리랑카, 동남아시아에서 크루즈가 운항한다고 했으므로 지문의 내용과 일치하지 않는다.

어휘 itinerary n. 여행 일정표 opening n. 빈자리, 공석

[Paraphrasing]
throughout the year 일 년 내내 → all year long 일 년 내내

12 추론 문제

해설 웹페이지에 따르면, 채용 과정에 대해 암시되는 것은?
(A) 일부 지원자는 답변을 받지 않을 것이다.
(B) 모든 면접은 대면으로 진행될 것이다.
(C) 모든 직책에서 언어 능력이 요구될 것이다.
(D) 급여는 사전에 공개되지 않을 것이다.

해설 웹페이지의 'We will contact applicants who pass the initial screening process.'에서 초기 심사 과정을 통과한 지원자들에게 연락을 줄 것이라고 했으므로 통과하지 못한 지원자들은 답변을 받지 않을 것이라는 사실을 추론할 수 있다. 따라서 (A)가 정답이다.

어휘 reply n. 답변, 대응; v. 대답하다, 응하다 salary n. 급여
disclose v. 공개하다, 밝히다

13 추론 문제 연계

해설 Mr. Manresa는 어느 배에서 일하기 위해 지원하는 것 같은가?
(A) Magnum Explorer
(B) Magnum Endeavor
(C) Magnum Adventure
(D) Magnum Pacifica

해설 질문의 핵심 어구인 Mr. Manresa가 작성한 첫 번째 이메일을 먼저 확인한다.
[단서 1] 첫 번째 이메일의 'I am interested in the assistant restaurant manager position.'에서 저, 즉 Mr. Manresa는 레스토랑 보조 매니저 자리에 관심이 있다고 했다. 그런데 어느 배에서 레스토랑 보조 매니저를 채용하는지 제시되지 않았으므로 웹페이지에서 관련 내용을 확인한다.
[단서 2] 웹페이지의 'As an assistant restaurant manager, work aboard the Magnum Pacifica'에서 레스토랑 보조 매니저로서 Magnum Pacifica에 탑승하여 일하라고 했으므로, Magnum Pacifica에서 레스토랑 보조 매니저를 구한다는 사실을 확인할 수 있다.
두 단서를 종합할 때, Mr. Manresa는 Magnum Pacifica에서 레스토랑 보조 매니저로 일하기 위해 지원한다는 것을 알 수 있다. 따라서 (D)가 정답이다.

14 육하원칙 문제

해설 Ms. Lewen은 Mr. Manresa에게 무엇을 제공할 것인가?
(A) 업무 목록
(B) 교육 계획서
(C) 비행기 표
(D) 일련의 안내 사항

해설 두 번째 이메일의 'To: Leo Manresa', 'From: Jessica Lewen', 'Detailed instructions will be provided'에서 Ms. Lewen이 Mr. Manresa에게 세부적인 안내 사항이 제공될 것이라고 했으므로 (D)가 정답이다.

어휘 job duty 업무 a set of 일련의 instruction n. 안내 사항, 설명

15 추론 문제 연계

해설 Mr. Manresa에 대해 추론될 수 있는 것은?
(A) 여러 지역에 배정될 수도 있다.
(B) 싱가포르로 출장을 가야 할 수도 있다.
(C) 현재 다른 크루즈 회사에 고용되어 있다.
(D) 인도와 스리랑카 근처의 배에서 일했다.

해설 채용 담당자가 Mr. Manresa에게 보낸 두 번째 이메일을 먼저 확인한다.
[단서 1] 두 번째 이메일의 'If successful, you will travel to our head office'에서 만약 합격한다면, 당신, 즉 Mr. Manresa는 본사로 출장을 갈 것이라고 했다. 하지만 Magnum 크루즈사의 본사가 어디에 있는지는 제시되지 않았으므로 웹페이지에서 관련 내용을 확인한다.
[단서 2] 웹페이지의 'our head office at ~ Singapore'에서 Magnum 크루즈사의 본사가 싱가포르에 있다는 사실을 확인할 수 있다.
두 단서를 종합할 때, Mr. Manresa가 합격하면 본사가 위치해 있는 싱가포르로 출장을 가야 할 수도 있다는 사실을 추론할 수 있다. 따라서 (B)가 정답이다.

어휘 assign v. 배정하다, 맡기다 employ v. 고용하다

16-20번은 다음 이메일, 광고, 후기에 관한 문제입니다.

수신: 모든 마케팅 직원 <marketingteam@fizzlespark.com>
발신: Irina Sokolov <i.sokolov@fizzlespark.com>
날짜: 4월 4일
제목: 마케팅 캠페인

모두 안녕하세요,

[16]회사의 새롭게 출시된 유기농 주스 라인인 Whole Renew를 위한 광고 캠페인을 마무리한 모두의 노고에 감사드리고 싶습니다. 최고경영자가 완료된 광고들을 검토했고 결과에 기뻐하고 있습니다.

상기시켜 드리자면, [18-(D)]곧 있을 프로모션에 대한 세부 내용은 다음 일정에 따라 홈페이지에 게시될 예정입니다:

[18-(D)]5월—하나 구매 시 하나를 무료로 제공
6월—20퍼센트 할인 프로모션
7월—향후 구매 건에 대한 5달러 할인 쿠폰

마지막으로, [17]저는 여러분에게 여러분의 직원 할인을 이용해 그 라인을 시음해 볼 것을 권장합니다. 제가 직접 제품들을 시음해 보았는데, 저는 그것들이 엄청나게 맛있다고 보장할 수 있습니다!

Irina Sokolov 드림
[16]마케팅 부서장, FizzleSpark National사

finalize v. 완료하다, 마무리하다 delighted adj. 기쁜
post v. 게시하다; n. 게시물 encourage v. 권장하다
sample v. 시음하다; n. 견본 guarantee v. 보장하다, 약속하다
incredibly adv. 엄청나게

FizzleSpark National사
Whole Renew

100퍼센트 유기농 재료들로 만들어진 맛있는 주스 라인 Whole Renew 한 병을 선택해 보세요. 비트와 사과부터 망고와 생강까지, [19]다양한 종류의 음료들 중에서 당신의 입맛에 맞는 것을 고르세요. 또한, [18-(D)]이 모든 신선한 선택지들은 이번 달에 하나의 가격으로 두 개가 제공됩니다.

특가는 여기서 끝나지 않습니다! [20]6월 10일에 어느 Victoria 카페 지점에서든 Whole Renew 음료를 구매하고 무료 유기농 간식을 받으세요. 추가적인 세부 사항을 위해서는 Victoria 카페 스마트폰 애플리케이션을 다운로드 받으세요.

reach for ~을 선택하다, ~에 손을 뻗다 ingredient n. 재료
suit v. 맞다, 어울리다 refreshing adj. 신선한, 상쾌한 deal n. 특가, 거래
pick up ~을 구매하다, 받다

Victoria 카페
평점: ★★★★★ (5점 만점)

[20]6월 10일에 Shearmont 쇼핑 플라자에서 새 옷을 사던 중, 저는 이

카페에 들르기로 결정했습니다. 전반적으로, 저는 매우 감명받았습니다. 분위기가 매력적이었고, 직원들은 친절했습니다. ²⁰종업원이 그날 프로모션이 있으니 Whole Renew 주스 중 하나를 마셔볼 것을 추천했는데, 마셔 보길 잘했습니다. 이는 기분 좋은 깜짝선물이었고, 신선하고 맛있었습니다! 다음에 Shearmont 쇼핑 플라자에 가시게 된다면, 이 카페를 방문해 보실 것을 추천드립니다. 후회하지 않으실 겁니다.

-Sarah Klein

어휘 impressed adj. 감명받은, 인상적인 atmosphere n. 분위기
inviting adj. 매력적인, 솔깃한 server n. 종업원
suggest v. 추천하다, 제안하다 regret v. 후회하다

16 추론 문제
해석 FizzleSpark National사는 어떤 종류의 회사일 것 같은가?
(A) 커피숍
(B) 음료 생산 회사
(C) 광고 대행사
(D) 슈퍼마켓 체인

해설 이메일의 'the company's newly launched line of organic juices'에서 회사가 새롭게 유기농 주스 라인을 출시했다고 했고, 'Marketing Department Head, FizzleSpark National'에서 이 이메일은 FizzleSpark National사의 마케팅 부서장이 작성한 것임을 알 수 있으므로 FizzleSpark National사가 음료 생산 회사라는 사실을 추론할 수 있다. 따라서 정답은 (B)이다.

어휘 producer n. 생산 회사, 생산자

Paraphrasing
juices 주스 → beverage 음료

17 육하원칙 문제
해석 이메일에 따르면, Ms. Sokolov는 무엇을 제안하는가?
(A) 평가와 관련하여 임원에게 연락하는 것
(B) 일정보다 빨리 프로젝트를 완료하는 것
(C) 직원 혜택을 활용하는 것
(D) 고객 회의 시간을 변경하는 것

해설 이메일의 'I encourage you to sample the line using your employee discount'에서 Ms. Sokolov가 직원 할인을 이용해 그 라인, 즉 유기농 주스 라인 Whole Renew를 시음해 볼 것을 권장한다고 했으므로 (C)가 정답이다.

어휘 executive n. 임원, 이사 ahead of ~보다 빨리 benefit n. 혜택, 이득
client n. 고객

Paraphrasing
employee discount 직원 할인 → employee benefit 직원 혜택

18 Not/True 문제 연계
해석 광고에서 다루어진 특가에 대해 언급된 것은?
(A) 멤버십 프로그램에 등록된 고객들에게만 제공된다.
(B) 회사의 회장에 의해 거절되었다.
(C) 한 지점에서의 구매로만 제한된다.
(D) 5월에 웹사이트에 게시되었다.

해설 특가에 대해 설명하는 광고를 먼저 확인한다.
단서 1 광고의 'all of these refreshing choices are two for the price of one this month'에서 이 모든 신선한 선택지들은 이번 달에 하나의 가격으로 두 개가 제공된다고 했다. 그런데 이러한 특가가 언제 게시되었는지는 제시되지 않았으므로 이메일에서 관련 내용을 확인한다.
단서 2 이메일의 'details about our upcoming promotions will be posted on our homepage according to the following schedule'과 'May–Buy one, get one free offer'에서 곧 있을 프로모션에 대한 세부 내용은 다음 일정에 따라 홈페이지에 게시될 예정이라고 한 후, 5월에 하나를 구매하면 하나를 무료로 제공한다는 내용이 게시될 것이라고 했다.

두 단서를 종합할 때, 광고에서 다루어진 하나의 가격으로 두 개가 제공되는 특가는 5월에 웹사이트에 게시되었음을 알 수 있다. 따라서 (D)가 정답이다.

어휘 reject v. 거절하다

Paraphrasing
homepage 홈페이지 → Web site 웹사이트

19 육하원칙 문제
해석 Whole Renew의 한 가지 특징은 무엇인가?
(A) 다양한 맛
(B) 무설탕 성분
(C) 다채로운 포장
(D) 충분한 비타민

해설 광고의 'Choose from a wide selection of drinks to suit your taste'에서 다양한 종류의 음료들 중에서 입맛에 맞는 것을 고르라고 했으므로 (A)가 정답이다.

어휘 packaging n. 포장 ample adj. 충분한

Paraphrasing
a wide selection of 다양한 종류의 → A variety of 다양한

20 추론 문제 연계
해석 Ms. Klein은 Victoria 카페에서 무엇을 했을 것 같은가?
(A) 무료로 식품을 받았다.
(B) 멤버십에 가입했다.
(C) 시설 관리자와 이야기했다.
(D) 기간이 한정된 쿠폰을 받았다.

해설 Ms. Klein이 작성한 후기를 먼저 확인한다.
단서 1 후기의 'on June 10, I decided to stop by this café'에서 6월 10일에 Ms. Klein이 이 카페, 즉 Victoria 카페에 들렀다고 했고, 'My server suggested that I try one of the Whole Renew juices ~, and I'm glad I did.'에서 종업원이 Ms. Klein에게 Whole Renew 주스 중 하나를 마셔볼 것을 추천했는데, 마셔 보길 잘했다고 했다. 그런데 그녀가 주스를 마시는 것 외에 무엇을 했는지에 대해 제시되지 않았으므로 광고에서 관련 내용을 확인한다.
단서 2 광고의 'Pick up a Whole Renew beverage at any Victoria Café location on June 10 and get a free organic snack.'에서 6월 10일에 어느 Victoria 카페 지점에서든 Whole Renew 음료를 구매하면 무료 유기농 간식을 받을 수 있음을 확인할 수 있다.

두 단서를 종합할 때, Ms. Klein은 6월 10일에 Victoria 카페를 방문하여 Whole Renew 주스를 구매하고 무료 유기농 간식을 받았다는 사실을 추론할 수 있다. 따라서 (A)가 정답이다.

어휘 free of charge 무료로

Paraphrasing
organic snack 유기농 간식 → food item 식품

21-25번은 다음 이메일, 신청서, 일정표에 관한 문제입니다.

수신: Marcus Dodd <mar_dodd@webbermail.com>
발신: Keisha Joubert <kjoubert@seafairresort.com>
날짜: 7월 24일
제목: 다가오는 여행

Mr. Dodd께,

저희는 8월 18일에 Seafair 리조트로의 귀하의 도착을 기대하고 있습니다. 귀하와 귀하 일행의 다른 두 명의 손님들이 나흘 동안 머무를 예정이기 때문에, ²¹귀하가 저희 측에서 제공하는 몇몇 활동들에 참여하시면 좋을 것입니다. 예를 들어, 저희의 테니스 코트는 사용하기를 원하는 누구든지 이용 가능합니다. 저희는 또한 선착순으로 이용될 수 있는 윈드서핑 장비를 구비하고 있습니다. 그러나, 만약 Grand Soeur섬에서의 인기 있는 하이킹 중 하나에 참여하고 싶으시다면, 최소한 하루 전에 미리 저희의 안내 데스크

또는 웹사이트에서 등록하셔야 합니다. 이것은 또한 ²⁵Coco섬으로의 스노클링과 스쿠버다이빙 여행뿐만 아니라 Petite Soeur섬과 Reynolds섬으로의 카약 여행에도 해당합니다. 이 활동들 중 어떠한 것에라도 참여하시려면, www.seafair.com/activities를 방문하십시오.

Keisha Joubert 드림
활동 관리자
Seafair 리조트

---

look forward to ~을 기대하다 **take part in** ~에 참여하다
first-come, first-served basis 선착순 **at least** 최소한 **excursion** n. 여행

Seafair 리조트—신청서 * 스노클링

손님 이름	Marcus Dodd
객실 번호	723
²²⁻⁽ᴬ⁾오늘 날짜	²²⁻⁽ᴬ⁾8월 19일
²²⁻⁽ᴬ⁾원하는 활동 날짜	²²⁻⁽ᴬ⁾8월 20일
²²⁻⁽ᴮ⁾필요한 장비 (해당하는 것에 모두 표시하세요)	²²⁻⁽ᴮ⁾☐ 물갈퀴 ☐ 마스크 ☐ 스노클
²²⁻⁽ᴰ⁾능력 수준	☐ 미숙 ☐ 능숙 ²²⁻⁽ᴰ⁾☑ 전문가

중요한 고려 사항
1. 저희는 수영복을 빌려주거나 판매할 수 없습니다. 참가자들은 자신의 것을 가지고 있어야 합니다.
2. 이 활동은 하루에 15명으로 제한됩니다.
3. ²³만약 같은 날 예정된 스쿠버다이빙 여행에 다섯 명 미만의 사람이 등록했다면, 그들은 *Waveroller* 배에서 귀하의 그룹에 합류할 것입니다.
4. 만약 기상 상태가 적합하지 않다면, 이 활동은 취소될 것입니다.
5. 건강상 문제가 있는 참가자들은 가이드에게 관련된 의료 정보를 제공해야 합니다.

fin n. 물갈퀴, 지느러미   **snorkel** n. 스노클(잠수용 호흡 기구)
inexperienced adj. 미숙한   **competent** adj. 능숙한
expert adj. 전문가의; n. 전문가   **consideration** n. 고려 사항
rent v. 빌려주다, 빌리다   **unsuitable** adj. 적합하지 않은
health condition 건강상 문제   **relevant** adj. 관련된

---

²³/²⁵8월 20일 스노클링 여행 계획
²⁵가이드: Terry Haide, Bluewater 자격증 소유자

활동	시간	참고
Seafair 리조트의 Leisure Hut에서 만남	오전 9시	
Seafair 부두에서 출발	오전 9시 10분	²³스쿠버다이빙 그룹들이 같은 이동 수단을 이용할 것입니다.
장소 1에 도착	오전 9시 30분	
안전 브리핑 참석	오전 9시 40분	
장비 사용에 대한 교육 이수	오전 10시	
Ombre Reef 주위에서 스노클링	오전 10시 15분	참가자들은 수중 투어를 받게 될 것입니다.
휴식	오전 11시	
Urchin Cove 주위에서 스노클링	²⁴오전 11시 30분	²⁴참가자들은 혼자서 탐험할 수 있을 것입니다.
점심 식사	오후 12시 15분	피크닉 구역에서 식사가 제공될 것입니다.
Seafair 리조트로 복귀	오후 1시 15분	

---

license n. 자격증   **holder** n. 소유자   **depart** v. 출발하다
transport n. 이동 수단; v. 이동시키다   **on one's own** 혼자서, 스스로
serve v. 제공하다

21 목적 문제
해석 Ms. Joubert는 왜 Mr. Dodd에게 연락했는가?
(A) 그에게 여가 선택지들을 알리기 위해
(B) 그가 예약을 변경하도록 설득하기 위해
(C) 숙소 관련 선호 사항에 대해 묻기 위해
(D) 동호회에 가입하는 것에 대한 장려책을 제공하기 위해

해설 이메일의 'you may want to take part in some ~ activities'에서 귀하, 즉 Mr. Dodd가 몇몇 활동들에 참여하면 좋을 것이라고 한 후, 다양한 활동들에 대한 정보를 제공하고 있으므로 (A)가 정답이다.

어휘 **leisure** n. 여가, 자유시간   **option** n. 선택지   **booking** n. 예약
accommodation n. 숙소, 숙박   **preference** n. 선호 사항, 선호
incentive n. 장려책, 혜택

22 Not/True 문제
해석 신청서에서 Mr. Dodd에 대해 언급된 것은?
(A) 며칠 전에 미리 등록했다.
(B) 자신의 장비를 가져올 것이다.
(C) 의료 서류를 제출했다.
(D) 처음으로 스노클링을 해볼 것이다.

해설 (B)는 신청서의 'Equipment Needed', '☐ Fins, ☐ Mask, ☐ Snorkel'에서 Mr. Dodd가 필요한 장비에 표시하지 않았으므로 지문의 내용과 일치한다. 따라서 (B)가 정답이다. (A)는 'Today's Date', 'August 19', 'Desired Date of Activity', 'August 20'에서 오늘 날짜, 즉 등록한 날짜가 8월 19일이 원하는 활동 날짜인 8월 20일보다 하루 전이므로 지문의 내용과 일치하지 않는다. (C)는 지문에 언급되지 않은 내용이다. (D)는 'Ability Level', '☑ Expert'에서 Mr. Dodd가 능력 수준으로 전문가에 표시했으므로 지문의 내용과 일치하지 않는다.

어휘 **gear** n. 장비   **medical** adj. 의료의

[Paraphrasing]
Equipment 장비 → gear 장비

23 추론 문제 연계
해석 8월 20일의 스쿠버다이빙 참가자들에 대해 암시되는 것은?
(A) 다섯 명 미만의 사람으로 구성되어 있다.
(B) Bluewater 자격증을 취득하려 하고 있다.
(C) 체크아웃 후에 추가 요금을 지불해야 할 것이다.
(D) Seafair 리조트로 저녁에 돌아올 것이다.

해설 질문의 핵심 어구인 8월 20일이 언급된 일정표를 먼저 확인한다.
[단서 1] 일정표의 'Plan for August 20 Snorkeling Excursion', 'Scuba diving groups will take the same transport.'에서 8월 20일의 스노클링 여행 계획에서 스쿠버다이빙 그룹들이 스노클링 그룹과 같은 이동 수단을 이용할 것이라고 한 것을 확인할 수 있다. 그런데 스노클링 여행에서 스쿠버다이빙 그룹들이 같은 이동 수단을 이용하는 이유가 제시되지 않았으므로 신청서에서 관련 내용을 확인한다.
[단서 2] 신청서의 'If fewer than five people have enrolled in the scuba diving excursion ~ for the same day, they will join your group on the boat, the *Waveroller*.'에서 만약 같은 날 스쿠버다이빙 여행에 다섯 명 미만의 사람이 등록했다면, 스쿠버다이빙 참가자들은 *Waveroller* 배에서 귀하의 그룹, 즉 스노클링 그룹에 합류할 것이라고 했다.
두 단서를 종합할 때, 스노클링 여행에서 스쿠버다이빙 그룹이 같은 이동 수단을 이용할 것이라고 했으므로 다섯 명 미만의 사람이 스쿠버다이빙 여행에 등록한 사실을 추론할 수 있다. 따라서 (A)가 정답이다.

어휘 **individual** n. 사람, 개인; adj. 개인의, 각각의
attempt v. ~하려 하다, 시도하다; n. 시도

24 육하원칙 문제

해석 일정표에 따르면, 자유 시간은 언제 일어날 것인가?
(A) 오전 9시 10분
(B) 오전 10시
(C) 오전 10시 15분
(D) 오전 11시 30분

해설 일정표의 '11:30 A.M.', 'Participants will be able to explore on their own.'에서 오전 11시 30분에 참가자들이 혼자서 탐험할 수 있을 것이라고 했으므로 (D)가 정답이다.

Paraphrasing
on their own 혼자서, 스스로 → independent 자유의, 독립된

25 육하원칙 문제 연계

해석 Mr. Haide에 의해 인솔되는 그룹은 어느 섬을 방문할 것인가?
(A) Grand Soeur섬
(B) Petite Soeur섬
(C) Coco섬
(D) Reynolds섬

해설 질문의 핵심 어구인 Mr. Haide가 언급된 일정표를 먼저 확인한다.
단서 1 일정표의 'Plan for ~ Snorkeling Excursion', 'Guide: Terry Haide'에서 스노클링 여행의 가이드가 Terry Haide라고 했다. 그런데 스노클링 그룹이 어느 섬을 방문할 것인지에 대해 제시되지 않았으므로 이메일에서 관련 내용을 확인한다.
단서 2 이메일의 'snorkeling ~ excursions to Coco Island'에서 스노클링 여행을 Coco섬으로 갈 것임을 확인할 수 있다.
두 단서를 종합할 때, Mr. Haide에 의해 인솔되는 스노클링 그룹은 Coco섬에 방문할 것임을 알 수 있다. 따라서 (C)가 정답이다.

MEMO

해커스잡·해커스공기업 누적 수강건수 700만 선택
취업교육 1위 해커스

합격생들이 소개하는 **단기합격 비법**

삼성 그룹
최종 합격!
오*은 합격생

정말 큰 도움 받았습니다!
삼성 취업 3단계 중 많은 취준생이 좌절하는 GSAT에서
해커스 덕분에 합격할 수 있었다고 생각합니다.

국민건강보험공단
최종 합격!
신*규 합격생

모든 과정에서 선생님들이 최고라고 느꼈습니다!
취업 준비를 하면서 모르는 것이 생겨 답답할 때마다, 강의를 찾아보며 그 부분을
해결할 수 있어 너무 든든했기 때문에 모든 선생님께 감사드리고 싶습니다.

해커스 대기업 / 공기업 대표 교재

GSAT 베스트셀러
279주 1위

7년간 베스트셀러
1위 326회

[279주 베스트셀러 1위] YES24 수험서 자격증 베스트셀러 삼성 GSAT 분야 1위(2014년 4월 3주부터, 1판부터 20판까지 주별 베스트 1위 통산)
[326회] YES24/알라딘/반디앤루니스 취업/상식/적성 분야, 공사 공단 NCS 분야, 공사 공단 수험서 분야, 대기업/공기업/면접 분야 베스트셀러 1위 횟수 합계
(2016.02.~2023.10/1~14판 통산 주별 베스트/주간 베스트/주간집계 기준)
[취업교육 1위] 주간동아 2024 한국고객만족도 교육(온·오프라인 취업) 1위
[700만] 해커스 온/오프라인 취업강의(특강) 누적신청건수(중복수강/무료 강의 포함/2015.06~2024.11.28)

| 대기업 | 공기업 |

최종합격자가
수강한 강의는?
지금 확인하기!

해커스잡 ejob.Hackers.com

*토익 온라인 모의고사 추가 1회분은 해커스토익 사이트(Hackers.co.kr)에서 제공됩니다.

한 권으로 끝내는
해커스 토익 800+plus
LC + RC + VOCA

실전모의고사

해커스 어학연구소

저작권자 ⓒ 2025, 해커스 어학연구소 이 책 및 음성파일의 모든 내용, 이미지, 디자인, 편집 형태에 대한 저작권은 저자에게 있습니다.
서면에 의한 저자와 출판사의 허락 없이 내용의 일부 혹은 전부를 인용, 발췌하거나 복제, 배포할 수 없습니다.

🎧 실전모의고사   MP3 바로 듣기

LISTENING TEST

In this section, you must demonstrate your ability to understand spoken English. This section is divided into four parts and will take approximately 45 minutes to complete. Do not mark the answers in your test book. Use the answer sheet that is provided separately.

PART 1

Directions: For each question, you will listen to four short statements about a picture in your test book. These statements will not be printed and will only be spoken one time. Select the statement that best describes what is happening in the picture and mark the corresponding letter (A), (B), (C), or (D) on the answer sheet.

Sample Answer

The statement that best describes the picture is (B), "The man is sitting at the desk." So, you should mark letter (B) on the answer sheet.

1.

2.

3.

4.

5.

6.

PART 2

Directions: For each question, you will listen to a statement or question followed by three possible responses spoken in English. They will not be printed and will only be spoken one time. Select the best response and mark the corresponding letter (A), (B), or (C) on your answer sheet.

7. Mark your answer on your answer sheet.
8. Mark your answer on your answer sheet.
9. Mark your answer on your answer sheet.
10. Mark your answer on your answer sheet.
11. Mark your answer on your answer sheet.
12. Mark your answer on your answer sheet.
13. Mark your answer on your answer sheet.
14. Mark your answer on your answer sheet.
15. Mark your answer on your answer sheet.
16. Mark your answer on your answer sheet.
17. Mark your answer on your answer sheet.
18. Mark your answer on your answer sheet.
19. Mark your answer on your answer sheet.
20. Mark your answer on your answer sheet.
21. Mark your answer on your answer sheet.
22. Mark your answer on your answer sheet.
23. Mark your answer on your answer sheet.
24. Mark your answer on your answer sheet.
25. Mark your answer on your answer sheet.
26. Mark your answer on your answer sheet.
27. Mark your answer on your answer sheet.
28. Mark your answer on your answer sheet.
29. Mark your answer on your answer sheet.
30. Mark your answer on your answer sheet.
31. Mark your answer on your answer sheet.

PART 3

Directions: In this part, you will listen to several conversations between two or more speakers. These conversations will not be printed and will only be spoken one time. For each conversation, you will be asked to answer three questions. Select the best response and mark the corresponding letter (A), (B), (C), or (D) on your answer sheet.

32. Where do the speakers work?

    (A) At a technology company
    (B) At an accounting firm
    (C) At a hotel
    (D) At a restaurant

33. Who is Freddy Cho?

    (A) A magazine editor
    (B) An interior decorator
    (C) A receptionist
    (D) A manager

34. According to the woman, what item should be purchased?

    (A) Tablecloths
    (B) Flower bouquets
    (C) Seat covers
    (D) Gift bags

35. What does the man have to do this afternoon?

    (A) Go to an airport
    (B) Book a room
    (C) Ride on a train
    (D) Open an account

36. What does the woman tell the man to update?

    (A) A budget
    (B) A device
    (C) A schedule
    (D) An application

37. What does the woman mean when she says, "I think that can wait"?

    (A) A client is willing to wait.
    (B) A worker may leave early.
    (C) A repair is not very urgent.
    (D) A flight has been canceled.

38. What are the speakers mainly discussing?

    (A) A manual
    (B) A business policy
    (C) An interview
    (D) A store opening

39. What did some employees recently do?

    (A) They made complaints.
    (B) They worked extra hours.
    (C) They transferred to another office.
    (D) They submitted some paperwork.

40. What does Ms. Kensington request?

    (A) An estimate
    (B) A report
    (C) A blueprint
    (D) A pamphlet

41. What does the man apologize for?

    (A) Arriving later than scheduled
    (B) Forgetting some documents
    (C) Entering the wrong building
    (D) Missing a training session

42. Who is Ms. Mendez?

    (A) A safety inspector
    (B) A personal assistant
    (C) A financial consultant
    (D) A corporate chairperson

43. What does the woman ask the man to do?

    (A) Revise some contracts
    (B) Update a Web site
    (C) Work with a partner
    (D) Bring some materials

GO ON TO THE NEXT PAGE

44. Where do the speakers work?
 (A) At a manufacturing plant
 (B) At an advertising company
 (C) At an investment firm
 (D) At a travel agency

45. Why does the woman say, "you've been doing very well here"?
 (A) To indicate surprise
 (B) To give encouragement
 (C) To express gratitude
 (D) To extend an offer

46. What will the woman probably do by next Monday?
 (A) Speak with a supervisor
 (B) Visit another branch
 (C) Provide a response
 (D) Turn in a vacation request

47. What department does the man most likely work in?
 (A) Legal
 (B) Finance
 (C) Human resources
 (D) Technical support

48. What problem does the woman mention?
 (A) Some colleagues are running late.
 (B) A security system is confusing.
 (C) Some equipment is not working properly.
 (D) A phone call was missed.

49. What does the man say he will do?
 (A) Update a schedule
 (B) Rearrange some desks
 (C) Move to a new area
 (D) Contact a coworker

50. What was the man asked to do?
 (A) Interview a candidate
 (B) Review a report
 (C) Lead a session
 (D) Submit a budget

51. What problem does the man mention?
 (A) He is unable to attend a meeting.
 (B) He took over a project.
 (C) He can't find a certification.
 (D) He is unfamiliar with a topic.

52. What does the woman suggest the man do?
 (A) Set up some furniture
 (B) Present a business card
 (C) Write an e-mail
 (D) Join a conference call

53. Why is the woman calling?
 (A) To conduct an interview
 (B) To confirm a schedule
 (C) To apply for a position
 (D) To offer a subscription

54. What did the man do last week?
 (A) He traveled to another country.
 (B) He completed a study.
 (C) He accepted a major prize.
 (D) He announced a new project.

55. What will the man talk about at a conference?
 (A) Benefits of a program
 (B) Methods of manufacturing
 (C) Uses of a technology
 (D) Sources of funding

56. According to the woman, what is taking place?

(A) A sports competition
(B) A business convention
(C) A holiday parade
(D) A music festival

57. What is mentioned about a receptionist?

(A) She provided check-in information.
(B) She has not returned a phone call.
(C) She required a confirmation number.
(D) She is not able to offer an upgrade.

58. What did the man do this morning?

(A) Purchased an item
(B) Visited a Web site
(C) Signed up for a newsletter
(D) Submitted a complaint

59. Where most likely are the speakers?

(A) At a residence
(B) At a laboratory
(C) At a police station
(D) At a furniture store

60. What does the woman want Donald to do?

(A) Conduct a survey
(B) Assist a coworker
(C) Clean out a vehicle
(D) Look up directions

61. What will Donald probably do next?

(A) Fill out some documents
(B) Bring products to a showroom
(C) Throw away some packaging
(D) Search for an appliance

Mountain Fitness Center	
Program	Instructor
Pilates	Ashley
Weightlifting	Jess
Swimming	Aaron
Yoga	Gerard

62. Look at the graphic. Who will lead the man's class?

(A) Ashley
(B) Jess
(C) Aaron
(D) Gerard

63. What does the woman tell the man to bring?

(A) A pair of shoes
(B) A membership card
(C) A water bottle
(D) A towel

64. According to the woman, what does the gym do each month?

(A) Send out invoices
(B) Post new class options
(C) Host a free event
(D) Request some feedback

GO ON TO THE NEXT PAGE

Sargent Community Center

Auditorium	Dance Room	Room 101	Lounge
		Room 102
Room 104		Room 103

65. Why did the man miss the last meeting?

(A) He had to take care of some work.
(B) He was not informed about the location.
(C) He did not like the book selection.
(D) He was away on a trip.

66. Look at the graphic. Where will a group meet?

(A) Room 101
(B) Room 102
(C) Room 103
(D) Room 104

67. What is the man concerned about?

(A) A colleague's opinion
(B) A room size
(C) A venue cost
(D) A discussion topic

Sun Dream Hotel
10438, Jasper Ave., Edmonton

Guest Name: Reggie Malstrom
Dates of Stay: July 7-9

Room Charge:	$308
Lunch:	$21
Room Service Dinner:	$24
Shuttle Service:	$12
Total Paid:	$353

68. Why did the man travel to Edmonton?

(A) To provide some staff training
(B) To research some competitors
(C) To attend a conference
(D) To meet with potential investors

69. What does the woman say about the company's travel expenses policy?

(A) It follows industry standards.
(B) It only covers accommodation.
(C) It was changed last month.
(D) It was explained in a meeting.

70. Look at the graphic. Which charge is incorrect?

(A) $308
(B) $21
(C) $24
(D) $12

PART 4

Directions: In this part, you will listen to several short talks by a single speaker. These talks will not be printed and will only be spoken one time. For each talk, you will be asked to answer three questions. Select the best response and mark the corresponding letter (A), (B), (C), or (D) on your answer sheet.

71. What is the topic of the podcast?
    (A) An educational program
    (B) An online service
    (C) A business opening
    (D) A charity event

72. What are the listeners encouraged to do?
    (A) Join a contest
    (B) Visit a Web site
    (C) Buy a pass
    (D) Download an app

73. What most likely will happen next?
    (A) A product will be reviewed.
    (B) A musician will perform.
    (C) A guest will answer questions.
    (D) A prize will be awarded.

74. Where most likely are the listeners?
    (A) At a fast food restaurant
    (B) At a movie theater
    (C) At a supermarket
    (D) At a gas station

75. What does the speaker mean when she says, "Tomorrow is the last day"?
    (A) A winner will be announced before long.
    (B) Some products should be purchased soon.
    (C) A business will change its hours.
    (D) Some samples are still available.

76. According to the speaker, what will happen next Sunday?
    (A) Some activities will be held.
    (B) A business will reopen.
    (C) Some awards will be given.
    (D) An evaluation will start.

77. Who most likely are the listeners?
    (A) Office personnel
    (B) Program designers
    (C) Installation specialists
    (D) Maintenance workers

78. According to the speaker, what must be done to activate the system?
    (A) A fingerprint has to be scanned.
    (B) A switch needs to be flipped.
    (C) A code needs to be entered.
    (D) A computer has to be turned on.

79. What should listeners do before they leave the building?
    (A) Obtain a security clearance
    (B) Verify that the building is empty
    (C) Turn off the control panel
    (D) Ensure that someone is on duty

80. What industry does the speaker most likely work in?
    (A) Fashion
    (B) Advertising
    (C) Architecture
    (D) Publishing

81. How did the speaker learn about the listener?
    (A) By watching a TV show
    (B) By visiting a Web site
    (C) By listening to a podcast
    (D) By reading a magazine

82. What does the speaker offer to do?
    (A) Make a recommendation
    (B) Submit some artwork
    (C) Meet at his office
    (D) Extend a contract

GO ON TO THE NEXT PAGE

83. What is the broadcast mainly about?
(A) A press conference
(B) A business merger
(C) A hiring announcement
(D) A product launch

84. What does the speaker mean when she says, "those predictions have been proven wrong"?
(A) A company performed better than expected.
(B) Customers were displeased with the service.
(C) An electronic device was released early.
(D) Investors agreed with a decision.

85. What did Damien Crenshaw do last week?
(A) He joined a new firm.
(B) He talked to some reporters.
(C) He met with corporate leaders.
(D) He led a marketing campaign.

86. What does the speaker say about the Corbyn Film Festival?
(A) It is going to be held over four days.
(B) It focuses on a specific genre.
(C) It has been widely publicized.
(D) It has never been hosted before.

87. According to the speaker, what will take place at 8 P.M.?
(A) A documentary film screening
(B) A question and answer session
(C) A private party
(D) An award ceremony

88. Why should listeners visit a festival booth?
(A) To take photos with a cast
(B) To buy some items
(C) To see a revised schedule
(D) To review movie options

89. Why is the speaker calling?
(A) To encourage participation in an event
(B) To provide information about a project
(C) To give feedback on a performance
(D) To offer praise for an achievement

90. What does the speaker say the listener can find online?
(A) A gym address
(B) A bus timetable
(C) A course route
(D) A ticket price

91. What is the listener asked to do?
(A) Pay a participation fee
(B) Bring a sign-up form
(C) Inform of a decision
(D) Rent an automobile

92. Why does Haley Cobb receive an award?
(A) She cleaned up a public area in the city.
(B) She provided training to volunteers.
(C) She helped people find housing.
(D) She organized a fundraising campaign.

93. Why does the speaker say, "The results have been quite surprising"?
(A) To praise the success of an organization
(B) To suggest that a government policy is popular
(C) To emphasize the results of a study
(D) To express shock at unexpected challenges

94. What will Ms. Cobb most likely do next?
(A) Lead an exercise
(B) Show a video clip
(C) Name a recipient
(D) Give a speech

Regan's Restaurant
Daily Special Menu

• Appetizer •
Crab roll

• Salad •
Greek salad

• Main Dish •
Lamb
or
Roasted vegetables with rice

• Dessert •
Chocolate cake

95. What problem does the speaker mention?

(A) A price is too high.
(B) A request has been denied.
(C) Some merchandise is sold out.
(D) Some items were damaged.

96. Look at the graphic. Which item will not be served?

(A) Crab roll
(B) Greek salad
(C) Lamb
(D) Chocolate cake

97. What should the listeners offer to do for guests?

(A) Park their vehicles
(B) Take some items
(C) Make reservations
(D) Distribute samples

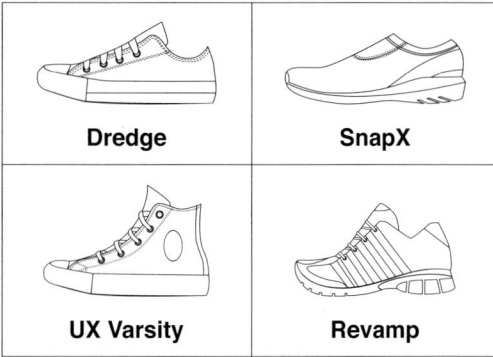

98. Look at the graphic. Which is the recently released product?

(A) Dredge
(B) SnapX
(C) UX Varsity
(D) Revamp

99. Who is Jackson Warner?

(A) A shoe designer
(B) A salesperson
(C) A business owner
(D) An athlete

100. What does the speaker encourage listeners to do on a mobile application?

(A) Download a coupon
(B) Find a store location
(C) Register for an event
(D) View a product list

This is the end of the Listening test. Turn to PART 5 in your test book.

GO ON TO THE NEXT PAGE

READING TEST

In this section, you must demonstrate your ability to read and comprehend English. You will be given a variety of texts and asked to answer questions about these texts. This section is divided into three parts and will take 75 minutes to complete.

Do not mark the answers in your test book. Use the answer sheet that is separately provided.

PART 5

Directions: In each question, you will be asked to review a statement that is missing a word or phrase. Four answer choices will be provided for each statement. Select the best answer and mark the corresponding letter (A), (B), (C), or (D) on the answer sheet.

PART 5 권장 풀이 시간   11분

101. Good speakers can usually ------- people's moods and change their tone accordingly.

(A) sense
(B) sensed
(C) sensing
(D) sensibly

102. Ms. Paget's flight doesn't arrive until Monday night, so ------- asked that the meeting be rescheduled.

(A) her
(B) herself
(C) hers
(D) she

103. Hartman Motors lowered its vehicle prices significantly ------- stay competitive.

(A) now that
(B) on account of
(C) in order to
(D) in spite of

104. Fruits and vegetables require ------- storage conditions to preserve their freshness and extend their shelf life.

(A) low
(B) ideal
(C) visible
(D) sincere

105. The merger ------- under negotiation for the past two years, but it is close to being concluded.

(A) to be
(B) has been
(C) will be
(D) is being

106. Many of Greenvale Hospital's charitable programs ------- with generous grants.

(A) supports
(B) to support
(C) supporting
(D) are being supported

107. Mears Incorporated is ------- the three largest manufacturers of farm equipment in the country.

(A) on
(B) among
(C) except
(D) against

108. Fit Trend's fitness tracker is without ------- the most advanced device of its kind on the market.

(A) trust
(B) means
(C) question
(D) value

109. Computer parts and accessories make up ------- 10 percent of total annual sales at Westwood Electronics.

   (A) simultaneously
   (B) merely
   (C) reluctantly
   (D) randomly

110. A committee ensured a smooth ------- when Haxpa Corp. took control of Brava Holdings.

   (A) transiting
   (B) transitory
   (C) transition
   (D) transitional

111. The Fifth Street Bistro focuses on local ingredient sourcing ------- importing products from distant suppliers.

   (A) up to
   (B) as though
   (C) each time
   (D) rather than

112. For a film with so much promotion, *Origin of Hope* did ------- poorly at the weekend box office.

   (A) surprise
   (B) surprised
   (C) surprising
   (D) surprisingly

113. Laura Hong is in charge of instructing the new intern, ------- will be employed this summer.

   (A) which
   (B) who
   (C) one
   (D) that

114. Some passengers may be asked to empty the ------- of their luggage if airport employees detect a security risk.

   (A) assets
   (B) subjects
   (C) contents
   (D) matters

115. At Arqua Furniture, all salaries ------- those of part-time employees are paid on the 10th of every month.

   (A) while
   (B) into
   (C) throughout
   (D) including

116. ------- interested in attending the Chamber of Commerce workshop should be directed to Ms. Moore in the administrative office.

   (A) Anyone
   (B) Whenever
   (C) Whom
   (D) Other

117. Mr. Chauncey's previous work experience at a Japanese software company was discussed ------- his interview.

   (A) about
   (B) aside
   (C) along
   (D) during

118. Adopting ------- approaches to product design allowed Hyde Enterprises to succeed.

   (A) thought
   (B) thoughtful
   (C) thoughtfulness
   (D) thoughtfully

119. At the weekly meeting, the supervisor reminded employees ------- that any violations of policies would have negative consequences.

   (A) repeats
   (B) repeatedly
   (C) repeated
   (D) repetition

120. Ms. Nielsen has agreed to lead the product launch presentation ------- she needs help with preparations.

   (A) after
   (B) since
   (C) unless
   (D) although

GO ON TO THE NEXT PAGE

121. Under the revised labor regulation, all foreign workers will be issued permits with a three-year ------- period.

(A) productivity
(B) partnership
(C) validity
(D) symbol

122. Ms. Wyman resigned three years ago, but still stops by ------- to catch up with former colleagues.

(A) jointly
(B) recently
(C) gradually
(D) occasionally

123. The Brentwood Trade Show provides appliance vendors the opportunity to promote their products to ------- buyers.

(A) prospect
(B) prospected
(C) prospector
(D) prospective

124. Transport officials sent out extra buses to ------- the impact of the subway line's closure.

(A) assess
(B) diminish
(C) intensify
(D) dismiss

125. The lineup of speakers ------- by organizers to take part in this month's lecture series has been modified.

(A) inviting
(B) invited
(C) will invite
(D) has been invited

126. ------- the movie is well received by fans, a sequel could start production with the same creative team and lead actors.

(A) Providing
(B) Likewise
(C) Due to
(D) Even if

127. Economic conditions over the past year have not been -------, so Avatech has decided to discontinue its line of tablet computers.

(A) optimize
(B) optimal
(C) optimally
(D) optimization

128. Puff Bakery offers an ------- of freshly made pastries each day that include only organic ingredients.

(A) acquisition
(B) amount
(C) assortment
(D) availability

129. Baxter Corporation is looking for ------- that will oversee its professional training courses.

(A) facilitate
(B) facilitates
(C) facilitators
(D) facilitation

130. The purchasing department has not decided ------- of the proposals received from suppliers it will recommend to management.

(A) those
(B) whatever
(C) why
(D) which

PART 6

Directions: In this part, you will be asked to read four English texts. Each text is missing a word, phrase, or sentence. Select the answer choice that correctly completes the text and mark the corresponding letter (A), (B), (C), or (D) on the answer sheet.

Questions 131-134 refer to the following e-mail.

From: Gail Rossey <g.rossey@quailcooling.com>
To: Peter Edmonds <pe880@tmail.com>
Subject: Re: Product complaint
Date: March 22

Dear Mr. Edmonds,

Your e-mail of March 21 indicated that your Quail Cooling air conditioner makes a loud noise every time you turn it on. -------.
                                                                                  131.

You asked whether you should take the product back to the shop where you purchased it.

-------, I recommend that you bring it to a Quail Cooling service center. The one closest to
132.
your house is at 147 Field Street. ------- having to wait, you may make an appointment in
                                    133.
advance by calling 555-2827. The technician will fix your air conditioner on the spot. No

------- fee will be charged.
134.

Gail Rossey
Customer Service Agent, Quail Cooling

---

131. (A) This problem is likely caused by a faulty part.
(B) A repairperson is scheduled to visit your home.
(C) I can help you as long as you present your receipt.
(D) Please follow the directions in the user manual.

132. (A) Instead
(B) Furthermore
(C) Nonetheless
(D) Otherwise

133. (A) Being avoided
(B) Avoid
(C) Avoids
(D) To avoid

134. (A) shipping
(B) monthly
(C) service
(D) transfer

GO ON TO THE NEXT PAGE

Questions 135-138 refer to the following invitation.

The Blackpool Chamber Music Society
proudly presents its spring concert
on May 3

You are cordially invited to attend the Blackpool Chamber Music Society's spring concert, which will be held ------- at Greenfield Auditorium. This venue, where last year's concert took place, can seat up to 300 people. The concert will include performances by a string quartet and a piano trio. The evening of entertainment will start at 7 P.M. and ------- until 9 P.M.
135. .... **136.**

On the night of the concert, tickets will be sold at the entrance for $20. Those with a season pass will not only be able to enter the building for free, but will also be able to attend the final rehearsal and after-party. These will ------- on May 2 and 4, respectively.
137.
-------. For further details, please visit our Web site.
138.

135. (A) weekly
(B) effectively
(C) last
(D) again

136. (A) continuation
(B) to continue
(C) continuing
(D) continue

137. (A) resume
(B) broadcast
(C) expire
(D) occur

138. (A) The reservation was confirmed on April 20.
(B) Both will be held at 5 o'clock in the afternoon.
(C) Your donation will be put to good use.
(D) It was a suitable venue for the banquet.

Questions 139-142 refer to the following review.

Emerald Island Resort, Australia ★★★★★

Review posted on February 12 by Agatha Henriksen

My husband and I were looking for a ------- getaway to end our month-long holiday. Emerald Island Resort seemed like the most suitable place for this. Situated in a remote marine park, the resort features detached villas with their own swimming pools. This resort also has a reputation for top-notch service. This is why it can be expensive. -------, we secured a deal at an affordable price. Apart from a free night's stay, the offer included wine tastings and massages. From the impressive surroundings to the superb customer service, Emerald Island Resort surpassed ------- expectation. For those wishing to go, the resort is 90 minutes by plane from Cairns. -------.

139. (A) traditional
(B) flexible
(C) private
(D) popular

140. (A) Once
(B) Nearly
(C) Fortunately
(D) Additionally

141. (A) every
(B) no
(C) these
(D) many

142. (A) We wish to provide the needed support.
(B) I would be happy to make your reservation.
(C) It is also possible to reach it by boat.
(D) Our return flight to Denmark was delayed.

GO ON TO THE NEXT PAGE

Questions 143-146 refer to the following instructions.

Before making your first cup of coffee with the Delux Home Brewer (DHB), the device needs to be -------. This eliminates any residue in the machine. Start by opening the lid on
143.
the top and pouring water inside. The amount should reach but not exceed the line marked FULL. -------, close the lid and plug the DHB into an electrical outlet. Make sure that the
144.
coffeepot is resting on the inner tray. Now, simply press the CLEAN button and wait until all the water has circulated through the DHB. -------.
145.

You are now ready to make your first batch of coffee. Refer to Page 7 of this manual for ------- directions about the process.
146.

143. (A) taken
(B) checked
(C) washed
(D) shaken

144. (A) Alternatively
(B) Likewise
(C) Eventually
(D) Next

145. (A) The filter was not made for such a purpose.
(B) Up to four different options can be selected.
(C) A standard serving consists of 10 ounces.
(D) This water should be poured down the drain.

146. (A) precise
(B) precisely
(C) precision
(D) preciseness

PART 7

Directions: In this part, you will be asked to read several texts, such as advertisements, articles, instant messages, or examples of business correspondence. Each text is followed by several questions. Select the best answer and mark the corresponding letter (A), (B), (C), or (D) on your answer sheet.

PART 7 권장 풀이 시간   54분

Questions 147-148 refer to the following advertisement.

Fiona's Haven!

Visit Fiona's Haven for all of your flower and plant needs! Choose from a wide variety!

- Customized floral arrangements of any size for weddings and other special occasions.
- A range of indoor plants and trees.
- Delivery services to all locations within the city limits. Free for orders of $100 or more.

Call us at 555-3049 to discuss prices and products. Fiona's Haven is located at 938 Colonial Drive in downtown Orlando. Our hours of operation are from 10 A.M. to 7 P.M., Monday through Friday.

---

147. What type of business is Fiona's Haven?

(A) A planner of events for special occasions
(B) A venue for private or business functions
(C) A supplier of plants and flowers
(D) A landscaper for homes and businesses

148. How can customers become eligible for free delivery?

(A) By ordering a new product
(B) By spending a specific amount
(C) By placing an order by phone
(D) By having an address in the downtown area

GO ON TO THE NEXT PAGE

Questions 149-150 refer to the following memo.

MEMO

To: Plant operation division, Cready Power Company
From: Millie Wickens, Assistant Plant Manager
Date: Monday, September 14
Subject: Access system

This Wednesday, the system for gaining entry to the plant operations room will be changed. This is because the plastic cards we currently use often need to be reissued on account of loss or damage. Instead of a card reader, we will begin using a fingerprint scanner. However, you still should bring your access card on Wednesday because the service person will not arrive until around 11 A.M. Please return from lunch before 1 P.M. because all of you will be required to register your fingerprints at that time.

---

149. Why will the current security system be changed?

(A) Sensitive information needs to be protected.
(B) Some machinery has been damaged.
(C) Additional employees have been hired.
(D) Some items must be replaced frequently.

150. What will members of the plant operation division do at 1 P.M. on Wednesday?

(A) Meet a client
(B) Fill out a questionnaire
(C) Conduct some training
(D) Provide some data

Questions 151-152 refer to the following text-message chain.

Greg Sawyer — 2:01 P.M.
How are the preparations going for the opening of the new branch of our restaurant? Any issues I should be aware of?

Denise Lewis — 2:04 P.M.
There's one complication. When I visited the location this morning, the head of the company we hired to do the renovations informed me that the kitchen ventilation system isn't functioning properly. We're going to have to get it replaced.

Greg Sawyer — 2:08 P.M.
Shouldn't the building owner pay for that?

Denise Lewis — 2:12 P.M.
Unfortunately, no. I reviewed the lease agreement a short while ago, and it states that we're responsible for this sort of expense. We need to address the problem before the municipal safety inspection next week.

Greg Sawyer — 2:14 P.M.
That doesn't leave us much time. How much will this cost us?

Denise Lewis — 2:16 P.M.
I'm meeting with Mr. Hwang from a restaurant supply company at 4 P.M. After he checks out the site, he'll give me an estimate.

151. What is indicated about the business the writers work for?

(A) It will soon have an additional location.
(B) It has undergone a leadership change.
(C) It will replace its current supplier.
(D) It increased its operating budget.

152. At 2:14 P.M., what does Mr. Sawyer mean when he writes, "That doesn't leave us much time"?

(A) A lease agreement is about to come to an end.
(B) Ms. Lewis should visit a municipal office shortly.
(C) A building improvement needs to be done immediately.
(D) Funds need to be secured for an unanticipated expense.

Questions 153-155 refer to the following e-mail.

To	Galina Kusnetsov <galinakus@postamail.com>
From	Jovin Medical Center <admin@jmc.com>
Subject	Our new mobile application
Date	September 18

Dear Ms. Kusnetsov,

You may be interested to know that Jovin Medical Center launched a mobile application last week that patients can use to manage appointments and make inquiries. We recognize that having to call clinic staff during working hours can be inconvenient since our phone lines are often busy. — [1] —. We therefore hope that most of our patients will use the application, which is accessible at all times, and free up our phone lines for those who urgently need to reach us.

Once you have downloaded the Jovin Medical Center application, sign in using your medical center ID number. — [2] —. Your patient profile will list your upcoming appointments and provide the option of requesting cancellations or modifications. A chat system also allows you to get answers to your questions about clinic procedures. — [3] —. While the application is currently limited to these functions, we plan to make it possible for patients to access other information, such as the results of medical tests. If you have any questions about the application, please respond to this e-mail or read the updated FAQ page on our Web site. — [4] —.

Jovin Medical Center

153. According to the e-mail, what is the purpose of the application?

(A) To provide follow-up advice to regular patients
(B) To reduce the volume of calls to the clinic
(C) To lower the number of appointment cancellations
(D) To allow patients to locate nearby clinics

154. What is true about the Jovin Medical Center application?

(A) It can be used to reach doctors and nurses directly.
(B) It may be updated to display medical records.
(C) It can be installed after paying a small fee.
(D) It has been functional for approximately a month now.

155. In which of the positions marked [1], [2], [3], and [4] does the following sentence best belong?

"You can use this feature to make new appointments and to ask any questions you might have."

(A) [1]
(B) [2]
(C) [3]
(D) [4]

Questions 156-158 refer to the following Web page.

www.organifresh.com

Organi Fresh – Making Mealtime Easier

About Us | Menu | Order | FAQ | Contact Us

Organi Fresh takes the hassle out of shopping for food and preparing healthy meals by doing the work for you. When you order an Organi Fresh meal delivery, you'll get a week's worth of delicious food prepared by our highly skilled professional chefs. All of our food is made using seasonal organic produce and natural ingredients. We never use preservatives, and we keep the use of oil, sugar, and salt to a minimum.

Simply take a look at our menu, which includes a mix of Asian, Mediterranean, and South American cuisine, then choose the meals you want for the week. With our Standard Plan, you'll get three meals a day for a week at a cost of $28 per day. Or order our Lunch & Dinner Plan to receive two meals a day for a week at a cost of just $22.50 per day. All of these prices include the cost of shipping!

Finally, all of our meals are packed in containers that are both microwavable and ovenproof. Your order for the week will be shipped fresh in a cooler packed with ice every Friday. Try us once, and we're certain you'll be back for more!

156. What is the topic of the Web page?

(A) An organic restaurant
(B) A pre-packed meal service
(C) A catering business
(D) A new diet program

157. What information is NOT mentioned on the Web page?

(A) Cuisine types
(B) Ordering options
(C) Product costs
(D) Storage suggestions

158. What is true about Organi Fresh meals?

(A) They must be consumed immediately.
(B) They can be ordered over the phone.
(C) They are delivered on the same day each week.
(D) They come with reusable containers.

GO ON TO THE NEXT PAGE

Questions 159-161 refer to the following article.

Wave Technologies Finalizes Uptron Acquisition

CINCINNATI (December 8)—Electronics company Wave Technologies has acquired appliance manufacturer Uptron. The move is seen as a demonstration of Wave Technologies' commitment to increasing its presence in the lucrative kitchen appliance market. Having already established itself as a leading producer of household electronics such as televisions, Wave Technologies entered into an agreement with the Bolton Department Store chain two years ago to provide dishwashers and refrigerators.

"The acquisition of Uptron will allow us to expand our product range and better serve our existing clients," said Karen Fowler, Wave Technologies' chief business strategist. The purchase provides Wave Technologies with access to Uptron's 12,000-square-meter Ohio plant, which meets international standards for product safety. However, Wave Technologies will continue to be based in Indiana.

159. What is indicated about Bolton Department Store?

(A) It will widen its product line in December.
(B) It had a business partnership with Uptron.
(C) It was established approximately two years ago.
(D) It sells products made by Wave Technologies.

160. The word "expand" in paragraph 2, line 1, is closest in meaning to

(A) prolong
(B) broaden
(C) cover
(D) postpone

161. What is suggested about Wave Technologies?

(A) It changed its product safety standards recently.
(B) It will be moving manufacturing equipment to Ohio.
(C) It increased its production capacity significantly.
(D) It has reduced the size of its workforce in Indiana.

Questions 162-163 refer to the following advertisement.

Time Out Vendors

Refresh D-02
Cold Drink Vending Machine

The all-new Refresh D-02 Vendor will give your customers wider drink selections in bottles and cans. The Refresh D-02 Vendor can now hold 10 types of drinks, ranging from sodas and fruit juices to bottled water. This machine is an update of our former D-01 model but still includes a removable back-lighted display which makes branding and pricing convenient. Stocking drinks is also very simple by using the machine's easy-loading product shelves.

Specifications	
Dimensions	Height 1.8 meters
	Width 0.8 meters
	Depth 0.8 meters
Weight	261 kilograms
Number of Drink Selections	10
Standard Capacity	20-ounce Bottle (200 pieces)
Payment Mechanism	Dollar Bill Acceptor
	Coin Acceptor
	Credit Card Reader

For more details on Refresh D-02 Vendor, call 555-8591 or visit www.timeoutvendors.com.

---

162. What details about the machine are NOT provided in the advertisement?

(A) Specifications about its size
(B) Its storage capacity
(C) The cost of renting it out
(D) A list of items it is capable of holding

163. What is stated about the machine's payment device?

(A) It accepts paper money.
(B) It identifies foreign currency.
(C) It uses a digital display.
(D) It does not take coin payments.

GO ON TO THE NEXT PAGE

Questions 164-167 refer to the following e-mail.

To	Christina Meister <chrismeister@gomail.com>
From	Martin Jedlika <mjedlikakey@translations.com>
Subject	Re: Document translation
Date	July 8

Dear Ms. Meister,

Thank you for contacting Key Translations about your need for an English-to-Greek document translation. We have reviewed the file you sent, and you can find our initial quote below:

Pages	4 pages priced at $40 per page
Duration	10 hours
Translation	$160
10% first-time customer discount	-$16
Total	$144

We can also provide a certified hard copy of the translation. This will include the translator's name and signature, as well as a statement that affirms the accuracy of the translation. We can send it to you by courier at the following rates:

- Domestic Standard (2-3 days): $16
- Domestic Express (1 day): $22
- International Standard (5-8 days): $25
- International Express (3-4 days): $33

If you require a certified hard copy, please send a reply stating which courier option you prefer, and I will adjust the estimate accordingly. Otherwise, simply make a bank transfer using the account information on our Web site. Once your payment has been received, we will proceed with the project.

Sincerely,

Martin Jedlika
Project Manager, Key Translations

164. Why was the e-mail written?

(A) To verify that a project is in progress
(B) To request a document translation
(C) To explain a project delay
(D) To specify a price for a potential client

165. What is indicated about Ms. Meister?

(A) She has never done business with Key Translations.
(B) She is comparing quotes from a number of companies.
(C) She will travel to Greece in July.
(D) She did not include the correct file in her e-mail.

166. How much does it cost for a one-day delivery of a document?

(A) $16
(B) $22
(C) $25
(D) $33

167. According to Mr. Jedlika, why should Ms. Meister reply to the e-mail?

(A) To confirm that a translation is accurate
(B) To make use of an additional service
(C) To provide information about a bank account
(D) To approve a revision to a file

Questions 168-171 refer to the following letter.

Dear Cost Smart Customers,

As you may have heard, several other large retail stores across the country were targeted by cyber criminals earlier this week. This may have resulted in the theft of customer information, including personal and payment details. — [1] —. Because we value you and know how much of a threat unauthorized access to your information can be, we promise to do everything we can to safeguard Cost Smart's system against similar attacks.

We have already upgraded our security and encryption software. — [2] —. We also plan to provide additional training to staff to make them aware of precautions they should take. While we believe that our actions will be effective in deterring cyber criminals, as a Cost Smart customer, we ask you to be cautious as well.

Please note that we will never contact you over the phone to ask for personal information. — [3] —. If you receive text messages from senders representing themselves as Cost Smart customer service associates, delete them immediately. — [4] —. Also, always visit our Web site directly rather than clicking on links in e-mails. The Web sites you are directed to may be designed to look exactly like ours. This is to trick you into entering your password, thereby revealing it to the operator of the site.

Thank you for your loyalty. If you have any questions, please call us at 555-8897.

Florence Stoddard
Cost Smart General Manager

168. What is the purpose of the letter?
(A) To suggest that online shopping should be avoided
(B) To describe some preventive measures
(C) To explain how criminals use stolen data
(D) To apologize for the loss of customer information

169. What is suggested about the text messages mentioned in the letter?
(A) They allow customers to confirm orders.
(B) They advertise upcoming sales events.
(C) They are not received during regular business hours.
(D) They are not sent by store employees.

170. According to the letter, why should customers not click on an e-mail link?
(A) It may infect a computer with a virus.
(B) It will disable security programs.
(C) It may lead to a fake Web page.
(D) It will delete important data.

171. In which of the positions marked [1], [2], [3], and [4] does the following sentence best belong?

"We are confident that these improvements to our system will help prevent your data from being transferred out of our systems illegally."

(A) [1]
(B) [2]
(C) [3]
(D) [4]

GO ON TO THE NEXT PAGE

Questions 172-175 refer to the following online chat discussion.

Zelda Coe	3:15 P.M.	I've been considering allowing my staff to work remotely. It's just an idea. But it may be a good way to boost employee satisfaction while also increasing productivity. What do you think?
Stuart Ojeda	3:16 P.M.	Well, I'm sure that many employees would love to be able to avoid commuting to the office each day. But I'm not sure that all of them would be able to take advantage of this opportunity. They may not have the necessary equipment.
Libby Schuster	3:17 P.M.	Right. Their home computers might not be powerful enough to run the graphic design software we use.
Zelda Coe	3:18 P.M.	I see. What if I just offered this option to anyone who has a suitable computer and prefers to telecommute then?
Stuart Ojeda	3:19 P.M.	I don't know. At my old job, I found that employees who worked from home contributed less during meetings. This issue had a negative impact on team cohesion and even led to some delays in the completion of projects.
Libby Schuster	3:20 P.M.	Plus, they may feel excluded if they don't see their coworkers regularly. In any case, coming into the office puts employees in the right state of mind to work.
Zelda Coe	3:21 P.M.	Thank you all for your thoughts. I'm going to send out an e-mail to our staff asking for their input on this matter.

172. At 3:15 P.M., what does Ms. Coe mean when she writes, "It's just an idea"?

(A) A decision has not yet been made.
(B) She wants a specific answer.
(C) A problem has been resolved.
(D) She had no time to develop a plan.

173. What do Mr. Ojeda and Ms. Schuster agree on?

(A) Those who work from home do not feel like part of a team.
(B) Employees commuting to the office are often late.
(C) Workers may not have what is needed to work remotely.
(D) Those who work outside the office are unreliable.

174. What is suggested about Mr. Ojeda?

(A) He thinks it is necessary to conduct performance evaluations.
(B) He has worked in an office where telecommuting was an option.
(C) He believes that some workers should receive salary increases.
(D) He has recently been promoted to a management position.

175. What will Ms. Coe probably do next?

(A) Create a presentation for a meeting
(B) Gather feedback from employees
(C) Submit a request to a superior
(D) Review current company policies

Questions 176-180 refer to the following notice and article.

Attention All Guests

The management of the Sunrise Resort Group would like to take this opportunity to remind everyone that our Key West location's grand opening is scheduled for July 25. Situated on beautiful South Beach, it will have all the amenities that you'd expect to find at a Sunrise Resort, including a spa, conference center, swimming pool, and golf course. We are also excited to announce that world-renowned chef David Mears has accepted our invitation to oversee the operation of the restaurant at this resort, and we are confident that the dishes produced by his team will please all of our guests.

To reward our loyal customers, we are offering registered guests at all Sunrise Resorts 25 percent off on a room at our Key West location. Stop by the front desk, and one of our staff members will be happy to give you a discount voucher you can present when you check in at our new establishment. If you want more information about any of our locations, be sure to visit www.sunriseresorts.com/branches.

Key West Residents Divided About New Resort

MIAMI (August 15)—The Sunrise Resort Group's newest establishment opened today, and some residents are not very happy about it. They argue that the resort, which has a maximum capacity of 400 guests, will have a negative impact on people living in the area. Valerie Collins, the head of a civic group called Beautiful Key West (BKW), argues that the influx of tourists will put a strain on local resources and contribute to the deterioration of marine and island ecosystems.

However, Mayor Justin Ingham, who was narrowly reelected in May, maintains that tourism is vital to the community's economy. "The Sunrise Resort will create many new jobs and expand our tax base," he stated during a recent appearance on the popular morning news program Key West Happenings. He also mentioned that the hotel will bring in a large number of potential customers for local businesses.

176. What has Mr. Mears agreed to do?

(A) Organize a grand opening
(B) Lead a tour of some facilities
(C) Promote a local dish
(D) Manage a dining facility

177. How can Sunrise Resort guests receive a discount?

(A) By signing up for a rewards program
(B) By entering a code on a Web site
(C) By calling a front desk clerk
(D) By picking up a coupon

178. What is indicated about the Key West Sunrise Resort?

(A) It received praise from a tourism organization.
(B) It has launched a spa brand in July.
(C) It began operations later than planned.
(D) It has merged with a large hotel chain.

179. In the article, the word "vital" in paragraph 2, line 2, is closest in meaning to

(A) refreshing
(B) essential
(C) consistent
(D) informal

180. According to the article, what happened in May?

(A) A televised interview was conducted.
(B) A civic group collected signatures.
(C) A mayor announced a tax policy.
(D) A municipal election was held.

Questions 181-185 refer to the following information and e-mail.

Bayweather Manufacturing
Employee Expense Account Categories

⇨ When filling out your monthly expense report, find the corresponding category for each expense and write its code in the "Type" column.

⇨ If you are unsure about what category a particular expense falls into, consult Chapter 12 of the employee handbook. Note that some categories have limits and restrictions in terms of the amount that can be reimbursed.

T43	Postage & courier services
T45	Printing & photocopying
P7	Equipment rental
B27	Fees for professional development courses
M30	Food & drink for company events
M31	Food & drink while meeting clients
J13	Food & drink during business travel
J14	Accommodations during business travel
J15	Transportation related to business travel
P11	Legal documents needed for business travel
X1	Other *

* For expenses in the "Other" category, provide a detailed description in the space provided on the expense report form.

To: Pedro Larson <plarson@bayweather.com>
From: Wendy Macintyre <wmacintyre@bayweather.com>
Date: October 11
Subject: Problem with expense report

Dear Mr. Larson,

I appreciate the care with which you completed your expense account report for September. It was much more accurate than your August report—the first one you submitted while working at this company. Nonetheless, there's a discrepancy I need you to look into before your expenses can be reimbursed. For the visa you had to get for your business trip to Pakistan, the cost indicated on your expense account report is $95. However, the receipt you provided is for $62. You will need to bring supporting documentation for the larger amount to my office by Thursday at the latest as that is the deadline for the submission of expense reports this month. Please let me know if you have any questions.

Regards,

Wendy Macintyre
Accounting department

181. Why will some employees have to refer to a handbook?

(A) To view a list of contact details
(B) To study a set of regulations
(C) To prepare for a training activity
(D) To classify an expense

182. What is implied about Bayweather Manufacturing?

(A) It provides each employee with a mobile phone.
(B) It pays for certain educational expenses.
(C) It requires that invoices be signed by a manager.
(D) It reimburses staff members at the end of each month.

183. What is indicated about Mr. Larson?

(A) He complained about a procedure at a meeting.
(B) He sent a report for August that contained errors.
(C) He traveled overseas with a group of coworkers.
(D) He was asked to fill out a new version of a form.

184. Which expense category does Ms. Macintyre refer to?

(A) T43
(B) M30
(C) B27
(D) P11

185. What does Ms. Macintyre ask Mr. Larson to do?

(A) Distribute some information
(B) Submit a report
(C) Provide some paperwork
(D) Extend a deadline

GO ON TO THE NEXT PAGE

Questions 186-190 refer to the following job advertisement, letter, and e-mail.

Multiple Positions Available—Quadra Realty

Are you interested in working for the largest commercial real estate agency in Los Angeles? Quadra Realty is a growing company that helps businesses find and manage workplace facilities. We are currently looking for people to fill the following positions:

Accountant / Fairfax Branch
Requirements: Bachelor's degree in accounting and three years of related experience

Real Estate Agent / Huntington Branch
Requirements: Realtor's license and four years of related experience

Receptionist / San Pedro Branch
Requirements: High school diploma and two years of related experience

Assistant Manager / Forest Grove Branch
Requirements: Bachelor's degree in business administration and six years of related experience

Please go to our homepage, www.quadrarealty.com, for more information about these positions and instructions on how to apply.

July 15

Brett Reynolds
Quadra Realty
1602 Delta Avenue
Los Angeles, CA 90293

Dear Mr. Reynolds,

I would like to express my interest in becoming an employee of Quadra Realty. I believe that I am well suited for the listed position. Although I have not worked for a real estate agency previously, I majored in accounting in college. In addition, I have spent the last four years in the accounting department of Blackwood Construction. I am looking for a new employment opportunity at this time because my company is planning to relocate to Oakland, and I wish to remain in the Los Angeles area.

You can reach me by phone at 555-0393 or by e-mail at j.quayle@digiquest.com if you have any questions. Unfortunately, I am only available to interview on weekday mornings because of my current work schedule. Thank you for considering my application.

Sincerely,

Jenna Quayle

To	Doug Stevens <d.stevens@quadra.com>, Laura Meyers <l.meyers@quadra.com>, Jeff Kim <j.kim@quadra.com>, Pauline Greer <p.greer@quadra.com>
From	Brett Reynolds <b.reynolds@quadra.com>
Subject	Hiring status
Date	September 8

Hi everyone,

I just wanted to update all of the branch managers on the hiring process. At this point, we have several promising candidates for the open positions. The interviews will take place on the following days:

Monday, September 15 (2 P.M.)   Wednesday, September 17 (10 A.M.)
Thursday, September 18 (4 P.M.)   Saturday, September 20 (11 A.M.)

If you have any specific questions you would like me to ask the applicants, please send them to me. I'll need this information by September 10 so that I will have time to prepare for my first meetings with the candidates. Once the interviews are completed, I will create summary reports on the most suitable applicants. These will be e-mailed on September 24 for you to review.

Sincerely,

Brett Reynolds
Human Resources Manager, Quadra Realty

---

186. What is indicated in the job advertisement about Quadra Realty?

(A) It recently modified its employee benefits package.
(B) It primarily provides services to corporate clients.
(C) It requires all employees to have a university degree.
(D) It intends to open offices outside the Los Angeles area.

187. Which branch is Ms. Quayle applying for a position at?

(A) The Fairfax branch
(B) The Huntington branch
(C) The San Pedro branch
(D) The Forest Grove branch

188. What is mentioned about Blackwood Construction?

(A) It will close some offices.
(B) It will begin a new building project.
(C) It will hire more staff members.
(D) It will move to a different city.

189. When will Ms. Quayle most likely be interviewed?

(A) On September 15
(B) On September 17
(C) On September 18
(D) On September 20

190. What can be concluded about Mr. Reynolds?

(A) He will conduct the interviews personally.
(B) He has already made an offer to a candidate.
(C) He is uncertain if a position is still available.
(D) He is in charge of training new employees.

GO ON TO THE NEXT PAGE

Questions 191-195 refer to the following e-mails and announcement.

TO: Windfield Art Gallery Staff <staff@windfieldart.com>
FROM: Martina Klancy <m.klancy@windfieldart.com>
SUBJECT: Handling Sculptures
DATE: November 23

Hi, Everyone.

As our gallery will be exhibiting a large number of sculptures next month, it is important that everyone know how to handle this type of artwork. Please take note of the following guidelines:

1. Put on protective cloth gloves prior to handling any sculptures.
2. Wipe down the base of a sculpted work using the cleaning spray stored in the maintenance closet. This must be done on Thursday afternoons. Please notify gallery visitors that the artwork cannot be viewed while it is being cleaned or dusted.
3. Any pieces weighing more than 15 kilograms must be placed on a cart before being transported through the gallery. Lighter artwork may be relocated by hand as long as gloves are worn.
4. Highly valuable pieces, such as Fragile Hands, need to be enclosed in glass cases. These cases must be dusted on Thursday mornings, when the gallery is least busy.

If you have any questions, please feel free to stop by my office.

Sincerely,

Martina Klancy
Owner, Windfield Art Gallery

Windfield Art Gallery

Gallery visitors should be aware that our building will be closed starting tomorrow, November 25, through Friday, November 29. This closure is happening to accommodate the installation of sculptures created by Kali Adisa that recently arrived at our facility from Nigeria. We appreciate your patience while we complete these arrangements.

During this period, we encourage our patrons to view information about Ms. Adisa's December exhibition on our mobile application. Advance tickets are available at a discounted rate exclusively through the application. Pamphlets about our gallery's winter exhibitions can also be picked up from the slot attached to our gallery's front door.

Martina Klancy
Owner, Windfield Art Gallery

TO: Martina Klancy <m.klancy@windfieldart.com>
FROM: Joshua Nero <j.nero@brexfordmuseum.org>
SUBJECT: Last week's visit
DATE: December 16

Dear Ms. Klancy,

I want to congratulate you on the success of last week's Kali Adisa exhibition at your gallery. I was delighted that I took your recommendation to purchase tickets for the exhibition at a reduced price. Overall, I was impressed by Ms. Adisa's work. They were excellent representations of contemporary Nigerian art.

I was disappointed, however, that one piece I had heard about from critics—*Fragile Hands*—was not available on the day I visited because its case was being dusted off. Luckily, the ticket I bought includes admission for multiple days, so I plan to come back and see that piece later.

Congratulations again, and I look forward to seeing you at our fundraiser next Friday.

Regards,

Joshua Nero
Curator, Brexford Art Museum

---

191. What should staff do with sculptures that weigh over 15 kilograms?

(A) Place them on the floor of the gallery
(B) Use a piece of equipment to move them
(C) Apply a cleaning spray to them twice a week
(D) Secure them to the wall with wires

192. According to the announcement, what happened recently?

(A) Some features were added to a mobile application.
(B) A sculptor gave a series of lectures about an exhibit.
(C) Some works were delivered from another country.
(D) A gallery informed patrons of a permanent closure.

193. What is available at Windfield Art Gallery's front entrance?

(A) Discount coupons
(B) Informational booklets
(C) Artwork prints
(D) Advance tickets

194. What recommendation did Ms. Klancy make to Mr. Nero?

(A) Purchasing a sculpture from the exhibition
(B) Taking some photographs of a popular sculpture
(C) Speaking to some art critics about an exhibition
(D) Using a mobile application to get passes

195. When most likely did Mr. Nero see the Kali Adisa exhibition?

(A) On a Thursday morning
(B) On a Thursday afternoon
(C) On a Friday morning
(D) On a Friday afternoon

GO ON TO THE NEXT PAGE

Questions 196-200 refer to the following information, Web page, and e-mail.

Westerburn Public Library Online Renewal Policy

All books owned by Westerburn can be renewed through your online account. Simply log in, click on the "View" menu, select "Checked out items," and mark the boxes next to the titles you wish to renew. Then press "Send" at the bottom of the screen. Members are allowed to renew our material for two-week periods provided there are no pending requests for them. If materials you have checked out have been requested in advance by any other member, the system will indicate that they cannot be borrowed again.

Interlibrary loans can also be renewed online. However, some restrictions may apply. Please check the sticker on the back of the book cover for the lending library's renewal policies, which may be different from our own.

List of Active Loans for Westerburn Public Library Member No. 0177634 - Melissa Terrance

Date: 08/08

Renew	Title	Call No.	Source	Due Date
Non-Renewable	*The Reign of King Jordanius* / Hans Schoffer	834.04 SCH	Westerburn Public Library	08/10
☑	*The Science of Memory* / Laurence Templeton	216.94 TEM	Westerburn Public Library	08/10
☑	*A History of Medicinal Plants* / Daniel Wu	147.09 WUD	(Interlibrary Loan) Highland Marsh Public Library	08/10
☐	*Tell Her: Short Stories* / Maya Teller	924.07 TEL	(Interlibrary Loan) Greenport University Library	08/15

SEND

*For interlibrary loans, you can return the books directly to us or to their library of origin.

To: Melissa Terrance <mellit@greatmail.com>
From: Agnes Featherstone <agnesf@westerburn.com>
Date: August 9
Subject: Re: Inquiry

Dear Ms. Terrance,

To answer your question, the reason your request was rejected is that the book you wanted to renew (Call No. 147.09 WUD) is from another library with different lending policies than our own, and our online renewal system is not set up to reflect them. If you check the sticker on the back of the book, you'll see that the library where the book is from allows reference materials to be renewed only once. Unlike the other items on your list of active loans, you have already renewed this item once before. Please note that it is due tomorrow.

Thank you.

Agnes Featherstone
Westerburn Public Library Staff

196. What is the information mainly about?
(A) Requesting items from other libraries
(B) Accessing library databases online
(C) Extending loans on the Web page
(D) Returning books after their due date

197. What is indicated about Westerburn Public Library?
(A) Its late fees can be paid through an online service.
(B) It prohibits new members from reserving materials.
(C) Its books can be renewed for a 14-day period.
(D) Its policies regarding interlibrary loans have changed.

198. What is true about *The Reign of King Jordanius*?
(A) It is a part of a special collection.
(B) Someone else made a request for it.
(C) Another copy of it is available at a partner library.
(D) Its sticker indicates renewal is forbidden.

199. What is indicated in the Web page?
(A) Maya Teller's book may be returned to Westerburn Public Library.
(B) The lending period of Highland Marsh Public Library is two weeks.
(C) Ms. Terrance holds a special type of membership at her library.
(D) *The Science of Memory* has been overdue for several days now.

200. Which book has Ms. Terrance already renewed once?
(A) *The Science of Memory*
(B) *A History of Medicinal Plants*
(C) *Tell Her: Short Stories*
(D) *The Reign of King Jordanius*

This is the end of the test. You may review Parts 5, 6, and 7 if you finish the test early.

실전모의고사 정답·해석·해설

PART 1
1. (A) 2. (B) 3. (C) 4. (A) 5. (D) 6. (B)

PART 2
7. (A) 8. (B) 9. (B) 10. (C) 11. (C) 12. (A) 13. (B) 14. (A) 15. (C) 16. (B)
17. (C) 18. (A) 19. (B) 20. (B) 21. (A) 22. (A) 23. (C) 24. (C) 25. (A) 26. (B)
27. (C) 28. (A) 29. (B) 30. (C) 31. (A)

PART 3
32. (C) 33. (D) 34. (A) 35. (A) 36. (C) 37. (B) 38. (B) 39. (A) 40. (B) 41. (A)
42. (C) 43. (D) 44. (B) 45. (A) 46. (C) 47. (D) 48. (C) 49. (D) 50. (B) 51. (D)
52. (C) 53. (A) 54. (B) 55. (C) 56. (D) 57. (A) 58. (B) 59. (D) 60. (B) 61. (A)
62. (B) 63. (C) 64. (A) 65. (A) 66. (D) 67. (B) 68. (C) 69. (C) 70. (B)

PART 4
71. (D) 72. (C) 73. (B) 74. (C) 75. (B) 76. (A) 77. (A) 78. (C) 79. (B) 80. (D)
81. (B) 82. (C) 83. (B) 84. (A) 85. (C) 86. (D) 87. (B) 88. (B) 89. (A) 90. (C)
91. (C) 92. (C) 93. (A) 94. (D) 95. (D) 96. (A) 97. (B) 98. (B) 99. (D) 100. (C)

PART 5
101. (A) 102. (D) 103. (C) 104. (B) 105. (B) 106. (D) 107. (B) 108. (C) 109. (B) 110. (C)
111. (D) 112. (D) 113. (B) 114. (C) 115. (D) 116. (A) 117. (D) 118. (C) 119. (B) 120. (D)
121. (C) 122. (D) 123. (D) 124. (B) 125. (B) 126. (A) 127. (B) 128. (C) 129. (C) 130. (D)

PART 6
131. (A) 132. (A) 133. (D) 134. (C) 135. (D) 136. (D) 137. (D) 138. (B) 139. (C) 140. (C)
141. (A) 142. (C) 143. (C) 144. (D) 145. (D) 146. (A)

PART 7
147. (C) 148. (B) 149. (D) 150. (D) 151. (A) 152. (C) 153. (B) 154. (B) 155. (C) 156. (B)
157. (D) 158. (C) 159. (D) 160. (B) 161. (C) 162. (C) 163. (A) 164. (C) 165. (A) 166. (B)
167. (B) 168. (B) 169. (D) 170. (C) 171. (B) 172. (A) 173. (C) 174. (B) 175. (B) 176. (D)
177. (D) 178. (C) 179. (B) 180. (D) 181. (D) 182. (B) 183. (B) 184. (C) 185. (C) 186. (B)
187. (A) 188. (D) 189. (B) 190. (A) 191. (B) 192. (C) 193. (B) 194. (B) 195. (A) 196. (C)
197. (C) 198. (B) 199. (A) 200. (B)

PART 1

1. 1인 사진

(A) He is looking at an item.
(B) He is setting up some shelves.
(C) He is paying for a product.
(D) He is pushing a cart in a store.

set up ~을 설치하다 push v. 밀다

해석 (A) 그는 제품을 보고 있다.
(B) 그는 몇몇 선반을 설치하고 있다.
(C) 그는 상품의 값을 지불하고 있다.
(D) 그는 가게에서 카트를 밀고 있다.

해설 (A) [○] 남자가 제품을 보고 있는 모습을 가장 잘 묘사한 정답이다.
(B) [×] setting up some shelves(몇몇 선반을 설치하고 있다)는 남자의 동작과 무관하므로 오답이다. 사진에 있는 선반(shelves)을 사용하여 혼동을 주었다.
(C) [×] paying for a product(상품의 값을 지불하고 있다)는 남자의 동작과 무관하므로 오답이다. 사진에 있는 상품(product)을 사용하여 혼동을 주었다.
(D) [×] 사진에서 카트를 확인할 수 없으므로 오답이다.

2. 2인 이상 사진

(A) A worker is opening a car door.
(B) A worker is leaning out of a vehicle.
(C) Some bricks are piled next to a building.
(D) Some people are positioning traffic cones.

lean v. 상체를 굽히다, 기대다 pile v. 쌓다, 포개다
position v. (특정한 장소에) 놓다, 두다; n. 위치
traffic cone 원뿔형 도로 표지

해석 (A) 한 작업자가 차 문을 열고 있다.
(B) 한 작업자가 차 밖으로 상체를 굽히고 있다.
(C) 몇몇 벽돌이 건물 옆에 쌓여 있다.
(D) 몇몇 사람들이 원뿔형 도로 표지를 놓고 있다.

해설 (A) [×] 사진에서 차 문을 열고 있는 사람을 확인할 수 없으므로 오답이다.
(B) [○] 한 작업자가 차 밖으로 상체를 굽히고 있는 모습을 가장 잘 묘사한 정답이다.
(C) [×] 사진에서 벽돌을 확인할 수 없으므로 오답이다.
(D) [×] positioning(놓고 있다)은 사람들의 동작과 무관하므로 오답이다. 사진에 있는 원뿔형 도로 표지(traffic cones)를 사용하여 혼동을 주었다.

3. 2인 이상 사진

(A) Some people are raking up leaves in a park.
(B) Some people are sitting on a bench.
(C) There are some trees along a trail.
(D) A lamppost has fallen across a path.

rake v. 갈퀴로 긁어 모으다 trail n. 길, 오솔길
lamppost n. 가로등

해석 (A) 몇몇 사람들이 공원에서 나뭇잎들을 갈퀴로 긁어 모으고 있다.
(B) 몇몇 사람들이 벤치에 앉아 있다.
(C) 길을 따라서 몇몇 나무들이 있다.
(D) 가로등이 길을 가로질러 넘어졌다.

해설 (A) [×] raking up leaves(나뭇잎들을 갈퀴로 긁어 모으고 있다)는 사람들의 동작과 무관하므로 오답이다.
(B) [×] sitting(앉아 있다)은 사람들의 동작과 무관하므로 오답이다. 사진에 있는 벤치(bench)를 사용하여 혼동을 주었다.
(C) [○] 길을 따라서 몇몇 나무들이 있는 모습을 가장 잘 묘사한 정답이다.
(D) [×] has fallen(넘어졌다)은 사물의 상태와 무관하므로 오답이다. 사진에 있는 가로등(lamppost)을 사용하여 혼동을 주었다.

4. 1인 사진

(A) A man is reaching out his arm.
(B) A man is organizing some eating utensils.
(C) All the boxes have been loaded onto a rolling cart.
(D) Some books are being displayed in a store window.

reach out ~을 뻗다 organize v. 정리하다 load v. 싣다
rolling cart 이동식 카트

해석 (A) 한 남자가 팔을 뻗고 있다.
(B) 한 남자가 몇몇 식기들을 정리하고 있다.
(C) 모든 상자들이 이동식 카트에 실어졌다.
(D) 몇몇 책들이 가게 창문에 진열되고 있다.

해설 (A) [○] 한 남자가 팔을 뻗고 있는 모습을 가장 잘 묘사한 정답이다.
(B) [×] 사진에서 식기들을 확인할 수 없으므로 오답이다.
(C) [×] 사진에서 이동식 카트를 확인할 수 없으므로 오답이다. 사진에 있는 상자들(boxes)을 사용하여 혼동을 주었다.
(D) [×] are being displayed(진열되고 있다)는 사물의 상태와 무관하므로 오답이다. 사진에 있는 책들(books)을 사용하여 혼동을 주었다.

5. 실외 사진 영국

(A) Some guests are lining up at an entrance.
(B) A courtyard is being prepared for a party.
(C) A flag is hanging from a balcony.
(D) Some plants have been placed in a row on steps.

line up 줄을 서다 entrance n. 입구 courtyard n. 안뜰
in a row 한 줄로, 잇따라

해석 (A) 몇몇 손님들이 입구에 줄을 서 있다.
(B) 안뜰이 파티를 위해 준비되고 있다.
(C) 깃발이 발코니에 걸려 있다.
(D) 몇몇 식물들이 계단 위에 한 줄로 놓여 있다.

해설 (A) [x] 사람이 없는 사진에 진행형(are lining up)을 사용하여 사람의 동작을 묘사했으므로 오답이다.
(B) [x] 사람이 없는 사진에 진행 수동형(is being prepared)을 사용하여 사람의 동작을 묘사했으므로 오답이다.
(C) [x] 사진에서 깃발을 확인할 수 없으므로 오답이다.
(D) [o] 식물들이 계단 위에 한 줄로 놓여 있는 모습을 가장 잘 묘사한 정답이다.

6. 2인 이상 사진 호주

(A) One of the women is stirring a beverage.
(B) One of the women is holding a cup in each hand.
(C) The women are picking up some flowers in a garden.
(D) The women are standing in a doorway.

stir v. 젓다 beverage n. 음료 doorway n. 출입구

해석 (A) 여자들 중 한 명이 음료를 젓고 있다.
(B) 여자들 중 한 명이 각 손에 컵을 들고 있다.
(C) 여자들이 정원에서 몇몇 꽃을 꺾고 있다.
(D) 여자들이 출입구에 서 있다.

해설 (A) [x] stirring a beverage(음료를 젓고 있다)는 여자의 동작과 무관하므로 오답이다. 사진에 있는 음료(beverage)를 사용하여 혼동을 주었다.
(B) [o] 여자가 각 손에 컵을 들고 있는 모습을 가장 잘 묘사한 정답이다.
(C) [x] 사진에서 꽃을 확인할 수 없으므로 오답이다.
(D) [x] standing in a doorway(출입구에 서 있다)는 여자들의 동작과 무관하므로 오답이다.

PART 2

7. Who 의문문 미국 → 캐나다

Who redecorated the waiting room?
(A) Margaret did.
(B) With special permission.

(C) I like it, too.

redecorate v. 다시 장식하다, 실내를 개조하다
permission n. 승인, 허가

해석 누가 대기실을 다시 장식했나요?
(A) Margaret이 했어요.
(B) 특별 승인을 받아서요.
(C) 저도 그것을 좋아해요.

해설 (A) [o] Margaret이 했다며 대기실을 다시 장식한 인물을 언급했으므로 정답이다.
(B) [x] 누가 대기실을 다시 장식했는지를 물었는데, 특별 승인을 받아서라며 관련이 없는 내용으로 응답했으므로 오답이다.
(C) [x] 누가 대기실을 다시 장식했는지를 물었는데, 자신도 그것을 좋아한다며 관련이 없는 내용으로 응답했으므로 오답이다.

8. How 의문문 영국 → 호주

How much did you spend on the television?
(A) That brand is my favorite.
(B) About $500, I think.
(C) At the park.

spend v. (돈을) 소비하다

해석 그 텔레비전에 얼마나 소비하셨나요?
(A) 그 브랜드는 제가 제일 좋아하는 브랜드예요.
(B) 약 500달러 정도인 것 같아요.
(C) 공원에서요.

해설 (A) [x] 텔레비전에 얼마나 소비했는지를 물었는데, 그 브랜드는 자신이 제일 좋아하는 브랜드라며 관련이 없는 내용으로 응답했으므로 오답이다.
(B) [o] 약 500달러 정도라며, 텔레비전에 소비한 금액을 언급했으므로 정답이다.
(C) [x] 텔레비전에 얼마나 소비했는지를 물었는데, 공원에서라며 관련이 없는 내용으로 응답했으므로 오답이다.

9. 부정 의문문 미국 → 호주

Isn't it a bit early to take a lunch break?
(A) Yes, that's my suggestion.
(B) I often eat around 11 A.M.
(C) Mike stopped by half an hour ago.

lunch break 점심시간 suggestion n. 제안
often adv. 보통, 자주

해석 점심시간을 갖기에는 조금 이르지 않나요?
(A) 네, 그것이 저의 제안이에요.
(B) 저는 보통 오전 11시 정도에 먹어요.
(C) Mike는 30분 전에 들렀어요.

해설 (A) [x] lunch(점심)에서 연상할 수 있는 점심 메뉴 제안과 관련된 suggestion(제안)을 사용하여 혼동을 준 오답이다. Yes만 듣고 정답으로 고르지 않도록 주의한다.
(B) [o] 자신은 보통 오전 11시 정도에 먹는다는 말로, 점심시간을 갖기에 이르지 않음을 간접적으로 전달했으므로 정답이다.
(C) [x] lunch break(점심시간)에서 연상할 수 있는 시간과 관련된 half an hour(30분)를 사용하여 혼동을 주었다.

10. What 의문문

🔊 캐나다 → 미국

What did you think of the client?
(A) I really enjoyed the party.
(B) A partnership deal.
(C) She is a good listener.

partnership n. 동업, 제휴   deal n. 계약

해석 그 고객에 대해 어떻게 생각하셨나요?
(A) 저는 파티를 매우 즐겼어요.
(B) 동업 계약이요.
(C) 그녀는 남의 말을 경청하는 분이에요.

해설 (A) [x] 그 고객에 대해 어떻게 생각했는지를 물었는데, 파티를 매우 즐겼다며 관련이 없는 내용으로 응답했으므로 오답이다.
(B) [x] client(고객)와 관련 있는 partnership deal(동업 계약)을 사용하여 혼동을 준 오답이다.
(C) [o] 그녀는 남의 말을 경청하는 분이라며, 고객에 대한 의견을 언급했으므로 정답이다.

11. 선택 의문문

🔊 영국 → 호주

Do you want to change your office or stay where you are?
(A) A new keyboard and a mouse.
(B) You can keep the change.
(C) I'm comfortable right here.

stay v. 지내다, 유지하다   change n. 잔돈, 거스름돈

해석 사무실을 바꾸고 싶으신가요, 아니면 지금 계신 곳에서 지내고 싶으신가요?
(A) 새로운 키보드와 마우스요.
(B) 잔돈은 가지셔도 돼요.
(C) 저는 바로 여기가 편해요.

해설 (A) [x] change(바꾸다)와 관련 있는 new(새로운)를 사용하여 혼동을 준 오답이다.
(B) [x] 질문의 change(바꾸다)를 '잔돈'이라는 의미로 사용하여 혼동을 준 오답이다.
(C) [o] right here(바로 여기)로 지금 있는 곳을 선택했으므로 정답이다.

12. Where 의문문

🔊 캐나다 → 미국

Where did you find the missing stapler?
(A) Behind the cabinet.
(B) I'm ready to begin the interview.
(C) Late yesterday morning.

missing adj. 분실된   stapler n. 스테이플러
cabinet n. 보관함

해석 분실된 스테이플러를 어디서 찾으셨나요?
(A) 보관함 뒤에서요.
(B) 저는 면접을 시작할 준비가 되었어요.
(C) 어제 아침 늦게요.

해설 (A) [o] 보관함 뒤라며, 분실된 스테이플러를 찾은 장소를 언급했으므로 정답이다.
(B) [x] 분실된 스테이플러를 어디에서 찾았는지를 물었는데, 자신이 면접을 시작할 준비가 되었다며 관련이 없는 내용으로 응답했으므로 오답이다.
(C) [x] 분실된 스테이플러를 찾은 장소를 물었는데, 시간으로 응답했으므로 오답이다.

13. 부가 의문문

🔊 영국 → 호주

The sales team increased their sales last quarter, didn't they?
(A) Some sales data.
(B) Yes. They doubled their previous numbers.
(C) Seven members in total.

increase v. 늘리다   double v. 두 배로 늘리다
previous adj. 지난

해석 영업팀은 지난 분기에 판매량을 늘렸죠, 그렇지 않나요?
(A) 몇몇 영업 데이터요.
(B) 네. 그들은 그들의 지난 수치에서 두 배로 늘렸어요.
(C) 총 7명의 구성원들이요.

해설 (A) [x] 질문의 sales(판매량, 영업)를 그대로 사용하여 혼동을 준 오답이다.
(B) [o] Yes로 영업팀이 지난 분기에 판매량을 늘렸다고 전달한 후, 지난 수치에서 두 배로 늘렸다는 부연 설명을 했으므로 정답이다.
(C) [x] sales team(영업팀)과 관련 있는 members(구성원들)를 사용하여 혼동을 준 오답이다.

14. 일반 의문문

🔊 캐나다 → 미국

Do you have the new issue of *Trend Magazine*?
(A) It hasn't come out yet.
(B) Several pages long.
(C) You'll find some photographs on the desk.

new adj. 최근의, 신작의
issue n. (잡지·신문 같은 정기 간행물의) 호   come out 출간되다

해석 *Trend*지 최근 호를 갖고 계신가요?
(A) 그것은 아직 출간되지 않았어요.
(B) 여러 페이지예요.
(C) 당신은 책상 위에서 사진들을 찾을 수 있을 거예요.

해설 (A) [o] 그것은 아직 출간되지 않았다는 말로, *Trend*지 최근 호를 갖고 있지 않음을 간접적으로 전달했으므로 정답이다.
(B) [x] *Trend*지 최근 호를 갖고 있는지를 물었는데, 분량으로 응답했으므로 오답이다.
(C) [x] *Trend*지 최근 호를 갖고 있는지를 물었는데, 책상 위에서 사진들을 찾을 수 있을 거라며 관련이 없는 내용으로 응답했으므로 오답이다.

15. When 의문문

🔊 영국 → 캐나다

When should I take down the store sign?
(A) Did you take the bus to the mall?
(B) She is not here.
(C) I'll go ask the manager.

take down ~을 내리다   sign n. 간판   mall n. 쇼핑몰

해석 제가 언제 가게 간판을 내려야 할까요?
(A) 당신은 쇼핑몰로 버스를 타고 갔나요?

PART 2 45

(B) 그녀는 여기 없어요.
(C) 제가 관리자에게 가서 물어볼게요.

해설 (A) [x] store(가게)와 관련 있는 mall(쇼핑몰)을 사용하여 혼동을 준 오답이다.
(B) [x] 언제 가게 간판을 내려야 할지를 물었는데, 그녀는 여기에 없다며 관련이 없는 내용으로 응답했으므로 오답이다.
(C) [o] 관리자에게 가서 물어보겠다는 말로, 언제 가게 간판을 내려야 할지 모른다는 점을 간접적으로 전달했으므로 정답이다.

16. 일반 의문문　　🔊 미국 → 호주

Are family members covered by your health plan?
(A) For my next dental appointment.
(B) Let me check my insurance agreement.
(C) Yes, he's planning it.

health plan 의료 보험　insurance agreement 보험 계약서

해설 가족들이 당신의 의료 보험에 포함되나요?
(A) 제 다음 치과 진료 예약을 위해서요.
(B) 제 보험 계약서를 확인해 볼게요.
(C) 네, 그는 그것을 계획하고 있어요.

해설 (A) [x] health plan(의료 보험)과 관련 있는 dental appointment(치과 진료 예약)를 사용하여 혼동을 준 오답이다.
(B) [o] 보험 계약서를 확인해 본다는 말로 가족들이 의료 보험에 포함되는지 모른다는 점을 간접적으로 전달했으므로 정답이다.
(C) [x] 질문의 plan(보험, 제도)을 '계획하다'라는 의미로 사용하여 혼동을 준 오답이다.

17. 평서문　　🔊 미국 → 캐나다

The purpose of the workshop is to improve communication skills.
(A) It will be very difficult to locate, however.
(B) The projector is still working well.
(C) It sounds similar to the last one.

improve v. 향상시키다　locate v. 위치를 찾다, 두다

해설 워크숍의 목적은 의사소통 기술을 향상시키는 것입니다.
(A) 하지만, 위치를 찾기가 매우 어려울 거예요.
(B) 그 프로젝터는 여전히 잘 작동하고 있어요.
(C) 지난번 것과 비슷하게 들리네요.

해설 (A) [x] 질문의 purpose(목적)를 나타낼 수 있는 It을 사용하여 혼동을 준 오답이다.
(B) [x] workshop(워크숍)과 관련 있는 projector(프로젝터)를 사용하여 혼동을 준 오답이다.
(C) [o] 지난번 것, 즉 지난번 워크숍과 비슷하게 들린다는 말로 의견을 추가했으므로 정답이다.

18. 부가 의문문　　🔊 영국 → 미국

Summer is the best time to visit the resort, isn't it?
(A) That's when most people go.

(B) I already packed for my vacation.
(C) Swimming is not my favorite sport.

pack v. 짐을 싸다

해설 여름은 리조트를 방문하기 가장 좋은 때죠, 그렇지 않나요?
(A) 그때 대부분의 사람들이 가죠.
(B) 저는 이미 저희 휴가를 위해 짐을 쌌어요.
(C) 수영은 제가 아주 좋아하는 스포츠는 아니에요.

해설 (A) [o] 그때 대부분의 사람들이 간다며, 여름이 리조트를 방문하기 가장 좋은 때임을 전달했으므로 정답이다.
(B) [x] resort(리조트)와 관련 있는 vacation(휴가)을 사용하여 혼동을 준 오답이다.
(C) [x] Summer(여름)와 관련 있는 Swimming(수영)을 사용하여 혼동을 준 오답이다.

19. When 의문문　　🔊 캐나다 → 영국

When will Nathaniel receive the certificate?
(A) He is an accountant.
(B) By the end of this month.
(C) We sent the pictures today.

certificate n. 자격증, 증명서

해설 Nathaniel이 언제 자격증을 받을까요?
(A) 그는 회계사예요.
(B) 이번 달 말에요.
(C) 저희가 오늘 사진들을 보냈어요.

해설 (A) [x] 질문의 Nathaniel을 나타낼 수 있는 He를 사용하여 혼동을 준 오답이다.
(B) [o] 이번 달 말이라며, 특정 시점을 언급했으므로 정답이다.
(C) [x] 질문의 receive(받다)와 반대 의미인 sent(보냈다)를 사용하여 혼동을 준 오답이다.

20. 제안 의문문　　🔊 호주 → 캐나다

Do you want me to save you a seat?
(A) Put it on the counter, please.
(B) That won't be necessary.
(C) Yes, it's under the passenger seat.

save a seat 자리를 맡다　passenger seat 조수석

해설 제가 당신의 자리를 맡아놓을까요?
(A) 이것을 계산대에 놓아주세요.
(B) 그럴 필요는 없을 거예요.
(C) 네, 그것은 조수석 아래에 있어요.

해설 (A) [x] 자리를 맡아놓을지를 물었는데, 이것을 계산대에 놓으라며 관련 없는 내용으로 응답했으므로 오답이다.
(B) [o] 그럴 필요는 없을 거라는 말로, 자신의 자리를 맡아놓지 않아도 됨을 간접적으로 전달했으므로 정답이다.
(C) [x] 질문의 seat(자리)를 그대로 사용하여 혼동을 준 오답이다.

21. Who 의문문　　🔊 호주 → 영국

Who knows how to use the new shipping software?
(A) I have the manual here.

(B) To change the settings.
(C) You don't have an account with us.

manual n. 설명서   setting n. 설정   account n. 계정

해석 누가 새로운 배송 소프트웨어를 사용하는 방법을 알고 있나요?
(A) 제가 여기 설명서를 가지고 있어요.
(B) 설정을 변경하기 위해서요.
(C) 당신은 저희 계정이 없어요.

해설 (A) [ㅇ] 자신이 설명서를 가지고 있다는 말로, 새로운 배송 소프트웨어를 사용하는 방법을 아는 사람이 없음을 간접적으로 전달했으므로 정답이다.
(B) [x] 누가 소프트웨어를 사용하는 방법을 아는지를 물었는데, 설정을 변경하기 위함이라며 관련이 없는 내용으로 응답했으므로 오답이다.
(C) [x] software(소프트웨어)와 관련 있는 account(계정)를 사용하여 혼동을 준 오답이다.

22. 일반 의문문   캐나다 → 영국

Have you been to Venice Library since it reopened?
(A) I didn't know it was closed.
(B) No, it's on the opposite side.
(C) Thanks for helping me during the renovation.

reopen v. 다시 문을 열다   renovation n. 보수

해석 Venice 도서관이 다시 문을 연 이후로 가본 적이 있나요?
(A) 저는 그것이 닫혔는지 몰랐어요.
(B) 아니오, 그것은 반대편에 있어요.
(C) 보수 기간 동안 저를 도와 주셔서 감사해요.

해설 (A) [ㅇ] 그것이 닫혔는지 몰랐다는 말로 Venice 도서관에 한동안 가지 않았음을 간접적으로 전달했으므로 정답이다.
(B) [x] Venice 도서관이 다시 문을 연 이후로 가본 적이 있는지를 물었는데, 장소로 응답했으므로 오답이다. No만 듣고 정답으로 고르지 않도록 주의한다.
(C) [x] reopened(다시 문을 열다)와 관련 있는 renovation(보수)을 사용하여 혼동을 준 오답이다.

23. Which 의문문   미국 → 캐나다

Which report did you revise?
(A) Ten more copies.
(B) Actually, I prefer to read online.
(C) The one about the marketing campaign.

report n. 보고서   revise v. 수정하다   copy n. (책 등의) 한 부   prefer v. 선호하다

해석 당신은 어느 보고서를 수정했나요?
(A) 10부 더요.
(B) 사실, 저는 온라인으로 읽는 것을 선호해요.
(C) 홍보 캠페인에 대한 것이요.

해설 (A) [x] 어느 보고서를 수정했는지를 물었는데, 10부 더라며 관련이 없는 내용으로 응답했으므로 오답이다.
(B) [x] report(보고서)와 관련 있는 read(읽다)를 사용하여 혼동을 준 오답이다.
(C) [ㅇ] 홍보 캠페인에 대한 것이라며, 어느 보고서를 수정했는지를 언급했으므로 정답이다.

24. Why 의문문   호주 → 미국

Why is Henry working overtime?
(A) Some training materials.
(B) I work out in the evenings.
(C) Because he is dealing with a complaint.

overtime n. 초과 근무   material n. 자료   work out 운동하다

해석 왜 Henry는 초과 근무를 하고 있나요?
(A) 몇몇 교육 자료요.
(B) 저는 저녁에 운동해요.
(C) 그는 불만 사항을 처리하고 있기 때문이에요.

해설 (A) [x] working(근무를 하고 있다)에서 연상할 수 있는 회사 업무와 관련된 training materials(교육 자료)를 사용하여 혼동을 준 오답이다.
(B) [x] 질문의 working(일하다)을 '운동하다'라는 의미로 사용하여 혼동을 준 오답이다.
(C) [ㅇ] 그는 불만 사항을 처리하고 있다는 말로, Henry가 초과 근무를 하고 있는 이유를 언급했으므로 정답이다.

25. 일반 의문문   호주 → 영국

Do any of your hotel rooms have balconies?
(A) Yes. All the rooms on the upper floors.
(B) Tell Mr. Yoshida about it.
(C) We're not offering a discount.

discount n. 할인

해석 당신의 호텔 방 중에 발코니가 있는 방이 있나요?
(A) 네. 위층에 있는 모든 방들이요.
(B) 그것에 대해 Mr. Yoshida에게 말씀해 주세요.
(C) 저희는 할인을 제공하고 있지 않습니다.

해설 (A) [ㅇ] Yes로 발코니가 있는 방이 있음을 전달한 후, 위층에 있는 모든 방들이라는 부연 설명을 했으므로 정답이다.
(B) [x] hotel – tell의 유사 발음 어휘를 사용하여 혼동을 준 오답이다.
(C) [x] 호텔 방 중에 발코니가 있는 방이 있는지를 물었는데, 할인을 제공하고 있지 않다며 관련이 없는 내용으로 응답했으므로 오답이다.

26. Where 의문문   캐나다 → 미국

Where is the film screening going to take place?
(A) I've been to that place before.
(B) Unfortunately, it's been canceled.
(C) From 5 P.M. to 7 P.M.

screening n. 상영   unfortunately adv. 불행하게도

해석 영화 상영이 어디에서 열릴 예정인가요?
(A) 저는 그곳에 전에 가본 적 있어요.
(B) 불행하게도, 그것은 취소되었어요.
(C) 오후 5시부터 오후 7시까지예요.

해설 (A) [x] 질문의 take place(열리다)에서 place를 '장소'라는 의미로 사용하여 혼동을 준 오답이다.
(B) [ㅇ] 그것이 취소되었다는 말로 영화 상영이 열리지 않을 것임을 간접적으로 전달했으므로 정답이다.
(C) [x] 영화 상영이 열릴 장소를 물었는데, 시간으로 응답했으므로 오답이다.

27. 부정 의문문　　🎧 호주 → 영국

Can't we park in this spot?
(A) Here are the keys.
(B) The parking garage across the street.
(C) Don't you know the regulations?

spot n. 자리, 장소　parking garage 주차장
regulation n. 규정

해석　이 자리에 주차할 수 없나요?
　　(A) 여기 열쇠들이 있어요.
　　(B) 길 건너편에 있는 주차장이요.
　　(C) 당신은 규정을 모르시나요?

해설　(A) [×] 이 자리에 주차할 수 없는지를 물었는데, 여기 열쇠들이 있다며 관련이 없는 내용으로 응답했으므로 오답이다.
　　(B) [×] park(주차하다)와 관련 있는 parking garage(주차장)를 사용하여 혼동을 준 오답이다.
　　(C) [o] 규정을 모르는지를 되물어 이 자리에 주차할 수 없음을 간접적으로 전달했으므로 정답이다.

28. 평서문　　🎧 영국 → 미국

This school has strict entrance requirements.
(A) I'm still going to submit an application.
(B) We need to lower our voices.
(C) A class with Professor Chavez.

strict adj. 엄격한　entrance requirement 입학 요건
application n. 지원서　lower v. 낮추다

해석　이 학교는 엄격한 입학 요건을 가지고 있어요.
　　(A) 저는 여전히 지원서를 제출할 예정이에요.
　　(B) 우리는 목소리를 낮춰야 해요.
　　(C) Chavez 교수의 수업이요.

해설　(A) [o] 여전히 지원서를 제출할 예정이라는 말로 학교의 입학 요건에 대한 의견을 제시했으므로 정답이다.
　　(B) [×] 이 학교는 엄격한 입학 자격을 가지고 있다고 말했는데, 목소리를 낮춰야 한다며 관련이 없는 내용으로 응답했으므로 오답이다.
　　(C) [×] school(학교)과 관련 있는 class(수업)와 Professor(교수)를 사용하여 혼동을 준 오답이다.

29. How 의문문　　🎧 호주 → 영국

How do I request reimbursement for my travel expenses?
(A) I took a trip with my family last weekend.
(B) The finance team recently updated the guidelines.
(C) I'll do it another time.

reimbursement n. 상환　travel expense 여행 경비
guideline n. 지침

해석　어떻게 제 여행 경비에 대한 상환을 요청하나요?
　　(A) 저는 지난 주말에 가족과 함께 여행을 했어요.
　　(B) 재무팀이 최근에 지침을 업데이트했어요.
　　(C) 다른 시간에 할게요.

해설　(A) [×] travel(여행)과 관련 있는 trip(여행)을 사용하여 혼동을 준 오답이다.
　　(B) [o] 재무팀이 최근에 지침을 업데이트했다며, 상황을 요청하는 방법을 모른다는 점을 간접적으로 전달했으므로 정답이다.
　　(C) [×] 어떻게 경비에 대한 상환을 요청하는지 물었는데, 다른 시간에 할 것이라며 관련이 없는 내용으로 응답했으므로 오답이다.

30. 제안 의문문　　🎧 캐나다 → 미국

Would you like a bag to carry your groceries?
(A) Try looking in the back room.
(B) It's the latest episode of the series.
(C) I brought one with me.

episode n. 회차, 에피소드

해석　당신의 식료품을 들 수 있는 가방을 드릴까요?
　　(A) 뒤쪽 방을 확인해 보세요.
　　(B) 이것은 그 시리즈의 최신 회차예요.
　　(C) 제가 하나 갖고 왔어요.

해설　(A) [×] 식료품을 위한 가방을 줄지를 물었는데, 뒤쪽 방을 확인해 보라며 관련이 없는 내용으로 응답했으므로 오답이다.
　　(B) [×] groceries − series의 유사 발음 어휘를 사용하여 혼동을 준 오답이다.
　　(C) [o] 하나, 즉 가방을 갖고 왔다는 말로 제안을 간접적으로 거절한 정답이다.

31. 평서문　　🎧 영국 → 캐나다

Ethan called while he was transferring in Madrid.
(A) Did he leave a message?
(B) OK, thanks for driving me home.
(C) Please show me your flight ticket.

transfer v. 환승하다

해석　Ethan이 마드리드에서 환승하는 동안 전화했어요.
　　(A) 그가 메시지를 남겼나요?
　　(B) 네, 저를 집에 태워 주셔서 감사해요.
　　(C) 당신의 항공권을 보여주세요.

해설　(A) [o] 그, 즉 Ethan이 메시지를 남겼는지를 되물어 그가 전화한 것에 대한 추가 정보를 요청했으므로 정답이다.
　　(B) [×] Ethan이 전화했다고 말했는데, 자신을 집에 태워 줘서 감사하다며 관련이 없는 내용으로 응답했으므로 오답이다.
　　(C) [×] transferring(환승하다)에서 연상할 수 있는 교통 수단과 관련된 flight ticket(항공권)을 사용하여 혼동을 준 오답이다.

PART 3

32-34 영국 → 캐나다

Questions 32-34 refer to the following conversation.

> W: ³²The next event being held at our hotel's reception hall is an employee appreciation dinner for Dynamic Technology. We've only got a few days to put up the decorations.
> M: Are we going to use our standard décor?
> W: No. ³³Freddy Cho, Dynamic Technology's lead director, specifically requested that we use maroon to match the firm's logo color.
> M: ³⁴Does that mean we'll need to buy new supplies?
> W: ³⁴Yes. We need tablecloths, and the event budget will cover the cost.

employee n. 직원 appreciation n. 감사
decoration n. 장식물 standard adj. 일반적인
décor n. 장식 maroon n. 적갈색, 밤색; adj. 적갈색의, 밤색의
cover v. (무엇을 하기에 충분한 돈이) 되다

해석
32-34번은 다음 대화에 관한 문제입니다.
여: ³²우리 호텔 연회장에서 열릴 다음 행사는 Dynamic Technology사의 직원 감사 만찬입니다. 우리는 장식물을 걸 시간이 며칠밖에 없어요.
남: 우리는 일반적인 장식을 사용할 건가요?
여: 아니요. ³³Dynamic Technology사의 수석 관리자인 Freddy Cho가 회사의 로고 색상과 어울리는 적갈색을 사용하도록 구체적으로 요청했어요.
남: ³⁴그것이 우리가 새 물품을 사야 하는 것을 의미하나요?
여: ³⁴네. 우리는 식탁보가 필요한데, 행사 예산으로 충분히 될 거예요.

32. 화자 문제
해석 화자들은 어디에서 일하는가?
(A) 기술 회사에서
(B) 회계 법인에서
(C) 호텔에서
(D) 식당에서

해설 대화에서 신분 및 직업과 관련된 표현을 놓치지 않고 듣는다. 대화 초반부에서 여자가 "The next event being held at our hotel's reception hall is an employee appreciation dinner(우리 호텔 연회장에서 열릴 다음 행사는 직원 감사 만찬입니다)"라고 한 것을 통해, 화자들이 호텔에서 일하는 것을 알 수 있다. 따라서 정답은 (C)이다.

어휘 accounting n. 회계

33. 특정 세부 사항 문제
해석 Freddy Cho는 누구인가?
(A) 잡지 편집자
(B) 실내 장식가
(C) 접수원
(D) 관리자

해설 질문의 핵심 어구(Freddy Cho)가 언급된 주변을 주의 깊게 듣는다. 대화 중반부에서 여자가 "Freddy Cho, Dynamic Technology's lead director(Dynamic Technology사의 수석 관리자인 Freddy Cho)"라고 하였다. 따라서 정답은 (D)이다.

[Paraphrasing]
lead director 수석 관리자 → manager 관리자

34. 특정 세부 사항 문제
해석 여자에 따르면, 어떤 물품이 구입되어야 하는가?
(A) 식탁보
(B) 꽃다발
(C) 의자 덮개
(D) 선물 가방

해설 질문의 핵심 어구(item ~ purchased)와 관련된 내용을 주의 깊게 듣는다. 대화 후반부에서 남자가 "Does that mean we'll need to buy new supplies?(그것이 우리가 새 물품을 사야 하는 것을 의미하나요?)"라고 하자, 여자가 "Yes. We need tablecloths(네. 우리는 식탁보가 필요해요)"라고 하였다. 이를 통해, 식탁보가 구입되어야 함을 알 수 있다. 따라서 정답은 (A)이다.

어휘 bouquet n. 꽃다발

35-37 호주 → 미국

Questions 35-37 refer to the following conversation.

> M: Excuse me, Ms. Bowen. Is it all right if I leave the office one hour early today? ³⁵I have to pick my mother up from the airport this afternoon.
> W: ³⁶That should be fine as long as you make sure to update your project schedule before you go.
> M: ³⁷I just took care of that, actually. I'm working on the budget request forms now.
> W: I think that can wait. Thanks, though.

as long as ~하기만 하면, ~하는 한 can wait 급하지 않다

해석
35-37번은 다음 대화에 관한 문제입니다.
남: 실례합니다, Ms. Bowen. 제가 오늘 1시간 일찍 사무실을 떠나도 괜찮을까요? ³⁵저는 오늘 오후에 공항에서 어머니를 모셔 와야 해요.
여: 가기 전에 ³⁶당신의 프로젝트 일정을 확실히 업데이트하기만 하면 괜찮을 거예요.
남: ³⁷사실, 저는 막 그것을 처리했어요. 지금은 예산 신청서에 관해 작업하고 있어요.
여: 그것은 급하지 않은 것 같아요. 그렇지만, 감사해요.

35. 특정 세부 사항 문제
해석 남자는 오늘 오후에 무엇을 해야 하는가?
(A) 공항에 간다.
(B) 방을 예약한다.
(C) 열차를 탄다.
(D) 계정을 만든다.

해설 질문의 핵심 어구(this afternoon)가 언급된 주변을 주의 깊게 듣는다. 대화 초반부에서 남자가 "I have to pick my mother up from the airport this afternoon.(저는 오늘 오후에 공항에서 어머니를 모셔 와야 해요.)"이라고 하였다. 따라서 정답은 (A)이다.

36. 특정 세부 사항 문제

해석 여자는 남자에게 무엇을 업데이트하라고 말하는가?
(A) 예산안
(B) 기기
(C) 일정
(D) 애플리케이션

해설 질문의 핵심 어구(update)가 언급된 주변을 주의 깊게 듣는다. 대화 중반부에서 여자가 "That should be fine as long as you make sure to update your project schedule(당신의 프로젝트 일정을 확실히 업데이트하기만 하면 괜찮을 거예요.)"이라고 하였다. 따라서 정답은 (C)이다.

어휘 budget n. 예산안, 예산

37. 의도 파악 문제

해석 여자는 "그것은 급하지 않은 것 같아요"라고 말할 때 무엇을 의도하는가?
(A) 고객이 기다릴 의향이 있다.
(B) 직원이 일찍 떠나도 된다.
(C) 수리가 아주 긴급하지 않다.
(D) 항공편이 취소되었다.

해설 질문의 인용어구(I think that can wait)가 언급된 주변을 주의 깊게 듣는다. 대화 후반부에서 남자가 "I just took care of that[project schedule], actually. I'm working on the budget request forms now.(사실, 저는 막 그것[프로젝트 일정]을 처리했어요. 지금은 예산 신청서에 관해 작업하고 있어요.)"라고 하자, 여자가 그것, 즉 예산 신청서 작업은 급하지 않은 것 같다고 하였으므로, 직원이 일찍 떠나도 된다는 의도임을 알 수 있다. 따라서 (B)가 정답이다.

어휘 urgent adj. 긴급한

38-40 [미국 → 캐나다 → 영국]

Questions 38-40 refer to the following conversation with three speakers.

> W1: A big snowstorm is expected in the region tomorrow. ³⁸Maybe we should encourage staff to work from home.
> M: I agree. And while we're on that subject, ³⁹several employees recently complained about our firm not having a better telecommuting policy.
> W2: I've heard that, too. Many workers feel that they can do their daily tasks remotely.
> W1: Hmm . . . Will that reduce productivity?
> M: Actually, ⁴⁰Ms. Kensington, other corporations have found that allowing telecommuting leads to higher efficiency and better employee morale.
> W1: ⁴⁰Interesting. Please e-mail me a summary of your research on that, and I'll consider the change.
>
> telecommuting n. 재택근무 remotely adv. 원격으로, 멀리서
> efficiency n. 효율성 morale n. 사기, 의욕
> summary n. 요약본

해석
38-40번은 다음 세 명의 대화에 관한 문제입니다.

여1: 내일 이 지역에 거대한 눈보라가 예상된다고 해요. ³⁸어쩌면 우리는 직원들이 집에서 일하도록 장려해야겠어요.
남: 동의해요. 그리고 우리가 그 주제에 관해 이야기하고 있으니, ³⁹몇몇 직원들이 최근에 우리 회사가 더 나은 재택근무 정책을 갖고 있지 않은 것에 대해 불평했어요.
여2: 저도 그것을 들었어요. 많은 직원들이 그들의 일상 업무를 원격으로 할 수 있다고 생각해요.
여1: 흠… 그것이 생산성을 감소시킬까요?
남: 사실, ⁴⁰Ms. Kensington, 다른 기업들은 재택근무를 허용하는 것이 더 높은 효율성과 더 나은 직원들의 사기를 끌어낸다는 것을 발견했어요.
여1: ⁴⁰흥미롭네요. 그것에 관한 당신의 조사의 요약본을 제게 이메일로 보내주세요, 그러면 제가 변경을 고려해 볼게요.

38. 주제 문제

해석 화자들은 주로 무엇을 이야기하고 있는가?
(A) 설명서
(B) 회사 정책
(C) 면접
(D) 가게 개점

해설 대화의 주제를 묻는 문제이므로, 대화의 초반을 주의 깊게 듣는다. 여자1이 "Maybe we should encourage staff to work from home.(어쩌면 우리는 직원들이 집에서 일하도록 장려해야겠어요.)"이라고 한 후, 회사의 재택근무 정책에 대한 내용으로 대화가 이어지고 있다. 따라서 (B)가 정답이다.

어휘 business n. 회사

39. 특정 세부 사항 문제

해석 몇몇 직원들은 최근에 무엇을 했는가?
(A) 불평을 했다.
(B) 추가 근무를 했다.
(C) 다른 사무실로 전근을 갔다.
(D) 몇몇 서류를 제출했다.

해설 질문의 핵심 어구(employees)가 언급된 주변을 주의 깊게 듣는다. 대화 중반부에서 남자가 "several employees recently complained about our firm not having a better telecommuting policy(몇몇 직원들이 최근에 우리 회사가 더 나은 재택근무 정책을 갖고 있지 않은 것에 대해 불평했어요)"라고 하였다. 따라서 (A)가 정답이다.

40. 요청 문제

해석 Ms. Kensington은 무엇을 요청하는가?
(A) 견적서
(B) 보고서
(C) 청사진
(D) 소책자

해설 질문의 핵심 어구(Ms. Kensington)가 언급된 주변을 주의 깊게 듣는다. 대화 후반부에서 남자가 "Ms. Kensington, other corporations have found that allowing telecommuting leads to higher efficiency and better employee morale(Ms. Kensington, 다른 기업들은 재택근무를 허용하는 것이 더 높은 효율성과 더 나은 직원들의 사기를 끌어낸다는 것을 발견했어요)"이라고 하자, 여자1[Ms. Kensington]이 "Interesting. Please e-mail me a summary of your research on that(흥미롭네요. 그것에 관한 당신의 조사의 요약본을 제게 이메일로 보내주세요)"이라고 하였다. 따라서 (B)가 정답이다.

어휘 estimate n. 견적서 blueprint n. 청사진

41-43 호주 → 영국

Questions 41-43 refer to the following conversation.

> M: ⁴¹I'm so sorry I didn't get here by 11 A.M. The meeting took a lot longer than expected.
> W: ⁴²You met with Ms. Mendez, our corporate financial advisor, right?
> M: Yes. It was a productive meeting. She has some great ideas about our firm's investment plan.
> W: Good to hear. Since you arrived a bit late, our meeting about the publicity campaign will have to be delayed until tomorrow. I've got to leave for a luncheon now.
> M: No problem. How does 10:30 A.M. sound to you?
> W: That'll work. ⁴³Could you bring your notes from last month's campaign?

advisor n. 자문 위원, 고문   investment n. 투자
publicity n. 홍보   delay v. 미루다   luncheon n. 오찬

해석
41-43번은 다음 대화에 관한 문제입니다.

남: ⁴¹오전 11시까지 이곳에 도착하지 못해서 정말 죄송해요. 회의가 예상보다 훨씬 더 오래 걸렸어요.
여: ⁴²당신은 우리 기업의 재정 자문 위원인 Ms. Mendez를 만났죠, 그렇죠?
남: 네. 그것은 생산적인 회의였어요. 그녀는 우리 회사의 투자 계획에 관한 좋은 아이디어들을 갖고 있어요.
여: 좋네요. 당신이 약간 늦게 도착했으니, 홍보 캠페인에 관한 우리 회의는 내일까지 미뤄져야겠어요. 저는 지금 오찬을 위해 출발해야 해요.
남: 문제없어요. 오전 10시 30분이 어떠세요?
여: 그때는 괜찮을 거예요. ⁴³지난달 캠페인의 당신의 메모를 가지고 와주시겠어요?

41. 특정 세부 사항 문제

해석 남자는 무엇에 대해 사과하는가?
(A) 예정보다 늦게 도착한 것
(B) 몇몇 서류를 잊은 것
(C) 잘못된 건물로 들어간 것
(D) 교육 세션을 놓친 것

해설 질문의 핵심 어구(apologize)와 관련된 내용을 주의 깊게 듣는다. 대화 초반부에서 남자가 "I'm so sorry I didn't get here by 11 A.M.(오전 11시까지 이곳에 도착하지 못해서 정말 죄송해요.)"이라고 하였다. 따라서 (A)가 정답이다.

42. 특정 세부 사항 문제

해석 Ms. Mendez는 누구인가?
(A) 안전 감독관
(B) 개인 비서
(C) 재정 자문 위원
(D) 기업 회장

해설 질문의 핵심 어구(Ms. Mendez)가 언급된 주변을 주의 깊게 듣는다. 대화 초반부에서 여자가 "You met with Ms. Mendez, our corporate financial advisor, right?(당신은 우리 기업의 재정 자문 위원인 Ms. Mendez를 만났죠, 그렇죠?)"

이라고 하였다. 따라서 (C)가 정답이다.

어휘 inspector n. 감독관   assistant n. 비서, 조수
consultant n. 자문 위원   chairperson n. 회장

43. 요청 문제

해석 여자는 남자에게 무엇을 하라고 요청하는가?
(A) 몇몇 계약서를 수정한다.
(B) 웹사이트를 업데이트한다.
(C) 동료와 함께 일한다.
(D) 몇몇 자료를 가져온다.

해설 여자의 말에서 요청과 관련된 표현이 언급된 다음을 주의 깊게 듣는다. 대화 후반부에서 여자가 "Could you bring your notes from last month's campaign?(지난달 캠페인의 당신의 메모를 가지고 와주시겠어요?)"라고 하였다. 따라서 (D)가 정답이다.

44-46 호주 → 미국

Questions 44-46 refer to the following conversation.

> M: Hello, Ms. Rhine. Can you spare a few minutes? ⁴⁴I'd like to discuss a job opening within our marketing firm. ⁴⁵I'm interested in the position at our San Antonio branch.
> W: ⁴⁵San Antonio? . . . But, you've been doing very well here.
> M: My parents live in that area, and I've wanted to be closer to them for a long time. So, here's my request form.
> W: I see. Well, ⁴⁶I'll go over it and e-mail you my response by next Monday.
> M: Thanks a lot.

spare v. (시간을) 내다   job opening 채용 공고
position n. 자리, 위치

해석
44-46번은 다음 대화에 관한 문제입니다.

남: 안녕하세요, Ms. Rhine. 몇 분 정도 시간 내 주실 수 있나요? ⁴⁴저는 우리 홍보 회사 내에서의 채용 공고에 대해 논의하고 싶어요. ⁴⁵저는 우리 샌안토니오 지점의 자리에 관심이 있어요.
여: ⁴⁵샌안토니오요?… 하지만, 당신은 이곳에서 매우 잘하고 있었잖아요.
남: 제 부모님이 그 지역에 살고 계시고, 저는 오랫동안 그들과 더 가까워지길 원했어요. 그래서, 여기 제 신청서예요.
여: 알겠어요. 음, ⁴⁶제가 이것을 검토해 보고 다음 주 월요일까지 제 답변을 이메일로 보내드릴게요.
남: 정말 감사합니다.

44. 화자 문제

해석 화자들은 어디에서 일하는가?
(A) 제조 공장에서
(B) 광고 회사에서
(C) 투자 회사에서
(D) 여행사에서

해설 대화에서 신분 및 직업과 관련된 표현을 놓치지 않고 듣는다. 대화 초반부에서 남자가 "I'd like to discuss a job opening within our marketing firm.(저는 우리 홍보 회사 내에서의 채용 공고에 대해 논의하고 싶어요.)"이라고 한 것을 통해 화자들이 광고 회사에서 일한다는 것을 알 수 있다. 따라서 (B)가 정

PART 3   51

답이다.

어휘 advertising n. 광고

> [Paraphrasing]
> marketing firm 홍보 회사 → advertising company 광고 회사

45. 의도 파악 문제

해석 여자는 왜 "당신은 이곳에서 매우 잘하고 있었잖아요"라고 말하는가?
(A) 놀라움을 나타내기 위해
(B) 격려해 주기 위해
(C) 감사를 표현하기 위해
(D) 제안을 하기 위해

해설 질문의 인용어구(you've been doing very well here)가 언급된 주변을 주의 깊게 듣는다. 대화 초반부에서 남자가 "I'm interested in the position at our San Antonio branch.(저는 우리 샌안토니오 지점의 자리에 관심이 있어요.)"라고 하자, 여자가 "San Antonio?(샌안토니오요?)"라며 하지만 당신은 이곳에서 매우 잘하고 있었다고 한 것을 통해, 놀라움을 나타내기 위한 의도임을 알 수 있다. 따라서 (A)가 정답이다.

어휘 surprise n. 놀라움 encouragement n. 격려
gratitude n. 감사 extend an offer 제안하다

46. 다음에 할 일 문제

해석 여자는 다음 주 월요일까지 무엇을 할 것 같은가?
(A) 관리자와 이야기한다.
(B) 다른 지점을 방문한다.
(C) 답변을 준다.
(D) 휴가 신청서를 제출한다.

해설 질문의 핵심 어구(by next Monday)가 언급된 주변을 주의 깊게 듣는다. 대화 후반부에서 여자가 "I'll go over it and e-mail you my response by next Monday(제가 이것을 검토해 보고 다음 주 월요일까지 제 답변을 이메일로 보내드릴게요.)"라고 하였다. 따라서 (C)가 정답이다.

어휘 turn in ~을 제출하다

47-49 🎧 영국 → 캐나다

Questions 47-49 refer to the following conversation.

W: Hi, Rodney. This is Jessica from the sales department. ⁴⁷Can you take a look at my computer? I'm having some issues.
M: ⁴⁷I'm trying to fix an ID card scanner right now. Is there something wrong with your computer?
W: Yeah, ⁴⁸it keeps shutting off while I'm working.
M: That doesn't sound good. I know you've got an older model, so it probably needs to be replaced. ⁴⁹I'll call my colleague and ask him to take a look at it.

---

shut off 꺼지다, 멈추다 colleague n. 동료

해석
47-49번은 다음 대화에 관한 문제입니다.

여: 안녕하세요, Rodney. 영업부 Jessica예요. ⁴⁷제 컴퓨터를 한번 봐주실 수 있나요? 저는 문제를 겪고 있어요.

남: ⁴⁷저는 지금 신분증 스캐너를 고치려는 중이에요. 당신의 컴퓨터에 무슨 문제가 있나요?
여: 네, ⁴⁸제가 작업하는 동안 이것이 계속 꺼져요.
남: 좋게 들리지는 않네요. 당신이 오래된 모델을 갖고 있는 것을 알고 있으니, 아마 교체되어야 할 것 같아요. ⁴⁹제가 동료에게 전화해서 그것을 봐달라고 요청할게요.

47. 화자 문제

해석 남자는 어느 부서에서 일하는 것 같은가?
(A) 법무
(B) 재정
(C) 인사
(D) 기술 지원

해설 대화에서 신분 및 직업과 관련된 표현을 놓치지 않고 듣는다. 대화 초반부에서 여자가 "Can you take a look at my computer? I'm having some issues.(제 컴퓨터를 한번 봐주실 수 있나요? 저는 문제를 겪고 있어요.)"라고 하자, 남자가 "I'm trying to fix an ID card scanner right now.(저는 지금 신분증 스캐너를 고치려는 중이에요.)"라고 한 것을 통해, 남자가 기술 지원 부서에서 일한다는 것을 알 수 있다. 따라서 (D)가 정답이다.

48. 문제점 문제

해석 여자는 무슨 문제를 언급하는가?
(A) 동료들이 늦는다.
(B) 보안 시스템이 헷갈린다.
(C) 장비가 제대로 작동하지 않는다.
(D) 전화를 놓쳤다.

해설 여자의 말에서 부정적인 표현이 언급된 다음을 주의 깊게 듣는다. 대화 중반부에서 여자가 "it[computer] keeps shutting off while I'm working(제가 작업하는 동안 이것[컴퓨터]이 계속 꺼져요)"이라고 하였다. 따라서 (C)가 정답이다.

어휘 equipment n. 장비

49. 다음에 할 일 문제

해석 남자는 무엇을 할 것이라고 말하는가?
(A) 일정을 업데이트한다.
(B) 책상을 재배치한다.
(C) 새로운 구역으로 이동한다.
(D) 동료에게 연락한다.

해설 대화의 마지막 부분을 주의 깊게 듣는다. 남자가 "I'll call my colleague and ask him to take a look at it.(제가 동료에게 전화해서 그것을 봐달라고 요청할게요.)"이라고 하였다. 따라서 (D)가 정답이다.

어휘 rearrange v. 재배치하다

> [Paraphrasing]
> call ~ colleague 동료에게 전화하다 → Contact a coworker 동료에게 연락하다

50-52 🎧 호주 → 미국

Questions 50-52 refer to the following conversation.

M: Kathy, ⁵⁰I was asked to proofread a report, but I'm having trouble understanding it.
W: Can you tell me what the report is about?
M: ⁵¹The report deals with banking regulations, which I don't have much experience with.
W: Honestly, I don't know a lot about that

field either. If I were you, I'd explain the situation to Mr. Wiley. He's our regulations expert.
M: Yes, I suppose you're right. Is he in his office right now?
W: Not at the moment. ⁵²Just send him an e-mail instead.

proofread v. 교정보다　**deal with** ~을 다루다
banking n. 은행 업무

해석
50-52번은 다음 대화에 관한 문제입니다.
남: Kathy, ⁵⁰저는 보고서를 교정봐 달라는 요청을 받았는데, 이것을 이해하는 데 문제를 겪고 있어요.
여: 보고서가 무엇에 관한 것인지 저에게 알려주시겠어요?
남: ⁵¹이 보고서는 은행 업무 규정을 다루는데, 저는 이것에 경험이 많지 않아요.
여: 솔직히, 저도 그 분야에 대해 많이 알지 못해요. 제가 당신이라면, Mr. Wiley에게 상황을 설명하겠어요. 그가 우리 규정 전문가예요.
남: 네, 당신 말이 맞는 것 같아요. 그가 지금 그의 사무실에 있나요?
여: 지금은 없어요. ⁵²대신 그에게 이메일을 보내세요.

50. 요청 문제
해석 남자는 무엇을 하도록 요청받았는가?
(A) 후보를 인터뷰한다.
(B) 보고서를 검토한다.
(C) 회의를 이끈다.
(D) 예산안을 제출한다.

해설 남자의 말에서 요청과 관련된 표현이 언급된 다음을 주의 깊게 듣는다. 대화 초반부에서 남자가 "I was asked to proofread a report(저는 보고서를 교정봐 달라는 요청을 받았어요)"라고 하였다. 따라서 (B)가 정답이다.

어휘 **candidate** n. 후보　**session** n. 회의, 시간

[Paraphrasing]
proofread a report 보고서를 교정보다 → Review a report 보고서를 검토하다

51. 문제점 문제
해석 남자는 무슨 문제를 언급하는가?
(A) 회의에 참석할 수 없다.
(B) 프로젝트를 인계받았다.
(C) 증명서를 찾을 수 없다.
(D) 주제에 익숙하지 않다.

해설 남자의 말에서 부정적인 표현이 언급된 다음을 주의 깊게 듣는다. 대화 중반부에서 남자가 "The report deals with banking regulations, which I don't have much experience with.(이 보고서는 은행 업무 규정을 다루는데, 저는 이것에 경험이 많지 않아요.)"라고 하였다. 따라서 (D)가 정답이다.

어휘 **take over** ~을 인계받다　**certification** n. 증명서

52. 제안 문제
해석 여자는 남자에게 무엇을 하라고 제안하는가?
(A) 가구를 설치한다.
(B) 명함을 제시한다.
(C) 이메일을 작성한다.
(D) 전화 회담에 참여한다.

해설 여자의 말에서 제안과 관련된 표현이 언급된 다음을 주의 깊게 듣는다. 대화 후반부에서 여자가 "Just send him[Mr. Wiley] an e-mail instead.(대신 그[Mr. Wiley]에게 이메일을 보내세요.)"라고 하였다. 따라서 (C)가 정답이다.

어휘 **set up** ~을 설치하다, 준비하다　**conference call** 전화 회담

53-55 [3인] 미국 → 캐나다
Questions 53-55 refer to the following conversation.

W: Dr. Lee, this is Elena Fritz from *Horizon Magazine*. ⁵³Thank you for agreeing to answer some questions for the article I'm writing on renewable energy.
M: Of course. ⁵⁴I'm excited to talk about the study I did with a group of other scientists. We finished it last week.
W: Before we get into that, I want to clarify something for my article. ⁵⁵You're planning to speak at the National Energy Conference in July, right?
M: That's right. ⁵⁵I'm going to talk about the various ways in which solar panels can be utilized to reduce energy costs.

renewable energy 재생에너지　**clarify** v. 분명히 하다
various adj. 다양한　**solar panel** 태양 전지판
utilize v. 활용하다

해석
53-55번은 다음 대화에 관한 문제입니다.
여: Dr. Lee, *Horizon*지의 Elena Fritz입니다. ⁵³제가 재생에너지에 대해 쓰고 있는 기사를 위해 몇몇 질문에 답해주시기로 해서 감사합니다.
남: 물론이죠. ⁵⁴저는 제가 몇몇 다른 과학자들과 함께 한 연구에 대해 이야기하게 되어 흥분됩니다. 저희는 그것을 지난주에 마쳤어요.
여: 그것에 관해 들어가기 전에, 제 기사를 위해 분명히 하고 싶은 것이 있어요. ⁵⁵당신은 7월에 국가 에너지 회의에서 연설을 할 계획이에요, 맞죠?
남: 맞아요. ⁵⁵저는 태양 전지판이 에너지 비용을 줄이기 위해 활용될 수 있는 다양한 방법에 대해 이야기할 거예요.

53. 목적 문제
해석 여자는 왜 전화를 하고 있는가?
(A) 인터뷰를 진행하기 위해
(B) 일정을 확인하기 위해
(C) 일자리에 지원하기 위해
(D) 구독을 제안하기 위해

해설 전화의 목적을 묻는 문제이므로, 대화의 초반을 주의 깊게 듣는다. 여자가 "Thank you for agreeing to answer some questions for the article I'm writing on renewable energy.(제가 재생에너지에 대해 쓰고 있는 기사를 위해 몇몇 질문에 답해주시기로 해서 감사합니다.)"라고 하였다. 따라서 (A)가 정답이다.

어휘 **confirm** v. 확인하다　**subscription** n. 구독

54. 특정 세부 사항 문제
해석 남자는 지난주에 무엇을 했는가?
(A) 다른 국가로 여행을 갔다.

(B) 연구를 완료했다.
(C) 큰 상을 받았다.
(D) 새로운 프로젝트를 발표했다.

해설 질문의 핵심 어구(last week)가 언급된 주변을 주의 깊게 듣는다. 대화 중반부에서 남자가 "I'm excited to talk about the study I did with a group of other scientists. We finished it last week.(저는 제가 몇몇 다른 과학자들과 함께 한 연구에 대해 이야기하게 되어 흥분됩니다. 저희는 그것을 지난주에 마쳤어요.)"라고 하였다. 따라서 (B)가 정답이다.

어휘 complete v. 완료하다 major adj. 큰, 주요한

55. 특정 세부 사항 문제

해석 남자는 회의에서 무엇에 관해 이야기할 것인가?
(A) 프로그램의 이점
(B) 제조 방법
(C) 기술의 사용법
(D) 자금의 출처

해설 질문의 핵심 어구(conference)가 언급된 주변을 주의 깊게 듣는다. 대화 후반부에서 여자가 "You're planning to speak at the National Energy Conference in July, right?(당신은 7월에 국가 에너지 회의에서 연설을 할 계획이에요, 맞죠?)"라고 묻자, 남자가 "I'm going to talk about the various ways in which solar panels can be utilized(저는 태양 전지판이 활용될 수 있는 다양한 방법에 대해 이야기할 거예요.)"라고 하였다. 따라서 (C)가 정답이다.

어휘 benefit n. 이점 method n. 방법 funding n. 자금

56-58 🎧 호주 → 영국

Questions 56-58 refer to the following conversation.

M: Our bus has been stuck in traffic for a long time. What's going on, Janine?
W: ⁵⁶I bet that everyone's here for the Upstate Jazz Festival. It's held in Albany every July.
M: Oh, right. I think we'll be arriving at our hotel later than planned.
W: That's for sure. I'm worried about our booking. ⁵⁷The receptionist at the hotel said that guests are encouraged to check in before 7 P.M. Do you think we'll have an issue?
M: I don't think so. ⁵⁸Guests can arrive any time before 11 P.M. I read it on the hotel's Web site this morning.
W: Oh, that's good to know.

stuck in traffic 교통 혼잡에 갇힌 booking n. 예약
receptionist n. 접수 담당자

해석
56-58번은 다음 대화에 관한 문제입니다.
남: 우리 버스가 오랫동안 교통 혼잡에 갇혀 있어요. 무슨 일 있나요, Janine?
여: ⁵⁶모든 사람들이 Upstate Jazz 축제를 위해 여기에 온 것이 틀림없어요. 이것은 매년 7월에 올버니에서 열려요.
남: 아, 그러네요. 제 생각에는 우리가 계획한 것보다 호텔에 늦게 도착하겠어요.
여: 확실히 그러네요. 저는 우리 예약이 걱정돼요. ⁵⁷그 호텔의 접수 담당자가 투숙객은 오후 7시 전에 체크인하도록 권장된다고 말

했어요. 우리에게 문제가 생길 거라고 생각하시나요?
남: 그럴 것 같지 않아요. ⁵⁸투숙객은 오후 11시 이전에 어느 때든 도착해도 돼요. 제가 오늘 아침에 호텔 웹사이트에서 이것을 읽었어요.
여: 아, 알게 돼서 다행이네요.

56. 특정 세부 사항 문제

해석 여자에 따르면, 무엇이 열리고 있는가?
(A) 운동 경기
(B) 사업 회의
(C) 공휴일 퍼레이드
(D) 음악 축제

해설 질문의 핵심 어구(taking place)와 관련된 내용을 주의 깊게 듣는다. 대화 초반부에서 여자가 "I bet that everyone's here for the Upstate Jazz Festival.(모든 사람들이 Upstate Jazz 축제를 위해 여기에 온 것이 틀림없어요.)"라고 하였다. 따라서 (D)가 정답이다.

어휘 convention n. 회의, 협약 parade n. 퍼레이드, 행진

57. 언급 문제

해석 접수 담당자에 대해 무엇이 언급되는가?
(A) 체크인 정보를 제공했다.
(B) 전화에 회신하지 않았다.
(C) 확인 번호를 요구했다.
(D) 업그레이드를 제공할 수 없다.

해설 질문의 핵심 어구(receptionist)가 언급된 주변을 주의 깊게 듣는다. 대화 중반부에서 여자가 "The receptionist at the hotel said that guests are encouraged to check in before 7 P.M.(그 호텔의 접수 담당자가 투숙객은 오후 7시 전에 체크인하도록 권장된다고 말했어요.)"이라고 하였다. 따라서 (A)가 정답이다.

58. 특정 세부 사항 문제

해석 남자는 오늘 아침에 무엇을 했는가?
(A) 제품을 구매했다.
(B) 웹사이트에 방문했다.
(C) 소식지를 신청했다.
(D) 불만을 제기했다.

해설 질문의 핵심 어구(this morning)가 언급된 주변을 주의 깊게 듣는다. 대화 후반부에서 남자가 "Guests can arrive any time before 11 P.M. I read it on the hotel's Web site this morning.(투숙객은 오후 11시 이전에 어느 때든 도착해도 돼요. 제가 오늘 아침에 호텔 웹사이트에서 이것을 읽었어요.)"이라고 하였다. 따라서 (B)가 정답이다.

어휘 newsletter n. 소식지 submit v. 제기하다, 제출하다

59-61 🎧 캐나다 → 미국 → 호주

Questions 59-61 refer to the following conversation with three speakers.

M1: Isn't this piece of furniture supposed to go to a customer in New York City?
W: Yes, ⁵⁹the sofa has to be transported from our furniture store to his house. In fact, it needs to be brought there this afternoon.
M1: Should I take care of that delivery now?
W: Yes. Hold on, though. ⁶⁰I'll ask someone to help you . . . Donald, do you have a

moment? I want you and Mike to load this furniture into our van.
M2: I'd be happy to, but ⁶¹I have to complete these order forms first. It won't take long.
W: OK. No problem.

transport v. 운송하다 take care of ~을 처리하다
order form 주문서

해석
59-61번은 다음 세 명의 대화에 관한 문제입니다.
남1: 이 가구는 뉴욕시의 고객에게 가기로 되어 있지 않나요?
여: 네, ⁵⁹그 소파는 우리 가구점에서 그의 집으로 운송되어야 해요. 사실, 그것은 오늘 오후에 그곳으로 배달되어야 해요.
남1: 지금 제가 그 배송을 처리해야 할까요?
여: 네, 그런데, 잠시만요. ⁶⁰제가 누군가에게 당신을 도와 달라고 부탁해 볼게요… Donald, 시간 있으신가요? 저는 당신과 Mike가 이 가구를 우리 밴에 실어 주었으면 좋겠어요.
남2: 기꺼이 그렇게 하겠지만, ⁶¹저는 이 주문서들을 먼저 작성해야 해요. 오래 걸리진 않을 거예요.
여: 알겠어요. 문제없어요.

59. 장소 문제
해석 화자들은 어디에 있는 것 같은가?
(A) 주택에
(B) 실험실에
(C) 경찰서에
(D) 가구점에

해설 장소와 관련된 표현을 놓치지 않고 듣는다. 대화 초반부에서 여자가 "the sofa has to be transported from our furniture store to his house(그 소파는 우리 가구점에서 그의 집으로 운송되어야 해요)"라고 한 것을 통해, 화자들이 가구점에 있음을 알 수 있다. 따라서 (D)가 정답이다.

어휘 residence n. 주택 laboratory n. 실험실

60. 특정 세부 사항 문제
해석 여자는 Donald가 무엇을 하길 원하는가?
(A) 설문조사를 진행한다.
(B) 동료를 돕는다.
(C) 차량을 청소한다.
(D) 길 안내를 찾아본다.

해설 질문의 핵심 어구(Donald)가 언급된 주변을 주의 깊게 듣는다. 대화 중반부에서 여자가 "I'll ask someone to help you... Donald, do you have a moment?(제가 누군가에게 당신을 도와 달라고 부탁해 볼게요. Donald, 시간 있으신가요?)"라고 한 후, "I want you and Mike to load this furniture into our van.(저는 당신과 Mike가 이 가구를 우리 밴에 실어 주었으면 좋겠어요.)"이라고 하였다. 따라서 (B)가 정답이다.

어휘 assist v. 돕다 clean out ~을 청소하다 look up ~을 찾아보다
direction n. 길 안내, 방향

61. 다음에 할 일 문제
해석 Donald는 다음에 무엇을 할 것 같은가?
(A) 문서를 기입한다.
(B) 전시실로 상품을 가져온다.
(C) 포장재를 버린다.
(D) 기기를 찾는다.

해설 대화의 마지막 부분을 주의 깊게 듣는다. 남자2[Donald]가 "I have to complete these order forms first(저는 이 주문서

들을 먼저 작성해야 해요)"라고 하였다. 이를 통해, Donald가 문서를 기입할 것임을 알 수 있다. 따라서 (A)가 정답이다.

어휘 fill out ~을 기입하다 showroom n. 전시실
packaging n. 포장재 appliance n. 기기

[Paraphrasing]
complete ~ order forms 주문서들을 작성하다 → Fill out some documents 문서를 기입하다

62-64 3ω 영국 → 호주
Questions 62-64 refer to the following conversation and schedule.

W: Hello, this is Mountain Fitness Center. How may I help you?
M: Hi. ⁶²I signed up for a weightlifting class that starts tomorrow morning, and I'm wondering what I should bring.
W: We provide towels, so you won't need to bring one of those. However, ⁶³you'll want to dress in comfortable clothes and have your own water bottle.
M: OK, great. And, what about paying for the course? Am I supposed to pay for the class before it begins?
W: No. ⁶⁴We send members their bills at the end of each month. You can pay for it then.

weightlifting n. 역도 comfortable adj. 편안한
bill n. 청구서

해석
62-64번은 다음의 대화와 일정표에 관한 문제입니다.
여: 안녕하세요, Mountain 헬스장입니다. 어떻게 도와드릴까요?
남: 안녕하세요. ⁶²저는 내일 아침에 시작하는 역도 수업을 등록했는데, 무엇을 갖고 가야 하는지 궁금해요.
여: 저희는 수건을 제공하므로, 그것은 가져오지 않아도 될 거예요. 하지만, ⁶³편안한 옷을 입으시고 회원님의 물병을 가져오시면 좋을 거예요.
남: 네, 좋아요. 그리고, 강좌에 대한 지불은 어떻게 하나요? 제가 수업이 시작하기 전에 수업료를 지불해야 하나요?
여: 아니요. ⁶⁴저희는 매월 말에 회원님들께 청구서를 보내드려요. 그때 지불하시면 돼요.

Mountain 헬스장	
프로그램	강사
필라테스	Ashley
역도	⁶²Jess
수영	Aaron
요가	Gerard

62. 시각 자료 문제
해석 시각 자료를 보아라. 누가 남자의 수업을 이끌 것인가?
(A) Ashley
(B) Jess
(C) Aaron
(D) Gerard

해설 일정표의 정보를 확인한 후 질문의 핵심 어구(lead the man's class)와 관련된 내용을 주의 깊게 듣는다. 대화 초반부에서

남자가 "I signed up for a weightlifting class that starts tomorrow morning(저는 내일 아침에 시작하는 역도 수업을 등록했어요)"이라고 하였으므로, 남자의 수업을 Jess가 이끌 것임을 일정표에서 알 수 있다. 따라서 (B)가 정답이다.

어휘 lead v. 이끌다

63. 특정 세부 사항 문제
해석 여자는 남자에게 무엇을 가져오라고 말하는가?
(A) 신발 한 켤레
(B) 회원 카드
(C) 물병
(D) 수건

해설 질문의 핵심 어구(bring)와 관련된 내용을 주의 깊게 듣는다. 대화 중반부에서 여자가 "you'll want to dress in comfortable clothes and have your own water bottle(편안한 옷을 입으시고 회원님의 물병을 가져오시면 좋을 거예요)"이라고 하였다. 따라서 (C)가 정답이다.

64. 특정 세부 사항 문제
해석 여자에 따르면, 헬스장에서 매달 무엇을 하는가?
(A) 청구서를 발송한다.
(B) 새로운 수업 선택권을 게시한다.
(C) 무료 행사를 개최한다.
(D) 의견을 요청한다.

해설 질문의 핵심 어구(each month)가 언급된 주변을 주의 깊게 듣는다. 대화 후반부에서 여자가 "We send members their bills at the end of each month.(저희는 매월 말에 회원님들께 청구서를 보내드려요.)"라고 하였다. 따라서 (A)가 정답이다.

어휘 invoice n. 청구서 host v. 개최하다

[Paraphrasing]
bills 청구서 → invoices 청구서

65-67 🇬🇧 영국 → 캐나다

Questions 65-67 refer to the following conversation and floor plan.

W: Are you coming to this month's book club meeting, Grant?

M: Yes, I plan to go. ⁶⁵I skipped the last meeting because I had a lot of work to do. I don't want to miss it again.

W: Great. We'll be discussing the latest novel by Arin Miller, *A Captain's Tale*.

M: I was informed. Are we meeting in our usual room at Sargent Community Center? The one by the lounge?

W: ⁶⁶Actually, we've arranged to use the room in front of the auditorium instead. That space has a TV, so we'll be able to watch part of the movie based on the book.

M: ⁶⁷But isn't that room too small for our group?

W: Not really. It's nearly as large as the others.

---

skip v. 건너뛰다, 빼먹다 miss v. 놓치다 inform v. 알리다
usual adj. 평소의 lounge n. 휴게실 auditorium n. 강당
based on ~을 기반으로 한

해석
65-67번은 다음의 대화와 평면도에 관한 문제입니다.
여: 이번 달 독서 모임에 오시나요, Grant?
남: 네, 저는 갈 계획이에요. ⁶⁵해야 할 일이 많아서 지난 모임을 건너뛰었어요. 저는 그것을 또 놓치고 싶지 않아요.
여: 좋네요. 우리는 Arin Miller의 최신 소설인 *A Captain's Tale*에 대해 이야기할 거예요.
남: 알고 있어요. 우리는 Sargent 시민 문화 회관의 평소 사용하던 방에서 모이나요? 휴게실 옆에 있는 그곳이요?
여: ⁶⁶사실, 우리는 대신 강당 앞의 방을 사용하도록 준비했어요. 그 공간에는 TV가 있어서, 그 책을 기반으로 한 영화의 일부를 볼 수 있을 거예요.
남: ⁶⁷하지만 우리 단체에 그 방은 너무 좁지 않나요?
여: 별로 그렇지 않아요. 그곳은 거의 다른 방들만큼 넓어요.

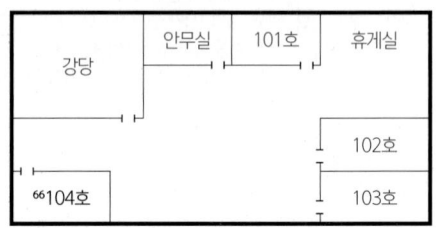

Sargent 시민 문화 회관

65. 이유 문제
해석 남자는 지난 모임을 왜 놓쳤는가?
(A) 업무를 처리해야 했다.
(B) 장소에 대해 알지 못했다.
(C) 책 선정이 마음에 들지 않았다.
(D) 여행을 가 있었다.

해설 질문의 핵심 어구(last meeting)가 언급된 주변을 주의 깊게 듣는다. 대화 초반부에서 남자가 "I skipped the last meeting because I had a lot of work to do.(해야 할 일이 많아서 지난 모임을 건너뛰었어요.)"라고 하였다. 따라서 (A)가 정답이다.

66. 시각 자료 문제
해석 시각 자료를 보아라. 단체는 어디에서 모일 것인가?
(A) 101호
(B) 102호
(C) 103호
(D) 104호

해설 평면도의 정보를 확인한 후 질문의 핵심 어구(group meet)와 관련된 내용을 주의 깊게 듣는다. 대화 중반부에서 여자가 "Actually, we've arranged to use the room in front of the auditorium instead.(사실, 우리는 대신 강당 앞의 방을 사용하도록 준비했어요.)"라고 하였으므로, 단체가 강당 앞에 있는 104호에서 모일 것임을 평면도에서 알 수 있다. 따라서 (D)가 정답이다.

67. 문제점 문제
해석 남자는 무엇에 대해 걱정하는가?
(A) 동료의 의견
(B) 방의 크기
(C) 장소 비용
(D) 논의 주제

해설 남자의 말에서 부정적인 표현이 언급된 다음을 주의 깊게 듣는다. 대화 후반부에서 남자가 "But isn't that room too small for our group?(하지만 우리 단체에 그 방은 너무 좁지 않나

요?)"라고 하였다. 따라서 (B)가 정답이다.

어휘 discussion n. 논의

68-70 호주 → 미국

Questions 68-70 refer to the following conversation and invoice.

> M: Hello. You've reached Reggie Malstrom.
> W: Hi. This is Annabel from the finance department. ⁶⁸I just want to check some hotel charges from your trip to Edmonton last month for the conference.
> M: Oh. ⁶⁹Did I exceed the maximum amount for travel expenses?
> W: ⁶⁹We raised our spending limit to $1,000 last month, and you're under that amount. However, I think Sun Dream Hotel may have overcharged you. ⁷⁰According to your billing statement, you ate lunch at the hotel on the day of the conference. Is that right?
> M: ⁷⁰No, it isn't. I had lunch at the convention center, not at the hotel.
> W: Thanks for clarifying. I'll call them up and ask about it.

charge n. 요금; v. 청구하다, 부과하다　exceed v. 초과하다
maximum amount 한도액　travel expense 여행 경비
spending limit 지출 한도　overcharge v. 과잉 청구하다
billing statement 대금 청구서

해석
68-70번은 다음의 대화와 청구서에 관한 문제입니다.
남: 안녕하세요. Reggie Malstrom입니다.
여: 안녕하세요. 저는 재무 부서의 Annabel입니다. ⁶⁸지난달 컨퍼런스를 위한 당신의 에드먼턴 출장에서 발생한 호텔 요금을 좀 확인하고 싶어요.
남: 아. ⁶⁹제가 여행 경비의 한도액을 초과했나요?
여: ⁶⁹우리는 지난달에 1,000달러로 지출 한도를 높였어요, 그리고 당신은 그 금액 이하예요. 하지만, Sun Dream 호텔에서 당신에게 과잉 청구한 것 같아요. ⁷⁰당신의 대금 청구서에 따르면, 당신은 컨퍼런스 당일에 호텔에서 점심을 드셨어요. 이것이 맞나요?
남: ⁷⁰아니요, 그렇지 않아요. 저는 호텔이 아니라, 컨벤션 센터에서 점심을 먹었어요.
여: 명확히 해주셔서 감사합니다. 제가 그들에게 전화해서 그것에 관해 물어볼게요.

Sun Dream 호텔	
에드먼턴, Jasper가, 10438번지	
투숙객명: Reggie Malstrom	
투숙일: 7월 7일-9일	
객실 요금:	308달러
⁷⁰점심:	⁷⁰21달러
룸서비스 저녁:	24달러
셔틀 서비스:	12달러
총액:	353달러

68. 이유 문제
해석 남자는 왜 에드먼턴에 갔는가?
(A) 직원 교육을 제공하기 위해
(B) 경쟁업체를 조사하기 위해
(C) 컨퍼런스에 참석하기 위해
(D) 잠재적인 투자자들을 만나기 위해

해설 질문의 핵심 어구(Edmonton)가 언급된 주변을 주의 깊게 듣는다. 대화 초반부에서 여자가 "I just want to check some hotel charges from your trip to Edmonton last month for the conference.(지난달 컨퍼런스를 위한 당신의 에드먼턴 출장에서 발생한 호텔 요금을 좀 확인하고 싶어요.)"라고 하였다. 따라서 (C)가 정답이다.

어휘 competitor n. 경쟁업체　potential adj. 잠재적인

69. 언급 문제
해석 여자는 회사의 여행 경비 정책에 대해 무엇이라 말하는가?
(A) 산업 표준을 따른다.
(B) 숙박 비용만 보상한다.
(C) 지난달에 변경되었다.
(D) 회의에서 설명되었다.

해설 질문의 핵심 어구(travel expenses policy)와 관련된 내용을 주의 깊게 듣는다. 대화 중반부에서 남자가 "Did I exceed the maximum amount for travel expenses?(제가 여행 경비의 한도액을 초과했나요?)"라고 하자, 여자가 "We raised our spending limit to $1,000 last month(우리는 지난달에 1,000달러로 지출 한도를 높였어요)"라고 하였다. 따라서 (C)가 정답이다.

어휘 industry standard 산업 표준　cover v. (비용 등을) 보상하다
accommodation n. 숙박

70. 시각 자료 문제
해석 시각 자료를 보아라. 어느 요금이 부정확한가?
(A) 308달러
(B) 21달러
(C) 24달러
(D) 12달러

해설 청구서의 정보를 확인한 후 질문의 핵심 어구(incorrect)와 관련된 내용을 주의 깊게 듣는다. 대화 후반부에서 여자가 "According to your billing statement, you ate lunch at the hotel on the day of the conference. Is that right?(당신의 대금 청구서에 따르면, 당신은 컨퍼런스 당일에 호텔에서 점심을 드셨어요. 이것이 맞나요?)"라고 하자, 남자가 "No, it isn't. I had lunch at the convention center, not at the hotel.(아니요, 그렇지 않아요. 저는 호텔이 아니라, 컨벤션 센터에서 점심을 먹었어요.)"라고 하였으므로, 점심 요금인 21달러가 부정확함을 청구서에서 알 수 있다. 따라서 (B)가 정답이다.

PART 4

71-73 미국

Questions 71-73 refer to the following podcast.

> ⁷¹In today's episode of Talk of the Town, I'll be discussing an upcoming concert to raise funds for the homeless. My guest is the talented drummer Louise Egan, who will be performing at the show and is one of the organizers. ⁷²If you're interested in supporting this great cause, make sure to get a ticket

soon. I'll provide details about how to do this later. But first, ⁷³Louise has offered to demonstrate a few basic rhythms, including some that are common in Irish folk songs.

upcoming adj. 다가오는   talented adj. 재능 있는
perform v. 공연하다, 연주하다   support v. 지원하다; n. 지원
cause n. 대의, 원인   demonstrate v. 시연하다

해석
71-73번은 다음 팟캐스트에 관한 문제입니다.

⁷¹오늘의 Talk of the Town 에피소드에서, 저는 노숙자들을 위한 모금을 모으는 다가오는 콘서트에 대해 이야기할 것입니다. 제 게스트는 재능 있는 드러머인 Louise Egan인데, 그는 이 쇼에서 공연할 것이고 주최자 중 한 명입니다. ⁷²만약 이 좋은 대의를 지원하는 것에 관심이 있으시다면, 빨리 티켓을 구매하도록 하세요. 저는 이것을 어떻게 할지에 대한 자세한 정보를 나중에 제공하겠습니다. 하지만 먼저, ⁷³Louise는 몇 가지 기본 리듬을 시연해 주기로 했는데, 이는 아일랜드 민속 음악에서 흔히 들을 수 있는 몇 가지를 포함합니다.

71. 주제 문제
해석   팟캐스트의 주제는 무엇인가?
(A) 교육 프로그램
(B) 온라인 서비스
(C) 사업체 개업
(D) 자선 행사

해설   팟캐스트의 주제를 묻는 문제이므로, 지문의 초반을 주의 깊게 듣는다. "In today's episode of Talk of the Town, I'll be discussing an upcoming concert to raise funds for the homeless.(오늘의 Talk of the Town 에피소드에서, 저는 노숙자들을 위한 모금을 모으는 다가오는 콘서트에 대해 이야기할 것입니다.)"라고 한 후, 자선 행사에 대한 내용이 이어지고 있다. 따라서 (D)가 정답이다.

어휘   educational adj. 교육의   charity event 자선 행사

72. 제안 문제
해석   청자들은 무엇을 하도록 권장되는가?
(A) 경연에 참가한다.
(B) 웹사이트를 방문한다.
(C) 표를 산다.
(D) 앱을 다운로드한다.

해설   질문의 핵심 어구(encouraged to do)와 관련된 내용을 주의 깊게 듣는다. 지문 중반부에서 "If you're interested in supporting this great cause, make sure to get a ticket soon.(만약 이 좋은 대의를 지원하는 것에 관심이 있으시다면, 빨리 티켓을 구매하도록 하세요.)"이라고 하였다. 따라서 (C)가 정답이다.

[Paraphrasing]
ticket 티켓 → pass 표

73. 다음에 할 일 문제
해석   다음에 무슨 일이 일어날 것 같은가?
(A) 제품이 검토될 것이다.
(B) 음악가가 연주할 것이다.
(C) 게스트가 질문에 답할 것이다.
(D) 상이 수여될 것이다.

해설   지문의 마지막 부분을 주의 깊게 듣는다. 지문 후반부에서 "Louise has offered to demonstrate a few basic rhythms, including some that are common in Irish folk songs(Louise는 몇 가지 기본 리듬을 시연해 주기로 했는데, 이는 아일랜드 민속 음악에서 흔히 들을 수 있는 몇 가지를 포함합니다)"라고 하였다. 따라서 (B)가 정답이다.

어휘   prize n. 상   award v. 수여하다; n. 상

74-76 영국
Questions 74-76 refer to the following announcement.

⁷⁴Attention all shoppers. Our supermarket is having a special buy-one-get-one-free offer on pints of ice cream. ⁷⁵This applies to all brands and flavors. Tomorrow is the last day, so ⁷⁵make sure you don't miss out. And ⁷⁶don't forget that next Sunday we'll be holding our 10-year anniversary! Various activities will take place in the plaza next to our building, including games for kids. Bring the entire family to celebrate with us!

offer n. 할인; v. 제공하다   brand n. 브랜드, 상표   flavor n. 맛
miss out 좋은 기회를 놓치다   plaza n. 광장

해석
74-76번은 다음 공지에 관한 문제입니다.

⁷⁴쇼핑객 여러분께서는 주목해 주십시오. 저희 슈퍼마켓에서는 파인트 아이스크림에 대해 하나를 사면 하나를 무료로 드리는 특별 할인을 진행하고 있습니다. ⁷⁵이것은 모든 브랜드와 맛에 적용됩니다. 내일이 마지막 날이므로, ⁷⁵좋은 기회를 놓치지 않도록 하세요. 그리고 ⁷⁶다음 주 일요일에 저희가 10주년 기념 행사를 개최할 것이라는 점을 잊지 말아 주세요! 아이들을 위한 게임을 포함하여 다양한 활동들이 저희 건물 옆의 광장에서 열릴 것입니다. 저희와 함께 기념하기 위해 모든 가족분들을 모셔 오세요!

74. 장소 문제
해석   청자들은 어디에 있는 것 같은가?
(A) 패스트푸드 음식점에
(B) 영화관에
(C) 슈퍼마켓에
(D) 주유소에

해설   장소와 관련된 표현을 놓치지 않고 듣는다. 지문 초반부에서 "Attention all shoppers. Our supermarket is having a special buy-one-get-one-free offer(쇼핑객 여러분께서는 주목해 주십시오. 저희 슈퍼마켓에서는 하나를 사면 하나를 무료로 드리는 특별 할인을 진행하고 있습니다)"라고 한 것을 통해, 청자들이 슈퍼마켓에 있음을 알 수 있다. 따라서 (C)가 정답이다.

어휘   movie theater 영화관   gas station 주유소

75. 의도 파악 문제
해설   화자가 "내일이 마지막 날이므로"라고 말할 때 무엇을 의도하는가?
(A) 우승자가 곧 발표될 것이다.
(B) 몇몇 제품들이 빨리 구매되어야 한다.
(C) 가게가 영업시간을 변경할 것이다.
(D) 몇몇 견본들이 여전히 이용 가능하다.

해설   질문의 인용어구(Tomorrow is the last day)가 언급된 주변을 주의 깊게 듣는다. 지문 중반부에서 "This[a special ~ offer] applies to all brands and flavors.(이것은 모든 브랜드와 맛에 적용됩니다.)"라고 했고, 내일이 마지막 날이라며 "make sure you don't miss out(좋은 기회를 놓치지 않도록

하세요)"이라고 하였으므로, 몇몇 제품들이 빨리 구매되어야 한다는 의도임을 알 수 있다. 따라서 (B)가 정답이다.

어휘 winner n. 우승자 before long 곧 soon adv. 빨리, 곧

76. 다음에 할 일 문제

해석 화자에 따르면, 다음 주 일요일에 무슨 일이 일어날 것인가?
(A) 몇몇 활동들이 열릴 것이다.
(B) 가게가 다시 개점할 것이다.
(C) 몇몇 상이 수여될 것이다.
(D) 평가가 시작될 것이다.

해설 질문의 핵심 어구(next Sunday)가 언급된 주변을 주의 깊게 듣는다. 지문 후반부에서 "don't forget that next Sunday we'll be holding our 10-year anniversary! Various activities will take place(다음 주 일요일에 저희가 10주년 기념 행사를 개최할 것이라는 점을 잊지 말아 주세요! 다양한 활동들이 열릴 것입니다)"라고 하였다. 따라서 (A)가 정답이다.

어휘 evaluation n. 평가

77-79 [3w] 캐나다

Questions 77-79 refer to the following instruction.

> ⁷⁷I would like to demonstrate to everyone here in our department the operation of our office's new security system. You may need to turn it on or off in the future, so you should know how to use it properly. ⁷⁹When you leave the building, ⁷⁸you must type a five-digit code into this control panel to activate the system. The alarm will turn on after the door has been locked. Once the system has been set, the alarm will ring if the door is opened. So, ⁷⁹please walk through the building to make sure there aren't any staff still inside before you type in the code.
>
> operation n. 작동 security system 보안 시스템
> properly adv. 제대로 code n. 암호 control panel 제어판
> activate v. 작동시키다

해석
77-79번은 다음 설명에 관한 문제입니다.

⁷⁷여기 계신 우리 부서 모든 분들께 사무실의 새로운 보안 시스템의 작동을 시연해드리겠습니다. 장차 여러분은 이것을 켜거나 꺼야 할 수도 있기 때문에, 제대로 사용하는 방법을 아셔야 합니다. ⁷⁹건물을 떠날 때, ⁷⁸시스템을 작동시키기 위해 이 제어판에 다섯 자리 숫자 암호를 입력하셔야 합니다. 문이 잠긴 후 알람이 켜질 것입니다. 시스템이 설정되면, 문이 열릴 경우 알람이 울릴 것입니다. 그러므로, ⁷⁹암호를 입력하기 전에 건물을 둘러보면서 아직 안에 있는 직원이 없는지 반드시 확인하시기 바랍니다.

77. 청자 문제

해석 청자들은 누구인 것 같은가?
(A) 사무실 직원들
(B) 프로그램 디자이너들
(C) 설치 전문가들
(D) 유지보수 작업자들

해설 지문에서 신분 및 직업과 관련된 표현을 놓치지 않고 듣는다. 지문 초반부에서 "I would like to demonstrate to everyone here in our department the operation of our office's new security system.(여기 계신 우리 부서 모든 분들께 사무실의 새로운 보안 시스템의 작동을 시연해드리겠습니다.)"이라고 하였다. 따라서 (A)가 정답이다.

어휘 personnel n. 직원 installation n. 설치
specialist n. 전문가

78. 특정 세부 사항 문제

해석 화자에 따르면, 시스템을 작동시키기 위해 무엇이 되어야 하는가?
(A) 지문이 스캔되어야 한다.
(B) 스위치가 눌러져야 한다.
(C) 암호가 입력되어야 한다.
(D) 컴퓨터가 켜져야 한다.

해설 질문의 핵심 어구(activate the system)가 언급된 주변을 주의 깊게 듣는다. 지문 중반부에서 "you must type a five-digit code into this control panel to activate the system(시스템을 작동시키기 위해 이 제어판에 다섯 자리 숫자 암호를 입력하셔야 합니다)"이라고 하였다. 따라서 (C)가 정답이다.

어휘 fingerprint n. 지문 flip v. (스위치를) 누르다
enter v. 입력하다, 들어가다

[Paraphrasing]
must type a ~ code 암호를 입력해야 한다 → A code needs to be entered 암호가 입력되어야 한다

79. 특정 세부 사항 문제

해석 청자들은 건물을 떠나기 전에 무엇을 해야 하는가?
(A) 보안 허가를 얻는다.
(B) 건물이 비어 있는지 확인한다.
(C) 제어판을 끈다.
(D) 반드시 근무 중인 직원이 있도록 한다.

해설 질문의 핵심 어구(before ~ leave the building)와 관련된 내용을 주의 깊게 듣는다. "When you leave the building, you must type a ~ code(건물을 떠날 때, 암호를 입력하셔야 합니다)"라고 한 뒤 "please ~ make sure there aren't any staff still inside before you type in the code(암호를 입력하기 전에 아직 안에 있는 직원이 없는지 반드시 확인하시기 바랍니다)"라고 하였다. 따라서 (B)가 정답이다.

어휘 obtain v. 얻다 verify v. 확인하다 ensure v. 반드시 ~하다
on duty 근무 중

80-82 [3w] 호주

Questions 80-82 refer to the following telephone message.

> I'm calling for Michael Garcia. My name is Greg Barnum, and ⁸⁰I'm the art director at Blue Stream Books. I'd like to hire you to make the illustrations for some of our firm's book covers. ⁸¹I found examples of your drawings on your blog. Your portfolio is really impressive, and the style is perfect for our books. If you are interested in doing some work for us, please contact me at 555-2987. ⁸²I'm more than happy to meet you to talk in my office. Thank you.
>
> illustration n. 삽화 impressive adj. 인상적인

해석
80-82번은 다음 전화 메시지에 관한 문제입니다.

저는 Michael Garcia에게 전화드립니다. 제 이름은 Greg Barnum이고, ⁸⁰Blue Stream Books사의 미술 책임자입니다. 저희 회사의 책 표지들 중 몇몇에 대한 삽화를 제작하기 위해 당신을 고용하고 싶습니다. ⁸¹저는 당신의 블로그에서 당신 그림의 예시들을 발견했습니다. 당신의 포트폴리오는 매우 인상적이고, 스타일은 저희 책에 완벽합니다. 만약 당신께서 저희를 위해 작업을 하시는 데 관심이 있으시다면, 제게 555-2987로 연락해 주세요. ⁸²기꺼이 제 사무실에서 당신과 만나 이야기를 나누고 싶습니다. 감사합니다.

80. 화자 문제
해석 화자는 어느 업계에서 일하는 것 같은가?
(A) 패션
(B) 광고
(C) 건축
(D) 출판

해설 지문에서 신분 및 직업과 관련된 표현을 놓치지 않고 듣는다. 지문 초반부에서 "I'm the art director at Blue Stream Books. I'd like to hire you to make the illustrations for some of our firm's book covers.(저는 Blue Stream Books사의 미술 책임자입니다. 저희 회사의 책 표지들 중 몇몇에 대한 삽화를 제작하기 위해 당신을 고용하고 싶습니다.)"라고 한 것을 통해, 화자가 출판 업계에서 일하는 것을 알 수 있다. 따라서 (D)가 정답이다.

어휘 architecture n. 건축 publishing n. 출판

81. 특정 세부 사항 문제
해석 화자는 어떻게 청자에 대해 알게 되었는가?
(A) TV쇼를 봄으로써
(B) 웹사이트를 방문함으로써
(C) 팟캐스트를 들음으로써
(D) 잡지를 읽음으로써

해설 질문의 핵심 어구(learn about the listener)와 관련된 내용을 주의 깊게 듣는다. 지문 중반부에서 "I found examples of your drawings on your blog.(저는 당신의 블로그에서 당신 그림의 예시들을 발견했어요.)"라고 했으므로 화자가 웹사이트를 방문했다는 것을 알 수 있다. 따라서 (B)가 정답이다.

82. 제안 문제
해석 화자는 무엇을 해 주겠다고 제안하는가?
(A) 추천을 한다.
(B) 몇몇 미술품을 제출한다.
(C) 그의 사무실에서 만난다.
(D) 계약을 연장한다.

해설 제안과 관련된 표현이 포함된 문장을 주의 깊게 듣는다. 지문의 중후반에서 "I'm more than happy to meet you to talk in my office.(기꺼이 제 사무실에서 당신과 만나 이야기를 나누고 싶습니다.)"라고 하였다. 따라서 (C)가 정답이다.

83-85 미국
Questions 83-85 refer to the following broadcast.

And now for our local business news. ⁸³The Minneapolis-based electronics firm DigitalSolar Incorporated announced its plans to merge with technology start-up GoTech. DigitalSolar was founded just five years ago. At the time, ⁸⁴many experts did not believe it would last more than a couple of years. However, those predictions have been proven wrong. To increase its product offerings, the company has now decided to expand. ⁸⁵Damien Crenshaw, CEO of DigitalSolar, discussed the proposal with executives from GoTech last week, at which point a deal was made. Financial details of the deal are expected to be released soon.

merge v. 합병하다 start-up n. 신생기업
last v. 존속하다, 유지되다 prediction n. 예측
prove v. 판명되다 offering n. 제공 executive n. 경영진
release v. 발표하다, 출시하다

해석
83-85번은 다음 방송에 관한 문제입니다.
자, 이제 우리 지역 산업 뉴스입니다. ⁸³미니애폴리스에 위치한 전자 회사인 DigitalSolar사는 기술 신생기업인 GoTech사와 합병할 계획을 발표했습니다. DigitalSolar사는 5년 전에 설립되었습니다. 그 당시, ⁸⁴많은 전문가들은 이것이 2년 이상 존속할 것이라고 믿지 않았습니다. 하지만, 그러한 예측들은 잘못된 것으로 판명되었습니다. 제품 제공을 늘리기 위해, 이 회사는 이제 확장하기로 결정했습니다. ⁸⁵DigitalSolar사의 최고 경영자인 Damien Crenshaw는 지난주 GoTech사의 경영진과 합병 제안에 관해 논의했으며, 이때 계약이 이루어졌습니다. 계약의 재정적인 세부 사항은 곧 발표될 것으로 예상됩니다.

83. 주제 문제
해석 방송은 주로 무엇에 관한 것인가?
(A) 기자 회견
(B) 기업 합병
(C) 채용 공고
(D) 제품 출시

해설 방송의 주제를 묻는 문제이므로, 지문의 초반을 주의 깊게 듣는다. "The Minneapolis-based electronics firm DigitalSolar Incorporated announced its plans to merge with technology start-up GoTech.(미니애폴리스에 위치한 전자 회사인 DigitalSolar사는 기술 신생기업인 GoTech사와 합병할 계획을 발표했습니다.)"라고 한 후, 기업 합병에 대한 내용으로 지문이 이어지고 있다. 따라서 (B)가 정답이다.

어휘 press conference 기자 회견 hiring n. 채용

84. 의도 파악 문제
해석 화자가 "그러한 예측들은 잘못된 것으로 판명되었습니다"라고 말할 때, 무엇을 의도하는가?
(A) 회사가 예상보다 잘 해냈다.
(B) 고객들이 서비스에 불만족했다.
(C) 전자기기가 일찍 출시되었다.
(D) 투자자들이 결정에 동의했다.

해설 질문의 인용어구(those predictions have been proven wrong)가 언급된 주변을 주의 깊게 듣는다. 지문 중반부에서 "many experts did not believe it would last more than a couple of years(많은 전문가들은 이것[DigitalSolar사]이 2년 이상 존속할 것이라고 믿지 않았습니다)"라고 한 후, 그러한 예측들은 잘못된 것으로 판명되었다고 한 것을 통해 회사가 예상보다 잘 해냈다는 것을 알 수 있다. 따라서 (A)가 정답이다.

어휘 perform v. 해내다, 수행하다
be displeased with ~에 불만족하다

85. 특정 세부 사항 문제

해석 Damien Crenshaw는 지난주에 무엇을 했는가?
(A) 새로운 회사에 들어갔다.
(B) 몇몇 기자들과 얘기했다.
(C) 기업 지도자들과 만났다.
(D) 마케팅 캠페인을 이끌었다.

해설 질문의 핵심 어구(Damien Crenshaw)가 언급된 주변을 주의 깊게 듣는다. 지문 후반부에서 "Damien Crenshaw, CEO of DigitalSolar, discussed the proposal with executives from GoTech last week, at which point a deal was made.(DigitalSolar사의 최고 경영자인 Damien Crenshaw는 지난주 GoTech사의 경영진과 합병 제안에 관해 논의했으며, 이때 계약이 이루어졌습니다.)"라고 한 것을 통해 Damien Crenshaw가 지난주에 기업 지도자들과 만났다는 것을 알 수 있다. 따라서 (C)가 정답이다.

86-88 [캐나다]

Questions 86-88 refer to the following talk.

> Thank you for attending the Corbyn Film Festival. ⁸⁶Although this is our organization's first festival, we hope to hold many more in the future. Over the course of the next three days, 20 films from around the world will be screened, including ones that have received recognition at other major festivals. Moreover, we are pleased to inform everyone that we will be joined by legendary director Luke Norris. ⁸⁷Mr. Norris, whose documentary *White Lines* will air this evening, has graciously offered to respond to questions during a meet and greet at 8 P.M. And ⁸⁸feel free to head to the festival booth at any point to purchase festival merchandise and film-related souvenirs.
>
> attend v. 참석하다 recognition n. 인정, 인지
> legendary adj. 전설적인 graciously adv. 감사하게, 관대하게
> meet and greet 팬미팅, 만남과 대화의 행사
> merchandise n. 상품 souvenir n. 기념품

해석
86-88번은 다음 담화에 관한 문제입니다.

Corbyn 영화제에 참석해 주셔서 감사합니다. ⁸⁶이번이 우리 단체의 첫 축제이지만, 저희는 미래에 더 많이 개최하기를 바랍니다. 다음 3일 동안, 다른 주요 영화제들에서 인정을 받았던 영화들을 포함하여, 전 세계 20편의 영화들이 상영될 것입니다. 게다가, 전설적인 감독 Luke Norris가 저희와 함께할 것이라는 것을 여러분께 알려드리게 되어 기쁩니다. 오늘 저녁에 방영될 다큐멘터리 *White Lines*의 감독인 ⁸⁷Mr. Norris는 감사하게도 오후 8시에 팬미팅 중 질문들에 응답하기로 하였습니다. 그리고 ⁸⁸축제 상품과 영화와 관련된 기념품을 사기 위해 언제든 축제 부스로 오십시오.

86. 언급 문제

해석 화자는 Corbyn 영화제에 관해 무엇을 말하는가?
(A) 4일에 걸쳐 열릴 것이다.
(B) 특정 장르에 집중한다.
(C) 널리 홍보가 되었다.
(D) 이전에 열린 적이 없었다.

해설 질문의 핵심 어구(Corbyn Film Festival)와 관련된 내용을 주의 깊게 듣는다. 지문 초반부에서 "Although this[Corbyn Film Festival] is our organization's first festival, we hope to hold many more in the future.(이번이 우리 단체의 첫 축제이지만, 저희는 미래에 더 많이 개최하기를 바랍니다.)"라고 하였다. 따라서 (D)가 정답이다.

어휘 specific adj. 특정한, 구체적인 publicize v. 홍보하다

87. 특정 세부 사항 문제

해석 화자에 따르면, 오후 8시에 무엇이 열릴 것인가?
(A) 다큐멘터리 영화 상영
(B) 질문 응답 시간
(C) 비공개 파티
(D) 시상식

해설 질문의 핵심 어구(take place at 8 P.M.)와 관련된 내용을 주의 깊게 듣는다. 지문 중반부에서 "Mr. Norris ~ has graciously offered to respond to questions during a meet and greet at 8 P.M.(Mr. Norris는 감사하게도 오후 8시에 팬미팅 중 질문들에 응답하기로 하였습니다.)"이라고 하였다. 따라서 (B)가 정답이다.

어휘 private adj. 비공개의, 사적인

88. 이유 문제

해석 청자들은 왜 축제 부스를 방문해야 하는가?
(A) 출연진과 사진을 찍기 위해
(B) 몇몇 물품을 구매하기 위해
(C) 변경된 일정을 보기 위해
(D) 영화 선택지를 살펴보기 위해

해설 질문의 핵심 어구(festival booth)가 언급된 주변을 주의 깊게 듣는다. 지문 후반부에서 "feel free to head to the festival booth at any point to purchase festival merchandise and film-related souvenirs(축제 상품과 영화와 관련된 기념품을 사기 위해 언제든 축제 부스로 오십시오)"라고 하였다. 따라서 (B)가 정답이다.

어휘 cast n. 출연진 option n. 선택지

89-91 [호주]

Questions 89-91 refer to the following telephone message.

> Hey, Lisa. It's Matthew calling. ⁸⁹The date of the Cleveland Marathon was just announced, and I really think you should sign up for it. As you've been training really hard, you are ready for your first marathon. ⁹⁰If you'd like to participate, you can go to their Web site and check the course route. I've already signed up, and I plan on driving down there the night before. You can ride with me if you want. ⁹¹Just let me know your decision by the end of the month.
>
> sign up for ~을 신청하다 train v. 훈련하다
> plan on ~할 계획이다

해석
89-91번은 다음 전화 메시지에 관한 문제입니다.

안녕하세요, Lisa. 저 Matthew예요. ⁸⁹클리블랜드 마라톤의 날짜가 막 발표되었고, 저는 당신이 그것을 신청해야 한다고 생각해요. 당신

은 정말 열심히 훈련해 왔으니, 당신의 첫 마라톤을 위해 준비되었어요. ⁹⁰참여하고 싶으시다면, 웹사이트에 가서 코스 경로를 확인하실 수 있어요. 저는 이미 신청했고, 전날 밤에 그곳으로 운전해서 갈 계획이에요. 원하시면 저와 함께 타고 가셔도 돼요. ⁹¹이번 달 말까지 당신의 결정을 제게 알려주세요.

89. 목적 문제
해석 화자는 왜 전화를 하고 있는가?
(A) 행사 참여를 장려하기 위해
(B) 프로젝트에 대한 정보를 제공하기 위해
(C) 실적에 대해 피드백을 주기 위해
(D) 성취에 대해 칭찬을 하기 위해

해설 전화 메시지의 목적을 묻는 문제이므로, 지문의 초반을 주의 깊게 듣는다. "The date of the Cleveland Marathon was just announced, and I really think you should sign up for it.(클리블랜드 마라톤의 날짜가 막 발표되었고, 저는 당신이 그것을 신청해야 한다고 생각해요.)"이라고 하였다. 이를 통해, 행사 참여를 장려하기 위해 전화했음을 알 수 있다. 따라서 (A)가 정답이다.

어휘 encourage v. 장려하다, 격려하다 performance n. 실적
achievement n. 성취

90. 특정 세부 사항 문제
해석 화자는 청자가 온라인에서 무엇을 찾을 수 있다고 말하는가?
(A) 체육관 주소
(B) 버스 시간표
(C) 코스 경로
(D) 표 가격

해설 질문의 핵심 어구(find online)와 관련된 내용을 주의 깊게 듣는다. 지문 중반부에서 "If you'd like to participate, you can go to their Web site and check the course route.(참여하고 싶으시다면, 웹사이트에 가서 코스 경로를 확인하실 수 있어요.)"라고 하였다. 따라서 (C)가 정답이다.

어휘 gym n. 체육관, 헬스장 timetable n. 시간표

91. 요청 문제
해석 청자는 무엇을 하도록 요청받는가?
(A) 참가비를 지불한다.
(B) 신청서를 가져온다.
(C) 결정을 알려준다.
(D) 차량을 빌린다.

해설 요청과 관련된 표현이 포함된 문장을 주의 깊게 듣는다. 지문의 중후반에서 "Just let me know your decision by the end of the month.(이번 달 말까지 당신의 결정을 제게 알려주세요.)"라고 하였다. 따라서 (C)가 정답이다.

92-94 [3w] 영국
Questions 92-94 refer to the following introduction.

It's my pleasure to introduce the recipient of the Purlin Citizen of the Year Award, Haley Cobb. ⁹²Ms. Cobb has been awarded this honor thanks to her volunteer work in the city. ⁹²/⁹³In particular, she has been helping people in need find housing through her organization, Housing Connection. The results have been quite surprising. ⁹³In 10 years, the group has arranged permanent housing for over 3,000 people. Now, ⁹⁴please join me in welcoming Ms. Cobb up here on the stage. She'd like to say a few things.

recipient n. 수상자 in particular 특히 in need 도움이 필요한
find v. 마련하다, 찾다 housing n. 주택
permanent adj. 영구적인

해석 92-94번은 다음 소개에 관한 문제입니다.
올해의 Purlin 시민상의 수상자인 Haley Cobb을 소개하게 되어 기쁩니다. ⁹²Ms. Cobb은 도시 내에서의 자원봉사 활동 덕분에 이 영예를 수상하게 되었습니다. ⁹²/⁹³특히, 그녀는 자신의 단체인 Housing Connection을 통해 도움이 필요한 사람들이 주택을 마련하도록 도와주었습니다. 결과는 꽤 놀라웠습니다. ⁹³10년 동안, 이 단체는 3,000명이 넘는 사람들에게 영구적인 주택을 마련해 주었습니다. 이제, ⁹⁴Ms. Cobb을 여기 무대로 함께 맞이해 주십시오. 그녀가 몇 가지를 이야기하고 싶어 합니다.

92. 이유 문제
해석 Haley Cobb은 왜 상을 받는가?
(A) 도시의 공공장소를 청소했다.
(B) 자원봉사자들에게 교육을 제공했다.
(C) 사람들이 주택을 마련하도록 도왔다.
(D) 모금 캠페인을 계획했다.

해설 질문의 핵심 어구(Haley Cobb)가 언급된 주변을 주의 깊게 듣는다. 지문 초반부에서 "Ms. Cobb has been awarded this honor thanks to her volunteer work ~. In particular, she has been helping people in need find housing(Ms. Cobb은 자원봉사 활동 덕분에 이 영예를 수상하게 되었습니다. 특히, 그녀는 도움이 필요한 사람들이 주택을 마련하도록 도와주었습니다)"이라고 한 것을 통해, Haley Cobb이 사람들이 주택을 마련하도록 도왔기 때문에 상을 받는다는 것을 알 수 있다. 따라서 (C)가 정답이다.

어휘 public area 공공장소 fundraising n. 모금

93. 의도 파악 문제
해석 화자는 왜 "결과는 꽤 놀라웠습니다"라고 말하는가?
(A) 단체의 성공을 높이 평가하기 위해
(B) 정부 정책이 인기 있음을 시사하기 위해
(C) 연구의 결과를 강조하기 위해
(D) 예상치 못한 어려움에 대한 충격을 표현하기 위해

해설 질문의 인용어구(The results have been quite surprising)가 언급된 주변을 주의 깊게 듣는다. 지문의 중반부에서 "In particular, she has been helping people in need find housing through her organization, Housing Connection.(특히, 그녀는 자신의 단체인 Housing Connection을 통해 도움이 필요한 사람들이 주택을 마련하도록 도와주었습니다.)"이라고 한 후, 결과는 꽤 놀라웠다며 "In 10 years, the group has arranged permanent housing for over 3,000 people.(10년 동안, 이 단체는 3,000명이 넘는 사람들에게 영구적인 주택을 마련해 주었습니다.)"이라고 한 것을 통해, 단체의 성공을 높이 평가하기 위함임을 알 수 있다. 따라서 (A)가 정답이다.

어휘 praise v. 높이 평가하다 emphasize v. 강조하다
applaud v. 칭찬하다, 성원하다

94. 다음에 할 일 문제
해석 Ms. Cobb은 다음에 무엇을 할 것 같은가?

(A) 훈련을 주도한다.
(B) 영상을 보여준다.
(C) 수상자를 호명한다.
(D) 연설을 한다.

해설 지문의 마지막 부분을 주의 깊게 듣는다. "please join me in welcoming Ms. Cobb up here on the stage. She'd like to say a few things.(Ms. Cobb을 여기 무대로 함께 맞이해 주십시오. 그녀가 몇 가지를 이야기하고 싶어 합니다.)"라고 하였다. 따라서 (D)가 정답이다.

어휘 name v. 호명하다, 지명하다

Paraphrasing
say a few things 몇 가지를 이야기하다 → Give a speech 연설을 하다

95-97 미국

Questions 95-97 refer to the following announcement and menu.

I've got a couple of updates to share with you all regarding the daily special menu. ⁹⁵First, there was a problem with our food shipment today. Some packages of ingredients were torn open and will need to be returned. So, ⁹⁶we aren't going to be able to serve tonight's appetizer. Instead, we will be serving a mushroom soup. Please let guests know of the change when you hand them their menus. Also, ⁹⁷once guests arrive, be sure to offer to take their umbrellas and coats. Remember to give them tags so they can get their belongings later.

shipment n. 수송, 배송 serve v. 제공하다
belongings n. 소지품

해석
95-97번은 다음 공지와 메뉴에 관한 문제입니다.
저는 일일 특별 메뉴에 관해 여러분 모두와 공유할 몇 가지 최신 정보가 있습니다. ⁹⁵먼저, 오늘 우리의 식품 수송에 문제가 있었습니다. 몇몇 재료의 포장이 찢어져서 환불되어야 할 것입니다. 따라서, ⁹⁶우리는 오늘 밤의 애피타이저를 제공할 수 없을 것입니다. 대신, 우리는 버섯 수프를 제공할 것입니다. 손님들께 메뉴를 전해드릴 때 이 변경 사항에 대해 알려주세요. 또한, ⁹⁷손님들이 도착하시면, 반드시 그들의 우산과 외투를 받아드리겠다고 제안해 주세요. 나중에 그들이 소지품을 받을 수 있도록 꼬리표를 드리는 것을 기억해 주세요.

Regan's 식당
일일 특별 메뉴

• 애피타이저 •
⁹⁶게살 롤

• 샐러드 •
그리스식 샐러드

• 주요리 •
양고기
또는
밥을 곁들인 구운 채소

• 후식 •
초콜릿 케이크

95. 문제점 문제
해석 화자는 무슨 문제를 언급하는가?
(A) 가격이 너무 비싸다.
(B) 요청이 거절되었다.
(C) 몇몇 상품이 매진되었다.
(D) 몇몇 제품이 손상되었다.

해설 화자의 말에서 부정적인 표현이 언급된 다음을 주의 깊게 듣는다. 지문 초반부에서 "First, there was a problem with our food shipment today. Some packages of ingredients were torn open and will need to be returned.(먼저, 오늘 우리의 식품 수송에 문제가 있었습니다. 몇몇 재료의 포장이 찢어져서 환불되어야 할 것입니다.)"라고 하였다. 따라서 (D)가 정답이다.

96. 시각 자료 문제
해석 시각 자료를 보아라. 어느 제품이 제공되지 않을 것인가?
(A) 게살 롤
(B) 그리스식 샐러드
(C) 양고기
(D) 초콜릿 케이크

해설 메뉴의 정보를 확인한 후 질문의 핵심 어구(not be served)와 관련된 내용을 주의 깊게 듣는다. 지문 중반부에서 "we aren't going to be able to serve tonight's appetizer(우리는 오늘 밤의 애피타이저를 제공할 수 없을 것입니다)"라고 하였으므로, 애피타이저인 게살 롤이 제공되지 않을 것임을 메뉴에서 알 수 있다. 따라서 (A)가 정답이다.

97. 특정 세부 사항 문제
해석 청자들은 손님들에게 무엇을 해 주겠다고 제안해야 하는가?
(A) 그들의 차량을 주차한다.
(B) 몇몇 물품들을 받는다.
(C) 예약을 한다.
(D) 샘플들을 나눠준다.

해설 질문의 핵심 어구(guests)가 언급된 주변을 주의 깊게 듣는다. 지문 후반부에서 "once guests arrive, be sure to offer to take their umbrellas and coats(손님들이 도착하시면, 반드시 그들의 우산과 외투를 받아드리겠다고 제안해 주세요)"라고 하였다. 따라서 (B)가 정답이다.

어휘 vehicle n. 차량 distribute v. 나누어 주다

Paraphrasing
umbrellas and coats 우산과 외투 → some items 몇몇 물품들

98-100 캐나다

Questions 98-100 refer to the following advertisement and product list.

MainActive Fashions is the world's best-selling athletic footwear brand. ⁹⁸We have just released our newest product. These new shoes allow for easy and comfortable movement. The secret behind their performance is the stringless design, making them easier to put on and take off than competing products. And don't miss our special event. On June 30, ⁹⁹tennis player Jackson Warner will sign pairs for 100 customers at Rushburn City Mall from 3 P.M. to 5 P.M. ¹⁰⁰Sign up for this on our

mobile application as soon as you can.
best-selling adj. 가장 잘 팔리는 **athletic footwear** 운동화
movement n. 움직임 **performance** n. 성능
competing product 경쟁 제품

해석
98-100번은 다음 광고와 제품 목록에 관한 문제입니다.
MainActive Fashions사는 세계에서 가장 잘 팔리는 운동화 브랜드입니다. ⁹⁸저희는 막 최신 제품을 출시했습니다. 이 새로운 신발은 쉽고 편안한 움직임을 가능하게 합니다. 그것들의 성능에 숨겨진 비결은 끈 없는 디자인으로, 경쟁 제품들보다 그것들을 신고 벗는 것을 더 쉽게 만듭니다. 그리고 저희의 특별 행사를 놓치지 마세요. 6월 30일에, ⁹⁹테니스 선수인 Jackson Warner가 Rushborn City몰에서 오후 3시부터 오후 5시까지 100명의 손님들을 위해 신발에 사인할 겁니다. ¹⁰⁰저희 모바일 앱에서 가능한 한 빨리 이것을 신청하세요.

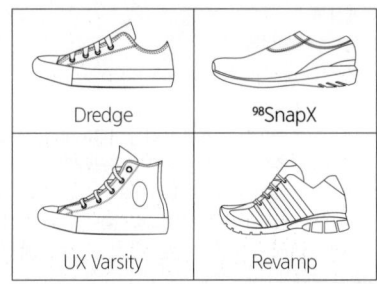

Dredge ⁹⁸SnapX
UX Varsity Revamp

98. 시각 자료 문제
해석 시각 자료를 보아라. 무엇이 최근에 출시된 제품인가?
(A) Dredge
(B) SnapX
(C) UX Varsity
(D) Revamp

해설 제품 목록의 정보를 확인한 후 질문의 핵심 어구(recently released)와 관련된 내용을 주의 깊게 듣는다. 지문 초중반부에서 "We have just released our newest product.(저희는 막 최신 제품을 출시했습니다.)"라고 한 후, "These new shoes allow for easy and comfortable movement. The secret behind their performance is the stringless design(이 새로운 신발은 쉽고 편안한 움직임을 가능하게 합니다. 그것들의 성능에 숨겨진 비결은 끈 없는 디자인입니다)"이라고 한 것을 통해, 끈 없는 디자인의 SnapX가 최근에 출시된 제품임을 제품 목록에서 알 수 있다. 따라서 (B)가 정답이다.

99. 특정 세부 사항 문제
해석 Jackson Warner는 누구인가?
(A) 신발 디자이너
(B) 판매원
(C) 가게 소유주
(D) 운동선수

해설 질문의 핵심 어구(Jackson Warner)가 언급된 주변을 주의 깊게 듣는다. 지문 중반부에서 "tennis player Jackson Warner(테니스 선수인 Jackson Warner)"라고 하였다. 따라서 (D)가 정답이다.

어휘 **salesperson** n. 판매원 **athlete** n. 운동선수

100. 특정 세부 사항 문제
해석 화자는 청자들에게 모바일 어플리케이션에서 무엇을 하라고 권장하는가?
(A) 쿠폰을 다운로드한다.

(B) 가게 위치를 찾는다.
(C) 행사에 신청한다.
(D) 제품 목록을 본다.

해설 질문의 핵심 어구(on ~ mobile application)가 언급된 주변을 주의 깊게 듣는다. 지문 후반부에서 "Sign up for this[tennis player Jackson Warner will sign pairs] on our mobile application as soon as you can.(저희 모바일 앱에서 가능한 한 빨리 이것[테니스 선수인 Jackson Warner가 신발에 사인할 겁니다]을 신청하세요.)"이라고 하였다. 따라서 (C)가 정답이다.

PART 5

101. 조동사 다음에 동사원형 채우기
해석 훌륭한 발표자들은 대개 사람들의 기분을 감지할 수 있고 그에 따라 그들의 말투를 바꿀 수 있다.

해설 조동사(can) 다음에 올 수 있는 것은 동사원형이므로 동사원형 (A) sense가 정답이다. 동사 또는 과거분사 (B), 동명사 또는 현재분사 (C), 부사 (D)는 조동사 다음의 동사원형 자리에 올 수 없다.

어휘 **mood** n. 기분, 분위기 **tone** n. 말투, 어조
accordingly adv. 그에 따라 **sense** v. 감지하다; n. 감각
sensibly adv. 현명하게, 현저히

102. 격에 맞는 인칭대명사 채우기
해석 Ms. Paget의 항공편은 월요일 밤이 되어서야 도착해서, 그녀는 회의가 일정이 바뀌도록 요청했다.

해설 so로 시작하는 절(so ~ rescheduled)에 동사(asked)만 있고 주어가 없으므로 주어 자리에 올 수 있는 소유대명사 (C)와 주격 인칭대명사 (D)가 정답의 후보이다. '그녀는 회의가 일정이 바뀌도록 요청했다'라는 문맥이므로 주격 인칭대명사 (D) she(그녀)가 정답이다. 소유대명사 (C)를 쓸 경우 '그녀의 것은 회의가 일정이 바뀌도록 요청했다'라는 어색한 문맥이 된다. 목적격 인칭대명사 (A)와 재귀대명사 (B)는 주어 자리에 올 수 없다.

어휘 **flight** n. 항공편, 비행

103. to 부정사의 in order to 채우기
해석 Hartman Motors사는 경쟁력을 유지하기 위해 그것의 차량 가격들을 상당히 낮추었다.

해설 이 문장은 주어(Hartman Motors), 동사(lowered), 목적어(its ~ prices)를 갖춘 완전한 절이므로, _____ ~ competitive는 수식어 거품으로 보아야 한다. 따라서 수식어 거품을 이끌 수 있는 모든 보기가 정답의 후보이다. 이 수식어 거품은 동사(stay)만 있고 주어가 없으며 '경쟁력을 유지하기 위해'라는 의미가 되어야 하므로, 목적을 나타내는 to 부정사를 만들기 위해 동사원형(stay) 앞에 to가 와야 한다. 따라서 목적을 나타내는 to 부정사 대신 쓸 수 있는 (C) in order to(~하기 위해)가 정답이다. 부사절 접속사 (A)는 뒤에 주어와 동사를 갖춘 완전한 절이 와야 한다. 전치사 (B)와 (D)는 뒤에 명사가 와야 한다. 참고로, to 부정사가 목적을 나타낼 때는 to 대신 in order to를 쓸 수 있음을 알아 둔다.

어휘 **lower** v. 낮추다 **significantly** adv. 상당히
now that ~이므로 **on account of** ~ 때문에
in spite of ~에도 불구하고

104. 형용사 어휘 고르기
해석 과일과 채소는 신선도를 유지하고 유통기한을 연장하기 위해 이상적인 저장 조건을 필요로 한다.

해설 '신선도를 유지하고 유통기한을 연장하기 위해 이상적인 저장 조건을 필요로 한다'라는 문맥이므로 (B) ideal(이상적인)이 정답이다. (A) low는 '낮은', (C) visible은 '눈에 보이는', (D) sincere는 '진실된'이라는 의미이다.

어휘 storage condition 저장 조건 preserve v. 유지하다
shelf life 유통기한

105. 올바른 시제의 동사 채우기
해석 합병은 지난 2년 동안 협상되어 왔지만, 곧 완료될 것 같다.

해설 but 앞의 절(The merger ~ years)에 주어(The merger)만 있고 동사가 없으므로 동사 (B), (C), (D)가 정답의 후보이다. 현재완료를 나타내는 시간 표현(for the past two years)이 있으므로 과거에 발생한 일이 현재까지 영향을 미치거나 방금 완료된 것을 표현할 때 사용되는 현재완료 시제 (B) has been이 정답이다. 미래 시제 (C)와 현재진행 시제 (D)는 현재완료 시간 표현과 함께 쓰일 수 없다. to 부정사 (A)는 동사 자리에 올 수 없다.

어휘 merger n. 합병 negotiation n. 협상
close to 곧 ~할 것 같은, ~에 가까운 conclude v. 완료하다

106. 태에 맞는 동사 채우기
해석 Greenvale 병원의 많은 자선 프로그램들은 넉넉한 보조금으로 지원되고 있다.

해설 문장에 동사가 없으므로 동사 (A)와 (D)가 정답의 후보이다. 복수 주어(Many of ~ programs)와 동사(support)가 '프로그램들이 지원되다'라는 수동의 의미가 되어야 하므로 복수 동사이면서 수동태인 (D) are being supported가 정답이다. to 부정사 (B)와 동명사 또는 현재분사 (C)는 동사 자리에 올 수 없다.

어휘 charitable adj. 자선의, 자선을 베푸는
generous adj. 넉넉한, 관대한 grant n. 보조금

107. 전치사 채우기
해석 Mears사는 국내에서 가장 큰 세 개의 농기계 제조업체 중 하나이다.

해설 빈칸은 명사구(the three largest manufacturers)를 목적어로 취하는 전치사 자리이므로 모든 보기가 정답의 후보이다. '가장 큰 세 개의 농기계 제조업체 중 하나'라는 의미가 되어야 하므로 전치사 (B) among(~ 중, ~ 사이에)이 정답이다. (A) on은 '~ 위에', (C) except는 '~을 제외하고', (D) against는 '~에 반대하여, ~에 기대어'라는 의미이다.

어휘 manufacturer n. 제조업체 farm equipment 농기계

108. 명사 관련 어구 완성하기
해석 Fit Trend사의 건강 추적 장치는 의심 없이 시장 내 같은 종류 중에서 가장 진보적인 기기이다.

해설 '건강 추적 장치는 의심 없이 가장 진보적인 기기이다'라는 문맥이므로 빈칸 앞의 전치사 without과 함께 '의심 없이, 이의 없이'라는 의미의 어구 without question을 만드는 명사 (C) question(의심)이 정답이다. (A) trust(신뢰), (B) means(수단), (D) value(가치)는 '의심 없이, 이의 없이'라는 의미의 어구를 만들 수 없다.

어휘 fitness n. 건강, 신체 단련 tracker n. 추적 장치, 추적자
advanced adj. 진보적인, 고급의

109. 부사 어휘 고르기
해석 컴퓨터 부품과 부대용품은 Westwood 전자 제품사 전체 연간 매출의 겨우 10퍼센트를 차지한다.

해설 '전체 연간 매출의 겨우 10퍼센트를 차지한다'라는 문맥이므로 (B) merely(겨우)가 정답이다. (A) simultaneously는 '동시에', (C) reluctantly는 '마지못해', (D) randomly는 '무작위로'라는 의미이다.

어휘 make up ~을 차지하다 annual adj. 연간의

110. 명사 자리 채우기
해석 Haxpa사가 Brava Holdings사를 인수할 때 위원회는 순조로운 변화를 보장했다.

해설 부정관사(a) 다음에 올 수 있으면서 형용사(smooth)의 꾸밈을 받을 수 있는 것은 명사이므로 명사 (C) transition(변화)이 정답이다. (A)는 동명사일 경우 부정관사(a) 다음에 올 수 없고, 현재분사일 경우 명사 자리에 올 수 없다. 형용사 (B)와 (D)는 명사 자리에 올 수 없다.

어휘 committee n. 위원회 ensure v. 보장하다
smooth adj. 순조로운, 매끄러운
take control of ~을 인수하다, 장악하다
transit v. 통과하다, 수송하다; n. 수송
transitory adj. 일시적인 transitional adj. 변천하는, 과도기의

111. 비교급 표현 채우기
해석 Fifth Street Bistro는 먼 공급업체로부터 제품을 수입하는 것보다는 지역 재료 조달에 중점을 둔다.

해설 '먼 공급업체로부터 제품을 수입하는 것보다는 지역 재료 조달에 중점을 둔다'라는 의미가 되어야 하므로 비교급 표현 (D) rather than(~보다는)이 정답이다. 전치사 (A) up to(~까지)는 어색한 문맥을 만든다. 부사절 접속사 (B) as though(마치 ~처럼)와 (C) each time(~할 때마다)은 절과 절을 연결한다.

어휘 focus on ~에 중점을 두다 sourcing n. 조달
import v. 수입하다 distant adj. 먼 supplier n. 공급업체

112. 부사 자리 채우기
해석 많이 홍보된 영화치고, Origin of Hope는 주말 박스 오피스에서 놀랄 만큼 저조한 성적을 기록했다.

해설 부사(poorly)를 꾸밀 수 있는 것은 부사이므로 부사 (D) surprisingly(놀랄 만큼, 대단히)가 정답이다. 동사 또는 명사 (A), 동사 또는 과거분사 (B), 동명사 또는 현재분사 (C)는 부사를 꾸밀 수 없다. 동사 did를 타동사로 보고 명사 (A)와 동명사 (C)를 타동사의 목적어로 본다 해도, 각각 '박스 오피스에서 놀라운 일을 저조하게 하다/놀랍게 하는 것을 저조하게 하다'라는 어색한 문맥을 만든다. did를 동사를 강조하는 조동사로 보고 동사 (A)를 주절(Origin of Hope ~ office)의 동사로 본다 해도, surprise(~를 놀라게 하다)는 타동사이므로 뒤에 목적어가 와야 한다.

어휘 promotion n. 홍보 poorly adv. 저조하게, 형편없이

113. 관계대명사 채우기
해석 Laura Hong은 그 새로운 인턴을 교육하는 것을 담당하며, 그는 이번 여름에 고용될 것이다.

해설 이 문장은 주어(Laura Hong), 동사(is), 보어(in ~ intern)를 갖춘 완전한 절이므로, ____ ~ summer는 수식어 거품으로 보아야 한다. 이 수식어 거품은 동사(will be employed)만 있고 주어가 없는 불완전한 절이며 빈칸 앞의 명사구(the ~ intern)를 선행사로 갖는 관계절이므로 관계절을 이끄는 관계대명사 (A), (B), (D)가 정답의 후보이다. 선행사(the ~

intern)가 사람이므로 주격 관계대명사 (B) who가 정답이다. 주격 또는 목적격 관계대명사 (A)는 선행사가 사물일 때 쓰인다. 주격 또는 목적격 관계대명사 (D)는 관계대명사일 때 콤마 (,) 바로 뒤에 올 수 없다. 부정대명사 (C)는 거품절을 이끌 수 없다.

어휘 in charge of ~을 담당하는 instruct v. 교육하다
employ v. 고용하다

114. 명사 어휘 고르기
해석 공항 직원이 보안상 위험을 감지하면 몇몇 승객들은 그들의 수하물 속에 든 것들을 비우도록 요구될 수 있다.

해설 '몇몇 승객들은 그들의 수하물 속에 든 것들을 비우도록 요구될 수 있다'라는 문맥이므로 (C) contents(속에 든 것들, 내용물)가 정답이다. (A) assets는 '재산, 자산', (B) subjects는 '대상, 주제', (D) matters는 '사안, 문제'라는 의미이다.

어휘 empty v. 비우다; adj. 비어 있는 luggage n. 수하물, 여행 가방
detect v. 감지하다, 발견하다

115. 전치사 채우기
해석 Arqua 가구점에서는, 시간제 근로자들의 것들을 포함하여 모든 급여는 매달 10일에 지급된다.

해설 이 문장은 주어(all salaries)와 동사(are paid)를 갖춘 완전한 절이므로, ____ ~ employees는 수식어 거품으로 보아야 한다. 이 수식어 거품은 동사가 없는 거품구이므로, 거품구를 이끌 수 있는 전치사 (B), (C), (D)가 정답의 후보이다. '시간제 근로자들의 것들을 포함하여'라는 의미가 되어야 하므로 전치사 (D) including(~을 포함하여)이 정답이다. (B) into는 '~안으로', (C) throughout은 '~ 동안, ~ 내내'라는 의미이다. 부사절 접속사 (A) while(~하는 동안, ~이긴 하지만)은 거품구가 아닌 거품절을 이끈다.

어휘 salary n. 급여, 봉급 part-time adj. 시간제의

116. 부정대명사 채우기
해석 상공 회의소 워크숍 참석에 관심이 있는 누구든지 행정실의 Ms. Moore에게 보내져야 한다.

해설 빈칸은 동사(should be directed)의 주어 자리이므로 주어 자리에 올 수 있는 부정대명사 (A) Anyone이 정답이다. 복합관계부사 (B), 목적격 관계대명사 (C), 부정형용사 (D)는 주어 자리에 올 수 없다.

어휘 attend v. 참석하다 direct v. 보내다, (길을) 안내하다
administrative office 행정실

117. 전치사 채우기
해석 Mr. Chauncey의 면접 동안 일본 소프트웨어 회사에서의 그의 이전 업무 경험이 논해졌다.

해설 빈칸은 명사구(his interview)를 목적어로 가지는 전치사 자리이므로 전치사 (A), (C), (D)가 정답의 후보이다. 'Mr. Chauncey의 면접 동안 그의 이전 업무 경험이 논해졌다'라는 의미가 되어야 하므로 기간을 나타내는 전치사 (D) during(~ 동안)이 정답이다. (A) about은 '~에 대해', (C) along은 '~을 따라서'라는 의미이다. 부사 또는 명사 (B)는 명사구를 목적어로 가질 수 없다.

어휘 previous adj. 이전의 discuss v. 논하다, 상의하다
aside adv. 한쪽으로, ~ 외에는

118. 형용사 자리 채우기
해석 제품 디자인에 대해 사려 깊은 접근법을 채택하는 것은 Hyde Enterprises사가 성공할 수 있게 했다.

해설 명사(approaches)를 꾸밀 수 있는 것은 형용사이므로 형용사 (B) thoughtful(사려 깊은)이 정답이다. 명사 또는 동사 (A), 명사 (C), 부사 (D)는 형용사 자리에 올 수 없다.

어휘 adopt v. 채택하다 approach n. 접근법; v. 접근하다
thoughtfulness n. 사려 깊음 thoughtfully adv. 생각이 깊게

119. 부사 자리 채우기
해석 주간 회의 동안, 관리자는 직원들에게 어떤 회사 규정 위반이라도 부정적인 결과가 있을 것이라고 반복적으로 상기시켰다.

해설 주절의 동사(reminded)를 꾸밀 수 있는 것은 부사이므로 부사 (B) repeatedly(반복적으로)가 정답이다. 동사 (A), 동사 또는 과거분사 (C), 명사 (D)는 동사를 꾸밀 수 없다.

어휘 supervisor n. 관리자 remind v. 상기시키다
violation n. 위반 consequence n. (발생한 일의) 결과
repeat v. 되풀이하다 repetition n. 반복

120. 부사절 접속사 채우기
해석 비록 Ms. Nielsen은 준비에 도움이 필요하지만 그녀는 제품 출시 발표를 진행하는 것에 동의했다.

해설 이 문장은 주어(Ms. Nielsen)와 동사(has agreed)를 갖춘 완전한 절이므로 ____ ~ preparations는 수식어 거품으로 보아야 한다. 이 수식어 거품은 동사(needs)가 있는 거품절이므로, 거품절을 이끌 수 있는 부사절 접속사인 모든 보기가 정답의 후보이다. '비록 그녀는 도움이 필요하지만 제품 출시 발표를 진행하는 것에 동의했다'라는 의미가 되어야 하므로 양보를 나타내는 부사절 접속사 (D) although(비록 ~이지만)가 정답이다. (A) after는 '~한 이후에', (B) since는 '~이기 때문에, ~한 이래로', (C) unless는 '만약 ~이 아니라면'이라는 의미이다.

어휘 lead v. 진행하다, 이끌다 presentation n. 발표

121. 명사 관련 어구 완성하기
해석 개정된 노동 규정 아래, 모든 외국인 노동자들은 3년 유효기간의 허가증을 발급받게 될 것이다.

해설 '모든 외국인 노동자들은 3년 유효기간의 허가증을 발급받게 될 것이다'라는 문맥이므로 빈칸 뒤의 명사 period(기간)와 함께 쓰여 '유효기간'이라는 의미의 어구인 validity period를 만드는 (C) validity(유효)가 정답이다. (A) productivity(생산성), (B) partnership(동업), (D) symbol(상징)은 '유효기간'이라는 의미의 어구를 만들 수 없다.

어휘 revised adj. 개정된 regulation n. 규정 permit n. 허가증

122. 부사 어휘 고르기
해석 Ms. Wyman은 3년 전에 사직했지만, 여전히 이전 동료들을 만나기 위해 가끔 들른다.

해설 'Ms. Wyman은 여전히 이전 동료들을 만나기 위해 가끔 들른다'라는 문맥이므로 (D) occasionally(가끔)가 정답이다. (B) recently(최근에)도 해석상 그럴듯해 보이지만, 주로 과거 또는 현재완료 시제와 함께 쓰이며 현재 시제와는 함께 쓰일 수 없다. (A) jointly는 '공동으로', (C) gradually는 '서서히, 점진적으로'라는 의미이다.

어휘 resign v. 사직하다, 물러나다 stop by 들르다
catch up with ~를 만나다, 따라잡다 former adj. 이전의
colleague n. 동료

123. 형용사 자리 채우기
해석 Brentwood 무역 박람회는 가전제품 판매업체들에게 장래 고객에게 자사 제품을 홍보할 기회를 제공한다.

해설 빈칸 뒤의 명사(buyers)를 꾸밀 수 있는 것은 형용사이므로 과거분사 (B)와 형용사 (D)가 정답의 후보이다. '장래 고객에게 자사 제품을 홍보할 기회를 제공한다'라는 의미가 되어야 하므로 형용사 (D) prospective(장래의, 유망한)가 정답이다. 과거분사 (B)를 쓸 경우 '답사되는 고객'이라는 어색한 의미가 된다. 동사 또는 명사 (A)와 명사 (C)는 형용사 자리에 올 수 없다.

어휘 trade show 무역 박람회 appliance n. 가전제품
vendor n. 판매업체, 노점상
prospect v. (금 등을 찾아서) 답사하다; n. 가망, 가능성
prospector n. 탐사자, 탐광자

124. 동사 어휘 고르기
해석 교통 당국 관계자들은 지하철 노선 폐쇄의 영향을 줄이기 위해 추가 버스들을 보냈다.

해설 '지하철 노선 폐쇄의 영향을 줄이기 위해 추가 버스들을 보냈다'라는 문맥이므로 (B) diminish(줄이다)가 정답이다. (A) assess는 '재다, 평가하다', (C) intensify는 '심화시키다', (D) dismiss는 '해고하다, 해산시키다'라는 의미이다.

어휘 transport n. 교통; v. 수송하다
official n. 관계자, 공무원; adj. 공식적인
send out ~을 보내다, 파견하다 extra adj. 추가의
impact n. 영향, 충격 closure n. 폐쇄

125. 현재분사와 과거분사 구별하여 채우기
해석 이번 달의 강의 시리즈에 참석하도록 주최자들에 의해 초대된 연설자들의 구성이 변경되었다.

해설 이 문장은 주어(The lineup of speakers)와 동사(has been modified)를 갖춘 완전한 절이므로 ____ ~ series는 수식어 거품으로 보아야 한다. 따라서 수식어 거품을 이끌 수 있는 현재분사 (A)와 과거분사 (B)가 정답의 후보이다. 꾸밈을 받는 명사(speakers)와 분사가 '주최자들에 의해 초대된 연설자'라는 의미의 수동 관계이고, 행위의 주체가 by 다음에 왔으므로 과거분사 (B) invited가 정답이다. 현재분사 (A)를 쓰면 '주최자들에 의해 초대한 연설자'라는 어색한 문맥이 된다. 동사 (C)와 (D)는 수식어 거품을 이끌 수 없다.

어휘 lineup n. 구성, 정렬 organizer n. 주최자, 조직자
modify v. 변경하다, 수정하다

126. 부사절 접속사 채우기
해석 오직 영화가 팬들로부터 좋은 평가를 받는 경우에만, 같은 제작진과 주연 배우들로 속편이 제작을 시작할 수 있다.

해설 이 문장은 주어(a sequel), 동사(could start), 목적어(production)를 갖춘 완전한 절이므로 ____ ~ by fans는 수식어 거품으로 보아야 한다. 이 수식어 거품은 동사(is ~ received)가 있는 거품절이므로, 거품절을 이끌 수 있는 부사절 접속사 (A)와 (D)가 정답의 후보이다. '오직 영화가 팬들로부터 좋은 평가를 받는 경우에만, 속편이 제작을 시작할 수 있다'라는 문맥이므로 (A) Providing(오직 ~하는 경우에만)이 정답이다. (D) Even if는 '비록 ~일지라도'라는 의미이다. 접속부사 (B)와 전치사 (C)는 거품절을 이끌 수 없다.

어휘 well received 좋은 평가를 받은 sequel n. 속편
production n. 제작, 생산 likewise adv. 마찬가지로
due to ~ 때문에

127. 형용사 자리 채우기
해석 지난 일 년 동안 경제 상황이 최적이 아니었으므로, Avatech사는 자사의 태블릿 컴퓨터 라인의 생산을 중단하기로 결정했다.

해설 빈칸은 be동사(been)의 보어 자리이므로 보어가 될 수 있는 형용사 (B)와 명사 (D)가 정답의 후보이다. '지난 일 년 동안 경제 상황이 최적이 아니었다'라는 의미로 보어가 주어(Economic conditions)의 상태를 설명하고 있으므로 형용사 (B) optimal(최적의)이 정답이다. 명사 (D) optimization(최적화)을 쓰면 주어(Economic conditions)와 동격 관계를 이루어 '지난 일 년 동안 경제 상황이 최적화가 아니었다'라는 어색한 문맥이 된다. 동사 (A)와 부사 (C)는 보어 자리에 올 수 없다.

어휘 condition n. 상황, 상태, 조건
discontinue v. (생산을) 중단하다 optimize v. 최적화하다
optimally adv. 최적으로

128. 명사 관련 어구 완성하기
해석 Puff 제과점은 유기농 재료만을 포함하는 여러 가지 신선한 페이스트리를 매일 판매한다.

해설 '여러 가지 신선한 페이스트리'라는 문맥이므로 빈칸 앞의 부정관사 an과 빈칸 뒤의 전치사 of와 함께 '여러 가지의'라는 의미의 어구 an assortment of를 만드는 (C) assortment(여러 가지, 모음)가 정답이다. (B)의 an amount of도 '상당한'이라는 의미로 해석상 그럴듯해 보이지만, 불가산 명사와 함께 쓰여야 하므로 답이 될 수 없다. (A) acquisition(습득), (D) availability(유효성)는 '여러 가지의'라는 의미의 어구를 만들 수 없다.

어휘 organic adj. 유기농의

129. 사람명사와 사물/추상명사 구별하여 채우기
해석 Baxter사는 그것의 전문적인 교육 강좌들을 감독해 줄 조력자들을 찾고 있다.

해설 전치사(for)의 뒤에 올 수 있는 것은 명사이므로 명사 (C)와 (D)가 정답의 후보이다. '교육 강좌들을 감독해 줄 조력자들을 찾고 있다'라는 의미가 되어야 하므로 사람명사 (C) facilitators(조력자)가 정답이다. 추상명사 (D) facilitation(편리화)은 '교육 강좌들을 감독해 줄 편리화를 찾고 있다'라는 어색한 문맥을 만든다. 동사 (A)와 (B)는 명사 자리에 올 수 없다.

어휘 oversee v. 감독하다 professional adj. 전문적인
facilitate v. 가능하게 하다

130. 의문사 채우기
해석 구매부서는 공급자들로부터 받은 제안들 중 어떤 것을 경영진에 추천할지 결정하지 않았다.

해설 빈칸 이하의 절은 동사(has ~ decided)의 목적어로 사용된 명사절로, 명사절을 이끄는 복합관계대명사 (B), 의문사 (C)와 (D)가 정답의 후보이다. 빈칸 뒤에 목적어가 없는 불완전한 절(it ~ to management)이 왔고, '제안들 중 어떤 것을 추천할지 결정하지 않았다'라는 문맥이므로 (D) which(어떤 것)가 정답이다. 복합관계대명사 (B)를 쓰면 '제안들 무엇이든 간에 추천할지 결정하지 않았다'라는 어색한 문맥이 된다. 의문부사 (C) 뒤에는 완전한 절이 와야 하므로 답이 될 수 없다. 지시대명사 (A)는 명사절을 이끌 수 없다.

어휘 purchasing n. 구매 proposal n. 제안, 제의
recommend v. 추천하다, 권고하다

PART 6

131-134번은 다음 이메일에 관한 문제입니다.

발신: Gail Rossey <g.rossey@quailcooling.com>
수신: Peter Edmonds <pe880@tmail.com>
제목: 회신: 제품 불만
날짜: 3월 22일

Mr. Edmonds께,

3월 21일 자 귀하의 이메일은 귀하의 Quail Cooling사 에어컨이 귀하가 그것을 켤 때마다 큰 소음을 일으킨다고 말했습니다. ¹³¹이 문제는 아마 결함이 있는 부품에 의해 발생되는 것 같습니다.

귀하는 그 제품을 귀하가 그것을 구매했던 가게로 다시 가져가야 하는지 여부에 대해 문의했습니다. ¹³²대신에, 저는 귀하께서 그것을 Quail Cooling사의 서비스 센터로 가져오시길 권장합니다. 귀하의 집에서 가장 가까운 곳은 147번지 Field가에 있습니다. ¹³³기다려야 하는 것을 피하기 위해, 귀하께서는 555-2827로 전화하여 사전에 예약을 할 수도 있습니다. 기술자가 현장에서 귀하의 에어컨을 수리해 줄 것입니다. ¹³⁴서비스 요금은 청구되지 않을 것입니다.

Gail Rossey 드림
고객 서비스 직원, Quail Cooling사

indicate v. 말하다, 명시하다 appointment n. 예약, 일정
in advance 사전에, 미리 on the spot 현장에서 fee n. 요금
charge v. 청구하다

131. 알맞은 문장 고르기

해석 (A) 이 문제는 아마 결함이 있는 부품에 의해 발생되는 것 같습니다.
(B) 수리공이 귀하의 집을 방문할 예정입니다.
(C) 귀하께서 귀하의 영수증을 제시하는 한 저는 귀하를 도울 수 있습니다.
(D) 사용자 설명서의 지시를 따르십시오.

해설 앞 문장 'Your e-mail ~ indicated that your Quail Cooling air conditioner makes a loud noise every time you turn it on.'에서 귀하의 이메일은 귀하의 Quail Cooling사의 에어컨이 그것을 켤 때마다 큰 소음을 일으킨다고 말했다고 한 후, 뒷부분에서 수리를 위한 서비스 센터 방문 방법에 관한 세부 사항을 설명하고 있으므로 빈칸에는 에어컨 문제의 원인과 관련된 내용이 들어가야 함을 알 수 있다. 따라서 (A)가 정답이다.

어휘 faulty adj. 결함이 있는 scheduled adj. 예정된
as long as ~하는 한 present v. 제시하다; adj. 현재의
direction n. 지시, 방향

132. 접속부사 채우기 주변 문맥 파악

해설 빈칸은 콤마와 함께 문장의 맨 앞에 온 접속부사 자리이다. 앞 문장에서 귀하가 그 제품을 구매했던 가게로 다시 가져가야 하는지 여부에 대해 문의했다고 했고, 빈칸이 있는 문장에서는 귀하가 그것을 Quail Cooling사의 서비스 센터로 가져오길 권장한다고 했으므로, 앞에 언급된 내용을 대체하는 내용을 언급할 때 사용되는 접속부사 (A) Instead(대신에)가 정답이다.

어휘 furthermore adv. 더욱이, 뿐만 아니라
nonetheless adv. 그럼에도 불구하고
otherwise adv. 그렇지 않으면

133. to 부정사 채우기

해설 이 문장은 주어(you), 동사(may make), 목적어(an appointment)를 갖춘 완전한 절이므로 _____ ~ wait는 수식어 거품으로 보아야 한다. 이 수식어 거품은 동사가 없는 거품구이므로, 거품구를 이끌 수 있는 분사구 (A)와 to 부정사 (D)가 정답의 후보이다. '기다려야 하는 것을 피하기 위해, 사전에 예약을 할 수도 있습니다'라는 의미가 되어야 하므로 목적을 나타내는 to 부정사 (D) To avoid가 정답이다. 3형식 동사 avoid는 수동태로 쓰일 경우 뒤에 목적어를 가질 수 없으므로 수동형 (A)는 답이 될 수 없다. 동사 (B)와 (C)는 거품구를 이끌 수 없다.

어휘 avoid v. 피하다

134. 명사 관련 어구 완성하기 주변 문맥 파악

해설 명사(fee) 앞에서 복합 명사를 만들 수 있는 명사 (A), (C), (D)와 명사를 꾸밀 수 있는 형용사 (B)가 모두 정답의 후보이다. 빈칸이 있는 문장만으로 정답을 고를 수 없으므로 주변 문맥이나 전체 문맥을 파악한다. '_____ 요금은 청구되지 않을 것이다'라는 문맥인데, 앞 문장에서 기술자가 현장에서 에어컨을 수리해 줄 것이라고 한 후, 빈칸이 있는 문장에서는 요금이 청구되지 않을 것이라고 했으므로 수리 서비스에 대한 요금이 청구되지 않을 것임을 알 수 있다. 따라서 빈칸 뒤의 명사 fee(요금)와 함께 쓰여 '서비스 요금'이라는 의미의 복합 명사 service fee를 만드는 명사 (C) service(서비스)가 정답이다.

어휘 shipping n. 운송(료) monthly adj. 매월의
transfer n. 이동; v. 이동하다

135-138번은 다음 초대장에 관한 문제입니다.

Blackpool 실내악 협회가 5월 3일에
자랑스럽게 봄 콘서트를 선보입니다

¹³⁵Greenfield 강당에서 다시 열리게 될 Blackpool 실내악 협회의 봄 콘서트에 당신을 정중히 초대합니다. 작년 콘서트가 열렸던 이 장소는 최대 300명의 사람들을 수용할 수 있습니다. 이 콘서트는 현악 4중주와 피아노 3중주의 공연들을 포함할 것입니다. ¹³⁶연회의 밤은 오후 7시에 시작해 오후 9시까지 계속될 것입니다.

콘서트 당일 밤에, 티켓은 출입구에서 20달러에 판매될 것입니다. 시즌권을 가지고 있는 사람들은 건물에 무료로 들어갈 수 있을 뿐만 아니라, 마지막 리허설과 뒤풀이에 참석할 수 있을 것입니다. ¹³⁷이것들은 각각 5월 2일과 4일에 일어날 것입니다. ¹³⁸두 가지 모두 오후 5시에 열릴 예정입니다. 더 자세한 내용을 위해, 저희의 웹사이트를 방문하십시오.

chamber music 실내악 society n. 협회
cordially adv. 정중히 auditorium n. 강당 venue n. 장소
entrance n. 출입구 after-party n. 뒤풀이
respectively adv. 각각

135. 부사 어휘 고르기 주변 문맥 파악

해설 'Greenfield 강당에서 _____ 열리게 될 것이다'라는 문맥이므로 모든 보기가 정답의 후보이다. 빈칸이 있는 문장만으로 정답을 고를 수 없으므로 주변 문맥이나 전체 문맥을 파악한다. 뒤 문장에서 이 장소는 작년에 처음 사용되었다고 했으므로 작년에 이어 이번에도 Greenfield 강당이 사용될 것임을 알 수 있다. 따라서 (D) again(다시, 한 번 더)이 정답이다.

어휘 weekly adv. 매주 effectively adv. 효과적으로, 사실상
last adv. 마지막으로

136. 동사 자리 채우기

해설 '연회의 밤은 오후 7시에 시작해 오후 9시까지 계속될 것이다'라는 의미가 되어야 하고, 등위접속사(and)가 동사(start)와 또 다른 동사인 빈칸을 연결하고 있음을 알 수 있다. 앞의 동사(start)가 조동사(will) 뒤에 오는 동사원형이므로 그와 같은 형태인 동사원형 (D) continue(계속되다)가 정답이다. 명사 (A), to 부정사 (B), 동명사 또는 현재분사 (C)는 동사 자리에 올 수 없다.

어휘 continuation n. 계속, 연속

137. 동사 어휘 고르기 _주변 문맥 파악_

해설 '이것들은 각각, 5월 2일과 4일에 _____ 것이다'라는 문맥이므로 모든 보기가 정답의 후보이다. 빈칸이 있는 문장만으로 정답을 고를 수 없으므로 주변 문맥이나 전체 문맥을 파악한다. 앞 문장에서 시즌권을 가지고 있는 사람들은 마지막 리허설과 뒤풀이에 참석할 수 있다고 했으므로, 리허설과 뒤풀이는 각각 5월 2일과 4일에 일어날 것임을 알 수 있다. 따라서 (D) occur(일어나다, 발생하다)가 정답이다.

어휘 resume v. 재개하다 broadcast v. 방송하다
expire v. 만료되다

138. 알맞은 문장 고르기

해석 (A) 4월 20일에 예약이 확정되었습니다.
(B) 두 가지 모두 오후 5시에 열릴 예정입니다.
(C) 당신의 기부금은 유용하게 사용될 것입니다.
(D) 그것은 연회를 하기에 적절한 장소였습니다.

해설 앞 문장 'These will (occur) on May 2 and 4, respectively.'에서 이것들, 즉 리허설과 뒤풀이가 각각 5월 2일과 4일에 일어날 것이라고 했으므로 빈칸에는 두 행사와 관련된 내용이 들어가야 함을 알 수 있다. 따라서 (B)가 정답이다.

어휘 reservation n. 예약 donation n. 기부금
put to good use ~을 유용하게 사용하다, ~을 잘 활용하다
suitable adj. 적절한, 알맞은 banquet n. 연회, 만찬

139-142번은 다음 후기에 관한 문제입니다.

Emerald Island 리조트, 호주 ★★★★★
2월 12일에 Agatha Henriksen에 의해 게시된 후기

139제 남편과 저는 저희의 한 달 동안의 휴가를 마무리하기 위해 조용히 있을 수 있는 휴가지를 찾고 있었습니다. Emerald Island 리조트는 이것을 위한 가장 적절한 장소로 보였습니다. 외딴 해양 공원에 위치해 있는 이 리조트는 그들만의 수영장이 딸린 독립된 저택들이 특징입니다. 이 리조트는 또한 최고의 서비스로 유명합니다. 이는 그것이 비쌀 수 있는 이유입니다. 140다행히, 저희는 적당한 가격에 상품을 확보했습니다. 1일 무료 숙박권 외에도, 이 할인은 와인 시음과 마사지를 포함했습니다. 141인상적인 환경에서부터 최고의 고객 서비스까지, Emerald Island 리조트는 모든 예상을 뛰어넘었습니다. 가고 싶은 이들을 위해, 이 리조트는 케언스에서 비행기로 90분이 걸립니다. 142배를 통해 그곳에 도착하는 것도 가능합니다.

getaway n. 휴가지, 도주 month-long adj. 한 달 동안의
situate v. 위치시키다 remote adj. 외딴, 먼
marine park 해양 공원 detached adj. 독립된
have a reputation for ~으로 유명하다
top-notch adj. 최고의, 일류의 secure v. 확보하다, 획득하다
affordable adj. (가격이) 적당한 apart from ~ 외에, ~을 제외하고
offer n. 할인, 제안 impressive adj. 인상적인
surroundings n. 환경 superb adj. 최고의
surpass v. 뛰어넘다, 능가하다 expectation n. 예상, 기대

139. 형용사 어휘 고르기 _전체 문맥 파악_

해설 '한 달 동안의 휴가를 마무리하기 위해 _____ 휴가지를 찾고 있었다'라는 문맥이므로 모든 보기가 정답의 후보이다. 빈칸이 있는 문장만으로 정답을 고를 수 없으므로 주변 문맥이나 전체 문맥을 파악한다. 뒷부분에서 이 리조트는 외딴 해양 공원에 위치해 있고, 독립된 저택들이 특징이라고 했으므로, Emerald Island 리조트가 조용한 휴가지임을 알 수 있다. 따라서 (C) private(조용히 있을 수 있는, 사적인)가 정답이다.

어휘 traditional adj. 전통적인 flexible adj. 유연한
popular adj. 인기 있는

140. 접속부사 채우기 _주변 문맥 파악_

해설 빈칸은 콤마와 함께 문장의 맨 앞에 온 접속부사 자리이다. 앞 문장에서 최고의 서비스가 그것, 즉 Emerald Island 리조트가 비쌀 수 있는 이유라고 했고, 빈칸이 있는 문장에서는 적당한 가격에 상품을 확보했다고 했으므로 앞 문장보다 긍정적인 상황을 나타낼 때 사용되는 접속부사 (C) Fortunately(다행히)가 정답이다.

어휘 once adv. 언젠가, 한 번 nearly adv. 거의
additionally adv. 게다가

141. 수량 형용사 채우기

해설 빈칸 뒤의 단수 가산 명사(expectation)를 꾸밀 수 있는 수량 표현 (A)와 한정사 (B)가 정답의 후보이다. '인상적인 환경에서부터 최고의 고객 서비스까지, 리조트는 _____ 예상을 뛰어넘었다'라는 문맥이므로 리조트의 많은 부분이 만족스러웠다는 것을 알 수 있다. 따라서 (A) every(모든)가 정답이다. 한정사 (B)를 쓸 경우 '인상적인 환경에서부터 최고의 고객 서비스까지, 리조트는 어떤 예상도 뛰어넘지 않았다'라는 어색한 문맥을 만든다. 지시형용사 (C)와 수량 형용사 (D)는 복수 가산 명사와 함께 쓰인다.

142. 알맞은 문장 고르기

해석 (A) 저희는 필요한 지원을 제공하기를 원합니다.
(B) 저는 기꺼이 당신의 예약을 해드릴 것입니다.
(C) 배를 통해 그곳에 도착하는 것도 가능합니다.
(D) 덴마크로 돌아오는 저희의 항공편이 지연되었습니다.

해설 앞 문장 'For those wishing to go, the resort is 90 minutes by plane from Cairns.'에서 가고 싶은 이들을 위해, 이 리조트는 케언스에서 비행기로 90분이 걸린다고 했으므로 빈칸에는 Emerald Island 리조트에 가는 방법과 관련된 내용이 들어가야 함을 알 수 있다. 따라서 (C)가 정답이다.

어휘 reach v. 도착하다, 닿다 delay v. 지연하다, 연기하다

143-146번은 다음 설명에 관한 문제입니다.

143Delux Home Brewer (DHB)로 당신의 첫 번째 커피 한 잔을 만들기 전에, 기기는 세척되어야 합니다. 이것은 기기 내 모든 잔여물을 제거합니다. 위에 있는 뚜껑을 열고 안에 물을 부음으로써 시작하십시오. 그 양은 '가득'이라고 표시된 선에 닿아야 하지만, 초과해서는 안 됩니다. 144다음으로, 뚜껑을 닫고 DHB의 플러그를 콘센트에 꽂으십시오. 커피포트가 내부 트레이에 얹혀 있는 것을 확인하십시오. 이제, 간단히 '청소' 버튼을 누르고 모든 물이 DHB를 통해 순환할 때까지 기다리십시오. 145이 물은 배수구에 흘려 보내져야 합니다.

당신은 이제 당신의 첫 번째 한 회분의 커피를 만들 준비가 되었습니다. 146이 과정에 대한 정확한 안내를 위해 이 설명서의 7쪽을 참고하십시오.

eliminate v. 제거하다, 없애다 residue n. 잔여물 lid n. 뚜껑

pour v. 붓다 exceed v. 넘다, 초과하다
plug v. (전기 기구에) 플러그를 꽂다; n. 플러그
electronic outlet 콘센트 rest on ~에 얹혀 있다
circulate v. 순환하다 batch n. 한 회분

143. 동사 어휘 고르기 | 전체 문맥 파악
해설 '기기는 _____되어야 한다'라는 문맥이므로 모든 보기가 정답의 후보이다. 빈칸이 있는 문장만으로 정답을 고를 수 없으므로 주변 문맥이나 전체 문맥을 파악한다. 뒤 문장에서 이것이 기기 내 모든 잔여물을 제거한다고 했고 뒷부분에 물을 붓고 '청소' 버튼을 눌러 물이 순환할 때까지 기다리라고 했으므로, 기기가 세척되어야 한다는 것을 알 수 있다. 따라서 동사 wash(세척하다)의 과거분사형 (C) washed가 정답이다. 참고로, (B) checked(점검하다)도 해석상 그럴듯해 보이지만, 기기를 점검하는 행위 자체가 기기 내 모든 잔여물을 제거할 수는 없으므로 답이 될 수 없다.

어휘 shake v. 흔들다

144. 접속부사 채우기 | 전체 문맥 파악
해설 빈칸은 콤마와 함께 문장의 맨 앞에 온 접속부사 자리이다. 앞부분에서 뚜껑을 열고 물을 부으라고 했고, 빈칸이 있는 문장에서는 뚜껑을 닫고 플러그를 콘센트에 꽂으라고 했으므로, 앞에서 말한 내용과 다음 단계로 이어지는 내용의 문장에서 사용되는 접속부사 (D) Next(다음으로)가 정답이다.

어휘 alternatively adv. 그 대신에 likewise adv. 비슷하게
eventually adv. 결국

145. 알맞은 문장 고르기
해석 (A) 그 필터는 그러한 목적으로 만들어지지 않았습니다.
(B) 최대 네 가지 다른 옵션들이 선택될 수 있습니다.
(C) 표준 1회 제공량은 10온스로 구성됩니다.
(D) 이 물은 배수구에 흘려 보내져야 합니다.

해설 앞 문장 'Now, simply press the CLEAN button and wait until all the water has circulated through the DHB.'에서 이제, 간단히 '청소' 버튼을 누르고 모든 물이 DHB를 통해 순환할 때까지 기다리라고 했으므로 빈칸에는 청소를 위해 사용된 물과 관련된 내용이 들어가야 함을 알 수 있다. 따라서 (D)가 정답이다.

어휘 standard adj. 표준의 serving n. 1회 제공량, 1인분
consist of ~으로 구성되다 drain n. 배수구; v. 물을 빼내다

146. 형용사 자리 채우기
해설 빈칸 뒤의 명사(directions)를 꾸밀 수 있는 것은 형용사이므로 형용사 (A) precise(정확한)가 정답이다. 부사 (B), 명사 (C)와 (D)는 형용사 자리에 올 수 없다.

어휘 precisely adv. 정확하게 precision n. 정확, 정밀
preciseness n. 명확함, 정확성

PART 7

147-148번은 다음 광고에 관한 문제입니다.

Fiona's Haven!
147당신의 꽃과 식물에 대한 모든 필요를 충족하기 위해 Fiona's Haven에 방문하세요! 폭넓은 종류에서 선택하세요!

- 결혼식과 다른 특별한 행사들을 위한 모든 사이즈의 주문 제작된 꽃꽂이들.
- 147다양한 실내 식물들과 나무들.
- 148시내 전 지역에 대한 배달 서비스. 100달러 이상 주문 시 무료.

가격과 상품을 상의하시려면 555-3049로 저희에게 전화하세요. Fiona's Haven은 올랜도 시내에 938번지 Colonial로에 위치해 있습니다. 저희의 운영 시간은 월요일부터 금요일까지, 오전 10시부터 오후 7시까지입니다.

variety n. 종류, 다양성
customized adj. 주문 제작된, 개개인의 요구에 맞춘
floral arrangement 꽃꽂이 occasion n. 행사, 경우
a range of 다양한 indoor adj. 실내의
discuss v. 상의하다, 논의하다 operation n. 운영

147. 육하원칙 문제
해석 Fiona's Haven은 어떤 종류의 사업체인가?
(A) 특별한 행사들을 위한 행사 기획 업체
(B) 개인 또는 기업 행사를 위한 장소
(C) 식물과 꽃들의 공급업체
(D) 가정과 사업체를 위한 조경 업체

해설 지문의 'Visit Fiona's Haven for all of your flower and plant needs!'와 'A range of indoor plants and trees.'에서 꽃과 식물에 대한 필요를 충족하기 위해 Fiona's Haven에 방문하라고 하며, 다양한 실내 식물들과 나무들이 있다고 했으므로, Fiona's Haven이 꽃과 식물을 판매한다는 사실을 알 수 있다. 따라서 (C)가 정답이다.

어휘 venue n. 장소 function n. 행사, 기능 supplier n. 공급업체
landscaper n. 조경 업체, 정원사

148. 육하원칙 문제
해석 고객들은 어떻게 무료 배달을 받을 자격을 얻을 수 있는가?
(A) 새로운 제품을 주문함으로써
(B) 일정 금액을 지불함으로써
(C) 전화로 주문함으로써
(D) 시내 지역에 주소를 가짐으로써

해설 지문의 'Delivery services to all locations within the city limits. Free for orders of $100 or more.'에서 시내 전 지역에 대한 배달 서비스가 제공되며, 100달러 이상 주문 시 무료라고 했으므로 (B)가 정답이다.

어휘 eligible adj. ~할 자격이 있는 specific adj. 일정의, 특정한

Paraphrasing
orders of $100 or more 100달러 이상 주문 → spending a specific amount 일정 금액을 지불하는 것

149-150번은 다음 회람에 관한 문제입니다.

회람
수신: 공장 운영 부서, Cready Power사
발신: Millie Wickens, 공장 부팀장
날짜: 월요일, 9월 14일
제목: 출입 시스템

이번 주 수요일, 공장 운영실에 입장하는 시스템이 바뀔 것입니다. 149이것은 우리가 현재 사용하고 있는 플라스틱 카드들이 분실 혹은 손상 때문에 자주 재발급되어야 하기 때문입니다. 카드 리더기 대신에, 우리는 지문 인식기를 사용하기 시작할 것입니다. 하지만, 수리공이 오전 11시쯤에야 도착할 것이기 때문에 150여러분은 여전히 수요일에 여러분의 출입 카드를 가져와야 합니다. 여러분 모두가 오후 1시에 여러분의 지문을 등록하도록 요구될 것이기 때문에 점심을 먹고 그 시간 전에 돌아오십시오.

```
plant n. 공장, 시설   gain entry 입장하다
reissue v. 재발급하다   on account of ~ 때문에
fingerprint n. 지문   register v. 등록하다
```

149. 육하원칙 문제

해석 현재의 보안 시스템은 왜 변화될 것인가?
(A) 민감한 정보가 보호되어야 한다.
(B) 몇몇 기계가 손상되었다.
(C) 추가적인 직원들이 고용되었다.
(D) 몇몇 물품들이 자주 교체되어야 한다.

해설 지문의 'This is because the plastic cards ~ often need to be reissued'에서 이것, 즉 입장하는 시스템이 바뀌는 것은 플라스틱 카드들이 자주 재발급되어야 하기 때문이라고 했으므로 (D)가 정답이다.

어휘 security n. 보안   sensitive adj. 민감한, 세심한
replace v. 교체하다, 대체하다   frequently adv. 자주

[Paraphrasing]
often need to be reissued 자주 재발급되어야 한다 → must be replaced frequently 자주 교체되어야 한다

150. 육하원칙 문제

해석 공장 운영 부서의 직원들은 수요일 오후 1시에 무엇을 할 것인가?
(A) 고객을 만난다.
(B) 설문지를 작성한다.
(C) 교육을 실시한다.
(D) 정보를 제공한다.

해설 지문의 'you still should bring your access card on Wednesday'와 'Please return ~ before 1 P.M. because all of you will be required to register your fingerprints at that time.'에서 여러분, 즉 공장 운영 부서의 직원들은 수요일에 여전히 출입 카드를 가져와야 하며, 그날 오후 1시에 지문을 등록하도록 요구될 것이기 때문에 그 시간 전에 돌아와야 한다고 했으므로, 수요일 오후 1시에 공장 운영 부서의 직원들은 지문 등록을 할 것임을 알 수 있다. 따라서 (D)가 정답이다.

어휘 questionnaire n. 설문지

[Paraphrasing]
register ~ fingerprints 지문을 등록하다 → Provide ~ data 정보를 제공하다

151-152번은 다음 문자 메시지 대화문에 관한 문제입니다.

```
Greg Sawyer                                오후 2시 1분
151-(A)우리 식당의 새 지점 개점을 위한 준비는 어떻게 되어 가고 있나요? 제가 알아야 할 문제가 있나요?

Denise Lewis                               오후 2시 4분
한 가지 문제가 있어요. 제가 오늘 오전에 그곳을 방문했을 때, 우리가 개조를 하기 위해 고용한 회사의 대표가 주방 환기 시스템이 제대로 작동하지 않는다고 제게 알려주었어요. 그것을 교체해야 할 것 같아요.

Greg Sawyer                                오후 2시 8분
건물 주인이 그것에 대한 비용을 지불해야 하지 않나요?

Denise Lewis                               오후 2시 12분
안타깝게도, 아니에요. 제가 조금 전에 임대차 계약서를 검토했는데, 그것은 우리가 이러한 종류의 비용에 책임이 있다고 명시해요. 152우리는 다음 주 시 안전 점검 전에 이 문제를 처리해야 해요.
```

```
Greg Sawyer                                오후 2시 14분
시간이 많지 않네요. 이 비용이 얼마나 들까요?

Denise Lewis                               오후 2시 16분
제가 오후 4시에 식당 설비 업체의 Mr. Hwang과 만날 거예요. 그가 현장을 확인한 다음, 제게 견적서를 줄 거예요.
```

```
be aware of ~을 알다   complication n. 문제
renovation n. 개조, 수리   ventilation n. 환기, 통풍
function v. 작동하다, 기능하다; n. 기능   properly adv. 제대로
unfortunately adv. 유감스럽게도   lease n. 임대차 계약
expense n. 비용   address v. 처리하다
municipal adj. 시(읍/군)의, 지방 자치제의   inspection n. 점검
supply company 설비 업체   estimate n. 견적서, 추정치
```

151. Not/True 문제

해석 작성자들이 일하는 사업체에 대해 언급된 것은?
(A) 곧 추가 지점이 생길 것이다.
(B) 경영진 교체를 겪었다.
(C) 현재 공급업체를 교체할 것이다.
(D) 운영 예산을 증가시켰다.

해설 지문의 'How are the preparations going for the opening of the new branch of our restaurant?'에서 식당의 새 지점 개점을 위한 준비는 어떻게 되어 가고 있는지 물었으므로 (A)가 정답이다. (B), (C), (D)는 지문에 언급되지 않은 내용이다.

어휘 undergo v. 겪다   current adj. 현재의

152. 의도 파악 문제

해석 오후 2시 14분에, Mr. Sawyer가 "That doesn't leave us much time"이라고 썼을 때 무엇을 의도하는가?
(A) 임대차 계약이 곧 끝날 것이다.
(B) Ms. Lewis는 곧 시청에 방문해야 한다.
(C) 건물의 개량 공사가 즉시 이루어져야 한다.
(D) 예상치 못한 비용을 위해 자금이 확보되어야 한다.

해설 지문의 'We need to address the problem before the municipal safety inspection next week.'에서 Denise Lewis가 다음 주 시 안전 점검 전에 이 문제, 즉 주방 환기 시스템이 제대로 작동하지 않는 문제를 처리해야 한다고 하자, Mr. Sawyer가 'That doesn't leave us much time'(시간이 많지 않네요)이라고 한 것을 통해 Mr. Sawyer가 다음 주 시 안전 점검 전에 문제를 처리하려면 시간이 많지 않으므로 건물의 개량 공사가 즉시 이루어져야 한다고 생각함을 알 수 있다. 따라서 (C)가 정답이다.

어휘 shortly adv. 곧, 얼마 안 되어   improvement n. 개량 공사, 개선
unanticipated adj. 예상치 못한

153-155번은 다음 이메일에 관한 문제입니다.

```
수신: Galina Kusnetsov <galinakus@postamail.com>
발신: Jovin 의료 센터 <admin@jmc.com>
제목: 저희의 새로운 모바일 애플리케이션
날짜: 9월 18일

Ms. Kusnetsov께,

당신은 154-(D)Jovin 의료 센터가 지난주에 환자들이 예약을 관리하고 질문을 하기 위해 사용할 수 있는 모바일 애플리케이션을 출시했다는 것을 알게 되어 흥미로울 수도 있습니다. 저희는 저희의 전화가 자주 통화 중이기 때문에 근무 시간 동안 병원 직원에게 전화해야 하는 것이 불편할 수 있다는 것을 알고 있습니다. ㅡ [1] ㅡ. 153따라서 저희는 저희 환자들의 대부분이
```

항상 접속 가능한 이 애플리케이션을 사용하여 저희에게 급하게 연락해야 하는 사람들을 위해 저희의 전화 회선을 원활하게 해 줄 수 있기를 바랍니다.

일단 당신이 Jovin 의료 센터 애플리케이션을 다운로드했다면, 당신의 의료 센터 ID 번호를 사용하여 로그인하십시오. — [2] —. 당신의 환자 프로필은 당신의 다가오는 예약들을 나열하고 취소 또는 변경을 요청할 수 있는 옵션을 제공할 것입니다. ¹⁵⁵또한 채팅 시스템은 진료 과정에 대한 당신의 질문에 대해 답을 얻을 수 있게 합니다. — [3] —. ¹⁵⁴⁻⁽ᴮ⁾애플리케이션이 현재는 이러한 기능들로 제한되어 있지만, 저희는 환자들이 건강 검진 결과와 같은 다른 정보에 접근하는 것을 가능하도록 만들 계획입니다. 애플리케이션에 관한 문의 사항이 있다면, 이 이메일에 답장하거나 저희의 웹사이트에 업데이트된 자주 묻는 질문 페이지를 읽어주십시오. — [4] —.

Jovin 의료 센터

launch v. 출시하다; n. 출시 appointment n. 예약, 약속
inquiry n. 질문, 문의 clinic n. 병원
inconvenient adj. 불편한 accessible adj. 접속 가능한
urgently adv. 급하게 reach v. 연락하다
cancellation n. 취소 modification n. 변경, 수정
procedure n. 과정, 절차

153. 육하원칙 문제

해석 이메일에 따르면, 애플리케이션의 목적은 무엇인가?
(A) 정규 진료 환자들에게 추가 조언을 제공하기 위해
(B) 병원으로의 통화량을 줄이기 위해
(C) 예약 취소 횟수를 줄이기 위해
(D) 환자들이 인근 병원들의 위치를 찾도록 하기 위해

해설 지문의 'We ~ hope that most of our patients will use the application, ~ and free up our phone lines'에서 저희, 즉, Jovin 의료 센터는 환자들의 대부분이 애플리케이션을 사용하여 자신들의 전화 회선을 원활하게 해 줄 수 있기를 바란다고 했으므로 (B)가 정답이다.

어휘 follow-up adj. 추가의, 후속의 volume n. 양, 부피
nearby adj. 인근의; adv. 인근에

[Paraphrasing]
free up ~ phone lines 전화 회선을 원활하게 하다 → reduce the volume of calls 통화량을 줄이다

154. Not/True 문제

해석 Jovin 의료 센터 애플리케이션에 대해 사실인 것은?
(A) 의사들과 간호사들에게 직접 연락하는 데 사용될 수 있다.
(B) 의료 기록들을 표시하도록 업데이트될 수도 있다.
(C) 소액의 비용을 지불한 후에 설치될 수 있다.
(D) 현재 약 한 달 동안 작동해 왔다.

해설 지문의 'While the application is currently limited ~, we plan to make it possible for patients to access other information, such as the results of medical tests.'에서 애플리케이션, 즉 Jovin 의료 센터 애플리케이션이 현재는 제한되어 있지만, 환자들이 건강 검진 결과와 같은 다른 정보에 접근하는 것을 가능하도록 만들 계획이라고 했으므로 (B)는 지문의 내용과 일치한다. 따라서 (B)가 정답이다. (A)와 (C)는 지문에 언급되지 않은 내용이다. (D)는 'Jovin Medical Center launched a mobile application last week'에서 Jovin 의료 센터가 지난주에 모바일 애플리케이션을 출시했다고 했으므로 지문의 내용과 일치하지 않는다.

어휘 display v. 표시하다, 보여주다 record n. 기록
functional adj. 작동하는 approximately adv. 약, 대략

[Paraphrasing]
the results of medical tests 건강 검진 결과 → medical records 의료 기록

155. 문장 위치 찾기 문제

해석 [1], [2], [3], [4]로 표시된 위치 중, 다음 문장이 들어갈 곳으로 가장 적절한 것은?

"당신은 새로운 예약을 하고 당신이 가질 수 있는 어떤 질문이든 묻기 위해 이 기능을 사용할 수 있습니다."

(A) [1]
(B) [2]
(C) [3]
(D) [4]

해설 주어진 문장에서 당신은 새로운 예약을 하고 당신이 가질 수 있는 어떤 질문들이든 묻기 위해 이 기능을 사용할 수 있다고 했으므로, 이 문장이 예약 및 문의를 할 수 있는 기능과 관련된 내용이 나오는 부분에 들어가야 함을 알 수 있다. [3]의 앞 문장인 'A chat system ~ allows you to get answers to your questions about clinic procedures.'에서 채팅 시스템은 진료 과정에 대한 당신의 질문에 대해 답을 얻을 수 있게 해준다고 했으므로, [3]에 제시된 문장이 들어가면 채팅 시스템은 진료 과정에 대한 질문들에 대해 답을 얻을 수 있게 하며, 새로운 예약을 하고 어떤 질문들이든 묻기 위해 이 기능, 즉 채팅 시스템을 사용할 수 있다는 자연스러운 문맥이 된다는 것을 알 수 있다. 따라서 (C)가 정답이다.

어휘 feature n. 기능, 특징

156-158번은 다음 웹페이지에 관한 문제입니다.

www.organifresh.com
Organi Fresh사 – 식사 시간을 쉽게 만들다

소개 | 메뉴 | 주문 | 자주 묻는 질문 | 연락처

Organi Fresh사는 당신을 위해 일을 함으로써 음식을 사고 건강한 식사를 준비하는 것에 대한 번거로움을 없애드립니다. ¹⁵⁶당신이 Organi Fresh사 식사 배달을 주문하면, 당신은 저희의 매우 숙련된 전문 요리사들에 의해 준비된 일주일 치의 맛있는 음식을 받게 될 것입니다. 저희의 모든 음식은 제철 유기농 농작물과 천연 재료들을 사용해 만들어집니다. 저희는 절대 방부제를 사용하지 않으며, 저희는 기름, 설탕, 그리고 소금의 사용을 최소한도로 유지합니다.

¹⁵⁷⁻⁽ᴬ⁾아시아, 지중해, 그리고 남미 요리의 조합을 포함하는 저희의 메뉴를 한 번 본 다음, 당신이 일주일 동안 원하는 식사를 고르세요. ¹⁵⁷⁻⁽ᴮ⁾저희의 표준 플랜으로, ¹⁵⁷⁻⁽ᶜ⁾당신은 하루 28달러의 비용으로 일주일 동안 하루에 세 끼의 식사를 받게 될 것입니다. ¹⁵⁷⁻⁽ᴮ⁾또는, 단돈 22.50달러의 비용으로 일주일 동안 하루에 두 끼의 식사를 받을 수 있도록 저희의 점심 & 저녁 플랜을 주문하세요. 이 모든 가격들은 배송비를 포함합니다!

마지막으로, 저희의 모든 식사들은 전자레인지 조리와 오븐 사용이 둘 다 가능한 용기들로 포장됩니다. ¹⁵⁶/¹⁵⁸⁻⁽ᶜ⁾당신의 일주일 치 주문은 얼음과 함께 냉장 박스에 포장되어 매주 금요일에 신선하게 배송될 것입니다. 저희를 한 번만 이용해 보시면, 저희는 당신이 더 많은 것을 위해 다시 돌아올 것이라 확신합니다!

take the hassle out 번거로움을 없애다 meal n. 식사, 끼니
seasonal adj. 제철의 organic adj. 유기농의
produce n. 농작물; v. 생산하다 preservative n. 방부제
minimum n. 최소한도 Mediterranean adj. 지중해의
cuisine n. 요리 pack v. 포장하다 container n. 용기
microwavable adj. 전자레인지로 조리할 수 있는

ovenproof adj. 오븐에 사용할 수 있는
cooler n. 냉장 박스, 냉장고

156. 주제 찾기 문제

해석 웹페이지의 주제는 무엇인가?
(A) 유기농 식당
(B) 사전 포장된 식사 서비스
(C) 출장 음식 공급업체
(D) 새로운 식단 프로그램

해설 지문의 'When you order an Organi Fresh meal delivery, you'll get ~ delicious food'에서 Organi Fresh 식사 배달을 주문하면, 맛있는 음식을 받게 될 것이라고 했고, 'Your order for the week will be shipped ~ in a cooler packed with ice'에서 일주일 치 주문이 얼음과 함께 냉장 박스에 포장되어 배송될 것이라고 했으므로 (B)가 정답이다.

어휘 pre-packed adj. 사전 포장된 catering n. 출장 음식 공급
diet n. 식단, 다이어트

157. Not/True 문제

해석 웹페이지에 언급되지 않은 정보는?
(A) 요리 종류
(B) 주문 옵션
(C) 제품 가격
(D) 보관 조언

해설 (D)는 지문에 언급되지 않은 내용이다. 따라서 (D)가 정답이다. (A)는 'our menu, which includes a mix of Asian, Mediterranean, and South American cuisine'에서 메뉴가 아시아, 지중해, 그리고 남미 요리의 조합을 포함한다고 했으므로 지문의 내용과 일치한다. (B)는 'With our Standard Plan, you'll get three meals a day ~. Or, order our Lunch & Dinner Plan to receive two meals a day.'에서 표준 플랜으로, 하루에 세 끼의 식사를 받게 될 것이며, 또는 하루에 두 끼의 식사를 받을 수 있도록 자신들의 점심 & 저녁 플랜을 주문하라고 했으므로 지문의 내용과 일치한다. (C)는 'you'll get three meals a day for a week at a cost of $28 per day'에서 하루 28달러의 비용으로 하루에 세 끼의 식사를 받게 될 것이라고 했으므로 지문의 내용과 일치한다.

어휘 storage n. 보관, 저장 suggestion n. 조언, 제안

158. Not/True 문제

해석 Organi Fresh의 식사에 대해 사실인 것은?
(A) 바로 먹어야 한다.
(B) 전화로 주문될 수 있다.
(C) 매주 같은 날에 배송된다.
(D) 재사용 가능한 용기와 함께 온다.

해설 지문의 'Your order for the week will be shipped ~ every Friday.'에서 당신의 일주일 치 주문은 매주 금요일에 배송될 것이라고 했으므로 (C)가 정답이다. (A), (B), (D)는 지문에 언급되지 않은 내용이다.

어휘 consume v. 먹다, 소모하다 reusable adj. 재사용 가능한

[Paraphrasing]
shipped ~ every Friday 매주 금요일에 배송되다 → delivered on the same day each week 매주 같은 날에 배송되다

159-161번은 다음 기사에 관한 문제입니다.

Wave Technologies사가 Uptron사 인수를 확정하다

신시내티 (12월 8일)—전자회사 Wave Technologies사는 가전제품 제조업체인 Uptron사를 인수했다. 이 움직임은 수익성이 높은 주방가전 시장에서 존재감을 높이려는 Wave Technologies사의 전념을 보여주는 증거로 여겨진다. 이미 텔레비전과 같은 가전제품의 선도적인 생산업체로서 자사의 입지를 확고히 한 ¹⁵⁹Wave Technologies사는 2년 전에 Bolton 백화점 체인과 식기세척기와 냉장고를 공급하는 계약을 체결했다.

"¹⁶⁰Uptron사 인수는 저희가 저희의 제품 범위를 확장하고 저희의 기존 고객들에게 더 나은 서비스를 제공할 수 있도록 할 것입니다."라고 Wave Technologies사의 최고 사업전략가인 Karen Fowler가 말했다. ¹⁶¹이번 매입은 Wave Technologies사에게 Uptron사의 12,000제곱미터 규모의 오하이오주 공장에 대한 접근권을 제공하며, 이 공장은 제품 안전성에 대한 국제 기준들을 충족시킨다. 하지만, Wave Technologies사는 계속해서 인디애나주에 기반을 둘 것이다.

acquisition n. 인수, 매입 acquire v. 인수하다, 획득하다
appliance n. 가전제품 manufacturer n. 제조업체
demonstration n. 증거, 입증 commitment n. 전념, 헌신
presence n. 존재감, 영향력 lucrative adj. 수익성이 높은
establish v. 확고히 하다, 설립하다 agreement n. 계약, 합의
chain n. (상점·호텔 등의) 체인 dishwasher n. 식기세척기
serve v. 서비스를 제공하다 purchase n. 매입, 구매
base v. 기반을 두다, 본거지를 두다

159. 추론 문제

해석 Bolton 백화점에 대해 암시되는 것은?
(A) 12월에 그것의 제품 라인의 폭을 넓힐 것이다.
(B) Uptron사와 제휴 관계를 맺었었다.
(C) 약 2년 전에 설립되었다.
(D) Wave Technologies사에 의해 만들어진 제품들을 판매한다.

해설 지문의 'Wave Technologies entered into an agreement with the Bolton Department Store chain two years ago to provide dishwashers and refrigerators'에서 Wave Technologies사는 2년 전에 Bolton 백화점 체인과 식기세척기와 냉장고를 공급하는 계약을 체결했다고 했으므로 Bolton 백화점이 Wave Technologies사가 만든 제품들을 공급받아 판매한다는 것을 추론할 수 있다. 따라서 (D)가 정답이다.

160. 동의어 찾기 문제

해설 2문단 첫 번째 줄의 "expand"는 의미상 -와 가장 가깝다.
(A) 연장하다
(B) 넓히다
(C) 포함하다
(D) 연기하다

해설 expand를 포함한 구절 'The acquisition of Uptron will allow us to expand our product range and better serve our existing clients'에서 expand는 '확장하다'라는 뜻으로 사용되었다. 따라서 (B)가 정답이다.

161. 추론 문제

해석 Wave Technologies사에 대해 암시되는 것은?
(A) 최근에 그것의 제품 안정성 기준을 변경했다.
(B) 오하이오주로 제조 장비를 옮길 것이다.
(C) 생산 능력을 크게 늘렸다.

(D) 인디애나주의 직원 규모를 줄였다.

해설 지문의 'The purchase provides Wave Technologies with access to Uptron's 12,000-square-meter Ohio plant'에서 이번 매입은 Wave Technologies사에게 Uptron사의 12,000제곱미터 규모의 오하이오주 공장에 대한 접근권을 제공한다고 했으므로, Wave Technologies사의 생산 능력이 크게 늘어났다는 것을 추론할 수 있다. 따라서 (C)가 정답이다.

어휘 production capacity 생산 능력
significantly adv. 크게, 상당히 reduce v. 줄이다
workforce n. 직원, 노동력

162-163번은 다음 광고에 관한 문제입니다.

Time Out Vendors사

Refresh D-02
청량음료 자판기

새로운 Refresh D-02 자판기는 여러분의 고객들에게 병과 캔 음료의 더 넓은 선택권을 제공할 것입니다. 162-(D)Refresh D-02 자판기는 이제 탄산음료와 과일 주스에서부터 생수에 이르는 10가지 종류의 음료를 수용할 수 있습니다. 이 기계는 저희의 예전 D-01 모델이 업데이트된 것이지만, 163-(C)브랜드와 가격 표시를 편리하게 해주는 분리형 후방 조명 화면을 여전히 포함합니다. 음료를 채우는 것 역시 기계의 제품 적재가 용이한 선반을 이용하면 매우 간단합니다.

상세 사항	
162-(A)크기	162-(A)높이 1.8미터 너비 0.8미터 깊이 0.8미터
무게	261킬로그램
음료 선택 개수	10
162-(B)표준 용량	162-(B)20온스 병 (200개)
163-(A)/(D)지불 장치	163-(A)달러 지폐 투입구 163-(D)동전 투입구 신용카드 리더기

Refresh D-02 자판기에 대한 더 자세한 사항을 원하시면, 555-8591로 전화 주시거나 www.timeoutvendors.com을 방문하십시오.

---

cold drink 청량음료 vending machine 자판기
vendor n. 자판기, (판매)업체, 행상인 hold v. 수용하다, 담다
range v. (범위가) 이르다, 미치다; n. 범위 soda n. 탄산음료
removable adj. 분리형의, 떼어낼 수 있는
convenient adj. 편리한 stock v. 채우다, 들여놓다
easy-loading adj. 적재가 용이한 shelf n. 선반
specification n. 상세 사항, 설명서 dimension n. 크기, 치수
width n. 너비 depth n. (앞에서 뒤까지) 깊이
weight n. 무게 standard adj. 표준의; n. 표준, 기준
capacity n. 용량, 용적 mechanism n. 장치, 방법
acceptor n. 투입구, 수용체, 수납자

162. Not/True 문제

해설 기계에 대한 어떤 정보가 광고에서 제시되지 않았는가?
(A) 크기에 대한 상세 사항
(B) 저장 용량
(C) 대여 가격
(D) 수용할 수 있는 제품들의 목록

해설 (C)는 지문에 언급되지 않은 내용이다. 따라서 (C)가 정답이다. (A)는 'Dimensions, Height 1.8 meters, Width 0.8 meters, Depth 0.8 meters'에서 높이, 너비, 깊이 등 제품의 크기에 대한 상세 사항을 확인할 수 있으므로 지문의 내용과 일치한다. (B)는 'Standard Capacity, 20-ounce Bottle (200 pieces)'에서 표준 용량이 20온스 병 200개라고 했으므로 지문의 내용과 일치한다. (D)는 'The Refresh D-02 Vendor can now hold 10 types of drinks, ranging from sodas and fruit juices to bottled water.'에서 Refresh D-02 자판기가 이제 탄산음료와 과일 주스에서부터 생수에 이르는 10가지 종류의 음료를 수용할 수 있다고 했으므로 지문의 내용과 일치한다.

Paraphrasing
Dimensions 크기 → size 크기

163. Not/True 문제

해설 기계의 지불 장치에 대해 언급된 것은?
(A) 지폐를 받는다.
(B) 외화를 식별한다.
(C) 디지털 화면을 사용한다.
(D) 동전 지불은 받지 않는다.

해설 (A)는 'Payment Mechanism, Dollar Bill Acceptor'에서 지불 장치로 달러 지폐 투입구가 있다고 했으므로 지문의 내용과 일치한다. 따라서 (A)가 정답이다. (B)는 지문에 언급되지 않은 내용이다. (C)는 'includes a removable back-lighted display which makes branding and pricing convenient'에서 브랜드와 가격 표시를 편리하게 해주는 분리형 후방 조명 화면을 포함한다고 했지 지불 장치가 디지털 화면이라고 한 것은 아니므로 지문의 내용과 일치하지 않는다. (D)는 'Payment Mechanism, Coin Acceptor'에서 지불 장치로 동전 투입구가 있다고 했으므로 지문의 내용과 일치하지 않는다.

어휘 identify v. 식별하다, 확인하다 foreign currency 외화

Paraphrasing
Bill 지폐 → paper money 지폐

164-167번은 다음 이메일에 관한 문제입니다.

수신: Christina Meister <chrismeister@gomail.com>
발신: 167Martin Jedlika <mjedlikakey@translations.com>
제목: 회신: 문서 번역
날짜: 7월 8일

Ms. Meister께,

Key 번역 회사에 당신의 영어-그리스어 문서 번역의 필요에 관해 연락해 주셔서 감사합니다. 저희는 당신이 보낸 파일을 검토했고, 164당신은 아래에서 저희의 최초 견적을 확인할 수 있습니다:

페이지	페이지당 40달러로 책정된 4페이지
기간	10시간
번역	160달러
165-(A)최초 고객 10퍼센트 할인	165-(A)−16달러
총액	144달러

저희는 또한 번역의 보증된 출력물을 제공할 수 있습니다. 이것은 번역의 정확성을 확인하는 문구뿐만 아니라, 번역가의 이름과 서명을 포함할 것입니다. 저희는 아래와 같은 요금으로 택배를 통해 당신에게 그것을 보내드릴 수 있습니다:

- 국내 표준 (2-3일): 16달러

- 국제 표준 (5-8일): 25달러
- ¹⁶⁶국내 특송 (1일): 22달러
- 국제 특송 (3-4일): 33달러

¹⁶⁷만약 당신이 보증된 출력물을 필요로 한다면, 당신이 어떤 택배 옵션을 선호하는지 명시한 답장을 보내주십시오. 그러면 저는 그에 맞춰 견적을 수정할 것입니다. 그렇지 않다면, 저희의 웹사이트의 계좌 정보를 이용해 간단히 계좌 이체를 하십시오. 당신의 지불액을 받자마자, 저희는 이 프로젝트에 착수할 것입니다.

Martin Jedlika 드림
프로젝트 담당자, Key 번역회사

translation n. 번역 contact v. 연락하다
initial adj. 최초의, 첫 번째 quote n. 견적 duration n. 기간
certified adj. 보증된, 증명된 hard copy 출력물
signature n. 서명 statement n. 문구, 성명
affirm v. 확인하다 accuracy n. 정확성
courier n. 택배, 배달원 accordingly adv. 그에 맞춰
bank transfer 계좌 이체 proceed v. 착수하다, 시작하다

164. 목적 찾기 문제

해석 이메일은 왜 쓰였는가?
(A) 프로젝트가 진행 중이라는 것을 입증하기 위해
(B) 문서 번역을 요청하기 위해
(C) 프로젝트 연기에 대해 설명하기 위해
(D) 잠재적인 고객에게 가격을 명시하기 위해

해설 지문의 'you can find our initial quote below'에서 아래에서 저희, 즉 Key 번역 회사의 최초 견적을 확인할 수 있다고 했으므로 잠재적인 고객에게 견적을 발송했다는 사실을 확인할 수 있다. 따라서 (D)가 정답이다.

어휘 verify v. 입증하다, 확인하다 in progress 진행 중인
potential adj. 잠재적인

[Paraphrasing]
quote 견적 → specify a price 가격을 명시하다

165. Not/True 문제

해석 Ms. Meister에 대해 언급된 것은?
(A) Key 번역 회사와 거래해 본 적이 없다.
(B) 많은 회사들의 견적들을 비교하고 있다.
(C) 7월에 그리스로 여행을 갈 것이다.
(D) 그녀의 이메일에 정확한 파일을 포함시키지 않았다.

해설 지문의 '10% first-time customer discount', '-$16'에서 최초 고객 10퍼센트 할인에서 Ms. Meister가 16달러를 할인받았음을 알 수 있으므로 (A)는 지문의 내용과 일치한다. 따라서 (A)가 정답이다. (B), (C), (D)는 지문에 언급되지 않은 내용이다.

어휘 compare v. 비교하다 a number of 많은, 다수의

166. 육하원칙 문제

해석 문서의 당일 배송에는 얼마나 비용이 드는가?
(A) 16달러
(B) 22달러
(C) 25달러
(D) 33달러

해설 지문의 'Domestic Express (1 day)', '$22'에서 국내 특송 (1일)이 22달러임을 알 수 있으므로 (B)가 정답이다.

어휘 one-day adj. 당일의

[Paraphrasing]
Express (1 day) 특송 (1일) → one-day delivery 당일 배송

167. 육하원칙 문제

해석 Mr. Jedlika에 따르면, Ms. Meister는 왜 이메일에 답장해야 하는가?
(A) 번역이 정확하다는 것을 확인하기 위해
(B) 추가적인 서비스를 이용하기 위해
(C) 은행 계좌에 대한 정보를 제공하기 위해
(D) 파일에 대한 수정을 승인하기 위해

해설 지문의 'Martin Jedlika', 'If you require a certified hard copy, please send a reply'에서 이메일의 발신자인 Mr. Jedlika가 만약 당신, 즉 Ms. Meister가 보증된 출력물을 필요로 한다면 답장을 보내달라고 했으므로 (B)가 정답이다.

어휘 confirm v. 확인하다, 확정하다 make use of ~을 이용하다

[Paraphrasing]
require a certified hard copy 보증된 출력물을 필요로 하다
→ make use of an additional service 추가적인 서비스를 이용하다

168-171번은 다음 편지에 관한 문제입니다.

Cost Smart사 고객님들께,

들으셨을지도 모르겠지만, 전국의 몇몇 다른 대형 소매점들이 이번 주 초에 사이버 범죄자들의 표적이 되었습니다. 이것은 개인 정보 및 지불 내역을 포함한 고객 정보의 절도를 야기했을 수 있습니다. — [1] —. 저희는 여러분을 소중하게 여기고 여러분의 정보에 대한 승인되지 않은 접근이 얼마나 위험이 될 수 있는지 알고 있기 때문에, ¹⁶⁸저희는 Cost Smart사의 시스템을 유사한 공격으로부터 보호하기 위해 저희가 할 수 있는 모든 것을 할 것이라고 약속드립니다.

¹⁷¹저희는 이미 저희의 보안 및 암호화 소프트웨어를 업그레이드했습니다. — [2] —. 저희는 또한 직원들에게 그들이 취해야 할 예방 조치를 알도록 추가적인 교육을 제공할 계획입니다. 저희의 조치들이 사이버 범죄자들을 막는 데에 효과적일 것으로 생각하지만, ¹⁶⁸저희는 여러분에게도 Cost Smart사 고객으로서 주의할 것을 요청드립니다.

¹⁶⁹저희는 절대 여러분께 개인 정보를 요청하기 위해 전화로 연락하지 않을 것이라는 점을 유의하십시오. — [3] —. ¹⁶⁹만약 여러분이 자신을 Cost Smart사 고객 서비스 직원으로 소개하는 발신자들로부터 문자 메시지를 받는다면, 즉시 그것들을 삭제하십시오. — [4] —. 또한, ¹⁷⁰이메일들의 링크를 클릭하기 보다는 항상 곧바로 저희의 웹사이트를 방문하십시오. 여러분이 안내된 그 웹사이트는 저희 것과 똑같이 보이도록 제작된 것일 수도 있습니다. 이것은 여러분을 속여서 여러분의 비밀번호를 입력하게 하려는 것이고, 그렇게 함으로써 그것을 그 사이트 관리자에게 보여주는 것입니다.

여러분의 신의에 감사드립니다. 질문이 있으시면, 555-8897로 저희에게 전화 주십시오.

Florence Stoddard 드림
Cost Smart사 관리자

retail store 소매점 target v. 표적으로 삼다, 겨냥하다
theft n. 절도, 도둑질 threat n. 위험, 위협
unauthorized adj. 승인되지 않은 safeguard v. 보호하다
attack n. 공격; v. 공격하다 encryption n. 암호화
precaution n. 예방 조치, 사전 대책 deter v. 막다, 저지하다
cautious adj. 주의하는, 신중한 direct v. 안내하다, 향하다
thereby adv. 그렇게 함으로써 reveal v. 보이다, 드러내다
operator n. 관리자, 경영자

168. 목적 찾기 문제

해석 편지의 목적은 무엇인가?
(A) 온라인 쇼핑을 피해야 한다는 것을 제안하기 위해
(B) 몇몇 예방책들을 설명하기 위해
(C) 범죄자들이 어떻게 도용된 정보를 사용하는지 설명하기 위해
(D) 고객 정보의 손실에 대해 사과하기 위해

해설 지문의 'we promise to do everything we can to safeguard ~ system against similar attacks'에서 저희, 즉 Cost Smart사는 시스템을 유사한 공격으로부터 보호하기 위해 자신들이 할 수 있는 모든 것을 할 것이라고 약속한다고 했고, 'we ask you to be cautious as well'에서 여러분, 즉 고객들도 주의할 것을 요청한다고 한 후 보호를 위한 방법들을 설명하고 있으므로 (B)가 정답이다.

어휘 preventive measure 예방책 stolen adj. 도용된, 훔친
apologize v. 사과하다

169. 추론 문제

해석 편지에서 언급된 문자 메시지에 대해 암시되는 것은?
(A) 고객이 주문들을 확정하도록 한다.
(B) 다가오는 판매 행사들을 광고한다.
(C) 정규 업무 시간 중에는 수신되지 않는다.
(D) 가게 직원들에 의해 발송되지 않는다.

해설 지문의 'we will never contact you over the phone'과 'If you receive text messages from senders representing themselves as Cost Smart customer service associates, delete them immediately.'에서 저희, 즉 Cost Smart사는 절대 고객들에게 전화로 연락하지 않을 것이며 만약 여러분, 즉 고객들이 자신을 Cost Smart사 고객 서비스 직원으로 소개하는 발신자들로부터 문자 메시지를 받는다면, 즉시 그것들을 삭제하라고 했으므로 문자 메시지의 발신자가 Cost Smart사의 직원이 아니라는 사실을 추론할 수 있다. 따라서 (D)가 정답이다.

어휘 upcoming adj. 다가오는

170. 육하원칙 문제

해석 편지에 따르면, 고객들은 왜 이메일 링크를 클릭하면 안 되는가?
(A) 컴퓨터를 바이러스로 감염시킬 수도 있다.
(B) 보안 프로그램들을 손상시킬 것이다.
(C) 가짜 웹페이지로 연결될 수도 있다.
(D) 중요한 정보를 삭제할 것이다.

해설 지문의 'always visit our Web site directly rather than clicking on links in e-mails. The Web sites you are directed to may be designed to look exactly like ours.'에서 이메일들의 링크를 클릭하기보다는 항상 곧바로 저희, 즉 Cost Smart사의 웹사이트에 방문하라고 하며, 여러분, 즉 고객들이 안내된 웹사이트는 Cost Smart사의 것과 똑같이 보이도록 제작된 것일 수도 있다고 했으므로 (C)가 정답이다.

어휘 infect v. 감염시키다 disable v. 손상시키다 lead v. 연결되다

171. 문장 위치 찾기 문제

해설 [1], [2], [3], [4]로 표시된 위치 중, 다음 문장이 들어갈 곳으로 가장 적절한 것은?

"저희는 저희 시스템의 이러한 개선들이 여러분의 정보가 저희 시스템의 외부로 불법적으로 전송되는 것을 예방하도록 도울 것이라고 확신합니다."

(A) [1]
(B) [2]
(C) [3]
(D) [4]

해설 주어진 문장은 보안 시스템 개선과 관련된 내용이 나오는 부분에 들어가야 함을 알 수 있다. [2]의 앞 문장인 'We have already upgraded our security and encryption software.'에서 저희, 즉 Cost Smart사는 이미 보안 및 암호화 소프트웨어를 업그레이드했다고 했으므로, [2]에 제시된 문장이 들어가면 Cost Smart사는 보안 및 암호화 소프트웨어 업그레이드와 같은 개선들이 고객의 정보가 시스템의 외부로 불법적으로 전송되는 것을 예방하도록 도울 것이라고 확신한다는 자연스러운 문맥이 된다는 것을 알 수 있다. 따라서 (B)가 정답이다.

어휘 confident adj. 확신하는, 자신감이 있는
prevent v. 예방하다, 막다 illegally adv. 불법적으로

172-175번은 다음 온라인 채팅 대화문에 관한 문제입니다.

Zelda Coe   오후 3시 15분

¹⁷²저는 저의 직원들이 원격으로 근무하도록 허용할지 고민해오고 있어요. 그저 하나의 아이디어일 뿐이에요. 하지만 그것은 직원 만족도를 올리면서 생산성도 증가시키는 좋은 방법일 수도 있어요. ¹⁷²어떻게 생각하시나요?

Stuart Ojeda   오후 3시 16분

음, 많은 직원들이 매일 사무실로 통근하는 것을 피할 수 있게 되는 것을 좋아할 것이라고 확신해요. 하지만 저는 그들이 모두가 이 기회를 이용할 수 있을지는 확실하지 않아요. ¹⁷³그들은 필요한 장비가 없을 수도 있어요.

Libby Schuster   오후 3시 17분

¹⁷³맞아요. 그들의 집에 있는 컴퓨터들은 저희가 사용하는 그래픽 디자인 소프트웨어를 실행하기에 충분히 강력하지 않을 수 있어요.

Zelda Coe   오후 3시 18분

알겠어요. 만약 제가 이 선택권을 적합한 컴퓨터를 가지고 있으면서 재택근무하기를 선호하는 사람에게 제공한다면요?

Stuart Ojeda   오후 3시 19분

잘 모르겠어요. ¹⁷⁴제 예전 직장에서, 저는 집에서 일한 직원들이 회의 중에 더 적게 기여했다는 것을 발견했어요. 이 문제는 팀 화합에 부정적인 영향을 미쳤고 심지어 몇몇 프로젝트의 완성이 지연되게 했어요.

Libby Schuster   오후 3시 20분

또한, 만약 그들이 동료들을 정기적으로 만나지 않으면 그들은 배제되었다고 느낄 수 있어요. 어쨌든, 사무실에 오는 것은 직원들이 일하기에 좋은 마음가짐을 갖게 해요.

Zelda Coe   오후 3시 21분

여러분 모두의 의견에 감사해요. ¹⁷⁵저는 저희 직원들에게 이 사안에 대한 그들의 의견을 요청하는 이메일을 보낼 거예요.

---

consider v. 고민하다, 고려하다 remotely adv. 원격으로
boost v. 올리다, 북돋우다 productivity n. 생산성
commute v. 통근하다 take advantage of ~을 이용하다
telecommute v. 재택근무하다 contribute v. 기여하다
negative adj. 부정적인 cohesion n. 화합, 결합
excluded adj. 배제된, 제외된 coworker n. (직장) 동료
state of mind 마음가짐 input n. 의견

172. 의도 파악 문제

해설 오후 3시 15분에, Ms. Coe가 "It's just an idea"라고 썼을 때 그녀가 의도한 것은?
(A) 결정이 아직 내려지지 않았다.
(B) 구체적인 답변을 원한다.

(C) 문제가 해결되었다.
(D) 계획을 발전시킬 시간이 없었다.

해설 지문의 'I've been considering allowing my staff to work remotely.'에서 Ms. Coe가 직원들이 원격으로 근무하도록 허용할지 고민해 오고 있다고 한 후, 'It's just an idea'(그저 하나의 아이디어일 뿐이에요)라고 하며, 'What do you think?'에서 동료들에게 어떻게 생각하는지 질문한 것을 통해, Ms. Coe가 원격 근무를 허용할지에 대해 아직 결정을 내리지 않았다는 것을 알 수 있다. 따라서 (A)가 정답이다.

어휘 decision n. 결정 resolve v. 해결하다
develop v. 발전시키다

173. 육하원칙 문제

해설 Mr. Ojeda와 Ms. Schuster는 무엇에 동의하는가?
(A) 집에서 일하는 사람들은 팀의 일원처럼 느껴지지 않는다.
(B) 사무실에 통근하는 직원들은 자주 늦는다.
(C) 직원들은 원격으로 근무하기 위해 필요한 것을 가지고 있지 않을 수도 있다.
(D) 사무실 밖에서 일하는 사람들은 신뢰할 수 없다.

해설 지문의 'They may not have the necessary equipment.'에서 Mr. Ojeda가 그들, 즉 직원들은 원격으로 근무하는 데 필요한 장비가 없을 수도 있다고 하자, 'Right. Their home computers might not be powerful enough to run the graphic design software we use.'에서 Ms. Schuster가 맞다고 동의하며 그들, 즉 직원들의 집에 있는 컴퓨터들은 자신들이 사용하는 그래픽 디자인 소프트웨어를 실행하기에 충분히 강력하지 않을 수 있다고 했으므로 (C)가 정답이다.

어휘 unreliable adj. 신뢰할 수 없는

174. 추론 문제

해설 Mr. Ojeda에 대해 암시되는 것은?
(A) 업무능력 평가를 실시하는 것이 필요하다고 생각한다.
(B) 재택근무가 선택지였던 사무실에서 일한 적이 있다.
(C) 몇몇 직원들이 급여 인상을 받아야 한다고 생각한다.
(D) 최근에 관리직으로 승진되었다.

해설 지문의 'At my old job, I found that employees who worked from home contributed less during meetings.'에서 Mr. Ojeda가 그의 예전 직장에서, 집에서 일한 직원들이 회의 중에 더 적게 기여했다는 것을 발견했다고 했으므로 그가 이전에 재택근무를 할 수 있는 회사에서 일했다는 사실을 추론할 수 있다. 따라서 (B)가 정답이다.

어휘 promote v. 승진시키다, 홍보하다

[Paraphrasing]
worked from home 집에서 일했다 → telecommuting 재택근무

175. 육하원칙 문제

해설 Ms. Coe는 다음에 무엇을 할 것 같은가?
(A) 회의를 위한 발표를 만든다.
(B) 직원들로부터 피드백을 모은다.
(C) 상사에게 요청서를 제출한다.
(D) 현재 회사 정책을 검토한다.

해설 지문의 'I'm going to send out an e-mail to our staff asking for their input on this matter.'에서 직원들에게 이 사안에 대한 그들의 의견을 요청하는 이메일을 보낼 것이라고 했으므로 (B)가 정답이다.

어휘 superior n. 상사 policy n. 정책

176-180번은 다음 공고와 기사에 관한 문제입니다.

모든 고객분들은 주목해 주십시오

Sunrise 리조트 그룹의 경영진은 이 기회를 통해 ^{178}저희의 Key West 지점의 개장이 7월 25일로 예정되어 있다는 것을 모두에게 상기시켜 드리고자 합니다. 아름다운 남해안에 자리잡은 이곳은 스파, 회의장, 수영장, 그리고 골프장을 포함해, 여러분이 Sunrise 리조트에서 찾을 것으로 기대하시는 모든 편의 시설을 갖출 것입니다. 저희는 또한 ^{176}세계적으로 유명한 요리사 David Mears가 이 리조트에서 레스토랑 운영을 감독해 달라는 저희의 초청을 받아들였다는 것을 알리게 되어 기쁘고, 저희는 그의 팀에 의해 제작된 요리가 저희의 모든 고객을 만족시킬 것이라고 확신합니다.

저희의 단골 고객분들께 보상해 드리기 위해, ^{177}모든 Sunrise 리조트의 등록된 고객분들께 Key West 지점의 객실에 대해 25퍼센트의 할인을 제공하고 있습니다. 프런트에 들르시면, 저희 직원 중 한 명이 기꺼이 귀하께 새로운 시설에서 체크인할 때 제시하실 수 있는 할인 쿠폰을 드릴 것입니다. 저희 지점들에 대해 더 많은 정보를 원하신다면, www.sunriseresorts.com/branches에 꼭 방문해 주십시오.

remind v. 상기시키다 grand opening 개장, 개점
amenity n. 편의시설 world-renowned adj. 세계적으로 유명한
oversee v. 감독하다 dish n. 요리, 음식
loyal customer 단골 고객 present v. 제시하다; adj. 현재의
establishment n. 시설

새 리조트에 대해 의견이 분열된 Key West 주민들

마이애미 ^{178}(8월 15일)—Sunrise 리조트 그룹의 최신 시설이 오늘 개장했는데, 몇몇 주민들은 이를 탐탁지 않아 하고 있다. 그들은 최대 수용 인원이 400명인 이 리조트가 해당 지역에 살고 있는 사람들에게 부정적인 영향을 줄 것이라고 주장한다. Beautiful Key West(BKW)라고 불리는 시민단체의 대표인 Valerie Collins는 여행객들의 유입이 지역 자원에 부담을 주고 해양과 섬의 생태계 악화의 원인이 될 것이라고 주장한다.

그러나, ^{180}5월에 가까스로 재선된 ^{179}Justin Ingham 시장은 관광업이 지역 경제에 필수적이라고 주장한다. "Sunrise 리조트는 많은 새로운 일자리를 창출하고 과세 기준을 확대할 것입니다"라고 그는 인기 있는 아침 뉴스 프로그램인 Key West Happenings의 최근 출연에서 말했다. 그는 또한 호텔이 지역 사업체들을 위한 많은 잠재적인 고객들을 끌어들일 것이라고 언급했다.

divided adj. 의견이 분열된 influx n. 유입 strain n. 부담, 압박
contribute to ~의 원인이 되다 marine adj. 해양의, 바다의
ecosystem n. 생태계 narrowly adv. 가까스로
maintain v. 주장하다, 유지하다 tax base 과세 기준

176. 육하원칙 문제

해설 Mr. Mears는 무엇을 하기로 동의했는가?
(A) 개장을 계획한다.
(B) 몇몇 시설의 견학을 이끈다.
(C) 지역 요리를 홍보한다.
(D) 식사 시설을 운영한다.

해설 공고의 'world-renowned chef David Mears has accepted our invitation to oversee the operation of the restaurant at this resort'에서 세계적으로 유명한 요리사 David Mears가 이 리조트에서 레스토랑 운영을 감독해 달라는 초청을 받아들였다고 했으므로 (D)가 정답이다.

Paraphrasing
oversee the operation of the restaurant 레스토랑 운영을 감독하다 → Manage a dining facility 식사 시설을 운영하다

177. 육하원칙 문제
해석 Sunrise 리조트 고객들은 어떻게 할인을 받을 수 있는가?
(A) 보상 프로그램에 등록함으로써
(B) 웹사이트에 코드를 입력함으로써
(C) 프런트 직원에게 전화를 함으로써
(D) 쿠폰을 얻음으로써
해설 공고의 'we are offering registered guests at all Sunrise Resorts 25 percent off ~. Stop by the front desk, and one of our staff members will be happy to give you a discount voucher you can present when you check in at our new establishment.'에서 모든 Sunrise 리조트의 등록된 고객들에게 25퍼센트의 할인을 제공하고 있다며, 프런트에 들르면 저희, 즉 리조트의 직원 중 한 명이 기꺼이 새로운 시설에서 체크인할 때 제시할 수 있는 할인 쿠폰을 줄 것이라고 했으므로 (D)가 정답이다.

178. 추론 문제 연계
해석 Key West Sunrise 리조트에 대해 암시되는 것은?
(A) 관광 단체로부터 찬사를 받았다.
(B) 7월에 스파 브랜드를 출시했다.
(C) 계획했던 것보다 늦게 운영을 시작했다.
(D) 큰 호텔 체인과 합병했다.
해설 새로운 Key West Sunrise 리조트에 대해 중점적으로 설명하는 공고를 먼저 확인한다.
단서 1 공고의 'our Key West location's grand opening is scheduled for July 25'에서 저희, 즉 Sunrise 리조트의 Key West 지점의 개장이 7월 25일로 예정되어 있다고 했다. 그런데 이 지점이 실제로 7월 25일에 개장했는지 제시되지 않았으므로 기사에서 관련 내용을 확인한다.
단서 2 기사의 '(August 15)—The Sunrise Resort Group's newest establishment opened today'에서 8월 15일에 Sunrise 리조트 그룹의 최신 시설이 오늘 개장했다고 했으므로 Sunrise 리조트의 Key West 지점이 8월 15일에 개장했음을 알 수 있다.
두 단서를 종합할 때, Sunrise 리조트의 Key West 지점이 계획했던 7월 25일보다 늦게 개장했다는 사실을 추론할 수 있다. 따라서 (C)가 정답이다.

179. 동의어 찾기 문제
해석 기사에서, 2문단 두 번째 줄의 단어 "vital"은 의미상 -와 가장 가깝다.
(A) 신선한
(B) 필수적인
(C) 일관적인
(D) 편안한
해설 vital을 포함한 구절 'Mayor Justin Ingham ~ maintains that tourism is vital to the community's economy'에서 vital은 '필수적인'이라는 뜻으로 사용되었다. 따라서 (B)가 정답이다.

180. 육하원칙 문제
해석 기사에 따르면, 5월에 무슨 일이 있었는가?
(A) 텔레비전으로 방송되는 인터뷰가 시행되었다.
(B) 시민 단체가 서명을 수집했다.
(C) 시장이 세금 정책을 발표했다.
(D) 시장 선거가 실시되었다.

해설 기사의 'Mayor Justin Ingham, who was narrowly reelected in May'에서 Justin Ingham 시장이 5월에 가까스로 재선되었다고 했으므로 (D)가 정답이다.
어휘 televised adj. 텔레비전으로 방송되는
municipal election 시장 선거

181-185번은 다음 안내문과 이메일에 관한 문제입니다.

Bayweather 제조사
직원 경비 계정 분류

⇨ 월간 경비 보고서를 작성할 때, 각각의 경비에 해당하는 분류를 찾아 "유형" 칸에 코드를 기입하세요.

⇨ ¹⁸¹특정한 지출이 어떤 분류에 해당하는지 불확실한 경우, 직원 안내서의 챕터 12를 참고하십시오. ¹⁸²몇몇 분류는 환급될 수 있는 금액에 관해 한도와 제한이 있다는 점을 유의하십시오.

T43	우편 및 배달 서비스
T45	인쇄 및 복사
P7	장비 대여
¹⁸²B27	¹⁸²전문성 개발 강좌를 위한 요금
M30	회사 행사를 위한 식음료
M31	고객과 만나는 동안의 식음료
J13	출장 동안의 식음료
J14	출장 동안의 숙소
J15	출장과 관련된 교통수단
¹⁸⁴P11	¹⁸⁴출장에 필요한 법률 문서
X1	기타 *

* "기타" 분류에 있는 비용에 대해서는, 경비 보고서 양식에 제시된 공간에 상세한 설명을 적으세요.

expense account 경비 계정(비용을 기록하고 정산하는 회계 항목)
corresponding adj. 해당하는   consult v. 참고하다, 찾아보다
restriction n. 제한   in terms of ~에 관해
reimburse v. 환급하다   postage n. 우편
accommodation n. 숙소   detailed adj. 상세한
description n. 설명

수신: Pedro Larson <plarson@bayweather.com>
¹⁸⁴발신: Wendy Macintyre <wmacintyre@bayweather.com>
날짜: 10월 11일
제목: 경비 보고서에 관한 문제

Mr. Larson께,

9월 경비 계정 보고서를 작성함에 있어 주의를 기울여 주신 것에 감사드립니다. ¹⁸³그것은 귀하가 이 회사에서 근무하는 동안 처음으로 제출하셨던 8월 보고서보다 훨씬 더 정확했습니다. 그럼에도 불구하고, 귀하의 경비가 환급될 수 있기 전에 살펴봐 주셔야 할 맞지 않는 점이 있습니다. ¹⁸⁴귀하가 파키스탄으로의 출장을 위해 취득해야 했던 비자의 경우, 경비 계정 보고서에 표시된 금액은 95달러입니다. 하지만, 귀하가 제시한 영수증은 62달러에 대한 것입니다. 목요일이 이번 달 경비 보고서의 제출 마감 기한이므로 ¹⁸⁵귀하는 더 큰 액수를 뒷받침하는 서류를 늦어도 목요일까지 제 사무실로 가져오셔야 할 것입니다. 무엇이든 질문이 있다면 알려주십시오.

Wendy Macintyre 드림
회계 부서

appreciate v. 감사하다 accurate adj. 정확한
discrepancy n. 맞지 않는 점, 불일치
look into ~을 (주의 깊게) 살펴보다 documentation n. 서류
deadline n. 마감 기한 submission n. 제출

181. 육하원칙 문제
해석 몇몇 직원들은 왜 안내서를 참고해야 할 것인가?
(A) 연락처 목록을 보기 위해
(B) 일련의 규정을 살펴보기 위해
(C) 연수 활동을 준비하기 위해
(D) 비용을 분류하기 위해

해설 안내문의 'If you are unsure about what category a particular expense falls into, consult Chapter 12 of the employee handbook.'에서 특정한 지출이 어떤 분류에 해당하는지 불확실한 경우 직원 안내서의 챕터 12를 참고하라고 했으므로 (D)가 정답이다.

어휘 contact detail 연락처 classify v. 분류하다

182. 추론 문제
해석 Bayweather 제조사에 대해 암시되는 것은?
(A) 각 직원들에게 핸드폰을 제공한다.
(B) 특정 교육 비용을 지불해 준다.
(C) 청구서가 관리자에 의해 서명되도록 한다.
(D) 매달 말에 직원들에게 환급한다.

해설 안내문의 'Note that some categories have limits ~ in terms of the amount that can be reimbursed.'에서 몇몇 분류는 환급될 수 있는 금액에 관해 한도가 있다고 하며 Bayweather 제조사가 특정 경비를 환급해 준다는 점을 언급했고, 'B27, Fees for professional development courses'에서 B27에 해당하는 경비가 전문성 개발 강좌를 위한 요금이라고 했으므로 Bayweather 제조사에서 직원들의 전문성 개발 교육 비용을 환급을 통해 지불해 준다는 것을 추론할 수 있다. 따라서 (B)가 정답이다.

어휘 educational adj. 교육의 invoice n. 청구서

183. 추론 문제
해석 Mr. Larson에 대해 암시되는 것은?
(A) 회의에서 한 절차에 대해 불평했다.
(B) 오류가 포함된 8월 보고서를 보냈다.
(C) 직장 동료 단체와 함께 해외여행을 갔다.
(D) 새로운 버전의 양식을 작성할 것을 요청받았다.

해설 이메일의 'It was much more accurate than your August report—the first one you submitted ~. Nonetheless, there's a discrepancy I need you to look into'에서 그것, 즉 Mr. Larson이 작성한 9월 경비 계정 보고서는 그가 처음으로 제출했던 8월 보고서보다 훨씬 더 정확했지만 그럼에도 불구하고 살펴봐야 할 맞지 않는 점이 있다고 했으므로, Mr. Larson이 작성했던 8월 보고서에도 오류가 있었다는 것을 추론할 수 있다. 따라서 (B)가 정답이다.

어휘 contain v. 포함하다, 가지고 있다

184. 육하원칙 문제 연계
해석 Ms. Macintyre는 어느 경비 분류에 대해 언급하는가?
(A) T43
(B) M30
(C) B27
(D) P11

해설 Ms. Macintyre가 작성한 이메일을 먼저 확인한다.

단서 1 이메일의 'From: Wendy Macintyre'에서 Ms. Macintyre가 보낸 이메일임을 알 수 있고, 'For the visa you had to get for your business trip to Pakistan'에서 귀하, 즉 Mr. Larson이 파키스탄으로의 출장을 위해 비자를 취득해야 했다고 했다. 그런데 출장을 위해 취득해야 했던 비자가 어느 경비 분류에 속하는지 제시되지 않았으므로 안내문에서 관련 내용을 확인한다.

단서 2 안내문의 'P11, Legal documents needed for business travel'에서 출장에 필요한 법률 문서 경비의 분류가 P11이라는 사실을 확인할 수 있다.

두 단서를 종합할 때, Ms. Macintyre가 언급한 출장을 위한 비자의 경비 분류가 P11이라는 것을 알 수 있다. 따라서 (D)가 정답이다.

185. 육하원칙 문제
해석 Ms. Macintyre는 Mr. Larson에게 무엇을 하도록 요청하는가?
(A) 몇몇 정보를 배포한다.
(B) 보고서를 제출한다.
(C) 몇몇 서류를 제시한다.
(D) 마감 기한을 연장한다.

해설 이메일의 'You will need to bring supporting documentation for the larger amount to my office by Thursday at the latest'에서 귀하, 즉 Mr. Larson은 더 큰 액수를 뒷받침하는 서류를 늦어도 목요일까지 제, 즉 Ms. Macintyre의 사무실로 가져와야 할 것이라고 했으므로 (C)가 정답이다.

어휘 distribute v. 배포하다 extend v. 연장하다

186-190번은 다음 구인 광고, 편지, 이메일에 관한 문제입니다.

여러 지원 가능한 일자리-Quadra 부동산

[186]당신은 로스앤젤레스에서 가장 큰 상업용 부동산 중개소에서 일하는 것에 관심 있으십니까? Quadra 부동산은 사업체들이 직장 시설을 찾고 관리하는 데 도움을 주는 성장하는 기업입니다. 저희는 현재 다음과 같은 일자리를 채워줄 사람들을 찾고 있습니다:

[187]회계사 / Fairfax 지점
[187]요건: 회계학 학사 학위 및 3년의 관련 경력

부동산 중개인 / Huntington 지점
요건: 부동산 중개인 자격증 및 4년의 관련 경력

접수원 / San Pedro 지점
요건: 고등학교 졸업장 및 2년의 관련 경력

부지점장 / Forest Grove 지점
요건: 경영학 학사 학위 및 6년의 관련 경력

이 일자리들에 관한 더 많은 정보와 지원하는 방법에 관한 설명을 위해, 저희의 홈페이지인 www.quadrarealty.com에 방문해 주십시오.

realty n. 부동산 **commercial** adj. 상업용의
real estate 부동산 **workplace** n. 직장
accountant n. 회계사 **bachelor** n. 학사
accounting n. 회계학 **realtor** n. 부동산 중개인
diploma n. 졸업장

7월 15일

Brett Reynolds
Quadra 부동산
1602번지 Delta가

로스앤젤레스, 캘리포니아주 90293

Mr. Reynolds께,

저는 Quadra 부동산의 직원이 되는 것에 저의 관심을 표하고자 합니다. ¹⁸⁷저는 제가 명단에 기재된 일자리에 아주 적합하다고 생각합니다. 비록 저는 이전에 부동산 중개소에서 일한 적은 없지만, ¹⁸⁷저는 대학에서 회계학을 전공했습니다. ¹⁸⁷/¹⁸⁸⁻⁽ᴰ⁾또한, 저는 지난 4년간 Blackwood 건설회사의 회계부서에서 근무했습니다. 저는 지금 새로운 고용 기회를 찾고 있는데, 이는 ¹⁸⁸⁻⁽ᴰ⁾제 회사가 오클랜드로 이전할 계획이고, 저는 로스앤젤레스 지역에 남길 원하기 때문입니다.

만약 질문이 있으시면 제게 555-0393으로 전화 또는 j.quayle@digiquest.com으로 이메일을 통해 연락할 수 있습니다. 유감스럽게도, ¹⁸⁹저는 저의 현재 근무 일정 때문에 평일 아침에만 면접을 볼 수 있습니다. 제 지원서를 고려해 주셔서 감사합니다.

Jenna Quayle 드림

suited adj. 적합한 **listed** adj. (명단에) 기재된
previously adv. 이전에 **major in** ~을 전공하다
relocate v. 이전하다, 옮기다 **remain** v. 남다

수신: Doug Stevens <d.stevens@quadra.com>, Laura Meyers <l.meyers@quadra.com>, Jeff Kim <j.kim@quadra.com>, Pauline Greer <p.greer@quadra.com>
발신: Brett Reynolds <b.reynolds@quadra.com>
제목: 고용 현황
날짜: 9월 8일

안녕하세요 여러분,

저는 모든 지점장들에게 고용 절차에 관해 최신 정보를 알려주고 싶었습니다. 현시점에서, 저희는 공석들에 대한 몇몇 유망한 지원자들이 있습니다. ¹⁸⁹면접은 다음의 날들에 이루어질 것입니다:

월요일, 9월 15일 (오후 2시)
¹⁸⁹수요일, 9월 17일 (오전 10시)
목요일, 9월 18일 (오후 4시)
토요일, 9월 20일 (오전 11시)

¹⁹⁰만약 제가 지원자들에게 묻길 바라는 구체적인 질문들이 있다면, 저에게 그것들을 보내주십시오. 저는 지원자들과의 제 첫 번째 만남을 준비할 시간을 가질 수 있도록 9월 10일까지 이 정보가 필요할 것입니다. 면접이 완료되면, 저는 가장 적합한 지원자들에 대한 요약 보고서들을 만들 것입니다. 이것들은 여러분이 검토할 수 있도록 9월 24일에 이메일로 발송될 것입니다.

Brett Reynolds 드림
인사부장, Quadra 부동산

branch manager 지점장 **promising** adj. 유망한
candidate n. 지원자, 후보자 **applicant** n. 지원자

186. 추론 문제

해석 구인 광고에서 Quadra 부동산에 대해 암시되는 것은?
(A) 최근에 직원 복지 혜택을 변경했다.
(B) 주로 기업 고객에게 서비스를 제공한다.
(C) 모든 직원이 대학 학위를 가지도록 요구한다.
(D) 로스앤젤레스 지역 외부에 사무실을 개설하고자 한다.

해설 구인 광고의 'Are you interested in working for the largest commercial real estate agency in Los Angeles?'에서 로스앤젤레스에서 가장 큰 상업용 부동산 중개소에서 일하는 것에 관심 있는지 물은 후, 'Quadra Realty is a ~ company that helps businesses find and manage workplace facilities.'에서 Quadra 부동산은 사업체들이 직장 시설을 찾고 관리하는 데 도움을 주는 기업이라고 했으므로, Quadra 부동산은 기업 고객을 대상으로 영업하는 부동산이라는 사실을 추론할 수 있다. 따라서 (B)가 정답이다.

어휘 **modify** v. 변경하다 **primarily** adv. 주로
intend to ~하고자 하다

187. 육하원칙 문제 연계

해석 Ms. Quayle은 어느 지점의 일자리에 지원했는가?
(A) Fairfax 지점
(B) Huntington 지점
(C) San Pedro 지점
(D) Forest Grove 지점

해설 Ms. Quayle이 작성한 편지를 먼저 확인한다.
[단서 1] 편지의 'I believe that I am well suited for the listed position.'에서 저, 즉 Ms. Quayle은 자신이 명단에 기재된 일자리에 아주 적합하다고 생각한다고 했고, 'I majored in accounting in college. In addition, I have spent the last four years in the accounting department'에서는 대학에서 회계학을 전공했으며 지난 4년간 회계부서에서 근무했다고 했다. 그런데 회계사 일자리가 어느 지점에서 필요한 일자리인지 제시되지 않았으므로 구인 광고에서 관련 내용을 확인한다.
[단서 2] 구인 광고의 'Accountant / Fairfax Branch', 'Requirements: Bachelor's degree in accounting and three years of related experience'에서 Fairfax 지점의 회계사 일자리의 요건이 회계학 학사 학위 및 3년의 관련 경력이라는 것을 확인할 수 있다.
두 단서를 종합할 때, Ms. Quayle은 Fairfax 지점의 회계사 일자리에 지원했다는 것을 알 수 있다. 따라서 (A)가 정답이다.

188. Not/True 문제

해석 Blackwood 건설회사에 대해 언급된 것은?
(A) 몇몇 사무실들을 닫을 것이다.
(B) 새로운 건축 프로젝트를 시작할 것이다.
(C) 더 많은 직원들을 고용할 것이다.
(D) 다른 도시로 이동할 것이다.

해설 편지의 'I have spent the last four years in ~ Blackwood Construction'과 'my company is planning to relocate to Oakland, and I wish to remain in the Los Angeles area'에서 저, 즉 Ms. Quayle이 지난 4년간 Blackwood 건설회사에서 근무했고, 자신의 회사가 오클랜드로 이전할 계획이며 자신은 로스앤젤레스 지역에 남길 원한다고 했으므로 (D)는 지문의 내용과 일치한다. 따라서 (D)가 정답이다. (A), (B), (C)는 지문에 언급되지 않은 내용이다.

[Paraphrasing]
is planning to relocate to Oakland 오클랜드로 이전할 계획이다 → will move to a different city 다른 도시로 이동할 것이다

189. 추론 문제 연계

해석 Ms. Quayle은 언제 면접을 볼 것 같은가?
(A) 9월 15일에
(B) 9월 17일에
(C) 9월 18일에
(D) 9월 20일에

해설 Ms. Quayle이 작성한 편지를 먼저 확인한다.

단서 1 편지의 'I am only available to interview on weekday mornings:'에서 자신, 즉 Ms. Quayle은 평일 아침에만 면접을 볼 수 있다고 했다. 그런데 평일 아침의 면접 날짜가 제시되지 않았으므로 이메일에서 관련 내용을 확인한다.

단서 2 이메일의 'The interviews will take place on the following days:'와 'Wednesday, September 17 (10 A.M.)'에서 면접이 9월 17일 수요일 오전 10시에 이루어질 것을 확인할 수 있다.

두 단서를 종합할 때, Ms. Quayle은 평일 아침인 9월 17일 수요일 오전 10시에 면접을 볼 것이라는 것을 추론할 수 있다. 따라서 (B)가 정답이다.

190. 추론 문제

해석 Mr. Reynolds에 대해 결론지을 수 있는 것은?
(A) 직접 면접을 진행할 것이다.
(B) 이미 지원자에게 제안을 했다.
(C) 일자리가 아직 채용 가능한지 확신할 수 없다.
(D) 신입 직원들의 교육을 담당하고 있다.

해설 이메일의 'If you have any specific questions you would like me to ask the applicants, please send them to me.'와 'I will ~ prepare for my first meetings with the candidates'에서 만약 자신, 즉 Mr. Reynolds가 지원자들에게 묻길 바라는 구체적인 질문들이 있다면, 자신에게 그것들을 보내 달라고 했고, 지원자들과의 첫 번째 만남을 준비할 것이라고 했으므로 Mr. Reynolds가 직접 면접을 진행할 것이라는 사실을 추론할 수 있다. 따라서 (A)가 정답이다.

어휘 **personally** adv. 직접, 개인적으로 **uncertain** adj. 확신이 없는
in charge of ~을 담당하는

191-195번은 다음 두 이메일과 공고에 관한 문제입니다.

수신: Windfield 미술관 직원 <staff@windfieldart.com>
발신: Martina Klancy <m.klancy@windfieldart.com>
제목: 조각품들을 다루는 것
날짜: 11월 23일

안녕하세요, 여러분.

우리 미술관이 다음 달 다수의 조각품들을 전시할 것이기 때문에, 모두가 어떻게 이러한 유형의 미술품을 다루는지에 대해 아는 것이 중요합니다. 다음 지시 사항을 주목해 주시기 바랍니다.

1. 어떤 조각품이든 다루기 전에 보호용 천 장갑을 착용해주십시오.
2. 관리 벽장에 보관된 청소용 스프레이를 사용하여 조각된 작품들의 밑 부분을 닦아 주십시오. 이것은 목요일 오후에 완료되어야 합니다. 미술관 방문자들에게 예술작품이 청소되거나 닦이는 동안에는 이것이 보여질 수 없다고 알려주십시오.
3. [191]무게가 15킬로그램 이상 나가는 모든 작품들은 미술관을 통과하여 이동되기 전에 손수레 위에 놓여야 합니다. 더 가벼운 예술작품들은 장갑이 착용되어 있는 한 손으로 옮겨질 수 있습니다.
4. [195]Fragile Hands와 같이 매우 귀중한 작품들은 유리 상자 안에 넣어져야 합니다. 이 상자들은 미술관이 가장 덜 바쁜 때인 목요일 아침에 닦여야 합니다.

만약 질문이 있으시면, 주저 말고 언제든지 제 사무실로 방문해주십시오.

Martina Klancy 드림
소유주, Windfield 미술관

handle v. 다루다 **sculpture** n. 조각품 **exhibit** v. 전시하다
protective adj. 보호용의 **wipe down** ~을 닦다
base n. 밑 부분 **maintenance** n. 관리, 유지
dust v. (먼지를) 닦다 **transport** v. 옮기다
valuable adj. 귀중한 **enclose** v. 넣다

Windfield 미술관

미술관 방문객들은 저희 건물이 내일 11월 25일부터 11월 29일 금요일까지 문을 닫을 것임을 아셔야 합니다. 이번 휴관은 [192]최근 나이지리아로부터 우리의 시설에 도착한, Kali Adisa가 만든 조각품들의 설치를 수용하기 위해 이루어지는 것입니다. 저희가 준비를 완료하는 동안 여러분들의 인내심에 감사 드립니다.

이 기간 동안, 저희는 저희의 고객들이 Ms. Adisa의 12월 전시회에 대한 정보를 저희의 모바일 애플리케이션에서 보는 것을 권장합니다. [194]사전 예매권은 오직 애플리케이션을 통해서만 할인된 가격에 이용 가능합니다. [193]저희 미술관의 겨울 전시회에 대한 팸플릿도 미술관 정문에 부착된 투입구에서 가져가실 수 있습니다.

[194]Martina Klancy
소유주, Windfield 미술관

closure n. 휴관, 폐쇄 **accommodate** v. 수용하다
installation n. 설치 **facility** n. 시설 **arrangement** n. 준비
patron n. 고객, 후원자 **exhibition** n. 전시회
advance ticket 사전 예매권 **exclusively** adv. 오직
slot n. 투입구 **attached** adj. 부착된

수신: Martina Klancy <m.klancy@windfieldart.com>
발신: Joshua Nero <j.nero@brexfordmuseum.org>
제목: 지난주의 방문
날짜: 12월 16일

Ms. Klancy께,

저는 지난주 당신의 미술관에서 열린 Kali Adisa 전시회의 성공에 대해 축하하고 싶습니다. 저는 [194]제가 할인된 가격에 전시회 티켓을 구매하라는 당신의 권유를 받아들인 것이 기뻤습니다. 전반적으로, 저는 Ms. Adisa의 작품에 감명을 받았습니다. 그것들은 현대 나이지리아 예술의 훌륭한 표현이었습니다.

그러나, 저는 비평가들로부터 들었던 한 작품인 [195]Fragile Hands가 제가 방문한 날 그것의 상자가 닦이고 있어서 볼 수 없었다는 것에 실망했습니다. 다행히, 제가 구매한 티켓이 며칠 동안 입장을 가능하게 해서, 저는 나중에 다시 와서 그 작품을 볼 계획입니다.

다시 한번 더 축하드리며, 저는 다음 주 금요일 저희의 기금 모금 행사에서 당신을 뵙길 기대합니다.

Joshua Nero 드림
큐레이터, Brexford 미술관

delighted adj. 기쁜 **recommendation** n. 권유, 추천
representation n. 표현, 묘사 **contemporary** adj. 현대의
critic n. 비평가 **luckily** adv. 다행히 **admission** n. 입장
fundraiser n. 기금 모금 행사

191. 육하원칙 문제

해석 직원들은 무게가 15킬로그램이 넘는 조각상들에 대해 무엇을 해야 하는가?
(A) 미술관의 바닥에 그것들을 둔다.
(B) 그것들을 옮기기 위해 장비를 사용한다.
(C) 2주에 한 번 청소용 스프레이를 바른다.
(D) 철사를 사용하여 그것들을 벽에 고정한다.

해설 첫 번째 이메일의 'Any pieces weighing more than 15 kilograms must be placed on a cart before being transported'에서 무게가 15킬로그램 이상 나가는 모든 작품들은 이동되기 전에 손수레 위에 놓여야 한다고 했으므로 (B)가 정답이다.

어휘 apply v. 바르다, 적용하다 secure v. 고정하다, 획득하다
wire n. 철사

> [Paraphrasing]
> cart 손수레 → equipment 장비
> being transported 이동되는 것 → move 옮기다

192. 육하원칙 문제

해석 공고에 따르면, 최근에 무슨 일이 있었는가?
(A) 몇몇 기능들이 모바일 애플리케이션에 추가되었다.
(B) 조각가가 전시에 대한 일련의 강의를 하였다.
(C) 몇몇 작품들이 다른 나라로부터 전달되었다.
(D) 미술관이 고객들에게 영구적인 폐쇄를 알렸다.

해설 공고의 'sculptures ~ recently arrived at our facility from Nigeria'에서 최근 나이지리아로부터 우리의 시설에 조각품들이 도착했다고 했으므로 (C)가 정답이다.

어휘 a series of 일련의 lecture n. 강의
permanent adj. 영구적인

> [Paraphrasing]
> arrived at ~ facility from Nigeria 나이지리아로부터 시설에 도착했다 → were delivered from another country 다른 나라로부터 전달되었다

193. 육하원칙 문제

해석 Windfield 미술관의 정문에서 무엇을 구할 수 있는가?
(A) 할인 쿠폰
(B) 정보 소책자
(C) 미술품 인쇄본
(D) 사전 예매권

해설 공고의 'Pamphlets about ~ exhibitions can ~ be picked up from the slot attached to our gallery's front door.'에서 전시회에 대한 팸플릿을 미술관 정문에 부착된 투입구에서 가져갈 수 있다고 했으므로 (B)가 정답이다.

어휘 print n. 인쇄본

> [Paraphrasing]
> Pamphlets about ~ exhibitions 전시회에 대한 팸플릿 → Informational booklets 정보 소책자

194. 육하원칙 문제 연계

해석 Ms. Klancy는 Mr. Nero에게 무엇을 권유했는가?
(A) 전시회에서 조각품을 구매하는 것
(B) 인기 있는 조각품들의 몇몇 사진을 찍는 것
(C) 전시회에 관해 몇몇 예술 비평가들과 이야기를 하는 것
(D) 입장권을 구매하기 위해 모바일 애플리케이션을 사용하는 것

해설 Mr. Nero가 작성한 이메일을 먼저 확인한다.
[단서 1] 두 번째 이메일의 'I took your recommendation to purchase tickets ~ at a reduced price'에서 저, 즉 Mr. Nero가 할인된 가격에 전시회 티켓을 구매하라는 당신, 즉 Ms. Klancy의 권유를 받아들였다고 했다. 그런데 어떻게 할인된 가격에 전시 티켓을 구매했는지 제시되지 않았으므로 공고에서 관련 내용을 확인한다.
[단서 2] 공고의 'Advance tickets are available at a discounted rate exclusively through the application.'과 'Martina Klancy'에서 사전 예매권은 오직 애플리케이션을 통해서만 할인된 가격에 이용 가능하다고 알리는 공고를 Ms. Klancy가 작성했음을 알 수 있다.
두 단서를 종합할 때, Ms. Klancy는 Mr. Nero에게 모바일 애플리케이션을 사용하여 입장권을 구매하는 것을 추천했음을 알 수 있다. 따라서 (D)가 정답이다.

어휘 pass n. 입장권

195. 추론 문제 연계

해석 Mr. Nero는 언제 Kali Adisa 전시회를 봤을 것 같은가?
(A) 목요일 아침에
(B) 목요일 오후에
(C) 금요일 아침에
(D) 금요일 오후에

해설 Mr. Nero가 작성한 이메일을 먼저 확인한다.
[단서 1] 두 번째 이메일의 'Fragile Hands—was not available on the day I visited because its case was being dusted off'에서 Mr. Nero가 방문한 날 *Fragile Hands*가 그것의 상자가 닦이고 있어서 볼 수 없었다고 했다. 그런데 *Fragile Hands*의 상자가 언제 닦였는지 제시되지 않았으므로 첫 번째 이메일에서 관련 내용을 확인한다.
[단서 2] 첫 번째 이메일의 'Highly valuable pieces, such as *Fragile Hands*, need to be enclosed in glass cases. These cases must be dusted on Thursday mornings'에서 *Fragile Hands*와 같이 매우 귀중한 작품들은 유리 상자 안에 넣어져야 하며 목요일 아침에 닦여야 한다고 한 사실을 확인할 수 있다.
두 단서를 종합할 때, Mr. Nero는 *Fragile Hands*의 상자가 닦였던 목요일 아침에 Kali Adisa 전시회를 봤다는 사실을 추론할 수 있다. 따라서 (A)가 정답이다.

196-200번은 다음 안내문, 웹페이지, 이메일에 관한 문제입니다.

> **Westerburn 공립 도서관 온라인 기한 연장 규정**
>
> [196]Westerburn 공립 도서관이 소유한 모든 책들은 온라인 계정을 통해 기한이 연장될 수 있습니다. 로그인만 하셔서 "보기" 메뉴를 클릭하고, "대여된 항목"을 선택하신 후, 기한 연장을 하기 원하는 책 제목 옆의 상자에 표시하시면 됩니다. 그러고 나서 화면 아래의 "보내기"를 누르세요. [197-(C)]회원들은 자료들에 대한 대기 신청이 없으면 2주씩 기한을 연장하는 것이 허용됩니다. [198-(B)]만약 본인이 대여한 자료들이 앞서 다른 회원에 의해 신청되었다면, 시스템은 그 자료들이 다시 대여될 수 없음을 알려줄 것입니다.
>
> 도서관 상호 대출도 온라인에서 기한 연장이 될 수 있습니다. 하지만, 몇몇 제약이 적용될 수 있습니다. 책 표지 뒷면에 있는 스티커에서 책을 대여해준 도서관의 기한 연장 규정을 확인해 주시기 바라며, 이 규정들은 저희 도서관과 다를 수도 있습니다.

어휘 renewal n. 기한 연장, 갱신, 복구 own v. 소유하다; adj. 자신의
renew v. 기한을 연장하다, 재개하다 material n. 자료, 재료
provided conj. 만약 ~이라면
interlibrary loan 도서관 상호 대출 restriction n. 제약, 규제

Westerburn 공립 도서관 회원의 진행 중인 대출 목록
회원 번호 0177634 – Melissa Terrance

199-(D)날짜: 8월 8일

기한 연장	제목	200도서 정리 번호	199-(A)출처	199-(D)반납일
198-(B)기한 연장 불가	198-(B) The Reign of King Jordanius / Hans Schoffer	834.04 SCH	Westerburn 공립 도서관	8월 10일
☑	199-(D) The Science of Memory / Laurence Templeton	216.94 TEM	Westerburn 공립 도서관	199-(D) 8월 10일
☑	200 A History of Medicinal Plants / Daniel Wu	200 147.09 WUD	(도서관 상호 대출) Highland Marsh 공립 도서관	8월 10일
☐	199-(A) Tell Her: Short Stories / Maya Teller	924.07 TEL	199-(A)(도서관 상호 대출) Greenport 대학 도서관	8월 15일
보내기				

* 199-(A)도서관 상호 대출의 경우, 책을 저희에게 바로 반납하시거나 원래 도서관에 반납하실 수 있습니다.

active adj. 진행 중인, 활동적인   **call number** 도서 정리 번호
source n. 출처, 근원   **directly** adv. 바로, 직접적으로
of origin 원래의, ~ 출신인

수신: Melissa Terrance <mellit@greatmail.com>
발신: Agnes Featherstone <agnesf@westerburn.com>
날짜: 8월 9일
제목: 회신: 문의

Ms. Terrance께,

문의에 답해드리자면, 귀하의 신청이 거절된 이유는 200기한 연장하기 원하시는 책(도서 정리 번호 147.09 WUD)이 저희와 다른 대여 규정들을 가진 다른 도서관의 책이고, 저희의 온라인 기한 연장 시스템은 그것들을 반영하도록 설정되어 있지 않기 때문입니다. 책 뒷면의 스티커를 확인하시면, 그 책을 대출해 준 도서관은 참고 문헌이 단 한 번만 기한이 연장되도록 허용한다는 것을 아실 수 있을 것입니다. 귀하의 진행 중인 대출 목록의 다른 항목들과는 달리, 200귀하께서는 이미 이 책을 이전에 한 번 연장하셨습니다. 반납일이 내일이라는 것을 참고해 주시기 바랍니다.

감사합니다.

Agnes Featherstone 드림
Westerburn 공립 도서관 직원

reject v. 거절하다, 거부하다   **reflect** v. 반영하다, 나타내다
reference n. 참고, 언급

196. 주제 찾기 문제
해석 안내문은 주로 무엇에 대한 것인가?
(A) 다른 도서관의 책 요청하기
(B) 도서관 데이터베이스에 온라인으로 접속하기
(C) 웹사이트에서 대출 연장하기
(D) 반납일 이후에 책 반납하기

해설 안내문의 'All books owned by Westerburn can be renewed through your online account.'에서 Westerburn 공립 도서관이 소유한 모든 책들은 온라인 계정을 통해 기한이 연장될 수 있다고 한 후, 구체적인 연장 방법 및 규정들을 안내하고 있으므로 (C)가 정답이다.

어휘 **access** v. 접속하다; n. 접근, 입장

197. Not/True 문제
해석 Westerburn 공립 도서관에 대해 언급된 것은?
(A) 연체료는 온라인 서비스를 통해 지불될 수 있다.
(B) 신규 회원이 자료를 예약하는 것을 금지한다.
(C) 책들은 14일의 기간 동안 연장될 수 있다.
(D) 도서관 상호 대출에 대한 정책이 변경되었다.

해설 안내문의 'Members are allowed to renew our material for two-week periods'에서 회원들은 2주씩 기한을 연장하는 것이 허용된다고 했으므로 (C)는 지문의 내용과 일치한다. 따라서 (C)가 정답이다. (A), (B), (D)는 지문에 언급되지 않은 내용이다.

어휘 **late fee** 연체료   **regarding** prep. ~에 대한

198. Not/True 문제 연계
해석 The Reign of King Jordanius에 대해 사실인 것은?
(A) 특별 소장품의 일부이다.
(B) 다른 사람이 대여 신청을 했다.
(C) 다른 한 권이 제휴된 도서관에서 이용 가능하다.
(D) 스티커에 기한 연장이 금지되어 있다고 나와 있다.

해설 질문의 핵심 어구인 The Reign of King Jordanius가 언급된 웹페이지를 먼저 확인한다.
단서 1 웹페이지의 'Non-Renewable', 'The Reign of King Jordanius'에서 The Reign of King Jordanius가 기한 연장 불가라는 사실을 알 수 있다. 그러나, 왜 기한 연장이 불가한지 제시되지 않았으므로 안내문에서 관련 내용을 확인한다.
단서 2 안내문의 'If materials you have checked out have been requested in advance by any other member, the system will indicate that they cannot be borrowed again.'에서 만약 본인이 대여한 자료들이 앞서 다른 회원에 의해 신청되었다면 시스템은 그 자료들이 다시 대여될 수 없음을 알려줄 것이라고 한 사실을 확인할 수 있다.
두 단서를 종합할 때, The Reign of King Jordanius가 기한 연장이 불가한 이유는 다른 회원에 의해 신청되었기 때문임을 알 수 있다. 따라서 (B)가 정답이다.

어휘 **collection** n. 소장품, 수집   **forbid** v. 금지하다

199. Not/True 문제
해석 웹페이지에 언급된 것은?
(A) Maya Teller의 책은 Westerburn 공립 도서관에 반납될 수 있다.
(B) Highland Marsh 공립 도서관의 대여 기간은 2주이다.
(C) Ms. Terrance는 도서관에 특별한 종류의 회원권을 갖고 있다.
(D) The Science of Memory는 현재 며칠간 연체되어 있다.

해설 웹페이지의 'Tell Her: Short Stories / Maya Teller', 'Source', '(Interlibrary Loan) Greenport University Library'에서 Maya Teller의 책이 도서관 상호 대출로 빌려진 것을 알 수 있고, 'For interlibrary loans, you can return the books directly to us'에서 도서관 상호 대출의 경우 책을

저희, 즉 Westerburn 공립 도서관에 바로 반납할 수 있다고 했으므로 (A)는 지문의 내용과 일치한다. 따라서 (A)가 정답이다. (B)와 (C)는 지문에 언급되지 않은 내용이다. (D)는 'Date: 08/08', 'The Science of Memory', 'Due Date', '08/10'에서 현재 날짜가 8월 8일이고 *The Science of Memory*의 반납일이 8월 10일이어서 책이 아직 연체되지 않은 것을 알 수 있으므로 지문의 내용과 일치하지 않는다.

어휘 **overdue** adj. 연체된, 기한이 지난

200. 육하원칙 문제 연계

해석 Ms. Terrance는 어떤 책을 이미 한 번 기한 연장을 했는가?
(A) *The Science of Memory*
(B) *A History of Medicinal Plants*
(C) *Tell Her: Short Stories*
(D) *The Reign of King Jordanius*

해설 Ms. Terrance에게 보내진 이메일을 먼저 확인한다.

단서 1 이메일의 'the book you wanted to renew (Call No. 147.09 WUD)'와 'you have already renewed this item once before'에서 당신, 즉 Ms. Terrance가 기한 연장하기 원하는 책의 도서 정리 번호가 147.09 WUD이고, 그녀가 이미 그 책을 이전에 한 번 연장을 했다는 사실을 확인할 수 있다. 그런데 도서 정리 번호가 147.09 WUD인 책이 무엇인지 제시되지 않았으므로 웹페이지에서 관련 내용을 확인한다.

단서 2 웹페이지의 '*A History of Medicinal Plants*', 'Call No.', '147.09 WUD'에서 도서 정리 번호가 147.09 WUD인 책이 *A History of Medicinal Plants*임을 확인할 수 있다.

두 단서를 종합할 때, Ms. Terrance가 *A History of Medicinal Plants*를 이미 한 번 기한 연장했음을 알 수 있다. 따라서 (B)가 정답이다.

점수 환산표

아래는 실전모의고사를 위한 점수 환산표입니다. 문제 풀이 후, 정답 개수를 세어 자신의 토익 리스닝/리딩 점수를 예상해봅니다.

정답 수	리스닝 점수	리딩 점수	정답 수	리스닝 점수	리딩 점수	정답 수	리스닝 점수	리딩 점수
100	495	495	66	305	305	32	135	125
99	495	495	65	300	300	31	130	120
98	495	495	64	295	295	30	125	115
97	495	485	63	290	290	29	120	110
96	490	480	62	285	280	28	115	105
95	485	475	61	280	275	27	110	100
94	480	470	60	275	270	26	105	95
93	475	465	59	270	265	25	100	90
92	470	460	58	265	260	24	95	85
91	465	450	57	260	255	23	90	80
90	460	445	56	255	250	22	85	75
89	455	440	55	250	245	21	80	70
88	450	435	54	245	240	20	75	70
87	445	430	53	240	235	19	70	65
86	435	420	52	235	230	18	65	60
85	430	415	51	230	220	17	60	60
84	425	410	50	225	215	16	55	55
83	415	405	49	220	210	15	50	50
82	410	400	48	215	205	14	45	45
81	400	390	47	210	200	13	40	40
80	395	385	46	205	195	12	35	35
79	390	380	45	200	190	11	30	30
78	385	375	44	195	185	10	25	30
77	375	370	43	190	180	9	20	25
76	370	360	42	185	175	8	15	20
75	365	355	41	180	170	7	10	20
74	355	350	40	175	165	6	5	15
73	350	345	39	170	160	5	5	15
72	340	340	38	165	155	4	5	10
71	335	335	37	160	150	3	5	5
70	330	330	36	155	145	2	5	5
69	325	320	35	150	140	1	5	5
68	315	315	34	145	135	0	5	5
67	310	310	33	140	130			

※ 점수 환산표는 해커스토익 사이트 유저 데이터를 근거로 제작되었으며, 주기적으로 업데이트되고 있습니다. 해커스토익 사이트 (Hackers.co.kr)에서 최신 경향을 반영하여 업데이트된 점수환산기를 이용하실 수 있습니다. (토익 > 토익게시판 > 토익점수환산기)

자르는 선

Answer Sheet

LISTENING (PART 1~4)

1	Ⓐ Ⓑ Ⓒ Ⓓ	21	Ⓐ Ⓑ Ⓒ	41	Ⓐ Ⓑ Ⓒ Ⓓ	61	Ⓐ Ⓑ Ⓒ Ⓓ	81	Ⓐ Ⓑ Ⓒ Ⓓ
2	Ⓐ Ⓑ Ⓒ Ⓓ	22	Ⓐ Ⓑ Ⓒ	42	Ⓐ Ⓑ Ⓒ Ⓓ	62	Ⓐ Ⓑ Ⓒ Ⓓ	82	Ⓐ Ⓑ Ⓒ Ⓓ
3	Ⓐ Ⓑ Ⓒ Ⓓ	23	Ⓐ Ⓑ Ⓒ	43	Ⓐ Ⓑ Ⓒ Ⓓ	63	Ⓐ Ⓑ Ⓒ Ⓓ	83	Ⓐ Ⓑ Ⓒ Ⓓ
4	Ⓐ Ⓑ Ⓒ Ⓓ	24	Ⓐ Ⓑ Ⓒ	44	Ⓐ Ⓑ Ⓒ Ⓓ	64	Ⓐ Ⓑ Ⓒ Ⓓ	84	Ⓐ Ⓑ Ⓒ Ⓓ
5	Ⓐ Ⓑ Ⓒ Ⓓ	25	Ⓐ Ⓑ Ⓒ	45	Ⓐ Ⓑ Ⓒ Ⓓ	65	Ⓐ Ⓑ Ⓒ Ⓓ	85	Ⓐ Ⓑ Ⓒ Ⓓ
6	Ⓐ Ⓑ Ⓒ Ⓓ	26	Ⓐ Ⓑ Ⓒ	46	Ⓐ Ⓑ Ⓒ Ⓓ	66	Ⓐ Ⓑ Ⓒ Ⓓ	86	Ⓐ Ⓑ Ⓒ Ⓓ
7	Ⓐ Ⓑ Ⓒ	27	Ⓐ Ⓑ Ⓒ	47	Ⓐ Ⓑ Ⓒ Ⓓ	67	Ⓐ Ⓑ Ⓒ Ⓓ	87	Ⓐ Ⓑ Ⓒ Ⓓ
8	Ⓐ Ⓑ Ⓒ	28	Ⓐ Ⓑ Ⓒ	48	Ⓐ Ⓑ Ⓒ Ⓓ	68	Ⓐ Ⓑ Ⓒ Ⓓ	88	Ⓐ Ⓑ Ⓒ Ⓓ
9	Ⓐ Ⓑ Ⓒ	29	Ⓐ Ⓑ Ⓒ	49	Ⓐ Ⓑ Ⓒ Ⓓ	69	Ⓐ Ⓑ Ⓒ Ⓓ	89	Ⓐ Ⓑ Ⓒ Ⓓ
10	Ⓐ Ⓑ Ⓒ	30	Ⓐ Ⓑ Ⓒ	50	Ⓐ Ⓑ Ⓒ Ⓓ	70	Ⓐ Ⓑ Ⓒ Ⓓ	90	Ⓐ Ⓑ Ⓒ Ⓓ
11	Ⓐ Ⓑ Ⓒ	31	Ⓐ Ⓑ Ⓒ	51	Ⓐ Ⓑ Ⓒ Ⓓ	71	Ⓐ Ⓑ Ⓒ Ⓓ	91	Ⓐ Ⓑ Ⓒ Ⓓ
12	Ⓐ Ⓑ Ⓒ	32	Ⓐ Ⓑ Ⓒ Ⓓ	52	Ⓐ Ⓑ Ⓒ Ⓓ	72	Ⓐ Ⓑ Ⓒ Ⓓ	92	Ⓐ Ⓑ Ⓒ Ⓓ
13	Ⓐ Ⓑ Ⓒ	33	Ⓐ Ⓑ Ⓒ Ⓓ	53	Ⓐ Ⓑ Ⓒ Ⓓ	73	Ⓐ Ⓑ Ⓒ Ⓓ	93	Ⓐ Ⓑ Ⓒ Ⓓ
14	Ⓐ Ⓑ Ⓒ	34	Ⓐ Ⓑ Ⓒ Ⓓ	54	Ⓐ Ⓑ Ⓒ Ⓓ	74	Ⓐ Ⓑ Ⓒ Ⓓ	94	Ⓐ Ⓑ Ⓒ Ⓓ
15	Ⓐ Ⓑ Ⓒ	35	Ⓐ Ⓑ Ⓒ Ⓓ	55	Ⓐ Ⓑ Ⓒ Ⓓ	75	Ⓐ Ⓑ Ⓒ Ⓓ	95	Ⓐ Ⓑ Ⓒ Ⓓ
16	Ⓐ Ⓑ Ⓒ	36	Ⓐ Ⓑ Ⓒ Ⓓ	56	Ⓐ Ⓑ Ⓒ Ⓓ	76	Ⓐ Ⓑ Ⓒ Ⓓ	96	Ⓐ Ⓑ Ⓒ Ⓓ
17	Ⓐ Ⓑ Ⓒ	37	Ⓐ Ⓑ Ⓒ Ⓓ	57	Ⓐ Ⓑ Ⓒ Ⓓ	77	Ⓐ Ⓑ Ⓒ Ⓓ	97	Ⓐ Ⓑ Ⓒ Ⓓ
18	Ⓐ Ⓑ Ⓒ	38	Ⓐ Ⓑ Ⓒ Ⓓ	58	Ⓐ Ⓑ Ⓒ Ⓓ	78	Ⓐ Ⓑ Ⓒ Ⓓ	98	Ⓐ Ⓑ Ⓒ Ⓓ
19	Ⓐ Ⓑ Ⓒ	39	Ⓐ Ⓑ Ⓒ Ⓓ	59	Ⓐ Ⓑ Ⓒ Ⓓ	79	Ⓐ Ⓑ Ⓒ Ⓓ	99	Ⓐ Ⓑ Ⓒ Ⓓ
20	Ⓐ Ⓑ Ⓒ	40	Ⓐ Ⓑ Ⓒ Ⓓ	60	Ⓐ Ⓑ Ⓒ Ⓓ	80	Ⓐ Ⓑ Ⓒ Ⓓ	100	Ⓐ Ⓑ Ⓒ Ⓓ

* 시험시간: **120분** (LC 45분, RC 75분)

READING (PART 5~7)

101	Ⓐ Ⓑ Ⓒ Ⓓ	121	Ⓐ Ⓑ Ⓒ Ⓓ	141	Ⓐ Ⓑ Ⓒ Ⓓ	161	Ⓐ Ⓑ Ⓒ Ⓓ	181	Ⓐ Ⓑ Ⓒ Ⓓ
102	Ⓐ Ⓑ Ⓒ Ⓓ	122	Ⓐ Ⓑ Ⓒ Ⓓ	142	Ⓐ Ⓑ Ⓒ Ⓓ	162	Ⓐ Ⓑ Ⓒ Ⓓ	182	Ⓐ Ⓑ Ⓒ Ⓓ
103	Ⓐ Ⓑ Ⓒ Ⓓ	123	Ⓐ Ⓑ Ⓒ Ⓓ	143	Ⓐ Ⓑ Ⓒ Ⓓ	163	Ⓐ Ⓑ Ⓒ Ⓓ	183	Ⓐ Ⓑ Ⓒ Ⓓ
104	Ⓐ Ⓑ Ⓒ Ⓓ	124	Ⓐ Ⓑ Ⓒ Ⓓ	144	Ⓐ Ⓑ Ⓒ Ⓓ	164	Ⓐ Ⓑ Ⓒ Ⓓ	184	Ⓐ Ⓑ Ⓒ Ⓓ
105	Ⓐ Ⓑ Ⓒ Ⓓ	125	Ⓐ Ⓑ Ⓒ Ⓓ	145	Ⓐ Ⓑ Ⓒ Ⓓ	165	Ⓐ Ⓑ Ⓒ Ⓓ	185	Ⓐ Ⓑ Ⓒ Ⓓ
106	Ⓐ Ⓑ Ⓒ Ⓓ	126	Ⓐ Ⓑ Ⓒ Ⓓ	146	Ⓐ Ⓑ Ⓒ Ⓓ	166	Ⓐ Ⓑ Ⓒ Ⓓ	186	Ⓐ Ⓑ Ⓒ Ⓓ
107	Ⓐ Ⓑ Ⓒ Ⓓ	127	Ⓐ Ⓑ Ⓒ Ⓓ	147	Ⓐ Ⓑ Ⓒ Ⓓ	167	Ⓐ Ⓑ Ⓒ Ⓓ	187	Ⓐ Ⓑ Ⓒ Ⓓ
108	Ⓐ Ⓑ Ⓒ Ⓓ	128	Ⓐ Ⓑ Ⓒ Ⓓ	148	Ⓐ Ⓑ Ⓒ Ⓓ	168	Ⓐ Ⓑ Ⓒ Ⓓ	188	Ⓐ Ⓑ Ⓒ Ⓓ
109	Ⓐ Ⓑ Ⓒ Ⓓ	129	Ⓐ Ⓑ Ⓒ Ⓓ	149	Ⓐ Ⓑ Ⓒ Ⓓ	169	Ⓐ Ⓑ Ⓒ Ⓓ	189	Ⓐ Ⓑ Ⓒ Ⓓ
110	Ⓐ Ⓑ Ⓒ Ⓓ	130	Ⓐ Ⓑ Ⓒ Ⓓ	150	Ⓐ Ⓑ Ⓒ Ⓓ	170	Ⓐ Ⓑ Ⓒ Ⓓ	190	Ⓐ Ⓑ Ⓒ Ⓓ
111	Ⓐ Ⓑ Ⓒ Ⓓ	131	Ⓐ Ⓑ Ⓒ Ⓓ	151	Ⓐ Ⓑ Ⓒ Ⓓ	171	Ⓐ Ⓑ Ⓒ Ⓓ	191	Ⓐ Ⓑ Ⓒ Ⓓ
112	Ⓐ Ⓑ Ⓒ Ⓓ	132	Ⓐ Ⓑ Ⓒ Ⓓ	152	Ⓐ Ⓑ Ⓒ Ⓓ	172	Ⓐ Ⓑ Ⓒ Ⓓ	192	Ⓐ Ⓑ Ⓒ Ⓓ
113	Ⓐ Ⓑ Ⓒ Ⓓ	133	Ⓐ Ⓑ Ⓒ Ⓓ	153	Ⓐ Ⓑ Ⓒ Ⓓ	173	Ⓐ Ⓑ Ⓒ Ⓓ	193	Ⓐ Ⓑ Ⓒ Ⓓ
114	Ⓐ Ⓑ Ⓒ Ⓓ	134	Ⓐ Ⓑ Ⓒ Ⓓ	154	Ⓐ Ⓑ Ⓒ Ⓓ	174	Ⓐ Ⓑ Ⓒ Ⓓ	194	Ⓐ Ⓑ Ⓒ Ⓓ
115	Ⓐ Ⓑ Ⓒ Ⓓ	135	Ⓐ Ⓑ Ⓒ Ⓓ	155	Ⓐ Ⓑ Ⓒ Ⓓ	175	Ⓐ Ⓑ Ⓒ Ⓓ	195	Ⓐ Ⓑ Ⓒ Ⓓ
116	Ⓐ Ⓑ Ⓒ Ⓓ	136	Ⓐ Ⓑ Ⓒ Ⓓ	156	Ⓐ Ⓑ Ⓒ Ⓓ	176	Ⓐ Ⓑ Ⓒ Ⓓ	196	Ⓐ Ⓑ Ⓒ Ⓓ
117	Ⓐ Ⓑ Ⓒ Ⓓ	137	Ⓐ Ⓑ Ⓒ Ⓓ	157	Ⓐ Ⓑ Ⓒ Ⓓ	177	Ⓐ Ⓑ Ⓒ Ⓓ	197	Ⓐ Ⓑ Ⓒ Ⓓ
118	Ⓐ Ⓑ Ⓒ Ⓓ	138	Ⓐ Ⓑ Ⓒ Ⓓ	158	Ⓐ Ⓑ Ⓒ Ⓓ	178	Ⓐ Ⓑ Ⓒ Ⓓ	198	Ⓐ Ⓑ Ⓒ Ⓓ
119	Ⓐ Ⓑ Ⓒ Ⓓ	139	Ⓐ Ⓑ Ⓒ Ⓓ	159	Ⓐ Ⓑ Ⓒ Ⓓ	179	Ⓐ Ⓑ Ⓒ Ⓓ	199	Ⓐ Ⓑ Ⓒ Ⓓ
120	Ⓐ Ⓑ Ⓒ Ⓓ	140	Ⓐ Ⓑ Ⓒ Ⓓ	160	Ⓐ Ⓑ Ⓒ Ⓓ	180	Ⓐ Ⓑ Ⓒ Ⓓ	200	Ⓐ Ⓑ Ⓒ Ⓓ

* 답안지 마킹은 **연필**을 사용하시기 바랍니다.
* 문제 풀이 후 p.85에 있는 **점수 환산표**를 확인해보세요.

맞은 문제 개수: ______ / 200

실시간 토익시험 정답확인&해설강의
Hackers.co.kr

한 권으로 끝내는
해커스 토익 800⁺
LC + RC + VOCA

시험장에도 들고 가는 토익 기출 VOCA 학습법

1. 매일 하루 분량의 단어를 암기합니다.
본인이 선택한 학습 플랜(본책 p.10~11)에 따라 20일 또는 10일 완성을 목표로 합니다.

2. 무료 단어암기 MP3와 함께 이동할 때나 자투리 시간을 활용하여 단어를 암기합니다.
단어암기 MP3는 www.HackersIngang.com에서 무료로 다운 받거나, DAY별 QR코드를 활용하세요.

목차		
DAY 01 PART 1 기출 어휘	**DAY 11** PART 5&6 기출 어휘
DAY 02 PART 2 기출 어휘	**DAY 12** PART 5&6 기출 어휘
DAY 03 PART 2 기출 어휘	**DAY 13** PART 5&6 기출 어휘
DAY 04 PART 2 기출 어휘	**DAY 14** PART 5&6 기출 어휘
DAY 05 PART 3 기출 어휘	**DAY 15** PART 5&6 기출 어휘
DAY 06 PART 3 기출 어휘	**DAY 16** PART 5&6 기출 어휘
DAY 07 PART 3 기출 어휘	**DAY 17** PART 7 기출 어휘
DAY 08 PART 4 기출 어휘	**DAY 18** PART 7 기출 어휘
DAY 09 PART 4 기출 어휘	**DAY 19** PART 7 기출 어휘
DAY 10 PART 4 기출 어휘	**DAY 20** PART 7 기출 어휘

저작권자 ⓒ 2025, 해커스 어학연구소 이 책 및 음성파일의 모든 내용, 이미지, 디자인, 편집 형태에 대한 저작권은 저자에게 있습니다.
서면에 의한 저자와 출판사의 허락 없이 내용의 일부 혹은 전부를 인용, 발췌하거나 복제, 배포할 수 없습니다.

DAY 01 PART 1 기출 어휘

☑ PART 1에 반드시 나오는 최신 기출 어휘들이므로, 확실히 암기해 둡니다. 🎧 VOCA_D01.mp3

0001	arrange	v 마련하다, 준비하다, 배열하다
0002	vehicle	n 차량, 운송수단
0003	merchandise	n 상품, 물품
0004	outdoor	adj 야외의
0005	examine	v 검사하다, 조사하다
0006	stack	v 쌓다, 포개다 n 더미, 무더기
0007	hold	v 잡고 있다, 개최하다
0008	assemble	v 모으다, 조립하다
0009	walkway	n 통로
0010	face	v 마주보다, 직면하다
0011	remove	v 제거하다
0012	rack	n 선반, 받침대
0013	suitcase	n 여행 가방
0014	mount	v 올라타다, 장착하다
0015	pour	v 붓다, 쏟다
0016	empty	adj 비어 있는, 빈 v 비우다
0017	field	n 들판, 분야
0018	suspend	v 매달다, 중단하다
0019	insert	v 삽입하다, 끼워 넣다 n 부속품
0020	visible	adj 보이는, 눈에 띄는
0021	drawer	n 서랍
0022	structure	n 구조, 건물
0023	block	v 막다, 차단하다 n 장애물
0024	bucket	n 양동이, 물통
0025	shed	n 창고, 헛간

0026	rest	v 쉬다 n 휴식, 나머지
0027	kneel	v 무릎을 꿇다
0028	stock	v 채우다, 구비하다 n 재고, 주식
0029	microwave	n 전자레인지 v 전자레인지로 조리하다
0030	sweep	v (바닥을) 쓸다, 청소하다
0031	potted	adj 화분에 심은
0032	storefront	n 가게 앞에 딸린 공간
0033	stroll	v 거닐다, 산책하다
0034	bin	n 쓰레기통
0035	select	v 선택하다, 고르다
0036	column	n 기둥, 열
0037	corridor	n 복도, 통로
0038	doorway	n 문간, 입구
0039	unoccupied	adj 비어 있는, 사용되지 않는
0040	railing	n 난간
0041	crouch	v 웅크리다, 쪼그리고 앉다
0042	interact	v 상호작용하다, 교류하다
0043	partially	adv 부분적으로
0044	walk through	~을 차근차근 설명하다, 안내하다
0045	take apart	~을 분해하다
0046	lean against	~에 기대다, 몸을 기울이다
0047	side by side	나란히, 옆으로
0048	in the distance	먼 곳에
0049	hold up	~을 떠받치다, 지연시키다
0050	vending machine	자동판매기

DAY 02 PART 2 기출 어휘

PART 2에 반드시 나오는 최신 기출 어휘들이므로, 확실히 암기해 둡니다.

🎧 VOCA_D02.mp3

0051	agenda	[n] 안건, 의제
0052	committee	[n] 위원회
0053	finalize	[v] 마무리 짓다
0054	postpone	[v] 연기하다, 미루다
0055	book	[v] 예약하다
0056	quarter	[n] 분기, 4분의 1
0057	hallway	[n] 복도, 현관
0058	projection	[n] 예측, 전망
0059	inbox	[n] 받은 편지함, 수신함
0060	generate	[v] 생성하다, 발생시키다
0061	inspector	[n] 조사관, 검사원
0062	caterer	[n] 출장 요리업자
0063	several	[adj] 여러, 몇몇의
0064	edit	[v] 편집하다, 수정하다
0065	carpenter	[n] 목수
0066	bulk	[n] 대량, 규모 [adj] 대량의
0067	headquarters	[n] 본사, 본부
0068	leftover	[n] 남은 것, 나머지 [adj] 남은, 잔여의
0069	acquisition	[n] 인수, 취득
0070	deadline	[n] 마감 기한
0071	short-staffed	[adj] 인력이 부족한, 인원이 모자란
0072	negative	[adj] 부정적인
0073	competent	[adj] 유능한, 적격의
0074	client	[n] 고객
0075	leather	[n] 가죽

0076 ☐	**fundraiser**	ⓝ 모금 행사
0077 ☐	**courtyard**	ⓝ 안뜰
0078 ☐	**portrait**	ⓝ 초상화, 인물사진
0079 ☐	**tradition**	ⓝ 전통, 관습
0080 ☐	**work from home**	재택근무하다
0081 ☐	**fill out**	~을 작성하다, 기재하다
0082 ☐	**national holiday**	국경일, 공휴일
0083 ☐	**business trip**	출장
0084 ☐	**in time**	늦지 않게, 이윽고
0085 ☐	**break down**	고장 나다, ~을 분석하다, 분해하다
0086 ☐	**open position**	공석, 빈자리
0087 ☐	**be ahead of**	~보다 앞서 있다, ~을 앞지르다
0088 ☐	**hardware store**	철물점, 공구점
0089 ☐	**hand out**	~을 나눠주다, 배포하다
0090 ☐	**be supposed to**	~하기로 되어 있다, 예정되어 있다
0091 ☐	**not until**	~할 때까지 ~않다, ~해야 비로소
0092 ☐	**sales representative**	영업 담당자, 판매 대리인
0093 ☐	**take care of**	~을 돌보다, 처리하다
0094 ☐	**in charge of**	~을 담당하는, 책임지는
0095 ☐	**science fiction**	공상 과학 소설
0096 ☐	**department manager**	부서장, 부장
0097 ☐	**on the way**	~에 가는 중인
0098 ☐	**security clearance**	보안 허가
0099 ☐	**artificial intelligence**	인공지능
0100 ☐	**right after**	~ 직후에, ~ 이후 바로

DAY 03 PART 2 기출 어휘

☑ PART 2에 반드시 나오는 최신 기출 어휘들이므로, 확실히 암기해 둡니다. ♪ VOCA_D03.mp3

0101	**administrator**	n 관리자, 행정관
0102	**repairman**	n 수리공, 정비사
0103	**compile**	v 수집하다, 편집하다
0104	**fundraising**	n 모금 활동
0105	**sweetener**	n 감미료, 달게 하는 것
0106	**avenue**	n 대로, 거리
0107	**well-attended**	adj 많은 사람이 참석한, 인기 있는
0108	**thoughtful**	adj 사려 깊은, 생각이 깊은
0109	**plug**	v (플러그를) 꽂다, 연결하다 n 플러그
0110	**part-time**	adj 시간제의 adv 시간제로
0111	**satellite**	n (인공) 위성
0112	**qualification**	n 자격, 자격요건
0113	**housekeeping**	n 가사, 살림
0114	**headlight**	n 전조등
0115	**undergo**	v 겪다, 경험하다
0116	**expressway**	n 고속도로
0117	**bottom**	n 바닥, 하부 adj 맨 아래의
0118	**stormy**	adj 폭풍우의, 격렬한
0119	**overbudget**	adj 예산 초과의
0120	**ride**	v 타다, 승차하다 n 탑승, 여행
0121	**packet**	n 소포, 꾸러미
0122	**persuasive**	adj 설득력 있는, 영향력 있는
0123	**downtown**	n 도심, 시내 adj 도심의, 번화가의
0124	**upgrade**	v 향상시키다 n 향상, 개선
0125	**due**	adj 예정된, 만기의

0126 vendor	[n] 판매 회사, 노점상
0127 warehouse	[n] 창고
0128 urgent	[adj] 긴급한, 시급한
0129 relocation	[n] 이전
0130 sales figures	매출액, 판매 수치
0131 print shop	인쇄소
0132 short of	~이 부족한, ~에 미치지 못하는
0133 human resources	인사부
0134 take charge	떠맡다, 책임지다
0135 plenty of	많은, 풍부한
0136 traffic congestion	교통 정체, 교통 혼잡
0137 cover letter	자기소개서
0138 be comfortable with	~을 편안하게 느끼다, ~에 익숙하다
0139 savings account	저축 예금
0140 out of office	(직장에서) 자리에 없는, 부재중인
0141 at that time	그 당시에, 그때
0142 electronic records	전자 기록, 디지털 문서
0143 electronics store	전자제품 매장
0144 career fair	취업 박람회
0145 be on vacation	휴가 중이다
0146 supply closet	비품 보관함
0147 executive summary	(보고용) 개요서
0148 budget surplus	예산 잉여금, 예산 흑자
0149 shipping address	배송지 주소
0150 sales pitch	구매를 유도하기 위한 말 또는 설명

DAY 04 PART 2 기출 어휘

☑ PART 2에 반드시 나오는 최신 기출 어휘들이므로, 확실히 암기해 둡니다. 🎧 VOCA_D04.mp3

0151	technician	[n] 기술자
0152	weigh	[v] 무게를 달다, 무게가 나가다
0153	mop	[n] 대걸레, 밀대 [v] 걸레질하다
0154	aggressive	[adj] 공격적인, 적극적인
0155	conductor	[n] 지휘자
0156	costume	[n] 의상, 복장
0157	complete	[v] 완료하다, 끝내다 [adj] 완전한, 전체의
0158	place	[v] 놓다, 배치하다 [n] 장소, 위치
0159	unlocked	[adj] 잠기지 않은
0160	on-hand	[adj] 보유 중인, 즉시 사용 가능한
0161	flyer	[n] 전단지, 광고지
0162	feed	[v] 먹이다, 공급하다 [n] 먹이, 사료
0163	demonstration	[n] 시연, 시위
0164	ship	[v] 배송하다, 운송하다
0165	aware	[adj] 알고 있는, 인식하는
0166	brighten	[v] 밝아지다, 빛나게 하다
0167	attendee	[n] 참가자
0168	rather	[adv] 오히려, 꽤
0169	misplace	[v] 잘못 두다, 분실하다
0170	operational	[adj] 운영상의, 작동하는
0171	prospective	[adj] 예상되는, 장래의
0172	assortment	[n] 모음, 종합
0173	bookcase	[n] 책장, 책꽂이
0174	personnel	[n] 직원, 인사
0175	finish	[v] 끝내다, 완료하다

0176	yard	n 마당
0177	lead	v 이끌다, 인도하다 n 선두, 우세
0178	briefcase	n 서류 가방
0179	approve	v 승인하다, 인가하다
0180	handle	v 처리하다, 다루다
0181	storage room	저장실, 창고
0182	take a break	휴식을 취하다
0183	express mail	속달 우편
0184	office supply	사무용품
0185	be in charge of	~을 담당하다, 책임지다
0186	tracking app	추적 앱
0187	stitch on	~을 꿰매다, ~에 박음질하다
0188	job description	직무 기술서, 업무 설명
0189	budget report	예산 보고서
0190	tracking number	추적 번호, 운송장 번호
0191	air conditioning	에어컨
0192	vote on	~에 투표하다, ~을 결정하다
0193	be intended for	~을 위한 것이다, 목적으로 하다
0194	slow reader	느리게 읽는 사람
0195	out of order	고장 난, 작동하지 않는
0196	connect to	~에 연결하다
0197	hiring initiative	채용 계획
0198	come up with	~을 생각해 내다, 제안하다
0199	finance department	재무부, 회계부
0200	company retreat	회사 야유회

DAY 05 PART 3 기출 어휘

☑ PART 3에 반드시 나오는 최신 기출 어휘들이므로, 확실히 암기해 둡니다.   ♫ VOCA_D05.mp3

0201	equipment	n 장비, 설비
0202	belongings	n 소지품, 소유물
0203	access	n 접근, 입장권 v 접근하다
0204	inquire	v 문의하다, 묻다
0205	pharmacist	n 약사
0206	colleague	n (직장) 동료
0207	location	n 위치, 장소
0208	vacant	adj 비어 있는, 공석인
0209	skyscraper	n 고층 빌딩
0210	conduct	v 수행하다, 지휘하다 n 행동, 품행
0211	conference	n 회의, 학회
0212	material	n 재료, 소재 adj 물질적인
0213	overseas	adj 해외의, 외국의 adv 해외로
0214	offer	v 제안하다, 제공하다 n 제안, 특가, 할인
0215	repair	v 수리하다, 고치다 n 수리, 보수
0216	warranty	n 보증, 품질보증서
0217	address	n 연설, 주소 v 다루다, 처리하다
0218	opportunity	n 기회
0219	discount	n 할인 v 할인하다
0220	retirement	n 퇴직, 은퇴
0221	document	n 서류, 문서 v 기록하다
0222	regulation	n 규정, 규제
0223	contact	v 연락하다, 접촉하다 n 연락, 접촉
0224	survey	n 조사, 설문 v 조사하다
0225	availability	n 이용 가능성

0226 ☐	**celebrate**	[v] 축하하다, 기념하다
0227 ☐	**adjust**	[v] 조정하다, 적응하다
0228 ☐	**permit**	[n] 허가증, 면허증 [v] 허락하다
0229 ☐	**reimburse**	[v] 변제하다, 상환하다
0230 ☐	**diner**	[n] (식사하는) 손님, 작은 식당
0231 ☐	**outdated**	[adj] 구식의, 시대에 뒤떨어진
0232 ☐	**identification**	[n] 신분증, 확인
0233 ☐	**measurement**	[n] 측정, 치수
0234 ☐	**applicant**	[n] 지원자, 신청자
0235 ☐	**shipment**	[n] 수송품, 발송
0236 ☐	**commitment**	[n] 헌신, 약속
0237 ☐	**ingredient**	[n] 재료, 성분
0238 ☐	**architect**	[n] 건축가, 설계자
0239 ☐	**malfunction**	[n] 오작동 [v] 오작동하다
0240 ☐	**negotiate**	[v] 협상하다, 교섭하다
0241 ☐	**merger**	[n] 합병, 통합
0242 ☐	**convention**	[n] 협의회, 관례
0243 ☐	**discuss**	[v] 논의하다, 토론하다
0244 ☐	**faulty**	[adj] 결함이 있는, 불완전한
0245 ☐	**notification**	[n] 통지, 알림
0246 ☐	**reject**	[v] 거절하다, 거부하다 [n] 불합격자
0247 ☐	**limited**	[adj] 제한된, 한정된
0248 ☐	**real estate agent**	부동산 중개인
0249 ☐	**count on**	~에 의지하다, ~을 믿다
0250 ☐	**set up**	~을 설치하다, 준비하다

DAY 06 PART 3 기출 어휘

☑ PART 3에 반드시 나오는 최신 기출 어휘들이므로, 확실히 암기해 둡니다.　🎧 VOCA_D06.mp3

0251	beverage	n 음료
0252	agreement	n 동의, 합의
0253	load	v 싣다, 적재하다 n 짐, 적재량
0254	harvest	n 수확, 추수 v 수확하다
0255	voucher	n 상품권, 쿠폰, 할인권
0256	thorough	adj 철저한, 완전한
0257	competition	n 경쟁, 대회
0258	desirable	adj 바람직한, 탐나는
0259	decline	v 감소하다, 거절하다 n 감소, 쇠퇴
0260	efficiency	n 효율성, 능률
0261	anniversary	n 기념일
0262	challenging	adj 도전적인, 어려운
0263	receptionist	n 접수원, 안내원
0264	leak	n 누수, 누출 v 새다, 누출되다
0265	gear	n 장비
0266	loan	n 대출, 대여 v 빌려주다
0267	inn	n 여관
0268	locate	v 위치시키다, 찾아내다
0269	organize	v 조직하다, 정리하다
0270	electrician	n 전기 기술자
0271	cuisine	n 요리, 음식
0272	agriculture	n 농업, 농경
0273	architecture	n 건축
0274	detergent	n 세제, 세정제
0275	aisle	n 통로, 복도

0276	conflict	n 갈등, 충돌 v 충돌하다, 상충하다
0277	laboratory	n 실험실, 연구소
0278	confirmation	n 확인, 승인
0279	article	n 기사
0280	recycling	n 재활용
0281	hospitality	n 환대, 접대
0282	invest	v 투자하다
0283	assure	v 장담하다, 확신시키다
0284	catering	n 음식 공급업, 음식 공급
0285	archive	n 기록 보관소 v 보관하다
0286	update	v 업데이트하다 n 업데이트, 최신 정보
0287	lighting	n 조명
0288	collaborate	v 협력하다, 공동 작업하다
0289	fee	n 수수료, 요금
0290	alternate	adj 번갈아 하는, 교대의 v 교대하다
0291	negotiation	n 협상, 교섭
0292	contractor	n 계약자, 도급업자
0293	real estate	부동산
0294	sign up	~에 등록하다, ~을 신청하다
0295	press conference	기자 회견
0296	public relations	홍보, 대외 관계
0297	public transportation	대중교통
0298	city official	시 공무원
0299	place an order	주문하다
0300	assembly line	조립 라인

DAY 07 PART 3 기출 어휘

☑ PART 3에 반드시 나오는 최신 기출 어휘들이므로, 확실히 암기해 둡니다. 🎧 VOCA_D07.mp3

0301	**assumption**	n 가정, 추정
0302	**forward**	v 전달하다, 발송하다 adv 앞쪽으로
0303	**physician**	n 의사
0304	**segment**	n 부분, 구간
0305	**furnace**	n 용광로, 난방기
0306	**customize**	v 맞춤 제작하다, 사용자화하다
0307	**treadmill**	n 러닝머신
0308	**stain**	n 얼룩, 오점 v 얼룩지게 하다
0309	**national**	adj 국가의, 전국적인
0310	**neighborhood**	n 이웃, 근처
0311	**stairway**	n 계단, 층계
0312	**pesticide**	n 살충제, 농약
0313	**utensil**	n 도구, 기구
0314	**advertisement**	n 광고, 선전
0315	**resolve**	v 해결하다, 결심하다 n 결심, 결의
0316	**interview**	n 면접, 인터뷰 v 면접하다
0317	**ownership**	n 소유권, 소유
0318	**residential**	adj 주거의
0319	**unnecessary**	adj 불필요한, 쓸데없는
0320	**instruct**	v 가르치다, 지시하다
0321	**fertilizer**	n 비료, 거름
0322	**protective**	adj 보호하는, 보호용의
0323	**artificial**	adj 인공적인, 인조의
0324	**activate**	v 활성화하다, 작동시키다
0325	**custom**	n 관습, 풍습 adj 맞춤형의

0326	latest	adj 최신의
0327	removal	n 제거
0328	irrigation	n 관개
0329	damaged	adj 손상된, 파손된
0330	imitate	v 모방하다, 흉내 내다
0331	adequate	adj 적절한, 충분한
0332	degree	n 학위, 정도
0333	inaccurate	adj 부정확한, 틀린
0334	mold	n 곰팡이, 틀 v 형성하다
0335	diversify	v 다양화하다
0336	conservation	n 보존, 보호
0337	election	n 선거, 당선
0338	paycheck	n 급여, 급료
0339	unpack	v 짐을 풀다
0340	soil	n 토양, 흙
0341	discussion	n 논의, 토론
0342	interest	n 관심, 이자 v 흥미를 갖게 하다
0343	analysis	n 분석
0344	manuscript	n 원고, 필사본
0345	floor plan	평면도
0346	time off	휴가, 휴무
0347	contact information	연락처 정보
0348	credit card	신용카드
0349	look for	~을 찾다
0350	out of stock	재고가 없는

DAY 08 PART 4 기출 어휘

☑ PART 4에 반드시 나오는 최신 기출 어휘들이므로, 확실히 암기해 둡니다. 🎧 VOCA_D08.mp3

0351	renovation	n 개조, 수리
0352	inventory	n 재고, 목록
0353	justify	v 정당화하다, 타당성을 입증하다
0354	dedicated	adj 헌신적인, 전념하는
0355	landscaping	n 조경
0356	transportation	n 교통, 운송
0357	donation	n 기부, 기증
0358	emphasize	v 강조하다
0359	prototype	n 원형, 시제품
0360	certification	n 증명, 증명서, 자격증
0361	assignment	n 과제, 임무
0362	insurance	n 보험, 보장
0363	evaluation	n 평가, 측정
0364	accounting	n 회계
0365	compliment	n 칭찬, 찬사 v 칭찬하다
0366	familiar	adj 친숙한, 잘 아는
0367	vegetarian	n 채식주의자 adj 채식의
0368	aviation	n 항공, 비행
0369	exhibition	n 전시회, 전시
0370	trial	n 재판, 시도
0371	itinerary	n 여행 일정
0372	refreshment	n 다과, 가벼운 식사
0373	contain	v 포함하다, 담다
0374	mayor	n 시장
0375	reassure	v 안심시키다, 확신시키다

0376	referral	n 소개, 위탁
0377	trail	n 길, 흔적 v 뒤따르다
0378	photograph	n 사진 v 사진 찍다
0379	résumé	n 이력서
0380	innovation	n 혁신
0381	artifact	n 인공물, 유물
0382	restoration	n 복원, 회복
0383	celebrity	n 유명인, 명성
0384	manual	n 설명서, 안내서 adj 수동의, 손으로 하는
0385	track	v 추적하다 n 자국, 경주로
0386	endorse	v 지지하다, 보증하다
0387	varied	adj 다양한, 변화가 있는
0388	persuade	v 설득하다, 납득시키다
0389	revised	adj 수정된, 개정된
0390	waste	n 낭비, 폐기물 v 낭비하다
0391	admission	n 입장, 입학
0392	sample	n 견본, 샘플 v 시식하다, 시도하다
0393	scent	n 향기, 냄새
0394	on time	제시간에, 정시에
0395	visitor pass	방문자 출입증
0396	take place	발생하다, 일어나다
0397	city council	시의회
0398	power outage	정전
0399	kitchen appliance	주방 가전제품
0400	sign up for	~에 등록하다, ~을 신청하다

DAY 09   PART 4   기출 어휘

☑ PART 4에 반드시 나오는 최신 기출 어휘들이므로, 확실히 암기해 둡니다.   🎧 VOCA_D09.mp3

0401	nearby	adj 근처의, 인접한 adv 가까운 곳에
0402	criticize	v 비판하다, 비난하다
0403	attire	n 복장, 의복
0404	electricity	n 전기, 전력
0405	footage	n 영상 자료
0406	clinical	adj 임상의
0407	facilitate	v 촉진하다, 용이하게 하다
0408	hands-on	adj 직접 해보는, 실무적인
0409	separate	adj 분리된, 별개의 v 분리하다
0410	insight	n 통찰력, 이해력
0411	outing	n 외출, 야외 활동
0412	wing	n 부속 건물, 날개
0413	grocery	n 식료품점, 식료품
0414	capability	n 능력, 역량
0415	athlete	n 운동선수
0416	overbook	v 초과 예약하다
0417	apron	n 앞치마
0418	probably	adv 아마도
0419	chemical	n 화학물질 adj 화학의
0420	engineering	n 공학, 기술
0421	wellness	n 건강
0422	accompany	v 동행하다, 동반하다
0423	filter	n 필터, 여과기 v 여과하다
0424	discounted	adj 할인된
0425	textile	n 직물, 섬유

#		
0426	wildlife	[n] 야생생물
0427	pursue	[v] 추구하다, 쫓다
0428	informal	[adj] 비공식적인, 편안한
0429	hesitant	[adj] 망설이는, 주저하는
0430	handy	[adj] 편리한, 유용한
0431	entertainment	[n] 오락, 오락물
0432	margin	[n] 판매 수익, 마진, 여백
0433	licensed	[adj] 허가된, 면허가 있는
0434	impact	[n] 영향 [v] 영향을 주다
0435	on track	정상적으로 진행 중인, 예정대로 진행되는
0436	have in common	공통점이 있다
0437	retail store	소매점
0438	market share	시장 점유율
0439	background information	배경 정보
0440	boarding pass	탑승권
0441	electrical outlet	전기 콘센트
0442	souvenir shop	기념품 가게
0443	trade fair	무역 박람회
0444	appliance store	가전제품 상점
0445	on foot	걸어서, 도보로
0446	loyal customer	단골고객
0447	step down	사임하다, 물러나다
0448	confirmation number	확인 번호
0449	access code	접속 코드, 접근 코드
0450	property manager	부동산 관리자, 자산 관리자

DAY 10 PART 4 기출 어휘

☑ PART 4에 반드시 나오는 최신 기출 어휘들이므로, 확실히 암기해 둡니다. 🎧 VOCA_D10.mp3

0451	watercolor	n 수채화, 수채물감
0452	handcraft	n 수공예품 v 손으로 만들다
0453	critic	n 비평가, 평론가
0454	arena	n 경기장
0455	overload	n 과부하 v 과부하를 주다
0456	raw	adj 날것의, 가공되지 않은
0457	headlamp	n 전조등
0458	integrity	n 정직성, 진실성
0459	corporation	n 기업, 법인
0460	freeze	v 얼다, 얼리다 n 동결
0461	agricultural	adj 농업의, 농경의
0462	kneepad	n 무릎 보호대
0463	exclude	v 제외하다, 배제하다
0464	resurface	v 다시 출현하다, (도로를) 재포장하다
0465	feasible	adj 실행 가능한, 타당한
0466	commemorative	adj 기념의, 추모의
0467	cliff	n 절벽, 낭떠러지
0468	precaution	n 예방책
0469	navigation	n 항해, 운항
0470	scented	adj 향기 나는
0471	wrist	n 손목
0472	voluntary	adj 자발적인, 자원의
0473	assessment	n 평가, 사정
0474	congestion	n 혼잡, 정체
0475	restock	v 재입고하다, 다시 채우다

0476 ☐	**conventional**	[adj] 관례적인, 전통적인
0477 ☐	**kite**	[n] 연
0478 ☐	**roadwork**	[n] 도로 공사
0479 ☐	**reveal**	[v] 드러내다, 밝히다
0480 ☐	**simplify**	[v] 간소화하다
0481 ☐	**confidentiality**	[n] 비밀, 기밀성
0482 ☐	**amusement park**	놀이공원
0483 ☐	**make a recommendation**	추천하다, 권고하다
0484 ☐	**pay rate**	급여율, 임금률
0485 ☐	**help oneself**	(음식 등을) 마음껏 먹다, 마음대로 하다
0486 ☐	**try on**	~을 입어보다, 착용해 보다
0487 ☐	**pass out**	기절하다, ~을 배포하다
0488 ☐	**sold out**	매진된
0489 ☐	**financial status**	재정 상태
0490 ☐	**non-profit organization**	비영리 단체
0491 ☐	**kick off**	시작하다, 개시하다
0492 ☐	**photo shoot**	사진 촬영
0493 ☐	**consent form**	동의서
0494 ☐	**food processing company**	식품 가공 회사
0495 ☐	**target customer**	목표 고객
0496 ☐	**panel discussion**	공개 토론
0497 ☐	**green space**	녹지 공간
0498 ☐	**water station**	식수대, 급수대
0499 ☐	**voice actor**	성우
0500 ☐	**assignment sheet**	과제지, 할당표

DAY 11 PART 5&6 기출 어휘

☑ PART 5&6에 반드시 나오는 최신 기출 어휘들이므로, 확실히 암기해 둡니다.   ♩ VOCA_D11.mp3

0501	feature	n 특징, 특성 v 특징으로 하다
0502	purchase	v 구매하다 n 구매, 구입
0503	replacement	n 교체, 대체품
0504	candidate	n 후보자, 지원자
0505	position	n 위치, 직책 v 배치하다
0506	production	n 생산, 제작
0507	expense	n 비용, 지출
0508	account	n 계정, 설명 v 설명하다
0509	acquire	v 획득하다, 습득하다
0510	request	n 요청, 의뢰 v 요청하다
0511	process	n 과정, 절차 v 처리하다
0512	participate	v 참여하다, 참가하다
0513	launch	v 출시하다, 시작하다 n 출시, 개시
0514	provide	v 제공하다, 공급하다
0515	previous	adj 이전의
0516	closely	adv 면밀히, 밀접하게
0517	policy	n 정책, 방침
0518	draft	n 초안, 초고 v 작성하다
0519	investor	n 투자자
0520	potential	adj 잠재적인, 가능한 n 잠재력
0521	complimentary	adj 무료의, 칭찬하는
0522	automatically	adv 자동으로, 저절로
0523	distribute	v 배포하다, 분배하다
0524	suggestion	n 제안, 추천
0525	initiative	n 계획, 주도권

0526	donate	v 기부하다, 기증하다
0527	delay	v 지연시키다, 연기하다 n 지연
0528	remain	v 남아있다, 계속하다
0529	accurate	adj 정확한, 정밀한
0530	extensive	adj 광범위한, 포괄적인
0531	remind	v 상기시키다, 일깨우다
0532	immediately	adv 즉시, 곧바로
0533	hire	v 고용하다
0534	serve	v 제공하다, (음식을) 차려 주다
0535	temporarily	adv 일시적으로, 임시로
0536	likable	adj 호감이 가는, 마음에 드는
0537	decision	n 결정, 판단
0538	recently	adv 최근에, 얼마 전에
0539	responsible	adj 책임이 있는
0540	expertise	n 전문 지식, 전문 기술
0541	include	v 포함하다, 내포하다
0542	significant	adj 중요한, 의미 있는
0543	selection	n 선택, 선정
0544	implement	v 시행하다, 실행하다 n 도구
0545	directly	adv 직접적으로, 곧바로
0546	remotely	adv 원격으로, 멀리서
0547	absorb	v 흡수하다, 이해하다
0548	rate	n 비율, 속도 v 평가하다
0549	manufacture	v 제조하다, 생산하다 n 제조, 생산
0550	ordinary	adj 보통의, 평범한

DAY 12 PART 5&6 기출 어휘

PART 5&6에 반드시 나오는 최신 기출 어휘들이므로, 확실히 암기해 둡니다.   VOCA_D12.mp3

0551	ideal	adj 이상적인 n 이상
0552	personal	adj 개인적인, 사적인
0553	expect	v 예상하다, 기대하다
0554	grateful	adj 감사하는, 고마워하는
0555	attendance	n 출석, 참석, 참석자 수
0556	organization	n 조직, 기관
0557	exception	n 예외, 이례
0558	modify	v 수정하다, 변경하다
0559	specification	n 설명서, 세부 사항, 사양
0560	considerable	adj 상당한, 중요한
0561	operation	n 운영, 작동
0562	share	v 공유하다, 나누다 n 몫, 지분
0563	guarantee	v 보증하다, 확약하다 n 보증, 보장
0564	accept	v 받아들이다, 수락하다
0565	exactly	adv 정확히, 꼭
0566	sponsor	v 후원하다, 지원하다 n 후원자
0567	transfer	v 이동하다, 옮기다 n 이동, 전송
0568	satisfaction	n 만족, 충족
0569	widely	adv 널리, 광범위하게
0570	receipt	n 영수증, 수령
0571	thoroughly	adv 철저히, 완전히
0572	carefully	adv 조심스럽게, 신중하게
0573	participation	n 참여, 참가
0574	evenly	adv 균등하게, 고르게
0575	completely	adv 완전히, 전적으로

0576 maintain	v 유지하다, 관리하다
0577 qualified	adj 자격 있는, 적격의
0578 productivity	n 생산성, 생산력
0579 direction	n 방향, 지시
0580 settlement	n 합의, 정착
0581 innovative	adj 혁신적인, 창의적인
0582 payroll	n 급여 명부, 임금대장
0583 respond	v 응답하다, 반응하다
0584 extremely	adv 매우, 극도로
0585 annually	adv 매년, 연간으로
0586 increase	v 증가하다, 늘리다 n 증가, 인상
0587 advanced	adj 고급의, 발전된
0588 durable	adj 내구성 있는, 오래가는
0589 report	v 보고하다, 알리다 n 보고서
0590 anticipate	v 예상하다, 기대하다
0591 frequently	adv 자주, 빈번하게
0592 quite	adv 꽤, 상당히
0593 current	adj 현재의, 최신의
0594 boost	v 증진하다, 향상시키다 n 증진, 향상
0595 monitor	v 감시하다, 추적 관찰하다
0596 approval	n 승인, 인가
0597 knowledge	n 지식
0598 capable	adj 능력 있는, 유능한
0599 reminder	n 상기시키는 것
0600 refer to	~을 참조하다, 언급하다

DAY 13   PART 5&6   기출 어휘

☑ PART 5&6에 반드시 나오는 최신 기출 어휘들이므로, 확실히 암기해 둡니다.   ♫ VOCA_D13.mp3

0601	submission	n 제출
0602	effective	adj 효과적인, 유효한
0603	regarding	prep ~에 관하여, ~에 대해
0604	follow	v 따라가다, 뒤따르다
0605	variety	n 다양성, 여러 종류
0606	service	n 서비스, 봉사 v 점검하다, 정비하다
0607	actually	adv 실제로, 사실상
0608	creative	adj 창의적인, 독창적인
0609	figure	n 수치, 인물 v 생각하다
0610	grant	v 허가하다, 승인하다 n 보조금
0611	rarely	adv 드물게, 거의 ~않다
0612	practice	n 연습, 실행 v 연습하다
0613	conditional	adj 조건부의, 조건적인
0614	responsibility	n 책임, 의무
0615	vary	v 서로 다르다
0616	further	adv 더욱, 더 멀리 adj 추가의
0617	eventually	adv 결국, 마침내
0618	technology	n 기술
0619	subscription	n 구독, 가입
0620	acceptable	adj 받아들일 수 있는, 용인되는
0621	arrangement	n 배치, 준비
0622	intend	v 의도하다, 계획하다
0623	predict	v 예측하다, 예상하다
0624	issue	n 문제, 쟁점 v 발행하다
0625	repetition	n 반복, 되풀이

0626	**highly**	adv 매우, 대단히
0627	**actively**	adv 적극적으로, 활발하게
0628	**revise**	v 수정하다, 개정하다
0629	**priority**	n 우선순위, 우선권
0630	**distribution**	n 배포, 분배
0631	**balance**	n 균형, 잔액 v 균형을 맞추다
0632	**reasonable**	adj 합리적인, 적당한
0633	**apologize**	v 사과하다
0634	**employee**	n 직원
0635	**packaging**	n 포장, 포장재
0636	**determine**	v 결정하다, 판단하다
0637	**necessary**	adj 필요한
0638	**electronic**	adj 전자의
0639	**easily**	adv 쉽게, 용이하게
0640	**fairly**	adv 꽤, 공정하게
0641	**specific**	adj 구체적인, 특정한
0642	**initial**	adj 초기의, 처음의
0643	**flavor**	n 맛, 풍미
0644	**demand**	n 요구, 수요 v 요구하다
0645	**description**	n 설명, 묘사
0646	**approach**	v 접근하다, 다가가다 n 접근, 접근법
0647	**clearly**	adv 명확히, 분명히
0648	**ongoing**	adj 진행 중인, 계속되는
0649	**continuously**	adv 계속해서, 연속적으로
0650	**productive**	adj 생산적인, 효율적인

DAY 14 PART 5&6 기출 어휘

☑ PART 5&6에 반드시 나오는 최신 기출 어휘들이므로, 확실히 암기해 둡니다. ♪ VOCA_D14.mp3

0651	last	v 지속되다 adj 마지막의
0652	contribute	v 기여하다, 공헌하다
0653	proposed	adj 제안된
0654	move	v 이동하다, 이사하다
0655	require	v 요구하다, 필요로 하다
0656	price	n 가격, 값 v 가격을 매기다
0657	specify	v 명시하다, 구체적으로 밝히다
0658	prepare	v 준비하다, 대비하다
0659	strictly	adv 엄격히, 정확히
0660	outline	n 개요, 윤곽 v 개요를 서술하다
0661	personable	adj 매력적인
0662	increasingly	adv 점점 더
0663	nearly	adv 거의, 약
0664	official	adj 공식적인 n 관계자, 공무원
0665	observe	v 관찰하다, 준수하다
0666	adjustment	n 조정, 적응
0667	impressive	adj 인상적인, 감동적인
0668	attraction	n 관광 명소, 매력
0669	permanent	adj 영구적인
0670	progress	n 진행, 발전 v 진전하다, 진행되다
0671	community	n 지역사회, 공동체
0672	minimize	v 최소화하다, 축소하다
0673	standard	n 기준, 표준 adj 표준의
0674	valuable	adj 가치 있는, 귀중한
0675	profit	n 이익, 수익 v 이익을 얻다

0676	recognize	v 인식하다, 알아보다
0677	conveniently	adv 편리하게, 손쉽게
0678	allow	v 허용하다, 허락하다
0679	shorten	v 줄이다, 단축하다
0680	efficient	adj 효율적인, 능률적인
0681	deserve	v 받을 만하다, 자격이 있다
0682	confident	adj 자신감 있는, 확신하는
0683	minimal	adj 최소한의, 극히 적은
0684	strongly	adv 강하게, 강력히
0685	suitable	adj 적합한, 알맞은
0686	contribution	n 기여, 공헌
0687	occasionally	adv 가끔, 때때로
0688	experience	n 경험 v 경험하다
0689	compensation	n 보상, 보수
0690	generous	adj 관대한, 후한
0691	customer	n 고객, 손님
0692	mention	v 언급하다, 말하다 n 언급
0693	brief	adj 짧은, 간결한
0694	show	v 보여주다, 나타내다
0695	financially	adv 재정적으로, 금전적으로
0696	comprehensive	adj 포괄적인, 종합적인
0697	attach	v 부착하다, 첨부하다
0698	check	v 확인하다, 점검하다
0699	calculate	v 계산하다, 산출하다
0700	exclusive	adj 독점적인, 배타적인

DAY 15 PART 5&6 기출 어휘

☑ PART 5&6에 반드시 나오는 최신 기출 어휘들이므로, 확실히 암기해 둡니다. ∩ VOCA_D15.mp3

0701	penalty	n 벌금, 처벌
0702	forecast	n 예측, 예보 v 예측하다
0703	up-to-date	adj 최신의, 최근의
0704	prompt	adj 신속한, 즉각적인 v 촉발하다
0705	tightly	adv 단단히, 꽉
0706	originate	v 기원하다, 유래하다
0707	obvious	adj 분명한, 명백한
0708	specialize	v 전공하다, 전문으로 다루다
0709	primary	adj 주된, 주요한, 기본적인
0710	randomly	adv 무작위로, 임의로
0711	authorization	n 허가, 권한 부여
0712	project	n 계획, 프로젝트 v 예상하다, 계획하다
0713	opposite	adj 반대의, 맞은편의 n 반대
0714	protection	n 보호, 방어
0715	method	n 방법, 방식
0716	residence	n 거주지, 주택
0717	fortunately	adv 다행히, 운 좋게
0718	entire	adj 전체의, 모든
0719	unavailable	adj 이용할 수 없는, 구할 수 없는
0720	reflect	v 반영하다, 숙고하다
0721	emergency	n 비상사태, 긴급 상황
0722	inconvenience	n 불편, 곤란 v 불편을 끼치다
0723	resource	n 자원, 자료
0724	analyze	v 분석하다
0725	consent	n 동의, 허락 v 동의하다

0726 ☐	**reliability**	n 신뢰도, 믿음직함
0727 ☐	**research**	n 연구, 조사 v 연구하다
0728 ☐	**typically**	adv 일반적으로, 전형적으로
0729 ☐	**appreciation**	n 감사, 인정
0730 ☐	**passenger**	n 승객
0731 ☐	**various**	adj 다양한, 여러 가지의
0732 ☐	**rise**	v 오르다, 일어나다 n 상승
0733 ☐	**leave**	v 떠나다, 남기다 n 휴가
0734 ☐	**securely**	adv 단단히
0735 ☐	**compensate**	v 보상하다
0736 ☐	**enable**	v 가능하게 하다, 할 수 있게 하다
0737 ☐	**buy**	v 구매하다, 사다
0738 ☐	**steady**	adj 안정된, 꾸준한 v 안정시키다
0739 ☐	**slightly**	adv 약간, 조금
0740 ☐	**despite**	prep ~에도 불구하고
0741 ☐	**enthusiastic**	adj 열정적인, 열심인
0742 ☐	**break**	v 깨다, 부수다 n 휴식
0743 ☐	**transform**	v 바꾸다, 변형시키다
0744 ☐	**impressed**	adj 감명받은, 인상 깊은
0745 ☐	**consideration**	n 고려, 배려
0746 ☐	**roughly**	adv 대략, 거칠게
0747 ☐	**sort**	n 종류, 유형 v 분류하다
0748 ☐	**at least**	최소한, 적어도
0749 ☐	**engage in**	~에 참여하다
0750 ☐	**deal with**	~을 처리하다, 다루다

DAY 16 PART 5&6 기출 어휘

☑ PART 5&6에 반드시 나오는 최신 기출 어휘들이므로, 확실히 암기해 둡니다.   ∩ VOCA_D16.mp3

0751	lately	adv 최근에, 요즘
0752	precisely	adv 정확히, 꼭
0753	accumulate	v 축적하다, 모으다
0754	solid	adj 단단한, 견고한
0755	transit	n 운송, 통과, 교통 체계
0756	affect	v 영향을 미치다
0757	achieve	v 달성하다, 성취하다
0758	rare	adj 희귀한, 드문
0759	seasonal	adj 계절의, 계절에 따라 다른
0760	nevertheless	adv 그럼에도 불구하고
0761	information	n 정보
0762	instead	adv 대신에
0763	additionally	adv 또한, 게다가
0764	salesperson	n 판매원, 영업사원
0765	propose	v 제안하다, 제의하다
0766	retain	v 유지하다, 보유하다
0767	portion	n 부분, 일부
0768	fill	v 채우다, 메우다
0769	confusion	n 혼란, 혼동
0770	merge	v 합병하다, 통합하다
0771	complicated	adj 복잡한, 어려운
0772	suggest	v 제안하다, 암시하다
0773	lack	v 부족하다 n 부족, 결핍
0774	remainder	n 나머지, 잔여물
0775	clear	adj 명확한, 분명한 v 치우다

0776	quickly	adv 빠르게, 신속히
0777	afford	v ~할 여유가 있다
0778	explanation	n 설명, 해명
0779	enroll	v 등록하다, 가입하다
0780	eagerly	adv 열심히, 간절히
0781	industry	n 산업, 업계
0782	represent	v 대표하다, 나타내다
0783	especially	adv 특히, 특별히
0784	entry	n 입장, 입국
0785	finalist	n 최종 후보, 결승 진출자
0786	reason	n 이유, 근거 v 추론하다
0787	halfway	adv 중간쯤에
0788	showcase	v 선보이다, 전시하다 n 진열장
0789	profitable	adj 수익성 있는, 유익한
0790	intentionally	adv 고의로, 의도적으로
0791	dedication	n 헌신, 전념
0792	diverse	adj 다양한, 여러 종류의
0793	durability	n 내구성, 지속성
0794	atmosphere	n 분위기, 대기
0795	restriction	n 제한, 규제
0796	neatly	adv 깔끔하게, 단정하게
0797	commence	v 시작하다
0798	carry out	~을 수행하다, 실행하다
0799	owing to	~ 때문에, ~으로 인해
0800	take on	~을 떠맡다, 착수하다

DAY 17 PART 7 기출 어휘

☑ PART 7에 반드시 나오는 최신 기출 어휘들이므로, 확실히 암기해 둡니다.   🎧 VOCA_D17.mp3

0801	**replace**	v 교체하다, 대체하다
0802	**additional**	adj 추가적인, 부가적인
0803	**supervisor**	n 관리자, 감독관
0804	**moderate**	adj 적당한, 중간의 v 완화하다
0805	**expand**	v 확장하다, 확대하다
0806	**secure**	v 확보하다, 보장하다 adj 안전한, 확실한
0807	**application**	n 지원, 신청서
0808	**excel**	v 뛰어나다, 탁월하다
0809	**property**	n 재산, 부동산
0810	**cover**	v 덮다, 다루다 n 표지
0811	**estimate**	v 추정하다 n 견적(서), 추정치
0812	**popular**	adj 인기 있는, 대중적인
0813	**recommend**	v 추천하다, 권하다
0814	**volunteer**	n 자원봉사자 v 자원하다
0815	**participant**	n 참가자, 참여자
0816	**feedback**	n 피드백, 의견
0817	**deliver**	v 배달하다, 전달하다
0818	**promotion**	n 승진, 홍보
0819	**charge**	n 요금, 책임 v 청구하다, 부과하다
0820	**affordable**	adj 감당할 수 있는, 저렴한
0821	**encourage**	v 격려하다, 장려하다
0822	**ensure**	v 보장하다, 확실히 하다
0823	**extend**	v 연장하다, 확장하다
0824	**attract**	v 끌어들이다, 매료시키다
0825	**alternative**	n 대안, 대체 수단 adj 대안의

0826 executive	n 임원, 경영진 adj 경영의
0827 representative	n 대표자 adj 대표적인
0828 direct	v 지시하다, 감독하다 adj 직접적인
0829 professional	adj 전문적인 n 전문가
0830 nutritious	adj 영양가 있는, 영양분이 풍부한
0831 perform	v 수행하다, 실행하다
0832 expert	n 전문가 adj 전문적인
0833 renovate	v 개조하다, 수리하다
0834 storage	n 보관, 저장
0835 multiple	adj 다수의, 여러 가지의
0836 annual	adj 연간의, 매년의
0837 district	n 지역, 구역
0838 in advance	미리, 사전에
0839 evaluate	v 평가하다, 심사하다
0840 expansion	n 확장, 팽창
0841 capacity	n 용량, 능력
0842 inform	v 알리다, 통지하다
0843 operate	v 운영하다, 작동하다
0844 local	adj 지역의, 현지의
0845 security	n 보안, 안전
0846 superior	adj 우수한, 뛰어난 n 상급자, 상사
0847 manufacturer	n 제조자, 제조업체
0848 intense	adj 강렬한, 극심한
0849 at no cost	무료로
0850 on schedule	예정대로, 일정에 맞게

DAY 18   PART 7   기출 어휘

☑ PART 7에 반드시 나오는 최신 기출 어휘들이므로, 확실히 암기해 둡니다.   ♫ VOCA_D18.mp3

0851	relocate	v 재배치하다, 이전하다
0852	fulfill	v 이행하다, 성취하다
0853	athletic	adj 운동의, 체육의
0854	resident	n 거주자 adj 거주하는
0855	host	n 주최자, 진행자 v 주최하다
0856	requirement	n 요구 사항, 필요조건
0857	condition	n 상태, 조건
0858	earn	v 획득하다, 벌다
0859	valid	adj 유효한, 타당한
0860	reach	v 도달하다, 연락하다 n 범위, 영향력
0861	present	v 제시하다 adj 현재의, 출석한
0862	benefit	n 혜택, 이점 v 이익을 얻다
0863	invoice	n 청구서
0864	commercial	adj 상업적인 n 광고
0865	shift	n 교대 (근무), 변화 v 이동하다, 바꾸다
0866	certificate	n 증명서, 자격증
0867	status	n 상태, 지위
0868	specialist	n 전문가
0869	upcoming	adj 다가오는, 곧 있을
0870	installation	n 설치
0871	honor	n 명예, 영예 v 존중하다, 존경하다
0872	exhibit	v 전시하다 n 전시품, 전시회
0873	encounter	v 마주치다 n 만남
0874	register	v 등록하다, 신청하다
0875	reserve	v 예약하다

0876 ☐	**accessible**	[adj] 접근 가능한, 이용 가능한
0877 ☐	**unusual**	[adj] 특이한, 보통이 아닌
0878 ☐	**satisfied**	[adj] 만족한, 충족된
0879 ☐	**value**	[n] 가치 [v] 평가하다
0880 ☐	**strategy**	[n] 전략, 계획
0881 ☐	**reliable**	[adj] 신뢰할 수 있는, 믿을 만한
0882 ☐	**preference**	[n] 선호, 기호도
0883 ☐	**deposit**	[n] 보증금 [v] 맡기다, 두다
0884 ☐	**carry**	[v] 운반하다, 지니다
0885 ☐	**improve**	[v] 개선하다, 향상시키다
0886 ☐	**technical**	[adj] 기술적인, 전문적인
0887 ☐	**award**	[n] 상 [v] 수여하다
0888 ☐	**identify**	[v] 식별하다, 확인하다
0889 ☐	**decade**	[n] 10년, 십 년간
0890 ☐	**qualify**	[v] 자격을 갖추다, 부합하다
0891 ☐	**involve**	[v] 포함하다, 관련시키다
0892 ☐	**financial**	[adj] 재정적인, 금융의
0893 ☐	**flexible**	[adj] 유연한, 융통성 있는
0894 ☐	**simply**	[adv] 단순히, 그저
0895 ☐	**join**	[v] 참여하다, 합류하다
0896 ☐	**properly**	[adv] 적절히, 제대로
0897 ☐	**fabric**	[n] 직물, 천
0898 ☐	**credit**	[v] 인정하다 [n] 명성, 신용
0899 ☐	**objective**	[n] 목표 [adj] 객관적인
0900 ☐	**pick up**	~을 가져가다, 구매하다

DAY 19   PART 7   기출 어휘

☑ PART 7에 반드시 나오는 최신 기출 어휘들이므로, 확실히 암기해 둡니다.   ♫ VOCA_D19.mp3

0901	coworker	n 동료
0902	order	n 주문, 순서 v 주문하다
0903	accommodate	v 수용하다, 적응하다
0904	collection	n 수집, 컬렉션
0905	interactive	adj 상호작용하는, 대화형의
0906	commute	v 통근하다 n 통근
0907	supervise	v 감독하다, 관리하다
0908	praise	v 칭찬하다 n 칭찬
0909	quality	n 품질, 특성 adj 고급의, 양질의
0910	experienced	adj 경험 있는, 숙련된
0911	management	n 관리, 경영
0912	meet	v 만나다, 충족하다
0913	virtual	adj 가상의, 사실상의
0914	aircraft	n 항공기, 비행기
0915	function	n 기능, 행사 v 기능하다, 작동하다
0916	luggage	n 수하물, 짐
0917	appropriate	adj 적절한
0918	transaction	n 거래
0919	critical	adj 중요한, 비판적인
0920	renew	v 갱신하다, 새롭게 하다
0921	inquiry	n 문의, 조사
0922	improvement	n 개선, 향상
0923	international	adj 국제적인, 세계적인
0924	regularly	adv 정기적으로, 규칙적으로
0925	summarize	v 요약하다, 정리하다

0926	recruit	ⓥ 모집하다, 고용하다 ⓝ 신입 사원
0927	appearance	ⓝ 외모, 출현, 등장
0928	successful	adj 성공적인, 성과가 있는
0929	customized	adj 맞춤형의, 주문 제작된
0930	component	ⓝ 구성요소, 부품
0931	opening	ⓝ 공석, 개장, 개관
0932	satisfy	ⓥ 만족시키다, 충족시키다
0933	form	ⓝ 양식, 형태 ⓥ 형성하다
0934	relatively	adv 비교적, 상대적으로
0935	recruitment	ⓝ 채용, 모집
0936	convenience	ⓝ 편의, 편리함
0937	enlarge	ⓥ 확대하다, 확장하다
0938	adapt	ⓥ 적응하다, 조정하다
0939	quantity	ⓝ 수량, 양
0940	enjoyable	adj 즐거운, 유쾌한
0941	lease	ⓝ 임대, 임대 계약 ⓥ 임대하다, 대여하다
0942	permission	ⓝ 허가, 허락
0943	procedure	ⓝ 절차, 과정
0944	purpose	ⓝ 목적, 의도
0945	training	ⓝ 훈련, 교육
0946	leading	adj 선두의, 주요한
0947	verify	ⓥ 확인하다, 검증하다
0948	machinery	ⓝ 기계, 장치
0949	competitor	ⓝ 경쟁 업체, 경쟁 상대
0950	willing	adj 기꺼이 하는, 자발적인

DAY 20 PART 7 기출 어휘

PART 7에 반드시 나오는 최신 기출 어휘들이므로, 확실히 암기해 둡니다.

0951	**substitute**	n 대체품 v 대체하다
0952	**reward**	n 보상, 상 v 보상하다
0953	**prolong**	v 연장시키다
0954	**extension**	n 확장, 연장
0955	**gardening**	n 원예, 정원 가꾸기
0956	**draw**	v 그리다, 끌어당기다
0957	**coordinate**	v 조정하다, 조직화하다
0958	**alert**	v 경고하다 adj 경계하는
0959	**clarify**	v 명확히 하다, 설명하다
0960	**redesign**	v 재설계하다
0961	**refund**	n 환불, 반환금 v 환불하다
0962	**association**	n 협회, 연계, 연관
0963	**outstanding**	adj 뛰어난, 미지불된
0964	**preserve**	v 보존하다, 유지하다
0965	**corporate**	adj 기업의, 법인의
0966	**biography**	n 전기, 자서전
0967	**investment**	n 투자, 투자금
0968	**amenity**	n 편의 시설
0969	**essential**	adj 필수적인, 본질적인 n 필수품
0970	**spread**	v 펼치다, 확산하다 n 확산
0971	**supplies**	n 물품, 공급품
0972	**satisfactory**	adj 만족스러운, 충분한
0973	**establish**	v 설립하다, 확고히 하다
0974	**recognition**	n 인식, 인정
0975	**reputation**	n 평판, 명성

0976 advancement	n 발전, 진보, 승진
0977 conclude	v 결론짓다, 마무리하다
0978 memorable	adj 기억에 남는, 인상적인
0979 detour	n 우회로 v 우회하다
0980 strengthen	v 강화하다, 견고하게 하다
0981 organic	adj 유기농의, 자연적인
0982 housing	n 주택, 숙박 시설
0983 revenue	n 수익, 수입
0984 waive	v (권리 등을) 포기하다, 면제하다
0985 ferry	n 나룻배, 연락선 v 나르다, 수송하다
0986 functional	adj 기능적인, 실용적인
0987 accommodation	n 숙박 시설, 숙소
0988 auction	n 경매 v 경매로 팔다
0989 seek	v 찾다, 추구하다
0990 assistance	n 도움, 지원
0991 railway	n 철도, 선로
0992 fine	n 벌금 adj 좋은, 섬세한
0993 lecture	n 강의 v 강의하다
0994 foundation	n 기초, 재단
0995 congratulate	v 축하하다, 축복하다
0996 recyclable	adj 재활용 가능한
0997 regional	adj 지역의, 지방의
0998 in person	직접, 대면으로
0999 focus on	~에 집중하다
1000 keynote speaker	기조연설자

MEMO

MEMO

MEMO